THESE UNITED STATES
The Questions of Our Past

Concise Edition · Combined Volume

Third Edition

Irwin Unger

New York University

PEARSON
Prentice
Hall

Upper Saddle River, New Jersey 07458

Library of Congress Cataloging-in-Publication Data

UNGER, IRWIN.
   These United States : the questions of our past / Irwin Unger. — Concise
ed., combined vol., 3rd ed.
      p. cm.
   Includes bibliographical references and index.
   ISBN 0-13-229965-8 (alk. paper)
   1. United States—History.   I. Title.
E178.1.U54 2006
973—dc22

                                                    2006015437

Vice President/Editorial Director: Charlyce Jones Owen
Associate Editor: Emsal Hasan
Senior Editorial Assistant: Maureen Diana
Senior Media Editor: Deborah O'Connell
Vice President/Director of Production and Manufacturing: Barbara Kittle
Senior Managing Editor: Joanne Riker
Production Liaison: Louise Rothman
Prepress and Manufacturing Manager: Nick Sklitsis
Prepress and Manufacturing Buyer: Benjamin Smith
Director of Marketing: Brandy Dawson
Senior Marketing Manager: Emily Cleary
Cover Art: May Day rally for immigrant rights, Thursday, May 1, 2003 at Boston's City
   Hall Plaza. AP Wide World Photos
Director, Image Resource Center: Melinda Reo
Manager, Visual Research: Beth Brenzel
Cover Image Specialist: Karen Sanatar
Composition and Full Service Project Management: Assunta Petrone/Preparé, Inc.
Printer/Binder: RR Donnelley/Harrisonburg
Cover Printer: Lehigh

Credits and acknowledgments borrowed from other sources and reproduced,
with permission, in this textbook appear on page PC1.

Pearson Education LTD.
Pearson Education Australia PTY, Limited
Pearson Education Singapore, Pte. Ltd.
Pearson Education North Asia Ltd.
Pearson Education Canada, Ltd.
Pearson Educatión de México, S.A. de C.V.
Pearson Education—Japan
Pearson Education Malaysia, Pte. Ltd.

PEARSON
Prentice
Hall

10 9 8 7 6 5 4 3 2 1

ISBN 0-13-229965-8

To *Rita and Mickey, Libby and Arnie,*
Phyllis and Jerry, and Norma and David
—once more

BRIEF CONTENTS

CONTENTS

MAPS

ABOUT THE AUTHOR

Pulitzer Prize winning historian Irwin Unger has been teaching American history for over forty years on both coasts. Born and largely educated in New York, he has lived in California, Virginia, and Washington State. He is married to Debi Unger and they have five children, now all safely past their college years. Professor Unger formerly taught at California State University at Long Beach, the University of California at Davis, and New York University. He is now professor emeritus.

Professor Unger's professional interests have ranged widely within American history. He has written on Reconstruction, the Progressive Era, and on the 1960s. His first book, *The Greenback Era*, won a Pulitzer Prize in 1965. Since then he has written *The Movement: The New Left* and (with Debi Unger) *The Vulnerable Years, Turning Point: 1968, The Best of Intentions* (about the Great Society), and *LBJ: A Life,* and *The Guggenheims: A Family History.*

PREFACE

This is the third edition of *These United States: Concise Edition*. Like its predecessors, it is a compact version of *These United States: The Questions of Our Past* and is designed to present all the essentials of the larger work in a briefer format to facilitate readability and reduce the price of the work to the student.

The condensing process has not, I believe, sacrificed essential material. Rather, redundant examples, overextended treatments, and marginal topics have been eliminated, a process that drew on reviewers' and adopters' evaluations. And to constrain costs, we have also reduced the number of illustrations and maps and removed the "Portraits" from the main body of the text and placed them in a separate booklet.

In most significant ways the book's plan remains the same, however. First, unlike virtually every other introductory text, it still has a single author and speaks in a single voice. I hope readers will agree that a book by a single individual has inherent advantages over one composed by a committee. Second, each chapter is still organized around a significant question, each designed to challenge students with the complexity of the past and compel them to evaluate critically different viewpoints. This plan, I believe, makes the learning of history a quest, an exploration, rather than the mere absorption of facts. Yet, at the same time, "the facts" are made available. *These United States* provides the ample "coverage" of standard texts.

The word "standard" here does not mean old-fashioned. Though *These United States* discusses political, diplomatic, and military events, it also deals extensively with social, cultural, and economic matters. It concerns itself not only with "events," moreover, but also with people, currents, and themes. It is not old-fashioned in another way: it expands the "canon" to include those who have traditionally been excluded from the American past and seeks to embrace the enormous diversity of the American people. The reader will find in *These United States* women as well as men, people of color as well as those of European extraction, youths as well as adults; the poor as well as the rich; artists, writers, and musicians as well as politicians, generals, and diplomats.

In this newest version of the work, I have added sections on various aspects of social history, particularly on slavery, on the Salem witch trials, and on daily life. I have also extended the story through the events of 2000 and 2005, including the collapse of the "bubble" economy of the 1990s, the World Trade Center and Pentagon attacks, the war on terrorism, the invasion of Afghanistan, and the war in Iraq.

I hope that, like its precursors, this edition meets with favor among faculty and students, and serves both as a successful teaching instrument and an absorbing introduction to the American past.

Irwin Unger
Department of History, Emeritus
New York University

TEACHING AND LEARNING PACKAGE

For the Instructor:

Instructor's Manual with Tests The Instructor's Manual includes chapter summaries, learning objectives, suggestions for lecture topics, essay or classroom discussion topics, and suggestions for projects or term papers. The Test Item File contains multiple-choice questions, essay questions, identification questions, and matching questions.

Prentice Hall and Penguin Bundle Program Prentice Hall is pleased to provide instructors using *These United States* with an opportunity to receive significant discounts when orders of the text are bundled together with Penguin titles in American history. Please contact your local Prentice Hall representative for details.

For the Student:

History Notes, Volumes I and II This study resource includes commentary, definitions, identifications, map exercises, short-answer exercises, and essay questions.

Historical Documents and Portraits This compilation includes excerpts from primary sources and biographical information about a representative figure from each chapter.

New!

U.S. Documents CD-ROM Bound into every new copy of *These United States* is the U.S. Documents CD-ROM, consisting of over 300 primary source documents with questions for discussion or homework assignment. The documents can be printed and the questions can be answered online.

ACKNOWLEDGMENTS

Every author incurs debts in writing or revising a book such as this. I have been the beneficiary of particularly generous help and advice and I would like to acknowledge it here.

My thanks to Charlyce Jones Owen and, especially, Senior Assistant Maureen Diana for their invaluable help on this new edition, Emily Cleary for her marketing skills, and Assunta Petrone and Louise Rothman for their expertise as production editors. Thank you also to the reviewers of this edition: James R. Goff, Jr, Appalachian State University and David Gerard Hogan, Heidelberg College (OH). A number of my fellow academics were generous enough to read and evaluate earlier manuscript for this concise edition. They include William M. Leary, University of Georgia; Michael Haridopolos, Brevard Community College; Stephen L. Hardin, The Victoria College; and David G. Hogan, Heidelberg College. My thanks also to the scholars and teachers who evaluated earlier editions: James F. Hilgenburg, Jr., Glenville State College; Johanna Hume, Alvin Community College; Robert G. Fricke, West Valley College; Steve Schuster, Brookhaven College; Kenny Brown, University of Central Oklahoma; Paul Lucas, Indiana University, James A. Page, Collin County Community College (TX); Kurt W. Peterson, Judson College; and Thomas A. Kinney, Case Western Reserve; and last, but assuredly not least, Irving Katz, Indiana University. Though I did not invariably follow their advice, I always took it seriously.

1

The New World Encounters the Old

Why 1492?

c. 38,000 BCE	America's first settlers begin to cross a land bridge connecting Siberia and Alaska
986 CE	Norwegian merchant Bjarni Herjulfsson becomes the first European to sight the mainland of North America
c. 1000	Leif Ericsson lands on Vinland
c. 1010–13	Thorfinn Karlsefni and others attempt to colonize Vinland
c. 1300	Venetian and Genoese merchants establish overland trade routes to the East
c. 1400	The invention of printing, advances in navigation and naval architecture, and the introduction of gunpowder increase possibilities for worldwide exploration by Europeans
1488	Bartolomeu Dias rounds Africa's Cape of Good Hope for the Portuguese crown
1492	Christopher Columbus lands on San Salvador in the Bahamas
1497	Henry VII of England sends John Cabot to find a short route to the Indies: Cabot reaches Newfoundland
1498	Vasco da Gama, Portuguese navigator, becomes the first European to reach India by sea around Africa
1519–22	Ferdinand Magellan's circumnavigation of the world proves that the Americas are new lands, not the Indies
1521	Hernando Cortés conquers the Aztec empire in Mexico for Spain
1523–28	France sends Giovanni da Verrazano to find a short route to the Indies; he explores the east coast of North America
1532	Francisco Pizarro conquers the Inca empire in Peru for Spain
1534	Jacques Cartier attempts to find a northwest passage to the Indies for France
1609	Henry Hudson establishes Dutch claim to the Hudson River region in his search for a northwest passage

Every schoolchild knows that Columbus "discovered" America in 1492. It is a "fact" firmly rooted in our national consciousness. Yet Columbus did not discover America, if by that we mean he was the first person to encounter the two great continents that lie westward between Europe and Asia. At least two other groups stumbled on the Americas before Columbus. Sometime between 40,000 BCE and

1

12,000 BCE people from northeast Asia reached the "New World" from across the Pacific and quickly spread across the vast new lands. We call their descendants Indians, though many prefer the name Native Americans. Then about 1000 CE, Norsemen, Scandinavians from northern Europe, happened on the Atlantic coast of North America.

Given these earlier encounters, is there any special significance to that famous year 1492? Should we drop it from our list of crucial dates and substitute 40,000 BCE or 1000 CE? If we keep 1492, how do we justify it? Did Columbus's landing in the Caribbean have a greater impact on the world than the two earlier events, or does our traditional emphasis simply mark our Europe-centered biases? What did Columbus's discovery mean, both to those in the Old World of Europe, Asia, and Africa and to those already living in the Americas? To answer these questions let us look at the first discovery and its significance.

The Native Americans

The Indian peoples of the Americas were relatively late arrivals from the Old World where the human species evolved. Archeological finds suggest that peoples of several sorts from the Old World may have settled the Americas in remote times, perhaps as far back as 40,000 years ago. Most Indian population descended from these first settlers, but there is evidence that a group of Athapasken-speakers arrived somewhat later and dispersed through western Canada and Alaska. Physically, both groups belonged to the same human stock as the modern Chinese, Japanese, and Koreans. The migrants were people who depended on roots, berries, seeds, fish, and game for food. Perhaps decreasing rainfall and reduced food supplies in their Asian homeland forced them eastward. Today their journey would be blocked by the Bering Sea, but in that distant era of lower sea levels a land bridge joined Alaska to Siberia. Once in North America the migrants moved southward, and within a few thousand years had spread from just below the Arctic Ocean to the stormy southern tip of South America. They had also increased enormously in numbers. From perhaps a few hundred original immigrants, by 1492 the Indian population of the Americas had swelled to some 50 million or more, a figure comparable to that of contemporary Europe.

As their numbers grew over the centuries, the descendants of these people diversified into many groups with distinct languages, cultures, and political and economic systems. By about 3000 BCE some had begun to practice agriculture, with "maize" (corn) as their chief crop and the staple of their diet. They also grew tomatoes, squash, various kinds of beans, and, in South America, potatoes. Surpluses from agriculture transformed Indian life. Abundant food led to larger populations and also to more diverse societies. Classes of priests, warriors, artisans, and chiefs appeared. In the most fertile agricultural regions great civilizations arose with a technological prowess, artistic sophistication, and political complexity comparable to the civilizations of Asia and Europe.

The Great Indian Civilizations.   The Mayan people, creators of one of these Indian civilizations, built great ceremonial and administrative cities in the dense rain forests of Yucatan and Central America. Mayan society was composed of

many separate urban centers, each independent and governed by a group of priests. It also developed a culture of great sophistication: The Mayans alone among the American Indian peoples had a written language and books, and their mathematicians adopted the idea of zero as a number place-holder long before Europeans did.

The Aztecs to the north, in central Mexico, were a more warlike people than the Mayans. Around 1300 CE they settled on the site of what is now Mexico City. Led by powerful rulers, the Aztecs conquered virtually all their neighbors, creating a great empire of more than 5 million inhabitants in central Mexico. In the course of their many wars the Aztec rulers took thousands of prisoners and enormous quantities of feathered headdresses, jade jewelry, and beautiful gold and silver ornaments. The treasure went into the coffers of the rulers and their nobles; the prisoners, by the thousands, had their hearts cut out in public ceremonies to appease the Aztec war god.

Further south, in the Andes mountains of South America, the Incas created an empire that paralleled the Aztec domain to the north. At its height, 7 million people lived within its borders. Strong rulers like the Aztec chiefs, the Inca emperors built fortresses on the mountainsides and a network of roads that held their far-flung Andean state together. The Inca people were among the most skilled metallurgists of the time, making weapons, tools, and ornaments of gold, silver, copper, and bronze. The Inca privileged classes lived comfortably, but the sick and handicapped were also provided for by the government. Inca society has sometimes been compared to a modern social welfare state.

This is a reconstruction of what Cortés and his men saw when they arrived at "the great city of Mexico." The structure at the center of the plaza is the altar where prisoners were sacrificed to the Aztec gods.

The Indians of North America.   North of these great Indian civilizations were less complex, smaller-scale cultures and societies. By 1492 there was a substantial population, perhaps as many as 7 million people, in what is now the United States and Canada. This population was diverse in culture, economy, and social organization. There were twelve distinct language groups in the present-day continental United States, each embracing numerous individual tribes. The various tribes also had differing economies. Some depended on hunting game and gathering food from the forests and meadows. Others cultivated maize, beans, squash, melons, and tobacco. Indian populations were dense in the well-watered eastern third of the future United States and along the Pacific coast. They were sparse in the arid Great Basin and desert areas of the West.

Indian dwellings ranged from tepees of skin-covered poles—the typical homes of the western Plains Indians—to the impressive lodges made of wooden beams covered with bark built by the Iroquois and other eastern woodland peoples. Among the Hurons and many southeastern tribes these structures were often grouped into towns surrounded by stockades. Although some Indian tribes were isolated and self-sufficient, others relied on traders who traveled long distances by canoe on the lakes and rivers to exchange goods with other tribes.

Many tribes sheltered skilled craftspeople who made beautiful pottery, light and swift birchbark canoes, and implements of copper. Others wove a kind of cloth from the inner bark of trees. The people of other tribes, however, lived very simply, with few artifacts. The numerous peoples of California, for example, blessed with a mild climate and abundant food, made do with minimal clothing and crude houses. Only their beautiful basketwork revealed their skills with materials. Typically, in Indian cultures, women were the cultivators, raising the crops that provided most of the food for the agricultural tribes. Men were the hunters and fishers and the warriors in societies that often resorted to war to settle disputes. The key food producing role of Indian women often gave them a higher relative status than their European sisters.

Politically, these peoples varied greatly. The Indians of the Iroquois Confederacy, or Six Nations, were a united and warlike league, the terror of its Indian neighbors and the scourge of later European settlers. On the other hand, the Chippewas of present-day Ohio lived in many small bands that had little in common besides language. Tribal government among them varied widely. The Natchez of the lower Mississippi River Valley were ruled by an absolute despot called the Great Sun, who was chosen collectively by the female Suns when his predecessor died. The Iroquois had a kind of representative political system. Female clan heads elected both the male delegates to the Confederacy council and the sachems, or chiefs, who governed the Six Nations.

Religion was an important aspect of life among virtually all Native Americans. Most believed in an ultimate being, the creator of nature, humankind, and all the good things of life. But, unlike Europeans who believed in one God, Indians held that spiritual forces resided in all living things. Even inanimate natural objects, in their view, were alive, imbued with *manitou*. Human beings were merely one part of the seamless web of live things. Like other religious peoples, they expressed their feelings about the change of seasons, hunting, death, love, and war

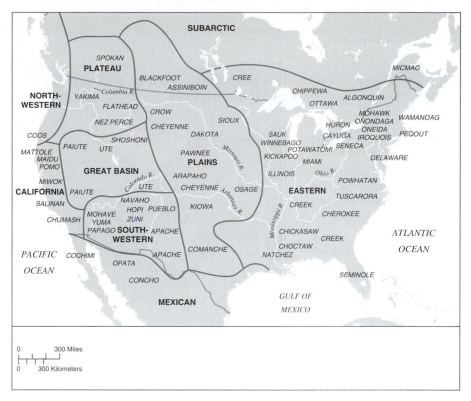

Indian Tribes of North America

in elaborate ceremonies that included dances, songs, feasts, and the wearing of vivid costumes and masks.

The Europeans, who would soon be arriving in North America, held very different views of nature and humankind's place in the natural world. As the Judeo-Christian Bible proclaimed, God had conferred on human beings "dominion over the fish of the sea and over the birds of the air and over every living thing that moves upon the earth." This view of "man the master" was reinforced by the contemporary European theme of raw nature as dangerous, a "wilderness" of threatening animals, insects, poisonous plants, and "savages," a place to be avoided or tamed to man's use. An even more powerful force guiding Europeans in their relations to nature was avarice. Nature represented latent wealth and opportunity for personal riches. To stand in the way of exploiting nature's bounty not only hobbled the enterprising individual but violated the laws of human progress. Associated with these attitudes were European views of property. The white settlers of America believed in exclusive individual possession of land, timber, minerals, and other natural resources and measured status by how much of these a person owned.

While Indians were not incapable of altering nature to meet their needs—their pursuit of big game in the earliest years following migration from Asia may have exterminated the mammoths and wild horses that then occupied the Americas—

they were not driven by a lust for limitless resource-consuming possessions and so were not generally willing to sacrifice present satisfactions for remote future ones. Nor did Native Americans accept the European concept of private land ownership. Land, they believed, belonged to the whole tribe, not the individual. Taken together, these differing attitudes toward nature and property would have significant consequences for future Indian-European relations.

The First European "Discovery"

Europeans first touched the eastern edge of the Americas long before Columbus. According to early Scandinavian sagas, in 986 CE a ship commanded by a Norwegian merchant, Bjarni Herjulfsson, on the way to European-settled Greenland, was driven off course by a storm and narrowly escaped being dashed to pieces on an unfamiliar coast. The land Herjulfsson and his crew encountered—probably Newfoundland or Labrador—was covered with "forests and low hills." The Europeans were not interested in this new land and did not disembark. When they finally reached Greenland, however, they reported their discovery to others.

Ever on the lookout for new lands to settle, other Scandinavians soon followed up on Herjulfsson's lead. In the year 1000, Leif Ericsson, a founder of the Greenland colony, sailed westward to investigate the reports of the new country. He and his party found it relatively warm, densely forested, with streams that overflowed with salmon. Finding what they later described as grapes, and hoping perhaps to encourage settlement, they dubbed the new country Vinland (Wineland) the Good.

Would-be Norse settlers followed Leif Ericsson to Vinland. In 1010 or thereabouts, three boatloads of Greenlanders set out to establish permanent communities in North America. Indian attacks drove them away, but the Norse apparently made other efforts to colonize the new country. In 1960 archaeologists discovered the remains of a small Norse village at L'Anse aux Meadows in northern Newfoundland. The find confirmed for the first time the sagas of medieval Scandinavian exploration. But the simple structures and the primitive tools uncovered also suggest how feeble and limited the Norse colonizing effort was.

Some garbled knowledge of the Norse discoveries spread to other parts of Europe. Yet nothing happened. The first European contact with the Americas simply did not "take." Europe quickly forgot the eleventh-century Norse voyages to North America. It was as if they had never taken place.

The Rise of Modern Europe

The isolation of the Americas, of course, did not last. The Old World eventually intruded into the New, and within a few generations the contact between these two different worlds completely transformed both. To the people of Europe this contact with the Americas seemed a "discovery"; actually, it was a meeting. As one scholar has written: "Columbus did not discover a new world; he established contact between two worlds already old."

Medieval Europe.   Why did Europe fail to follow up on the Norse voyages of the eleventh century? Why did it respond differently after 1492? What had happened during the centuries separating Leif Ericsson from Columbus to change the way Europeans reacted to the momentous meeting of the two worlds?

Eight hundred years before the Norse voyages, the Roman Empire had joined all parts of the Western European world into a peaceful, prosperous, civilized whole. Then, during the period 500–700 BCE the Germanic invasions, the Muslim conquest of the southern and eastern Mediterranean, and the devastating attacks on settled Europe by the Scandinavian Vikings brought turmoil to the continent. Europeans turned to barons, armed nobles, to protect life and property within their castles against raiders and brigands. Before long, however, the barons themselves became the source of disorder as they battled one another for land and power. By the eighth or ninth century all long-range travel and trade within Europe and between Europe and other parts of the world had become unsafe. Goods, except for a few high-profit luxury items, ceased to move over the Roman roads left over from ancient times, or along now pirate-infested sea routes.

Not surprisingly, Europe declined in wealth. Italy retained its cities and trade, but elsewhere each small neighborhood was forced to become self-sufficient. By the year 1000, particularly north of the Alps, a fragmented, localized economic system had replaced the unified, complex organization of the Roman Empire. Europe was now poor, politically divided, beset by local wars and civil disorder, its people largely illiterate and unfree. Each nobleman's estate or manor—with its castle or manor house, peasants' village, and surrounding fields—had to provide all the food, implements, and other commodities it needed. With each manor supplying its own needs, there was little reason to produce a surplus or find new ways to increase the output of crops or other goods. Cities that had once been great centers of commerce and industry declined, with many disappearing entirely.

Most Europeans during this era were unfree peasants or serfs. Like farm animals, they went with the land when it was passed on from one baron to another through inheritance or conquest. In return for the right to till the soil, the peasant family gave the lord of the manor part of its crop plus various other payments in the form of work. Money seldom changed hands. Instead, exchanges and obligations were discharged through crops, animals, or services. Illiterate, superstitious, and often malnourished, as well as exploited, the serfs of Europe were a severe brake on economic change.

Even during the darkest of the "Dark Ages" Europe retained a small merchant class. But in the centuries from 700 to 1000 these traders wielded little economic power and suffered from low social status. Neither serfs nor priests nor feudal lords, they did not fit into the medieval social order, which presupposed a rural society composed of tilling peasants, praying clergymen, and fighting noblemen. Nor did Roman Catholicism, the religion of virtually all Western Europeans, find commerce and merchants congenial. The Church held that all economic relations must be subject to moral guidelines and was suspicious of those who looked only to profits. These attitudes undoubtedly reinforced the economic backwardness of Europe.

By the year 1000, Europe had disintegrated politically as well as economically. Kings reigned in France, England, Portugal, and other realms, but they were not like later monarchs. They did not have armies, navies, or corps of civil servants. Instead, they relied on their vassals—the feudal nobility—to supply them with men and arms in emergencies and to administer the customary law in their districts. Nor did the monarchs of this era have large financial resources. No European kingdom imposed uniform national taxes. Although theoretically supreme, kings were often inferior in wealth and power to one or more of the feudal lords who supposedly owed them allegiance.

The one institution that held Western Europe together during the early Middle Ages was the Roman Catholic Church. Retaining many features of the Roman imperial government—the Latin language, a corps of literate officials, and a supreme head, the pope, residing in Rome—the Church preserved many of the values and much of the culture and organizational skill of the ancient world. Possessing a virtual monopoly of literacy, priests and church officials provided essential services to kings and nobles as scribes and administrators. But the medieval church was no substitute for powerful secular rulers.

Nor was the Church's learning as useful for practical affairs as it might have been. Indeed, its attention to the salvation of the individual's soul focused Europeans' minds on the afterlife rather than on worldly matters. This emphasis discouraged the creative curiosity about nature and the physical world felt by men and women of ancient times.

In the year 1000, in short, Europe could not rise to the challenge of the new-found world to the west. It did not have the economic or technical resources, the political and social cohesion, or even the interest to do so. The disorganized, politically feeble, largely illiterate Europe of Leif Ericsson's time was incapable of responding to the Norse encounter with America.

The Lure of the East.   Five hundred years later, when Columbus returned from the Caribbean to report the discovery of a new route to "the Indies," Europe reacted powerfully and decisively. The continent's response reflected the remarkable revival of trade and commerce in the half millennium between Leif Ericsson and Columbus. This revival would eventually undermine feudalism and the self-sufficient manor-based economy on which it rested.

In part the change followed contact with the Islamic civilization that rimmed the eastern, southern, and western shores of the Mediterranean Sea. For centuries Western Christians were content with their limited knowledge and rough material sufficiency. But then, at the very end of the eleventh century, thousands of Europeans set out as Crusaders for Palestine to recover the Holy Sepulcher, Jesus' tomb, from the Muslim "infidels" who occupied the Holy Land. After the Crusaders captured Jerusalem in 1099, Europeans settled in the newly conquered Levant on the eastern edge of the Mediterranean. Compared with the rude commodities of France, England, and Germany, the silks, cotton, spices, cabinetwork, pottery, and weapons of the Muslims were marvels of delicacy and sophistication. Many Europeans appreciated the skills and artistry of Muslim craftsmen, developed a taste for sugar, silks, fine leatherwork, and other luxury goods of the Islamic world and came to respect Muslim science and philosophy. This was the beginning of a change in European attitudes and an awakening to the opportunities of commercial relations with distant lands and cultures.

Even more intriguing than the civilization of Islam were the riches of the distant Orient. By the eleventh century a lucrative trade had sprung up between Europe and remote China and India. Italian textiles, arms, and armor, along with north European copper, lead, and tin, moved eastward to these destinations; silk, jewels, and spices came westward in return. Asian merchants—Chinese, East Indians, and Arabs—handled the first leg of the trade to the West. The final phase to Europe's consumers was conducted largely by Italians from Venice and Genoa. Their immense profits soon made the Venetians and Genoese the envy of other European traders.

The most important sector of this East–West exchange was the spice trade. In the Middle Ages spices seemed indispensable to civilized living. They retarded decay, relieved the blandness of daily fare, and disguised the poor quality of unrefrigerated meat. Europeans used many locally grown herbs to flavor their food, but none of these could compare to pepper, cloves, nutmeg, and cinnamon, which came from India, Ceylon, and the "Spice Islands" of present-day Indonesia.

The revival of long-distance trade was accompanied by a change in European attitudes toward money and money-makers. Monarchs and nobles learned they could no longer afford to revile and oppress traders for they were now rich capitalists whose wealth might be needed to pay debts or procure arms. New rules granted merchants privileges and provided them with protection. Before long the Church relaxed its ban against charging interest for lending money. Banking soon became both a respectable and a highly profitable enterprise.

The contact with the East also helped break down the self-sufficient manorial system. The nobility soon acquired a passion for the luxuries of Islam and the Orient. But to buy them they needed cash, and cash, in an era when almost all economic relations were based on payment in locally produced commodities or in services, was scarce. The need for cash soon changed these economic relations. Now serfs might be permitted to buy their freedom and purchase land and become independent freeholders. Meanwhile, up-to-date nobles tried to improve their own cultivation methods to guarantee a surplus that they could sell for money in the growing towns. By the thirteenth or fourteenth century the revival of trade had led to the breakdown of the manorial system in many parts of Western Europe and the disappearance of serfdom.

The revival of trade also encouraged the growth of cities and the flowering of urban life. As trade returned, new cities sprang up and old ones expanded. Former serfs flocked to the towns with their markets, warehouses, docks, and shops to work for wages, as laborers, artisans, and craftsmen, and to enjoy the greater freedom and variety of city life. Besides the older centers of Italy, newer towns arose along the Baltic and North seas to distribute the goods of the East and to serve the growing commerce of northern Europe.

The Nation-State.   The urban merchant class was a powerful force for change in early modern Europe. The burghers, or bourgeoisie (from *burgh* or *bourg*, meaning "town"), were natural foes of the unruly barons whose constant wars made travel unsafe and who levied expensive tolls on trade. What the burghers wanted was peace, order, and economic unity to permit goods and people to move safely and freely over long distances. Only a friendly and powerful central authority could ensure such conditions.

The interests of the merchants made them the natural allies of feudal kings. And the kings quickly found uses for the merchants. They were the source of borrowed money needed to impose internal order and support challenges to the king from other rulers. Their literacy could free monarchs from reliance on priests and bishops as administrators. The revival of trade and subsequent creation of a money economy made it possible to impose national taxes. Before long, the modern nation-state, with its dedicated civil servants, its armies and navies, and its capacity to mobilize capital and resources to achieve national goals, had emerged in place of the disjointed, hidebound, feeble feudal kingdoms of the past.

These political changes had immense implications for European relations with the rest of the world. The new nation-states were powerful instruments of European policy and ambition. The new rulers could marshal, organize, and focus large forces to serve European ends and project these forces thousands of miles across the seas. In quest of wealth, the new centralized national states would finance exploration and conquest. Their early successes would reinforce the expansion process until it came to feed on itself.

Revolutions in Thought and Communication.   Intellectual and cultural shifts also made 1492 different from 1000 CE. People in the Middle Ages had little sense of historical change. To medieval Christians all that had preceded the birth of Jesus was a prelude to that great event; all that followed was a long epilogue that would culminate in Christ's Second Coming and the "end of days." Before about 1300 CE Europeans gave the ancients little credit for their contributions to civilization and, in fact, knew little about them. Then, in fourteenth-century Italy, scholars began to discover that the Greeks and Romans knew many things that they did not. This new realization was probably sparked by the interchange with Greek-speaking Constantinople and the Muslim Mediterranean world, which had preserved and translated many ancient Greek and Latin authors and thinkers. It was reinforced by the discovery of hundreds of ancient manuscripts hidden in monasteries, churches, and libraries for almost a thousand years.

The new contact with classical antiquity was a wonderfully stimulating experience. Encountering a new civilization, even one long dead, made European culture richer and more complex. At the same time it gave Europeans a new confidence in their own society and in themselves. The ancients were great and creative people, surely, but their achievements were not beyond reach of the moderns.

The interest in history and literature inspired by contact with the Greek and Roman world (the new "humanism") secularized the way many people thought; that is, it deflected their attention from religion and salvation toward the things of this world. The humanism of the era we call the Renaissance was not the irreligious, materialistic, and pleasure-obsessed set of attitudes we once believed it was. But it did create new concern with the laws of physical nature and new appreciation of the beauties of form, color, and line.

The new attitudes were immeasurably helped by the invention of printing. In ancient and medieval times books had to be copied laboriously by hand and so were scarce and expensive. By the end of the Middle Ages the revival of trade had created a new class of literate men and women, but the high cost of recording people's thoughts and experiences inevitably slowed the spread of ideas and knowledge. Then, in the middle of the fifteenth century, Johann Gutenberg of Mainz, Germany perfected a way to print pages from movable type, and the new technique soon spread throughout Europe. By 1500, about 1,000 printers were working in the trade, and they had published 30,000 separate book titles in some 6 million copies.

Many of these books were devoted to religion, but there were also scientific works, books on navigation, and numerous accounts of discoveries in the Far East and West. Columbus's description of his first voyage to the "Indies" was quickly printed and widely circulated and read. The new, inexpensive printed book created a large audience for new information and guaranteed that Europeans would not forget America a second time.

New Technology.   Advances in navigation and naval architecture also helped Europe exploit its encounter with the Americas after 1492. In the year 1000 the Norse captains had located their position on the open sea by sighting the sun with the naked eye and guessing their speed through the water. By 1492 Europeans had adopted the compass, consisting of a magnetized needle attracted to the north magnetic pole attached to a card marked with directions. Now a ship captain could calculate his direction even when the pole star was obscured by clouds and pinpoint his location more accurately than by sighting the sun. By the fifteenth century, European navigators were also beginning to calculate latitude with the quadrant and astrolabe.

Improvements in navigation were accompanied by advances in ship design. The merchant ship of medieval Europe was a tubby vessel with a rudder at the side and a single, large square sail useful only when the wind blew directly from behind. Gradually these ships were modified to carry adjustable sails and mount their rudders at the stern. Now, by "tacking"—following a zigzag course toward one's destination—vessels could sail without the wind directly at the rear. Faster, more maneuverable, and more stable ship types such as caravels, carracks, and galleons also expanded Europe's reach. These nautical changes gave Europeans the equipment needed to undertake long ocean voyages with relative confidence.

One more innovation was needed before Europeans were equipped to subdue the world: gunpowder. First used to propel missiles from cannons early in the fourteenth century, it was mostly employed in siege operations against walled cities. Cannon were soon installed aboard ships as well. With time, guns were miniaturized so that by 1360 soldiers could wield primitive handheld small arms. When combined with the horse, pike, metal armor, and steel sword, these weapons would prove devastating against the native peoples of the Americas.

European Expansion

By the 1400s, fueled by advances in navigation, trade, and the rise of the bourgeoisie and nation-state, Europeans were launched on a campaign to explore the world and make contact with other lands and peoples. The quest began with the

A Portuguese galleon, of the sort that enabled Europeans to conquer the oceans and helped create the Portuguese empire in the sixteenth century. The gun ports on the sides and stern are realistic in this contemporary engraving, but the men on deck—and the fish—are exaggerated in size.

effort of Prince Henry of Portugal, later known as Henry the Navigator, to seek out new lands to the south and west of Europe. Henry was not a fully modern man impelled by curiosity or hope of profits. Rather, his chief concern was to find the legendary Christian kingdom of Prester John and reunite him and his people with the main body of Christendom.

To advance his goals Henry financed a program of exploration along the Atlantic coast of Africa. Each year ships left Portugal to venture ever farther south, their captains spurred on by Henry's financial rewards for progress. By 1445 Dinis Dias had rounded Cape Verde and reached the humid, fertile part of the African coast below the Sahara. Ten years later Alvise da Cadamosto sighted the Senegal and Gambia rivers and discovered the Cape Verde Islands.

After Henry's death his work was taken over by the kings of Portugal who now focused their efforts on finding an all-sea route to India, Cathay (China), and Xipangu (Japan) that would pass around the southern end of the African continent and cross the Indian Ocean. If the Portuguese could bypass the Italian and Muslim middlemen, who controlled the land routes, and go to the source of the precious products of Asia, all the profits of trade would be theirs.

In 1488 Bartolomeu Dias finally rounded the tip of the African continent. Encouraged by Dias's report, Vasco da Gama set out from Portugal for India in July 1497. The following May his four ships arrived at Calicut, where he collected a valuable cargo of pepper, ginger, cloves, and cinnamon. He returned home safely in 1499, the first European to sail directly from Europe to India and back.

Once opened, the route around Africa became a busy thoroughfare. To expedite the trade in spices, silks, drugs, and other precious goods, the Portuguese established trading posts in Africa, along the Malabar coast of India, in Ceylon, and on the islands of Indonesia. The Portuguese commercial empire soon expanded to the western Pacific. By 1550 the small Atlantic nation had established a virtual monopoly of the European spice trade.

Columbus and the Spanish Explorations.

The success of the Portuguese aroused the envy of the rulers of Europe's other new nation-states. Eventually the Dutch, the French, and the English would challenge Portugal's stranglehold on the all-water Eastern spice trade around Africa. But meanwhile, a Genoese adventurer and visionary named Cristoforo Colombo (Christopher Columbus) had arrived at an alternative that not only promised a shorter route to the East but also seemed likely to avoid a direct confrontation with the Portuguese. Columbus's scheme was simple, though based on false premises. Only a narrow body of water, he believed, lay between Europe and the Indies. So a ship sailing west, after only a few weeks, should reach Asia and its riches.

After unsuccessfully peddling his idea to every prince of Western Europe, Columbus finally caught the interest of Ferdinand of Aragon and Isabella of Castile. The joint rulers of Spain had just concluded a centuries-long crusade to push the Muslim "Moors" out of the Iberian peninsula and were looking for new worlds to conquer. Pledging her jewels as security, Isabella borrowed from a Spanish religious order some of the money Columbus needed. The rest came from the small city of Palos, whose burghers, as punishment for an infraction of Spanish law, she ordered to supply "the Admiral" with three small vessels. The total cost of the expedition was about 2 million maravedis (today about $50,000), a great fortune that could not have been gathered for such a purpose 500 years earlier, in Norse times. With this sum Columbus fitted out his three small ships and on August 3, 1492, he and his crew of ninety left Palos. They arrived at the Caribbean island of San Salvador ten weeks later, almost exactly five centuries after the first European had sighted North America (though they believed they had reached the Indies).

Columbus's first voyage was followed by three others, each better equipped than the first. The "Admiral of the Ocean Sea" explored the Caribbean, surveyed its major islands, and touched the mainland of the Americas at several points. He also established the first permanent European communities in the New World. Columbus's expeditions were followed by many more whose leaders established European settlements on the Caribbean islands. From these settlements in turn Spanish commanders launched expeditions to the mainland. One of these, under Vasco Nuñez de Balboa, crossed the Isthmus of Panama in 1513, its members becoming the first Europeans to see the eastern shore of the Pacific Ocean.

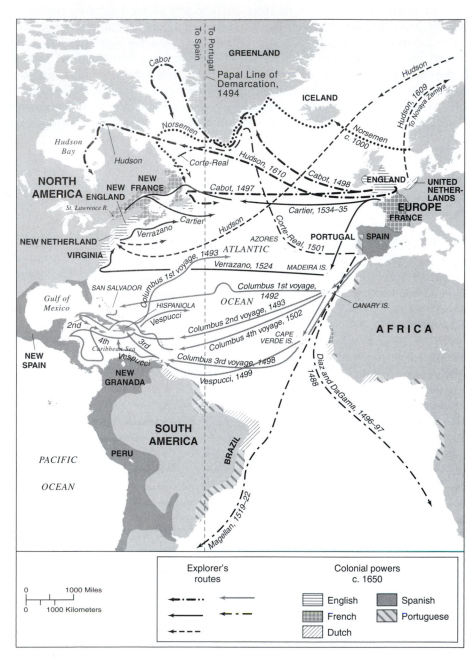

Voyages of Exploration

Having discovered new lands between Europe and Asia, Spain did not abandon hope of finding an all-water route to the Far East. In 1519 the Spanish crown sent the Portuguese navigator Ferdinand Magellan to find a way around the Americas. Sailing south, in November 1520, Magellan discovered the stormy strait at the southern tip of South America that bears his name, sailed through it, and launched his small fleet onto the vast Pacific. Months later, after harrowing experiences with hunger, scurvy, and thirst, he arrived in the Philippines, off the Asian mainland. There he was killed in a skirmish with the natives. Eventually one of his vessels reached Spain by sailing westward around Africa. Though the route was far too long to be practical for the Europe–Asia trade, Magellan's voyage proved that the Americas were not part of the Indies. It was also the first circumnavigation of the globe, a milestone for humankind.

Spain Encounters the Indian Civilizations.   Spain's bounding energies soon made it master of the two new continents its explorers had encountered. In 1519 Hernando Cortés set out from Cuba with 600 men, 17 horses, and 10 cannons, landed at present-day Veracruz, and marched overland to the Aztec capital of Tenochtitlán (Mexico City). The Aztec ruler, Moctezuma II, believed that the invaders were gods returned to the world of men. His warriors, moreover, were startled and demoralized by the Spaniards' strange horses and firearms. Taking advantage of this combination of trust and fear, the Spaniards seized Moctezuma and plundered the overflowing Aztec treasury. After Moctezuma's death, his successors sought to rally the people of Mexico against the invaders, but few Indian nations, unwilling to aid their Aztec oppressors, would cooperate. The final blow to Aztec hopes was a devastating epidemic of smallpox caught from the Europeans. By 1521 all resistance was over. The mighty Aztec empire had fallen to a few hundred Europeans.

The conquest of Mexico was soon followed by the fall of the Inca empire in Peru. The conquistador this time was Francisco Pizarro, a young man of lowly Spanish birth, who, while in Panama, had heard of a rich native empire along the Pacific coast of South America. In 1532, after a 45-day climb up the high wall of the Andes from the coast, Pizarro and his 102 men and 62 horses reached the frontier of Peru. The Inca ruler, Atahualpa, confident of his own strength, allowed them to advance unchecked. When he finally met the Europeans, they attacked, cut down 5,000 Indian warriors, and took the Inca emperor prisoner. The royal captive offered the Spaniards a roomful of silver and gold to buy his freedom. Pizarro accepted. Then, with the treasure safely in his hands, he had Atahualpa bound to a stake and strangled. Inca resistance continued for some time after this, but over the next few years the Europeans extended their control over the whole of the vast Inca domain, from modern Colombia to what is now central Chile.

The conquest of the third great existing Native-American civilization, the Mayans, was slower and less dramatic. There was no single Mayan state whose collapse would assure Spanish rule. Not until about 1550 were the Mayan communities of middle America subjugated and placed firmly under the control of the Spanish king. The last great native civilization of the Americas was now gone.

Meanwhile Spanish explorers, priests, soldiers, and settlers—moved by greed, curiosity, ambition, and Christian zeal to save souls—pushed their reconnaissance of the Americas into what is now the United States. In 1565 they established the first European settlement on the North American mainland at St. Augustine, in present-day Florida. Thirty years later Don Juan de Oñate, moving north from Mexico, brought settlers to present-day New Mexico. In 1609 these European colonists founded the city of Santa Fe.

Spain's Rivals.

By 1600 Spain had conquered virtually all of Central and South America except for Brazil. This eastward extension of South America had been awarded to Portugal by the Treaty of Tordesillas in 1494, which, with the sanction of the Pope, divided the non-European world between the two Iberian nations.

At first Spain's claims in America were unchallenged. Gold and silver confiscated from the Indians poured into Spain, soon joined by additional streams of precious metals from newly opened mines in Peru and Mexico. From 1500 to 1650 Spain extracted almost 20,000 tons of silver and 200 tons of gold from its American colonies. In addition, cocoa, tobacco, dyes, and other American products found ready markets throughout Europe, providing another source of Spanish income. All this New World bounty made Spain the richest and most powerful nation in Europe.

But the Spanish monopoly could not last indefinitely. Other European rulers questioned the pope's decision to divide the non-European world between Spain and Portugal. As the French king Francis I remarked to the Spanish ambassador in 1540, "The sun shone for him as for others," and where, he wondered, in "Adam's will" had the Americas been divided between Spain and its Iberian neighbor?

England was the first northern European country to join the scramble for a share in the New World. In 1496 King Henry VII authorized a Venetian captain, John Cabot, to sail west "to seeke out, discouer, and finde whatsoeuer isles, countryes, regions or prouinces of the heathens and infidels whatsoeuer they be. . . ." Cabot made two voyages to North America, sighting either Nova Scotia or Newfoundland, and sailing down the Atlantic coast as far as the Delaware or Chesapeake bays. The English government did not follow up on these voyages, but Cabot's report of codfish in Newfoundland waters attracted many fishermen from France and England to the area. More important, his voyages became the basis for English claims to North American territory.

France joined the quest for overseas wealth in 1524, when Francis I dispatched the Florentine mariner Giovanni da Verrazano to find a more practical sea route to the Far East than Magellan's. Verrazano touched land probably somewhere along the Carolina coast and sailed north as far as Nova Scotia fruitlessly seeking a gap to the Pacific in the North American continent. Later Francis sent mariner Jacques Cartier on a similar quest. On his first voyage to America Cartier explored the coasts of Newfoundland, Prince Edward Island, and the Gaspé Peninsula. On a second voyage he sailed up the St. Lawrence River to the site of present-day Montreal. Cartier's voyages, of course, did not reveal the long-sought sea route to Asia , but they gave France a claim to part of North America.

The Dutch began exploring America relatively late. By the beginning of the seventeenth century most of modern Holland had achieved autonomy from Spain and was developing into a prosperous country dominated by aggressive merchants and bankers. In 1609 a group of these capitalists, joined as partners in the Dutch East India Company, hired Henry Hudson, an English sea captain, to find the elusive water route to the Far East through North America. Hudson failed to find this "Northwest Passage," but he added to Europe's geographical knowledge and Holland's claim to part of North America by sailing down the Atlantic coast from Newfoundland to Virginia. During this trip Hudson explored Cape Cod and Delaware Bay and sailed partway up the broad river that now bears his name.

These expeditions were only a small part of the sixteenth- and early seventeenth-century exploration of the Americas. There were scores of other expeditions along every coast and into every accessible bay, inlet, and navigable river of the two western continents. Meanwhile, Spanish captains like Hernando de Soto and Francisco Vásquez de Coronado, and the Frenchman Samuel de Champlain, pushed overland deep into the heartland of North America. By about 1650 Europeans knew the essential outlines of the two New World continents and had even learned much about their remote interiors.

The Columbian Exchange

Writing in 1552 the Spanish historian Francisco López de Gómara claimed "the greatest event since the creation of the world (excluding the incarnation and the death of Him who created it) is the "discovery" of the Indies." If we discount the word "discovery" and allow for some exaggeration, López was correct: Few if any events have so changed the history of the world as the encounter of Europeans and Native Americans at the end of the fifteenth century. The resulting interaction of culture, products, ideas, and diseases—the "Columbian Exchange"—altered human destiny.

In Central and South America, Europeans quickly swept away all traces of Indian self-rule, save for a few remote interior regions. North of Mexico the process of conquest was slower but no less thorough. Vicious warfare against the Indians was part of the history of every European colonial power. At times, the kings of Spain, France, and England sought to protect their new Indian subjects. Friars, priests, and ministers sometimes denounced the cruel treatment of the Native Americans. Yet even when Europeans refrained from outright murder, they treated the native peoples harshly. In the Spanish colonies Indians were enslaved and sometimes worked to death. Well into the nineteenth century Indians in Spanish-held lands remained "peons" whose lot resembled that of medieval serfs. In the English colonies the more nomadic North American tribes generally escaped forced labor only by slipping away into the forest.

Contact with Europeans injured the native peoples even when whites intended no harm. Because of their long geographic separation, humans of the Old and the New Worlds had developed immunities to different diseases. As a result, neither people could fend off the infections of the other. Europeans encountered a virulent form of syphilis in America, and it quickly spread over all of Europe. Thousands broke out in horrible sores and died before anyone knew how to deal with the malady. The Indians suffered far more. Even European childhood diseases such as measles became killing scourges among populations without protective antibodies in their blood. Smallpox, too, along with tuberculosis and cholera, hit the native populations hard. In Mexico the 25 million Indians of 1519 were reduced, primarily by disease, to 2.5 million by 1600. Along the Atlantic coast of North America a similar grim process took place. In 1656 Adriaen Van der Donck reported that the Indians of New Netherland, the Dutch colony, claimed "that before the arrival of the Christians, and before the small pox broke out amongst them, they were ten times as numerous as they now are. . . ." Indeed, the English and Dutch occupations of the eastern coast were greatly facilitated by the European plagues that had spread to North America from the south and decimated the native population even before the Europeans themselves appeared on the scene.

Disease was only part of the damage that Europeans inflicted on Indian societies. In many areas, especially drier regions, native agriculture was destroyed by the great herds of sheep and cattle the conquerors introduced. European manufactures swamped native crafts and undermined native skills. European "fire water"—brandy, wine, whisky—created serious alcoholic dependence among many. Even efforts to implant the Christian faith often did harm. The European missionaries hoped to benefit the Indians by bringing them the blessings of Christianity. Some friars and priests won converts by their example of humility, kindness, and courage; others, however, fiercely attacked every aspect of the Indians' religion. Bishop Diego de Landa of Yucatán destroyed thousands of Mayan books in his effort to root out the sin of idolatry, impoverishing both the Mayans themselves and our knowledge of their civilization and history.

Europe Benefits.   The transatlantic encounter after 1492 was no less momentous for Europeans than for Native Americans. But the effects were almost diametrically opposite. With few exceptions (such as the scourge of syphilis), the contact between the Americas and Europe benefited Europe dramatically. Its fabulous treasure from the Americas catapulted Spain into the first rank of European powers. Simultaneously, the deluge of American gold and silver stimulated European trade, commerce, and industry. Rising prices produced by the influx of precious metals further weakened the feudal system by accelerating the conversion of labor services into cash payments. The treasure also provided national rulers with enormous new incomes, giving them and the nation-state an additional edge over unruly and disobedient vassals. Finally, the events following 1492 accelerated the rise to wealth and influence of the merchant-capitalists who entered the American trade. In short, the "discovery" of America speeded the "modernization" of Europe that was already underway when Columbus sailed from Palos.

The transatlantic contact also provided Europeans with an enormously expanded and improved diet. Potatoes and Indian corn would eventually become staples consumed by millions of Europeans. Tomatoes, pumpkins, a wide assortment of beans, and many new fruits were also brought eastward to be widely grown in Europe. Rubber and chicle (the raw material for chewing gum) were other useful American borrowings. Not all the plant imports were seen as blessings: Some would consider tobacco almost as serious a scourge as syphilis, and

Syphilis fell like a scourge on Europe shortly after Columbus returned from the New World. It was the real "Montezuma's Revenge." The picture of a victim was drawn by the German artist Albrecht Dürer in 1496.

there are those who have their doubts about chicle. Yet it is clear that America was a botanical, as well as a mineral, treasure trove.

The New World also influenced the intellectual climate of Europe. The relative ease with which Europeans conquered the New World peoples encouraged European arrogance—on the theory, apparently, that strength and ferocity equaled virtue. After observing the Aztecs' mass sacrifices of war captives, the Spanish were certain that the native religions were bloodthirsty superstitions. But not all Europeans found their prejudices reinforced. Some felt wonder at the variety of the world's cultures. Some saw Native Americans as "noble savages" living in the same state of simplicity and grace that Adam and Eve had enjoyed in the Garden of Eden. It is not surprising that the first modern utopia was conceived by Sir Thomas More in 1516, soon after the Spanish discoveries. This contact with new cultures widened Europe's horizons and produced new fields of knowledge and new intellectual disciplines, including the predecessors of anthropology and sociology.

Conclusions

We focus on 1492 as the date of America's discovery for several good reasons then. One of these, no doubt, is that we tend to accept a Europe-centered view of the world. But from any cultural perspective, Columbus's landing at San Salvador in 1492 was a transforming event. For the millions living in the Americas, the change was a social disaster marked by disease, misery, bondage, and cultural disintegration. For Europe as a whole, 1492 marked the beginning of a new era of geographic, intellectual, and economic expansion.

By 1500 Europeans were also about to embark on the greatest mass migration of all time, one that would eventually pull 100 million humans westward across the Atlantic. We have seen something of the "forces" that led to this momentous occurrence. Let us now consider the personal motives that impelled countless ordinary (and not-so-ordinary), individuals to risk their lives and their fortunes to create new communities in the strange lands across the ocean.

ONLINE RESOURCES

"Spanish Exploration and Conquest of Native America" *http://www.floridahistory.com* Containing text and analysis of conquest records, maps, and illustrations, this site explores the movements and experiences of the Spanish conquistadors. It also offers an in-depth look at the impact Spanish exploration had on the Native-American population.

"Hippocrates on the Web: Plagues and Peoples: The Columbian Exchange" *http://www. umanitoba.ca/faculties/medicine/history/histories/plagues.html* Read the words of sixteenth- and seventeenth-century Europeans and Native Americans describing the devastating impact of disease.

Feudal Life in Europe *http://www.learner.org/exhibits/middleages/feudal.html* A good review of life in Medieval Europe before Columbus.

The Norse in the North Atlantic *http://www.heritage.nf.ca/exploration/norse.html* A good review of the Norse Voyages before Cabot, including the Vin land discovery and attempted settlement. Includes maps and pictures.

2

The Old World Comes to America

What Brought Europeans and Africans to the New World?

1517–21	Martin Luther launches the Protestant Reformation
1527–39	Henry VIII of England defies the pope and declares himself head of a new Church of England
1577	Elizabeth I of England privately begins to promote exploration and colonization in America
1587–88	Sir Walter Raleigh founds England's first American settlement on Roanoke Island
1607	The London Company establishes the first permanent English settlement at Jamestown
1619	The first Africans in British North America arrive at Jamestown; The House of Burgesses is established as Virginia's legislature
1620	The Pilgrims settle at Plymouth on Cape Cod Bay
1624	The Dutch establish New Netherland in the Hudson Valley
1629	Puritans receive a charter for Massachusetts Bay Colony
1632	Lord Baltimore is granted a charter to found Maryland
1635	Roger Williams establishes Rhode Island at Providence
1636	Bostonian Thomas Hooker founds a colony at Hartford, Connecticut; Dissenter Anne Hutchinson is banished from Massachusetts
1664	New Netherland becomes the English colony of New York
1681	William Penn receives a charter to found the Quaker colony of Pennsylvania
1701	East Jersey and West Jersey are united as a single province
1701–03	Delaware is separated from Pennsylvania and becomes a separate colony
1732	James Oglethorpe founds Georgia as refuge for English debtors

As we have seen, North America was not an empty continent when Columbus first stumbled on San Salvador in the Caribbean in October 1492. Yet today the Indian population of the United States represents only a small percentage of the total; the rest are descendants of men and women who crossed the oceans from some part of the Old World after 1492.

Immigration to America is one of the great sagas of world history and a central part of our national experience, lasting for hundreds of years, and continuing today. Here, we will consider the first wave of Old World settlement that began in the early seventeenth century and continued to American independence in the 1770s.

Early explorers of the Americas by sea often claimed they had found an earthly paradise, a "fruitful and delightsome" land with "most sweet savours" wafting from its shores. But most ordinary Europeans apparently took these descriptions with a large grain of salt. Repelled by raw, untamed nature, many perceived America, with its vast gloomy forests, its wild beasts, and its painted "savages," a dubious place to make a new home. Besides, there was the ordeal of getting there. During the two to four months the average transatlantic passage took in the seventeenth and eighteenth centuries, crews and passengers were packed into tiny ships, confined below deck in bad weather, and fed on salt meat, worm-infested ship's biscuit, and foul water. "Ship fever," a form of typhus, frequently raged through these vessels, carrying off old and young alike. During the age of sail, thousands went to watery graves without ever seeing their new homeland. As for America's great potential resources, finding and successfully exploiting them was both risky and time-consuming.

Yet despite the dangers, the discomforts, and the uncertainties, both promoters and settlers staked their money and their lives on the gamble of America. Promoters conceived, organized, financed, and led expeditions to the coast of North America and then guided them through their formative years. Settlers, both men and women, actually risked themselves personally, contributing to new colonies with their own lives. What moved these people? Was their goal wealth? Did they crave adventure? Were they seeking prestige? Were they primarily in quest of religious or political freedom?

The Aristocratic Impulse

Many early colony promoters were driven by the desire for glory, adventure, status, and power. England about the year 1600 was full of young gentlemen and aristocrats who found life at home uninteresting and confining. Under the English laws of primogeniture ("the first born"), the eldest son of a "gentle" family alone inherited his father's estate and the family title if any. Younger sons turned to the army or the professions; others, swallowing the typical disdain of "gentlemen" for mere trade, entered business. Still others sought out rich wives. None of these alternatives fully compensated for the accident of being born in the wrong birth order, and by the early years of the seventeenth century many younger sons had begun to look to America to escape their limitations at home. They often envisioned a New World version of England as it once was, where they might reign as feudal noblemen amidst the trappings of chivalry and hereditary privilege.

The English gentleman of this period did not enjoy soiling his hands with physical labor. He also typically disdained the bourgeois virtues of prudence, patience, and frugality and valued and cultivated boldness, passion, and openhanded hospitality. Such men saw exploration and colonization of the New World as a bold adventure.

The Roanoke Attempt.   The noble promoters of English settlement in America learned too slowly that successful colonization required more substantial virtues than aristocratic gallantry and courage. In 1587 Sir Walter Raleigh sent an expedition to present-day North Carolina under the immediate command of John White. Women and children went along, but the enterprise included a large group of gentlemen with coats of arms to identify them and their descendants as members of the new feudal aristocracy to be established in America.

The colonists arrived at Roanoke Island off North Carolina too late to plant a crop and had to rely on the Indians for food. White went back to England for supplies soon after the birth in the colony of his granddaughter, Virginia Dare. His return to America was delayed by Spain's dispatch of the Spanish Armada to conquer England. When White finally returned to the small settlement he found no survivors. The English had disappeared, apparently killed by the local Indians, who probably had lost patience with the Europeans' dependence on them.

Aristocratic Entrepreneurs.   The aristocratic yearning for adventure and disdain for work continued to handicap English colonists long after Raleigh's failure. The first permanent English settlement in North America, established at Jamestown in 1607, for instance, would also suffer from the idleness of gentlemen more interested in finding gold, carving out personal estates, or despoiling the Indians than in clearing the land, raising crops, and founding self-sustaining communities. Still, we must not dismiss the contribution of aristocratic impulses to settlement of the New World. In a number of colonies royal charters conferred on a "proprietor" the powers of a great feudal lord. The 1632 royal charter for Maryland, for example, gave George Calvert (Lord Baltimore) the right to create special titles of nobility and confer them on his friends and associates. These vassals, in turn, would rule over a population of tenants, the American equivalent of serfs, who would pay "quit rents" that resembled medieval labor services. The Carolina colony, established in the 1660s, was slated to have "landgraves," a new kind of titled nobleman, ruling over rent-paying commoners. Even the Dutch tried a feudal plan in their colony along the Hudson River. Any Dutch gentleman who brought fifty settlers to New Netherland could claim a sixteen-mile tract of land along any navigable river. Here he might reign as "patroon," or lord of the manor.

All these attempts to establish a feudal system in America failed. There were simply too many applicants for the position of manor lord and too few for the entry-level job of serf. The proprietors and would-be landgraves quickly found that they could not compete with colonies where land was cheap and distinctions of rank not so sharp. The schemes to recreate a feudal world in America had to be abandoned. The aristocratic impulse soon flagged.

The Profit Motive

A more effective motive for colony promotion was the simple yen for wealth. Whether we consider the role of national governments or of private promoters, the lust for riches overshadowed the desire for rank and titles in summoning forth colony-founding energies.

Mercantilism and the Nation-State.

Few Europeans were more eager to exploit the wealth of the New World than kings and princes. Rulers were obviously inspired by Spain's successful example. But they were also influenced by a group of thinkers called mercantilists, whose goal was to strengthen their own nation and elevate it above the others. The key to international supremacy, these men held, was treasure, gold and silver. These "sinews of war" enabled rulers to hire soldiers, buy weapons, build navies, and conduct an ambitious foreign policy.

The English mercantilists hoped, of course, that their own nation, like Spain, would discover fabulous deposits of silver and gold in its overseas possessions. But even if England were not so lucky, an overseas empire would provide vital products—sugar, tobacco, dyewoods, tropical fruits, furs, and timber—that it would otherwise have to buy from foreign countries by exporting gold and silver to pay for them. England, moreover, would be able to sell surpluses of colonial goods for hard cash and so draw coin from other nations. The colonies might also become ready markets for English goods. Mercantilist Richard Hakluyt the Younger, in his *Discourse Concerning Westerne Planting* (1584), pictured the North American Indians clothed in English woolens, sleeping in English beds, and using English tools. Eventually hundreds of ships would criss-cross the ocean, carrying American products to Britain and British products to America. Employment would leap, turning the thousands of dangerous jobless "sturdy beggars" who roamed the English countryside into busy artisans and seamen.

Hakluyt addressed his book directly to Elizabeth, England's shrewd and ambitious queen. But at first the queen avoided directly challenging Spain's claim to sole possession of North America. She encouraged Sir Walter Raleigh's attempts at settlement of Virginia in the 1580s, but preferred to work behind the scenes. In 1577 she financed the half-exploratory, half-piratical around-the-world expedition of "sea dog" Sir Francis Drake, which established England's claim to present-day California and British Columbia and made Drake and the queen rich from the proceeds of a captured Spanish treasure galleon.

After Elizabeth's death in 1603, the English crown proved more willing to defy Spain openly. Yet none of the Stuart monarchs who followed her used public funds to finance a colonization project directly. Rather, under James I and his successors, the crown provided exclusive charters and land grants to proprietors and commercial companies; suspended laws that restricted emigration from England; and, as we shall see, conferred various economic privileges on producers of colonial products needed in Britain. Finally, it provided military and naval protection to new settlements. All told, it is hard to see how British North America could have been created and successfully nurtured without the aid of the English nation-state.

Merchants and Profits.

English merchants too were directly moved by the profit motive, hoping to get rich by trading in the furs, timber, metals, and tropical products that the colonies could supply, by transporting passengers to the new settlements, and by speculating in land.

Unfortunately, few individual merchants could afford the large sums needed in the early stages of exploration and settlement. Few foresaw just how difficult it would be to make a colony a profitable enterprise, but commercial investors recognized the wisdom of reducing the risk by pooling their capital with others. Accordingly, merchants sold shares in "joint-stock" companies that resembled modern corporations. These shares entitled investors to profits in proportion to their investment and spread the risk if the company's ventures failed. Shareholders were often granted other privileges as well, such as a personal claim to a certain amount of land in the New World, or the right to trade with the Indians on their individual accounts.

Jamestown: A Commercial Enterprise. The first of the commercially inspired colonies following Raleigh's earlier failure—and the first permanent English "plantation" in the New World—was Jamestown in Virginia. Backed by two groups of merchants, one from London and the other from Plymouth and Bristol, in 1606 the promoters of the enterprise secured a charter from the crown that established two Virginia companies.[1] One of these, the Plymouth Company, could plant settlements anywhere between the Potomac and what is now Bangor, Maine. The second, the London Company, could settle between Cape Fear in present-day North Carolina and the site of what is now New York City. The overlapping strip was open to both.

Both groups got off to a shaky start. In the summer of 1607 the Plymouth Company deposited forty-four men at Fort St. George, on a rocky projection of the Maine coast, as the preliminary to a larger effort the following year. After one cruel winter the Maine settlers had had enough; when spring came, the survivors returned home. Discouraged, the Plymouth group abandoned its colonization efforts. In early 1607 the better-financed Londoners dispatched three vessels and 105 passengers to the Virginia coast. The promoters hoped that the new settlement—called Jamestown after James I—would be self-sustaining. When the vessels departed for home with a cargo of clapboards soon after landing settlers and supplies, it seemed that all would be well.

It was not to be. Not a single one of the first settlers was a woman, obviously a fatal flaw in what was meant to be a self-sustaining colony. Thirty-six, moreover, were gentlemen who could not be expected to soil their hands with manual labor. Besides, the site of the town near the James River was swampy and malarial.

During the first summer the colonists—employees of the company—planted orange trees, cotton seed, and exotic melons rather than the grain and vegetables they needed for food. Meanwhile, despite the efforts of John Smith, head of the seven-man governing council, to get them to cooperate, they squabbled and fought. The winter was still worse. In January a company ship arrived from England, bringing 120 new settlers to reinforce the surviving 38. This further strained the settlement's limited resources. Soon after, a fire destroyed all the houses and storehouses. The colonists were now virtually without food, but instead of foraging for supplies, they threw themselves into a frantic search for gold.

Fortunately, Smith was able to keep the settlers alive. He stopped the gold hunt and put men to work building, planting crops, and producing pitch, tar, and wood

---

[1] "Virginia" was the name Raleigh had given to the entire eastern seaboard of the present-day United States in honor of his patron Elizabeth, the "virgin queen."

ashes. To tide the settlers over until harvest time, he negotiated with Powhatan, the local Indian chief, for food. The game, corn, fish, and other supplies Powhatan gave them cut the death toll to fewer than a dozen during the winter of 1608–1609.

Smith's successors failed to maintain good relations with the Indians. Powhatan's warriors soon attacked settlers on the colony's outskirts and drove them back to Jamestown proper, where overcrowding and bad sanitation killed many. The winter of 1609–1610 was Jamestown's tragic "starving time." Food was so scarce that some colonists resorted to cannibalism. In the spring, when another contingent of settlers arrived, the supply situation became even more critical; at one point the colony's leaders decided to abandon the settlement altogether.

The following year, 1611, was the turning point. Under Sir Thomas Dale strong leadership was restored. When, after a few years of experimenting with different kinds of plants, in 1616 John Rolfe developed a variety of native tobacco palatable to Europeans, the colonists now discovered their true vocation: tobacco growing. In a few years English smokers were paying premium prices for "Virginia leaf."

However unhealthy we today know smoking to be, the new tobacco crop saved the colony. Jamestown quickly became a boom town. Small fortunes were quickly made and quickly lost; gambling, drunkenness, and crime became rampant. Yet tobacco provided a solid base for growth even when tobacco prices came down after 1630. For the remainder of the colonial period Virginia and its neighbor, Maryland, provided most of the better tobacco Europeans consumed.

The London Company's policies contributed to the colony's continued growth and stability after 1612. In 1616 the company began to grant land to settlers, previously merely company employees. Individual effort would now confer benefits on the worker himself. A year later the company started to grant large tracts of land called "Hundreds" to enterprising people willing to buy stock in the company for the sake of establishing their own "particular plantations." In 1619 the company created a legislative assembly consisting of a governor-appointed council and an elected House of Burgesses, the first representative political body in the New World. To cap the campaign to build a self-sustaining colony, the company also began to pay the ship passage of young women from England to become wives of the settlers.

In the midst of these gains, Virginia was plunged into a devastating Indian war. Until 1622 Powhatan had used the Europeans to offset his tribal enemies; they in turn had counted on him for food during lean times. Neither side much liked the other. A few company officials believed in the possibility of an integrated community, but most settlers despised the Indians. As a Jamestown official noted, "There is scarce a man amongst us that doth soe much as afforde them [the Indians] a good thought in his hart and most men with their mouthes give them nothinge but maledictions and bitter execrations."

For a while Powhatan's successor, Opechancanough, ignored the insults. But when the expanding white population threatened Indian claims, he decided to strike. In March 1622 Opechancanough's warriors attacked the unsuspecting Virginia settlers, killing 357 men, women, and children. The English struck back with a war of extermination, wiping out whole communities and resorting to such tactics as setting out casks of poisoned wine for unsuspecting Indians to drink. When

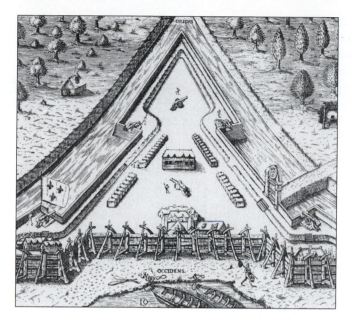

A very early view of the fort at Jamestown by an artist rather indifferent to rules of perspective. Still, it captures the primitive nature of this first successful European settlement in British America.

the smoke of their campaign had cleared, the English had virtually destroyed the tribes of coastal Virginia and ended the "Indian menace."

Still, profits eluded the London Company. Between 1607 and 1624 it declared not a single dividend and indeed kept calling for additional funds from its shareholders to stave off bankruptcy. In 1624 the crown intervened, annulled the company's charter, and made Virginia a royal colony under a governor appointed by the king.

The Virginia experience was not unique. Few joint-stock colonizing ventures made money for their investors. The Plymouth Company effort along the Maine coast, as we saw, failed dismally. Dutch investors in the joint-stock Dutch West India Company established several settlements along the Hudson River from 1624 on, but the Dutch never considered their colony much of a commercial success. When the English captured New Netherland in 1664 (and renamed it New York), the Dutch did little to get it back, although they briefly resumed control in 1673–1674. Few people made money from these merchant-promoted settlements. Nevertheless, the joint-stock company proved to be an invaluable way of pooling economic resources and harnessing the profit motive to the task of founding colonies in America.

"The Best Poor Man's Country"

Aristocrats and merchants, though useful as promoters and leaders, could scarcely populate the new English settlements by themselves. Few chose to leave the wealth and comfort of Britain, and in any case, there were not enough of them to begin with. Immigrants in large numbers had to be drawn from the "common" people; America had to be made attractive to laborers, artisans, servants, shopkeepers, and farmers—both men and women—if the new settlements were to take root and prosper.

And attractive it became. In the seventeenth century some 155,000 people came to North America from England alone. In the eighteenth century the number of European arrivals increased. During the fifteen years preceding the American Revolution (1760–1775), 125,000 emigrants left the British Isles (England, Scotland, Wales, and Ireland) for mainland North America, while another 12,000 immigrants arrived from Germany and Switzerland. The majority of immigrants were young. Youth, with its physical strength, adaptability, and sense of adventure, was required by the new land, and the infant settlements received them gladly.

Mixed Motives.   Most immigrants to America during the seventeenth and eighteenth centuries came willingly, though not always wisely. Some were propelled by boredom, some fled from the law or from unpleasant jobs or difficult family circumstances. In 1732 philanthropists led by James Oglethorpe founded Georgia as a haven for English debtors, who in that era were often jailed when they could not pay their creditors. (Georgia was the last British colony to be established in North America and was still a sparsely settled community at the time of the Revolution.)

Only a small number of immigrants were feckless runaways, lawbreakers, or debtors, however. According to the surviving lists of seventeenth-century immigrants from London and Bristol, many were orphan boys sent to the colonies by the church authorities to relieve British taxpayers of the burden of supporting them. The adult males emigrating through Bristol were mostly farmers; those departing through London mostly artisans and tradesmen—carpenters, weavers, shipbuilders, wheelwrights, barrelmakers, and cobblers. All in all, scholars believe, a disproportionate number of departing English were craftspeople and artisans from the cities and towns. Propelling these people from their homeland were low wages, increasingly high rents, bad harvests, and severe depression in the woolen industry.

About a quarter of the immigrants on the London and Bristol emigration lists are women. Most were in their early twenties, the usual age of marriage in Britain. They were probably fleeing an environment where husbands were scarce as were economic opportunities for unmarried women. The proportion of women immigrants to colonial America varied according to the development stage of the particular colony, with more women immigrants arriving when a community had passed beyond the pioneer phase. At the same time, some colonies—Massachusetts, Connecticut, and Pennsylvania, for example—were the destination of whole families, even in the early years, including wives, mothers, daughters, and sisters.

High Wages and Cheap Land.   In addition to the forces pushing people from Europe, other forces were pulling them to America. During the seventeenth and early eighteenth centuries colony promoters hired agents to travel through Britain and the European continent recruiting colonists. These "Newlanders," wearing jewels and fancy clothes, circulated among the peasants, telling the ignorant that America's mountains were full of precious metals and that its springs gushed milk and honey.

It was not all humbug. The New World was no paradise, but ordinary people could expect to make real gains by moving to America. Success required hard work, but hard work paid richer dividends than in Europe. The reason was simple. North America was a vast continent bursting with resources that could be turned into wealth. The missing ingredient was labor, and those who could supply it were certain to receive a higher economic reward than at home.

For Europeans, then, colonial America promised high wages. Still better, it promised cheap land. This fact was well understood by seventeenth-century colony promoters, who soon began offering a free "headright" of fifty or a hundred acres to settlers who paid their own way to the New World, and even more to those who subsidized additional settlers. Where land was not actually given away, it was sold cheaply. Proprietor William Penn, for example, sold 15,000 acres in Pennsylvania to a group of Germans for £300, less than five cents an acre.

Indentured Servants.   Though America exerted a strong pull on the peasants and laborers of Europe, cost of the Atlantic passage for a single person in the seventeenth century—about $100 in today's money—was far more than any laborer or landless husbandman could afford. The solution for most would-be settlers was a labor contract (an indenture) whereby, in exchange for passage, immigrants agreed to work for an employer in America for a specified time at a certain wage or a specified amount of food, clothing, and shelter.

There were several kinds of indentured servants. The most fortunate possessed a needed or uncommon skill and therefore could get favorable terms from an employer before leaving home. These "servants" normally agreed to work for four years, with their labor contract describing the trade they would work at and defining acceptable working conditions. The indenture frequently also promised "freedom dues"—clothes, tools, and even land—when the contract expired. "Redemptioners" were less fortunate. Most of these were German and Swiss refugees from war and hard times during the eighteenth century. Redemptioners usually moved as whole families. They arranged for merchants to pay their fare and agreed to reimburse them when they arrived in America. If they could not somehow find the passage money immediately upon arrival, the merchant or his agent could sell their services for a time sufficient to recover the debt. This arrangement sometimes led to the heart-wrenching breakup of families.

The life of an indentured servant was often hard. They usually worked from ten to fourteen hours a day, six days a week. Masters had the right to whip them for disobedience or laziness. Normally, they could not marry, vote, or engage in trade. Their indenture and their persons could be transferred from one master to another without their permission. If they ran away, their terms of service could be extended. Many failed to survive the difficult indenture period and were buried in unmarked graves.

Yet many did attain success in America, working off their contracts and establishing themselves as free farmers or craftspeople. News of their achievements drifted back to Europe and inspired others to follow, thus ensuring the indenture system's survival despite its risks and uncertainties. While most of New England was peopled by free families who either paid their own way or were sponsored by the community, by 1750 a large part of the white population from Pennsylvania southward was composed of indentured servants or their descendants.

Involuntary Immigrants

Many thousands of men and women were brought across the Atlantic against their will. Involuntary immigration was an unadorned product of greed. The inducements colonial promoters offered to would-be settlers were often not enough to attract the laborers needed to do the heavy work of the colonies. Especially in the southern colonies, planters without abundant labor could not take advantage of cheap land and a ready market for their crops of tobacco, rice, and indigo in Europe. Rather than forgo profits, they were willing to pay good prices for forced labor from whatever source they could find.

Involuntary European Immigrants. Some of the involuntary immigrants were Europeans. During the seventeenth and eighteenth centuries kidnappers operated in every English port, enticing the young, the naive, or the intemperate aboard ship to carry them to America to sell as indentured servants. More numerous were "His Majesty's Seven Year Guests"—convicts given the choice of going to America as seven-year indentured servants or facing a hangman's noose at home. Those who accepted "transportation" were pardoned and turned over to merchants, who bore the expense of the transatlantic trip in exchange for the right to sell the convicts' labor to the colonists. Every colonial legislature protested this dumping of England's "fellons and other desperate villaines" on America. Parliament remained unmoved, however, and the planters of Maryland and Virginia, where most felons were sent, were generally happy to have their labor. Historians estimate that some 20,000 convicts were sent to America during the eighteenth century alone.

Black Slaves. Indentured servants, convicted felons, and kidnapped youths notwithstanding, labor remained in short supply in America, especially in the regions south of Pennsylvania. Europe, it seemed, simply could not send enough workers to satisfy the needs of the New World's profit-making enterprises.

But Africa could in the form of captive slaves. Though slavery no longer existed in Christian Europe, it survived in Islamic lands and existed in Africa itself among the indigenous peoples. The Portuguese, the Spanish, and later the French, Dutch, and English responded to the lure of profits and readily adopted the system for their labor-short American colonies. Many Europeans rationalized slavery by arguing that the African peoples were "heathens" who worshiped idols, or "naked savages" who might benefit from contact with Christian, "civilized" people.

The Africans brought to the Americas were plucked primarily from peoples and nations along Africa's Atlantic coast, largely between present-day Guinea and Angola. These people practiced agriculture and had brought to high levels the arts of weaving, metalworking, pottery making, and wood and ivory carving. The bronze sculptures of Benin, the silver and gold jewelry of the Yoruba, and the rugs and carpets of the Asante were beautiful artifacts. West Africans were also talented in the arts of government. Powerful states such as Benin, Congo, Dahomey, and Ghana brought order and prosperity to large areas of Africa, conducting foreign affairs in much the same way as contemporary European kingdoms.

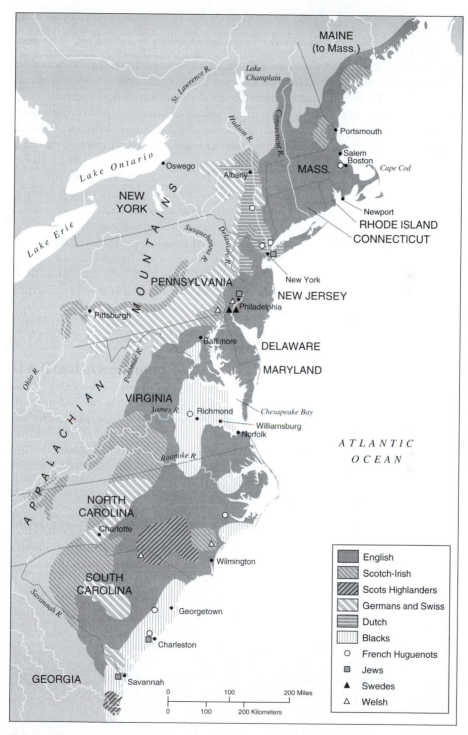

Colonial Settlements by Nationality, 1770

Legend:

- English
- Scotch-Irish
- Scots Highlanders
- Germans and Swiss
- Dutch
- Blacks
- ○ French Huguenots
- ■ Jews
- ▲ Swedes
- △ Welsh

Map labels:

MAINE (to Mass.)

St. Lawrence R.

Lake Champlain

Hudson R.

Connecticut R.

Portsmouth

Salem
Boston

Cape Cod

Lake Ontario

●Oswego

Albany

NEW YORK

MASS.

Newport

RHODE ISLAND
CONNECTICUT

Lake Erie

APPALACHIAN MOUNTAINS

Susquehanna R.

Delaware R.

PENNSYLVANIA

●Pittsburgh

Philadelphia

New York

NEW JERSEY

●Baltimore

DELAWARE

MARYLAND

Ohio R.

Potomac R.

VIRGINIA

James R.

○ Richmond

Chesapeake Bay

Williamsburg

●Norfolk

Roanoke R.

ATLANTIC OCEAN

NORTH CAROLINA

●Charlotte

Wilmington

SOUTH CAROLINA

Savannah R.

○ Georgetown

Charleston

GEORGIA

Savannah

0   100   200 Miles

0   100   200 Kilometers

The slave trade that ripped these people from their homes was a well-organized system by the end of the seventeenth century. At first Europeans themselves captured slaves along the Guinea coast. But whites could not withstand West Africa's tropical diseases and by 1700 the white slavers had come to rely on African merchants and chiefs as middlemen to supply them with prisoners of war or with victims snatched by raiders from the interior of the African continent. Men and women accused of crimes were also enslaved and sold. Chained together, these unfortunate people were brought overland to the coast by the merchants or by war parties. There they were sold to the European traders for guns, powder, cloth, beads, and rum.

Once aboard ship, the next step in the African slave trade was the infamous "middle passage" to America. "Slavers" as small as ninety tons—ships scarcely bigger than a modern fishing boat—were sometimes packed with 400 slaves besides the crew and supplies. The captives were chained together to prevent rebellion. Wise captains attempted to keep them healthy, but slaves lived in filth below deck where temperatures rose into the nineties, and inevitably the death rate was appalling. Some slave vessels arrived in the Americas with well over half their passengers dead from dysentery, smallpox, or some European disease to which Africans had little natural resistance.

The first slaves reached the English mainland colonies in 1619 when a Dutch vessel unexpectedly put in at Jamestown with a cargo of twenty Africans. Over the next thirty or forty years a small trickle of blacks were brought to the Chesapeake region and most, it seems, were kept as bondservants for a few years and then freed, much like indentured servants. At first the market for slaves in the plantation colonies was limited despite the labor shortage. The mortality rates of all immigrants to the southern plantation colonies were extremely high during the early years of settlement, and so the lifetime service of a black slave offered little advantage over short-term white servitude. By the 1660s or 1670s, however, life expectancies in the southern colonies rose as settlers learned how to deal with American diseases and as food supplies improved. At this point high-priced slaves for life began to promise an economic advantage over cheaper four-year indentured servants.

Racial attitudes as well as economics played a part in establishing slavery in North America. White indentured servants were protected by law from the worst physical abuse; women servants could not be exploited sexually. If the master of an indentured servant violated the custom of the country or the terms of the contract, he or she could be sued by the servant. Except briefly in the earliest period, Africans enjoyed no such rights. The English were prejudiced against the physical characteristics of Africans and viewed them as lesser beings. Brutally torn away from all that was familiar, brought among strangers, surrounded by other captives who did not speak their language, and confronted with an alien landscape and an unfamiliar climate, blacks were in no position to protect themselves.

As the slave system fully matured, its victims were subject to ever more elaborate "slave codes" that defined their legal position in detailed ways and placed severe restrictions on their movements and conduct. Under these codes they became "chattel property," to be bought, sold, inherited, and bequeathed like houses, horses, or plows. As slaves became more valuable as property, the planters sought to increase their number. Prices rose and each year more and more were imported from Africa or from the Caribbean islands, which frequently served as way stations for laborers brought directly from Africa. Some 300,000 Africans were landed at the docks of the mainland colonies during the seventeenth and eighteenth centuries. More than ten times as many slaves were brought to the Caribbean and Latin America during this period. There, the high profits on the sugar plantations permitted the owners to bring in few women, work the males to death, and then replace them by importing new male slaves. The Chesapeake planters, who made smaller profits on tobacco, could not afford such an extravagant system, and from the beginning they imported female slaves as well. The relatively high proportion of women, plus the healthier conditions of the North American mainland compared to the New World tropics, resulted in a rapid increase in the slave population through an excess of births over deaths. By 1759 more than one-fifth of the inhabitants of mainland British America were black slaves, and many of these were native-born Americans.

America as a Religious Haven

Americans like to think of their country as a haven for the oppressed. And while the yearning for land and a better living standard pulled more people from the Old World to the New than any other force, America did serve as a refuge for thousands of transatlantic migrants fleeing Old World oppression. In the seventeenth century most of these were refugees from religious intolerance, and they came primarily to the settlements north of the Chesapeake, especially to New England and Pennsylvania, imprinting on these communities many of their values and characteristics.

Religious refugees came from every class of European society. At the top were rich nonconformist merchants and landed gentlemen who sought to aid their poorer co-religionists. In the case of Massachusetts, many of the gentry actually joined the migration to America. Most of those who came to escape persecution at home, however, were ordinary laborers, artisans, farmers, housewives, servants, and shopkeepers, much like those who came to escape poverty. Most of those fleeing religious oppression had no interest in freedom of worship for its own sake. They were often as intolerant toward others as their persecutors were toward them. Their complaint was merely that the wrong people were dictating the religious rules. It is not surprising, then, that such refugees would often become persecutors in turn when they found themselves in a position to dictate religious beliefs and practices.

The Reformation.   To understand the flight from persecution we must look at the religious scene in sixteenth- and seventeenth-century Europe. Until the 1520s virtually all Western Europeans were Roman Catholic Christians who believed that men and women achieved salvation and avoided eternal damnation through accepting Jesus, participating in the church's sacraments, performing "good works," and embracing the Catholic creed. Through its rituals, ceremonies, ministries, and confessionals, the all-embracing Catholic Church provided solace and hope for the multitude and cloistered refuge for those with a contemplative bent.

Its spiritual authority was reinforced by its stewardship of the Bible, which was available only in Latin, the language of the ordained clergy and a small lay elite. The supreme head of the Catholic Church, the pope, the Vicar of Christ, seated in Rome, was the final authority in matters of faith and morals. He also sought at times to assert temporal power over the rulers of the European states.

By 1500 many Europeans had become critical of the Catholic Church. Some objected to church governance through a hierarchy of priests, bishops, and cardinals as unwarranted by the original Gospels. Some believed Church doctrines had drifted far from the views of Jesus and the early Church Fathers. Many found the Church too worldly or even immoral. Popes, bishops, and even ordinary priests, they said, were obsessed with wealth and secular power. Monasteries and convents no longer were centers for the contemplative life, but havens for the idle and the dissolute. To the growing number of skeptics it seemed that the Church had become hypocritical, venal, corrupt, and in need of fundamental reform.

In 1517 Martin Luther, an Augustinian friar, attacked the Church's sale of papal letters remitting punishment for sin to raise money for building the magnificent new St. Peter's basilica in Rome. He soon moved on to deny the Church's claim to be the guardian of the gates of heaven and asserted in its place that salvation was a transaction between God and the individual, needing no priest as intermediary. Luther also denounced the self-imposed isolation of monks and nuns and insisted that all Christians participate in the world's affairs. In theology he denied the Catholic emphasis on "good works," such as the papal letters, as the road to salvation and substituted the idea of faith: Only God could confer salvation; it could not be earned by deeds, however pious or numerous.

Luther's demands for change touched a receptive chord and quickly spread through Europe. Before long the reform movement expanded into a thorough assault on Church ceremony, worldliness, papal power, and the belief that the sacraments of the Church were essential to salvation. The attack begun by Luther against the established religious order eventually touched many other aspects of life, producing the continent-wide upheaval known as the Protestant Reformation.

For a while the Reformation scarcely affected England. King Henry VIII accepted the Catholic Church's doctrines and forms of worship. But when the pope refused to annul Henry's marriage to Catherine of Aragon and excommunicated him in 1533 for marrying Anne Boleyn, the king declared himself supreme head of the Church of England. He also authorized an English translation of the Bible so that it might be read by all literate people, and dissolved the monasteries, confiscating their vast property.

For the next century England became a battleground between the forces of Catholicism and the new Protestantism. Under Elizabeth I a Protestant Church of England (the Anglican Church) emerged, controlled by the English crown but retaining many of the old religion's ceremonies and beliefs. This outcome did not please everyone. Some English people refused to accept Anglicanism and remained loyal Catholics. Others sought to go beyond Anglicanism to embrace the tenets of John Calvin, a French Protestant reformer, who had established his headquarters at Geneva in Switzerland.

Calvinists insisted that all humans were in essence sinful and wicked. As one English Calvinist vividly expressed it, "every natural man and woman is born as full of sin as a toad of poison, as full as ever his skin can hold." Such beings obviously deserved eternal damnation and could not ransom themselves through good works. But God, in his mercy and out of regard for Jesus' sacrifice of His earthly life, would save a few. These few "elect" were predestined to be saved from hell, since God, who knew all and determined all, had selected them at the beginning of time.

English Calvinists demanded that the Church of England "purify" itself entirely of Catholic belief and ceremonies and abandon the bishop-run church-governing structure that it still retained from the old religion. At first these "Puritans" were content to remain within the official Anglican Church as "dissenters" or "nonconformists," working to change it from the inside. Eventually, after being harassed and persecuted, many became "separatists" who renounced the Church of England entirely.

Elizabeth managed to tread a narrow path between the religious extremes but in the half-century following her death in 1603, England experienced a religious churning that threatened to tear the country apart. New sects rose to prominence, each, it seemed, more extreme and unusual than the preceding one. Some of these "sectaries" were intensely hostile to the existing social system, despising and denouncing political absolutism, class deference, intellectual authority, and even private property. But even the more moderate Nonconformists and the remaining Catholics seemed to deny the authority of the crown and the unity of the nation, besides endangering their own souls and infecting with error all who came in contact with them.

The Pilgrims of Plymouth.
By the early 1600s several religious minorities had abandoned hope of change in England and begun to consider emigration. The first to depart was a small body of radical Puritan separatists, the Pilgrims. In 1608 this group moved to Leiden in Holland, a refuge for religious minorities from all over Europe. For a while they prospered, but as time passed the little congregation began to fear for its survival and its purity of belief in the face of the easygoing religious ways of the Dutch. In 1617 the Pilgrim leaders decided to move the congregation to "Virginia," where they could maintain their preferred mode of life and form of worship without distraction. After selling their possessions in Holland and securing loans from the London Company and from Thomas Weston, a London merchant, about thirty of the Pilgrims departed for England. At Southampton they joined a larger group of nonseparatists hired to work in the colony by the profit-seeking Weston. On September 16, 1620, after many difficulties and much delay, the 180-ton *Mayflower*, with 149 passengers and crew, sailed from Plymouth harbor for America.

The Pilgrims' original destination was the region near the mouth of the Hudson River, but severe storms drove them to the north and they decided to stay at Cape Cod Bay where they had touched land. Fearful that the nonseparatists ("strangers") among them might dominate the community, and worried that their charter might not have legal force because the region was outside the London Company's grant, the Pilgrims adopted the Mayflower Compact before leaving ship. This short document established a civil government with powers "to enact, constitute, and frame such just and equal Laws, Ordinances, Acts, Constitutions, and Offices, from time to time, as shall be thought most meet and convenient for the general Good of the Colony."

During the first winter the colonists, who called their settlement Plymouth after their port of departure, suffered grievously from disease. Fortunately, the weather was relatively mild and the Indians proved helpful. One, Squanto, had been seized by a European trader years before and taken to England, where he had learned the English language. He and Massasoit, the grand sachem of the local Wampanoags, befriended the colonists, teaching them how to plant maize and other native plants and showing them the best fishing streams. In spite of this aid, the Pilgrim community, like almost all early English settlements, went through a "starving time" that first winter. By spring nearly half the colonists were dead. During the summer, however, the survivors put the Indians' teachings to good use; by fall their storehouses were well stocked. In November 1621 they celebrated their success with a harvest festival that has come down to us, after many twists and bypaths, as Thanksgiving.

The Plymouth colony expanded slowly, reaching a population of about 1,000 in 1640 and 3,000 in 1660. Although life in the small settlement was hard, William Bradford and the other Pilgrim leaders never forgot that their mission was to found a godly colony. Yet Plymouth's religious orthodoxy was never intolerant or harsh. For seventy years the "Old Colony" modestly prospered. Then, in 1691 it was absorbed into the larger Massachusetts Bay community.

The Massachusetts Bay Puritans.   Until the 1620s the Puritan dissenters in Britain had hoped to reform the established Church of England. By the middle of that decade, however, they feared for the future of the godly in a nation ruled by Charles I and Anglican Archbishop William Laud. Laud considered Puritan doctrines wicked and erroneous and, in cooperation with the king, he suppressed Puritan books, forbade Puritans to preach, and attempted to impose Anglican practices and beliefs on all dissenters. In 1629 when Charles dissolved the Puritan-friendly Parliament and assumed personal rule of England, it was clearly time to leave.

A few Puritans had already departed. In 1625 forty had emigrated to the fishing colony of Salem, north of present-day Boston. Now a number of prominent Puritan gentlemen procured a royal charter for a new colony, establishing the Massachusetts Bay Company, a corporation authorized to own and govern all land between the Merrimack and Charles rivers, from the Atlantic to the Pacific. The charter also prescribed a structure for the new Massachusetts Bay Company that omitted the provision, common to such grants, that the governor, assistants, and freemen of the company had to remain in England to do business.

In the summer of 1629 the promoters of emigration persuaded John Winthrop, a Cambridge University-educated gentleman and attorney, to accept the governorship of the company. Winthrop agreed on condition that the settlers bring the company's charter to New England, where it would be out of reach of the English authorities, enabling the colonists to enjoy virtual autonomy in their political and religious affairs. Reflecting on the hard fate of the Virginia colonists to the south, Winthrop noted the differences between the two ventures. The Virginia settlers, he wrote, had fallen into "great and fundamental errors" because, among other

John Winthrop expected the Massachusetts Bay Colony to be an example of order, morality, and conformity for wayward humanity. "We shall be as a City upon a Hill, the eies of all people are uppon us." *(Courtesy of American Antiquarian Society)*

things, "their mayne end was Carnall and not religious." The new community would avoid that mistake and be an example to all humanity. It would be "as a City upon a Hill, the eies of all people [will be] uppon us."

In fact there were "carnall" reasons for the Puritan migration as well. In addition to Winthrop's appeals and the desire to escape Laud's harassment, a depression in the English wool industry in the late 1620s helped push the Puritans to the New World. Men and women facing both persecution and hunger sold their property, paid their debts, and signed up for Massachusetts. In the early spring of 1630 four well-equipped, crowded vessels left for New England. They were soon followed by seven more. The Puritan settlers were generally more prosperous and more socially prominent than the Pilgrims and other separatists.

In a few months 1,000 settlers were building cabins, clearing fields, and planting crops in the Shawmut (Boston) area. Despite some sickness and a few untimely deaths the first year, settlers continued to arrive and the population grew quickly. By 1640 Massachusetts had about 9,000 inhabitants, almost as many as Jamestown, founded 33 years earlier.

Offshoots of the Massachusetts Bay Colony.

Religious oppression in America itself would soon become a colonizing force. Under John Winthrop and the other learned Puritan "magistrates," Massachusetts Bay was dominated by religion. All adult male family heads who were full-fledged members of the church were considered "freemen" and allowed to participate in political decisions. Women were denied all political rights, as were many men who were not church members or who owned no property. The leaders of the colony did not welcome those who did not accept Puritan religious views. As John Cotton, a prominent

Puritan minister later noted, "the design of our first planters was not toleration, but [they] were professed enemies of it. . . . Their business was to settle, and (as much as in them lay) secure Religion to Posterity according to that way which they believed was of God." Before long, political and religious intolerance had begun to drive independent-minded people out of the Bay Colony itself.

One of the first to go was the Reverend Thomas Hooker. Though himself a minister, Hooker demanded that church membership not be a requirement for voting. When the Massachusetts authorities refused to yield, Hooker joined with others who were leaving the Bay Colony to find better land. Hooker's group established a colony at Hartford and adopted the Fundamental Orders, a form of government that, though scarcely democratic, gave the magistrates less power than they had in the Bay Colony and imposed a more lenient religious test for full citizenship. Soon after, other former residents of Massachusetts established New Haven on the north shore of Long Island Sound. Still other communities, peopled from Plymouth, Massachusetts Bay, and the Connecticut River settlements themselves, sprang up nearby. In 1662 the new river communities and those on the Sound were merged as the self-governing colony of Connecticut.

Roger Williams, another Puritan minister, also helped the fission process. Arriving in Massachusetts in 1631, Williams promptly quarreled with the Bay Colony's religious leaders over whether the community had fully separated from the Church of England and whether its charter was legal. He also denounced the practice of requiring church attendance and the payment of taxes to support the Puritan clergy. In 1635 the Massachusetts authorities ordered his arrest and Williams fled to Narragansett Bay, just east of Connecticut. There he bought land from the Indians and established the community of Providence Plantation, becoming the father of the Rhode Island colony. The new colony's key principles were the complete separation of religion and government (separation of church and state), toleration of all religious beliefs, and the sovereignty of the people.

Other dissenters soon flocked to the Narragansett area. One of the most remarkable was Anne Hutchinson, "a woman of ready wit and bold spirit," who, like Williams, had tangled with the leading clergymen of the Bay Colony over religious doctrine. Hutchinson espoused the idea that only those infused with the Holy Spirit could preach the word of God and that only a few, herself included, could determine to whom the Holy Spirit had been revealed. Besides threatening the leadership of the Bay Colony ministers, Hutchinson's outspokenness also defied the principle of female subordination. The church leaders summoned her to a hearing and demanded that she retract her views and cease to preach. She refused and threatened that if they continued to persecute her, God would ruin them, their posterity, and "this whole State." Shocked by her boldness and presumption, the leaders expelled Hutchinson from the church and declared her a heretic. She and some of her followers soon moved to Aquidneck near Providence.

Other exiles and dissenters also came to the Narragansett region, enlarging the population of the little cluster of towns. In 1663 King Charles II granted Rhode Island and Providence Plantation a royal charter as a separate colony.

Penn's Woods.   Pennsylvania, too, was the offshoot of religious persecution— in this case of the Quakers, as outsiders called those belonging to the Society of

Friends. Quakers believed that to understand God's will people needed only to consult their "inner light"; there was no necessity for an elaborate credo and a trained clergy. In the 1640s and 1650s Quaker "enthusiasts" traveled through England passionately preaching their message of the inner light and advising their listeners to throw off the vanities of the world and renounce war and excessive respect for authorities.

The Anglican clergy, and many orthodox English people, considered Quaker behavior and teachings even more offensive than those of the Puritans. One contemporary called them "a new fanatic sect, of dangerous principles, who show no respect to any man, magistrate, or other, and seem a melancholy, proud sort of people. . . ." The English government feared the Quakers' contempt for a "hireling ministry" and their refusal to take oaths or pay church tithes. In 1655 the government ordered the Quakers to desist from their disorderly practices and enforced the command by a flock of legal prosecutions.

During the 1650s Quaker missionaries fanned out from England, many going to the British colonies. Here, too, they were attacked and persecuted. Except in Rhode Island, their emotional preaching and breaches of religious decorum resulted in savage punishment. For refusing to desist from preaching, several Quakers were whipped and imprisoned in Massachusetts. Between 1659 and 1661, four were hanged.

In the 1670s a few Quaker families from England settled along the Delaware River in an area that in 1701 would join with Puritan-settled East Jersey to form the royal province of New Jersey. In 1681 William Penn, who had become a "Friend" against his influential father's strong wishes, secured a charter from Charles II for a giant block of land along the Delaware River to repay a debt the crown owed Admiral Penn. In addition, the king's brother gave Penn a strip of land along the lower Delaware River which would become the separate colony of Delaware in 1701.

Even before this grant Penn had prepared the way for a mass migration of Quakers to Pennsylvania (Penn's Woods) by constructing a "frame of government" for the colony and a set of laws. The result was one of the most enlightened political systems in the contemporary world. In Pennsylvania any male who owned or rented a small amount of land or who paid any taxes would be allowed to vote. No taxes would be imposed on anyone without the approval of the elected colonial legislature. All trials were to be before juries. In place of the long list of crimes punishable by death in England, Pennsylvania would condone only two capital crimes: treason and murder. No atheists were to be admitted to the colony, but all who believed in God, regardless of their denomination, were welcome and would be allowed to worship in peace.

In 1682 Penn visited his new colony to observe the laying out of Philadelphia, one of the first modern planned cities. During this visit he also cemented cordial relations with the local Indians by paying generously for their land. Settlers soon began arriving in large numbers, drawn by Penn's policies of selling land at low prices and extending religious liberty to all Christians. Pennsylvania attracted not only thousands of British Quakers, but also French Protestants (Huguenots), who were in disfavor in Catholic France, and many German Pietists (radical Protestants), victims of persecution by German Catholics and Lutherans alike. By 1689, with 12,000 inhabitants, the colony was already a going concern.

The Limits of Religious Toleration.   Seventeenth-century religious dissidents from Europe also settled in Maryland, the Carolinas, and New Netherland. Maryland was a particular refuge for George Calvert's Catholic co-religionists, though it also attracted Puritan and Anglican Protestants. In New Netherland the tolerant Dutch attracted religious minorities from almost every part of the Western world—Huguenots from France, Jews from the Portuguese colony of Brazil, and assorted religious refugees from Germany, England, Massachusetts, and elsewhere. By the end of Dutch rule in 1664, the small colony—and especially its chief town, New Amsterdam on Manhattan Island—had become a cosmopolitan community inhabited by a score of nationalities and a wide assortment of religious groups.

America, then, served as a refuge for religious dissenters from Europe. Pennsylvania, New Netherland, Rhode Island, and, for a while, Maryland, accorded the right to worship to a wide array of faiths. But religious toleration was far from universal even in the mainland British colonies. In few places were Catholics or Jews allowed to practice their religion openly. Toleration, if accorded at all, generally meant toleration only for Protestants of various kinds.

In many colonies, as we have seen, even Protestants who differed from the founding denomination suffered disabilities. In most of New England only Puritans were welcome. In southern New York, after Britain took it over, and most of the colonies south of Pennsylvania only Anglicans enjoyed full civil and religious rights. In both Calvinist and Anglican colonies ministers of the favored ("established") churches received support from the provincial treasury through tithes—religious taxes—imposed on all residents of the colony regardless of their religious preferences. All other clergy had to rely on their parishioners to support their churches and pay their salaries, if allowed to preach at all. Yet taken as a whole, religious toleration was more complete and general in the British mainland colonies than elsewhere in the Western world.

Conclusions

The motives, then, of those who promoted and those who settled the American colonies present a mixed picture. Americans may prefer to see their country as founded primarily on freedom, a refuge for those fleeing oppression and bigotry, but at best this view is only partly true. New England, Pennsylvania, and, to a lesser extent, Maryland, New Jersey, and Delaware assuredly served as havens for religious dissenters. But they themselves exhibited religious tolerance only for select groups. Nowhere, except perhaps in Rhode Island and New Netherland, were those of every religious persuasion welcome. Nor should we forget that for many men and women who crossed the Atlantic America was the opposite of a haven: It was a prison. For thousands of transported European felons and for an even larger number of Africans, America was a place of bondage.

For those who came voluntarily, moreover, the strongest lure was not freedom; it was economic and social opportunity. Capitalists could make profits from trade, land speculation, and commercial agriculture; gentlemen could raise their status and restore their diminished fortunes; rulers could enrich their realms and make themselves more powerful than their rivals. The expectations of Europeans who had only their lives to invest were more modest, perhaps, but they, too, were primarily economic. Most ordinary men and women crossed the Atlantic to acquire the economic independence and decent comfort that the social and economic systems of England and continental Europe denied them. Opportunity was America's basic premise in the beginning and would remain so throughout its history.

ONLINE RESOURCES

"Thomas Harriot's A Brief and True Report of the New Found Land of Virginia" *http://www.nps.gov/fora/raleigh.html* The primary account describes the first English colony, including the natural environment, provisions for the colonists, and their experiences with Native Americans.

"Religion and the Founding of the American Republic. America as a Religious Refuge: The Seventeenth Century" *http://lcweb.loc.gov/exhibits/religion/rel01.html* Through this Library of Congress Web site, discover the role of religion in the founding of the New England colonies. This site details the religious persecution religious "nonconformists" experienced in their European homelands and the promise of religious freedom the New World held out to these men and women.

"From Indentured Servitude to Racial Slavery" *http://www.pbs.org/wgbh/aia/part1/1narr3.html* Read about Virginia's recognition of slavery, slave codes, and the need for African slave labor. The site also contains scholarly commentary on the earliest African Americans and their experiences.

"William Penn: Visionary Proprietor" *http://xroads.virginia.edu/~CAP/PENN/pnhome.html* By examining Penn's plans for the city of Philadelphia and his relationships with Native Americans, this site provides great insight into Penn's religious, political, and social ideology, both as a Quaker and as a member of the elite class.

"Immigrant Communities in Maryland" *http://raven.umd.edu/~mddlmddl/791/communities.html/* In addition to exploring the origins of Maryland and its social, political, and cultural characteristics, this site offers a detailed look into the colonial immigrants from Germany and enslaved Africans. Of special interest is the story of a slave named Job, who tells of his capture in Africa and his enslavement in Maryland.

Reformation Europe *http://www.fordham.edu/halsall/mod/modsbook02.html#ProtestantReformation* Containing the writings and sermons of Martin Luther and John Calvin, this site examines the effects of the Protestant Reformation on European thought and culture. Also, the site explores the impact of the Reformation on women.

Religion and the Founding of the American Republic. America as a Religious Refuge: The Seventeenth Century *http://www.loc.gov/exhibits/religion/rel01.html* This Library of Congress Web site explores the role of religion in the founding of the New England colonies. It details the religious persecution "nonconformists" experienced in their European homelands and the promise of religious freedom the New World held out to these men and women.

A Brief History of Jamestown *www.apva.org* Sponsored by the Association for the Preservation of Virginia Antiquites, this site contains the writings of John Smith and lists early Jamestown settlers and their occupations. It also provides a useful timeline of the Virginia Company and the founding of Jamestown and includes names of key individuals involved.

The Terrible Transformation: Africans in America *http://www.pbs.org/wgbh/aia/part1/narrative.html* This interactive Web site details the history of European slave traders in West Africa and the growth of slavery in North America through its use of primary documents, illustrations, and commentary by preeminent historians.

Olaudah Equiano: The Life of Gustavus Vassa *http://www.wsu.edu:8000/~dee/Equiano.html* Read an excerpt from this former slave's autobiography. Learn of his and other slaves' experiences in the late eighteenth century, including experiences on slave ships and the conditions on West Indies plantations.

Gottlieb Mittelberger on the Misfortunes of Indentured Servants (1784) *http://www.historical documents.com/GottliebMittelberger.htm* A church organist making his way from Germany to Pennsylvania, Mittelberger wrote of his observations of the conditions and status of white indentured servants bound for the New World. Read his first-hand account at this site.

Economic and Imperial Relationships *http://www.ucalgary.ca/applied_history/tutor/migrations/four2.html* This site contains information on mercantilism and economy.

3
Colonial Society

How Did Old World Life and Culture Change in the Wilderness?

1636	Harvard, in Massachusetts, is the first college to be founded in the colonies
1642, 1647	Massachusetts Bay Colony enacts compulsory school laws
1662	The Half-Way Covenant allows the children of Massachusetts Bay church members to join the congregation without a conversion experience
1675–78	Indian–white tensions erupt into King Philip's War in New England
1675	Bacon's Rebellion in Virginia
1692	Twenty men and women are hanged in the Salem, Massachusetts witch trials
1705	Virginia's legislature establishes a Propositions and Grievances Committee to receive public petitions proposing new laws
1732	Publication of the first issue of Benjamin Franklin's *Poor Richard's Almanack*
1734–37	Congregationalist minister Jonathan Edwards sparks a religious revival in New England
1739	Stono Rebellion of South Carolina slaves
1740	George Whitefield's Methodism leads to a "Great Awakening" throughout the colonies
1746–52	Benjamin Franklin's experiments with electricity earn him international fame

In 1782, shortly after American independence, J. Hector St. John de Crèvecoeur, a French gentleman who had settled in the American colonies, asked a question that would be posed in various forms again and again: "What, then, is the American, this new man?" Crèvecoeur's answer was that the American was a mixture of the old and the new:

> "He was an individual who leaving behind all his ancient prejudices and manners, receives new ones from the mode of life he has embraced, the new government he obeys, and the new rank he holds. . . . Americans are the western pilgrims, who are carrying along with them that great mass of arts, sciences, vigour, and industry which began long since in the east; they will finish the great circle. . . ."

Americans, then, Crèvecoeur was saying, were not simply transplanted Europeans. They had surely brought with them to the new land many of the habits and much of the cultural heritage of the Old World. But they had also left behind a good deal, and much of what they had taken with them had been transformed in their new circumstances.

Were Crèvecoeur's conclusions correct? Had the cultural mixture of the colonies blended into a new type? Was there a distinctive American culture by the eve of the Revolution? Or were Americans merely transplanted Europeans with attitudes, values, and institutions solely traceable to the European continent? In what sense and in what ways were Americans "new," and if they were new, how had they become so?

A New Mixture in a New Land

Two powerful factors clearly worked to transform immigrants to colonial America: a different physical environment, and a different mixture of human types.

A New Physical Environment.   Unlike Europe, America, as late as the Revolution, was still almost entirely a forested wilderness. Most of the population of the British colonies was confined to a narrow strip of coast between the Appalachian Mountains and the sea. Beyond the coastal "tidewater" region tongues of settlement extended along the rivers that flowed from the mountains, but much of the rest was a vast expanse of forest dotted by a few clearings and threaded by Indian trails. Even in the 1770s only five American towns had more than 10,000 inhabitants—Boston, Newport, New York, Philadelphia, and Charleston. Nor did the settled countryside much resemble its European counterpart with its trim fields, neat fences and hedgerows, stone barns, and well-built farmhouses. Everywhere in colonial America there were more woods than cleared land, and even established farms with their timber dwellings and scraggly wood fences seemed impermanent and ill-tended by European standards.

Travel in this great wilderness was slow and uncomfortable. Roads were dirt tracks through the forest; bridges were logs laid across stones. The mounted riders of the colonial postal service took three weeks to cover the 310 miles from Boston to Philadelphia. Inns were scarce and generally squalid.

Diversity Among the Europeans.   The population mix of the colonies was far more hetereogeneous than that of any European country. Even in its European ingredients the colonial population was diverse. In the seventeenth century streams of French, Dutch, Swedes, and Germans joined the largely English population. Between 1700 and 1775 about 100,000 Germans crossed the Atlantic to the mainland British colonies. Many went to Pennsylvania; others settled in western Maryland and western Virginia. Presbyterians from Scotland had displaced the conquered Catholics in northern Ireland in the early seventeenth century, prospering in their new homes by raising cattle and weaving linen until the British government imposed duties on imports from Ulster, severely damaging the Scotch-Irish economy. Masses of Ulster Protestants soon flocked to America. Many went to the Pennsylvania backcountry to the west of the older settled regions. Others moved into western Virginia and then down through the Great Valley (the Shenandoah) and the frontier counties of the Carolinas as far as northern Georgia.

Crèvecoeur claimed that in America "individuals of all nations are melted into a new race of men." But even white Europeans often refused to mingle, much less melt. The result was a lumpy demographic stew rather than a smooth purée. Most groups retained their characteristics generation after generation, practicing their own religion, speaking their own language, pursuing their own customs, and marrying within their own fold.

Distinctive groups were often intolerant of others. The Germans, because they were numerous and slow to assimilate, aroused the suspicion of English-speaking Pennsylvanians. In the 1750s Benjamin Franklin penned an exasperated outburst against the "Palatine boors" that expressed a widely held view among British Pennsylvanians of the dangers they posed:

> "Advertisements intended to be general are now printed in Dutch [German] and English. The signs in our streets have inscriptions in both languages, in some places only German. They begin of late to make all their . . . legal instruments in their own language . . . which . . . are allowed in our courts, where the German business so increases that there is continued need of interpreters; and I suppose within a few years they will also be necessary in the Assembly, to tell one half of our legislators what the other half say. In short, unless the stream of importation can be turned from this to other colonies . . . they will so outnumber us that . . . we . . . will . . . not be able to preserve our language, and even our government will become precarious."

The Scotch-Irish were not always warmly welcomed either. In Pennsylvania the authorities feared that they would violate the rights of the Indians and set off a major Indian war. These fears were not unfounded. The newcomers were the very image of the frontiersmen of legend: tall, red-haired, quick to anger, hospitable, fiercely independent. Such hot-blooded people did not get along well with their white neighbors and were constantly embroiled in disputes and quarrels with the Indians. Yet they made valuable additions to the American population. Herdsmen and hunters rather than farmers, they filled in the colonial backcountry, where their qualities made them useful, if sometimes troublesome, pioneers.

Native Americans.

From the beginning, European–Indian contacts affected both sides in profound ways. Generally the two societies remained distinct although they interacted where they touched.

Some of the interactions were benign. The early settlers of New England had learned Indian farming techniques and borrowed from the Native Americans many food plants and recipes whose Indian names—squash, hominy, and succotash, for example—entered the English language. For their part, the Indians acquired the colonists' muskets, cloth, iron implements, and other goods through trade in beaver pelts and deerskins.

More commonly, however, the transfer from European to Indian proved damaging to the latter. The Indians were quickly entangled in the transplanted economy of the Europeans, especially the fur trade. Though not the perfect ecological heroes posited by sentimentalists, Indians usually did not, in this era, place too heavy a burden on the animal life of the forest. But when whites appeared, ready to trade metal tools, guns, cloth, and "fire water" for animal pelts, many succumbed to temptation. Wherever the fur trade flourished it decimated the beaver and other animal populations. Increasingly, moreover, the Indians became dependent on trade with whites and less able to do without the white man's goods. The "fire water" proved particularly harmful. Drunkenness and alcoholism became a corrosive part of Indian life, damaging the health of individuals and tearing at the very fabric of Indian society.

From a strict cultural perspective, however, the exchange between Indian and European was relatively superficial in the British colonies. Colonists of English and Scottish extraction did not mix as readily with the Indians as did the Spanish in Mexico and Florida and the French in Canada. In addition, people of northern European origins intermarried less often with the Indians than did whites of southern European extraction. Protestants, moreover, lacked the zeal for saving heathen souls displayed by their Catholic rivals in Canada, Brazil, and New Spain. In the 1660s the Reverend John Eliot, a Bay Colony Puritan minister, translated the Bible "into the Indian tongue." In all, Eliot established 14 towns of "praying Indians" with over 1,000 Indian converts. By the mid-1670s there were perhaps 4,000 Christian Indians in New England. In the 1740s the Moravians, German Protestant Pietists, set out to convert the Indians in Pennsylvania without destroying their culture. Still, the total conversion effort in Protestant America was relatively feeble.

Indeed, rather than Christian love, Indian–white relations in British America were generally marked by hostility and violence. The competing view of land ownership often led to troubles. Outside Pennsylvania, where the white Quaker officials respected Indian rights, Indian–white contacts produced constant warfare. We have already seen how, in 1622, tensions between the Jamestown settlers and the Virginia coastal tribes tripped off a massacre of white colonists and a war that destroyed the power of the Indians in the region. In the 1630s the Pequot War decimated the Indian population of eastern Connecticut. Most serious of all, during the first century of settlement, was King Philip's War which erupted in the mid-1670s. In this conflict the tribes of southern New England, under the leadership of Philip (Metacomet), son of the Plymouth colony's benefactor, Massasoit, attacked the settlers of Massachusetts for encroaching on their lands and hunting grounds. The Narragansetts of Rhode Island and the Nipmucks of Connecticut soon joined Philip's Wampanoag warriors in the struggle.

Armed for the first time with guns, the Indians devastated the white settlements with their hit-and-run tactics. Before long the colonists adopted Indian methods of warfare: surprise raids, ambushes, and even scalping. Eventually the war against the "savages" made the colonists savage. Soon they were torturing prisoners and deploying large dogs to tear the Indians apart. In the end the Europeans' superior numbers and organization prevailed. By 1676 the southern New England tribes were defeated and subdued.

King Philip's War exacted an enormous toll of both sides. According to one estimate, one sixteenth of the white male population of New England died in the fighting. One casualty of the war was Eliot's praying Indians. Although they had remained loyal to the whites, they were interned for three years on Deer Island, where they were forced to live on shellfish. Many died. Philip himself was captured and shot, and many of his followers were sold into slavery in the Caribbean

This is a contemporary drawing of
Metacomet, usually called King Philip.
He looks rather gentle here, but he proved
a formidable enemy of the New England
settlers.

or indentured as servants to whites. Indian lands were awarded to the victorious
white soldiers. After 1676 the New England Indians ceased to be a challenge to
the white population except on the remote frontiers.

Colonial Blacks.   In 1760 about 325,000 of the approximately 1.6 million people
in British North America were black. Of these, 12,000 lived in New England, another 25,000 in the middle colonies (New York, New Jersey, and Pennsylvania),
and the remainder in the southern colonies, with Virginia and South Carolina far
in the lead. Almost all of these people were slaves. But a few thousand were "free
people of color" some of whom, in both North and South, were able to achieve a
surprising prosperity. We know, for example, of Anthony Johnson, an early Maryland slave who earned his freedom and became a rich planter owning slaves
himself. Johnson's family continued to be a respected part of the colony's Eastern
Shore society well into the eighteenth century.

    Black workers were a vital part of the laboring class in colonial America.
Though relatively few in number, in New England and the middle colonies, slaves
were employed as day laborers, seamen, house servants, or craftsmen's assistants
in the ports and towns. They worked in tanneries, salt works, lead and copper
mines, and iron foundries. In the Chesapeake region and the Carolinas, where
slaves formed the backbone of the labor force, they labored on plantations and
farms producing the tobacco, rice, indigo, and grain that were the bases for the
regions' economies. Even in the southern plantation colonies, however, many
blacks worked as house servants and artisans.

This forced labor on colonial farms, plantations, and in towns transformed the culture of enslaved Africans. Slaves had to learn occupations that were not part of their African culture. In South Carolina, Virginia, and elsewhere they quickly acquired trades such as bricklaying, "plaistering," wig-making, silversmithing, and gunsmithing. The cultural exchange was not all one way, however. Slaves brought skills and knowledge from Africa and used them in America. West Africans were familiar with boats and the sea; in South Carolina many of them worked as fishermen. They introduced the West African perriauger—a kind of canoe—for transportation along the Sea Islands and through the many rivers and streams of the Carolina coastal lowlands. Slaves also introduced West African agricultural products to South Carolina, including melons, gourds, and probably even rice. Black cooks learned the techniques of European cuisine, but they contributed their own ingredients such as sesame seeds and red pepper. In fact, much of the South's distinctive cooking is derived from the merger of African and European elements.

The African family and kinship systems also survived for a time the transplant to America. In most of the slaves' original homelands each individual was tied to the community through elaborate kinship networks. In their new homes husbands and wives, parents and children were often separated against their will. But the inherited networks made it possible for slaves to remain in touch with distant relatives for many years, despite infrequent chances for face-to-face contact.

Little is known about the religion of the first generation or two of American slaves. Most West Africans worshiped the spirits of the dead, who were believed to remain close by, protecting their descendants. It seems likely that the first slaves tried to practice their religion much as they had at home, though far from the graves of their venerated ancestors. There is evidence that transfer to America was destructive to the African religious system as a whole. But it is also clear that many discrete practices—belief in amulets, conjurers, faith healing—survived the Atlantic leap and flourished on the new soil.

In most of the colonies few efforts were made at first to convert Africans to Christianity, in part because Christians were not supposed to enslave their fellow Christians. Nonetheless, by the mid-eighteenth century the Anglican Society for the Propagation of the Gospel had made converts among the slave population. Still more effective were the evangelical Protestant groups like the Methodists and the Baptists whose "enthusiasm" and emotionalism made Christianity more attractive to many slaves.

Everywhere in this era the lives of the lowly were harsh by modern standards. White servants, for example, worked long hours at menial, grueling, and often degrading jobs and submitted to strict discipline from their employers. The treatment of slaves was not much worse. Yet the lot of the colonial slave, as of other workers, varied from place to place, from time to time, and from master to master. In New England, where slaves were few, they were relatively well treated because they often lived in close contact with whites in a family setting. In the South—a "slave society," not merely a "society with slaves"—the system was harsher. The slaves' housing was often minimal. One eighteenth-century white Virginian, forced to take shelter one evening in a "Negro cabin" with six slaves, reported that the shack "was not lathed or plaistered, neither ceiled nor lofted above . . . one window, but no glass in it, not even a brick chimney, and as it stood on blocks about a foot above the ground, the hogs lay constantly under the floor, which made it swarm with flies." Some masters abused their slaves cruelly. The Virginian Robert Carter underfed his slaves and expected them to make up the deficiency by raising their own food in their spare time. "King" Carter, one of Virginia's largest tobacco planters, at one point petitioned the courts to chop off the toes of "two incorrigible negroes . . . named Barbara Harry and Dinah. . . ." The court gave him "full power to dismember" the uncooperative women. Colonial slaves were harshly disciplined and tightly controlled. In seventeenth-century South Carolina, slaves judged guilty of offenses such as murder, striking a white person, or plotting an insurrection could be castrated, branded, and burned alive. In the eighteenth century whipping replaced most of the earlier punishments, but whipping too was a brutal and terrifying experience. Slaves who left their plantations were required to carry "tickets" indicating their owners' permission to be away from home. Mounted patrols stopped blacks on the roads, entered black homes for inspection, and confiscated black-owned firearms.

It was during the last years of the seventeenth century and the early years of the eighteenth, when the plantation system was putting down firm roots along the Carolina coast and in the Chesapeake region, that the colonial slave regime in the South was harshest. During this period most of the slaves were still native-born Africans and, in the throes of adjusting to an alien land, were unable to resist the planters' single-minded demands for productivity. By the middle of the eighteenth century, after American-born slaves became predominant, they were able to force masters to ease oppressive rules and practices and allow some privileges. Using tactics that included destroying their masters' tools, injuring cattle and crops, running away, and feigning illness, they forced masters to accept a reasonable work day; to allow some family privacy; to guarantee a Sunday day of rest; to permit trade with other slaves and with whites in items like chickens, melons, eggs and other self-raised products.

Yet despite these concessions colonial blacks resented slavery and found ways to express their hatred of the system. South Carolina slaves often escaped to the Spanish settlements in Florida. Some slaves fled to the Indian frontier. To discourage flight, Virginia allowed anyone who encountered a runaway to kill him on sight without penalty.

The most serious slave protest was group rebellion. Nowhere in the mainland English colonies did slaves mount a large-scale uprising or set up independent black communities as they did in Brazil, Surinam, and places in the Caribbean. But there were several organized slave rebellions during the colonial period. In New York City in 1712 twenty-five slaves armed with knives, axes, and guns set fire to a white man's outhouse. When whites rushed to save the burning structure, the slaves attacked them, killing nine. The authorities called out the militia, who quickly rounded up the insurrectionists. Twenty-one were executed. The Stono Rebellion in South Carolina—a far more serious threat to white rule—began near Charleston in September 1739 when a group of slaves broke into a storehouse and seized arms and supplies. Fleeing south toward Spanish Florida, the rebels gathered recruits as they went and attacked any whites who got in their way.

The militia soon caught up with the fugitives and killed them all. Thirty whites and forty-four blacks lost their lives. The Stono Rebellion sent a shock wave through South Carolina. White South Carolinians would never feel entirely safe again.

Regions

New England, Middle Colonies, the South.   Diversity in colonial America also extended to patterns of settlement. Much of New England was divided into "towns," small communities of about 500 with a central village and adjacent fields and woods. The New England town was a relatively homogeneous community. All of its members belonged to the same Puritan faith; most came from the same part of east-central England. Most town residents were members of farm families, but each community also had a minister, a schoolmaster, artisans, and craftspeople of various kinds. The dwellings within the village center were distributed around the perimeter of the "common," an open space where sheep and cattle grazed and where the community held its militia "musters" and conducted other collective outdoor activities. The village church, with its austere white exterior and tall steeple, usually bordered the common. Each family normally had a small garden parcel close to its dwelling and larger fields, more distant from the town center, where it grew its chief bread crops.

Life in the typical New England town was generally placid and orderly. Community decisions were made through the monthly town meeting. Though women, minors, servants, and nonchurchgoers were disenfranchised, a sizable proportion of the adult males voted. These towns, one scholar has said, were "peaceable kingdoms," where disputes were readily resolved and a wide consensus achieved by discussion. They were also ideal settings for community activities, whether educational or religious. Some of the edge that New England has enjoyed over the years in science, literature, and business enterprise has been ascribed to the compact settlement of the colonial New England town, which made schools more practical than where settlement was more scattered.

In the middle colonies (New York, New Jersey, and Pennsylvania), on the western border, and in the South, such tight-knit communities were rare, except in a few places, like Long Island, where New Englanders had put down roots. Instead, families lived on detached farms, often separated from their neighbors, especially on the western frontier, by large stretches of forest. In the middle colonies commerce helped create a sprinkling of small cities, but in the Chesapeake region (Maryland and Virginia) and the Carolinas, these were uncommon. Aside from a few provincial capitals such as Williamsburg, Virginia and Annapolis, Maryland and the port of Charleston in South Carolina, little approaching a true city could be found in the region south of Pennsylvania until almost the very end of the colonial era.

Given these patterns of land occupation, it is not surprising that historians have supposed that the life of the typical Pennsylvanian or Virginian, say, entailed far less intense community involvement than that of the contemporary New Englander. But did it? A study by Darrett and Anita Rutman of Middlesex County, Virginia, in the period 1659–1750 demonstrates that communities in the Chesapeake region were not the chaotic, impersonal places often assumed. Though the people of Middlesex County did not come together each month in a formal legislative town meeting as in New England, they had their equivalent social, if not political, occasion in the monthly county court day. On court days not only were criminal and civil cases heard by the magistrates, but people without court business came for the horse racing, the liquor refreshment, the gossip, and the chance to renew acquaintanceships and do business.

Studies such as the Rutmans' have narrowed the gap between New England and the colonial South. Moreover, there is reason to think that we have exaggerated the communal solidarity of many towns in New England. A study of Marblehead and Gloucester, both in Massachusetts, shows, for example, that community solidarity and homogeneity were often lacking even in the Bay Colony, especially in the ports and the fishing communities.

Though we can no longer draw such sharp contrasts between the social texture of New England and that of the South, it remains true that differences did affect the course of regional development.

East–West Differences.
Among the regional divisions that marked colonial society, East–West differences were especially troublesome. Much of the sectional tension involved the Indians. On the frontier the white population brushed against Indian groups unwilling to surrender additional lands or permit Europeans to settle among them. In the clashes that ensued, the authorities in the older coastal areas, preferring to preserve order at all costs, sometimes sided with the Indians against the western frontiersmen. This response created resentment between East and West.

These East–West tensions first appeared in Virginia, where by the 1670s settlers had pushed beyond the Tidewater into the Piedmont, the hilly plateau region immediately to the west. Piedmont settlers soon came to feel that the Tidewater planters who generally controlled the provincial government were unconcerned with their problems. They especially resented the easterners' indifference to Indian attacks.

In 1675 and 1676, when Indian warfare broke out on the frontier, Virginia governor Sir William Berkeley called for restraint. The frontiersmen, under the leadership of Nathaniel Bacon, craving vengeance, ignored him and attacked local Indian villages, wiping several out. Berkeley marched to the scene with 300 armed men determined to "call Mr. Bacon to accompt." By the time he arrived, Bacon and his followers had disappeared into the forest, where they mounted further attacks on the local tribes, friendly and hostile alike. Now a hero in the Piedmont, Bacon was elected to the House of Burgesses and took his seat in Jamestown, accompanied by armed partisans to see that he was not arrested.

The rebellious delegates, gaining control of the Burgesses, passed measures to liberalize voting, open offices to small property holders, make taxes less burdensome for poorer colonists, and improve defenses against the Indians. Bacon soon demanded to be made commander of all the colony's armed forces. Berkeley refused, but the assembly, intimidated by Bacon's armed supporters, yielded. Bacon soon departed with his men for the frontier, intent on killing more Indians. A series of maneuvers between militia loyal to the governor and Bacon's partisans ended with the burning of Jamestown in September 1676. In this moment of triumph Bacon suddenly died of a "Bloody Flux," ending his cause. Berkeley was not forgiving and hanged thirty-seven of Bacon's followers. Bacon's Rebellion was over.

Pennsylvania too began to experience Indian–white and East–West tensions as white settlers moved westward. The Scotch-Irish settlers had complained for years that the Quaker-dominated government in Philadelphia did not support them adequately against the Indians. In December 1763 a mob of frontiersmen from the towns of Paxton and Donegal took the law into its own hands and attacked a group of peaceful Conestoga Indians, killing six. When the horrified Pennsylvania assembly ordered the "Paxton Boys" arrested, the enraged westerners marched on Philadelphia, prepared to get "justice" at the point of a gun. For a while it looked as if the colony would be thrown into civil war. Fortunately, Benjamin Franklin intercepted the rebels and negotiated a solution. Though further violence was avoided, this near-rebellion left a legacy of sectional antagonisms within Pennsylvania that lasted to the end of the century.

Families

The diverse ethnic and cultural ingredients in British North America continued to be separate, and new regional differences inevitably developed. But this does not mean that the New World environment did not broadly affect transplanted Old World institutions, attitudes, and practices. On the contrary, the new setting profoundly modified many Old World social and cultural forms, helping to produce a society identifiably American.

Birth Rates, Death Rates, and Family Size.   Even the most fundamental institution of all, the family, was altered by the new American environment. Exposed to New World conditions, the European family became both larger and more egalitarian than it had been in the mother country.

Famines, plagues, and wars ravaged seventeenth-century Europe and cut down thousands of men, women, and children before their time. By itself this situation would have limited European family size. It was also typical of early modern Britain that, except for the aristocracy, the nuclear family consisted of parents and young children. Once grown, children were expected to establish their own households. This custom, coupled with the high death rates in this period, made for relatively small families, not more than four or five people.

The new American environment created a different family pattern. From the beginning, people in New England lived longer than their counterparts in Britain. During the seventeenth century the average life expectancy for men in Plymouth Colony came close to that of our own day. In Dedham, in the Bay Colony, death rates were half those of contemporary Europe. At the same time, in most of the New England towns birth rates were high, usually higher than in Europe. The net effect of these low death rates and high birth rates was to create larger families in New England than on the other side of the Atlantic.

At first the family history of the southern colonies was quite different. Most early immigrants to Maryland and Virginia were single men who came either as planters or as servants. The authorities tried to attract women by paying their passage, but their success was limited. In 1704, for example, only about 7,200 of the 30,000 Europeans in Maryland were women. Most male Virginians and Marylanders were forced to remain bachelors.

The generally unhealthy state of the Chesapeake region also held down family formation. Malaria and dysentery killed many people in early colonial Virginia and Maryland and hit pregnant women particularly hard. In addition, European diseases were carried to the Chesapeake region by the tobacco-collecting vessels that came directly to each planter's dock. In South Carolina the rice-growing lowlands with their "agues" continued to be unhealthy well into the 1800s.

Still, as time passed, an ever-larger proportion of the Chesapeake and Carolina population consisted of the native-born, a development that equalized the numbers of males and females. This return to a normal sex ratio made more marriages possible, so that by the eighteenth century the family became the normal household unit even in the South. Meanwhile, because of closer commercial contact with other parts of the world, smallpox, malaria, and other illnesses invaded New England, increasing mortality rates. By the later years of the colonial period the disparity in size between the southern and northern colonial family had virtually disappeared.

The difference between European and American demographic characteristics, however, never entirely vanished during the colonial period. As late as 1790 American families were larger than their European counterparts. Population grew faster, too. Because land was cheaper and more abundant in America than in Europe, young people could afford to marry early. In the absence of birth control they usually had many children. Even without heavy immigration this would have made for a rapid population increase. But the flood of European immigrants magnified the effects.

Women and Family Roles.

In colonial America the family served many functions. It was, for one thing, the center of education and training. Parents taught young children their first "letters" and their earliest religious precepts. A father taught his sons how to farm, repair tools, hunt, and fish. If he was a craftsman, he taught his son his trade. Girls learned from their mothers how to cook, bake, sew, weave, and spin.

The family was also a "little commonwealth," within which people's lives were prescribed and regulated and acceptable social behavior taught and enforced. In their current theory, as expounded by the social philosopher Robert Filmer, the family was a small state. Even more than in England, in the early colonies fathers were the rulers in these small political units. He enforced discipline and prescribed the rules. The law in the Puritan colonies even allowed them the power of life and death over their children. This absolute authority was not always effective. Adolescent children then, as now, could be outrageously disobedient. One seventeenth-century Boston lad was convicted by the courts of reviling his father "by Calling him a Liar and a Drunckard & holding up [his] fist against him." Girls seldom threatened their parents physically; their disobedience often took the form of "lewd and disorderly" behavior—that is, sexual misconduct. Not infrequently, this led to pregnancy, and the birth of what that era frankly referred to as a "bastard" child.

QUEBEC
(French
until 1763)

Quebec

Montreal

MAINE
(part of
Mass.)

*Lake
Champlain*

Falmouth
NEW HAMPSHIRE
Portsmouth
Newburyport
Salem
MASSACHUSETTS

Lake Huron

Lake Ontario

Oswego

Hudson R.

Boston

Albany

Connecticut R.

Fort Niagara
IROQUOIS
CONFEDERATION

NEW
YORK

Newport

Hartford

RHODE ISLAND

Lake Erie

Fort Detroit

New Haven

CONNECTICUT

Delaware R.

MOUNTAINS

New York
Perth Amboy

NEW JERSEY

PENNSYLVANIA

Susquehanna R.

Philadelphia
New Castle

Pittsburgh

York

DELAWARE

Fort Cumberland

Alexandria

MARYLAND

Ohio R.

Stanton

Richmond

Chesapeake Bay

VIRGINIA

Williamsburg
Norfolk

James R.

Roanoke R.

Fort
Chiswell

Hillsboro

Cape Hatteras

WATAUGA
SETTLEMENTS

Salem

Bath

NORTH CAROLINA

New Bern

*Cape
Fear R.*

Charlotte

SOUTH
CAROLINA

Camden

Wilmington

*ATLANTIC
OCEAN*

APPALACHIAN

Savannah R.

Augusta

GEORGIA

Charleston

Savannah

	Settled before 1650
	Settled between 1650 and 1700
	Settled between 1700 and 1770
○	Cities over 10,000 in 1770

0   100   200 Miles

0   100   200 Kilometers

FLORIDA

GULF OF MEXICO

Colonial Settlement, 1650–1770

The patriarchal system was reinforced by the father's control over the family land and property. In the southern colonies, with their looser settlement patterns and their more abundant fertile land, this arrangement was probably not a serious problem for children. In early New England, however, where towns were limited in size and where fathers usually lived to ripe old age, grown sons were often forced to live in their parents' household, subject to continued patriarchal control, or to become tenants on their father's land. Fortunately, New England sons had an escape route. By the beginning of the eighteenth century an ever-larger number were leaving the crowded Massachusetts and Connecticut towns to move to cheap land in the Berkshire Hills, the Green Mountains, New Hampshire, and Maine.

Within the colonial family the roles of fathers and mothers differed distinctly. Fathers typically carried on the family's public functions—such as casting its vote, serving in the militia, filling governmental positions—and its work outside the home. Men were the tillers of the soil; women of European ancestry eschewed agriculture. This arrangement was distinctly different from that of the Indian population and Algonkian men claimed that by keeping their women from planting, and weeding, and harvesting, English men were "spoiling good working creatures." Mothers were responsible for private domestic matters and for acting as "helpmeets" to their husbands. Within this limited domain women had considerable power. Mothers were expected to supervise the children, particularly the youngest ones. But in addition to their household duties, many married women supplemented family income by helping in the family business, by running their own small businesses, or by selling surplus produce or handmade goods. They were also organizers of church functions.

However inferior their status to American men, American women had greater privileges than women in Europe. Colonial men often recognized the value of women's work. In one Plymouth community a man was denied a license to run a tavern because he had no wife to help him in the business. Laws of the times granted American women higher legal status than their English sisters. Divorce was easier for wronged wives. Husbands who abused their spouses, especially in New England, were often reprimanded by the authorities. And colonial widows were entitled to a larger fixed amount of their husbands' estates than was common in the mother country. Some colonial women, especially mature widows, and above all those of wealth and high family status, even asserted themselves politically or in the realm of religious belief. As we have seen, Anne Hutchinson defied the Massachusetts ministers and authorities early in the Bay colony's history. Another case was Anne Eaton of New Haven colony, wife of the colonial governor, who began to question the Puritan doctrine that children should be baptized at birth rather than when they had experienced God's grace. Mistress Eaton was admonished to recant by both her husband and her minister but refused. During a sermon by the Reverend Davenport, seeking to refute her views, she muttered to the other congregants: "it is not so."

Yet it remains true that the colonial woman's role and status were inferior to the man's. Even their services as wives and mothers conferred little freedom or prestige on colonial women, and many keenly felt their subordination. Their response was more often resignation than rebellion, however. As one South

Carolina woman noted, her "self-denying duties" were "a part of the curse pronounced upon Eve" and nothing could be done about it.

Servants, who usually lived with their employers or masters, were often treated as part of the family. Masters had the authority to discipline them and sometimes were obliged to provide them with an education. In the South slaves were in
some ways members of the master's family, too. Legally, slaves were treated as the
children of their masters or mistresses, who, like parents, were expected to provide food, clothing, and shelter and to mete out rewards and punishments.

The structure and power relations of colonial families were not static. They
evolved over time, and by the eighteenth century a new pattern, according to historian Philip Greven, had begun to emerge, though the older, patriarchal one remained very much alive. This new "genteel" type flourished among richer,
better-educated, and less pious Americans. It appeared late because wealth, comfort, and a secular outlook were relatively late developments in America.

Genteel families were bound together by affection rather than by authority
and fear; they were more child-centered. Fathers were less insistent on their
despotic rights and were more likely to accept the autonomy of their wives and
children. One effect was the greater freedom of adult children to choose their
spouses rather than have their parents select them. Scholars have theorized that
the soaring rate of premarital pregnancy in the late eighteenth century may have
reflected the desire of grown daughters and sons to force the consent of fathers to
marriages they would otherwise have forbidden.

Everyday Life

To describe coherently how colonial Americans lived day-to-day presents many
problems. The colonial era lasted 170 years by conventional measure (from 1607 to
1776). During that interval habits, customs, styles, and values changed. They were
not the same at the end as at the beginning. Daily life in the colonial era also differed among classes, races, nationalities, and regions. Yet some common qualities
of that life can be extracted from the immense diversity.

Housing among the earliest settlers was generally primitive. The first Europeans to touch shore in North America dug caves in the hillsides or put up lean-
tos and canvas tents. But as soon as possible the settlers built dwellings in styles
familiar at home. Until well into the eighteenth century, farmhouses in the northern colonies were made by driving posts into the ground, siding the structures
with clapboard, and capping them with a wood–shingled roof. Many of these
were no larger than twenty-by-twenty feet and rose a story-and-a-half, the "half"
being a loft reached by an inside ladder. Each of these structures had a fireplace,
often of logs partially protected from fire by clay plastering. They were usually
unpainted, as paint was imported and expensive. In the absence of glass, householders used wooden shutters to cover windows. These kept out the rain and
wind, but they also excluded the daylight, and such dwellings were often dark,
dank places.

Even in the eighteenth century rooms in colonial homes were seldom
differentiated by function. People slept, washed, dined, sat, and entertained in

whatever room was handy, though there were sleeping lofts in houses with more than one story and most homes had kitchens with a table and fireplace for cooking. Sanitary facilities were primitive. People often bathed—when they bathed at all—outdoors. They used privies set some distance from the house to keep the flies away. There were no window screens in those days, and mosquitoes and flies often made life in summer an ordeal. Rooms lacked closets. Clothes were folded away in chests or hung on pegs on the wall. Furniture was generally sparse and crude. Meals were consumed on tables made of boards set on trestles. Benches and stools were more common than chairs. Beds were hard mattresses stuffed with grass or feathers laid over a web of rope attached to a wood frame. Tableware— bowls, plates, trenchers—were made of hollowed-out wood at first and then later of pewter, a silver-gray alloy of tin and lead. Spoons were common, but forks were rare until late in the colonial period.

Housing in the towns was generally better than in the countryside. Town structures were more often of brick or stone than farm houses. As dwelling places for the colonies' prosperous merchants, shopkeepers, and skilled artisans, the towns also had many of America's largest and most luxurious private houses, buildings with two or three stories, many bedrooms, parlors, and multiple fireplaces. Professional architects designed some of these. In the South a few "show" plantation homes matched the luxury of the best townhouses in Salem, Newport, Boston, and Philadelphia.

Food was plentiful but plain in the colonies. The forests and waters provided game, fish, fowl, berries, fruits, and nuts in abundance. The settlers planted European parsnips, turnips, carrots, cabbage, and onions in their kitchen gardens. They also sowed wheat where it would grow and raised hogs, sheep, cattle, and chickens. They borrowed maize and beans from the Indians. These ingredients they consumed roasted, stewed, or in the form of breads and various sorts of mushes or porridges. Frying with lard was a common way to prepare meats, especially in the South. Breakfast often consisted of a porridge of grain mixed with milk and flavored with molasses. The main meal was dinner served in the afternoon and often featuring a stew with meat and vegetables. Supper often repeated breakfast or was leftovers from dinner. In the towns, especially of New England, fish such as cod and herring was a common article of diet. Cuisine, generally, was not very flavorful, at least by our standards. Most cooks used few spices and did little to preserve natural flavors. None of this was especially healthy. The fat content of colonial food was high; the vitamin content undoubtedly low. Still, its variety and abundance made it superior to the diet of contemporary Europe. Americans were on average taller and heavier than were Western Europeans as early as the 1770s, a fact attesting to their superior nutrition.

Colonial Americans scorned water as a thirst-quencher. At the outset milk was one of the few alternatives, but as soon as possible the colonists turned to beer, wine, hard cider, and distilled liquors, the latter mostly rum made from West Indies molasses. By the eighteenth century tea had become common, but through most of the colonial era beverages containing alcohol were the drink of choice. This practice cannot have contributed to longevity, and drunkenness was a common colonial problem.

American dress modes were tied to class and occupation. The male farmer wore, on workdays, a linen shirt under a tight jacket called a "doublet." Below the waist he wore knee breeches, usually of wool but often of leather, ending in long cotton or linen stockings. His feet were shod either in moccasins or in boots, depending on the season. The city artisan often supplemented this dress with a leather apron. Women of the farm or artisan class typically wore a three-piece outfit: a long skirt, a bodice, and sleeves attached to the bodice by ties at the armholes. Headgear for men consisted of woolen caps; for women, hoods or scarves.

Needless to say, the dress of the colonial elite was fancier. Breeches and bodices were often of velvet or satin; leather shoes had silver buckles. In later years men wore three-cornered hats of beaver felt. Wigs became the almost universal head covering among "gentlemen" during the early eighteenth century, though at times, in the towns, even slaves wore them. Heavy, hot, and expensive, wigs eventually were replaced by longish hair whitened with chalk and tied in a queue behind. Rich women wore slippers of satin or morocco leather and donned long skirts over several layers of petticoats. In the eighteenth century they adopted the hoop-petticoat, an outside skirt stiffened with whalebone. Women often wore their bodices low-cut. Slim waists were prized, and the middles of prosperous young women and matrons were frequently compressed by tight-laced corsets.

The workweek was a six-day affair for most colonial people. Only on Sunday did work cease, and for the pious that did not mean leisure but church-going that took up long hours followed by sedate occupations such as visiting, reading, and conversation. Life revolved around the seasons more than today. Most men were farmers and their year was governed by the crop-growing cycle of spring plowing and planting, summer weeding and hoeing, and fall harvesting. Winter on the farm was devoted to fence and house repair, handicrafts, and the like. Women's tasks were less affected by the season. Each week, whether summer or winter, brought the same routine of washing, cooking, nursing, and house cleaning.

The colonists, except for the most devout, craved amusement for their leisure hours. In the South people enjoyed horse racing and indulged in "blood sports," such as cockfighting and bull baiting. Colonial boys played games with a ball and a bat that resembled modern baseball. In the winter, northern children ice-skated and sledded. Males in general hunted and fished for amusement as well as food.

Government

Colonial Political Structure.   British immigrants to America brought with them the political ideas, customs, and practices of the mother country. On the local level, for example, both the town in New England and the church vestry in the South were political units transplanted from Britain. Beginning with Virginia in 1619, settlers were empowered one by one to set up legislatures resembling Parliament in each of the British mainland colonies. These were given different names in different colonies (General Court, House of Burgesses, General Assembly), and like Britain's Parliament usually had a lower and an upper house.

Each colony also had a chief executive, the equivalent of the English monarch. In royal colonies (in 1776 New Hampshire, Massachusetts, New York, New Jersey,

Maryland, Virginia, North Carolina, South Carolina, and Georgia) the governor was appointed by the British sovereign. In proprietary colonies (Pennsylvania and Delaware, and New York, Maryland, and the Carolinas before they became royal colonies) the governor represented the proprietor, the man who held the original charter. Only in Connecticut and Rhode Island was the governor elected by the local enfranchised citizens. No matter how he was chosen, the governor usually could veto acts by the colonial legislature, much as, in theory at least, the English sovereign could acts of Parliament.

As time passed, the governors were forced to give up some of their power to the assemblies. At first the British authorities refused to consider these bodies true legislatures. One official in London described them as only "so many Corporations at a distance, invested with an Ability to make Temporary By Laws for themselves." But the distance from England, official British policy of ignoring restrictions on the colonies to allow them to prosper and thus enrich England, and inefficiency in administering colonial affairs encouraged the colonial legislatures to expand their powers. Early in the eighteenth century the colonial lower houses forced the governors to allow them to debate freely without executive interference, to judge the qualifications of their own members, to exclude crown officials from their deliberations, and to meet when and for as long as they wished. Most important, they forced the governors to surrender to them "the power of the purse." By the middle of the eighteenth century the assemblies had moved from granting an annual lump-sum appropriation to the governor to spend as he saw fit to earmarking appropriations for specific periods. They also began to pay the governors' salaries for a single year—and only at the end of it—to guarantee their good behavior. In several colonies these efforts to control the governors touched off furious battles. By the 1750s most of these struggles had been decided in favor of the legislatures.

By the end of the colonial era the provincial assemblies were miniature parliaments exercising almost all the hard-won rights of their English model, including control over taxation, expenditures, the salaries of officials, military and Indian affairs, and everything that affected religion, education, and what we today would call welfare. The legislatures' power was not unlimited, however. Governors continued to veto laws they opposed. And even if the governor approved a measure, it could be "disallowed" by the Privy Council in England. Especially during the early years of the eighteenth century, however, the English government did little to restrain the colonial assemblies, and during this period of "salutary neglect" much real political power slipped into the hands of the colonists.

Voters and Their Representatives.

Although the framework of the colonial governments was similar to that of Great Britain, political power was more widely diffused in the colonies than in Britain. The upper houses of the colonial legislatures, the councils, were appointed and were composed typically of landed gentlemen, prosperous lawyers, and rich merchants. But membership was not hereditary, as it was in the English House of Lords.

More significant was the relatively broad electorate that chose the colonial lower houses. By modern democratic standards the colonial franchise was severely limited. Slaves, of course, could not vote, nor could indentured servants.

Though at times some women exercised considerable, usually informal, public authority, no colonial female had the right to vote. Even free white adult males had to own land or houses, or lease them for a long period, to qualify as voters. This was only one side of the picture, however. Property was so easily acquired and so widely held in America that the election laws disqualified relatively few free adult males from voting. Furthermore, traditional requirements linking church membership to voting privileges were undermined by the growing diversity of religions in America. The end result was a relatively broad franchise. In various Rhode Island towns in the mid-eighteenth century, for example, 60 percent or more of the total adult male population was eligible to vote. In some New York districts up to 80 percent of all adult males had the vote. In Massachusetts, according to conservative Governor Thomas Hutchinson, "anything with the appearance of a man" was allowed to exercise the franchise.

Though many ordinary people could vote, colonial officials were not carbon copies of the colonial population. Colonial voters generally preferred to send the local squire, a prosperous merchant, or a rising young lawyer to the House of Burgesses or House of Assembly rather than a farmer, craftsman, or small shopkeeper. Local officials were also members of the elite. Southern vestries appointed their own successors and were dominated by the "squirearchy" of rich planters, who resembled the county gentry of England. The town, the basic governmental unit in New England, was not entirely democratic, either. Virtually all adult males participated in the town meeting, but town leaders were generally men of high status. In a word, the political system of colonial America was not democratic.

On the other hand, political deference—submission to social superiors—was decidedly weaker in America than in England. When the local squire ran for office, he had to campaign hard and promise to abide by the wishes of the voters. Candidates were expected to act democratically and avoid aloofness. During election campaigns they made it a point to mingle with the electors and offer them "refreshment," liquid or otherwise.

All-in-all, we must conclude that colonial government was neither predominantly democratic nor predominantly aristocratic; it displayed both tendencies. Democracy as we know it did not exist anywhere in the seventeenth- and eighteenth-century world. But as political institutions were transferred from England to America, they were changed in ways that allowed greater popular freedom and self-determination.

Religion

Organized religion was another institution that changed in the New World. White settlers brought with them a great variety of faiths—Presbyterian, Quaker, Baptist, Anglican, Lutheran, Congregational, Mennonite, Catholic, Jewish, and others. Before long, under the special conditions in America, the practices of many of these groups began to diverge from their European norms.

Guarding the Flame in New England.   The Puritans who immigrated to Massachusetts did not come to found a separate church. Rather, they came to escape the harsh repression of a powerful state and the Anglican bishops who

administered the state religion. But once free of these restraints, they created the New England Way, a distinctive pattern that differed from both the Puritanism and the Anglicanism of Old England.

One of the differences involved church structure. In the Old World, bishops or a council of church elders (presbyters) ruled the church. But in America the sparseness of the white population and the relative isolation of settlements encouraged church government by individual, self-governing congregations. Each group of Christians, led by their ministers, developed, in the words of the Reverend John Cotton, "complete liberty to stand alone." This system was called Congregationalism.

The New England Way also changed Puritan doctrine. At the heart of the Puritan faith as it evolved in Britain was the Calvinist notion that since Adam's fall only the "elect" (the "saints"), solely through God's mercy, would be saved from hell. But in New England the alternate idea of the "covenant" appeared: People could effect their salvation by entering into a kind of contract with God by which the Lord would agree to guarantee them the faith needed for salvation. Thus "saints" were not predestined, but "reborn," or converted.

These saints, the Puritans believed, would not only behave virtuously, but would also avoid wicked thoughts. Their faith thus placed a tremendous moral and emotional burden on the New England Puritans. Some became tortured souls obsessed with a sense of their own sinfulness. Michael Wigglesworth, a Congregational minister at Malden, kept a diary between 1653 and 1670 in which he constantly lamented his depravity. A typical entry noted:

> Peevishness, vain thoughts, and especially pride still prevail in me. I cannot think one good thought; I cannot do anything for God but presently pride gets hold of me. . . . I fear there is much sensuality and doting upon the creature in my pursuit of the good of others.

New England Puritans closely linked religion and government. The law required everyone to attend church services and pay taxes to support the Congregational ministry, regardless of their religious preference. But not all church attenders were church members: Only those who had experienced conversion—felt the infusion of "divine grace"—could belong to the "church" of "visible saints" and partake of the rite of baptism. And only converted males could vote or hold office, although all were expected to obey the laws. Massachusetts was a community where God was considered the ruler and his will was expressed through the church leaders. Though clergymen did not hold office, they advised the secular rulers and were consulted in all matters that pertained to public life and community policy. Questions that today we would consider matters of personal preference were treated as public issues subject to strict law. Sexual behavior in all its aspects fell under close public control; so did family concerns, such as children's disobedience. Blasphemy was a serious crime punishable by the authorities, as was breaking the Sabbath by game playing, drinking, or levity. Public education was intended not only to transmit skills and secular culture but also to imbue religious principles.

For a time it seemed possible to establish in Massachusetts a truly godly community—that famous "City upon a Hill"—where holiness would guide every aspect of life and people might avoid the corruptions of England. But as time passed New Englanders increasingly turned to worldly affairs and shifted their attention from God to gain. By the middle of the seventeenth century the pious Puritan was already giving way to the get-ahead, enterprising Yankee. Before long many church members failed to experience conversion and so their children could not be admitted to full church membership. This shrinking of the elect left many people without civil rights and threatened the churches with much-diminished membership. The answer was the Half-Way Covenant, which provided that persons who had been baptized and who led virtuous lives could become "half-way" church members. No conversion experience was necessary. These people could not participate in the Lord's Supper, one of the few sacraments remaining in Calvinism, but they were no longer disqualified from normal civil rights.

The Salem Witch Hunt.   The new policy eased the crisis, but it did not check the erosion of orthodoxy in the Puritan colony. In 1692 a new challenge to the colony's ministerial leadership erupted when a group of young girls in Salem, north of Boston, began to display "odd postures," "fits," "distempers," and "foolish, ridiculous speeches." One of these was the nine-year-old daughter of the Reverend Samuel Parris, minister of the Salem village congregation. The girls accused others of consorting with the devil and engaging in witchcraft, a crime in Massachusetts derived from the Old Testament injunction that witches deserved death. Before many months the circle of women, with a few men, accused of being witches or wizards expanded to over one hundred. Tried by special provincial courts, nineteen were hanged in the end, including the Reverend George Burroughs, a former Salem Village minister.

At first the colony's leaders, political and religious, supported the witchcraft prosecutions. Few doubted that witches existed and were capable of harming their enemies physically and destroying their possessions. Nor did they doubt that witches intended "to pull down the kingdom of Christ and set up the Devil's Kingdom." But they began to question the reliability of witnesses against the accused and the evidence the prosecutors had gathered. Among the skeptics was Increase Mather, the most powerful clergyman in the colony. In October 1693 Mather preached a powerful sermon in which he cast doubt on the testimony of the accusers. Mather's essential message was, "It were better that ten suspected witches should escape, than that one innocent person should be condemned."

Mather's opposition rallied other prominent clergy as well as Governor Sir William Phips to the side of sanity. Their pressure ended the trials and led to the release of the remaining accused. While it is true that the man who stopped the witch hunt was himself a religious leader, some historians believe the panic may have been fanned by the earnest efforts of some of the Massachusetts clergy to raise a new fear of sin and thus revive the orthodox church. An alternate explanation connects the hysteria to conflicts within the Salem community between those who felt powerless and wronged and their more successful neighbors.

The High Church in the Wilderness.   The American environment affected other Protestant denominations as well. In the Anglican communities on the Chesapeake local circumstances wore down traditional religion even more than in

New England. With its elaborate ceremonies and complex organization, the Anglican Church was less suited to early America than Puritanism, a condition made more trying by the distance between settlements and plantations in the Chesapeake area and the absence of cities and towns.

It was especially difficult to maintain the traditional governance of the Anglican Church. In England bishops ruled but no bishop came to America during the colonial period. Low salaries, isolation from the amenities of civilization, and the absence of substantial towns made English Anglican ministers reluctant to accept parishes in America. And with no bishop in the colonies, young Americans who desired to become clergymen had to travel to England for ordination. Because few were willing to make the voyage, many parishes were forced to do without an ordained spiritual leader or to accept an inferior one. The net effect was that in Virginia, Maryland, and elsewhere the Church of England moved toward a congregational system, placing control of religious matters in the hands of the vestry, the ruling lay group of the parish.

The Congregationalists and the Anglicans were not the only troubled religious bodies. By the beginning of the eighteenth century most of the transplanted European denominations were losing ground. On the frontiers of New York, New Jersey, and Pennsylvania the German Lutherans and Pietists and the Scotch-Irish Presbyterians were slow to form congregations. In eastern Pennsylvania, as the Quaker community grew richer, its members replaced piety with worldliness.

The Great Awakening.

The general decline of orthodoxy created a vacuum in the lives of many people. Among farmers, craftspeople, and other ordinary men and women, religion came increasingly to seem remote and unsatisfying. This attitude eventually triggered a religious resurgence that we call the Great Awakening.

The movement began in the 1720s as a series of revivals among the Presbyterians and Dutch Reformed groups in the middle colonies. During the next decade it was infused with new power by the Congregational minister Jonathan Edwards of Northampton, Massachusetts. In 1729 Edwards began to preach the old Calvinist doctrine of predestination, calling people back to God and threatening them with eternal damnation for their sins. Edwards's theology was old-fashioned, but his emotional preaching style was new, and his sermons shocked the traditionalists, who considered them unseemly. Ordinary people, however, flocked to hear him preach at his Northampton church. Before long clergymen throughout New England were emulating Edwards's hellfire-and-damnation sermons.

In 1738 the English preacher George Whitefield visited America and turned the Great Awakening into a religious event of continental proportions. Whitefield was a spellbinder who, like Edwards, preached the traditional old-time Calvinism of predestination and damnation for all but an elect. Benjamin Franklin, skeptical of organized religion in general and of Whitefield's appeals for money to found an American orphanage in particular, went to hear the preacher when he visited Philadelphia but was resolved not to contribute to his cause. "I had in my pocket, a handful of copper money, three or four silver dollars, and five pistoles in gold," Franklin later wrote. "As he proceeded I began to soften, and concluded to give the copper, another stroke of his oratory determined me to give the silver; and he finished so admirably that I emptied my pocket wholly into the collector's dish, gold and all."

The doctrines of the revivalists varied. Some were strict Calvinists who believed most souls damned. Others—Arminians—assumed a more forgiving God. But most of their followers embraced their passionate appeal for surrender to Jesus and a commitment to live an exemplary Christian life rather than their theology. Whitefield, Edwards, and the other revivalists presented these views so simply and with such emotional effect that thousands were brought back to religion. Attacked by educated people as "shouters," "enthusiasts," and disturbers of the peace, the revivalists of the Great Awakening were immensely successful among common people. Many joined, or rejoined, the older denominations. Within these churches congregations and clergy soon divided between those who followed the decorous old way—the Old Lights—and those who followed the emotional new way—the New Lights. Many more people flocked to newer denominations such as the Baptists and later the Methodists. Thus, by producing new sects and dividing congregations and ministers, the Great Awakening further diversified religious expression in America.

The Enlightenment.   The Great Awakening lured many ordinary people back into the traditional religious fold. But by the middle of the eighteenth century many educated men and women in America were turning not to traditional religion but to a new set of secular beliefs we call the Enlightenment.

This major alteration in the way Western thinkers perceived the world was rooted in the scientific revolutions of the day, especially in the ideas of Sir Isaac Newton. In the new view the world appeared a rational, orderly place, operating not according to the immediate will of God but by changeless natural laws. Several important concepts followed from this view: First, that as members of this rational universe, human beings were good, not sinful; second, that by use of their reason, human beings could discover the natural laws of the universe; third, that knowledge of these laws would enable people to control their environment and society; and finally, that the inevitable result of this control would be "progress" toward a happier, more virtuous and prosperous society. Science played a significant role in this world picture because it was by means of scientific method—observation and experiment—that natural laws could be discovered.

A few members of the "enlightened" elite rejected all religion and became agnostics or even atheists. Most, however, chose deism. Deists continued to believe in God, but theirs was a god who operated through natural laws, not miracles. He showed himself through nature, not Christian revelation. God's role in the world was much like that of a clockmaker—a being who makes a clock, winds it up, and then leaves it to work by its own mechanical laws.

Deism developed late in the colonial period and affected only a small group of Americans. The deists, however, were an influential group—including Benjamin Franklin, Thomas Jefferson, Ethan Allen, and Thomas Paine—who would have an impact on the world of ideas disproportionate to their numbers.

Intellectual America

The conditions that changed the social, political, and religious institutions transplanted from Europe also molded colonial science, education, and the professions. For better or worse, intellectual development in America diverged from the Old World experience.

Science.   The seventeenth century was an era of immense progress in the natural sciences. It was the time when Galileo first used the telescope to observe the solar system, William Harvey detected the circulation of the blood, Johannes Kepler formulated the laws governing the orbits of the planets, and Isaac Newton discovered the basic laws of motion and the role of gravity. These scientists were all Europeans, however; Americans made no contributions to basic scientific theory.

Neither the social nor physical environment of colonial America encouraged deep theoretical science. Engaged in a day-to-day struggle to earn a living, the colonists tended to be interested in practical, not theoretical, matters. Moreover, even at the very end of the colonial era the scaffolding necessary for a flourishing scientific enterprise was absent. Theoretical science requires laboratories, patronage, centers of learning, and stimulating contact among thinkers. Colonial America— lacking large accumulations of wealth, inhabited by a sparse and scattered population, and far from the intellectual centers of the Western world—was not a likely birthplace for a Harvey, a Galileo, a Kepler, or a Newton. Twenty-five Americans were elected before 1776 to the prestigious British scientific body, the Royal Society of London, but they were honored for their acute observations of natural phenomena, not for grand theories or major intellectual breakthroughs.

Only one colonial scientist deserves comparison with the top echelon of Europe: Benjamin Franklin. Franklin's experiments in the 1740s and 1750s contributed to an early understanding of electricity and won him an honorary doctorate from a European university. Yet among the practical Americans "Doctor" Franklin was largely famous for his invention of the lightning rod to protect buildings from electrical storms and for the efficient parlor stove that bears his name.

Education.   In America education also took on a distinctive cast. At the lower levels American education was advanced for its day. Primary schools, staffed by both men and women, existed in every colony by the mid-eighteenth century, but educational opportunities varied greatly. More boys than girls attended schools, a fact reflected in the higher literacy rate of colonial men than women. Slaves received no formal education, though a few learned to read and write. There were also strong regional inequalities in access to education. Because of the scattered settlement pattern in the southern colonies, it was hard to bring together a concentration of pupils sufficient to support a local school. Rich planters hired private tutors for their sons and daughters, and occasionally these tutors also instructed the sons and daughters of the planter's poorer neighbors. But educational opportunities in the southern colonies were generally limited, especially for the children of common farmers.

The more densely settled northern colonies, particularly New England, did better by their young people. The Dutch in New Netherland were quick to establish schools supported by the colonial treasury. Still more conscientious were the Massachusetts Puritans, who believed that it was essential to salvation for individuals to be able to read and understand the Scriptures for themselves. In 1647 the Massachusetts General Court required each town in the province with fifty families to establish a "petty" school to teach children to read and write. Any town with at least one hundred households was also required to establish a "grammar" school (high school) to prepare students for college and the learned professions. The purpose of the law, the legislators noted, was to defeat "ye ould deluder, Satan"; but its most important effect was to create in New England a body of literate people probably unique among contemporary Western communities.

Educated Americans tried to nurture higher education even in the crude early settlements. In 1636, just six years after the Puritans settled Massachusetts, Bay Colony authorities established Harvard College in Cambridge, to create the literate, educated ministry the Puritans considered vital to religion. Massachusetts's example was soon followed by other colonies. By the time of the Revolution eight other institutions of higher learning had been established in America: the College of William and Mary (1693); Yale (1701); the College of New Jersey, later called Princeton (1746); Queen's College, later called Rutgers (1766); King's College, later called Columbia (1754); the College of Philadelphia, later called the University of Pennsylvania (1754); Rhode Island College, later called Brown University (1764); and Dartmouth (1769). Like Harvard, most of these colleges were sponsored by religious denominations. They turned out men with "liberal" educations who either became clergymen or, after further training, entered one of the other traditional learned professions—law or medicine.

Law and Medicine.   Colonial conditions molded professional education, too. In England members of the legal profession endured a long and elaborate training process at the old and respected Inns of Court. English lawyers included attorneys to start the legal machinery going, solicitors to offer legal advice, notaries to prepare legal documents, and barristers to plead cases. The structure resembled England's class system: an elite at top with lesser folk beneath.

The struggling colonists could not support this elaborate and expensive system. In America there was only one all-purpose attorney, who drew up documents and briefs, advised clients, and pleaded cases in courtrooms. Instead of listening to lectures in law schools, lawyers learned by working in law offices, reading standard law books, attending court, and performing minor legal chores for senior attorneys. Toward the end of the colonial period, however, the legal profession drew closer to its English model. Some Americans began to go to London for legal training. But despite America's growing exposure to English forms, the English legal structure remained too cumbersome for America, with its weaker system of higher education and its more open class structure.

A similar simplification took place in the colonial medical profession. Despite scientific advances in medicine in seventeenth-century Europe, medical men still embraced theories of disease expounded by ancient or medieval authorities.

These theories usually ascribed disease to some imbalance in the four "humors"—choler, blood, bile, and phlegm. The physician's task was to determine the nature of the imbalance and restore equilibrium—often, as it happened, with harsh and ineffective remedies. Fortunately for Americans, the European physicians' learned ignorance could not be transplanted easily to North America. In Europe doctors trained at the universities. Few cared to surrender the high fees and status they enjoyed in Europe to come to the American wilderness, nor did American colleges teach medicine until the eve of the Revolution. Moreover, the exotic drugs and preparations European doctors used were hard to duplicate in America.

The dilution of European practices in the colonies probably improved medical care. Colonial medical practitioners, like colonial legal practitioners, learned by apprenticeship and from day-to-day contact with patients. Without mistaken theories to lead them astray, doctors relied on experience, observation, and common sense. Instead of purges, poultices, bleeding, and the foul potions prescribed in Europe, they turned to local herbs, often ones recommended by the Indians, for cures. Even when these did no good, they generally did little serious harm.

The American medical profession was also structured more democratically than the European. The shortage of trained personnel created opportunities for people who could not have practiced in England. Many medical practitioners in the colonies were women, and a number of slaves and free blacks were respected for their medical knowledge. Cotton Mather, who became a crusader for smallpox vaccination over the objections of European-trained physicians, first learned about the procedure from his black slave, a man named Onesimus.

Harvard College in the mid-1700s, a century after its founding

The Arts

In the fine arts colonial American accomplishments generally fell well below the best of Europe. Early American writing was predominantly nonfiction with an emphasis on biography, travel descriptions, religious exposition, and history. Much of it is today of interest only to academic students. At times, however, these works achieved some distinction. William Bradford's *Of Plimmoth Plantation,* an account of the founding and early days of the Pilgrim colony, was a heartfelt and effective narrative, though it was not published until many years after its author's death. The *Magnalia Christi Americana* (1702), by New Englander Cotton Mather, the scion of a distinguished Bay Colony ministerial family, is a rich encyclopedic review of New England's early history, replete with biographies, descriptions of wondrous happenings, and defenses of the New England way. In the South, Robert Beverley, an American-born planter, wrote the epically proportioned *The History and Present State of Virginia* (1705), a work that reveals the author's compassion for the Indians and his hope that Virginia would become a pastoral paradise.

Fiction was sparser. The first American novel did not appear until after independence, but there were several talented colonial poets. The best perhaps was Edward Taylor, an English-born minister educated at Harvard College. Taylor wrote more than 200 devotional poems full of rich imagery and subtle nuances. Unfortunately, almost none of his poetry was published until the 1930s. Anne Bradstreet of Andover, Massachusetts—a "Tenth Muse lately sprung up in America," her publisher called her—was more fortunate. Bradstreet had come to Massachusetts as a bride with the first Puritan wave in 1630 at the age of eighteen. Like many pioneer women, she had been dismayed by the crude frontier environment. But, as was expected of colonial women, she accepted her fate. "I changed my condition and was married," she later wrote, "and came into this country, where I found a new world and new manners, at which my heart rose [that is, was stirred against it]. But after I was convinced it was the way of God, I submitted to it. . . ." During the next forty years, amid the cares and labors of raising eight children and attending to her busy husband, she wrote reams of verse. Her later work, with its unaffected language and faithful images of the American landscape, is the first authentic American poetry.

Although imaginative literature did not flourish in colonial America, newspapers, broadsides, pamphlets, instructional books, and almanacs were produced in abundance. The colonists read widely because they needed practical information. Newspapers were read by proportionately more Americans than Europeans; they contained vital information about colonial affairs. Almanacs were useful to farmers and merchants, who had to know about prices and the weather. In the hands of Benjamin Franklin, the famous *Poor Richard's Almanack* came close to being a form of creative literature. Besides the usual data on planting times, seasonal changes, tides, eclipses, and the like, *Poor Richard's* contained entertaining little word sketches by "Richard Saunders" (Franklin's pseudonym) and pithy maxims that have become part of America's folk heritage.

Though Americans lagged badly behind Europeans in the fine arts, they excelled in the production of functional objects. This bent helps to explain the relatively high level of painting in the colonies. Colonial artists did not, like their European counterparts, paint dramatic landscapes, cavorting gods and goddesses, or heroic battle scenes. Instead, they focused on portraits, the most practical genre of painting. Here they could count on a ready market for their efforts. In the absence of photography, wealthy merchants and planters, who had little interest in art for art's sake, turned to painters to glorify their affluence and preserve their likenesses and those of their families for posterity.

The earliest American artists were amateurish daubers who often paid the rent by painting signs for merchants or inn keepers. Then, toward the end of the colonial era, John Singleton Copley and Benjamin West, of Boston and Philadelphia, respectively, began to attract wealthy patrons. But even in the second century of settlement, America could not hold onto its most talented artists. In 1760 West left for Rome and soon after settled in England. In 1775 Copley too left for Britain, in part to escape attack as a Loyalist, but also to expand his artistic horizons.

American architecture was also primitive and limited at first. As we saw, the earliest settlers lived in lean-tos, dugouts, and tents. Later in the first century of settlement, they began to imitate European models. Upper-class seventeenth-century houses in Massachusetts and Virginia resembled Tudor English buildings, replete with gables and small-paned leaded windows. Even the log cabin was a European borrowing, brought to the Delaware Bay region in the seventeenth century by Swedes and Finns.

In time, American architecture became more original. The new elite style of the eighteenth century took its name—Queen Anne or Georgian—from the English monarchs of the day. With its regularly spaced rows of windows, white-trimmed brick, and fine detailing at doors and openings, Georgian architecture was not, strictly speaking, a native genre at all. But it was adapted to American needs and circumstances in ways that frequently transcended mere imitation. The best of eighteenth-century colonial architecture blended admirably with the American environment; to this day Independence Hall in Philadelphia and domestic buildings like William Byrd's Virginia mansion, Westover, convey a sense of a vigorous provincial society evolving a distinctive cultural tradition.

A similar progression from imitation to innovation can be observed in the minor arts and the crafts. In the seventeenth century there were few skilled craftsmen in the colonies, and the settlers either used English artifacts or made their own crude ones. But by the eighteenth century many talented workers in brass, pewter, glass, silver, clay, and wood had immigrated to America from England and the Continent. Meanwhile, the skills of both white and black Americans had matured to a high level. Paul Revere of Boston combined native inspiration with imported forms and designs to create exquisite bowls, trays, and tea services in silver. At his glassworks at Mannheim, Pennsylvania, the German entrepreneur Henry William Stiegel produced glassware that is still eagerly collected. Skill and creativity marked the approach of colonial women to functional crafts, such as recycling bits of material into boldly designed quilts. Their work is now recognized and appreciated as the expression of artistic sensitivities that transcended the drudgeries of primitive life in the New World.

Conclusions

Crèvecoeur was right. By the eve of the Revolution America was no longer a carbon copy of Europe, and Americans were not simply transplanted Europeans.

Several factors had contributed to the change. British North America included a mixture of racial and ethnic components unknown in Europe; even the European ingredients of this mix were present in different proportions and existed in different relationships to one another than in the Old World. The Indian and African elements in the New World mixture were completely unknown to Europeans; yet they affected the military practice, technology, language, and customs of the new society.

In addition to the changes that accompanied the mingling of diverse cultures, there were those produced by the special physical and social environment of the New World. The abundance of land relative to the population made for better health, larger families, and ultimately a larger electorate and a more democratic political system. The relative scarcity of women allowed them some freedom to take on nontraditional roles and helped improve their legal status. A more scattered population and a less elitist social structure made it difficult to implant complex European institutions intact; as a result, the legal and medical professions were simplified and transformed. Meanwhile, the absence of a substantial leisure class, of great universities, and of private and government patronage altered the character of the arts and learning, pushing them toward greater practicality.

Nevertheless, we must qualify Crèvecoeur's announcement of a "new man" in America. Many of the distinctive national and cultural groups existed side by side without blending. In the case of blacks and Indians, their contributions were deliberately inhibited by the European majority. It would take generations before the blending process could produce a uniform new cultural mix, and the process is not complete today, nor will it ever be.

And there is another qualifier to add to the Crèvecoeur formula. At the end of the colonial period, as wealth increased and transatlantic communication improved, the culture of the colonial elite began to move closer to Britain's. In many ways, by the eve of the Revolution, religion, the professions, the arts, and political life had begun to take on the characteristics of the mother country. In 1775 American society was becoming a provincial offshoot of Europe. Yet the differences remained and the convergence would soon slow. By the mid-eighteenth century the actual interests of Americans and English people had begun to draw apart. British–American differences would soon produce a crisis that would sever the imperial connection and create a separate American nation and with it a still more distinctive culture.

ONLINE RESOURCES

"Famous American Trials: Salem Witchcraft Trials, 1692" *http://www.law.umkc.edu/faculty/ projects/ftrials/salem/SALEM.HTM* This comprehensive site contains various sources about this infamous incident in American history including excerpts from trial transcripts, biographies of key accusers and the accused, copies of arrest warrants for alleged witches, and illustrations. Also, read Cotton Mather's primary account of the events titled "Memorable Providences."

"The Exercise of a School Boy" *http://www.history.org/Almanack/life/manners/rules2.cfm* This site lists the text of the etiquette book entitled *Rules of Civility and Decent Behavior in Company and Conversation.* As a youth, George Washington transcribed these rules as a lesson of colonial gentility.

"The European Enlightenment" *http://www.wsu.edu/%7Edee/ENLIGHT/ENLIGHT.HTM* On this comprehensive site, read about the general tenets of Enlightenment philosophy, excerpts from the works of Enlightenment thinkers, and a glossary of terms and concepts. This site links to several others on the subject.

"Religion and the Founding of the American Republic" *http://www.loc.gov/exhibits/ religion/rel02.html* This Library of Congress site explores religion in eighteenth-century America and chronicles the coming of the religious movement known as the Great Awakening. It features many of the best-known religious leaders of this movement, including Jonathan Edwards and George Whitefield. The site also offers the views of critics of this movement.

"Albion's Seed Grows in the Cumberland Gap" *http://xroads.virginia.edu/%7EUG97/ albion/albion3.html* Discover the patterns of settlement and law and order of new immigrants to the backcountry of the Cumberland Gap, an area encompassing the present-day states of Kentucky, Tennessee, and Virginia.

4

Moving Toward Independence

Why Did the Colonists Revolt?

1651	England passes the first Navigation Act to prevent Dutch intrusion into the colonial trade
1688	The overthrow of James II begins the Glorious Revolution in England
1699	The Wool Act; France establishes the settlement of Louisiana on the Gulf of Mexico
1721–48	The period of salutary neglect
1732	The Hat Act
1733	The Molasses Act
1750	The Iron Act
1754	Benjamin Franklin proposes the Albany Plan of Union to the colonies, but it is never adopted
1754–63	The French and Indian War; Colonists disobey England's ban on all trade with France and its colonies; War with France ends with the Treaty of Paris; Colonial settlement west of Appalachians prohibited by the Proclamation of 1763
1764	The Sugar Act; The Currency Act
1765, 1766	The Quartering Acts
1765	The Stamp Act; The Intercolonial Stamp Act; Congress resolves that colonists should be taxed only by a representative legislature
1765–66	New York and other cities respond to the Stamp Act by adopting nonimportation agreements
1766	Parliament repeals the Stamp Act, but reaffirms with the Declaratory Act its right to legislate for the colonies
1767	The Townshend (or Revenue) Acts provoke another boycott of British goods
1770	Parliament repeals Townshend duties, except those on tea; The Boston Massacre
1773	The Tea Act threatens to undercut the colonial smuggling trade; East India Company tea is destroyed in the Boston Tea Party
1774	Boston Harbor is closed by the Coercive (or Intolerable) Acts; The First Continental Congress attacks Britain's restrictions on colonial trade
1775	Armed confrontation at Lexington and Concord

Few events in American history are as momentous as the great struggle that ended with independence in 1783. Yet the causes of that crucial upheaval have long been controversial. Thomas Jefferson believed that Britain's "deliberate, systematical plan of reducing us to slavery" had spurred Americans to take the drastic step of declaring their freedom. John Adams recalled many years later that the British threat to send Anglican bishops to America had "spread a universal alarm against the authority of Parliament." A third group of contemporaries stressed economic strains in the imperial relationship. In 1766 British customs officials in Rhode Island complained bitterly that the interests of "the Mother Country & this Colony" were "deemed by the People almost altogether incompatible, in a commercial View. . . ." Any official who attempted to defend British trade policies had been "threatened as an Enemy to this Country. . . ."

Which of these explanations is correct? Is each partly correct? Is one fundamental and the others secondary? Are there others that are valid? Let us consider the economic one first.

The Colonial Economy

What was the colonial economy like; what were its strengths and weaknesses? Did British policy foster prosperity or hinder it? Did Americans have valid economic grievances against the mother country?

Agriculture.   On the eve of the Revolution agriculture employed 80 percent of the colonial working population and created most of the wealth produced. A majority of American cultivators were small farm owners, "yeomen," engaged in mixed agriculture—growing corn, rye, wheat; raising cattle, sheep, horses, hogs; and planting fruit trees, potatoes, and vegetables. The farmer's own family consumed most of these products, but except on the distant frontier, cultivators sold a part of their output to townspeople or even to customers overseas. In most places the farmer's labor force consisted almost entirely of himself and his family.

American farmers were not especially efficient or innovative by the best European standards. Except for the German settlers of Pennsylvania, the colonists impressed foreign visitors as slovenly cultivators who neglected the fertility of the soil and the care and improvement of their livestock. The critics were right, but there was a simple reason for their behavior: American farmers could rely on the sheer abundance of fresh, fertile land to carry them through. As Thomas Jefferson remarked, "We can buy an acre of new land cheaper than we can manure an old one." In later years Americans would learn to regret this wasteful attitude, but in colonial America it suited the circumstances of the time and place.

Colonial agriculture varied by region. In New England the soil was so rocky almost everywhere except in the Connecticut Valley and a few other favored spots that local farmers, it was said, had to shoot the seed into the unyielding ground with a gun. Connecticut produced some surplus livestock, grain, and dairy products for export, and Rhode Island raised horses for the Caribbean trade. But with these exceptions New England agriculture had mostly local importance.

In contrast, New York, New Jersey, and Pennsylvania were the "bread colonies," harvesting large surpluses of wheat from their fertile fields. They converted this grain to flour in the region's many gristmills and exported much of it to the Caribbean or southern Europe. In addition, the bread colonies exported potatoes, beef, pork, and other farm products.

The Chesapeake region, including the colonies of Virginia and Maryland, was British America's great tobacco-growing area. By the mid-eighteenth century tobacco cultivation had moved from the Tidewater region to the Piedmont plateau, where the soils were fresher and more productive, forcing the remaining coastal farmers to switch to grain. The Piedmont planters faced more difficult transportation problems than their Tidewater predecessors. Located above the "fall line," where the eastward-flowing streams dropped sharply to the coastal plain, they could not put their crops directly aboard ships tied to their own dock. Instead, they sold their tobacco to local merchants who packed the leaf into huge hogsheads. They rolled these to towns like Richmond or Petersburg, which lay along the fall line, and loaded them aboard ships for transport to foreign buyers. By the 1770s Maryland and Virginia were shipping about 100 million pounds of tobacco annually—worth £1 million, or about $50 million in modern money—to the pipesmokers and snuff-takers of Europe. The Chesapeake region also became a major grain exporter, with most going to the south of Europe and the West Indies.

Rice was the major crop of the South Carolina lowlands, although some was also grown in North Carolina and Georgia. Requiring vast amounts of water, as well as a long growing season, rice was suited to the swampy coastal regions of the most southerly colonies and proved highly profitable there. In 1710 South Carolina exported 1.5 million pounds. By 1770 the rice-growing colonies, with South Carolina far in the lead, exported almost 84 million pounds. Most of it went to England, the sugar plantations of the Caribbean, and southern Europe.

The lowland areas of South Carolina and Georgia also produced the indigo plant from which was extracted a blue dye widely used for coloring woolen cloth. The crop was introduced in the 1740s by Eliza Lucas Pinckney, an enterprising young woman newly arrived from the Caribbean island of Antigua. Helped by a British government bounty of six pence a pound, the production and export of indigo quickly leaped. By 1770 almost 600,000 pounds of indigo were shipped from the port of Charleston each year. Tar, pitch, resin, and turpentine, extracted from pine trees and widely employed in the shipping and paint industries, were other extractive products of the southern colonies. The British encouraged naval-store production within its overseas empire by offering a bounty, and by 1770 North Carolina was exporting naval stores worth about £35,000 each year, almost all of it to Great Britain.

Fishing and Whaling.
The sea was one of the earliest sources of food and wealth for New England. The first Massachusetts settlers caught hake, haddock, halibut, and mackerel in local waters for their own tables. By the mid-1630s they were beginning to sell the preserved catch to distant customers. By the eighteenth century the cod fish had become the major haul.

Each season hundreds of vessels sailed from the towns of Gloucester, Marblehead, Salem, and other ports to fish for cod at the Grand Banks off Newfoundland. These small craft were manned by crews who received between a sixth and a tenth of the season's catch as their share, with the rest going to the boat owners. The cod was an important item in the Massachusetts economy. Salted and dried, the best grades were sent to Catholic southern Europe and to the "Wine Islands" of Madeira and the Canaries off Africa, while the worst went to the West Indies to feed the sugar planters' slaves. The trade in dried fish represented a large part of the Bay Colony's total exports.

Whaling was another profitable enterprise of the northern colonies. At first whaling was confined to small New England and Long Island ports. In the eighteenth century, as the local whale supply declined, capitalists fitted out larger vessels for trips well out into the Atlantic. The whalers from Nantucket, New Bedford, and Sag Harbor were not interested in the flesh of the great mammals. Their goal was whale oil, the liquid rendered from whale blubber, which supplied much of the lighting fuel for colonial lamps, and spermaceti, a waxy substance from the heads of sperm whales, used to make fine candles.

Colonial Industry.   Besides the 80 percent who tilled the soil, perhaps 5 percent of the colonial work force were full-time craftsmen, "mechanicks," or artisans, in the cities, towns, and villages. In addition, thousands of rural colonists produced finished or semifinished goods at home for sale on a part-time basis.

Almost all colonial manufactured goods were produced by hand. Colonial farm women spun wool and flax fiber into yarn and then wove it on hand looms into cloth. Farm women also molded candles from wax extracted from bayberries. They churned butter and made cheese from milk supplied by the family cow, and pressed cider from apples, and perry from pears. Rural men also used the home as a workshop. Farmers often devoted the long winter evenings to carving ax handles, gunstocks, and other wooden articles.

In the towns, full-time craftsmen, using hand tools, manufactured items for customers in their workshops. Coopers made barrels as containers for flour, tobacco, sugar, rum, and other bulk goods. Wheelwrights crafted wheels for carts, wagons, and coaches. Cordwainers produced shoes; blacksmiths made nails, horseshoes, shovels, and edged tools; tanners produced the leather that others made into shoes, aprons, saddles, and other items. Every growing colonial village needed housing, and the demand was met by carpenters, masons, bricklayers, and various laborers. As communities became richer and more populous, colonial craftspeople became ever more skilled. By the eve of the Revolution they were producing beautiful silverware and fine furniture. In addition, the small cities were full of barbers, tailors, milliners, and other skilled providers of services for the prosperous consumer.

Even in the cities the typical manufacturing establishment was a small workshop run by the owner with the help, perhaps, of a young apprentice and an older journeyman who had not yet set up shop for himself. The urban master craftsman generally lived above his shop, which was both a little manufacturing establishment and a retail store. Much of his work was done on direct order from a customer, but he usually made additional wares in slack times to have ready for buyers coming to the door. Sometimes he sold his surplus to traveling peddlers. Often the craftsman's wife handled the selling in the front of the establishment while he and his helpers turned out the product in the back.

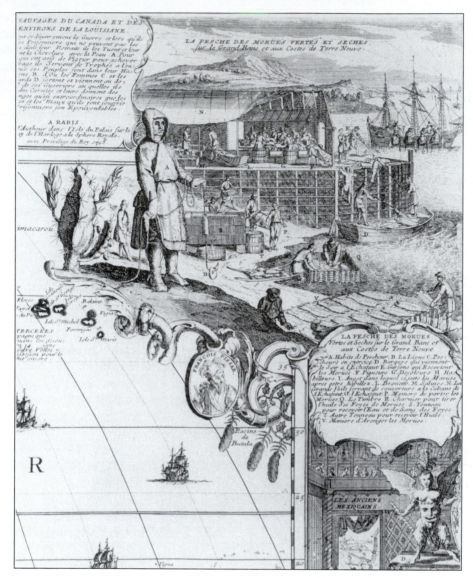

A French illustration of the colonial Grand Banks cod fishery. The racks in the background were used for drying the fish.

Only a very few colonial enterprises resembled the modern factory with hired labor, expensive machinery, and the separation of workplace from home. With water power widely available, mills with waterwheels and machinery, often made of wood, sprang up in every colony to do especially heavy work. There were few settled localities without sawmills to cut boards and gristmills to grind grain into flour. A few of the most successful grain millers—merchant millers—established large-scale operations and overseas markets for their flour.

Shipbuilding was one of the largest-scale industries in colonial America. By 1670 Massachusetts had turned out 730 vessels, and between 1696 and 1713 the colony built more than 1,000 ships of almost 70,000 tons total displacement. Besides the shipyards along the Charles River, there were large ship-building establishments in Salem; Portsmouth, New Hampshire; Newport, Rhode Island; and Philadelphia, each employing scores of workers. In addition to the shipyards themselves, the major ports acquired scores of sail-making establishments and ropewalks to provide rigging for the vessels.

Another relatively large-scale, factorylike colonial manufacturing enterprise was iron-making. By the middle of the eighteenth century its center was Pennsylvania, though New Jersey, Maryland, and Virginia also had large furnaces producing pig iron from ore. By 1700 the American colonies were producing about 2 percent of the world's total pig iron; by the 1770s they accounted for 15 percent.

Commerce.   Commerce or trade was the final and, next to agriculture, the most important, leg of the colonial economy. Ultimately, foreign markets drove the colonial economy. Foreign buyers provided the means for raising the colonial economy above the subsistence level. Commerce sustained the bread colonies, which relied on the Caribbean market to absorb their surplus grain and provisions. Without markets in Britain and Europe the southern tobacco, rice, indigo, and naval-stores colonies would have been far poorer. Both overseas and intercolony trade supported the shipbuilding, sail-making, and rope-making industries and encouraged flour milling, lumbering, barrel-making, and iron manufacture.

Exports helped Americans pay for the paper, hardware, pottery, and cloth, as well as wines, the latest books, fine furniture, and scientific instruments that came only from Britain, the European continent, or the Wine Islands. To pay for these goods, Americans needed coin or commercial credits from sales of their own goods abroad. Unfortunately, colonial trade relations were out of balance geographically. England needed the tobacco, rice, indigo, and naval stores of the Chesapeake region and the Carolinas; these colonies, accordingly, easily earned the credits needed to pay for what they imported from the mother country. But the major northern products—fish, grain, and cattle—were not wanted in Great Britain since it produced its own. Because each year the northern colonies bought more from Britain than they sold to it, they were forced to find other customers whose purchases would offset the British deficit.

The Caribbean served this role. In the West Indies the planters concentrated all their energies on growing sugar cane for the European market. Their neglect of everything but sugar made them excellent customers for cheap food, horses, lumber, and barrels from the northern mainland colonies. By 1700 hundreds of vessels from northern ports sailed to the islands each year, laden with provisions, flour, and dried fish to feed the slaves and their masters, and with lumber, wooden hoops, and staves to build structures and to package sugar, rum, and molasses.

Once he had found buyers for his miscellaneous cargo, the New England or middle-colony merchant accepted payment in several forms. The colonies acquired a wide assortment of shillings, doubloons, guilders, and pieces of eight in the West Indies. But molasses and sugar were also acceptable. These could be

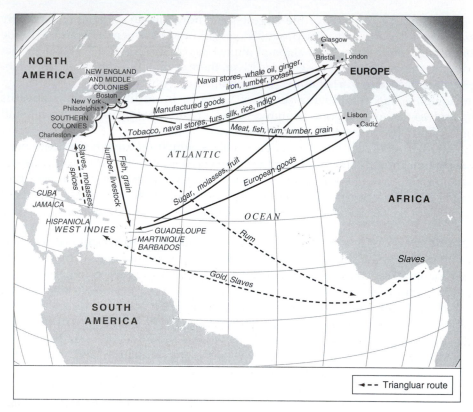

Colonial Trade Routes

consumed directly at home, or the molasses could be converted into rum and traded with the Indians for furs, or exported overseas. The trader could also accept bills of exchange on England—receipts that the planters received when they sold their sugar in England. These represented credits that could be used like cash to pay for English goods or clear debts owed to English creditors. With their holds full of molasses and some West Indies cotton or citrus fruit, and the captain's strongbox stuffed with coin or bills of exchange, the ship sailed home to Boston, Providence, New York, or Philadelphia.

The transatlantic slave trade also helped offset the commercial deficit with the mother country. Most of the slaves carried from Africa to America in the eighteenth century were transported by the French, the British, or the Dutch. But some were carried by slavers out of Boston and Newport. The typical New England slave trader sent a small vessel with a cargo of rum distilled from West Indies molasses to the west coast of Africa. There the Yankee captain exchanged some rum for British goods, such as iron, cloth, gunpowder, cheap jewelry, and glass with a trader from London or Bristol. With this mixed stock of goods he bought slaves from an African middleman and loaded the human cargo aboard his vessel. He then returned to the Caribbean, where he sold the captives for the same coin, molasses, or bills of exchange that other cargo brought. Only a small proportion of the slaves stolen from Africa were transported directly to the Carolinas or the Chesapeake on the mainland. Many came first to the Caribbean.

Wealth and Inequality.   How did Americans fare, overall, under this evolving economic system? And did its benefits fall on each person equally?

By one measure—population growth—the American community prospered mightily during the colonial era. Benjamin Franklin was right when he claimed that Americans doubled in numbers every twenty-five years. In 1680 there were fewer than 80,000 settlers along the Atlantic coast of British North America. By 1700 there were about a quarter of a million. Fifty years later the population had passed the 1 million mark and by 1770 had soared above 2 million. This surge in part marked the heavy immigration from the Old World to America, itself a sign of prosperity. But it also marked the abundance of land and food that encouraged early marriage and large families and prevented the malnutrition and famine that cruelly pruned population elsewhere in the contemporary world. Brisk population growth is in some ways the most convincing measure of sustained colonial prosperity.

And despite the explosion of people, during each decade average per capita income grew. Output, that is, expanded even faster than population. The best estimate that we have suggests that overall per person growth of output in colonial America ran about 0.6 percent a year. This was unusually high for a preindustrial society and was fast enough to double the average colonial's income over the course of 120 years. By the eve of the Revolution, Alice Hanson Jones has said, the standard of living in British North America, was "probably the highest achieved for the great bulk of the population in any country up to that time."

Of course, not everyone benefited equally from the high and growing prosperity. The group most obviously excluded from the benefits of an advancing economy was the slaves. By 1770 there were about 460,000 black slaves in the mainland colonies out of a total population of some 2.1 million. Clearly they did not receive very much of the wealth that their labor produced. For free rural Americans, the location of land and how it was held and the size of landholdings determined individual levels of prosperity. Yeoman farmers who grew crops only to supply their own family needs seldom were rich. Commercial agriculture made for prosperity, but it also encouraged inequality. In towns close to the Boston market, for example, where farmers sold to urban consumers, a sharp division existed between rich and poor. In 1771 about one-quarter of the taxpayers in Milton and Roxbury were landless, while the wealthiest 10 percent owned 46 percent of the real estate. In general, both less wealth and greater equality were to be found in the frontier regions of each colony, where land per person was abundant and major markets too distant to support commercial agriculture. In the South the picture was similar: Regions of subsistence farming had many landowners and a high degree of equality. By contrast, the commercial rice- and indigo-growing Carolina coast and the tobacco-growing Chesapeake tidewater were the realms of the great slaveholding gentry.

Surinam was a Dutch sugar-growing colony on South America's Atlantic coast.
It was an important trading partner for British North America, and especially for
Rhode Island. In this 1758 John Greenwood painting we see a group of Rhode Island
sea captains—including a future governor of Rhode Island and a future commander
in chief of the Continental Navy—rowdily enjoying their layover in Surinam before
returning home with sugar, molasses, and rum. Note the black servants at lower
right and upper left.
*(John Greenwood, "Sea Captains Carousing in Surinam," 1758. Oil on bed ticking,
95.9 × 191.1 cm. The Saint Louis Art Museum, Museum Purchase)*

In the towns marketable skills counted as much as real estate in determining
an individual's prosperity. Apprentices, journeymen, laborers, and seamen made
up the urban lower class. Fully trained craftsmen and shopkeepers did better; at
the top of the pyramid were the merchants and professionals. Those merchants
who sold goods door to door in nearby rural areas were poor by comparison with
the great overseas traders who sent their ships to Europe, Africa, or the West
Indies. It was difficult to break into the ranks of the overseas traders, but the class
was not completely closed to the energetic, ambitious, or lucky.

Obviously, economic inequalities existed in the American colonies. But were
these inequalities growing or diminishing in the years before the Revolution?
Were the rich getting richer and the poor getting poorer?

The most recent studies seem to show that inequality was increasing in the
larger cities and in rural parts of the older settled regions. The opening of new settlements, however, offset this trend to some extent, for the colonial frontier remained a region where there were few rich and few poor. And even in the older
sections, we must not forget that the overall income trend was upward. Almost all
free Americans were getting richer. The growing gap was not because the poor
were getting poorer in absolute terms. It resulted from the fact that those at the top
were increasing their wealth and incomes faster than those at the bottom. All in
all, as Robert Beverley had written of Virginia early in the eighteenth century,
America was "the best poor Man's Country in the World."

Costs and Benefits of Empire Before 1763

How did America's place in the British Empire affect its economic circumstances? And did its economic place within the empire, in turn—or the colonists' perception of that place—influence how they felt about their political ties to Great Britain?

The Economic Balance Sheet.

As we look at the colonial economy it is clear that there were both benefits and losses from the imperial relationship. From the 1650s on the colonists were forced to accept a multitude of restrictions on their trade with other parts of the world. Though frequently violated or circumvented, these restrictions limited their ability to work out their own economic destiny.

As we saw in Chapter 2, colonies were supposed to enrich the mother country by supplying it with exotic commodities and hard-to-get raw materials, by consuming its surplus manufactures, and by providing jobs to a host of people engaged in the colonial trade. With these potential benefits in mind, beginning in 1650 Parliament enacted measures called the Navigation Acts. To keep the enterprising Dutch from profiting from the carrying trade within the empire and between the empire and other nations, they decreed that all ships engaged in such trade must be owned by either Britons or Americans, built in either Britain or America, captained by a subject of the British crown, and manned predominantly by such subjects. Other Navigation Acts established lists of "enumerated articles" that had to be shipped to England first whatever their ultimate destination. The lists included the most valuable colonial exports such as sugar, tobacco, rice, naval stores, and indigo. Another law provided that, except for salt for the New England fisheries, wine from Madeira and the Azores, and servants and horses from Scotland and Ireland, all European commodities sent to the colonies had to be shipped from England, rather than from their place of origin, and in English-built ships.

Besides excluding foreigners from the imperial trade and encouraging shipping and shipbuilding, these measures were intended to make England the distribution center for goods entering or leaving the colonies. They would guarantee British merchants a key role in the colonial overseas trade and allow the British government to levy a tax on all goods passing through Great Britain. To enforce the Navigation Acts and collect duties imposed on overseas trade, the British government stationed a host of customs commissioners in the colonial ports.

The British also sought to limit the manufactures of the mainland colonies to preserve them as markets for British producers and prevent colonial competition with home producers. The Wool Act of 1699 forbade the export of wool yarn or cloth from any American colony either to Europe or to any other American colony. The Hat Act of 1732 prohibited the export of American hats from one colony to another and imposed strict limits on the number of workers in any hat-making shop. Finally, two Iron Acts, of 1750 and 1757, sought to encourage the production of American bar and pig iron—raw materials for the British iron and steel industry—but to restrict the colonial iron-finishing industry that the British wanted to keep for themselves. This measure forbade the construction in the colonies of rolling and slitting mills, of forges, and of steel furnaces.

Americans undoubtedly were penalized by these trade regulations. The enumerated tobacco sent to Europe, mostly from Maryland and Virginia, had to be unloaded and then reloaded in England first. The charges for this roundabout method of export to Europe were high, and the planters lost money because of it. American consumers, in turn, were forced by the rule that European goods must first be sent to England before crossing the Atlantic to pay higher prices for such items.

Were the impediments imposed on the colonies by these regulations severe? To answer this question fairly, we should consider not just costs such as these, but the overall economic benefits to America of the empire as well. The foremost benefit was that Britain assumed the expense of the empire's defense. During the seventeenth and eighteenth centuries, as we shall see, four great European wars placed the colonies in danger. The British army and navy often proved indispensable to colonial safety. Recognizing their stake in the outcome, the colonists contributed money and men themselves to the military effort; but most of the cost by far was borne by the British. Without the mother country's contribution to imperial defense, the colonies would have been forced to lay out millions of pounds in extra taxes, a financial burden that would have lowered their incomes and retarded their economic growth.

It is also important to recognize that in restricting the imperial trade to subjects of the king, Parliament meant Americans as well as Britons. American-built ships, owned by American merchants, with American crews, were as much entitled under the Navigation Acts to protection against Dutch competition and the privileges of the imperial trade as their counterparts in England, Scotland, or Ireland. Under this arrangement American shipbuilding flourished so that by the 1763–1775 period the thirteen continental colonies produced vessels worth £300,000 each year. About half this output was sold to British merchants. During these same years American ship owners earned an estimated £600,000 annually by carrying cargo and passengers to and from various points within the empire.

America received other economic benefits as part of the empire. The British paid bounties to encourage production of items that did not compete with English-made goods and for raw materials that English manufacturers needed; these brought thousands of pounds a year to American indigo growers, pig-iron manufacturers, and naval-stores producers.

The measures to restrict colonial manufacturers do not fall in either the debit or credit columns. The Iron Act, aimed at finished iron products, did little to restrain the colonial iron industry because it was not rigorously enforced. As for the Wool and Hat acts, they did not, as we might suppose, kill off promising industries. The intention of these measures was clear: They were designed to limit future growth that might injure British producers. Still, in their day they probably had little effect.

On the whole, the American experience within the mercantile system was positive. And Americans recognized, generally, how much they gained economically from the imperial relationship. Before 1763 only one economic measure, the Molasses Act of 1733, caused serious friction. This imposed a high tax on molasses, sugar, and rum brought into the colonies from the Dutch, French, and Spanish West Indies. Intended to protect the British Caribbean sugar planters from the competition of lower-cost foreign producers, the act threatened the profitable trade between New England and the foreign West Indies. Yankee merchants responded by turning the smuggling of foreign sugar and molasses into a fine art. The law, never strictly enforced, became a virtual dead letter.

The Political Ledger.   When we measure the political pluses and minuses of the British–American relationship, we encounter a similar even balance through the 1760s. There were indeed periods of rather strict imperial governance. During the reigns of Charles II (1660–1685) and James II (1685–1688), the British authorities tried to tighten imperial control. In 1684 they revoked the Massachusetts Bay charter and soon after merged New England, New York, and New Jersey into the Dominion of New England. Under the stern rule of Governor Sir Edmund Andros, residents of the northern colonies were denied the right to tax themselves or to make laws regulating their day-to-day concerns. In the proprietary colonies farther south, the crown sought to impose direct royal control.

This effort at tight imperial regulation, while stirring deep fears among the colonists, proved short-lived. In 1689 a coalition of Whig leaders, champions of Protestantism, and partisans of Parliament, inspired by the liberal political ideas of John Locke and other Whig thinkers, deposed the Catholic ruler James II in Britain. They then invited Mary, James's Protestant daughter, and her husband, William of Orange, to rule England in his place. Accompanying the offer was the Declaration of Rights, establishing Parliamentary supremacy in England and bolstering the rights of individuals as against the crown.

This so-called Glorious Revolution echoed loudly in America. Led by the Puritan clergy, Massachusetts rebels arrested Governor Andros and his subordinates and shipped them all back to England. The Dominion of New England was dissolved and the individual colonies separated once more, though Massachusetts absorbed Plymouth colony and the sparsely settled region of Maine. Efforts to restore the former Bay Colony charter, allowing virtual self-rule, failed, however. Despite loud protest, in 1691 Massachusetts had to accept a new charter with a royal governor at the top, a royal review of all legislation, and a property qualification for voting to replace the old religious test. Notwithstanding the Massachusetts experience, the thrust of the Glorious Revolution was to guarantee to the crown's subjects on both sides of the Atlantic a large measure of self-government through powerful representative legislatures and assemblies.

By the early eighteenth century, then, the colonists had achieved a large measure of political autonomy. The English Privy Council was still permitted to "disallow" measures the colonial legislatures passed and the colonial governors approved; but of some 8,500 colonial laws submitted to the council, only 469 were declared null. Nor was the Board of Trade, which shared colonial administration with the governors and the Privy Council, any more coercive. From 1721 to 1748, when Sir Robert Walpole and the Duke of Newcastle were the crown's chief advisers, the English government gave higher priority to colonial economic growth than to tight and tidy English rule. This era of "salutary neglect" helped encourage an even greater sense than before that the colonists were self-governing in all internal matters.

The Issue of Religion.   Before 1763, then, Americans had little reason to complain of British political or economic oppression. But what about the religious oppression John Adams spoke of?

A majority of colonists were Protestant nonconformists of some kind. Some of these charged that the Anglicans intended to establish "a tyranny over the bodies and souls of men," destroy the religious liberties of Americans, and restrict public office to members of the Anglican Church. Most of all they feared the British would create Anglican bishops for the colonies, who would rule over American religious affairs as they did those of England.

In fact, British officials recognized that American religious dissenters were often firm supporters of the crown. Such people, in the words of one, "should not be provoked or alienated" by imposing bishops on them. The British government did occasionally interfere in colonial religious matters, but it was usually to insist that toleration be extended to some unpopular denomination, rather than to restrict religious expression. Though intolerant Americans sometimes were offended by such intrusion, few ever felt seriously threatened. In religion, as in politics and economics, the conflicts between mother country and colonies remained muted before 1763.

The Crisis of Empire

Whatever was true during the first century and a half of British settlement, after 1763, many of the most influential and articulate people in the colonies would begin to find the system of imperial administration galling and the actions of the British government intolerable. Before long they would demand that they be changed. The dramatic change of heart would be linked to the end of the French threat to English America.

The English–French Confrontation.   French Canada (New France) and English America had been planted at approximately the same time. Thereafter the two communities had evolved in different ways. By the mid-eighteenth century Canada was a sparsely settled region with some 55,000 farmers cultivating the lands of the gentry, ruled autocratically by a royal governor. Pious and conservative, the French Canadians accepted the dominance of the seigneurs, the Church, and the appointed royal officials without serious question.

Friction between English America and New France was almost preordained. Both communities were political extensions of their respective mother countries and inevitably became enmeshed in the quarrels of the two European archrivals. Both were also religious antagonists. Before long Catholic New France and Protestant English America took up the fierce political and religious conflicts that had beset the European world for two centuries.

Just as important as these transplanted European quarrels were the tensions native to America itself. New France and "new England" vied over control of the fishing trade in Newfoundland and over competing claims in the Caribbean. Even closer to home was rivalry over the fur trade with the Indians. The British had the advantage of cheaper and better trade goods; the French, on the other hand, were more effective in winning the personal allegiance of the Indians. Canadian traders went to the Indians for furs rather than waiting for the Indians to deliver them to the European settlements. They lived with the Indians and often married. Indian women. Their half-European, half-Indian children in turn forged bonds that the English seldom could match. French religious institutions also gave them an advantage with the Indians. Unlike the Protestants to the south, French Catholics were effective in converting Indians to Christianity.

In the late 1680s Britain and France confronted one another in the first of four major wars that would extend over several continents simultaneously. In King William's War (1689–1697), Massachusetts colonial troops captured the French stronghold of Port Royal in modern Nova Scotia. The post was returned to France, however, by the Treaty of Ryswick (1697), which ended the conflict. The French soon moved to occupy the vast Mississippi Valley, a region also claimed by the American colonists under their provincial charters. In 1699 the French established an outpost at Cahokia, near present-day St. Louis; in 1703 they placed a fort at Kaskaskia in southern Illinois. They also planted settlements on the Gulf Coast and along the shores of the Great Lakes. When war broke out again in 1702 (Queen Anne's War, 1702–1713), French troops and their Indian allies clashed with the Anglo-Americans in a vast arc from Maine to the outskirts of Louisiana, as the French called their new colony in the North American interior. By the Treaty of Utrecht (1713), ending this conflict, England acquired Newfoundland, Acadia (renamed Nova Scotia), and the Hudson Bay region.

Following the Treaty of Utrecht, the French sought to consolidate their hold on Louisiana by establishing new posts and settlements in the disputed region. In 1718 they established New Orleans near the mouth of the Mississippi. The British countered by constructing Fort Oswego on Lake Ontario and fortifying the northern frontier against the pro-French Abenakis. When war between Britain and France broke out again (King George's War, 1740–1748), both sides once more clashed in North America. New England troops captured the French strong point of Louisbourg in Nova Scotia, while in New York William Johnson, the province's commissary of Indian affairs, induced the Iroquois to attack the French. In retaliation the French and their Indian allies raided Albany and burned Saratoga.

The French and Indian War.

These three wars were extensions of disputes that originated in Europe. The most destructive and momentous of all the colonial wars, however, started over an issue of more immediate concern to many Americans.

French expansion into the Mississippi Valley seemed to threaten the very existence of the British colonies as self-governing Protestant communities. Besides, a string of interior French colonies promised to block westward expansion. Colonial farmers looking for fresh, fertile lands for themselves and their children would be walled off and confined to the dwindling acres east of the mountains. Would-be speculators in western lands, who were especially prominent and vocal in Pennsylvania and Virginia, would be denied their expected windfall profits from land sales.

The crisis came in what is now western Pennsylvania and Ohio. Here, Pennsylvania fur traders had established a string of trading posts to collect pelts from the Indians. Hoping to head off further English encroachment, the French, under the Marquis Duquesne, determined to construct a chain of forts from Lake Erie to the Forks of the Ohio at what is now Pittsburgh. In 1753 a party of several hundred Frenchmen and Indians built three stockades along Lake Erie and on French Creek. Still left unfinished when winter came was the projected post at the strategic Forks, where the Allegheny and Monongahela join to form the Ohio River.

News of the French project alarmed Governor Robert Dinwiddie of Virginia. Dinwiddie responded by dispatching a tall, young Virginia squire, George Washington, with a force of armed men to warn the French to leave. Washington failed in his mission. The following year, after the French had completed Fort Duquesne at the Forks, Washington returned to oust them by force. The young Virginian foolishly allowed himself to engage the French though outnumbered ten to one. At Fort Necessity, a hurriedly constructed American stockade, the French took the intruders prisoner. When released from captivity, Washington and his little force returned to the Virginia capital, Williamsburg, carrying news that the French were on the verge of making good their claim to the great interior valley.

The confrontation of a few hundred armed men in western Pennsylvania triggered the French and Indian War, a struggle lasting from 1754 to 1763. In 1756 the conflict spread to Europe itself when Britain and Prussia concluded an alliance against France, which in turn allied itself with Austria and then, in 1762, with Spain. Because Britain, France, and Spain were all great imperial nations, the struggle quickly turned into a "world war." Before it was over, armies and fleets had grappled in the Mediterranean, the Caribbean, the Far East, India, and on the European continent, as well as in the dense forests of North America. At first the war went badly for the English. But then, in 1757, William Pitt the Elder took over its management and brought Britain a series of brilliant victories that changed the course of history.

In America, as elsewhere, the war started badly for the Anglo-Americans when, during the summer of 1755, the British general, Edward Braddock, suffered a serious defeat at the hands of the French and their Indian allies in an attempt to capture Fort Duquesne. On July 9 Braddock's small force of 1,400 British redcoats, 450 Virginia militiamen under Washington, and 50 Indian scouts, after hacking their way through the dense Pennsylvania forest, encountered 600 French and 200 Indians seven miles from the French post. With flags flying and bagpipes playing, the British advanced in a line in the approved European fashion. But the battle quickly degenerated into a wild melee with the French and Indians pouring deadly fire into the advancing redcoats and Americans from concealed positions on either side. Wounded mortally, Braddock ordered a retreat. As the combined Anglo-American force limped back to their base, they were attacked by the enemy from behind every tree and rock. Of the 1,900 men who had set out, only 500 arrived home safely.

Other British commanders were more successful. In the fall of 1758 General John Forbes resumed the effort to oust the French from the Forks of the Ohio. Seeing Forbes' powerful Anglo-American army approaching, the Indians of the Ohio country deserted the French. On November 24 the handful of French soldiers remaining at Fort Duquesne blew it up and fled, leaving it to the British, who reconstructed it as Fort Pitt. Impressed by this British victory, the Indians turned on their former French allies and virtually drove them out of the upper Mississippi Valley.

A still more brilliant British triumph came in the summer of 1759 when General James Wolfe and an army of 4,500 redcoats scaled the heights above the St. Lawrence River and deployed on the Plains of Abraham outside the walls of Quebec, the political and religious capital of French Canada. The French commander was the able Marquis de Montcalm, but his force consisted only of ill-trained provincial troops. They bravely attacked but, in the face of the redcoats' deadly musket volleys, fell back to the town and soon after surrendered. Both commanders died in the battle. With the fall of Quebec, followed later by the capture of Montreal, French power in Canada collapsed.

The war dragged on for many months following the fall of New France. In 1761 Prime Minister Pitt, despite his successes, resigned. The new king, George III, replaced him with Lord Bute and other "Tory" advisers who were more friendly to the idea of royal power than Pitt and his fellow Whigs. By this time the British people were weary of the war, which had cost them well over £100 million and had pushed taxes to record levels. In February 1763 the British, French, and Spanish signed the Treaty of Paris ending the war.

The treaty made sweeping changes in the political map of North America. By its terms France ceded Cape Breton Island and all of Canada to Great Britain and recognized the region from the Appalachians to the Mississippi and from the Great Lakes to Florida as British territory. Spain, France's ally, gave Florida, including much of the eastern Gulf Coast, to England. In return for this loss, Spain gained from the French what they had retained of Louisiana; that is, the portion west of the Mississippi. Other territory changed hands in India, Africa, and the Caribbean. To the Americans the crucial matter was that powerful France was now virtually eliminated from the entire North American continent.

The end of the French presence abruptly altered American attitudes toward the British Empire. As long as the French were nearby, the Americans clung to the protection of England. Now that the French menace was gone, the colonists could afford to consider the disadvantages of their subordinate relationship within the Empire. Moreover, the French and Indian War had created serious tensions between the British government and its American subjects that now clamored to be resolved.

British–American Relations During the War.

From the British point of view, the Americans had not been the best of subjects during the war. Defying the Rule of 1756 forbidding wartime trade between the colonies and France, American vessels had sailed to the French Caribbean islands, carrying, in exchange for sugar, needed supplies excluded by the British naval blockade. American merchants had also exchanged American flour and fish for French wines and gold at Hispaniola, initially a neutral Spanish port, despite Pitt's complaint that this trade enabled the enemy "to sustain and protect" the "long and expensive War."

The British government sought to stop the illegal wartime commerce with France by issuing writs of assistance, general search warrants allowing customs officials to inspect private property to determine whether smuggled goods were present. Though such writs had been issued before, they now angered colonial merchants, who saw them as a dangerous violation of the rights of private citizens. In 1760 several Boston traders hired attorney James Otis to argue against the legality of the writs. In a fiery address that John Adams later called the "first scene of the first act of opposition" to British authority in America, Otis denounced the writs as "against the fundamental principles of law" and the British constitution, and hence void. In the end the writs were upheld by the Massachusetts court and confirmed by the later Townshend Acts, but they were never effectively used in the Bay Colony.

Besides flouting wartime trade regulations, the colonists had also resisted paying their share of war expenses. To help meet war costs, Pitt had imposed a "requisition" system whereby each colonial assembly would share with the British treasury the expense of recruiting and supplying troops. In addition, the British would reimburse the colonial legislatures for part of their initial outlays in the following year. This was a generous scheme, British officials said, since the Americans were fighting the French as much for themselves as for the mother country. Yet time and again, it seemed to British officials, the Americans had failed to do their part. They had delayed voting money for defense or even refused outright to do so. According to Lord Loudon, British commander in chief in America, it had been "the constant study of every province . . . to throw every expense on the Crown and bear no part of the expense of this war themselves."

Then there was the serious friction between colonial and British troops in camp and on the battlefields. British officers and even common soldiers had little respect for the colonial militia. Nor could American officers in colonial units rise to high command. At one point early in the war Washington was denied a colonelcy in the British forces because he was a "provincial."

Problems with the Indians also created bad feeling between Britain and the colonists. The British blamed Americans for their failure to cooperate in a common policy toward the Indians. In 1754 the British Board of Trade had issued a call for a colonial congress to consider Indian–white relations generally and find a way to induce the tribes south of the Great Lakes to support the Anglo-American cause against the French. Only New England, New York, Pennsylvania, and Maryland sent delegates to the meeting at Albany. The results were not impressive. The congress recommended a number of measures to meet Indians complaints against American fur traders and land speculators and charges that the British government had failed to protect them against the French. It also adopted a proposal Benjamin Franklin made for a political union of all the continental colonies to exercise jurisdiction over Indian affairs and deal with the overall problem of western development. Yet none of the separate colonies wished to surrender control over western policy. The congress's recommendations were not adopted, and Indian–white relations remained chaotic.

Indian problems soon worsened. In the wake of the British conquest of the West, hundreds of American traders crossed the Appalachian Mountains. They cheated the Indians and plied them with drink. At the same time scores of American, Scottish, and English speculators besieged Parliament, demanding land grants in the West that could be sold to eager would-be settlers. A flood of small farmers was already pouring into the Pittsburgh region, displacing the local Indians. British officials in the West were no more sensitive to Indian feelings than the Americans. Lord Jeffrey Amherst despised the "savages" and advised spreading smallpox among them. In 1762 Amherst abruptly cut off the food and ammunition traditionally supplied to the Indians during the winter.

To the northern tribes Amherst's act seemed the last straw. By this time a major Indian renewal movement was underway, inspired by a religious leader called the "Prophet," who urged his people to abandon white ways and reassert their independence. In May 1763, led by Pontiac, one of the Prophet's disciples, the Indians attacked Fort Detroit, triggering a fierce Indian uprising throughout the West that in two months drove virtually all the whites back over the mountains. The British struck back and by the summer of 1764 had put down Pontiac's rebellion. But the affair highlighted the chaos in Indian affairs and, more generally, Britain's problems in controlling its empire.

The Proclamation of 1763.

With the French and Indian War over, British as well as American attitudes toward the empire changed. In general, the Whig leaders who had governed England had accepted the validity of colonial claims to autonomy in managing local affairs. Philosophically, they had opposed the assertion of royal power at home, and this attitude had carried over to their view of how to govern America. But the Tory government of Lord Bute and Chancellor of the Exchequer George Grenville supported the crown against Parliament and had little use for colonial "pretensions" to self-rule. Given the experience of the war and the Indian problem, tighter administration of the empire, they felt, was clearly needed.

The first move to tighten colonial control was the Proclamation of 1763. This measure prohibited colonists from settling west of the Appalachians and required all those already there "forthwith to remove themselves." East of the mountains, colonists were forbidden to purchase land directly from the Indians. The entire trans-Appalachian region was to be placed under the control of the British commander in chief and to remain an exclusive Indian preserve until further notice. Through the proclamation the British hoped to pacify the Indians and to give themselves time to contrive a rational permanent policy for disposing of the crown's lands, especially in the West. Eventually colonists would be allowed to move across the mountains, but not before Indian claims had been dealt with and an orderly system of land transfer and settlement worked out.

However rational its goals, the proclamation dismayed many Americans. Those who had anticipated profits from land speculation, fur trading, and farming saw their hopes for gain go up in smoke. Among the influential land promoters of Virginia, the check on western settlement seemed designed to permit Englishmen to grab an unfair share of speculative profits in the American West. For small farmers, the new western policy, by closing the frontier escape hatch, seemed likely to widen the gap between rich and poor.

Changes in British Tax Policy.

Even more disturbing to most Americans, however, was Parliament's new effort to raise revenue in America. The British government had long imposed duties on certain imports through laws like the Molasses Act, but the primary purpose of these had been to regulate commerce, not to extract money from the Americans. Now there were other considerations. Britain after 1763 labored under an immense debt that cost it £4.5 million a year in interest alone. Military costs, too, were certain to continue. Britain would have to maintain an expensive army to protect the colonists against the Indians and prevent the return of the French. The solution was obvious: Make the Americans pay part of the bill.

The first revenue measure of the Grenville ministry was the Sugar Act (1764). This law imposed import duties on non-English cloth, indigo, coffee, wine, sugar, and molasses. The tax on molasses was especially offensive. Even though the new duty was actually lower than the earlier Molasses Act rates, the money was now really to be collected. Smuggling had made the old law a sham; the new law forced American merchants to pass through a thicket of certificates, affidavits, oaths, and inspections and added a new vice-admiralty court to try suspected smugglers under rules that put more of the burden of proof than previously on the accused.

Most American merchants balked at this renewed effort to exclude them from the profitable foreign West Indies market. The Navigation Acts had pressed only

North America, 1763

lightly on the colonies thus far, largely because the Americans had offset their disadvantages through trade with the Caribbean. By cutting off trade with the foreign West Indies, the Sugar Act not only threatened profits but also endangered the northern colonists' overall adjustments to the requirements of the imperial economy.

The Stamp Act.   The Proclamation of 1763 injured Virginians primarily; the Sugar Act promised to hurt New England and the middle colonies. The Grenville ministry next proposed a measure that angered powerful groups in every one of the colonies and threatened the political autonomy that Americans as a whole had gained over a century of struggle.

During the summer of 1763 Grenville decided to impose on America a tax on legal documents and other items, to be paid with stamps purchased from the British treasury. Under the new law a revenue stamp would have to be affixed to all professional licenses, court documents, papers concerning land transfers or exports or imports, all private contracts, newspapers, and even college diplomas. These stamps were to be paid for in gold or silver, and the money collected set aside for exclusive use in the colonies. Violations of the law would be tried in both the ordinary and the admiralty courts.

Before proceeding with the measure, Grenville had the foresight to consult with agents who represented colonial interests in London at the seat of empire. The American agents were dubious about such a tax, but the colonial legislatures, Grenville learned, would not accept the alternative of taxing themselves. Under the circumstances, he refused to abandon his scheme. In early 1765, after a brief debate, Parliament passed the momentous Stamp Act.

Two other measures supplemented Grenville's program of tightening imperial control. The Quartering Act (actually two separate measures of 1765 and 1766) required colonial authorities to provide barracks and supplies for British troops or, in lieu of barracks, to make provision for billeting troops in inns or unoccupied dwellings. The Currency Act (1764) forbade colonial legislatures to issue paper money as legal tender. Previously applied only to New England, the prohibition was now extended to all the colonies. The Quartering Act seemed a dangerous extension of British military power in America; the Currency Act hampered the colonial legislatures' efforts to provide a circulating medium in place of scarce coin. Neither law, however, produced the wave of outrage that greeted the Stamp Act.

The Stamp Act touched almost every aspect of colonial social and economic life—the professions, commerce, the press, and education. It penalized two of the most articulate and influential groups in the colonies—lawyers and newspaper publishers. It also threatened the hard-won authority of colonial assemblies, which had previously exercised the power to levy taxes. Furthermore, the Stamp Act raised profound and disturbing constitutional issues. First, were the colonies subordinate to Great Britain, or equal partners in the empire? Second, must American colonists pay taxes imposed by Parliament, where they were not formally represented? Few colonists expected their representatives to be seated in the English Parliament; rather, they wanted Parliament to recognize the authority of colonial assemblies, including their exclusive authority to tax Americans. Unlike most of the post-1763 British measures, by jeopardizing all the colonies equally, the

Stamp Act created a common bond of opposition to British policies. It was probably one of the most foolish and inexpedient bills passed by the British Parliament in its long history.

News of the Stamp Act reached the colonies in mid-April 1765. In May the Virginia House of Burgesses, goaded by the young firebrand lawyer Patrick Henry, boldly resolved that Americans had all the rights of Englishmen and that only their own legislatures could tax them. Virginia's action electrified Americans everywhere. Newspapers all over the colonies praised the resolutions and denounced British policy. Other colonial assemblies quickly joined the House of Burgesses in attacking the act, and the Massachusetts General Court called for a colonial congress to meet in October to consider united action in the crisis.

But outraged citizens did not wait until the congress met. In almost every colony the new law stirred up violence. Mobs of artisans, shopkeepers, sailors, and merchants, some organized as "Sons of Liberty," burned effigies of Grenville and royal officials in America and physically attacked tax collectors and partisans of the new tax. In Boston the protesters set fire to the house of Lieutenant Governor Thomas Hutchinson. So effective was this intimidation that almost all the official stamp distributors resigned their royal commissions.

By the time the Stamp Act Congress convened in New York (October 7–25, 1765), the act was a dead letter in every colony except Georgia, where an unusually firm governor succeeded in making the citizens obey it. The congress adopted petitions addressed to the king, the House of Lords, and the House of Commons. Although mild in tone, they insisted once again that Americans could be taxed only by bodies that represented them directly.

The petitions did little to move the British government, and mob violence only angered Grenville and other English conservatives. A few English Whig leaders, such as Edmund Burke, supported the Americans on the grounds of justice, but in the end economic pressure killed the tax. The merchants of England, skeptical of the Stamp Act from the outset, grew increasingly hostile to the measure when it became clear that the law was disastrous for trade with America. In some places in the colonies, legal processes for enforcing commercial contracts stalled. Still more dismaying were the Nonimportation Agreements initiated by New Yorkers and widely adopted in the other colonies by which citizens pledged not to buy British goods, and merchants agreed not to import them. The resulting drop in transatlantic trade soon brought many British manufacturers and exporters to the brink of bankruptcy.

Parliament yielded to the complaints of the English merchants. On March 18, 1766, it repealed the detested measure but simultaneously adopted the Declaratory Act, affirming its right to legislate for the colonies "in all cases whatsoever." In effect, the English government was telling the Americans that it acknowledged the stamp tax as a practical mistake, but that it would not accept the principle of "no taxation without representation" that had been marshaled to oppose it.

The Townshend Acts.

The rejoicing that followed news of the repeal of the Stamp Act was short-lived. In January 1766 the New York assembly refused to contribute support for British troops as required by the Quartering Act. Over the summer hostile feelings arose between New York citizens and British soldiers, and several Americans were injured in violent clashes between redcoats and members of the Sons of Liberty, the secret organization formed to protest the Stamp Act. At the urging of Charles Townshend, Grenville's successor, Parliament suspended the New York legislature's powers in mid-1767.

During the debate over taxation, Townshend had noticed that Americans made a distinction between a tax for raising revenue and one intended to regulate commerce. The first, they said, was a dangerous novelty; the second was traditional and acceptable. "Champagne Charlie"—a witty, charming, but shallow man—now seized on this distinction as a way around American resistance to revenue taxes. In May 1767 he proposed legislation that proved almost as foolish and inept as the Stamp Act: the Revenue Act of 1767.

Commonly referred to as the Townshend Acts, the law imposed new import duties on glass, red and white lead, painters' colors, paper, and tea. The imposts were to be paid in coin and the money used to pay royal officials in the colonies, thereby ending their dependence on colonial legislatures for their salaries. The Townshend Acts also authorized the colonial higher courts to issue writs of assistance to help customs officers search private property for violations of the new law. A companion measure established a board of customs commissioners with headquarters in Boston and new vice-admiralty courts in Halifax, Philadelphia, and Charleston to enforce both old and new trade regulations.

"Patriots," as the opponents of Britain's policies were now called, once more demanded a boycott of British goods through Nonimportation Agreements. This time the colonial merchants were determined to keep the violence under control, and for a while they succeeded. Before long, however, the public began to defy the customs commissioners openly. In a number of places mobs rescued ships and cargoes held for suspected smuggling. In Rhode Island the courts were intimidated into acquitting accused smugglers.

The disorder never became as widespread as it had during the Stamp Act crisis, but it seemed sufficiently alarming to the royal governor of Massachusetts, Sir Francis Bernard, to require drastic action. Responding to Bernard's reports, the British government ordered the military commander in chief, Thomas Gage, to move troops from New York to Boston. At the same time the British ministry sent the governor two more regiments of redcoats from Britain. The troops were greeted with hostility and deep suspicion by Bostonians, who were convinced that the soldiers were there to intimidate the colony and arrest Patriot leaders.

Meanwhile in Britain, pressure mounted to repeal the Townshend duties. They had brought relatively little revenue and by encouraging a second boycott had led to another drastic drop in Anglo-American trade. Once more adopting an expedient course, Parliament canceled the duties in 1770, except for a three-penny tax on each pound of tea. By now, even such firm friends of America as William Pitt were beginning to fear that the colonists were determined to overturn the basic laws governing commercial relations between Britain and the colonies.

Fears for Colonial Religious Autonomy.

The tightening of imperial bonds was not confined to the political and economic spheres. In religion, too, the advent of the crown's Tory advisers tripped off efforts to limit colonial autonomy. In March 1763 the archbishop of Canterbury, head of the Church of England, wrote that he and his fellow bishops finally intended to "try our utmost for bishops" at the next session of Parliament. The colonies did not have an episcopal structure; this void, the archbishop said, would have to be remedied.

The archbishop's scheme to attach the colonies more securely to Anglicanism eventually failed. Yet controversy over the religious issue continued to rage, constantly fed by rumors that the effort to establish Anglican bishops in America had not ended. Especially in New England, where hostility to Anglicanism had always been intense, many colonists came to believe that there was a plot to impose upon them bishops, tithes for the Church of England, and even laws restricting public office to Anglicans. Inevitably the religious and political issues merged. The link between these issues seemed confirmed by the role of the Anglican clergy in America. Unlike the dissenting ministers, who were often the most vehement enemies of the Grenville and Townshend programs, clergy of the Church of England generally opposed active resistance to the stamp tax and Townshend duties, urging their flocks to obey the law and show respect for royal officials.

Patriot Insecurity.   Before 1763 most Americans had been proud of their British heritage, and even those whose ancestors came from other lands had acknowledged their allegiance to Britain. Thereafter, they drifted away from this loyalty and eventually developed a rationale for autonomy that would carry them all the way to independence.

In part the process reflected American social insecurity. Yes, Americans were affluent and relatively free, but this condition, unusual among societies of the day, seemed precarious. As historian Gordon S. Wood has noted, "the people were acutely nervous about their prosperity and the liberty that made it possible." He also describes the resentment that many colonists felt against those who, owing to their connections with the British royal government, had special advantages in the scramble for wealth and "preferment," favors in the form of office or lucrative business arrangements. The patriot leaders were not modern democrats, but neither did they favor a system that conferred permanent privilege on a few. Above all they despised the hereditary principle entrenched in the British monarchy— that birth to the right parents conferred permanent and unchallengeable advantages regardless of merit.

Patriot Ideology.   During the imperial crisis of 1763–1776 some of the best minds of America were devoted to the task of justifying colonial "rights." At various stages of the British–American conflict such men as John Dickinson, Thomas Jefferson, John Adams, and Benjamin Franklin published letters, pamphlets, and editorials that indicted British policies in the name of fundamental political principles. At times their writing was important largely for its immediate political utility. Dickinson's *Letters from a Farmer in Pennsylvania to the Inhabitants of the British Colonies* (1767–1768) for example, was an attack on the Townshend duties that emphasized the illegality of collecting internal taxes in America as opposed to merely regulating commerce. But there were also more searching and thorough defenses of American freedom and the right to resist authority that, taken together, announced a new philosophy of government and a new perspective on the individual's relations to it.

Few of the pamphleteers and writers were entirely original thinkers. They borrowed widely from European, especially English, sources, particularly from the radical Whig publicists of the late 1680s and 1690s, who had sought to justify the Glorious Revolution against James II and later had worked out arguments to limit the power of the crown. John Locke's *Treatise of Civil Government* was a particularly important source of ideas. Society, said Locke, was based on an agreement between ruler and ruled to preserve the natural rights of man inherent in the order of the universe. Although obedience to a just ruler was required by this "social contract," defiance of tyranny was also an obligation.

Patriots almost always maintained that they were defending traditional rights guaranteed under the unwritten British constitution and endangered by either the king or his chief ministers. Far from demanding what was legitimate obedience from their subjects, they argued, the tyrants in Britain were attempting to subvert rights sanctioned both by history and by the laws of nature. Such arguments became vital weapons in the Patriot arsenal; as incorporated in the Declaration of Independence, they would be handed down to later Americans as part of their political heritage.

The Whig thinkers also provided Americans with a moral rationale for independence. In England political dissenters during the early eighteenth century had come to regard English society as corrupt. Compared with the past, royal officials were mere "placemen" who served royal power with no other aim but to grow rich. England itself had grown grossly wealthy, its people a prey to luxury and vice.

Americans seized on this bleak picture enthusiastically, using it to support the Patriot position. In contrast to corrupt Britain, American society was pure and unspoiled. The colonists still lived honestly and simply. But would all this not end if Bute, Grenville, and the rest had their way? If Americans did not resist, surely a horde of locusts in the shape of royal officials would descend on America and consume its substance, meanwhile exposing the colonists to the dissipations and moral laxity that the young society until now had been spared. If for no other reason than to preserve American virtue, then, British policies must be resisted at all costs.

Massacre in Boston.   As the journalists, pamphleteers, and lawyers learnedly or passionately argued the extent of natural rights, ordinary men and women grew ever more hostile to British policy and restless at the visible symbols of British authority. Some outburst of violence was probably inevitable in Boston. The city in 1770 was a hotbed of anti-British feeling, and townspeople and redcoats had been trading insults ever since the soldiers had arrived from New York. To make matters worse, many Boston artisans deeply resented the fact that off-duty British soldiers were taking part-time jobs and so depriving them of scarce work. Then, one evening in March, a mob attacked a British sentry at his post. The soldier called for help, and when the squad dispatched to rescue him arrived, they encountered a rapidly growing, angry crowd. At some point someone gave the command for the redcoats to fire. When the smoke from the muskets cleared, three Americans lay dead and several wounded, two of whom later died.

The incident threatened to touch off a major uprising. The townspeople, Governor Hutchinson reported, were in a perfect frenzy and might attempt to drive out all 600 redcoats stationed in Boston. If they attacked, it would plunge the colony into full-scale rebellion against the crown, the consequences of which would be too horrible to contemplate. Although unsure of his authority, Hutchinson quickly ordered the arrest of the soldiers involved in the "massacre" and directed that the British troops be removed from their barracks in town to Castle William in Boston Harbor. From there they could continue to guard the city but would no longer be in direct contact with the irate citizens. Eventually seven of the redcoats were tried for the massacre. Ably defended by John Adams and Josiah Quincy, five were acquitted and two received light sentences.

The Gaspée Incident.   Repeal of the Townshend duties in April 1770 cooled the argument between Britain and America. Yet the next two or three years were not without jarring incidents of American defiance and British reprisal.

The most serious of these was the Gaspée incident, involving a British revenue cutter operating out of Narragansett Bay. On June 9, 1772, while pursuing a suspected smuggler, the vessel ran aground on the Rhode Island coast near Providence, a hotbed of Patriot sentiment. That evening a group of the town's prominent citizens boarded the vessel, wounded its commander, disarmed the crew, and burned the ship to the keel. This was not only a crime against the king's property, but also a blatant attack on a royal officer. Royal officials immediately posted a large reward for information leading to the conviction of the guilty parties and convened a commission of leading American Loyalists to investigate the affair. But no one chose, or dared, to come forward with information, and royal officials could only fume with frustration.

The Tea Act.   The Gaspée affair notwithstanding, the period between 1771 and 1773 was one of relative calm. During these years the Patriot cause, with few new outrages to feed on, went into eclipse. The militant Sons of Liberty pledged to compel the British government to rescind the remaining duty on tea and tried to force merchants to continue the Nonimportation Agreements. They failed. Instead, British–American trade revived—to the joy of the merchants, who no longer saw any purpose in boycotting English wares now that the other Townshend duties were dead. Meanwhile, Americans evaded the tea duty by smuggling in their favorite beverage from Dutch sources.

Now the government in England blundered once more and set in motion the final phase of the British–American confrontation. After decades of growing profit in trade with India and the Far East, the British East India Company had been brought to the edge of ruin by mismanagement and fraud. Its last remaining asset, 18 million pounds of tea, could not be sold because taxes in Britain and America made smuggled Dutch tea cheaper. To help the company, the British government, under the Tea Act of 1773, eliminated an export duty on British tea. Though the new law retained the existing three-pence-a-pound import duty on tea brought to America, this new arrangement would allow the East India Company to undersell American merchants who sold smuggled tea. By allowing the company to forgo the auction of its product in Britain and sell directly to various favored American consignees, the new law meant it could bypass or undersell even the "fair traders," those American merchants who obeyed the law and bought only English tea.

The scheme, it seemed, might be the beginning of a new policy to favor those merchants in the colonies who supported British policies and penalize those who did not.

In each major port artisans, shopkeepers, and merchants gathered to condemn this latest threat to American liberty. Information was passed from cities to villages and from colony to colony through the Committees of Correspondence, building a broad and organized resistance. The radicals urged all Americans to abstain from drinking tea. Patriot women responded by turning to native concoctions that Patriot drinkers loyally pronounced "vastly more agreeable" than anything out of India.

In Boston during the winter of 1773 the Tea Act finally triggered a military confrontation. Leading the Boston radicals were the fiery Samuel Adams, organizer of the Massachusetts Sons of Liberty, and John Hancock, a prominent merchant. In late November the first tea-carrying vessels arrived in Boston. On the evening of December 16 a group of Patriots dressed as Mohawk Indians boarded the ships and dumped the contents of 342 chests of tea—worth £10,000—into the harbor. Hundreds of people watched from the wharf as a thick layer of tea leaves spread over the water. They did not know it, but they were watching part of Britain's American empire sink beneath the waves.

The Intolerable Acts.

Between March and May 1774, following other attacks on tea-carrying vessels, an angry Parliament passed the so-called Intolerable or Coercive Acts. The first of these punished Boston by closing the port to all commerce until the East India Company had been paid for its tea. The second, intended to prevent local juries from frustrating enforcement of imperial trade regulations, allowed royal officials accused of crimes while stopping a riot or collecting revenue to be sent to Britain for trial. The third modified the charter of Massachusetts by giving the royal governor enlarged appointive powers and limiting the authority of the town meetings, which had served as forums for anti-British radicals.

Patriots considered two other measures passed at this time, though not reprisals for the Boston Tea Party, equally "intolerable." The first extended the provisions of the Quartering Acts so that troops might be lodged in private dwellings. The second, the Quebec Act, established a highly centralized administration for the province of Quebec, Canada, won during the French and Indian War, and granted toleration for the Catholic religion that most of the French population embraced. The law also extended the boundaries of Quebec south to the Ohio River. Protestant Americans, revealing their age-old prejudices, objected to this acceptance of Catholicism. Citizens of Virginia, Connecticut, and Massachusetts denounced the extension of Canada into the area south of the Great Lakes as violating provincial claims to the region under founding charters.

The First Continental Congress.

In response to widespread demand for a united colonial front against the Intolerable Acts, fifty-five delegates representing all the colonies except distant Georgia met at Philadelphia in early September 1774. This First Continental Congress was composed of men with widely differing views. There were radicals who claimed that American rights were founded on natural law and that, accordingly, Parliament could not abridge them in any way. There were also moderates who argued that American liberties came ultimately from the

British constitution and that Parliament had the right to legislate at least on matters of imperial trade. Conservatives, led by Joseph Galloway of Pennsylvania, proposed establishing a political union between Britain and America under a crown-appointed "president-general" and a kind of super Parliament. It was narrowly defeated.

During the debate a copy of the Suffolk Resolves, recently drafted in Massachusetts, arrived in Philadelphia. These condemned the Intolerable Acts and urged the people of Massachusetts to establish an armed militia, boycott British goods, and withhold taxes from the royal government. Presented to the delegates, the Suffolk Resolves were endorsed as the congress's own resolutions. In its own Declaration of Rights and Grievances the congress sharply attacked virtually all British trade legislation since 1763 and established a Continental Association, which forbade the importation or consumption of British goods and urged an embargo on colonial exports as well. The congress resolved to meet the following May if American grievances had not been redressed by then.

The First Continental Congress was a milestone on the road to American solidarity. Until this time provincial legislatures had acted independently to protest British actions; there had been no body that could claim to speak for Americans as a whole. Now, in 1774, another and greater crisis had finally broken through the selfish localism that had so often governed colonial relations. Americans would continue to resist surrendering local political autonomy to a collective government. But they had taken the first step toward political union.

Lexington and Concord.   In the next months the Patriot leaders prepared for the worst. In every colony men joined militia units, collected arms, ammunition, and gunpowder, and began to engage in military drill. In Massachusetts these groups were called Minute Men because they were expected to "Stand at a minute's warning in Case of alarm." In other provinces the assemblies voted to send money and supplies to the people of Massachusetts, who were suffering economically under the Intolerable Acts. Meanwhile, General Gage, now installed as governor of Massachusetts, prepared his forces to repel a Patriot attack. Gage particularly feared the Boston Committee of Safety, headed by John Hancock, which had been formed to coordinate Patriot military actions and to call out the Minute Men at the first sign of further British provocation.

In mid-April Gage received orders to enforce the Intolerable Acts, by military action if necessary, and to stop Patriot preparations for armed defense. He immediately dispatched a force of 700 men to Concord to destroy Patriot arms caches. Learning of the redcoat destination, the Boston Committee of Safety sent Paul Revere and William Dawes to alert the countryside and warn Hancock and Sam Adams, staying at nearby Lexington, to escape. When the redcoats arrived at Lexington at dawn on April 19, 1775, they found seventy Minute Men waiting for them. After repeated British commands to disperse, the outnumbered Americans complied. At this point someone fired a shot. The British then let off several volleys, killing eight Americans. The Americans replied but got the worst of the exchange. At the end of the skirmish the British occupied Lexington Common.

The redcoats now marched to Concord, where they destroyed some Patriot supplies. By this time the countryside had been thoroughly aroused, and as the British troops returned to their base, they were attacked on every side by colonial militia. The twenty-one miles back became a murderous gauntlet as Minute Men fired at the redcoats from behind walls, barns, and trees. By the time the British reached the safety of Charlestown, 250 had been killed or wounded. Also dead were almost 100 Americans.

Conclusions

Lexington and Concord turned a disagreement into a war. For the next eight years North America would be the arena for struggling armies. At the end there would be an independent United States.

In one sense this momentous result was the climax of the long process we observed in Chapter 3 that had helped to create a distinctive society and culture in America and a feeling among the colonists that they were not simply transplanted Europeans. It was also related to the growing economic and political maturity of British North America. Here, ironically, British policy was itself largely responsible. Unlike the other European colonial powers, Britain had done much to foster colonial political autonomy and economic prosperity. By 1763 British North America had the population, the material resources, and the political self-confidence to defy one of Europe's most powerful nations.

But cultural, political, and economic maturity by themselves were not enough for revolution; the ties to Britain remained too strong. The actual imperial crisis was precipitated by the special circumstances after 1763. One crucial matter was the French and Indian War. By relieving the colonists of a long-standing danger, it weakened American dependence on Britain. At the same time it loaded the British taxpayer with debt and demonstrated to Pitt's Tory successors that the Americans could not be counted on to bear the burdens of empire in an acceptable way.

However justified from the British perspective, the policies adopted after 1763 were foolishly conceived and executed. A few in Britain saw that the American colonies had become a mature society fast approaching England in wealth and numbers; but most Englishmen and, most crucially, King George's Tory ministers could see them only as disobedient children. Charging ahead blindly, Britain imposed measures that threatened many occupational and economic groups, deeply disturbed the elite merchants, lawyers, and planters, and aroused fears among many thousands of ordinary people that they were about to be enslaved and exploited by harpies in the shape of bishops and royal officials.

In short, we cannot separate the economic, religious, and political strands of causation. All these factors motivated the colonists, who eventually sought independence; and in each of these areas we find a common anxiety: fear of oppression. A fierce colonial attachment to self-determination in all spheres was the ultimate source of the American Revolution.

ONLINE RESOURCES

"Two Divergent Accounts of the Boston Massacre" *http://www.let.rug.nl/~usa/D/1751-1775/ bostonmassacre/prest.htm* From both the British and colonists' perspectives, these two documents help to show the growing ideological rift between England and the colonies.

"Resolutions of the Stamp Act Congress" *http://www.let.rug.nl/~usa/D/1751-1775/stampact/ sa.htm* With an introduction and background on colonial resistance, this site contains the full text of the resolutions of the Stamp Act.

"Chief Pontiac's Siege of Detroit" *http://info.detnews.com/history/story/index.cfm?id=180& category=events* This site contains the story of Pontiac, chief of the Ottawas, and chronicles his leadership in taking control of the Fort of Detroit. The site is enriched with illustrations, photos, and archival materials including a copy of Pontiac's surrender.

"Declaration and Resolves" *http://www.ushistory.org/declaration/related/decres.htm* Read the Declaration and Resolves of the first Continental Congress. Under the "related information" link, read biographical sketches on colonial leaders and descriptions of events that led to the colonists' quest for freedom.

"Laws and Resolutions" *www.ushistory/org/declaration/index.htm* On this informative Web site, you can read historical documents such as the Mayflower Compact, the Pennsylvania Charter of Privileges, and find out more about the signers of the Constitution.

5

The Revolution

How Did It Change America?

1775	The Second Continental Congress meets in Philadelphia; It declares war on Britain, organizes the Continental Army under George Washington, authorizes a navy, and appoints a Committee of Secret Correspondence; Ethan Allen captures Fort Ticonderoga; The Battle of Breed's (Bunker) Hill in Boston
1776–79	Main theater of war is in middle colonies; Philadelphia and Yorktown occupied by the British
1776	Paper money "continentals" printed; Thomas Paine's *Common Sense*; in Congress Richard Lee of Virginia introduces a resolution of independence from Britain; Congress approves the Declaration of Independence; Congress appoints a committee to plan for a permanent constitution
1777	Congress recommends that states sell Loyalist property; Horatio Gates defeats General Burgoyne at Saratoga, the turning point of the war; Congress approves a draft of the Articles of Confederation
1778	France and the American colonies establish a military alliance
1779	Spain declares war on Great Britain
1779–81	Main theater of war shifts to the southern colonies
1781	Final victory at Yorktown; Articles of Confederation ratified; the colonial monetary system collapses; Congress appoints Robert Morris to organize Bank of North America to strengthen public credit
1782	Americans and British agree on a preliminary peace treaty dealing with the states' western boundaries, fishing rights off Newfoundland, British garrisons in the West, colonial debts, and payment for Loyalist property
1783	The Treaty of Paris brings full independence; Massachusetts court interpretation of the state constitution prohibits slavery; thereafter slavery is illegal in the Bay State
1786	Virginia legislature adopts the principle of separation of church and state in an act drafted by Jefferson

Writing in the summer of 1775, shortly after Lexington and Concord, John Adams described an encounter with a person he had defended in court as an attorney. The man—"a common Horse Jockey," Adams called him—greeted the Founding Father on the road. "Oh! Mr. Adams," he exclaimed, "what great Things have you and your Colleagues done for us! We can never be grateful enough to you. There are no Courts of Justice now in this Province, and I hope there will never be another!" Adams was appalled. Would the future of America be as the "common

Horse Jockey" hoped? Would the colonies, in the course of changing govern-ments, jettison all law to protect lives and property and turn their entire social structure upside down? "If the Power of the Country should ever get into such hands," remarked Adams, "and there is great danger that it will, to what purpose have we sacrificed our Time, Health, and every Thing?"

Adams and other moderate Americans worried throughout the war about a takeover of power by the less respectable people of the colonies. Their concern, especially once actual war commenced, was understandable. Eight years of bitter fighting followed the skirmishes at Lexington and Concord. During that time the American community expended vast amounts of energy and wealth and sacrificed thousands of lives. Surely a struggle of this magnitude—one, moreover, fought in the name of freedom from tyranny—could be expected to undermine conventional values, transform traditional relationships, and weaken long-standing institutions. Did it? The obvious and fundamental result of the American Revolution was inde-pendence. But how profoundly did the Revolution change American society? Did Adams's fears prove justified?

American Prospects

However much they feared the consequences of military confrontation, Ameri-cans could not predict what lay ahead in the days following Concord and Lexing-ton. Ties of memory, habit, interest, and affection, and anxieties about the unknown all acted as deterrents to a complete break with England. Few as yet wanted independence. Even among the most ardent Patriots the common hope was that Britain would see the light, abandon its punitive policies, and reconsider its fundamental relations with America. This hope was reflected in John Dickin-son's Olive Branch Petition adopted by the Second Continental Congress in July 1775, declaring that the colonists remained loyal to King George and asking him to intervene to protect his American subjects against Parliament's tyranny. Loyalists, needless to say, were even less willing to break with the past. Whether Loyalist or Patriot, virtually all Americans in the spring of 1775 recoiled at the thought of complete independence.

Whatever their ultimate goals, Americans recognized that armed resistance to the mighty British Empire was a risky policy. Britain was probably the strongest nation on earth in 1775. On the face of it, the British had an enormous advantage over the Americans in numbers, military experience, and political cohesion. But they also labored under great difficulties. British military and naval power had declined since the end of the French and Indian War in 1763. Meanwhile, France had rebuilt its military forces and was in a position to challenge Britain again. More serious, Britain's victories in the recent French and Indian war had left it iso-lated. France, Spain, Holland, and Russia all feared British power and had griev-ances that they hoped to redress. These nations, especially France, were potential American allies in 1775. Their hostility to Great Britain would prove indispensable to the American cause.

Britain also faced enormous strategic problems in fighting a war in America. The British Isles were 3,000 miles from the military scene, and troops and supplies sent to the battlefields would take two or three months to arrive. When they finally did, the troops would have to fight on unfamiliar terrain, often surrounded by a hostile populace. Americans were on their home ground, close to supplies and manpower, and able to apply the strength they had to the battle at hand.

Yet the "rebels," too, faced colossal difficulties. Several hundred thousand Americans were not only opposed to the Patriot cause but were willing to risk their lives and fortunes to defeat it. The Loyalists would be a great source of strength to the British. Several regiments of Loyalists would fight ferociously against their own countrymen. Loyalist troops would be widely feared and detested by Patriots for their zeal in the crown's cause.

Military Forces.

The French and Indian War notwithstanding, relatively few Americans had military experience, let alone the knowledge required for raising, equipping, and leading a large army. A number of colonials had served as officers during that earlier war, but none, not even George Washington, had held a rank higher than militia colonel. And the professional foreign soldiers who soon flocked to America seeking military appointments for professional or ideological reasons were often incompetent. The French nobleman, the Marquis de Lafayette, the Germans Johann Kalb (known as Baron de Kalb) and Baron Friedrich Wilhelm von Steuben, and the Pole Thaddeus Kosciusko were skilled soldiers. But there was no officer on the American side who had the experience of commanding large bodies of troops in the field or of planning military strategy for a whole continent.

The colonists were better off in ordinary military manpower. Americans believed then, and would continue to believe for most of their history, that a volunteer soldier was better than a hired mercenary. British redcoats, and still more the Hessians—German soldiers hired by the British king to help put down the rebellion—supposedly lacked the spirit of those fighting for their homeland with freedom in their hearts.

The variety of uniforms in Baron Von Closen's watercolors of colonial troops suggests the fragmentation of Patriot forces during the Revolution. Note the black soldier at the far left.

In reality, American soldiers lacked the rigorous training of the redcoats, and this difference often strongly favored the British. On the other hand, most Americans knew how to use a rifle or musket, and in fact, their lack of traditional European military experience helped as much as it hurt. At the outset of a battle, British soldiers were trained to fire volleys in the general direction of their opponents and trust to the sheer volume of lead to shock and disrupt the enemy. The ranks would then charge the foe with drawn bayonets. These tactics worked well enough on the open fields of Europe, where opposing armies faced each other in full view. But in the forests that covered so much of the colonies, where men could hide behind every tree and bush, they were unsuitable. Colonial troops equipped with accurate Kentucky rifles, deployed behind cover, were often far more effective. The British tried to modify their tactics to suit American conditions. Loyalist troops, moreover, were familiar with guerrilla fighting and were valuable auxiliaries to the British army. But on the whole, American commanders and enlisted men remained better adapted to war in the colonies than the British.

The Patriot leaders could not count on a consistent and stable supply of manpower. It was one thing for a young man to turn out with his gun for a local skirmish or a few weeks of soldiering. It was another, however, to enlist as a regular in the Continental Army, fight battles against professional soldiers, subject himself to military discipline, and spend months or possibly years away from home and family. It proved hard for the Continental Congress and the individual states to raise troops. At first patriotism was enough to bring in recruits; later, cash bounties and promises of land were necessary to induce men to enlist. Once in the army, the new recruits were hard to keep. Many served just a few months and then, with or without official leave, returned to civilian life. Almost 400,000 men passed through the Continental armies during the war, but George Washington never had more than 20,000 troops under his command at one time.

Supplying the army was another problem for the Americans. There were many fine gunsmiths in the colonies, but they produced so many types and sizes of weapons that securing the proper ammunition was difficult. There was also a shortage of gunpowder and shot, and the dearth at times threatened to put the entire American army out of action. Artillery was in especially short supply, for the country was not yet capable of manufacturing cannon. American shipyards could not build ships of the line, the battleships of the day, and the Continental navy could scarcely challenge the British fleet in direct battle. But Americans could produce excellent small craft that served effectively as privateers—armed private ships legally commissioned to attack the enemy. Privateers provided most of the American naval punch. Licensed by Congress with "letters of marque" to prey on British commerce, they attacked enemy merchant ships even within sight of the British coast. During the war privateers captured 3,200 British ships, at immense cost to Great Britain and its citizens. Privateering helped to balance the great losses suffered by northern shippers from the British blockade of American harbors and seizure of hundreds of American merchant vessels on the high seas.

Creating a Government.   At the beginning, the Second Continental Congress was the country's only central political authority. Although it regularly passed resolutions and proposed emergency measures, the congress was not an effective government. Sovereignty continued to reside in the individual state governments; in fact, the assemblage in Philadelphia was more like a diplomatic conference of sovereign states than a government. In the end, implementation of every proposal Congress made depended on the support of the thirteen state legislatures, and these as often ignored its wishes as obeyed them.

Despite its limitations, for many months the Second Continental Congress acted as the government for the American people. It created the Continental Army with George Washington as commander in chief. On May 29, 1775, it adopted an address to the people of Canada asking them to join in resisting British tyranny. In July it approved the Olive Branch Petition; and after that was rejected by the king, it disavowed American allegiance to Parliament. That same month Congress established a post office department and appointed commissioners to negotiate peace treaties with the Indians. In the fall of 1775 it authorized a navy for the "United Colonies," and soon after appointed a five-man Committee of Secret Correspondence to approach Britain's European enemies for aid.

Wartime Finance.   Still the Americans lacked a strong, effective central government. One of Congress's chief weaknesses was that it had no power to tax. Americans were unused to heavy taxation and during the various colonial wars of the past the individual colonies had met the problem by issuing paper money. Now, once more, Congress and the states resorted to the printing press to pay military contractors, the army, and public officials. The paper money issued by Congress was called "continentals," and by 1780 notes with a face value of $200 million had been circulated. The states individually issued almost as much during the same period.

The American folk expression "not worth a continental" suggests the fate of this paper money. At first the continentals and state notes kept their face value surprisingly well. But as the volume of issues grew, their purchasing power fell. By 1780 $40 in continentals was worth less than $1 in gold and silver coin. Paper money prices soared so high that a bushel of corn that had sold for $1 in Massachusetts in the spring of 1777 sold for $80 by the summer of 1779.

In a modern nation such hyperinflation is likely to produce social and economic disaster. And the inflation during the struggle for independence did harm some Americans. Patriots who bought Congress's bonds ("loan office certificates") or who accepted "commissary" or "quartermaster certificates"—government IOUs—in payment for supplies and services lost money when prices soared. Inflation also hurt officers and men of the Continental Army and the state forces, whose pay plummeted in value. Still, the effects were limited. No one in those days had bank accounts or life insurance, and in this predominantly rural, agricultural economy relatively few worked for money wages or paid cash for the food they ate or the clothes they wore. Inflation, then, had far milder effects than it would today. And in any event, neither Congress nor the state governments had any real alternative to paper money given the tax-avoidance traditions of America and Congress's inability to impose taxes.

The Road to Independence

Early Battles.　Following the skirmishes at Lexington and Concord, General Gage found himself besieged in Boston by several thousand New England troops. In early June 1775 he prepared to dislodge the rebels from Dorchester Heights. The Americans countered by fortifying Breed's Hill (not Bunker Hill, as legend has it) in Charlestown, across the harbor from Boston. On June 17 British naval vessels began firing on the Americans, and at noon 2,400 redcoats landed on the Charlestown peninsula. Twice the heavily laden "lobster-backs" trudged up Breed's Hill into the murderous fire of the Americans entrenched on top; twice they retreated. The third time General William Howe ordered them to drop their packs and charge with fixed bayonets. This time the redcoats swept the Americans off their perch and off nearby Bunker Hill as well. At the end of the day the British held the field, but at the cost of over 200 dead. Though technically an American defeat, the Battle of Bunker Hill was a moral victory that helped convince Americans they could stand up to British regulars.

Bunker Hill had been preceded by Ethan Allen's daring capture of the small British garrison at Fort Ticonderoga on Lake Champlain. It was followed by a double American thrust northward, led by Benedict Arnold and Richard Montgomery, against Montreal and Quebec, designed to deprive Britain of its Canadian base of operations. The expedition was dogged by bad luck and nearly led to disaster for the Americans. Montgomery took Montreal, but Quebec, defended by British regulars and Canadians who had rejected Congress's invitation to join the struggle against England, held out. In the battle to capture Quebec, Montgomery was killed, Arnold wounded, and several hundred Americans killed or captured.

In the South the early fighting went better for the Americans. There a force of Virginians and North Carolinians encountered the royal governor of Virginia, Lord Dunmore, and his army of white Loyalists and black slaves. The blacks had been promised their freedom if they supported the king. Lord Dunmore's small force fought enthusiastically but was overwhelmed by the Patriots.

The year 1776 began well for the Patriot cause. In a series of actions in the Carolinas between February and June, the Americans beat off the attacks of generals Sir Henry Clinton and Charles Cornwallis. In March, after Continental troops had dragged the artillery captured at Ticonderoga down to within range of Boston, General Howe evacuated the city. The British never seriously threatened New England again.

Turning Points.　As the months of fighting passed, many of the remaining emotional ties to Britain snapped. The use of Hessian mercenaries, the king's contemptuous rejection of the Olive Branch Petition, the December 1775 British proclamation declaring the colonies in open rebellion, and the closing off of all formal commerce with the rebellious Americans—these acts made it increasingly clear to Patriots that reconciliation was impossible. A critical event in the South was Lord Dunmore's arming of the slaves, a move that violated one of the South's strongest racial taboos. Chesapeake planters who had previously held back now rushed to support the Patriot cause.

With each passing day, then, Patriots found it easier to consider independence from Britain as their goal. Their need for allies provided an additional push toward independence. The French leaders viewed the British troubles in America with glee. Resentful of their defeat in the French and Indian War, they hoped to see proud Britain humbled and France restored to an important place in North America. Both France and Spain considered Britain a threat to their Caribbean possessions and expected a weak, independent America to be easier to deal with than the mighty British Empire. Early in 1776 the French foreign minister, the Count de Vergennes, sounded out Spain on aid to the Americans. Soon both countries began to funnel secret money and supplies to the colonists. Americans welcomed the aid but realized that all-out French and Spanish support depended on their own willingness to fight for independence, for only independence would accomplish what the two continental powers wanted: a crippled Britain.

Yet something more was needed to convince most Patriots that they should take the final step. Though disillusioned with Parliament and the king's ministers, Americans retained a touching faith in the king himself and hoped he would see the light. A forty-seven-page pamphlet called *Common Sense,* published in early 1776 by a recent immigrant from England, Thomas Paine, destroyed their last illusions. In bold and ringing phrases Paine denounced King George and the British government and insisted that the time had come to sever completely the ties with Britain. Calling George the "royal brute," Paine helped to destroy the colonists' awe of the crown and respect for the king. Far from being a benevolent father to his people, George had unleashed the wrath of redcoats, Hessians, Indians, and desperate slaves on them. He was not worthy of their esteem. Furthermore, monarchy was a form of government condemned by God; kings were "crowned ruffians." Concluded Paine: "The blood of the slain, the weeping voice of nature cries, 'tis time to depart'."

Independence Declared.   Paine's stirring polemic sold 120,000 copies in three months and was read throughout the colonies. Tories denounced it as treasonous and certain to encourage "republican" views—that is, ideas of popular government. *Common Sense* had an immense impact on Patriots. Washington found it "working a powerful change in the minds of many men." In April a convention of North Carolinians authorized the colony's delegates in Congress to support independence. Virginia, the most populous colony, did the same the following month. Then, on June 7, 1776, Virginia delegate Richard Henry Lee introduced a resolution in the Continental Congress that the United Colonies "are, and of right ought to be, free and independent States." In response to this motion, Congress appointed Thomas Jefferson, Benjamin Franklin, John Adams, Roger Sherman, and Robert Livingston to prepare a document declaring and justifying American independence. At the end of June a draft of the proposed statement, composed largely by Jefferson, was sent to Congress. On July 2, Congress voted unanimously for the principle of independence, and on July 4 it formally approved the revised Declaration of Independence.

The declaration contained a detailed indictment of King George for cruelties, crimes, and illegal political acts against humanity and America. George was made into a villain who personified British wrongdoing. It was also a statement of the principles governing the drastic action proposed. The signers adopted Paine's radical antimonarchism and the views of the 1689 Whig publicists to justify independence. The people's consent, not the divine right of kings, was the ultimate source of political authority, they declared. Governments were established to assure citizens of "certain unalienable rights," including the rights to "Life, Liberty and the pursuit of Happiness." These words were borrowed from Locke, but significantly changed. Locke had written "life, liberty, and property." Jefferson and his colleagues, though deeply respectful of property, shifted the emphasis to the dignity of individuals and their right to personal fulfillment. The declaration also asserted boldly and bluntly that "all men" were "created equal."

The words that followed these expressed the view, borrowed from the English Whigs, that the people had the right to overthrow a government not based on the "consent of the governed." Revolution should not be resorted to "for light and transient causes." But when, as in this case, "a long train of abuses and usurpations" had been committed, with the goal of an "absolute Despotism," then it was the people's right "to throw off such Government, and to provide new Guards for their future security." Though written in the heat of military and political crisis, the declaration was a moving defense of human freedom, and it would inspire millions around the globe for generations to come.

The Fight for Independence

The Declaration of Independence was greeted throughout the nation with bonfires, toasts, fireworks, and pealing bells. But there was still a long way to go before the reality of independence could be established. The British, certainly, did not take the declaration at face value. In September 1776 General Howe and his brother, Admiral Richard Howe, met on Staten Island with Benjamin Franklin, John Adams, and Edmund Rutledge, representing Congress, and offered the Americans reconciliation. But first they would have to rescind the Declaration of Independence. The three Americans listened and then firmly rejected the terms. The fighting went on.

The War in the East, 1776–1777.   The war was not going well for the Americans. Howe, in fact, had opened the September negotiations only after trouncing the Americans soundly. Foreseeing Howe's move to make New York the base for British operations in America, Washington had moved his victorious troops south from Boston soon after the British evacuated that city. In July of 1776 Howe landed his forces on Staten Island opposite New York City. At the end of August, with 20,000 men under his command, he attacked Washington's troops on Long Island (Brooklyn Heights) and forced them to flee first to Manhattan, then to White Plains, and then across the Hudson to New Jersey. Howe occupied New York City, and the British kept it until the end of the war. At the very end of the year Washington partly redeemed his defeat in New York by attacking a force of Hessians at Trenton. The German troops, their vigilance impaired by too much Christmas cheer, were taken by surprise, and almost a thousand surrendered to the Americans.

The year 1777 held mixed fortunes for the rebels. Washington won an important victory at Princeton in January and cleared the British out of much of New Jersey. But in the summer Howe and Cornwallis routed the American general Anthony Wayne and occupied Philadelphia, forcing Congress to flee to avoid capture.

Still, 1777 brought the turning point of the war. During the summer, while Howe was moving on Philadelphia, British troops under General John Burgoyne were advancing south from Canada. The British plan was to split the colonies in two along the line of Lake Champlain and the Hudson River. As Burgoyne moved south, General Clinton in New York was to advance up the Hudson. Clinton did move north but failed to link up with the force coming south. In late June Burgoyne's army of 8,000 British, Canadians, Indians, and Germans left Quebec and advanced on Fort Ticonderoga. They captured the fort but were soon struggling through the dense forests of northern New York, using up their supplies and getting farther and farther from their Canadian base. Near Lake George, Burgoyne's troops encountered stiff resistance from the troops of Horatio Gates. Gates's army consisted of Continental regulars and New England militia who had flocked to his ranks to avenge the brutal killings of civilians by Burgoyne's Indian allies. Burgoyne tried to retreat northward, but the move to escape was futile. At Saratoga he was surrounded, and on October 17, 1777, "Gentleman Johnnie" surrendered his remaining 6,000 men.

The French Alliance.

The victory at Saratoga convinced the French that the Americans might well make good their claim to independence. In September 1776 Congress had dispatched Silas Deane, Benjamin Franklin, and Arthur Lee to Europe to negotiate treaties with Britain's enemies. Progress at first was slow. Not until January 1778 did Vergennes, the French minister of foreign affairs, tell the American envoys that France was prepared to ally itself with the United States. Soon after that he and the American representatives negotiated two important treaties. The first guaranteed each nation free trading rights with the other. The second was an alliance for joint military effort against Britain, to last until the United States had won its freedom. Each party promised not to conclude a peace with England without the other's consent.

In early May Congress ratified the French treaties. France was now in the war as America's ally. Spain declared war on Britain the following year. The Dutch, too, having clashed with the British over their smuggling of munitions to the rebels through their Caribbean possessions, broke relations with Britain in early 1781, though they never formally declared war. Soon French, Spanish, and later Dutch money—both gifts and loans—began to pour into America, enabling Congress to pay for much-needed arms, food, and equipment. Several other northern European nations, including Russia, Sweden, Prussia, and Denmark, organized the League of Armed Neutrality to keep their vessels supplying the Americans from being stopped by Britain. In all, by the end of the Revolution, Britain had been isolated and placed on the diplomatic defensive. European aid proved indispensable to America.

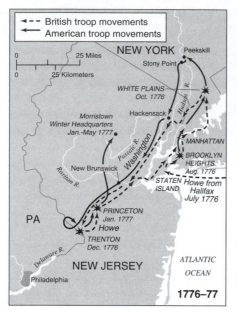

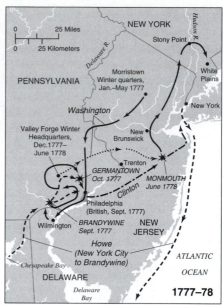

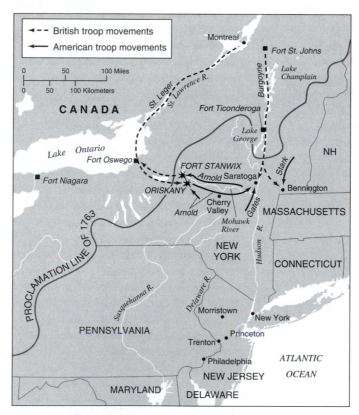

Central Campaigns, 1776–1778

War in the West.   The war that engulfed the older communities of the East also cast its lurid light across the West. On almost every colonial frontier Americans competed with the British for the friendship and aid of the Indians. In this struggle the British often had the advantage: They possessed the trade goods that the Indians wanted and, unlike the American settlers, posed no threat to the Indians' possession of ancestral lands.

In 1775, the Cherokees proclaimed their allegiance to George III and attacked the settlers of western North Carolina only to be fought off successfully. The infant settlements in eastern Kentucky, established by Richard Henderson and Daniel Boone only months before Lexington and Concord, were more exposed to British-inspired Indian attack. In the summer of 1776 bands of Shawnee and Delaware forced the Kentuckians to flee from their isolated homes to the settlement's three main villages. These remained havens for many whites throughout the war, but away from the log walls of the village stockades, hostile Indians pounced on isolated travelers, stole livestock, and prevented farmers from planting crops.

On the New York frontier the plight of the Americans was even worse. There the British had the support of the powerful Iroquois, under their chief Joseph Brant, and many Loyalists, organized as the Tory Rangers. In the first clash in the region in August 1777, American militia at Fort Stanwix stopped a British advance designed to reinforce Burgoyne, but soon afterward a supporting party of Americans under General Nicholas Herkimer was caught in an ambush at Oriskany, losing 200 men to a force of Indians, Loyalists, and Hessians under Colonel Barry St. Leger. During 1778 the Loyalists attacked the inhabitants of the Wyoming Valley in Pennsylvania and massacred hundreds while the Iroquois spread panic throughout upper New York.

By this time it was clear that defensive policies in the West had not worked. In the summer of 1778 the Kentuckians, led by George Rogers Clark, determined on their own to go on the attack. Clark and his men soon seized most of the northwestern settlements established by the French a generation before. In 1779 Congress itself finally sent several expeditions to nail down the West for the United States. Forays led by Clark himself and by Colonel Daniel Brodhead and General John Sullivan succeeded, but others failed and threatened to undo much of their work. By the time the war ended, the Americans were in firm possession of the frontier in the South, but the British controlled the Northwest. The war in the West ended in a draw.

Eastern Battles, 1778–1780.   It was in the older settlements that the war was finally won. At news of the British defeat at Saratoga in 1777, Lord North, now prime minister, expressed his heartfelt desire to get out of the "damned war." By now British taxpayers were complaining of the war's high costs, and British merchants, badly hurt by the loss of American trade, were in desperate straits. Hoping to avert the impending alliance between France and America, North dispatched a commission under the Earl of Carlisle to offer the Americans new terms for reconciliation, including ending all efforts to impose revenue taxes on America and suspending all parliamentary acts for America passed since 1763. When this effort failed, North offered to resign; but the king, who remained stubbornly and bitterly opposed to American independence, insisted that he remain.

The Americans, too, had their problems after Saratoga. In fact, the winter of 1777–1778 is generally considered the low point for Washington's army. Worn down by sickness and losses, the Continental Army withdrew to winter quarters at Valley Forge, just twenty miles from Philadelphia, where the British were living in comfort. The encampment was a wretched place. Recent fighting had left the area denuded of supplies. Food and clothing might have been brought in, but a breakdown of supply services left the men cold, hungry, and ill-clothed. To make matters worse, discontent was rife among the officers, whose salaries were small and often unpaid. Eventually Congress improved the pay situation, and a new quartermaster general, Nathanael Greene, established a more efficient supply service. Even so, the Continental Army barely survived the awful winter.

For the next three years the fighting went on intermittently and inconclusively. In the winter of 1778–1779 the British won control of Georgia by taking Savannah and Augusta. In 1780 General Sir Henry Clinton captured Charleston, South Carolina, along with 5,000 American troops and 300 guns. Heartened by Clinton's victory, suppressed South Carolina Loyalists now rushed to take up arms against their countrymen. Horatio Gates, the hero of Saratoga, attempted to retake the state for Congress, but was badly beaten by Cornwallis at Camden.

Fighting continued in the north as well. In August 1778 a joint Franco-American operation to capture Newport failed when a storm drove off the French fleet under Admiral d'Estaing. In New Jersey, New York, and the West the Americans were more successful. In July 1779 Anthony Wayne's troops captured a British garrison of 700 at Stony Point on the Hudson at the cost of only 15 American lives. In August "Lighthorse Harry" Lee drove the last British troops out of New Jersey.

Victory at Yorktown.
The years 1780 and 1781 were full of confused advances and retreats, and American morale sank almost as low as during the Valley Forge winter. In May 1780 Washington's troops near Morristown, New Jersey, nearly mutinied. Restlessness among front-line regiments continued through the following year. In January 1781 troops on the Pennsylvania and New Jersey lines did rebel.

The lowest ranks of the army were not the only ones disaffected. In the fall of 1780, papers carried by captured British Major John André revealed that General Benedict Arnold, now commanding the American troops at West Point, planned to surrender his vital post to the British. When Arnold learned of André's capture, he fled to the British lines and eventually became an officer in the king's forces.

Although initially discouraging, the year 1781 brought final military victory at Yorktown. The Yorktown campaign opened in April 1781, when General Cornwallis marched north from his base in North Carolina, hoping to crush the American forces in Virginia. He soon collided with troops under Lafayette. For four months Cornwallis and Lafayette danced around one another without reaching a showdown. When Wayne came to Lafayette's aid, the British commander retreated to the coast, hoping to establish a base where the Royal Navy could protect and supply him.

Washington heard of Cornwallis's move while he was besieging the British at New York. He quickly abandoned his effort to recapture the city and moved south. The moment was especially favorable because the French fleet under Count de Grasse could now join the attack. De Grasse soon stationed his ships off the Virginia coast, where Lafayette had pushed Cornwallis onto the narrow Yorktown peninsula. On September 14 Washington's troops and 5,000 French soldiers led by the Count de Rochambeau arrived at Yorktown. Bit by bit, remorseless French and American pressure reduced the area under British control. Cornwallis had counted on help from the sea, but the French fleet was at this point too strong for the British navy. Under relentless attack, Cornwallis notified Henry Clinton, his superior in New York: "If you cannot relieve me very soon, you must prepare to hear the worst."

General Clinton set out on his rescue mission on October 19. But he was too late. Three days earlier Cornwallis had made a desperate attempt to escape across the York River and had been frustrated by a storm. Seeing all hope for his army gone, the British general resolved to surrender. On October 19, 1781, 7,000 British and Hessian troops laid down their arms. Legend has it that as the defeated army marched out of its camp, the British military bands played a tune called "The World Turned Upside Down." The musicians' choice was prophetic. Yorktown was not only the last important battle of the war; it was also the end of the old British Empire.

The Articles of Confederation

Victory had come not a moment too soon for the American cause. By the fall of 1781 the United States was in serious financial trouble, its monetary system collapsing and prices and wages soaring out of sight. In the last months of the war Congress appointed Robert Morris, a shrewd Philadelphia businessman, as superintendent of finance. He proceeded to reorganize the government's financial affairs, strengthen the public credit, and eliminate waste in the budget. Soon after taking office he also organized the Bank of North America, the first commercial bank in the United States.

The closing months of the war also saw the beginning of a new American government. It had taken the states almost five years to agree on a new political structure. In the meantime, as we have seen, the Continental Congress had acted as the American government. Little more than a convention of sovereign powers, it had not been effective, and since the beginning of the war it had been clear to most American leaders that the country needed a more formal and permanent central authority. In June 1776 Congress had appointed a committee led by John Dickinson of Delaware to establish a constitution for the United States that would end all doubt about congressional authority to conduct war and provide the structure for a permanent union. The committee's proposal called for a legislature in which each state would have one vote. The new congress would have fairly broad powers, but not the power to tax—Americans remained tax-shy. Instead, it might ask the states for contributions proportional to their population.

The Dickinson scheme immediately came under attack. Delegates from large states complained that small states would be overrepresented since each, regardless of population, would have one vote in the proposed congress. At the same time, southern states with large slave populations thought that basing financial contributions on total population was unfair. Slaves, they pointed out, were only property, not citizens, and so should not be counted.

The major stumbling block, however, was that the plan gave the proposed congress the power to set westward limits to the states, to grant lands to private parties in regions beyond those limits, and to create new states in the West. This scheme stepped on many toes. Seven states claimed that their boundaries extended well into the trans-Appalachian region. Six states, on the other hand—New Hampshire, New Jersey, Rhode Island, Pennsylvania, Delaware, and Maryland—had no claims to western lands and favored Congressional control. Why, they asked, should the common struggle to win independence lead to a few states grabbing the western domain that all had fought for? Maryland and Pennsylvania investors had added worries: They had bought lands in the northwest from the Indians and feared that Virginia's claims would nullify their purchases.

The opponents of the initial plan delayed its consideration until the fall of 1777. This time, with the provision that each state would have one vote, it passed Congress. To go into effect the plan now needed acceptance by all the states. It won the support of twelve by the end of 1778, but Maryland refused to go along with it because her big neighbor, Virginia, still retained title to the lion's share of the upper Mississippi Valley. Months of jockeying followed until the Virginia delegates agreed to accept congressional control of the western region. Finally, in March 1781, with Maryland's objections withdrawn, Congress announced the formal adoption of the Articles of Confederation.

The Articles were a clear improvement over the existing government arrangements. Most important, they formalized the union of the American states. In specific terms, they gave legal standing to several powers that the Continental Congress had exercised earlier. The Confederation Congress could conduct war and foreign affairs, make commercial treaties, and negotiate with the Indians. It could borrow and coin money and issue bills of credit. The Articles also gave Congress the new power to manage public lands in the West.

Yet many imperfections remained. The new government consisted of only a legislature; it had no separate executive or judicial branches. And not all of the new Congress's powers were exclusive. The states could continue to deal directly with foreign governments and engage in war with Congress's consent. They could borrow money, maintain mints, and issue bills of credit even without Congressional approval. The states also had the sole right to legislate in matters concerning debts, contracts, and private affairs. Most important of all, they alone could levy taxes. And if experience showed that changes in the Articles were desirable, they would be hard to make; amendments required the consent of every state.

Still, the Articles of Confederation were a substantial move toward American national unity. The Continental Congress had been a makeshift, purely voluntary association entered into to deal with the imperial crisis. Now, with the Articles of Confederation, for the first time there was a permanent American government, one that would speak for the citizens of all the states.

Social Change

The growing sense of a common nationality was only one of many changes that the war initiated. As Americans looked around them between 1775 and 1783, many were certain that they were also witnessing a social revolution. American Loyalists, particularly, believed the rebels were more intent on overthrowing the existing social order than in righting the wrongs of imperial government. The Reverend Samuel Peters of Connecticut called the Patriots "ungovernable, right-eous and high-handed moberenes." Another Yankee Loyalist saw Patriot control of Massachusetts after 1775 as the triumph of the rabble: "Everything I see is laughable, cursable, and damnable; my pew in the church is converted into a pork tub; my house into a den of rebels, thieves, and lice; my farm in possession of the very worst of all God's creatures; my few debts all gone to the devil with my debtors." The suffering these Tories had endured at the hands of their rebel fellow Americans doubtless colored their attitudes. But even Patriots felt uneasy about the class resentment and the "levelling spirit" that disorder and change had brought to the surface. Langdon Carter of Virginia worriedly reported to Washington that some Patriots in his neighborhood wanted "a form of government that, by being independent of rich men, every man would then be able to do as he pleased." John Adams, after recounting his meeting with the disrespectful "Horse Jockey" described earlier, exclaimed: "Surely we must guard against this Spirit and these Principles or We shall repent of all our Conduct. . . ."

Carter, Adams, and other moderates feared that what had begun as a dispute over the governing of the empire was turning into a social revolution. A number of modern historians, too, have seen the War of Independence as an internal revolution. As one, Carl Becker, famously expressed it some years ago, the war with Britain was as much over "who shall rule at home" as over "home-rule."

A Revolutionary Experience?   The French Revolution of 1789 and the Russian Revolution of 1917 are prototypes of what most of us consider social revolutions. These events are abrupt and often violent overthrows by new rulers, claiming to speak for the poor and the powerless, of an elite that has monopolized power and enjoyed much of a society's wealth and privileges. The victors then usually expel or exterminate the old "oppressors," seize their property, and distribute it among "the people." Let us consider whether this model resembles the course of events in America between 1775 and 1783. Was the American struggle for independence a social revolution?

The term "revolution" does fit some of the change during these years. The fate of the American Loyalists, about 20 percent of the population, resembles the fate of the French elite at the end of the eighteenth century and the Russian at the beginning of the twentieth. During and immediately after the Revolutionary War, some 80,000 Loyalists fled the United States to settle in Upper Canada (present-day Ontario), the Canadian Maritime Provinces, England, and the West Indies.

Often they left hurriedly, just before the Patriot mob intent on hanging or tar-and-feathering arrived. Many abandoned their property—which the Patriot state governments usually confiscated—or sold it in a panic at knockdown prices. This exile and confiscation or forced sale of property look very much like social revolution. By removing an elite of rich landowners, prosperous attorneys, and successful merchants and dividing their property among those presumably poorer Americans who remained, surely America became more democratic and more equal.

The facts only partially support such a conclusion, however. Loyalists were not all from the upper crust. They came from every sector of colonial society. Many of the leading Tories certainly were "high-toned" folk. Rich merchants and landlords, successful lawyers, royal officials, and many of the Anglican clergy supported the British cause. On the other hand, many poor people, especially in rural areas, also chose to fight for the king. In New York the tenants of the Hudson Valley landlords were promised the lands of Patriot patroons if they remained loyal, and many did. In the backcountry of the Carolinas, where small farmers bitterly resented the political domination by the rich Patriot leaders on the seaboard, there were many yeoman Loyalists. There were even black Tories. Lured by promises of freedom if they deserted their masters and fought the rebels, thousands of blacks joined the crown's forces. So alarming was this defection that, to counter it, Congress reversed Washington's policy of rejecting black enlistees in the Continental Army. Thereafter, black soldiers, both slaves and free men, fought in the American army. Nevertheless, many blacks continued to prefer the king. When the war ended, hundreds of them refused to remain in the land where they had been enslaved and departed for Canada or the Caribbean with other Loyalists.

Patriots, too, came from both the highest and lowest ends of colonial society. Slaves, as we noted, fought for the Patriot cause, as did seamen, apprentices, artisans, and journeymen of the port towns. But so did a large portion of the colonial elite, from the planters of the South to the great merchants of New England and the middle colonies. As for the middle class of small farmers and shopkeepers, they, or at least their sons, formed the backbone of the Continental Army. In short, the Patriots were anything but "a rabble," as some Tories claimed. They were a cross section of the American people.

So there were only marginal differences between the social standing of those who supported independence and stayed in America and those who fought it and left. The Tory exodus did not deprive the country of a ruling class as did the departure of emigrés from France in the 1790s and "white Russians" from the land of the czars in 1917–1918. The exodus, accordingly, lends little support to the idea of an American social revolution between 1775 and 1783.

And what of the redistribution of wealth, the second standard by which we may identify a social revolution? The property of many Loyalist grandees, especially those who fled to the British lines during the war, was indeed taken by state governments. Did these seizures revolutionize existing property-holding patterns? Probably not. Late eighteenth-century America was not, after all, a society of a few great landlords and a vast landless peasantry, like France in 1789 and Russia in 1917. Many people already owned land, and the amount confiscated from the Tories could not have affected the overall balance very much. Even if every acre seized had been handed over to the landless, it would not have done much to equalize land-holding. Besides, when the states sold the confiscated farm acres and town lots, they did not generally go to the "common folk." Much of it, it seems, was snapped up by Patriot landholders or speculators. Existing inequalities, if anything, were probably magnified by the resale of confiscated Loyalist real estate.

It seems clear, then, that the expulsion and expropriation of the Loyalists did little to change the social profile of the community or the nature of property-holding in America. But this is not to say that the Revolution did not liberalize American life. Indeed, there is good evidence that it helped in many ways to make America a more democratic community.

Democratization. Even if the Tory exiles included members of the "lower orders" and the middle class, historian Gordon Wood believes that a large proportion of the families at the very apex of colonial life departed en masse. Though not numerous, they were particularly powerful and their departure, he believes, broke the crust, allowing new families to rise. This new upper class depended more on merit and achievement and less on "connections" for its wealth and power.

More significant, perhaps, was the growing concern for equity and social justice that accompanied the Revolution. Even slavery, the most blatant social inequity in America, was weakened by the Revolution.

Although white Americans were mostly concerned with their own rights and freedoms, the dispute with Britain following 1763 forced them to ponder the issue of human liberty. Not all Patriots were able to protest colonial servitude to Britain and at the same time ignore the slaves' bondage. How can we "reconcile the exercise of slavery with our professions of freedom," Richard Wells, a Philadelphia Patriot, asked pointedly. John Allen, a Baptist minister in Massachusetts, accused his fellow Americans of hypocrisy in refusing to admit the evil of slavery. "Blush . . . ye trifling patriots! who are making a vain parade of being advocates for the liberties of mankind, [and] . . . are . . . thus making a mockery of your profession by trampling on the sacred and natural rights and privileges of Africans."

Happily, the attack on slavery went beyond words. In 1775 the Quakers in Philadelphia established the first antislavery society. Five years later Pennsylvania passed the first law providing for the gradual freeing of slaves. In 1783 the Massachusetts courts interpreted the state constitution as prohibiting slavery, and thereafter slavery was illegal in the Bay State. Other northern states soon followed these leaders, ending slavery either by judicial act or by adopting gradual emancipation laws for slaves who reached a stipulated age. Even in the South slavery was affected by the Revolutionary ferment of egalitarianism. Prominent Patriots such as Jefferson and Henry Laurens, imbued with the ideals of the Enlightenment, attacked the system. Several southern legislatures passed laws making it easier for masters to free (manumit) their own slaves and restricting the domestic slave trade in various ways. By the end of the century, in every state from Pennsylvania northward, slavery was on the way to extinction, and it seemed to some Americans that even in the South it was in decline.

Another sign of the revolutionary zeal for freedom was the decline of indentured servitude, the system of unfree labor that had met the work needs of the colonies and helped facilitate the transfer of people across the Atlantic from Europe. In the new atmosphere of challenge to authority many Americans began to think that keeping people in near bondage, even if only for a period of years, was anachronistic. Believing that indenture was "contrary to . . . the idea of liberty" America had "so happily established," in 1784 a group in New York raised a public subscription for a shipload of servants so they would not have to accept the condition of indentured servitude.

Lawbreakers, too, benefited from the changes in attitudes awakened by the struggle for independence. Before the Revolution, and for years after, men and women convicted of felonies were often subject to brutal penalties. Criminals were placed in stocks, branded, whipped, and mutilated. The list of crimes with death as the penalty was appallingly long. After 1776, however, several states reduced the number of crimes punishable by hanging and replaced torture and the lash with imprisonment. In Pennsylvania, soon after independence, some effort was even made to replace harsh punishments with reformation of offenders. The purpose of sentencing, said the state legislature, should be "to reclaim rather than destroy. . . ." Years would pass before other states would imitate Pennsylvania, but clearly in this area too the Revolution was a minor watershed.

Finally, there was improvement in the status of women. During the war American women had contributed to the Patriot cause in age-old ways. They made blankets and shirts for Washington's army and spun woolen cloth to offset restricted British imports. They took over jobs and businesses in the absence of male family heads. "I find it necessary to be directress of our husbandry," Abigail Adams wrote John in 1776, and "I hope in time to have the reputation of being as good a farmer as my partner has of being a good statesman." They also expanded their horizons. Some became active in fund-raising for the Continental Army or participated in other Patriot causes. Others developed interests in public issues they had neglected before and joined political discussion groups. A very few women actually engaged in combat. Mary Ludwig Hays McCauley, better known as Molly Pitcher, took her husband's place behind a cannon at the Battle of Monmouth when he was overcome by the heat.

Some women expected their sex to benefit as a group from the war. The spirited Abigail Adams wrote her husband in 1776 that "in the new code of laws" then being considered by Congress—that is, the Articles of Confederation—it was important for the legislators to "remember the ladies and be more generous and favorable to them" than their predecessors had been. "Do not," she urged, "put such unlimited powers in the hands of the husbands."

Abigail Adams and those who thought like her would not fully realize their hopes. And yet the war and the forces it released did have some effect on women's circumstances. In New England the rhetoric of freedom led to liberalized divorce laws that placed women on virtually the same plane as men in seeking legal separation from an abusive or unfaithful spouse. In many states, the laws for the first time recognized the equal right of sons and daughters in inheritance and gave women greater control over their property. The years of debate over American rights also stimulated the first feminist questioning of existing female education. Most of the great battles for female "emancipation" lay in the future. Yet we must not ignore the revolutionary impulse entirely as a force for female liberation.

New Politics.

The political system also felt the liberalizing effects of the great upheaval. As they transformed themselves from provinces to "states," the former colonies changed royal charters to constitutions. In some the structural shifts were relatively modest. In others, however, there were more sweeping changes. Virginia, Pennsylvania, North Carolina, and Massachusetts ended or reduced the gross underrepresentation of their frontier counties in their legislatures. Pennsylvania, Delaware, North Carolina, Georgia, and Virginia liberalized their franchises so that almost any white male taxpayer, no matter how poor, could vote. Most states reduced the power of the executive branch, considered aristocratic, by taking away the governor's veto over laws passed by the assemblies. Pennsylvania entirely eliminated the legislature's upper house, thereby concentrating all power in the lower one, and fragmented the executive branch, considered too powerful, by replacing the governor with an executive council of thirteen members. Virginia and several other states pioneered an important democratic advance by adopting formal written bills of rights guaranteeing freedom of speech, conscience, assembly, petition, and privacy, as well as the right to trial by jury and other legal safeguards for the individual.

A final democratic innovation of these years was the constitutional convention, a meeting called for the specific purpose of altering the fundamental frame of government. Only such a convention, it was now believed, could validly express the wishes of the people. Its decisions, especially when confirmed by a direct vote of the electors (a referendum), took precedence over actions of a mere legislature. First put in practice by Massachusetts during the Revolutionary era, the concept that a convention best expressed the will of the people governed the call for the federal Constitutional Convention in 1787. It was a major contribution to democratic theory and practice.

The use of conventions to frame instruments of fundamental law reflected the new idea that in some ultimate sense "the people" alone were the source of power. Republicanism was a related concept. Republicans wished to reduce the role of birth, breeding, rank, and family influence in political life. These seemed relics of colonial days and royal government when, despite the widespread franchise, Americans had acknowledged hereditary authority and shown deference to officials. Now, said republicans, only talent, virtue, and devotion to the common good should qualify a person for political advancement and high office.

We must qualify the view that the Revolution liberalized political ideology, however. The leaders of the Revolution were carried by the logic of their opposition to royal government to condemn hereditary privileges, but few of them ever got over their fear of pure democracy, in which numbers alone counted and everyone was politically equal. Though they acknowledged that "the people" were the source of power, they did not include women, blacks, Indians, and men without some property in the term. Moreover, except for a few "violent men"—or, as we would say, radicals—republicans did not believe that elected representatives should submit totally to the wishes of the voters. Instead, they typically favored a "mixed" government in which the popular voice representing "numbers" would be tempered by "talent" of superior leaders.

Privilege.   Colonial law had upheld the privileged position of several specific institutions and individuals; here, too, the Revolution had a liberalizing effect. In those states with an established Anglican Church there was progress toward the complete religious toleration and separation of church and state that we have come to consider peculiarly American. It was inevitable that Anglicanism, the denomination most closely associated with the English crown, should lose standing after the Declaration of Independence. But the whole idea of an established church had become increasingly distasteful to Patriots. During the war Jefferson, allied with Virginia's Baptists, Methodists, and other dissenters, fought to disestablish Anglicanism in the state. Afterwards, he and his allies secured passage of the Bill for Establishing Religious Freedom (1786). Other states also disestablished the Anglican church, and several of them removed the remaining restrictions on non-Protestant voting and office-holding.

The Congregationalists' privileged position in New England was a tougher nut to crack. Though many New Englanders had become Baptists, the religious outsiders at first made little progress toward ending the special status of the region's Congregational churches. Unlike the Anglicans, Congregationalism was not identified with the mother country. In fact, the Congregational clergy had been among the most ardent defenders of the Patriot cause. This close association with the fight against Britain gave the Congregational establishment an extended lease on life. Connecticut did not disestablish the Congregational church until 1818. In Massachusetts its privileged position lasted until 1838. It took more than half a century, then, before New England finally achieved the separation of church and state that came elsewhere during the 1780s and 1790s. Yet on the whole, in religious matters too, the Revolution was a major liberalizing force in American life.

The Revolution also ended entail and primogeniture, two practices that reinforced economic inequality and privilege. Entailing was a legal procedure that allowed a property holder to forbid his heirs to sell their inheritances even after his death. Primogeniture was the practice of favoring the firstborn son in inheritances in the absence of a will providing for a more equal property distribution. Together these two practices were designed to preserve large landholdings and buttress the power and wealth of aristocratic families. In 1776 Jefferson drafted a law that abolished entail in Virginia. Similar laws were soon adopted in other states. In 1777 the Georgia legislature prohibited primogeniture, and by 1800 the practice was dead everywhere in America.

Making the Peace

Much of this liberating change took place against the background of war. But the terms of peace had to be settled before their effects could be felt.

France and the United States had agreed not to negotiate a separate peace with Great Britain, but both countries found it hard to resist working out their

At Versailles a lady offers Benjamin Franklin a laurel wreath, perhaps to replace the fur cap he often wore to charm the French court. Franklin, a marvelous diplomat, secured formal recognition of the United States and a military and commercial alliance with France; later he helped negotiate the Treaty of Paris, which brought the war to a close.

own peace arrangements. By 1781 the French were tired of the war and beset by financial problems so serious that they would soon threaten the French monarchy's very survival. Having achieved their prime goal of humbling the arrogant British, they saw little reason to continue the fighting. The Americans, too, if conceded their independence, had little reason to fight on. However, there was stubborn Spain. The 1778 treaty with France that brought Spain into the war promised that it be given Gibraltar—the great British fortress guarding the Atlantic entrance of the Mediterranean—if Spanish troops could capture it. But month after month the British defenders held out against the Spanish siege, depriving the Madrid government of its goal. If France stuck by its European ally, it looked as if peace—and American independence—depended on the transfer of a pile of rock.

Fortunately, the American peace negotiators proved adept. In early 1782 Lord North, discredited by the defeat at Yorktown, finally resigned as prime minister and his successor, the Marquis of Rockingham, prepared to concede independence to America. When Rockingham suddenly died, negotiations with the Americans were taken over by Lord Shelburne, a man willing to accept American independence only as a last resort. But Shelburne miscalculated. He sent to Paris as British negotiator Richard Oswald, a philosophical Scottish gentleman, an old friend of Benjamin Franklin from the Philadelphian's London days. Oswald proved to be exceptionally accommodating. When Franklin proposed a settlement that included as "necessary" terms independence "full and complete in

every sense," the total evacuation of all British troops from American soil, bound-
aries for the new nation that extended to the Mississippi in the west and the Great
Lakes to the north, and free access for American fishermen to the Grand Banks off
Newfoundland, Oswald saw no objections. Nor did he even balk at one of
Franklin's secondary, but "desirable," terms: the concession of Canada to the new
American nation!

But difficulties with France soon intervened. Franklin trusted Vergennes, the
French foreign minister, but Franklin's colleague, John Jay, who had joined in the
Paris negotiations, did not. Jay correctly believed that the French did not intend to
make peace until Spain, France's other ally, got what it wanted from the war. But
beyond its obligations to its ally, France wanted different things from the peace
than the United States. Seeking to protect their own rights on the Grand Banks, the
French were unwilling to stand behind American claims to fishing rights off Newfoundland. Vergennes even seemed ready to accept boundaries for the United
States that surrendered much of the lower Mississippi Valley to Spain and conceded the northwest to Great Britain.

Hoping to divide its enemies and save Gibraltar, Britain pushed its separate
negotiations with the United States. On October 5, 1782, Jay and Oswald, without
France, agreed on a draft for preliminary articles of peace, not to go into effect,
however, until France and Britain had entered into a similar preliminary agreement. The terms at their core included all of Franklin's earlier primary demands.
In London the British ministry insisted that compensation for Loyalist property
confiscated during the war and repayment in British money for all debts owed by
Americans to British creditors be added to these terms. John Adams, now in Paris
to join the negotiations, urged acceptance of these features, and they were included in the final draft.

As finalized, the peace articles acknowledged American independence. The
new nation's boundaries would be generous: in the west the Mississippi; to the
south Spanish Florida; to the northwest the Great Lakes; and in the northeast an
ill-defined line roughly corresponding to the present Canadian–American boundary. The British agreed to allow Americans to fish off Canadian territorial waters
and promised to evacuate American territory still under British occupation "with
all convenient speed." In return, the United States promised to place "no lawful
impediment" in the way of repayment by Americans of debts owed British creditors and agreed to recommend that the states restore to the Loyalists their civil
rights and their confiscated property.

Before signing, the American negotiators considered whether to first inform
the French of the peace terms and ask their permission to proceed. Besides the
moral obligation enjoined by the 1778 Franco-American treaty, Congress had so
instructed them. They decided against it for fear that France, with its own agenda,
would scuttle the agreement. Yet they could not cut France out entirely. After the
treaty was initialed, Franklin went to tell Vergennes of their action. Sheepishly admitting some "impropriety" to the French Foreign Minister, he urged him strongly to accept the agreement. The French by now were thoroughly tired of the war,
and Vergennes chose not to be offended. Instead, he approached the Spanish

ambassador in Paris and told him that American perfidy had left France unable to support Spain's claims to Gibraltar any longer. The Count de Aranda saw the light. With this hurdle pushed aside, Spain and France concluded a peace with Great Britain. On September 3, 1783, all these preliminary negotiations, including the Anglo-American articles of agreement, were incorporated into the Treaty of Paris. The great struggle for independence was over.

Conclusions

At news of the peace, a wave of elation and thanksgiving surged through the country. So intense was the joy in Philadelphia that prudent citizens urged the city fathers to restrain the celebration to keep it from getting out of hand. The jubilant mood could not last. Americans now confronted the problems of repairing the damage of seven long years of war and learning how to function as citizens of an independent nation. The difficulties would be formidable. The war had caused extensive physical destruction to both the cities and the countryside. In the South the British had carried off hundreds of slaves and destroyed dikes and dams. New Jersey, "cockpit of the Revolution," where so many battles had been fought, had been ravaged by advancing and retreating armies. All this damage would have to be repaired.

There would be social mending to do as well. Loyalists—those who had not fled for good—would have to be reconciled to the new regime and recompensed for their property losses. Several thousand free blacks in the North would have to be absorbed into the larger society. But on the whole, these adjustments would be minor. American society had not undergone a true social revolution. The war had accelerated processes that had long been moving the American community toward greater democracy, legal equality, and religious toleration. Between 1776 and 1783, religious establishments had been severely undercut, slavery had been eroded, the treatment of women and prisoners had improved, and the few surviving vestiges of feudalism had been swept away. Yet compared with the fundamental upheaval that marked the great French Revolution of 1789 and the Russian and Chinese revolutions of the last century, these were relatively small changes.

But if America had not experienced a major social revolution, it did undergo a political one. From a colony it became an independent nation. The Revolutionary War was primarily a colonial war of independence. If it resembles any upheaval of recent times, it is the decolonization struggles of African and Asian peoples after World War II. And the problems that the new nation would face belonged largely in the same realm: the political. Though the war had advanced the unity of English-speaking America and helped create a sense of shared nationality, it had not forged a cohesive nation. Previous republics had always been small, homogeneous city-states. Never had one been so huge in extent. Could this unusual creation called the United States, with its 900,000 square miles and 3 million people, survive and prosper as an independent republic? In the next few years the issue would be put to the test.

ONLINE RESOURCES

"The History Place American Revolution" *http://www.historyplace.com/unitedstates/revolution/index.html* This Web site provides a chronology of the American Revolution that is linked to copies of full-text documents such as the Articles of Confederation, the Declaration of Independence, and Thomas Paine's *Common Sense.* It also contains a portrait gallery featuring paintings of revolutionary actors.

"Essays on the Revolution" *http://revolution.h-net.msu.edu* Under the icon "essays," discover numerous scholarly articles including several that discuss the negotiation and controversy over the U.S. Constitution.

"Chronicling the Revolution" *http://www.pbs.org/ktca/liberty/chronicle.html* This site addresses a wide range of topics concerning the American Revolution, including songs of the revolutionaries, details of women's and Native Americans' involvement, and revolutionary events that took place in the urban landscape.

Liberty! The American Revolution *http://revolution.h-net.msu.edu* The official companion site to the PBS "Liberty!" series, this rich resource provides bibliographies of principal figures and a collection of essays concerning the social and political concerns that emerged during the war.

African-American Soldiers of the Revolution *http://docsouth.unc.edu/nell/nell.html* Part of the University of North Carolina at Chapel Hill Libraries' program "Documenting the American South," this site contains a full-text version of William Cooper Nell's 1885 work titled "The Colored Patriots of the American Revolution, With Sketches of Several Distinguished Colored Persons." This work offers a brief survey of the condition of black Americans and the prospects of black men who had served in the Revolutionary War effort.

Saratoga National Historical Park *http://www.nps.gov/sara/f-batles.htm* On this site, learn about the battle of Saratoga, and take a virtual tour through the landscape of the battle.

Internet Modern History Source Book *http://www.fordham.edu/halsall/mod/modsbook2.html#revol18c* In the section titled "American and French Revolution," this site compares the American and French conflict. Also, through its presentation of primary source materials, it provides an insight into contentious American opinions on the radicalism of the French Revolution.

6

The Origins of the Constitution

By Popular Demand?

1781	Articles of Confederation ratified; Congress proposes a duty on imports to raise revenue, but Rhode Island defeats it
1783	Congress proposes another import duty, which New York defeats; Fearing attack by unpaid American troops, Congress flees Philadelphia; Robert Morris sends Empress of China to open trade with China
1784	Spain refuses to allow Americans to transship their goods from New Orleans
1785	Congress adopts the Land Ordinance of 1785, a model for future federal land policy; Maryland and Virginia sign an agreement about navigation rights on the Potomac River and Chesapeake Bay
1785–87	Shays' Rebellion in Massachusetts
1787	The Ordinance of 1787 prohibits slavery in the Northwest Territory and establishes that new states carved from it will be fully equal to the original states; Constitutional Convention meets at Philadelphia; State delegations approve the completed draft of the Constitution
1788	Delaware, Pennsylvania, New Jersey, Georgia, and Connecticut ratify the Constitution; Massachusetts ratifies with a request for a Bill of Rights; Rhode Island rejects; Maryland, South Carolina, and New Hampshire ratify; Congress certifies adoption of the Constitution; Virginia ratifies with a request for a Bill of Rights; New York ratifies; Congress adopts the first ten amendments to the Constitution (the Bill of Rights); Rhode Island and North Carolina ratify
1789	George Washington becomes president; John Adams, vice president

The great nineteenth-century English statesman William Gladstone once described the American federal Constitution as "the most remarkable work—in modern times—to have been produced by the human intellect at a single stroke in its application to political affairs." Clearly the Constitution is not a perfect document, for we have amended it twenty-seven times. But few citizens today would deny that our frame of government has served the nation extraordinarily well over more than two centuries.

It required a prodigious act of faith and will to abandon the Articles of Confederation and replace them with a new political framework for the federal union. The states had ratified the Articles only six years earlier, and although by no means perfect, they had established the sort of political entity most Americans wanted: a weak union of near-sovereign states that avoided the centralized power that many citizens associated with British tyranny. Indeed, to the end of the Confederation period, the Articles would have many loyal supporters. Obviously the influential Americans who assembled in Philadelphia in the summer of 1787 to create a new constitution for the United States must have had a change of heart. Who were these people and what caused them to alter their views?

The origins of the federal Constitution have interested historians for many years. In the nineteenth century it was usually held that the failings and inadequacies of the Articles were so obvious that all could see them. John Fiske called the Confederation period—the time between the British surrender at Yorktown in 1781 and the establishment in 1788 of the new federal government under the Constitution—the "Critical Period." He believed that during these years the nation was "rapidly drifting toward anarchy." Because the Articles were unable to provide the political and social glue to hold the country together, the calling of the Constitutional Convention and the adoption of the document it produced were merely the logical and valid results of broad public concern. The Constitution, in effect, carried to its natural conclusion the nationalistic trend of the Revolution itself.

Fiske's view reflected the patriotic self-congratulation that was common among nineteenth-century Americans. Later this would give way to greater skepticism. Just before World War I, Charles A. Beard attacked Fiske's interpretation. The Critical Period, he said, was not very critical. The United States was "in many respects steadily recovering order and prosperity" and "the economic condition of the country seemed to be improving." Ultimately, Beard wrote, the only important group suffering under the Articles had been those who held the wartime securities of the Continental and state governments. These few but powerful individuals wanted the public debts fully repaid and feared that the state governments and the Confederation Congress would yield to pressure from taxpayers to scale down or repudiate the debts. A democratic system would favor the taxpayers. To protect their interests, creditors had to establish a strong central government that could check the power of majorities and also had sufficient taxing power to pay the public debts. The American federal Constitution of 1787, Beard and his disciples insisted, was a reactionary document intended to restore the power an elite had lost during the Revolution. It was not justified by broad national need or demanded by popular majority; instead, it was intended to protect the economic interests of the powerful.

Let us examine the state of the nation in the 1780s to see which of these interpretations is more convincing, to see how and why the Constitution replaced the Articles of Confederation and became the fundamental law under which Americans have lived for more than two centuries.

America in the 1780s

Agriculture.   Peace with Britain brought economic troubles to American farmers. During the war years armies had swept across the countryside, destroying fences and barns, burning crops and farmhouses. On the frontier Indian raids had pushed back the line of settled farming. In the Carolinas the dikes that controlled the tidal streams in the rice country had been damaged by hostile troops and by neglect. In Virginia the flight of Loyalist slaves and the removal of others by the British had seriously depleted the labor force on the plantations. In 1783 rural America faced a major repair job.

In time the physical damage and the labor disruption were mended, but political changes continued to cause difficulties for American agriculture. The severing of imperial ties had unforeseen consequences for farmers. Once the war ended, the British government rescinded the bounty that it had paid indigo planters, and indigo virtually disappeared as a crop from the Carolina coast. The bounty on naval stores also ceased. At the same time Britain imposed a high tax on imported American tobacco. Before independence, when Americans had been subjects of King George, American agricultural commodities had found a ready market in the British West Indies. Now, as foreigners, Americans could no longer expect special rights in British-controlled markets. Shortly before the war ended, the English government clamped down on the export of many mainland commodities to their Caribbean possessions. Farmers of Massachusetts, the Connecticut and Hudson valleys, eastern Pennsylvania, and the grain-growing areas of the Chesapeake were thus deprived of markets for their surpluses. Unsold crops piled up; farm prices fell.

Frontier farmers beyond the Appalachians also faced difficult times after 1783. By the war's end thousands of settlers had crossed the mountains to live in what are now Kentucky and Tennessee. These people raised the food they consumed but relied on the eastern states or Europe for salt, guns, powder, shot, plows, cloth, notions, and small luxuries. They could pay for these imports with surplus grain or meat or with furs, skins, and lumber gathered from the surrounding forests. But how could they get these goods to market? As the crow flies, the farmers of eastern Kentucky and Tennessee were not very far from the seaboard. Unfortunately, the trip by pack animals across the Allegheny and Blue Ridge mountains was hard, slow, and expensive.

The Mississippi and its tributaries were the natural links between the western farmers and the outside world. The westerners could load their products on rafts or flatboats, float them south with the current, and land them at New Orleans to be shipped to the East Coast or the Caribbean by oceangoing vessels. But under the 1763 treaty ending the French and Indian War, Spain controlled the mouth of the Mississippi, and Spain demanded payment of a stiff tax to allow Americans to land their wares at New Orleans. Although the Spanish had supported the Americans during the Revolution, they considered the revolt a dangerous example to their own discontented colonies and feared the Americans would one day seize the weakly held Spanish lands in the West. Why help them prosper? The potentially busy Mississippi waterway accordingly remained closed, while surplus crops went unsold and western farmers did without coveted manufactured goods.

Commerce.   The imperial Navigation Acts had restricted direct American trade with many parts of the world, with Americans forbidden to export directly to northern Europe, and most European imports coming only by way of Britain. Enumerated articles had to go to Britain on the way to their ultimate destination. Though there had been no legal impediments to colonial voyages to Asia, English merchants had been so dominant in the trade with China, India, and the East Indies that Americans had, in effect, been excluded. With the Navigation Acts gone and newly independent Americans more confident of their prowess, enterprising men jumped at the chance to develop trade with new customers and to open new trading routes. For the first time American ships visited places such as Copenhagen, Rotterdam, Stockholm, Bremen, and even the Russian trading posts on the west coast of North America. In 1783 Robert Morris opened direct trade with China when he and his associates sent the "Empress of China" on a voyage to Canton that brought extraordinary returns to the promoters. Thereafter, American vessels from Boston, Salem, New York, Philadelphia, and other East Coast ports regularly rounded "the Horn" or "the Cape" on the way to the East Indies and China. Trade with France, much restricted before 1776, swelled under the Franco-American treaty of 1778, which gave Americans special privileges in French dominions. American commerce with the French, Dutch, and Danish West Indies also grew.

Yet the new trade routes did not compensate for the loss of British imperial customers. Americans were excluded from commerce with the British West Indies and could no longer trade with the Newfoundland and Nova Scotia fisheries. Nor could New England and middle states shipbuilders count on a protected market for their vessels in the empire. American-built ships were now "foreign" and no longer given a privileged position in the imperial trade. Britain also placed a high duty on American whale oil. The results of all these changes were damaging. By the end of the 1780s, American foreign commerce had partly recovered from wartime and immediate postwar disruption. By 1790 Americans exported more than they had in 1772. But measured on a per capita basis, American exports were 30 percent lower in 1790 than in the average year just before the war for independence.

Other problems beset the country's commercial interests. After 1783 the agents of British firms set up offices and warehouses in every American port and began to out-compete Americans in the large transatlantic trade in British goods. Before long British vessels were even carrying British products from port to port along the Atlantic coast at the expense of American coastal traders. American merchants demanded that the United States favor imports carried by American ships and exclude foreigners from the coastal trade. Such laws would be American navigation acts, no different from the British restrictions against which colonial Americans had rebelled. But few Americans saw the irony; self-interest was enough to overcome consistency.

Industry.   The livelihoods of city artisans, mechanics, and craftspeople—the "manufacturers" of the day—were also uncertain in the immediate postwar era. During the war consumers in many areas had been forced to turn to domestic artisans for goods formerly imported from Great Britain. American manufacturers had flourished until, with the return of peace, consumers went on a spending spree for British wares. Suddenly the American cabinetmakers, weavers, hat makers, tailors, silversmiths, and cobblers found their shops empty of customers.

The "manufacturers" appealed to the state legislatures for help. One Massachusetts petition sought relief for "persons out of employ who have wives and children asking for bread." Several states came to the rescue. They exempted some industries from taxes, lent money to others, and offered premiums to investors and inventors. What the artisans really wanted, however, was tariff protection—high

A 1790 view of Mississippi commerce in New Orleans. In the center of the picture is a keelboat; to the right a flatboat. The river's width in this picture is greatly reduced.

duties that would make foreign imports expensive and thus force American consumers to buy the home product. Massachusetts, Rhode Island, New Hampshire, Connecticut, Pennsylvania, New York, and several southern states did impose taxes on imports.

Unfortunately for the new nation's industries and their workers, the piecemeal system of state duties was ineffective. The states tried to avoid conflicts with one another by exempting goods imported from other states. This practice simply nullified the duties. Importers in states without tariffs sent foreign goods into neighboring states disguised as American-made commodities. New York engaged in a preposterous trade war against New Jersey and Connecticut over this evasion. In 1787 the New York legislature decreed that foreign goods coming through the two neighboring states must pay four times the duties of American goods. New Jersey retaliated by making New York pay £30 a month for the privilege of maintaining the Sandy Hook lighthouse on New Jersey property. Connecticut imposed duties on goods coming from New York.

The economic warfare among the states never went very far, but it could have led to a system of commercially insulated, competing states that would have thrown away the blessings of continent-wide free trade. Before long, alert citizens were asking how the country could avoid such an outcome and still protect itself against the superior industry of Great Britain.

Creditors and Debtors.   Unable to impose taxes, Congress ceased paying the interest and principal of the national debt. Thereafter, the value of government securities—Congress's promises to pay back money it had borrowed during the Revolution—dropped sharply. Speculators willing to take the chance that Congress might eventually pay its obligations bought up government IOUs at a fraction of their face value and soon held a large part of the total amount. The original holders of the securities thus got something for their money, but many felt cheated. Many state creditors felt the same way. After the war some states had taxed themselves heavily and paid their debts. Others did not, and their depreciated securities, like Congress's, soon passed into the hands of speculators.

Nor were private creditors much better off. The postwar years brought a sharp drop in general prices. Imports, as we noted, had boomed briefly after 1783 as American consumers, starved for British goods during the war, snapped up every cargo from Bristol, London, and Liverpool. To pay for this merchandise merchants and customers shipped overseas the gold and silver coin left behind by the French army or lent to Congress during the war by Dutch bankers. But there was a limit to the available cash, and the country soon reverted to its normal condition of currency dearth.

When money is scarce, it becomes more valuable relative to the things it buys. Thus prices for domestic goods soon fell sharply. This deflation hurt farmers and artisans, who produced goods for sale. It also hurt debtors, who found it hard to get money to pay their creditors. To relieve their distress, debtors demanded paper money, and in several states the legislatures passed measures to oblige them. Most states printed only moderate amounts of the new paper currency and did not make it "legal tender" that forced creditors to accept it for debts even if they did not want to. These issues caused few problems. New York and Pennsylvania businessmen actually supported their state's paper money issues to help end the currency famine and make business easier to conduct. The situation was very different in Rhode Island. In that turbulent state the debtors were in political control and seemed determined to defraud their creditors. In 1786 the legislature, acting under debtor pressure, issued £100,000 of legal tender paper money and declared that everyone must accept it at face value whatever its actual purchasing power. A creditor who resisted was breaking the law, and the debt would be canceled. Soon debtors were pursuing their creditors and paying them without mercy. Creditors complained bitterly, but to no avail.

The evidence thus confirms the economic difficulties of the Confederation period. And it also suggests that they were widespread, not confined just to creditors, as Charles Beard argued. Merchants, farmers, and craftspeople, as well as creditors, had good reason to complain in these early postwar years.

The distress had important political repercussions. Citizens began to ask pointed questions. Who was to blame for the problems? Why had prices dropped? Why did the British refuse to make trade concessions to Americans? Why could Spain close the port of New Orleans without retaliation? Why were American craftspeople not protected against cheap foreign goods? Why could Rhode Island debtors arbitrarily scale down their debts? Why must national creditors sell their government securities to speculators at a fraction of their face value? The fault in every case seemed the weak national government established by the Articles of

Confederation. Before long a growing segment of the most enterprising voters had concluded that something must be done to strengthen the national frame of government if the country was to recover and fulfill its economic promise.

Confederation Finances.   Beard was right to identify Confederation finance as part of the background for the constitutional convention of 1787. Congress had not paid Revolutionary soldiers, security holders, or any of its other creditors—and could not deal with many of its other pressing problems—because it lacked financial resources. Under the Articles of Confederation, as we saw, the central government had no power to tax and could do no more than assign revenue quotas to the states. Raising these funds then became the responsibility of the thirteen state legislatures. Under this scheme money came in very slowly because the states, with their own expenses, were reluctant to fulfill their national obligations.

To meet its needs Congress offered large blocks of western land for sale to speculators. Under one such arrangement, 1.5 million acres of land were sold for less than eight cents an acre in hard money to a group of Boston businessmen and promoters. Congress also resorted to borrowing money from abroad as well as from Americans. But these loans were a mere stopgap, since the government could not expect bankers to continue to lend to it when it had no means to repay them. Meanwhile, though the fighting had ended, a part of Washington's restless army remained unpaid and undischarged in its camp at Newburgh, New York.

Hoping to solve the government's revenue problems, in 1781 some members of Congress proposed an amendment to the Articles allowing Congress to levy a duty of 5 percent on all goods entering the country. The revenue from this "impost" would be used to pay the defaulted debt. Amending the Articles, however, required the unanimous consent of the states. Twelve states quickly ratified the amendment, but Rhode Island rejected the proposal. Another impost amendment, put forward in 1783, failed when New York ratified it with such crippling conditions that the other states would not accept it.

These failures had serious consequences. As we have seen, many people were forced to sell their government securities to speculators for whatever they would bring. Veterans were denied the cash bonuses Congress had promised them. Continental officers, who believed they were entitled to half-pay for life in retirement, were especially angry and were soon muttering of rebellion in the army's camp at Newburgh.

Nationalism.   Another important source of political change in this period was nationalism. This feeling links individual happiness to the interests and welfare of the nation as a whole; it is the emotional bond that joins citizens of a country to one another. Nationalism is a powerful force that can overwhelm individual and group interest and at times inspire sacrifice of life itself.

The active nationalists of the period were mostly young men who had served in the Continental Army or in Congress. They had fought and sacrificed for the United States. They had seen many parts of the continent, had met men like themselves from every region, and had shared with them their hopes for a new national future. Their experiences had broadened their perspectives into a "continental" view and had made them aware of the inadequacies of localism. Many former officers of Washington's army belonged to the Society of the Cincinnati, an organization formed in 1783 and dedicated to preserving the bonds forged in war and promoting the interests of the new nation. In later years the Jeffersonian Republicans would accuse its members of seeking to create an aristocracy in the United States.

The heightened continental consciousness could be seen in many areas in the immediate postwar period. Before 1776 Americans had looked to Britain and Europe for religious, cultural, and intellectual leadership. In the first years of independence they sought to end this subordination. In these years Americans established religious autonomy from Europe. American Anglicans (who took the name Episcopalians), led hitherto by church superiors in distant England, now acquired their own bishops and a separate church government. In 1784 the Methodists left the British-controlled Methodist Conference and organized an independent American Methodist Episcopal Church. In 1789 the pope selected the first resident American Catholic bishop, a move that recognized American independent nationhood.

Americans also declared their cultural independence from the Old World. In 1780 a group of Bostonians formed the American Academy of Arts and Sciences to encourage "every art and science" that might add to "the interest, honor, dignity, and happiness of a free, independent, and virtuous people." Five years later a reinvigorated American Philosophical Society issued its first volume of scientific transactions. A leader of the new movement for cultural independence was Noah Webster, a Connecticut-born Yale graduate. Soon after Yorktown Webster set out to create a distinctive intellectual life for "the confederated republics of America." In 1783 he published his *Blue-Backed Speller,* a volume, he proclaimed, that would help make America "as independent in literature as she is in politics." In the next few years he also published a grammar and a reader that used stories and examples drawn from American life as exercises for children learning their letters. Another sign of the new cultural nationalism—a dubious one perhaps—was the publication in 1787 of the first American history textbook.

To the growing body of nationalists the Confederation's political feebleness seemed humiliating. Everywhere they looked they found distressing signs of their country's plight. In June 1783 Congress had made itself look ridiculous by fleeing Philadelphia in fear of attack by unpaid and mutinous Continental troops. During the next months it wandered from town to town trying to find a decent resting place. When the new Dutch minister to the United States arrived to present his credentials, Congress was ensconced in Princeton, a small college town without proper facilities for state occasions. The embarrassed president of Congress, Elias Boudinot, wrote the representative of the nation's former ally to apologize for the inadequacy: "We feel ourselves greatly mortified that our present circumstances in a small Country village prevent us giving you a reception more agreeable to our wishes. But I hope these unavoidable deficiencies will be compensated by the sincere Joy on this occasion." In the end the ceremony went off creditably, but few who observed Boudinot's plight were proud of their country's government.

Though alert enough when threatened by physical attack, Congress seemed indifferent to everything else. In the six weeks following ratification of the 1783 peace treaty it was difficult to gather a quorum to do business. In mid-February 1784 James Tilton of Delaware wrote a fellow member that "the situation of Congress is truly alarming; the most important business pending and not states enough to take it up. . . ." Another member declared: "The Congress is abused, laughed at and cursed in every company." Is it any wonder that sincere patriots feared for their country's future?

Foreign Affairs

Even more disturbing to nationalists than the domestic weakness of the Confederation was its feebleness in foreign affairs. Almost everywhere the United States was treated with contempt. France remained friendly and honored the trade privileges specified by the treaty of 1778; but Spain and Britain were antagonistic, and even minor powers felt they could defy American interests. As Jefferson, serving as American minister in Paris, wrote in 1784: "All respect for our government is annihilated on this side of the water from an idea of its want of energy."

The British, in particular, took advantage of American weakness. Besides excluding Americans from the profitable West Indies trade, they refused to evacuate a flock of forts and trading posts on American soil. They had good commercial reasons for thus violating the 1783 peace treaty: With British troops garrisoned at Michilimackinac, Detroit, Niagara, Oswego, and other posts, American fur traders were forced to surrender the trade of the Northwest to their Canadian rivals from Montreal. But the continued occupation was also a political response. The Americans had failed to live up to two provisions of the Treaty of Paris: They had not fully compensated Loyalists for their property losses, and they had not paid all prewar debts owed British merchants. Although Congress earnestly recommended that the states encourage both actions, the plea had been largely ignored. Loyalist groups and British creditors complained bitterly, but it did little good. The American government could not force its own citizens to comply with its treaty agreements.

The American minister to London, John Adams, pleaded with the British to adopt a more generous policy toward American trade and to evacuate the northwestern posts. Royal officials treated the American envoy with a "dry decency" and cold "civility," but refused to budge. Britain might have dealt more generously with the United States if Congress had been able to impose duties on British imports. As Jefferson noted, the United States "must show" the English that "we are capable of foregoing commerce with them, before they will be capable of consenting to equal commerce." But of course Congress lacked the power to exclude foreign goods, and the British knew it. As Lord Sheffield, a defender of British shipping interests, remarked, it would "not be any easy matter to bring the American states to act as a nation. They are not to be feared as such by us."

American relations with Spain during the Confederation era also revealed Congress's weakness. Besides restricting America's Mississippi commerce, Spain refused to allow United States ships to trade with its colonies in Latin America, thus cutting off a profitable relationship that had developed during the war. These blows to American interests finally goaded even the sleepy Congress to act. In 1785 it authorized John Jay, the secretary for foreign affairs, to open negotiations with Spain over these issues.

Once more the feckless American government proved incapable of achieving results. The Spanish minister, the lady-pleasing Don Diego de Gardoqui, was willing to make concessions on trade with Spanish-American ports, since these did not threaten his nation's control over territory. He refused, however, to yield on the right of tax-free deposit at New Orleans. His position suited some influential easterners, who feared that a too-rapid growth of the West would draw off population from the older states and eventually lead to western secession from the United States. It also coincided with the interests of northeastern merchants, who stood to gain by enlarged trade opportunities with Spanish America but saw little advantage in the right of deposit. Yet it was just this right to unload their cargo at New Orleans and transfer it to oceangoing ships that was the crucial matter to westerners.

A stronger government might have forced each group to accept a compromise for the national good. As it was, the treaty finally negotiated with Spain outraged the West. In exchange for Latin American trade concessions, the United States agreed to forgo the right of deposit for twenty-five years. Unrepresented as yet in Congress, the westerners received the support of southern congressmen, who saw little gain for their section in the trade provisions and so could afford to take a nationalist position. Voting solidly against adoption, the southern representatives defeated the treaty. No one got anything. Once again, American weakness had betrayed American interests.

In the Mediterranean, too, the feeble American government was humiliated during the immediate postwar years. For centuries the Barbary states in North Africa—Morocco, Algiers, Tunis, and Tripoli—had prospered by preying on the commerce of Europe. Swift Barbary corsairs would swoop down on merchant ships and seize their cargoes; the pirates would then remove passengers and crews and hold them for ransom. Most European powers either paid tribute to the Barbary beys and bashaws in return for safe passage or provided their citizens with naval protection. Before 1776, English men-of-war had guarded American commerce against the corsairs. Now that Americans were independent, they could no longer rely on the Royal Navy, and their merchant ships soon became fair game for the raiders in the Mediterranean and off the coasts of Spain and Portugal. In 1787 the United States signed a treaty in which Morocco agreed to respect American rights. But negotiations with the other Barbary states failed because they insisted on bribes, which Congress could not pay. Unable either to pay tribute or to provide naval protection for its shipping, the United States suffered continuing harassment from the North African pirates.

The Public Domain

In one important area of national concern—the administration of the vast public domain—the Confederation government gets at least a mixed review. When Virginia finally surrendered its claims to the Northwest in 1784, Congress found itself in possession of almost a quarter of a billion acres of some of the finest land on earth. What should be done with this princely realm? How should it be disposed of? Who should get it? Should it be considered primarily a source of revenue for the central government, or an opportunity to shape American society in some desirable way? And how should the communities carved out of this land be governed? Should they be equal politically to the original states? If the problems were immense, so were the stakes, for the course chosen would profoundly affect the nation's future.

One issue never in serious doubt was whether the "West" should be subject to the needs of white Americans. Imbued with the new "romantic" sensibility that swept Europe and America toward the end of the eighteenth century, a few sensitive souls came to appreciate untamed nature. During the 1780s Philip Freneau, a Patriot poet, sang of the "wild genius of the forest" and contrasted it with the corruption of civilization. The prominent Philadelphia doctor Benjamin Rush noted about this time that "man is naturally a wild animal, and . . . taken from the woods, he is never happy." But few others in this era questioned the goals of clearing the forests and plowing the prairies of the region beyond the Appalachians and converting them into farms and towns. Even if the romantic views had been stronger and more widespread, they could not have overcome the enormous pressure to acquire cheap land and the ethic that human progress depended on resource exploitation.

The Land Ordinance of 1785.

The first public land issue Congress tackled was how to transfer real estate to private individuals. As yet no one seriously considered giving the land away without cost, if for no other reason than Congress needed some source of revenue. But there remained many other unanswered questions. Should the price be high or low? Should the land be sold in large blocks to speculators, or in small parcels to farmers? One crucial issue was whether to adopt the New England system of first surveying the land and then selling it in compact parcels or, the scheme more common in the South, of selling a receipt for a particular number of acres and then allowing the buyer to choose his land more or less where he pleased with the survey to follow. The New England plan had the advantages of encouraging orderly and compact settlement and of avoiding overlapping land claims. But it was likely to slow the pace of settlement by forcing people to buy bad land along with good and by requiring that each section opened be filled before others became available. The New England pattern also promised to avoid the sort of pell-mell rush to the West that was certain to disturb the Indians. On the whole, however, westerners favored the southern scheme, for all its potential for trouble, because it promised faster settlement.

The Land Ordinance of 1785 was Congress's attempt to choose a course among these conflicting alternatives. It provided that all government lands be surveyed and divided into square townships six miles on an edge. Each township in turn would be cut into thirty-six sections, each of a square mile, or 640 acres. Half the townships would be sold as complete units of over 23,000 acres each. The other half would be sold in 640-acre sections. Some land was reserved for Revolutionary veterans after the land was surveyed; all the rest would be sold at auction at a minimum price of a dollar an acre.

The Land Ordinance followed more closely the New England than the southern settlement tradition. As in New England, it mandated orderly surveying and compact tracts. Southerners, preferring relatively small tracts, got part of what they wanted in the provision for sale of single sections. On the other hand, the measure also allowed for the large block sales that speculators preferred. All in all, the scheme favored the principles endorsed by northeasterners over those desired by the rest of the country. Westerners, in particular, would not find it satisfactory. Over the next century they would agitate to alter the public land laws to favor the small farmer and the family farm over the land speculator and the large holding.

Congress's Indian Policy. Congress was no more successful in dealing with the Indian tribes than with foreign powers. In 1784 it dispatched commissioners to induce the Northwestern tribes to surrender a major portion of their lands to white settlers. At Fort Stanwix in central New York they compelled the Iroquois to give up all claims to the region for a few presents. Soon after, at Fort McIntosh in western Pennsylvania, they persuaded the Chippewa, Ottawa, Delaware, and Wyandot Indians to make a similar concession. The two treaties did not accomplish their aim. Several tribes rejected them and at the same time, they opened the door to renegade whites from Kentucky, Virginia, and Pennsylvania to stake out claims on Indian lands still in dispute. By the spring of 1786 it looked as if a major Indian war was about to erupt in the Northwest.

At this point western settlers, in a pattern that would be repeated many times in later years, decided to take matters into their own hands by hiring the Indian fighter George Rogers Clark to lead an offensive against the Ohio Indians. The attack failed when the western volunteers recruited by Clark mutinied. The Indians now repudiated the two treaties and declared that white settlers would be excluded from the whole Northwest. The "line now cutting Pennsylvania," they announced, "shall bounde them on the sunrising, and the Ohio shall be the boundary between them and the Big Knives." Congress refused to accept this Indian barrier, but in its usual feeble way, could do nothing to prevent it.

The Ordinance of 1787. Despite its weakness, the Confederation Congress could claim one major political accomplishment: the Northwest Ordinance providing government for the region north of the Ohio River and west of Pennsylvania.

In 1784, following Thomas Jefferson's suggestion, Congress proposed to divide the trans-Appalachian region into ten political communities. When the population of any of these reached 20,000, the inhabitants could adopt a constitution and apply for admission to the Union as a state equal in status to the states already comprising the Confederation. Although this measure was never put into effect, it served as the model for the Northwest Ordinance adopted three years later.

Section One of the 1787 Northwest Ordinance mandated that no fewer than three nor more than five states be formed out of the Northwest Territory. In its political provisions it was less liberal than Jefferson's plan. Section Two, instead of allowing the people of a new territory self-rule from the outset, required a three-step process toward autonomy. At the outset the territory would be governed by a governor, a territorial secretary, and three judges appointed by Congress. Then, when the adult male population had reached 5,000, it could elect a legislature to share power with a council of five chosen by the governor and Congress. It could also elect a territorial delegate to Congress, though he could not vote. Finally, when the territory's total population had reached 60,000, it could apply for admission to the Union as a self-governing state equal to all the others. Section Three of the Ordinance prohibited slavery in the new communities and provided a bill of rights for their inhabitants.

The Northwest Ordinance was a momentous piece of legislation. Its exclusion of slavery ultimately ensured that the entire North would be free territory. Equally important, the ordinance determined the future of the West and the Union by establishing the principle that new states would be equal to the original thirteen.

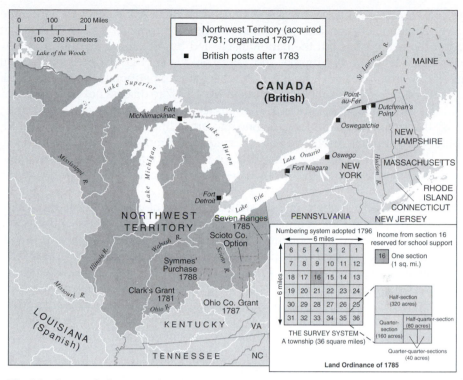

The Northwest Ordinance of 1787

If we consider the possible alternative of holding new territories in colonial thralldom, we can see how beneficial a precedent the ordinance was. Ray Billington, a historian of the American West, has declared: "The Ordinance of 1787 did more to perpetuate the Union than any document save the Constitution. Men could now leave the older states assured that they were not surrendering their political privileges. [By enacting the Ordinance] Congress not only saved the Republic, but had removed one great obstacle to the westward movement."

The Constitutional Convention

The Confederation government, then, was not without accomplishments. But they were outweighed by its failures to meet the needs—political, economic, emotional—of many citizens. By 1785 it seemed clear to many vocal Americans, not just a small elite, that the nation needed a more powerful and effective central government to serve its interests and fulfill its hopes.

The road to the Constitutional Convention was not direct, however. The process of revising or replacing the Articles began in 1785 when Maryland and Virginia signed an agreement over navigation rights on the Potomac River and Chesapeake Bay. The success of this pact induced Maryland to call for a broader arrangement that would include Pennsylvania and Delaware and cover disputes over import duties, currency, and other commercial matters. Nationalists in the

Virginia legislature quickly proposed that all thirteen states meet in September 1786 at Annapolis to consider common commercial problems. Only five states attended the conference, but the nationalists—led by Alexander Hamilton of New York, James Madison of Virginia, and John Dickinson of Delaware—took advantage of the situation. They convinced the delegates to petition Congress for a full-scale convention to meet at Philadelphia in May 1787 to discuss not only economic problems but fundamental political changes as well.

By this time, Congress's long decline had brought it close to paralysis. The Annapolis Convention's resolution was referred to a committee of three, which proposed to submit it to another committee of thirteen, which the legislators never got around to appointing. Congress, it seemed, intended to let the proposal die.

Shay' Rebellion.

Events in Massachusetts, a center of political turbulence since the 1760s, jolted the country and Congress into action. Massachusetts was one of those states that had obligated itself to pay its war debt. To meet this commitment the Bay State legislature had imposed on its citizens the heaviest taxes in New England. To farmers already suffering from low crop prices, the taxes were a disaster. Debts and bankruptcies soon mounted in the western counties, and many yeomen fell behind in their tax payments. As if this were not enough, Massachusetts law required that the pettiest commercial transactions be recorded by a court, necessitating the payment of high fees to lawyers and court officials. The large volume of legal business resulting from hard times thus added to the heavy tax load imposed on the state's rural citizens.

By the summer of 1786 discontent among farmers in the western counties had reached the flash point. In late August they convened in Worcester and condemned the taxes and heavy legal fees. Shortly afterward, an armed mob of 1,500 men, eager to end property foreclosures for tax delinquency and debt default, stopped the convening of the Hampshire County court. In early September three more county courts were kept from sitting by groups of angry men.

Although the Massachusetts legislature made some effort to ease the burden of debtors, disaffected westerners began to arm and drill as if they expected to take on King George's redcoats once again. Led by Daniel Shays, a former Continental Army officer, they formed a committee to resist what they considered intolerable conditions. Meanwhile, in the eastern part of the state, people had begun to panic. In Boston, Governor James Bowdoin decided to raise a military force to suppress the dissenters. Rather than impose new taxes to support this small army, Bowdoin appealed to the city's rich men, who, in their fright, promptly came up with $25,000. In January 1787 a rebel force of 1,200 met the smaller group of Bowdoin's militia at Springfield. The state troops fired a single artillery volley, and the rebels fled in panic. The uprising was over by spring.

Shay' Rebellion was actually not much of a threat to the social order, yet it frightened many people. One citizen later insisted that if the rebels had won, there would have been "an abolition of all public and private debts" followed by "an equal distribution of property." The rebellion particularly dismayed the country's nationalists. He was "mortified beyond expression" by the disorders, Washington wrote. For the country "to be more exposed in the eyes of the world and more contemptible" than it already was seemed "hardly possible." Congress at last took heed of the restless mood of many citizens, and on February 21 it voted to ask the states to send delegates to a constitutional convention at Philadelphia. All except maverick Rhode Island complied.

The Challenge. The convention in stately Independence Hall opened on May 14, 1787. It was an assembly of political giants. Leading the rest in prestige were George Washington, Benjamin Franklin, James Madison, Robert Morris, James Wilson, John Dickinson, and Alexander Hamilton. There was also a large contingent of less famous but notably able men: George Mason, George Wythe, and Edmund Randolph, all of Virginia; John Rutledge and Charles Pinckney of South Carolina; William Paterson of New Jersey; Roger Sherman and Oliver Ellsworth of Connecticut; and Rufus King of Massachusetts. The rest of the fifty-five delegates made lesser contributions to the convention's work, though most enjoyed high standing in their states and had played important roles in national events.

Seldom has any group taken on so momentous a task. Western governments have usually been the products of historical accident and the gradual evolution of tradition and experience. The idea of a written frame of government, of a structure of fundamental law put down in precise words at one time, is an American invention. The practice began, as we saw in Chapter 5, with the making of state constitutions after 1775. Its finest expression is the federal Constitution of 1787.

The "Founding Fathers" (or "Founders," as many say today) did, of course, draw on the traditions of the colonies and Great Britain; the English experience is embedded in every legal and governmental institution of the United States. They also relied on their understanding of the ancient world, especially Rome, and on the views of the great political and legal thinkers of modern times including Locke and Montesquieu. But in the end they were guided primarily by their own practical experience of government.

Though a number of the men at Philadelphia owned substantial amounts of unpaid public debt, a more important bond among them was their nationalism, or continentalism. Few doubted that the years after 1781 were indeed critical, that America had been treated with contempt abroad and threatened with mob rule at home. There were some defenders of states' rights at Philadelphia—Robert Yates of New York, George Mason of Virginia, and Luther Martin of Maryland, for example—but most delegates were sure that the Articles of Confederation had failed as an instrument of government and that the United States needed a stronger central authority.

Few of the delegates, however, wished to strengthen the government at the expense of freedom. The goal of the majority was balance, an end much harder to achieve. They wished to establish a "mixed" government, combining popular and aristocratic elements, that would protect private property, but also preserve personal liberty. They intended to construct a strong government, but one that would respect local autonomy and local rights. In a nation of continental proportions the diversity of interests, opinions, and philosophies made the task formidable. During the deliberations small states would clash with large states, slave states with free states, commercial interests with agrarian interests, democrats with aristocrats, champions of local rights with nationalists. In the end, compromise would be unavoidable.

The Debate on Representation.[1] Following some preliminary skirmishing over procedural rules, the convention began its real work when Edmund Randolph, acting for James Madison, submitted a proposal that has come to be known as the Virginia Plan. Randolph advocated not merely a revision of the Articles of Confederation, but a completely new government, with separate legislative, executive, and judicial departments. Congress would have two houses, and the states would be represented in each in proportion to their population. In each house the elected members would vote as individuals, not as part of a single state unit, as they did under the Articles. They would, in effect, represent themselves or their constituents, not their states. The new legislature would be all powerful and choose the persons to fill positions in the executive and judicial branches of government.

The Virginia Plan emphasized the central government as opposed to the states. Randolph hoped to establish a "strong consolidated union, in which the idea of states would be nearly annihilated." The Articles had created a league of virtually independent states; the new plan would confer broad powers on the central government, which would "legislate in all cases to which the separate States are incompetent"—that is, in every area where it chose to assert its power. But Randolph's proposal did not spell out precisely the new government's powers.

The Virginia Plan was countered by the New Jersey Plan, submitted by William Paterson. Paterson recommended that the Articles be revised, not replaced. His new government was to be a "federal," not a truly centralized one; that is, there would be a central government, but the states would retain independent authority in some spheres. The New Jerseyite, speaking for a smaller state than Randolph, endorsed the one-house legislature of the Articles, in which each state was represented equally, regardless of its wealth or population. States would continue to vote as units in Congress, so that the states, rather than the people, would be represented in the new government. But the New Jersey Plan did improve on the Articles by granting the national government the power to tax and regulate foreign and interstate commerce. It also made federal laws and treaties superior to all state laws, another advance over the Articles.

It is easy to see that the New Jersey Plan would benefit states with small populations more than the Virginia Plan. If Paterson's proposal was adopted, they would have representation in Congress equal to that of the more populous ones. If, on the other hand, the Virginia Plan prevailed, the small states' voices would be drowned out by those of their larger neighbors. For this reason it is often said that the two plans represented a conflict between large and small states. But the disagreement was just as much between the strong centralists and their more locally oriented colleagues.

The two plans became the basis for debate, and both were modified in the discussions. On the whole, the centralizers came out ahead. The new government would have greatly enlarged powers, but they would be specified and not left to Congress to decide. It would also be a true central government. Congress would represent the citizens of the United States, not the states as entities. Members of Congress would therefore vote as individuals, and not merely to decide how the

---

[1] The text of the complete Constitution may be found in the Appendix.

The small room in Independence Hall, Philadelphia, where the debates on
the Constitution were held in 1787.

vote of their state should be cast. On the other issues of representation, a compromise was adopted. In one house, the Senate, each state would have equal representation regardless of population; in the other, the House of Representatives,
population would determine the size of state delegations.

Slavery.   At this point the delegates had to consider the issue of what constituted "population." Were slaves property, or were they people? If they were property, they might be the basis for levying taxes but could not be considered in
calculating a state's representation in the lower house of Congress. If they were
people, they should be counted for determining representation. But slaves were
not free and could not vote, so treating them as people would give the southern
states a voice in Congress disproportionate to the actual number of their voters.
Each voter in the South, where slaves were numerous, in effect would have more
power than each voter in the North, where they were few. Northerners naturally
objected to such a scheme. Southerners, noting that their wealth in slaves would
force them to pay a heavy tax bill, insisted on some political compensation for the
burden they would bear.

The issue was very sensitive, for it touched on the continued existence and
prosperity of slavery in the South. And slavery, the South's "peculiar"—that is,
special or unique—institution, was entangled in every aspect of southern life.

True, ever since the Revolution had proclaimed that "all men are created equal," the supporters of slavery had been on the defensive. The northern states, as we have seen, were beginning to emancipate their slaves. And even in the South, under the influence of the Revolution's liberating ideology, slavery's bonds were loosening somewhat. But slaves still tilled the South's fields, built its fences, and performed its household chores. Though slavery was fast disappearing in the North, only a handful of enlightened southerners were willing to contemplate its abolition in their own section. Even men like Jefferson, Madison, and Washington, though admitting to moral doubts about slavery, saw no alternative to the peculiar institution so long as thousands of blacks lived among them.

The men at Philadelphia carefully avoided the slavery issue wherever they could. Nowhere in the document they composed is the word "slavery" ever used. They did include, however, as essential to southern approval, provisions postponing any prohibition of the foreign slave trade until after 1808 and permitting Congress to pass measures allowing states to recover slave runaways (fugitives) from other states. On the issue of representation, the delegates elected to compromise. Taxes and representation in the lower house of Congress would be based on "the whole number of free Persons," excluding Indians but including indentured servants, and "three-fifths of all other Persons." Thus, with the "three-fifths compromise," America's Founding Fathers managed the neat trick of simultaneously treating a slave both as property and as three-fifths of a human being.

Freedom or Order?   The delegates desired both the representative principle on the one hand, and order and rule by the "best men," a kind of elitism, on the other. Some leaned strongly to one side, some to the other, with most somewhere in the middle.

The give-and-take among these principles resulted in several important features of the Constitution, particularly the separation of powers. Borrowing from Montesquieu, the French political philosopher, the delegates assigned to each branch of government—executive, legislative, and judicial—distinct powers, and directed that members of each be selected in a distinct way. This separation would ensure the independence of each branch. In addition, the Founders adopted the idea that each branch must be able to "check and balance" the others. By such an arrangement the greatest freedom would be ensured, for if one branch grew too powerful and sought to dominate the others, it could be constitutionally stopped.

To this end, the chief executive was to have a veto over acts of Congress, the most democratic part of the new government. But the president was not to be all-powerful. His veto could be overridden by a two-thirds vote of Congress. The chief executive could make treaties with foreign powers, but they would have to be confirmed by a two-thirds vote of the Senate. He was to be commander in chief of the army and navy, but only Congress could declare war. Finally, he could appoint a host of high officials, but these appointments would have to be confirmed by the Senate. As a final check on the president—and his appointees—the House of Representatives could bring impeachment charges against federal officials and, if convicted by the Senate, they could be removed from office.

Standing guard against the excesses and abuses of Congress and the president was to be the third branch, the federal judiciary, capped by a Supreme Court.

Although it is nowhere stated in the Constitution, legal scholars believe that the delegates at Philadelphia assumed the right of the federal courts to declare acts of Congress contrary to the Constitution and so void. To protect the judges against political pressure, they gave them lifetime tenure and declared that during their terms of office Congress could not reduce their salaries.

Checks and balances offered one way to combine strong and stable government with a popular voice. The mixture of democratic and aristocratic methods of choosing the officers of each branch was another. The president would be selected not by the direct vote of the people but by an electoral college chosen by the states as they individually saw fit. The number of electors from each state would be equal to the number of representatives and senators it sent to Congress. State law would determine how they would be chosen, but it was assumed that they would not be elected directly by the people. Nor was the Senate, the upper house of Congress, to be a stronghold of democracy. Senators would be selected by their state legislatures. To limit popular control of Congress further, senators were to have long terms of six years; only one third would be seeking reelection in each congressional election held every two years. Finally, the federal judiciary, including the Supreme Court, was to be appointed by the president and confirmed by the Senate, and thus far removed from popular pressure. To temper these aristocratic features, the House of Representatives would be directly controlled by the voters. Representatives would be elected for two-year terms by the same liberal rules that governed the selection of members of the lower houses of the state legislatures.

Powers of the New Government.

Besides establishing a new structure, the Constitution greatly enlarged the powers and scope of the national government. The new government, as we have seen, would impose its authority on the people directly, not through the states. It would also fuse the nation into a single legal whole. Under the new charter each state was required to give "full faith and credit" to all laws and court decisions of the others and to surrender to any other state criminals fleeing across state lines to avoid prosecution. To protect property rights, states were forbidden to pass laws "impairing the Obligation of Contracts." The new government could also do many specific things its predecessor could not do. It could impose and collect taxes from citizens, though by the Constitution's original terms these taxes had to be proportionate to each state's population. It could regulate foreign and interstate commerce, although at the behest of the southern states which shipped large amounts of rice and tobacco abroad, it was forbidden to tax exports. The new government had sole control over the coinage of money and could establish a postal system, build post roads, and pass laws of naturalization. It was also endowed with the power to establish a system of uniform weights and measures, a uniform bankruptcy law, and, to encourage invention and the arts and sciences, patent and copyright systems. Finally, the Constitution declared that the new government could "make all laws which shall be necessary and proper for carrying into Execution the foregoing Powers, and all other Powers vested by this Constitution in the Government of the United States." This provision, which is known as the "elastic clause," later became the justification for greatly expanded federal authority. In sum, a strengthened national government was to exercise broad authority over economic and political affairs, and over a single economic and legal unit.

Still, the Constitution created not a unitary but a "federal" government; it left the states with independent authority in many spheres. Crime and breaches of the peace were in the states' jurisdiction, except when a state legislature or governor specifically requested federal help to put down local violence. Social relations, including marriage, divorce, and education, were also left to the states, as were laws regarding purely local commercial relations and most business affairs.

Although slavery was considered a "domestic" institution much like the family, it could not be left solely to the states' jurisdiction. Conflict over representation had resulted in the three-fifths compromise, and the problems of slaves escaping to free states as well as the foreign slave trade also had to be considered. After much debate the Philadelphia delegates agreed that Congress could not forbid the foreign slave trade until 1808, but thereafter it might do so if a majority wished. Congress could, however, pass laws to deal with runaway slaves who crossed state lines and guarantee slaveholders the right to recover such fugitives regardless of local antislavery laws.

All through the summer and into September the delegates debated every issue. The discussion, like the weather, was often heated. To quiet ruffled tempers and encourage goodwill among the delegates, Benjamin Franklin at one point proposed that a chaplain be invited to open each morning session with a prayer. Washington, the presiding officer, also worked to maintain peace; and although he said little, his dignity and calm demeanor helped to keep the delegates' differences from getting out of hand.

Nothing could prevent disagreement, however. A number of the delegates considered the completed draft of the Constitution far too centralizing. New York's Robert Yates and John Lansing, George Mason of Virginia, Luther Martin and John Mercer of Maryland, and Elbridge Gerry of Massachusetts denounced the work of the convention for that reason. Lansing, Yates, and Mercer went so far as to quit Philadelphia in protest. On the other hand, the most extreme centralizers believed the proposed constitution did not go far enough. Alexander Hamilton wanted the states abolished outright in favor of a strong, unitary government. The views that had ultimately prevailed were those of James Madison, Oliver Ellsworth, and Roger Sherman, who succeeded in mobilizing the majority around the compromise proposals.

On September 8 the convention sent the completed draft to the Committee of Style and Arrangement. This group of five polished the convention's paragraphs and rearranged them in logical order. One of its members, Gouverneur Morris of Pennsylvania, wrote a preamble that described the promotion of "the general welfare" as one of the purposes of the new framework of government. On September 17, 1787, each of the state delegations voted its approval, and the convention adjourned.

Ratification

Now the Constitution's friends faced the problem of securing its adoption, and it seemed likely that the battle would prove difficult. The Confederation Congress had authorized the Philadelphia convention only to "revise" and "amend" the Articles of Confederation, not to propose a wholly new form of government. Would Congress reject the convention's work? On September 29 the Constitution was presented to Congress. That body was almost dead and had no heart for resistance. After some minor debate it recommended the plan to the separate states for consideration by convention. The more difficult task was winning state-by-state ratification.

The opposition was formidable. Certain groups of debtors, aware that state-issued paper money would be illegal under the new government, were naturally opposed to it. So were some taxpayers in states that had paid their debts and feared that through new federal taxes they would pay someone else's as well, and those who considered a strengthened national government a retreat from "true republicanism." Finally, there were the temperamentally cautious people, inclined to stick to the ills they were familiar with rather than fly to others they knew not of.

At one time scholars described the battle to get the Constitution adopted as a fierce struggle. In part, this view projects back into the adoption period attitudes that gelled in the years following, when political parties were beginning to form. It also reflects the fact that in a few states the adoption issue was indeed hard fought. Because it would have been difficult to achieve a successful Union without them, the debates that took place in these states were important. Still, it is clear that the "federalists"—those who favored the new federal government—won with relative ease.

The delegates at Philadelphia had decided that the new government would go into operation when nine states had ratified the Constitution by special conventions. Delaware, Pennsylvania and New Jersey were won over almost immediately, the first and third by unanimous votes in their conventions. In Pennsylvania the delegates from Philadelphia and the towns had to overcome opposition from the rural areas but won a two-to-one victory. Early in 1788 Georgia's convention also ratified unanimously. Connecticut soon followed with a heavy federalist majority. In Massachusetts the friends of the Constitution encountered their first serious opposition. By early estimates the state convention had a solid antifederalist majority. Among the initial opponents were the influential Sam Adams and John Hancock, for years leaders of the state's popular party. If these men could be converted, enough delegates would follow them to carry ratification. Fortunately for the Constitution, Adams was induced to change his mind by a mass meeting of Constitution supporters staged by Paul Revere. Convinced that the rally expressed the views of the state's common folk, Adams agreed to support the Constitution. Hancock, now the state's governor, was coaxed and flattered by federalists into believing he was in line for high federal office under the new Constitution.

One of the federalists' problems in Massachusetts and a number of other states was that the Constitution lacked a bill of rights to protect citizens against federal tyranny and violations of civil liberties. Some opponents of the Constitution used this primarily to delay or defeat adoption. But others, such as Hancock, were sincere in their concern. When Hancock agreed to endorse ratification, he proposed simultaneously that nine amendments be added to protect citizens against possible federal oppression. With this request tacked on to its motion, the Massachusetts convention voted 187 to 168 for adoption.

In March the federalists suffered their first actual setback when nonconformist Rhode Island overwhelmingly rejected the Constitution by a popular referendum. The state, as we saw, had been the center of debtor-imposed paper money schemes and had not even sent a delegation to Philadelphia. During the ratification battle the state's federalists did not stand a chance, so they boycotted the vote. The results were as expected: The supporters of the Constitution received only 10 percent of the votes cast.

Rhode Island's rejection did not stop the federalists' forward momentum, however. In April and May, Maryland and South Carolina joined the parade of adoptions, and by large convention majorities. Then, by a close vote on June 21, New Hampshire became the ninth state to ratify the Constitution. Under the rules that the convention had prescribed, the Constitution was now officially in force. But New York and Virginia had not acted. If these two large states voted no, it would be almost impossible to maintain a workable federal system.

Federalist forces in Virginia were strong and well organized. Among them were some of the most prestigious men in the state, including James Madison, Edmund Pendleton, George Wythe, Edmund Randolph, and John Marshall. Also working in the federalists' favor was the general assumption that the first president under the Constitution would almost certainly be the state's greatest son, George Washington. Not yet the "father of his country," he was nevertheless a commanding figure in the new nation and seemed to embody the finest type of patriotism. On the antifederalist side, however, there was an impressive array of talent, too, including Patrick Henry, Richard Henry Lee, James Monroe, and George Mason. Henry was the spearhead of the antifederalist attack. In an impassioned speech to the state convention he portrayed the new Constitution as dangerous to liberty.

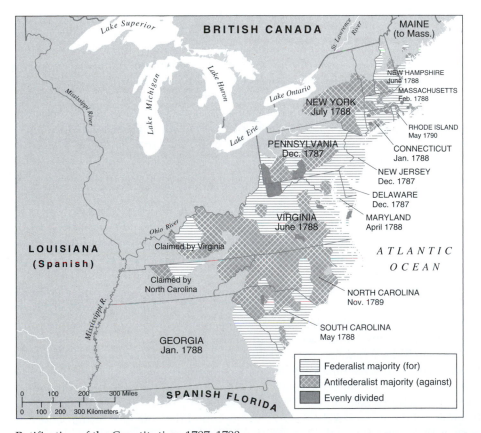

Ratification of the Constitution, 1787–1790

Under it the citizen would be abused, insulted, tyrannized. Henry also appealed to localism and the self-love of his listeners. "The Constitution reflects in the most degrading and mortifying manner on the virtue, integrity, and wisdom of the state legislatures," he declared. It assumed "that the chosen few who go to Congress will have more upright hearts, and more enlightened minds, than those who are members of individual legislatures." Many in his audience believed it was the finest address of his distinguished career as an orator. In the end, though, Henry's eloquence was not enough. The convention voted to ratify narrowly with the proviso that a bill of rights be added to the new frame of government.

The battle now shifted to New York. Without that state the Union would be physically split in half; with it, the Union would be complete in all essentials. For weeks the federalists had been bombarding New York newspaper readers with articles written by Hamilton, Madison, and Jay. These *Federalist Papers*, explaining, defending, and praising the new Constitution, were, of course, partisan expositions of the federalist position. But they were more than propaganda; they were also brilliant analyses by unsentimental men of the way politics was practiced in the real world. Ordinary men were not equipped to govern the country directly, they stated; they did not have the necessary knowledge or understanding. The country could be well ruled only by those who recognized that government was a "complicated science" requiring "abilities and knowledge of a variety of other subjects, to understand it." Every just and successful government must respect the wishes of ordinary people, but wisdom must temper the decisions of majorities. Majorities were frequently temporary and more often moved by passion than by mature judgment. In the future, moreover, when social inequalities had become greater than at present, majorities were certain to attack property rights. Government must be strong enough to guard against the natural but mistaken leveling tendencies of democracy.

The persuasiveness of the *Federalist Papers* and Hamilton's impassioned presentation of the federalist position at the state ratifying convention gave the adoption drive a great boost. But the pro-Constitution people had more than eloquence on their side. If New York State did not join the Union, New York City might choose to join anyway to avoid losing the lucrative commerce that flowed through it to New Jersey and southern New England. What would the state do then? In the end the logic of circumstances prevailed. On July 26, 1788, the New York convention voted 30 to 27 to adopt the Constitution.

The new Union was now secure. Early in 1789 national elections were held for the first time under the Constitution, and federalist candidates won a majority in the new Congress. In January the electoral college voted unanimously for Washington as president and settled on John Adams as his vice president. Rhode Island and North Carolina were still outside the Union, and their citizens did not participate in the election.

Soon after the elections the new government, as promised, adopted the first ten amendments to the Constitution, now commonly called the Bill of Rights. The first nine guaranteed the rights of free speech, press, and assembly and forbade the federal government to make any law "respecting the establishment of religion or prohibiting the free exercise thereof." They affirmed the right of the people "to bear and keep arms," protected citizens against "unreasonable searches and seizures," required jury trials in criminal and major civil cases, and forbade "excessive" bail or fines and "cruel and unusual punishments." The tenth amendment "reserved" to the states all powers not given the United States by the Constitution. Note that these ten amendments placed limits on Congress and the federal government; they did not apply to the state governments. As most states already had similar restraints in their own constitutions, it was considered at this time unnecessary to restrict them in the same way.

With their last objections gone, and fearful of being treated as foreign nations if they did not join the Union, North Carolina and Rhode Island reversed their earlier stands and ratified the Constitution in 1789 and 1790, respectively. The United States was now a nation; it had ceased to be a league of petty states.

Conclusions

Between Yorktown in 1781 and Washington's inauguration in 1789 the country underwent a constitutional transformation of startling dimensions. The end of fighting did not bring the blessings of peace and freedom to the American people. Instead, it ushered in a period of declining trade, falling prices, and unemployment. It also brought national humiliation. In foreign affairs the United States was treated with contempt; even minor powers felt free to disregard American rights.

Thousands of ordinary citizens found the period deeply disappointing. Farmers, planters, craftspeople, creditors, and merchants—easterners as well as westerners, northerners as well as southerners—looked on in dismay as material conditions worsened; they longed for a way to protect their interests and improve their circumstances. Patriots, who saw their dreams of a glorious national future fading, felt despair, and demanded a more effective government to assert their country's position in the world community.

All of these groups turned to constitutional revision as their solution, and the great convention at Philadelphia was the result. Predictably, the Constitution that emerged from the deliberations reflected the feelings of the nationalists and all those who blamed weak central government for their plight. One can almost deduce the political and economic problems of the "Critical Period" from the specific grants of power to the new federal government. No doubt, that government was supported by the country's elite and the defenders of strong restraints on debtors and social levelers. But it was also endorsed by thoughtful and politically active citizens of every social persuasion. We will never be able to say for certain whether a majority of adult Americans in 1788 supported the Constitution. Yet it is likely that the federal Constitution was indeed written and adopted "by popular demand."

ONLINE RESOURCES

"The Federalist Papers" *http://www.yale.edu/lawweb/avalon/federal/fed.html* This site contains the text of the influential Federalist Papers.

"We the People *http://usinfo.state.gov/topical/rights/structur/constitu.htm* Read the full text of and commentary on the U.S. Constitution. This site also offers biographical sketches of each of the signers, which are classified in state order.

7

The First Party System

What Issues Divided the New Nation?

1789	The French Revolution; Congress adopts the Tariff and Tonnage acts to raise the first federal revenues; Congress establishes the State, Treasury, and War departments, and prescribes the structure of the Supreme Court and the federal courts in the Federal Judiciary Act
1790–91	Hamilton presents his financial program to Congress
1790	Congress enacts Hamilton's plan for public credit in the Funding Act
1791	Congress charters the Bank of the United States
1793	War breaks out between France and Britain, Spain, and Holland; France sends Citizen Genêt as minister to the United States; Jefferson resigns as secretary of state and is replaced by Federalist Edmund Randolph
1794	Britain authorizes the seizure of neutral ships trading between the French West Indies and Europe; The United States and Britain sign the Jay Treaty; General Anthony Wayne crushes the Indians at Fallen Timbers; rapid settlement of the Northwest Territory follows; The Whiskey Rebellion in Pennsylvania
1795	The Pinckney Treaty concluded between the United States and Spain; With the Treaty of Greenville the Indians cede territory in what will later be Ohio
1796	Washington's Farewell Address; Adams elected president
1797	The French order American ships carrying British goods confiscated
1797–98	The "XYZ Affair"
1798	Congress votes to triple the size of the army and enlarge the navy; The Federalist Congress passes the Alien and Sedition Acts; Secretary of State Timothy Pickering prosecutes opposition leaders under the laws; Kentucky and Virginia declare their right to nullify acts of the national government
1800	The Convention of 1800 between France and the United States nullifies the Treaty of 1778; Jefferson elected president

Americans had every reason to expect that, under the newly adopted Constitution, the nation finally had the political machinery needed to deal with its public business. But did it?

Today every representative government operates through a political party system based on organizations of people with roughly similar views on political issues who create platforms, choose candidates for office, and formulate legislative programs. Political parties are essential attributes of modern democratic nations in which free elections select those who make and carry out the laws.

149

The delegates at Philadelphia in the summer of 1787 did not perceive parties in this way. They had established offices for the new federal government with defined powers and modes of selection, but they had supposed that these positions would be filled by men whose only concern would be disinterested public service, not the furthering of a particular political group or viewpoint. Public officials, moreover, would be chosen by citizens who placed the common good above their own special needs. Each issue would be decided on its own merits, not on the basis of ideology or preconceived positions. When the Philadelphia delegates considered political parties, the word they commonly used was "factions," by which they meant groupings around particular political chieftains for purely selfish reasons, such as the rewards of political office or the favor of the leader. Factions or parties, they believed, would divide citizens into hostile camps. They were not part of the legitimate machinery of government; they were dangerous growths on it. Government by party, then, seemed a disruptive, selfish, and often corrupt way to conduct a nation's political affairs.

And yet within a decade two great national parties had emerged in the United States. Many thoughtful citizens were dismayed that the country should so quickly fall from political virtue. But this "first party system," which lasted until about 1815, became an essential part of the young republic's political life. Without it, Americans learned, it was difficult to get anything accomplished; indeed, free government itself was rendered ineffective.

What produced this momentous change of heart? Were the new parties the result of differences over ideology? Did opposing views of the Constitution create the party divisions? Were the parties deliberately planned to meet administrative or political needs? Were they the outgrowth of personality clashes among leaders driven by opposing ambitions? Let us look at the circumstances under which the parties emerged, for events often determine the shape of evolving institutions.

But first one confusing matter should be clarified. One of the two parties that appeared during the 1790s was called Federalist; the other was often referred to as Anti-Federalist, though it was also called Republican or Democratic-Republican, or sometimes Jeffersonian. These two groups must not be confused with the federalist and antifederalist partisans of the period when the Constitution was being debated. The issues that divided the two political parties of the "first party system" went beyond the disputes of 1787–1789.

The New Government Launched

National Finances.   Congress convened for the first time in New York early in 1789 and in its first session adopted two important tax measures: the Tariff Act of 1789, which placed duties on a wide range of imported articles; and the Tonnage Act, which taxed foreign vessels entering American ports. Congress also established three executive departments—State, Treasury, and War—and passed the Federal Judiciary Act, prescribing the structure of the Supreme Court and the federal court system.

The debate on the Tonnage Act revealed differences between Northerners, who conducted most of the nation's foreign trade, and Southerners, who exported tobacco and rice, but the disagreements were muted. It is the measure of the relative political peace of these early months that Washington could appoint Jefferson, soon to be the leading Republican, and Hamilton, soon to be the leading Federalist, as his first secretary of state and secretary of the treasury, respectively.

Yet even in this first session of the First Congress there were signs of trouble to come. One hint was the farcical dispute over how the president should be addressed. Was Washington to be called "His Elective Majesty," "His Highness the President," "His Excellency," or merely "Mr. President"? The first three titles had overtones of British monarchy; the last suggested plain American republicanism. The argument seems trivial, but it divided people into temperamental aristocrats and temperamental democrats, and foreshadowed later party differences.

Relative harmony became loud discord when, in its second session, the First Congress confronted the pressing issue of the unpaid war debts. As we have seen, millions of dollars of state and national obligations were overdue. Failure to pay overseas creditors made it difficult for the American government to borrow from foreign bankers. Most of the debt, however, was owed to American citizens, including war veterans, former army suppliers, and those who had directly lent money to Congress or the states. The public creditors also included many businessmen and speculators who had bought up securities and debt certificates in the hope that they would rise in value when the government was finally able to repay them. How were all these people to be paid? And were they to be paid fully and equally?

Hamilton's Plan for America.

The man chosen to provide practical answers to these questions was Treasury Secretary Alexander Hamilton of New York. Born illegitimate in the West Indies, he lacked the advantages of "good birth" and family wealth so useful in getting ahead in eighteenth-century America. But he made up for this by enormous charm, drive, and intelligence. The young man had so impressed prominent men on St. Croix that they sent him to college on the mainland. Hamilton arrived in New York in 1773 in the midst of the imperial crisis and promptly joined the Patriot cause and then the Patriot army. His skill as an artillery officer soon brought him to the attention of Washington, who appointed him his aide-de-camp. After Yorktown Hamilton returned to his adopted city and set up as a lawyer.

Hamilton believed in strong government and had been instrumental in getting New York to adopt the Constitution. He thought the new Union was still too weak, but it was better than the old Confederation. When offered the job of secretary of the treasury, Hamilton leaped at the chance to help forge a strong national government and transform the United States into a unified and prosperous nation.

Hamilton was a political innovator with an expansive vision of America's future. The United States of 1790 was a nation of 4 million people, most of them farmers or farm workers. The first national census (1790) showed that only about 3 percent of the population lived in cities with more than 8,000 people. Hamilton recognized the importance of agriculture in America and understood that it would remain the country's economic mainstay for many years to come. But he believed that the United States must turn to manufacturing for its future prosperity. Industry would free the nation from foreign dependence. It would also transform it in positive ways. Looking at England, then fast becoming the workshop of the world, Hamilton perceived the wealth and power that might lie in store for

Alexander Hamilton at about the time of his leadership of the
Treasury Department.

America. As a public servant, he hoped to do more than just straighten out the
country's tangled finances. In many ways the first secretary of the treasury was
the first great national planner. He sought to encourage economic growth and social modernization. Although today we can see many of the environmental and
human drawbacks of unrestrained industrialization, for its time Hamilton's was a
progressive vision.

Hamilton incorporated these goals into three major reports submitted to Congress between January 1790 and December 1791. The *First Report on the Public Credit*
proposed a plan for putting national finances on a sound basis. Now that the government had a guaranteed revenue from taxes and duties, let it pay its own creditors. It should also take over ("assume") the remaining state debts incurred during
the war for independence. Hamilton knew that even with its newly acquired taxing
power the government could not simply pay off these debts in one lump sum. His
solution was a new issue of federal bonds that would bear an attractive interest rate.
Holders of the old, defaulted debt could exchange it for the new "funded debt."

Hamilton's motives here were in part political. He hoped to strengthen the national government by winning the support of the rich and powerful, the country's chief creditors. But he also believed that a public debt would be a "blessing" rather than a "curse." The new funded debt could be used to back a new national money supply, which in turn would stimulate commerce and provide investment capital for a capital-poor nation. The new funded debt, he noted, would be "an engine of business, an instrument of industry and commerce."

The secretary spelled out the way this process would operate in the *Report on a National Bank*. Congress should charter a commercial bank (the Bank of the United States). Besides handling federal tax collections and disbursements and aiding private business transactions, a federally chartered bank would provide money for circulation and credit for investment. Investors in the Bank of the United States could use the new funded debt bonds, instead of gold and silver, to buy bank stock. These bonds would then become the backing for an issue of "bank notes" that could then be lent to manufacturers and merchants and used as the normal cash of the country. By such means, Hamilton theorized, banks in general and the proposed federal bank in particular could become "nurseries of national wealth."

In his final important state paper, the *Report on Manufactures,* Hamilton urged Congress to support industry with subsidies, a tariff, and a system of roads, canals, and other "internal improvements." America's high labor costs and shortage of investment capital put it at a disadvantage against the better-developed European countries, but these handicaps could be overcome by government action. So long as given industries were weak, the government should nurture them. The benefits of supporting "infant industries," Hamilton claimed, would be felt not only by promoters of industry and the laboring classes but also by farmers, who would find new markets for their products in the manufacturing cities and towns that the government's protective policies would foster. Of Hamilton's three major reports, only this one on manufactures failed to result in immediate action by Congress. But it planted the seeds for later government protection of American industry.

Enacting the Hamiltonian Program.

The Funding Act of 1790 sought to enact the first portion of Hamilton's program. Part one allowed all existing holders of national securities to convert them into federal bonds at face value, though at varying rates of interest. Under part two the federal government would "assume" the outstanding state debts.

The measure aroused the ire of James Madison, now a leader in the House of Representatives. Hamilton and his allies, Madison said, were not showing enough consideration for "original holders," who had helped the government during the war and had received securities in exchange. Many of these patriots had been forced to sell their securities at large discounts to speculators. Why should they not receive some part of the gain that would come when the debt was funded? Though he dwelt on the ethical aspects of the issue, Madison was also concerned about the interests of his constituency—just as his opponents were. The southern states had already paid most of their debts. Now, under the assumption provision, burdened southern taxpayers would be asked to pay federal taxes to redeem the debts of delinquent northern states. Though it took a sectional form, the debate also reflected economic differences. To Madison and his supporters the North represented trade and commerce, the South, agriculture. The Funding Act, accordingly, seemed designed to benefit the commercial interests at the expense of the agricultural interests. After all, southerners declared, most of the speculators who would gain from the act lived in the port towns of New England, New York, and Pennsylvania.

The first part of the Funding Act passed after a bitter battle. But the assumption section seemed certain to go down to defeat until, with Jefferson's approval, Madison and Hamilton arranged a deal. In exchange for yielding on assumption, the new national capital, after moving to Philadelphia for ten years, would be constructed at a site on the Potomac between Maryland and Virginia. Thus sugarcoated the Funding Act, with both sections intact, passed. In the end principle had yielded to sectional pride.

Early in 1791 Congress received Hamilton's bank bill. Madison attacked this measure, too. Once again, he was reluctant to advance commerce and industry at the expense of agriculture, but he preferred to raise constitutional objections. A strong nationalist in the 1780s, Madison now asked where in the Constitution Congress was authorized to incorporate such a bank. He rejected Hamilton's answer that certain powers of the federal government were "implied" in the Constitution.

Despite Madison's resistance, Congress established the Bank of the United States with a twenty-year federal charter. The new institution would accept deposits, make commercial loans, and perform other familiar banking services. But it would also handle the government's financial business, including its tax collections and disbursements, and issue up to $10 million in paper money, backed partly by gold but largely by the funded debt. In this way, as Hamilton intended, the federal debt would become the basis for money circulation and a source of credit for a capital-poor land. In structure the bank would combine public and private features. Five of the twenty-five directors of the bank were to be appointed by the government, the rest by the private stockholders.

Washington was undecided about signing the bank bill. He would eventually become the Federalists' hero, but the president was not yet a strong political partisan. He understood his symbolic role as a just father who must rise above the fray, and to take an obviously partisan stand without very good reason might destroy the image. In his dilemma he turned to his cabinet—Hamilton, Jefferson, and Attorney General Edmund Randolph—for advice. Two written statements resulted, presenting the classic arguments for "loose construction" and "strict construction" of the Constitution. Hamilton defended the bank with his doctrine of implied powers. Jefferson and Randolph argued that powers not explicitly granted Congress by the Constitution were beyond its authority. Washington accepted Hamilton's views and approved the bill.

The Beginnings of Parties

The Economic Division.
The Hamiltonian program drove a wedge through the nation, dividing Americans into opposing political camps. On one side were the emerging Federalists—speculators in government securities, merchants, manufacturers, and would-be manufacturers. Employees of the merchants and manufacturers— merchant seamen, artisans, clerks, bookkeepers, and all who worked in trade—also

tended to support Hamilton's program. On the emerging Republican or Antifederalist side were many small farmers and southern planters, especially those of middle rank.

The division along occupational lines transcended mere geography. The "commercial" classes were particularly numerous in New England and the Middle Atlantic states; southerners mostly belonged to the "cultivator" class. This situation largely accounts for the sectional split in Congress over the bank and funding. But in the South, wherever large pockets of people were engaged in finance, trade, and industry, Federalists found numerous supporters. Similarly, in the North, where surplus crops were produced for export, the farmers were Federalists, while in more isolated farm areas cultivators expressed Republican sentiments.

The Ideological Division.

Economic interest, however, was not the only element that separated Federalists from Republicans. There were also differences in attitudes toward freedom, human nature, majority rule, and the role of government.

Republicans such as Jefferson, Madison, and John Taylor of Virginia regarded the Hamiltonian-Federalist dream as misguided and dangerous. Committed libertarians, they deplored paternalistic government. Individuals were far better judges, in general, of their own interests, they felt, than any set of government officials. Tyranny was more to be feared than chaos. Unless checked, government would grow excessively powerful and end by destroying freedom. However unfairly, they saw their opponents as disguised monarchists who were scarcely different from King George III and his ministers. Strictly limit the power of the national government, they exhorted, and assign as many functions as possible to the states.

Recent scholarship has made it clear that the Jeffersonian Republicans were believers in free markets (laissez-faire) rather than naive anticapitalists. Yet they were also "agrarians," people who cherished a society composed of small freeholders. Jefferson called the nation's farmers "the chosen people of God, if he ever had a chosen people." John Taylor proclaimed that "divine intelligence" had "selected an agricultural state as a paradise." The Jeffersonians were suspicious of the urban masses. City "artificers," wrote Jefferson, were "the panderers of vice & the instruments by which the liberties of a country are generally overturned."

The fear of the urban "mob" was the fear of the propertyless who had no stake in society and could easily be corrupted and used by demagogues. It also reflected the Jeffersonian view that social virtue inhered in fields and flocks, not in factories, shipyards, and offices. Shadowy forms of urban wealth—stocks and bonds—were even more dubious. Drawing on views deeply embedded in Western consciousness, the agrarians attached a moral stigma to money lending and "stockjobbing." Republican prejudices logically extended to home-grown industry. In 1781 Jefferson would declaim: "While we have land to labour, then, let us never wish to see our citizens occupied at a work-bench or twirling a distaff. Carpenters, masons, smiths, are wanting in husbandry; but, for the general operations of manufacture, let our work-shops remain in Europe." The preference for "husbandry" did not preclude commerce; obviously American farmers would want to trade their crop surpluses for foreign manufactures. Yet it was primarily as an adjunct to agriculture that commerce deserved favor.

Whatever their economic preferences, the Jeffersonians were optimists who believed in the ability of human intelligence to improve people's lot. They were also conservatives, in the original sense of the word: they wished to conserve what already existed. America must remain a nation of farms and forests. Their motto could have been "Keep America Green!" By contrast, for all their social and political caution, the Federalists sought to alter the economic status quo in fundamental ways.

Federalists and Republicans disagreed, too, over the value of majority rule. Federalists were elitists. They distrusted human nature and feared the rule of mere numbers. Such a regime denied power to the trained and the able, the "well-born," and gave it to their inferiors. To Hamilton, the people were "a great beast." Harrison Gray Otis of Boston called the voters a "duped and deluded mob." John Jay of New York, first chief justice of the Supreme Court, reflected that "the mass of men are neither wise nor good, and virtue . . . can only be drawn to a point and executed by . . . a strong government ably administered." Republicans, by contrast, proclaimed human nature to be inherently good. That human vices "are part of man's original constitution," announced one New York Jeffersonian, had been shown to be false. The evil deeds that people at times committed should be traced rather "to the errors and abuses that have at every period existed in political establishments." Jefferson himself regarded the people as eminently trustworthy. "I am," he announced, "not among those who fear the people; they, and not the rich, are our dependence for continued freedom." At moments Jefferson even sounded like a radical. In letters to friends and associates he wrote that "the tree of Liberty must be watered periodically with the blood of tyrants" and "a little revolution

Rembrandt Peale, a famous American artist, painted
this portrait of Jefferson in 1805. It was completed in time
to be displayed at the president's second inauguration.
(*Rembrandt Peale (1778–1860), "Thomas Jefferson"*
(1743–1826), 1805. The New-York Historical Society Museum)

every twenty years is an excellent thing." In his public statements and acts he was far more reserved. We should also remember that he and his political allies tended to limit the "people" to the white tillers of the soil. Of the "mobs of great cities" they were far more suspicious. It is clear, nevertheless, that philosophically the Republicans were more democratic than their opponents.

We must not draw the distinctions between Federalist aristocracy and Republican democracy too sharply, however. Many southern Jeffersonians were slaveholders. Many deplored slavery in the abstract but considered it indispensable. Jefferson himself did not believe in absolute human equality but in "natural aristocracy," an elite based on talent and ability, rather than birth. Nor should we assume that Hamilton and his followers were unqualified aristocrats or "monocrats," as their enemies called them. Generally they accepted representative government as unavoidable in America and never seriously intended to establish a monarchy.

Yet when all these qualifications are noted, it remains true that Federalists had less faith in majority rule than their opponents. The Republicans, in turn, had less confidence in persons of wealth and position than in "the people."

The Role of Religion.

Religion also separated the two emerging parties. In the 1790s the Federalists attracted Congregationalists in New England and Episcopalians in the Middle Atlantic states and the South. Leading Federalists were often outspoken defenders of traditional Christian beliefs. The Republicans won the support of a hodgepodge of Baptists, Methodists, Roman Catholics, nonbelievers, and deists. These groupings may not appear to make much sense—Roman Catholics and nonbelievers do not seem to have much in common. If we take a second look, however, we can see the pattern: Members of long-established churches, which had received financial support from state governments and so had privileged positions, voted Federalist; the others tended to prefer the Jeffersonian-Republicans.

The Republican appeal to nonbelievers is easy to understand. Jefferson himself was a deist whose religious creed rejected many orthodox Christian elements. As for the Republican appeal to Catholics and evangelical Protestants, such as Baptists and Methodists, these groups had long been victims of legal discrimination. By the 1790s they were still disqualified from holding office in some areas, and in parts of New England where Congregationalism was still the established church, they remained second-class citizens. The role of Jefferson and Madison in securing the Virginia Statute for Religious Freedom, which disestablished the Anglican church, earned the Republican leaders the gratitude of all those outside the established religious order everywhere. In Connecticut and Massachusetts the Republicans confirmed this attachment by leading the fight to end the preferred status conferred on Congregationalism. It is not surprising, then, that people who thought of themselves as religious outsiders should find Republicanism more congenial than Federalism.

Religion served to offset economic interest as a factor in party support. A Congregational farmer in Massachusetts, for example, would seem to be represented by Republicans agrarian interests, but might well vote Federalist on the basis of religion. A rich Catholic lawyer from New York, whom we would expect to vote for the Federalists on the basis of occupation, might well support the Republicans for religious reasons. On the whole the religious factor seemed to help the Federalists more than their opponents.

Relations with Europe

The first party system was not only a response to domestic events and attitudes. It was also derived from America's complex relations with the rest of the Atlantic world.

In 1790 Spain controlled the mouth of the Mississippi and still denied Americans the right of free deposit at New Orleans. The British continued to restrict American trade with their empire and refused to abandon the military posts they occupied in the Northwest. And even France had begun to limit American trade with its colonies, despite the commercial treaty of 1778.

Revolution in France.   The outbreak of the French Revolution of 1789 would make these problems infinitely worse. That great political convulsion in France aroused strong passions in the United States. At first most Americans rejoiced at the overthrow of the corrupt, aristocratic, and worn-out Old Regime in the most powerful nation on the European continent. One enthusiastic Yankee orator saw the fall of the Bastille, the hated prison that symbolized French tyranny, as a "spark from the altar flame of liberty on this side of the Atlantic, which alighted in the pinnacle of despotism in France and reduced the immense fabric to ashes in the twinkling of an eye." In Boston streets were renamed for revolutionary ideals—Royal Exchange Alley, for example, became Equality Lane. Some Americans replaced "mister" with the revolutionary "citizen" and "Mrs." with the awkward "citess." At first even men of conservative temper welcomed the change. President Washington graciously received from Lafayette the key to the Bastille as a link between the American and French struggles against tyranny.

But the fall of the Bastille was followed by the overthrow of the French monarchy, the execution of King Louis XVI and his queen, Marie Antoinette, the bloody Reign of Terror, confiscation of the property of French nobles, and ever more violent attacks on the church and traditional Christianity. American public opinion quickly split. Fisher Ames, a Massachusetts Federalist, was soon denouncing revolutionary France as "an open hell, still ringing with agonies and blasphemies, still smoking with sufferings and crimes, in which we see . . . perhaps our future state." Other Federalists warned that the French "moral influenza" was to be more dreaded than a "thousand yellow fevers." Jefferson, Madison, and their allies, however, continued to admire the revolutionaries, cheering the end of "superstition" and applauding the "rule of reason." Many approved of the execution of Louis XVI and even saw virtue in the Reign of Terror.

When war broke out in 1793 between the new revolutionary French Republic and England, Spain, and Holland, Americans were uncertain how to respond. France was America's formal ally, and although it had not lately taken the friendship seriously, the new French Republic needed American support now that it was fighting for its life. The French saw the United States as a source of food and supplies for itself and the French colonies in the Caribbean and a possible base of operations against British and Spanish possessions in North America.

Citizen Genêt.   Seeking American aid, in 1793 the French government dispatched "Citizen" Edmond Genêt to the United States. Genêt immediately became a magnet for controversy. Secretary Hamilton opposed receiving him for fear that it would involve the nation in the war. Secretary Jefferson believed that if we refused, we would be repudiating our alliance with France. Neither man wished to see the United States enter the war in Europe, but Hamilton believed that it was the president's task to proclaim neutrality, and he should do so at once, while Jefferson favored a congressional announcement, but only after the United States had squeezed concessions out of both the British and the French. Washington took his treasury secretary's advice and in April 1793 issued a proclamation of neutrality asking Americans to be "impartial" toward the belligerents and forbidding actions favorable to either side. Republicans found the proclamation too even-handed. "The cause of France is the cause of man," declared one protesting Jeffersonian.

Meanwhile, hoping to make the United States a base for operations against Britain and Spain, Genêt hired George Rogers Clark, the Indian fighter and a hero of the Revolution, to lead an expedition against the Spanish in Louisiana and Florida. He also issued commissions in the proposed army and authorized privateers to sail from American ports to attack British and Spanish shipping. In midsummer of 1793 Genêt demanded that Washington call Congress into special session to decide what the United States would do to aid the French Republic. If the president refused, he arrogantly declared, he would take his case to the American people over Washington's head.

Genêt's activities further polarized American opinion. The Republicans at first befriended him, and Jefferson filled the Frenchman's ears with the misdeeds of his Federalist opponents. The Federalists despised him and used his dubious activities on American soil as a stick with which to beat their opponents. The English-born Federalist journalist William Cobbett labeled the Republicans the "bastard offspring of Genêt, spawned in hell, to which they will presently return."

Before long Genêt's activities had so embarrassed the American government that even Jefferson agreed he must be sent home. France, however, was now in the hands of the radical Jacobins, who despised the moderates who had sent Genêt to America. Rather than send the amiable but foolish emissary to certain execution, Washington granted him asylum in the United States.

The Partisan Press.   Differences over foreign policy, combined with the disagreements over the Hamiltonian program, had by now produced a combative party press that further inflamed the political rivalry. Federalist and Republican newspapers published scathing attacks on their opponents. John Fenno's *Gazette of the United States* treated Hamilton as a demigod and spewed out insults against his enemies. These "Jacobins" were working to corrupt the nation's youth and "make them imbibe, with their very milk . . . the poison of atheism and disaffection." The *General Advertiser*, edited by Franklin's grandson, Benjamin Franklin Bache, and Philip Freneau's *National Gazette* denounced the Federalists as outright monarchists and dupes of British policy. Bache even maligned Washington as the "scourge of all the misfortunes of our country," a man who had given currency "to political iniquity and to legalized corruption."

Within Washington's cabinet the relations between Jefferson and Hamilton became so bad that at the end of 1793 Jefferson resigned as secretary of state and was replaced by Edmund Randolph, a Virginia Federalist. But Jefferson's departure did not end his leadership of the Republicans. From Monticello, his hilltop home in Virginia, he continued to issue political advice, remaining in close touch with Madison, the party's chief tactician in Congress.

Relations with England. Just before Jefferson's departure, European affairs once more reached a crisis. This time the United States found itself pitted against the world's greatest naval power, England. The difficulty concerned neutral rights on the high seas in time of war, an issue that would fester unsettled for generations.

Basically the two nations disagreed over whether the United States could trade freely with France, England's enemy. The French, unable to protect their shipping against the powerful British navy, had opened their imperial trade, normally restricted to French vessels, to neutral commerce. The British, rightly, saw this as a maneuver to evade their naval advantage and invoked the Rule of 1756, which declared that trade forbidden in time of peace could not be legally pursued in time of war. In effect, a weak naval power could not protect itself by hiding behind a neutral. Britain and the United States also argued over "contraband." International law recognized the right of one nation to blockade its wartime enemy's ports and prevent neutral nations from delivering certain war goods—contraband—through the blockade. But contraband was not clearly defined, nor was the legal status of neutral trade in other goods.

Soon after Anglo-French hostilities began, Britain proclaimed a blockade of France and its colonies and deployed its navy to destroy French shipping and commerce. The French immediately lifted all restrictions on foreign imports and opened their ports to foreign ships. Neutral America seized the opportunity to supply French shipping needs. For the next two decades, as Britain and France struggled to dominate Europe, French demand stimulated American trade beyond all previous measure. Salem, Boston, Providence, New York, and Philadelphia boomed between 1790 and 1796 as the annual value of foreign trade leaped from $46 million to $140 million.

The British denounced the Americans for profiting from Britain's troubles by supplying their chief enemy with needed commodities. Even more galling, Britain was unintentionally supplying many of the seamen for the bloated American merchant fleet. Some of these were deserters from the Royal Navy, who preferred the lenient treatment and good pay of American merchant seamen to the harsh discipline, bad food, and physical dangers faced by sailors in the British navy. British merchant seamen, too, jumped ship for the higher pay and better working conditions of the American merchant marine.

To offset the loss of sailors, British men-of-war began to stop American vessels to inspect the crews for deserters, "impressing" both those deemed guilty and those who merely looked like apt recruits for the depleted Royal Navy. Americans were outraged by impressment, but their anger was tempered by fear that worsening relations with Britain would entirely destroy the lucrative trade with France. To New Englanders and residents of the middle states' ports—the chief beneficiaries of this trade—it seemed wiser to submit to British practices, however arbitrary, than to defy Britain, provoke war, and see the new trade completely shut down.

The British and the Indians. In one area of Anglo-American relations, however, almost all Americans agreed that British policies were deplorable. In the Northwest British garrisons remained on American soil and British fur traders still monopolized business with the Indians. Americans were also certain that the British were encouraging the Indians south of the Great Lakes in their policy of harassing American settlers. During the winter of 1791–1792, after defeating two American military expeditions sent against them, the Indians forced the Ohio settlers to retreat to the region's two well-defended villages. President Washington now decided to settle the conflict by overwhelming force and dispatched a new army under Anthony Wayne to the Ohio region. Wayne, an abler strategist than his predecessors, trained and seasoned his troops through the winter and spring of 1793–1794. In August 1794 he confronted the Indians at Fallen Timbers and decisively defeated them.

The Jay Treaty.   In the fall of 1793 the crisis between England and the United States came to a head when a British order in council—an executive proclamation—authorized English naval commanders to seize neutral vessels trading with the French Caribbean islands. In short order 250 American ships were boarded by British naval parties, escorted to British ports, and confiscated. The seizures infuriated Americans, and it soon seemed like 1775 all over again. Mobs roamed the streets of American seaport towns, denouncing Britain and insulting and threatening Englishmen. British tempers were equally hot and it looked as if war was imminent. To avoid a military showdown, for which the United States was ill prepared, in 1794 Washington sent Chief Justice John Jay to London to negotiate a settlement.

The British drove a hard bargain with the upstart Americans. They agreed to surrender the western posts and pay for American ships recently confiscated. They also agreed to arbitrate American merchants' claims for confiscated cargoes and yielded slightly on the long-festering issue of trade with the British Empire. The United States would be allowed to trade with British India, and small American vessels would be permitted to enter British West Indies ports. But in most other matters they refused to budge. They rejected American demands for full commercial equality with British subjects. They denied liability for the slaves they had removed from the South during the Revolution. The final agreement contained a broad definition of contraband that made many American goods liable to seizure, as well as a proviso that the United States must close its ports to French privateers. To satisfy long-standing English complaints, the United States also agreed to refer all unpaid American private debts owed English creditors to a joint commission for settlement. On western problems, too, the United States made concessions. In return for surrendering the Northwest posts, Britain would be allowed to exploit the resources of the region south of the Canadian border as in the past.

Historians today believe the treaty to have been a wise move. It hitched the United States, they say, to the victor in the generations-long world rivalry between Britain and France. But to France's friends and England's enemies the Jay Treaty seemed a sellout. Jay was denounced as an "archtraitor" and hanged in effigy by irate crowds all across the country. Popular opinion denounced the Federalists. Hamilton was hit in the head by a rock when he attempted to defend the treaty before an irate crowd. The president's home in Philadelphia was surrounded by "an innumerable multitude . . . demanding war against England, cursing Washington, and crying success to the French patriots and virtuous Republicans." The agreement itself was referred to widely as "that damned treaty." For a while there was doubt that the Senate would confirm it or the president sign it. But the Senate's strong Federalist majority passed the treaty after striking out one of the more unfavorable trade provisions. Washington hesitated but approved it when he realized that the alternative might well be war with England. Even after adoption the treaty continued to rankle, and Washington was reviled for endorsing it. Jefferson claimed that he had "undone the country," and a bitterly partisan Virginian ventured the shocking toast: "A speedy death to General Washington."

Hostility to the Jay Treaty powerfully reinforced the ongoing process of party formation. In the House of Representatives—the body that would have to appropriate money to carry out several provisions of the pact—Republicans organized the first congressional party caucus ever held to consider ways to defeat the treaty. In the end their attempt failed, but the close House vote revealed the new strength of the opposition and the extent to which foreign affairs had polarized Congress along party lines.

The Whiskey Rebellion; The Pinckney Treaty.
The major disputes with Great Britain now settled, however unsatisfactorily, the Washington administration turned to differences with Spain.

In the Northwest Britain's surrender of the military posts meant the abandonment of its Indian allies. Chastened by their defeat at Fallen Timbers, the Indians signed the Treaty of Greenville in 1795, surrendering all of Ohio except for a small strip along Lake Erie. Before many months a mass movement of white pioneer farmers into the Northwest was underway. In the Southwest, where Indian resistance to the whites was weaker, by 1796 there were already two new states—Kentucky and Tennessee—carved out of a region that had had no permanent white inhabitants twenty years earlier.

The western pioneers were a restless and unruly lot. For years frontier farmers had been angry over federal tax policy. Unable to sell their grain to distant urban customers because of high transportation costs, they had found an ingenious alternative. To make their grain portable, they made it potable, distilling it into whiskey, which could be easily carried to market in barrels. When the government imposed a tax on distilled liquors in 1791 to raise money for Hamilton's funding plan, westerners defied the authorities and threatened tax collectors with physical harm.

In 1794 the farmers of western Pennsylvania carried defiance to the point of open rebellion. The "Whiskey Rebels" closed down federal courts and stole the mails. They attacked federal troops guarding the tax collector for the Pittsburgh district. Washington quickly ordered out the militia of Virginia, Maryland, New Jersey, and Pennsylvania. With the bellicose Hamilton as second in command, this small army marched on the rebels. The insurgents surrendered without a shot. Two were convicted of high treason and then pardoned.

The incident confirmed westerners' disgust at the trigger-happy Federalists. At the same time it showed the government that westerners were not to be trifled with. Now they were demanding that the federal government do something about Spain's refusal to allow the right of deposit at New Orleans. If the United States government did not give them what they wanted, they would take matters into their own hands and negotiate directly with Spain.

At this point Washington ordered Thomas Pinckney to Spain to arbitrate the differences between the two nations. Fortunately for the United States, Spain was ready to negotiate. In short order Pinckney and the Spanish foreign minister concluded a treaty granting the United States free navigation of the Mississippi and the right of tax-free deposit at New Orleans for three years, subject to renewal. The treaty also set the boundary between the United States and Florida at the thirty-first parallel, conceding the Yazoo Strip of southern Georgia and Mississippi to the Americans. The Jay Treaty had left many issues unresolved. The Pinckney Treaty, for the moment at least, settled the nagging problem of Mississippi navigation at virtually no cost to the United States.

Washington's Farewell.   In 1796 Washington decided to retire after two terms to his plantation home at Mount Vernon on the Potomac. Before leaving, however, he delivered a formal farewell to his fellow Americans, not as an address, but in the form of a letter published in the newspapers. We remember the departing president's "Farewell Address" for its warning against "permanent alliances with any portion of the foreign world." But most of his message cautioned against the "spirit of party" and a tribute to the virtues of "fraternal affection" and national unity. Toward the end of his administration Washington had been drawn into the ranks of the Federalists. Still, he did not believe in the party system, and he told the American people that factionalism served to "distract the public councils and enfeeble the public administration."

With Washington gone, the Federalists were now deprived of an immense political asset. In the election of 1796 they would not have the nation's greatest popular hero at the head of their ticket. This time there would be a real contest for the presidency.

The Election of 1796.   No one was quite sure how the presidential candidates would be selected in 1796 and how, once chosen, one would be elected to office. Washington had faced no opposition as nominee or candidate and had not campaigned. Now things were different. In a few states there were already permanent party organizations and a nominating procedure. In others, and at the national level, party machinery was primitive. In the end the leaders of each party informally consulted with one another and decided who to support as their party's candidates. The Republicans' choice of Jefferson was never in doubt. Among the Federalists, however, the leaders disagreed. The "High," or extreme, Federalists supported Thomas Pinckney, the treaty negotiator. Moderates preferred Vice President John Adams. Because the party leaders were unable to settle on a single nominee, there were two Federalist candidates.

The contest was fought over the unpopular Jay Treaty and general foreign policy, though the Republicans tried to make the supposed monarchism of their opponents a major issue. Presidential electors were chosen by popular vote in only half the states; in the others the state legislatures made the choice. The Federalists won a majority in the electoral college, carrying most of the states from New Jersey north. But since they were divided between High Federalists and Adams men, the Federalist electors could not coordinate their votes. Adams received the highest number of votes and became president. Enough Federalists refused to support Pinckney, however, to give Jefferson the second highest number of votes, thereby making him vice president under the existing terms of the Constitution.

The XYZ Affair.   Adams no sooner took office than the United States found itself in an undeclared war with its recent ally, France. The French government, now
in the hands of the Directory, a new ruling group, considered the Jay Treaty a virtual Anglo-American alliance, and the election of Adams, the candidate of the pro-
British Federalists, seemed to confirm American sympathies for France's chief
enemy. In 1797 the French authorities ordered that impressed American sailors
taken from captured British ships be hanged and that any intercepted American
ship carrying British goods be confiscated. They also refused to receive the American minister, Charles Cotesworth Pinckney.

Adams might have used these insults to break relations with France. But unlike the more inflexible High Federalists he preferred to negotiate. As commissioners to settle with the French, he appointed the previously rejected Charles C.
Pinckney; John Marshall, a Virginia Federalist; and Elbridge Gerry, a Massachusetts leader with Republican leanings. At the same time, as a precaution, the administration asked Congress to provide funds to expand the army and navy.

In France, the American commissioners were received by Charles Talleyrand,
the French foreign minister. A wily and corrupt man, Talleyrand made them cool
their heels for days and then turned them over to three of his agents. These men—
mentioned in the diplomatic dispatches as X, Y, and Z—promised to speed up negotiations if the Americans paid Talleyrand and other French officials $250,000, made a
loan to France of $12 million, and apologized publicly for harsh words President
Adams had recently hurled their way. The commissioners refused to comply. They
had not been instructed to pay a bribe, they said, and lending France so much
money would seriously damage relations with England. Besides, how could they
know whether, after paying, the United States would gain a favorable treaty?

When news of the negotiations reached the United States, it produced a
tremendous uproar. Americans considered the French demands corrupt and an
unforgivable insult to their nation. The Federalists attacked the French and their
Republican friends with renewed fury and made Pinckney and Marshall, the two
Federalist commissioners, into heroes. One Federalist journalist proudly boasted
that when the French had asked to be bribed, Pinckney had retorted: "Millions for
defense, but not one cent for tribute!" (What he actually said was far less eloquent:
"No, no, not a six-pence!")

The XYZ Affair ignited a naval war between the former allies. French raiders
from the Caribbean began attacking American vessels in United States coastal waters. Congress responded by voting money to triple the size of the army and build
forty new ships for the navy. In May 1798 it created the Navy Department with a
secretary of cabinet rank to head it. Washington was recalled to public service and
placed in charge of the army, with Hamilton, yearning, as always, for military
glory, second in command. In July Congress nullified the French alliance of 1778,
ending the pretense of special friendship for that country. For the next few years
American and French ships attacked one another in the Caribbean. The Americans
also helped the British and their ally, the black patriot Toussaint L'Ouverture,
overthrow the French regime on the island of Hispaniola and establish Haiti as the
first black nation in the New World.

The pressure on Adams to formally declare war on France was immense. But the president, aware of American unpreparedness, refused. In 1799 the French government began to show a more conciliatory attitude. Late in the year Adams sent three new emissaries to Paris to reopen negotiations. The president wanted the French to compensate Americans for their recent "spoliations" of American commerce, and insisted that France formally accept nullification of the 1778 treaty. Now led by Napoleon Bonaparte, the French refused the first condition but accepted the second. On that basis the two countries signed the Convention of 1800. The United States had again avoided war.

Republican Triumph

The crisis with France improved Anglo-American relations and won considerable popular support for the Federalists. But it also set in motion a train of events that ultimately led to the emergence of the Republicans as the majority party.

As yet, few Americans understood the role of a "loyal opposition." Opposing the administration in power seemed disloyalty, if not treason, and they could not see the value of a second party in keeping the first honest. Partisan hostility often went beyond the bounds of decency. The Republican *General Advertiser* called the president the "old, querulous, bald, blind, crippled, toothless Adams." Vermont Congressman Matthew Lyon was almost expelled from Congress for spitting in a Federalist member's eye and wrestling with him on the floor of the House of Representatives chamber.

The Alien and Sedition Acts.   Deep ideological differences, certainty that they were the nation's bulwark against foreign evil, and the surge of patriotism in the face of French danger all help to explain (though they do not excuse) the extreme actions that the Federalists now took. In 1798 the Federalist Congress, claiming national security as justification, passed four laws known collectively as the Alien and Sedition Acts. The Naturalization Act extended the residence requirement for naturalization as a citizen from five to fourteen years, thereby keeping the vote from recent pro-French Irish and French immigrants. The Alien Act gave the president power to expel from the country any alien considered dangerous or suspected of treasonable acts. Under the Alien Enemies Act, the president was authorized to arrest, imprison, or expel enemy aliens in the event of war. The Sedition Act made it illegal for both aliens and citizens to (1) impede the execution of federal laws; (2) bring the federal government, Congress, or the president into disrepute; (3) instigate or abet any riot, insurrection, or unlawful assembly; or (4) prevent a federal officer from performing his duties.

Under the Sedition Act Secretary of State Timothy Pickering prosecuted four leading Republican newspapers and several individuals. Ten of the indictments resulted in convictions, and a flock of foreign political activists fled the country rather than face almost certain prosecution. Despite these "successes," the Alien and Sedition Acts were a tremendous political blunder. The Federalists had their opponents on the run until the passage of these laws. Unable to support the

France of the XYZ Affair and the undeclared naval war, many moderate Republicans had defected to the side of the administration. Now the government's vindictiveness and disregard of free speech propelled the waverers back to the Republican side.

To meet this challenge to civil liberties and to the power of the states relative to the national government, Jefferson and Madison induced the legislatures of Kentucky and Virginia to denounce the recent Alien and Sedition Acts on constitutional grounds. The Virginia and Kentucky Resolutions held that the Constitution was a "compact," or agreement, among the states to confer only limited powers on the national government. Whenever the national government exceeded these powers—as in the Alien and Sedition Acts—the states had the right to oppose it. The Kentucky legislature later asserted the right of states to resort to "nullification . . . of all unauthorized acts" by the national government.

Both states called on their sister commonwealths to join their protest. Few did. Where the Federalists were in control, the legislatures rejected the idea that the states were the proper judges of constitutionality. And even Republican legislatures were reluctant to approve the nullification doctrine. Nevertheless, the Virginia and Kentucky Resolutions gave effective voice to widespread rank-and-file Republican outrage at the administration's disregard of civil liberties. They were also significant precedents for the later southern position on states' rights.

The Transfer of Power.   By the time Congress ratified the Convention of 1800, Adams was out of office and Thomas Jefferson had become the third president of the United States. The 1800 presidential contest that ended in Republican victory was the precedent for peaceful and orderly surrender of power by one political party to another that America has followed ever since.[1]

When the 1800 campaign opened, notwithstanding the Alien and Sedition acts, Adams's peace policy was popular with the moderate public and Federalists had made gains in the state elections of 1799. But the party was actually in trouble. Washington's death at the end of the year deprived it of a powerful unifying force. Soon the personal rivalry and temperamental differences between Adams and Hamilton, though both of the same party, became an open scandal. Moreover, Republican efforts to woo northern business interests and town laborers had begun to produce results. Few contemporaries as yet saw these weak spots. In May 1800 a caucus of Federalist congressmen chose Adams and Charles Cotesworth Pinckney of the XYZ Affair as their candidates. The Republicans nominated Jefferson and Aaron Burr of New York by the same congressional caucus system. Both caucuses pledged to support each candidate equally, even though this commitment created the risk that the House of Representatives, under the existing constitutional rule, would have to choose between them for president and vice president if there should be a tie in the electoral college.

And a tie, in fact, was what happened. During the campaign Federalists and Republicans employed such modern tactics as printed party tickets, appeals to party loyalty, and public speechmaking. When it was over, Adams had 65 electoral votes; Pinckney 64. Jefferson and Burr received 73 votes each.

---

[1] Except in 1860 when Lincoln was elected and the lower south seceded in protest.

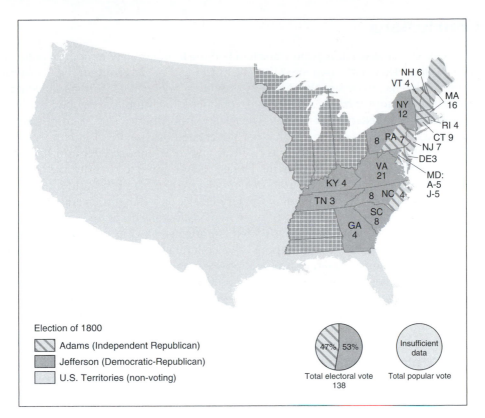

Election of 1800

Election of 1800

NH 6
VT 4
MA 16
NY 12
RI 4
CT 9
PA 7
NJ 7
DE3
VA 21
MD: A-5 J-5
KY 4
TN 3
NC 4
SC 8
GA 4

Election of 1800

Adams (Independent Republican)

Jefferson (Democratic-Republican)

U.S. Territories (non-voting)

47% 53%
Total electoral vote 138

Insufficient data
Total popular vote

Who would be president and who vice president? The law said that the candidate with the highest number of votes was elected president; the second highest number vice president. No one doubted that the Republicans had intended Jefferson to be their candidate for the top office; but as the law prescribed, the House of Representatives would have to decide the question, with each state casting one vote. The Federalists would be in a position to veto whichever candidate they wished. But would they? To some Federalists it seemed that if Jefferson was bad, Burr was even worse. Hamilton admitted that Jefferson "had some pretentions to character," but Burr was a complete rogue, a man "bankrupt beyond redemption." "Mr Burr is one of the most unprincipled men in the United States," Hamilton wrote John Rutledge of South Carolina. He must not be allowed to attain the "chief magistracy." When Jefferson's friends gave the Federalist congressman from Delaware, James Bayard, assurances that the Virginian would allow most Federalist civil servants to keep their jobs, Bayard, the only Delaware member in the House, threw his state's vote to the Virginian. This shift encouraged other Federalist states to yield, and on the 36 ballot Jefferson received the votes of ten states with four for Burr and two abstentions. The transfer of power was now complete. Jefferson, the arch-Republican, would be the third president of the United States.

Conclusions

In little more than a decade, Americans had laid the foundation of a modern political party system. They had discovered that the machinery of government the Constitution provided had to be supplemented by voluntary political institutions called parties. But they had not made a deliberate, considered decision; parties had evolved through the circumstances of the day. The need to put America's economic house in order and deal with its unsettled finances had created passionate disagreements between people with commitments to agriculture and those engaged in trade, banking, and manufacture. Differences over the French Revolution had divided the country between those who felt the exhilaration of a freer, more democratic, and more secular Europe, and those who saw revolutionary France as a dangerous enemy of religion and social order and perceived Britain as a bastion of stability.

Constitutional biases had also divided Americans. During the years of Washington's and Adams's administrations, the Federalists had, understandably, favored a broad interpretation of national powers; and they had stretched these to the limit to achieve their legislative ends. The Jeffersonians, by contrast, had fought centralized, concentrated national power and favored protection of the states' authority. Time would show that much of this difference depended on which party was "in" and which was "out." And yet we must not be too cynical about the parties' professions of constitutional principles. What started as rationalization often ended as sincere conviction.

However it came about, by 1800 the country had acquired two great national parties. Neither had a monopoly of virtue or wisdom. The Republicans had shown greater sensitivity to personal rights and freedom; ideologically, they would point the way to a more open and democratic society. But their vision of the nation's social and economic future was cramped and naive. The Federalists had seen that America's greatness could not be limited by the past. They had recognized that the United States was fated to become a land of busy workshops as well as fertile farms and pastures. Yet they had failed to understand the average person's yearning for equality and the immense value of personal liberty and free expression in a progressive society. It remained to be seen now if the party of Jefferson could avoid the excesses of its opponents and find a workable balance for the nation.

ONLINE RESOURCES

"The Whiskey Rebellion" *http://www.earlyamerica.com/earlyamerica/milestones/whiskey/index.html*
   In addition to general reading about this uprising in the Pennsylvania backcountry, read George Washington's original instructions to the militia to reinstate order.

Fracas in Congress: The Battle of Honor between Matthew Lyon and Roger Griswold *http://etext.virginia.edu/journals/EH/EH41/Neff41.html* This site offers an in-depth look at the notions of political honor and the rise of partisanship. See this site for one of the most well-known political battles in early American history.

8

The Jeffersonians in Office

How Did Power Affect Republican Ideology?

1800	Jefferson elected president; Washington, D.C., becomes the national capital
1801	President Adams appoints midnight judges to tighten Federalist control of the courts
1802	The federal government sells its shares in the Bank of the United States; The Republican Congress repeals the Judiciary Act of 1801
1803–06	Lewis and Clark explore the West
1803	*Marbury v. Madison;* The Louisiana Purchase
1805	The Essex decision: Congress retaliates with the Nonimportation Act
1805–06	The Wilkinson–Burr conspiracy
1806–07	England and France issue decrees limiting neutral trade in Europe
1807	The *Chesapeake–Leopard* affair; Jefferson activates the Nonimportation Act of 1806; The Embargo Act
1808	James Madison elected president
1809	The Nonintercourse Act
1810	Macon's Bill Number Two
1811	Southern and western War Hawks dominate the House of Representatives; American naval ship *President* attacks English navy's *Little Belt;* Congress defeats an attempt to recharter the Bank of the United States; Battle of Tippecanoe
1812	Congress provides for a 35,000-man regular army, gives Madison the power to call up state militias, and declares war on England
1814	Napoleon defeated in Europe; British troops are transferred to America and move on Washington; The Hartford Convention; The Peace of Ghent provides settlement of minor disputes between United States and Britain, leaves major issues of war untouched
1815	Andrew Jackson's victory over the British at New Orleans
1817	Rush–Bagot Agreement provides for demilitarizing United States–Canada border

In December 1815 James Madison sent his seventh annual message to Congress. The president reported Captain Stephen Decatur's defeat of the Dey of Algiers, a victory that finally forced the Barbary pirates to cease their demands for tribute and their attacks on American ships. He also reported progress in concluding peace with the Indian tribes in the West and described the still-disturbed state of the country's finances in the wake of the recent war. But the most arresting portion of the message was its last paragraphs. In these Madison recommended a national bank to solidify the nation's finances, a protective tariff to encourage domestic industry, a program for building roads and canals, and "a national seminary of learning" within the District of Columbia, to be financed by the federal government. This national university would serve as "a central resort for youth and genius from every part of the country, diffusing on their return [to their homes] those national feelings, those liberal sentiments, and those congenial manners which contribute cement to our Union and strength to the great political fabric of which it is the foundation."

These proposals were startling. Madison was the man who had fought Hamilton's scheme to establish a national bank and drafted the Virginia Resolution of 1798, which proclaimed the limited power of the federal government under the Constitution. His party was the party of states' rights and strict construction. Now leader of that party, he was asking Congress for some of the very things he had strongly opposed!

What had produced this about-face? Only fourteen years had elapsed between the election of 1800, which made Thomas Jefferson president, and Madison's seventh annual message. What had taken place in this decade and a half to cause such a drastic change of direction among Republicans?

President Jefferson

Part of the answer is Republican adaptability. Once in office, Jefferson proved to be less dogmatic than many of his opponents had feared. In his inaugural speech he sought to quiet fears and disarm his enemies. The recent presidential campaign had been bitter, he noted, but now that it was over, the country must unite. His party would respect the funded debt established by Hamilton and the rights of the Federalist minority. Though the two parties called themselves by different names, their members were "brethren of the same principle." "We are all Republicans, we are all Federalists," he declared. Nor would the victorious Republicans return the country to its feeble state before the Constitution. It was important, he said, to support "the State governments in all their rights"; but it was also necessary to preserve "the General Government in its whole constitutional vigor, as the sheet anchor of our peace at home and safety abroad."

A New, Republican Spirit.
Despite Jefferson's conciliatory professions, he intended to introduce "republican" principles into the conduct of the government. The new president reduced the stuffy formalities that had surrounded Washington and Adams. In place of his predecessors' regal ceremonial visits to Congress to express their wishes on new legislation or policy, Jefferson sent written messages. Instead of formal "levees," occasions at which members of the government and uniformed diplomats paid court to the president in strict order of rank, or lavish formal state banquets, Jefferson gave private dinners at which guests took whatever seat they could find. Still more characteristic of Jefferson were his small private suppers, with guests seated at a round table where no one could claim precedence over anyone else. For these informal gatherings the red-haired president often wore carpet slippers and a threadbare scarlet vest, his shirt not always

perfectly clean. The guests at these affairs, discussed philosophy, the arts, literature, and science while eating food prepared by an excellent French chef, though often served by the president himself.

Jefferson's "republicanism" must be seen in historical context, however. The principal author of the Declaration of Independence undoubtedly believed that "all men were created equal," in some philosophical sense. But he was a large slaveholder who could not dispense with slave labor on his show plantation Monticello in the Virginia hills. He also could not envision how slavery could ever be abolished in the South without somehow removing the freed blacks to other lands. The "two races, equally free, cannot live in the same government," he announced at one point. The new president welcomed talent among black people when called to his attention but ultimately, like most white Americans, considered blacks "inferior to the whites on the endowments both of body and mind." To be fair, he advanced this idea, he added, "as a suspicion only." Jefferson's views on race did not, it seems, prevent him, a widower, from maintaining a liaison with Sally Hemings, a young black slave. During the party battles before 1800 James Callender, a scandal-mongering journalist, had attacked Jefferson as a hypocrite and a debauchee for taking advantage of the master–slave relationship. Jefferson and his friends would deny the charge, but recent historians, using the evidence of DNA from both Jefferson's and Hemings' descendants, agree that either Jefferson or a close relative probably did father children with the slave woman.

Federalist Legislation Repealed.

Jefferson tried to break with the Federalist past in more fundamental ways than public style. At first he labored to contract the role of the national government, and he was partially successful. The secretary of the treasury, Albert Gallatin of Pennsylvania, reduced the detested national debt by cutting down appropriations for the army and the navy, which the Republicans neither liked nor considered essential. At the same time the new administration was able to do away with several unpopular internal taxes the Federalists had imposed. The Republicans attacked or eliminated other Federalist policies or programs. They repealed some of the Alien and Sedition Acts, allowed others to expire, and pardoned all those the Federalists had imprisoned for sedition. Because it had a twenty-year charter, the Bank of the United States could not be dismantled until 1811, but in 1802 the federal government sold its shares of bank stock at a profit and got out of the banking business.

A Strong Executive.

The initial Republican attack on "big government" soon gave way to a more pragmatic approach. The third president was by temperament a vigorous leader who did what was needed to advance the national interest as he saw it. Although he had earlier condemned a powerful central government, after 1801, when he passed from opposition to power, he shifted ground. As president he decided that he could not be overburdened with constitutional scruples if he was to get things done. His critics charged him with hypocrisy, but we can see his inconsistencies as growth.

Though willing to reassure his opponents, Jefferson had no intention of allowing them to dominate the national government or tie his hands. As yet, the politicians had not raised to a lofty democratic principle the "spoils system" of replacing government personnel of the defeated party with members of the victorious one.

Jefferson believed that the measure of fitness to hold appointive office should be merit. But not all the Federalist officeholders, he felt, could be counted on to administer fairly the laws passed by a Republican Congress and approved by a Republican president. Some of them, moreover, were corrupt or incompetent. Besides, he could not deny that many Republicans deserved jobs as rewards for loyal service to the president and the party. Jefferson would have preferred to allow positions to become available by retirement or death. Unfortunately, he noted, the vacancies "by death are few; by resignation none." During Jefferson's first two years in office he replaced almost 200 Federalist officials with members of his own party. Federalist leaders, who believed that the new president had promised to leave all positions below cabinet rank alone, protested, but to no avail.

The Attack on the Judiciary.   A particularly thorny problem for the incoming president was the national judiciary. United States judges were virtually all Federalists, and these men were not impartial or disinterested. Because they were appointed for life, the president could not remove them. Matters were made particularly acute, from the Republican point of view, by the Judiciary Act of 1801, passed during the final days of the Adams administration. The act relieved Supreme Court justices of the burden of having to travel from place to place to hear lower court cases; it gave that job to sixteen new circuit judges. The law improved national legal enforcement, but it also gave the Federalist party even tighter control over the federal court system. On the evening of March 3, 1801, the very day before Jefferson's inauguration, Adams signed the commissions of the new circuit judges along with those of a flock of new federal marshals, attorneys, and justices of the peace. All the "midnight appointees" were Federalist party members, and it now looked as if the opposition party had locked up control of at least one branch of the government for decades to come, despite the Republican victory of 1800.

The Republicans were outraged by Adams's action. Jefferson noted that the Federalists had "retired to the judiciary . . . and from that battery all the works of Republicanism are to be beaten down and destroyed." To keep the new appointees from assuming office, Secretary of State James Madison refused to deliver their commissions. Soon after, the Republican Congress repealed the 1801 Judiciary Act and replaced it with the Judiciary Act of 1802.

What would the Federalist opposition now do?

At this point the commanding figure of John Marshall, chief justice of the Supreme Court, enters the picture. A Virginian of strong Federalist views, Marshall believed that the Supreme Court had the right to check the fickle and headstrong representatives of the people by declaring acts of Congress unconstitutional. Judicial review, as this process is called, had been talked about earlier, but it had never been conclusively established. Republicans considered it "unrepublican" and claimed that the power to judge constitutionality belonged to either the executive or the legislative branch or both. Early in 1803 Marshall saw a way to establish his precious principle by adjudicating the case of the midnight judges, but do so in a way the Republicans would find difficult to oppose.

His opportunity came in the case of *Marbury v. Madison*, involving a man nominated as justice of the peace for the District of Columbia by Adams and refused his commission by Madison. Marbury had sued to have the commission delivered by the secretary of state. Speaking for the Court, Marshall denied Marbury's claim

Chief Justice John Marshall's ruling in *Marbury v. Madison* helped entrench Federalist principles in American law. Marshall had fought at Valley Forge; his experience there, he wrote later, had confirmed him "in the habit of considering America as my country and Congress as my government."

by declaring the federal law under which he had sued to be unconstitutional. In effect, Madison and the administration had won on the question of Marbury's appointment, but the administration's victory depended on accepting the right of the Supreme Court to decide whether a law passed by Congress was in conflict with the Constitution and therefore void. An important claim held by many Federalists had been established: The Supreme Court, whose members were beyond easy reach of popular opinion, was to be the final judge of constitutionality.

The midnight judges case did not end Jefferson's attack on the existing Federalist-dominated court system. In 1803 the administration turned to impeachment to remove the most ardent Federalist partisans from the federal bench and replace them with Republicans. They initially selected two targets: John Pickering, a federal district judge in New Hampshire, and the notorious Judge Samuel Chase of the Supreme Court. Both men were outrageously partisan Federalists; Pickering, besides being an alcoholic, was probably insane. He was impeached by the House of Representatives and removed by the Senate with little difficulty. But Chase— however ill-tempered and partisan—convinced enough senators that he had not committed the "high crimes and misdemeanors" that were the specified constitutional grounds for removal from office. Chase's acquittal virtually ended the Republican assault on the Federalist judiciary.

International Politics and Republican Policy

More than any other single factor, the need to deal effectively with foreign powers pushed Jefferson and his successor toward Federalist principles of activist central government.

Jefferson Buys Louisiana.   In 1801 the United States was still entangled in the complicated issues that had grown out of the French Revolution. Britain and France were briefly at peace following the Treaty of Amiens in 1802. But then in May 1803 hostilities between the French, under Napoleon Bonaparte, and their enemies erupted once more and darkened the Atlantic world for another dozen years.

Once again America was sucked into the international whirlpool. The first warning came in 1800 when Spain and France signed the Treaty of San Ildefonso allowing France to resume sovereignty of Louisiana. News of the deal caused great alarm in the United States. Jefferson feared that France intended to reestablish an empire in North America. It was one thing for a weak Spain to occupy New Orleans. It was far worse for a powerful and arrogant France to control the mouth of the Mississippi and be in a position to choke off American commerce from the great river and its tributaries.

Even more than in the previous decade the United States had vital interests in the Mississippi Valley. Hundreds of thousands of Americans now lived beyond the Appalachians. Over 150 vessels regularly plied the great central river, carrying over 20,000 tons of freight annually. As Jefferson was painfully aware, whoever controlled the Mississippi wielded enormous power over the United States. If France gained control of the river and the region, he noted, "from that moment we must marry ourselves to the British fleet and nation."

When rumors of the French deal with Spain reached the United States, Jefferson dispatched Robert R. Livingston to Paris to buy both West Florida and New Orleans from Napoleon. From the outset Livingston encountered difficulties. Talleyrand, the French foreign minister, would not let him see Napoleon. The devious Frenchman was waiting to see what would happen in Santo Domingo, where a French army was struggling to put down the slave revolt led by General Toussaint L'Ouverture. Only if Toussaint were defeated could France protect Louisiana. The black liberator was eventually captured by trickery, but the Haitians refused to surrender, and a combination of black guerrillas and the yellow fever mosquito in the end defeated the French army.

News of the growing French disaster soon trickled back to Paris, making it clear to Napoleon that France must give up all thought of a new North American empire. Besides, it looked as if hostilities were about to break out again in Europe, and war with England, the First Consul realized, would expose Louisiana to British attack from Canada or military conquest by the Americans. The property, however, might be converted into cash, which could help finance French imperial ambitions in Europe. On April 11, 1803, Napoleon told his minister of finance, Francois de Barbé-Marbois: "I renounce Louisiana. It is not only New Orleans that I will cede, it is the whole colony without reservation. . . ."

Napoleon's new attitude completely altered the negotiating picture. Livingston, now joined by James Monroe, was confronted with a remarkable and totally unexpected proposition. Instead of only New Orleans, Barbé-Marbois asked, why not take all of the immense Louisiana territory? Another 20 million francs would pay for outstanding claims of American citizens against France dating back to the naval war of the 1790s. This offer exceeded the expectations and instructions of the American emissaries, but they seized it. On May 2, 1803, the American negotiators signed the treaty transferring Louisiana to the United States for $15 million.

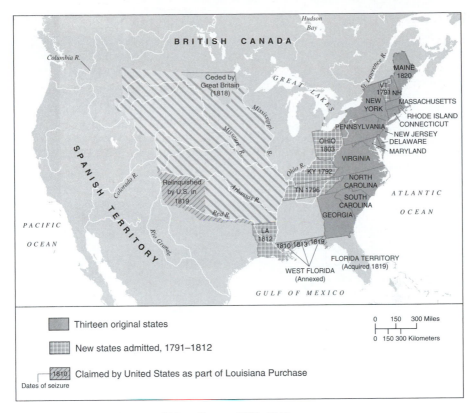

The Louisiana Purchase and New States, 1791–1812

The deal was a wonderful piece of good luck. But it left many questions unanswered and many problems unsolved. Spain had actually never formally surrendered the province to France and could be expected to cause trouble. There was also uncertainty about the territory's precise boundaries. When Livingston questioned Talleyrand on the colony's limits, the Frenchman had remarked cynically that the Americans had "made a noble bargain" for themselves and would no doubt "make the most of it." They would indeed; but in the meantime the unclear borders with Mexico and Canada were sure to complicate relations with Spain and Great Britain.

Most difficult of all, perhaps, were the constitutional problems raised. Fifty thousand French and Spanish descendants of the original European settlers, and French-speaking exiles from Acadia in Canada ("Cajuns"), inhabited the colony. Under the treaty they were all to become American citizens. Did the United States have the constitutional right to incorporate these people without their consent? And what about the fact that nowhere did the Constitution confer authority on anyone to buy new territory for the nation? Federalists denounced these assumptions of powers. Each side called the other hypocritical for reversing its usual position on implied powers under the Constitution.

Jefferson himself was troubled by constitutional scruples, and for a while hesitated. But it seemed certain that the Louisiana Territory would support millions of small land-holding farmers, and that prospect was dear to the president's heart.

The battle of the U.S.S. *Constitution* and H.M.S. *Guerrière* as depicted in a contemporary painting. Single encounters like this one were among the few naval victories the United States could claim in the War of 1812. They scarcely affected the outcome of the war, but they did help American morale.
(Michel Felice Corne, "Battle between the U.S.S. Constitution and H.M.S. Guerrière," 1812. Oil on canvas, 32.75 × 47.75 inches. New Haven Colony Historical Society)

Trying to get a bargain and preserve his principles at the same time, Jefferson proposed that Congress should simultaneously confirm the treaty and adopt a constitutional amendment expressly authorizing such territorial acquisitions. But Napoleon would not wait for the president to overcome his philosophical misgivings. Warned that the First Consul was becoming restless, Jefferson abandoned the idea of a constitutional amendment and pushed the treaty through the Senate. On December 20, 1803, in a simple ceremony at New Orleans, the French flag was lowered and the Stars and Stripes raised in its place. Louisiana, a region almost equal in extent to the original United States under the 1783 peace treaty with Britain, was now American.

The Lewis and Clark Expedition.   Even before Napoleon had made his startling offer, Jefferson had engaged his private secretary, Meriwether Lewis, and a former soldier, William Clark, to explore the vast Louisiana region. His motives were both political and commercial. Before the purchase, he had hoped the exploration would establish an American claim to the region. He also believed that it might expedite his plan to gather the eastern Indian tribes into reservations where they could be induced to abandon their "savage" ways and settle down as "civilized" farmers. In his view this required drawing to regions further west the white traders who encouraged the Indians' nomadic ways. Lewis and Clark, accordingly, were charged with investigating the fur resources of the new region and with establishing commercial relations with the western tribes. News of the Louisiana Purchase added to these goals an intense curiosity about what exactly the United

States had bought for $15 million. The expedition, the president directed, must make careful observations of the flora, animal life, minerals, soils, and geography of the regions they crossed.

The Lewis and Clark party left St. Louis in the spring of 1804. After wintering in the Dakotas, they set off for the Pacific the following April with thirty-seven men and a woman, Sacajawea, a Shoshone captive of the Dakota tribes, who was given her freedom in exchange for guiding the expedition across the Rockies. Sacajawea took them as far as the Lemhi Pass on the Continental Divide, where they were met by Shoshone tribesmen. Grateful for the return of their kinswoman, the Indians provided the expedition with horses and guides for the next stage of the journey, over the remaining ranges of the Rockies to the valley of the Clearwater River. By mid-November, after traversing the rapids of the Clearwater and the Columbia, the weary explorers arrived at the shores of the Pacific where they spent the winter. When they returned to St. Louis in September 1806, they were received with wild enthusiasm. At the cost of only a single life and some $50,000, they had established relations with several important Indian nations; discovered usable passes through the Rockies; and provided important botanical, zoological, geological, and anthropological data about a vast stretch of western North America. Their expedition helped to open the trans-Mississippi region and was soon followed by others that laid the groundwork for the wave of settlement that would carry millions of Americans across the continent.

The Wilkinson–Burr Conspiracy.

Acquisition of Louisiana had finally ended one source of western troubles: farmers' difficulty in sending their goods to market through New Orleans. But the West was still not sure that it could entrust its future to the government in Washington. Many easterners, the people of the trans-Appalachian region knew, were suspicious of growing western power and numbers. In Massachusetts, for example, extreme Federalists, members of the so-called Essex Junto, were talking of detaching New England, New York, and New Jersey from the Union and forming a new confederation of states that would insulate the commercial Northeast from the power of the allied agricultural South and West. Western resentments and suspicions offered opportunities for ambitious and unscrupulous men to carve careers for themselves as champions of the trans-Appalachian region.

Two of the most dangerous of these adventurers were General James Wilkinson, governor of the Louisiana Territory, and Vice President Aaron Burr of New York. Though a trusted lieutenant of every American president from Washington through Madison, Wilkinson was in the pay of the Spanish government as Agent Number 13. Burr, a far more talented man, though descended from a long line of Puritan ministers, was a compulsive womanizer, a reckless pleasure seeker, and a cynic, driven by ambition and the desire to win fame and glory. He might still have attained the presidency if he had not made a fatal misstep. In 1804, angered by Hamilton's role in helping to defeat him when he ran for governor of New York, Burr challenged the former treasury secretary to a duel. The two men met on the Hudson Palisades opposite New York. Hamilton held his fire; Burr shot to kill. Mortally wounded, Hamilton was carried back to New York where he died the next day. People called Burr's action murder. From that point on, a conventional course to power was closed to Burr, and he turned to intrigue and conspiracy to achieve his ends.

Though the exact truth is still in dispute, it appears that he and Wilkinson sought British and Spanish support for a scheme to detach the West from the United States, combine it with parts of Spanish Mexico, and set up an independent nation with themselves as rulers. To raise money Burr connived with the British minister in Washington, who seemed interested in any plan that promised to diminish American strength. Deciding that his former arrangements with Spain were more profitable, Wilkinson betrayed Burr. Posing as an American patriot anxious to defend his country's interests, he told Jefferson of Burr's scheme. The administration indicted Burr. Tried before Chief Justice Marshall, he was acquitted of treason but, rather than face various state charges against him, fled to Europe.

Neutral Rights Once More.

Impressment, blockades, neutral rights, contraband, and Indian incitements continued to disturb America's relations with the two leading European powers after 1803. The country's foreign involvements during 1803–1812 seemed like a replay of 1793–1800 with the volume turned up.

Soon after France and England resumed their interminable war in 1803, the British reactivated their impressment policy. Before long, British ships were hovering off East Coast ports, ready to swoop down on American vessels and remove seamen from their decks for the Royal Navy. In July 1805, in the Essex decision, a British admiralty court declared illegal the American practice of carrying French West Indian produce to American ports and then shipping it to France. These commodities were not neutral goods, the court said, they were really French, and under the Rule of 1756 could be confiscated like other enemy goods if intercepted by the British navy.

Congress retaliated in April 1806 by passing the Nonimportation Act. Designed to force the British into a more acceptable response, this measure forbade the importation of many goods that Americans normally bought from Britain but could, if necessary, produce at home. Jefferson held the law in abeyance while British and American negotiators tried to hammer out an accommodation. These talks in fact produced an agreement but, embarrassed by how little it conceded to the United States, Jefferson refused to submit it to the Senate for confirmation.

Meanwhile, American commerce and pride continued to suffer under a barrage of measures and countermeasures by Napoleon and his chief European adversary. In May 1806 Britain announced a blockade of the European continent from the Elbe River in Germany to the port of Brest in France. Napoleon retaliated with the Berlin Decree, placing Britain under blockade and forbidding all British commerce with France. The British then threatened to confiscate all ships engaged in French coastal trade or entering those European continental ports still not off limits unless they paid British duties and secured British clearance. Napoleon replied with the Milan Decree, which declared that all vessels that obeyed his enemy's new rulings would be subject to French seizure.

The British–French war of regulations seemed designed to produce maximum irritation in America. If American merchants bowed to the British, they would offend the French, and vice versa. To make matters worse, the regulations contained large loopholes in both their provisions and their enforcement. These continued to entice Americans into the lucrative trade with Europe and the West Indies, but made it hazardous and uncertain.

The *Chesapeake–Leopard* Affair.

While the fusillade of French–British decrees and Orders in Council flew through the air, the impressment issue became acute. Sir George Berkeley, British naval commander at Halifax, Nova Scotia, blamed American officials for encouraging the desertion of British seamen, and resolved to stop the practice. He was especially irked by the situation in the Chesapeake Bay region, where many deserters from the Royal Navy had taken refuge and a number had enlisted in the American navy. One of these deserters, Jenkin Ratford, now a sailor on the U.S.S. *Chesapeake,* was reported to be swaggering through Norfolk insulting British officers on leave.

On June 1, 1807, Berkeley directed his subordinates to stop the *Chesapeake,* if they should encounter it beyond American territorial waters, and search it for deserters. Soon after, H.M.S. *Leopard* overtook the American frigate as it left for the Mediterranean on a shakedown cruise. The American captain, Commodore James Barron, suspecting nothing—for the British had never attempted to impress from an American naval vessel before—allowed a British officer to come aboard. He handed Barron a demand that the deserters be surrendered. When Barron refused, the *Leopard* fired three broadsides into the American ship, killing three Americans and wounding eighteen. Not yet fully outfitted for combat, the *Chesapeake* was able to fire back only a single token shot before it surrendered. A British search party then boarded the vessel, lined up its crew, and removed Ratford and three other deserters. Ratford was later hanged.

Never before had the British so blatantly violated American sovereignty. Indignation swept the country, and protesters organized mass meetings in dozens of cities to condemn British high-handedness. The British consul in New York had to be given police protection and a mob attacked and almost demolished a British vessel at its pier in the harbor. Many Americans expected war; many demanded it.

The Embargo.

Jefferson could easily have brought a united nation into war at this point, but instead, after issuing a proclamation closing American waters to the Royal Navy, he sent an emissary to negotiate the impressment issue with the British. Unfortunately, the American representative accomplished little. Not until 1811 did the British make acceptable reparation for the *Chesapeake–Leopard* affair. Meanwhile, the clamor in America abated and war enthusiasm cooled.

Jefferson had mixed motives for taking a moderate course in the *Chesapeake* affair. The president was conscious of American military weakness. He and his fellow Republicans were themselves responsible for this condition. Ever since the undeclared naval war with France in 1798–1800—which many Republicans believed a pro-British, Federalist venture—they had denounced standing armies and a strong navy as "dangerous to liberty" and conducive to "the spirit which leads to war." Militarism, they said, went along with Federalist faith in centralized political power. Jefferson was not indifferent to American defense, but he thought a citizen militia and small, lightly armed coastal vessels using oars and sails were sufficient. This would spare the country a large and expensive military establishment.

Jefferson also believed the United States had a better weapon against British and French high-handedness than an army and navy. Americans had wielded economic weapons effectively against Britain during the great imperial crisis before independence, and now, in December 1807, he activated the first Nonimportation Act and soon after asked Congress to place an embargo on all exports from the United States. Congress responded with the 1807 Embargo Act, which forbade American vessels to sail to foreign ports without special permission and forbade foreign vessels to carry off American goods. American ships could continue to engage in the coastal trade between domestic ports, but the owners of such vessels had to post bonds twice the value of the ships and their cargoes to guarantee that they would not sail off to foreign ports once at sea. The law did not explicitly prohibit imports in foreign ships; but if foreign ship owners could not carry American cargo on their return trips, they had little incentive to trade with the United States. The law also restricted overland trade to British Canada. In effect, Congress had sealed off the country from foreign commerce on the theory that Europe needed America more than America needed Europe.

Theory was one thing; reality was another. The law was impossible to enforce. Some state governors took advantage of its loopholes to peddle exemptions to merchants for cash or political support. Merchants, on their own, found ways to get around the law. Many risked the loss of their bond by directing their ships to Europe or the Caribbean once out of sight of land. Others conducted illegal commerce with Canada across the Great Lakes. Defiance was greatest in New England, where Jefferson was denounced as a tyrant executing an unconstitutional law. Equally opposed, however, were the merchants of New York and Philadelphia.

For a while, wholesale evasion made the law tolerable. But the Giles Enforcement Act of 1809 closed the loopholes, and foreign trade virtually ceased. Farmers saw the prices of their export crops plunge dramatically. But more seriously hurt were the traders of the port towns and all who depended on them. New York in 1809, one contemporary reported, "looked like a town ravaged by pestilence." The city's waterfront streets were deserted, its ships dismantled, and its counting houses closed and boarded up. Boston and seaboard New England were hardest hit of all, with thousands of seamen, dock laborers, sail-makers, and rope-makers idle.

And to top it all, the law failed to achieve its ends. It hurt some British manufacturers, but English wage earners, Caribbean planters, and slaves suffered the most, and none of these groups carried sufficient political weight in Parliament. Even when the embargo finally began to pinch important British commercial interests, sheer stubbornness kept the British government from yielding to American pressure.

For a year and a half the administration tried to enforce its unpopular policy, using militia and regulars to halt the overland trade with Canada and the navy to stop violations by sea. Driven by frustration, the president, a great defender of liberty while in the opposition, proposed to declare whole communities in rebellion and subject to prosecution for treason. At one point he told a Republican congressman that in times of emergency "the universal recourse is a dictator."

Popular opposition to the infamous embargo soon reached a crescendo. In the shipping states, even Republicans pleaded that the policy be abandoned. Faced by this overwhelming pressure and the obvious failure of its policy to alter British and French behavior, the administration finally yielded. In March 1809, as one of his last official acts, Jefferson signed the Nonintercourse Act, repealing the embargo and reopening foreign trade except with Britain and France, but allowing the president to restore trade with either country, or both, if they ceased violating American rights.

Madison Takes the Helm.

Soon after, Jefferson left Washington for Monticello, never again to serve in high political office. He was not proud of his presidency, but he underestimated it. He had successfully guided the United States through a major transition from the rule of one party to the rule of another; had doubled the physical size of the country; and had brought a new, more democratic tone to the nation's political culture. These were accomplishments that few presidents would match.

His successor, James Madison, was a man in the Jeffersonian mold. Co-founder of the Republican party, Jefferson's secretary of state, and one of the chief architects of the Constitution, Madison had earned the right to be his party's choice. He went on to defeat Federalist Charles Cotesworth Pinckney in the 1808 election.

Historians have generally considered Madison's presidency a failure. Although a profound student of government, an effective legislative leader, and a charming conversationalist, he lacked executive ability. In peace and war he would prove irresolute; and when he did bring himself to act, he would often blunder.

Madison's first misstep came in the second month of his presidency, when he made arrangements with David M. Erskine, the British minister in Washington, to suspend the Nonintercourse Act in exchange for British withdrawal of the 1807 Orders in Council. Unfortunately, Erskine had exceeded his instructions, and the British foreign secretary in London repudiated the agreement when he heard of it. Madison, now believed by many to be the dupe of the British, felt compelled to restore the prohibition on British–American trade.

The Nonintercourse Act having put too great an economic strain on the country, Congress in 1810 replaced it with Macon's Bill Number Two. This was a curious measure. The United States, it stated, would immediately reopen commerce with both Britain and France. If either country, however, should cease to violate American commercial rights, the president could then reimpose trade prohibitions on the other, after a three-month wait to give the slower-acting power a chance to rescind its trade restrictions. In effect, as an inducement to cease attacks on American trade, the United States promised to support against its enemy the first nation to act.

The wily Bonaparte quickly saw that he might trap America into becoming his unwitting ally against England. The Duc de Cadore, the French foreign minister, informed the American minister in Paris that the Berlin and Milan decrees had been revoked. It was a deception. In fact, on the very day Cadore told the American ambassador of the supposed French change of heart, Napoleon signed the Decree of Trianon, which ordered the confiscation and sale of all American vessels that had called at French ports after May 20, 1809. The president, however, swallowed the bait. On November 2 he announced that trade restrictions against Great Britain would be reimposed early in 1811. Without surrendering a thing, Napoleon had gotten the United States to strike a blow against France's archenemy.

Further Western Troubles.

Anglo-American tensions were further aggravated by events in the West. Though the British had finally removed their troops from American territory, western settlers and their spokesmen remained convinced that England, though actually innocent of the charge, was stirring up troubles with the Indians. The continued presence of British-Canadian fur traders in the Northwest, as allowed under the Jay Treaty, created further antagonisms and suspicion of British intrigue.

Actually, Americans themselves were responsible for the Indian troubles. At the behest of land speculators, frontier officials, many of them Jefferson's appointees, had for years taken over vast tracts of land from the native Americans, giving them little in return. In 1802 Governor William Henry Harrison of the Indiana Territory, using the threat of military force, had compelled the Kickapoo, Wea, and Delaware tribes to cede to the United States several million acres in what is now southern Indiana. The Treaty of Vincennes became the evil precedent for a rash of coerced agreements that compelled the northwestern and southwestern tribes to surrender millions of acres of choice lands for a few thousand dollars and a few baubles.

Ignoring Harrison's provocative actions, by 1810–1811 settlers throughout the West were certain that "British gold" was being used to encourage Indian militancy. Many of the fears and complaints centered on the activities of the Shawnee chief Tecumseh and his brother, "the Prophet," a chieftain believed to possess supernatural powers. These two remarkable men recognized that Harrison's success at land grabbing depended to a large extent on the disunity of the Indian tribes. To defeat Harrison and his kind, they proposed creating a tribal confederation that would present a united front to white officials. But beyond this, reviving the old dream of Pontiac, Tecumseh told his people that the whites must be driven "back whence they came, upon a trail of blood. . . ." Tecumseh at first urged his followers to exercise restraint as long as Harrison did not try to take possession of the Indian lands the whites had inveigled. Then, when Harrison indicated that he intended to proceed with the takeover, Tecumseh exhorted all-out war against the American settlers. "Burn their dwellings," he urged a meeting of Creeks, Cherokees, and Choctaws. "Destroy their stock. The red people own the country. . . . War now. War forever. War upon the living. War upon the dead; dig up their corpses from the grave; our country must give no rest to the white man's bones."

In September 1811 Harrison and a thousand troops set out to suppress the Indian rebellion. The small army reached Prophetstown and camped nearby. Just before daylight on November 7 the Indians attacked while the Americans still slept. Harrison's seasoned troops held, however, and when the American cavalry charged the Indians broke and fled.

Though the Battle of Tippecanoe would help make Harrison's reputation as successful Indian fighter, it was actually a kind of defeat. The vanquished Indian rebels abandoned their capital and scattered throughout the West. Wherever they went, they carried their pan-Indian vision and their hatred of the white man. Before long the whole West, north as well as South, was in flames.

Besides the largely unfounded claims of Indian agitation, Westerners had other grievances against the British. British policies, it was said, had cut off the European market for western grain and created large unsold surpluses. Prices had dropped, causing distress to many western farmers. Though the American embargo had only made matters worse, Westerners hoped it would eventually force Britain to back down, and western representatives in Congress were among the law's staunchest supporters.

Western attitudes would have been an important element in the decision to finally go to war against Britain in any case. But western views were given added weight by the skillful maneuvering of the War Hawks, some forty western and southern representatives elected to the Twelfth Congress that met in 1811. Led by Henry Clay, the group included such notable men as John C. Calhoun, William

Lowndes, and Langdon Cheves of South Carolina; Felix Grundy of Tennessee; Richard M. Johnson of Kentucky; and Peter Porter of western New York. Marked off from other members of the Twelfth Congress by their aggressive nationalism and their resolve to shake the nation loose from subservience to Great Britain come what may, the War Hawks succeeded in electing Clay speaker of the House and packing the important foreign relations and naval committees with their members. Thereafter every move to condemn Britain or to appropriate money for the army and navy received their enthusiastic support.

Congress Votes for War.   No single dramatic event finally pushed the country into war. All through 1811 relations with Britain deteriorated. The British government did not take kindly to Madison's proclamation reimposing the embargo on Anglo-American trade. British cruisers were soon gathering in increasing numbers off the Atlantic coast, stopping more American vessels than ever and removing suspected British deserters in droves. Once more, impressment set off a major naval incident. In May Commodore John Rodgers, commanding the frigate *President*, stumbled on the British corvette *Little Belt* off Virginia. Rodgers chased the British vessel, overtook it, and attacked, inflicting severe damage. The *President* did not sink the smaller British ship, but most Americans felt satisfied that the disgrace of the *Chesapeake* defeat had finally been avenged.

Matters now moved swiftly to a head. In April 1812 Congress gave President Madison power to call up the state militias for six months' service. On the same day British Foreign Secretary Lord Castlereagh rejected the American demand that the 1807 Orders in Council be withdrawn. The British economy was now finally beginning to feel the bite of the embargo, and continued pressure might have forced England to back down had a madman not shot Prime Minister Spencer Perceval, throwing the London government into turmoil. By the time it began to function again, Castlereagh was ready to suspend the Orders in Council. But news of his announcement arrived too late in America to influence events. On June 18, Congress declared war on England.

Who Wanted War?   The declaration of war against Britain was not unanimous. Of 128 representatives in the House voting, 49 voted no. In the Senate 13 out of 32 members refused to support the war declaration. Historians have tried to determine the motives for war by analyzing the vote, but the picture remains murky. Representatives of coastal New England clearly opposed war, but those from interior New England favored it. New York, too, opposed the war, but Pennsylvania, including the port of Philadelphia, voted to fight. The South, especially the Carolinas and Georgia, was almost solidly in support of the war, as was the West beyond the Appalachians.

More important perhaps than whether a congressman lived in the North, the South, or the West was whether his constituents exported farm products (in which case he tended to support the war declaration) or engaged in ocean commerce (in which case he probably voted against it). In other words, pocketbook considerations seem to have been more important than geography in determining the way individual representatives voted. Sectional factors in this view seem significant mostly because many westerners and southerners were certain that their prosperity depended on teaching the British that they must not interfere with America's export trade, whereas many New Englanders feared that war with Great Britain would lead to the complete destruction of American commerce by the powerful British navy.

Perhaps the most workable analysis of the war vote, however, connects it to politics and party. Generally speaking, the Federalists and John Randolph's dissenting Quid Republicans voted against the war; administration Republicans, including, of course, the War Hawks, favored it. Professor Bradford Perkins estimates that fully 90 percent "of the real, available Republican membership [of the House of Representatives] backed the bill" to declare war. Despite misgivings, the strong anti-British stand of the party ever since the 1790s, and particularly since Jefferson's embargo, committed the Republicans to taking this step.

If we look behind the vote in Congress, we can identify something more fundamental than economic interest and party, however. The War of 1812 was the result of an upsurge of nationalism among Americans. By 1812 many citizens were determined to avenge the humiliations the United States had suffered at British hands for almost a generation. Though their country had won its formal independence in 1783, it still seemed to be under Britain's thumb. Impressment, Orders in Council, incitement of Indians, confiscation of American ships—whether real or imagined—all contributed to the anger and hurt pride these Americans felt. Many Federalists and New Englanders might have preferred to ignore the incidents, believing it better to suffer these ills for the sake of profit and safety. Some westerners, as John Randolph charged, might have supported the war out of lust for British Canada to add to western land and wealth. But for many Americans, the prospect of continued submission to haughty Britain seemed ample reason for military resistance.

The War of 1812

The war was bungled. Owing in part to Republican hostility to peacetime armies, American military and naval forces were feeble. Congress had provided for a 35,000-man regular army in January 1812, but at the beginning of June it consisted of only 6,700 officers and men. Worse, the troops were not stationed close to Canada, the most accessible part of British territory, but were scattered throughout the country. Although he was authorized to bring 100,000 militia into federal service, the president was effectively deprived of the best-trained state troops by New England's virtual neutrality during the war. Facing the motley American army would be an uncertain number of equally nondescript Canadian militia plus 7,000 British and Canadian regulars. But behind them—once Napoleon surrendered in Europe—were thousands of tough veterans of the Duke of Wellington's Spanish campaign against the French.

The Americans were even worse off on the high seas. In June 1812 the American navy consisted of only seven seaworthy frigates and over one hundred almost worthless gunboats. By contrast, Britain had over two hundred frigates and ships of the line, most with twice the firepower of the largest American vessels. Americans would add ships to their navy during the war and would send out scores of privateers against British ocean commerce, yet the American naval effort would resemble a scrappy minnow nipping at a shark's tail.

In financial matters, too, the United States was handicapped. In 1811 Congress had defeated by a close vote an attempt to recharter the Bank of the United States. The bank, as Hamilton had predicted, had helped the government manage its financial operations and had provided businessmen with much-needed credit and capital. Although hostile at first, Albert Gallatin and other Republicans eventually came to favor it. But the bank had not converted all its opponents, and it had made new enemies among some business groups. These forces had defeated renewal. Now, without a central bank to make loans to meet the government's extraordinary wartime needs, the treasury found itself in difficulties. The situation was made worse by New England's reluctance to lend to the treasury from its large reserves of available capital.

The president also faced the problem of poor communications within the country. Contact with the interior, especially across the mountains, was slow and difficult. Roads were few throughout the nation; those crossing the Appalachians were no more than Indian trails. The Great Lakes were potentially useful, but nowhere on American territory were they connected by water to the country's major population centers. Bad communications imposed serious handicaps on military commanders, who were forced to move supplies and men along crude trails hacked out of the forest.

The Hartford Convention.   Almost the whole area east of the Hudson River sat out the war. Many New Englanders regarded Great Britain as the world's last hope against the tyrant Napoleon, and they condemned Madison for having made the United States France's ally. In 1814, after seeing their commerce virtually swept off the seas by the British navy, antiwar Yankees forced the calling of a convention at Hartford, Connecticut. There they planned to discuss how to deal with the war and to consider whether the discontented states should secede from the Union. Fortunately, the extremists at Hartford were outmaneuvered by the moderates, and the convention took no action beyond endorsing the right of states to nullify federal acts and proposing constitutional amendments limiting the power of the president and Congress over foreign relations. New England disaffection stopped short of outright disloyalty, yet the hostility to the war in the Northeast would be a dead weight around Madison's neck.

The Early Years of the War.   After we acknowledge all of these difficulties, however, Madison still must bear much of the blame for the failures of the American war effort. As commander in chief, he appointed the generals, and his initial choices were abysmal. Major General William Hull was sent to attack the British in Upper Canada (Ontario), but was forced to surrender to the British near Detroit. General Harrison, ordered to retake Detroit, instead gave up much of the Northwest to the British and their Indian allies. An American invasion of the Niagara peninsula under Generals Stephen Van Rensselaer and Alexander Smyth was turned into a tragic farce when the New York militia, ordered to cross into Canada to fight the enemy, refused on the grounds that they had no obligation to fight outside their home state, and stood idly by watching the U.S. regulars across the Niagara River being slaughtered by British troops. Only the famous victories of the frigates *Constitution* and *United States* in single-ship combat with the *Guerrière* and *Macedonian* kept up American spirits in the first year of war.

Despite the disasters in the field, Madison was reelected for a second term in 1812 over De Witt Clinton of New York, the Federalist candidate. The president's 128 electoral votes represented the prowar sections, largely in the South and West; Clinton's 89 represented the antiwar regions of New England, with New York, New Jersey, and part of Maryland thrown in.

The second year of the war went only a little better than the first. In January 1813 Harrison's lieutenants were defeated in a series of battles south of the Great Lakes. Because the British seemed likely to be successful so long as they could move freely on Lake Erie, the government ordered Captain Oliver Hazard Perry to construct a small navy on the south shore of the lake. On September 1 Perry's fleet met a somewhat smaller flotilla under Captain Robert Barclay. In a fierce exchange Perry sank or captured the entire British force. "We have met the enemy and they are ours," read Perry's succinct dispatch to Harrison.

With Lake Erie under American control, Harrison moved against the British in Upper Canada. In the Battle of the Thames in early October he and his Kentucky militia encountered a small force of British regulars, Canadian militia, and some 1,500 Indians, these last led by the notorious Tecumseh. The shock of the first volley scattered the British and Canadians. The Indians held out longer, but they, too, soon turned and ran. Tecumseh was presumed dead, though his body was never found. This defeat led to the collapse of the Shawnee chief's confederation and the desertion of many tribes from the British cause.

The year 1813 also saw the outbreak of Indian troubles in the Southwest. The Creek War brought on the grim ambushes, scalpings, and indiscriminate murder of women and children often perpetrated by both sides in Indian–white wars. In August a Creek force of 1,000 slaughtered 250 white settlers jammed for safety into Fort Mims in southern Alabama. Later that year the Tennessee militia avenged the deed by killing 186 Indians near Jacksonville, Alabama.

The Indian fighting marked the rise to prominence of Andrew Jackson, a Tennessee planter-politician who commanded the government's forces as major general of the state militia. Early in 1814 Jackson marched on the Creeks in what is now Alabama. At Horseshoe Bend he attacked and massacred 800. The surviving Creeks were forced to sign a peace treaty at Fort Jackson surrendering a giant slice of territory in southern Georgia and central Alabama. For his services Jackson was made a major general in the regular army.

The Last Campaigns.   Meanwhile, in Europe Napoleon Bonaparte had finally been defeated and in April 1814 was sent into exile on the Mediterranean island of Elba. Bonaparte's surrender freed thousands of seasoned British troops for the American war, and in late summer 1814, some 11,000 of these veterans under General George Prevost set out from Canada headed for New York City. But all hopes of cutting the United States in two along the old Champlain-Hudson route ended when American gunboats under Captain Thomas McDonough defeated an English fleet at Plattsburgh on Lake Champlain. With the Americans in control of the lake, Prevost hurriedly retreated, leaving behind a mountain of supplies and hundreds of deserters.

The second prong of the planned British knockout campaign, aimed at Chesapeake Bay, proved more successful. In June the British navy transported 4,000 troops directly from France to the Patuxent River. From there they advanced on Washington, the nation's capital, and at Bladensburg, Maryland, defeated a hastily gathered force of militia, sailors, and a few regulars sent to stop them. The British veterans then marched into Washington unopposed. Congress and the president had already fled the city, leaving behind the spirited first lady, Dolley Madison, to save Gilbert Stuart's portrait of the city's namesake. The British burned the Capitol, the presidential mansion, and almost all the city's public buildings, sparing only the Patent Office.

The redcoats now turned north to Baltimore, the country's third-largest city. Here they were checked. Fort McHenry and the defense fortifications quickly thrown up were manned by thousands of militia, sailors, and some regulars. The British fleet bombarded the fort for two days, but it held out. To commemorate the heroic defense, the lawyer Francis Scott Key wrote a poem, the "Star-Spangled Banner," and set it to the tune of an old British drinking song. It is appropriate that the only serious literary work evoked by this mismanaged war is associated with befuddlement.

As the third prong of the British knockout campaign, in late November a British army of 7,500 under Sir Edward Pakenham landed at Lake Borgne, forty miles from New Orleans. Andrew Jackson and his troops sped south and engaged the enemy in skirmishes east of the city, slowing the British advance. On New Year's Day Jackson's skilled artillerymen severely punished the British, compelling Pakenham to wait for reinforcements.

On January 8, 1815, the British resumed their advance against Jackson's force of U.S. regulars, Kentucky and Tennessee riflemen, and New Orleans and Louisiana militiamen composed of Bayou pirates, free blacks, and young blue-bloods from the city. In a dense morning fog the British regulars advanced on the Americans lined up behind a low wall. The fog lifted before the red-clad troops had gone very far and at 500 yards the American artillery opened fire with devastating effect. When the remaining redcoats reached rifle range, Jackson ordered his men to blaze away with small arms.

The combination of rifle and artillery fire was too much for the British. In less than an hour one third of their force was cut down, another third was milling about in confusion, and three of the highest-ranking British officers, including Pakenham, were dead. Facing reality, General John Lambert ordered retreat. On January 27 the surviving British troops sailed for home.

The Peace of Ghent.   The Battle of New Orleans would never have taken place if transatlantic communications had been swifter in these years. On December 24 British and American negotiators had concluded a peace at Ghent in what is now Belgium. The peace treaty, signed before Jackson's stunning victory, was an ambiguous and tentative document that brought the United States few gains. It said nothing about impressment, ignored the neutral rights and Indian issues that had bedeviled British–American relations for years, and left the Canadian–American boundary where it had been before the war. None of the goals that had prompted Americans to action were realized by the treaty.

It did not satisfy the British either. For them the war had begun as a defensive struggle, but their early military successes had led the English leaders to hope for territorial concessions from the Americans and perhaps an Indian buffer state between the United States and Canada. War weariness and fear that fighting might shortly resume in Europe led the British to abandon these goals at Ghent.

Little was accomplished by the treaty, then, except for the restoration of peace. It provided for a commission to settle the disputed boundary with Canada in the far northeast and mentioned future settlement of differences over navigation of the Great Lakes and the Newfoundland fisheries. In 1817, to implement the treaty at

Ghent, Britain and the United States signed the Rush–Bagot Agreement by which both nations accepted almost total disarmament along the Canadian–American border. Applied at first solely to the Great Lakes region, it eventually converted the whole of the Canadian–American boundary into the longest unarmed frontier in the world.

Yet the fact remains that the document ending the war was less significant than the victory at New Orleans. Weeks after the Ghent negotiations had concluded, the British government ordered reinforcements to Pakenham—a move that suggests that if their army had defeated Jackson, they would have refused to confirm the treaty. The British had never formally recognized the legality of the Louisiana Purchase, and it is possible that if their troops had captured New Orleans, they would have tried to carve out a sphere of influence along the lower Mississippi. Jackson's triumph ended the possibility of a new British Empire in North America at the expense of the United States.

More important, however, the victory at New Orleans left Americans with a sense that they had defeated British tyranny a second time. It created a new national hero in the person of testy, rough-hewn Andy Jackson, and a proud new national mythology. Unspoiled, sturdy, and independent, American frontiersmen, so the myth went, had taken on Europe's best and defeated them decisively. Jackson's triumph produced a surge of patriotism that all but obliterated the disunity that had afflicted the country at the beginning of the war. However it had begun, by its glorious ending the war reaffirmed American self-respect and pride. "The war," Albert Gallatin would write a colleague, "has renewed and reinstated the national feelings and character which the Revolution had given, and which were daily lessened. The people have now more general objects of attachment. . . . They are more American; they feel and act more as a nation."

Gallatin's view is confirmed by the facts. President Madison's 1815 message to Congress expressed the new spirit that had captured the nation: Even the party of states' rights must now devote its energies to forging closer national bonds and stronger national institutions. Republicans had learned their lesson. The country had been severely handicapped by poor communications and the absence of a central bank. Perhaps Hamilton and his friends had been right after all. Why not give their ideas a try?

Ironically, although the war made the Republicans into nationalists, it destroyed the party that formerly had had a virtual copyright of the nationalist label. Had the war ended on a sour note, the Federalists might have come out of it with enhanced prestige. As it was, New Orleans made the party of Washington and Hamilton seem unpatriotic and even treasonous. After 1815 the Federalists would never again be a serious threat to the Republicans on the national level.

Conclusions

Between the 1800 presidential campaign and James Madison's seventh annual message to Congress, American political attitudes had taken a 180-degree turn. Jefferson's election had been a repudiation of Federalist excesses and a mandate for the party that represented local as opposed to national power. The public undoubtedly exaggerated Jefferson's differences from his opponents. Nevertheless, the Republican victory of 1800 represented an endorsement of a less activist national government and a repudiation of the strong centralizing bent of the Federalists.

The American people could not have foreseen that they and their leaders would do an about-face. Events would overtake everyone's theories. In the decade and a half that followed Jefferson's inauguration, the growing confrontation with France and England invoked an ever more active and effective central authority. The clash also created a new sense of national priorities, especially among southerners and westerners, whose agricultural interests, as opposed to the commercial interests of New Englanders, did not conflict with a strong stand against the country's foreign enemies. The war itself made clear to many former opponents of Federalist "follies" that to function, the country must accept much that Hamilton and his allies had proposed. Finally, with the splendid climax at New Orleans, the country experienced a new sense of unity and a self-confidence that would last until immense new issues once again reactivated the divisive forces of localism.

The Battle of New Orleans and the Treaty of Ghent closed one important chapter of American history. For fifty years the United States had been embroiled in Europe's remote affairs. Now, with Napoleon gone, Europe settled down to a long period of relative international calm. For almost a century the United States would be spared the clash of empires that had unsettled its affairs for so long. And with peace, Americans could go about the business of exploiting their bounteous human and natural resources and converting them into tangible wealth.

ONLINE RESOURCES

"Pro-Slavery Petitions in Virginia" *http://www.pbs.org/wgbh/aia/part2/2h65.html*

"Banneker's Letter to Jefferson" *http://www.pbs.org/wgbh/aia/part2/2h71.html* View these two Web sites to see divergent views of slavery—one based on property rights and citizenship and one on the desire for racial equality and freedom.

"Thomas Jefferson on Politics and Government" *http://etext.virginia.edu/jefferson/quotations* Containing over 2,700 quotes from Thomas Jefferson, this site contains, in his own words, Jefferson's thoughts on the theory and structure of Republican government, citizens' rights, and judicial review. Also, this site offers numerous links to other resources that contain additional writings of Jefferson.

"The Louisiana Purchase Treaty, April 30, 1803" *http://www.yale.edu/lawweb/avalon/diplomacy/france/louis1.htm* Read the full text of this historic treaty that greatly enlarged the nation and helped to fulfill the Republican hopes for westward expansion of territory.

"Lewis and Clark: The Journey of the Corps of Discovery" *http://www.pbs.org/lewisandclark* Trace the discoveries of Lewis and Clark in what was the Jeffersonian West through this Web site. Timelines, maps, academics' assessments of their journey, and a question-and-answer section put Lewis and Clark's important trek in historical perspective. The site also contains portions of Lewis and Clark diaries that are searchable online.

9

The American Economic Miracle

What Made It Possible?

1793	Eli Whitney invents the cotton gin
1794	The Philadelphia–Lancaster Turnpike opens; West Point established
1803	The Louisiana Purchase
1807	Robert Fulton's steamboat *Clermont* makes a round trip between Albany and New York
1811	The federal government begins work on the National Road at Cumberland, Maryland; Fulton-Livingston interests awarded an exclusive charter from the Louisiana territorial legislature to operate steamboats on the Mississippi
1815	Entrepreneur Francis Cabot Lowell's Boston Manufacturing Company produces cotton cloth on a new power loom
1816	The Second Bank of the United States chartered
1817	New York's legislature approves funds for the Erie Canal
1818	The National Road reaches the Ohio River
1819	Financial panic and economic depression
1825	Completion of the Erie Canal: Shipping rates between Buffalo and New York fall more than 75 percent; Rensselaer Polytechnic Institute founded
1827	Mechanics Union of Trade Associates founded in Philadelphia
1828	The Baltimore and Ohio Railroad chartered
1830	Congress passes Pre-emption Act for the public domain
1837	Financial panic and economic depression
1844	Samuel F. B. Morse transmits the first intercity telegraph message
1847	Lawrence Scientific School established at Harvard
1853	The Gadsden Purchase secures an important southwestern railroad pass for the United States
1857	Financial panic and economic depression
1859	Edwin Drake drills the first successful oil well at Titusville, Pennsylvania

In 1833 Michael Chevalier, a French mining engineer, arrived in America to study the young republic's canals and railroads. A keen student of the industrialization process then well underway in Europe, Chevalier was amazed at what the Americans had accomplished. One arresting sight was the city of Pittsburgh, where eighty years earlier the French had established Fort Duquesne amid the solitude of the unbroken forest. Now, Chevalier wrote,

> Pittsburgh was a manufacturing town which will one day become the Birmingham of America. . . . It is surrounded . . . with a dense black smoke which, bursting forth in volume from the foundries, forges, glasshouses, and the chimneys of all the factories and houses, falls in flakes of soot upon the dwellings and persons of the inhabitants. It is, therefore, the dirtiest town in the United States. . . . Nowhere in the world is everybody so regularly and continually busy as in Pittsburgh. I do not believe there is on the face of the earth a single town in which the idea of amusement so seldom enters the heads of the inhabitants.

The rest of the country, the French visitor found, had not changed as much from its eighteenth-century condition. The majority of Americans were still farmers, and almost all the rest were employed in petty trade and handicrafts. But, as Pittsburgh demonstrated, immense changes were taking place. By 1860, a generation after Chevalier's visit, the United States would have a dozen Pittsburghs, beehives of industry belching black smoke into the air. It would also have clusters of factories humming with the sound of looms and spindles. Meanwhile, crisscrossing the fields and woods, "iron horses" would carry the products of the new mills and factories, along with a deluge of commodities created by a surging agriculture. On the eve of the Civil War the United States would be one of the world's economic giants, ahead of all but Britain.

We today recognize that unrestrained economic growth has its drawbacks, but it would be difficult to exaggerate the importance of this transformation. It would influence the entire course of American history as well as the world's. For good or ill, America would eventually become a superpower and its people on average the most affluent in the world. How did this "economic miracle" come to pass?

Factors of Production

From the point of view of individual well-being, economic development requires not just the expansion of a nation's total output, but of expansion exceeding the growth of population. Rapid increase of *total* goods and services may make a nation richer and augment its overall power relative to other nations. But if we are interested in the material prosperity of individuals, then it is *per capita* expansion that we must consider.

Historians and economists disagree over the causes of economic growth. Some emphasize the various "factors of production"—the "inputs" of labor, natural resources, skills, capital, and technology—that must be added to the economic mix to increase "output." Other experts assume that the most dynamic element in economic expansion is the increasing "demand" for goods and services that comes with population growth, changing consumption patterns, and government tax and spending policies. A third school is especially impressed by the cultural elements

Pittsburgh in 1796 and 1857. Located at the junction of three navigable rivers, the village thrived before 1800. In 1799 businessmen set up a nail factory there, and by the 1850s Pittsburgh's population worked in coal mines, steel mills, and glass factories under an ever-present cloud of industrial soot.

that encourage societies to alter their investment and consumption patterns and their attitudes toward profit, wealth, and private property. In reality, to understand how the United States increased its output enough to create relative abundance for its people, we must look at each of these, for all seem to have contributed to the outcome.

Resources.   From the outset the United States was richly endowed by nature. The nation in 1815 stretched over one billion acres. No other country in the world possessed so much level, well-watered, fertile agricultural land in the earth's temperate zone, where the growing season is relatively long yet the advent of frost checks excessive growth of harmful bacteria and their insect carriers. The nation's forests, although they initially impeded farming, were a unique resource, for virtually everything in the nineteenth century was made of wood—houses, fences, wagons, even clocks and machinery. Wood, moreover, was a major source of fuel, used by steamboats, locomotives, factory steam engines, and by most householders to cook their food and heat their homes. America was also rich in minerals. The ores of the Appalachian region from central Vermont to the Carolinas formed an "iron belt" that as early as 1800 was dotted with forges, smelters, and mines. Copper and lead deposits were found in Michigan and Missouri. Pennsylvania and Ohio had excellent coal and—though as yet unused—the country possessed vast petroleum reserves.

In water power, too, the United States was blessed. The Appalachian chain was the source of many rivers that emptied into the Atlantic. Along the fall line, where the Piedmont plateau drops abruptly to the Atlantic coast plain, scores of swift cascading streams offered a vast reserve of water power to turn mill wheels.

In 1815 relatively little of the country's land was being farmed. In the West white farmers were found only in the regions adjacent to the Ohio Valley and a few other pockets. Almost all of the Mississippi valley was forest except some tracts in present-day Indiana, Illinois, and Iowa, covered with tall prairie grass. Even in the Atlantic coast states forests and unused farm woodlots covered the landscape, especially in northern New England, New York, western Pennsylvania, and the mountain regions of the southern states.

Nor were the nation's power resources much used. Aside from some gristmills for grinding wheat and corn into flour and meal, and sawmills for slicing logs into boards, the waterpower of the fall line went largely to waste. Also neglected was the coal of eastern Pennsylvania; as long as wood was cheap, people had no incentive to exploit the unfamiliar black stone for fuel. As for petroleum, though people knew "rock oil" would burn, they did not know how to guarantee a steady supply, so it remained a curiosity sold by quacks and hucksters as medicine.

In the forty-five years following the War of 1812, the accessible and usable resources within the country's 1803 boundaries were greatly expanded. Growing population and easier access to consumers induced farmers to expand their cultivated acreage. Increasingly, similar incentives moved businessmen to build water-powered mills and exploit coal deposits. In 1859 Edwin L. Drake, backed by New Haven capitalists, found that by drilling into the ground, an abundant supply of petroleum could be assured. Drake's well at Titusville, Pennsylvania, set off a "rush" to the oil regions that resembled the earlier gold rush to California.

But besides learning to exploit its existing resources, the country added to these resources by enlarging its boundaries. Between the Louisiana Purchase in 1803 and the Gadsden Purchase fifty years later, the United States grew by 830 million acres. A large part of the new territory was arid, but it also included great tracts of fertile land in the Central Valley of California, in east Texas, and in Gulf Coast Florida; vast deposits of copper, silver, gold, lead, and zinc in the Rocky Mountain area; and unique timber resources along the coasts of California and Oregon.

Labor.   But natural resources, of course, would have been meaningless without men and women to utilize them. The United States was a sparsely populated country in 1815. With 8.5 million people spread over 1.7 million square miles, it had under 5 inhabitants for every square mile (640 acres) of land, compared with over 90 per square mile today. In 1820 the population reached 9.6 million, including some 1.8 million blacks. Though legal importation of slaves had ceased in 1808 (when Congress implemented the constitutional provision allowing it to end the Atlantic slave trade), African Americans remained about 19 percent of the country's population.

With so few people spread over so much land, the United States suffered from a chronic labor shortage. The shortage was alleviated somewhat by the youth of the population. In 1817 the median age was 17. In an era when people began to work for a living at 13 or 14, such a young population was a distinct economic asset. Offsetting this demographic advantage, however, were the problems of disease and ill health. There were major cholera epidemics in 1832 and again in 1849–1850 that killed thousands and disrupted economic life. In low-lying, swampy areas many people suffered each summer from "fevers" or "agues," probably mosquito-borne malaria. In addition, typhus, typhoid, whooping cough, and tuberculosis killed or disabled vast numbers of working people every year. After 1815 the potential labor force was further reduced by individual efforts to limit family size. The American birth rate dropped sharply, so that by 1850 it was below that of many countries in Europe.

As in the past, the Old World helped to offset the New World's labor shortage. Between independence and 1808 the South's labor force was augmented by a large number of slave imports. Then, on January 1, 1808, the African slave trade became illegal. Some smuggling of captive Africans continued, but the number of slaves who arrived in the United States from abroad was drastically cut. Europe added to America's population, however, with each passing year. In the period 1776–1815 no more than 10,000 Europeans had entered the United States annually. In the next 25 years the number rose to over 30,000 each year. Then, in the 1840s and 1850s, economic dislocations in Germany and Scandinavia and the potato blight in Ireland made life hard, in some cases intolerable, for hundreds of thousands of European peasants. During the 1840s and 1850s a staggering average of 200,000 Europeans arrived each year at American Atlantic and Gulf Coast ports. Many of these immigrants were in their most productive early adult years. Europe had nurtured them through their dependent childhood period, and they added their brawn and their skill to the American labor pool at scarcely any cost to their adopted nation. Almost all of these additions accrued to the North. European newcomers perceived the South as an alien place where slaves competed with free labor and the chances of economic success were limited. They avoided Dixie. All told, by 1860, the nation's labor force, as a result of both natural increase and transatlantic immigration, had grown to over 11 million people.

Public Schools and Economic Growth.   Modern economic development has depended as much on the improvement of labor force quality—the enhancement of "human capital," as economists call it—as on the sheer growth of workers' numbers. In America the upgrading of labor force skills, literacy, and discipline was the result of the system of public education.

Educational standards had been relatively high in colonial America, especially in New England, but they had declined during the half-century following the Revolution. In 1835 Professor Francis Bowen of Harvard complained that New England's once-celebrated school system "had degenerated into routine . . . [and] was starved by parsimony." In the West, if we can believe the students of one small rural school, the teaching level was still lower. At the end of the academic year these pupils inscribed this verse on the wall of their schoolhouse:

> Lord of love, look from above
> And pity the poor scholars.
> They hired a fool to teach this school
> And paid him fifty dollars.

But even as Bowen—and the "scholars"—wrote, labor leaders, philanthropists, businessmen, and concerned citizens were struggling to improve the country's educational system. The most effective worker for better schools after 1835 was Horace Mann, a lawyer who gave up a successful legal practice to become secretary of the Massachusetts Board of Education in 1837. Mann believed that an educated body of citizens was essential for a healthy democratic society. His colleagues also believed, as one of his successors on the state Board of Education noted, that "the prosperity of the mills and shops is based quite as much upon the intellectual vigor as the physical power of the laborers." During Mann's twelve years as secretary of the board, Massachusetts doubled teachers' salaries, built and repaired scores of school buildings, opened fifty public high schools, and established a minimum school year of six months. Other states, especially in the North, soon followed the lead of the Bay State. The new school systems taught useful values as well as useful skills. Children learned punctuality, good hygiene, industriousness, sobriety, and honesty—all valuable qualities for an emerging industrial society.

Many gaps remained in the country's educational system even after the advent of the state-supported primary school. Secondary education, except in Massachusetts, remained the privilege of the rich who could afford the tuition of private "academies" for their children. One of the most serious deficiencies was in the education of girls and young women. At the elementary level young girls were treated the same as boys. Beyond the first few grades, however, female education was often inferior. American women could not attend college until Oberlin admitted its first female student in 1833. The typical secondary school or academy for young women in 1815 was a "finishing school" where the daughters of businessmen, professionals, and wealthy farmers or planters were taught French, music, drawing, dancing, and a little "polite" literature. Then, in the period of 1820–1840, educational reformers, both men and women, began to conceive of a new sort of secondary schooling for women.

These reformers attacked the idea that women should be mere ornaments or drudges. In a bustling progressive society, they said, women had a vital role to play as mothers and teachers, educating the leaders of the nation in all areas of life. This "cult of domesticity" did not assert women's equality with men. But it did insist that in their own "spheres" women were an immense neglected resource and that this waste must not continue. The new idea that women's role was important transformed female education, especially in the Northeast. Under the leadership of Emma Willard, Mary Lyon, Joseph Emerson, and Catharine Beecher, female "seminaries" were established throughout the region. Schools such as Willard's Troy Female Seminary (1821) and Lyon's Mount Holyoke Female Seminary (1836), unlike the earlier finishing schools, taught algebra, geometry, history, geography, and several of the sciences. These more "muscular" subjects were now thought appropriate for the mothers-to-be of statesmen, soldiers, and captains of industry. The most important role of these schools, however, was to provide a flood of trained women to fill the ranks of the burgeoning teaching profession.

Though the educational system still had many failings, by 1860 the United States had a highly skilled and literate labor force. It was ahead of every nation in the world except Denmark in the ratio of students to total population, and New England was even ahead of the advanced Danes. Literacy made it possible for workers to read plans and compose written reports, and gave them access to new ideas and new ways of doing things. It is no accident that the ingenious Yankee tinkerer became a legendary figure or that New England, with the best educational system in the country, became a beehive of shops, mills, and factories, producing cloth, clocks, shoes, hardware, and machinery for the rest of the nation.

By mid-century, Americans made the world's best farm machinery. Eli Whitney's gin, shown in a mid-century version, cleaned cotton fifty times faster than a hand laborer and incidentally increased the demand for slaves.

Technology.   During the years between independence and the Civil War, the United States became a world leader in useful invention. In the 1780s Oliver Evans invented a new flour mill that introduced grain at the top and automatically cleaned, ground, cooled, sifted, and barreled it as it descended to the bottom of the structure. In the 1790s Eli Whitney perfected the "gin," a machine that cleaned the sticky seeds from the cotton boll and revolutionized cotton growing in the United States. In 1787 John Fitch first hitched steam power to navigation, creating the first steam boat. Twenty years later, Robert Fulton's paddle-wheeled steamboat, the *Clermont*, made the trip from New York to Albany in a record-breaking 32 hours. In the 1840s a New York University professor, Samuel F. B. Morse, developed a practical telegraph system to transmit information instantaneously over long distances.

While the men who advanced technology in these years were well educated in the arts and humanities, few had formal technical education. Most of the country's first civil engineers, for example, learned their trade by working on the early turnpikes and canals. Gradually, however, more formal means to train technicians and scientists were developed. West Point (founded in 1802), Norwich University (1820), Rensselaer Polytechnic Institute (1825), and the Lawrence Scientific School at Harvard (1847) eventually established engineering schools to train men to build the canals, bridges and railroads that would knit the country together.

Growing Markets.   We can treat the expanding and ever-more-skillful population of the country as an addition to the supply side of the economic growth equation. It was also a factor on the demand side, however. As population increased, so did the market for everything from babies' cribs to old folks' canes. Americans were already well supplied with food, clothing, and shelter, and each addition of family income provided additional money for modest luxuries. Before the Civil War the finer industrial goods were commonly obtained from Britain or France, but with each passing year American industry expanded to meet the growing home market for jewelry, furniture, carriages, carpets, writing paper, clocks, fine cloth, and a thousand other sophisticated manufactured articles.

Capital.   The growing labor force of the United States was matched by a growing supply of physical capital. Capital, as economists use the term, is not money as such, but money transformed into machines, barns, factories, railroads, mines—that is, money invested in "tools" that produce other commodities. It comes ultimately from the savings of society, what it sets aside out of its total income. When employed productively, capital becomes the basis for increasing the output of goods and services and the rate of economic growth.

During the colonial period, most capital came from abroad in the form of implements, credits, and cash brought by immigrants or lent to Americans by European promoters and merchants. After independence the United States continued to rely on foreign sources of capital. The increasing flood of immigrants brought some capital to America, but loans extended by British, French, Dutch, and German bankers and businesspeople were a larger source of foreign capital. The total amount of the nation's outstanding foreign loans went from under $100 million in 1815 to $400 million by the eve of the Civil War.

Foreign trade was yet another source of capital. The United States in this peri-od exported vast quantities of raw materials and farm products to foreign nations. Cotton from the South alone represented almost half the value of the country's total annual exports in the mid-1850s. Profits from these sales enabled the country to buy not only European consumer goods, but also machinery, iron rails, loco-motives, and other tools. At the same time the American merchant marine earned income for the United States. Europeans often preferred to hire America's swift clipper ships to send their exports to Australia, South America, and the Far East. Foreign trade created fortunes for American merchants, particularly in the middle states and New England, much of which was reinvested in domestic industry. And finally, as a source of capital, after 1849 there was gold from California. The millions of dollars of precious metals extracted from the streams and hills of the gold rush country also helped pay for the capital goods imported from the advanced industrial nations of Europe.

Banks and Banking.

The country's commercial banking system also con-tributed to the growth of private capital in these years. They did so by creating money or credit and lending it to business borrowers. Commercial banks keep only a small reserve of money against the debts they owe to their depositors and the loans they make to borrowers. On a small amount of paid-in capital or de-posited savings, they can lend a large amount to investors. In effect, commercial banks are money machines that transmit the cash or credit they create to business-people who need it and can put it to productive use.

This system depended on prudence to work successfully. If bankers lent to un-reliable borrowers or made loans far beyond what a cautious reserve policy re-quired, they jeopardized their firms and often the economy as a whole. Depositors, or other creditors, fearing for the safety of their savings, might de-mand immediate repayment. If enough of a bank's creditors simultaneously asked for their money back, the bank might be forced to "suspend payments" and close its doors. That in turn could trip off a broad "panic," with everyone de-manding cash and insisting their creditors pay their debts. Serious national panics occurred in 1819, 1837, and 1857, and each ushered in a long economic downturn. For a time businesspeople would not invest and consumers would not buy. Eco-nomic activity slowed, and workers lost their jobs.

In the pre-Civil War period, banks also provided the paper money that people used in their daily buying and selling. The United States Treasury issued gold, silver, and copper coins, but this was not enough to do the people's business. Instead, in all but minor transactions, the "bank note," issued by some banking corporation, served the public as money. By law these notes were usually backed by a reserve of gold to redeem each note when presented, but the requirement was often laxly enforced. The Second Bank of the United States, chartered in 1816, had little trouble keeping its circulation of paper notes "as good as gold." Many of the state-chartered banks, however, issued excessive amounts to maximize their profits. When a bank could not redeem its notes—as when it could not pay its depositors—it was forced to suspend operations. Those who held the bank's notes now found themselves with worthless paper, much as depositors in defaulted banks found themselves with worthless bank accounts.

Growth of the Banking System.   Despite these failings, the country's banking system proved adequate to the job of increasing the nation's pool of capital. The
first modern American commercial bank was the Bank of North America, chartered
by Congress in 1781 and located in Philadelphia. In 1784 the legislatures of New
York and Massachusetts chartered two additional banks. Congress, acting on
Hamilton's financial program, chartered the first Bank of the United States (or
BUS). Like any other commercial bank, the BUS lent money, but before its demise
in 1811, it took on some of the functions of a central bank. That is, it sought to control and stabilize the entire economy by providing extra funds to state bank lenders
when credit was scarce and by limiting their loans when credit was excessive.

The Second Bank of the United States, chartered in 1816, was even larger than
the First, with $35 million in capital compared to the $10 million of its predecessor.
It, too, sought to provide a balance wheel for the economy. At times, however, it
blundered badly. Under its first president, it initially followed an easy-credit policy, lending freely to businessmen and speculators. This practice helped fuel a
western land boom after 1815. Then, when it tightened credit in 1819, the Bank
triggered a major panic and depression.

Meanwhile, a large state banking system was growing up alongside the BUS.
In 1820 there were 300 state banks; in 1860, almost 1,600. At first most state banks
were established by charters granted individually by state legislatures. By the
1840s, however, banks could secure charters by applying to designated state
officials and meeting general legal requirements (free banking). In some states,
especially in the Northeast, these requirements were strict. In the newer parts of
the country they were often slack. There the need for capital to clear land, build
barns, construct railroads, and lay out towns was most acute, and interest rates—
the price of money—was therefore high. Under the circumstances, it is not surprising that many western states' banking laws were lax and enforcement even
more lenient. This led to large issues of "wildcats," paper money backed by hope
and faith rather than "specie" (gold and silver). The practices of western banks encouraged a boom-and-bust pattern, but their free-and-easy policies undoubtedly
facilitated rapid capital growth in the emerging parts of the country. All told, economic historians conclude, the banking system of this period, for all its faults,
worked well for an enterprising people.

Government Actions.   Americans disagreed about the role of the government
in the American economy. Jeffersonians continued to fear federal and state intrusion into private affairs as a danger to political freedom. Citizens influenced by the
laissez-faire ideas of Adam Smith believed that government intervention would
only hamper economic progress. And private capital was in fact the predominant
source of economic growth during the pre-Civil War period, but we must not ignore the role of government in the country's pre-Civil War expansion. Through
laws favorable to the easy chartering of banks and corporations, the states encouraged private capitalists to pool their savings for investment purposes. The federal
tariff system, proposed by Hamilton and implemented by the Republicans in 1816,
by making imports more expensive, protected American manufacturers against
foreign competition and so encouraged capitalists to risk their money in factories
and mills. The legal system, buffered by lawyers, contributed to the growth surge

that marked these years. Never far removed from the commercial realm, lawyers came to identify ever more closely with the entrepreneurial spirit. Increasingly, judges and lawyer-dominated legislatures proved more attentive to the right to earn a profit than to individual rights under the common law.

Governments also contributed to capital formation more directly. Many investments, such as canals, required so much capital and posed so many risks that private investors hesitated to undertake them. Yet they promised to confer economic benefits on many people or whole regions. Profit on a railroad through a wilderness area, for example, might take years to realize, though the road might open an undeveloped region for settlers and eventually benefit the whole nation. To encourage growth in these instances, state and local governments in the years before 1860 joined with private promoters to build roads, canals, and railroads. Sometimes the states lent money to private capitalists; in the case of the canals, they often financed projects directly. New York State put up the $7 million for the Erie Canal after efforts to secure federal funds failed. Federal revenues built the National Road, begun in 1811 and completed in 1850, from Cumberland, Maryland, to Vandalia, Illinois, a distance of 700 miles. The federal government also financed the St. Mary's Falls ship canal linking Lake Huron and Lake Superior, built coastal lighthouses, dredged rivers and harbors, and, in the 1850s, contributed millions of acres of land to promoters of the Illinois Central Railroad connecting the Great Lakes with the Gulf of Mexico.

All told, the government contribution to pre-Civil War investment was enormous. One scholar has estimated that by 1860 states, counties, and municipalities had spent about $400 million toward building the country's transportation network alone. And the federal government spent at least as much. If we add to this sum the millions expended by governments on schools, hospitals, and other vital public facilities, and the value of the tariff and land grants, we can see that we must qualify strongly the myth of private enterprise as the sole engine of economic growth in pre-Civil War America.

The Course of American Economic Growth

America, then, was endowed with stupendous natural resources, a skilled, acquisitive, and disciplined population, and values and institutions conducive to hard work, saving, and capital growth. How did these elements combine to produce an economic miracle?

The Birth of King Cotton.   Most people associate nineteenth-century economic growth with factories, forges, and mines. But agricultural progress was a vital part of the process.

The outstanding advance in American agriculture before the Civil War was the opening of the "cotton kingdom." Toward the end of the eighteenth century several ingenious Englishmen developed machines to spin cotton yarn and weave it into fabric. By the 1790s the mills of Lancashire in northwest England were producing cheap cotton cloth for an ever-expanding world market. But where was the raw cotton to come from for the hungry mills? A small amount of cotton was grown on the Sea Islands off the South Carolina and Georgia coasts. Sea island

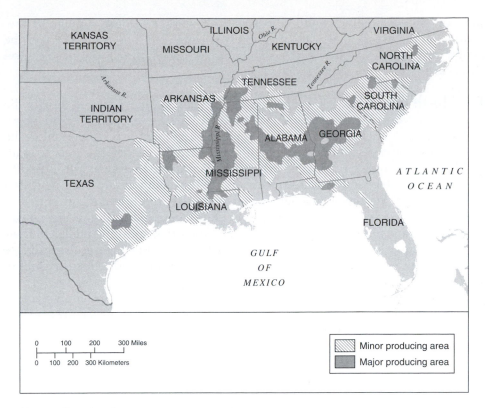

Cotton-Growing Areas

cotton has smooth fibers; its seeds could easily be removed by hand. But the region where it flourished was limited. Short-staple cotton would grow throughout the South's vast upland interior, but it had burr-like green seeds that required much hand labor to remove. It was not economical to grow, even in the slave South. Cotton cultivation remained confined to the narrow band of Carolina–Georgia coast.

Yet the South badly needed a new cash crop. Tobacco, rice, and indigo had all suffered declining markets after independence. What could be done to make short-fiber cotton a practical replacement for the slumping older staples? The answer was provided by the Yankee Eli Whitney. In 1793, while visiting the Georgia plantation of Mrs. Nathanael Greene, widow of the Revolutionary War general, Whitney learned about the problem confronting southern planters. As a gesture of gratitude to his gracious hostess, he put together a simple machine that would efficiently remove the sticky seeds from the upland cotton boll. Now a single laborer, using Whitney's new "gin" (from "engine"), could do the work of fifty hand cleaners.

The gin, and cotton culture, quickly spread throughout the lower South. Thousands of planters, white farmers, and slaves migrated into western Georgia, Alabama, Mississippi, Louisiana, Arkansas, and east Texas to clear fields and plant cotton. From about 2 million pounds in 1793, short-fiber cotton output shot up to 80 million pounds by 1811. In 1859 the United States produced 5 million bales of 400 pounds each and had become the world's leading supplier of raw cotton. On the eve of the Civil War cotton was "king," and its realm spanned the region from North Carolina on the Atlantic coast, 1,300 miles westward to central Texas, and from the Gulf of Mexico to Tennessee.

The North and West.

If cotton was king in the South, wheat was king in the agricultural North. Grown since colonial times in almost every part of North America except New England and the deep South, it continued to be important in the Middle Atlantic states and the upper South after 1815. Thereafter, as canals and railroads made the prairies accessible, wheat growing moved westward. By 1859 Illinois, Indiana, Ohio, and Wisconsin had become the chief wheat-producing states.

The soils of the new wheat region were especially fertile and the prairies that covered large parts of several northwestern states were practically treeless; farmers did not have to clear forest cover, an occupation that consumed much of their time in the middle states. The shift of wheat growing to the Midwest accordingly increased the output per capita of American agriculture and helped to supply expanding national markets at ever-lower costs.

Labor was a problem in northern agriculture. There were generally enough hands for plowing, planting, and cultivating. But at harvest time, when the crop had to be gathered quickly, there was not enough labor to go around. In the 1830s Obed Hussey and Cyrus McCormick invented horse-drawn mechanical reapers to speed the process. A man with a hand-operated "cradle" could cut from three to four acres of ripe wheat a day; with the new machines he could harvest more than four times as much. By 1860 there were some 80,000 reapers worth $246 million, at work on the fields of the North and West, more than in the rest of the contemporary world.

Land Policy.

Land policies too encouraged agricultural productivity. Congress in these years was under constant pressure to provide family farms for the growing population by accelerating the conversion of public lands to private use. In 1800 it allowed settlers to buy land in tracts of 320 acres, or half the smallest parcel previously permitted, at a minimum of $2 an acre. The same law also gave the buyer four years to pay and provided a discount of 8 percent for cash. The Land Act of 1804 lowered the minimum price to $1.64 an acre and reduced the smallest amount purchasable to 160 acres.

Federal land policies, however, were not consistent. The states and the federal government occasionally sold public land in large blocks, some of 100,000 acres or more. But these were not worked as great estates. Rather, they were bought by speculators, often on credit, and resold in small parcels to settlers. The system allowed free-wheeling businesspeople to make large profits, but even that did not prevent widespread ownership of land by people of small and middling means.

Low land prices and easy credit combined to set off periodic waves of speculation in the West. Buyers with little capital placed claims to much larger amounts of land than they could ever expect to farm themselves in hopes of selling most of it for profit later. Meanwhile, they met their payments to the government by borrowing from the banks. To prevent widespread default Congress passed periodic relief acts that delayed collection of overdue payments. Such measures did not always help, however. When speculation got out of hand in 1819, the country experienced a major depression set off by panicky speculators trying to unload their land at a time when no one wanted to buy. The Panic of 1837 also stemmed in part from western land speculation.

Not every would-be farmer waited for land to be surveyed and put up for sale. Many cleared some unsurveyed acres and farmed illegally. Such "squatters" risked losing fences, barns, houses, and the land itself when the tract they had settled and "improved" was finally offered for sale by the government. In 1830 champions of the squatters, led by Senator Thomas Hart Benton of Missouri, convinced Congress to pass the Pre-emption Act to allow those who had illegally occupied portions of the public domain on or before 1829 to buy up to 160 acres of land at the minimum price of $1.25 an acre before others were allowed to bid. In 1841 the time restrictions on the Pre-emption Act were removed.

Land policy remained relatively unchanged for more than a decade after 1841. Benton and his colleagues, joined at times by working-class leaders, continued to fight for a "homestead act" that would give land free to all bona fide settlers. But many easterners feared that free western lands would drain off eastern labor; southerners feared it would give the government an excuse to raise the tariff to offset the loss of land-sale revenues and also that it would encourage the growth of free states. The continued opposition of the South blocked a homestead law until 1862. Still, federal land policies overall accelerated the geographical expansion of the economy's agricultural sector.

Farm Productivity.

If agriculture had remained stagnant, rapid overall economic growth would not have been possible. While the reaper made farm labor more efficient and newly opened "virgin" lands yielded far more for each outlay of labor and capital than the older lands of the East, there was a serious downside to this agricultural expansion. It depleted centuries-long accumulations of top-soil nutrients wastefully. But it also churned out ever-cheaper wheat, pork, beef, fruits, vegetables, and fiber in a profusion seldom attained anywhere, anytime. Without this development there would not have been an "economic miracle."

Steamboats and Roads.

In some ways American geography favored the efficient, cheap transportation necessary for growth. The Mississippi River system combined with the Great Lakes made it possible for ships to penetrate deep into the vital interior of North America. But the lakes lacked lighthouses and port facilities and at several points were connected only by unnavigable rapids. As for the Mississippi system, flatboats and rafts could easily be floated down to New Orleans propelled by the current, but the trip upstream by poled keelboats required backbreaking labor and took far longer.

Capitalists and inventors had been working on schemes to apply steam power to river navigation for some time, but not until Robert Fulton took up the quest, backed by the powerful Livingston family, did it become economically feasible. Soon steamboats were operating on schedule up and down the Hudson River. In 1811 the Fulton-Livingston interests, having already secured a legal monopoly of steamboat traffic in New York State waters, received an exclusive charter from the Louisiana territorial legislature to operate steamboats on the lower Mississippi. If unchecked, the Fulton group might have monopolized steamboat navigation on all the inland waters. However, the Supreme Court struck down these monopoly privileges in the case of *Gibbons v. Ogden* and opened up steamboat navigation to all investors. Entrepreneurs were not long in seizing the opportunity. By 1855 there were 727 steamboats on the western rivers with a combined capacity of 170,000 tons; many more plied the Great Lakes as well as the streams and coastal waters of the Gulf and the Atlantic. It had taken four months to pole a boat upstream from New Orleans to Louisville; by 1853 steamboats made it in under four and a half days. Freight rates on the same route in this period fell from an average of $5 per hundred pounds to under 15 cents.

Impressive as the advances in inland navigation were, there still remained the problem of transportation where there were no natural waterways. Overland travelers during the colonial period had been forced to use narrow, muddy, circuitous trails to move themselves and commodities. After 1800 a network of surfaced, all-weather roads for horses, carriages, and wagons began to appear, financed by tolls on users. The first major "turnpike" in the country was the Philadelphia–Lancaster Road in Pennsylvania opened in 1794. The entire country soon caught the road-building fever. In the Northeast private capital built most of the turnpikes; in the South and West state governments built the roads directly or bought stock in private turnpike companies. The federal government also joined in the rush, investing $7 million in the construction of the National Road.

Locks such as these on the Erie Canal near Albany made it possible for canal boats to ascend and descend from one level to another. The motive force for the boats was provided by mules walking a towpath and attached by ropes, as seen at right. *(John Hill (1830–32), "Junction of the Erie and Northern Canals," c. (1770–1850). Engraving. Courtesy of the New-York Historical Society, New York City)*

Canals. Though turnpikes reduced the cost and time of moving people and goods, transportation by land remained more expensive than by water. Where there were no navigable streams or lakes, the solution was canals. A few miles of artificial waterway were constructed in the Northeast just before the War of 1812. The real boom got under way in 1817, when the New York State legislature appropriated funds for constructing an enormously long canal between the Hudson River and Lake Erie, bypassing the Appalachian barrier to connect the Great Lakes with the Atlantic Ocean.

The project was an impressive technical achievement. The state engineers learned on the job and improvised a score of new tools and techniques. In the end they moved millions of cubic yards of earth, constructed 83 locks, scores of stone aqueducts, and 363 miles of "ditch" 4 feet deep and 40 feet wide. The completed Erie Canal, opened by a colorful ceremony in 1825, was an engineering marvel that astounded the world. Power for the canal boats was provided by horses and mules that treaded towpaths on either side of the waterway. A man or a boy led the animals; another man at the tiller kept the boat in mid-channel and signaled passengers seated on top of the cabin to duck by blowing a horn when the vessel approached a low bridge.

The canal was also an immense economic success. In 1817 the cost of shipping freight between New York City and Buffalo on Lake Erie was 19.2 cents a ton. By 1830 it was down to 3.4 cents. Freight rates to and from the upper Mississippi Valley also plummeted. By 1832 the canal was earning the state well over one million dollars yearly in tolls. The canal deflected much of the interior trade that had gone down the Mississippi and its tributaries and redirected it eastward to New York City, reinforcing its existing economic advantage over the nation's other business centers.

New York's experience inevitably aroused the envy of merchants in the other Atlantic ports. Baltimore, Boston, Philadelphia, and Charleston businessmen now demanded that their states follow New York's lead. At the same time, promoters, speculators, farmers, and merchants in the Northwest saw that their region's prosperity depended on constructing canals to link up with the waterways built or proposed. The pressure on state governments soon got results. By the 1830s the dirt was flying all over the Northeast and Northwest as construction crews raced to create a great network of canals. In 1816 there were 100 miles of canals in the United States; by 1840 over 3,300 miles of artificial waterways criss-crossed the Middle Atlantic states, southern New England, and the Old Northwest.

Few canals built after 1825 were as successful as the Erie. Some never overcame difficult terrain and other engineering problems; others never attracted sufficient business to repay investors. Still others were built too late and were overtaken by the railroads, which provided quicker and less easily interrupted service. Nevertheless, the sharp decline in freight and passenger rates was a great boon to interregional trade. Western farmers found new outlets in the East for their wheat, corn, pork, beef, and other commodities. With transportation costs lower, the price of manufactured goods in the West fell, enabling eastern manufacturers to sell more to western customers. Everyone benefited.

The Railroads Arrive. The railroads, too, encouraged growth. The early steam railroads were plagued by technical problems. Engines frequently broke down; boilers exploded. And even on a normal trip, passengers emerged from the cars nearly suffocated by smoke or with holes burned in their clothes from flying sparks. Rails were at first flat iron straps nailed to wooden beams. When these came loose, they sometimes curled up through the floors of moving passenger cars, maiming or killing the occupants. Cattle that got in the way of trains caused derailments. Trains moving rapidly over lightly ballasted rails and around sharp curves did not always stay on the track. Some of these problems were inevitable in so new a system, but accidents were also the result of makeshift construction imposed by the shortage of capital and the desire to build quickly.

Gradually, railroad technology improved. All-iron rails, more substantial passenger cars, the "cow catcher" in front of the locomotive to push aside obstructions, more dependable boilers, and enlarged smokestacks to contain the hot sparks all made the railroads more efficient and more comfortable. To deal with the hairpin curves characteristic of American railroads, engineers developed loose-jointed engines and cars with wheels that swiveled to guide trains around turns.

The first major American railroad was the Baltimore and Ohio, chartered in 1828. In 1833 the Charleston and Hamburg in South Carolina reached its terminus 136 miles from its starting point, making it the longest railroad in the world. By 1860 the country boasted some 30,000 miles of track, and passengers and freight could travel by rail from the Atlantic coast as far west as St. Joseph, Missouri, and from Portland, Maine, to New Orleans. The system was far from complete, and many communities remained without rail connections. Nevertheless, the accomplishment was impressive.

The Factory System.   Advances in agriculture and transportation contributed immensely to the pre-Civil War economic surge. But the most dynamic development of the antebellum economy was the rise of the factory system, initially in southern New England.

There had been large workshops here and there in the colonial period, but none of these had brought together hundreds of "operatives" and expensive power-driven machinery under one roof to produce a single uniform product. The modern factory, copied from eighteenth-century English inventors and entrepreneurs in cotton textile manufacture, arrived in the United States soon after independence and in a rudimentary form. The first mill using water power to spin cotton yarn was probably the Beverly Cotton Manufactory of Massachusetts incorporated in 1789. In 1790 a skilled English mechanic, Samuel Slater, linked up with Almy and Brown, a concern with capital to invest descended from colonial candle-makers and West Indies traders. In 1790–1791 the firm opened the nation's first cotton spinning mill at Pawtucket, Rhode Island. Before long, the small state was covered with spinning mills that employed whole families, including women and young children, to tend the water-powered spindles.

The Rhode Island mills produced only cotton yarn. For finished cloth skilled hand weaving was still needed, a labor-intensive and expensive process. The deficiency was made up in the second decade of the nineteenth century when Francis Cabot Lowell, a Boston merchant hard hit by Jefferson's embargo, visited Lancashire, center of the flourishing British textile industry. Lowell took careful note of the latest power looms and carried the plans home in his head, prepared to build a loom superior to the original.

The Railroad Networks, 1850–1860

Joining with other merchants, Lowell secured a corporation charter for the Boston Manufacturing Company. With their combined capital the promoters built a mill at a water power site in Waltham on the Charles River. The first cotton cloth came from the company's power looms in 1815 and proved superior to British imports. Between 1816 and 1826 the Boston Manufacturing Company averaged almost 19 percent profit a year.

The promoters soon found they could not produce enough cloth at the limited Waltham power site to satisfy the demand and made plans for a complete new textile community along the swift-flowing Merrimack. The new mills at Lowell, Massachusetts, were much larger than either the Waltham factory or the earlier spinning mills in Rhode Island. How could they attract enough labor for the new factories? The promoters turned to New England farm girls drawn to Lowell by promises of good wages and cheap, attractive dormitory housing built at company expense. The company also provided a lyceum, where the literate and pious young women could hear edifying lectures, and paid for a church and a minister. By the mid-1830s Lowell was a town of 18,000 people with schools, libraries, paved streets, churches, and health facilities. The mills themselves numbered some half-dozen, each separately incorporated, arranged in quadrangles surrounded by the semidetached houses of the townsfolk and the dormitories of the female workers.

The Lowell system became famous even across the Atlantic. Distinguished foreign visitors made pilgrimages to the town and were invariably impressed by what they saw. The British novelist Charles Dickens, who had encountered at home the worst evils of industrialism, noted that the girls at Lowell wore "serviceable bonnets, good warm cloaks and shawls. . .,[were] healthy in appearance, many of them remarkably so. . .,[and had] the manners and deportment of young women, not of degraded brutes." What a contrast they made with the beaten, sickly workers and child laborers of the mills of Lancashire and Birmingham!

Unfortunately, the halcyon days did not last. During the "hungry forties," when the nation's economy slowed, conditions in the mills worsened. The girls' wages were cut, and when they protested, they were replaced with newly arrived Irish immigrants who were not so demanding. But for a time the Lowell system served as a showcase for the benefits of industrialization.

Industrial Workers

Unequal Gains.   In 1815, well before Lowell, the Erie Canal, and the Baltimore and Ohio Railroad, Americans were already a rich people by the standards of the day. During the next thirty-five years their average wealth and income increased impressively. One scholar believes that between the mid-1830s and the Civil War alone, annual GNP (gross national product, a dollar measure of all goods and services produced) more than doubled. Growth in per capita GNP was also high, as much as 2.5 percent a year in the 1825–1837 period, for example.

Yet it is clear that all Americans did not benefit equally from the economic surge. Clearly it enlarged the urban middle class by creating jobs not only for laborers and factory operatives but also for engineers, clerks, bookkeepers, factory managers, and others. Most of these "white-collar" workers were native-born Americans whose familiarity with the English language and American ways gave them the pick of the new jobs. The industrial leap also created a new class of rich manufacturers, bankers, and railroad promoters. Many were "new" men who used the industrial transformation to lift themselves out of poverty. Samuel Slater, for one, had come to America in 1789 with almost nothing; he was worth $700,000 by 1829.

But in fact, the economic growth of the 1815–1860 period was accompanied by growing inequality of economic condition. Studies of wealth ownership between the end of the colonial era and 1860 show a considerable increase in the proportion of houses, land, slaves, bank accounts, ships, equipment, factories, and other kinds of property, owned by the richest 10 percent of the American people, compared with everyone else.

Wages and Working Conditions.

Did these growing inequalities mean that the people doing the actual hard physical labor of the nation failed to benefit from the economic growth of the period?

Leaving aside the South's slaves (see Chapter 13), taken as a whole, American wage earners made real economic gains during the generation preceding 1860. But while getting better individual circumstances varied widely. Relatively few married women worked for wages, but those who did were badly paid. When women teachers flocked to the new public schools, teachers' average wage levels fell. For traditional "women's work" the situation was similar. Female household servants in 1850 received, typically, a little over a dollar a week plus their room and board. Manufacturers of straw hats, ready-made clothes, and shoes relied on a large pool of poorly paid female workers, many employed part-time at home and paid "by the piece." These women often earned no more than 25 cents a day. (The Lowell girls were relatively affluent at $2.50 to $3 a week.)

Many men were not much richer. In 1850 common laborers—ditch diggers, stevedores, carters, and the like—received 61 cents a day with board, or 87 cents without board. Skilled labor was in shorter supply and so better rewarded. Blacksmiths earned about $1.10 a day in 1852. In 1847 a skilled iron founder in Pennsylvania could make as much as $30 per week. The Boston Manufacturing Company paid machinists up to $11 a week.

To put these earnings in perspective, the *New York Tribune* estimated in 1851 that a minimum budget of about $10 a week was needed to support a family of five in expensive New York City. This meant that an unskilled worker needed help from other family members, and they generally got it. In many families children were put to work at ten or twelve and earned enough to push total family incomes past the bare subsistence point. One scholar estimates that just after the Civil War family heads in Massachusetts earned just 57 percent of total family income; the rest came from the employed children.

Though the income picture for labor is mixed, wage earners were clearly better off in the United States than in Europe. We know of one Irish immigrant construction worker who received wages of 75 cents a day plus board, including meat three times a day. Writing to his family in Ireland, however, he told them he ate meat three times a *week*. When asked why he hid the truth, the man replied, "If I told them that, they'd never believe me." In fact, the abundance of cheap food, especially items seldom part of working-class diet in Europe, invariably astonished people accustomed to foreign practice. One immigrant expressed amazement at what his New York boardinghouse offered its patrons. Breakfast included "beef steaks, fish, hash, ginger cakes, buckwheat cakes etc such a profusion as I never saw before at the breakfast tables." And at dinner there was even "a greater profusion than breakfast."

But wages and income were not the whole story. Wage earners' lives were not easy. Work hours were long. The Lowell girls spent twelve hours a day, six days a week, at their machines. Outdoor workers averaged eleven hours a day, fewer in winter, more in summer. Foreigners, seeking to explain superior American wages, believed that Americans worked harder than their own compatriots. And they probably did. Though the pace of factory labor was more leisurely than today, it was difficult for people used to the slow rhythms of the nineteenth-century farm to adjust to the remorseless pace of the factory machines.

Pre-Civil War workers and their families also experienced great insecurity. Occupational accidents were common, and when workers were injured, they usually lost their jobs. Men killed in the mines or factories left behind families who had to turn to meager private charities or begrudging public support. Besides industrial disaster, there was the uncertainty of employment. A bad harvest or a particularly hard winter often left agricultural workers destitute. Severe periodic depressions produced acute hardship among laborers and factory workers. During the hard times that began in 1819, an English traveler through the East and Northwest noted that he had "seen upwards of 1,500 men in quest of work within 11 months past." Again, following the 1837 and 1857 panics, unemployment forced many wage earners to ask for city and state relief for themselves and their families. In 1857 there were food riots in several northern cities.

Still another source of distress among workers was the downgrading of skills and the loss of independence that sometimes accompanied mechanization and the factory system. The fate of the Massachusetts shoemakers is a case in point. In the opening years of the nineteenth century they had been skilled, semi-independent craftsmen. Merchants brought them cut leather and paid them a given sum for each pair of shoes they sewed and finished in their "ten-footers," the ten-by-ten sheds they worked in behind their homes. These skilled craftsmen owned their own tools and often employed their wives and grown children to help with the work. Not only were they well paid; they also enjoyed a sense of independence since they were subcontractors, not wage earners, and were the heads of their households, not only in a social and legal sense, but also in a direct economic way.

Gradually, as the market for ready-made shoes, especially for southern slaves, expanded, the shoemakers' independence and incomes declined. Merchants divided the shoemaking process into smaller and simpler parts and "put out" the simplified work to unmarried young women in New England country villages. Eventually entrepreneurs introduced power-driven machines that sewed heavy leather, enabling the merchants to establish factories where wage workers could use the expensive, capitalist-owned machines. By the eve of the Civil War the independent master craftsman working in his ten-footer had been replaced with semiskilled labor working for weekly wages in factories.

The Labor Movement.   Clearly, many wage earners were unhappy with the new aggressive capitalism and the new factory system. In 1836 the young women at Lowell went on strike to protest a wage cut. In the end the owners won and the wage cut stuck. In 1860 the shoemakers of Lynn, Massachusetts, "turned out" to protest declining wages; before the strike ended, some 20,000 Massachusetts shoemakers had left their places at the machines.

All through the antebellum period workers struck for higher wages or better working conditions. Most of the strikes were unplanned uprisings in response to some unexpected blow such as a wage cut. But some grew out of long-standing grievances such as the sheer drudgery of factory life or the loss of worker independence. These grievances created a labor movement of considerable dimensions.

The small community craft societies organized in the early 1800s expanded over the next thirty years into citywide labor unions, each representing a whole trade. Later, such local unions joined together into national organizations. But after the Panic of 1837 employers usually defeated the strikers by threatening to hire the many unemployed. Trade unions thereafter declined, and in the next two decades labor discontent generally was diverted from union organizing to political action and various reform movements.

We must not exaggerate the extent of labor discontent during these years, however. The school system, as well as the churches, worked hard to instill the "work ethic" into the labor force, and on the whole they were successful. By and large the American workforce cooperated with economic growth. As one pre-1860 observer noted, in New England "every workman seems to be continually devising some new thing to assist him in his work, and there [is] a strong desire both with masters and workman . . . to be 'posted up' [that is, kept informed] in every improvement." Skilled English workingmen who came to American machine shops in the 1830s and 1840s were often startled to find that their American counterparts, rather than fighting the shop owners, were "fire eaters" whose "ravenous appetites for labor" made their own performance look bad. Several eminent students of American economic development are convinced that this cooperation was one of the most important elements in creating the pre-Civil War American economic miracle.

Conclusions

Many things contributed to the nation's impressive economic performance during the antebellum period. Nature had endowed the United States with uniquely rich resources. History had given it a vigorous, frugal, hard-working people. After 1815 Americans vastly improved on what they had inherited from nature and their own colonial past. During the succeeding decades European immigrants added their brains and brawn to the working population and its accumulated skills. Foreign investors, seeing the United States as a land of opportunity, sent their capital across the Atlantic. Government encouraged enterprise by passing general incorporation laws and tariffs, constructing schools, and investing directly in canals and roads. Skillful entrepreneurs, benefitting from low wages and low taxes, threw themselves into the task of making their communities—and themselves—rich. The country's values and ideals also contributed to material progress by creating a work ethic that made wage earners feel they had a share in the nation's economic progress.

Whatever the causes, the economic growth of this era was not an unrelieved blessing. Though many Americans benefited, the contrast between rich and poor became more pronounced. A byproduct of America's spectacular economic surge, these inequalities would assume greater importance in the generations ahead. And there is also the environment to consider. Undoubtedly the industrial processes, though still at an early stage, degraded the land, the water, the air, and the forests. Michael Chevalier's view of Pittsburgh in 1833 is a vivid case in point. Still, as of 1860, the changes were still in an early stage. The worst–and the best–was yet to come.

ONLINE RESOURCES

"Eli Whitney" *http://eliwhitney.org* This site contains information about Whitney and his invention of the cotton gin, which made cotton and slavery even more viable staples in the southern economy.

"Samuel Slater: Father of the American Industrial Revolution" *http://www.woonsocket.org/ slaterhist.htm* Containing text and photos of Slater's Rhode Island mill operation and his mill villages, this site provides information on the textile workers, adult and children, and how early industrialization shaped their lives. You can also take a virtual tour of the Slaterville Mill and Industrial Villages.

"History of the Erie Canal" *http://www.history.rochester.edu/canal* See how, in the era of great internal improvements, the opening of the canal had an impact on New York and the country. The site contains a chronology of the building of the canal, the evolution of boats used, biographical sketches of key players in the canal's history, and a link to searching primary documents about the canal.

"The Great Migration to the Mississippi Territory" *http://mshistory.k12.ms.us/features/ feature9/migrate.html* Through this site trace the great migration of whites and slaves to the West through this feature story, "Mississippi History Now."

"The Five Points Site" *http://r2.gsa.gov/fivept/fphome.htm* Explore this site, which utilizes both urban archaeology and history, to learn about the famous nineteenth-century New York neighborhood that was home to working-class Irish immigrants.

"Andrew Jackson and the Bank War" *http://odur.let.rug.nl/~usa/E/bankwar/bankwarxx.htm* Investigate every aspect of the debate over the power and privileges of the Second Bank of the United States, including key political actors and their points of view, through this site.

"A Treatise on Domestic Economy—A Mission" *http://xroads.virginia.edu/~CAP/UTC/ bchaps.html* Known as an authority on middle-class domesticity, Catharine Beecher explains, in her 1841 volume, the areas that were proper and suitable pursuits for middle-class women of the era—domestic issues ranging from home care to cooking to childcare. Here, read one chapter of her guidebook for women titled *Peculiar Responsibilities of American Women*.

"Men and Women in the Early Industrial Era" *http://www.albany.edu/history/history316* This site provides excellent links to numerous primary-source documents that address the early struggle for labor reform and life on the shop floor.

"Inland Navigation: Connecting the New Republic, 1790–1840" *http://xroads.virginia.edu/ ~HYPER/DETOC/transport/intro.html* This site documents the way in which Americans sought to join the expansive land and rivers through internal improvements like roads, canals, and railroads.

10
Jacksonian Democracy

What Was It and How Did It Change Political Life?

1810	The United States claims more land as part of the Louisiana Purchase; *Fletcher v. Peck*
1812	James Madison reelected president
1816	Congress incorporates the Second Bank of the United States (BUS); Tariff Act for the first time protects American industry from foreign competition; James Monroe elected president
1818	Andrew Jackson's raid on Spanish Florida
1819	*Dartmouth College v. Woodward*; *McCulloch v. Maryland*; The Adams–Onís Treaty with Spain
1821	*Cohens v. Virginia*
1823	The Monroe Doctrine announced
1824	Henry Clay's American System becomes the Whig platform; John Quincy Adams is elected president by the House and Jackson's supporters suspect a "corrupt bargain"
1828	Congress passes "Tariff of Abominations"; John Calhoun writes *Exposition and Protest*; Andrew Jackson elected president
1830	Indian Removal Act
1832	Tariff Act lowers 1828 duties only slightly; South Carolina declares the new tariff null and void; *Worcester v. Georgia* upholds Cherokee land claims; Jackson vetoes the bill renewing the BUS charter; Jackson removes government deposits from the BUS
1832–34	Biddle reduces and calls in BUS loans
1833	Congress passes the Force Bill; South Carolina agrees to a compromise tariff but nullifies the Force Bill
1835–42	Florida Seminoles forcibly resist removal west
1836	Jackson issues Specie Circular; Martin Van Buren elected president
1838	Cherokees leave Georgia for Oklahoma on the "Trail of Tears"
1840	Whig William H. Harrison elected president

March 4, 1829, was moving day in Washington. Andrew Jackson was to be inaugurated seventh president of the United States, and for weeks many of the city's oldest inhabitants had been packing their possessions and preparing to leave for new residences. To Margaret Bayard Smith, the elegant hostess who had presided over Washington society for twenty-five years, the change was a tragedy. "Never before did the city seem ... so gloomy," she wrote. "Drawing rooms in which I have so often mixed with gay crowds, distinguished by rank, fashion, beauty, talent, ... now empty, silent, dank, dismantled. Oh! 'tis melancholy!"

While some were leaving the still-raw capital on the Potomac, others were moving in. The city had filled with visitors, and the hotels overflowed. Washington endured a flood of new people every four years, of course, but this time there were more of them and they were different. Besides the usual frock-coated dignitaries and bureaucrats, rough-looking men in leather shirts and coonskin caps and equally unfamiliar types with Irish lilts to their voices strolled the capital's streets. The crowd was playful and good-humored, but also fiercely determined. Every face, according to Mrs. Smith, bore "defiance on its brow." "I never saw anything like it before," wrote the new senator from Massachusetts, Daniel Webster. "They really seem to think the country is rescued from some dreadful danger."

The determined mood of the newcomers was understandable. For fourteen years—ever since his great victory over the British at New Orleans—Andy Jackson's admirers had fought to make their hero president. The general was the most magnetic political leader since Washington; to many his personal qualities of bluntness, courtliness, and charm, combined with his stature as a military leader, would always be his chief political assets. But was hero worship the only reason for the excitement? Or was there more than personal loyalty behind the defiant brows? Was something important taking place in Washington that day? Would Old Hickory's election make a difference in the way the country was run? Would it bring new groups to power with new ideas and new programs? Obviously Webster and Mrs. Smith believed they were witnessing some sort of revolution. So did the rough-hewn men who wandered the streets of the capital in March 1829. Were they right? Was a major political change in the air? And if so, what was it? To answer these questions we must look first at the era before Jackson's election.

The Era of Good Feelings

By 1817, when James Monroe was inaugurated as fifth president, the "first party system" had run its course. The bad judgment that had led the Federalists to oppose the War of 1812, along with the limited appeal of their aristocratic ideology, virtually destroyed them as a significant political force. Though it continued to show strength in New England, Delaware, and a few other places, the party of Washington, Hamilton, and John Adams never challenged the Republicans in a national election again.

Federalist principles lived on, however. The War of 1812, as we saw in Chapter 8, taught the Republicans the value of banks, roads, and national self-sufficiency; in 1815 President Madison had asked for a new national bank, a protective tariff, and a system of internal improvements. In Congress Henry Clay, John C. Calhoun of South Carolina, and other "new Republicans" who had learned from Hamilton, supported the president. Madison got most of what he had asked for without serious opposition. In April 1816 Congress passed a measure to incorporate a second

Bank of the United States with a larger capitalization than its predecessor. A few weeks later it approved the Tariff Act of 1816, which for the first time protected American manufacturers against the lower costs and greater efficiency of European industry. Early the following year Congress enacted a major internal improvements bill. The old Federalist leader Gouverneur Morris watched this Republican turnaround with amazement. "The Party now in power," he mused, "seems disposed to do all that Federal men ever wished. . . ."

With the Federalist party gone, ideological tensions declined. Historians have called the decade following the War of 1812 the Era of Good Feelings. This is a useful label if we consider only presidential elections, contests without clashes of parties with distinct ideologies. It is a misnomer if it is intended to mean that political conflict had ceased. Political disagreements continued during these years, but they took the form, as in colonial times, of intraparty squabbling and personal rivalry. Within the states there were frequent battles between one Jeffersonian Republican faction and another. Nationally, the differing factions looked to Calhoun, Clay, John Quincy Adams, or Senator William H. Crawford of Georgia for leadership. But none of these men was as yet capable of evoking great enthusiasm among the voters. Moreover, the issues debated were obscure—if there were issues at all. Public indifference was widespread and the voter turnouts were small.

National elections continued, of course, but they merely confirmed the choices of Republican leaders. Every four years the Republican chieftains in Congress "caucused"—got together in closed session—and nominated the party's presidential candidate, and in the fall their choice was duly ratified by the voters. Making matters even more cut and dried, the caucus leaders invariably chose either the incumbent or, if he had served two full terms, his secretary of state. Thus Secretary of State Madison succeeded Jefferson, Secretary of State Monroe succeeded Madison, and Secretary of State John Quincy Adams would succeed Monroe. To top off the whole cozy arrangement—and turn off the voters—four of the first six presidents were Virginians, and the other two were from Massachusetts. With so little real choice, it was no wonder that voter participation in elections declined so sharply.

The Virginia Dynasty.   The presidents from Jefferson to Monroe (1800–1825) were part of what is known as the Virginia dynasty. (John Quincy Adams, who followed Monroe in office, belonged to this group in most respects in spite of his Massachusetts origins.) They were all cultivated gentlemen, but they were also colorless and withdrawn, and they proved surprisingly timid in domestic affairs.

John Quincy Adams, the sixth president, was a learned, intelligent man and the boldest innovator of the group, Jefferson excepted. In his first annual message to Congress he recommended federal support for a national university and a national observatory, a system of uniform weights and measures, a new Department of the Interior, reformed patent laws, and a massive program of internal improvements. But Adams, like most of the others, lacked leadership ability. However intelligent and able, he was also aloof and humorless. One associate said of him, "It is a question whether he ever laughed in his life." It is not surprising that he found the normal roughhouse of national politics distasteful. Controlled by Adams's political enemies, Congress ignored his recommendations, and the president, too fastidious to use his influence or the power of patronage to gain its support, accomplished little.

John Marshall's Court.   There would have been little innovation on the polit-ical front during the Era of Good Feelings if not for Chief Justice John Marshall. Marshall was a throwback to the earlier, confident Federalism of Hamilton. Unlike the new Republicans, he did not waiver in the cause of strengthening federal power and encouraging a climate attractive to business and enterprise. In 1810 under his leadership the Supreme Court for the first time struck down a state law as unconstitutional in *Fletcher v. Peck,* on the grounds that it violated a state con-tract with private parties. Nine years later, in the *Dartmouth College* case, the Mar-shall Court again upheld the inviolability of a private contract when it forbade the state of New Hampshire to amend the royal charter of Dartmouth College. A gov-ernment charter to a private corporation, Marshall pronounced, was equivalent to a contract and so protected by the Constitution. As Justice Joseph Story, one of Marshall's colleagues, remarked, the decision would protect "private rights" against "any undue encroachment . . . which the passions of the popular doctrines of the day may stimulate any State Legislature to adopt."

Meanwhile, at the same time, Marshall fought to expand the authority of the federal government over the states. In 1819 Maryland placed a tax on the paper money issues of the unpopular Second Bank of the United States. Marshall declared the Maryland law unconstitutional and hence void. The issue, he an-nounced in *McCulloch v. Maryland,* was twofold: Did Congress have power to charter a federal bank in the absence of a specific provision to that effect in the Constitution; and could states tax federal property? His decision was yes on the first question and no on the second. The right of Congress to charter a bank could be readily deduced from the Constitution's "necessary and proper clause," he pro-nounced. "Let the end be legitimate and all means which are appropriate. . ., which are not prohibited, but consist with the letter and spirit of the Constitution, are constitutional." As for state taxation of federal agencies, the "power to tax" in-voked "the power to destroy." No state could destroy a legal creation of Congress, and so the Maryland law was unconstitutional. In *Cohens v. Virginia* (1821) Mar-shall asserted that state court decisions were subject to review by the federal courts when they involved violation of federal law.

Foreign Affairs.   The Virginia dynasty presidents may have been indifferent leaders in domestic affairs, but they were vigorous and successful champions of America's international interests. In 1810 and again in 1812, while both Spain and England were preoccupied with Napoleon, the United States took possession of the western portion of Spanish West Florida on the dubious grounds it had been included in the Louisiana Purchase. Spain protested vigorously but, weakened by the international turmoil of the previous decades, could do little.

This serving of Spanish territory did not satisfy the American appetite. A remnant of the Florida panhandle still remained in Spanish hands, and still more enticing was the great southern loop of the peninsula itself. Acquiring this would not only round out the southeastern corner of the nation; it would settle the problem of escaped slaves, hostile Indians, and white renegades who periodically staged raids from Florida into Georgia and then fled back across the border into Spanish jurisdiction.

Secretary of State John Quincy Adams offered to buy Florida and at the same time settle the uncertain boundary between the Louisiana Purchase territory and the Spanish provinces in Mexico. Spain was not interested. Andrew Jackson's impetuous behavior as commander of American forces patrolling the Florida–Georgia border brought the situation to an unexpected head in 1818. Jackson was authorized by the administration to cross into Spanish territory to suppress the raiders but told to avoid attacking Spanish posts and settlements in the colony. The general had little patience with such a namby-pamby policy. Jackson crossed the border, captured the Spanish fort of St. Marks, executed two suspected British troublemakers—Alexander Arbuthnot and Robert Ambrister—and went on to occupy Pensacola, deposing the Spanish governor in the process.

Ordinary Americans cheered Jackson's bold acts; in Washington, London, and Madrid there was consternation. The only cool head was that of Secretary of State Adams, who saw that the general's rash behavior could be turned to America's advantage. Adams took the offensive. He dismissed Spain's loud protest, charged the Spaniards with failure to protect their own possessions, and enlarged United States' claims to Spanish territory in the Far West under the Louisiana Purchase treaty.

Adams's brazen tactics worked. The Spanish minister in Washington, Luis de Onís y Gonzales, blustered and complained, but his government recognized that it could no longer hold Florida and came to terms with the United States. In February 1819, in the Adams–Onís Treaty, Spain ceded Florida to the United States and surrendered its claim to Oregon. In return, the United States assumed the payment of $5 million in debts owed by Spain to American citizens and agreed to accept the Sabine Rivers as the southwestern boundary of Louisiana, thereby excluding the Mexican province of Texas.

The Monroe Doctrine.   Spain's weakness created hazards as well as opportunities for the United States. By 1820 all of Spanish America, except some Caribbean islands, had won independence. But Spain still hoped to regain control of its former possessions. These hopes were encouraged by France, Prussia, Austria, and Russia, whose monarchs in 1815 had established the Holy Alliance to resist the new forces of democracy and liberalism wherever they appeared. Among the European powers, only Great Britain opposed the alliance for fear that France might regain her lost influence in the Americas and that a revived Spanish-American empire would exclude Great Britain from the profitable trade that had developed with Latin America since its independence. To counter these dangers, the British foreign secretary, George Canning, proposed that his nation and the United States work together to prevent Spain from regaining control of her former colonies.

The American government, like the British, was dismayed at the prospect of Spanish restoration and the intervention of the great European powers in the Americas. It also feared the spread of Russian trading posts in California. But Secretary Adams was skeptical of any joint arrangement. For the United States to cooperate with Great Britain would put it in the position of "a cockboat in the wake of the British man-of-war." Far better for America to go it alone without relying on Britain's uncertain backing.

On Adams's recommendation President Monroe included a statement regarding Latin America in his December 1823 message to Congress. We now call this the Monroe Doctrine. Four principles would guide the United States in its relations with Europe and the rest of the Western Hemisphere, Monroe announced. First, no part of the American continents were "to be considered as subjects for future colonization by any European powers." Second, the new Latin American nations must remain independent republics; any attempt of the European powers "to extend their system [that is, monarchy] to any portion of this hemisphere" we would consider "as dangerous to our peace and safety." Third, the United States would respect existing European colonies in America and stay out of purely European concerns. The fourth component of the Monroe Doctrine—actually announced in a separate diplomatic note to the Russian minister in Washington—asserted that the United States would oppose any transfer of existing colonies in the Americas from one European country to another.

Monroe's statement appeared to the nations of continental Europe to be "blustering," "arrogant," and "monstrous." And it was. The United States was asserting rights unrecognized by international law or treaty—rights it also could not yet defend. The pretensions of the puny American nation seemed ludicrous. "Mr. Monroe, who is not a sovereign," scoffed the French foreign minister, "has assumed in his message the tone of a powerful monarch whose armies and fleets are ready to march at the first signal. . . . Mr. Monroe is the temporary President of a Republic situated on the east coast of North America. . . . Its independence was only recognized forty years ago; by what right then would the two Americas today be under its immediate sway from Hudson's Bay to Cape Horn?"

The United States was counting on Great Britain to stand behind it in case of challenge. Nevertheless, it took courage for a nation of scarcely 10 million to defy the powers of Europe. It also took idealism. No matter how the United States might later twist the Monroe Doctrine to serve its own interests, it was originally a generous statement in defense of international freedom and republican institutions.

The Missouri Compromise.   One event late in Monroe's administration carried hints of serious internal political troubles ahead. In February 1819 the Enabling Act, a measure to admit Missouri to the Union, came before Congress. Carved out of the Louisiana Purchase, Missouri had been settled predominantly by southerners, and the bill accepted it into the Union as a slave state. Soon after the bill was submitted, Representative James Tallmadge of New York proposed an amendment prohibiting any further introduction of slaves into the proposed new state and providing for the emancipation of all adult children of slaves born after the date of its admission. The halls of Congress echoed with angry debate for two sessions as members attacked or defended the Tallmadge amendment. Southerners warned that if slavery were excluded from Missouri, the Union would be torn apart. Even the aging Jefferson considered the Tallmadge amendment and the attitude of the northern congressmen ominous. The Missouri debate was a "fire bell in the night," he wrote, that warned of grave danger for the Union ahead.

After months of heated wrangling, the voices of moderation prevailed. Under the Missouri Compromise of 1820 Congress admitted two states to the Union— Maine and Missouri. Maine, carved from Massachusetts, would be free; Missouri would be slave. The balance of free and slave states in the Union would thus be preserved. The compromise further provided that the southern boundary of Missouri (36° 30′ north latitude) would be the dividing point between future slave and free territory within the remaining Louisiana Purchase territory.

Jackson Comes to Power

By this time the politicians were hard at work considering Monroe's successor. If precedent had remained a guide, there would have been little dispute; as secretary of state, John Quincy Adams would be the choice in 1824. But the voters were tired of being "King Caucus's" rubber stamp.

Democratic Reforms in the States.   The new attitude fueled a quiet political revolution. Between 1820 and 1840 the last vestiges of state property qualifications for voting disappeared. Several states in this period also ended "stand-up" voting, which revealed voters' preferred candidates, and replaced it with printed ballots to protect privacy and independence. Most states eliminated the remaining property qualifications for officeholding and reapportioned their legislatures to give underrepresented areas the political weight they deserved. By 1832 every state except South Carolina had also transferred the power to choose presidential electors from the legislatures to the voters themselves. Many states also changed appointive offices into elective ones. The convention system, in which the party rank and file had a voice, soon replaced the elitist caucus as a method of nominating candidates for office. First adopted in the states, the convention soon became the norm in national politics as well.

It used to be said that these changes originated in the West and only later spread to the East. The evidence shows that it was often the other way around. In political affairs, at least, the East was the pioneer and eastern practices were carried west by emigrants. It was also at one time commonly held that Andrew Jackson and his supporters were responsible for many of the changes. In fact, most of the changes preceded rather than followed the Jackson movement.

The Election of 1824.   There was no opposition party in 1824. Everyone called himself a Republican, and in the end the campaign turned out to be primarily a popularity contest. Jackson, alone among the contenders in 1824, was a genuine popular hero. Adams, however able, was associated with the old Virginia dynasty and his reserve hurt him with the voters. Clay and Calhoun were endorsed as candidates by local groups in Kentucky and South Carolina, respectively; but despite their prominent roles as national leaders during and immediately following the War of 1812, neither had national support. Calhoun soon dropped out of the race.

No candidate won a majority of the electoral college vote. Jackson was first in both the electoral and popular vote; Adams was second; and Clay trailed well behind both. The Constitution, as provided in the Twelfth Amendment, declared that in the event no candidate received an electoral vote majority, the selection of a president would rest with the House of Representatives, where each state would cast a single vote for one of the top three candidates. Jackson's supporters believed that members of the House had a moral obligation to endorse their candidate as the man who had won the most popular votes. When thirteen state delegations gave Adams a majority and the victory, they denounced the result as a denial of the people's will. When the new president appointed Clay his secretary of state, the Jackson supporters proclaimed that the two men had struck a "corrupt bargain."

Adams's administration was dogged by the "corrupt bargain" charge and by the rancor of Jackson's supporters. The country had seen nothing like this for ten years, and the effects were unfortunate. As we have noted, almost nothing in President Adams's domestic program passed Congress. Even in foreign affairs, where his great experience should have been an advantage, he accomplished little.

The Tariff of Abominations.

All through his administration Adams fought Jackson and his supporters. A major focus of their battle was the tariff.

By 1828 the last important tariff revision was already twelve years old. Now increasing numbers of wool growers, textile manufacturers, ironmasters, and even farmers were demanding higher duties on imports to protect them from foreign competition. The "protectionists" were concentrated in the Northeast and to a lesser extent in the Northwest. Southerners of virtually all economic classes opposed any increase in duties because they had little industry to protect and their major crop, cotton, had no competition. Indeed, the South was happy to rely on Great Britain, the cheapest producer of manufactured goods, for its imports. In 1816, when their region's economic future was still in doubt, many southerners had endorsed the tariff. In 1828, after it had become clear that the South's fate was to be supplier of raw materials for a world market, its leading spokesmen saw the protective tariff as an instrument for increasing northern profits at the South's expense.

The issue was highly charged, and most politicians would have preferred to avoid it. But Martin Van Buren of New York's Albany Regency believed that a major tariff revision would help get his friend Jackson elected president by winning him support in the North and West. It did not work as he expected. The tariff bill, when it finally emerged from the pro-Jackson Congress, injured the manufacturers of New England by raising rates on raw materials they needed to produce their goods. At the same time, it promised that southerners would pay higher prices for many English imports. Only Middle Atlantic industrialists and the producers of hemp, raw wool, and a few other farm products got anything positive out of the bill. So objectionable was the measure that puzzled contemporaries assumed that the wily Van Buren had intended to raise the political stock of the Jackson men by giving them a universally unpopular bill they could loudly denounce. Most scholars now agree that Van Buren honestly favored the tariff of 1828. He did not intend to offend northerners; that was the doing of Congress, which, in the give-and-take of tariff making, had twisted the measure out of its original shape.

The southern outcry against this "Tariff of Abominations" was universal, but it was John C. Calhoun who took it upon himself to make a constitutional case against it and for his region's interests. Published anonymously by the South Carolina legislature, Calhoun's *Exposition and Protest* denied that Congress had the right to levy a tariff so high that it would exclude imports. The Founding Fathers had intended to impose only moderate duties on imported goods as a means to raise revenue. Calhoun went beyond those familiar low-tariff arguments to insist that if Congress persisted in taking such an unconstitutional course, any state had the right to call a convention and declare such a measure null and void. *Exposition and Protest* revealed that its author, once a confirmed nationalist, was well on his way to becoming the great southern sectional champion.

The Election of 1828.   Despite Van Buren's hopes, the 1828 presidential election revolved around personalities rather than issues. Adams, with Richard Rush
of Pennsylvania as his running mate, was nominated by the "National Republican" convention at Harrisburg, the first major-party presidential convention. Jackson and Calhoun were selected by the Tennessee legislature and then placed on
the ballot by their supporters in the various states. Although President Adams
alone had the endorsement of the new, more democratic convention procedure, he
was actually the weaker candidate. His partisans were numerous only in New
England and other areas settled by New Englanders.

The contest was one of the dirtiest on record. The Jackson men, brooding over
their defeat in 1824, revived the "corrupt bargain" charge to discredit Adams and
resorted to blatant scandal-mongering. The Jackson press claimed that Adams's
wife, Louisa, had been born out of wedlock and he had lived in sin with her before
they were married. Equally scandalous stories were spread by the other side.
Rachel Jackson, the Adams people said, had not been divorced from her first husband when she married the general. As for Jackson, he was a brutal man who had
ordered the execution of six innocent militiamen during the campaign against the
Creek Indians a decade before.

There was almost no discussion of issues. Few principles seemed to separate
the candidates. One contemporary noted that no one in the New York State convention that confirmed Jackson's nomination for president knew the candidate's
views on public matters. A Pennsylvanian observed that "the great mystery of the

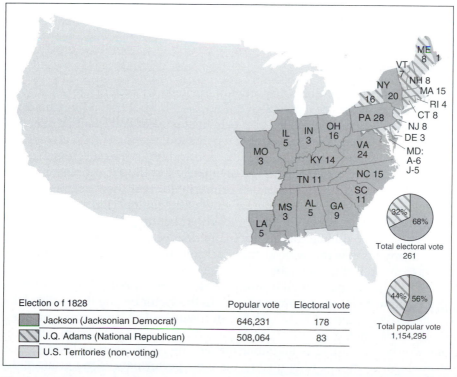

Election of 1828

case" was that "the South should support General Jackson avowedly for the purpose of preventing tariffs and internal improvements and that we should support him for a directly opposite purpose." Adams's positions were a little easier to discern. He stood for an active and paternalistic national government, if he stood for anything, and in New England the surviving Federalists clearly found him the more congenial candidate. Yet he also received the support of many Yankee Republicans, who saw him as the spiritual descendant of Jefferson.

Only the Anti-Masons seemed to have a clear program. This curious group had appeared in New York State following the mysterious disappearance of William Morgan, a former Mason who in 1826 had written a book exposing the Masonic order's rituals and other "secrets." Morgan was presumed murdered by the Masons, and the public's indignation led to the formation of a political organization dedicated to reducing the power of secret groups in national affairs. In 1828 the new party generally supported Adams, but in later years the Anti-Masons would nominate their own candidates and mount an attack on privilege in government and the economy that would be far more wide-ranging than anything undertaken by the reputedly radical Jackson party.

The 1828 contest, the Anti-Masons notwithstanding, did not contribute very much to reestablishing well-defined and competing party ideologies. Yet in several states it aroused political instincts dormant for over a decade. A two-sided contest, particularly one that included the colorful Jackson, was more gripping than either the rubber stamps of 1816 and 1820 or the multisided competition of 1824. In much larger numbers than four years before, voters came out to cast their ballots. Jackson won decisively, receiving 178 electoral and 646,000 popular votes to Adams's 83 electoral and 509,000 popular votes.

King Andrew

The Spoils System.   Jackson's first order of business was distributing the political loaves and fishes. The new president did not eject his political opponents from office wholesale, as scholars used to believe. In his first year and a half he removed 900 of over 10,000 federal employees, only 9 percent of the total. Yet Jackson's appointment policy was something new on the political stage. The Virginia dynasty presidents had favored members of their own party in filling vacancies, but they had seldom fired opposition officeholders primarily to create new openings. Jackson and his friends took no such moderate view of the federal civil service. Loyalty to the president, they quickly made clear, would be the prime consideration in retaining office. If the number of those actually dismissed was small, it was only because so many bureaucrats were already Jackson supporters or quickly became supporters to avoid losing their jobs.

At times the Jacksonians frankly admitted the narrow political reasons for removing long-time civil servants from office. "To the victor belong the spoils of the enemy," declared the candid New York Senator William L. Marcy, a Jackson man, in 1832. Generally, however, they tried to pass it off as political reform. Since, in Jackson's words, "the duties of all public officers are . . . so plain and simple that men of intelligence may readily qualify for their performance," no group need be excluded from serving the nation. Scholars, accepting the Jacksonians at their own word, have often treated the spoils system as a democratization of the political process.

In fact, as practiced by Jackson, the spoils system was not particularly democratic. The privileged social position of Jackson appointees differed little from that of their predecessors. The Jacksonians chief purpose was to provide political muscle to the party system. The lure of office would be a powerful incentive to ambitious men to work for party causes, while officeholders could be assessed for party contributions out of their government salaries. The spoils system would be a useful and important component of the emerging second party system, but it should not be taken as evidence that Jackson and his party were more democratic than their predecessors.

Whatever the deficiencies of the Virginia dynasty presidents, they had maintained a high level of honesty and efficiency in the public service. The Jackson men—and their successors—undoubtedly lowered the moral and intellectual tone of American political life. The spoils system damaged civil service morale and reduced efficiency. It also encouraged corruption. In one famous instance, in the New York customhouse, the collector Samuel Swartwout embezzled over one million dollars and escaped to England before he could be arrested.

At the same time, however, the ordinary American male began to feel a sense of participation. This new mood was not at first reflected in the voting statistics, except in the 1828 presidential election. Larger election turnouts would have to wait until real two-party contests had appeared in all the states and the voters had been caught up in the rivalries of close elections. But the Jackson party did infuse a new, more open spirit into political life—a spirit essential to the success of the second party system.

Jackson's Style.   Jackson was a strong president. A military man accustomed to command and unwilling to brook defiance by Congress, state legislatures, or the chief justice of the Supreme Court, he inspired either hatred or intense affection among the voters. He was not learned or even a clear and consistent thinker and acted on the prejudices he had acquired as a young man and never abandoned. A southerner and slaveholder, he had few objections to slavery and despised abolitionists. A man from the frontier state of Tennessee and a leader in the Indian wars, he had little love for Native Americans. Having been almost ruined in 1819 by the tight credit policies of the Bank of the United States, he hated banks in general and the Bank of the United States in particular. Jackson personalized almost all his political attitudes, turning political opponents into enemies who had to be destroyed lest they destroy him. Many Americans thought Old Hickory principled and spirited, but his opponents condemned his irascibility and high-handedness and called him "King Andrew." Their adoption of the name Whigs identified them as opponents of arbitrary power, much as the English Whigs had opposed royal absolutism in the late seventeenth century.

The Nullification Crisis.   Jackson's imperiousness surfaced during the tariff controversy that marked his first term. Though he had criticized the Tariff of Abominations during the election campaign, he disappointed the South by refusing to sponsor a substantial reduction in import duties. When, in 1832, Congress passed its own measure reducing the 1828 rates only slightly, South Carolinians, led by Vice President Calhoun, precipitated a political crisis by calling a convention and declaring the tariff void in the Palmetto State.

The South Carolina Ordinance of Nullification reflected more than southern economic discontent. By 1832, as we shall see in Chapter 12, slavery had become a major social and political issue in the nation. Just two years before, firebrand Massachusetts editor and reformer William Lloyd Garrison had begun to demand "immediate and complete emancipation" of southern slaves and had used angry language to denounce slaveholding and slaveholders. Garrison's attack frightened the South Carolina planter elite, who saw it as a serious threat to the stability and profitability of their slave-linked society. Nullification, they believed, was an appropriate weapon by which to defend the South's interests against an aggressive North that seemed likely to rally around the new antisouthern movement.

South Carolina's action was a constitutional challenge to the Union. But Jackson characteristically took it as a personal affront as well. The president called Calhoun a madman and denounced the state's move as "without parallel in the history of the world." Yet this time, at least, he sought to avoid a direct confrontation. In his December 1832 message to Congress he pointed to imminent changes in the tariff duties and told South Carolinians that their reaction was exaggerated. Yet soon after, he induced Congress to pass the Force Bill granting him additional powers to enforce the customs laws. Fortunately, Clay was able to patch together a compromise tariff bill that saved protection for nine years, until 1842, in exchange for dropping protection thereafter.

Finding no support in other states, the South Carolina planter elite backed down. The state legislature rescinded the Ordinance of Nullification against the 1832 Tariff Act, but at the same time, as a gesture of defiance, it claimed the Force Bill to be null and void. In the relief at getting past the crisis, few complained about the state's refusal to abandon the principle of nullification.

Indian Policy.   Jackson's position on nullification seems to confirm his strong nationalism. But he was perfectly willing to undermine the federal government's power when it suited his purposes or accorded with one of his fundamental prejudices. A blatant instance of this was his defiance of John Marshall over Indian policy.

In 1817, as agent for the War Department, Jackson had coerced a treaty out of the Cherokees of Georgia, by which they agreed to exchange their tribal lands for an equal amount of land in the West. Those Indians who did not want to go west might remain and settle down as farmers. Though the Georgia lands would have to be surrendered as tribal property, each Indian family might have 640 acres as an individual holding. To Jackson's disgust, virtually every Cherokee chose to remain in Georgia; indeed, many bought slaves and began to raise cotton on their new 640-acre plantations.

Meanwhile, Indian policy in general remained in a state of flux. In the North in 1818 and 1819, the government had induced the Wyandot, Chippewa, and Delaware tribes to surrender enormous areas in Indiana and Illinois. But the remaining Indian tribes, both north and south of the Ohio River, threatened to impede the rush of settlers pouring into the Great Lakes Plain, the Ohio Valley, and the Gulf Plain by the thousands. In 1825 President Monroe announced that henceforth

Jackson's use of the veto, his tightening of executive control,
and his personal approach to the presidency led Republicans to
dub him "King Andrew." As proper for the enemies of kings,
they called themselves "Whigs."

all the tribes of the eastern portion of the nation would be removed beyond the
ninety-fifth meridian to a "permanent Indian frontier." There they could live in
peace, he declared, unmolested by whites and free to preserve their ancestral ways.

Under the direction of Jackson's Secretary of War, Calhoun, Congress soon set
about removing the remaining tribes of the Northwest and South. The Indians resisted, and the new policy could only be carried out by unsavory tactics. Government

agents bribed chiefs to sign treaties that committed their tribes to move, passing these off as the collective will of the Indian people. Recalcitrant tribes were "persuaded" by military threats and force. In 1825 the Osage and Kansas tribes surrendered all of Kansas and northern Oklahoma except for two reservations. Over the next fifteen years the Shawnee, Kickapoo, Sauk, Fox, Potawatomi, Ottawa, Iowa, Miami, and Peoria were similarly moved.

The Indians of the Southeast proved more stubborn. In Georgia, the Carolinas, Alabama, and Mississippi the Five Civilized Nations—the Cherokees, Creeks, Choctaws, Chickasaws, and Seminoles—owned some 33 million acres of valuable land. These Indians had become a settled agricultural people with a sophisticated political and social system and a high level of literacy. They had conformed to the white man's ways, and by all the professed principles of contemporary white Americans, they should have been left alone to enjoy their unusual blend of European and Indian cultures. But their holdings aroused the greed and envy of their white neighbors. In 1827, hoping to head off Georgia's effort to oust them, the Cherokees wrote a constitution at New Echota establishing an independent republic. The outraged Georgians called this a violation of the federal Constitution and demanded that Washington evict the Cherokees as punishment. Congress responded by offering a bribe. The tribe would receive lands in the West and each Cherokee family that agreed to leave would get $50 in cash as well as a blanket, rifle, five pounds of tobacco, and other supplies. During the summer of 1828 federal agents pressured the Cherokees to accept this offer. There were few takers.

Jackson's election, and the discovery of gold on Cherokee lands, goaded the Georgians to harsher action. A new state measure provided that beginning in 1830 the tribe would be under the jurisdiction of state rather than federal law. The Indians would now have little or no protection against unprincipled whites coveting their land. The Cherokees protested to the federal government, which responded sternly with the Removal Bill, allowing the president to send any eastern tribe beyond the Mississippi if he wished, using force if needed. When the Indians asked the U.S. Supreme Court for an injunction to stop Georgia's repressive laws, the Court refused on the grounds the Cherokee were not, as they claimed, a foreign nation and so could not sue before the Supreme Court.

Now followed an orgy of greed and brutality at the Cherokees' expense. The Georgia government canceled debts owed the Indians, stopped payment of subsidies, and seized their property. State agents sought to stir up tribal animosities to undermine the Cherokees' morale. Christian missionaries who protested this ill-treatment were clapped in jail. A renewed appeal to the U.S. Supreme Court this time produced a favorable opinion from Chief Justice Marshall in *Worcester v. Georgia* (1832). The Indians did possess the status of a "domestic dependent nation," he declared, and were therefore entitled to federal protection against the state. But Jackson refused to enforce the chief justice's opinion, supposedly retorting: "John Marshall has made his decision, now let him enforce it!"

During the months that followed federal agents found a turncoat Indian leader who, in late 1835, agreed to abandon all the tribal lands for $5.6 million and free transportation to the West. The Cherokees denounced the agreement but realized they could no longer resist. For the next three years thousands of Indian families, grieving for their ancestral homes, set out on the "Trail of Tears" for what is now Oklahoma. The last holdouts were driven away by federal troops in the dead of winter. Many died on the way west.

Humane Americans, especially easterners, denounced Jacksonian Indian policies. The New England press labeled it "an abhorrent business." But it continued unabated. Few instances of white–Indian relations in North America exhibit the total callousness of the removal of the Civilized Tribes by Jackson and his successors.

The Attack on the Bank.

Andrew Jackson came to hate banks—especially "The Bank"—even more than he hated Indians. After its inauspicious start, when it helped trip off the Panic of 1819, the Second Bank of the United States had settled down to a useful existence under its third president, Nicholas Biddle. The bank lent money to merchants, helped expedite foreign trade, handled private and business checking accounts, issued paper money backed by gold, held the deposits of the federal government, and transferred government funds from one part of the country to the other as needed. Most important, it served as a central bank and the economy's balance wheel. As the nation's largest commercial bank, it could force the state banks to limit their credit when it felt the economy was overheated or encourage them to lend more readily when the economy was in the doldrums.

Many businesspeople supported the BUS, as did nationalist politicians. This support was not always disinterested, however. Newspaper editors and some of the most prominent men in government—including Daniel Webster, Henry Clay, and some Jacksonians—were in the bank's pay. The "God-like Daniel," who was frequently in debt, was a particularly shameless dependent of the bank, constantly asking that his "retainer" be "renewed or refreshed."

The bank also made some fierce enemies in the business community. Speculators, for one, found its conservative credit policies a hindrance to their expansive goals. Its most important opponents, however, were agrarians primarily from the South and West, such as Senator Thomas Hart Benton of Missouri, who disliked all banks, favored "hard money," and believed that the paper notes that banks issued were unwise and immoral. Agrarians also held that banks in general, and the Bank of the United States in particular, endangered free government. With its $35 million in capital, Biddle's "monster bank" was the largest corporation in the country by far. Such size by itself gave it a potential power over the economy that was frightening. Given Biddle's sense of its regulatory responsibilities, and its influence on politicians, it seemed to many that the bank had to be destroyed or it would destroy the country's democratic system.

The bank's twenty-year charter was due to expire in 1836. Wishing to ensure its continuity, Biddle applied for renewal in 1832. The measure passed Congress, but Jackson vetoed it. In a stinging attack, the president denounced the bank as a privileged monopoly controlled by foreign investors and warned that it would wield its great powers to punish its enemies if it became entrenched. The president undoubtedly believed that the Bank of the United States was a dangerous institution in a nation composed of many small economic units, but he also had a strong personal motive. "The Bank is trying to kill me," he told Van Buren, "but I will kill it."

The veto unleashed a storm of protest. Biddle called Jackson's veto message a "manifesto of anarchy." Webster, of course, also denounced it, as did two thirds of the nation's press, much of the business community, and many state bankers. The

Nicholas Biddle, the powerful head of the Second Bank of the United States. Under his direction, the bank loaned business money prudently and helped smaller banks survive temporary setbacks.
(James Barton Longacre (1786–1844), "Portrait of Nicholas Biddle." National Portrait Gallery, Smithsonian Institution/Art Resource, NY)

veto immediately became the chief party issue during the 1832 presidential election, with Jackson's supporters treating it as an attack on monopoly and privilege and his foes condemning it as an example of King Andrew's tyrannical temperament.

Whigs and Democrats.   By this time the second party system was rapidly taking shape. The Jackson party, now beginning to be called the Democrats, was a heterogeneous group that differed in its programs and principles from one part of the country to another. Most Democrats tended to favor low tariffs, hard money, antimonopoly, and a government hands-off policy toward the economy. But in New York, New England, and Pennsylvania the Jackson men favored banks, protective tariffs, and government aid for internal improvements. The Whigs were less divided in their economic principles. Their "American System" called for protective tariffs, federal aid for internal improvements, and a strong national bank. First announced by Clay in 1824, the American System projected a paternalistic national government that would nurture business, protect industrial workers from cheap foreign competition, and provide a secure market for farmers in America's growing cities.

The Whigs and the Democrats also differed somewhat in their political ideologies. The Democrats claimed to be the party of the "common man," and there
was some truth to their claim. James Silk Buckingham, an aristocratic English visitor to Ameerica, constantly heard the Democrats attacked by their opponents as
"agrarians, incendiaries, men who . . . desire to . . . seize the property of the rich
and divide it among the poor." The Jackson men, wrote William Seward, a New
York anti-Jackson leader, considered the parties distinctly different in their class
orientation: "It's with them the poor against the rich."

Yet the differences between the parties must not be exaggerated. Each attracted
voters from various classes, sections, and occupations. In the cities many "mechanics" voted for the Whigs or for various "workingmen's parties," which advocated
"radical" measures such as laws limiting the workday to ten hours and abolishing
the inconvenient militia service required of male voters. Farmers, too, were split,
with many rural voters, especially in New England and the Yankee-settled areas of
the Old Northwest, voting for the Democrats' opponents. In New York the regular
Democratic party often attacked the "Locofocos," a radical equal-rights wing of
their own party, as "infidels," "agrarians," and the "scum of politics." Moreover, the
Jackson Democrats—as much as the Whigs—were led by successful and prosperous
lawyers, businessmen, and gentlemen. The high and mighty "silk-stocking" element of the Whigs may have often expressed contempt for the "rabble" that supposedly made up the political opposition, but the leading Whigs—Clay, Webster,
and Seward—were popular figures who cultivated the voters and flattered them as
effectively as Jackson, Van Buren, Marcy, and the other leading Democrats.

The Whigs were strongest in New England and those places where New Englanders had settled, but they had supporters in every part of the country. In the
South small farmers voted Democratic; but large planters—despite their hostility
to the tariff favored by Whigs—voted Whig largely because they needed cheap
bank credit to market their cotton. Farmers in the West, eager for internal improvements, were also attracted to the Whigs. And in the cities the Whigs' American System attracted manufacturers and many industrial wage earners.

According to some scholars, what truly set Whigs and Democrats apart were
distinctive cultural and religious styles. There is evidence that in some states, such
as Michigan and New York, the Democrats were the party of laissez-faire in religion and morals as well as in economic affairs, whereas the Whigs saw nothing
wrong in government officials policing the public's personal habits and behavior.
Thus the Whigs often endorsed Sunday closing laws for businesses, opposed government deliveries of mail on the Christian Sabbath, and favored laws encouraging temperance. By contrast, Democrats generally believed that drinking and
doing business on Sundays were private, not public, matters. These divergent
attitudes also made the Whigs in the North more hostile to slavery than northern
Democrats. Northern Whig voters often saw slavery as sinful and, like other sinful
practices, within reach of government control; most northern Democrats believed
that, however deplorable slavery was, it was none of the government's business
what southerners did with their local institutions.

These outlooks in turn appealed to different cultural and religious groups. Whig
policies attracted evangelical Protestants, who considered politics a valid arena for
moral reform. Democratic laissez-faire appealed to Catholics, Episcopalians, and free

thinkers—all groups that preferred government to pursue a hands-off policy toward personal behavior and rejected politics based on morality. Because many New Englanders belonged to evangelical denominations, areas with a New England stamp voted Whig. Many of the recent immigrants were Catholics, and they generally joined the party of Jackson.

The Election of 1832.

But as the election of 1832 approached, these distinctions were only beginning to emerge. Jackson's opponents nominated Clay at their Baltimore convention. The Jackson supporters in turn renominated their hero, but selected Martin Van Buren as his running mate in place of Calhoun, who had defended South Carolina's nullification ordinance. Besides the two major parties, the Anti-Masons were in the field with William Wirt of Maryland as their candidate.

The chief issue in the campaign was ostensibly the Bank of the United States and the Jackson veto of the Bank recharter bill. Actually, personalities also counted. The voters were either charmed by Clay—"Old Coon," "Harry of the West," "The Mill Boy of the Slashes"—or repelled by his easygoing ways, drinking, and card playing. Jackson was to some a great national hero and to others the imperious and impetuous King Andrew. In the end the president won a decisive victory, with Clay second and Wirt a poor third.

Economic Ups and Downs.

The outstanding political event of Jackson's second term was the slow, agonizing death of the Bank of the United States. The president interpreted his election victory as a mandate to proceed immediately against the bank, even though its charter left it four more years of life. Disregarding the advice of two successive secretaries of the treasury, he removed government deposits from the bank and placed them in twenty-three state-chartered banks Whigs promptly labeled as "pet banks."

Biddle determined to fight back no matter what the cost. "All the other Banks and all the merchants may break," he wrote a friend, "but the bank of the United States shall not break." In the next months the BUS reduced its loans and called in those already outstanding, creating a credit squeeze that caused business severe hardship. Actually, with the treasury's $10 million in deposits removed from its reserves, the bank had to contract. But to demonstrate the bank's importance to the country's prosperity, Biddle contracted faster and further than necessary.

Worse was soon to come. With the Bank of the United States no longer regulating the country's credit and money supply, a major source of financial restraint was gone. The pet banks, with millions in government money in their reserves, began to lend extravagantly. Businessmen and speculators promptly invested their borrowed money in western lands, while states initiated ambitious canal-building schemes. The nation experienced a runaway boom that drove all prices, especially those of land, to record heights.

Jackson had not struck down Biddle's "monster" only to see it replaced by a state bank system that was even more irresponsible and dangerous. Nor did he wish to see the notes of the Bank of the United States, which were backed by gold, replaced by "wildcats" of a hundred banks that were little more than vague promises to pay. To halt the unhealthy boom, in July 1836 the president issued the

Specie Circular announcing that the federal government henceforth would accept only gold and silver in payment for public lands.

The Specie Circular pricked the bubble. The public abruptly lost confidence in the notes issued by the state banks and fought to convert them into specie. Hoping to hold on to their gold, the banks in turn called in their loans. Other creditors, fearful of the future, refused to lend further and clamped down on debtors. The result was a severe panic that halted business and brought down prices with a resounding crash. A decade of hard times followed.

Recent scholarship has absolved the Specie Circular of some of the blame for the panic and ensuing economic depression and has pointed to the collapse of international cotton prices as a major culprit. Jackson's supporters blamed the panic on "overbanking and overtrading." But many contemporaries condemned the president and criticized his hard-money and antibank policies. Fortunately for the Democrats, the full force of the economic collapse did not make itself felt until 1837, and so did not affect the 1836 presidential election.

Whigs and Democrats After Jackson

The Van Buren Administration.
The 1836 presidential contest was a confused affair. The Whigs, not yet a solid party, selected several regional candidates, including Webster of Massachusetts and Hugh Lawson White of Tennessee. The better-organized Democrats, required by the two-term tradition to pass over their leader, nominated Vice President Martin Van Buren. Van Buren pledged to follow in Jackson's footsteps and won a comfortable victory in the fall.

Scarcely was the new president installed in office than the full force of the economic storm broke. Van Buren called Congress into special session to deal with the emergency, but in a classic statement of the laissez-faire position, he noted that government was "not intended to confer special favors on individuals or on any classes of them to create systems of agriculture, manufacturers, or trade, or to engage in them. . . . The less government interferes with private pursuits the better for the general prosperity." The timid response of the new Democratic president lent support to the label "laissez-fairist" attached to the Jacksonians. But as one witty scholar has said, in many parts of the country Jackson men had "feet of Clay" and had few scruples against supporting business enterprise.

For the rest of Van Buren's ill-starred term the politicians remained preoccupied with the economy and economic legislation. To aid the treasury during the crisis, Congress ended the government's recently adopted policy of distributing to the states federal surpluses derived from excise taxes, the tariff, and land sales. In 1837 Van Buren proposed a scheme for a separate federal financial depository not dependent on banks. The proposal expressed Jacksonian suspicion of banks and paper money, and it seemed to the Whigs a crude system that would leave the country without a financial balance wheel or an effective means for regulating the state banks. Whigs and Democrats fought over the issue until 1840, when the Democrats in Congress managed to establish the Independent Treasury System. This required the treasury to collect and keep federal revenues and disburse them at need from its own vaults without relying on private banks. Moreover, government transactions with the public—salaries, taxes, bounties, and so forth—would now be confined to gold and silver. It was a primitive arrangement that handicapped business and commerce.

The Whigs Take Power.

As the 1840 presidential election approached, Van Buren, despite his spotty record and the bad times, had few opponents among the Democrats. On the Whig side the logical choice was Henry Clay, but the Whigs were reluctant to select a man too closely identified with the political battles of the past. At their first national convention, the delegates passed over Clay and turned instead to a man without strong political commitments: William Henry Harrison.

Harrison, though now sixty-seven, had a number of distinct advantages. A southerner by birth and sure to win many votes in the South that might otherwise go to the Democrats, he was also the hero of the 1811 battle of Tippecanoe. Most important of all, Harrison had no known political principles. For a party that had lost once by running its most representative figure, the obscurity of his views was a distinct asset.

The campaign revealed how well the Whigs had adapted to the sharp political partisanship that had appeared since 1828. Their candidate, the party leaders concluded, must be kept from expressing his ideas on any controversial issue. Let Harrison "say not one single word about his principles or his creed," advised Nicholas Biddle. The Whigs' major disadvantage, besides their candidate, was their aristocratic image. Fortunately, a careless remark by a prominent Democrat—that if Harrison were given a pension, a barrel of hard cider, and a log cabin to live in, he would never run for president—bailed them out. The Whigs immediately seized on the snobbery implied by the characterization. Picturing the wealthy Harrison as a simple man and a true democrat, they painted Van Buren as an aristocrat who lived in lordly style on his estate in Kinderhook, New York.

The "Log Cabin and Hard Cider" campaign was the first time a political party successfully marshaled the powerful forces of ballyhoo and propaganda to sell a presidential candidate to the American voters. The Whigs dressed up supporters as Indians to advertise Harrison's victory over Tecumseh. They distributed oceans of cider to thirsty voters. Whig party workers organized enormous parades with bands, giant banners, flaming torches, and flags.

The vote was huge—almost 60 percent greater than in 1836—and it was Whig. Harrison and his running mate, John Tyler of Virginia, carried nineteen of the twenty-six states and received 53 percent of the popular vote, an unusually high proportion for this period. The opposition had succeeded in the difficult task of turning an incumbent president out of office and had demonstrated the vitality of the newly revived party system.

Conclusions

By 1840 two new political parties had come into being. After a long gap that saw government become the preserve of public-spirited gentlemen, the people once more insisted on being heard. The change was not Jackson's doing: It had begun years before, in the states. Jackson was its beneficiary, not its author.

The two new parties seemed to parallel those of Hamilton's and Jefferson's time. Whigs and Democrats superficially resembled Federalists and Jeffersonian Republicans, respectively—without the powdered hair, velvet knee breeches, and silver shoebuckles. But on closer examination we see that the reality was different. Neither party was as closely associated with a single class as their predecessors. There was a difference in the parties' social focus: Democrats probably won the support of more small farmers than the Whigs, and because small farmers were a majority of Americans, this made them in some sense the party of the common people. But we should not make too much of this tendency. In an age that professed to be democratic, both parties had to appear to accept the voice of the "sovereign people."

The two new party organizations were not as clearly different in ideology as the old parties were, either. They disagreed over banks, tariffs, and internal improvements; but their leaders were apt to be more practical and accommodating than the Federalists and Jeffersonians. The emergence of the second party system marked the development of a pragmatic political consensus: Both parties would avoid extreme ideological positions and try to stand close to the political center. Jackson's victory did not set off a revolution in the social and political order, but it did loosen the rigid political framework of the day. By refusing to accept the gentlemanly procedures of the Virginia dynasty, the Jacksonians revitalized American political life. After 1828 the country would once more have a lively and effective two-party system, and the change would make the nation's government more responsive to public needs and public wants. It was the return of two-party government to American political life.

ONLINE RESOURCES

"Indian Removal and Its Aftermath" *http://www.synaptic.bc.ca/ejournal/jackson.htm*
   Read Andrew Jackson's messages to Congress addressing Native Americans and his policies toward them. This site contains the full text of the Indian Removal Act of 1830.
"John C. Calhoun: A Brief Introduction" *http://xroads.virginia.edu/~CAP/CALHOUN/ jcc1.html* This site offers an excellent introduction to the world and mind of Calhoun. It also provides instructive information on the Nullification Crisis and the growing sectionalism that gripped the nation.
"The American Whig Party" *http://odur.let.rug.nl/~usa/E/uswhig/whigsxx.htm http://www.let. rug.nl/~usa/E/uswhig/whigs01.htm* These sites offer information on the founding of the party and its subsequent demise. They also provide numerous links to pages that discuss Democrat Andrew Jackson's politics, presidency, and policies.
Missouri Compromise *http://www.pbs.org/wgbh/aia/part3/3h511.html* See the full text of this historical document, and read a narrative about this divisive chapter in the nation's history.
Trail of Tears *http://www.cviog.uga.edu/Projects/gainfo/trailtea.htm* This Web site provides numerous and diverse links to both Euro-American and Native American primary accounts of Indian removal, as well as artwork depicting the plight of the Indians and informative timelines.
Indian Surrender *http://www.mtholyoke.edu/acad/intrel/black.htm* Read the full text of Black Hawk's surrender speech after losing a battle with the Americans.

11

The Mexican War and Expansionism

Greed, Manifest Destiny, or Inevitability?

1803–06	Lewis and Clark Expedition to Pacific
1812	Astor establishes fur-trading post on Pacific in Oregon
1818	A treaty between Great Britain and the United States provides for joint occupation of Oregon Territory
1819	Adams–Onís Treaty establishes the western boundaries of the Louisiana Purchase
1823	Mexico grants Stephen Austin the right to settle in Texas with 300 American families
1836	Texas declares its independence from Mexico; Texans force captured Mexican leader Santa Anna to recognize the Texas Republic
1841	President Harrison dies and John Tyler becomes president
1842	Webster–Ashburton Treaty signed by Great Britain and the United States
1844	James K. Polk elected president
1845	Congress admits Texas into the Union; Anticipating war, Polk sends General Zachary Taylor and 4,000 troops to occupy Mexican territory on north bank of Rio Grande; Polk secretly authorizes American consul Thomas Larkin to encourage the secessionist movement in California; The Slidell Mission discusses Texas's southern boundary and offers to buy New Mexico and California for $30 million
1846	Mexico declares defensive war on the United States; Congress votes for war; The Oregon dispute with Great Britain is settled by treaty
1847	Polk authorizes General Winfield Scott to attack Vera Cruz and Mexico City
1848	The Mexican-American War ends with the Treaty of Guadalupe Hidalgo; Mexican Cession adds 339 million acres to the United States
1850	Congress admits California into the Union

On May 11, 1846, the clerk of the House of Representatives read the war message of President James K. Polk to a solemn joint session of Congress. The message was expected. Rumors had been circulating for weeks that a diplomatic break with Mexico was imminent. Just two days before, people in Washington had learned that Mexican troops had crossed the Rio Grande del Norte and attacked American army units on its eastern bank. Several Americans had been killed, others wounded.

"The cup of forbearance had been exhausted before the recent information from the frontier of the Del Norte," the president declared. "But now, after reiterated menaces, Mexico has passed the boundary of the United States, has invaded our territory and shed American blood upon American soil. She has proclaimed that hostilities have commenced, and that the two nations are now at war." "By every consideration of duty and patriotism," the president concluded, Americans must "vindicate with decision the honor, the rights, and the interests of their country."

Congress voted for war by an overwhelming majority, yet many representatives and senators were uneasy with the decision. During the next weeks and months, United States armies would go from triumph to triumph in a crescent of territory stretching 2,000 miles from the Gulf of Mexico to the Oregon boundary; but many Americans would denounce the war. In Congress Senator Thomas Corwin of Ohio would declare: "If I were a Mexican I would tell you 'Have you not room in your own country to bury your dead men? If you come into mine we will greet you with bloody hands, and welcome you to hospitable graves'." In the House a young Illinois Whig, Abraham Lincoln, would call the president "a bewildered, confounded, and miserably perplexed man" with a "painful" conscience. Lincoln would spend much of his single term in Congress demanding that Polk prove his allegations that the Mexicans had provoked the war by attacking Americans on their own soil.

Outside Congress were other harsh critics. New Englander James Russell Lowell's fictional Yankee spokesman, Hosea Biglow, called the attack on Mexico "a national crime committed on behoof of slavery." An ardent enemy of slavery, Lowell was certain that the "slave power" was determined to seize Mexican territory "so's to lug new slave states in." Henry Thoreau, the writer, who admired Mexico for giving refuge to escaped slaves, believed the American invasion justified "honest men to rebel and revolutionize."

Different theories of the war's origins are implied by these charges. Lincoln and Corwin view the conflict as naked United States aggression against a weaker neighbor. Thoreau and Lowell's Hosea Biglow see the war as a southern slaveholders' plot. Modern scholars, too, have advanced competing theories of causation. Historian Eugene Genovese perceived the cotton South as forced to expand territorially or suffer from declining profits as its soils lost their fertility and cotton ceased to produce abundant wealth. Other scholars have been are more inclined to see Americans as inspired in 1846 by the ideological attitude of continentalism, or Manifest Destiny, which justified United States dominion over the continent—indeed, made it seem inevitable—on grounds of supposed American cultural, political, or even racial superiority. Mexican scholars agree in ascribing the war to America's sense of superiority, though they also blame it on Yankee greed. In either case, they insist, the United States was a blatant aggressor.

A final school of interpretation seeks to avoid simple praise or blame. In this view the pre-Civil War expansionist impulse was the expression of what was almost a physical law. To the west of the growing, vibrant United States, it says, lay a sparsely populated and loosely governed expanse of territory. It was almost an empty region in a political and social sense, and American expansion into it resembled the rush of air to fill a vacuum. The war, in this view, was an inevitable event arising out of the unavoidable circumstances of history and geography.

The Mexican War marked the last phase of continental expansion that carried the American people to the Pacific. The war itself added 530,000 square miles of territory to the United States, and the related settlement of the Oregon boundary dispute with Great Britain added another 258,000. The total addition was truly imperial in extent, but was it also imperialist in origin? Was it greed that led President Polk to send his war message to Congress that day in early May? Was it misplaced idealism? Or was it still some other force that brought the two neighbors to war in 1846?

The Oregon Country

In 1830 the line marking the western edge of dense agricultural settlement in the United States did not extend much beyond the bottomlands of the Mississippi River. Almost all of the trans-Mississippi West remained the domain of the Indian tribes. Beyond the western boundary of the Louisiana Purchase was a vast region of mountain, desert, plateau, and rugged ocean coast still barely touched by European culture and institutions.

Political title to much of this region was uncertain. In 1819 the Adams–Onís Treaty had settled the boundary between American and Spanish possessions and surrendered Spanish claims in the Oregon country to the Americans. But title to the vast expanse of what was called "Oregon"—including present-day Oregon, Washington, Idaho, British Columbia, and parts of Montana and Wyoming—remained in dispute between Great Britain and the United States. British claims rested on the voyages of Captains James Cook in the 1770s and George Vancouver in the 1790s and on the activities of Canadian and British fur companies. American claims derived from the April 1792 discovery of the Columbia River by Captain Robert Gray, Lewis and Clark's encampment near the Pacific in 1805–1806, and the American merchant vessels that periodically visited the northern Pacific coast.

Stretching from the northern boundary of California to the southern boundary of Russian America (Alaska) at 54°40′ north latitude, the region had only a few hundred American inhabitants in 1840. Yet the United States guarded its claim jealously. In 1818 Secretary of State John Quincy Adams negotiated a convention with the British providing for joint occupation of Oregon for ten years. In 1827 the Anglo-American occupation was extended for an indefinite period, subject to termination by either party on a year's notice.

The Far Western Fur Trade.   Ultimately, the dispute over Oregon was resolved by actual settlement, not diplomacy. But as with so many other American frontiers, the fur traders came first, preparing the way for the settlers.

Several groups of entrepreneurs were involved in the far western fur trade. In Oregon the impresario was John Jacob Astor, a German-born entrepreneur who had come to the United States in 1783 and soon became a successful fur merchant. Astor entered the Oregon trade shortly after the United States acquired the Louisiana Territory and in 1811 established a trading post at the mouth of the Columbia, which he modestly named Astoria. The post flourished briefly until the threat of British attack during the War of 1812 induced Astor to sell it to a Canadian firm.

After the war the British-owned Hudson's Bay Company and the American-owned North West Company competed bitterly in the Oregon country for a while and then, in 1821, merged. Soon afterward the new company established Fort Vancouver on the north bank of the Columbia River in what is now Washington state. Head of the new settlement was Dr. John McLoughlin, who sought to exclude the Americans and nail down Britain's claim to the Oregon region.

Meanwhile, in the Rocky Mountain region, other Americans, under Missourian William Ashley, were uncovering new fur-bearing regions in what is now southwestern Wyoming. Ashley saw that he needed not only a new source of furs but also a new method of collecting them. In the past, white agents had bought the furs from Indian trappers. But beginning in 1825 Ashley sent his own employees to forage the newly opened region for furs. Under Ashley's successors in the Rocky Mountain Fur Company, as many as 600 "mountain men" of American, French, Mexican, black, and mixed Indian-European backgrounds spent the year in the mountain wilds, many of them with their Indian wives and half-Indian children. In the spring the trappers hunted beaver along the streams. In July they gathered at a "rendezvous," where they exchanged their "hairy bank notes" for cloth, rifles and shot, trinkets, food, liquor, and other commodities the company brought west. Cut off from others for months at a time by the deep snows and fiercely cold winters, the mountain men turned the July meetings into wild debauches. After a week or two of heavy drinking, gambling, fighting, and general hell-raising, the trappers and their families staggered off to rest up for the coming hard year. The company agents returned east with furs worth twenty times their cost.

The Way West.   The western fur trade helped open the trans-Missouri region for white settlement. Fur company agents and officials—Kit Carson, Jim Bridger, Milton and William Sublette, and others—marked out useful routes, explored unknown rivers, and discovered new mountain passes through the Great Plains, Rocky Mountain, and Great Basin regions. In 1823 one of Ashley's agents, Jedediah Smith, found South Pass, a major break in the towering mountain wall that blocked the overland route west. The following year Peter Ogden, of the Hudson's Bay Company, was the first white man to view the Great Salt Lake.

Not all the trans-Missouri expeditions furthered settlement. In 1806 Zebulon Pike returned from a government-authorized trip through the High Plains and judged the area too dry for cultivation. In 1820 Stephen Long, another explorer, called the region "wholly unfit for cultivation, and . . . uninhabitable by a people depending upon agriculture for their subsistence." His account of a "Great American Desert" just to the east of the mountains helped delay Plains settlement for decades and turned people's eyes to the well-watered, forested lands of Oregon farther west.

The journey of the pioneers to Oregon was a rugged overland trek across hundreds of miles of dangerous, inhospitable country. Each spring, beginning in 1841, eager Oregon-bound families assembled in Independence, Missouri, the jump-off point for the trip west. The settlers traveled in canvas-covered farm wagons, into which they crammed supplies and as much equipment as they could carry. Oxen in teams of six drew these wagons, while women and older children—at least in good weather—walked. The men either drove or rode saddle horses to scout for game and potential danger.

Each party, moving typically in a broad column several wagons wide, was commanded by a captain elected by the men. Some of these were skilled guides who had made the trip before or were natural leaders. Others, however, were incompetents who had to be replaced in mid-journey.

The going at first was easy. The lush green lands of the eastern portion of the Trail were level and pleasant to cross. Three hundred miles from Independence, the pioneers reached the Platte River, in present-day Nebraska, a shallow stream "too thick to drink and too thin to plow." Following the low banks of the river for another 500 miles, the travelers encountered the Rocky Mountains. Here the real challenges began. At times the wagons bounced over terrain so rough that the trail was covered with blood from the oxen's lacerated hooves. At many spots the men were forced to put their own shoulders to the wagons and push them along by brute strength. At this point, usually, over the side would go all the heavy gear—plows, stoves, tables, sofas, even pianos—that optimistic emigrants had stowed in hopes of making their new lives more comfortable. Finally, at the Dalles in what is now central Oregon, the travelers reached the Columbia River. After caulking the wagons' seams to make them watertight, they floated down the great river to their destination, the fertile valley of the north–south-flowing Willamette River.

In the 1830s many of the emigrants were American Methodist missionaries and their families bringing the Christian God and the white man's notions of morality to the Indians. During the hard times of the 1840s reports of cheap Oregon land and of

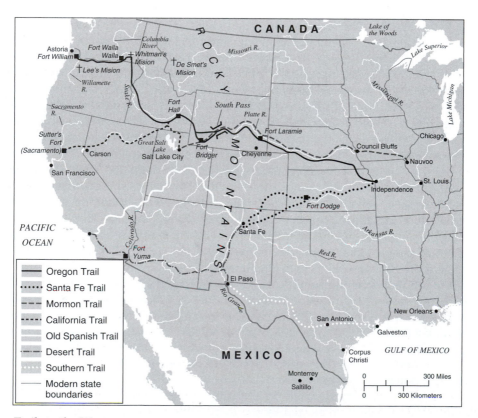

Trails to the West

insatiable markets for agricultural produce in Asia created an "Oregon fever" throughout the West. By 1845 there were over 5,000 Americans living in Oregon.

The British in Oregon watched this American influx uneasily at first. The settlers were clearly reinforcing the American claim to the Oregon country. The resident British were virtually all employees of the Hudson's Bay Company, and nowhere could they match the Americans in numbers. It soon became clear that Britain had lost the population competition south of the Columbia, where in any case the beaver had been trapped out. At this point McLoughlin generously helped the settlers in the Willamette region by providing jobs and other aid. In effect, the company surrendered what is now the state of Oregon to the Americans, though it continued for a while to oppose American entry into the region further north. Before long, excluding Americans from that area began to seem pointless too. In 1845 the Hudson's Bay director moved the firm's chief base to Vancouver Island in what is now British Columbia. The British had conceded to the Americans control of the whole block of territory between Puget Sound and the California boundary.

The Mexican Borderlands

For a generation preceding the migration to Oregon a few Americans had been drawn to the Southwest, where Mexico, formerly a Spanish colony, loosely held a million square miles of territory. The Mexican borderlands from Texas to California were generally arid, but within their limits were tracts where the land was well watered and enterprising farmers could raise lush crops. The Mexican capital city was comfortably far away, hundreds of miles to the south.

The Native People.   About half the population of the borderlands was Indian. In Texas the Comanche, Apache, and Kiowa were nomadic peoples who for centuries had hunted buffalo on foot with bow and arrow. During the late seventeenth century they had acquired horses from Spanish Mexico, and then rifles. These new possessions made them formidable foes of both their Indian neighbors and the Spaniards who began to push up from Mexico after 1700.

Farther to the west, in what is now New Mexico and Arizona, were the Zuñis, Acomas, Hopis, and several other tribes grouped under the name Pueblo Indians. Dependent on agriculture, they lived in densely populated, settled communities (pueblos) with mud-brick (adobe) structures that resembled modern apartment houses. The Pueblo tribes were generally peaceful people; they seldom waged offensive war against their neighbors, though they were capable of fighting fiercely for their homes and rights.

Along the Pacific coast in what is now California, when whites arrived in the eighteenth century as many as 350,000 Indians were spread through the narrow coastal plain, in the interior valleys, and along the lower reaches of the region's rivers. Though the material possessions of the California tribes were meager, they had developed a complex religious and ceremonial life, and a rich oral literature of songs, stories, and myths passed on from generation to generation.

Spanish Penetration.   The earliest Spanish settlers had come to the interior of the Southwest around 1600, when parties of soldiers from Mexico established Santa Fe in what is now central New Mexico. But the clergy were the chief agents of Spanish penetration. A Spanish friar of the Dominican, Franciscan, or Jesuit order would set off with a few Indian dependents for an unsettled region. When he had located a favorable spot, he returned to "civilization" and gathered a few soldiers, several families of Christianized Indians, and some fellow friars. Back on the new frontier, the "padres" recruited local Indian labor and, if all went well, in a decade or so they had created a "mission" with vineyards, cultivated fields of grain, herds of cattle, and clusters of Indian huts, all dominated by a church, elaborately decorated to beautify Christian worship and hold the attention of the Indian converts. Before long this new pocket of Spanish colonial civilization would send out other shoots to repeat the process and contribute to the steady advance of the European cultural frontier.

California.   In California the missionary process began in 1769 when Franciscan friar Junípero Serra and 14 brown-robed brothers led a party of 126 Indians and soldiers from present-day Arizona to San Diego Bay. Intended by the Spanish authorities to forestall Russian designs on California, the move combined imperial self-interest with the hope of gathering souls for the Lord. Over the next half-century the friars established another twenty missions, along with two garrisoned towns (presidios), in what is now the state of California.

In many ways these missions were immensely successful enterprises. By 1800 they sheltered some 13,000 Indians and had taken on the attractive physical form that tourists see today: whitewashed churches with red-tiled roofs, courtyards with arched colonnades and fountains, and ingenious workshops containing the artifacts of skilled Indian artisans. It is also easy to imagine the nearby vineyards, grain fields, fruit and olive orchards, and vast grazing herds that no longer exist.

But there was another, grimmer side. Mortality in the crowded missions was high among both children and adults. The Europeans, as usual, brought their diseases and their almost equally lethal culture. The former killed directly; the latter destroyed by undermining Indian morale and family life. Demographic disaster was visited on the California Indians. All told, between 1769 and 1846 the Indian population of California dropped to about 100,000—less than one third of what it had been when the friars first arrived.

The mission era ended in the 1830s when the Mexican government, prodded by would-be landowners, divested the missions of thousands of acres and ended the friars' paternal but stern control over the Indians. In the next few years aggressive entrepreneurs established some 700 *ranchos,* each covering thousands of acres. Devoted largely to cattle raising, each giant estate was headed by a *ranchero,* usually of Spanish descent, who supervised groups of *vaqueros* (cowboys) doing the hard common labor of herding, fence-mending, branding, and slaughtering.

Life in California in the years immediately preceding American occupation was colorful and, for the rancheros, almost idyllic. Little news came from the outside world to disturb the few thousand Spanish-Mexicans. Government in Mexico City was remote, and its hand rested lightly on the inhabitants. If we can believe the accounts of visitors, the life of the small Spanish elite was a round of fiestas, races, dancing, and courtship rituals.

Americans began to drift into California in small numbers in the 1830s. Some established themselves as merchants in Monterey, San Diego, and other towns. Others, arriving overland by way of the California Trail, became successful ranchers. There were immigrants directly from Europe, too. The Swiss John Augustus Sutter talked the Mexican governor into granting him a vast domain near present-day Sacramento, which he named New Helvetia in honor of his homeland. Many of the newcomers converted to Catholicism and married into prosperous Mexican families.

For the former mission Indians life was little better than before. Working for the *rancheros*, they spent long days purifying tallow, tanning hides, and loading skins onto ships for markets in the United States and Europe. They were paid nothing for their labor beyond their food, clothing, and shelter. If they left the ranch, they were hunted down like runaway slaves. It is not surprising that the California Indian population continued to fall at an appalling rate.

New Mexico.   Separated from the nearest settlements of northern Mexico by 600 miles of barren plains and rugged mountains, New Mexico, like California, had been settled by friars who planted missions as centers of Christian civilization and incidentally as outposts to protect New Spain against the French in Louisiana.

Unlike the indigenous peoples of California, the Indians of the New Mexico region were not easy to dominate. The Pueblo Indians were able to keep their tight-knit agricultural communities intact, and to this day preserve a distinctive and strongly defined culture. Their warlike qualities protected the nomadic Apache, Navaho, and Comanche tribes in the New Mexico–Arizona–west Texas region from the Europeans. These tribes had long preyed on the Pueblo Indians, stealing slaves and booty. They also attacked the Spaniards, who arrived about 1700, though the Europeans provoked them by enslaving captured Indians and offering bounties for their scalps. Once the Indians acquired horses from their enemies, they became formidable mounted warriors whose swift raids and quick retreats made them difficult to subdue. Indeed, not until the advent of the repeating revolver in the mid-nineteenth century would the European become the military equal of the Apache or Comanche horseman.

Despite these difficulties, the Spaniards succeeded in establishing several permanent communities in the New Mexico–Arizona region. By the 1820s New Mexico had 40,000 settled inhabitants, many of them clustered around the provincial capital, Santa Fe. These were self-sufficient in food but starved for manufactured goods, which distant and economically undeveloped Mexico could not supply. To fill the gap, in the early 1820s a Missouri merchant, William Becknell, launched a lucrative trade in textiles, rifles, tools, and other goods between St. Louis and New Mexico by way of the Santa Fe Trail. By 1824 parties of wagons and animals were using the trail blazed by Becknell to carry goods to and from New Mexico.

Texas.   The American presence in Texas, then an ill-defined region between Louisiana and the northern desert of Mexico, was far weightier than in New Mexico and California. Americans in small numbers began to cross the Sabine River into Spanish-held territory early in the nineteenth century. In 1820 the newly independent Mexican Republic, hoping to develop the region, gave Moses Austin a land grant and the right to settle 300 American families as permanent inhabitants. In 1823 Moses's son, Stephen, established the first American colony on the banks of the Brazos River in east Texas. By 1825 the colony had 1,800 inhabitants, including 443 black slaves.

Austin's settlement was followed by others launched by various American impresarios under contracts with the Mexican state of Texas-Coahuila. Settlers also came as individuals and in single families, attracted by reports of the region's fertile land. Some brought slaves. Fearful of the flood of Americans, in 1830 the Mexican government prohibited further United States immigration and established military garrisons in the state. The law was not enforced, however, and by 1835 about 20,000 transplanted Americans were living in Texas.

The Annexation of Texas

The inherent tensions between the Americans and Mexicans could not easily be resolved. The Americans were mostly Protestant and resented efforts by Mexican officials to convert them to the Catholic faith. Most were southerners determined to grow cotton with slave labor, and they resisted Mexico's laws forbidding slavery. Many transplanted Americans disdained Mexicans as culturally or racially inferior. Yet at first the American settlers in Texas proved remarkably loyal to their adopted country. When, in 1826, a small band of dissident Americans led by Haden Edwards revolted against the central government, the main body of settlers under Austin helped the Mexican authorities put down the insurrection.

The Texas Revolution.   Unfortunately, neither the citizens of the United States nor the Mexican government could let the Texan-Americans alone. Many Americans regretted the surrender of Texas to Spain in the Adams–Onís Treaty of 1819. Six years later, as president, John Quincy Adams tried to undo his own work by offering Mexico $1 million for Texas. His successor, Andrew Jackson, raised the bid to $5 million and sent Anthony Butler to Mexico City to induce the Mexican government to accept it. When this effort failed, Butler urged Jackson to take Texas by force.

The Mexican government, too, stirred up trouble. Almost never was there a peaceful succession of administrations in Mexico City, where two competing philosophies of government produced constant changes of policy and turmoil. "Federalists" advocated local autonomy for the individual Mexican states and weak control from Mexico City. This allowed the states to pursue policies favorable to immigration. "Centralists," on the other hand, demanded tight, centralized government from Mexico City to hold the unwieldy country together. They opposed immigration and, when in power, sought to prevent liberal state colonization grants to Americans.

The shifts of factions and leaders within the Mexican government had serious effects on the relations between Mexico and her newest citizens, the Texans. In 1834 Antonio Lopez de Santa Anna became the nation's leader for a second time. As a Centralist, he rescinded the autonomy his predecessors had allowed the Mexican states and established a harsh dictatorship in Mexico City.

His rise to power worsened an already uncomfortable situation for the Texans. For some time the American settlers had been unhappy with their limited self-rule. Texas was part of the Mexican state of Coahuila, with its capital at Satillo, 300 miles to the west, a great inconvenience to those in the distant northern region subject to its authority. Under the Mexican Federalists the Texans had hoped to achieve separate

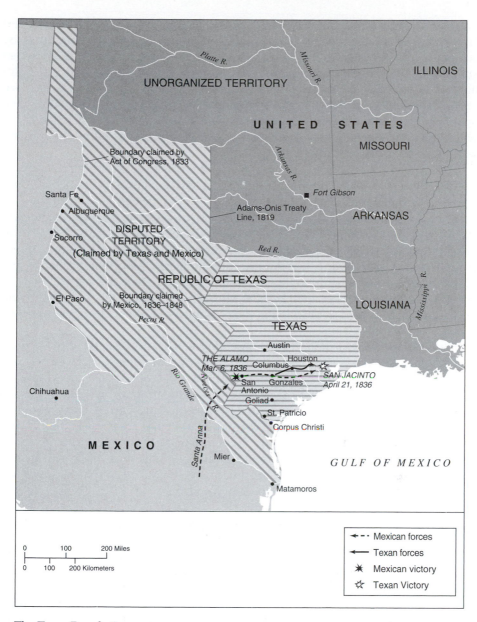

The Texas Revolution

statehood for themselves, but now these hopes were dashed, and in fact there seemed a distinct possibility that the Mexican government might try to expel all Americans from Texas. When Santa Anna sent troops to garrison several points within Texas, these fears seemed vindicated. Sporadic fighting soon broke out between Texans and Mexican troops. Though there were special reasons for Mexican–Texan tensions, hostility to the Santa Anna government was widespread in Mexico generally, and other outlying parts of the republic rose in revolt against the dictator as well.

In 1835 Santa Anna marched north with an army to punish the Texans and confiscate their arms. Prepared to challenge him were 187 Texans commanded by William B. Travis, holed up in the Alamo, an adobe-walled former mission in San Antonio. In late February 1836 Santa Anna and 4,000 troops arrived at San Antonio and surrounded the small American force. The Americans held out for two weeks, but on March 6 they were overwhelmed by the Mexicans. Every defender, including Travis and the frontier heroes Jim Bowie and Davy Crockett, died in the siege. Resentment against the Mexicans was soon being expressed by the rallying cry: "Remember the Alamo!"

Soon after, fifty-nine delegates met in the little village of Washington, adopted a declaration of Texas independence, named former governor of Tennessee, Sam Houston, commander in chief of the Texas army, and created a constitution that recognized slavery and granted each citizen a square league of land. In the next few weeks Houston and his men retreated before Santa Anna's army. As Mexican forces pursued the Texans eastward, their fighting effectiveness dwindled. Meanwhile, Houston grew stronger as American volunteers crossed the border to join his small army. At San Jacinto, Houston finally turned to face the enemy. At noon on April 21, 1836, his troops attacked the Mexicans and decisively defeated them. More than 600 Mexicans were killed in the fighting and 730, including Santa Anna himself, were captured.

San Jacinto brought Texas its independence. Houston forced the Mexican leader to sign treaties ending the war and accepting the independence of Texas. When news of Santa Anna's defeat and capture reached Mexico City, the Mexican Congress promptly repudiated the agreements on the ground that they had been coerced. Little attention was given at this point to the question of Texas's boundaries. The Mexicans would claim that it stopped at the Nueces; the Texans would insist that it reached farther west to the Rio Grande. But from the Mexican standpoint, Texas was still part of Mexico and the whole issue was irrelevant. In any event, Mexico was in no position to resume the war, and Texas settled down uneasily to a brief existence as an independent republic.

Expansionism: Advocates and Opponents

The knotty problems of Oregon, the Mexican borderlands, and indeed of virtually all the boundaries of the United States, fell into the lap of John Tyler when, in April 1841, William Henry Harrison contracted pneumonia and died a month after his inauguration. This was the first time a president had died in office, and it was not clear whether "His Accidency" should exercise the full powers of a duly elected chief executive. The Whigs' skepticism was magnified by their knowledge that Tyler was really a Democrat who had been placed on the party ticket to win southern Democratic votes. Tyler refused to accept an inferior status and stubbornly and successfully asserted his full presidential prerogatives.

In domestic matters Tyler's doggedness accomplished little. The Whigs had looked forward after their 1840 victory to rechartering a federal bank, raising the tariff, and carrying out other nationalist measures. Congress did pass a new federal bank bill, but Tyler, true to his Jeffersonian states' rights principles, promptly vetoed it. In short order his entire cabinet, except Secretary of State Daniel Webster, who still had important diplomatic business to complete, resigned in protest. Thereafter, Tyler and the Whig leaders in Congress remained at loggerheads. The president vetoed two Whig efforts to raise the tariff and signed the Tariff Act of 1842 only after Henry Clay's pet scheme to distribute surplus federal revenues to the states had been eliminated from the bill.

In foreign affairs, where the Constitution allows the chief executive a freer hand, Tyler was more effective. The president was a moderate expansionist. As a southerner, he craved new territory within slavery's supposed "natural limits"—the region where cotton, sugar, rice, and other warm-climate, slave-grown crops could flourish. Tyler was indifferent to expansion elsewhere.

The president's attitude affected the course of negotiations with Britain over the disputed boundary between Canada and the states of Maine, New York, Vermont, and New Hampshire. In 1838 the Maine authorities tripped off a violent clash between American and Canadian lumbermen and fur trappers when they tried to eject British subjects from parts of the Aroostook district claimed by the Canadian province of New Brunswick. Fortunately, the Maine and New Brunswick authorities agreed to a truce, but the boundary dispute continued to fester while other arguments with Britain accumulated, including the unwillingness of the United States to cooperate with Britain in suppressing the illegal Atlantic slave trade and the Caroline affair involving an American ship that had been used by Canadian rebels to mount a revolt against Britain.

Tyler and Secretary of State Daniel Webster chose to be conciliatory toward Britain. The British, too, preferred compromise and sent Lord Alexander Ashburton, a banker married to an American woman, to negotiate with Webster. In a few short weeks the two men hammered out the Webster–Ashburton Treaty (1842). Under its terms the United States would keep about 4.5 million acres of the 7.7 million in dispute along the Canadian–American boundary; the province of New Brunswick would get the rest. In addition, the United States government agreed to join Britain in supporting a naval squadron stationed off the African coast to capture slave ships attempting to bring Africans to the Americas. In a supplementary exchange of notes Ashburton in effect also apologized for the Caroline incident.

Tyler's tepid interest in northern real estate carried over to Oregon. Many Americans insisted that the United States rightfully owned all the Oregon country from the northern boundary of California at 42° north latitude to the southern boundary of Russian-America at 54°40′. Tyler offered to divide Oregon with the British at the forty-ninth parallel and to take even less territory if Britain forced Mexico to hand over to the United States the port of San Francisco. The British declined the offer and the Oregon dispute remained unsettled.

Victory for Tyler.   Tyler's major foreign policy success came in Texas. No sooner had they achieved independence than the Texans sought admission to the American Union. Many Americans, however, fervently opposed the annexation of Texas. Though eager to augment federal power within the existing limits of the United States, Whigs traditionally opposed dispersion of that power over a broader area. Many northerners, moreover, feared that Texas, which would surely enter the Union as a slave state or even a number of slave states, would reinforce the "slave power" in the national government. A group of antislavery congressmen, led by former

President John Quincy Adams, called the effort to annex Texas a plot by the "slavocracy" to add to southern strength in Congress. Still other citizens feared war. Annexation might well goad the Mexicans into attacking the United States.

With so many Americans hostile to slavery, skeptical of expansion, or afraid of war, Texas annexation became a political hot potato. In early 1837, just before leaving office, Jackson granted official diplomatic recognition to the Texas Republic, and during the next few years Americans established trade relations with the young nation. Annexation, however, remained stalled.

Events soon goaded the United States to action. Discouraged by American indifference, the Texans began to dicker with England and France for diplomatic recognition and for loans in exchange for free trade in cotton and generous land grants to French and British subjects. This flirtation with the European powers disturbed Americans, who recoiled at allowing the Lone Star republic to be absorbed into the British Empire, at this point no friend of the United States. Slaveholders were particularly concerned that once Britain acquired Texas it would abolish slavery there, exposing the South's western flank to abolitionist influence. Pro-annexation sentiment was further reinforced by an influential group of capitalists who owned Texas bonds and Texas lands and believed that making Texas a state of the Union would guarantee the safety and profits of their investments.

Tyler cleverly played on the interests and fears of all these groups to secure annexation. To southerners he emphasized the dangers of British abolitionism. To Anglophobes and patriots he suggested that British interest in Texas was part of a plot to encircle the United States. His personal friend, Senator Robert J. Walker of Mississippi, dangled the promise of Pacific ports in front of Northeastern commercial men interested in the China trade.

Despite Tyler's and Walker's efforts, the Senate defeated an annexation treaty in 1844, and Texas remained outside the Union almost to the end of Tyler's term. Annexation and Oregon became major issues in the 1844 presidential contest. The Whigs chose Henry Clay, who opposed annexation on the grounds that it would mean war with Mexico. To maintain party harmony, they avoided any mention of Oregon or Texas in their platform. The Democrats, as was their habit, became embroiled in a lengthy and public battle over men and policies. Martin Van Buren considered himself the party's titular leader despite his defeat in 1840, but he was opposed to annexation, and most of the party favored it. Annexationists successfully blocked his nomination, but they deadlocked the convention in the process. Maneuvering went on for days until, on the ninth ballot, James K. Polk of Tennessee, former speaker of the House of Representatives, received the prize. The Democratic platform called for the "reoccupation of Oregon and the reannexation of Texas at the earliest practicable period." The suggestion that the United States was merely exerting clear existing rights in these regions was dubious history, but it accurately expressed the expansionists' convictions. The Democrats went on to victory, but just barely. It is possible that Polk won only because James Birney, candidate of the tiny Liberty party, drew enough antislavery voters from Clay to give Polk New York by 5,000 votes and with it a paper-thin electoral majority.

Polk's election was not, then, a strong mandate for annexation. Nevertheless, many formerly undecided citizens, now concluding that annexation was inevitable, gave it their support. To Tyler this was a cue to renewed efforts. Rather

The Oregon Controversy, 1818–1846

than submit yet another annexation treaty, which would require the approval of two thirds of the Senate, he asked Congress for a joint annexation resolution, which would need only a bare majority of both houses for adoption. This approach worked. By heavily Democratic majorities in both houses, Congress approved the resolution. On March 1, 1845, in the closing hours of his administration, Tyler signed the joint resolution. Texas entered the Union as a slave state in December 1845, but only after another heated debate in Congress, with antislavery Whigs leading the opposition.

Moving Toward War

For many months the Mexican government had been threatening retaliation if the United States absorbed Texas. Now, in the wake of the joint resolution, the Mexican minister to Washington asked for his passport and returned to Mexico City eager to report that the Americans had no stomach for war and could be easily intimidated.

The minister had not taken the correct measure of James K. Polk. A slight man of forty-nine, the new president was not impressive physically. Nor did he loom much larger intellectually. But he was a remarkably strong-willed man, resembling his hero and patron Andrew Jackson in his aggressive spirit and willfulness. Determined to make his mark, Polk mastered the details of government through sheer energy.

Manifest Destiny.   Like many Americans of his day, Polk was imbued with the mystique of Manifest Destiny. A term coined by John L. O'Sullivan, a New York magazine editor, it asserted the God-given right of Americans to "overspread and to possess the whole of the continent which Providence has given us for the great experiment of liberty and federated self-government." "Make Way for the Young American Buffalo," declaimed a bombastic New Jersey defender of American destiny:

> He has not got land enough. . . . I tell you we will give him Oregon for his summer shade, and the region of Texas as his summer pasture. Like others of his race, he wants salt, too. Well, he shall have the use of two oceans—the mighty Pacific and the turbulent Atlantic shall be his.

As a sense of special American "mission," Manifest Destiny can be traced back as far as the Puritans of colonial Massachusetts Bay. Reinforced by the tremendous national energies unleashed following independence and by the aggressive economic opportunism and buoyant confidence that accompanied pre-Civil War economic growth, it reached a climax in the 1840s. It was undoubtedly a self-serving ideology. Like the French, British, German, and Japanese rationalizations of territorial ambitions at other times, it sought to justify policies based on selfish national interest. Certainly the peoples and nations who stood in the path of America's expansionist urge found it difficult to see it as divinely inspired and benevolent. And all too often, Manifest Destiny would excuse the harshest disregard of the rights of others. It also reeked of cultural and racial arrogance that implied the superiority of American civilization and "Anglo-Saxon" stock to any other in North America.

Yet American expansionism differed from its Old World equivalents. Americans have never been comfortable with colonies. The precedent of the Northwest Ordinance of 1787 was that all new territory acquired by the United States would eventually be organized into self-governing states of the Union equal to the others. This principle served as a check on American expansionism. Whether out of prejudice against other cultures and races or merely in recognition of irreducible cultural differences, Americans have been reluctant to annex densely populated regions of peoples with foreign traditions, customs, and beliefs. In 1846 this attitude would help put a damper on the "All Mexico!" movement that followed the war.

Polk and his cabinet endorsed the premises of Manifest Destiny. In Oregon the president seconded his followers' cry of "Fifty-four forty or fight." He also coveted the rich Mexican province of California which, he feared incorrectly, Britain was planning to seize. Polk's expansionism also led him to support the Texas claim to territory reaching southwestward to the Rio Grande. The Mexican government insisted that the province extended only to the Nueces River, and the precedents for this position were strong. Polk never questioned the Texans' claims, however, and was willing to use force to make them good.

Debate on Expansionism.   Not all Americans accepted Polk's ambitious territorial goals. In New England and parts of the Northeast where antislavery sentiment was strong, the expansionists were a minority. Whig voters tended to see politics as an extension of morality: Because expansion favored slavery, it was unethical. Moreover, their party had traditionally opposed expanding U.S. boundaries.

Expansionist feelings were strongest in the Mississippi Valley and among the business classes of the Northeast. In Pennsylvania and New York commercial men and industrialists looked forward to continental markets and the ready access to east Asia that Pacific ports might bring. In the Mississippi Valley land hunger was the fuel for expansionism. Many people in this vast, lightly settled region already feared the disappearance of cheap land and looked to the Far West as a reserve for future generations.

Expansionism was also associated with Democratic affiliation. Democrats were less inclined to treat politics as a moral arena: They either considered the extension of slavery into new regions an irrelevant issue or, in the South, actually welcomed it. Expansionists were generally youthful. The "Young America" group among the Democrats led the movement for a totally American continent. Led by men like the thirty-two-year-old Stephen A. Douglas of Illinois and journalists such as the twenty-six-year-old Walt Whitman, Young America exhibited all the enthusiasm for great, bold deeds traditionally associated with youth. President Polk, at forty-nine the youngest man until then to hold presidential office, identified with this group.

Compromise with England.   Although he coveted new territory, Polk was not anxious to go to war for it. In his inaugural address he repeated the claim of the 1844 Democratic platform that the American title to Oregon was "clear and unquestionable." But in later months he blew hot and cold on Oregon, alternately threatening and appeasing Britain. Soon after his inauguration he proposed settling the Oregon dispute by extending the existing Canadian–American boundary, the forty-ninth parallel, all the way to the Pacific. When the British minister haughtily rejected this proposal, the angry Polk withdrew it. Several months later, in his first message to Congress, the president again demanded all of Oregon to the 54°40′ line and asked Congress to give the required one-year notice to Britain ending joint occupation of the region.

The threat of a direct confrontation with the United States startled the British, and they asked the American government to renew its forty-ninth parallel offer. The touchy president refused, but allowed Secretary of State James Buchanan to tell the British that if they suggested a compromise, the American government would reconsider. In early June 1846 the British proposed extending the boundary beyond the Great Lakes along the forty-ninth parallel to the Pacific, but reserving all of Vancouver Island for themselves. Polk now submitted the plan to the Senate. The bellicose Young Americans denounced it as a betrayal of American interests, but by a vote of 41 to 14, the Senate adopted it. The Oregon question, which had dragged on since the days of John Quincy Adams a generation before, had finally been settled by good sense and compromise.

And not a moment too soon. Polk had not expected war with Mexico when he first proposed a settlement to the British; but by the time the Senate approved the Oregon treaty, Americans and Mexicans were killing one another along the entire border from Texas to California.

Columbia brings a new day to North America, laying railroad tracks, plowing fields, and stringing telegraph wire, as Indians, buffalo, and other wild animals flee before her advance. Americans believed they were ordained by God to farm Oregon and Texas, mine California, and build ports on the Pacific coast. This is a telling symbolic depiction of the "development" ethic that prevailed.

The Slidell Mission.   Polk blundered into war. In the fall of 1845 he had dispatched John Slidell to Mexico to see if the United States could get what it wanted by negotiation. Mexico had broken diplomatic relations with the United States at the time of the Texas annexation, and Mexican patriots were still outraged at what they considered the theft of one of their country's choice provinces. Nevertheless, Polk remained hopeful of a peaceful settlement. Slidell was to say that if Mexico recognized the Rio Grande as the southwestern boundary of Texas, the United States would pay the $3.25 million that Mexico owed to American citizens as compensation for disorders and defaults in that chaotic country. He was also to offer another $5 million for the province of New Mexico and $25 million more for California. He did not expect these negotiations to fail, Polk informed his envoy; but if they did, he would ask Congress "to provide proper remedies." Historians have interpreted this phrase as a threat of war, and it probably was. But Polk considered the use of force unlikely.

The Slidell mission went wrong from the beginning. The government of President José Herrera was inclined to negotiate, but when news got out of Slidell's purpose hostile public opinion made it difficult for Herrera to pursue a consistent policy. Although Slidell was permitted to enter Mexico, he was held at arm's length and not allowed to present his proposals.

Soon after, the Federalist Herrera government fell. The new Centralist administration under Mariano Paredes attacked its predecessor for "seeking to avoid a necessary and glorious war" and began to negotiate with Great Britain for support against the United States if war should come. Disgusted with what he considered Mexican bad faith, Polk ordered General Zachary Taylor to move his troops to the north bank of the Rio Grande to occupy the disputed Texas border region and protect Texas against possible attack. The Mexican government soon gave Slidell his walking papers.

By the spring of 1846 Polk concluded that war was inevitable. So did the Mexicans. Confident that they would have the support of Britain, that the American war effort would be shackled by New England and abolitionist opposition, and that Mexicans, man for man, were better soldiers than Americans, they were not averse to conflict. On April 23 Paredes announced that Mexico had declared "defensive war" on the United States.

News soon reached Washington that the Mexicans were preparing to attack Taylor's army. Early in May Polk discussed a war declaration with his cabinet, but before Secretary of State Buchanan could prepare a statement of grievances against Mexico, news reached Washington that Mexican troops had crossed the Rio Grande and attacked a unit of Taylor's troops in the disputed region. Two days later Polk's war message was read to Congress. War was declared by a vote of 40 to 2 in the Senate and 174 to 14 in the House.

War with Mexico

The war lasted almost two years, cost 13,000 American lives, and $100 million. It was a remarkable triumph for American arms. This time the combination of a small regular army and a mass of volunteers worked well. Young men flocked to the recruiting offices. Many enlistees came from the Mississippi Valley and especially the newer slave states, where the spirit of Manifest Destiny was at its most fervent. Leading these spirited troops was a cadre of well-trained officers from the military academy at West Point. Besides skilled military leadership, the country also enjoyed excellent morale. Many Whigs remained skeptical of the war, and antislavery citizens strongly opposed it. But it was a short and relatively popular war. Most Americans eagerly followed accounts of the armies in the field and cheered each victory.

Taking the Borderlands.   Never before had American soldiers fought over so vast an area. In June the small Army of the West under Stephen Watts Kearny set out from the Missouri River for Santa Fe, the capital of New Mexico and the major commercial town of the Southwest. On August 18, 1846, Kearny's men took the city without a fight. A month later Kearny's force departed for California, reaching San Pascual near San Diego with 100 half-naked, half-starved, and exhausted men in December.

By this time major battles had been fought in northern Mexico where the main American force under Old Rough-and-Ready—Zachary Taylor—confronted a Mexican army of poorly trained soldiers under General Mariano Arista. At Palo Alto, on May 8, 1846, American artillery blew great holes in the Mexican ranks. When Arista launched his mounted lancers against the American infantry, they were repulsed with heavy losses. Once more the Mexicans attacked, this time with infantry. The Americans replied with devastating fire from their eighteen-pounder

The Mexican War, 1846–1848

cannon. The fighting stopped at darkness, and the next morning Taylor awoke to discover the Mexicans had disengaged. At Resaca de la Palma, the next day (May 9, 1846), the two armies clashed once again. This time the Mexican defeat was decisive and Arista and his army retreated across the Rio Grande. On May 17 the American troops occupied Matamoros, the major Mexican gulf port at the mouth of the river.

Taylor's two battles made him an instant hero at home. Congress awarded him two gold medals, and war enthusiasm soared. A recruiting poster of these early months caught the mood of the nation: "Here's to Old Zach! Glorious Times! Roast Beef, Ice Cream, and Three Months' Advance!" Volunteers poured into the recruiting offices. A call by the Tennessee authorities for 2,800 men brought a response of 30,000. By August Taylor's army on the border had swelled to 20,000 troops.

On August 19 Old Rough-and-Ready began to move on Monterrey, capital of the Mexican state of Nuevo León. Once more the American artillery proved devastating. After several days of fighting in and around the city, the Mexicans agreed to withdraw after extracting an armistice that allowed them to keep their sidearms and remain unmolested for eight weeks. On September 25, 1846, Taylor raised the Stars and Stripes over Monterrey. He had lost 800 killed and wounded.

This fierce-looking man is Zachary Taylor, "Old Rough-and-Ready," the American commander in northern Mexico. Though a soldier, unskilled in politics, he proved to be a competent president during the two years he served in office before his death.

Although another American victory, Monterrey damaged Taylor's reputation. Critics charged that he should not have allowed the Mexicans such generous terms. President Polk's skepticism was reinforced by his fear that the Whig general would be a political rival in 1848. In January 1847 he ordered Taylor to remain at Monterrey while four fifths of his troops were transferred to General Winfield Scott for an invasion of the Mexican heartland by way of Vera Cruz, the port on the Gulf of Mexico east of Mexico City.

Conquest of California.

Meanwhile, in California, important events were unfolding even before formal hostilities. In 1845 Polk had secretly authorized Thomas O. Larkin, the American consul in the California capital, to help stir up a secessionist movement among the numerous American residents. In June, however, before Larkin's plans could mature, a group of Americans proclaimed the "Republic of California" and adopted a national flag emblazoned with a star, a stripe, and a crudely drawn grizzly bear. By coincidence, at this point Captain John C. Frémont arrived in California with a contingent of American troops supposedly sent for exploring purposes. The hotheaded young officer took over leadership of the Bear Flag Revolt, and he and his men soon clashed with a force led by the Mexican governor, and routed it. On July 1 Frémont occupied the Mexican fort at San Francisco while Governor Jose Castro fled south to Los Angeles.

Now officially at war with Mexico, the United States prepared to conquer the province. In early July a naval squadron under Commodore John D. Sloat arrived in Monterey and raised the U.S. flag over the Mexican custom house. The next day Sloat read a proclamation stating that "henceforth California will be a portion of the United States." In ill health, he was soon replaced by Robert Stockton, who joined with Frémont to impose American authority over the province.

The task proved more difficult than expected. Mexican troops drove the Americans out of Los Angeles, Santa Barbara, and San Diego. Virtually the whole of southern California was in Mexican hands when Stephen Kearny arrived outside San Diego with his small force from New Mexico. Kearny attacked the Mexican troops defending the town and was beaten off. He was rescued by Stockton; together the two leaders, with larger forces, retook the towns previously lost, occupying Los Angeles on January 10. As Stockton and Kearny moved north, the California Battalion under Frémont moved south from Sacramento. On January 13 the remaining Mexican forces in California signed the Capitulation of Cahuenga. The beautiful province was now American territory by right of conquest.

Victory in Mexico.   The United States now controlled all the Mexican borderlands from the Gulf of Mexico to the Pacific Ocean. But the war was far from over. Santa Anna was once more back in the picture, having inveigled the *Norteamericanos* into allowing him safe conduct through the naval blockade by promising to make peace on their terms. Once home he reneged and took command of the Army of Liberation. By February the erratic strong man was leading an army of 20,000 troops against Taylor still holed up in Monterrey with an army one quarter the size. The two forces met at Buena Vista, and once again American artillery proved decisive. After three days of fighting, the badly bloodied, hungry Mexican army retreated southward to meet a new American threat, this time coming from the east.

Winfield Scott ("Old Fuss and Feathers"), commanding 12,000 men, had arrived off Vera Cruz in early March, hoping to take the steamy tropical city quickly to avoid the summer yellow-fever scourge. Scott surrounded Vera Cruz and pounded it with big guns manned by naval crews. On March 29 the city surrendered and Scott quickly turned it into his base of operation for the advance on the Mexican capital high up on the country's cool central plateau.

In early April American troops began their march to the "Halls of Montezuma." At Cerro Gordo, 50 miles inland, Scott's men routed the larger Mexican army in hand-to-hand fighting with bayonets and muskets used as clubs at a cost of 63 killed and 337 wounded. In the fierce heat of the lowlands many of the Americans had thrown away their blankets and warm clothing, and as they now climbed into the cold of the highlands they suffered severely. They were also harassed by Mexican guerrillas who picked off stragglers, couriers, and isolated detachments. In mid-May Scott occupied Puebla, eighty miles from the capital, and remained there until reinforcements, under General Franklin Pierce, arrived from the United States in August. Fighting soon resumed, with the Americans defeating Santa Anna once more at both Contreras and Churubusco.

Santa Anna now withdrew to Mexico City and requested an armistice while he and the U.S. peace commissioner attached to Scott's army, Nicholas Trist, parlayed. Meanwhile, the Americans camped outside the capital waiting for Mexican surrender. Negotiations soon broke down, and the fighting resumed. The final American assault on the capital took place in early September with a series of battles culminating in the American attack on the fortified hill of Chapultepec, bravely defended by a thousand Mexican troops including the young cadets of the Mexican military academy. The Americans scaled the rocky hill with ropes and ladders, and on the evening and early morning of September 13–14 fought their way into the capital. The formal capture of Mexico City was marked by the raising of the American flag by the U.S. marine battalion.

But Santa Anna refused to capitulate. As the Americans were entering the capital, he and a force of 8,000 men attacked the small American garrison left behind at Puebla. When this operation failed Santa Anna fled the country, leaving the unavoidable surrender and peace negotiations to the ad interim president, Pedro Anaya.

The Peace.   As wars go, the Mexican conflict was brief; the actual fighting lasted about a year and a half. The peace negotiations, however, dragged on for months. With Santa Anna gone neither President Anaya nor any other Mexican leader could at first muster the will and authority to accept defeat and the inevitable loss of territory. In the United States, indecision about American territorial goals further delayed settlement. At the outset of fighting the territorial ambitions of Americans had been relatively modest: California and New Mexico. But with each new dazzling victory the national appetite grew until the cry "All Mexico!" became a powerful slogan and movement.

For a while the "All Mexico!" surge seemed unstoppable. It was attractive to the country's commercial interests, which saw an opportunity to build a canal across the Isthmus of Tehuantepec, a narrow part of the North American continent. By absorbing all of the defeated nation, American enterprise, progress, glory, and greatness might all be furthered simultaneously. Manifest Destiny would be fulfilled!

But the "All Mexico!" advocates did not reckon with the Mexicans themselves. In New Mexico and California, and in the Mexican heartland, the occupying American troops were soon facing attacks by Mexican irregulars. At Taos, New Mexico, Mexican and Indian guerrillas killed the American governor, Charles Bent, and had to be subdued by soldiers hastily brought in from Santa Fe. If the United States insisted on all of Mexico, it could expect more of this resistance. Who knew how long the fighting might last?

The issue was ultimately decided by the reluctance of most Americans to take on the responsibility of governing a large non-English-speaking population with different institutions and traditions. Meanwhile, peace negotiations proceeded slowly. In October 1847 Polk recalled Trist, but the headstrong, ambitious Virginian, on the advice of General Scott, continued to negotiate with Mexican officials. Fortunately for Trist, Santa Anna's successors finally concluded that they could not avoid concessions. On February 2, 1848, they signed an agreement with Trist at Guadalupe Hidalgo.

The Treaty of Guadalupe Hidalgo gave the United States the provinces of California and New Mexico and confirmed the Rio Grande as the southwestern boundary of Texas. The Mexican Cession included the present states of California, Nevada, and Utah, and parts of Arizona, New Mexico, Wyoming, and Colorado. In return, the United States agreed to pay Mexico $15 million and to assume the $3.5 million of American citizens' claims against the Mexican government.

These terms differed only marginally from those Slidell had proposed before the war, and some Americans opposed them. After a costly and total military victory, why take only as much as you had asked for in the first place? President Polk himself disliked the treaty because it had originated with Trist, whom he had relieved of his commission. But most Americans were inclined to accept it. "Admit all [the treaty's] faults," wrote one newspaper editor, "and say if an aimless and endless foreign war is not far worse. . . . We are glad to get out of the scrape even upon these terms." This accommodating spirit prevailed when the treaty came before the Senate, and it was ratified by 38 votes to 14.

Conclusions

And so the war ended on a relatively moderate and conciliatory note. The Mexican government could consider the $15 million an acknowledgment of American guilt; Americans could see themselves as forbearing and generous.

But what were the causes? The war was part of a process of territorial expansion over which Americans—and even more clearly their government—had relatively little control. Greed (or acquisitiveness, if one prefers) was part of the American character and could not easily have been checked by laws or moral exhortation, even if the United States government had wanted to. No agency could have kept American citizens from moving into the loosely held Mexican borderlands. Whatever Washington had done, it is likely that New Mexico and California would have taken the same course as Texas. American migration would have been followed by secession, demands for annexation, and eventual incorporation into the United States. No doubt war would have been part of the process.

The Mexican War, then, was in some ways almost inevitable. Had Mexico been a strong and stable country, Mexican–American relations would undoubtedly have taken a different turn. We cannot blame the victim for his misfortunes, but it is hard not to conclude that Mexico's history, which found it after independence a poor, disorganized nation, racked periodically by violence, with a powerful, dynamic, and materialistic neighbor to the north, was a crucial factor in its fate. A wise Mexican has observed: "Poor Mexico, so far from God, so near the United States!"

The joke, however, was on the Americans. At the war's start the writer Ralph Waldo Emerson predicted that the United States would conquer Mexico, but that the victory would "poison us." As we shall see in Chapter 14, it almost did.

ONLINE RESOURCES

"The End of the Oregon Trail Interpretive Center" *http://www.endoftheoregontrail.org/mambo/* Read about the plight of men and women on the Oregon Trail. At this site, learn about the logistics of wagon travel and settling the countryside. Short sketches give specifics about the lives of settlers. A site link explores the syncretic jargon that white settlers and Native Americans developed to communicate with one another.

"The U.S.-Mexican War" *http://www.pbs.org/kera/usmexicanwar/index_flash.html* The text of this Web site, in both English and Spanish, offers varied perspectives on the war, commentary from historians about the importance of the conflict, and valuable chronologies.

National Park Service's "Salina Pueblo Missions" *http://www.nps.gov/sapu/hsr/hsrt.htm* Through this site of the National Park Service, learn about the Pueblo Indians prior to their cultural clash with Spaniards and the establishment of missions. Maps, narratives, and illustrations tell of the social, political, and religious ideologies of the Pueblos and how they differed from those of Europeans.

"Early California History: An Overview" *http://lcweb2.loc.gov/ammem/cbhtml/cbintro.html* This Library of Congress site includes excellent information on California, its geography, the impact of people on the state, and the California missions' effect on its native people.

12
Americans Before the Civil War

What Were They Really Like?

1790	The geographic center of American population is east of Baltimore
1793	Congress adopts first fugitive slave law
1794	Black preacher Richard Allen establishes the congregation that becomes the first African Methodist Episcopal Church
1821	Emma Willard founds the Troy Female Seminary (the Emma Willard School) in New York
1825	Robert Owen founds New Harmony (Indiana)
1831	First issue of William Lloyd Garrison's *The Liberator*; Nat Turner's Rebellion in Virginia: 57 whites and about 100 slaves die
1833	American Antislavery Society organizes; Oberlin becomes the first college to admit women as full degree candidates
1837	Abolitionist editor Elijah Lovejoy, defending his printing press against a mob, is murdered in Illinois; Mary Lyon founds a women's academy, now Mount Holyoke College, in Massachusetts
1838	Sarah Grimke publishes *Letters on the Equality of the Sexes*
1840s	Potato famine sends hundreds of thousands of Irish to the United States
1844	Protestants riot against Irish Catholics in Philadelphia
1848	John Humphrey Noyes founds Oneida Community (New York); Lucretia Mott and Elizabeth Cady Stanton organize the first Women's Rights Convention at Seneca Falls, New York
1849	Elizabeth Blackwell receives a medical degree from Geneva College
1850	Hawthorne's *The Scarlet Letter* published
1851	Maine passes the first state prohibition law; Melville's *Moby Dick* published
1855	First edition of Walt Whitman's *Leaves of Grass*
1865	The first all-women's college, Vassar, is established

In the decades before the Civil War, the United States and its people fascinated foreigners. Hundreds of educated Europeans visited the new country to see for themselves what manner of society was emerging on the North American continent. Most European travelers were impressed by the relative equality they encountered here. Harriet Martineau, an English writer and intellectual, observed after her 1834 visit that few in America were "very wealthy; few are poor; and every man has a fair chance of being rich." Frances Trollope, another Englishwoman, who spent the years 1827–1830 in Cincinnati, noted that in America household maids and other domestics refused to consider themselves inferior to their employers, referring to themselves as "help" rather than "servants." Not every visitor agreed that Americans were democratic. Some detected a deep streak of snobbery in the United States. Isidor Löwenstern, a Viennese scholar who traveled through the country in 1837, observed that "distinctions of rank have their defenders in America as zealous as in the Old World. . . ." Women, he wrote, were especially snobbish. The ladies of Philadelphia, for example, took "infinite pains and all their cleverness to differentiate themselves, and as much as possible to avoid contact with inferior classes."

Foreign observers also argued over the much-touted American individualism. The Swedish novelist Fredrika Bremer considered it a prominent American characteristic that "every human being must be strictly true to his own individuality— must stand alone with God, and from this innermost point of view must act alone according to his own conscientious convictions." On the other hand, Martineau complained that Americans suffered from a "fear of singularity"; and the French visitor Alexis de Tocqueville believed that public pressure to conform constituted a "tyranny of the majority" in America almost as stifling as European despotism.

Still another disagreement among the foreign observers of pre-Civil War America was whether Americans were practical, hardheaded, and materialistic or romantic, sentimental, and idealistic. Trollope, no slouch herself at seeking wealth, wrote that she never met an American who was not trying to increase his fortune. "Every bee in the hive is actively employed in search of that honey. . . vulgarly called money; neither art, science, learning, nor pleasure can seduce them from its pursuit." Yet Bremer noted that Americans respected books and learning, and she was surprised by how much social and charitable work they performed. Nor did all observers believe that Americans worshiped money above all other things. Of all the cities of the world, wrote the Hungarian politician Ferencz Pulszky after his 1852 visit, Boston was "the only one where knowledge and scholarship" had "the lead of society." There a "distinguished author, an eminent professor, an eloquent preacher, are socially equals of the monied aristocracy."

What a confusing set of contrasts! Visitors saw equality; they saw snobbery. Americans were individualists; they were conformists. A practical, materialistic people, they also seemed to be scholars, poets, and philanthropists. How can we reconcile these conflicting views of antebellum Americans? Let us examine American culture, institutions, social structure, and values between 1815 and 1860. In this chapter we focus primarily on the pre-Civil War North and the West, saving the South for separate attention in Chapter 13.

The Moving Frontier

Generations of scholars have seen the West, where the older society and culture of the East touched the still unsettled frontier, as the key to American character and institutions. In the forty-five years following 1815, the West, defined as the region beyond the Appalachians, was the fastest-growing part of the nation. During this period it became home to 15 million Americans. By 1860, eleven years after the great Gold Rush, even distant California had almost 380,000 people. The country had over 31 million inhabitants when the first shots of the Civil War were fired, and half of the residents lived in states and territories where settled white communities had not existed at the time of Washington's inauguration seventy years before.

Americans generally moved west along lines of latitude. Thus the heavy migration from New England first crossed the Berkshire Hills to central New York, then swept through the Mohawk Valley into northern Ohio, northern Illinois, and southern Michigan. One branch of the Yankee exodus reached out to distant Oregon. New Yorkers and Pennsylvanians tended to settle the middle portions of the trans-Appalachian region. Most southerners moved to the lower parts of the Old Northwest, close to the Ohio River, and to the newer slave states of Kentucky, Tennessee, and the Gulf region. Southern blacks as well as whites moved westward. Most blacks accompanied their masters to the cotton fields of the interior; others, however, were transported in gangs by slave dealers and sold to cotton planters in the new region. Meanwhile, the Indians were continually pushed westward, ahead of the powerful flood of white and black settlers.

The Migrants' Motives.

Reasons for moving west of course varied from person to person, group to group, and region to region. Some western pioneers were the "loners" of traditional romantic accounts who could not stay put once they had seen the smoke of a neighbor's hearth fire on the horizon. But people "lit out for the territories" for other reasons as well. Some were refugees—fleeing the law, their creditors, their spouses, or their own pasts. Married women and children went west without much choice because their husbands or fathers did. On the other hand, many single women regarded the West as a land of opportunity. Western farmers needed wives, and unmarried women could easily find in the West the husbands and the security and social status that only marriage and a family of one's own could then confer.

Economic considerations, however, probably outweighed personal and social motives. New England's first emigrants streamed to the cheap lands of the Genesee country of western New York in the 1790s following the rapid rise in the cost of land at home. In the 1820s there was another New England exodus as tenants and agricultural laborers, dislodged by conversion of arable land to sheep pasture, joined the movement west. In the next few decades, unable to undersell the cheap commodities of the fertile Mississippi Valley, many Yankee farmers from Massachusetts or Connecticut simply gave up and joined the westward exodus.

The people of the Middle Atlantic region, where soils were good, had less reason to move than their Yankee neighbors. But by the 1840s and 1850s, many New Yorkers, children of transplanted New Englanders or the transplants themselves, began a second migration to Wisconsin and Iowa, responding once again to the lure of cheap, fertile land.

The older South also felt the economic attraction of the West. Declining soil fertility pushed people out of the Chesapeake region and the older cotton areas of South Carolina and Georgia, while the more fertile cotton lands across the mountains exerted a simultaneous pull. The rich lands of the free prairie states also saw an influx. Many Southerners, mostly slaveless farmers, preferred southern Ohio, Indiana, and Illinois to the new western Cotton Kingdom.

The Frontier Type. Many scholars believe the western environment transformed eastern migrants. The West, according to Frederick Jackson Turner, the late
nineteenth-century historian of the frontier, was "productive of individualism. . . .
It produced antipathy to control, and particularly any direct control." The West was
also egalitarian, he said. Among the pioneers, "one man is as good as another. . . .
An optimistic and buoyant faith in the worth of the plain people, a devout faith in
man prevailed in the West." It also encouraged idealism. "From the beginning of
that long westward march of the American people America has never been the
home of mere contented materialism. It has continually sought new ways and
dreamed of a new perfected social type."

The truth is more complex than Turner's western myth. Western individualism
was not unqualified. Community cooperation and intrusive social control could be
found on the frontier. Westerners joined in social activities and mutual-aid efforts
such as barn raising, fence building, cooperative harvesting, quilting bees, and assisting in childbirth. In politics westerners, like other Americans, rejected unqualified laissez-faire and seldom hesitated to pass laws to control the economic and
social practices of their neighbors when regulation suited their purposes.

Turner also exaggerated the extent to which the movement westward involved
individuals and isolated families. New Englanders often settled in compact communities modeled on the traditional "towns" of Massachusetts and Connecticut. At
times entire eastern communities pulled up stakes as entities and headed west. The
migration of the persecuted Latter-day Saints (Mormons) from upstate New York
ultimately to the intermountain region near the Great Salt Lake is a particularly
striking instance of group migration. The new Mormon "Zion," moreover, scarcely
conformed to the stereotype of a community dominated by rugged individualists.
In Utah, the Mormons established a closely regulated society in which decisions
were made by elders and by Brigham Young, the charismatic Mormon leader.

Still, westerners were probably more individualistic than easterners. Spread
more thinly over the land, without the steady support of close neighbors, they
faced an untamed physical environment and had to be self-reliant or perish. But individualism had another, less attractive side: lawlessness. Westerners were much
given to brawling and violent behavior. During the 1840s Iowans' use of the bowie
knife made them world-famous for bloodthirstiness. Cutting, eye gouging, and
nose biting were common ways of settling disagreements in the antebellum West.
Although the use of vigilantes was an effort to impose law on lawless communities, it also expressed westerners' penchant for taking the law into their own hands.

In general, western compliance with social norms was rather poor by eastern
or European standards. "I have rarely seen so many people drunk," wrote a traveler in the West in the 1830s. Tobacco chewing, spitting, and swearing were almost
universal. Charles Dickens concluded after his American visit in the 1840s that
westerners could scarcely speak without "many oaths. . . as necessary. . . words."

Turner's assertions about western egalitarianism and the lack of concern for
materialism must also be qualified. It is true that outside the Southwest, where
slavery left its deep impression, the rural West achieved a rough equality of material condition. As we saw in Chapter 9, abundant land and a democratic, if imperfect, system of land distribution created a large body of farm owners of middle
rank by 1860. Even more significant, however, is the fact that western *attitudes*

were egalitarian. One westerner did not regard another as superior merely because he possessed a better education or a more impressive pedigree. But communities in the Southwest were also full of "cotton snobs" and newly minted gentlemen. In the fast-growing western cities class distinctions developed very quickly. And no matter how indifferent they were to ancestry, westerners were generally impressed by money. Pioneer farmers had come west to achieve modest independence at least; to get rich if they could.

Turner's agreeable, positive picture, then, is an overstatement. Real westerners were cruder, more materialistic, and less egalitarian and individualistic in their behavior than he claimed. But their values were indeed individualistic and egalitarian, and values affect actions.

New Pressures in the Northeast

What about Americans in the rest of the country, or at least its northern edge? Did the West's qualities mark Americans elsewhere as well? Turner claimed that they did. The West, he said, was the ultimate source of the democratic values of the nation as a whole. Attitudes and institutions developed on the frontier were carried back east, helping to make the entire country (especially the North) an open, democratic society.

Such an interpretation, however, leaves many things out of account. In the pre-Civil War years the Northeast was engulfed in a rush of economic changes that turned farm people into factory wage earners living in cities and large towns and brought to America's shores thousands of newcomers from Europe. These changes had vital effects unrelated to the frontier experience of the West.

Problems of Urbanization.   One social force that Turner ignored was urbanization. In 1800 only five towns—New York, Philadelphia, Boston, Charleston, and Baltimore—had over 10,000 inhabitants. These small cities were primarily centers of foreign trade, and even inland urban communities were mostly distribution centers for buyers and sellers.

As the economy changed and grew, the new factories and mills attracted a wave of people to the older towns and created new ones in the Northeast. Cities also sprouted or expanded in the new West. Wherever located, they brought people together in schools, concert halls, theaters, clubs, churches, libraries, political parties, and other associations, creating a sense of community and shared interests and values. But cities were also places with many physical problems and troubling social difficulties. One was the lack of transportation. At first cities were so small that people could get around on foot. By the eve of the Civil War, however, Baltimore, Boston, Chicago, Cincinnati, St. Louis, and New Orleans all had over 100,000 people; Philadelphia had over 500,000; and New York-Brooklyn, over a million. Such metropolises required public transportation systems. Omnibuses—elongated wheeled carriages pulled by horses—arrived in the 1830s. But not until the appearance two decades later of the horse-drawn streetcar running on rails did the major towns acquire reasonably good transit systems.

Housing was another major urban problem, and it was never adequately solved. As middle-class people abandoned the city centers to move to newer neighborhoods, their dwellings were cut up into small apartments. Sometimes landlords built shacks in the gardens and backyards of older middle-class houses for the newcomers. By the 1850s most large cities had acquired the latest urban development: the slum.

Poor housing was matched by poor water supply, poor waste disposal, and poor health services. Early in the nineteenth century, Philadelphia, Cincinnati, and Pittsburgh built aqueducts to bring pure country water to their citizens, but it was mid-century before the inhabitants of New York, Boston, and other towns abandoned use of polluted wells and streams. Waste disposal in most American cities was primitive. Waste water from baths (infrequently taken), sinks, and "necessary houses" was often merely dumped into the streets. Where sewers existed, they were often connected to the same stream that supplied the community's drinking water. Scavenging pigs took care of much of the cities' garbage disposal. Although the pigs performed a civic duty, their droppings, along with those of horses by the thousands, were a major source of urban pollution. On a sweltering August day in 1852, one New Yorker noted, "The streets smell like a solution of bad eggs in ammonia."

It is not surprising that health was poor in antebellum cities. Typhoid fever and typhus were common. The devastating cholera epidemics of 1832 and 1849–1850 came from the infected local water supplies. Smallpox, yellow fever, and malaria were other common urban afflictions. Not all these diseases were actually water-borne, but doctors believed they were, and the alarm they caused moved public-spirited citizens to improve water supplies and establish boards of health.

Crime and Violence.

Traditional rural social restraints often broke down in the antebellum cities. Cities became catch basins for the antisocial with weak ties to families and other groups. Those who failed or found only marginal places in the urban economy, moreover, often succumbed to temptations or turned to antisocial occupations. Inevitably cities were full of burglars, footpads, pickpockets, and ruffians who preyed on law-abiding citizens. Cities were often nurseries of vice as well. One 1858 estimate claimed that there was one prostitute for every fifty men in American cities.

Even small communities were not exempt from the violence and disorder of antebellum American life. No Fourth of July or election day passed without broken heads and blood in the streets of America's villages and hamlets. The metropolises were worse, of course. City slums, like New York's notorious Five Points, fostered gangs that conducted full-scale wars with one another and with the police. Crammed with the poor and outcast, districts of urban immigrants were especially violence-prone, a fact that led many native Americans to conclude that the foreign-born were a danger to society. Riots were frequent in antebellum cities. In 1837 Boston volunteer firemen and Irish mourners clashed violently at a funeral procession on Broad Street, and state militia had to be called out to quell the mayhem. Still worse was the Astor Place Riot in New York in 1849 when twenty-two people lost their lives and the new, luxurious Astor Place Opera House was severely damaged by a working-class mob.

At first, American cities had few means to deal with disorder. Until the 1840s the law was enforced by elected constables by day and a part-time "watch" at night. The increasing violence and rioting that marked these years of tensions between the native- and foreign-born and the urban erosion of rural-derived social controls made this antique system inadequate. In 1838 Boston established a

Troops in Philadelphia attempt to stop a riot between Catholics and bitterly anti-Catholic "nativists" in 1844. Fierce nationalists, the nativists objected to the Catholics' tie to a foreign authority: "the bloody hand of the Pope."

professional daytime police force to supplement the night watch. In the following decade New York gave up the night watch entirely and established a twenty-four-hour-a-day police force. Before long most other large eastern cities had taken the same road to a modern city police system.

Surging Immigration.   Increasing tensions between native-born Americans and recent immigrants clearly challenged the principle of equality. Immigration from Europe, as we saw, had been light during the half-century following the Revolution. Then, in the 1830s, the number of new arrivals grew to almost 600,000; in the 1840s, to 1.7 million; and in the 1850s, to 2.3 million. Most of the newcomers came from Britain, Germany, and the southern part of Ireland.

The two largest groups, the Irish and the Germans, did not fare equally well in America. For centuries the Catholic Irish peasants had been denied economic and political rights and had lived as impoverished tenants on lands owned by rich English Protestant landlords. In the late eighteenth and early nineteenth centuries the introduction of the potato permitted peasant families to raise more food on their small plots of ground, and Ireland's population soared. When the potato crop failed during the mid-1840s, hundreds of thousands of Irish fled to escape starvation. With their paltry possessions, many crossed the Atlantic to America. Too poor to buy land or pay the fare to the West once they arrived, Irish families usually stayed in the eastern cities, where they took the lowest-paying jobs—as construction workers, day laborers, factory hands, porters, handymen, and teamsters. Many Irish women and girls worked part-time as laundresses or garment workers or became maids, cooks, and charwomen in the homes of middle-class native-born Americans.

The Germans were more fortunate. Though they too were seeking better lives in America, many had owned their own land at home, and they brought with them to their new country the money they received from its sale. They were also, on the whole, more skilled than the Irish. Some were even members of the middle class—lawyers, doctors, musicians, soldiers, college professors, and businesspeople—who were fleeing the antiliberal persecutions that followed the failure of the liberal German Revolutions of 1848. (The educated German immigrants of this period are often referred to as "Forty-eighters.")

Many of the German arrivals could afford to leave the crowded labor markets of the large port cities for the cheap lands of Illinois and Wisconsin. Those who stayed in the East were often able to do better for themselves than the Irish. Every American city had German mechanics, printers, and craftsmen. Many Forty-eighters made their mark in business, medicine, academic life, and even politics. Carl Schurz, Gustav Koerner, and other German political refugees quickly rose to prominent positions in American public life.

Discrimination.   Most immigrants found America a mixed blessing. True, there were jobs, and for some, land. No one starved. Immigrant children could go to free schools. The more fortunate and enterprising could pull themselves up from unskilled laborers to the level of small businesspeople, often providing services for their compatriots or selling them the imported old-country goods they craved.

Still, the social environment of their adopted land was not ideal. Americans talked about equality and took pride in the openness of their borders, but they disliked the immigrants and often treated them harshly. During the fifty-year period of slack immigration following the Revolution, native-born white Americans had become unused to large bodies of aliens in their midst and felt overwhelmed by the deluge of newcomers after 1830. Many viewed the immigrants as lawbreakers, tipplers, and clannish people who refused to adopt the customs of their new country. Confusing causes with consequences, native-born Americans also held the immigrants responsible for their squalid housing, their raggedness, their bad health, and the unsanitary conditions in which they lived.

Native-born Americans also deplored the immigrants' religion. Virtually all the Irish, and many of the Germans, were Catholic. Protestant Americans had a long tradition of anti-Catholicism derived from the religious conflicts of the sixteenth-century English Reformation. Before 1830 the American Catholic community had been small, unobtrusive, and assimilated. With the deluge of the 1830–1860 period, however, there suddenly appeared in every town and city Catholic churches, schools, convents, hospitals, and seminaries. A central Catholic hierarchy soon took shape. For the first time Americans encountered the unfamiliar sight of priests and nuns in black clerical garments on their streets. They also experienced the newcomers' relaxed "Continental Sunday," which turned the sober Protestant Sabbath into an exuberant day of visiting, picnicking, playing, and imbibing.

Latent anti-Catholicism soon became active anti-Catholicism. Protestant laymen and ministers accused the highly centralized Catholic Church of antidemocratic tendencies. Catholics, moreover, were undermining the public school system, Protestants said, by establishing parochial schools and demanding that the state support them. A few bigoted extremists revived the time-worn accusations of rampant vice and immorality among Catholic priests and nuns.

Encouraged by such propaganda, between 1830 and 1860 the nation's cities witnessed violent confrontations between immigrant Catholics and militant native Protestants. More common, however, was the day-to-day discrimination that immigrants encountered. Landlords often would not rent to foreigners, especially the Irish. During the 1850s newspaper help-wanted ads frequently carried the warning "Irish Need Not Apply." Many immigrants achieved a tolerable economic life only because the chronic American labor shortage often gave employers little alternative to offering them jobs though seldom better than low-skilled physical work.

In the 1850s, when immigration was at its height, antiforeign, anti-Catholic feelings spawned a political movement based on bigotry. During the 1840s various antiforeign "nativist" societies sought to exclude foreigners from America or to reduce their influence in American life. About 1850, one of these, the secret Order of the Star-Spangled Banner, began to be called the Know-Nothings from the guarded response of its members when asked to describe the organization. In the next few years the Know-Nothings abandoned their secrecy and became a force in American political life. The new party fell as quickly as it rose, splitting into factions and losing members when it was unable to deal with the overriding issue of slavery in the territories (see Chapter 14). By 1858 it was all but dead, but it left behind a harsh legacy of political nativism that has never completely disappeared from America.

Free Blacks.   Even more than religion and nationality, race challenged America's egalitarian ideals. Two hundred thousand free blacks lived in the northern and western states in 1850. The free black community of the North included many talented men and women. Some of the most stylish restaurants, barbershops, and catering establishments in northern cities were run by blacks. The larger cities also sheltered able black ministers and journalists. But these people were exceptional. The great majority of northern free blacks were unskilled laborers at the bottom of the social pyramid. Both north and south, white Americans generally treated blacks with disdain. The one notable exception was northern abolitionists, especially the followers of William Lloyd Garrison, many of whom truly embraced an ethic of human equality.

Bigotry harshly affected the life of almost every free black. They were denied admission to white schools, refused jobs they were qualified to perform, and deprived of even elementary civil rights in most northern states. In many northern communities, Jim Crow laws (the name derived from the popular "blackface" minstrel show) mandated separate public facilities for blacks and whites. Several states in the northwest, pandering to white wage earners' fears of job competition, sought to exclude blacks from taking up residence within their borders. Those already resident were disqualified by "black laws" from serving on juries, testifying against whites in court, or joining the militia.

Their ostracism from many spheres of life inspired some free blacks to creative solutions. When in 1794 the St. George Methodist Church of Philadelphia tried to segregate blacks, the popular black preacher, Richard Allen, established the African Methodist Episcopal Church, which eventually had thousands of communicants all through the North and South. Free black Christians of other denominations likewise established separate churches rather than accept inferior status within white ones. Blacks also founded separate Masonic, Odd Fellows, and other fraternal lodges when they were not admitted to full equality in existing white associations.

As the years passed, conditions got worse rather than better for free black Americans. Before the 1830s there had been a place, if a marginal one, for blacks in the northern economy. With the influx of immigrants, their lot deteriorated. Employers would hire newly arrived Germans and Irish before free blacks. The immigrants, especially the Irish, were hostile to blacks, seeing them as competitors in the labor market. Tensions between blacks and Irish sometimes erupted into savage riots in which scores of people were injured.

Women.   American equality was also marred by discrimination based on gender. Antebellum America, like every other Western society, was male-dominated. It was difficult for any woman, except perhaps a strong-willed and self-sufficient widow, to live independently of a man, whether father, husband, or brother. Under the law the earnings and property of married women belonged to their husbands. Their spouses could beat them without the law's intervention except in aggravated cases. Their children were not their own in a strict legal sense, and in a divorce they usually lost all claim to their offspring. Nor were matters better in public realms. Women could not hold office or vote. Virtually all the professions were closed to them except schoolteaching, and as we have seen, women schoolteachers were paid lower salaries than men. Indeed, most women's work outside the home tended to be unskilled and poorly paid.

Few married women worked for wages in this era. Those who did were usually either young, unmarried girls waiting for future husbands and families, or older spinsters or widows who had no choice but to support themselves. Consequently, the life of a typical American woman was conditioned largely by her role and function in her family household. Here matters were improving somewhat, at least for the middle class, in these pre-Civil War years. For the wives of businessmen, professionals, and highly skilled workers, there were servants, usually young immigrant women, to help with the heavy chores of the typical household in the pre-electric, pre-running water, pre-telephone era. In addition, falling birth rates lessened the burden of raising children. Although birth-control methods were crude, by the eve of the Civil War, the numbers of children born each year per family had dropped about 40 percent from 1800 levels.

Other improvements came as new working conditions took men out of the household. Increasingly, among middle-class city people, fathers went to distant work in the morning, leaving wives and children at home. This emerging pattern encouraged acceptance of a distinct women's "sphere"—the family circle—where their role was supreme. Reinforced by the idea that in a free republic women educated the sons who eventually led the nation, the concept of a distinct women's sphere raised the status of women within the family. Women were still their husband's inferiors, but in the nursery and the kitchen they were supreme.

Despite some advances in status, however, women continued to suffer from male condescension. Male-dominated society claimed to honor women but often treated them as emotional and physical invalids. Women were thought to be frail creatures, nervous and sickly, and not competent to bear the full burdens of adulthood. Society surrounded them with a wall of stifling conventions and expectations, epitomized in the "cult of true womanhood." A "true" woman was sweet and gentle, modest and nurturing, pious and reverent, and irreproachably chaste. Even within the bonds of marriage, women were expected to be "pure" and deny their "animal" urges.

There were perhaps some advantages to these misconceptions and myths. Some women, especially those of the middle class, were spared heavy physical chores and the pressures of making a living. But no matter how intended or used, the practice of treating women like children diminished their lives and deprived society of their talents.

The Arts in Antebellum America

Though foreign travelers often condemned Americans for their crude materialism and indifference to the "finer things," there was another side to the nation's values. Americans were also an artistic, imaginative, and creative people who made important contributions to the arts in the antebellum era.

An American Literature.   "Who reads an American book?" sneered the English critic Sydney Smith in 1820. By the time he uttered his famous insult, many educated Europeans were doing that very thing.

In 1800 Americans were apologetic about their lack of literary achievement. During the earliest years of the Republic the air resounded with voices clamoring for a distinguished national literature that would use American themes and avoid slavish imitation of Europe. Energy and enthusiasm were not enough to produce such a literature, however; genius was required. Abruptly, in the opening years of the new century, two New Yorkers—Washington Irving and James Fenimore Cooper—provided it.

Irving leaped to international fame in 1819 with publication of a set of assorted short pieces, *The Sketch Book of Geoffrey Crayon, Gent.* These were written in England primarily on English themes. But included in *The Sketch Book* were two brilliant stories, "The Legend of Sleepy Hollow" and "Rip Van Winkle," that had as their setting the picturesque Hudson Valley with its stolid Dutch burghers and the misty green Catskill Mountains steeped in myths and legends. Though in reality based on German sources, this seemed to be authentic American material that answered the call for a native literature.

More truly "American" than Irving's short stories were the novels of James Fenimore Cooper. The first of these, *The Pioneers* (1823), set in the rapidly changing upstate New York of Cooper's childhood, recounted the struggles to impose "civilization" and the forces of "progress" on the pristine wilderness. Its cast of characters includes the untutored but wilderness-wise Natty Bumppo (Leatherstocking), his noble Indian friend, Uncas, and the symbol of change, Judge Marmaduke Temple. Bumppo is the hero of four other Leatherstocking Tales, including *The Last of the Mohicans* (1826). In these he personifies the "natural" man pitting his skills and sinews against the dangers of wild nature and wild men as he resists the corrosive effects of civilization.

The New England Renaissance.   Irving and Cooper made New York the nation's first literary capital. By the following decade there were major writers elsewhere as well. In the South, William Gilmore Simms's novels dealt with the South during the Revolution and paralleled the work of Cooper. The poets Paul Hamilton Hayne and Henry Timrod were southern nationalists who sought to carve out a specific southern poetic genre. The one southern writer of undisputed stature was Edgar Allen Poe, born in Boston but raised in Virginia.

Poe began his writing career as a poet, imitating Byron, Shelley, and the other great English romantics. But his short stories—including "The Gold Bug," "The Fall of the House of Usher," "The Murders in the Rue Morgue," and "The Pit and the Pendulum"—have fascinated and beguiled generations of readers in Europe and America. To us, the somber Poe often seems less "American" than less introspective writers such as Irving and Cooper. Yet in his fondness for hoaxes, mysteries, and violence, he was very much in the national mood.

Far more consistent with American pride were the literary giants who burst forth in New England, especially in and around Boston. In the generation before the Civil War the Massachusetts capital was the ideal seedbed for a literary flowering. With only 100,000 people in 1840, Boston was a city where face-to-face contact among those of like mind and taste was easily achieved. The city, moreover, had a tradition of learning based on the proximity of Harvard College and the heritage of a scholarly and intellectual New England clergy.

Boston's literary renaissance owed much to transcendentalism—an approach to God, humanity, and nature compounded of diverse elements of European romanticism, German philosophy, and oriental mysticism. Although they borrowed from foreign sources, the transcendentalists were distinctly American in their views and values: Humans were perfectible, God was forgiving, each person must follow his or her own inspiration, and all men and women had within them part of the divine spark. High-minded and humane, the transcendentalists rejected mere material gain.

The transcendental mood was best expressed in the essays of Ralph Waldo Emerson. Emerson's calm optimism, reasonable and humane views, social generosity, pure motives, and high-mindedness seemed noble and reassuring. He respected American practicality and praised self-reliance, but at the same time he deplored excessive concern with material progress.

In Concord, outside Boston, Emerson was surrounded by a group of talented and idealistic men and women, including Bronson Alcott, Henry David Thoreau, George Ripley, William Ellery Channing, Margaret Fuller, Elizabeth Peabody, and, for a time, Nathaniel Hawthorne. At Emerson's Tuesday evenings these bright people discussed their host's ideas and those of congenial European writers and thinkers. Their thoughts reached the cultivated public through a small magazine, *The Dial,* first published in 1840. In the early 1840s Ripley and a few others of the Emerson circle established Brook Farm, a cooperative experimental community at West Roxbury, Massachusetts, a venture that tested their utopian belief in human perfectibility and innate goodness.

If Emerson was the theorist of transcendentalism, Thoreau was its practitioner. Thoreau was far more sensitive than his contemporaries to the primacy of nature. "Wildness is the preservation of the World," he told an audience in Concord. In 1845 he put his own precepts to the test by going to live in the woods at Walden Pond. There he discovered the essentials of existence and concluded that human beings needed very little of a material sort to be happy. Thoreau was also a courageous individualist, defying the authorities during the Mexican War by refusing to pay his taxes to support what he felt was an unjust attack on America's weaker neighbor.

Nathaniel Hawthorne, the most creative of the Boston group, was, unlike his Concord acquaintances, a sardonic, skeptical man with a strong sense of the human capacity for evil. These qualities and perceptions he incorporated into many memorable short tales, and into the longer works, *The Scarlet Letter* (1850) and *The House of the Seven Gables* (1851). Hawthorne's disagreements with some members of Emerson's group prompted him to satirize the impracticality of their social experiments in *The Blithedale Romance* (1852), a novel about Brook Farm.

Melville and Whitman.
Emerson's transcendentalism was even less acceptable to another great American writer: New Yorker Herman Melville. Melville's first novels related his adventures among the natives of the South Seas. In 1850 he began *Moby Dick,* in outward form a sea adventure, but actually a far more profound book. In his study of Captain Ahab and Ahab's single-minded determination to destroy the white whale, Melville created a powerful allegory of human obsession. *Moby Dick,* with its dark and complex themes, was not as enthusiastically received by antebellum American readers as Melville's earlier work, but today it is thought to be one of America's greatest novels.

Like Melville, Walt Whitman was not fully appreciated until the 1900s. A writer of distinctly American character, Whitman carried individualism to the point of egotism. His "Song of Myself" begins with the famous lines:

> I celebrate myself and sing myself,
> And what I assume you shall assume,
> For every atom belonging to me as good belongs to you.

In this mood he reveals the boastfulness that we associate with the American frontier, although he himself spent much of his life in Brooklyn and Camden, New Jersey. Whitman was also a sensualist; whatever Americans of this generation did in private, few if any ever publicly proclaimed their lustiness, their admiration of personal beauty, and their delight in physical love as he did.

The People's Literature.
The Boston and New York writers appealed primarily to the educated middle class. The best were skeptical of American materialism, and several exhibited a streak of pessimism that ran against America's postcolonial tendency to envision a bright future. They were the first group of American intellectuals at odds with the dominant values of their society. The literature of the masses, however, was unapologetically upbeat and frankly endorsed get-ahead materialism and conformity. During the antebellum period, presses poured out a flood of inexpensive novels that reinforced positive American folk attitudes.

Much of the audience for literature of any sort in these years was female; American men were too busy with practical matters to read books. Convinced that only women writers could tap this audience successfully, publishers sought out women skilled with words. A genteel occupation that could be practiced at home, writing presented one of the few opportunities besides teaching for middle-class women to earn their living in a respectable way, and they quickly took advantage of it.

Much of the output was potboiler literature. Mary Agnes Fleming, Catharine Maria Sedgwick, Susan Warner, Sarah Payson Willis, and other women churned out countless novels praising domesticity, chastity, true love, and assorted household virtues. These were often cloyingly sentimental. To sustain interest the authors included such melodramatic stock types as the "other woman," the weak husband, and the martyred wife. In the end justice triumphed, and no one but the villain—or villainess—got hurt. Meanwhile, on the way to the denouement, the reader was exposed only to the sweetest, noblest, and most conventional sentiments.

The literature of antebellum America thus expressed many of the contradictions of the nation. Most of the better writers were skeptical of commercial values. They celebrated the individualism of the nonconformist who resisted the dominant teachings of the day or defied nature. In Melville, Poe, and Hawthorne we also detect despair and pessimism, attitudes scarcely approved by Americans or ascribed to them by most foreign observers. Popular literature, on the other hand, sang the praises of family, country, and traditional virtue and refused to carp at darker American characteristics.

Painting and Architecture.

The other arts are equally suggestive of the nation's inner contradictions. Many American painters considered their fellow citizens unappreciative materialists with philistine attitudes toward art. John Vanderlyn, a painter of elegant nudes, insisted that "no one but an artistic quack would paint in America." Washington Allston, like Vanderlyn trained in Europe, returned to the United States to experience the frustration that eventually led to his emotional breakdown and the collapse of his promising career. Later critics of the United States would cite Allston as a victim of the blighting effect of American materialism and lack of true appreciation for "culture" and the fine arts.

On the whole, however, the dissenters among the artists were outnumbered by the celebrators. Thomas Cole, Asher B. Durand, and the lesser artists of the Hudson River school chose as their subjects the American countryside, especially the scenery of the Northeast. Still closer to the popular taste were painters such as William Sidney Mount and George Caleb Bingham, whose scenes of rural life and homey anecdotes in paint resembled the sentimental popular novels but excelled them in quality. George Catlin and John Audubon were less mannered and less sentimental about the American environment. Catlin's superb pictures of American Indians have enough accuracy and detail to delight an anthropologist. Audubon, of course, was a great naturalist as well as an excellent draftsman, and his watercolor and crayon sketches of American birds are scientific documents as well as objects of great beauty.

Americans between 1815 and 1860 were both practical house builders and romantic artists in stone, brick, and wood. The practical side was to be found in the innovative "balloon frame" house that abandoned the heavy joined timbers of earlier house construction, and substituted a light skeleton of uprights and cross pieces attached by nails encased in siding of boards or shingles. The resulting structure was well suited to a fast-growing society that needed enormous amounts of new housing, had abundant timber, and was willing to sacrifice individuality and permanence for speed and cheapness.

Of course, there were people in both town and country who could afford more than a box with a roof in which to live. In this era they commissioned workers in the Greek-revival style to build gracious mansions with white pillars and public buildings indebted to the ancient Greeks and Romans. The Capitol and White House in Washington are both examples of the style. A competing genre was the nostalgic romanticism of the Gothic style. Gothic was better suited to churches and homes than to secular public buildings, though James Renwick's Smithsonian Institution is a distinguished exception. For churches Gothic was a natural style, and the traditions of the great European cathedrals and English parish churches were continued beautifully in such structures as Richard Upjohn's Trinity Church and Renwick's Grace Church in New York. It was in private homes, however, that the Gothic style flourished best. It lent itself not only to mansions; in some ways it was even more suitable for wooden cottages.

The Perfect Society

The social scene of the pre-Civil War North, like the cultural flowering, contained elements that contradicted the charges of American materialism and conformity. Northern society exhibited a degree of dissent, a willingness to confront established social institutions, and a zeal for replacing them with new ones, that could be found almost nowhere else in the contemporary world. This was a time, according to Emerson, when "madmen, madwomen, men with beards, Dunkers, Muggletonians, Comeouters, Groaners, Agrarians, Seventh Day Baptists, Unitarians and Philosophers—all came successively to the top, and seized their moment, if not their hour, wherein to chide, or pray, or preach, or protest."

Religious Roots of Reform.   The social reform movements of the years preceding 1860 drew some of their energy and substance from the new religious spirit that swept the nation. At the beginning of the nineteenth century American Protestantism was languishing. Piety had declined drastically both on the frontier and in the East. In New England and in those parts of upstate New York and the Great Lakes states where Yankees had immigrated, ministers worried that "the Sabbath would be lost, and every appearance of religion vanish."

Then, during the years preceding 1860, traveling bands of Methodist, Baptist, and Presbyterian evangelists fanned out across the nation intent on convincing thousands of Americans to ponder their sins, consider a new life, affirm or reaffirm their faith, and join the church. During the "Second Great Awakening" outdoor revivals drew hordes of rural citizens to marathon preaching sessions where eloquent preachers such as Charles Grandison Finney, Francis Asbury, and Peter Cartwright exhorted sinners to abandon their evil ways and find salvation in God's everlasting love. In the wake of each visiting evangelist, new members poured into the Methodist, Presbyterian, and Baptist churches; many of the "saved" joined new denominations. Western New York, called the "burnt-over" district for the wave after wave of revivalism that swept across it, became a religious hothouse that fostered a score of new sects, among them the Latter-day Saints (Mormons), Adventists, and Shakers.

Leaders of more traditional groups such as the Episcopalians and Congregationalists often attacked the new preachers as ranters; orthodox Calvinists deplored their rejection of predestination. But orthodox Calvinism was also at war during these years with Unitarianism, an offshoot of Congregationalism that had divested itself of Calvinist pessimism along with Christian belief in the Trinity. Heirs of Enlightenment rationality, Unitarians rejected what they considered the supernatural and irrational elements in traditional Christianity.

Unitarianism and evangelicalism attracted different sorts of followers. The first appealed to educated merchants and professional people, especially in the Boston area; the second made greater headway among farmers and lower-middle-class artisans and tradespeople. For all their social differences, however, Unitarians and evangelicals agreed that men and women could effect their own salvation and perfect both themselves and their society. The converted, proclaimed the evangelist Finney, "should aim at being holy and not rest till they are as perfect as God." Sin was selfishness; virtue, selflessness and benevolence toward others. Sin, said the new breed of religious leaders, was voluntary; humanity could reject it; and collective sin—social evils—could be rooted out by human will, education, and cooperative public action.

This "Perfectionist" doctrine quickly penetrated organizations already involved in efforts to improve society. By 1820 these groups were in close contact with one another in an informal "benevolent empire" that devoted its attention to world peace, temperance, foreign missions, antislavery, and other good causes. The benevolent societies usually had limited, practical goals. But perfectionism gave a passion, and at times a fanaticism, to the wave of humanitarian reform that swept the North and the West.

The Desire for Social Control.   Many reformers were also inspired by a belief that society was experiencing a severe breakdown and by fears that social chaos would result if steps were not taken to check the collapse. Reformers of this sort often blamed crime, insanity, and alcoholism on family failure in an industrializing, urbanizing environment. To men and women who held such views, "asylums," where victims of family collapse could find havens from the harsh new world and learn to cope with their difficulties, seemed the solution.

Penitentiaries were one form of asylum. Existing jails and prisons were unsanitary places with wretched food and squalid physical surroundings, where first offenders were mixed with hardened criminals. They did nothing to rehabilitate lawbreakers. The reformed system of penitentiaries endorsed by Louis Dwight, Elam Lynds, and others separated first offenders from repeaters, provided better sanitation, and allowed prisoners some privacy. But as a would-be substitute for family discipline, it also imposed solitary confinement, hard physical labor, and regimentation. In the Auburn system of New York, established in 1816, prisoners were marched to and from work in tight lockstep and flogged for violating prison rules. In the end the penitentiary system failed in its primary aim of rehabilitating criminals. Yet the changes were considered models of enlightenment in their day, and dozens of European observers came to view the American penal system and learn from it.

Another sort of asylum was envisioned by Dorothea Dix. In an earlier era "lunatics" had been kept at home in the care of their families. Increasingly, however, geographic mobility and the growing reluctance of families to carry the burden of unproductive relatives forced the community to care for the mentally disturbed. Unfortunately, there were few mental hospitals, and the insane were often treated like animals. Mental patients in Massachusetts, Dix reported, were kept in "cages, closets, cellars, stalls, pens!" They were "chained, naked, beaten with rods, and lashed into obedience." Dix petitioned her state to establish hospitals to provide the insane with humane treatment. With the aid of Samuel Gridley Howe, Horace Mann, and Dr. Luther Bell, by 1860 Dix had induced almost every state legislature to provide improved facilities for the mentally impaired and the insane.

Not every social ill the reformers attacked lent itself to the asylum solution. Antebellum America had a serious alcohol problem. Captain Basil Hall, an English visitor of the 1820s, noted the "universal practice of sipping a little at a time, but frequently. . .during the whole day." Americans themselves worried about their fellow countrymen's drinking habits. Ministers asserted that drunkenness and "lewdness" went hand in hand. The guardians of public morals believed that alcoholism was especially prevalent among the working class and immigrants; but in fact, all classes had their share of drunkards who squandered their wages, beat their wives, neglected their children, and committed vicious crimes while under the influence of "demon rum."

The temperance reform movement developed two wings. The moderates wished to educate society on the evils of alcohol in order to reduce excessive drinking. The "total abstainers" condemned all drinking as a sin and demanded state prohibition laws to outlaw the production, transport, and consumption of alcoholic beverages. In the 1840s, the prohibitionists, under the leadership of Neal Dow, gained control of the movement. Dow's first success came in 1851 when Maine, his native state, passed the first statewide prohibition law. In the next few years a dozen states, mostly in the North and West, adopted "Maine Laws."

Women Become Assertive.

At one time scholars ascribed the large number of women within the reform movements to the "natural tenderness" or the intrinsic nurturing quality of women. Today we are more likely to seek an explanation in the social setting of the day, especially in the experience of middle-class women.

The cult of domesticity had given mothers higher prestige and sanctioned better education for women than in previous eras. Yet society still believed that women's proper sphere was the home and family. To the young women pouring out of the new seminaries, or otherwise affected by the new partial liberation, the countless remaining restraints on women's public role seemed increasingly galling.

At first women activists found it very difficult to assert their own rights. Striving for the betterment of others seemed more acceptable, for these efforts were related to women's traditional helping role. Many reform-minded middle-class women turned to the problems of working girls forced into prostitution in order to eke out a living in the cities. Hundreds of middle-class women during these years also joined missionary societies to bring the message of Christ to the benighted frontier and to the "heathen" Chinese, Hawaiians, Burmese, and Africans across the oceans. Women also participated in record numbers in the ranks of the American Peace Society, which opposed recourse to war as a means of settling disputes among nations. They were also active in the movement against "demon rum," which they saw as a potential danger to families and to children.

The antislavery movement also attracted women reformers, and their experience in the momentous attack on black bondage was a catalyst in overcoming their reluctance to aid themselves. Within the antislavery movement few objected to women helping to raise money through such activities as bazaars or cake sales. But at least a few bolder women wanted to take more active roles as speakers and organizers. The first woman to put such urges into practice was Angelina Grimké, a young woman who left the South in 1829 with her more retiring sister, Sarah, when they could no longer stand the scourge of slavery. In 1837, after becoming Quakers, the sisters began to give antislavery talks to small groups of women who came to hear about the "peculiar institution" from those who knew it firsthand. Before long Angelina was addressing large gatherings of both men and women in New York and New England.

For women to speak before mixed audiences was a shocking break with tradition. Many moderate antislavery leaders decried Grimké's speeches and deplored the growing participation of women in the movement. But not the abolitionist radicals. Frederick Douglass, a black antislavery leader who felt discrimination based on biology with special poignancy, praised Grimké and endorsed female activism. So did the firebrand William Lloyd Garrison. "As our object is universal emancipation," wrote Garrison, "to redeem women as well as men from a servile to an equal condition—we shall go for the rights of women to their utmost extent."

Despite, or perhaps because of, her opponents, Angelina Grimké evolved into one of the earliest feminists. In 1838 she published *Letters on the Equality of the Sexes*, in which she denounced the traditional education and indoctrination of women designed to keep them in an inferior status. Women should be treated as full human beings. "Whatsoever it is morally right for a man to do," she announced, "it is morally right for a woman to do."

Other women, too, were propelled by the antislavery movement into grappling with their own social and political inferiority. When the 1840 World's Antislavery Convention in London excluded nine American female delegates from its sessions, two of these, Lucretia Mott and Elizabeth Cady Stanton, resolved to launch a new movement dedicated to improving the status of American women. In the summer of 1848 Mott and Stanton brought together 250 people in a women's rights convention at Seneca Falls, New York. The meeting marked the true beginning of the women's rights movement in the United States. The delegates issued a Declaration of Sentiments modeled after the Declaration of Independence, replacing King George III with "man" as the oppressor. It demanded a series of changes to reduce women's legal inferiority and denounced male efforts to diminish women's "confidence in [their] own power" and lessen their "self-respect." The most radical demand, one that clearly violated the notion that women's "proper sphere" was domestic life, was for the "elective franchise"—votes for women!

Seneca Falls did not create a national women's rights organization. Instead, it energized a flock of local and state groups, often informal and temporary, and produced several rounds of state and national conventions where the Seneca Falls Declaration was refined and augmented. The informal networks of women's rights advocates during the 1850s continued to fight for state laws to eliminate gross legal discrimination against women and scored some further successes. They also succeeded in securing new recruits for feminism. They made little impression on resistance to female voting, however. Even women reformers doubted the wisdom of the drive for woman suffrage. It seemed so extreme as to likely stigmatize the entire movement.

Besides group efforts to defeat male domination of society, many middle-class women strove individually to improve their conditions. Amelia Bloomer took up the issue of women's health and became an advocate of less constricting clothing for women, including use of the undergarment named after her. Access to higher education was a part of the self-improvement drive of women reformers. The unavailability of higher education to women was ended when first Oberlin, in 1833, and then other colleges, admitted women as full degree candidates. In 1865 the first all-women's college, Vassar, was established.

With degrees in hand, women could now take on the professions. In 1850 Antoinette Brown earned a theology degree at Oberlin and became the first ordained woman minister. The female breakthrough in medicine came with the Blackwell sisters, who earned their degrees at Geneva College in Pennsylvania, the only school that would admit them for medical training. Other women began to take law courses and set up practices as attorneys. In almost every case women professionals encountered resistance and ridicule in these years. But by the Civil War women had at least broken the crust of male domination of the public sphere, and it was apparent that more advances would follow.

Antislavery Sentiments.

Antislavery not only served to energize women reformers; it was a momentous and controversial reform movement in its own right.

In the decades following the Revolution the Quakers continued to oppose slavery, although they avoided harsh attacks on slaveholders. For a time after 1783 there were antislavery societies even in the South itself.

One expression of antislavery sentiment in this early period was the colonization movement dedicated to returning free blacks to Africa. Some members of the American Colonization Society (founded in 1817), especially southerners, saw their movement primarily as a means of getting rid of a dangerous group that threatened the survival of slavery. Others, however, believed that returning blacks to Africa could serve as a first step in eventually freeing all the slaves. Whatever their motives, promoters of colonization did not take into account the costs of transporting millions of people to Africa, or the feelings of black Americans themselves that America was their native land. Under the auspices of the Colonization Society, a few thousand free blacks, former slaves, and Africans rescued from intercepted illegal slave ships were sent to Liberia, a new black republic founded on the West African coast. But as a serious solution to the slavery problem, colonization remained not only mistaken, but unworkable.

During the late 1820s the antislavery movement took on a new dimension when it linked up with religious Perfectionism and was converted into a crusade for immediate and total abolition. The instigator of the change was William Lloyd Garrison, a pious young printer from Newburyport, Massachusetts, who developed a white-hot determination to drive slavery from the land. Garrison's "immediatism" rejected the quiet tone and step-by-step approach of the Quakers as dealing too gently with sin. Now was the time to demand abolition—if necessary in a way that did not spare people's feelings.

On January 1, 1831, the first issue of Garrison's *Liberator* appeared. It rang with the fervor for liberty and the righteous determination to end the evil of slavery that would make its editor the hope of the oppressed and the despair of moderates. In words that still inspire, Garrison wrote:

> I will be as harsh as truth, and as uncompromising as justice. On this subject, I do not wish to think, to speak, or write with moderation. . . .I am in earnest—I will not equivocate— I will not excuse—and I will not retreat a single inch—and I will be heard.

Despite its militant tone the *Liberator* at first attracted little attention. Then in August 1831 Nat Turner, a slave preacher, instigated a slave uprising in the Virginia tidewater region that led to 57 white and 100 slave deaths. A wave of horror rolled across the South. Though Garrison had had nothing to do with the revolt, southerners were certain that he had inspired Turner. They demanded that he and his fellow abolitionists be stopped by every means possible. Garrison was not deterred. As the years passed, he became even more uncompromising and intransigent.

A thorough Perfectionist, he became convinced that the criminal code, war, and government itself were all efforts to coerce human beings and were equally evil. By condoning slavery, the federal Constitution seemed particularly wicked, and in 1843 Garrison began to place at the head of his editorial column the words:

> Resolved, that the compact which exists between the North and South is a "Covenant with Death, and an Agreement with Hell,"—involving both parties in atrocious criminality,—and should be immediately annulled.

Not all abolitionists were as militant as Garrison. Led by the dynamic Theodore Weld, western abolitionists refused to adopt the extreme positions and language of the Garrisonians. They were also not as certain as Garrison that women's rights and other reforms were the proper concern of the antislavery movement. In 1840 the Weld group, joined by eastern moderates under the Tappan brothers of New York, split from the Garrisonians to form the American and Foreign Antislavery Society with headquarters in New York, leaving the Garrisonians in possession of the American Antislavery Society with headquarters in Boston.

Many conservative white Americans, even in the North, saw the abolitionists as dangers to social and political order. Mobs attacked Garrison in Boston and murdered antislavery leader Elijah Lovejoy in Alton, Illinois, when he refused to shut down his antislavery printing press. When not subject to physical violence, abolitionists were denounced as fanatics, dangerous agitators, and heretics. They were frequently denied basic constitutional rights. When Prudence Crandall attempted to admit a black girl to her Connecticut private school in 1833, local whites broke her windows and poisoned her well. Eventually she was driven from the state. Antiabolitionist feeling penetrated to the highest levels of public life. President Andrew Jackson attacked the antislavery advocates as extremists bent on instigating slave insurrections; his postmaster general denied abolitionists the use of the mails to distribute their newspapers, books, and pamphlets. In 1836 the House of Representatives adopted the "gag rule" placing all antislavery petitions of abolitionists "on the table," where they were simply ignored.

The physical, verbal, and legal assaults did not keep men and women from joining the antislavery movement. In fact, by creating antislavery martyrs and converting abolitionism into an issue of free speech, the attacks may have created sympathy for the movement and attracted recruits. Hundreds of men and women—many of New England ancestry, with occasional southerners such as the Grimké sisters and Alabama planter James G. Birney—flocked to the antislavery organizations. A majority of prominent abolitionists were white, but many free blacks also joined the movement. Unfortunately, blacks within the antislavery societies were often snubbed by white abolitionists who, though they defended human equality in the abstract, could not always overcome their actual prejudice against black people. Despite such prejudice, Frederick Douglass, the brilliant black editor of the antislavery *North Star*; Henry Highland Garnet, an eloquent black preacher; and Sojourner Truth, an illiterate former slave who spoke with effective simplicity for the cause of freedom, all became prominent members of abolitionist societies.

Utopian Socialism. Each of these reform movements was an attempt to cure some perceived ill of American society while leaving the main structure untouched. Some Americans, however, rejected the very foundations of their society and chose to withdraw from it almost entirely or to demand drastic change from the bottom up.

These militants considered America too competitive and individualistic, too given over to the pursuit of wealth, and too severely marred by inequality and exploitation. Yearning for a society closer to human scale where men and women could deal with one another face to face, eager to erase the distinctions between rich and poor, hopeful of replacing competition with cooperation, and determined to eliminate human drudgery, they went off to the woods or the frontier to found communities based on some idealistic economic, social, or religious philosophy.

Several of the new utopian communities were inspired by the writings of Charles Fourier, a French thinker who opposed capitalism as inhumane and competitive. Fourier proposed in its place a system of small cooperative communities—"phalanxes"—scattered about the countryside where men and women could work at farming and industry while living in a communal structure. No one would own the community's capital; all would share both the labor and the profit. Government of each phalanx would consist of a Council of Seven, five of whom would be women.

A communitarian experiment that owed as much to religious as to political principles was Oneida, led by John Humphrey Noyes, a Yale-educated minister who settled with his followers in western New York in 1847. At Oneida, Noyes preached against what he called "the Sin system, the Marriage system, the Work system, and the Death system," combining religious evangelism and socialist economics. All work at Oneida was reduced to what seemed essential and unavoidable. Women, particularly, were freed from drudgery by simplified methods of housekeeping.

Noyes's most radical experiment was "complex marriage." He and his followers believed that monogamy was selfish and interfered with a true sense of community. Instead, every man at Oneida was considered the husband of every woman, and vice versa. Outsiders called this "free love" and reviled it as an utter breakdown of morality. But the Oneidans responded that no one in the community was forced to accept sexual relations he or she did not desire. Though Oneida members practiced birth control, some children were born into the community; they were treated in an unusually permissive way, being allowed, for example, to sleep mornings until awakened by the natural rhythms of their bodies.

The Oneida community avoided the bickering that destroyed so many other communitarian experiments by a scheme of self-criticism whereby members could air their grievances before the whole group and work them out. Oneida also developed a firm economic foundation. Recognizing that a community such as his was better suited to industry than agriculture, Noyes trained members in embroidery and silk making and mobilized their ingenuity in developing manufactures. The community basked in prosperity for many decades, becoming, ironically, the basis for a major commercial cutlery firm still in business today.

There were many other experimental communities in this era. It is estimated that more than 100 such establishments with 100,000 members were formed in the United States between 1820 and 1860. As Emerson wrote an English friend in 1840: "We are all a little wild here with numberless projects of social reform. Not a reading man but has a draft of a new community in his waistcoat pocket."

Most communities founded on some sort of political or philosophical plan were short-lived. New Harmony, a socialist experiment on the banks of the Wabash sponsored by the British philanthropist Robert Owen, lasted two years and then disbanded when internal bickering destroyed all chance of harmony. Icaria, designed as an experiment in communal ownership and use of capital, attracted a small group of French people to the new state of Texas in 1847. A year later it was defunct. The longest-lived of the Fourierist communities—at Red Bank, New Jersey—lasted only a dozen years.

Communities with a religious base were generally more successful than ones founded on a political ideal. Among the most enduring "utopian" communities were those established by the English Quaker Mother Ann Lee, who came to America in 1774 and organized her first small "Shaker" settlement soon after. By the late 1840s about 6,000 Shakers were living in a score or more communities scattered across the northern states. In their trim, spare, simple villages the Shakers followed a life that combined economic cooperation with a pursuit of spiritual perfection that precluded sexual relations. Shakers prospered collectively by selling seeds, medicinal herbs, bonnets, cloaks, and cabinetwork, and lasted as a group well into the twentieth century.

The commercial success of the religious communities illustrates the paradoxes of antebellum America. Secular faiths were unable to deal with the craving for brotherhood and cooperation. During the pre-Civil War era no political or economic philosophy could overcome the acquisitiveness and individualism of the larger society. A religious perspective was more effective. But to survive, the religious communities found it necessary to become successful economic enterprises.

Conclusions

What were pre-Civil War Americans in the North and West truly like, then? Americans were competitive and individualistic; they were crude, bad-mannered, violent, and bigoted. They were also humane, romantic, creative, and socially speculative. It seems fitting to call them, as one historian has, a "people of paradox."

These inconsistencies can be traced to the special circumstances of the northern part of the nation in these years. The whole region north of Dixie was in a state of extraordinary flux. Still agricultural and rural, it was rapidly becoming commercial, industrial, and urban. Still largely composed of native-born Protestants whose forebears had arrived in the colonial era, it was experiencing a deluge of newcomers from Europe, many of them Catholic. Besides the tensions these changes created, there were antagonisms between East and West. Easterners often disliked western manners and practices, yet they themselves were moving west in vast numbers and learning to adjust to western economic competition. These transplanted easterners were undoubtedly influenced by the western practices they deplored.

One important fact should be kept in mind as we consider the country's evolution: Virtually all the changes we have described in this chapter followed lines of latitude. In shifts of people, institutions, values, and problems, Northeast mixed with Northwest. This is not to say that the two sections did not retain many distinctive features, but by 1860 Northeast and Northwest were far more like each other than either was to the South. This development of distinctive North–South sectional identities would soon have momentous consequences for the nation.

ONLINE RESOURCES

"The Shakers—Another America" *http://www.shakerworkshops.com/shakers.htm#* This richly detailed article describes the Shakers' beliefs, daily reflections, and rules and ordinances governing their lives.

"Hope of Reclaiming the Abandoned" *http://sadl.uleth.ca/nz/collect/whist/import/complete/womhist.binghamton.edu/fmrs/doc1.htm* An excerpt from a report of the Female Moral Reform Society of New York, this document illustrates how reformers used ideas about female "purity" to argue for an activist social role for women.

"Free Blacks in the Antebellum Period" *http://lcweb2.loc.gov/ammem/aaohtml/exhibit/aopart2.html* Read about the struggles and accomplishments of free African Americans during this era. Rare books and pamphlets illustrate the free African-American press and their own quest for nationwide freedom.

"The Seneca Falls Convention" *http://www.npg.si.edu/col/seneca/senfalls1.htm* In addition to a general overview of the Seneca Falls convention, this site features from the National Portrait Gallery portraits of the key women involved in the quest for equal rights. To read the full text of the Seneca Falls Convention and Declarations of Sentiment/Report of the Women's Rights Convention, consult *http://www.luminet.net/~tgort/convent.htm.* Choose the link for the dates of July 19–20, 1848.

Evangelicalism, Revivalism, and the Second Great Awakening *http://www.nhc.rtp.nc.us:8080/tserve/nineteen/nkeyinfo/nevanrev.htm* This site contains links about the conversion practices of evangelicals during the Second Great Awakening. For an eyewitness account of an evangelical revival by a female traveler, read Frances Trollope's full text entry at *http://xroads.virginia.edu/%7EHYPER/DETOC/Fem/religion.htm#trollope.*

Cult of Domesticity "Discussion: What Were Women's Roles in the Early Republic?" *http://www.library.csi.cuny.edu/dept/history/lavender/386/truewoman.html* In addition to a brief overview of the cult of true womanhood, this site contains the work of one of the time period's bestknown female writers discussing the "proper role" of women in the nineteenth century.

The Mary Anne Sadlier Archive *http://xroads.virginia.edu/~HYPER/SADLIER/IRISH/Sadlier.htm.* The site presents a critical introduction to Sadlier's writing.

Influence of Prominent Abolitionists *http://www.loc.gov/exhibits/african/afam006.html* On this site, discover the influence that abolitionists such as Frederick Douglass and Susan B. Anthony had on some Americans' thoughts on slavery. Connect to links for primary-source documentation such as speeches and printed antislavery tracks.

The Oneida Community Collection in the Syracuse University Library *http://libwww.syr.edu/digital/guides/o/OneidaCommunityCollection/* With books, pamphlets, serial publications, and more than 140 photographs, this site provides an in-depth look at the Oneida commune. It also contains a general history of the group and its founder, John Humphrey Noyes.

African-American Odyssey: Abolition, Antislavery Movements, and the Rise of Sectional Controversy *http://lcweb2.loc.gov/ammem/aaohtml/exhibit/aopart3b.html* On this site, see the text of the Fugitive Slave Law, learn of the growing sectionalism in America and its causes, and read Frederick Douglass's tribute to John Brown's actions in the Harper's Ferry uprising.

13

The Old South

What Is Myth and What Was Real?

1807	Congress prohibits the slave trade with Africa, but illegal importation of black slaves continues
1822	Denmark Vesey and thirty-five slaves are hanged for planning a slave rebellion in South Carolina
1831	Nat Turner leads an unsuccessful slave rebellion in Virginia; "Tariff of Abominations" precipitates nullification crisis in South Carolina
1832	In response to Turner's rebellion, the Virginia legislature debates the abolition of slavery
1836	Under pressure from southern congressmen, the House of Representatives adopts a gag rule prohibiting discussion of all abolitionist petitions
1849	John Calhoun writes *Disquisition on Government*: He states his theory of the concurrent majority in the Senate the following year
1852	Harriet Beecher Stowe's *Uncle Tom's Cabin* is published
1857	Hinton R. Helper's *The Impending Crisis of the South* is published
1858	In a famous speech James Hammond declares there has to be a mud sill upon which to erect a civilized cultured life
1860	Abraham Lincoln elected president; Slaves in the South number about 4 million, sixteen times the number of free blacks; South Carolina secedes from the Union

Magnolias and moonlight; white mansions with tall colonnades; beautiful hoop-skirted ladies and handsome, dignified white-suited gentlemen; thoroughbred horses; rich laughter and song drifting up from the slave quarters; waltzes and entrancing talk in the big plantation house—this was the Old South, a society that achieved for a brief moment a brilliance and happy harmony based on mutual respect of classes and races, an ideal of excellence, and good prices for cotton.

Or was it? There is another picture that is almost the complete opposite. In this view the Old South—the slave states in the half-century before 1860—was an abhorrent region where a privileged white minority lorded it over millions of black slaves and "poor white trash." The typical elite planter was a coarse, philistine, newly rich "cotton snob," who abused his black chattels and showed contempt for the nonslaveholding class he himself had so recently left behind. The poor whites, in turn, were shiftless, slovenly, violent, and ignorant people who lived by a little desultory farming and trading whiskey with the slaves for stolen

280

plantation goods. Beneath the poor whites were the exploited slaves. Oppressed by a regime of terror and physical violence, they fought back by contrived laziness, deceit, flight, or violence. The land of the South as a whole was unkempt, with fields badly cultivated, and housing, even for whites, crude and squalid.

What was the Old South really like? Are both descriptions essentially fables? Is one depiction truer than the other? Or is there some truth in both?

An Unexpected Diversity

One myth about the Old South is that it was utterly distinct in its climate and geography. Climate did make a difference. The lower South was indeed warmer than the rest of the nation, and this enabled it to grow short-fiber cotton successfully. It was too warm for wheat; its chief grain crop was corn. It had poor pasturage and so the corn-eating hog, rather than the grass-eating cow, was the basis of its animal husbandry. But there was little to separate the climate of Maryland from that of Pennsylvania—and yet the first state was part of the Old South, the second of the North. Nor was the South's topography unique. The Appalachian plateau, the Atlantic coastal plain, and the Mississippi Valley were geographical features shared by the nation's two sections. In short, it was not primarily the natural environment that defined the Old South.

Southern Agriculture.   Another myth is that the Old South was a single agricultural unit. When we think of Dixie in this period, we imagine a gigantic cotton field. Yet cotton was only one of the region's many crops, and not even the most valuable. Corn, which grew everywhere, fattened the section's farm animals and, in the form of "pone," "hominy," and "roasting ears," fed most of its people. The southern corn crop was valued at $209 million in 1855; the cotton crop at only $136 million. Other staple crops brought in cash. Kentucky hemp, Louisiana sugar, Carolina rice, and Virginia, North Carolina, and Kentucky tobacco were important in their regions. Although none even came close to cotton as a source of cash income, they contributed to the South's remarkable diversity.

Industry.   Another myth about the Old South is that it was economically backward. Until fairly recently, historians believed that cotton growing was actually an unproductive enterprise. It exhausted the soil, so that only by constant expansion into virgin land could the planter ensure himself a decent profit. Cotton also supposedly deflected capital from more productive enterprise. Southerners poured their money into new land and slaves rather than into machines and factories. And even if they had been willing to invest in industry, the older view went, the slave system would have prevented it. Slaves lacked the necessary skills, incentives, and education for industrial work. Moreover, to set up successful industrial enterprises where the labor force itself was property was too great a burden for would-be investors. Finally, a slave society inevitably encouraged aristocratic values and contempt for hard physical work—attitudes at odds with successful industrialization. Given all these qualities of a slave society, it was not surprising, said critics, that the South remained bound to agriculture and achieved a slower rate of economic growth than the rest of the nation.

Few scholars today accept these ideas without major qualifications. It is true that the Old South developed its manufacturing potential more slowly than the Northeast. But the reasons have little to do with slavery. True, most slaves were unskilled laborers, yet they were capable of performing many of the tasks required by industry. Some served as "drivers" or even overseers supervising large work gangs. Many were skilled craftspeople. On the cotton plantations there were coopers, masons, carpenters, brickmakers, gardeners, and the like. On the sugar plantations of Louisiana black experts supervised most of the delicate operations of sugar refining. Slave women were often expert seamstresses, weavers, cooks, and midwives. Some even practiced medicine, on white as well as black patients. Clearly, slaves could have supplied the workforce for an industrial economy.

Nor did prospective factory owners in the South have to tie up capital by buying their employees. Many planters hired their slaves out at prevailing wage rates. Hired slaves worked as municipal workers in southern cities; they worked by the day for southern householders. They also worked in southern factories and industries. Hired slaves were miners in Virginia, Kentucky, and Missouri. Deck hands on the river steamers of the Old South were generally black bondsmen, as were the construction workers on railroads and canals. Cotton mills in South Carolina, Alabama, and Florida used slave "operatives," and in Virginia slaves were employed in tobacco factories and at the Tredegar iron mills of Richmond, which would produce most of the Confederacy's artillery.

Clearly, then, the slave-labor system did not exclude industry and business from the Old South. Neither did southern values. Dixie planters were generally practical men who studied agriculture as a business, encouraged experimentation in crops and animal breeding, and organized their labor force efficiently. In fact, according to some historians, the "gang" system of labor they developed on the cotton and sugar plantations was one of the most efficient work patterns for agriculture ever devised. While the hours were moderate, the intensity of the effort was high and the output of the slaves impressive. All told, one scholar writes, the pre-Civil War southern plantation was "a modern business organization, and possibly even a leading business organization of its time."

A final demonstration of plantation slavery's efficiency was the actual overall economic performance of the antebellum South. The Old South, taken as a whole, was a remarkably productive community. Its industrial development was ahead of all but a very few European countries in cloth output and railroad mileage. In 1860 there were almost 200 textile mills scattered through the region, plus hundreds of tobacco factories, flour and lumber mills, and other manufacturing establishments that, primarily, processed the section's agricultural products.

Most interesting are the comparative figures of sectional income. In 1860 the average per person income for the entire United States was $128 (in 1860 dollars). For the North as a whole it was $141. For the South, if we include both slave and free people, it was only $103, less than either. But if we only include the free population, the South's per capita income rises to $150, a figure higher than both the North and the national average. And it was also growing at a faster rate than the country as a whole. Between 1840 and 1860 the economy of the entire United States grew at the average yearly rate of 1.4 percent for each man, woman, and child. The Old South's growth rate was 1.7 percent.

Taken together, then, it is clear that the gap between the Old South and the North in the matter of industrialization did not arise from slavery or aristocratic disdain for "trade." Rather, it resulted from a rational estimate of profits on investment that induced planters to put their capital into agriculture rather than manufacturing.

Social Diversity.   The Old South's social system has also been misperceived. In the past, few scholars questioned the existence of a well-defined three-tiered society of rich planters, poor whites, and black slaves. But in reality each layer was far more complex than this view suggests.

The top layer was very thin indeed. In 1860 only 2,200 southerners owned 100 or more slaves, and these 2,200 made up less than 1 percent of the 383,000 slaveholding families in that year. The lordly domain, and the lordly planter aristocrat, were a rarity in the Old South.

The typical slaveholder was a member of the middle class. Seventy-one percent of slaveholders in 1860—almost 200,000—had fewer than 10 slaves. These farmers ate plain food and lived in houses that were little more than enlarged wood-frame structures or even modified log cabins. Although aspiring to wealth and gentility, they were often plain in their speech and rough in their ways.

Even more numerous were the white yeomen farmers who worked their acres themselves, helped by their grown sons and some occasional hired labor. As described by Professor Frank Owsley and his students, they were independent, democratic, and lived comfortably but simply.

The white yeomanry was particularly numerous in hilly upland regions and the "pine belts," away from the rich bottomland of the Mississippi, Tombigbee, Pearl, and other rivers where the great plantations flourished. The bottomland was both malarial and expensive, and the yeomen gave it a wide berth. Yet even in the delta region of Mississippi and the "black belt" of Alabama, small farmers could be found.

The yeoman class was not without political power. Voting qualifications were almost as broad in the Old South as elsewhere in the country, and southern politicians had to heed the yeomen's wishes. Moreover, in some areas the yeoman-small planter class was able to manipulate election districts so that counties where the white population was proportionately greatest—and where the small farmers predominated—could dominate the state legislatures.

But in revising the traditional view, we must not go too far. Wealth in the South was more concentrated than in the North. Few northern farms equaled the thousands of acres of some cotton plantations. Moreover, with a "prime" male field hand selling for about a thousand dollars in 1850, any owner of a half-dozen slaves was a wealthy person. If we include only nonslaveholders, southern yeomen were poorer than their northern counterparts.

Nor can we deny that there was a class of very poor rural southern whites. Where infertile soils and steep terrain made farming difficult, small groups of white families made a precarious living by growing corn, raising hogs, and hunting. These rural poor were often despised. Fanny Kemble, a visiting English actress, called them "the most degraded race of human beings claiming an Anglo-Saxon origin that can be found on the face of the earth." Kemble hated slavery and sought to demonstrate that it demeaned whites as well as blacks. But it is clear that whether explained by slavery, isolation, nutritional diseases like pellagra, or natural selection, there was indeed a group of destitute whites who inhabited the rural nooks and crannies of pre-Civil War southern society.

We must also qualify Owsley's view of the Old South's yeoman democracy. Although the South's white farmers had to be heeded politically, they did not wield most of the region's political power. In the Carolinas, Georgia, Maryland, and Virginia voting was rigged in favor of the plantation areas. In the newer states slaveholders often enjoyed special advantages such as relatively low property taxes. And even where the yeomen made their numbers felt, the planter aristocracy often occupied positions of influence far beyond their formal power. Talented sons of the yeomanry with political ambitions had to acquire land and slaves to succeed in public life.

The South's white, nonslaveholding yeomen often resented both slavery and planter leadership. Their spokesman was Hinton R. Helper of North Carolina, whose book, *The Impending Crisis of the South* (1857), is a blistering attack on the planter class. The planters, he claimed, had retarded the South's growth and oppressed its yeomen. As a group, they were "so depraved that there ... [was] scarcely a spark of honor or magnanimity to be found among them." Helper, like many whites of his class, also despised blacks, but he was willing to use fire to fight fire. To destroy the power of the planters, he proposed to rally the nonslaveholders against them—with the help, if need be, of the slaves.

Life Under Slavery

The black South, too, has long been covered by a thick crust of myths. The older legend depicts "happy darkies" singing in the fields. Lovable but childlike creatures, they did not feel the oppression of slavery the way white people would. Indeed, on a day-to-day basis, slavery was a rather benign institution, and masters and slaves found it possible to develop mutual respect and to live comfortably with inequality. A newer picture is the diametric opposite. Slavery, it says, was a system of organized terror that either broke the spirit of black people or drove them to blind fury against their oppressors. Slaves were often whipped or maimed and were consigned to an incessant round of brutal, degrading labor. Worst of all, masters broke up the slaves' families and violated black women.

The truth is more complex than either description allows. Slave life was very diverse. Like most southern whites, most blacks were employed in agriculture. Only a small portion of the southern population in 1860 was urban, and only about 17 percent of the total city population of the slave states was black. Yet black urbanites provided the black community with much-needed leaders and were an important element in the general cultural life of cities such as New Orleans and Charleston.

Most southern blacks were slaves; but on the eve of the Civil War about 250,000 (the same number as in the North) were free. Free blacks lived predominantly in the upper South. Many were urban. In 1860 Baltimore's free black population outnumbered its slaves ten to one; Washington, D.C., had over 9,000 free blacks and fewer than 1,800 slaves.

Wherever free blacks lived in the South, their lot, as in the North, was not enviable. A few were successful in business, the skilled trades, the professions, or agriculture. Some free blacks even owned slaves of their own, and a tiny number were planters with considerable property, including slaves. Most, however, were unskilled laborers who huddled in the slums of the large southern towns, worked at menial tasks, suffered the contempt of whites, and, though nominally free, were denied fundamental civil rights.

The South's slaves numbered about 4 million in 1860, sixteen times the number of free blacks. The great majority worked the soil. Whereas whites were mostly associated with small farm units, almost three-fourths of the South's slaves were found on relatively large plantations.

Working on a large plantation had some advantages for slaves. Where there were many slaves, there were many different jobs. On the large plantations slave

This sketch by the English-born architect Benjamin Latrobe shows Virginia slaves working under the eye of an overseer. We are repelled by the arrogant and indolent pose of the overseer, a response that the artist, who hated slavery, was probably trying to encourage.

women found employment as seamstresses, cooks, nurses, or maids in the master's house; slave men worked as butlers, coachmen, and valets. Black house servants were not free, but they were the envy of other slaves. Their jobs kept them out of the fields and brought them into contact with the more interesting world of the "big house." It also enabled them to control their working conditions to some degree. Abusing a good cook or laundress might ruin dinner or make it impossible to get a clean shirt, after all. Even slaves who were not house servants enjoyed some advantages on large plantations. Besides working in the field, they might serve as drivers, skilled mechanics, or craftsmen. Because skilled workers were often hired out in towns and were sometimes allowed to negotiate their own terms of hire, these slaves were unusually free—for slaves.

Even the field hands on the large plantations were often better off than those on smaller establishments. It is true that the labor was intense. Worked in gangs under close supervision, the slaves were expected to be productive, and they were. The output per worker on large plantations was consistently higher than on small ones. Planters usually perceived that generosity was a more effective means to encourage hard work than force, and acted accordingly. But where an absentee master employed a white overseer to manage his plantation, slaves were sometimes treated more severely. Still, the overall estimate that the workload was seldom excessive on large plantations remains valid.

Finally, the physical comfort of slaves on large plantations was better than on small ones. Every slaveholder interested in making money understood that profits depended in part on maintaining a healthy, contented, well-nourished labor force. But only large plantations could provide medical services, weather-tight cabins, and the varied diet needed to maximize the efficiency of slave workers.

And we must consider the alternative. The one out of four slaves living on farms or small plantations no doubt had closer contact with the white owner and his family. They often ate at the same table with the master and sometimes even slept in the same cabin. But slaves who lived in such close quarters with their owners were constantly subject to white scrutiny, were always made aware of their inferior social status, and had less opportunity to meet other blacks. In addition, small farmers were more likely to run into financial problems and be forced to sell their slaves. Blacks then faced the grim prospect that their families would be broken up.

Slave Culture.

We now know that slavery did not prevent the development of a distinctive black American culture. This culture achieved a remarkable flowering in music and oral literature particularly. Slaves sang about God and salvation, about their work, about love and passion, and about their daily lives. They composed humorous songs, bitter songs, and even rebellious songs that explicitly called for freedom. Talented black storytellers drew on the West African tradition of oral history, fable, and legend; combined it with Bible stories; and filled their tales with the animals and people of the southern environment. The stories, like the songs, often expressed the slaves' true feelings about their condition. One of the best-known group of tales featured Brer Rabbit, who manages to outwit stronger animals with his resourcefulness and trickery.

The slaves' religion helped them forge a group identity. West Africans accepted a supreme God, though they did not think of him as a jealous, exclusive deity.

This belief enabled transplanted slaves to accept the Christian faith of their European masters. Blacks found the enthusiastic Protestantism of the Baptists and Methodists especially congenial, though they never fully accepted the Protestant emphasis on sin and culture of guilt.

Observers of the Old South never failed to comment on the deep religious commitments of black men and women and often noted that their piety put "their betters" to shame. Southern whites generally welcomed these religious feelings, and many planters employed white ministers to preach to their slaves, who seized the chance to attend religious services on the plantation. In the towns they often went to white churches, though they had to sit in separate places in the back or in the gallery. But blacks preferred religious autonomy. Throughout the antebellum period black preachers, most of them self-taught, ministered to the needs of their people, sometimes in secret. During slave days, as in more recent years, black clergymen served as the social and political leaders of their people.

Masters hoped that slaves learned from Christianity the messages of submission, humility, and sobriety. Black Christianity actually had very different consequences. Like black music and literature, it helped preserve a sense of black independence. Blacks found in their version of Christianity a theme of hope and freedom. The popularity of spirituals like "Go Down Moses" suggests how closely the slaves identified with the Children of Israel, enslaved in Egypt, and how eagerly they awaited liberation from bondage. Perceptive whites understood the subversive quality of black Christianity, and during times of slave unrest slaveowners often forbade religious meetings on the plantations.

Yet however lenient in some places and at certain times, slavery remained grounded on coercion. Slaves were punished by having privileges withdrawn or extra work piled on. They were also subject to physical punishment. Slaves were flogged for stealing, for disobeying orders, for running away, for fighting, and for drinking. Young men were more likely to be lashed than other slaves, but no group was exempt from physical punishment. At times slaves were whipped without apparent cause. Mary Boykin Chesnut, wife of a South Carolina planter-politician, admitted that "men and women are punished when their masters and mistresses are brutes, not when they do wrong." Even slaves who were not themselves physically chastised were deeply affected by it; to witness grown men or women being flogged was an intimidating experience that drove home the lesson that the white owner was indisputable master.

Slavery and the Family.

One of the most affecting parts of Harriet Beecher Stowe's famous antislavery novel, *Uncle Tom's Cabin* (1852), is the description of how Arthur Shelby, a kindly Kentucky master, is forced to sell the little slave boy Harry to a coarse and brutal slavetrader in order to pay his debts. Harry's mother, Eliza, flees with him before the sale and mother and child escape to free territory across the ice-choked Ohio River. *American Slavery as It Is,* an important abolitionist tract, denounced slavery's disregard of black family life, its encouragement of moral laxity, and the opportunity it afforded for the sexual exploitation of black women.

Everything recorded in the antislavery novels and tracts about the destructive impact of slavery on black families took place. Slave families were indeed broken up by sale; the experience of Eliza and Harry was not unique. The threat of separation was always a powerful weapon of social discipline. And slavery was at war with black family life in other ways. Nowhere in the Old South did the law recognize the sanctity of slave marriages; to have done so would have limited the power of slaveholders to dispose of slaves as they wished. On the other hand, the reality was not totally bleak. Masters often found it advantageous to encourage strong marriage ties among their slaves because they reduced rivalries and made for a more efficient workforce. Generally speaking, slaves preferred the married to the single state. But whether the initiative came from the master or from the slaves themselves, the result was a surprisingly large number of strong, loving, and permanent slave unions and stable slave families.

One of the most lurid charges leveled by abolitionists against the slave system is that it allowed white men to exploit black women sexually. There is truth to this accusation. Some slaveowners and white overseers had virtual harems. Less sensational, but more telling, the 1860 census records that 10 percent of the slave population had partly white ancestry. We must assume, given the disparity in power between white men and slave women, that the relationships that produced racially mixed offspring were frequently imposed on black women. Yet as Professor Eugene Genovese remarks: "Many white men who began by taking a black girl in an act of sexual exploitation ended by loving her and the children she bore. They were not supposed to, but they did. . . ."

Miscegenation—mating across racial lines—was rare on the well-run plantation, though less unusual in cities and towns. Wherever it took place, it was considered scandalous. Even a beloved black partner could never expect to be recognized and respected by the white community. Harmful to slave discipline and deeply resented by both slave men and women, it was also condemned by white society, which held that all sexual relations outside marriage were deplorable. Slave families, whose solidarity was formidable considering the trying conditions, were disrupted by the practice. White women, particularly, considered it a threat to their families, which explains why southern white women were often hostile to slavery. But miscegenation did take place, and it must be considered another count in the indictment of slavery.

The "Bottom Line" of Slavery.

Slaves, then, were scarcely the "happy darkies" of myth. The most obvious evil of slavery was its denial of individual freedom. Ultimately, the slaves' lives were not their own. Slaves were not free to move. They could not withhold their labor or maximize the benefits from it. They could not express their personalities fully. The peculiar institution directly repudiated those sacred rights of life, liberty, and the pursuit of happiness that all Americans professed to cherish. Slaves knew of white America's professions, and the disparity between principles and performance undoubtedly made the pain of bondage all the greater.

And there was much else. Slavery provided no effective remedy for cruelty. There were laws against sadistic torture and mutilation of slaves; but the laws could not be easily enforced because the slave was a legal nullity who could not testify against whites in court. Masters might prefer to preserve slave families, but because nothing required them to do so, they seldom kept families intact if it conflicted with their pressing financial interests. Slavery also denied black people the full use of their abilities. Opportunities to become drivers or to acquire some skill were no substitute for the ability to reach the highest reaches of business or the professions. In addition, it was illegal to teach slaves to read and write. Some masters ignored the law and themselves instructed their slaves to read or permitted literate blacks to teach their fellow bondsmen. Yet in 1860 more than nine out of ten slaves could not read, a condition that severely limited their access to many areas of knowledge and experience. When talented slaves like Josiah Henson, Solomon Northrup, and Frederick Douglass were free to tell their stories, they utterly condemned the system that denied them their humanity. Slavery, wrote Frederick Douglass in his *Autobiography*, "could and did develop all its malign and shocking characteristics." It was "indecent without shame, cruel without shuddering, and murderous without apprehension or fear of exposure, or punishment."

Finally, slavery reinforced racism. It was a mark of inferiority that affected all black men and women and did not disappear even when black people secured their legal freedom. Slavery, accordingly, amplified the original racial antipathies of white Americans and made black skin a stigma strong enough to survive even the destruction of the peculiar institution itself.

The Southern Mind

Perhaps the most beguiling myth about the Old South is that it was a genial, cultivated society. Again the picture is not entirely false. Among the planters were kindly and charming ladies and gentlemen who read the classics, appreciated music, and kept in touch with the best thought of England and Europe. The region also had many literate, upright yeomen whose natural dignity, independence, and generous hospitality would have warmed the heart of Jefferson. Nor were all southern whites hostile to change. The South, for example, joined the crusade against demon rum and against mistreatment of convicted felons. It was even a little ahead of the North showing concern for the insane. Yet by 1860 the white South had also become a land of fear and suspicion where dissent seemed treason and those who denied the region's superiority over all other societies were cruelly ostracized or brutally driven out. In such an atmosphere culture languished or became the servant of self-defense, and all chance of reform ended.

Slave Revolts.   The South's fears were directly related to slavery. Although most southerners refused to acknowledge publicly that slavery was a cruel and exploitative system, many privately recognized that the slaves resented their bondage and would end it if they could. Slaves revealed their hatred of the system by the day-to-day resistance of ignoring directions, engaging in work slowdowns, abusing equipment, and running away. Occasionally a male slave would attack his master or overseer.

The most feared of all forms of slave resistance was the slave revolt, eruptions of collective racial violence that sent shock waves through white society. Several of these occurred in the Old South era. In 1800 a slave named Gabriel Prosser was foiled in his attempt to organize an army to capture the city of Richmond. A decade later, 500 slaves began a march on New Orleans and had to be dispersed by troops. In 1822 Denmark Vesey, a free black from Charleston, organized a slave insurrection that was betrayed by a slave. Vesey and thirty-four other blacks were hanged. Most frightening of all, however, was the Nat Turner uprising in the Virginia Tidewater region in 1831. In late August, Turner, a slave foreman and preacher, aided by several other slaves, killed his owner and his owner's family. Then, with seventy fellow bondsmen gathered along the way, he marched through the countryside, killing and burning. Before the rebellion was put down by state and federal troops, over fifty whites had lost their lives. Most of Turner's band were either captured or killed in skirmishes with the soldiers during the first forty-eight hours, and thirteen slaves and three free blacks were later hanged. It took an additional two months to capture the resourceful Turner, who was then tried and executed.

Though slave revolts were far less common in the American South than in other New World slave societies, they revealed the true feelings of blacks in a particularly dramatic way and chilled the hearts of white southerners. There were times when southerners seemed positively obsessed with the fear of a "servile insurrection" that might lead to massacres of whites and wide destruction of property. This nervousness fed on itself; for each instance of actual slave unrest in the antebellum South, there were a hundred rumors of slave plots.

Quieting the Opposition.   Occasionally, fears led to honest soul-searching among southerners. Soon after Nat Turner's insurrection, before slavery had become sacred and untouchable, the Virginia legislature conducted a frank debate on the possible abolition of slavery in the state. Representatives from the state's western, nonslaveholding districts attacked the peculiar institution as "offensive to the

A classic Old South plantation house. This one is in Louisiana.

moral feelings of a large portion of the community," "ruinous to the whites," degrading to labor, and a danger to the social order of the South. Others defended it passionately. In the end, unfortunately, the debate led nowhere; slavery in Virginia, as elsewhere, was by now so intertwined with the culture and economy of the community that to a majority of whites abolition seemed a cure worse than the disease.

This 1832 debate was the last serious public discussion of abolition in the South. Thereafter the response to slave unrest was unqualified repression. Laws requiring slaves to carry passes when they were away from their masters were more carefully enforced. The patrol system—posses of white men traveling about checking on slaves found off the plantation—was tightened. After 1831, in scores of southern communities, innocent slaves were jailed or even executed in panicky reaction to rumored slave uprisings.

These fears cast a pall over the political and intellectual life of the South. Many southerners became convinced that the restlessness of the slaves was the work of outside agitators: free blacks, black merchant seamen, and, above all, northern abolitionists. To deal with the problem southern legislatures passed laws that made manumissions (owners freeing their slaves) increasingly difficult and restricted the rights and movements of free blacks. Several states even sought to expel free blacks from within their borders. In Maryland and Missouri the state legislatures appropriated sums for the purpose of returning ("colonizing") free blacks to Africa. South Carolina tried to prevent slaves from being "contaminated" by black merchant seamen working for northern and foreign firms by forbidding black sailors to set foot on the state's soil.

The fiercest southern response was reserved for the abolitionists. Of all the outside groups that endangered the peace and safety of the South, they seemed the worst. Governor John Floyd of Virginia accused these "unrestrained fanatics" of fomenting the Nat Turner revolt. Other southerners called them "a pestilent sect," "ignorant and infatuated barbarians." Even though they were federal employees, postmasters throughout the South refused to deliver abolitionist newspapers and books. When antislavery activists denounced this as censorship of the mails, Postmaster General Amos Kendall, a Kentuckian by adoption, refused to intervene. "We owe an obligation to the laws," he conceded, but "we owe a higher one to the communities in which we live."

De facto censorship of the mails was the mildest of the South's efforts to preserve its system by cutting off the free exchange of ideas. After the Virginia debate of 1832 the subject of abolition was considered closed. Almost everywhere in the slave states toleration for social and intellectual dissent weakened. White southerners who refused to go along with the majority view, such as James G. Birney of Alabama, the Grimké sisters of South Carolina, and Cassius M. Clay of Kentucky, were denounced, threatened, and eventually driven from the South. Southern leaders sought to suppress abolitionist agitation elsewhere as well. In 1836, as we have seen, the southern delegation in Congress, annoyed at the barrage of petitions asking for abolition of slavery in the District of Columbia, induced the House of Representatives to adopt a rule automatically laying such petitions "on the table" without action. This "gag rule" remained in force for eight years despite attacks by antislavery advocates and civil liberties champions, who assailed it as a denial of free speech and a violation of the constitutional right of petition.

Arguments in Favor of Slavery.   The South also mounted a counterattack against its critics that produced some interesting—and generally deplorable—intellectual results. In the eighteenth century, southerners seldom defended slavery in the abstract. Indeed, the southern-born Founding Fathers often conceded that, ideally speaking, slavery was a violation of human rights. Its ultimate justification was necessity: The South could not survive without black laborers, and as it was unthinkable that blacks could be anything but social and economic subordinates, they must remain slaves. However unavoidable, slavery seemed clearly wrong to many thoughtful southerners during these years.

After about 1820, however, southern leaders and publicists ceased to question the institution and began to defend it. Slavery, they said, was sanctioned by the Bible and the Christian faith. In the Old Testament God made Ham, the second son of Noah, into a servant of his two brothers. Ham's descendants, the dark races, must therefore serve the light-skinned progeny of Shem and Japheth. As for the New Testament, it enjoined "servants" to be obedient and dutiful to their masters. It is difficult to tell how seriously white southerners took the biblical defense of slavery. It was possible to extract other, more hopeful, meanings from the Bible, as both black and white abolitionists had reason to know. For those already disposed to defend the peculiar institution on more practical grounds, it was nevertheless comforting to have the Scriptures' reinforcement.

The most sophisticated proslavery argument, however, was sociological. In the writings of Virginian George Fitzhugh, slavery was converted from a necessary evil to a "positive good." Fitzhugh considered the North's vaunted freedom a failure. It had not brought comfort and security to the white masses: It had brought them slums, social dislocation, and "wage slavery." By rejecting egalitarianism and individualism and accepting the idea of social hierarchy, the South had avoided the cruelty of a competitive society. Slaves, unlike free white laborers, were not tossed on the human rubbish heap after they had ceased being useful to their employers. The South, moreover, was free of such intellectual and moral taints as Mormonism, Perfectionism, Fourierism, trade unionism, and other disgusting and deplorable consequences of freedom. "In the whole South," Fitzhugh proclaimed, "there is not one Socialist, not one man rich or poor, proposing to subvert and reconstruct society."

Fitzhugh's attack on northern society and its turbulent democracy quickly became a commonplace of southern opinion. Calhoun rehearsed it on the floor of the Senate. It filled the pages of newspapers, books, and pamphlets and was heard from pulpits throughout Dixie. Senator James Hammond of South Carolina gave it classic form in his famous speech of 1858, in which he declared that there had to be a "mud sill" in each society upon which to erect a civilized, cultured life. This mud sill was a class "to do the menial duties, to perform the drudgery of life. . .a class requiring but a low order of intellect and but little skill." Far better, said Hammond, that these people be black, as in the South, than white, as in the North.

Romance and Culture.   The need to justify the South's way of life profoundly affected southern culture and social values. Influenced by the novels of Sir Walter Scott, literate southerners came to equate their society with the rigidly ordered and conservative social systems of pre-modern Europe. Southerners of the best sort, they asserted, were true gentlemen whose forebears were the Cavaliers who fled

England after the defeat of Charles I by the Puritan leader Oliver Cromwell. They were, claimed one Alabaman, "directly descended from the Norman Barons of William the Conqueror, a race distinguished . . . for its warlike and fearless character, a race at all times . . . renowned for its gallantry, chivalry, honor, gentleness and intellect. . . ." Northerners, by contrast, were descended from Cromwell's Puritan Roundheads, people without breeding or gentility who, to top it all, exhibited the "severe traits of religious fanaticism."

This romantic fantasy held a strange grip on upper-class southern life. In the Old South's cultural imagination, plantations became feudal manors, planters became chivalrous knights, slaves became respectful serfs. Many southerners came to idealize the warrior virtues. They esteemed horsemanship and adopted fox hunting as a plantation sport. They held medieval tournaments where young gallants jousted for prizes while lovely belles showered them with roses from the sidelines. In time only a military career could compete with planting as a proper calling for a gentleman.

Upper-class southern women were an essential part of the cult of chivalry. Southern "ladies" were placed on pedestals and treated with elaborate gallantry and outward deference. But the southern white woman's life was often quite different in reality. Most were not plantation mistresses, but the wives and daughters of common farmers. There was little pampering or chivalry in the lives of these women. And even the mistress of a great plantation often worked hard. Managing a large household and many house slaves was a complex and demanding job full of emotional turmoil. The house slaves were often "part of the family" and the tension between women's familial feelings for their servants and their need to exploit them for their own comfort was evident in the diaries of southern ladies. Meanwhile, the myth of female helplessness and need for protection limited the freedom and autonomy of southern white women even more than "women's sphere" restricted their contemporary northern sisters.

It is not surprising that the forces that encouraged the flowering of this elaborate social mythology tended to stifle artistic growth in the antebellum period. William Gilmore Simms and Edgar Allan Poe aside, no southern writer rose above mediocrity. After Thomas Jefferson's death in 1826 there were few creative southern architects. All the important American painters of the antebellum years either were northerners or lived in the North or Europe. Although many popular songs—like Stephen Foster's "Swanee River," "My Old Kentucky Home," "Old Black Joe," and "De Camptown Races"—had southern themes, the composers, including Foster, were mostly northerners. Even the minstrel show, which fused theater, comedy, and music into a unique form of entertainment, was basically a northern white commercialization of southern black folk culture and owed little to the white South.

Southern defensiveness also affected intellectual life. On the whole, the colleges and universities of the Old South were not great centers of learning, though for a while, in the 1830s, the best university in the country was Jefferson's University of Virginia, and South Carolina College had the most distinguished social science faculty. Many young southerners at the time went to Harvard, Yale, or Princeton. By the 1850s the growing fear of dissent had brought hundreds of southern students back home. The increasing restrictions on free inquiry meanwhile drove such interesting social thinkers as Francis Lieber of South Carolina

College and Henry Harrisse of the University of North Carolina to move north. Harrisse, before his departure, trenchantly attacked the intellectual intolerance he saw all around him.

> You may eliminate all the suspicious men from your institutions of learning, you may establish any number of new colleges which will relieve you of sending your sons to free institutions. But as long as people study, and read, and think among you, the absurdity of your system will be discovered and there will always be found some courageous intelligence to protest against your hateful tyranny.

By contrast with the fertile, innovative contemporary North, the South, then, was a cultural backwater. It was a region turned inward and intent on building up a false self-image and a false self-confidence.

Southern Political Ideology.

Yet defensiveness has its uses. Southerners were able to detect the flaws in the individualistic, tumultuous society of the North and raise questions about democratic political assumptions. This conservative critique was a defense mechanism, but it called attention to the inconsistencies and hypocrisies of free society.

Southern thinkers seriously questioned majoritarian democracy. Although most southern states had established universal white male suffrage, some of the most articulate southerners continued to doubt the wisdom of voter majorities. Pure and simple majority rule was obviously a disadvantage to the South as a section within the Union. If mere numbers were considered in making national political decisions, the South would be consigned to certain defeat. Well before 1860 it had fallen behind the North in population and hence in congressional representation. Sectional parity had been maintained in the United States Senate, if not in the House, by admitting into the Union one slave state for each free one. But almost certainly more free than slave states would eventually be carved out of the western territories; and when this took place, the South would lose its fragile political equality with the North in Congress.

Southerners worried about their section's decline and sought to discover its causes. A number, including J.D.B. De Bow, William Gregg, and Edmund Ruffin, concluded (contrary to fact) that the cause was slow economic growth due to the South's vassalage to the North. During the late 1830s, when southern political victory had removed the tariff from center stage, the attack shifted to the North's commercial dominance. According to the apostles of sectional commercial independence, virtually every aspect of the South's economy except the raising of crops was controlled by northern business interests. Much of the South's shipping was done in northern vessels. Almost all imports came through New York, and until the 1850s even the cotton crop generally went to New York before being shipped to Europe. Northern capitalists and their agents also controlled most of the South's banking. Northern cotton "factors" (agents) residing in the South dominated agriculture, extending credit to planters and farmers, sending crops to market, and buying supplies their customers wanted.

The picture of northern dominance the critics painted was exaggerated. Not all of the South's business was handled by outsiders; the section produced a substantial crop of home-grown merchants, bankers, and manufacturers who often combined town business with plantation ownership. Yet most southerners assumed northern dominance, chafed under it, and periodically determined to end it. Gregg, a successful textile magnate, constantly urged his fellow southerners to invest their capital in manufactures to make their section independent of the North and Europe. The publicist and editor De Bow used his *Review* to call for southern economic independence. "Action, Action, Action!!!" the *Review* demanded. "Not in the rhetoric of Congress, but in the busy hum of mechanism, and the thrifty operators of the hammers and anvil." Ruffin condemned southern farming practices and advocated improved agricultural methods to stem the flow of yeomen from the South and to help equalize free- and slave-state populations.

Beginning in 1837, southern merchants and publicists convened in various cities to consider ways to liberate their section from its supposed economic bondage to the North. Delegates discussed at great length how to end "the abject state of colonial vassalage" to the North by such devices as direct shipping of cotton to Europe from southern ports. The conventions achieved few concrete results, but they were effective forums for the display of anti-northern feelings. Toward the end of the 1850s, when sectional antagonisms exploded, the conventions went on record against northern books, magazines, and teachers and passed resolutions demanding the reopening of the transatlantic slave trade, which had been closed since 1808.

The growing imbalance of population and potential power between the two sections of the country was an unpleasant fact of life that southerners had to face. How could the South remain a part of the Union and, as the weaker partner, defend its unique and controversial interests?

This problem obsessed John C. Calhoun in his later years. During the tariff crisis of 1831–1832 Calhoun had resurrected the theory of nullification first raised in the 1790s as part of the Virginia and Kentucky Resolutions. But nullification seemed more and more inadequate. Between the 1830s and his death in 1850, the South Carolinian sought a new formula to protect his section's minority interests. In a succession of treatises, speeches, and letters, Calhoun's solution evolved into a critique of the democratic concepts of the age. People were not all equal, he concluded. The Declaration of Independence expressed a noble theory, but an invalid one. The best societies, like those of classical Greece and Rome, recognized the inherent inequality of human beings and exploited the inferior groups to construct great civilizations. If people were unequal, it stood to reason that some should lead and others follow; otherwise the inferior many would impose their will on the superior few, and the result would be a tyranny of the ignorant. In the United States, a despotism of numbers would result in sectional oppression: The North with its greater population would trample on the rights of the South.

How could those rights be protected? A "concurrent majority" was Calhoun's solution. Before any federal law that vitally concerned the interests of either section went into effect, let it be ratified by both sections of the country. This arrangement could be guaranteed by a dual presidency, with one president selected by the North and the other by the South. Both would have to approve any important measure passed by Congress before it became law. In this way the South could exercise a veto over a domineering North and check the normal tendency of a majority to ride roughshod over the rights of a minority.

Calhoun died before the inner logic of his theories was expressed in deeds. He had not wished to see the Union destroyed; he hoped to preserve it by finding an accommodation with which the South could live. It is fitting, however, that when the people of Charleston received news of South Carolina's secession from the Union in 1860, they unfurled a banner bearing Calhoun's image.

Conclusions

The Old South was not a moonlight and magnolias society; it was too diverse for that. The happy harmony of that fabled state was marred by regional, class, and economic divisions. The South was not all multi-acred delta estates. It consisted of small farms in the backcountry and the mountain regions and poor whites living from hand to mouth by grazing, hunting, and foraging. Though upper-class southerners sought to create a fantasy land of medieval chivalry, they were at best marginally successful. The Old South was ruled by a planter elite, but only with the consent of a substantial yeomanry and through the mechanism of universal white male suffrage. And even the life of the planter was not what the South's spokesmen and writers sought to make it. Under the veneer of an aristocratic indifference to money was the firm reality of hard striving and profit maximizing that made the chivalrous pose possible.

The Old South, despite its economic success, was not a serene and confident society. Even if it was not solely the land of "the whip and the lash" as depicted by its opponents, it lived on the coerced labor of millions of black men, women, and children. Most of these slaves were able to accommodate to the system. They managed to snatch some satisfactions from the life of bondage and maintain a degree of personal and cultural autonomy. Yet there was some basis for the fear of white southerners that they lived on the edge of a social volcano that could erupt at any time. The fear begat a degree of defensiveness that imposed conformity and intolerance of change and dissent.

To the very end of the slave era southerners would continue to share with other Americans memories, political values, and cultural attributes. Yet with each passing year the South diverged more and more from the liberal mainstream of the United States and the values of the Atlantic world. Before long many southerners would consider themselves people with distinct interests and a separate destiny. The consequences would be tragic.

ONLINE RESOURCES

American Slave Narratives: An Outline Anthology *http://xroads.virginia.edu/~Hyper/wpa/wpahome.html* In their own voices and words, African-American former slaves discuss their experiences before emancipation. Recordings of their WPA interviews are available on this site as sound files. Written transcripts are also available. For a more extensive collection of these narratives, consult the Web site for the American Life Histories Project of the Library of Congress at *http://memory.loc.gov/ammem/snhtml/snhome.html*

14
The Coming
of the Civil War

What Caused the Division?

1780	Pennsylvania becomes the first state to prohibit slavery
1787	The Northwest Ordinance prohibits slavery north of the Ohio River and west of Pennsylvania
1812	Louisiana is admitted into the Union as a slave state
1820	The Missouri Compromise
1832–34	The South Carolina nullification crisis
1839	Antislavery leaders found the Liberty party
1846	Congressional debate on the Wilmot Proviso worsens sectional controversy
1848	The California Gold Rush; Formation of the Free-Soil party; Zachary Taylor elected president
1850	The Compromise of 1850, including passage of the Fugitive Slave Act
1852	Harriet Beecher Stowe's *Uncle Tom's Cabin* published; Franklin Pierce elected president
1854	The Kansas–Nebraska Act; The Republican party is formed by antislavery Whigs and Democrats
1856	John Brown murders five proslavery settlers in Kansas; James Buchanan elected president
1857	Dred Scott decision; Buchanan accepts Kansas; fraudulent constitution
1858	The Lincoln–Douglas debates focus national attention on the Illinois election for United States Senator
1859	John Brown's raid on Harpers Ferry
1860	The Democratic party breaks up at its national convention; Abraham Lincoln is nominated by the Republican national convention, and elected president
1860–61	South Carolina, Georgia, Louisiana, Mississippi, Florida, Alabama, and Texas secede from the Union
1861	Delegates of six seceded states adopt a constitution and elect Jefferson Davis president; Lincoln says the federal government will hold its property in the South; Confederates fire on Union-held Fort Sumter; Arkansas, North Carolina, Virginia, and Tennessee secede

Stephen Douglas, the "Little Giant," sought to prevent southern secession by endorsing the principle of popular sovereignty. Although "the great persuader" managed a compromise in 1850, southern and northern Democrats were unwilling to allow the question of slavery to be resolved by popular votes in each new state. *(Matthew Brady (1823–1896), "Stephen Arnold Douglas" (1813–1861), c. 1860. Albumen silver print, 8.6 × 5.4 cm. National Portrait Gallery, Smithsonian Institution/ Art Resource, NY)*

The Civil War was the greatest political crisis that ever befell the United States, the only one that threatened its very survival as a nation. No sooner had the fighting broken out than thoughtful citizens on both sides urgently asked: Why? Why had a union so promising, so prosperous, so self-confident, so triumphant, come to this terrible state? Students of American history still ponder the question today.

A House Dividing

On the eve of the American Revolution in the 1770s an outspoken Massachusetts citizen would not have felt seriously out of place in the social or intellectual environment of South Carolina. Similarly, southerners visiting the North could speak their minds without shocking or offending their hosts. North and South were not so far apart in their economic or labor systems. Agriculture was the chief occupation of all Americans from New Hampshire to Georgia by a wide margin. Slavery existed in every colony. There were more slaves in the South, but a considerable part of the workforce north of the Mason-Dixon Line were half-free indentured servants. By 1800 even the religious differences that had separated Puritan New England from the Anglican South had receded as both regions felt the effects of evangelical revivalism and the breakdown of established churches.

Then, in the generation and a half following the War of 1812, differences between North and South multiplied. As we saw in Chapters 9 and 12, the North began to industrialize and evolve into an open, culturally diverse society. The South, meanwhile, confirmed its stake in plantation agriculture and embraced the social conformity and defensiveness described in Chapter 13. These structural differences were essential elements in sectional estrangement, but they are abstract and tell us little about the texture and daily reality of North–South conflict.

Ideological Differences.   We must not exaggerate the sectional contrasts. Both North and South were complex societies with a variety of dissenters from the prevailing orthodoxies. Only a minority of northerners were abolitionists, transcendentalists, or Perfectionists; many considered such people meddlers or fanatics. And the North was full of "doughfaces"—"northern men with southern principles"— who supported the South's positions in the emerging sectional debates. Even the conformist South was not homogeneous. Southerners such as J.B.D. De Bow and William Gregg urged their section to emulate the North's success in commerce and manufacturing, while among the small farmers in the upland regions and the backcountry were those who despised both slavery and the slaveholding class.

Yet there gradually emerged two distinct sectional outlooks, which each year grew further apart and more militant and antagonistic. Southern political and intellectual leaders increasingly glorified a society based on slavery, condemned dissent, rejected commercial values, endorsed inequality, and resisted social change. It became ever more difficult as the years passed for dissenters to defy the overwhelming weight of sectional opinion. The North also adopted distinctive guiding beliefs in these years, though more slowly and never so universally as the South. The heart of the emerging northern ethos was freedom, though this term meant different things to different people. To northern reformers it meant freedom to engage in social experiment. To northern intellectuals and writers it meant freedom to speculate and criticize. To northern manufacturers it meant freedom from government control, though not exemption from government aid. To northern farmers it meant freedom to take up cheap land in the West. To northern wage earners it meant freedom to move wherever opportunity offered and to advance in life. Northern opinion leaders and officials never attempted to impose these sentiments on the people. Nevertheless, the whole thrust of northern society created an increasing agreement on the importance of "free" values and attitudes, especially in contrast to the South and what it represented.

Economic Conflict.   The widening gap between the northern and southern value systems has been seen as a reflection of competing economies: northern commerce and industry versus southern agriculture. There is no question that the differing economic interests of the antebellum North and South pushed them into political conflict along a wide front. We saw in Chapter 10 how, during Jackson's presidency, the northern-sponsored tariff provoked South Carolina into angry reaction that threatened the Union. In 1846 southern political leaders, through their powerful influence in the Democratic party, were able to secure the Walker Tariff lowering duties on imported goods and the tariff of 1857 reducing rates still further. By the eve of the Civil War, the tariff had become a hot political issue in Pennsylvania and New England; this time northern groups felt aggrieved.

Nor was the tariff the only economic issue dividing the sections. Northern commercial interests favored federal subsidies to the American merchant marine to enable it to compete with foreign carriers; southerners saw little benefit to themselves in such measures and opposed paying the taxes required. Northern merchants and manufacturers favored federal appropriations for dredging rivers and harbors to improve navigation; many southerners, some Whigs excepted, believing that they would benefit from such measures less than northerners, fought the appropriations.

But the two most important economic issues disturbing the sectional waters during the generation preceding 1860 were a Pacific railroad and a homestead act. By the 1850s most Americans, North and South, endorsed building a railroad to connect the settled and developed portions of the United States with the newly acquired Mexican Cession and the Pacific coast. The location, however, triggered sharp sectional controversy. Southerners wanted to link New Orleans with San Diego or Memphis with San Francisco. Northerners demanded a route farther north to connect the Great Lakes with either San Francisco or the Puget Sound.

Building a railroad across hundreds of miles of empty country required a large federal subsidy, but the sectional bickering produced an impasse. In 1853 Mississippian Jefferson Davis, secretary of war in the pro-southern administration of Franklin Pierce, arranged to buy a 30,000-square-mile slice of northern Mexico. The move in part derived from southern yearning for more real estate. But the Gadsden Purchase also contained within its limits one of the better passes through the Rocky Mountains and was intended to improve the chances of a southern route for a Pacific railroad. The scheme did not work as intended. After the United States acquired the property, northern congressmen vetoed the route. Southerners, in turn, were able to frustrate the choice of a central or northern connection.

The two sections also battled over a homestead bill. Many ordinary southerners were interested in acquiring free farms in the West, and some southern political leaders responded by favoring a homestead act. A more substantial portion of southern opinion feared that free land would draw farmers from the South to regions where slavery could not take root and so would benefit the free states. In the 1854 debate over a homestead bill, one southern congressman insisted bluntly that the proposed legislation was "tinctured with Abolitionism." Eventually, in 1860, a coalition of northeastern and northwestern congressmen passed a homestead measure over the opposition of a virtually united South. President James Buchanan, a "northern man with southern principles," vetoed it.

The Role of Slavery.   These clashes over economic policies are not sufficient, however, to explain why the sections eventually came to blows. Not all the battling over tariffs, railroad subsidies, and internal improvements pitted the sections against one another. Often the divisions were within each section—pitting Whigs against Democrats, for example—not between them. Furthermore, sectional conflict over economic policy had raged before 1840 and would continue after 1865; yet only after 1848 did divisive forces actually threaten the Union. In the nullification crisis of 1832, the Tariff of Abominations failed to arouse strong disunionist sentiment outside South Carolina. A generation later eleven states left the Union when confronted with a similar threat to the South's "rights." Clearly, in the decade following the Mexican War, the bonds among the slave states grew stronger while those attaching them to the Union as a whole weakened. It was only in the decade following the Mexican War that grievances were converted to outrage and outrage to secession. What events and forces reinforced southern cohesion and loosened the South's ties to the rest of the nation?

The Dilemma of Territorial Expansion

The country's territorial expansion was a critical element in the escalating North–South struggle. If the nation had not confronted the question of slavery extension after 1846, the sections might have remained at peace. But it was not to be. In the past, as the country added new territory it became necessary to redraw the boundary between slavery and freedom first established by state emancipation acts and by the Northwest Ordinance of 1787 (slavery excluded from the Northwest) and the Southwest Ordinance of 1790 (slavery allowed in the Southwest). Slavery already existed in parts of the Louisiana Purchase when the United States bought it in 1803. Then, in 1819–1820, as we saw, another part of the Louisiana Purchase, Missouri Territory, was admitted to the Union as a slave state, while the remainder of the purchase was divided by Congress along the line of 36°30' north latitude into slave and free regions.

The Wilmot Proviso.   As of 1820 the whole of the existing United States had been assigned to one labor system or the other either by Congress or by individual states. For the next fifteen years the territorial limits of slavery ceased to trouble Americans very much. Then, in 1835, Texas revived the issue. Many opponents of annexation feared that admitting Texas to the Union would tip the balance in favor of slavery. Southerners, on the other hand, considered admission of Texas "as indispensable to their security." Despite much northern opposition, Texas was admitted to the Union in 1845.

The events of 1846–1848 reopened the slavery extension issue with a vengeance. Besides Oregon, the United States acquired by conquest the vast Mexican Cession in the far Southwest. While many southern leaders considered the region uncongenial to slavery, they denounced the idea that slavery should be arbitrarily excluded by law from a region that had been won by the exertions of an army two-thirds of whose volunteers came from slave states. When, in August 1846, only three months into the Mexican War, Democratic Congressman David Wilmot of Pennsylvania submitted a resolution requiring that a "fundamental condition" of acquiring "any territory from the Republic of Mexico" be that "neither slavery nor involuntary servitude shall ever exist in any part of said territory," he triggered a political explosion.

Wilmot belonged to a group of northern Democrats hostile to the Democratic Polk administration for its sacrifice of northern interests by supporting tariff reduction, surrendering half of the Oregon region to the British, and vetoing rivers and harbors improvement legislation. The South, they feared, totally controlled the Democratic party, treating its northern members as outcasts. Some of this same group felt that Martin Van Buren, the former president, had deserved the party presidential nomination in 1844, and resented the desertion of their hero by southern Democrats in favor of Polk.

The Wilmot Proviso produced a fever of sectional excitement. The aging Calhoun countered the proviso with resolutions denying that Congress had the power to exclude slavery from the territories. Southerners were soon denouncing the North. The "madmen of the North and the Northwest have . . . cast the die," proclaimed the *Richmond Enquirer,* "and numbered the days of the glorious Union." On the other side, every northern legislature but one endorsed the proviso. By solid northern votes, both Whig and Democrat, the House passed the proviso, but it was kept from coming to a vote in the Senate. In February 1847 the House once more approved it, but then, under administration pressure, a contingent of northern Democrats reconsidered, and the bill was defeated.

The issue of slavery or freedom in the Mexican Cession territory remained very much alive, with public opinion divided into several distinct positions. Many northerners continued to favor total exclusion of slavery from the newly acquired region. Northern and southern moderates endorsed extending the Missouri Compromise 36° 30′ line to the Pacific coast to separate slavery from freedom. Calhoun and his supporters demanded that slaveholders have equal access to all the territories. The southern elder statesman considered it a matter of life or death for the South. "If we flinch we are gone," he wrote a friend.

A new compromise position soon emerged that middle-of-the-road politicians, especially northern Democrats, rushed to support. "Popular sovereignty" proposed "leaving to the people of the territory to be acquired, the business of settling the matter [of slavery] for themselves." Associated particularly with Democrats Lewis Cass of Michigan and Stephen Douglas of Illinois, the scheme appealed to many Americans as an expression of grass-roots democracy: Let the people of the local community, rather than Congress, decide. But the details were not so

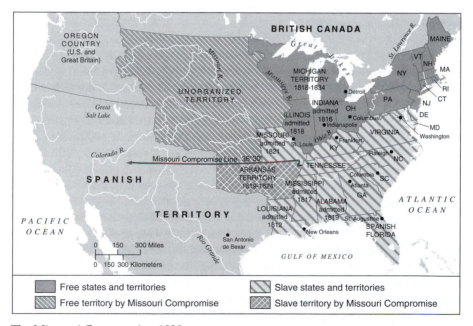

The Missouri Compromise, 1820

clear. When would the people decide? When the territory entered as a state? During the territorial stage by vote of the territorial legislature? And did popular sovereignty supersede Congressional enactment regarding slavery in the territories entirely? All this was puzzling. But its very ambiguity was the great virtue of the formula: It could please many people simultaneously and give the appearance of agreement when there really was none.

Free Soil.   Slavery extension inevitably colored the 1848 presidential campaign. Within both the Whig and Democratic parties there was a range of views from pro-Wilmot Proviso, through popular sovereignty, to the Calhounite position. The Whigs nominated as their candidate "Old Rough-and-Ready," Zachary Taylor, the hero of Buena Vista, and eschewed a party platform entirely. The antislavery "conscience Whig" faction denounced the choice of Taylor, a slaveholder, as an alliance between the "lords of the lash" (the southern planters) and the "lords of the loom" (the New England textile manufacturers).

The Democrats' differences over slavery extension were amplified by the split in the large New York delegation between the Barnburners, who opposed southern dominance in the party, and the Hunkers, who favored conciliating the South. The Barnburners were also loyal followers of Van Buren; the Hunkers, his enemy. When the presidential nominating convention refused to exclude their Hunker opponents, the Barnburners left in a huff and nominated Van Buren in a separate convention. Meanwhile, led by southern and western moderates, the regular Democratic convention chose Cass of Michigan on a vague pro-slavery plank that satisfied virtually no one. When the convention voted down the proposal by Alabaman William Lowndes Yancey endorsing southern rights in the territories, Yancey too walked out.

A third political group soon began to coalesce out of the discontented pro-Wilmot Proviso elements of both parties and joined with the minuscule Liberty party. Formed in 1839 by abolitionists, the Liberty party had nominated Senator John P. Hale of New Hampshire on a platform that demanded prohibition of slavery wherever federal power over the institution extended. Its leaders soon arranged a coalition with the Van Burenites that promised to combine Van Buren's vote-getting power with a strong platform against slavery extension. Meeting at Buffalo in August 1848, the rebels nominated Van Buren for president with Charles Francis Adams, son of the sixth president, as his running mate. The new Free-Soil party adopted a platform calling for "free soil, free speech, free labor, and free men."

The new party covered a range of positions. A minority were outright abolitionists who hoped to see slavery ended throughout the United States. A larger group was more interested in preserving the territories for free labor than destroying slavery in the South. Their position was summarized by Senator Preston King of New York: "If slavery is not excluded by law" from the national territories, he declared, "the presence of the slave will exclude the laboring white man." Yet many delegates at Buffalo saw the free-soil position as the first step toward ending slavery and left Buffalo convinced that the new party's showing in the fall would mark the start of slavery's downfall.

Unfortunately, the slaves' deliverance would have to wait until a later day. Taylor achieved an electoral as well as a popular majority, doing particularly well in the South. Van Buren won only a meager 300,000 votes, 14 percent of the northern popular vote. But the Free-Soil campaign was a portent. The new organization elected ten members to Congress, who would be outspoken antislavery advocates in the bitter debates just ahead. It also broke new political ground. Most northern voters were not yet ready for a single-issue, purely sectional, party, but the outlines of such an organization were now coming into view.

Gold in California.

Though a southerner and a slaveholder, as president, Zachary Taylor proved to be a bulwark of the Union. The immediate problem was California. In January 1848 a laborer working for John Augustus Sutter, a Swiss businessman long settled in the Mexican province, found gold while constructing a water mill channel near Sacramento. Sutter tried to keep the discovery a secret, but the news soon leaked out. In December, after California was safely American, President Polk confirmed the lucky strike in his annual message to Congress, setting off a stampede to the gold fields. By the early months of 1849 over sixty ships packed with gold seekers were on their way to the Pacific Coast by way of Cape Horn or Panama. In the spring thousands of others set out overland on the California Trail established by settlers earlier in the decade.

The Gold Rush forty-niners were usually disappointed. Hundreds sickened and died aboard ship or along the trail. By the fall, the route across the plains was strewn with the skeletons of horses and cattle and the graves of gold seekers. Among those who reached the diggings, few struck it rich. Some gave up and straggled home. Others settled down in the new country to farm, labor, keep store, or practice professions. By mid-1849 thousands of people from every state, section, race, and nationality had made California their home.

President Taylor understood that California would soon need some better form of government than the existing military regime. He also saw that allowing a lengthy territorial phase to precede statehood was potentially disruptive, for it would permit the free-soil forces in Congress to raise the Wilmot Proviso issue once again. To avoid another bitter debate over slavery in the territories, the president urged the Californians, and also the residents of New Mexico, to apply directly for admission to the Union as states. The Californians quickly complied under a constitution that excluded slavery. New Mexico, more sparsely settled and in turmoil over its Texas boundary, failed to heed his call.

Taylor's scheme offended the proslavery forces. California's admission as a free state would give the North a majority in the Senate. The change would be largely symbolic, but it seemed a dangerous precedent. "Our only safety," announced Southern firebrand James Hammond, "is in equality of POWER." Responding to the perceived danger, southern extremists called for a convention to meet in Nashville in June 1850 to discuss southern rights and consider the possibility of secession from the Union.

Divisive Issues in Congress.

California was not the only sectional friction point in 1850. Opponents of slavery for years had demanded that the capital of the nation not be disgraced by the presence of slave pens and auction blocks. For their part, southerners fumed over "personal liberty laws," attempts by northern states to nullify the federal fugitive slave law of 1793 by forbidding state officials to help federal authorities capture southern runaway slaves. Many of these escapees were actually aided by northern abolitionists through the "underground railroad," a network of houses, barns, and cellars stretching from slave territory to Canada, where slaves could hide while escaping to freedom. In truth, probably no more than a thousand slaves a year ever escaped from bondage, but many southerners believed that their countrymen in the North were scheming to destroy slavery by attrition.

Texas, too, figured in the reemerging sectional conflict. It claimed part of eastern New Mexico, and militant southern rights advocates supported the new slave state's claim, while Free-Soilers opposed it. Moreover, the Lone Star State had joined the Union with millions of dollars of unpaid public debts. Texas's creditors included some leading politicians and businessmen, many open to any deal that would protect their interests. Finally, there was the status of New Mexico. That vast region was not really ready for statehood, but it too needed some sort of government. Should Congress decide the slave question while the region was still in a territorial stage? Or should some version of the popular-sovereignty formula be applied?

The Compromise of 1850.

Fortunately for the Union, two Senate leaders—the veteran Henry Clay of Kentucky and Stephen Douglas of Illinois—quickly took matters in hand and forged a sectional armistice.

In his seventies, Clay did not intend to see his beloved Union torn apart. Across the Senate aisle, on the Democratic side, was another devoted unionist, Stephen A. Douglas of Illinois. Thirty-seven years old, Douglas was at the prime of his career. Historians have often judged this stubby, dynamic man an opportunist, but events would show that the ambitious "Little Giant" sincerely loved the Union and, when necessary, would put its welfare before his own. In their effort to prevent a disruptive sectional showdown, Clay and Douglas would have the help of Daniel Webster, the Whig elder statesman from Massachusetts.

Most members of the Thirtieth Congress desired a peaceful settlement, but several took positions that made a confrontation unavoidable. On the extreme southern side, looming above the rest, was the ailing John Calhoun, a fierce partisan for his beloved South. On the militant northern side were Senators Salmon Chase of Ohio and Charles Sumner of Massachusetts, both newcomers and ardent Free-Soilers, and the former Whig governor of New York, the diminutive, affable, cigar-smoking William Henry Seward. The veteran Seward was a militant antislavery man who seemed more devoted to freedom than the Union.

In the end, the Union cause proved stronger than southern rights, antislavery, or free soil. In January 1850 Clay presented a set of proposals to the U.S. Senate designed to settle all outstanding sectional issues simultaneously. His package included eight resolutions. Six were paired, half to satisfy the North, half to please the South. California was to be admitted to the Union as a free state; the rest of the Mexican Cession would be organized as territories "without . . . any restriction or condition on the subject of slavery." Texas was to surrender its boundary claims in New Mexico, and the federal government would assume its public debt. The slave trade in the District of Columbia would be ended; slavery itself in the District would be made inviolate. Two final resolutions favored the South: Congress would never interfere with the interstate slave trade; it would enact a more effective fugitive slave law. Under the urging of friends, Clay agreed to combine his proposals into a single "omnibus" bill.

It soon became clear that the Clay bill would not win easy support. The venerable Calhoun was too feeble to address the Senate himself, but he denounced the Clay proposals through a Virginia colleague while he, wrapped in flannels to

Abe Lincoln was a very young man when this portrait was painted. He became better looking!

keep his ravaged frame warm, looked on from his seat on the Senate floor. Northern aggressiveness was dividing the Union, Calhoun charged, and the only way to save it was to guarantee the South's right to veto unfriendly northern action. William Seward spoke for the militant northern side. Clay's compromise was "radically wrong and essentially vicious" for it failed to check slavery extension. The Constitution sanctioned excluding slavery from the territories, but beyond the Constitution there was a "higher law," the law of God, and under it all men were free and equal. The voice of the middle, the compromisers and peacemakers, was heard on March 7 when Daniel Webster, in one of his finest speeches, defended the Clay measure. Geography itself excluded slavery from the Mexican Cession; why antagonize the South by excluding it by law? "I would not take pains to reaffirm an act of nature, nor reenact the will of God." The temporizing address earned Webster angry denunciation in his own strongly antislavery state.

Webster's support was not enough. In late July, after almost six months of debate, the omnibus bill went down to defeat. By this time President Taylor had died of a stomach complaint. A southerner, he had nevertheless worked behind the scenes for his own plan to admit both California and New Mexico as free states without a trade-off for the South. His death placed Millard Fillmore of New York in the White House. Though a northerner, Fillmore favored the compromise. Another gain for the compromise forces was the failure of the Nashville convention to take disunionist actions. Instead, the delegates had adjourned to see what Congress would finally do.

Stephen Douglas took over management of the sectional issues after the defeat of Clay's omnibus bill. A skilled parliamentarian, he split the measure into five separate bills: California would enter the Union as a free state; the Texas border would be adjusted in favor of New Mexico; New Mexico would be organized as two territories—New Mexico and Utah—and when admitted as states they could decide either for slavery or freedom; the slave trade would be abolished in the District of Columbia; there would be a new, stricter, fugitive slave law. With the help of Fillmore, Douglas convinced a group of northern Democrats and upper-South Whigs to support all the measures. When combined with southern or northern partisans who would support those particular measures that favored their section, these moderate center votes were enough to pass the whole package of bills. What Clay could not achieve with a single measure had now been accomplished with five.

The Compromise of 1850 heartened unionists all over the country. Profoundly relieved at having escaped disunion, Congress celebrated the end of the unruly session with an enthusiasm that left many members with hangovers the next day. Jubilant crowds surged through the streets of Washington toasting Clay, Douglas, and Webster. In the country at large moderates gained confidence; many citizens agreed with Cass that the slavery question was finally "settled in the public mind." Soon after, the Nashville convention finally adjourned without taking a disunionist position.

Fugitive Slaves and Northern Sympathies.   It seemed that the Union had been saved. But as the months passed, it became clear that the Compromise of 1850 would not put an end to sectional discord. Indeed, its Fugitive Slave Act component seemed only to inflame sectional antagonisms.

The new fugitive slave law deprived suspected runaway slaves of virtually every right normally granted in American jurisprudence to those accused of violating the law. By merely submitting an affidavit to a federal commissioner, a person could claim ownership of an alleged black runaway. The commissioner might, on investigation, reject the affidavit, but if he did, he received a fee of only $5; if he ordered the suspect's return, he pocketed $10. During the investigation, the accused could not testify on his or her behalf. Still worse, the law required that any free citizen could be forced to join in the pursuit of any fugitive on pain of stiff fines and jail sentences. In effect, the law made every American a potential slave-catcher.

Anger at the law's disregard of civil liberties was amplified by its enforcement. The sight of black men and women, many long-time residents of the North, being dragged off to jail in chains and taken south to bondage by federal authorities converted hundreds of indifferent northerners to antislavery overnight. In Syracuse, Boston, Oberlin (Ohio), New York City, and even Baltimore, people hid escapees, attacked slave-catching officials, rescued fugitives from jail and whisked them away to Canada.

Public outrage prompted nine northern states to enact new personal liberty laws providing state attorneys to defend fugitives, appropriating funds to pay their defense costs, and denying the use of public buildings to detain accused escapees. At the South's behest, the federal government challenged the state personal liberty laws, and in *Ableman v. Booth* (1859) the Supreme Court declared the laws unconstitutional. Obviously, in the heat of sectional rivalry, both sections were sacrificing venerable constitutional scruples.

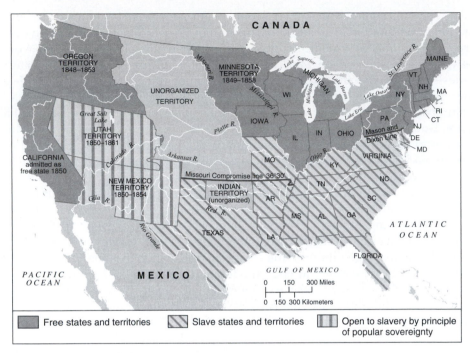

The Compromise of 1850

One northerner appalled by the Fugitive Slave Act was Harriet Beecher Stowe. As a little girl she had wept when her father, the Reverend Lyman Beecher, prayed for "poor, oppressed, bleeding Africa," and as a young woman she had been shocked at the sight of escaped slaves being plucked off the streets of Cincinnati by slave-catchers. In 1851 she wrote a series of slave-life sketches for the *National Era,* an abolitionist journal. She soon expanded these into a novel that appeared in 1852 as *Uncle Tom's Cabin.* The book was a huge success. In the sentimental style of the day, it recounted the story of a lively and vivid cast of characters, black and white, enmeshed in the tragic web of slavery and victimized by its inherent cruelty. By the end of its first year the book had sold 300,000 copies, and eight presses were running day and night to keep up with the demand.

Southerners denounced *Uncle Tom's Cabin* as inaccurate and biased. Stowe, they said, was an ignorant and dangerous woman. But in Europe and the North the book was acclaimed a masterpiece. It aroused such strong sympathy for slaves and such utter detestation of slavery that it could not help but heighten sectional antagonism. Legend has it that when President Lincoln met Harriet Beecher Stowe during the Civil War, he remarked: "So this is the little lady who wrote the book that made this big war!"

Worsening Tensions

If, in 1850, it seemed that Clay, Webster, and Douglas had finally checked the mounting sectional antagonism, appearances were deceiving. Within three years the two older men would be dead. Douglas would remain, but events would show that he lacked the political skill that had enabled his seniors to hold the nation together.

Meanwhile, there was a new occupant of the White House. In 1852 the Democrats nominated Franklin Pierce, Mexican War general, U.S. senator from New Hampshire, and a doughface Democrat who had long supported the South. The Whigs, badly divided on the slavery issue, chose as their candidate their own Mexican War hero, Winfield Scott. With the Barnburners now back in the Democratic fold, Pierce won a resounding victory in both sections. The Whigs carried only four states, two in the North and two in the South. They managed to garner only 35 percent of the lower South's popular vote compared to 50 percent for their candidate Taylor four years before. They had been reduced to a northern party almost entirely, though feeble even in the free states. As Alexander Stephens, a prominent southern Whig proclaimed: "The Whig party is dead."

Southern Dreams of Empire.

For four years, fugitive slaves notwithstanding, the nation avoided further sectional crisis. The Compromise of 1850 had put to rest the slavery expansion question in the Mexican Cession, the only part of the country where the legality of slavery had been uncertain. The entire country appeared once again to be staked out for all time as either slave or free. The slavery expansion issue in existing U.S. territory seemed solved.

But there remained the destabilizing possibility of further geographical expansion. Southerners had never abandoned the yearning for new territorial acquisitions, especially to the south. The United States had already wrenched immense chunks out of Mexico; why not more from that chaotic country? Also tempting were the Central American republics and the rich island of Cuba, the latter still feebly held by Spain. Through most of the 1850s southern political leaders continued to lust for more territory to extend the nation's imperial reach and, perhaps, incorporate more slave states to balance off the growing North. In the view of some contemporaries (whatever modern historians may believe) expansion also seemed necessary for the South's economic health. As Mississippi Senator Jefferson Davis expressed it, "Slave labor is wasteful labor, and it therefore requires a still more extended territory than would the same pursuits if they could be prosecuted by the more economic labor of white men."

This sectional version of Manifest Destiny sometimes took private forms. In the 1850s American "filibusterers" launched military raids into Mexico, often for private gain, but also for the purpose of carving out new slave states to the south. The most famous of these soldiers-of-fortune was William Walker, a "grey-eyed man of destiny" who, in 1856, invaded Nicaragua with a small army and overthrew its government. Walker was soon ousted by a coalition of Central American states, but tried twice more and eventually was executed by a Nicaraguan firing squad.

In these years, strongly influenced by southern attitudes and values, the American government itself went hunting after loose real estate to the south. Mexico was an obvious target, and the Gadsden Purchase was originally a more ambitious scheme to acquire Mexican land, drastically scaled down by skeptical northern senators. But successive American administrations coveted Cuba even more. The "Pearl of the Antilles" already possessed a flourishing slave-plantation economy based on sugar and would be a congenial addition to the South. It was owned by Spain, but Spain was weak and perhaps could be induced to surrender its distant island colony. The Pierce administration made acquiring Cuba its major foreign policy goal and in 1854 dispatched Pierre Soulé, a flamboyant Louisianan, to Madrid as minister to try to buy the island. Soulé was to offer the Spanish government $130 million for Cuba. If the offer was rejected, Secretary of State William Marcy instructed, Soulé should direct his "efforts to the next desirable object, which is to detach that island from Spanish dominion."

When Spain refused to sell, Soulé met at Ostend, Belgium, with the other major American diplomats in Europe, John Mason and James Buchanan, to consider what to do. The three men composed a memo to Marcy that bristled with arrogant self-assertiveness. Cuba was "as necessary to the North American republic as any of its present . . . family of states," they wrote. If Spain refused to sell the island to the United States, then "by every law, human and Divine, we shall be justified in wresting it from Spain." When it became public, the Ostend Manifesto created an uproar. Antislavery groups attacked it as a "manifesto of Brigands." Many northerners considered it an outrageous assertion of American power. Embarrassed by the incident, Pierce recalled Soulé and abandoned the attempt to acquire Cuba.

The Kansas–Nebraska Act.
The most damaging blow to sectional harmony during the 1850s, ironically, was the work of Stephen Douglas, a devoted unionist. The Little Giant had done much to cool sectional anger in 1850, but he undid most of his good work in January 1854 when he introduced a bill to establish a territorial government in the Nebraska country, a part of the Louisiana Purchase.

Douglas was moved by several considerations. An ardent expansionist, he hoped to accelerate western settlement by fostering community building on the frontier. Related to this goal was his interest in a transcontinental railroad that would link Chicago to the Pacific coast and bring prosperity to his home city and, incidentally, increase the value of his Chicago real estate holdings.

By the 1820 Missouri Compromise Congress had excluded slavery from the Nebraska country. Douglas's new bill, as originally submitted, declared, as had the Utah and New Mexico territorial acts of 1850, that at the point of admission to statehood the people of the region could accept or reject slavery notwithstanding the Missouri Compromise. This was not enough for southern senators David Atchison of Missouri, James Mason and Robert M. T. Hunter of Virginia, and Andrew Butler of South Carolina, who perceived that if slaves were excluded from a region during the territorial period, the new communities would probably enter as free states. Douglas sought to placate the group by agreeing to allow the people of the territory to deal with slavery before the point of statehood. This "popular sovereignty" would open the possibility of at least one new slave state in the Louisiana Purchase territory, a region seemingly closed by law to slavery for all time.

But the powerful southern bloc insisted on even more: that the new measure include a specific repeal of the Missouri Compromise. Knowing that his bill could not pass without southern support, Douglas complied. The revised bill explicitly repealed that part of the Missouri Compromise that forbade slavery in the Louisiana Purchase north of 36°30'. It also divided the region into two territories: Kansas to the south, Nebraska to the north. In effect, Douglas had opened a door once closed to slavery by Congress in a large slab of the unsettled west.

For four raucous months Congress debated the Kansas–Nebraska bill. Douglas defended the repeal provision by the specious claim that the 1850 Utah and New Mexico territorial bills had implicitly repealed the 36°30' provision. Moreover, he said, echoing Daniel Webster in 1850, there was little likelihood that geography and climate would allow slavery to take root in the Nebraska country. Southerners supported the bill as an overdue recognition of their rights to the common territory of all the American people paid for by common sacrifice and taxes.

The Kansas–Nebraska bill outraged many Northerners. In the words of the *Appeal of the Independent Democrats,* a manifesto authored by two Ohio Free-Soilers, Senator Salmon Chase and Congressman Joshua Giddings, the Kansas–Nebraska bill was "a gross violation of a sacred pledge," a "criminal betrayal," and "part and parcel of an atrocious plot" to make the Nebraska country "a dreary region of despotism inhabited by slaves and masters." At one point feelings about the measure ran so high that northern and southern partisans came close to blows in Congress.

Douglas, with President Pierce's support, pushed the bill through Congress over the determined opposition. But it was an ominous victory. The bill split the northern Democrats in two; it was passed by a solid South plus those northern Democrats who stayed with the Pierce administration. A large bloc of anti-administration northerners deplored it. The law, a clear victory for the South, reopened wounds thought closed, if not fully healed.

National Parties Break Up.

The Kansas–Nebraska Act put unbearable strains on an already weakened party system. From Maine to California Democratic newspapers screamed with outrage at the actions of Douglas and Pierce. The Kansas–Nebraska bill, announced one, was "a triumph of Slavery [and] Aristocracy over Liberty and Republicanism." Democratic party loyalists defended Douglas and the administration, but many northern Democrats worried that their angry constituents would repudiate them at the polls. Whig divisions went even deeper. The Whigs had lost most of their southern support and were in trouble in the free states as well. Now, Kansas–Nebraska further divided the party's two wings. The pro-Nebraska stand of the southern Whigs in Congress had profoundly disillusioned such men as Horace Greeley, editor of the influential *New York Tribune,* and he proclaimed the North's "indignant resistance" to the measure.

The times seemed ripe for a new nativist party that could shift attention to alien and Catholic "plots" and away from slavery, and during 1854–1855 the Know-Nothings seemed likely to become a formidable player on the political stage. With a platform calling for extending the time required for naturalization from five to fourteen years, permitting only citizens to vote, and restricting office-holding to native-born Americans, the Know-Nothings expressed the rampant xenophobia and anti-Catholic feelings of the decade. But they also expressed the disenchantment with the existing party system.

Many contemporaries expected the Know-Nothings to replace the Whigs as the other major party. And indeed Whigs, north and south, joined the new organization in large numbers, further draining Whig strength. But many American voters despised their nativist attitudes. As the Illinois "Conscience Whig" Abraham Lincoln noted,

> Our progress in degeneracy appears to me to be pretty rapid. As a nation, we begin by declaring that "all men are created equal." We now practically read "all men are created equal, except negroes." When the Know-Nothings get control, it will read "All men are created equal except negroes, and foreigners, and Catholics."

Happily for those stranded northern Whigs who like Lincoln could not stomach bigotry, an alternative soon appeared. In 1854–1855 anti-Nebraska political organizations sprang up all through the North in the wake of Douglas's ill-advised bill. At a meeting at Ripon, Wisconsin, in February 1854, one of these groups adopted the name Republican. Several months later another anti-Nebraska group met at Jackson, Michigan, and gave the Republicans their new platform: no slavery in the territories, repeal of the Kansas–Nebraska and Fugitive Slave acts, and abolition of slavery itself in the District of Columbia. The new party grew rapidly in strength, recruiting many northern Whigs and a portion of northern Democrats. After 1856, many erstwhile northern Know-Nothings, seeing their party losing strength, also joined the Republicans, convinced that it was more reliably Protestant and native American than its Democratic rival.

"Bleeding Kansas."

"Bleeding Kansas."   The Republican surge was accelerated by the outbreak of a vicious guerrilla war in Kansas. From the outset leaders of the two sections recognized that settlers would soon pour into Kansas and their origins would determine whether Kansas became a slave or a free state. Both sides threw down the gauntlet. "We will engage in competition for the virgin soil of Kansas," Seward told his Senate colleagues, "and God give the victory to the side which is stronger in numbers as it is in right." Senator Atchison, from Missouri, the slave state adjacent to Kansas, responded in kind: "We are playing for a mighty stake; if we win we carry slavery to the Pacific Ocean, if we lose we lose Missouri, Arkansas, and Texas and all the territories; the game must be played boldly."

In fact, a majority of Kansas-bound settlers were relatively indifferent to the sectional confrontation. Most free-staters were from the Midwest and were more interested in free farms than free soil. The contingent of Yankees financed by Eli Thayer's New England Emigrant Aid Society was exceptional in its antislavery zeal. The other side, too, consisted largely of men and women seeking better lives rather than a particular social system. Most of the slave-state people came from Missouri; a few brought their slaves with them. Their opponents called them "border ruffians," but most were ordinary white southern yeomen.

Yet within weeks of passage of the Kansas–Nebraska Act, friends and foes of slavery in the territory were at each other's throats: Ambushes, arson, and murder quickly became the order of the day in "Bleeding Kansas." The struggle over Kansas was not over slavery alone. The government's failure to properly extinguish Indian claims or make essential land surveys created confusion and conflict. There were also disputes over water rights, town-site locations, and other issues connected with establishing new communities. But obviously differences in social philosophy made things worse. Men who disagreed over such mundane issues were more prone to fight when they also held irreconcilable views on slavery. In any case, Americans elsewhere viewed the struggle as a bitter confrontation of the nation's two social systems and responded accordingly.

The early maneuvers favored the South. In late 1854 and early 1855, Kansas territorial governor Andrew Reeder called elections for territorial representative to Congress and the territorial legislature. The results were rigged. Though free-state residents by this time probably outnumbered their opponents, several thousand Missourians crossed the river to vote illegally, giving the slave-state forces majorities. Reeder recognized the fraud, but he refused to authorize new elections. In short order, the proslavery legislature passed a harsh slave code and disqualified from office citizens who did not support slavery. In response, the free-state forces fortified the town of Lawrence and organized their own free-state party. Soon after, at a convention held in Topeka, they drew up a constitution prohibiting slavery in Kansas and convened a free-state legislature in opposition to the one recognized by Reeder. In time, Governor Reeder declared his sympathy for the free-state group. President Pierce, responding to southern pressure, replaced him with William Shannon, a more reliable proslavery man.

The struggle soon took a more dangerous turn. In the spring of 1856 a small army of proslavery men descended on Lawrence, destroyed the free-state printing press, tore down the hotel, burned several private homes, and ransacked the town. Southern newspapers depicted the raiders as gallant knights battling for a holy cause. Northern Free-Soilers denounced the "border ruffians." In New Haven, Connecticut, the popular Brooklyn minister, Henry Ward Beecher, urged an antislavery congregation to send more settlers to Kansas equipped with Sharps rifles. Thereafter many Kansas-bound northerners carried the deadly repeater rifles, now dubbed "Beecher's Bibles."

Among those who turned to violence in Kansas was one John Brown of Osawatomie, a stern, latter-day Old Testament patriarch who had failed in virtually everything he attempted and identified his own suffering with that of the slaves. He soon came to see himself as an instrument of an avenging God to smite the slaveholders in Kansas. Angered by the attack on Lawrence, in May 1856, Brown, several of his sons, and a small band of followers took revenge by hacking to death in cold blood five slave-state settlers at Pottawatomie Creek.

The Pottawatomie massacre set off a virtual war in Kansas. Spring planting was neglected while bands of southern "border ruffians" and northern "bushwhackers" roamed the territory pillaging, burning, and killing. Scores died and millions of dollars of property was destroyed in the disorders. The events in Kansas raised sectional tensions in the rest of the country. As atrocity succeeded atrocity, even moderate citizens found it difficult to check mounting resentments of people from the other section.

The Brooks–Sumner Incident.

One of the more militant antislavery leaders in Congress was the junior senator from Massachusetts, Charles Sumner. No one was a more courageous and consistent defender of blacks. At the same time, few men in public life were as dogmatic, as certain of the unfailing rectitude of their positions, or as unwilling to give their opponents credit for honesty or good intentions as he. Sumner had watched the struggle over Kansas with growing dismay and on May 19, 1856, he rose in the Senate to deliver a blistering two-day denunciation of the South in a speech he called "The Crime against Kansas."

Elaborately prepared, sonorous, full of learned allusions, the address descended to crude personal attacks on Douglas, the president, Senator Atchison, and others. But Sumner reserved his sharpest barbs for Andrew Butler, the venerable senator from South Carolina, calling him a Don Quixote, a foolish blunderer, and a liar, and cruelly alluding to his physical infirmities. Two days later, Butler's young kinsman, South Carolina Congressman Preston Brooks, entered the Senate chamber as Sumner was sitting at his desk writing letters and struck him over the head repeatedly with a cane until the senator was bloody and unconscious.

The South considered Brooks's attack the just chastisement of a blackguard. Several southern communities presented Brooks with replacements for his shattered walking stick. The assault and the South's response shocked most northerners. The Massachusetts legislature denounced it as "a gross breach of Parliamentary privilege—a ruthless attack upon the liberty of speech—an outrage of the decencies of civilized life, and an indignity to the Commonwealth of Massachusetts." Northerners who prized free speech noted that, having suppressed dissent everywhere on their home ground, southerners were now trying to squelch it in the sacred halls of Congress itself. A small incident in itself, the Brooks–Sumner affair confirmed many northerners' skepticism of southern "chivalry" and convinced them that it was time to curb "the arrogant and aggressive" demands of the "slave power."

Republicans and the Worsening Crisis

Bleeding Kansas, the Brooks–Sumner affair, and *Uncle Tom's Cabin* all garnered recruits for the emerging Republican party. The new organization was a purely sectional party. It had virtually no support in the lower South and little in the border slave states. Its heartland was the "upper North" where the population was predominantly Yankee- (New England) derived. In the "lower North"—southern New York, Pennsylvania, New Jersey, and the southern parts of the Old Northwest—Republicanism competed with strong remaining attachments to the Democrats. Only a small minority of Republicans were out-and-out abolitionists. All believed that the federal government could and should prevent slavery from expanding. Many agreed with Lincoln that slavery, if contained, would retreat and eventually die. Others were indifferent to the eventual fate of the "peculiar institution"; it was sufficient that the western territories be kept open to free labor. Those businessmen who supported the Republicans at this stage were putting ideology ahead of economic advantage, as most merchants, bankers, and manufacturers saw the new party as a divisive influence that would upset the country's economy along with its politics.

The Republicans ran their first presidential candidate in 1856 when they nominated the California hero John C. Frémont. That year their platform demanded a free Kansas and congressional prohibition of "those twin relics of barbarism—Polygamy,* and Slavery." As an afterthought, it also endorsed government aid for a Pacific railroad and for internal improvements. The Democrats chose former Pennsylvania Senator James Buchanan of Ostend Manifesto fame, largely because he had been serving as U.S. minister to London and was one of the few prominent Democratic politicians free of "bleeding Kansas" taint. A third candidate, ex-President Fillmore, ran on the flagging Know-Nothing ticket and received the support of surviving Whigs.

In the campaign the Republicans depicted Frémont as the champion of the "laboring classes" against the slaveholders. The Democrats appealed to white fears of black equality and of political disunity if Frémont and the "black Republicans" won.

---

*Polygamy, as practiced by some Mormons in Utah, offended many traditional Christians and had become a political issue.

In the end, Buchanan carried the entire lower North, plus California, and fourteen of the fifteen slave states (Maryland supported Fillmore). Frémont won the rest of the North, a showing that alarmed southerners and filled them with foreboding.

Buchanan's Policies. Buchanan was a well-meaning but indecisive leader whose talents lay in the maneuvering of American politics as usual. Republicans sized him up as just another doughface Democrat, subservient to the South, and his choice of many southerners and proslavery northerners as advisers confirmed their judgment.

Even before his inauguration, Buchanan set out to undermine the Free-Soil position by intruding into the pending case of a Missouri slave, Dred Scott, then before the Supreme Court. Through the sponsorship of antislavery activists, Scott was suing for his freedom on the grounds that his former owner had taken him to free territory, including a portion that had been closed to slavery by the 1820 Missouri Compromise measure. The case was that long-awaited opportunity to have the federal courts settle once and for all the divisive question of whether Congress or the people of a territory—as opposed to the people of a fully sovereign state—could exclude slavery from part of the United States.

Southerners anticipated that the decision would go their way. The chief justice, Roger Taney, was a proslavery Marylander, and four of the associate justices were also southerners. But the southern leaders wanted at least one free-state judge to support their side to give it credibility. President-elect Buchanan now induced his fellow Pennsylvanian, Justice Robert Grier, to side with the proslavery majority. Knowing the certain Dred Scott outcome, on March 4, in his inaugural address, Buchanan noted that whatever the court's decision, "in common with all good citizens" he would "cheerfully submit" to it.

The actual decision two days later was a bombshell. Taney's opinion covered a number of issues that did not seem necessary to decide. First, said the chief justice, Scott was still a slave. His freedom was denied. Second, as a black person and a slave Scott was not a citizen and therefore had "no rights which the white man was bound to respect." Third, his stay in Wisconsin territory did not make him free since Congress did not have the power to exclude slavery from a territory and the law that had supposedly permitted it, the Missouri Compromise, was unconstitutional. Because Congress could not exclude slavery from a territory, neither could a territorial legislature, which was merely a creation of Congress. Most scholars today agree with the dissenting opinion of Justice Benjamin Curtis of Massachusetts, noting that some blacks had been legal citizens of the United States in past periods and that in no way did a congressional prohibition of slavery in the territories violate the Constitution. But the Supreme Court had spoken: Only the people of a state could keep slavery out of any part of the United States; the hands of Congress and a territorial legislature were tied. And some antislavery partisans feared that the Dred Scott decision even called into question whether a state could exclude slave property within its borders.

The Dred Scott ruling promised drastic political consequences. It annulled the core Republican principle that it was the right and, indeed, the duty of Congress to ban slavery from the territories. It also appeared to void the Douglas popular-sovereignty position that the local populace had the right to exclude slavery from an organized territory.

Buchanan soon gave the Republicans and the Douglas wing of his own party further grounds for dismay when he approved the Kansas state constitution adopted by a proslavery convention at Lecompton in late 1857. By the convention's terms, this document was to be submitted to the Kansas voters with a choice of two clauses regarding slavery. One recognized the full rights of slaveholders and, in effect, made Kansas a slave state. The other stated that "slavery shall no longer exist" in Kansas, but "the right of property in slaves now in this Territory shall in no manner be interfered with." The voters could choose one or the other; in effect, there would be no way to exclude slavery from Kansas totally.

Republicans denounced the Lecompton proposal as "the Great Swindle." Douglas charged it was a perversion of true popular sovereignty. Even Robert Walker, Buchanan's choice as Kansas's territorial governor, called it "a vile fraud, a bare counterfeit." In Kansas most free-state partisans boycotted the referendum and, not surprisingly, the more extreme proslavery version passed overwhelmingly.

When the Lecompton constitution came before Congress for approval as part of the Kansas statehood bill, the Buchanan administration rallied behind it as did virtually the entire House and Senate delegations from the South. In his message transmitting the bill to Congress, Buchanan noted that Kansas "is at this moment as much a slave state as Georgia or South Carolina." Douglas and most northern Democrats fought the bill as a travesty of popular sovereignty and a measure that would sink them and their party generally in the upcoming elections. At one point a free-wheeling fistfight broke out on the floor of the House with "fifty middle-aged and elderly gentlemen pitching into each other like so many . . . savages."

By wielding his patronage power aggressively, President Buchanan managed to eke out a victory for Lecompton in the House, but in the Senate Douglas Democrats joined the Republicans to defeat the bill by a narrow vote. A compromise bill, including a generous federal land grant to the state and a provision allowing acceptance or rejection of the entire constitution, was soon resubmitted to the Kansas voters. In August 1858 they rejected it by a vote of 11,300 to 1,788. Kansas would not enter the Union until 1861, after secession of the southern states.

The Emergence of Lincoln.   The troubles of the Buchanan presidency were compounded by the Panic of 1857 and the economic slump that followed. Although the downturn was probably to be expected after ten years of buoyant economic growth and speculation, the North blamed it on southerners in Congress for lowering their tariff protection. Southerners, on the other hand, largely unaffected by a falling stock market and urban unemployment, saw the panic as a vindication of the slave economy. Enjoying high world prices for cotton, they gloated at the misfortunes of northern commerce and industry.

Midway through Buchanan's term, the politicians were already looking ahead to 1860. Douglas was the obvious presidential front-runner for the Democrats. But the Little Giant had hurt his chances with southerners by his stand on the Lecompton constitution and his view that, under Dred Scott, slaveholders might have the right to take their slaves into the territories, but it would be a "barren and worthless right" unless the people of the territory provided a slave code and the other supportive laws the peculiar institution needed to survive. In effect, by

Fort Sumter, April 1861, soon after the Confederate attack.

refusing to act on slavery at all, the people of a territory could exclude it. The formula dismayed states' rights defenders. Before long, southern Democrats were demanding a federal slave code to get around the Douglas position.

Among the Republicans there was no lack of political talent or ambition as 1860 approached. But more and more people were beginning to hear the name of Abraham Lincoln of Illinois.

We who recognize Lincoln's greatness may find it difficult to see him as he was in the 1850s. The lanky, homely prairie lawyer was pithy, shrewd, and folksy and combined keen realism with an idealistic strain. But as yet he gave little sign that he was capable of leading a great nation through trying times.

Only gradually did he become politically "available." Following his single term in the House of Representatives (1847–1849), Lincoln had returned home to Springfield, Illinois, and private law practice. For the next few years he devoted his professional life to defending slanderers, petty thieves, and the Illinois Central Railroad in the courts. All the while, however, he kept up his connections with the Illinois Whigs and shared their doubts and anxieties when their party began to disintegrate. He did not formally become a Republican until his law partner, without authorization, signed his name to a call for a local Republican convention. In 1856 Lincoln campaigned for Frémont.

In 1858 Illinois Republicans gave Lincoln the party's official endorsement for U.S. Senate. The move was unusual. Senators were then chosen by the state legislators and there was no reason to campaign among the voters and no need for a formal nomination. This time, however—in hopes of defeating the formidable Douglas—the state Republican leaders decided to make the year's election for state officials hinge on the victory or defeat of their senatorial choice. The voters would be casting their ballots, actually, for individual state legislators, with the senatorial candidates, in effect, standing in for each party.

The campaign format, too, was unusual. At first the two candidates went their separate ways, speaking to individual audiences. Lincoln's acceptance speech, the famous "House-Divided" address, made slavery a moral issue by contrast with Douglas's purely political focus. The country, he announced, could not remain permanently half-slave and half-free. "A house divided against itself cannot stand." Under the Democrats it would become all slave; under the Republicans all free, for the Republicans intended to "arrest the further spread of [slavery], and place it where the public mind shall rest in the belief that it is in the course of ultimate extinction."

Before long the candidates agreed to conduct a direct face-to-face debate. Beginning in late August 1858 in the northern Illinois city of Ottawa, they would meet on the same platform in seven towns, ending in Alton in mid-October. In each they would fire questions at one another while the public watched and listened. The contest attracted national attention because it had national implications. To be a serious contender in the 1860 presidential race, Douglas had to defeat his opponent. People from all over the country followed the debates in the newspapers, and their interest gave Lincoln invaluable national exposure.

Although the format was unusual, the open-air political rally had long been a midwestern diversion, and thousands came to watch and listen to the speakers. The banners, the marching cadets, the glee clubs, and the general holiday atmosphere encouraged the candidates to banter and name-calling, but generally the level of discourse and discussion was high.

The debates zeroed in on race and slavery in the territories. Douglas at times appealed to crude white racism and fear of a mass invasion of Illinois by blacks if slavery were abolished. If, in the House-Divided speech, Lincoln sounded a bit like an abolitionist, at other points, especially in the southern part of the state where many of the voters were of southern descent, he pandered to the anti-black prejudices of his audience. When Douglas accused the "Black Republican party" of favoring racial equality and full civil rights for blacks, Lincoln said he did not believe that black people were the equal of whites, and as long as there were differences he expected the white race to have the superior position. Nevertheless, Lincoln's moral revulsion against slavery came through clearly. At Alton, in the last debate, he announced that "the sentiment that contemplates the institution of slavery . . . as a wrong is the sentiment of the Republican party." Slavery was "a moral, social, and political wrong."

The Dred Scott decision inevitably engaged the debaters. At Freeport, Lincoln tried to embarrass his opponent by asking him to reconcile his popular-sovereignty doctrine with Chief Justice Taney's decision in Dred Scott denying the right of the people of a territory to exclude slavery. Douglas repeated the formula he had already advanced: All a territorial legislature needed to do was refuse to enact a slave code and slavery was effectively kept out. Though not new, this Freeport Doctrine publicized Douglas's differences with his southern colleagues and increased the tension between him and his party's southern wing.

On election day the voters of Illinois gave the Republican candidates for the legislature more total popular votes than they gave the Democrats. But the

Democrats won more counties than their opponents, and the new Democratic legislature reelected the Little Giant to the Senate. Having survived the challenge, Douglas was now clearly the front-runner for his party's presidential nomination in 1860. Lincoln, though he had lost, was now a national figure. In February 1860 he traveled to New York to speak before the city's wealthy and influential Republicans. His Cooper Union address impressed his distinguished audience. Old Abe would now be a presidential contender, too, on the Republican side.

Harpers Ferry.   But first the country would have to undergo another ordeal of violence over slavery, and once again John Brown would be the instigator. Though many people knew of his role in the Pottawatomie massacre, Brown was never indicted and remained free to concoct other schemes to scourge the slaveholders. Between 1856 and 1859 he worked out a mad plan to foment a slave revolt that would bring down the institution of slavery. Starting with a nucleus of armed escapees in the inaccessible Virginia Blue Ridge, he and his band would advance south along the Appalachians attracting runaways and spreading slave insurrection all through the eastern slave country. Brown solicited money for his scheme from New England abolitionists and antislavery philanthropists. Not all approved. Frederick Douglass, for one, believed that invading Virginia with two dozen men was harebrained and told Brown as much.

Warnings did no good. In the fall of 1859 Brown, his sons, and a small band of black and white supporters bought guns and drew up plans for an assault on the federal armory at Harpers Ferry in what is now West Virginia. The armory would provide the weapons and light the spark for his insurrection. On the night of October 16 the rebels seized the armory and all its rifles and ammunition. But the slaves did not rise at the news. Instead, Brown and his small band remained holed up in the armory building not knowing what to do next. On October 18 a detachment of U.S. marines led by Colonel Robert E. Lee stormed the building and captured the surviving members of the implausible revolt.

Brown's raid raised sectional antagonisms to fever pitch. To southerners it was proof that the North would stop at nothing to undermine slavery, including igniting a dreaded servile insurrection. Hundreds of southern students at northern colleges packed their bags and returned home in protest. Georgians attacked the crew of a northern ship at Savannah and a New Yorker, newly installed as president of an Alabama college, was forced to flee for his life.

Brown was tried for treason, convicted, and sentenced to hang. During the trial and in the weeks between sentencing and execution, he conducted himself with great dignity. Many northerners had initially condemned the attack, and even Lincoln and *New York Tribune* editor Horace Greeley believed Brown tragically misguided. But Brown's bearing and eloquent words after his capture made him a hero to many in the North. Henry David Thoreau compared him to Jesus, and novelist Louisa May Alcott named Brown "Saint John the Just." When he was hanged on December 2, he became, in the eyes of antislavery advocates, a martyr to the cause of human freedom. In two short years Union soldiers, advancing against the slave South, would be singing the words: "John Brown's body lies a-moldering in the grave but his truth is marching on."

The Party Conventions of 1860.

Harpers Ferry kept the country in an uproar well into 1860, and by that time the nation was in the throes of the most fateful presidential election of its history.

The Democratic convention convened in April 1860 at Charleston, South Carolina, in the heart of "Secessia." Led by the fiery William Yancey of Alabama, the southern leaders threatened to walk out unless the convention endorsed a federal territorial slave code plank. The Douglas majority, certain that such a plank would ensure Democratic defeat in November, refused to yield. When the Douglasites won the platform fight, Yancey and forty-nine other southern rights' delegates marched out of the convention hall. Meeting elsewhere in town, the minority adopted their cherished plank and waited to see what their adversaries would do. The majority continued to meet, but were unable to give Douglas the nomination by the required two-thirds of the delegates still present despite fifty-seven ballots. Frustrated, they adjourned, promising to convene at Baltimore six weeks later to try again.

At Baltimore, unity still could not be achieved. The southern rights' bolters, some now back, as well as some newly chosen southern delegates, once again walked out. This time they held their own convention and nominated Vice President John C. Breckinridge of Kentucky on a federal slave code platform. Meanwhile, the remaining Baltimore delegates chose Douglas on a popular-sovereignty platform. On May 9 the remaining Whigs organized the Constitutional Union party with a fuzzy platform that endorsed the Union and "the enforcement of the laws." They chose as their candidates John Bell of Tennessee and Edward Everett of Massachusetts.

The Republicans met in Chicago confident of victory. As the delegates crowded into the dynamic young metropolis on the lake, the Republican front-runner seemed to be Senator William Seward of New York. But Seward was the author of "the higher law" doctrine, and in 1858 had made another provocative speech declaring that the two sections of the country were doomed to an "irrepressible conflict." Many Republicans considered him too radical to carry the lower North. Salmon Chase, the antislavery senator from Ohio, did not appear much better. At the other end of the Republican scale was Edward Bates of Missouri. But Bates was too moderate, and colorless besides. Simon Cameron of Pennsylvania, another possible nominee, was weighed down with a reputation for both party inconsistency and shady financial dealing.

The Lincoln forces made much of their rivals' weaknesses and pictured their candidate as the perfect balance between moderation and radicalism. He was also from the Midwest, they emphasized, a disputed region the Republicans had to carry to win in November. Skilled maneuverers, the Lincoln managers packed the galleries with enthusiastic, leather-lunged Lincoln supporters. Old Abe won the nomination on the third ballot. His running mate was Hannibal Hamlin of Maine.

The party platform, like the candidate, represented the more moderate Republican position. It demanded the exclusion of slavery from the territories, but endorsed the right of each state to "order and control its own domestic institutions." It also condemned the John Brown raid. At Chicago, the Republicans proved more sensitive to the economic interests of the North and West in 1860 than four years before. The party platform endorsed a homestead law, a protective tariff, a northern-route Pacific railroad, and federal aid for internal improvements.

The Union Dissolves.   None of the candidates favored disunion. Douglas, of course, was a passionate unionist, and the platform of John Bell's party was little more than an assertion of national unity. The Republicans, for their part, soft-pedaled the slavery extension issue, especially in the lower North, to avoid frightening off moderate and timid voters. Even John Breckinridge decried secession, though, as Douglas correctly noted, every secessionist voter was also a Breckinridge supporter.

The Republican campaign was marked by enthusiastic marches, banners, parades, and rallies. The young party emphasized the "free labor" theme, with Lincoln, the humble "rail-splitter," depicted as the perfect exemplar of its message. Lincoln's opponents sought various fusion arrangements to deny the Republicans victory by carrying the entire South plus several crucial northern states. These efforts failed except in a few localities, and it was soon clear that the nation faced the probability of a Republican president representing an exclusively northern constituency.

Weeks before the results were in, the Charleston Mercury predicted that if Lincoln won, "thousands of slaveholders will despair of the institution." Other southern journals and politicians warned that the Republican administration would appoint abolitionist federal officials in the South who would work to undermine slavery. If slavery collapsed, white farmers and wage earners would be forced to compete with the cheap labor of freed blacks. The prospect of a Black Republican victory seemed intolerable. One Atlanta editor announced: "Let the consequences be what they may, whether the Potomac is crimsoned in human gore, and Pennsylvania Avenue is paved ten fathoms deep with mangled bodies . . . the South will never submit to such humiliation and degradation as the inauguration of Abraham Lincoln."

The election results did not endorse extremism of either sort. Lincoln won a clear electoral college majority over his combined opponents, carrying every free state except New Jersey, where he split the electoral vote with Douglas. Yet he won only 39 percent of the popular vote, virtually all from the free states. Douglas was second in popular votes with 29 percent, but in every state but Missouri he was second to someone else, and so could only claim 12 electoral votes. Together, the Little Giant and Bell, both strong unionists, won more popular votes in the slave states than Breckinridge. Even if we judge Breckinridge's support to be mainly secessionist, the 1860 election was scarcely a mandate for disunion.

Nevertheless, when the South Carolina legislature, then in session, learned of the election outcome it declared by unanimous vote, that the "union now subsisting between South Carolina and other States . . . is hereby dissolved." In the next few weeks conventions in six more states—Alabama, Mississippi, Florida, Georgia, Louisiana, and Texas—voted to leave the Union. Few outright opponents of secession were to be found at the secession conventions of the lower South, though in each there was a contingent of "cooperationists," people who favored waiting until the South as a whole decided to leave the Union. The largest fraction of all consisted of "immediate secessionists," who demanded secession without delay and without qualifications. All through the lower South the immediate secessionist group represented the counties that were richer, more closely tied to slavery and cotton, and traditionally more Democratic than Whig.

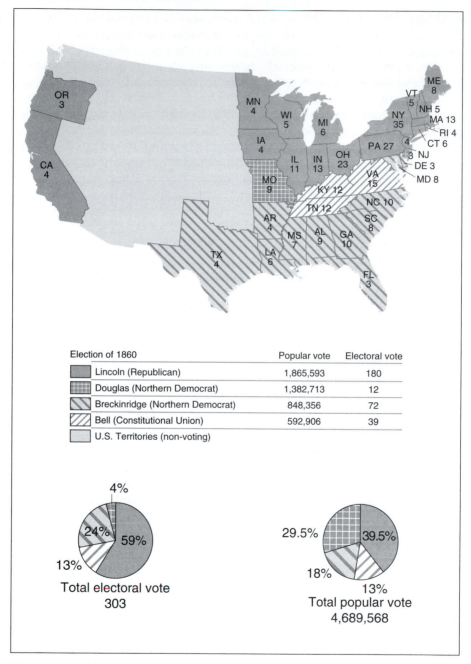

Election of 1860	Popular vote	Electoral vote
Lincoln (Republican)	1,865,593	180
Douglas (Northern Democrat)	1,382,713	12
Breckinridge (Northern Democrat)	848,356	72
Bell (Constitutional Union)	592,906	39
U.S. Territories (non-voting)		

4%
24%
59%
13%

Total electoral vote
303

29.5% 39.5%
18% 13%

Total popular vote
4,689,568

The Presidential Election of 1860

Secession Winter.
People who lived through the months between the election and Lincoln's inauguration in March remembered it vividly as a time of acute public anxiety. Southerners hovered between hope and despair, not knowing how

the federal government would respond to secession and fearful that the confusion of the time would encourage slave revolt. Meanwhile, officials of the seceded states seized federal customs houses, post offices, mints, arsenals, and forts; army officers, members of Congress, and other federal officials of southern birth declared their allegiances to their native states.

In early February delegates from six of the seceded states met in Montgomery, Alabama, and organized a new federation to replace the old. Choosing Jefferson Davis of Mississippi and Alexander Stephens of Georgia as provisional president and vice president, respectively, they adopted a frame of government for the Confederate States of America that in most ways resembled the old federal Constitution. The Confederate constitution, however, declared slavery everywhere protected by law, forbade protective tariffs, gave the president the right to veto specific portions of bills passed by Congress, and confined him to a single six-year term of office.

Northerners, too, felt confused and apprehensive in those "secession winter" months. In Washington rumors circulated that southern sympathizers intended to seize the capital. In New York City, where merchants and bankers had close business ties with the South, and where most of the white working class were Democrats, there was disturbing talk from the Democratic mayor, Fernando Wood, about taking the city out of the Union. Many northern moderates supported compromise to close the sectional breach before it became irreparable.

President Buchanan did not approve of secession, but neither did he believe that the federal government had the right to take coercive steps to save the Union. As Seward would express it, his position seemed to be that "no state has a right to secede unless it wishes to." Buchanan hoped above all that violence would not erupt during his remaining weeks in office; thereafter secession would be his successor's problem. Surrounded at first by southern advisers, the president was unable to check the progressive disintegration of the Union.

Republicans were divided and indecisive. A few strong antislavery partisans, like Horace Greeley, advised letting "the erring sisters depart in peace," thereby freeing the Union of the taint of slavery. Some Republican moderates favored compromise on the territorial issue, perhaps by extending the Missouri Compromise line to the California border. Other Republicans, confusing "conditional Unionism" in the South with true Unionism, advised going slow until the forces of unity reasserted themselves in Dixie.

The core of the party, however, refused to compromise with secession. It was wrong and dangerous. If the lower South could leave the Union, why not the other slave states, and then perhaps the West? Once allowed, could anything stop total dissolution of the Union? And for what purpose? The South had lost a political contest played by the rules; could it now cry foul? Secession was not rebellion against tyranny, as in 1776, but an attack on the most benign, most democratic government the world had ever known. And how could the separation be effected without serious harm? The new Confederacy would control the mouth of the Mississippi. Could that vital spot be allowed to fall into unfriendly hands? And who would get the territories? No, the only option was to resist secession.

The eyes of the country during these tense months inevitably turned to the president-elect. Many sincere unionists urged Lincoln to make some major conciliatory gesture on the slavery extension issue. Lincoln was willing to support a constitutional amendment forbidding the federal government to meddle in slavery in the states and even agreed to enforce the Fugitive Slave Act if it was made fairer. But he would not surrender exclusion of slavery from the territories. If he did, the issue would only have to be fought all over again in the future. As he told a fellow Republican: "The tug has to come, and better now than any time hereafter."

Meanwhile, desperate efforts were underway in Congress and the states to patch together another sectional compromise. The most promising proposal was the scheme of Kentucky Senator John J. Crittenden to extend the Missouri Compromise line through the remaining federal territory. But it, along with several others, required that the Republicans abandon their core issue. The Crittenden plan also opened the door for slavery to be extended to territories "hereafter acquired." Republicans in Congress rejected the Crittenden compromise as well as the others.

Major Anderson's Ordeal.

With each passing day the crisis deepened. Increasingly, the attention of the country focused on the two southern military posts still in federal hands—Fort Sumter in Charleston harbor, and Fort Pickens at Pensacola, Florida. Their status, like so many issues of the preceding decade, had become charged with tremendous emotional and symbolic importance. Even Buchanan was unwilling to give up the forts, though he had done little to prevent other southern seizures of federal property. In January he despatched the merchant steamer *Star of the West* with munitions and troops to reinforce the beleaguered Union army commander at Sumter, Major Robert Anderson. The South Carolina militia forced the steamer to turn back, leaving Anderson's garrison as desperate as ever.

By inauguration day, March 4, 1861, the issue of the forts had still not been settled. Lincoln's inauguration address adopted a conciliatory tone. The Union was "perpetual"; secession was the "essence of anarchy." The government would "hold, occupy, and possess" federal property and "collect the duties and imposts." On the other hand, the new president declared, he would not insist on delivering the federal mails if such service were "repelled," nor would he appoint "obnoxious strangers" to federal offices in the South. Ultimately, the "momentous issue of civil war" was in the hands of the South. The federal government would not assail the South, but at the same time he, as president, was sworn to "preserve, protect, and defend" the government. Lincoln ended with an appeal to "the mystic chords of memory" that joined the North and South in a common history and heritage.

Once in official charge, Lincoln was compelled to grapple with the question of the forts. Pickens could be reinforced by sea without difficulty. The issue of Sumter, under the direct guns of Confederate forces on shore, continued to fester. William Seward, now secretary of state, advised that it be evacuated and let Confederate commissioners in Washington believe that it would be done. But Lincoln was under great pressure from Republicans around the country to save Sumter. And if he was going to do it, it would have to be quickly. Major Anderson reported in early March that his supplies were running low and he could not hold out much longer.

On March 20 the president ordered an expedition to reinforce Anderson. Seward still objected, and composed a memorandum advising abandonment of Sumter. Hoping to take charge of the nation's affairs from a man he considered weak and vacillating, he went beyond this suggestion, however, and made the preposterous proposal that the United States provoke a diplomatic crisis with Britain and France that would induce still patriotic southerners to rush to the Union's defense. Lincoln quickly and firmly put Seward in his place. He alone, he told his puffed-up subordinate, must execute the nation's policies.

Lincoln proceeded with the Sumter relief expedition but took care to notify southern officials of his intentions. As a further precaution against provoking the South, he divided the expedition into two parts. One would only be for resupplying Major Anderson. The federal government would hold troop reinforcements in reserve to be used only if the supply ships were fired on. If the southern authorities did that, the onus of war would be on the South's head. The upper South, he hoped, would not see the expedition as an attack.

To Jefferson Davis and his colleagues the continued presence of U.S. property in the middle of Charleston harbor was a reproach to the very idea of Confederate independence and sovereignty. On April 9 Davis ordered the Confederate general in command at Charleston, Pierre Gustave Beauregard, to demand Anderson's surrender before the relief expedition arrived. If he refused, the Confederate batteries should open fire. Anderson rejected the ultimatum, but told the Confederates frankly that his supplies were low and he would have to surrender soon in any case. Beauregard decided that this reply was unsatisfactory.

At 4:30 A.M., on April 12, 1861, the first cannon shot arced over Charleston harbor to land on Fort Sumter. For thirty-four hours the bombardment continued, breaching the fort's walls and starting fires. True to his pledge to hold his post, Major Anderson returned the fire. On the afternoon of April 13, his ammunition exhausted, he lowered the Stars and Stripes and surrendered.

Conclusions

And so the war came. For the next four years the nation would suffer the agonies of fratricidal strife and skirt the edge of dissolution. What had brought the United States to this disastrous result?

Slavery comes closest to explaining the origins of the Civil War. But it was not moral outrage over the peculiar institution primarily that set northern armies on the march to crush the Confederacy. At the outset, only a small minority of northerners saw the war as a crusade against a fundamental social evil. The actual role of slavery was more subtle and indirect. Southerners had developed a deep stake in the peculiar institution and feared both social and economic cataclysm if it failed. And that failure seemed the goal of the "Black Republican" party and the northern majority that brought it to power in 1860. Southerners were also infuriated by the evident intent of their northern fellow citizens to deny them their "rights" in the common territory of the nation. Northerners, for their part, had come to fear and despise an aggressive and demanding "slave power" that sought to trample the rights of free men.

Slavery defined the South and set it off against the North. Deeply woven into the fabric of southern life, it helped to create a southern sense of distinctiveness. This sense took the form of a combined sectional aggressiveness and defensiveness, and these, in turn, made the clash of economic interests more bitter than it need have been. Slavery also converted the Mexican Cession into a source of constantly escalating friction that could not be contained by the existing party system or the other institutions that transcended section.

Yet we must also allow for the role of individuals and of accident. Sectional conflict might have been contained if this generation of Americans had possessed the statesmanship necessary for compromise. Douglas, who could have filled the role played by Webster and Clay in the past, badly miscalculated in 1854 and helped wreck the Union. The other leaders of the decade, many of them talented men, were far too closely tied to sectional interests to bridge the chasm opening between the sections. Whatever the route taken, the nation's greatest ordeal now began.

ONLINE RESOURCES

"Politics and Sectionalism in the 1850s" *http://odur.let.rug.nl/~usa/E/1850s/polixx.htm* This site contains interpretations of and excerpts from the Fugitive Slave Act and the Kansas–Nebraska Act. It also details the political debate over slavery in Congress and the influence of abolitionist leader such as Frederick Douglass.

"The Dred Scott Case: A Summary" *http://www.umsl.edu/virtualstl/phase2/1850/events/resources/documents/dscs.html* This site provides the background on the case and a discussion of the case and its impact. To read the full text version of the Supreme Court decision, see *http://odur.let.rug.nl/~usa/D/1851-1875/dredscott/dredxx.htm.*

"Lincoln–Douglas Debates" *http://www.founding.com/library/index.cfm?parent=64* On this Web site, read the actual text of these famed debates between presidential candidates Abraham Lincoln and Stephen Douglas. These debates cast into sharp relief the growing differences between North and South.

"SCARTOONS: Racial Satire and the Civil War" *http://xroads.virginia.edu/~CAP/SCARTOONS/cartoons.html* On this site, explore the growing sectionalism, the Civil war years, and the aftermath of the war through political cartoons of the era.

"Secession Era Editorials" *http://history.furman.edu/~benson/docs/index.htm* Read about perspectives of both the North and the South through hundreds of contemporary newspaper editorials that address issues such as John Brown's raid and the Nebraska Bill.

15

The Civil War

How Did the War Change the Nation?

1861	Confederates fire on Fort Sumter; President Lincoln calls up 75,000 state militia; Lincoln suspends habeas corpus for the first time and endorses severe penalties for treason; The First Battle of Bull Run; Congress grants Lincoln power to take over railroads and telegraphs, imposes internal revenue taxes on manufactures, and passes an income tax law; The Second Confiscation Act
1862	The Union treasury begins to issue $450 million of greenbacks; Ironclads *Monitor* and *Merrimac* battle; Albert S. Johnston stops Grant's advance in the West at the battle of Shiloh Church, Tennessee; Union forces capture New Orleans; The Confederate States of America institute a draft; The Homestead Act; George McClellan's Peninsular Campaign is checked by Robert E. Lee; The Morrill Land Grant College Act; The first black Union regiments are authorized; Congress passes the first of two Pacific Railway acts; The Second Battle of Bull Run; McClellan stops Lee's advance at Antietam Creek, Maryland; Lincoln issues the Emancipation Proclamation
1863	The Emancipation Proclamation goes into effect; Congress adopts a draft for the Union army; Joseph Hooker is defeated by Lee and Stonewall Jackson at Chancellorsville, Virginia; Democratic Congressman Clement Vallandigham is arrested and eventually banished to the South; Fifty pro-Union counties in Virginia are admitted into the Union as West Virginia; Battle of Gettysburg, Pennsylvania, the turning point of the war; Grant captures Vicksburg, Mississippi, and ensures Union control of the Mississippi River; The New York draft riots
1863, 1864	National Banking Acts establish uniform banking and currency practices
1864	Sherman captures Atlanta, Georgia, and marches to the sea; Second Pacific Railway Act passed by Congress; Lincoln reelected
1865	Lee asks Grant for terms of surrender and they conclude a peace at Appomattox Court House; Lincoln is assassinated by John Wilkes Booth, and Andrew Johnson becomes president

Looking back at the events of 1861–1865, most former Unionists and Confederates alike were certain that they had witnessed a profound transformation of the nation. Vast armies had struggled and many thousands had died. Immense wealth had been annihilated. The two warring governments had spent billions of dollars on arms, supplies, and services. The war had destroyed slavery and decisively shifted political power to the North. It seemed to mark a great divide between a sleepier agrarian nation and a bustling America of great factories and teeming cities.

Yet some scholars have had doubts about how much the Civil War changed the nation. The war, they say, may have formally ended slavery, but the nation's black people had to wait until almost our own day for anything resembling real freedom. The war, moreover, did not promote the economic growth of the United States, nor was it the great watershed between an agrarian and an urban-industrial world. In fact, many historians believe, the Civil War retarded economic development and slowed the shift from agriculture to industry, from country to city.

How did the war affect the nation? As we discuss the awesome "brothers' war," we must, if we are to answer the question, consider not just the battles and campaigns but also the social, political, and economic changes that accompanied the strife and carnage.

North Versus South

The Civil War was a confrontation of two armies, two economies, two ideologies, and two governments. With the advantages of hindsight, we might conclude that in each of these areas the Union had the advantage. But not all Americans living in 1861 perceived it this way, and the fact that the war lasted so long and cost the Union so dearly confirms contemporary perceptions that the sides were evenly matched.

The Balance of Forces.   An objective, neutral observer drawing up a sectional balance sheet in April 1861 might in fact have given the edge to the South. It is true that with 9 million people, the seceded states had less than half the population of the North, and 3 million of its inhabitants, moreover, were blacks, whom the Confederacy was unwilling to arm. The South was also outclassed economically. In 1860 the whole of what became the Confederate States of America had only 18,000 manufacturing establishments, employing 110,000 workers. The North had over 100,000 factories and shops, with 1.3 million employees. In transportation facilities the North was also far ahead with more than 70 percent of the nation's railroad track and twice as many horses and mules as the Confederacy.

Yet the South seemed to many contemporary observers to have immense assets too. The southern economy produced an abundance of food to feed its citizens, its draft animals, and its armies. Cotton seemed a major strength. It was useful for cloth and uniforms, but more importantly, it promised to energize Confederate diplomacy. Without cotton, southerners thought, Europe's great textile industry, particularly Britain's, would shut down. To restore a dependable supply of American cotton and save itself from industrial ruin, England would have to intervene on the South's behalf. To guarantee that Britain felt the pinch, early in the war southern states embargoed cotton, and patriotic Confederate citizens pressured growers to limit the amount of cotton they planted. Some cotton was even burned. The campaign cut the South's 1862 cotton output to a third of its prewar volume.

In any war the Confederacy also appeared to have important strategic advantages. For the South to win, it need only survive. For the North to win, it had to conquer. The Confederacy would enjoy "interior" lines of communication; retreat from its borders would only shorten the distance between the South's core and its armies in the field, making it easier to supply and deploy troops. The North faced the opposite situation. As its attacking armies advanced farther and farther into enemy territory, they would experience the problems of constantly lengthening lines of communication. In the end, if only the North's difficulties and costs could be made painful enough, southern independence seemed assured.

The key was whether the North's will to fight could survive the strain. Many at the time believed that here, too, the Confederacy had the edge. The South was fighting for its rights, its freedom, insisted its supporters. As Jefferson Davis proclaimed in his farewell speech to the United States Senate, Mississippi had left the Union only "from the high and solemn motive of defending and protecting the rights we inherited, and which it is our duty to transmit unshorn to our children." By contrast, southerners declared, only the North's desire to dominate, to achieve selfish economic and political ends, could explain its refusal to grant the South its due. A better cause, then, guaranteed better morale and better morale promised victory.

The South seemed also to possess superior military talent. Secession deprived the United States Army of a third of its officers, and the best third at that. Men such as Joseph E. Johnston, Edmund Kirby-Smith, and above all Robert E. Lee took commissions in the Confederate armed forces only after great personal anguish. Their choice made, however, they supported the southern cause with dedication and skill; especially in the months before the Union discovered its own talented military leaders, they contributed immeasurably to Confederate successes.

At the level of the common soldier, too, the Confederacy appeared to be ahead. Southerners, it was said, were an outdoor people, who knew how to use rifles, and were better adapted to physical hardship. Confederate sympathizers had little doubt that young southern farm boys would make better soldiers than the wan, hollow-chested Yankee clerks from the counting-houses and shops of the northern cities.

Leadership.   Yet despite appearances, we can now see that almost all the real advantages lay with the North. Abraham Lincoln was the North's greatest single asset. Leading the Union for four of the most dangerous years it ever faced, he managed to make the essentially right political decisions. The mobilization of Union resources to fight a great—and in many quarters unpopular—war required prodigious political juggling. Northern state governors, even Republicans, at times clashed with the federal authorities, especially over military recruiting. Within his own party Lincoln had to deal with both radicals and conservatives. At times he felt compelled to limit civil liberties to preserve order and to prevent "agitators" from discouraging enlistment. He also faced the dilemma of the border states, which remained in the Union only precariously and had to be dealt with deftly to avoid pushing them into the Confederate camp. Finally, there was slavery: Emancipation was the North's moral trump card, but should it be played? And if so, when?

The president often had better military instincts than his generals. His chief claim to military leadership, however, was his choice of men. He was not always right, but he was capable of learning. Eventually he recognized the military genius of Ulysses S. Grant and William T. Sherman and gave them a free hand in managing the Union armies. The combination of their talents was an important step toward victory.

Lincoln's selection of civilian subordinates was also, on the whole, wise and successful. William Seward, once he recognized that he was not the prime minister, served the administration admirably as secretary of state. Though secretary of the treasury Salmon Chase had no previous experience in finance, he guided the government through some of the most difficult financial shoals it would ever encounter. Lincoln's choice of Simon Cameron, the powerful Republican leader of Pennsylvania, as secretary of war was a mistake. Cameron was both corrupt and incompetent. Fortunately, Lincoln quickly discovered his error, sent Cameron to Russia as American minister, and chose Ohio Democrat Edwin Stanton for the post. Often caustic and intolerant, Stanton was a prodigious worker and a passionate and skilled defender of the Union cause.

Lincoln's chief success, however, was as a symbol of the Union's will to survive and an articulator of goals beyond mere survival. His major state papers and speeches rank among the most inspiring evocations of the democratic spirit. Taking what could easily be interpreted as a war of conquest, Lincoln transformed it into a struggle for the finest aspirations of the American people. The war was a "people's contest," a "struggle. . .to elevate the condition of men—to lift artificial weights from all shoulders—to clear the paths of laudable pursuit for all—to afford all an unfettered start and a fair chance in the race of life." The Union's survival, Lincoln told his fellow citizens, was humanity's "last, best hope." If it should be defeated, democracy would fail, and the forces of darkness and tyranny triumph. If, however, the Union prevailed, government "of the people, by the people, for the people" would "not perish from the earth."

And what of the Confederacy's leader, Jefferson Davis? A West Point graduate, Franklin Pierce's secretary of war, and former United States senator from Mississippi, Davis seemed eminently suited to guide the besieged Confederacy.

During the weeks following Fort Sumter, the martial spirit affected everyone: Notice the enthusiasm as New York's Seventh Regiment leaves for the front. So many northerners tried to enlist that the United States turned down thousands.

He was honest, courageous, and intelligent; and his sharply etched, lean features and dignified bearing gave him the look of a national leader. Davis, however, had to have his hand in everything, both civilian and military, and often he botched the job. According to Stephen R. Mallory, Davis's secretary of the navy, the Confederate president "neither labored with method or celerity himself, nor permitted others to do so for him." He was also argumentative and, unlike his northern counterpart, insensitive to public opinion.

The War Begins

The first responsibility of each president was to raise an army. Immediately after the attack on Fort Sumter, Lincoln had called for 75,000 state militia to join the small regular army for three months' service. The war, he expected, would be brief, and the troops would be home for late spring planting. Except in the border states, the public response was quick and enthusiastic. Young men regarded the war as a glorious lark, and they flocked to recruiting offices. State quotas were quickly oversubscribed; and militia regiments, many composed of untrained youths without rifles or proper uniforms, rushed off for Washington to meet their country's call.

Lincoln's move to put down the rebellion tripped off a furious reaction in the still uncommitted slave states. Between April 17 and May 20 four more—Virginia, Arkansas, Tennessee, and North Carolina—seceded and joined the Confederacy, bringing with them more of the South's manpower and much of its agricultural and industrial capacity. Meanwhile, war fever also seized the South and thousands of young southerners rushed to join the army to defend southern rights. The Confederacy had the opportunity to make a formidable force out of this raw material, but it let the chance slip. Like Lincoln, the Confederate Congress believed the war would end by winter, and it accepted many short-term volunteers who soon had to be replaced.

Bull Run. The fighting would be bloody, bitter, and seemingly interminable. Many of the early clashes took place in the strategically important border regions—Kentucky, Missouri, eastern Tennessee, and western Virginia—where the two sections touched one another and where the people were deeply divided in their allegiances. The battle of Bull Run in July 1861, twenty miles from Washington, was the first major military confrontation. There, 30,000 men under Union General Irvin McDowell met a smaller force commanded by Confederate General Beauregard. The Confederates were outgunned and outnumbered, but better led and better coordinated. For a time the Union forces held the upper hand, but when the Confederates, screaming their shrill "rebel yell," counterattacked, the Federals panicked, abandoning their rifles and artillery, and fleeing pell-mell to the safety of Washington. Accompanying them in their headlong retreat was an array of civilians, including several congressmen and many ladies, who had come out from the Union capital on a warm summer's day to watch the expected rebel rout.

The defeat at Bull Run (called the battle of Manassas in the South) seemed to confirm Confederate claims that southerners were superior fighters. On the other hand it provided a healthy antidote to northern overoptimism. Republican governors from all over the North telegraphed the War Department offering new state regiments to protect the capital and prepare for resuming the march south. These men, moreover,

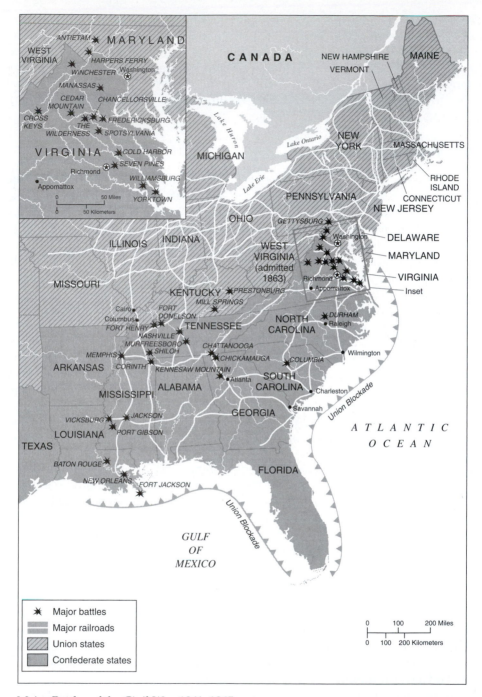

Major Battles of the Civil War, 1861–1865

would be enlisted for three years. Patriotism, the glamor of a uniform, and the love of adventure were still potent stimulants to enlistment; another 75,000 volunteers streamed into training camps near Washington prepared to put down the "rebellion."

Lincoln's Early Commanders.   The man who took charge of this force was George B. McClellan, a small, wiry man with a bristling black moustache and a Napoleonic complex. As a young officer, "Little Mac" had served in the Mexican War; but he had spent most of his military career in the Corps of Engineers, and when the war broke out in early 1861 he was a civilian railroad director. His training and experience as an organizer and administrator helped him pull the army together. McClellan drilled his troops rigorously, welding the new arrivals and the ragged, dispirited mob that had fled to Washington from Bull Run into a confident, spit-and-polish army. He was soon being hailed as a savior.

McClellan, however, lacked the needed daring and drive of a good field commander. As a Democrat, moreover, he was suspicious of the president and his party. He took months to equip and train his men before resuming the attack. Finally in March 1862, after insistent goading by Lincoln, McClellan's magnificent army of 130,000 set out for Richmond from Hampton Roads, where they had arrived by sea. At Williamsburg, in early May, McClellan first encountered the enemy. The engagement was inconclusive. For the next two months McClellan fought a series of battles—the Peninsular Campaign—against two of the South's ablest military leaders, Robert E. Lee and Thomas J. ("Stonewall") Jackson. He managed to avert defeat; but his army returned to Washington in June bruised and badly battered. Nothing had been achieved.

In the West, Union forces under the Virginian George H. Thomas and the shaggy, hard-drinking Ulysses S. Grant were having better luck. In late January Thomas defeated the Confederates at the Battle of Mill Springs in Kentucky. Several weeks later Grant captured Fort Donelson on the Cumberland River, taking 14,000 Confederate prisoners. Soon Nashville fell to Union forces. Grant believed that he was now in a position to crush the Confederate army in the West decisively, but he underestimated the recuperative powers of his foe. On April 6, 1862, Albert Sidney Johnston attacked the exposed Union position near Shiloh Church, Tennessee, and pushed back the federal troops commanded by William Tecumseh Sherman. A confused two-day battle brought heavy casualties to both sides, including the death of the Confederate commander. Ultimately, the Confederate attack was repulsed, but Grant's men, exhausted and hungry, could not muster the energy to pursue the beaten Confederates.

McClellan's lack of offensive zeal disturbed Lincoln. In addition, the general was thoroughly detested by the emerging circle of "Radicals" in the Republican party, who advocated abolition of slavery and a more aggressive policy to defeat the South. In July 1862 the president replaced McClellan as field commander in the East with General John Pope.

For the next year the tide of war swept back and forth, with Lincoln unable to find a field commander to match Lee. When Pope was beaten by Lee and Jackson in the Second Battle of Bull Run (August 29–30, 1862), Lincoln turned once again to McClellan, who once again disappointed him. McClellan stopped Lee's advance into Maryland at Antietam (September 17, 1862) but lost the opportunity of decisively defeating the far smaller Confederate force. In November Lincoln decided to replace McClellan with Ambrose E. Burnside. The choice was unwise. In December 1862 at Fredericksburg, Virginia, the new Union commander sent massed infantry against entrenched Confederate troops, whose rifles and artillery slaughtered the charging blue-clad Federals. Lincoln replaced Burnside with Joseph Hooker, who quickly demonstrated that he was no better. At Chancellorsville, Virginia (May 2–4, 1863), Lee and Jackson severely mauled Hooker's Army of the Potomac. The only consolation for the Union forces was that Jackson was accidentally killed by his own men.

Union Strategy.   The Union was not only slow in finding a competent military leader; it also had difficulty evolving a clear, overall military strategy. To many northerners "On to Richmond!" seemed at first plan enough. Others considered it simple-minded, though in fact, to the very end the Union concentrated excessively on capturing the Confederate capital. In 1861 the aged commander in chief, Winfield Scott, proposed that, like the great anaconda snake, the North seize its victim in its coils and squeeze it to death. Union forces would contain the South along its borders, blockade the Confederate coast, and cut the South in half along the Mississippi River. Seeing that its cause was hopeless, the South would surrender, without much blood shed on either side. The Anaconda Plan was greeted with derision by the northern press and never adopted as such.

The passive containment feature of the anaconda plan was rejected, yet several parts of the scheme were in fact incorporated into Union strategy. In April 1862 Union forces under General Benjamin F. Butler took New Orleans, the South's largest city and control point for access to the Mississippi. Bit by bit the Union forces advanced up and down the banks of the river. In the summer of 1863 the final Confederate positions fell when Grant, aided by Admiral David Porter's river gunboats, took Vicksburg and Port Hudson. The Confederacy was now cut in two by a Union-controlled north–south corridor.

The Naval War.   The squeeze tactics were especially effective at sea, where each month the northern naval blockade grew tighter. In early 1862 the *Merrimac,* a Confederate ironclad converted from a scuttled United States naval vessel, threatened to break the Union blockade of Hampton Roads, Virginia. The federal navy rushed its own brand new ironclad, the *Monitor,* to the scene. The two vessels battled to a draw, and the southern ship retired, never again to challenge Union naval supremacy.

Its naval advantage was to stand the North in good stead. In the western theater federal gunboats on the Mississippi and its tributaries supported Union military operations with their cannon and kept river supply lines open. Along the Atlantic and Gulf coasts the seagoing Union fleet made possible successful amphibious attacks against southern ports such as New Orleans, Mobile, Savannah, and Port Royal. Most useful, however, was the coastal blockade. Each month the sea noose around the South drew tighter. In 1861 the federal navy captured one Confederate vessel in ten that tried to escape to the open sea; by 1865 its record had improved to one in two, and growing Confederate shortages of many products hitherto imported from Europe attested to the mounting effectiveness of the blockade.

The Confederates also had their moments of glory at sea. Many Confederate blockade-runners evaded Union cruisers and dashed to Bermuda or some other British-American port and returned with weapons, medicines, foodstuffs, and luxuries. On the high seas the *Alabama* and other Confederate raiders destroyed Union shipping worth millions of dollars. Despite these successes, the Confederates were never able to challenge the Union navy on the waters, and each month saw the northern advantage grow as its shipyards turned out scores of new vessels to augment Union naval strength. In June 1864 the United States Navy's *Kearsarge* finally caught up with Captain Raphael Semmes of the *Alabama* off Cherbourg, France, and put an end to his spectacular commerce-raiding career.

The Diplomatic War.

Europe's need for cotton had promised the Confederacy a chance to win diplomatic recognition and possibly military help from Britain and France. The South also hoped that Britain would seize the opportunity to cut the United States down to size by helping to divide it in half. The South counted on support from Europe's upper classes, who admired the southern planter elite more than the supposedly crude, money-mad Yankees. The French, for the most part, followed Britain's anti-Union lead. But, after establishing a puppet regime in Mexico that challenged the Monroe Doctrine, they had their own reasons for favoring a Yankee defeat and an enfeebled, distracted United States.

In the end King Cotton diplomacy proved to be a disappointment. Britain was overstocked with cotton in 1861 and for a time felt no pinch from the Confederate de facto embargo. Thereafter, the British imported cotton from Egypt and India to replace some of the lost southern supply. The North also had several high cards. Britain at the time needed northern grain almost as much as southern cotton. But more than this, the North could offer the British public something that its enemy could decidedly not: the prospect of emancipation. Though they were not averse to southern independence, the British middle and working classes could not morally support the slave system. If the North could convince the British people of its true antislavery intentions, the London government would find it difficult to throw its weight against the Union.

For three years the Union and the Confederacy fought desperately to curry favor with the British. The South won the early diplomatic rounds when, in November 1861, the U.S.S *San Jacinto* stopped the British merchant vessel the *Trent*, removed the Confederate commissioners to France (John Slidell) and England (James M. Mason), and brought them as prisoners to Boston. Furious at this violation of their high seas rights, the British demanded their release, as well as reparations and an apology. Lincoln and Secretary of State Seward sat on the situation for a time and then, concluding that war with Great Britain was not expedient, quietly returned the commissioners with an apology. But the Trent affair gave the Confederates a diplomatic edge. Early in 1862 the British government permitted the Confederates to use British shipyards to build and outfit the *Alabama* and other sea raiders, and soon after allowed the Confederate navy to contract with the Laird shipbuilding firm in Scotland for several powerful, ironclad "rams." For a while, too, English investors were receptive to lending money to the Confederacy.

The tide turned, however, when British friends of the United States, Richard Cobden and John Bright, appealed to antislavery opinion and succeeded in creating a strong pro-Union current. The efforts of these sympathetic Britons, the tireless maneuvering of Lincoln's minister to England, Charles Francis Adams, and, above all, Union victories on the battlefield combined to shift British opinion away from the Confederacy. In October 1863 the British government seized the Laird rams before the Confederates could take delivery, ending their threat to the Union blockade. Though the North's worst diplomatic fears were allayed by the end of 1862, the possibility of a falling-out between Britain and the Union gave hope to the South almost to the end of the war.

War and Society

The military, naval, and diplomatic drives of North and South were sustained by stupendous efforts of their respective home fronts. The raising of troops, the marshaling of financial and economic resources, and the containment of internal dissent were all vital parts of the great struggle on both sides to achieve victory.

Conscription.   Throughout the war both combatants relied primarily on volunteers to fill their military ranks. For the first year the system worked well. Typically, in the North, a prominent local citizen who craved adventure, influence, or a military reputation opened a recruiting office and issued a call for volunteers. When enough men had signed up they formed a company; ten companies equaled a regiment. The men of the company chose their own junior officers, who in turn chose the senior regimental officers. Usually the senior officers included the sponsors of the regiment. The regiment then joined the Union forces.

The pure volunteer system did not last. A few months of bitter fighting and growing casualty lists dampened youthful enthusiasm and patriotism; fewer and fewer volunteers turned up at the recruiting offices. Yet the war consumed manpower at a frightful rate. More than 2.1 million men fought for the Union and about 800,000 for the Confederacy. Over half of all northern men of military age eventually wore the Union blue; over four-fifths of the South's young white males donned Confederate gray. Relatively few combatants escaped wounds or death. Some 360,000 Union men lost their lives; about 260,000 Confederates did not survive. Union wounded totaled another 275,000; Confederate wounded, at least 100,000.

By the middle of 1862 both governments were forced to resort to conscription. The South's April 1862 draft law made all able-bodied white males between 18 and 35 liable for military service, but exempted civil servants, militia officers, clergymen, and teachers. A supplemental measure that fall, intended to prevent slave disorders and encourage agricultural output, exempted an adult white male on each plantation with twenty slaves or more. Finally, the southern draft allowed any draftee to hire a substitute to go in his place.

In the Union, the March 1863 Enrollment Act made every healthy male aged 20 to 45 subject to a federal draft with the exception of those who were the sole support of widows, motherless children, or indigent parents. The law also allowed a potential draftee to pay someone else to take his place or to pay a $300 commutation fee exempting him from service. Because the law was intended primarily to stimulate flagging enlistment, each congressional district could fill an assigned quota with volunteers. Only if state and local officials could not raise the necessary numbers within fifty days would the draft be invoked locally to make up the difference.

Conscription in both sections produced anger, resentment, and a multitude of abuses. In the North officials offered large bounties to anyone who would enlist to avoid the drafting of local citizens. "Bounty jumpers" made a business of accepting hundreds of dollars from several districts, one after the other, and then failing to report for duty. In both sections, critics charged that the draft benefited the rich. The "twenty-slave clause" in the Confederate draft supposedly favored the planter class over small farmers. The provision for buying substitutes in both draft systems, though intended primarily to soften the harsh law, also seemed tilted toward those with ready cash. Under the North's Enrollment Act, moreover, rich

The wounded near Fredericksburg. The emptiness and despair on these soldiers' faces contrast with the confidence and optimism of the early volunteers. With inadequate food, shelter, and sanitation, the ideals of glory and victory gave way to the realities of pain and death.

districts were able to outbid poorer ones for able-bodied substitutes and so spare more of their citizens from military duty. These provisions led to charges in both North and South that it was "a rich man's war and a poor man's fight."

Recent research into the social makeup of Union and Confederate armies, however, casts doubt on the charge of class bias in Civil War military recruitment. Allowing for the youth of most soldiers, the occupations and class affiliations of the boys in blue and the boys in gray resembled those of their societies as a whole. In both sections the sons of the rich and the sons of the poor apparently risked their lives in proportionate numbers. Both armies had many foreign-born soldiers. In the Union the foreign-born troops reached 26 percent of the total.

Still, the draft acts aroused deep resentments and led to resistance in both sections. In the South young men escaped to the remotest mountains and often joined with deserters from the Confederate army to defy the authorities. Union draft resistance took an especially violent form in New York City where the working class, Democratic in its politics and often resentful of blacks, blamed the draft on the despised Republican administration. Soon after federal officials in New York began to select draftees in July 1863, mobs of whites attacked symbols of the Union cause, looting the homes of prominent Republicans, destroying the offices of the *New York Tribune*, burning down the city's Colored Orphan Asylum, and lynching a half-dozen innocent black people. The federal government rushed troops from the Gettysburg battlefield to end the anarchy, and General George Meade's veterans fired volleys into the mob. When, after four days, the ghastly riots finally ended, more than a hundred people were dead.

Conscription did not raise many soldiers directly. In the North only 46,000 men were actually drafted into service. But many thousands more volunteered rather than accept the stigma of forced recruitment. All told, a recent student of the draft system concludes, it worked moderately well to get the job done.

Whatever its failings, conscription was a novel exercise of central government power. The three previous American wars had been fought by volunteers. Now, under the goad of necessity, both Union and Confederate governments had asserted a right never claimed before—to compel men to risk their lives for the nation. But this innovation was only one of many pointing to enhanced power for the national government and to the physical and social consolidation of the country.

The Beginnings of Modern National Finance.   Paying for the war was a major challenge for both governments. At one point the Union treasury was disbursing $2 million a day for munitions, supplies, military pay, and other war-related expenses.

The Confederacy initially tried to meet most of its costs with money borrowed from foreign and domestic sources. This approach yielded little, for few capitalists at home or abroad would lend money to the South except at outrageous interest rates. A "produce" loan of cotton and other crops was equally disappointing. As early as 1861, following the precedent of the Revolution, the Confederate treasury turned to paper money, unbacked by gold, mere IOUs.

Though the Confederate printing presses spewed out over $1.5 billion in paper money during the war, even that sum proved inadequate. Before many months the value of Confederate currency had fallen so low that the government was forced to adopt other means for meeting the costs of war. In early 1863 the Confederate Congress authorized the impressment of slaves for the building of fortifications and for other government work. It also empowered the government to detail soldiers for work in vital war factories. In April 1863 it assumed the authority to take from farmers a tenth of all the major crops they produced.

In the North the need to supply the military forces led to a parallel, though less drastic, inflation of national power, and because it was the Union government that survived, that growth was momentous for the country's future. With access to the markets of Europe, the gold of the West, and most of the country's banking capital, Union Secretary of the Treasury Salmon Chase was better able than his Confederate counterpart to tax and borrow. By 1865 Congress had imposed internal revenue taxes on hundreds of manufactured items, created a Bureau of Internal Revenue to administer the tax laws, and established America's first income tax. Using the excuse that heavily taxed American manufactures must be protected against cheaper foreign wares, the Republican Congress also raised tariff rates to levels never before reached, drastically reversing the prewar trend under the Democrats.

Internal taxes and import duties were not enough, however, and the Union, too, resorted to borrowing. Under Chase's prompting, Congress authorized the sale of several hundred million dollars of bonds, paying 6 percent interest in gold. The treasury's chief agent, Philadelphia banker Jay Cooke, advertised this issue in every northern newspaper and sent his agents to peddle the securities from door to door. Eventually he sold $362 million in bonds. By the war's end these bond sales and other loans had pushed the Union debt to the immense figure of $2.5 billion.

The treasury's financial needs produced a major revolution in the country's banking system. The state banks that had supplied the country's currency and credit since the demise of the Second Bank of the United States in 1836 proved inadequate to meet the country's political emergency. Matters were brought to a crisis in December 1861, when public hoarding of gold and excessive treasury borrowing forced the banks to cease redeeming their notes in specie. Without a gold reserve imposing a limit on their paper money issues, the banks were free to turn on the printing presses. The country now faced the prospect of a deluge of worthless paper bank notes to meet its currency needs.

To avoid this chaotic situation and at the same time tap the banks for funds, Chase proposed a national currency backed by government bonds and issued by a new system of federally chartered banks. Under the National Banking Acts of 1863 and 1864, businesspeople who bought a specified amount of federal bonds could organize new banks under federal charter and issue bank notes backed by the government securities. Now, instead of a multitude of privately issued bank notes unsecured by gold, the country would have a uniform paper money system under strict federal control. And after the war these notes would be doubly safe, for then, it was assumed, gold would once more return to normal circulation and the government and the banks would be able to redeem their obligations in "specie" on demand. The measure also sought to put the state banks out of business or force them to convert to national banks by taxing their note issues.

The national banking system did help the treasury finance the war. By June 1863 there were 450 national banks in existence, with millions of dollars' worth of federal bonds in their reserves, representing large revenues to the federal government. More important, however, for the first time in a generation Washington was back in the business of regulating the country's banking affairs.

Still, this was not enough to pay the Union's bills, and there seemed no alternative to treasury-issued paper money, as in the South. The Union's "greenbacks" would be "legal tender" with its value further shored up by a promise to redeem them in gold after the war. Limited in amount to $450 million, they did not depreciate drastically. By late 1864 northern prices were about two and a half times those of 1860. In the South prices had risen fiftyfold.

Government Becomes Big Business.   The demands of war enormously swelled the size of the Union government. Disbursements and tax collections brought an army of clerks to the Treasury Building across from the White House, while in the field hundreds of treasury agents fanned out to regulate the illegal cotton trade between northern buyers eager for scarce fiber and southerners avid for the means to pay for scarce imported goods. The War Department's scale of operation became even greater than the treasury's. Under Quartermaster General Montgomery Meigs, it performed prodigious labors in supplying the army. During the year ending June 30, 1865, alone, the Quartermaster Department purchased 3.4 million trousers, 3.7 million pairs of drawers, and 3.2 million flannel shirts, laying out for these and countless other articles over $431 million. In 1861 the federal civil service had employed 40,000 people; by 1865 there were 195,000, a fivefold increase.

Government orders invigorated the North's economy. The giant War Department procurement effort lowered costs in private armories. It also stimulated production in a wide array of businesses directly connected to the war effort. By 1864 output of coal, iron, copper, and leather was greater than before the war. Frequently the scale of government orders encouraged standardization and mechanization of production, establishing a model for postwar development. The canning industry was stimulated by government orders: When Gail Borden's condensed milk factory opened in early 1861, its entire output was "immediately commandeered" for the army. All told, the index of manufacturing for the North alone by 1864 was 13 percent higher than for the whole nation in 1860.

Organizing Agriculture.

In the South invading armies, the breakdown of transportation, and the erosion of the slave labor system led to agricultural decline. In the North agriculture burgeoned under wartime need. The departure of thousands of young men from the farms precisely when the demand for farm products reached an all-time peak accelerated the acceptance of horse-drawn mechanical harvesters and mowers. During the entire decade of the 1850s American farmers had bought 100,000 of these machines; in 1864 manufacturers were turning out that many each year.

The expansion of northern farm output during the war was only obliquely a consequence of government action. But the government had an important direct impact on the social side of American agriculture as well. For years various northern and western farming groups had demanded favors of the federal government. Now, with the obstructive South out of the Union and the Republicans in control, the barriers came down. In 1861 Congress authorized a department of agriculture within the Patent Office to be headed by a commissioner. In 1862 it enacted the Morrill Land Grant College Act, setting aside several million acres of federal land for support of agricultural and industrial higher education. The 1862 Homestead Act provided that any citizen or any alien who declared his intention of becoming a citizen and who was also head of a family and over 21 might claim 160 acres of land on specified surveyed portions of the public domain. After residing on this land, adding improvements, and paying a small registration fee, he would become its owner, with no further strings except the usual local taxes. The law would be less than perfect in the way it was administered, yet it represented a triumph of the ideal of a free family farm and a fulfillment of Republican promises to western farm groups.

The War and Economic Growth.

The war undoubtedly stimulated the northern economy in many ways. At one time scholars believed that it accelerated overall American economic growth and marked the basic shift of the American economy from an agricultural to an industrial base. It is now clear, as we saw in Chapter 9, that the structural transformation from rural-agricultural to urban-industrial was already well underway by 1860; it did not require the trigger of the Civil War. But the issue of the war's stimulating effect on the economy is less clear. Figures that lump together data for both sections show a slowing down of the American economy during the 1860s, the war decade. Total commodity output in the United States was growing at the average rate of 4.6 percent a year in 1840–1859; during the period 1870–1899 it would increase annually by an average of 4.4 percent. In 1860–1869, however, it was only 2.0 percent, less than half these rates.

Given the economic surge in so many wartime northern industries, this is puzzling. But these figures add South to North, and during the war the South's economy suffered devastating blows from northern invasion and from the failure to repair and replace factories, railroads, barns, livestock, and other items that make up a nation's capital stock. Any gains in northern output, then, must be set against large declines in the South. But there are other good reasons for this outcome. With a million or so young men in the army, the Union lost a vast pool of productive labor, and total output inevitably suffered. Labor and capital were already fully employed in 1861, and government outlays for war were mostly at the expense of the private sector with little addition to the net output of the economy.

There is a related question to consider here. Did the political effects of the war have significant economic consequences? With the South out of the Union, it proved possible to at least agree on the building of a Pacific railroad, to pass a protective tariff, and to restructure the nation's banking system. Clearly, the Union government under the Republicans was more friendly and helpful to economic "progress" than its southern and Democratic-dominated predecessor. And this shift of power and ideology would persist for years beyond 1865, with inevitable effects on the country's future economic development. It is difficult to avoid the conclusion that although the war may not have been caused by sectional economic rivalry, its consequences may well have favored the predominant interests of the business-industrial classes over the agrarian classes.

Dissent.   Despite the war-kindled patriotism, dissent flourished in both the Union and the Confederacy. In each it would create serious difficulties for the government. Ironically, repression would be stronger in the North, which prided itself on its intellectual freedom, than in the South, with its tradition of intolerance.

Dissent in the North ranged from mild disagreement with Republican policies to violent opposition that bordered on treason. The so-called War Democrats often differed with Lincoln and the Republicans over the best way to achieve victory, but they followed the lead of Stephen Douglas in offering their whole-hearted support to the Union. The Little Giant died in June 1861, depriving the War Democrats of their outstanding leader; but to the end of the struggle, they were among the Union's staunchest supporters.

More critical of the administration's positions were the Peace Democrats. As the months passed, a segment of the opposition party became convinced that the Union must accept a negotiated peace that would restore the prewar sectional balance. At the depths of Union fortunes a substantial fringe of Peace Democrats even talked of letting the seceded states go, in effect conceding victory to the South.

Called Copperheads by their enemies, the Peace Democrats were especially numerous among immigrants in the urban centers and among the southerners who had settled in the free states of the Midwest before 1860. Ideologically, especially in the Midwest, they were often opponents of the centralizing tendencies of the Republicans and of the new powers of the federal government. Men such as Clement Vallandigham, Samuel S. Cox, George Pendleton, and Daniel Voorhees regarded the Lincoln administration as the agent of "revived Whiggery." They, along with most other Democrats, also denounced the administration's efforts to make slavery's abolition a part of the Union cause and to abridge freedom of speech and of press. They were dissenters as well against the cultural values that the Republicans represented. The Lincoln party, they held, was the embodiment of moralistic New England puritanism. Congressman Cox blamed the war on the New England "tendency to make government a moral reform association."

The Copperheads were not the only opponents of the Lincoln administration's policies. Anti-Union feelings in the slave states that remained in the Union—Delaware, Maryland, Kentucky, and Missouri—were often intense. In several border states during the war pro-Union neighbor fought pro-Confederate neighbor with a viciousness that sometimes went beyond anything found on the battlefields. In Missouri guerrilla war made the state resemble "Bleeding Kansas" during the 1850s as roving bands of irregulars attacked innocent and not-so-innocent citizens of the opposite persuasion. In suppressing the disorders in the border region, Union commanders frequently alienated the prosouthern populace and stirred up even greater dissatisfaction.

Inevitably, Lincoln had to consider how much dissent was permissible in a nation threatened with dissolution. The president was strongly committed to free speech. But his first responsibility, he felt, was to preserve the Union.

To head off his opponents and those he considered dangerous to the Union cause, Lincoln employed a combination of guile, persuasion, and coercion. Within his own party he had to contend with the Radicals, Republicans who fervently opposed slavery and believed that the president was not moving fast enough or firmly enough against the South. They particularly deplored his reluctance to use the war as an opportunity to destroy slavery and his unwillingness to employ blacks in the armed forces. Republican conservatives pulled the other way, insisting that the war to restore the Union must not be "abolitionized." To attack slavery would only drive the border states out and confirm southern determination to resist. Lincoln dealt with the opposing wings of his party, as he explained at one point, by carrying "a pumpkin in each end of the bag." In his cabinet this meant balancing Seward against Chase and seeing to it that neither prevailed. In Congress this meant listening to all Republican voices, keeping his options open, and moving only when it helped the Union cause.

Dealing with dissenters outside the party was more difficult. The remaining Democrats in Congress were often a thorn in the president's side. Several historians believe that a functioning two-party system during the war was a significant northern advantage over the South. It kept opposition to the administration within the bounds of party conflict, they say, and prevented it from becoming destructive and irresponsible. On the other hand, in the South, without a working party system, attacks on the Davis administration quickly turned into damaging personal assaults on the president, which seriously undermined his authority. Whatever the case, to Lincoln, Democratic opposition at times seemed indistinguishable from disloyalty, and it was hard for him to resist wielding his authority as commander in chief to suppress his critics.

Civil Liberties During Crisis.

Lincoln's first response to the dangers of disloyalty came in mid-1861 when, to contain anti-Union sentiment in several districts of the country, he suspended the writ of habeas corpus, a fundamental constitutional protection against unlawful imprisonment. In September 1862 he expanded the area in which the suspension applied and authorized the arrest by military commanders of all "Rebels and Insurgents, their aiders and abettors within the United States, and all persons discouraging volunteer enlistments, resisting militia drafts, or guilty of any disloyal practice." All told, the Union government arrested about 15,000 civilians during the war for disloyal activities, espionage, sabotage, or some other action detrimental to the Union cause. A number of times it also interfered with freedom of the press by excluding "disloyal" newspapers from the mail and on a few occasions shut down papers accused of hurting the Union cause. None of this was admirable behavior for a democratic government. Yet, all told, given the serious danger to the nation's survival, the government and the military avoided excess in suppressing dissent.

The most famous, or infamous, breach of civil liberties by the Lincoln administration was the arrest of Clement Vallandigham. In May 1863 the former congressman, campaigning for the Democratic nomination for governor of Ohio, deliberately provoked the government by denouncing the war as a failure, demanding repudiation of the Emancipation Proclamation, and calling for a negotiated peace with the Confederacy. General Burnside, then military commander in Ohio, promptly arrested Vallandigham and a military commission sentenced him to prison for the duration of the war.

The incident embarrassed Lincoln. It made the administration seem despotic while at the same time converting the ex-congressman into a free-speech martyr. On the other hand, the president did not see how he could ignore those people who threatened Union survival. "Must I shoot a simple minded soldier boy who deserts," he wrote a group of Democrats who protested the Vallandigham arrest, "while I must not touch the hair of a wily agitator who induces him to desert?" Lincoln solved the problem by banishing the Ohio Democrat to the Confederacy. Vallandigham soon escaped to Canada and resumed his campaign for governor long distance. But he was no longer an embarrassment to the administration.

The Emancipation Proclamation.

The Lincoln administration's willingness to invade civil liberties is a further instance of war-inflated government power. Fortunately, repression did not become a permanent feature of American political life. And in race relations, the use of government war powers worked a profound, permanent, and beneficent change.

Lincoln and the Radicals of his party differed on the question of slavery. As part of a Union-first policy, the president initially tried to steer clear of the issue. As long as the border slave states might join the Confederacy, Lincoln sought to focus the public mind on reuniting the nation rather than on ending the "peculiar institution." When General John C. Frémont, the former Republican presidential candidate, proclaimed in August 1861 that all slaves held by rebels within his Missouri command were free, Lincoln overruled him. The president also refused to use a feature of the Second Confiscation Act of 1861 that allowed the emancipation of captured slaves employed by the Confederacy against the Union. When Horace Greeley publicly criticized him for his inaction against slavery, Lincoln replied that his "paramount object" in the struggle was "to save the Union,. . .not either to save or destroy slavery."

But Lincoln and the Radicals were both at the mercy of circumstances. To begin with, blacks were not passive observers of emancipation. In the North black abolitionists joined their white colleagues in asserting that the war was a struggle over slavery and that to win it the Union must destroy the hateful institution. Slavery, Frederick Douglass proclaimed, was "a tower of strength" to the Confederacy. "The very stomach of this rebellion is the negro in the condition of a slave. Arrest that hoe in the hands of the negro and you smite the rebellion in the very seat of its life."

Even more compelling than the words of free northern blacks were the deeds of southern slaves. Despite the absence from the farms and plantations of thousands of young white men, slaves generally continued to work at their accustomed tasks: They did indeed serve as "the very stomach" of the rebellion. They failed to rebel because resistance in the heavily armed and militarized wartime South would have been suicidal. But they did not acquiesce. When Union armies drew near, the odds changed dramatically, and blacks showed their real feelings. Black refugees in the thousands fled to the Union lines. At first federal officials did not know what to do with these homeless and destitute people, since slavery was still legal and they were still the property of white owners. Faced with this situation, General Benjamin F. Butler shrewdly called them "contraband of war" and paid them to work as free laborers on military fortifications. Other military commanders, following Butler's lead, employed thousands of "contrabands" at military jobs. Other refugees were set to work growing cotton for northern mills or took jobs with private employers for money wages. Long before the end of the war a substantial part of the South's slaves had, in effect, liberated themselves from bondage.

More than informal self-liberation, however, was required to demolish the pernicious institution as a legal system beyond all possibility of resurrection. Lincoln originally hoped that compensated emancipation and colonization in either Africa or Central America would finish slavery. At one point he pushed a measure through Congress appropriating a half million dollars to settle freed slaves on an island off Haiti. But blacks were hostile to colonization, and in the border states slaveholders proved unwilling to consider freeing their slaves even if paid. Lincoln now had to consider simply ending slavery—an institution representing $4 billion worth of private property—by direct action under presidential war powers. However much he despised slavery, it was a momentous step to take, and he was reluctant to act.

The hope that the destruction of slavery would shorten the war finally tipped the balance in favor of emancipation by federal proclamation. Three considerations worked powerfully on the president. One was Frederick Douglass's point: the reliance of the Confederacy on slave labor. If the slaves knew that the federal government intended to set them free, they would cease to be a source of strength for the Confederacy. Another consideration was the potential value of black soldiers. If the North could tap this human reservoir, it could offset the immense losses on the battlefields and the declining zeal of white volunteers. A final factor was the moral advantage of turning the war for the Union into a war for human freedom. If the Union cause were identified with the destruction of slavery, it would be difficult for any European power to aid the Confederacy.

By July 1862 Lincoln had concluded that a proclamation of emancipation was "absolutely essential for the salvation of the Union." He postponed making his intentions known, however, fearing that if the news came at a time of military difficulties, it would be taken as an act of desperation. On September 22, following Lee's defeat at Antietam, he issued a preliminary emancipation proclamation declaring that on January 1, 1863, in every part of the South then still in rebellion, all slaves would be "thenceforward and forever free." As scheduled, on New Year's Day, 1863, the final Emancipation Proclamation took effect. Technically, it affected only those places where federal law could not be enforced—the Confederacy. It said nothing about slavery in the border states, and had the Union lost the war, it would have become a symbol of futility. But the Union won, of course, and the proclamation in the end effectively sounded the death knell for slavery all over the United States.

It also, as hoped, favorably affected the Union's standing abroad. Henry Adams, serving as his father's secretary at the American legation in London, wrote home after news of the proclamation reached Britain: "The Emancipation Proclamation has done more for us here than all our former victories and all our diplomacy."

Behind the Lines.

The war caused dramatic changes in civilians' lives. In the South it produced great hardship for virtually every citizen. As prices rose, as transport broke down, as the blockade took effect, southern living standards deteriorated. In Richmond a clerk in the Confederate War Department complained bitterly in 1863 that the inhabitants of the city were "almost in a state of starvation" though there was abundant food in the Confederacy as a whole. In Mobile, food riots, led by women carrying banners reading "Bread or Blood" and "Bread and Peace," broke out in 1863. All through the South tea and coffee, both imported items, became scarce; and southern consumers turned to parched wheat, corn, peanuts, and even acorns as substitutes. When commodities were available, they often sold at prices far beyond the means of the average consumer.

The North, too, experienced an inflationary surge. Prices rose faster than money wages, reducing the average worker's real income by about 20 percent and causing some labor unrest behind northern lines. But the effects were less extreme and never seriously threatened social order.

Women and the War.

Northern women were significant beneficiaries of the war. Before 1861, employment opportunities for women had been limited. With thousands of able-bodied men now in the Union armies, traditional sex barriers weakened. Many women joined the vastly expanded War and Treasury departments as secretaries, copyists, and clerks. In the private sector the number of women factory operatives, schoolteachers, and clerical workers also increased. Unfortunately, unskilled women workers were among those most seriously hurt by rising prices.

One of the most important breakthroughs for women was the creation of a female nursing profession. Though Florence Nightingale, an Englishwoman, had already proved the competence of women as military nurses during the 1850s Crimean War in Europe, male authorities resisted their use in Union military hospitals. They did not count on the determination and patriotism of strong-willed women such as Clara Barton and Dorothea Dix, who insisted on sharing the work and sacrifices of the war effort. In the end some 10,000 white women served as nurses in the North receiving $12 a month. About 4,000 black women worked for the Union as practical nurses, cooks, laundresses, and orderlies at $10 a month. Dix was appointed superintendent of women nurses for the Union army. Though women on both sides organized societies to aid the war effort, only in the North were these carried beyond the local level.

Many of the gains in paid employment for northern women were temporary. After 1865, as government departments contracted and men returned to civilian life, women were forced back into their parlors or kitchens. But the Civil War did much to establish nursing as a profession for women and to develop formal training and certification in that field. Clara Barton, who founded the American Red Cross twenty years after the Civil War, noted that by the time the war ended, "Woman was at least fifty years in advance of the normal position which continued peace. . .would have assigned her."

The lives of southern white women were altered by the war even more than those of their sisters in the North, though not primarily through long-term institutional change. With such a large proportion of white males off to war, southern women had to take over more and more of the management of the region's farms. They also flocked to the South's factories to take up the slack. When, as the war wound down, Union troops approached their neighborhoods, slaves fled the farms, plantations, and cities, leaving white women from slaveholding families without the help they had always counted on. Even before the fighting ceased, white southern women had begun to experience the drastic collapse of living standards that would mark the defeated region for many decades after 1865.

The Last Years of Battle

Lee's defeat of Hooker at Chancellorsville in May 1863 lifted the spirits of the entire Confederacy. Yet the South's situation, taken as a whole, did not seem encouraging. In the West, Grant was advancing on Vicksburg and would soon place that strategically important Mississippi city under siege. Along the Atlantic coast the Union was preparing to attack Charleston. All through the Confederacy, prices were soaring; the blockade's noose was growing tighter. Something must be done to prevent the South's collapse.

With some misgivings, the Richmond government adopted Lee's plan to invade the North. This move could relieve the pressure in the West, skim much-needed supplies from the prosperous northern countryside, encourage the peace forces in the North, and perhaps even lead to the capture of Washington or Philadelphia. On June 15 General Robert Ewell's corps, under Lee's overall command, forded the Potomac heading north. The remainder of the Army of Northern Virginia soon joined it, and together the combined Confederate force swept across the Mason-Dixon Line into Pennsylvania. As the Confederates advanced they levied tribute on local storekeepers, farmers, and bankers, and destroyed railroad property and Republican Congressman Thaddeus Stevens's iron works. Lee's advance alarmed the entire Union. Having lost faith in Hooker, Lincoln placed George G. Meade in command of the Army of the Potomac to face the threat.

Gettysburg.   The choice was a good one: Meade was solid, though neither colorful nor aggressive. Moving north parallel and to the east of Lee, Meade and the Confederates accidentally converged at Gettysburg, a small town fifty miles from the Pennsylvania state capital at Harrisburg. Meade's men dug in on ridges both to the south and to the north of town and prepared to face the Confederate attack. The 88,000 Federals not only outnumbered Lee's 75,000 but also had superior artillery.

The battle was a seesaw affair lasting three full days (July 1–3, 1863). Lee's forces came close to sweeping the Federals off their position several times. The fighting was exceptionally bloody, some of it hand to hand. Union artillery was devastating and so were Union rifles. The replacement of the smooth-bore musket by the far more accurate rifle as the standard infantry weapon gave the defense a tremendous advantage. Masses of infantry charging an entrenched enemy were ripped to pieces by the minié balls (lead bullets that expanded to fit the rifled barrel) of the defenders' weapons. It was the misfortune of the Confederates that Lee believed in the concept of the offensive-defensive—fighting what was at heart a defensive war by aggressive attacks on the enemy to discourage his effort to destroy the Confederacy. In the new era of the rifle this approach produced ferocious casualties, and so it was at Gettysburg. Each brave charge of the gray-clad Confederates was sent stumbling back after fearful carnage.

On the last day of battle the Confederates launched forty-seven regiments, 15,000 men, under General George Pickett of Virginia against the Union center perched on ominously named Cemetery Ridge. The men in gray advanced across the open field against murderous artillery fire and swept to the top of the Union emplacement. Then, their momentum exhausted, they reeled back, leaving behind several thousand dead and wounded in the field.

Pickett's charge was the last spasm of Confederate strength. Lee expected Meade to counterattack, but the Federals were almost as exhausted as the Confederates and sat tight. Seizing this opportunity to disengage safely, Lee ordered a general retreat. Soon he and his ragged army were safely back in Virginia.

Lee's defeat at Gettysburg coincided with Grant's capture of Vicksburg following a long campaign and costly siege. Then, in the fall of 1863, Grant and General George H. Thomas won the battles of Lookout Mountain and Missionary Ridge and finally pushed the Confederates out of ravaged Tennessee. Called to command all the Union forces, Grant came east in March 1864 to confront Lee. In the next months he aimed sledgehammer blows at Lee and his lieutenants in the densely forested country between Washington and Richmond. The gains in ground were negligible, and the losses on both sides were appalling. Yet Grant realized that the attrition was easier for the Union to bear than for the enemy. Southern manpower was by now all but exhausted; the North, though weary, still had human reserves.

"Johnny Reb" and "Billy Yank."   Although Gettysburg had been the war's turning point, many dismal months of fighting remained. The chief sufferers toward the end, as in the beginning, were the common soldiers of the Union and the Confederacy. Of the two, "Billy Yank" had the easier time, especially after the North's factories began to operate at high gear. The resources of the Union assured him enough food and clothing to keep the inner and outer man reasonably content. But his life was no picnic. Being a Union soldier involved long periods of hard foot-slogging over rough roads in every sort of weather, days of boredom in bivouac, followed, finally, by terrifying exposure to flying lead and iron. If wounded, his chances for survival were poor. The medical profession did not use anesthesia and was ignorant of the sources of infection. Many of the injured died of sepsis, shock, gangrene, or loss of blood. Many who survived battle were swept away by diseases picked up in unsanitary camps or as a result of exposure and exhaustion.

"Johnny Reb" experienced all these afflictions and several more besides. The southern soldier often lacked adequate shoes, clothing, and food. Despite Confederate ingenuity in manufacture and supply, much of his equipment, including his rifle and ammunition, was captured from the Yankees. There was seldom enough to go around.

The men of both armies had their good moments. Within units, many lifelong friendships were forged in camp and in the heat of battle. But however warmly veterans later recalled their fighting days, soldiering was not an occupation that many men cared to stay at indefinitely, and in both armies the desertion rates were stupendous. In all, 200,000 Union men and 104,000 Confederates deserted, almost 10 percent of all Yankees and 13 percent of all "Rebs."

Black Soldiers.   One source of northern strength denied the South was the manpower of black Americans. Defenders of equality strongly favored the use of black troops. As Frederick Douglass declared: "Once let the black man get upon his person the brass letters, U.S.; let him get an eagle on his button, and a musket on his shoulder, and bullets in his pocket, and there is no power on earth which can deny that he has earned the right to citizenship." But many white Northerners were immovable bigots who feared the very consequences that Douglass welcomed. In February 1863 forty-three Democratic congressmen signed a statement condemning Republican plans to enlist black soldiers as a plot to establish "the equality of the black and white races."

As it became more and more difficult to fill the depleted ranks of the Union Army, however, the opposition faded. Why not share the burden of dying for the Union with one of the chief beneficiaries of the war, many whites began to ask. By early 1863, with Lincoln's enthusiastic support, the War Department authorized the creation of black regiments composed of northern free blacks and, in larger numbers, of ex-slaves freed by the Emancipation Proclamation. At first the Confederate government declared that any captured member of a black regiment, whether white officer or black private, would be severely punished. But when Lincoln threatened to retaliate against captured Confederates, the Richmond government backed down. Still, the Confederates never accepted the legitimacy of black troops fighting against them and often treated captured black soldiers brutally. At Fort Pillow in Tennessee black soldiers who had surrendered were massacred by their Confederate captors.

Black troops fought bravely in many bloody engagements. In June 1863 black soldiers recruited from among "contrabands" beat back a Confederate attempt to break through Union defenses at Milliken's Bend near Vicksburg, Mississippi. A month later, two days after the New York draft riots, the 54th Massachusetts, a black regiment, attacked the Confederate earthworks at Fort Wagner outside Charleston. The attackers failed but sustained heavy casualties in what every observer called a valiant effort. Declared the *Atlantic Monthly*: "Through the cannon smoke of that dark night the manhood of the colored race shines before many eyes that would not see."

Yet black troops were often prevented from serving in combat. Placed almost invariably under white officers and treated initially as second-class soldiers in matters of pay, bounties for service, and other benefits, black troops nevertheless established a record for courage and enterprise equal to any group in the Union army. In March 1863 Lincoln called black troops "very important, if not indispensable" to the Union war effort. By the end of the fighting the Union armed forces had enrolled 179,000 black soldiers and another 20,000 black sailors.

The valor of foreign-born and black fighting men had favorable effects on ethnic and racial attitudes in the North. Antiforeign sentiment declined. Racial bigotry continued, but the legal and social positions of northern blacks improved. Midwestern legislatures repealed state laws discriminating against free blacks or denying them the right to reside within state borders. Several cities ended the common practice of segregating blacks on streetcars and in schools. America scarcely became a racial paradise, but the shining record of black troops fighting for the Union made many white citizens reconsider their prejudices.

The Election of 1864.   The lessening of ethnic conflict in the North was not matched by a decline in political strife. Nobody proposed passing over the presidential election of 1864 in the interest of national harmony. At Baltimore the Republicans renominated Lincoln and chose Andrew Johnson, the Tennessee Unionist Democrat, as his running mate. Johnson's selection was intended to reach out to non-Republicans, and to reinforce this strategy the delegates renamed their party the National Union Party. The Democrats turned to General McClellan as their presidential candidate. McClellan was a war Democrat, but his running mate, George Pendleton of Ohio, supported a negotiated peace with the South, as did the Democratic platform. During the campaign the Republicans charged their opponents with disloyalty, and they were not completely wrong. The Richmond government yearned for Democratic victory, and southern agents secretly poured money into the campaigns of midwestern Democrats. For a time the Democrats believed they could ride to victory on the wave of discouraging northern defeats during the late spring—the Wilderness, Spotsylvania, Petersburg, and the Crater. Lincoln himself was pessimistic and thought it "exceedingly probable that this Administration will not be reelected."

But then the military tide turned. In early May a Union army of 100,000 men led by William T. Sherman cut south from Tennessee and advanced on Atlanta, Georgia, a major rail junction and manufacturing center. Through much of July and all of August Sherman halted before the city while he and his Confederate foe, John B. Hood, maneuvered for advantage. Then on September 2, Union troops marched into the abandoned city. Sherman telegraphed the president: "Atlanta is ours, and fairly won." On August 23, meanwhile, the Union navy under Admiral David G. Farragut captured Mobile, shutting down a major port for Confederate blockade runners. In the Shenandoah Valley of Virginia, the Union cavalry commander, Philip Sheridan, won a smashing victory against Jubal Early's troops in late September. These victories were reflected in the polls. On November 8 the Lincoln–Johnson ticket swept the electoral college by 212 to 21 and won a popular majority of 400,000 votes.

Last Battles, the Last Casualty.   The months following the election saw the rapid collapse of southern hopes. On November 15 Sherman and his veteran army left Atlanta heading east for Savannah on the Atlantic coast. Before departing the city, the general ordered everything of military worth burned. The flames got out of control, and a third of Atlanta went up in smoke.

Sherman's "march to the sea" was considered foolhardy by many military experts. Cutting himself off from his supply bases and advancing through the core of "secessia" could spell disaster. Sherman rejected the doubters: He would survive by living off the country while cutting a swath of destruction through the heart of Dixie. The general had a theory of warfare that, alas, would see much application in our own day. Winning wars, he believed, was not merely a matter of winning battles and killing enemy soldiers. It was also instilling fear into the enemy people and destroying their morale. Fortunately, in 1864–1865, this did not yet mean brutal extermination of civilians. But it did mean massive destruction of property. Sherman's men demolished everything in a fifty-mile belt on either side of their march. One of their favorite targets was southern railroads. Yankee foragers ("bummers") also destroyed fences, crops, and farmhouses. Another Yankee target was slavery. Union troops marching to Savannah liberated every black person in sight. Before long Sherman's troops were being trailed by a column of thousands of liberated slaves, the able-bodied and lame, the young and old, men and women.

On December 22 Sherman reached Savannah and turned north, heading for a rendezvous with Grant and the Army of the Potomac. Through South Carolina he continued to apply his "total war" tactics. One result was the destruction by fire of Columbia, the capital of the state. In the West, meanwhile, General George Thomas had smashed Hood's army at Nashville. Grant, too, was finally able to achieve the breakthrough he had long sought south of Washington. During the early weeks of 1865 Grant pressed hard against Lee in Virginia. In early April, with the help of Sheridan's cavalry, he took the important center of Petersburg, which had eluded him for many months. Lee and his army slipped away, but by now southern morale had virtually collapsed. President Davis proposed to recruit black troops to shore up the faltering Confederate cause, promising these men freedom for themselves and their families in exchange for risking their lives. It is doubtful if many black men would have fought for the Confederacy under these terms, but the issue was now moot. On April 2 Confederate officials began to flee Richmond to avoid capture by Grant's army. The following day, with the city burning, the Federals arrived in the Confederate capital. The first blue-clad troops to enter were the men of the all-black Fifth Massachusetts Cavalry.

On April 7 Robert E. Lee—his army hungry, demoralized, and encircled—asked Grant for terms. On Sunday, two days later, the two commanders met at the crossroads hamlet of Appomattox Courthouse and agreed on surrender terms. Grant was generous. The Confederate officers and men were to be released on their promise not to take up arms again. The Confederates would surrender all weapons and war materiel, but the men might keep their personal equipment, including their horses and mules. These, Grant said, they would need to help them "work their little farms." The brief ceremony over, 26,000 Confederates laid down their arms.

Lincoln came to the Confederate capital in early April to view the prize of four years' outlay of Union blood and treasure. In the next few days his mind ran much to the problems of political reconstruction, and after his return to Washington he made a major address on the subject. On April 14, 1865, the happy though tired chief executive went with his wife, Mary, and some friends to the theater in Washington to see the British comedy *Our American Cousin*. During the third act a dark-haired man entered the presidential box, fired a single shot at Lincoln, and leaped to the stage. Amid the confusion and the shrieks, he shouted something that sounded like *"Sic Semper Tyrannis"* ("Thus always to tyrants"), the Virginia state motto, and escaped. Early the next morning Abraham Lincoln died.

The assassin was John Wilkes Booth, an actor and Confederate sympathizer who, with a few other disgruntled southerners, had concocted a plot to destroy the man they held responsible for Confederate defeat. The plotters also intended to assassinate Seward, Vice President Johnson, and other high Union officials. Booth was cornered in Virginia on April 26 and either shot himself or was shot by a zealous Union soldier. He died before disclosing the full conspiracy; false rumors of complicity by Secretary Stanton or the Confederate leaders soon gained wide circulation.

Conclusions

The war was over; but was an era also over? Had the war transformed American life?

The war did not change the United States from an agricultural to an industrial society. That process was already underway before 1860 and would not be completed until well after 1865. Meanwhile, the events of 1861–1865 did fuse the country into a more coherent social and economic whole. It made possible a transcontinental railroad and created a national banking system and a new national currency. It trained thousands of men to manage large-scale operations and mass movements of people and goods—talents that when applied to private enterprise would help to create modern "big business" and further integrate the country. Though it took years beyond 1865 for the full effects to work themselves out, the war also helped to universalize the commercial values of the Northeast. The South would be slow to embrace fully the new ethos; southern intellectuals well into the twentieth century would resist Yankee acquisitiveness. But for good or ill the rest of the country would find the North's hustle and "get-ahead" more acceptable after 1865 than before. Even the intellectuals who had been emphatically critical before 1860 found liberal capitalist society more palatable after the experience of 1861–1865.

The war also ended for all time the threat of secession. States' rights would continue to be an issue in American political life, but never again would one part of the nation threaten to leave the Union.

Finally, and most important, the war destroyed slavery. It did not end problems of racial adjustment; they are still with us today. But it did sweep away a benighted, oppressive institution that rigidly prescribed the relations of the races and replaced it with alternatives that, however imperfect, permitted reform and improvement.

ONLINE RESOURCES

"The Civil War and Emancipation" *http://www.pbs.org/wgbh/aia/part4/4p2967.html* On this site, read about the plight of slaves and African-American freed people, the impact of the Emancipation Proclamation, and the experiences of African-American Civil War soldiers. On the "related entries" section is a link to the full text of the Emancipation Proclamation and a personal account of a former slave in an Army camp.

"Selected Civil War Photos" *http://memory.loc.gov/ammem/cwphtml/cwphome.html* Over 1,100 photos of the Civil War fill this Web site. These photos depict military units, battle preparation, and the aftermath of warfare.

"Civil War Women: Primary Sources on the Internet" *http://scriptorium.lib.duke.edu/women/ cwdocs.html#1* This site contains a wealth of primary-source documents that address women's experiences during the Civil War. These documents include diaries, letters, memoirs, photos, and prints.

"The Emancipation Proclamation" *http://www.archives.gov/exhibits/featured_documents/ emancipation_proclamation/index.html* See the original document and read the full text transcript of the important document. Also, this site contains one scholar's view on the proclamation's meaning and significance.

Hearts at Home: Southern Women in the Civil War *http://www.lib.virginia.edu/small/exhibits/ hearts/* On this online exhibit, explore the world of southern women during the Civil War by reading letters to and from the home front, poetry, and newspaper clippings. Learn about women's work during the war, their feelings about the war, and ways in which it affected their daily lives.

The Strain of War *http://docsouth.unc.edu/leconteemma/leconte.html* This diary entry of a South Carolina woman describes the social conditions of the war including lack of goods, high prices, and the emotional and financial losses she experienced as a result of the war.

Illinois Alive: Illinois and the American Civil War *http://history.alliancelibrarysystem.com/ IllinoisAlive/cw.cfm* Learn the impact the Civil War had on a northern state through extant military correspondence, letters from soldiers, and description of Illinois towns.

The Civil War in Georgia *http://www.cviog.uga.edu/Projects/gainfo/civilwar.htm* With primary documents, maps, and eyewitness accounts, this site gives information on Sherman's decisive Atlanta Campaign and his "March to the Sea." Of special interest are the full text of his original field orders and his letters to Union General Ulysses S. Grant.

Assassination of President Abraham Lincoln *http://lcweb2.loc.gov/ammem/alhtml/alrintr.html* This site offers a general overview of President Lincoln's assassination. A timeline details the event, and a gallery section provides contemporary artwork and newspaper accounts reflecting American's reaction to the death.

16
Reconstruction

What Went Wrong?

1863	Lincoln announces his Ten-Percent Plan for Reconstruction
1863–65	Arkansas and Louisiana accept Lincoln's conditions, but Congress does not readmit them to the Union
1864	Lincoln vetoes Congress's Wade-Davis Reconstruction Bill
1865	Johnson succeeds Lincoln; The Freedmen's Bureau overrides Johnson's veto of the Civil Rights Act; Johnson announces his Reconstruction plan; All-white southern legislatures begin to pass Black Codes; The Thirteenth Amendment
1866	Congress adopts the Fourteenth Amendment, but it is not ratified until 1868; The Ku Klux Klan is formed; Tennessee is readmitted to the Union
1867	Congress passes the first of four Reconstruction Acts; Tenure of Office Act; Johnson suspends Secretary of War Edwin Stanton
1868	Johnson is impeached by the House and acquitted in the Senate; Arkansas, North Carolina, South Carolina, Alabama, Florida, and Louisiana are readmitted to the Union; Ulysses S. Grant elected president
1869	Woman suffrage associations are organized in response to women's disappointment with the Fourteenth Amendment
1870	Virginia, Mississippi, Texas, and Georgia are readmitted to the Union
1870, 1871	Congress passes Force Bills
1875	Blacks are guaranteed access to public places by Congress; Mississippi "redeemers" successfully oust black and white Republican officeholders
1876	Presidential election between Rutherford B. Hayes and Samuel J. Tilden
1877	Compromise of 1877: Hayes is chosen as president, and all remaining federal troops are withdrawn from the South
By 1880	The share-crop system of agriculture is well established in the South

Almost no one has had anything good to say about Reconstruction, the process by which the South was restored to the Union and the nation returned to peacetime pursuits and relations. Most contemporaries judged it a failure. To many southern whites it seemed a time when Dixie was subjected to a cruel northern occupation and civilization itself was buried under an avalanche of barbarism. For the freedmen—as the former slaves were collectively called—the period started with bright promise but ended in bitter disappointment, with most blacks still on the bottom

353

rung of society. Contemporary northerners, too, generally deplored Reconstruction. They had hoped it would remake the South on the national model. But it did not, and many were relieved when the last federal troops withdrew in 1877 and the white South once more governed itself.

Nor have later Americans generally thought well of Reconstruction. A half century ago most historians accused the Republicans who controlled Reconstruction after the Civil War of being blinded by vindictiveness and botching the job. Scholars of the next generation rejected this view, but believed the chance to modernize and liberalize southern society had been missed because the North had neither the will nor the conviction to take the bold steps needed. More recently some historians have declared that by failing to guarantee the political rights of the freedmen and provide them with land, the North sold out the black people, leaving them little better off than before the Civil War.

Obviously, then, from many points of view, Reconstruction has seemed a failure. Were the results as bad as most critics have believed? And if so, what went wrong?

The Legacy of War

A month after Appomattox, Whitelaw Reid, a correspondent for the Republican paper, the *Cincinnati Gazette,* went south to see what the war had done to Dixie. Reid was struck by the devastation he encountered. Hanover Junction, near Richmond, he reported, "presented little but standing chimneys and the debris of destroyed buildings. Along the [rail]road a pile of smoky brick and mortar seemed a regularly recognized sign of what had once been a depot." Not a train platform or water tank had been left, he wrote, and efforts to get the road in running order were often the only improvements visible for miles. Elsewhere the picture was the same. Interior South Carolina, despoiled by General Sherman's army, "looked for many miles like a broad black streak of ruin and desolation." In the Shenandoah Valley of Virginia between Winchester and Harrisonburg, scarcely a horse, pig, chicken, or cow remained alive. Southern cities, too, were devastated. Columbia, capital of South Carolina, was a blackened ruin with not a store standing in the business district. Atlanta, Richmond, Selma, and other southern towns were also ravaged. All told, over $1 billion of the South's physical capital had been reduced to ashes or twisted wreckage.

Human losses were even more appalling. Of the South's white male population of 2.5 million in 1860, a quarter of a million (10 percent) had died of battle wounds or war-induced disease. Most of these were young men who represented the region's most vigorous and creative human resource. Of those who survived, many were physically maimed and many others were worn out emotionally.

The South's economic institutions were also shattered. Its banking structure, based on now-worthless Confederate bonds, had collapsed. Personal savings had been wiped out when Confederate currency lost all its value. Even more crushing, the region's labor system was in ruins. Slavery as an economic institution was dead, but no one knew what to replace it with. Many blacks remained on the farms and plantations and continued to plant, cultivate, and harvest. But many

THE FALL OF RICHMOND Vᵃ ON THE NIGHT OF APRIL 2ᴺᵈ 1865.

Richmond, Virginia, the Confederate capital, being abandoned by the Jefferson Davis government in the last days of the war.

others—whether to test their new found freedom, hunt for long-lost relatives, or just to take their first holiday—wandered the roads or fled to the towns, abandoning the land on which the South's economy was based.

The war had also left behind damaging resentments. After struggling for independence against the "tyrannical government in Washington" and "northern dominance" for four years, white southerners could not help feeling apprehensive, angry, and disappointed. Now, even more than in 1860, a weak South would be oppressed by the North, its arrogance reinforced by victory. Northerners, for their part, would not easily forget the sacrifices and losses they had suffered in putting down what they considered the illegal and unwarranted rebellion; nor would they easily forgive the "atrocities" committed by the Confederacy. At Andersonville, Georgia, for example, during July 1864, 31,000 Union prisoners had been confined in a sixteen-acre stockade, protected from the weather only by flimsy tents and fed on scanty rations. As many as 3,000 prisoners had died in a month, a rate of 100 a day. To the northern public the Confederate prison officials, and especially the camp commandant, Captain Henry Wirz, seemed beasts who must be punished.

The American people, then, faced a gigantic task of physical, political, and psychological restoration. By the usual measure, the period of revival, or Reconstruction, lasted for some twelve years, until 1877. It was a time of upheaval and controversy, as well as new beginnings. In its own day the problems associated with Reconstruction dominated the political and intellectual life of the country, and they have fascinated and repelled Americans ever since.

Issues and Attitudes

During the years of Reconstruction all Americans agreed that racial and political readjustments were necessary. But what changes should be made and how to make them deeply divided contemporaries, North and South, black and white, Republican and Democrat. People's views tended to cluster around five major positions: Radical Republican, northern conservative, southern conservative, southern Unionist, and southern freedman. Let us examine each of these.

Radical Republicans.   The group we call Radical Republicans, though never very large, was highly influential especially in the "upper North." Successors to the hard-liners who had pushed Lincoln to pursue the war more vigorously and attack slavery more forcefully, they believed that the defeated South must be made to recognize its errors, and forced to acknowledge that now it could no longer decide its own fate. Southerners could avoid northern wrath and show they deserved to be readmitted as citizens of the United States in a number of ways. At the very least, they must reject their former leaders and choose new ones who had not been connected with the Confederacy. They must take oaths of loyalty to the United States. They must reject all attempts to repay the Confederate debt incurred in an unjust cause. Most important of all, they must accept the fact that the former slaves were now free citizens and must be treated as the political equals of whites.

Many former slaves, Radicals felt, had worked and fought for the Union, and the nation must now help them through the difficult transition to full freedom. As to how this end could best be accomplished, not all Radicals agreed. A few held that it would be necessary for the freedmen to get land so they could support themselves independently. But at the very minimum they must be given the right to vote and, during the early stages of the change, must be protected against privation and exploitation. No doubt they would be grateful for the efforts of their Republican friends in defeating the slave power, destroying slavery, and defending them against those who do not accept the new situation. This gratitude would undoubtedly incline them to vote Republican. But that was all to the good. The Republican party was the great hope of the nation. It was the party of freedom and economic progress and not afraid to use government to encourage that progress. In a word, it was the party that had, since its founding, proved that it was the best embodiment of both the nation's moral and practical sense.

Northern Conservatives.   Northern conservatives were generally recruited from the prewar Democratic party. Most had opposed secession and supported the war, but now that it was over and secession defeated, the country, they held, must forget the past. Let southerners—white southerners, that is—determine their own fate. It was in the best American tradition to let local communities decide their own future without undue interference from the national government. The nation must confirm this great principle of local self-determination, and let the South back into the Union on its own terms.

As to the freedmen's question, the victorious North must not force black suffrage or social equality down the throats of the former Confederates. Almost all white Americans, they noted, believed that "Negroes" were ill-equipped to exercise the rights of citizens. The Radicals insisted on giving them the vote only because they wanted to secure continued control of the national government and guarantee the predominance of the values and goals of the Northeast, the nation's commercial-industrial region, against the very different interests and goals of the country's agricultural West and South. It was clearly hypocritical of the supposed champions of the freedmen, they noted, to be so timid in supporting Negro suffrage in the northern states, where such a stand was politically unpopular and where there were too few blacks to add to their voting strength. The country must reject such hypocrisy and restore peace and tranquility as quickly and completely as possible.

Southern Conservatives.

White southern conservatives could not condemn the "lost cause." Though vanquished by superior force, it was a noble cause and it had brought out the best in the southern people. The South must never forget the sacrifice and heroism of the gallant men in gray. Perhaps secession was a mistake, but that would never diminish the grandeur of the Confederate struggle.

But it was obviously necessary now to get back to the business of daily living. The South must be allowed to resume its traditional political relations with the rest of the states. It must be free to determine its own fate with a minimum of conditions. Above all, it must be permitted to steer its own course on race relations. The "carpetbaggers" who were descending from the North looking for easy money, and the southern renegade "scalawags" willing to betray their own people for the sake of power, were self-serving and contemptible. They did not understand or refused to accept southern traditions.

Admittedly, some changes had to be allowed. The South must recognize that blacks were no longer slaves and white southerners must make certain concessions to their private rights. But at least in the public realm these must be limited by their capacities. Above all, they must not be permitted to exercise political power. They were not the equal of whites. They could be duped and deceived by their professed "friends" into supporting the Republican party, but actually their interests would be best served by those who had always been the leaders of southern society and who remained their natural protectors.

Southern Unionists.

Another group who played a significant role in the debate over Reconstruction were Southern Unionists, who had rejected secession and often been persecuted in the Confederacy. They were, after 1865, at long last free to speak their minds. Now that the secessionists had been defeated, they felt they deserved recognition and favor. Unfortunately the ex-rebels were still in the majority. They said they had accepted the new circumstances of the South, but many of them had not, and the Unionists remained in a vulnerable position. At the very least it was necessary that they be protected by their northern friends against hostile unreconciled rebels. Moreover, they should be rewarded for their loyalty to the Union with an important place in the new southern order.

Southern Freedmen.   Southern freedmen believed that they deserved all the rights and privileges of free people as expressed in the Declaration of Independence. They had contributed to Union victory in war and had earned, they felt, the right to be treated as equals. They were also the largest group in the South truly loyal to the Union. Southern whites, with some exceptions, could not be trusted. They were unreconciled to defeat, and if the North failed to protect the freedmen and guarantee their rights as free men and women, these ex-Confederates would once more seize power and nullify the Union victory. The federal government, then, must continue for an indefinite period to take an active role in the process of southern Reconstruction.

Most did not expect white southerners to treat them as social equals; but they felt that they must have equality before the law and full civil rights, including, of course, the right to vote. They must also have economic independence, which meant not only the right to sell their labor in the open market but also to own their own land. Thousands of the South's best acres, abandoned by disloyal owners during the war, were controlled either by the Freedmen's Bureau or by the army. Giving the freedmen this land would enable them to secure their independence and prevent them from being kept in permanently subordinate positions. They also craved access to education. Literacy was an important tool for achieving economic independence. If the cost of a public school system meant that southern state taxes must rise, so be it.

Several of these positions overlapped. But it would clearly be difficult to reconcile those people who wanted to return to prewar conditions as quickly as possible and those who hoped to make social transformation a requirement for readmitting the South to the Union. In the next dozen years there would be fierce battles between the contending parties, some almost as passionate as the war itself.

Presidential Reconstruction

Even before Lee's surrender in 1865 the Lincoln administration confronted the problem of how to govern the conquered territory and subdued people. In 1862 the president appointed military governors for those parts of four Confederate states under federal control. But while military administrators might suffice for a while, they ran counter to the American tradition of civilian rule and could only be considered a temporary resolution of the problem.

Lincoln's Ten-Percent Plan.   Lincoln sought to keep in his own hands the process of restoring southern self-rule and normalizing the South's relations with the rest of the country. He believed this would be more efficient, but he also predictably preferred guiding the final stage of reuniting the Union himself. The president favored a lenient process, one that would not create too many hurdles to the South's readmission to the Union, impose severe punishment on white southerners, or require unrealistic changes of heart. He agreed, however, that any scheme had to guarantee the South's acceptance of slavery's demise.

Lincoln waited almost a year from the time of the Emancipation Proclamation to announce his plan for reconstruction. Issued on December 8, 1863, his Proclamation of Amnesty and Reconstruction, usually called the Ten-Percent Plan, offered full pardon and full restoration of all rights to white southerners who pledged future loyalty to the Union and accepted the abolition of slavery. Excluded from the pardon and restoration were high-ranking Confederate political and military leaders. When loyal southerners in any rebel state equaled at least ten percent of the number of voters in the 1860 elections, this group could convene and establish a new state government to supersede the old. The new state constitution adopted must accept emancipation, but it could also temporarily allow laws for the freed slaves "consistent . . . with their present condition as a laboring, landless, and homeless class." The state governments that met these conditions would be entitled to admission to the Union and to representation in Congress.

The Ten-Percent Plan did not please several important groups. Blacks and their allies condemned it for ignoring black suffrage and permitting southern governments to limit their full civil rights. The powerful Radical Republican faction in Congress deplored the easy requirements for amnesty of former rebels. The government should impose an "ironclad oath" on southerners, requiring them to declare that they had never willingly helped the Confederacy. Under the president's scheme far too many Confederate collaborators would be restored to full rights.

The differences between the president and Congress came to a head in early 1864 when Louisiana applied for readmission under terms close to Lincoln's blueprint. The state's March 1864 constitutional convention produced a new frame of government establishing a minimum wage and nine-hour day on all public works, adopting a progressive income tax, and creating a system of free public education. The delegates, however, also rejected black suffrage despite the president's suggestion that the vote be given to "some of the colored people . . . as for instance, the very intelligent, and especially those who have fought gallantly in our ranks."

The exclusion of all blacks from suffrage angered the Republican majority in Congress. In July 1864 they pushed through the tough Wade-Davis Manifesto, proposing to delay the reconstruction process until a majority of a given state's white males had pledged to support the United States Constitution. At that point, it said, elections would be held for a state constitutional convention with only those who had taken the Ironclad Oath permitted to vote. In addition, though it stopped short of requiring black suffrage, Wade-Davis proposed that the freed slaves be guaranteed equality before the law. Lincoln feared that the measure would force him to repudiate the Louisiana government and so pocket-vetoed it. But, he said in mock innocence, he had no objection if other southern states chose Wade-Davis rather than his own plan. Despite the disagreement with Congress, by the time of Appomattox Unionist governments recognized by Lincoln were operating in Louisiana, Arkansas, and Tennessee.

Johnson Takes Charge.   Lincoln's assassination profoundly altered the course of political reconstruction. Had he lived, his popularity, prestige, and flexibility might have induced Congress to accept major portions of his plan. And yet

Congress resented the war-swollen powers of the president, even Lincoln, and would certainly have insisted on playing a major role in restoring the Union. It seems unlikely that either side would have gotten its own way entirely. Lincoln's successor, however, had to confront this inevitable struggle with Congress without the martyred president's skills and popularity.

Like Lincoln, Johnson was an ambitious, self-made man from southern yeoman stock. He was not a Republican and had been put on the Union party national ticket in 1864 to attract War Democrats. He did not share the nationalist principles of the Republicans. Rather, he was a defender of local power, even states' rights. Nor did he share the antislavery views of many Republicans. He despised his state's privileged planter class and considered secession a plot to perpetuate the elite's power, but at the same time, he had little respect for blacks. A fierce democrat when it came to the rich and powerful, he drew the equality line at the white race.

Johnson lacked most of Lincoln's winning personal qualities. Lincoln was confident in his own abilities. Johnson suffered from severe self-doubts, a weakness that made him susceptible to flattery. Lincoln was gregarious. Johnson was a loner with few friends or close advisers. Lincoln was flexible, a natural compromiser. Johnson was a rigid man who could be cajoled out of a position, but when defied directly, refused to budge. This stubbornness, in turn, often drove potential allies into the waiting arms of Radical Republicans. The president's characteristics became apparent only gradually, however. At first the Radical Republicans, tired of dealing with the wily Lincoln, had rejoiced at Johnson's succession. As military governor of Tennessee during the war he had declared that "treason . . . must be made infamous and traitors . . . punished," and they concluded that he would be harder on the South than his predecessor.

During his first eight months in office Congress was not in session and the president had a relatively free hand in formulating Reconstruction policy. Johnson formally announced his Reconstruction plan in two proclamations issued on May 29, 1865. The first offered pardon and amnesty to participants in the rebellion who pledged loyalty to the Union and support for the end of slavery. All who took the oath would have returned to them all property confiscated by the Union government during the war, except for slaves. Exempted from this blanket pardoning process were fourteen classes of southerners who were required to apply individually for pardons from the president. These included most high Confederate officials and owners of taxable property worth more than $20,000. This last proviso reflected Johnson's southern yeoman prejudice against the old planter class as the source of disunion and secession.

The second proclamation designated William Holden as provisional governor of North Carolina and directed him to call a convention to amend the state's existing constitution so as to create a "republican form of government." Voters would be restricted to those who had taken the oath of allegiance; they would not include ex-slaves or any blacks. Johnson soon extended the same process to six other southern states while also recognizing the new governments of Louisiana, Arkansas, and Tennessee, three states Lincoln had already accepted back into the

An idealized portrait of Andrew Johnson. His photographs show a
coarser-featured man, an image more in keeping with his actual
origins and early life.

Union. Johnson made it clear that he expected the conventions to accept the abolition of slavery and pledge not to repay any public debts incurred in the Confederate cause. He also asked them to consider giving voting rights to a few educated
and property-holding blacks in order to "disarm" those clamoring for full civil
rights for ex-slaves. Otherwise they could decide for themselves what sort of government and laws they would adopt.

In the next few months Johnson chose provisional governors from among
each unreconstructed state's "loyalists" to manage the process he had prescribed.
He often turned to members of the old Whig elite. These men typically had been
skeptical of secession but had gone with their states when the decision to leave the

Union was made. Few favored any changes in the undemocratic and unprogressive systems of the prewar era; none supported civil equality for blacks. The governors wielded broad patronage power and, during their months in office, used it to win the support of the Old South's planter and merchant class regardless of their Unionism or willingness to accept a new social and political order.

Meanwhile, each of the unreconstructed states held elections for a convention and adopted new state constitutions. Each acknowledged the end of slavery and all, except stubborn South Carolina, pledged to repudiate its Confederate debts. No state conceded blacks the vote, however, though several revised their formulas for representation to favor the white small farmer counties over the plantation regions. Soon afterward, they held statewide elections for permanent governors and other officials and chose state legislators and congressional delegates.

During the summer and fall of 1865, conservative white southerners had reason to feel reassured that, despite Johnson's tough talk about disunionists and his disdain for the planters, the president did not intend to disturb their region's social and political systems. In August he overruled Freedmen's Bureau Commissioner Oliver Howard's Circular 13 setting aside forty-acre tracts of land for the freedmen to farm and ordered the return of land confiscated during the war from disloyal southerners. He also yielded to southern demands for removing black troops, whose presence whites considered a "painful humiliation" and a force for undermining plantation labor discipline. At the same time the president scattered pardons wholesale to those who applied to him directly. By 1866 he had given out almost 7,000 of these. Whatever his initial response to the old planter elite, the president had become the protector of the South's old social order.

The Johnson Governments.

During the months the "Johnson governments" operated without restraint from Washington, their deeds strengthened the Radicals and destroyed any possibility that Congress would accept the president's Reconstruction policy.

Several actions especially offended northern Republicans. In the elections for new state and federal officials southern voters selected few real Unionists. Chosen to represent the former Confederate states in the upcoming Congress were four Confederate generals, five Confederate colonels, six Confederate cabinet officers, fifty-eight former Confederate congressmen, and Alexander H. Stephens, former vice president of the Confederate States of America. Many of the newly elected state officials were also tainted with secession. It was natural for white southerners to turn to former secessionists for their leaders. But this blatant display of Confederate sympathies outraged many northerners.

The new state legislatures compounded the offense. Despite the president's recommendations, several refused to ratify the Thirteenth Amendment, passed by Congress in January 1865, that placed the abolition of slavery, hitherto based on Lincoln's Emancipation Proclamation, on a sound constitutional foundation. Mississippi and South Carolina also refused to repudiate their wartime state debts. None of the Johnson governments allowed even a handful of blacks to vote. But worst of all, each of them enacted a set of laws to govern race relations that jarred Union sensibilities.

These (Black Codes) did extend to the freedmen several rights of normal citizens. They legalized marriages between blacks, including earlier slave-era relationships; permitted ex-slaves to buy, own, sell, and otherwise transfer property; and gave the freedmen the right to appear, plead, and testify in court in cases involving fellow blacks. But the codes also sought to relegate the ex-slaves permanently to second-class legal, economic, and political status. Under the Black Codes, African American southerners could not offer their labor freely on the market. Mississippi required black workers to produce each January a written document showing they had a contract to work for the coming year. Laborers who left their jobs before a contract expired forfeited any wages already earned and could be arrested. "Vagrants"—defined as the idle, disorderly, and those who "misspend what they earn"—could face fines or forced plantation labor. The South Carolina code demanded a stiff annual tax for blacks working as anything other than farmers or servants. In Florida, blacks who broke labor contracts could be whipped, sold into indenture for up to one year, or placed in the pillory. In several states blacks were forbidden to bear arms, were subject to more severe punishment for given offenses than whites, and could not live or buy property in specified locations. Most states prohibited interracial marriage. Most rankling of all were apprenticeship laws, which allowed the courts to "bind out" black minors to employers for a period of time without their own consent or that of their parents. These seemed thinly disguised attempts to reinstate slavery.

One of the real advances afforded by the emancipation was the legal recognition of black marriages. After 1865, black men and women seized the opportunity to solemnize relationships begun under slavery or to contract new ones. Officiating at this wedding is a chaplain from the Freedmen's Bureau.

African Americans eloquently denounced the codes. One black man wrote the Freedmen's Bureau: "I think very hard of the former owners for Trying to keep my Blood when I kno that Slavery is dead." A black Union veteran exclaimed: "If you call this Freedom, what do you call Slavery!" Inevitably many white northerners considered the president's version of Reconstruction deplorable. Wendell Phillips prophetically noted that without the right to vote, blacks in the South would be consigned to "a century of serfdom." But nothing so offended northern Republican opinion as the Black Codes. The *Chicago Tribune* declared that the people of the North would turn one of the worst offending states, Mississippi, into a "frog pond" before they would allow its laws "to disgrace one foot of soil in which the bones of our soldiers sleep and over which the flag of freedom waves." Another critic called the codes "an outrage against civilization." Meanwhile, many northern congressmen were receiving almost daily reports from white southern Unionists that the former secessionists were crowing about how they once again had the upper hand and would make life difficult for their opponents. Simultaneously, northern travelers in Dixie recounted unpleasant experiences with unreconstructed "rebels." Hotels and restaurants often refused them service and individual southerners insulted them.

The outrage over the Johnson governments' policies and the Black Codes should not deceive us about the extent of racial liberalism in the nation at large. Northern Democrats were often blatant racists who had no scruples against appealing to the voters' prejudices and resisted every attempt to confer the franchise on blacks. Republicans, generally, were less bigoted and, in any case, believed that the freedmen's votes were needed to keep former rebels from regaining power in the South. But even many Republicans were reluctant to accord black Americans the full rights of citizenship, at least where they themselves lived. In the fall of 1865 three northern states—Connecticut, Wisconsin, and Minnesota—placed constitutional amendments on their ballots to allow the handful of black males within their borders to vote. A substantial minority of Republican voters opposed the changes, and together with the Democrats, helped defeat the black franchise in all three. In effect then, a majority of all northern white voters opposed letting blacks vote and this reality inevitably tempered the radical ardor of Republican politicians in districts where elections were closely contested.

Congress Takes Over

By the time the Thirty-Ninth Congress assembled on December 4, 1865, the Republican majority was determined to take over the process of southern reconstruction to assure that rebels would not get their way. Its first act was to reject the Congressional delegations sent by the Johnson governments to Washington. Prompted by the Radicals, the Clerk of the House, Edward McPherson, skipped the names of the newly elected southern congressmen as he called the roll. Immediately after, the two houses established a Joint Committee on Reconstruction to look into conditions in the South and consider whether any former

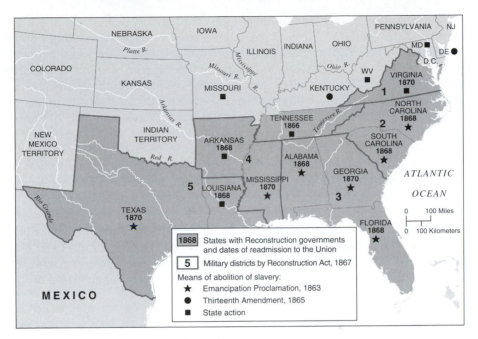

Reconstruction of the South, 1865–1877

Confederate states were entitled to representation. Consisting of fifteen Senators and Representatives, three of them Democrats, their views stretched across the political spectrum, although the "too ultra" Radical Charles Sumner was deliberately excluded.

Despite his policies, Johnson had still not completely alienated the Republican moderates and they listened to his conciliatory annual message with respect. For a time the Republican congressional centrists took charge. This changed abruptly when moderate Lyman Trumbull of Illinois introduced a bill to extend the life of the Freedmen's Bureau and broaden its authority.

Established in March 1865, just before the war ended, the bureau aided war refugees, both white and black, found employment for freedmen, and supplied transportation home for those displaced by the war. It had established hospitals and schools and drawn up guidelines for bringing ex-slaves into the free labor market. In enlarging the bureau's scope, the Trumbull bill gave Congress the additional power to protect freedmen against discrimination, including the right to punish state officials denying blacks their civil rights, and authorized it to build and run schools for the ex-slaves. It was generally considered a moderate measure.

The Civil Rights bill of 1865, on the other hand, was far-reaching in scope. It declared all persons born in the United States, including blacks (but not Indians), citizens, and specified their rights regardless of race. These included the right to make contracts, bring lawsuits, and enjoy the "full and equal benefit of all laws and proceedings for the security of person and property." To ensure that no state denied citizens these rights, it authorized federal district attorneys and marshals, as well as the Freedmen's Bureau, to sue in the federal courts. In many ways the law foreshadowed the civil rights measures of the mid-twentieth century.

Johnson refused to sign either bill. The Freedmen's Bureau, he said in his veto message, was a vast patronage boondoggle that would create a horde of bureaucrats to oppress ordinary citizens. Moreover, it violated the Constitution; never before had the federal government been called on to provide economic relief to individuals. The president soon after attacked the Civil Rights bill as another unwarranted extension of federal power. The bill was a "stride toward centralization and the concentration of all legislative powers in the national Government."

In the end Congress was unable to muster the two-thirds majority needed to pass the Freedmen's Bureau bill, though it managed to override the Civil Rights veto. The fight over the Freedmen's Bureau destroyed the hope of moderates that Johnson could be trusted with Reconstruction. It was the opening round of a struggle that lasted until the end of Johnson's term, with each new battle driving more and more moderates into the Radical camp.

The Fourteenth Amendment.

While Congress and the president fought for supremacy, the Joint Committee on Reconstruction set to work on its own comprehensive plan to restore Dixie to the Union. Even with the Thirteenth Amendment finally approved by the states and the Civil Rights bill enacted into law, Radicals worried that the rights of black Americans were vulnerable. Certainly, if it proved necessary to rely on the federal courts, they would have little security. Although it was not until April 1866 that the Supreme Court, in the case of *Ex Parte Milligan*, voided the Lincoln administration's wartime imposition of martial law on civilians in Indiana, the justices already seemed hostile to the Republican philosophy of federal supremacy. What would prevent them from striking down the Civil Rights Act or any other measure that Congress passed to protect the freedmen? With this in mind, the first initiative of the Joint Committee was to propose another amendment to the Constitution to put the principles of the Civil Rights bill beyond the reach of the president, the states, and unfriendly federal judges.

As finally hammered out and submitted to the states for adoption, the Fourteenth Amendment contained four clauses, the first two of which were of major significance. The original Bill of Rights had limited only the federal government's power over citizens. Now the Constitution would place restraints on the states as well. The first clause defined citizenship to include all those born or naturalized in the United States. It then declared that no state could make or enforce any law that abridged the rights of American citizens, or deprived any person of "life, liberty, or property without due process of law." Nor could any state "deny to any person within its jurisdiction the equal protection of the laws." In effect, individuals could not be executed, imprisoned, or fined by the states except through the normal processes of law with all their constitutionally protected procedures and safeguards, nor could the states treat any individual or class of individuals as inferior to others. Clause one vastly expanded federal power over the states and served in the end many purposes besides ensuring racial justice in the South.

Clause two, concerning suffrage, was not what the most radical of the Republican leaders wanted. Congress might have bluntly declared unconstitutional all political discrimination on racial grounds. Instead it deferred to continuing northern racial prejudice by a series of evasions. Rather than giving the vote outright to all adult male citizens, it merely declared that whenever a state denied any age-qualified male citizen the right to vote, that state's representation in Congress would be reduced proportionately. The South, with its large black population, would now have a strong incentive to grant full voting rights to black males. (Otherwise it would send far fewer representatives to Congress than its total population warranted.) Northern states, however, with few black residents, could continue to deny them suffrage without serious penalty. Not until after the adoption of the Fifteenth Amendment (1870) were "race, color, or previous condition of servitude" completely eliminated as legal grounds for denying adult men the vote, though, to the dismay of women activists, women were not admitted to the franchise.*

Congressional Reconstruction

To assure adoption of the new constitutional amendment, Congress made its passage by the southern state legislatures a condition of readmission to the Union. But this incentive did not work. By the end of 1866 the legislatures of Texas, South Carolina, Georgia, Florida, North Carolina, Arkansas, and Alabama had all rejected it. In fact, the ratification process dragged even in the North, and not until well into 1867 did the amendment receive the necessary approval by three-fourths of the states.

By now the president's abrasive personality and backward-looking views had alienated almost all the Republicans in Congress. But there still remained a nub of conservative Republicans. In April 1866 these leaders joined with moderate Democrats to form the National Union Executive Committee. In August they held a National Union Convention in Philadelphia to form a third party based on sectional reconciliation and immediate return of the southern states to the Union. The highlight of the convention was the affecting ceremony of Massachusetts and South Carolina delegates, representing the two sectional poles, marching into the convention hall in pairs, arm and arm.

Though the president gave the National Union movement his blessing, it came to little. For one thing, the conservative forces could not overcome the escalating southern intransigence confirmed by news from the South. In May an angry white mob invaded the black section of Memphis, killing forty-six people. In late

---

*The proposed amendment's two minor clauses (1) denied public office to those who had taken oaths of allegiance as state or federal officials and then served in the rebellion; and (2) repudiated any state debt incurred in aid of the Confederate cause.

July another white mob assaulted delegates to a black suffrage convention in New Orleans. Before federal troops could arrive, the attackers had murdered thirty-seven blacks and three of their white supporters. Here was proof, if any were needed, that the South would never accept the consequences of defeat without northern coercion.

Despite its poor prospects, the president campaigned aggressively for the National Union movement in the 1866 off-year elections. Against the advice of friends, he set out on a "swing around the circle," giving speeches attacking the Radicals as the country's real traitors, defending the South as loyal, justifying his generous pardoning policy, and even offering his life to save the Union and the Constitution. Wherever he went, his critics heckled him unmercifully and goaded him into rash, undignified replies. He probably did his cause more harm than good. Radical Republicans won a decisive victory almost everywhere. The new Congress would retain its three-to-one Republican majority.

But even before the Fortieth Congress convened, the second session of the Thirty-Ninth, its Republican leaders encouraged by the 1866 election mandate, passed the First Reconstruction Act (also called the Reconstruction Act of 1867). By December 1866 Johnson had lost all Republican support and the Radicals felt the time was ripe to replace all the Johnson state governments by a system that would finally express the will of the Union's most progressive forces.

The First Reconstruction Act swept aside the existing state regimes in the former Confederacy and divided the South into five military districts, each under a general who was empowered to use troops if necessary to protect life and property. The military commanders would supervise the choice of delegates to state conventions that would write new constitutions and establish new state governments. All adult males would be eligible for voting for the conventions regardless of race, except those excluded for participating in the rebellion. The new constitutions had to provide for a similar broad electorate for legislature, governor, and other public officials, and required that their work be accepted by a majority of the same, color-blind, pool of voters. When the new constitutions had been so ratified, when Congress had approved them, and when the new state legislatures had ratified the Fourteenth Amendment, the states would then be admitted to the Union and their delegations to Congress seated.

Johnson Impeached.
Radicals feared Johnson would use his appointment authority and general executive powers to frustrate their plans. And before long he did, removing several of the military commanders as too radical and issuing orders to others intended to negate Congress's intentions.

To hedge him in, Congress passed a series of additional measures in 1867. To prevent Johnson from again taking advantage of an interval between congressional sessions, in January it approved a bill that called the new Congress into special session immediately after the old one had expired. In March it passed, over Johnson's veto, the Tenure of Office Act requiring Senate consent for the dismissal of all federal officeholders appointed with Senate approval. A third measure required that all presidential orders to the army be issued through the general of the army. This happened to be war hero Ulysses Grant, a man who had come to support the Radical Republican position on Reconstruction. At the same time, to goad dilatory southern voters to take steps under the First Reconstruction Act, Congress passed the Second Reconstruction Act. A Third Reconstruction Act in July tightened control by the five military commanders over the provisional governments in the South and sought to broaden the rules excluding ex-Confederates from the Reconstruction process.

For some Radicals these measures still seemed insufficient to stop Johnson, and in January 1868 they attempted to remove him from office through impeachment. Not yet ready for such a drastic procedure, the moderates quashed the move in committee. But then Johnson handed his opponents their opportunity for a more serious impeachment effort. In August, during a congressional recess, the president suspended from office Secretary of War Edwin Stanton, a Radical inherited from Lincoln, and appointed Grant as interim secretary. In January 1868 the Senate refused to accept Stanton's dismissal, and Grant, against the wishes of Johnson, stepped down. Defiant, the president once more removed Stanton and replaced him with Lorenzo Thomas. But Stanton, egged on by congressional Radicals, barricaded himself in his office and refused to leave or to allow Thomas to enter. However ludicrous, the Stanton affair seemed to provide grounds for

In August 1866 President Johnson announced that "peace, order, tranquility, and civil authority now exist . . . in the United States." Dissatisfied with Johnson's idea of peace and order, the House voted his impeachment less than two years later. Here a packed gallery follows the trial of the century.

impeachment that had not existed before. The president, exclaimed one moderate, had "thrown down the gauntlet and says to us plainly as words can speak it: 'Try this issue now betwixt me and you: either you go to the wall or I do'." On February 24, 1868, the House formally voted to impeach the president by a strict party vote of 126 to 47.

The impeachment trial, conducted before the Senate sitting as a court, was the show trial of the century. The major charge against the president was his "unlawful" removal of Stanton. Attorney General Henry Stanbery, the president's counsel, argued that Stanton had been appointed by Lincoln, not Johnson, and so was not covered by the Tenure of Office Act. The law, moreover, was unconstitutional, and it was the right of the president to challenge it to bring it before the courts.

During the six weeks of the trial intense excitement reigned in Washington and the country. Radicals insisted that acquittal would be a victory for rebels and traitors. Democrats, and Johnson's few remaining moderate supporters within Republican ranks, claimed that conviction would mean that Congress had successfully usurped the power of the executive branch. The president's defenders also noted that the man next in line for the presidency was the president pro tempore of the Senate, the truculent Radical, Benjamin Wade.

On May 16, 1868, Johnson was acquitted by one Senate vote. Most historians believe that he should not have been impeached in the first place. There can be no question that he was stubborn and at times boorish, and that he used his executive power to impede Congress. Nor is there much dispute among scholars today that his racial policies were misguided. In a parliamentary system such as Britain's he would have been removed by a legislative vote of "no confidence." But the Founders had deliberately created an independently elected executive with the right to disagree with Congress. It seems unlikely that they intended impeachment to serve as a way to remove an official from office except for breaking the law or for gross incapacity. The Radicals in effect, then, were seeking implicitly to change the Constitution in a vital aspect.

Reconstruction in the South

The Election of 1868. Johnson still had almost a year to go before his term ended, but achieved little in the months remaining. During this period he spent much of his time maneuvering for the Democratic presidential nomination. The Democrats did not want him. In the West many preferred George Pendleton of Ohio, a Democratic senator who favored the "Ohio Idea," a scheme to relieve taxpayers' burdens and stimulate the economy by paying the large federal debt in paper money ("greenbacks"). Eastern Democrats claimed the Ohio Idea would call into question all debts, public and private, shake the financial markets, and set loose the forces of social anarchy. It took twenty-two ballots before Governor Horatio Seymour of New York, a "hard money" man, nosed out Pendleton. The "soft money" group was able to get the Ohio Idea incorporated into the party platform but, as soon as nominated, Seymour repudiated it.

The Republicans turned, not to their most militant wing, but to the center. The acquittal of Johnson had weakened the Radicals and they could not stop the nomination of Grant. General Grant had not opposed the Radicals' policies after 1865 but he was a pragmatist, rather than a zealot, and reassured the moderates. The Republican platform denounced the Ohio Idea as "repudiation" and a "national crime," and defended the civil rights of the freedmen in the South.

The election was remarkably close. In the South, armed and violent whites succeeded in intimidating many blacks from going to the polls. In eleven Georgia counties with black majorities no votes at all were recorded for Grant. But the Republicans did manage to carry all but two states in Dixie thanks to black voters and won most of the North. With 53 percent of the popular vote, Grant won the election.

By the time the new president was inaugurated in March 1869, the governments organized under the congressional reconstruction acts—composed of white and black Republicans and decidedly Radical in temper—had been admitted to the Union, and the Fourteenth Amendment had been incorporated into the Constitution. In a narrow legal sense, Reconstruction was now complete. But, in fact, the situation in the newly restored states remained uncertain and tense.

The Southern Radical Governments.

In many ways, the most serious deficiency of the Reconstruction process was its failure to create a democratic political culture. Blacks fully participated in the formation and running of the state governments established by the five military commanders under the terms of the Reconstruction Acts. They voted in the elections for state constitutional conventions, served in those conventions, voted in the state elections for state and federal office that followed, and served in these offices. Participation did not mean domination, however. Even where the Republicans were in control, and even in South Carolina and Mississippi, where the black population outnumbered the white, they held only a minority of political offices. The rest were filled by native-born southern whites and northern-born white immigrants to Dixie.

One of the persistent myths of Reconstruction is that black political officials during the years of Republican rule in the South were unusually corrupt and incompetent. But that was not the case. Among the fifteen black southerners elected to Congress were a number of exceptionally able, honest, and well-educated men. Maine congressman James G. Blaine, who served with many of the black legislators, said of them: "The colored men who took their seats in both Senate and House . . . were as a rule studious, earnest, ambitious men, whose public conduct . . . should be honorable to any race." On the level of state government, black officeholders ranged from excellent to poor. All in all, as legislators and officials, their successes did not fall noticeably behind those of their white colleagues.

Native-born white Republican leaders in the South have also been unduly disparaged. "Scalawags" were denounced by their opponents as "the vilest renegades of the South," as men "who have dishonored the dignity of white blood, and are traitors alike to principle and race." In fact, many were former Unionists and members of the South's prewar Whig business class who were attracted to the Republican party because of its pro-business, pro-growth policies. And they were not the tiny minority of the white population that we would expect if they were merely renegades. In 1872, for example, 20 percent of the South's white voters cast their ballots for Republican candidates.

Nor were the northern whites who participated in the southern Republican state governments the "itinerant adventurers" and "vagrant interlopers" that southern conservatives charged. Called "carpetbaggers," after the cheap carpet-cloth suitcases carried in those years by travelers, many were former Union soldiers who had served in Dixie during the war and come to like it as a place to live. Others were sincere idealists committed to establishing a new social order. Obviously many white southern Republicans—scalawags and carpetbaggers alike—hoped to take personal advantage of new circumstances, but there is no reason to consider them any more venal, corrupt, or self-serving than other ambitious politicians.

On the whole the Radical-dominated southern state governments were remarkably effective and reasonably honest. Of course, measured by the standards of the tight-fisted prewar South, they seemed to be big spenders that ran up large debts. But the new governments took on functions not required of their predecessors. They sought to help railroads and other businesses. They established the South's first state-supported school systems and sharply increased public spending for poor relief, prisons, and state hospitals. Though still far behind the North in providing social services, under Radical rule the South began to catch up with the rest of nineteenth-century America.

The new Radical governments were also more democratic and egalitarian than were the prewar southern state regimes. The constitutions adopted under congressional Reconstruction made many previously appointive offices elective and gave small farmers better representation in the legislatures than before the war. They also extended the vote to white males who did not meet the surviving old property qualifications. The new state governments reduced the number of crimes punishable by death and granted married women more secure control over their property, reforms most northern states had adopted before 1860. They swept away the unequal treatment of black workers that had been incorporated into the Black Codes. Some of the Radical regimes even pursued policies that foreshadowed the modern social welfare state. South Carolina financed medical care for its poor citizens. Alabama paid legal fees for poor defendants. Not for another century would the South—or the nation as a whole—see anything like this again.

Economic Recovery.

While the politicians fought over the political future of the southern states, important economic and social changes were underway in Dixie. Damaged southern railroads were quickly rebuilt after Appomattox and the rail system extended to new regions. Much of the needed capital was supplied by investors from the North and from Britain, who anticipated a favorable business climate in the South. The southern state governments, both the Johnson regimes and the ones established under Congress's aegis, also contributed capital, going heavily into debt to lend money to railroad enterprises. Industry too recovered.

Between the 1860s and 1880, southern manufactures increased in value almost 55 percent. In agriculture cotton became even more important after 1865 than before the war. By 1878 the South's cotton output had almost reached its prewar peak. By the 1890s the region was producing twice as many bales as in 1859.

Tenantry and Sharecropping.

But the most important change in the post-1865 southern economy was its social transformation. Before 1861, defenders of slavery had denied that blacks could function in a free labor market. During the war the Treasury Department put this theory to the test in the South Carolina Sea Islands near Port Royal and demonstrated that when ex-slaves were given land and incentives they made successful farmers. The Port Royal venture collapsed when the Treasury Department failed to transfer legal land titles to the freedmen as it had promised, selling the abandoned Sea Island property to the highest bidder instead.

Efforts to create a class of black farm owners in the South resumed after the war. Thaddeus Stevens and other Radicals in Congress introduced legislation to transfer confiscated rebel estates to newly enfranchised blacks. Only landowning, they believed, could protect blacks against exploitation and keep them from being virtually re-enslaved. The former slaves themselves yearned to become landowners. "We all know that the colored people want land," a South Carolina carpetbagger noted. "Night and day they think and dream of it. It is their all and all." Whitelaw Reid quoted an elderly black man he had met on his trip to the South: "What's de use of bein' free if you don't own land enough to be buried? Might juss as well stay slave all yo days."

Yearnings often became expectations. Many freedmen came to believe that the government intended to give them "forty acres and a mule," and they were bitterly disappointed when it proved untrue. In the end, a large black yeomen class failed to appear. Ultimately the Radicals were not so very radical, and their respect for private property rights—even those of ex-rebels—took precedence over their concern for the freedmen. Most were certain that the ballot offered sufficient protection to the freedmen; a social revolution was not needed.

Black southerners might have accumulated some money by painful saving and then purchased land. Southern land prices were low in the 1870s, and a few hundred dollars could have bought a black family a small farm. In 1865 Congress chartered the Freedmen's Bank to support such black self-help efforts. But the bank was poorly managed and could not withstand the financial panic of 1873. When it closed its doors the following year, it took with it over $3 million of hard-won savings from thousands of black depositors. And there was another impediment to the freedmen buying land: White southerners, believing that if blacks had land of their own they would not work for white landlords and employers, discouraged freedmen from buying farms even when they could pay cash.

Though only a minority of southern blacks ever became independent farm owners, most continued to be cultivators. For a while after Appomattox they worked for cash wages under contracts supervised by the Freedmen's Bureau. But it was difficult for landlords to find cash in the months following the war.

The freedmen, for their part, resented the harshness with which some bureau agents enforced labor contracts against them. Still more unsatisfactory from the ex-slaves' point of view was the return to gang work and the planters' close supervision of every aspect of their labor and their lives. The system reminded them too much of slavery and seemed a mockery of freedom.

Out of this mutual dissatisfaction with wage-paid farm labor emerged a tenant system that by 1880 had become characteristic of much of the cotton-growing South. Tenantry included whites as well as blacks. Thousands of Confederate privates returned home to become, not successful planters, but tenants on lands owned by former slaveholders. Many were forced into tenantry by high property taxes; others by inability to pay their debts.

Tenantry took many forms. Tenants might pay rent either in cash or in part of the crop. Though the system was not as desirable as ownership, a cash tenant was at least free from constant supervision and sometimes could save enough to buy land for himself. The greater number of tenant farmers, however, especially among the freedmen, were either sharecroppers or share renters. The former contributed only their labor, and in return for use of the land and a house, usually divided the crop equally with the landlord. A share renter could provide his own seed, mule, and plow as well, and usually got three-fourths of what he produced. By 1900 three-quarters of black farmers were tenant farmers of one sort or another as were over 35 percent of white farmers.

Linked to tenantry, and making it worse, was the crop-lien system, a credit arrangement by which a storekeeper (who sometimes was the landlord as well) would extend credit to the tenant for supplies during the crop-growing season. When the harvest came and the cotton was sold, the tenant would then repay the debt. Buying on credit was expensive, since it included an interest charge. It also gave dishonest storekeepers a chance to cheat. Tenants who could not meet their debts could not change the merchant they dealt with; they became virtual "debt-peons," tied to him almost like serfs.

However imperfect, the new labor regime that emerged in the South during Reconstruction was an advance over slavery. Some blacks managed to become landowners despite all the difficulties. By 1880 twenty percent of black farmers owned some land, though their holdings were generally smaller and less fertile than those of whites. And even tenantry was better than slavery. It released ex-slaves from the degradation of close personal work supervision by whites. And tenants, even sharecroppers, were better off economically than slaves. The economists Roger Ransom and Richard Sutch conclude that whereas slaves received in food, clothing, housing, and medical attention about 23 percent of what whites received, the freedmen after 1865 obtained a full half of average white income. In addition to these economic advances, blacks were now able to make decisions about their economic lives that they never could before. Almost all decided that black women would no longer work in the fields; like white women, they would stay home and become proper housewives and mothers. Many black children too left the labor market to attend school.

Yet the freedmen's fate represented a missed opportunity for the nation. Many of the gains were a one-time advance, made just after the war. Thereafter, while

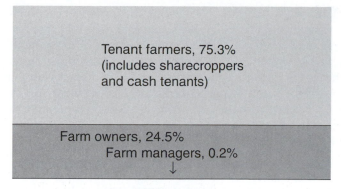

Black Status

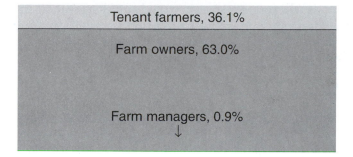

White Status

The status of farm operators in former slave states, 1900

the country as a whole became richer, black living standards in the South stagnated. Indeed, the sharecrop–crop-lien system proved to be an economic trap for the entire lower South. Because they did not own the land, sharecroppers had no incentive to improve it. Landlords, too, had little incentive, for they could only hope to recover a limited portion of the greater output that might come from additional capital investment. Tenantry also tied the South to a one-crop system and prevented diversification. As one sharecropper complained in the 1880s: "We ought to plant less [cotton and tobacco] and more grain and grasses, but how are we to do it; the man who furnishes us with rations at 50 percent interest won't let us; he wants money crops planted." This failure to diversify had serious consequences for the southern economy. One effect was soil exhaustion only offset by expensive additions of fertilizers. Worst of all, it tied the region to cotton at a time when world cotton prices were in a drastic slide that would last an entire generation. All told, after 1865 the South as a section fell further behind the rest of the nation in almost every measure of material abundance and social well-being: literacy, infant mortality, longevity, health, and per-capita income. By 1890, the section had become America's problem area.

Social and Cultural Change.   Yet despite the imperfect economic adjustment, the end of slavery brought considerable social and cultural gains for black Americans. Black men and women enjoyed a new freedom of movement, which some exercised by going to the cities or departing for more prosperous parts of the country. At the end of Reconstruction several thousand blacks left the lower South and moved north or west. A particularly large movement of "exodusters" to Kansas after 1878 alarmed southern white leaders, who feared that the South might lose its labor force.

The end of slavery freed blacks to express themselves in ways never before possible. Slavery had not destroyed black culture, but it had made it difficult for blacks to demonstrate the full range of their talents and to exercise their organizational abilities. Emancipation released energies previously held in check. Blacks withdrew from white churches in large numbers and formed their own. These churches gave talented former slaves an opportunity to demonstrate leadership beyond anything previously possible. Unlike politics, which was largely closed to talented black men after 1877, the Protestant ministry continued to provide leadership opportunities.

The end of slavery also expanded educational opportunities for blacks. Before the war slaves had been legally denied education. After 1865 northern educators and philanthropists seized on Dixie as missionary territory to be converted to "civilization." In the months after Appomattox hundreds of Yankee teachers,

The first African-American senator and representatives in the 41st and 42nd Congress of the United States. As a group they acquitted themselves competently.

hoping to uplift a benighted region, went South to establish schools and bring the blessings of literacy. The Freedmen's Bureau also labored to end illiteracy and sought to train blacks in trades. The most permanent impact was achieved by southern self-help. Before long every southern state, under Radical guidance, had made some provision for educating black children. The southern educational system long remained poor and segregated (except for a time in the cosmopolitan city of New Orleans); yet the schools managed to make a dent in ignorance. By 1880 a quarter of all blacks could read and write; twenty years later the figure had risen to half. College training for blacks, nonexistent in the South before 1860, became available as well. Southern state governments founded separate black colleges and universities. Meanwhile, the Freedmen's Bureau and white philanthropists helped charter such black private colleges as Atlanta University in Georgia, Fisk University in Tennessee, and Howard University in Washington, D.C.

The gains notwithstanding, segregation by race became a central fact of life in the South after 1865. In 1875 Congress passed a strongly worded Civil Rights Act guaranteeing to all persons, regardless of color, "the full and equal enjoyment of all the accommodations . . . of inns, public conveyances . . . , theaters, and other places of public amusement"; but separation and social inequality persisted; in fact, the separation of the races became more complete than before the war. In most communities, trains, buses, and theaters had white and black sections. In private life the racial spheres were still more exclusive, and blacks almost never entered the homes of white people except as servants. Even southern Radicals seldom treated blacks as social equals.

Redemption.   Regardless of their accomplishments, many white southerners despised the Radical regimes and accused them of corruption. Some were in fact corrupt, but generally no more than was normal in state affairs during those years. Southern conservatives also disliked the reforms they initiated, because they were new, because they seemed Yankee-inspired, and because they were expensive. Landlords, in particular, denounced the new programs for raising taxes on real estate, which before the war had been lightly taxed. But above all, conservatives found it difficult to accept the Republican-dominated state governments because they were part of the new racial regime. After 250 years of slavery, the white South found it virtually impossible to consider a black person the political equal of a white one.

After 1867 the southern states became arenas for ferocious struggles between the political forces of the new era and those of the old. For a while the Radical governments succeeded in holding onto political office, especially in states where they were most firmly entrenched—Alabama, Mississippi, Texas, Florida, Louisiana, and South Carolina. But in the end they could not match the experience, self-confidence, and ruthlessness of the defenders of bygone times, who hoped to "redeem" the South from "Black Republicanism."

A major weapon of the "redeemers" was the Ku Klux Klan. Formed in 1866 in Tennessee by young Confederate veterans primarily as a social club, the Klan quickly evolved into an antiblack, anti-Radical organization. To intimidate black voters, hooded, mounted Klansmen swooped down at night on isolated cabins, making fearsome noises and firing guns. They also torched black homes, attacked

When the Freedmen's Bureau set up schools for blacks, former slaves of all ages
flocked to them. Wrote Booker T. Washington, "It was a whole race trying to go to
school." The Show Hill School, here, abandoned classical education in favor of
industrial training, which was deemed more appropriate to black needs.

and beat black militiamen, ambushed both white and black Radical leaders, and
lynched blacks accused of crimes. During the 1868 presidential campaign Klansmen assassinated an Arkansas congressman, three members of the South Carolina
legislature, and several Republican members of state constitutional conventions.
Some conservative apologists dismissed the Klan as an organization composed of
white riffraff, but in fact, as one Radical newspaper noted, it included "men of
property . . . respectable citizens."

At its height in the late 1860s, the Klan's outrages went virtually unchecked.
Law enforcement officials felt impotent to deal with the violence. Witnesses of
Klan misdeeds were often scared off from testifying against it. In several southern
states the Klan created a reign of terror and lawlessness that threatened to undo
the entire Reconstruction process. Then in 1870 and 1871 Congress passed three
Force Bills, which declared "armed combinations" and Klan terrorist tactics illegal. The bills gave the president the right to prosecute in federal courts all those
who sought to prevent qualified persons from voting. For the first time the federal government had defined certain crimes against individuals as violation of federal law. President Grant invoked the measures in nine South Carolina counties,
and soon hundreds of Klansmen were indicted for illegal activities.

The Klan quickly declined, but not the determination of southern conservatives to cow the black population and take control of the South away from Radicals and their supporters. The "redeemers" abandoned hooded robes, flaming
crosses, and night rides, but not other forms of intimidation. In their successful

Secret societies like the Knights of the White Camelia, the Pale Faces, and the Knights of the Ku Klux Klan organized to frustrate Reconstruction. Describing itself as an "institution of Chivalry, Humanity, Mercy, and Patriotism," the Klan violently intimidated blacks.

effort in 1875 to "redeem" Mississippi, conservatives used the powerful weapon of ostracism to force white Republicans to change their party. One who succumbed to their tactics, Colonel James Lusk, told a black fellow Republican: "No white man can live in the South in the future and act with any other than the Democratic party unless he is willing and prepared to live a life of social isolation and remain in political oblivion."

Even tougher tactics were deployed against black voters. Blacks who voted Republican were denied jobs or fired from those they had. More stubborn black Republicans were threatened with violence. During the 1875 Mississippi state election thousands of white Democrats armed themselves with rifles and shotguns, and then, to make the message clear, entered the names of black Republicans in "dead books." In Vicksburg, Yazoo City, and other Mississippi towns blacks were shot and killed in preelection fights.

In that campaign the Democrats captured the Mississippi legislature and elected the only state official running for statewide office. The Republican governor, Adelburt Ames, faced with impeachment by the new legislature, agreed to resign. Mississippi had been "redeemed." Similar processes took place in other southern states, so that by 1876 only Louisiana, Florida, and South Carolina remained under Republican administrations—and these regimes stayed in power solely because they were protected by federal troops.

The End of Reconstruction.   Clearly, the redeemers were effective tacticians and organizers. But their success also depended on the weakening commitment of northerners to Radical rule in the South.

The decline of northern resolve had several sources. Many honest Republicans came to see the defense of the black man as an excuse for continued domination of their party by its most corrupt wing. Whenever a new scandal was uncovered in the Grant administration, for example—and there would be many—it was buried under an appeal for Republican unity against the ex-rebels who had committed atrocities against "the boys in blue" during the war. The process came to be called "waving the bloody shirt." By the middle of the 1870s many Republicans had concluded that abandoning blacks and their friends in the South was better than continuing to uphold the unscrupulous element in their own party.

Fatigue and racism also played their parts. How long, many northerners asked, could the country invest energy and money to sustain a system that the "best elements" of southern society opposed? The ex-slaves would never make good citizens, and there was no point in continuing the hopeless battle. Such arguments were reinforced by a growing conviction among northern commercial and industrial groups that stability in the South would be better for business than the political agitation that constantly disturbed the nation.

The end came in 1876. In the presidential election of that year the Democrats nominated Samuel J. Tilden of New York, an honest but colorless corporation lawyer. The Republican candidate was Rutherford B. Hayes, the aloof but upright governor of Ohio. The Democratic platform promised to withdraw federal troops from the South and endorsed traditional Democratic low-tariff, small-government positions. The Republicans declared that they would never abandon the black man and would continue to support positive government, a protective tariff, and "sound money."

The election was so close that the results were immediately challenged. The Democrats claimed they had carried New York, New Jersey, Connecticut, Indiana, and the entire South. The Republicans insisted that the votes of Florida, Louisiana, and South Carolina—the still "unredeemed" states—rightfully belonged to them. They also challenged one Democratic vote in Oregon, where electors had split between the two candidates. As in 1824, the election was thrown into the House of Representatives. For the next four months the country's political life was in an uproar as the politicians scrambled to settle the election issue before Inauguration Day in March 1877.

Southern black voters after 1865 were alternately courted and coerced by white politicians. The Democrats found force more necessary than the Republicans did to win black votes. In this Radical Republican cartoon two Democrats (the one at right looking remarkably like Jefferson Davis) make no pretense of winning "hearts and minds."

Both sides brought every weapon possible to bear on the dispute—propaganda, legal maneuvering, congressional commissions, and threats of violence. Some historians believe that one hidden issue during the disputed election period was railroads. Southerners, they say, believed that only the Republicans would approve a land grant to the Texas and Pacific Railroad, designed to connect New Orleans and other important southern cities with the Pacific Coast. This reasoning led influential southern leaders, many former Whigs with little love for the Democrats, to seek a bargain with the Republicans. What seems more likely than this "Compromise of 1877" was something less devious: that southerners merely traded electoral votes for removing federal troops from the South. But whoever is right, soon after Hayes's inauguration as nineteenth president of the United States, the last federal soldiers were withdrawn from Dixie. The redeemers quickly moved in. Reconstruction was over.

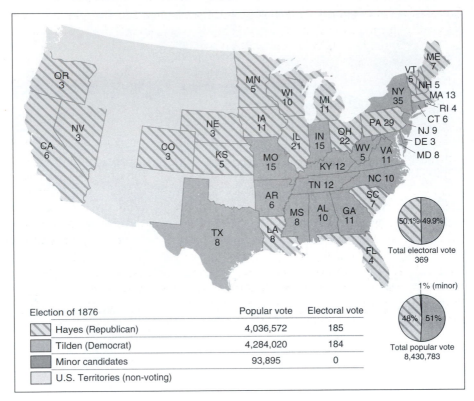

Election of 1876	Popular vote	Electoral vote
Hayes (Republican)	4,036,572	185
Tilden (Democrat)	4,284,020	184
Minor candidates	93,895	0
U.S. Territories (non-voting)		

Total electoral vote 369 — 50.1% / 49.9% — 1% (minor)

Total popular vote 8,430,783 — 48% / 51%

Presidential Election of 1876

Conclusions

The process by which the South readjusted to the new circumstances after 1865 was not an unrelieved disaster. During these momentous years southerners repaired the physical devastation of the war and reestablished their states' constitutional relations with the Union. Meanwhile, black southerners were able to create for themselves important new islands of freedom—freedom to move, freedom to create social and cultural institutions of their own, freedom for black women to leave the fields. They also improved their material well-being. As sharecroppers, blacks kept a larger share of the wealth they produced than as slaves. Also on the credit side were the Radical-sponsored Fourteenth and Fifteenth amendments. Once embedded in the Constitution, they would become the bases for a "second Reconstruction" in the mid-twentieth century.

Yet much is dismaying about Reconstruction. Americans of this era failed to meet the great challenges that faced them. Instead of a prosperous black yeomanry, the South would be left with a mass of impoverished semipeons who for generations would be a reproach to America's proud claims of prosperity and equality. Instead of political democracy, Reconstruction would bequeath a legacy of sectional fraud, intimidation, and shameless racial exclusion. Rather than accelerating southern economic growth, Reconstruction would chain the South to a declining staple crop agriculture and leave it ever further behind the rest of the nation.

Who was to blame for these failures? One answer is that Americans were trapped by the past. Deep-seated prejudices and memories of slavery blinded most white southerners (and many northerners) to the need for racial justice. Traditional individualism and the commitment to self-help obscured the fact that the special circumstances of black dependence resulting from slavery called for imaginative government aid. And there were the accidents of events and personalities. Would Lincoln have seen realities more clearly? Certainly the accession of Andrew Johnson, a stubborn man of limited vision and conventional racial views, did nothing to solve the unique problems of the day. Refusing to recognize the North's need to exact some penance from the defeated South, he needlessly antagonized even moderates and drove them into the Radical camp. The result was a legacy of sectional hatred that poisoned American political life for generations.

Meanwhile, the nation was turning away from the "everlasting southern problem" to what many citizens believed were more important matters. The South and Reconstruction became increasingly remote as the country experienced a surge of economic expansion that dwarfed anything of the past.

Online Resources

"Finding Precedent: The Impeachment of Andrew Johnson" *http://www.andrewjohnson.com* By examining the impeachment of President Andrew Johnson, this Web site explores the major issues behind the impeachment debate and describes the political factions vying to determine Reconstruction policy. The site employs Reconstruction-era editorials and provides biographical sketches and portraits of many of the key figures involved.

"The Black Codes and Reaction to Reconstruction" *http://chnm.gmu.edu/courses/122/recon/ code.html* This site contains the text of the Mississippi Black Code and other Reconstruction policies. The site also chronicles citizens' reactions to these policies through contemporary newspaper editorials, magazine articles, and congressional testimony, and it discusses the impact of these reforms on African Americans.

"Civil War and Reconstruction, 1861–1877: Reconstruction and Rights" *http://lcweb2.loc.gov/ ammem/ndlpedu/features/timeline/civilwar/civilwar.html* In addition to a good overview of the Civil War and Reconstruction eras, read transcripts of oral histories from whites who actually experienced Reconstruction in the South. Their stories include eyewitness accounts of racially motivated violence in regard to African-American voting.

Toward Racial Equality: *Harper's Weekly* Reports on Black America, 1857–1874 *http://blackhistory.harpweek.com* This site includes contemporary editorials, illustrations, and advertisements that address the status of African-Americans after the Civil War. These primary documents focus specifically on racial violence in both the North and the South, the work of the Freedman's Bureau, and debates on black civil rights.

Reconstruction: A State Divided *http://lsm.crt.state.la.us/cabildo/cabildo.htm* Providing an in-depth look at how the Reconstruction policy debate affected one particular place in time, this site offers a window into Reconstruction in the state of Louisiana.

Sharecropping: "After Freedom, We Worked Shares" *http://historymatters.gmu.edu/d/6377/* Illuminating the hardships that African-American sharecroppers faced during the Reconstruction period, this site contains the words of Henry Blake, formerly enslaved, who tells about his life as a freed man on the farm.

The Mississippi Black Codes *http://afroamhistory.about.com/library/blmississippi_blackcodes.htm* This site has an actual text copy of the harsh Black Codes from the state of Mississippi. Like those adopted by many state legislatures in the South, these codes bear witness to the legal limitations imposed on African-Americans following emancipation.

Railroads and the New South *http://xroads.virginia.edu/~CLASS/am485_98/hall/newsouth.html* This site depicts the history of the New South through the lens of Roanoke, Virginia. It details how the introduction of the railroad affected one town economically, socially, and politically and created a more urban landscape. It is representative of the influences of technology throughout the New South.

"Still Livin' Under the Bonds of Slavery" *http://historymatters.gmu.edu/d/82* Download and listen to the audio recording of Minnie Whitney, who describes sharecropping in the late nineteenth century. Hear tales of hard times and oppression as well as agency and self-sufficiency.

17

The Triumph of Industrialism

What Were the Causes, What Were the Costs?

In the half-century following the Civil War the United States became the largest and richest industrial nation in the world. As late as 1880 agriculture still represented a larger share of Americans' income than any other source. Ten years later its contribution was surpassed by industry, and by 1900 the total value of goods produced by factories and shops in the United States was twice that of goods produced on farms. In the mid-1890s America's output of industrial commodities surpassed every other nation's. In 1913 one-third of all the world's manufactures came from American factories.

The explosive surge in industry was the major force behind the country's impressive gains in GDP (gross domestic product), the simplest overall measure of economic growth. Between 1865 and 1908 total GDP grew at an average rate of more than 4 percent a year, considerably faster than for most of the period since then. By 1908 total economic output was eight times that of the year Robert E. Lee surrendered at Appomattox. Population was also increasing in this period. Still, at its end, Americans were producing twice the total of goods and services per person each year as at the beginning. Unfortunately, this did not mean that every American was twice as rich on the eve of World War I as he or she—or, more likely, their forebears—had been in 1865. As we will see, the gains were unequally distributed. But the extraordinary performance provided the foundation for broad affluence by the standards of the day.

What caused the industrial leap and the economic surge after 1865? Was there some single, predominant factor, or were there a number of separate ones? And was growth essentially cost-free? Or did the American people pay a price for the impressive advance? Let us start with the causes. We shall then consider the costs.

Captains of Industry

The quality of contemporary business leadership is one explanation for the economic advance. According to this view, tycoons such as Andrew Carnegie, John D. Rockefeller, and "Commodore" Vanderbilt were the principal agents transforming America into an economic colossus.

And, in fact, it would be difficult to ignore their role in the economic life of this era. Even against the gaudy and boisterous background of the period we call the Gilded Age, these "captains of industry" stand out vividly. In some ways their historical image is a negative one. They have been likened to "robber barons" who held the nation up for ransom to amass their great fortunes, or depicted as heartless employers who cruelly exploited their workers. They have also been attacked as crude and vulgar men who flaunted their wealth and conspicuously displayed their bad taste. Still, it is also true that in our national mythology they are often given credit for singlehandedly converting the United States into an industrial giant. What role did they actually play in this process of economic transformation?

A close look at the extraordinary economic achievement of the Gilded Age shows that the great entrepreneurs—the risk-takers, managers, and organizers—were indeed important contributors to the nation's spectacular economic success. Entrepreneurship is a large element in virtually all economic growth. To increase an economy's output, it is not enough to unimaginatively add more materials, labor, and machines to the prevailing economic mix. Growth also requires deploying the initiating, coordinating, and managerial functions to start new firms and expand existing ones. The entrepreneurial skills necessary to detect an important economic need, cut costs, tap new sources of savings, recruit and direct labor, recognize and inspire new talent are not universal. Those societies abundantly endowed with these skills will inevitably advance more rapidly than ones that are not.

Gustavus Swift and the Organizing Function.

To understand the role of entrepreneurship in the economic transformation following the Civil War, let us consider several examples. A good place to start is the meat-packing industry. Though modern sensibilities may find the processing of animal foods a dubious enterprise, to Americans of a century or more ago it was a vital part of the nation's industrial output.

Before 1860 most fresh meat came from local butchers. Dressed carcasses spoiled too quickly to come from distant sources, while shipping live animals created large losses in weight. But in the generation following the Civil War, three developments helped transform the business of supplying the public with meat. First, an increasing proportion of Americans came to live in cities, remote from the farms where meat animals were fattened. Second, an expanding rail network made the products of the prairies and plains of the West more accessible to urban consumers. Third, in the 1870s, the railroads introduced refrigerated cars, allowing chilled fresh beef and pork to be shipped long distances without spoilage.

One of the first men to recognize the new possibilities opened for the meat industry was Gustavus Swift. Swift saw the advantages of slaughtering cattle close to the grass and corn of the West and shipping the dressed product to eastern consumers. This would not only eliminate the losses in shipping live cattle; it would allow cheaper centralized processing. Much of the slaughtering could be mechanized. As the industry evolved, it came to employ a "dis-assembly line." As carcasses passed on a moving line they were quickly skinned, dismembered, and prepared for shipping. Labor costs were thereby reduced. The scale of the operations also made for efficiencies. Animal parts that were normally discarded could be sold to make medicines, sausage casings, fertilizers, leather, and other byproducts. (It would be said of the great hog butchers of the late nineteenth century that they used every part of the pig but the squeal.)

Swift sent his first dressed, chilled beef east by refrigerator car in the mid-1870s. Consumers at first resisted the unfamiliar product; local butchers who feared the competition sought to have it legally excluded. But in a few years—joined by other packers such as Armour, Cudahy, and Morris—he was shipping millions of pounds of meat annually from his Chicago plants and marketing it through a network of branch houses and agents. In 1875 the Chicago packers slaughtered 250,000 cattle; in 1880, 500,000; in 1890, a million.

Thomas Edison and Technological Innovation.

Swift contributed primarily to improving the organization of an existing industry. Thomas Edison created several whole new branches of manufacture.

We think of Edison today as an inventor of gadgets, and indeed he was. He improved the telephone and the telegraph, and created the motion picture camera, the phonograph, and the incandescent light bulb. Yet he was far more than a tinkerer; he was also a first-rate entrepreneur whose skills launched several giant new businesses.

In developing the electric light bulb Edison and his associates met a vital public need. At the beginning of the nineteenth century, Americans worked and played almost entirely during daylight hours and the rhythms of life corresponded closely to the seasonal length of the day. At night city streets were dark. Private homes were often unlighted after daylight except on special occasions. Gaslight arrived during the 1850s, but its use was confined to city streets and to the middle and upper classes of the larger urban centers, where it was economically feasible to install costly pipes and meters.

The new petroleum industry changed this picture. In the 1840s and 1850s, "rock oil" was a substance extracted in small amounts from streams and used as a medicine. Its value as the source of an illuminant was understood, but no one was certain that it could be collected in large enough quantities to be useful for mass lighting. Then, in 1859 a group of businessmen hired E. L. Drake to dig for oil in western Pennsylvania. After several weeks Drake struck a major oil pool, proving that there was an abundant supply of the substance underground. Before long, what had been a quack medical remedy became a household necessity. Refined into kerosene, petroleum quickly replaced whale oil lamps and candles as the nation's major source of home lighting.

From the outset, kerosene, like gas, raised the risks of fire and explosion, especially in congested urban centers. By the 1870s the use of electricity seemed the solution. In the form of the arc light, it was already in limited use for illuminating stage productions and city streets. But arc lights were too brilliant and too wasteful of power for private homes. This is where Edison saw his opportunity. If electric light could be produced in small units, it would replace kerosene and gas for home use. Many scientists at the time believed that the feat could not be accomplished, but, at his laboratory in New Jersey, Edison pushed ahead to develop a practical home electric lighting system.

The story as usually told emphasizes Edison's quest for a durable filament for a light bulb. In fact, Edison hoped to develop an entire system similar to gas lighting. This would require a centrally located source of electric power that could serve many lamps, a means to transmit the power efficiently to each lamp, lamps that could be turned on and off without affecting other lamps on the circuit, and, finally, a metering arrangement to measure each customer's use of current. Edison had to lure customers from an established workable system to his own, and at the same time make a profit for private investors.

This difficult enterprise aroused Edison's impressive talents as both businessman and inventor. After securing dependable financial backing, he worked out the technical specifications for an efficient and economically feasible lighting system. Once he had developed a usable carbon filament for his glass lamp, he created a simple metering system that enabled the Edison Company to assess charges against users. In September 1882, he opened a central generating station on Pearl Street near New York City's financial district, where his success would be sure to attract the attention of the nation's money men. During the next few years the Edison Company opened other stations in Boston, Philadelphia, and Chicago. In a few years the nation's cities were alive with light, and urban Americans stayed up later to read, talk, dine, and generally enjoy themselves. A whole way of life had been revolutionized by one man's skill, insight, and enterprise.

Andrew Carnegie and Cost Consciousness.

Careful cost analysis and ruthless cost cutting were the hallmarks of Andrew Carnegie's entrepreneurship.

Carnegie was the classic self-made man. Arriving in the United States with his family in 1848, the thirteen-year-old Scottish lad first worked in a Pittsburgh textile factory replacing broken threads on the spinning spools for $1.20 a week. In the 1850s he became an assistant to Thomas A. Scott, vice president of the Pennsylvania Railroad. From Scott, Carnegie learned how to deal with a large-scale enterprise and how to save thousands by squeezing pennies.

Carnegie was not an inventor like Edison. He worked with existing technology and processes, but made them show a profit. When he moved from railroading to bridge building and then to iron and steel making during the 1860s, the new Bessemer and open-hearth processes were already being used to make steel. Carnegie adopted the new methods for his Pittsburgh-based Edgar Thomson Works, but he seized on improvements as they appeared, disregarding the costs of scrapping his older but still usable equipment. Carnegie ran his furnaces, hearths, and converters full-blast regardless of replacement costs, and did not let up even when orders tumbled during hard times. He also cut expenses ruthlessly and kept down labor costs by mechanizing as many processes as he could. Carnegie recruited a corps of driving young executives and then held them strictly accountable for every penny spent producing steel. One of these men later said: "You [were] expected always to get it ten cents cheaper the next year or the next month." Within a few years Carnegie and his associates had lowered the price of steel so much that it could be used to replace iron, wood, and stone in construction, thus paving the way for marvels of engineering never before possible.

Of all the so-called robber barons, Carnegie was probably the most civic-minded. Like the others, he fought to keep his employees' wages low, but he also believed that rich men were custodians of wealth for society at large. Before he died, the "Star-spangled Scotsman" gave away much of his immense fortune to charitable institutions, research foundations, endowments for peace and international understanding, and to establish public libraries.

Capital Creation and J. P. Morgan.

Where did the funds to invest in meat-packing plants, power stations, and steel mills come from? Ultimately the source of any money for capital investment must be savings. Swift and Carnegie relied largely on the retained profits of their own enterprises. Many businesspeople, however, were happy to tap the pools of savings set aside by other people.

In the 1880s the American savings rate was about 25 percent, far higher than today. People saved because thrift and prudence were morally approved and because there was no other way to provide for old age, disease, or accident.

Rich men and women were particularly able to save because their incomes far exceeded their day-to-day needs. A society with substantial inequalities of wealth and income meant that a large proportion of the public involuntarily contributed to economic growth.

Piling up personal savings is not enough, however. These savings must be channeled to entrepreneurs who have the will and the skill to use them effectively. When the saver and the investor are the same person—as in the case of Carnegie and Swift—there is little problem. But what if the two are different individuals? It is here that various investment institutions come into play.

One of those institutions was the stock market located on New York's Wall Street, where stocks and other securities issued by corporations and governments had been bought and sold since the late eighteenth century. Those who bought "shares" in a business corporation were part owners of the firm and received a portion of its profits without risking losses beyond the extent of their share purchase (limited liability). This system should have been an effective way for entrepreneurs to raise capital, but its value was seriously undercut by the fact that the stock exchange had become a sort of gambling casino where speculators—"bulls" and "bears"—bought and sold shares, not to gain profits from corporate earnings, but to make killings in "corners," "raids," and other get-rich-quick maneuvers. Prudent people with savings looked aghast at these risky and shady doings and stayed away from the stock market.

A more successful way to channel savings to investors during these years was through the banks. But the nation's banking structure had serious weaknesses. The national banking system, as created by the National Banking Acts of 1863 and 1864, was a major advance over the old state bank system, but it had substantial drawbacks. Banks with federal charters were not allowed to take land as security for loans, a restriction that limited their value for farmers who only had their land to offer as collateral. Nor could they readily increase the country's money supply to take care of seasonal needs or the steady, long-term growth of the economy, since the amount of their paper money issues depended on their holdings of a limited volume of government bonds. Lacking a central bank of last resort that might provide extra funds when needed, the national banking system was also unable to deal effectively with financial panics or other sudden crises.

Despite these flaws the national banks served to bring savers and investors together satisfactorily, at least where smaller amounts of capital were needed. For large-scale capital investment, however, the most effective agent was the investment banker. The need for investment bankers was especially urgent during the Gilded Age, when explosive urban growth and rapidly expanding railroads and industry created an extraordinary demand for capital.

Investment banks did not normally engage in the day-to-day business of commercial banking. Instead, they dealt with large borrowers, either government agencies or industrial and transportation promoters interested in raising large amounts of capital.

Before 1860 a few banking firms had begun to serve as middlemen between the government and savers. During the Civil War Jay Cooke and Company had assumed many of the risks of selling the giant treasury issues of "five-twenty" bonds that had financed the Union army and navy. In the 1870s Cooke became the

J. P. Morgan. He had a bulbous red nose—carefully obscured in this portrait. Yet his forceful personality comes through.

financial agent of the giant Northern Pacific Railroad. When the public lost confidence in Northern Pacific securities, Cooke and Company went bankrupt, triggering the panic of 1873 and the six years of hard times that followed.

The public's experience in 1873 did little to encourage investor confidence in stocks. But by the 1880s attitudes began to change, largely because of J. P. Morgan. Morgan often said that his chief asset was trust. The public believed that any promotion he orchestrated was apt to succeed. Building on this trust Morgan was able to put together a flock of corporation mergers that combined competing, inefficient, small firms into giants that promoted greater productivity and above all promised managed, tolerable competition. This required inducing hundreds of investors of the constituent firms to accept stock in the new, consolidated firm. Convinced that a Morgan-organized-and-run company was certain to be profitable, they usually complied.

Morgan, and the other investment bankers of the day, accustomed prosperous Americans to think of the stock market as a safe place to invest their savings, not merely an arena for risky speculation. By the end of the century the stock exchange had become a vital money market where those with savings came together with those who needed funds to invest in industry. By 1910, billions of dollars of stock were bought and sold annually on Wall Street. Much of this trading remained speculative. But a good deal of it represented the constructive meeting of savers who wanted secure returns and promoters who could put these savings to productive use.

The Spoilers

Clearly the entrepreneurship of Swift, Edison, Carnegie, Morgan, and others like them benefited the American people by providing new or cheaper products or by encouraging investment. Though most nineteenth-century businessmen had limited social sympathies and few scruples against sharp dealing, their efforts helped to increase the income of Americans generally. Not all business leaders, however, were constructive innovators. Some were primarily spoilers who got rich by manipulating finance while cheating investors, bribing politicians, ruining competitors, or rigging prices. Among these spoilers were Jay Gould and John D. Rockefeller.

The Railroads and Jay Gould.   The Civil War slowed the exuberant railroad construction of the 1850s, but after 1865 the country turned with a will to conquering time and distance with rails and steam locomotives. In 1865 there were about 35,000 miles of rail in the United States. By 1890 the country had 167,000 miles of track, and by 1910, when the network was largely complete, America was tied together by 240,000 miles of steel rails.

After 1865, promoters consolidated smaller companies into trunk lines such as the New York Central and the Baltimore and Ohio. Chicago, St. Louis, Kansas City, and Omaha became major rail centers, and from these points other promoters began to push west and south over the rapidly developing prairies. The most spectacular growth, however, was the spread of the transcontinentals. In 1869 construction teams from the Central Pacific, driving east from Sacramento, and from the Union Pacific, driving west from Omaha, met at Promontory Point in northern Utah, completing the first Atlantic–Pacific railroad connection. By 1890 five major railroads crossed the Great Plains, linking the Atlantic to the Pacific Coast.

Railroad efficiency was also vastly increased. Relatively cheap steel rails soon replaced the older iron trackage allowing the railroads to run larger, more efficient locomotives and cars. Braking problems on these heavier trains were solved with the adoption of George Westinghouse's air brake in the 1880s. Track gauges were standardized in these years so that passengers and freight need not be shifted from one set of cars to another. Meanwhile, George Pullman developed a new passenger car that was an ordinary coach by day but could be converted into a comfortable sleeping car by night.

Scholars have warned against exaggerating the impact of the railroads on the late-nineteenth-century American economy, but most interpreters believe it was immense. Cheap, all-weather transportation accelerated the decline in shipping costs that had begun during the pre-Civil War period, opening vast new regions to economic exploitation. Lower transport costs allowed commodities to be produced in the most efficient locations and by the most efficient firms and then shipped to consumers all over the country. They enabled each region to specialize in what it did best and exchange its products for those of other regions, further lowering consumer costs. The creation of an integrated national market raised the country's total output per capita substantially.

Some of those who helped bring this process about were farseeing, creative individuals who risked their own fortunes in opening new areas to settlement.

James J. Hill, for example, the promoter of the Great Northern railroad connecting St. Paul with Puget Sound, built his road without the great federal subsidies behind the other transcontinentals. Many of the railroad promoters of the age, however, were neither as civic-minded nor as creative as Hill. Most notorious of all was Jay Gould.

Gould made a fortune by manipulating railroads' financial structures and leaving them debt-ridden and gutted. In 1867 Gould and his friend James Fisk became directors of the Erie Railroad, supposedly as allies of the New York railroad promoter, Cornelius ("Commodore") Vanderbilt, who hoped to achieve a dominant position in New York City's western traffic by adding the Erie to his New York Central. Vanderbilt began secretly to buy up Erie stock to gain a controlling interest.

The new directors, joined by the notorious speculator Daniel Drew, betrayed Vanderbilt. Drew, especially, was a master of "stock watering," a term borrowed from shady cattle dealing. He and his confederates issued vast amounts of new Erie securities unjustified by any increase in the railroad's earning capacity, and quietly dumped these shares on the market. The unsuspecting Commodore bought and bought, but could not manage to buy enough to gain control of the railroad. Eventually Vanderbilt discovered the deception and sought help from the courts; the Erie ringleaders did the same. For months the two groups fought bitter legal battles, culminating in Gould's wholesale bribery of the New York State legislature to legalize his acts. Gould soon lost interest in the Erie. But the railroad, stuck with millions of shares of watered stock, was never the same. As he turned to new endeavors, Gould jeered, "There ain't nothing more in Erie."

John D. Rockefeller and Monopoly.

The career of John D. Rockefeller illustrates another form of business abuse common during these years: monopoly. His manipulations also highlight the permissive legal atmosphere, with rules either unclear or unformulated, characteristic of business operations of the era.

Rockefeller's business stage was the oil-refining industry. After E. L. Drake's successful oil strike in western Pennsylvania, the industry had boomed, spreading through the East and Midwest and even to California. The new sources of supply soon generated spectacular growth in the refining industry, which converted crude oil into kerosene, wax, and lubricants. By the early 1870s the refining companies had begun to concentrate near Cleveland, Ohio, a region close to the eastern oil fields and with unusually good transportation connections to the country's major population centers.

The refining industry was risky. For a few thousand dollars anyone could set up a simple plant to produce kerosene. As more and more firms entered the business, profits fell to the vanishing point, and many refineries went bankrupt. The intense competition undoubtedly kept prices low and benefited the consumer, but from the refiners' point of view, the results were agonizing.

Rockefeller's campaign to reduce competition in his own industry was a spectacular success. In 1870 he and his partners established the Standard Oil Company of Ohio, which soon became one of the largest refining companies in the country. Admittedly the technical and managerial skills of the Standard managers were important factors in their firm's prosperity. Equally significant, however, was Rockefeller's ability to squeeze cheap rates from the railroads for shipping crude and refined oil. Rockefeller's success here depended on the distress of the railroads. In the 1870s they, too, found themselves facing cutthroat competition and were slashing rates on competitive lines to stay solvent. Railroad officials tried consolidation of several firms under one controlling firm to reduce competition. They also tried "pools," agreements among several competing roads to divide the traffic according to a set formula to avoid rate cutting. Invariably these agreements broke down when one firm or another found it advantageous to violate the pool agreements which, because their legality was at best dubious, could not be enforced by law.

Taking advantage of the railroads' own fierce competition, Rockefeller arranged to provide large-scale shipments of Standard products by a given railroad in return for rebates that would reduce Standard's shipping charges far below the published rates. So competitive was the refining business that even a small saving on transportation costs could give one producer a vital edge over the others. As a result, Standard Oil grew at the expense of its competitors—many of whom were forced to sell out to their aggressive opponent—and with each spurt of growth the firm further increased its ability to squeeze favorable terms out of the railroad companies.

By 1880 the Standard Oil Company controlled between 90 and 95 percent of the country's refining capacity and 92 percent of the crude oil supply of the Appalachian area, the major oil region at the time. In 1882 Rockefeller and his associates formed the first "trust," a company that owned the securities of subsidiary firms and controlled their operations.

The Ohio courts dissolved Rockefeller's trust on the grounds that it violated the rights of owners of the individual firms and was "a virtual monopoly of the business of producing petroleum . . . to control the price." But the Standard Oil people reorganized under a New Jersey law that legalized a rather similar device, the holding company, enabling a super-company to own stock in several subordinate firms and so control their operations. Thereafter, Standard's share of the industry declined somewhat, but as late as 1911, when the United States Supreme Court ordered the parent holding company dissolved into thirty separate firms, it was still by far the largest producer of refined oil and crude petroleum in the world.

The post-Civil War business leaders were, then, both wreckers and builders. If all had resembled Jay Gould or John D. Rockefeller, it would be difficult to consider them a positive factor in late-nineteenth-century economic growth. But the Carnegies, the Edisons, the Swifts, and the Morgans assuredly helped speed up the process of transforming America into a rich industrial society.

The Intellectual Foundation

Entrepreneurship was only one component of the economic advances of the Gilded Age. Another was a system of values congenial to material growth. Undoubtedly some American workers, as well as others, were reluctant participants in the era's economic developments. Yet, to a considerable degree, the American public accepted as fundamentally good private profit, hard work, and economic growth.

In part this support can be explained by the realities of American society. As we shall see, the growing economy, however imperfect, did permit a fair degree of improvement in the economic status and income of average wage earners, and a certain amount of movement up the social ladder for their children. These improvements reinforced the faith of ordinary people in the process. But actual experience was not the whole of it. Faith in the system was buttressed by a mass of ideology, myth, and propaganda that sang the praises—and the inevitability—of the social and economic changes underway.

The Work Ethic.

An important cultural accelerator of economic change was the work ethic. In part a residue of Puritan teaching that the elect would reveal themselves by hard work and worldly success, it was reinforced by popular writers, preachers, the schools, and opinion makers generally. The work ethic proclaimed the virtues of reliability, thrift, sobriety, respectability, honesty, and conscientious performance of duties and obligations. These were rewards in themselves, but they also promised other rewards: Those who sowed would inevitably reap. According to the famous *McGuffey Readers,* used by generations of American schoolchildren, "He who would thrive must rise at five; he who has thriven, may lie to seven." Popular biographies and novels made heroes of successful strivers. In the potboiler fiction of William M. Thayer and Horatio Alger, the heroes are usually ambitious poor boys who overcome adversity to achieve social respectability and economic security. Alger's 119 naive formula novels for young people were particularly successful in the Gilded Age. Though obsessed by achievement, in truth Alger's heroes often prosper more by sheer luck than by persistent labor. Yet the ultimate lesson Alger conveyed was that toil was both good in itself and profitable. His heroes are youths who glory in work. Tom Thatcher is "a sturdy boy of sixteen with bright eyes and smiling, sun-burned face. His shirt sleeves were rolled up, displaying a pair of muscular arms. His hands were brown, and soiled with labor. It was clear that here was no white-handed young aristocrat." Raised on a steady diet of such edifying tales and myths, millions of Americans were prepared to accept the virtues of the contemporary economic system.

The Defense of Inequality.

Among its other functions, the work ethic justified unequal rewards, for if hard work was the way to achieve riches, then what divided rich from poor was the quality and intensity of their effort, not birth or good fortune. But there were more direct defenses of the inequalities of wealth as well.

Until close to the end of the century the Protestant ministry often defended the disparities between rich and poor. Henry Ward Beecher told an audience during the 1870s depression: "I do not say that a dollar a day is enough to support . . . a man and five children if a man would insist on smoking and drinking beer. . . . But the man who cannot live on bread and water is not fit to live." In his famous lecture Acres of Diamonds, Baptist minister Russell Conwell delivered the message that material riches were a sign of God's approval, if honestly earned. For the Christian to reject riches was a mistake, for riches allowed the Christian to aid others. During the Gilded Age Conwell gave his standard talk 6,000 times to many thousands of listeners.

The leading writers, academics, and journalists of the day also defended the economic inequalities of the time and praised the competitive spirit of the age.

Many of these people drew on the ideas of Adam Smith and other economists of eighteenth- and early-nineteenth-century Britain, who sought to demonstrate how the unrestricted pursuit of private gain by individuals must maximize the profit of all. Through a process Smith called the "invisible hand," free play for personal acquisitive drives would ultimately generate abundance for all. Laissez-faire ("hands off") was by far the best policy for government to follow if its goal was economic progress.

After 1865, defenders of inequality could also turn to social Darwinism to make their case. In his monumental 1859 work *The Origin of Species,* the English naturalist Charles Darwin had concluded that competition among living creatures was the engine of species diversity. Individuals that were stronger, tougher, fiercer, quicker, more intelligent, or more aggressive—in a word, "fitter"—survived to reproduce and perpetuate their lines. The others died out. To many of Darwin's interpreters the process seemed "progressive" in that "lower" creatures gave way to "higher" ones. But in any case it was the law of nature.

Social Darwinists claimed that what applied to the biological world also applied to society: Competition and the "survival of the fittest" was the only way to achieve progress. For humankind to advance, competition of all kinds must be allowed a free hand. Every attempt of soft-hearted philanthropists to interfere with the social evolutionary process by curbing the strong and bolstering the weak was shortsighted and regressive. "Let it be understood," wrote Yale professor William Graham Sumner, "that we cannot go outside this alternative: liberty, inequality, survival of the fittest; not liberty, equality, survival of the unfittest."

Given that business leaders often bustled to create pools and trusts to reduce competition and frequently demanded government aid to protect their profits, it is not clear how sincerely they took laissez-faire or social Darwinist ideas. Yet at times they echoed the slogans of the professors and philosophers. Even Andrew Carnegie, an atypical business tycoon in so many ways, accepted the necessity for inequality on Darwinian grounds. In his famous essay, "The Gospel of Wealth," he memorably startled the reading public by declaring that rich men were only "stewards of wealth" who must give it all back to society. But Carnegie also wrote: "We accept and welcome . . . great inequality of environment; the concentration of business, industrial and commercial, in the hands of a few; and the law of competition between these as being not only beneficial, but essential to the future of the race."

Students of society cannot prove that ideas such as social Darwinism strongly influence human actions and social change. They may merely be rationalizations of urges and ambitions derived from simple self-interest. Yet in many cases, at least where such ideas did not fly in the face of clear, first-hand experience, defense of hard work and inequality and propaganda regarding the self-made man were accepted by workers and the middle class, helping to create a disciplined labor force that contributed to economic growth after 1865.

The Role of Government

Though the entrepreneurs of this era were certainly instrumental in economic progress, the federal government also stimulated the economy by direct investment, by grants, by tariffs, and by tax policies favorable to savers and investors. Without this help, growth would undoubtedly have been slower.

Government Aid. At times the federal government invested directly in the physical improvements the nation needed, appropriating funds for post offices, docks, canal locks, and dredged river channels. Each year Congress supported such enterprises by a flock of "rivers and harbors" bills. In 1867 these took $1.2 million from the taxpayers' pockets; by 1895 they cost almost $20 million. Local governments, too—by paving streets, constructing sewers, and building hospitals, schools, reservoirs, and aqueducts—contributed to the country's capital growth.

An especially important federal contribution to Gilded Age economic growth was friendly tax policy. After the 1870s the tariff—in effect a tax on consumers—rose in steps virtually without pause until the twentieth century, providing a wall behind which investors could initiate new industries without fear of more efficient foreign competition. Internal taxes also favored investors. For most of this period, import duties and excises on tobacco, whiskey, beer, wine, and other items were the main sources of federal funds.

This tax system was quite regressive; that is, it took a larger percentage of the income of the poor than of the rich. Between 1861 and 1872 the federal government imposed an income tax, a progressive tax that rose proportionately with higher income. But this was dropped as part of the postwar retreat from heavy taxation; when it was revived in 1894, it was declared unconstitutional by the Supreme Court. Local governments raised most of their revenues by taxing property, an equally regressive practice. All told, the tax burden fell disproportionately on farmers and people on the lower rungs of the income ladder, constituting a kind of subsidy to business and the rich. The system clearly was not egalitarian. Many would consider it unfair. But by leaving the rich with substantial surpluses to invest in land, securities, or business enterprises, it probably contributed to growth.

Federal subsidies also helped encourage growth. The wartime Morrill Land Grant College Act (1862), which provided federal land to endow agricultural colleges, undoubtedly stimulated greater farm productivity after 1865. Federal railroad legislation had even weightier consequences. By 1871, under the terms of the Pacific Railroad Acts (1862 and 1864) and several later railroad land grant measures, the federal government gave private railroad companies over 130 million acres of land in the trans-Mississippi West, about one tenth of the entire public domain. This vast empire included timber, minerals, and some of the most fertile soil on earth. Individual states contributed 49 million additional acres from their public lands. All told, this huge block of real estate—larger than the state of Texas—was a vital source of funds for the railroads.

The wisdom of the railroad land-grant policy has been debated for many years. Some historians call it a giant giveaway that deprived the American people of a large part of their heritage in order to benefit a few. In fact, railroad promoters certainly made money from the land grants beyond their costs of construction. But the government and the public also benefited: The grants accelerated growth of the West, reduced charges for transporting government goods (a requirement written into each of the grants), and enhanced prices of the land retained by the government adjacent to the railroads. Most important, the policy speeded the process of linking the country together by rail with the result of accelerating regional diversity. If the railroads had not had land to sell, few private capitalists would have put their money in ventures so risky as railroads thrown across hundreds of miles of empty space, much of it—until the railroads arrived—virtually worthless. Without the land grants, then, economic development would undoubtedly have been slower.

Hands Off.   Each of these examples—tariffs, taxes, railroad land grants—is an instance of government contributing directly to economic development. But government also helped by refusing to impose restraints on practices business favored, even when such restraints were endorsed by many voters. It was often through the federal courts that this hands-off policy was promoted.

Between 1865 and 1880, federal judges took the position that the states could restrict the exercise of private property rights in order to protect the health, welfare, or morals of citizens. In the Slaughterhouse cases of 1873, for example, the Supreme Court rejected the contention that the Fourteenth Amendment, which had been passed to safeguard the political rights of black freedmen against state encroachment, also protected the profits and property of individuals and corporations against state regulation. In the Granger cases (notably *Munn v. Illinois*) of 1877, it upheld the right of Illinois to establish maximum rates for storing grain on the grounds that a state, under its legitimate police powers, could regulate any business that embraced "a public interest."

In the 1880s, however, the federal courts began to limit the power of state legislatures to intervene in the operations of business. In the San Mateo (1882) and the Santa Clara (1886) cases—both involving efforts by California to regulate railroad practices—the Supreme Court now asserted that the Fourteenth Amendment did apply to those injured by state economic regulation. Moreover, the amendment's protections applied not just to individuals, but to corporations, which were "persons" under the Constitution. In effect, corporations too could claim that they had been deprived by states of "property" without "due process of law" and appeal for federal protection against regulatory laws. Thereafter, it became more difficult for state legislatures to intrude into the transactions between business and individuals to further what was perceived as the public interest against the misdeeds of business. *Wabash Railroad v. Illinois* (1886) struck down an Illinois law prohibiting discrimination between long-haul and short-haul costs in transportation contracts. The decision created a "twilight zone" where the states could not regulate and the federal government had no legal right to do so either.

To end this oddity, the next year Congress passed the Interstate Commerce Act creating the Interstate Commerce Commission. Designed to regulate interstate railroads, the law gave the commission, the first regulatory commission in the country, only limited powers. And these regulatory powers were soon further diminished by the courts. In the Maximum Freight Rate case (1897), for example, the Supreme Court allowed the Interstate Commerce Commission the right to determine only whether an existing freight rate was reasonable, not to set future rates. In the E. C. Knight case (1895) it emasculated another federal regulatory law, the Sherman Antitrust Act, by making it inapplicable to manufacturing businesses.

By 1900, the federal courts had subordinated state regulatory power to federal law and crippled Congress's right to regulate, imposing a virtual hands-off-business policy on the nation. The federal government would be allowed to help business in various ways but it could not limit business for the sake of perceived public need.

Railroads, 1850–1900

Later generations would often condemn these policies harshly. But they did create an environment in which those with capital felt confident of high returns with limited risk, undoubtedly accelerating the pace of economic expansion.

The Wage Earners

In discussing the triumph of industry after 1865, we have considered causes. What about consequences? We know that it created great personal fortunes for some. But how did American laboring men and women fare as the nation accelerated its output? And how did they respond to what they experienced?

If we look only at the cold statistics, the fate of Gilded Age wage earners appears moderately good. Average real wages and annual earnings rose substantially in the half-century following the Civil War. One economist has estimated that hourly wages and earnings of American industrial workers, allowing for changes in the purchasing power of the dollar, increased by 50 percent between 1860 and 1890. Another concludes that during the next twenty-five years the increase was another 37 percent. Even omitting individual improvements in skill and increasing experience, then, industrial workers between 1865 and 1914 almost doubled their real income.

But these statistics tell only part of the story. They are only averages, and so mask a great deal of variation. They also disregard many other aspects of the working person's life in this era of pell-mell economic change.

Steam-driven trip-hammers stamped out metal parts for reapers and other farm machinery at the McCormick factory in Chicago. Machines like these increased workers' productivity, but they also added immeasurably to the hazards of wage earners' lives.

Social Mobility and Financial Rewards.

White males made up the majority of the labor force in this era, and we will consider them first. When they took their first jobs, most received the wages typical of unskilled "laborers." But generally they raised their skill levels over the years, and by their forties or fifties were earning more than thirty years before regardless of the general trend of wage levels. This improvement took place even without a change in the occupation category they began with. But many workers could count on movement up and out of the occupation where they started the "race of life." The data on occupational mobility among white American working men suggest overall that movement from unskilled to semiskilled and even skilled jobs was not uncommon. A study of Boston in the period 1880–1930 shows that, of those who began as common laborers, between 35 and 40 percent ended up higher on the occupational scale, largely in the better-paid, more prestigious, white-collar group.

We must not exaggerate the improvement, however. Horatio Alger and the other mythmakers were defending a system that did not invariably pay off. Mobility and success depended on more than individual effort and merit. We know that the extent of mobility varied, for example, by decade, by ethnic group, and by religious identification. And it was certainly difficult for a poor boy to leap to the very top of the pile. The great tycoons of the Gilded Age were almost all native-born Protestants of colonial stock who received far better educations than did the average American of the day. Their fathers, moreover, were themselves middle class or well off. On the other hand, the popularity of the rags-to-riches myths depended on a substantial number of Americans seeing mobility as a fact of daily life. As the social historian Herbert Gutman has said in a study of late-nineteenth-century mobility in Paterson, New Jersey: "So many successful manufacturers who had begun as workers walked the streets of the city. . .that it [was] not hard to believe that 'hard work' resulted in spectacular material and social improvement."

We must keep in mind, in assessing the fate of Gilded Age working people, that we are dealing with a "segmented" class. Although the average wage in 1900 was $483 a year, carpenters, masons, and other skilled construction workers often earned as much as $1,250 annually. In 1880, when "laborers" were getting an average of $1.32 a day, blacksmiths received $2.31, locomotive engineers $2.15, and machinists $2.45. The wages of federal employees, clerical workers, and western miners were also above the national average. Agricultural workers, even when we take into account that they were commonly fed and housed by their employers, were always poorly paid. In the aptly named "sweated trades" of the big-city garment industry, working people were squeezed hard by their employers—struggling small businessmen who often showed little consideration for those whose wages represented their major cost of production.

One reason for low wages in the garment industry was the presence of many female workers. Very few women in these years received wages comparable to those of adult men. A typical woman's wage was the dollar or two a week earned by female domestics who washed, cooked, sewed, and ironed in middle-class homes; women piece-workers in New York and Chicago garment loft factories received less than a dollar a day. Fortunately, the picture was not as bleak as these figures suggest. Most women eventually married and ceased to be part of the labor market. Yet for the "spinster," the unmarried woman who had to support herself, or the widow with young children, such wages were scandalous.

Black Americans were also paid well below average. Most were sharecroppers in the South, but the few who had left the farms for the mills or factories were almost all relegated to low-paying, dead-end jobs regardless of their education, skills, or talents. Immigrants, too, received lower wages than skilled and native-born white workers, at least until they acquired skills and an adequate command of English.

Living and Working Conditions.

For families at the bottom of the wage pyramid, life was undoubtedly hard. Many wage earners fought a constant battle to maintain a decent living standard and achieve a little comfort. In 1883 the large family of a railroad brakeman in Joliet, Illinois, reportedly ate chiefly bread, molasses, and potatoes. The family's clothes, a contemporary investigator noted, were "ragged" and the children "half-dressed and dirty." A witness before a Senate committee in 1883 described the home of the typical Pennsylvania coal miner as consisting of two rooms, one upstairs and one down. "The houses are built in long rows without paint on the outside," he reported. "The kitchen furniture consists of a stove and some dishes, a few chairs and a table. They have no carpets on the floor. . . ."

Material living conditions improved over the next generation, but despite advances the quality of the wage earner's life remained unsatisfactory from a modern viewpoint. Factory hours dropped from about sixty-six a week in 1850 to sixty in 1890. Between 1860 and 1890 the daily hours worked by non-agricultural workers as a whole declined from eleven to ten. Yet the length of the workday remained a trial for most workers. "I get so exhausted that I can scarcely drag myself home when night comes," exclaimed a woman worker in a Massachusetts mill. A working man knew "nothing but work, eat, and sleep," and was "little better than a horse," declared one Pennsylvania factory employee.

There was often dreary monotony to contend with as well. Much industrial work consisted merely of repetitive, simple manipulations. At one Chicago packing house at the end of the century, five men were needed to handle just the tail of a steer—two to skin it, another two to cut it off, and one to throw it into a box. How could such mindless work provide any satisfaction? One middle-class reformer who tried factory work as an experiment in the 1890s summed up the feelings of most industrial wage earners: "There is for us in our work none of the joy of responsibility, only the dull monotony of grinding toil, with the longing for the signal to quit work, and for our wages at the end of the week."

In some ways "progress" made the worker's life worse, not better. Rapid technological change made many skills obsolete. Although the job market as a whole expanded enormously in this period, skilled hands often found themselves replaced by machines. In the iron industry, for example, Andrew Carnegie pushed relentlessly for new ways to reduce the number of skilled workers in the mills. The mills succeeded in bringing down production costs, but only at a high price to their workers. Some were discharged; many who remained were forced to accept semiskilled or unskilled work, which reduced their income and made their jobs still more monotonous. Some employers applied the principles of Taylorism, the ideas of Frederick W. Taylor, an industrial engineer who had developed his theories while trying to increase the efficiency of the workforce at the Midvale Steel Company. Taylor was certain that machine-tenders, like machines, could be made more productive if wasted motion could be eliminated. Workers often charged that Taylorism resulted in speed-ups that made their lives on the job more hectic and difficult.

Industrial work was also unsafe and unhealthy. Thousands died young from silicosis (a lung ailment caused by inhalation of rock dust), from tuberculosis, cancer, heart conditions, and other work-induced diseases. Unsafe machinery, mine gases, and explosive, dust-laden air maimed and killed many. Between 1870 and 1910 there were almost 4,000 injuries or deaths at Carnegie's South Works alone. In 1917 the nation's industrial casualty list was 11,000 killed and 1.4 million wounded.

Society did little or nothing to offset the fearful toll. Before 1900, common law held that if a "fellow servant" was responsible for a job injury, the employer was not liable for damages. And even if injury resulted from direct employer neglect or carelessness, injured workers or their families had to sue to receive compensation. Few could take such an expensive course. Some prosperous working people were able to buy private insurance; but when the chief wage earner was killed or lost the ability to hold a job, most families faced a grim future indeed.

In addition, workers had to contend with periodic business downturns. Between 1870 and 1900 there were two serious slumps and several lesser ones. In the first and last of these (1873–1879 and 1893–1897) the proportion of the labor force unemployed ran to over 12 percent, a figure not equaled until the 1930s. During these lean years many working-class families had difficulty keeping a roof over their heads and decent clothes on their backs. Beggars swarmed the streets, and hoboes and tramps rode the freight rails from town to town looking for work.

Averaged out throughout the Gilded Age, unemployment reduced workers' total income only about 7 percent below a full-employment level. But this burden, too, was not equally shared. For older workers, for blacks, for many unskilled immigrants, depressions were especially disastrous. Considered marginal by employers, they were the first to be fired and the last to be rehired. For the least employable members of the labor force, hard times sometimes meant permanent idleness.

Old age also presented economic hazards for working people. There were virtually no pension systems. Men and women who became too old to work usually had little to fall back on if they lacked personal savings. Private charity was often degrading and stingy. Many aging parents were forced to move in with their children. If retired workers presented a less serious burden for society as a whole during this period than today, it was because men and women had more children to support them, and fewer lived to their later, nonworking years.

To understand the circumstances of the American wage earner during the Gilded Age, it is essential, then, to make distinctions. White, male, native-born skilled workers were the nation's "labor-aristocrats"; many lived in decent comfort, owned their own homes, ate well, and enjoyed some comforts, even a few luxuries, though like other workers they were subject to job insecurity and danger and worked long hours. It is difficult to calculate the size of this labor elite, but it probably represented about a third of the total nonfarm labor force. For the other members of the armies of labor—women, blacks, and unskilled, recent immigrants—life was not only precarious but often meager and harsh. The families of the unskilled made up for the primary breadwinner's low wages to some extent by sending everyone to work, young and old, male and female. The prevalence of child labor was one reflection of this need. But this arrangement was a high price to pay for survival. In sum, the lives of the unskilled and semiskilled were not only insecure but also pinched. Life was getting better, but there was still a long way to go before people at the base of the income pyramid could say that America had fulfilled its age-old promise of abundance.

Working-Class Protest

Horatio Alger and the work ethic notwithstanding, it is not surprising that wage earners felt, and often expressed, discontent. Much protest undoubtedly took the form of angry sounding off to fellow workers, and absenteeism. But workers expressed themselves in collective ways as well, in the form of trade unionism, political reform, and utopianism.

Trade unionists typically accepted both the capitalist and industrial systems—though sometimes with reservations—and sought higher wages, shorter hours, and better working conditions within them through collective bargaining. If negotiation did not work they were willing to resort to picketing, slowdowns, strikes, and boycotts of employers' goods. The political reformers came in two varieties. The moderates favored separate labor parties to fight for the eight-hour day, workers' compensation laws, safety legislation, and child-labor laws. The militants favored radical parties—socialist or anarchist—that would replace capitalism and private property with some version of the "cooperative commonwealth," either by electoral processes or, if needed, by some sort of revolution. Neither of these sorts of political activists, however, sought to dismantle the system of large-scale industry and return to a simpler form of production. But there were those who did. A third approach to transforming the existing labor system—utopianism—aimed to turn back the clock to before the factory system and convert the industrial worker into a small producer.

Before 1860 most trade unions had been local organizations, enrolling workers within a given city. During the prosperous years immediately following the Civil War the national trade union movement appeared in response to the new coast-to-coast labor market that exposed local wage earners to competition from workers in distant cities. By 1873 there were forty-one national unions with between 300,000 and 400,000 members.

These early post-Civil War years witnessed the rise and fall of the National Labor Union (NLU), the first nationwide labor federation. Formed by Boston machinist Ira Steward in 1866, the NLU at first focused on securing the eight-hour day through state action. Steward believed the eight-hour principle would not only make the worker's job more tolerable; it would also help free workers from the exploitive wage system. Under William Sylvis, Steward's successor, the NLU turned to Greenbackism, a scheme for the government to issue paper money and lend it to workers. By this means workers could become self-employed small producers in their own right. In 1872 the NLU transformed itself into the National Labor Reform party and nominated Supreme Court Justice David Davis as its presidential candidate.

Depression of the Seventies.   The panic of 1873 and the depression that followed made jobs precious and hard to get. Employers, finding that they could hire desperate unemployed men and women willing to accept any terms, became less tolerant of "troublemakers." Union membership nationwide plummeted from about 300,000 in 1873 to some 50,000 in 1878.

The mid-1870s was a time of violent labor strife. In January 1874 New York City police charged into a crowd of unemployed workers assembled in Tompkins Square to protest hard times, injuring many. The following year was marked by the sensational trial of the so-called Molly Maguires for the murders of coal mine managers in eastern Pennsylvania and for acts of violence against the mine owners' property. Some scholars believe that the sensational evidence against the Mollies, collected by an agent of a private detective agency employed by the owners, was invented so that the principal mine owners could break a miners' union. In any case, when ten Mollies were hanged and another fourteen sent to jail, many middle-class Americans saw their deep suspicions of labor organizations confirmed.

The middle-class public suffered a still-worse shock in 1877 when striking workers turned to violence. After four years of hard times the eastern and midwestern railroads cut their workers' wages and lengthened their hours. In Baltimore, when angry workers picketed the Baltimore and Ohio Railroad, the local police dispersed them with nightsticks. Soon after, B & O workers seized the railroad's terminal and yards at Martinsburg, West Virginia. Similar seizures took place in Pittsburgh, Chicago, Buffalo, and points west, involving several major railroads and thousands of workers. For two weeks it looked as if the country was on the verge of a revolution. In Baltimore state militia fired at a mob of workers and youths, killing ten. In Pittsburgh rioters looted stores; burned machine shops, hundreds of freight cars, and the Union Depot; and engaged in a pitched gun battle with militia. Frightened by these signs of "red revolution," governors and local officials called out state troops and deputized volunteers. When the governor of Maryland called for federal help, President Hayes dispatched several army regiments to protect life and property. By early August the violence had ended, but not before many conservative Americans concluded that they had narrowly escaped a complete overthrow of the established order.

The Knights of Labor.   With the return of prosperity in 1878–1879, labor unions revived. At the forefront was the Noble Order of the Knights of Labor, a body created in 1869 by a group of Philadelphia tailors led by Uriah S. Stephens.

At first the Knights operated more like a secret lodge or fraternal order than an ordinary trade union. They provided an environment for members' social activity and offered life insurance, burial plots, and other benefits to compensate for the uncertainties of the wage earner's life. If they had any general labor policy, it was to encourage producers' cooperatives.

In the early 1880s, under the leadership of Terence V. Powderly, the Knights responded to improved times and the enhanced leverage it produced. Abandoning their longer-range reform goals, they confronted employers with wage demands backed by strikes or threats of strikes. In March 1885, the Knights forced Jay Gould's Southwest Railroad to cancel a 10-percent wage cut. On the strength of this victory over the hated Gould, the union attracted throngs of new members. In the next two years membership leaped from a little over 100,000 to almost 730,000.

Here was an opportunity to create a powerful labor movement, but the chance was missed. Powderly and the Knights' other leaders never could decide whether they were organizing a trade union, a lodge, a reform association, or a political pressure group. Nor could they decide whether to recruit black members. Powderly favored organizing black workers, but he denied that he endorsed racial equality and insisted that black members be confined to segregated locals. The Knights could not sustain the momentum of the mid-1880s and soon lost many of its new members.

The final blow to the trade union movement of the era came with the 1886 Haymarket Riot in Chicago. During the spring of that year, McCormick Harvester Company officials had locked out 1,400 members of the Knights of Labor for demanding an eight-hour day and a $2 daily wage. On May 3, when the company tried to bring in "scabs" to replace the union men, the workers attacked the strikebreakers; the police in turn fired on the workers. The McCormick dispute marked the climax of a five-year citywide struggle for the eight-hour day that had deeply disturbed Chicago's labor relations. One element in the inflammable mixture was the anarchists, a group of radicals dedicated to destroying all government, along with private property and the wage system. Though few in number, the anarchists had supporters among the city's large German population. Following the police attack at the McCormick company, August Spies, a leading anarchist, issued a circular in German calling on the city's wage earners to "rise in your might . . . and destroy the hideous monster [of capitalism] that seeks to destroy you." The response of the conservative daily press was equally alarmist and overwrought. "A Wild Mob's Work; Wrought Up to a Frenzy by Anarchist Harangues, They Attack Employees" was the headline in the *Chicago Tribune*.

On the evening of May 4, at the anarchists' call, 3,000 men and women gathered at Haymarket Square on the city's West Side. Many who might have come had been frightened away by Spies's inflammatory words. The meeting was relatively orderly, and the crowd had begun to thin out when the police tried to disperse the remnant. Suddenly a bomb exploded among the advancing police. When the smoke cleared, seventy policemen lay wounded. Eventually seven died from the blast.

The forces of law and order reacted blindly. No one ever discovered who planted the bomb, but the public and the authorities immediately blamed the anarchists and, by extension, all "labor agitators," whether radical or not. Hundreds of men were hustled off to jail, and ten anarchists were indicted for conspiracy to commit murder. Seven were sentenced to death after a trial that failed to establish their direct connection with the massacre. In late 1887, four were hanged.

The public outrage at the Chicago bombing shook the entire labor movement. Middle-class people now condemned all unions, even the most moderate and peaceful. To the already weakened Knights, the Haymarket affair was disastrous. Recruiting dried up; timid members quit. The Knights survived for another decade and a half, but after 1886 the union became a shadow of what it had been at its peak.

American Federation of Labor.   As the Knights sank, the American Federation of Labor (AFL) rose. Established in 1886 by ex-socialists, including Adolph Strasser, Peter J. Maguire, and Samuel Gompers, the AFL concentrated its efforts on native-born workers in the skilled crafts. As its name suggests, the AFL was a federation of unions. Each of the members belonged to the AFL only through his own trade union–carpenters, machinists, printers, or some other group.

The AFL prospered for several reasons. First, it confined its organizing efforts to skilled workers. These were the most easily organized because they were difficult to replace and so could afford to take risks. The AFL also abandoned utopian goals and avoided politics. Samuel Gompers and his lieutenants, though they had once been socialists, believed that political radicalism was dangerous to the labor movement. Skilled workers, they noted, were profoundly wary of radical politics, and any hint of extremism frightened the middle class. The blow that Haymarket had dealt the Knights of Labor convinced the AFL leaders that direct action, radical or not, was unsafe. Moreover, government intrusion into labor–management relations might be less beneficent than socialists imagined. The authorities might favor measures harmful to labor or seek to impose their decisions on labor disputes.

Gompers, who served as AFL president almost continuously until his death in 1924, endorsed "volunteerism" and "pure and simple" trade unionism as the best policies for the AFL. Unions would improve labor conditions by collective bargaining, resorting to strikes if necessary. Workers would be encouraged to vote for labor's political friends and against its enemies, but beyond that, should avoid political involvement. As for socialism, it was foolish, Gompers declared, to suppose that people could

. . . go to bed one night under the present system and tomorrow morning wake up with a revolution in full blast, and the next day organize a heaven on earth. That is not the way that progress is made; that is not the way . . . social evolution is brought about. We are solving the problem day after day. As we get an hour's more leisure every day it means millions of golden hours of opportunities to the human family. As we get 25 cents a day wage increase, it means another solution, another problem solved, and brings us nearer the time when a greater degree of social justice and fair dealing will obtain among men.

Joined with this moderate philosophy was a pragmatic program. The AFL fought to extract an eight-hour day from employers along with higher wages and better job conditions. It worked to get employers to recognize the union as the "collective bargaining" agent for their employees. It sought to establish a "union shop"—that is, get management to hire only union members.

Armed with this philosophy and program, the AFL forged ahead, particularly when prosperity returned after the depression of the mid-1890s. Despite strong opposition by employers, who considered collective bargaining an interference with the rights of private property, the federation made substantial gains. In 1904 it claimed 1.6 million members out of a total of some 2 million union members in the country. By 1914 it had over 2 million workers in its affiliated unions out of 2.7 million union members altogether. A large majority of blue-collar industrial work-ers, particularly the unskilled, remained outside the protection that unions con-ferred; so did most black workers and women. But by the eve of World War I, Gompers and the AFL were powers to be reckoned with in national life.

The Socialist Alternative.

The socialism of the late nineteenth century was built on a body of political beliefs and a theory of society that would exert enor-mous influence over the years. In *Das Kapital* (1867) and other works, Karl Marx, a German social theorist, had asserted the material, or economic, basis of all human interests and actions. Religion, family structure, government, literature, arts, and philosophy reflected each era's fundamental economic institutions. Each era, more-over, was marked by a dominant class. Those were the people who controlled the means of production and so exercised the power and enjoyed the wealth produced by society. In the Middle Ages the dominant class had been the feudal nobility. By the nineteenth century it was the bourgeoisie, the capitalist class.

According to Marxism, as the capitalist class amassed more and more of soci-ety's wealth and power, it would reach a point of crisis. Already, Marx and his dis-ciples noted, capitalist societies were finding themselves with goods that no one would buy and they would soon experience ever more frequent and serious de-pressions. These crises would further undercut the workers' material circum-stances. Eventually the proletariat, or working class, would realize their common interests; abandon the ethnic, cultural, religious, and national differences that had kept them apart; and turn to revolution. The masses would seize the factories, farms, and banks and nationalize the means of production and distribution.

The world would be a far better place after the revolution, Marx and his disci-ples insisted. Profits formerly skimmed off by the capitalists would be used to benefit the masses. Under the new socialist system there would no longer be exploiter and exploited, powerful and powerless. Instead, there would be only one class, the working class, and within it all would be equal. With the class struggle ended and capitalist "contradictions" eliminated, humanity would prosper as never before under a regime of economic and social justice for all.

Thousands of men and women were inspired by this Marxist vision. It held out hope to the oppressed of a world where they would enjoy the abundance and freedom seemingly reserved for the rich under capitalism. Its promise of a harmonious society after capitalism appealed to intellectuals by offering a substitute for their lost religious faith. It spoke to artists, writers, and romantic rebels by promising an antidote to what they saw as the crude and vulgar world of bourgeois values.

At the turn of the century the Marxists competed with several other socialist groups for the allegiance of wage earners and middle-class dissenters. For a while educated Americans were attracted to the Nationalist clubs organized by the journalist Edward Bellamy who, in *Looking Backward* (1888), described a society in the year 2000 where abundance, cooperation, and leisure had superseded scarcity, competition, and drudgery. Also prominent for a while were the anarchists, whose activities in the Haymarket riot have been mentioned. Members of the so-called Black International (in contrast with the Marxist Red International), they believed that every effort to regiment or coerce human beings was an evil denial of freedom. Anarchists favored rule by voluntary associations of people organized around their jobs. Although noncoercive in their philosophy, the anarchists were anything but gentle in their tactics. In both Europe and America they were notorious for assassinating public officials and throwing bombs to make their antiauthoritarian point.

Prior to the Haymarket bombing the anarchists and socialists had won small working-class followings in the major industrial centers. At first there were several competing socialist groups; but after its founding in 1877, the Socialist Labor party, under the brilliant but abrasive Daniel De Leon, became the chief socialist organization. As we have seen, the public reaction to the Haymarket riot injured trade unionism; it also damaged the various anticapitalist parties, and for several years they languished as little more than debating societies.

The Homestead Strike.   The labor movement's worst defeat during these years was the Homestead Strike in the summer of 1892. The dispute with management started as a confrontation with the Carnegie Steel Company management at the firm's plant at Homestead, Pennsylvania, where Carnegie's lieutenant, Henry Clay Frick, had introduced the most modern labor-saving machinery. Claiming that the new equipment would enhance productivity and hence wages for those who worked by the piece, Frick simultaneously announced that piece rates would be reduced. The Amalgamated Association of Iron and Steel Workers, representing the most skilled men, refused to accept the new terms. At the end of June 1893, joined by the unskilled workers, they went on strike and sealed off the plant.

Frick advertised for strikebreakers. To get the new employees to the idle plant, he hired 300 armed Pinkerton agents and sent them in two barges up the Monongahela River, which ran along the edge of the Homestead works. Early on the morning of July 6 the Pinkertons tried to slip by the guards posted by the strikers, but they were detected. The strikers let go with rifles and pistols; the Pinkertons returned the fire until the strikers poured oil on the water and lit it. At this point, rather than face incineration, the Pinkertons surrendered in return for safe conduct. As they departed for the railway station, however, they were badly beaten. All told, five strikers and three Pinkertons died in the savage melee.

Five days later the governor of Pennsylvania sent 8,000 militiamen to the plant and returned it to the company. The Amalgamated then offered to surrender its economic demands in return for recognition of its right to serve as the bargaining agent for the workers. Frick refused. "Under no circumstances will we have any further dealings with the Amalgamated Association," he declared. "This is final." This unyielding attitude, combined with the use of Pinkertons, brought public opinion to the side of the strikers. Though he supported Frick, Carnegie was dismayed by the mayhem and might have forced concessions, but a young anarchist, Alexander Berkman, barged into Frick's office and shot and stabbed him repeatedly. Frick survived, but public opinion now turned against the strikers, ending all possibility of compromise.

Depression, Pullman, and Socialist Revival.

The depression following the panic of 1893 encouraged further labor violence and gave socialism a renewed impetus. As in the 1870s, unemployment soared and thousands of idle workers tramped the streets looking for work. Employers sought once again to maintain profits and avoid losses by cutting wages. Like all depressions in capitalist societies, that of the 1890s weakened confidence in the system and aroused dissent. By creating a new charismatic leader, Eugene V. Debs, the Pullman strike of 1894 became an important turning point in the history of American socialism.

The focus of the affair was the Pullman Company. George Pullman, the inventor of the railroad sleeping car, had established his giant factory outside Chicago and surrounded it with a model community for his employees. With its tree-lined streets, cream-colored brick houses, its gardens and parks, the town of Pullman was a physically attractive place. It was also a repressive place. Pullman insisted on making his town moral, obedient, and profitable. He forbade liquor, spied on his employees, fired workers for running against the candidates he favored for local office, and charged high rents and utility rates. Pullman considered himself a benevolent man, but he acted like a feudal lord.

In the summer of 1893, when orders for new Pullman "palace cars" started to fall off, Pullman began to fire workers and cut wages while refusing to reduce rents and utility rates. To defend themselves, Pullman workers joined the newly organized American Railway Union (ARU) led by a tall, lanky Indianian, Eugene V. Debs. On May 11, 1894, after several unsuccessful attempts to negotiate with Pullman officials, over 3,000 employees walked off the job and asked for ARU support. Debs tried to persuade the Pullman management to negotiate. When his efforts failed, he reluctantly ordered the ARU switchmen to refuse to attach Pullman cars to trains. The railroad officials responded by dismissing the defiant switchmen. The ARU struck back. By July 1 all twenty-four railroads operating out of Chicago, the nation's chief rail hub, had shut down.

Despite their anger, the strikers were restrained and orderly. Yet the shutdown of the country's major transportation system dismayed the middle-class public. Hoping to break the strike and smash the union, the General Managers Association, representing the major railroads entering and leaving Chicago, hired strikebreakers and asked the federal government for aid, claiming that it was

Washington's responsibility to guarantee delivery of the mail, which had stopped in many places when the trains ceased to run. In Attorney General Richard Olney the railroad had a friend in government. A hot-tempered former railroad lawyer who despised labor leaders, Olney quickly ordered federal marshals to Chicago. He also convinced a federal judge to issue an injunction that ordered the union to cease the strike or be "in contempt of court." The following day, July 3, over the protests of Illinois governor John P. Altgeld, who denied that there was sufficient disorder to require federal intervention, President Grover Cleveland ordered the entire garrison of Fort Sheridan to the city to prevent violence.

The presence of troops and federal marshals infuriated the strikers, and the railway yards were swept by a wave of shootings and arson. The federal authorities cracked down, arresting Debs and other ARU officials on July 17 for violating the court injunction. Deprived of their leaders, the men gave up and gradually drifted back to work.

Debs went to prison for six months and thereafter turned against capitalism. In 1901 he became a founder of the Socialist Party of America, an organization that would win a larger following than Daniel De Leon's Socialist Labor party. During the remainder of his life, Debs would embody both the best and the worst in American socialism. Generous, humane, and fiery in defense of justice, he was also a stubborn visionary who lacked the ability to manage a party racked by bitter internal disagreements.

Despite his failings, under Debs's leadership the Socialist Party of America grew rapidly before World War I, winning the support of many German and Jewish wage earners and even some rural and small-town people in the Midwest. It also attracted a following of authors, ministers, and professional people. Between 1904 and 1912 the party increased its dues-paying membership from 20,000 to 130,000; in 1912 Debs received 900,000 votes, 6 percent of the total, when he ran for president on the Socialist ticket. The party did even better on the local level, electing several congressmen and a half-dozen mayors in cities such as Scranton, Milwaukee, and Syracuse.

Still, the Socialist Party of America never captured the support of a majority of American wage earners and, unlike its counterparts in Europe, never truly challenged the mainstream parties for control of the political system. To explain this failure we must contrast American workers to European workers. Native-born American wage earners were not class conscious. Well paid by comparison with industrial workers in other lands and just a generation or two off the farm, they expected to prosper and move up the social ladder. Many owned some property and could not accept a philosophy that predicted inevitable class conflict and the increasing misery of wage earners under capitalism. Immigrant workers were not much better as potential recruits for socialism. Most had difficulty enough adjusting to American cities and American industry without making further trouble for themselves, and they avoided "agitators." Despite their initially low status, they too expected to rise socially and economically. All told, the relative prosperity of the United States and people's expectations for improvement were strong antidotes to radical politics. As the German sociologist Werner Sombart noted with some exaggeration at the turn of the century, socialist "utopias" in America inevitably foundered "on the reefs of roast beef and apple pie."

Conclusions

As we explore the nation's climb to industrial preeminence a century ago, several factors come into view. Clearly, the skill, intelligence, drive, and even ruthlessness of America's industrial tycoons helped to propel the Great Republic past its rivals. But the captains of industry could not have created the world's industrial leader alone. Working people, accepting the conventional wisdom of the age, labored hard, believing that success and security would reward their efforts. And without government's substantial contributions, despite the theories of laissez-faire and social Darwinism, progress would have been far slower.

Clearly, many of the men and women who lived through these tumultuous years were ground down by the great economic machine they were helping to build. The pain they experienced was expressed in the violence of the Pullman, Homestead, and the 1877 railway strikes, and in the organized political efforts meant to effect change. Yet we must not exaggerate the extent or depth of discontent among wage earners. Many found their lives satisfactory and, with reason, looked forward to better times. Despite the agitation and the occasional violence, it remains true that most Americans retained their faith in the "system" and refused to accept radical solutions to the problems they faced. This ultimate faith was expressed in the continued vitality of the economy and the mainstream political parties and in the growth of cities and the nation as a whole.

ONLINE RESOURCES

"African American Mosaic—Migrations" *http://www.loc.gov/exhibits/african/afam009.html* Maps, illustrations, genealogical charts, and photos depict the African-American quest of the "Exodusters" who migrated West, especially to Kansas, in search of a better life.

"Looking Backward" *http://xroads.virginia.edu/~HYPER/BELLAMY/toc.html* This site provides access to the full text of Edward Bellamy's famed 1888 utopian novel *Looking Backward*.

"The Dramas of Haymarket" *http://www.chicagohistory.org/dramas/overview/main.htm* Produced by the Chicago Historical Society, this site details the events leading up to the Haymarket riot, including the radicalization of many American workers and class tensions in America. The site includes both essays and primary-source material.

"Taylorism and Scientific Management" *http://www.fordham.edu/halsall/mod/1911taylor.html*
Read Frederick Taylor's essays in his work, The Principles of Scientific Management. These principles of work had a dramatic effect on industry, the way work was performed, and the lives of workers.

Obstacles Faced by African Americans *http://www.pbs.org/wgbh/amex/1900/filmmore/reference/interview/washing_obstaclesfaced.html* This portion of PBS's "The American Experience" Web site details the status of and challenges faced by African-Americans in the areas of education, public accommodations, and voting at the turn of the century.

The Greatest Tyrant in the State of Pennsylvania: A Late Nineteenth-Century Rail Worker Describes Management *http://historymatters.gmu.edu/d/79* In the testimony recorded on this Web site, railroad worker Joseph Cahill tells the U.S. House of Representatives about his role in a labor union and management's mistreatment of workers in the late nineteenth century.

18

Age of the City

What Did Cities Offer? And to Whom?

1860–1910	American cities, as defined by the Census, increase in number from 392 to 2,220
1871	The Great Chicago Fire
1872	New York's Boss Tweed is indicted and jailed
1878	Asphalt paving introduced in Washington, D.C.
1880	Salvation Army introduced from England; James A. Garfield elected president
1881	Garfield assassinated; Chester A. Arthur becomes president
1882	Chinese Exclusion Act passed in response to organized labor's fear of cheap labor
1884	Grover Cleveland elected president
1888	Benjamin Harrison elected president
1892	Cleveland elected president for the second time
1894	Immigration Restriction League; Coxey's Army marches on Washington to protest unemployment
1896	William McKinley elected president
1897	First subway line is built, in Boston
1899–1904	Mayor Samuel "Golden Rule" Jones institutes municipal ownership of utilities in Toledo
1900–10	Eight million immigrants arrive
1901	McKinley assassinated; Theodore Roosevelt becomes president
1907	Congress appoints Dillingham Commission to investigate immigration
1914	Birth-control advocate Margaret Sanger is forced to leave the country

The city has been a central component of civilization for perhaps 5,000 years. In fact, cities seem to equal civilization, for it has been in urban settings that humanity has produced most of the ideas, artifacts, art, and science that we identify as essential marks of civilized life.

Throughout much of history, however, city dwellers have been a minority; until the years following the Civil War, the United States was no exception to this rule. As late as 1860 only 20 percent of the nation's people were urban. The most heavily urbanized sections of the nation on the eve of the Civil War were the New England and Middle Atlantic areas. Elsewhere, particularly in the West and the South, most Americans continued to live on villages and farms.

The Civil War slowed city growth somewhat, but thereafter it resumed at a rapid clip. Between 1860 and 1910 the number of census-defined "urban places" increased from 392 to over 2,200. In 1860 New York and Philadelphia were the only American cities with more than half a million inhabitants. By 1910 these communities, along with the "prairie colossus," Chicago, had over a million residents each, and five other cities had grown to populations of 500,000. During that fifty-year stretch the urban share of the country's population went from 20 to 46 percent. The Northeast remained the most urban part of the nation in 1910, but urbanization had spread far beyond the areas that had first felt the pull of industry and commerce.

What brought millions of people from the farms of America and from distant regions of the world to the cities of the United States in these years? And how did the millions of new urban dwellers prosper in their new homes?

Immigration

One source of soaring urban populations in the half-century following the Civil War was foreign-born newcomers. In the 1880s more than 5 million people entered the United States. The depression of the 1890s reduced the number of immigrants substantially, but between 1900 and 1910 over 8 million more foreigners arrived. Some of these people eventually returned home, either disappointed with America or so successful that they could live well in the "old country" on the fortunes they had made here. Yet most immigrants, by far, remained in the United States, and by the end of the century a majority of them made the cities their home.

America's Attractions.   Like previous immigrants, Gilded Age arrivals were moved by both "pushes" and "pulls." The chief "pull" of America for immigrants of this era, as for their predecessors, was economic. Immigrants from every land were attracted by the possibility of improving themselves in some material way; only a minority were drawn by America's reputation for religious and political freedom. Immigrants were remarkably well informed about American economic conditions. During hard times in the United States, such as the mid-1890s, foreigners stayed home. During good times, such as the 1880s and the first decade of the twentieth century, the current of immigrants became a flood.

American business actively encouraged immigration in these years. During the 1850s western mining companies had brought in Chinese workers to dig for gold in California and Nevada. In the 1860s the Central Pacific Railroad imported 10,000 Chinese to help construct the first transcontinental line. After its completion many of these laborers remained to build other western railroads and to swell the populations of San Francisco, Sacramento, Denver, and other western towns. In Texas, Arizona, New Mexico, California, and Colorado, railroad employers recruited many Mexicans to work on repair and construction crews. Truck farmers and fruit-growers in the Southwest and on the Pacific Coast recruited others to harvest fruit, cotton, lettuce, and tomatoes.

The railroads, endowed with enormous land grants, were also eager for settlers to convert their acreage into cash. The Illinois Central, the Northern Pacific, and other railroads scattered colorful brochures advertising their lands across Europe and established offices in major European cities where railroad representatives offered advice to would-be immigrants and described the favorable terms available to those willing to come. Thousands took the bait.

In 1864 Congress provided business with a means to recruit workers from abroad. Designed to remedy an anticipated labor shortage, the Contract Labor Law authorized employers to hire foreign workers under an agreement that guaranteed passage money, a specified wage, and defined working conditions. The law was not effective. Though only a few hundred skilled workers were brought to the United States under its provisions, trade union pressure induced Congress to repeal it in 1885 (the Foran Act).

A more fruitful source of foreign labor was the padrone system used to recruit Italian labor for eastern mines, factories, and construction projects. *Padroni* were Italian-American middlemen, frequently connected with small immigrant banking firms, who signed up gangs of Italian laborers in southern Italy at fixed wages and paid for the workers' passage. In the United States the padrone arranged with an American employer to supply workers at a sum that gave him a profit. In the early years, when the United States was still an unfamiliar destination for Italians, the system was useful in providing immigrants with food, board, and advice. The padroni, however, often took advantage of the trusting men they recruited, charging them high prices for what they provided while keeping them in virtual slavery. Fortunately, when the Italian-American community had put down firm roots and would-be immigrants could turn to relatives and friends for advice and help, the system declined.

Though sponsorship and active recruiting contributed to the immigration stream, the great majority of European arrivals needed little personal incentive to join the booming American economy. Letters from relatives and friends, talks with townspeople back in the old country for a visit, or information supplied by government agencies and shipping companies were enough to draw people by the thousands to embarkation ports to take ship for the United States.

Immigration in this period was also spurred by plummeting cost of ocean passage and the growing speed of ocean travel. During the 1860s the introduction of large and fast steam vessels with auxiliary sail reduced transatlantic crossing times from as long as three months to as little as ten days. A dozen shipping companies—British, German, Italian, Dutch, and French, as well as American—soon entered the transatlantic trade in people, and their fierce competition quickly brought passenger rates down even more.

The Push: The New Immigrants.   Like the "pull" to America, the "push" from other lands was predominantly economic. Until the 1890s most immigrants came from northern Europe—Britain, Germany, and Scandinavia. In each of these places agriculture had been hurt by competition from the newer grain-growing regions of Canada, the United States, Argentina, and Australia. Unable to compete with the lower production costs in these new lands, European landlords replaced peasants with machines. Thousands of north European farmers sought haven in the United States.

The push from northern Europe soon slackened. Industrialization, plus falling birth rates throughout northern Europe, provided new opportunities for displaced farm people in their own nations' factories and mines. British emigration more and more turned to the British "dominions"—Canada, Australia, New Zealand, and South Africa.

After 1890 a wave of immigrants from southern and eastern Europe more than offset this north European decline. These so-called New Immigrants were a diverse lot. Many were Slavs—Bohemians, Poles, Ukrainians, Slovaks, Serbs, Croatians, Ruthenians, Russians, and others—from the Hapsburg Empire (Austria-Hungary) or from Russia, the empire of the Romanov czars. Many came from Europe's south, the largest number from Italy, though there were many Greeks as well. Other eastern Europeans included Hungarians and Rumanians. From the Turkish dominions came Armenians and Syrians. Jews from either Austria-Hungary or imperial Russia formed another large group of New Immigrants. Many of the Slavs and virtually all the Italians were Roman Catholic, and for the first time there were substantial numbers of Orthodox Catholics among the new arrivals.

Until this time, America had seemed too far away, too alien, and too expensive for many of these people. Besides, their own governments often refused to allow them to leave for fear of reducing their military manpower or their tax rolls. But toward the end of the century Austria, Russia, and Turkey abandoned their opposition to emigration, ocean passage rates and travel time declined sharply, and overseas agricultural competition spread to eastern Europe.

Though the push was largely economic, political and religious factors also played a part in propelling people from the czarist and Ottoman lands across the Atlantic. The czars in St. Petersburg often treated their non-Russian subjects harshly. After 1870 thousands of German Pietists, who had settled in southern Russia during the

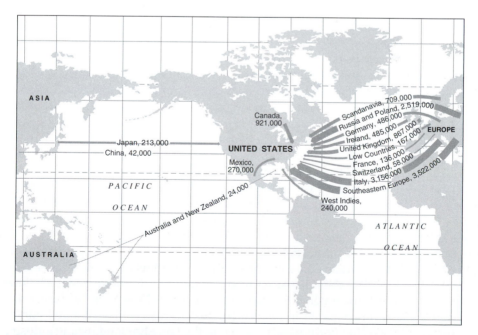

Sources of Immigrants, 1900–1920

eighteenth century, fled when the Russian government withdrew their privileges. A much larger group of refugees from the czars' domain were Jews who had resided in Russian-occupied lands since the Middle Ages. After 1880 a wave of discriminatory laws excluded them from public office, universities, agricultural pursuits, the professions, and other activities. The bigoted Russian government also incited anti-Jewish riots (pogroms) that resulted in hundreds of deaths and the devastation of whole communities. Meanwhile, in the Ottoman Empire, the Turkish government began to brutally persecute its Christian Syrian and Armenian minorities.

These changes, taken together, produced a drastic shift in the source of the immigrant streams from Europe. In 1880 a mere 17,000 immigrants to the United States came from Austria-Hungary; in 1907 there were almost 340,000. Only 5,000 Russian subjects immigrated to America in 1880; in 1907 over 225,000 arrived. In 1880 some 12,000 Italians came to the United States; in 1907, over 285,000.

From Farms to Cities.   The ocean crossing remained unpleasant for poorer immigrants until well into the twentieth century. They usually traveled below deck in "steerage," jammed into large open spaces with bunks for hundreds of others. Rough seas produced misery and at times cholera swept the ships, killing scores and so frightening American officials that the federal government imposed quarantines when they arrived shutting down all transatlantic immigration for substantial periods.

Most European immigrants came through the ports of New York, Boston, New Orleans, Baltimore, or Philadelphia, with New York far in the lead. Before 1892 most New York-bound immigrants passed through Castle Garden, a facility established at the tip of Manhattan Island by New York State officials. In 1892 the federal government assumed responsibility for receiving immigrants and replaced Castle Garden with a new facility at Ellis Island in New York Harbor. Here immigrants were asked their names, ages, occupations, places of origin, literacy, and financial status. They were also examined by doctors to see that they were not carriers of infectious diseases. Some were turned back to their homelands for health reasons or because they had mental problems or had been convicted of some crime. It was at Ellis Island that immigrants generally first made contact with the many societies established by their compatriots to offer advice and services and to keep them out of the hands of swindlers eager to cheat "greenhorns" of their money and possessions.

Once in America, immigrants had to chose their ultimate destinations. During the 1870s and 1880s thousands of Germans, Scandinavians, Poles, and Bohemians went to the wheat regions of Minnesota, the Dakotas, Nebraska, and Kansas, where they bought land from the railroads and became grain farmers. Then, as the nation shifted from agriculture to industry, many were increasingly drawn to the cities and their shops, factories, and construction sites.

Immigrants tended to concentrate in certain industries and occupations by nationality. French Canadians crossed the border from Quebec to the nearby New England towns, where they displaced many of the Irish in the textile mills. Jews from Russia and Poland entered the garment industry of New York, Rochester, and Chicago. Italians concentrated in the construction industry; Slavs entered mining and heavy industry; the Portuguese moved into the New England fishing industry.

Nativism.

Nativism.   The new pattern of immigration that emerged toward the end of the nineteenth century disturbed many Americans. Some deplored the "New" immigrants' excessive urban concentration, seeing it as a deterrent to their assimilation into American life. Concentrated in tight-knit ghettos, they would be slow to lose their alien ways and become "good Americans." Immigrant organizations themselves were concerned about the problem and Jewish and Catholic societies sought to deflect recent arrivals among their co-religionists to rural areas. Many native Americans were appalled by the unfamiliar look and ways of the newcomers. The novelist Henry James, while strolling on fashionable Beacon Hill in Boston one Sunday, observed groups of men and women in their best clothes "enjoying their leisure." "No sound of English . . . escaped their lips; the great number spoke some rude form of Italian, the others some outlandish dialect unknown to me. . . . The types and faces bore them out; the people before me were gross aliens to a man, and they were in serene and triumphant possession."

The resentment was not confined to elite, old-stock Americans like James, however. The New Immigrants frequently clashed with the Old Immigrants of the pre-Civil War generation or with their half-assimilated children. In 1877, during the hard times that followed the panic of 1873, Irish-American workers in San Francisco attacked Chinese businesses and the docks of the Pacific Mail Steamship Company, the firm they held responsible for importing the "coolies" from East Asia to undercut their wages. Soon afterward Denis Kearney, a native of Ireland's County Cork, helped organize the Workingmen's Party of California. Kearney denounced the rich railroad and mining magnates of California, but his speeches usually ended with the cry: "And whatever happens, the Chinese must go!"

The anti-Chinese movement in California was not unique. Spokesmen for organized labor elsewhere also feared "coolie labor," and indeed any cheap labor, whether from Europe or Asia. Passage of the Foran Act in 1885, repealing the Contract Labor Law of 1864, was, as we noted, largely the result of trade-union pressure. In 1882 lobbying by labor groups induced Congress to pass the Chinese Exclusion Act prohibiting the immigration of Chinese laborers for ten years. Renewed several times, the law was made permanent in 1902. Not until 1943 were foreign-born Chinese allowed to take up legal permanent residence in the United States.

Anti-immigrant sentiment in these years, however, was not solely economic in origin; nativist feelings also had cultural roots. Many native-born Americans were certain that the newest immigrants were inferior to those of the past. They came, it was said, from more backward lands where democratic institutions were unknown. They were often illiterate. A larger proportion of them were Catholic or Jewish, and hence further removed than earlier arrivals from the American Protestant tradition. The New Immigrants, moreover, did not intend to stay, the critics said. Many were birds of passage, men without wives or families, who would make their fortunes in America and return to their native lands. They refused to go to the farms, the indictment continued, congregating instead in the big cities, where they retained their foreign ways, turned to crime, and succumbed to insanity, epilepsy, or other nervous or emotional disorders that severely strained local health facilities and raised taxes for real Americans.

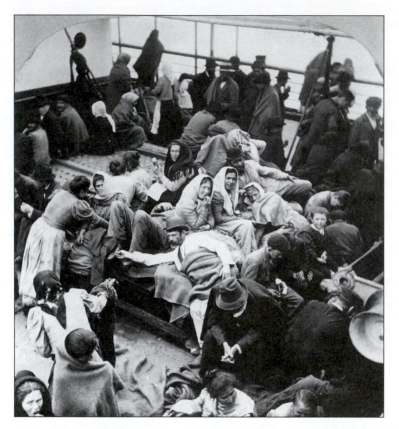

Were poor immigrants a resource? Steel king Andrew Carnegie, himself
an immigrant, believed they were. In fact, he estimated that each one was
worth $1,500. Immigrants labored in mines and mills, built railroads and
bridges, farmed the land, and bought products of the nation's factories.
(Courtesy of the Library of Congress)

The hostile response to these immigrants was reinforced at the turn of the century by the racist theories of men such as Josiah Strong and Madison Grant, who
proclaimed the natural superiority of "Nordics" over darker-haired, darker-eyed
white people of southern and eastern Europe. Racist ideology and traditional prejudice against foreigners led in 1907 to the appointment by Congress of the Dilling-
ham Commission to investigate immigration. Its voluminous report confirmed all
the common negative stereotypes of the day. The commission described the
Old Immigrants as "ideal farmers" and people "imbued with sympathy for our
ideals and . . . democratic institutions." By contrast, the more recent arrivals were
"different in temperament and civilization from ourselves." Generally speaking,
the report endorsed the common view of the inferiority of the New Immigrants
and branded them undesirable.

Given these hostile attitudes it is not surprising that nativist organizations,
dedicated to reducing the flow of immigrants or to limiting their role in American public life, drew broad support in these years. In the 1880s and 1890s, the

American Protective Association (APA) demanded that noncitizens be excluded from political office and attacked "the diabolical works of the Roman Catholic church." In 1894 a group of New England bluebloods organized the Immigration Restriction League with a program to impose literacy tests on the new arrivals, many of whom, the League believed, could not pass such a test.

The League failed in its main goals before the 1920s. In 1896, and again in 1913 and 1915, Congress passed measures requiring that all immigrants admitted to the United States be able to read and write either English or their own language. Each time, however, the president in office vetoed the measure. Though many Americans feared the foreign deluge, others opposed restriction. Businessmen resisted cutting off the inexhaustible supply of cheap labor, and the National Association of Manufacturers constantly lobbied against restrictions on immigration. Old-fashioned liberals, who prized America's tradition as a haven for the world's poor and oppressed, also fought efforts to end free immigration. Before the 1920s the doors remained open. Though Congress passed laws excluding immigrants with chronic diseases, those with records as criminals or prostitutes, and those with known anarchist views, drastic limitations on transatlantic immigrants would wait until a later day.

Buckwheats and Hayseeds.

City streets and neighborhoods were not only crowded with the foreign-born; they were also thronged with men and women straight off the nation's farms. In the exodus from the nation's farms and villages to Gilded Age cities, there were also both pushes and pulls.

The lure of the city for rural people is a persistent theme in the history of the Western world. Cities were no doubt wicked; they were dangerous. But compared with the sleepy village or farm, the city, with its well-stocked stores, its bustle, its amusements, its street life, and its brilliant lights, was a joy. The novelist Hamlin Garland recalled that everything about Chicago was interesting when he arrived there as a young farm boy: "Nothing was commonplace, nothing ugly." In *The City*, a 1909 play by Clyde Fitch, one character, recently arrived in New York, exclaims: "Who wants to smell new-mown hay, if he can breathe gasoline on Fifth Avenue instead!" And there were irresistible economic pulls. Thousands of young rural people came to the cities to work as clerks, secretaries, bookkeepers, and salespeople. Farm boys also were drawn to the mills and factories to tend machines, stoke furnaces, and supervise. At his plants in Pennsylvania Andrew Carnegie liked to hire "buckwheats," lads from the nearby countryside. These young men, he believed, made the best workers in the mills. For young Americans with special career interests, the cities were meccas. To talented musicians, artists, writers, actors, or performers of any kind, only the largest cities of the land could provide the training, the experience, and the appreciative audience they needed and craved.

The push also applied to rural youths—"hayseeds" in the vernacular of the day. If the cities were fascinating, the farms and villages often were not. Hamlin Garland wrote about the "sordidness, dullness, triviality, and . . . endless drudgeries" of rural life. In his short story "Up the Coulee" one of his characters complains: "Anything under God's heavens is better'n farmin'." But even if a farm youth wanted to stay and till the soil, it was often difficult. Farm families were large, and rural fathers could not provide land for all their sons. There was the option of going west, but as we shall see, through much of the late nineteenth century, agriculture was a troubled industry even on the newer western lands. In the Northeast, movement to the cities resembled a mass exodus. With the completion of the transportation network, it became ever more difficult for the old, rocky fields of New England and the Middle Atlantic states to compete with the rich soils of the Great Plains and the prairies. As the census of 1890 showed, the counties in two-fifths of Pennsylvania, one-fourth of New Jersey, about five-sixths of New York, and a very large part of New England had declined in population during the 1880s. Most of these missing people were now living in the region's cities.

The Urban Environment

The Physical Setting.   Whether from Italy or Iowa, Austria or Alabama, newcomers found urban life in the Gilded Age replete with problems. American cities in the years immediately following the Civil War were generally harsh, dirty, congested places. City streets were dusty in summer, muddy in winter, and filthy at all times. Nor was the sky above any better. The soft coal widely used for heating and industrial fuel darkened city air with soot. In the 1890s the ash from its steel and glass factories often brought twilight at midday to Pittsburgh.

Until the end of the century few American cities had adequate public water supplies or decent sewers or street-cleaning services. In 1880 Baltimore, with 330,000 people, had "no sewers to speak of. . ., all chamber slops [being] deposited in cesspools or privvy vaults." A newspaper report on Chicago in the same year declared with unusual directness that "the air stinks." Just after the Civil War, Memphis's streets were described as an open sewer.

Newcomers to the city struggled to find decent dwellings at affordable prices. Many were forced to take the dilapidated houses formerly occupied by the middle class who had fled the growing squalor and congestion of the inner city. Others found rooms in shoddily constructed new buildings. In New York at the end of the century over a million people lived in tenements of five to six stories with shallow air shafts on either side to provide a little light to interior rooms. These structures, called "dumbbell tenements" because of the long, narrow waist where the air shafts were placed, had only one bathroom for every twenty inhabitants. In Chicago, although the Great Fire of 1871 had created new housing opportunities, the city permitted builders to throw up block after block of shanties and ugly two-decker flats for the working class on the burned-over land.

Even before the Civil War the country's largest urban centers had ceased to be "walking cities," in which everything was accessible on foot, and had adopted the horse-drawn "omnibus" and, a little later, the horse-drawn streetcar on rails. After the war many more communities adopted animal power for transportation. Horse-drawn vehicles were faster than walking, but they had many drawbacks. In 1864 a newspaper described a typical streetcar trip as an experience of "martyrdom." Public transportation also compounded the sanitation problem. The thousands of horses slogging the city streets created enormous piles of droppings, and the resulting smells and clouds of flies made summers, particularly, an ordeal for city dwellers.

The Immigrant Adjustment.   Newcomers to the city also faced a harsh and disruptive social environment. Most eastern and southern European immigrants were rural peasants who found the cities of America alien places. Here there were no one-story cottages, but multifloor apartment dwellings. Lighting did not come from candles or an oil lamp; wood logs did not fuel cooking stoves; water did not come from a well. Instead you bought coal from a supplier, or turned on a switch or faucet and paid utility bills to the gas, water, or electric company. In Chicago, Cleveland, or New York, you did not throw your garbage to the pigs; you placed it in refuse cans for the sanitation department. And how different it was to earn a living and get from place to place! Immigrants, in a word, had to abandon the familiar customs and practices of Europe's rural villages and learn to survive in the vast, impersonal metropolis.

How to earn a living was the most urgent problem for immigrants to America's "urban wilderness." Most groups of newcomers included a small professional and business class. The Jews in the garment industry not only worked as cutters and sewing machine operators but also owned many of the shops. Italians became building contractors employing Italian workers. Because all groups retained a strong loyalty to the customs, cuisine, and language of their native land, enterprising immigrants with a little capital established restaurants, groceries, theaters, bookstores, and assorted businesses catering to their compatriots. The newcomers also preferred to turn to their own kind for professional help, and immigrant doctors, lawyers, and clergymen found ample demand for their services. By 1914 the typical American city was crowded with street signs in Polish, Italian, Yiddish, Chinese, Spanish, and other languages that advertised the wares of ethnic shopkeepers and the services of ethnic professionals.

Most of the cities' foreign-born remained unskilled or semiskilled workers for most of their lives. They worked in factories, as construction, as house servants, as day laborers. They performed the thousands of menial tasks required in this age preceding modern machines. Yet in Boston the British and other northern Europeans, as well as the Jews, moved up rather rapidly from unskilled to skilled jobs; some even graduated into the ranks of the business class or the professions. The Irish and Italians, in contrast, lagged behind both native American newcomers to Boston and more mobile immigrant groups. In New York, on the other hand, according to one study, both Jews and Italians moved ahead almost equally fast and both achieved large gains in income and status in a rather short time. In Atlanta immigrants raised their status with remarkable speed, says one scholar, far faster than the city's large black population, a group oppressed by deeply embedded racism.

The crucial factor affecting the immigrants' economic progress apparently was education. Those who were illiterate or who could not speak English were easily exploited. People who had nothing to sell but physical brawn stayed on the bottom rungs of the economic ladder. Immigrants understood the importance of education very well and flocked to night schools where, after a hard day's work, they attempted to learn English and reading and writing. The more enterprising or energetic succeeded. Others failed, defeated by age, bad luck, or personal inadequacy. Those who did not, or could not, acquire a basic education generally remained part of the large mass of urban poor.

Pressures on the Family.   The traditional father-dominated, home-centered rural family of a century ago changed substantially in the new city environment. On the farms and in the rural villages, whether of America or Europe, fathers worked close to their families. Even in the smaller cities of America this proximity was uncommon, and as the urban centers grew, the physical distance between home and work became ever greater. The advent of the horse-drawn streetcar enabled many more prosperous working-class men to commute to their jobs. Although the "streetcar suburbs" provided space for recreation and some contact with the beauty of the countryside, the long commuting time meant that a man spent longer periods than ever away from his wife and children. With fathers so often absent, young men, in particular, lost close touch with adult role models, and many found the process of adjusting to work and adulthood more difficult than in earlier days.

The gap between generations encouraged by city life was even greater among immigrants than among the native-born. The children of European peasants and laborers encountered very different customs and habits from those their parents had known in the old country. Growing up in the city streets and attending American schools, the "second generation" often developed different values. Girls picked up attitudes toward dress, courtship, demeanor, that were at odds with strict European views of the proper role for young, unmarried women. Boys were less obedient towards parents. Children who knew English and were familiar with American life fared better in the new environment and could use the language more effectively than their parents. Adolescence is at best a turbulent time of revolt against parental control; in the cultural clash between foreign-born parents and native-born children, families were frequently shaken to their foundations.

The city not only weakened the structure of the family but also reduced its size. It was expensive to raise children in the city. The cost of shelter in the country was modest. Farmhouses were large and cheap to build. But in the cities working-class families could not afford large apartments and painful overcrowding was common. Nor were children as much of an economic asset in the city as in the country, where they were an important part of the workforce. Working-class urban families were forced to put their children to work at odd jobs. Some city children worked alongside their parents at garment making or some other "sweated" trade conducted in the home. But compulsory education laws and the difficulties of finding wage-paying work for city boys and girls meant that they did not contribute as much to family support as rural children. The cost of raising a family in the city encouraged family limitation. Fertility rates in the United States had been declining for generations in both towns and countryside. Toward the end of the nineteenth century the constraints of the urban environment provided new incentives to family limitation, and birth rates dropped still further.

The growing trend toward smaller families disturbed social conservatives. Moralists and religious leaders frequently denounced efforts to disseminate birth-control information as sinful. In 1873, at the urging of "purity" crusader Anthony Comstock, Congress classified birth-control information as obscene and excluded it from the mails. Toward the end of the century, however, Margaret

Sanger, a visiting nurse on New York's Lower East Side, launched a campaign to provide poor women with scientific birth-control information. Defenders of old-fashioned morality attacked Sanger and denounced the whole family-limitation movement as "race suicide." Sanger persisted but was forced to flee the country in 1914 for publishing her journal *Woman Rebel,* which the authorities considered obscene. She later returned and organized the leading agency of the birth-control movement in the United States, the American Birth Control League.

Margaret Sanger's efforts, initially directed at the slum family, achieved their greatest success among middle-class women and those working-class women most anxious to move into the middle class. The effect on their lives was profound. With fewer children in the family, they were relieved from long years of childbearing and child nurture. Together with new labor-saving devices for the home such as the gas range and hot piped-in water, the decline in family size eventually freed many women from lifelong household drudgery. Some directed their released energies to civic work or self-improvement. Others were enabled to join the labor force in growing numbers. Where previously jobs available to women were largely in domestic service or low-paid factory work, by the 1890s, urban commercial jobs were expanding rapidly, and thousands of middle-class women could become retail salesclerks, bookkeepers, typists, bank tellers, and secretaries. By 1914 city streets were thronged with working women going to and from their jobs in downtown offices and stores.

Family limitation had mixed social consequences. In smaller families children were less often neglected. And with fewer mouths to feed, the family had more "discretionary income." Children could be allowed to stay in school until they were better prepared for the "race of life." The family had more money for leisure activities. Married women often found their lives more rewarding and the bonds of marriage less confining. But the change in family size also had a darker side. The family as an institution lost some of its cohesion. In 1867, when divorce laws were strict and divorced people often ostracized, only 10,000 divorces were granted in the entire country. By 1907, as a result of divorce-law reforms and the more permissive moral climate, there were 72,000 divorces, a rate over three times as great per capita. Whether viewed as a social calamity or liberation, divorce had become a more widely accepted feature of American life.

Crime, Vice, and Loneliness.
All newcomers to the American Gilded Age city encountered social pathologies. Cities were schools of crime and disorder, with gangs of cardsharps, pickpockets, purse snatchers, and thieves. Then as now, poor people were the major victims of city crime. They were also its chief perpetrators, especially of violent crimes. A city disease, crime was also a way of "making it" in America. Street boys stole from stores, passers-by, and drunks. In Chicago, an observer noted, the newsboys who gathered in the courtyard of the Hearst Building to pick up the evening papers were also petty thieves. Those young men, it seems, usually gambled away what they stole, but other slum dwellers used their illegal gains to get ahead. Crime, in sociologist Daniel Bell's phrase, was a "queer ladder of social mobility" for some of the urban poor.

Prostitution also plagued the cities of this period. The Gilded Age was a particularly prudish era in sexual matters. "Good" women were expected to be indifferent to sex. By itself this attitude might have encouraged prostitution; but in addition the cities attracted multitudes of young women looking for jobs and respectable marriages. Although many achieved their goals, others failed and fell prey to madams, shady saloon keepers, and others who took them in and led—or forced—them into prostitution. Periodically, reformers and crusaders would close the brothels and chase the prostitutes off the street, but the trade in sexual favors would quickly resume again.

Respectable people deplored the city saloon as a haunt of vice and drunkenness, but it met an urgent urban social need. American cities were lonely places for the thousands of men and women who arrived without family or friends. To offset the isolation of their lives, newcomers to the city joined lodges, church organizations, ethnic societies, and veterans' groups. In the 1890s settlement houses, where the poor could find educational and recreational facilities, helped create community feeling in the city neighborhoods. But the local tavern often served the same purpose. Church leaders and moralists might rail, yet to many isolated men the saloon was a place where they could find companionship for the price of a glass of beer.

The saloon, the settlement house, the fraternal order, and the ethnic society proved inadequate in providing moral and emotional support for city dwellers, especially those without families. Even the churches often failed. Catholics and Jews were quick to provide for their own religious needs, but Protestants often neglected their less-fortunate members. With their base in older rural America and the prosperous urban middle class, the Protestant denominations frequently found it difficult to understand or cope with the problems of poor city dwellers.

Disturbed by the demoralization in the city centers, in the 1880s Protestant reformers launched the Charity Organization movement. Hundreds of middle-class women became volunteer "friendly visitors" to slum families to advise them how to save, how to use their money, how to dress, and how to keep clean. They made little headway against the vast social ills that afflicted the city poor. The Salvation Army was more successful in aiding the cities' outcasts. Its soup kitchens, shelters, lodging houses, and "rescue missions" in the run-down areas of many cities provided meals and a place to stay for thousands of homeless. The YMCA and YWCA also sought to help. But none of these efforts solved the problems created in the cities by the breakdown of traditional ties to family, neighbors, and other social groups. By the end of the century every city had its "skid row," where lonely men and women lived out narrow hopeless lives amid squalid surroundings.

City Government

Contemporaries might disagree over the social and physical virtues of cities, but few cared to defend their politics. James Bryce, a prominent English observer of Gilded Age America, in fact considered American cities "the worst governed in Christendom."

The critics' chief target was the city machines—political organizations created to wield power and perpetuate a faction or party in office. Each machine was led by a "boss," who might or might not serve as mayor but who, regardless of his official title, dominated the city government. Beneath the boss was a collection of faithful aides—the ward or precinct captains ("ward heelers") and various rank-and-file hangers-on—who performed the machine's essential function of mobilizing the vote for its mayoral and city council candidates. The machines seldom ruled by force or outright coercion. They kept the loyal support of their constituents and retainers by providing them with jobs, often sinecures that paid well but did not require serious effort or any demonstrated competence.

The purpose of the machine was to win and retain office. But for what? Reformers, the champions of "good government," insisted that the machine's only goal was to drain the city treasury or to confer under-the-counter favors on businesspeople and purveyors of vice for the personal gain of its members. The boss and his henchmen, they said, were at heart little more than racketeers. And their methods were no more savory than their goals. Machines, the reformers noted, won the support of voters by wholesale bribery and corruption. They paid the poor $5 or $10 each for their votes; they stuffed ballot boxes with false returns; they brought in "floaters" from other communities to vote in city elections; they illegally naturalized aliens to cast ballots for the machine and against its opponents. In short, as good-government people saw it, the machines were essentially diseased organs that should be cut out of the body politic if city life was to be improved.

The Machines in Action.   The reformers were not entirely fair. The machines were often corrupt, but they performed important functions that could not be handled by the more formal institutions of the day. New York in the 1870s illustrates how they operated and why they became so deeply entrenched.

In the years immediately following the Civil War, the country's largest city was governed by a confused jumble of overlapping agencies. It had a board of aldermen, a board of councilmen, twelve supervisors, and a separate board of education—all with power to make decisions in various spheres without the mayor's approval. The police commissioners were appointed not by the mayor or by any city agency but by the governor of the state, as were the commissioners of Central Park and of the fire department. The system was a "hodgepodge," declared a contemporary critic, that made New York virtually ungovernable.

Into this confusion stepped William Marcy Tweed. Tweed was not the gross, predatory figure depicted in the savage cartoons of reformer Thomas Nast. Neither was he the model of an upright public servant. Tweed and his henchmen bilked the city treasury of millions of dollars collected largely in the form of kickbacks from private contractors who provided the city with supplies and services at rigged prices and then secretly returned some of their take to the machine and its leaders. One estimate puts the total thefts of Tweed's Tammany Hall, the New York City machine, at between $45 million and $200 million.

But Tweed and his henchmen did not take without giving. The Boss made the chaotic, aimless political system of New York respond to the pressing needs of its citizens. Did shippers need improved docks? Tweed would get new powers for the city to build them. Did working people need a rapid transit system? Tweed would see that transit promoters could acquire private property for the right-of-way. Did households need new sewers or a better water supply? Tweed would use his influence in the state capital so that the city could borrow to provide them. Other cities—St. Louis, Philadelphia, San Francisco, Cincinnati—had versions of Tweed.

The machines were not only useful devices for getting new sewers, improved lighting, and transit lines; they were also informal welfare organizations. Official almshouses, orphanages, and hospitals for the insane were dreary and oppressive places avoided by the poor. Churches and private philanthropic organizations could not provide adequately for such large numbers of needy. The machines helped offset the failings of the contemporary "safety net." Because they controlled massive amounts of patronage, they could find jobs for the unemployed in the police department, the fire department, the schools, or the sanitation service. Civil service rules seldom applied to these jobs, and the local ward captains reserved them for their favorites. The machines also supplemented the incomes of the poor—coal during the winter, turkeys at Thanksgiving and Christmas, and free medical services—and fed money into private charities. During his term as state senator, Tweed, though a Protestant, pressured the New York legislature into appropriating funds for the Catholic charities and parochial schools that many of his poor city constituents relied on.

The city machines were also buffers between poor citizens and the law. Much of what was accounted illegal in contemporary American cities was "victimless crime": gambling, drinking on Sunday, "blood" sports such as cockfighting or bare-knuckled boxing, and sex for money. Not all Americans approved of making these activities illegal, and many continued to engage in them, regardless of the law. When, during a sudden surge of civic virtue, the authorities clamped down on saloons, gambling, or vice, people were arrested for practices that they considered at worst venal sins. Where could they turn for help? The obvious answer was the precinct captain, who could "speak to" the judge. Even better, the machine could quash the spasm of virtue before it developed. City machines were understanding of human weaknesses, as reformers seldom were, and overlooked transgressions that did not unduly disturb public order.

The machines, then, often functioned both as social service organizations and as shields between city people and the barbs of city life. As Tammany leader George Washington Plunkitt explained, a ward captain was always obliging: "He will go to the police courts to put in a good word for the drunks and disorderlies or pay their fines, if a good word is not effective. He will feed the hungry and help bury the dead." Martin Lomasney, a Boston machine leader, explained it more philosophically: "I think that there's got to be in every ward somebody that any bloke can come to—no matter what he's done—and get help. Help, you understand; none of your law and justice, but help."

Goo-Goos.   Of course, the machines were not purely altruistic. In return for these services they expected gratitude that could be turned into votes at election time, as well as tolerance of graft and corruption. The public's patience was finite, however. In Tweed's case, the machine eventually ran up bills that the voters were no longer willing to pay. When a disgruntled former Tammany heeler decided to tell all, the commercial and financial leaders of the city, joined by good-government reformers ("goo-goos" to their enemies) and an outraged citizenry, mounted a campaign to cut Tweed down. In 1872 the reformers elected to the mayor's office William F. Havemeyer, a wealthy sugar refiner and one of their own. Tweed was indicted on criminal charges and sent to jail. On his release he was rearrested to stand trial in a civil action to recover the sums he had stolen. He fled to Spain, was returned to New York, and sent to jail again, where he died in disgrace in 1878.

Under Havemeyer the reformers attempted to run the city on economical and honest principles. They cut back on hundreds of patronage positions in the city services departments and eliminated many construction projects. Thousands of workers lost their jobs. With Tweed no longer in Albany to manage the necessary legislation, the state ceased to appropriate money for private and religious charities. Ticket-fixing, "speaking to" judges, and gifts of coal and turkeys also stopped, as did the tolerance for the petty law-bending of working-class life. This moralism and the cuts in patronage and services cost the reformers the support of the poor, and bossism soon returned in the form of "Honest" John Kelley. As leader of Tammany Hall, Kelley was a more scrupulous man than Tweed; but he, too, anchored the machine squarely on the support of the city poor and dispensed favors and services with a ready hand.

The pattern of spendthrift machine followed by tight-fisted reformers and spendthrift machine once again was repeated over and over in American cities during the Gilded Age. The working class often preferred open-handedness to economy, ethical tolerance to the moralism of the reformers. If municipal reform movements before the 1890s were generally short-lived, it was due as much to the reformers' limitations as to any perversity on the part of city voters.

A Better Place to Live

Many of the difficulties city dwellers faced after the Civil War were the result of extraordinary growth that outran the capacity of cities to solve their problems. By the 1890s, when the cities finally began to catch up, city life improved.

Physical Improvement.   A measure of progress was the upgrading of the physical environment. The introduction of asphalt in the 1870s made city streets cleaner and safer. It soon became the standard paving material for cities. Waste-disposal problems were also conquered as the years passed. In 1887 Los Angeles, a city without a major river to use for dumping waste, built a sewage treatment plant. Chicago stopped the pollution of Lake Michigan, the source of its drinking water, by reversing the direction of the Chicago River so that it flowed into the Mississippi. In the landlocked Midwest several cities turned to incinerators to dispose of waste. Most of these schemes only postponed the difficulties or imposed them on some other community downstream. But they were better than those that had preceded.

One of the great urban triumphs of the age was the provision of pure water. By the time of the Civil War many cities had systems for piping water into homes. After the war, following the discoveries of Robert Koch and Louis Pasteur that bacteria are powerful disease-causing agents, cities began to filter and chlorinate their water. By the time of World War I (1914), virtually every American city had pure drinking water, and death rates from cholera, typhoid, dysentery, and other water-borne diseases plummeted. Combined with milk pasteurization and other new health measures, these advances drastically reduced urban mortality rates, especially among the young.

New Ideas in Housing and Architecture.   The most intractable urban problem—the lack of adequate housing for the working class—became a concern of philanthropists during the 1870s. In that decade Alfred T. White, a successful Brooklyn businessman and engineer, became convinced that landlords' profits and decent housing for the poor were compatible. Pursuing "philanthropy and 5 percent," he completed his Home Buildings near the Brooklyn waterfront. These attractive structures accommodated forty families in apartments two rooms deep, ensuring good light and ventilation; they included a bathroom for each apartment. White's experiment, unfortunately, failed to revolutionize building practices. Developers continued to throw up jerry-built structures that crammed human beings into dank, dark apartments with few amenities.

Clearly, better design was not enough; but until the 1890s philanthropists had no other approach. Then, as part of the emerging "progressive" mood, reformers began to mobilize the power of government to protect urban citizens against the unrestrained profit motive. In New York, the legislature adopted a series of state tenement laws culminating in the measure of 1901, which outlawed the dumbbell structure and established more stringent minimum housing guidelines. Chicago, too, revised its housing code in 1898 and 1902 to impose higher standards on builders. Still, housing for the poor continued to be overcrowded and squalid.

Architects, philanthropists, and reformers upgraded other urban physical facilities as well. Before the 1890s American cities had few parks and open spaces. Office buildings, city halls, and courthouses were often ugly structures scattered about the downtown areas without plan or order. Above the city streets unsightly tangles of telegraph and telephone wires crisscrossed the sky. Many city streets were blighted by elevated trains that clattered overhead and plunged the ground below into shadow.

The "White City" at the 1893 Chicago World's Fair imitated ancient Rome and inspired countless "civic centers" in American cities.

Toward the end of the century new attitudes began to alter the cities' appearance and comfort. Inspired by the gleaming neoclassical structures of the White City, erected in Chicago to house the great Columbian Exposition of 1893, architects and urban planners sought to bring aesthetic order and distinction to American cities. During the next generation the City Beautiful Movement induced scores of American cities to build elaborate civic centers of neoclassical buildings to house city agencies. These structures, usually grouped around a large landscaped plaza, provided spacious open areas for urban dwellers in Cleveland, San Francisco, St. Louis, San Diego, and other cities.

This period also saw the birth of the skyscraper as a characteristic American architectural expression. The offspring of engineering and economics, the skyscraper conserved downtown land by combining the new technology of steel, which permitted tall structures without space-wasting thick walls, and the electric elevator. Although it started as an engineering innovation, it soon became a distinctive architectural style, worthy of aesthetic consideration.

City Transit.

Transportation also improved as the century approached its end. In the 1870s New York had built its first "el" (short for "elevated railway"), a commuter steam railroad raised on columns above the city streets. Chicago and other cities had quickly followed suit. The el was fast, but it was also dirty and unsightly. Pedestrians on the street below were subjected to a steady rain of soot and ash, while the el structure created a ribbon of blight along every avenue it traversed.

Help came during the 1870s. The cable car, attached to a moving cable between the rails, was adopted in San Francisco in 1872 to meet the special needs of that hilly city. Then, in the late 1880s, Frank Sprague, a naval engineer and former colleague of Edison's, built the first electric streetcar system in Richmond, Virginia. The Sprague streetcar drew its power from an overhead "trolley" held against a power wire by a spring arrangement. Fast, smooth, and nonpolluting, the electric trolley car was an immediate success. By 1895, some 850 lines were operating, carrying passengers from home to office, stores, factory, and amusement parks. Many longer interurban lines connected towns and cities in a dense network that blanketed the populous East and parts of the metropolitan West. Especially admired was the system of "red cars" whose tracks stretched like spokes from the central hub of Los Angeles to the surrounding satellite communities of southern California.

The final improvement was the subway, which combined electric traction with an underground right-of-way unobstructed by pedestrians or other traffic. Boston became the first city to acquire an underground transit system when it dug a mile-and-a-half tunnel for its trolleys under its downtown streets in 1897. New York opened the first true underground railroad in the United States in 1904 when it completed the first fifteen-mile stretch of what would eventually become the most extensive subway system in the world. Philadelphia and Chicago, too, acquired subways before World War I.

Schools for Newcomers.

As the country approached the new century, cities also began to cope better with assimilating the mass of newcomers who poured in from every part of the world. The major agency for Americanizing the new arrivals was the city school system.

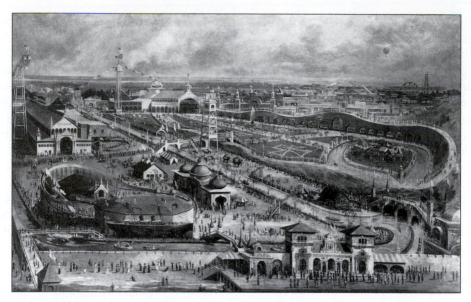

New Yorkers in the 1890s amused themselves at Steeplechase Park in Coney Island.
Almost every city in America had its equivalent in this era.
(Leo (?) McKay, "Steeplechase Park, Coney Island" (1898–1906). Oil painting.
Museum of the City of New York. 54.167.)

When we look back at urban schools of the 1890s and beyond, we are struck
by their strict discipline, narrow range of subject matter, and limited physical facilities. Nonetheless, they were successful in teaching the basic skills that society
needed. By contrast with our own day, the schools in large cities during the early
twentieth century often performed better than those in rural or suburban areas.

Americanizing the immigrants and their children was a difficult and impressive accomplishment of the schools. A cultural gap often existed between the children in city classrooms and their teachers. At times the teachers literally did not
speak the pupils' language, and textbooks made no concessions to the pupils' cultural backgrounds. Yet many immigrant children overcame this gap. Mary Antin,
a young Russian-Jewish immigrant, writing in 1912, told how the Boston schools
had made her into a "good American." Mary sat "rigid with attention" as her
teacher read the story of the Revolutionary War. As she learned "how the patriots
planned the Revolution, and the women gave their sons to die in battle, and the
battle led to victory, and the rejoicing people set up the Republic," it dawned on
her "what was meant by my country." She, too, was an American citizen, and the
insight changed her life. Mary went on to become a successful writer.

Not every immigrant child was so successfully Americanized. Many, finding
the schools alien and uncongenial, resisted their influence. Some dissenters believed the schools were taking away the children's sense of their own heritage
and leaving them stranded between two cultures. Horace Kallen, a prominent
teacher and social philosopher, conceived an alternative approach to the problem

of American social and cultural diversity. His "cultural pluralism" celebrated a "democracy of nationalities, co-operating voluntarily and autonomously in the enterprise of [American] self-realization through the perfection of men according to their kind." Kallen hoped men and women of diverse backgrounds could retain their heritages while sharing important common American values and attitudes. Few schools in these years heeded his advice, yet they managed on the whole to ease the transition from immigrant to American.

Reform with a Heart.

The schools' contribution toward easing the cities' social problems was supplemented by other agencies. The most comprehensive effort took the form of a new kind of humane political reform.

During the 1870s and 1880s, as we have seen, urban reformers had emphasized economy and efficiency over social justice and had often offended the urban poor. If any group of city politicians was concerned with the well-being of the city masses, it was the bosses who ran the machines. This division—shady politicians with a heart and honest reformers with a balance sheet—did not entirely cease with the advent of the new century. During the Progressive Era that began in the mid-1890s, one group of reformers continued to be more concerned with economy and efficiency than with social justice, as we shall see in Chapter 23.

But there was another thread to the urban reform movement that developed in the 1890s. As public-spirited citizens became aware of the failings of the Gilded Age city and of previous reform philosophies, they began to acquire a more sophisticated understanding of what had to be done. The result was compassionate urban reform and movements for social justice in cities such as Detroit, Cleveland, Toledo, and Milwaukee.

In Detroit, Mayor Hazen Pingree, the agent of the new reform, rode to office as mayor following the indictment of several Democratic aldermen for taking bribes. At first Pingree differed from the traditional reformers more in style than in substance. Although he emphasized reducing "the extravagant rate of taxation," he was not a rigid puritan. He avoided the usual goo-goo attacks on the voters' cultural preferences. In the style of the old ward leaders, he launched his first campaign by a round of drinks with the boys at Baltimore Red's Saloon.

Pingree learned, however, that his constituents also demanded that he acknowledge their economic needs. He soon became their champion against "the interests." He attacked the street-railway monopoly for its high fares and harsh labor policies. During an 1891 street-railway strike, the mayor sided with the strikers against the company. Following the panic of 1893, he initiated a much-publicized "potato-patch" plan under which the city turned over vacant lots to needy families so that they could raise vegetables to help support themselves. The mayor also shifted some of the city's tax burden from Detroit's citizens to the corporations that did business with the city.

Toledo's equivalent of Pingree was the colorful Samuel ("Golden Rule") Jones. Jones began a program of city ownership of water, gas, and electric utilities; put to a popular vote such questions as extending city franchises to private companies; and inaugurated a major expansion of the system of parks, playgrounds, and municipal baths. Like Pingree, Jones refused to go along with the conventional reformers' prejudice against working-class customs, amusements, and presumed vices. He rejected demands that he close the saloons and put drunks in jail. When local ministers asked him to drive prostitutes out of the city, he asked them pointedly: "To where?"

In Milwaukee, too, the city's reformers had been of the traditional goo-goo type. But during the hard times following 1893, when the utility companies tried to raise their rates while refusing to pay local taxes, reformers' attitudes changed. Outraged by the arrogance of the state's utility tycoons, they sought allies among the working class in a concerted attack on privilege. A decade and a half later the Socialists took control of the city from the middle-class reformers when Emil Seidel became mayor and instituted a reform regime that combined good government and social justice without socialist dogma. During the years of Socialist control the city enacted a minimum wage for all city employees and established a permanent committee on unemployment. In addition, Seidel expanded the public concert program, established commissions on tuberculosis and child welfare, and encouraged the use of the public schools for after-hours social, civic, and neighborhood clubs.

Conclusions

In the half-century following the Civil War, American cities exerted a powerful pull on the peoples of the world. Glamour, culture, excitement, and, above all, jobs drew millions of rural men and women, foreigners and natives, to the cities of the United States. For a while the deluge overwhelmed many urban services and facilities, making life for the newcomers uncomfortable, unsafe, and unhealthy.

American cities never became paradises. But by the early years of the twentieth century, they were better places to live than they had been fifty years before. Billions of dollars were spent for sewers, streets, aqueducts, and other municipal services, improving the health and comfort of citizens. Electric streetcars and subways brought fast, clean, and relatively comfortable transportation. Best of all, new leadership by people with a strong sense of responsibility toward the voters made government more efficient without sacrificing the values and interests of the great mass of working-class citizens. Many problems remained; in later years much that was gained would be lost. But for a while, around the year 1910, the American city had become an interesting, relatively livable, place. In 1905 the reformer Frederic C. Howe could call the American city "the hope of democracy."

ONLINE RESOURCES

"How the Other Half Lives" *http://www.yale.edu/amstud/inforev/riis/title.html* Explore the world of immigrants in New York in the late nineteenth century by viewing the full text and illustrations of Jacob Riis' work. To see a collection of over a dozen photographs depicting tenement life, see *http://www.masters-of-photography.com/R/riis/riis.html*.

"Metropolitan Lives" *http://nmaa-ryder.si.edu/collections/exhibits/metlives/index2.html* See the Ashcan artists' scenes of the realism of the city. Informative essays that discuss class relations, immigration, and changing gender norms accompany the paintings.

On the Lower East Side: Observations of Life in Lower Manhattan at the Turn of the Century *http://www.tenant.net/Community/LES/contents.html* Articles, documentaries, and first-person accounts found on this site provide rich details of the neighborhoods and living conditions of working-class immigrants in an urban American environment. Learn about their social networks and enduring folkways.

"The Gilded Age and the Titans of Industry" *http://www.pbs.org/wgbh/amex/carnegie/gildedage.html* On PBS's "The American Experience" Web site, learn about the experience of Americans during the so-called Gilded Age. Timeline features and a picture gallery provide links to a biography of industrialist Andrew Carnegie and photos of the industrialists' New York homes known by many as "Millionaires' Row."

19

The Trans-Missouri West

Another Colony?

1849	Bureau of Indian Affairs formed
1851	Federal government begins negotiating treaties for small Indian reservations in place of the Indian Frontier
1862	The Homestead Act; The Morrill Land Grant College Act
1864	The Chivington Massacre at Sand Creek; Lincoln reelected
1865	Sioux War on the Plains; Lincoln assassinated; Andrew Johnson becomes president
1866	Long drive of cattle from Texas to railroad sites to expand market to East begins
1867	Federal Peace Commission creates reform policies to assimilate Indians to white civilization; Patrons of Husbandry founded
1868	Ulysses S. Grant elected president
1873	The Timber Culture Act
1876	Custer's Last Stand at Little Big Horn
1877	Rutherford B. Hayes becomes president; The Desert Land Act
1880	James A. Garfield elected president
1881	Garfield assassinated; Chester A. Arthur becomes president
1884	Grover Cleveland elected president
1887	The Dawes Severalty Act designed to make Indians individual landowners; Severe winter destroys cattle boom on the Great Plains
1888	Benjamin Harrison elected president
1890	Massacre at Wounded Knee Creek
1892	Cleveland elected president for the second time
1893	Financial panic begins depression
1896	Presidential election between "goldbugs" and "silverites"; McKinley elected president over Bryan
1901	McKinley assassinated; Theodore Roosevelt becomes president
1902	The National Reclamation (Newlands) Act is passed to develop irrigation
1904	Roosevelt elected president
1905	The California Fruit Growers' Exchange introduces Sunkist products

America has had many "Wests." The colonial West was the forested region just beyond the settled Atlantic coastal plain. On the eve of the American Revolution, the West was the eastern half of the great Mississippi Valley across the Appalachian Mountains. For the generation preceding the Civil War, it was the land between the

Mississippi and the Missouri. The "Last West" of 1865 to 1910 was the broad expanse of territory stretching from the Missouri River to the Pacific Ocean.

In the Last West, as on America's previous frontiers, people with a basically European culture came into contact with an unfamiliar human and natural environment. As they adapted to western realities, the settlers often came to resent the power the East held over the country and over their lives. Easterners, they felt, did not understand the country's newest region or its problems; they were only interested in milking the frontier and its people. Many western Americans came to view themselves as inhabitants of a colony, exploited by people who lived hundreds of miles away. Meanwhile, they themselves often callously exploited the land and brutalized its native inhabitants.

To an extent, the Last West was indeed treated as a colony of the East. Western mining companies held their board meetings in New York or Chicago, not in Denver, Butte, or Boise. The great cattle ranches of the Great Plains and Great Basin were often owned by Bostonians, New Yorkers, or even French and British investors. Indian policies and land policies were not made in "the territories"; they were made in Washington, D.C., by people who did not seem to understand either Indians or western needs or wishes. When a cartoonist in the 1890s pictured America straddled by a huge cow grazing on the Great Plains and being milked in New York, westerners knew what he meant.

The men and women who settled the trans-Missouri West would eventually feel almost as alienated from Washington, D.C., Boston, and Chicago as had the white colonists of Massachusetts and Virginia from the England of George III. Howard Lamar, a historian of the West, notes that by 1889 "every territory in the West was calling its federal officials colonial tyrants and comparing its plight to that of the thirteen colonies." Eventually, in alliance with the South, they would rise up in a major political revolt against the urban East.

How did this antagonistic East–West relationship develop? What was the basis for western discontent following the Civil War?

Settlement of the Last West

The Land. The Last West was a vast and diverse area of some 1.2 million square miles, approximately two-fifths of the entire nation. Its eastern third, the Great Plains, is a level plateau gradually rising toward the west like a table tilted upward at one end. In its eastern portion rainfall in normal years is twenty inches or more, sufficient for grain crops. West of this band a few elevated spots such as the Black Hills of South Dakota catch the moisture-laden winds coming from the Pacific. Elsewhere the rainfall is usually too scanty for ordinary farming. Before the land was settled by whites, the ground was mainly covered with grass—long grass in the more humid eastern parts, short "buffalo" grass in the drier western half. Without trees or hills, the area lacked shelter from constant winds that often brought fierce blizzards in winter and turned grass and grain to dry straw in a few days during blazing hot summers.

As settlers moved westward across the Great Plains, 600 miles beyond the Missouri River they abruptly encountered a great escarpment rising like a wall—the lofty, forested Rocky Mountains. The Rockies in turn form the eastern rim of several shallow but extensive "basins." The largest is the Great Basin, consisting of most of present-day Nevada, western Utah, northern Arizona, and the extreme southeast of California. This region is arid, some of it true desert. Besides the Colorado, there are few rivers with outlets to the oceans. Before the advent of dams and irrigation, water flowed only briefly after occasional cloudbursts. Rivers generally petered out into "sinks" or ended in shallow lakes that evaporated during the dry season, leaving behind white alkaline "flats."

The narrow band of the Cascade and Sierra Nevada mountains form the western rim of the harsh basin region. Their eastern slopes are dry, but their western slopes catch the moisture-laden Pacific winds and are heavily forested. Between the Cascade–Sierra range and the coastal hills of Oregon, Washington, and California are several broad valleys: to the north, the valleys of Puget Sound and the Willamette River; to the south, in California, the great Central Valley.

Beyond the coast ranges, a narrow coastal plain, scarcely more than a thin ribbon of beach in many places, borders the Pacific. From San Francisco Bay northward, the climate of the Pacific Coast region resembles that of northwestern Europe, with rainy, relatively warm winters and cool, drier summers. South of San Francisco, the climate is Mediterranean: warm all year with little cloud cover and only sparse winter rains.

The Exploitation Ethic.   In the years following Appomattox, few Americans perceived the virtue of pristine wilderness in itself. Yet in 1872, Congress managed to set aside 2 million acres of northwestern Wyoming as Yellowstone National Park, the first of the nation's national parks. During the discussion of the Yellowstone bill, Ferdinand Hayden, sometimes called father of the national park system, emphasized the value of the region primarily as the site of natural curiosities—"decorations" such as geysers—rather than as a specimen of unspoiled nature. But with the possible exception of the national parks, most Americans perceived the West as a treasure trove awaiting human exploitation. Eastern entrepreneurs hoped to turn western resources into corporate profits. New settlers were eager to wrest livelihoods as ranchers, farmers, and miners from the new region. For most contemporaries, the West was a great cornucopia of timber, gold, grass, oil, and copper to be skimmed off its surface or extracted from its bowels. These people often resented even minor federal interference with their right to exploit the land. In 1883 Senator John J. Ingalls of Kansas declared "the best thing the Government could do with the Yellowstone National Park" was "to survey it and sell it as other public lands are sold."

Settlement Patterns.   The earliest part of the Last West to be occupied by whites was the Pacific Coast. The fertile soils of the Willamette Valley of Oregon attracted midwestern farmers in the 1840s, and in the 1850s gold brought thousands to California by ship around Cape Horn or overland by wagon train. By 1860 two Pacific Coast states had entered the Union: Oregon with 52,000 people and California with 380,000.

The Great Basin and Rocky Mountain regions were peopled as much from the West as from the East. By the mid-1850s the easy pickings in the Sierra gold streams of California had ceased. Gold remained, but it was either buried under many layers of silt or embedded in quartz rock. Ordinary prospectors did not have the capital or expert knowledge to extract the metal from these deposits and were forced to leave gold mining to large corporations. Through the next decades, displaced California miners and prospectors scattered through the Great Basin and Rocky Mountain regions from Mexico to Canada, their bedrolls, shovels, pans, supplies, and rifles piled on a burro or mule, ready to dig again. News, or even rumors, of a strike brought prospectors rushing from all directions to stake claims along reported gold streams. There they would join crowds of men, and a few women, from the East who were new to the game. Many of the gold-seekers were black; many more, especially among the Californians, were Mexican or of mixed Indian-white parentage; and there were many "Celestials," as the Chinese were called. As in California, only a few struck it rich. Most of the others soon drifted off in quest of new bonanzas.

The settlement pattern in the Great Plains was more conventional. The Plains population came predominantly from the agricultural Mississippi Valley immediately to the east. These people were farmers and farmers' children seeking lands cheaper than those available in the Midwest. During the 1880s Iowa, Missouri, and the five states of the Old Northwest lost a million of their sons and daughters to the Great Plains region. Joining these ex-midwesterners were immigrants from Ireland, Canada, Germany, and Scandinavia, as well as former black slaves fleeing southern sharecropping.

Plains settlers usually came as individuals or members of family units, but part of the migration was sponsored or even subsidized by outside agencies. In the Great Basin, for example, Mormon missionaries were responsible for drawing thousands from the East and from Europe to Utah and the so-called Mormon Corridor, stretching south from Idaho to Arizona. The transcontinental railroads attracted easterners and Europeans to their lands on the Plains by colorful brochures advertising $4-an-acre land, free seed, and free agricultural advice.

Native Peoples of the Last West

To the Indian tribes of the trans-Missouri West, the whites were unwelcome intruders. The Great Plains alone were inhabited by over 125,000 Native Americans in mid-century. About 75,000 of these were former woodland Indians—including the Blackfoot, Assiniboine, Sioux, Cheyenne, Arapaho, Crow, Shoshone, Pawnee, Kiowa, and Comanche—who had moved into the Great Plains from the East and adopted nomadic ways several hundred years before whites arrived. These tribes shared the region with an almost equal number of Indians of the so-called Five Civilized Tribes (Cherokee, Choctaw, Chickasaw, Creek, and Seminole), who had been forced to move by government order before the Civil War from their traditional homes in the Southeast. In the Oregon region there were some 25,000 Nez Percé, Spokane, Yakima, Cayuse, Chinook, Nisqually, and other peoples. Texas contained 25,000 Lipan, Apache, and Comanche Indians. In California and New Mexico Territory there were 150,000 Native Americans, distributed among the Ute, Pueblo, Navajo, Apache, Paiute, Yuma, Mojave, Modoc, and a flock of smaller coastal tribes, collectively called "Mission Indians," who had been gathered by the Spanish friars into settlements centering around mission churches during the preceding century.

The Western Cultures.   These Indians were diverse in their cultures, economies, religion, and political institutions. The Navajo and Apache of the Far Southwest were mostly nomadic hunters, though they practiced some agriculture as well. Along the Rio Grande and its tributaries were the Hopi, Zuñi, and other "Pueblo" peoples, who used irrigation to grow crops and lived in villages of adobe and stone, structures that resembled modern apartment houses. The Hopi and Zuñi had repulsed the Spaniards and the Mexicans during the eighteenth and early nineteenth centuries and would fend off American influences, too. Unlike other peoples, they were able to avoid the social and cultural breakdown that contact with whites generally brought.

The Indians of the Northwest—the Oregon–Washington region—included the coastal fishing peoples, who consumed salmon, traveled the sea in great canoes of hollowed-out tree trunks, lived in timber lodges, wore clothing made of pliant inner tree bark, and engaged in elaborate social ceremonies (potlatches) that involved competitive destruction of physical wealth to establish social status. To their east the Nez Percé lived in brush lodges, wore skin garments, and both fished for salmon and hunted elk, deer, and mountain goats for food.

The Plains Indians were the classic "Indians" of American "wild West" legend: tall, bronzed, with straight black hair, high cheekbones, and prominent, often curved, noses. At the eastern fringes of the Plains some tribes practiced agriculture. Farther west, where the rainfall diminishes, they were nomadic hunters.

These Plains Indians were formidable opponents. They traveled light. Their homes were skin-sided teepees that could be folded up in minutes and loaded on a pony to be set up quickly again miles away. Unlike the Indians of the East, people such as these could not be subdued by burning their crops and destroying their villages; they grew no crops, and did not live in settled communities.

The vast buffalo herds provided the Plains Indians with almost everything they needed to survive. They ate buffalo steaks and buffalo tongues; they made their clothing and their teepees of buffalo hides; buffalo "chips" (droppings) were their fuel; and buffalo sinews provided their cord and string. The guns and horses they had acquired from Europeans enabled the Plains Indians to increase their range and prosperity and made them formidable adversaries. By the time the westward-moving Americans encountered the Plains tribes, the Americans' only military advantage was sheer numbers.

Conflicting Views.   Indian and non-Indian societies were separated by a wide cultural gulf. Among whites, the individual took precedence over the group. By contrast, Indians generally subordinated personal ambitions to the tribe's needs and goals, and merged individual identity with that of the collectivity. The tribe came first even in adult–children relationships. As one Indian shaman told a French Jesuit missionary: "You French people love only your own children; but we love the children of our tribe."

Indian attitudes toward the land and resources were also different. The white settlers conceived of the land as a source of wealth, a means to an end. It could be bought, sold, bequeathed, and exploited by an individual owner. Most Indians saw land as part of the sacred, superhuman, world. Men must live in balance with nature. Land was also the collective possession of either tribe, family, or clan. If an individual had any special claim to a piece of land, it was only because he or she used it. Land left idle could be redistributed among other members of the tribe.

The nomadic ways of the western Plains tribes compounded Indian–white differences over real estate. Nomads must wander far and wide in search of food and cannot respect artificial boundaries established by treaties, property deeds, and land laws. Because they exploit the land extensively for hunting and food gathering, rather than intensively for farming, they need vast amounts of space. What seemed to whites an enormous surplus of land was barely enough to provide a Cheyenne or a Sioux tribe with sufficient food.

Federal Government, the Indians, and the Settlers.

In dealing with the Indians, the federal government often showed no more understanding of Indian realities than white settlers who went west. Until 1871 the federal authorities accepted the fiction that the tribes were independent Indian "nations" that, like other sovereign states, could be dealt with through diplomatic negotiations and treaties. This view was useful to white Americans because the disparity in power between the United States and the individual tribes made it possible to impose conditions that favored whites. In exchange for some blankets, food, tools, a few rifles, or a little cash, the Indians were often pressured into surrendering by treaty vast stretches of valuable land. If the government could not extract a favorable agreement from the current Indian leaders, it would find some dissident group to deal with that could be bribed or coerced. But the federal government did not respect the treaties it signed with the Indians as it did those concluded with foreign nations. When local western interests found a treaty inconvenient, they could often induce the government to abrogate it. At times the whole treaty system seemed nothing more than a facade for exploitation. As a governor of Georgia at one point expressed it: "Treaties were expedients by which ignorant, intractable, and savage people were induced without bloodshed to yield up what civilized people had the right to possess. . ."

Until the 1850s the federal government tried to maintain a permanent Indian frontier beyond the Mississippi where no whites could trespass. But the opening of California and Oregon to settlers soon made a shambles of the plan, and the government replaced it with the "reservation" policy. In place of a solid wall of Indian communities blocking off white settlement and passage westward, the tribes would be concentrated in widely spaced compact tracts. Here, supposedly, they would be protected from white exploiters and taught the ways of agriculture and other "civilized" arts and practices. The reservation policy was accompanied by serious troubles. White settlers on the scene often begrudged the Indians even the reduced areas the treaties gave them, while many of the Indians fiercely resisted the government's efforts to deprive them of their traditional range.

The most important treaties with the Plains tribes were those concluded at Forts Laramie and Atkinson in 1851 and 1853, respectively. Under their terms, the Indians promised to dwell in peace with the whites and with one another forever and to allow whites to build roads through their territory. The treaties also defined precisely the boundaries of each tribe's lands. These boundaries would later become the bases of the Plains reservations.

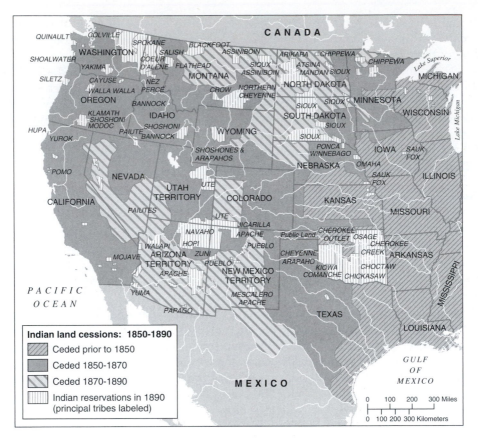

Indian Relations Beyond the Mississippi, 1850–1890

The Indians and the Civil War.

The Civil War converted the Last West into a battleground between Indians and whites and among the Indians themselves. Meanwhile, despite the war, whites continued to enter the region, drawn by a series of gold strikes in the Pacific Northwest, the eastern flank of the Sierra Nevada range, and the foothills of the Rockies.

No group suffered as much from disturbed wartime conditions as the Civilized Tribes of Indian Territory (Oklahoma). Many owned slaves and sympathized with the South. A minority, however, favored the Union. Both groups tried to avoid the white man's quarrels, but failed. At one point Cherokees wearing Union blue slaughtered Cherokees wearing Confederate gray. Several regiments of Creek, Seminole, and Cherokee fought with the Confederate forces at the Battle of Pea Ridge in 1862.

Nor did the remainder of the West escape the bitter turmoil of the war period. In Minnesota seething Sioux discontent with the reservation policy boiled over into a major Indian war that cut a bloody swath through the new state. Meanwhile, in the far Southwest, General James Carleton and Kit Carson, colonel of the New Mexico territorial volunteers, clashed with the restless Navajo and forced them to settle down at Bosque Redondo reservation, a barren region where many died of exposure, disease, and malnutrition. The worst disaster of the wartime Indian "troubles" was the notorious Chivington Massacre in Colorado Territory.

This dark page of Indian–white relations opened in the spring of 1864 when Cheyenne chief Black Kettle defied a government order to remove his tribe to a small reservation and began to raid mining camps and attack mail coaches. By the fall the Indians decided that they had done enough damage and sued for peace. But whites were not satisfied that the culprits had paid the full price for their offenses. Pressed by vindictive Coloradans, at dawn on November 29 the Third Colorado Volunteers under Colonel J. M. Chivington swooped down on 500 sleeping Cheyenne at Sand Creek. Black Kettle tried to surrender, but the volunteers ignored the Indians' white flag. The soldiers shot and killed 450 Cheyenne, two-thirds of them women and children, and scalped and mutilated many. The fearless victors of Sand Creek soon after paraded through the streets of Denver to the cheers of the citizens. "Colorado soldiers have again covered themselves with glory," trumpeted the Denver paper, the *Rocky Mountain News*.

Developing an Indian Policy.

The end of the Civil War marked a watershed in the government's Indian policy. The Republicans who dominated federal policy-making after 1865 were more strongly committed than their Democratic predecessors to racial justice. They were also strong nationalists who believed in the integration of all racial elements into the community. The Chivington Massacre, moreover, had shocked many sensitive men and women and convinced them that major reforms were needed.

These new attitudes opened a major gap between the sections over how to deal with the Native Americans. Easterners were now convinced that a "peace policy" was the best approach to the Indian problem, but recent events only confirmed western convictions that the government in Washington, D.C., was too feeble to suppress the Indian menace. When Senator James R. Doolittle of Wisconsin arrived in Denver in the summer of 1865 to represent the Senate Indian Committee, he quickly learned how wide the East–West disagreement was. At a public meeting in the city's opera house Doolittle attempted to explain the peace position that was now winning approval in the East. Should the Indians, he asked his audience, be firmly placed on reservations and taught to support themselves or should they be exterminated? Doolittle assumed that the question answered itself. But, as he later reported, his rhetorical question was followed by "such a shout as is never heard unless upon some battle field"—"Exterminate them! Exterminate them!"

The new "peace" approach also created a rift between civilians and the military. Having seen what force could do against an implacable white enemy, the victorious Union generals saw no reason why it should not be used against a lesser foe, the Indians. The divisions in opinion widened when Chief Red Cloud's Cheyenne, Arapaho, and Sioux warriors ambushed a detachment of U.S. troops under Captain William Fetterman in late 1866 near Fort Philip Kearny in Wyoming. Fetterman and his whole force of eighty-two men were killed.

In the end the peace advocates and reformers prevailed. In 1867 Congress established a commission to end violence on the Plains. The commissioners' attitudes typified those of reformers for the next half-century. They wanted peace with the Indians and hoped to see them prosperous and content. But the tribes must surrender their nomadic life, settle down on reservations as farmers, and shift from "barbarism" to "civilization." To help the Indians assimilate white culture, the government would provide schools to teach them English, agriculture, and mechanical skills, and would bring them the blessings of the Christian faith. Until they became self-supporting, they would be supplied with food, blankets, tools, and clothing.

The commissioners met with the Kiowa, Comanche, Cheyenne, and Arapaho in 1867 and, after bribes, threats, and cajolery, induced them to accept reservations in western Oklahoma on lands confiscated from the Civilized Tribes as punishment for their support of the Confederacy. The next year the Sioux signed the Treaty of 1868 at Laramie, Wyoming. In exchange for the government's abandonment of a mining road through their lands and the usual promise of blankets, rations, and other handouts, they agreed to lay down their arms and accept a reservation in western South Dakota. Federal officials extracted similar agreements from the Shoshone, the Bannock of Wyoming and Idaho, and the Navajo and Apache of Arizona and New Mexico.

The peace policy did not work any better than previous strategies. Whites continued to covet Indian lands and encroached on the reservations. The government itself violated its agreements, often failing to come through with the promised food and blankets. The efforts to Christianize the Indians offended their religious sensibilities. To make matters worse, the Bureau of Indian Affairs soon became a hotbed of corruption. The commissioner of Indian affairs, a political appointee, was almost always a party hack. He and his agents used money allotted for Indian supplies to line their own pockets. Effective administration of Indian affairs was further undermined by the division of responsibility between civilian officials and the army. In the end, violent confrontation between the army and the Indians continued to be a chronic element in Indian–white relations in the Last West.

The Final Indian Wars.

One of the gravest blows to the Indians' autonomy was the destruction of the Great Plains buffalo herds. The slaughter of the buffalo was not, as some claim, a deliberate effort to subdue the Indians. Many animals were killed to supply meat for the crews building the transcontinental railroads that began to cross the Plains soon after the Civil War ended. Others fell to "sportsmen" who came to the Plains to hunt the great beasts for the thrill of it. Eventually, random slaughter gave way to more purposeful and profitable hunting to satisfy the consumer demand for leather and buffalo robes. During the 1870s buffalo hunting became a major Plains industry, and it was soon clear to everyone that the buffalo were on their way to extinction. "From the way the carcasses are strewn over the vast plains," wrote a traveler in these years, "the American bison will soon be numbered among things of the past." He was almost right. By 1883, 13 million animals had been destroyed. When an eastern museum expedition arrived on the Plains that year to obtain live specimens for its collection, it found only 200 animals still alive.

The destruction of the buffalo virtually ended the Plains Indians' nomadic ways. The Indians became more dependent than ever on the government for handouts, or else were forced to take up an alien agricultural way of life to support themselves. For a generation more, however, the Indians resisted giving up their traditional life while resentment against the reservation policy festered.

The last years of the nineteenth century were marked by a chain of white provocations against the western Indian tribes. In the mid-1870s, gold prospectors invaded the Sioux reservation in the Black Hills of South Dakota. At first the federal authorities tried to exclude the whites. When the prospectors persisted, the government attempted to buy back or lease Sioux lands containing the gold diggings. The Indians defied the authorities and were declared renegades.

The Sioux turned for leadership to Sitting Bull, a chieftain of imposing appearance and fierce determination. Sitting Bull had only contempt for the Sioux who had accepted life on the reservations. "You are fools to make yourselves slaves to a piece of fat bacon, some hardtack, and a little sugar and coffee," he taunted his weaker-willed brothers. Allied with Chief Crazy Horse, he encouraged the rebels and was soon being pursued by soldiers under the command of General Alfred Terry. On June 25, 1876, a detachment of Terry's troops led by the reckless Colonel George Custer walked into a trap at the Little Bighorn River. Sitting Bull's warriors pounced on Custer's men and by the time Terry's remaining forces came to the rescue, Custer and all 264 of his men were dead.

Though an immense moral victory for the Sioux, Custer's defeat ultimately hurt the Indians' cause. The government sent more soldiers to the Plains and forced the Sioux to surrender much of the Black Hills region to whites. During the next fourteen years almost all the tribes as yet untamed were compelled to accept

In this vivid portrait of Sitting Bull we can see the determination and strength that led to the United States cavalry's greatest defeat—Custer's disaster at Little Big Horn in 1876.

confinement on the reservations. But discontent continued to seethe. The final pitched battle—though not the last violence—of the 400-year Indian–white war in North America took place in December 1890 at Wounded Knee Creek on the Sioux reservation in South Dakota.

As in the past, the brutal incursion by whites into Indian territory and Indian life had encouraged a surge of "renewal" among the affected tribes. Among the Plains groups this new mood was spread by a Paiute Indian prophet named Wavoka. Wavoka promised the Indians a paradise where they would be free of the whites and where they would live forever amidst their ancestors in peace and prosperity, without sickness or suffering. This Indian Garden of Eden could be attained by practicing love, hard work, and peace with the whites, and by participating in the Ghost Dance, a ceremony of spiritual renewal emphasizing singing and dancing to the point of trance.

The Ghost Dance religion worried the white authorities, who, despite its professions of peace, saw it as a possible incitement to violence. Their nervousness converted a possibility into a reality. When the commander of the U.S. Seventh Cavalry tried to disarm a group of Sioux at Wounded Knee, someone fired several shots. A bitter hand-to-hand fight ensued. When the Indians broke through the army's line, the troops fired at them with Hotchkiss repeating guns, killing at least 150, including many women and children.

The New Reformers.   During the closing years of the century, influential congressmen and their constituents, particularly in the East, were alerted to the Indians' plight and the whites' atrocities by the writings of Helen Hunt Jackson. Her 1881 book, *A Century of Dishonor*, recounted the doleful record of American Indian policy since independence and created a large body of public opinion in favor of reform. The active Indian reformers of this period were well-meaning men and women who found the western Indians worthy objects of their compassion and social consciences. But like the peace commissioners of 1867, they had little regard for traditional Indian ways and believed assimilation was the solution of the Indian problem.

The reformers' views, however flawed, were soon incorporated into new legislation. Congress established special Indian schools both on the reservations and off, where Indian children were taught to read and write English and learn trades that presumably would help them prosper on the reservations. The reformers also succeeded in changing the land laws to suit their theories. The Dawes Severalty Act of 1887 gave the president the power to order Indian lands surveyed and divided into 160-acre plots to be allotted to each Indian head of family, with additional amounts for minor children.

The new law broke with Indian tradition. Each adult male Indian was to become an individual landowner; the tribe would no longer own the land collectively. Indians would, it was hoped, become independent farmers on the white American model. To help ensure that the Indians would not quickly lose their land to sharpers, it was to be held in trust tax-free for twenty-five years. Individuals who took the allotments would in time become citizens of the United States and no longer be considered members of autonomous Indian "nations." The Dawes Act did not cover the Five Civilized Tribes, but under the Curtis Act of 1898 similar policies were applied to them.

Easterners and westerners generally welcomed the Dawes and Curtis acts, but for different reasons. The humanitarian reformers, with their assimilationist views, called the Dawes Act the "Emancipation Proclamation for the Indian." Westerners rejoiced because the laws reduced tribal holdings and allowed them to acquire additional Indian lands. For the Indians, the results were almost entirely negative. Government agents often prevented them from claiming the best lands for their individual plots. The long-term exemption of Indian lands from local taxation led several states to refuse to provide schools and other services to Indians, and despite its promises, Congress did not come through with adequate funds to offset this loss.

As agencies of "civilization," too, the acts were failures. The tribes lost their culture and cohesion yet not many Indians became strong, self-sustaining individuals as, presumably, Congress intended. Caught between two cultures, Indians often turned to drink, petty crime, and idleness. Though the twenty-five-year trust period written into the original laws supposedly protected the Indians from confidence men, the laws were amended so often that many Indians lost their property to speculators for a song. Between 1887 and 1934, Indian-owned lands were reduced from 139 million to 47 million acres. Without means or livelihoods, many Indians became charges on the public authorities.

Looking ahead, by the 1920s it had become clear to a number of white Americans that forced assimilation deprived the Indians of their heritage without providing a satisfactory alternative. Working through the American Indian Defense Association, the social reformer John Collier and his supporters demanded that the Dawes policy be replaced. The government should guarantee basic civil rights to Indians, confer limited self-government on the reservations, end paternalism, and encourage the preservation of Indian traditions and culture. Commissioner of Indian affairs after 1933, Collier secured passage of the Wheeler–Howard Act of 1934, which repealed the allotment policy, recognized the right of Indians to organize for "the purposes of local self-government and economic enterprise," and stated that the future goal of Indian education should be to "promote the study of Indian civilization, arts, crafts, skills, and traditions."

Passage of the act, once again, failed to solve the Indians' problems or satisfy their grievances. Yet it could be said that mainstream America was finally beginning to reverse the damaging trends of the past.

The Mining Frontier

There had been mining and mineral booms in the United States before the Gilded Age—in California during the 1850s, and in the Pennsylvania oil regions a few years later. But none had been so extensive or would leave so deep an imprint on regional social development and on the collective American imagination as the post-Civil War far western mining frontier.

Mining Communities.   The late 1850s spillover of prospectors from the California gold streams first reached north into British Columbia. In 1859 the search was deflected to the region around Pike's Peak in western Colorado. In a few months a new town, Denver, appeared in the shadow of the Rocky Mountains.

Soon afterward two gold prospectors in northwestern Nevada Territory hit "pay dirt." Their find, called the Comstock Lode after a drifter who claimed to be its discoverer, was one of the richest gold strikes on record. The district became an instant magnet for thousands of California miners, and Virginia City—a settlement of tents, lean-tos, and prefabricated frame structures—rose mushroom-like from the desert in a few weeks.

The Comstock Lode discovery was followed by strikes on the Snake River in northwestern Idaho. In 1863 gold was found at Last Chance Gulch in west-central Montana. The next strike was in the Black Hills of South Dakota during the 1870s. Coeur d'Alene in northern Idaho followed in the early 1880s. This was the last of the major gold rushes in the contiguous forty-eight states. But at the very end of the century fabulous finds would be made in the Canadian Yukon and in Alaska, marking the last episodes of the North American gold mining frontier.

The mining communities that grew up around the strikes have become a vivid part of the American Wild West legend. They were places of great variety, where every nation, race, and class could be found. The California diggings, reported Louisa Clappe, were "a perambulating picture gallery" where one could hear English, French, Spanish, German, Italian, and many Indian tongues spoken on the streets. They were also violent. The gamblers and hangers-on who followed the gold frontier were often unruly dissolute men and women. But violence and crime also flowed from the federal government's slow response to providing either new laws or law enforcement. The western answer was the vigilance committee, a group of local worthies who, without benefit of legal trial, hunted down and hanged the worst of the troublemakers as an example to the rest.

Creede, Colorado, a silver boom town in the Rockies, sprang up in a canyon so narrow there was only room for one main street. During the flush times of the early 1890s, Creede grew by several hundred people a day; by 1900 it was a virtual ghost town.

The federal government was also remiss in responding to demands for statehood in the mining regions. When Congress failed to act on Colorado's statehood petition, settlers in 1859 organized the Territory of Jefferson with an elected governor and legislature. Congress rejected this initiative, and not until 1876, when the community was well beyond the frontier stage, did it admit Colorado to statehood.

Big Business and Mining.

The tent camps and the vigilance committees were only passing phases of the western mining boomtowns. In some cases the next stage was abandonment. In scores of communities, when the richer ores gave out, the miners, storekeepers, and camp followers departed, leaving ghost towns of rusting machinery, decaying buildings, and empty mine shafts. Many mining communities, however, became permanent towns and cities. Denver, Lewiston, Coeur d'Alene, Pueblo, and Butte developed into substantial places with schools, churches, opera houses, and police forces. The mining industry also stimulated the growth of regional supply, shipping, and outfitting centers such as Seattle, Spokane, and Tucson.

The change from raw mining camp to sedate city seldom took place without a major shift in the mining business that sustained the local economy. As in California in an earlier period, after the loose nuggets and flakes had been skimmed off by men panning the streams and washing earth through cradles, gold mining became a heavily capitalized industry that required deep shafts and expensive machinery.

Gold was not the only mineral that drew people and capital to the Last West. The region also was rich in silver, copper, lead, zinc, and other valuable metals. These ores required deep mines, rock crushers, and complex chemical processes—operations that depended on heavy infusions of capital, trained mining engineers, technicians, and chemists, and a permanent force of wage-earning miners and smelter workers. The capital needed by the postpioneer mining industry was seldom available from local sources. Much of the costs of sinking shafts and erecting smelters and refineries in the fabulous Comstock Lode district, for example, came from San Francisco capitalists. These men extracted millions in profit from the Comstock Lode, and with the proceeds built great mansions on Nob Hill overlooking San Francisco Bay. One Californian who made a fortune in Nevada silver was George Hearst, whose son, William Randolph, would become a powerful New York press lord at the end of the century. In the 1880s Meyer Guggenheim, a lace manufacturer of Philadelphia, began to invest in the Leadville silver district of Colorado and soon became a major economic force in the state and the West. In 1907 one of his sons, Simon Guggenheim, official of ASARCO, the "Smelter Trust," came to Washington as a Republican senator from Colorado. In Montana the copper kings—William A. Clark, Marcus Daly, and Frederick Heinze—built Butte into a major copper-smelting center. Clark represented local capital, but Daly was allied with the Anaconda Copper Company, an eastern corporation with many English investors. Phelps Dodge, a New York firm, owned large copper mines and refineries in Arizona.

Although outside control over local resources would later fan westerners' discontent, the opening of the western mines added enormously to the country's resources. By 1900 the United States was one of the world's largest producers of gold, silver, copper, lead, and zinc. The production of gold and silver would also have immense political repercussions. The flood of gold would facilitate the adoption of the international gold standard in the last half of the century. But at the same time, the even greater proportional increase in silver production would depress its price relative to gold and profoundly disturb the nation's monetary—and political—affairs.

The Cattle Kingdom

Just east of the mining regions another economic frontier was taking shape. During the two decades that followed the Civil War, cattle raising became the basis of the Great Plains's economy, attracting eastern and even European investors. Even more than the mining frontier, the cattle kingdom would become an American legend.

Longhorns and Long Drives.   The Plains cattle industry originated in the Texas grasslands. Before the Civil War, Mexican ranchers had pastured immense herds of wild, rangy animals there. When Americans entered the south Texas area, they brought new breeds of cattle with them. These mingled with the Spanish-Mexican variety to produce the famed Texas longhorn, a wiry, resourceful creature that could survive winter on the open grasslands by digging through the snow with its sharp hooves to the nutritious dried grass beneath.

The Civil War cut off the Texas cattle industry from its major markets. During these fallow years the cattle ran wild on the Texas grasslands, and by 1866 there were an estimated 5 million head grazing on the Texas plains. Meanwhile, the rest of the country, having depleted its cattle stock to meet the Union army's needs, was starved for beef. In Texas cattle were selling for $4 a head, while in the eastern cities they were worth as much as $40 and $50.

Returning Confederate veterans were soon pondering ways to get Texas cattle to eastern consumers. The answer seemed clear. By this time the Missouri Pacific Railroad had reached Sedalia, Missouri, 700 miles north of San Antonio, in the heart of the Texas cattle country. If cattle could be driven on the hoof to the railroad, they could then be shipped east. In March 1866 a group of Texas ranchers and Iowa and Kansas businessmen launched the first of the classic "long drives" of range cattle north to railhead to satisfy the eastern market for beef and hides.

The Texas cattle drives soon became annual affairs. In a standard drive, a half-dozen mounted "cowboys" under a "trail boss" guided each band of a thousand or so unruly longhorns across open country accompanied by "chuckwagons" to carry food and equipment and a "horse wrangler" to care for the mounts. The route was dangerous. The Sedalia Trail passed through Indian territory where resentful tribesmen often stampeded the herds. Missouri farmers feared that the invading longhorns carried the dread Texas fever and sometimes engaged in shootouts with the Texans. Despite these obstacles, cattle that got through sold for $35 a head in Sedalia, providing a clear profit for the ranchers.

It did not take long for an enterprising businessman to see how the system could be improved. In 1867 a cattle dealer from Illinois, Joseph G. McCoy, established a depot at Abilene in central Kansas along the Kansas-Pacific Railroad. There ranchers could pen their animals and arrange for their sale to eastern buyers. Between 1867 and 1871 some 1.5 million head of Texas cattle were driven to Abilene for shipment east. When the area around Abilene became too densely settled, the drive was deflected farther west to Ellsworth on the Kansas-Pacific line. Later the "cow towns" of Newton and Dodge City were developed along the Santa Fe Railroad.

The Kansas cow towns, like the mining camps, were rowdy places. It was hard to maintain law and order among the transient "cow poke" population. Cowboys were a diverse lot of ex-Confederate and ex-Union soldiers, former slaves, Mexicans, and Indians who rode the range twelve hours a day looking for strays. At spring roundup they worked hard roping and branding the unmarked calves. On the long drives they spent as many as four months in the saddle, keeping the cattle moving and preventing stampedes. The work was dirty, hard, lonely, and unhealthy. No wonder that when paid several months' wages in Dodge City or Abilene at the end of the long drive, cowboys often went on roaring sprees—drinking, gambling, debauching, and sometimes shooting up the town.

Boom and Bust.   As the railroads penetrated farther into the central and northern Plains, thousands of Texas cattle were driven north to stock the newly accessible region. By the early 1870s these regions were covered with ranches.

During the late 1870s and early 1880s, the range cattle industry of Colorado, Wyoming, Montana, Idaho, and the western Dakotas relied on free use of the public land and on weather mild enough for the cattle to graze outdoors on the open range all year. The cattle used the public domain at no cost to the ranchers, who, in effect, were subsidized by the government with free land, grass, and water. All the ranchers

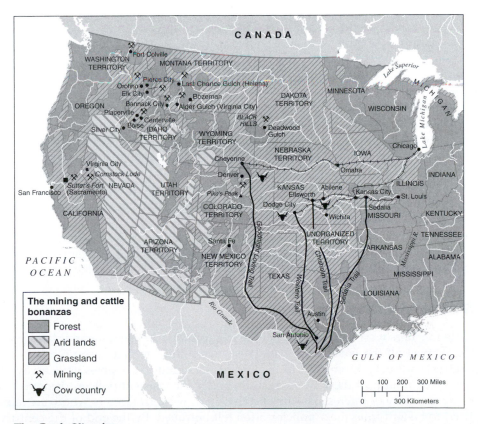

The Cattle Kingdom

had to do was wait as their cattle multiplied and put on weight. In the spring they rounded up their herds and shipped the mature animals east for a good profit.

For a decade the cattle kingdom flourished, sustained by high prices for beef and low cost of production. "Cotton was once crowned king," exulted a contemporary western editor during the open range heyday, "but grass is now." The free, adventurous, and individualistic life of the Plains rancher proved a powerful magnet for outsiders. Easterners, like the impetuous young New Yorker, Theodore Roosevelt, bought land on the Plains and became ranchers. So did Europeans, especially Englishmen and Scots. And many outsiders who did not come themselves sent their capital to the Plains. In 1883 twenty cattle-raising corporations capitalized at $12 million were formed in Wyoming alone.

By 1885 farsighted people began to suspect trouble ahead. Each year the range grass became sparser as more and more cattle grazed the Plains. To prevent personal disaster, ranchers began to fence off areas with barbed wire (invented in 1874) though this was illegal on publicly owned land. They also formed livestock associations to regulate the number of cattle grazed, exclude intruders, and protect the herds against rustlers and wolves. Despite these efforts, by the mid-1880s the Plains were overstocked. So numerous were cattle shipments that prices began to tumble.

Then nature struck. In 1886 the unusually mild winter weather the northern Plains had enjoyed for a decade abruptly changed. That summer was hot and dry; by fall the cattle, lacking decent forage, were weak. In November the blizzards came. January 1887 was the worst winter month that anyone could remember, with record snows and temperatures dipping at times to seventy degrees below zero. Thousands of cattle were buried alive by the snowdrifts. Others froze to death standing upright. Unable to get to the grass beneath the snow, crazed animals poured into the streets of several Plains towns and tried to eat everything in sight. When the terrible winter ended, hundreds of cattle carcasses were carried down the streams by the spring freshets, bearing with them the fortunes of their owners.

The cattle industry survived on the Plains, but it was never the same. Many of the cattle corporations went bankrupt. Now usually under the control of local people, the industry was transformed. Even more land than before was fenced in. Ranchers began to raise hay for winter feed and replace the wiry longhorns with Herefords and other breeds that would produce more meat per animal. Some ranchers, recognizing that sheep were hardier than cattle, turned to wool production, though others fought the sheep invasion as a threat. Meanwhile, wheat farmers began to intrude from the east, driving the cattlemen into the more isolated portions of the Plains. The ranching industry survived, but as a smaller, more localized, and more rational industry than during the heyday of the open range.

Western Land Policies

Cattle ranchers were not the only people to capitalize on liberal federal land policies. Almost all the land in the Last West was public domain, acquired by war, purchase, or treaty. From 1862 to the end of the century, Congress gave away or sold vast amounts of these western lands under inconsistent policies designed to satisfy a variety of interests. In the end the small western farmers who were supposed to benefit from these policies often felt betrayed. By the end of the century many of them were convinced that outside speculators and the government's remoteness from western realities were responsible.

Land Acts of the 1860s.

The passage of the 1862 Homestead Act fulfilled the dream of Jeffersonian agrarians by providing that any adult head of family or person over 21 who was a citizen or intended to become a citizen, could acquire, free of cost, 160 acres of surveyed federal land if they resided on the land for five years and "improved" it. In reality, however, only a fraction of the immense public domain ever got into the hands of small farmers free of charge. At the same time it was giving land to bona fide settlers under the Homestead Act, the government was distributing large parcels for other public purposes. The 1862 Morrill Land Grant College Act conferred on each state a portion of the public domain in proportion to its congressional representation to be used for state-run agricultural colleges. Most of the land went to populous eastern and midwestern states, where agriculture was subordinate to industry, and then sold or leased. The railroad land grants of the 1860s and 1870s were another instance of land excluded from homestead entry. In addition the federal government handed out land to encourage the construction of wagon roads and gave away millions of acres to states that entered the Union after 1862. Nor did it cease outright land sales. In 1862 some 84 million acres of federal lands were on the market for customers with cash.

Spokesmen for small farmer groups complained that free homesteads were largely an illusion; much of the best land was available only by cash purchase. And they were right. Between 1862 and 1904 only some 147 million acres of free land passed to farmers under the Homestead Act; in that same period more than 610 million acres were sold.

Acts Tailored to Western Realities.

The Homestead Act took no account of the special land problems of the arid Great Plains and Great Basin. The 160-acre allotment was too small for the "dry farming" cultivator on the eastern edge of the Plains; for the rancher who grazed hungry cattle in the drier portions of the region, it was impossible; each animal required 40 acres of grazing land to survive.

Following the Civil War, Congress passed a series of measures to deal with the special land problems of the West. One, the Timber Culture Act of 1873, allowed farmers with 160-acre homesteads to take out papers on another 160 acres of adjacent land if they agreed to plant trees on some portion of it. Trees, contemporaries believed, would encourage rain and so make the plains less arid. In reality, the tree-planting provision was largely ignored; the effect was to give Plains farmers about 10 million additional acres of dry land.

The Desert Land Act of 1877 was also designed to accommodate the land laws to the arid West. Most scholars, however, consider it a giveaway to the cattle companies. Under its provisions lands could be bought for a down payment of 25 cents per acre if the purchaser agreed to irrigate a full section (640 acres) within three years. After meeting the requirement the purchaser could pay an additional dollar per acre and own the whole parcel. Unfortunately, the law allowed purchasers to assign the acreage to others even before they had met the irrigation requirement. Large tracts thus passed to the cattle companies with few public benefits.

The Timber and Stone Act of 1878 also violated the spirit of the Homestead Act. The law applied to lands "unfit for cultivation" and "valuable chiefly for timber or stone." After declaring that the land in question contained no useful minerals, any citizen could buy up to 160 acres at $2.50 an acre. Few small farmers benefited from the law. Instead, through various sorts of fraud, large tracts ended up in the hands of timber companies.

In dealing with the climatic realities of the arid West, federal policy inevitably reflected the knowledge and values of the day. Today we are skeptical of large dams and irrigation systems. They may for a time "make the deserts bloom," but their long-term effects on desert ecology are often disastrous and, in many cases, they produce only temporary benefits. After years of being soaked with alkaline river water, the irrigated soil becomes chemically poisoned and unproductive.

Still, we should not blame our forebears for what they could not know. In the National Reclamation, or Newlands, Act of 1902 the federal government believed it was adding to the West's, and the nation's, wealth. And, in the short run, it was. The law established a reclamation fund from the proceeds of federal land sales in the arid states and territories, to be used for building dams, water channels, and other irrigation facilities in these states. Under the act a score of dams were constructed and thousands of acres were irrigated and reclaimed from the desert. Less successful than the engineering feats were the social results. Many settlers found that they could not pay the government's charges. Much of the land passed to large holders, despite periodic government efforts to provide relief for the hard-pressed small farmers.

Farming in the Last West

Indians, miners, and cattlemen could all show how imposed eastern policies were inappropriate to western needs. For the Indians, certainly, the mistakes were devastating. But ultimately it was the farmers' grievances that became the most unsettling to the nation.

Plains Agriculture. The Great Plains presented special difficulties for the would-be farmer. In most places rainfall was sparse and new agricultural approaches were required. In some regions pumps, powered by the unobstructed winds of the flat plains, could tap underground aquifers for water. During the 1880s windmills raised on pylons became a characteristic feature of the Plains landscape. Another solution was "dry farming," a system based on planting seeds far apart and covering plant roots with a dust mulch after each rainfall to preserve moisture. Dry farmers also adopted new drought-resistant grain types, some brought from Russia.

Even in regions of adequate rainfall, transplanted easterners faced difficulties not encountered at home. Given the absence of stone and timber, what could settlers use to fence their fields and build their barns and dwellings? During the 1860s agricultural experts touted hedges as fencing for cultivated fields. But before hedging could come into wide use, barbed wire appeared. A barbed-wire fence required only a few timber uprights; the rest was iron wire, a few rolls of which could enclose hundreds of acres. One contemporary listed the advantages of barbed wire: It "takes no room, exhausts no soil, shades no vegetation, is proof against high winds, makes no snowdrifts, and is both durable and cheap."

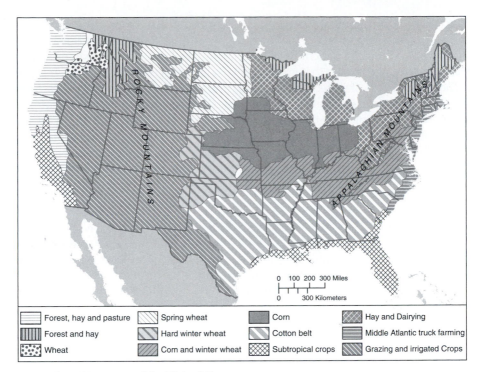

Agricultural Regions of the United States

To solve the shortages in housing material, early Plains settlers used squares of sod cut from the thick Plains turf. These were piled up to make walls along the edges of deep excavations in the ground that served as basements. The roof of such a house was also sod, placed on brush and cottonwood rafters. Warm in winter and cool in summer, these half-buried structures were also dirty, and during heavy rains leaked badly. Yet they served some families for many years and were even used for schoolhouses and other public buildings. Eventually, when the railroads came, timber from the East and Far West made frame structures possible. In time the houses of the Plains began to resemble those in the Midwest.

The Plains environment presented still other problems. In 1874 swarms of grasshoppers descended on the region from the Dakotas to Texas, consuming grain, vegetables, bark, clothes, and even the handles of plows and pitchforks. During the 1870s and early 1880s, however, rainfall was generally sufficient in the region, and with the confinement of the Indians to reservations and the arrival of the railroads, people flocked to western Kansas, Nebraska, and the Dakotas to grow grain for the East and Europe. Then the late 1880s ushered in a decade of extremely dry conditions. Crops drooped and died, and whatever survived the parching winds was consumed by insects. Farmers and their families fled the searing sun during the early 1890s and returned east with the sides of their wagons sardonically inscribed: "In God We Trusted; In Kansas We Busted!"

Yet many farmers persisted and ultimately prospered. Once labor shortages—another chronic problem on the Plains—had been solved by the invention of special harvesting and threshing machines, Plains farming became enormously productive. It was extensive agriculture that cultivated vast acreages using little labor. It focused on wheat, the crop best suited to grasslands and, due to its durability, to production in regions far from consumers. By 1899 the United States was producing over 600 million bushels of wheat a year, much of it from the Great Plains. In 1870 the wheat belt had been centered in the older Midwest. By 1899 Minnesota, North Dakota, South Dakota, and Kansas were among the top five wheat producers.

Pacific Coast Agriculture.   As the Plains became the nation's wheat belt the Pacific coast emerged as the nation's fruit and vegetable belt. Taking advantage of the region's mild climate, Oregon began to supply the San Francisco market with apples, pears, peaches, plums, and grapes. In Washington the arrival of the Northern Pacific Railroad in the 1880s stimulated the production of apples and pears in the state's eastern valleys. Meanwhile, California was developing into a significant specialty agricultural region. Grapes had been grown there long before Americans arrived. By 1900 California produced 19 million gallons of wine, over 80 percent of American output. In the 1870s Brazilian navel oranges were introduced on irrigated fields in southern California. When refrigerated railcars became available in the 1880s, navels picked during the early winter could be shipped all the way to the East Coast. Summer-ripening Valencia oranges, introduced somewhat later, enabled the growers to produce year-round.

The citrus industry at first was plagued by haphazard marketing. Shipments spoiled or got lost; at times the market was glutted, at other times undersupplied. To deal with these problems, in 1893 the growers organized the Southern California Fruit Exchange, which later became the California Fruit Growers' Exchange and marketed its product under the brand name Sunkist. The Exchange brought stability to the industry.

Farm Discontent and Western Revolt

In quantity, acreage, output per person and per acre, the advances of American agriculture were spectacular. Largely because of the mechanized farms of the Great Plains, wheat production tripled between 1860 and 1899. In the older Midwest, states such as Illinois and Iowa shifted from wheat to hogs and cattle, feeding them on the country's huge corn harvests—840 million bushels of corn in 1860, 2.7 billion bushels in 1900. In cotton and livestock the increases were equally dramatic. The nation's farm labor force continued to rise in absolute numbers until 1910, but the increase in farmers was far smaller than the expansion in their output, for new technology, new plant science, the land-grant colleges, and the Department of Agriculture all helped to increase productivity per worker at a rapid pace. The result was that the United States became an agricultural horn of plenty, capable of producing cheap grain, meat, and fiber, not only for its own exploding urban population, but also for much of the industrializing Atlantic world.

Yet another, darker tale competed with this agricultural success story: Post-Civil War American farmers felt oppressed, exploited, and ill-used by the rich and powerful residing in the eastern and midwestern cities.

Farm Problems.

According to farm spokespersons, farmers were victimized by bankers and mortgage companies that kept interest rates high and squeezed farmers and other borrowers and debtors through "hard money" policies that restricted the country's money supply and relentlessly forced down prices. The typical American farm, they claimed, was mortgaged to the hilt, and the moneylenders and bankers showed no mercy in foreclosing when the farmer could not pay. The prices of the goods that cultivators bought, moreover, were kept artificially high by tariffs and business monopoly practices, whereas prices they received for their unprotected crops fell steadily. Middlemen—bankers, millers, grain elevator operators—skimmed off profits, leaving little for farmers. Beyond these economic grievances, spokespersons for "agrarianism" expressed fears that those who "fed them all," the nation's cultivators, were losing influence and the new "money power" was in the driver's seat.

Today, economic historians consider the charges leveled by farm advocates during these last years of the nineteenth century exaggerated. For one thing, they note, farmers did not all fare alike economically. Pacific coast farmers prospered by adopting fruit and vegetable crops. Prairie farmers of Iowa and Illinois switched from wheat to corn and hogs and made decent profits. East coast and Great Lakes truck and dairy farmers found profitable markets in the cities.

As for claims of financial oppression, this too may be overstated. Interest rates were higher in the West and South—the country's prime farm areas—than in the Northeast. But this difference can be explained by the shortage of savings in the two staple-crop regions and the higher risks of farming compared to manufacturing or commerce. Nor were American farm borrowers poor peasants turning to moneylenders to stave off starvation. Most of the money that farmers borrowed was for barns, fences, plows, harvesters, and other capital items needed to increase productivity and income. The loans were, in effect, no different from the loans of any other small businessperson. Nor were the oppressive farm mortgages as universal as the critics claimed. Even in the wheat belt, no more than 39 percent of the farms were burdened with mortgages in 1890, though the figure was higher in Kansas and Nebraska. As for the bankers' wicked urge to foreclose, this was not common. The banks and the mortgage companies that lent farmers money were not interested in acquiring farm acreage; they often extended the repayment terms of loans more than once to avoid having to foreclose.

The claims that falling prices were contrived deliberately by a cabal of bankers and money power monopolists to squeeze the nation's "producers" are equally exaggerated. All prices fell during the generation following the Civil War. This meant the prices the farmers paid as well as those they received. There is no good evidence that the "terms of trade" between the producers of food and fiber and the providers of the services and manufactured goods that they used shifted significantly against the nation's tillers in these years. Moreover, the price declines were not only an American phenomenon; they were common to the entire world. If there was a conspiracy to force down prices, the conspiracy was evidently worldwide in its scope.

Nor is it clear that monetary forces were responsible for the great deflation of the late nineteenth century. This was an era when real costs were going down as a result of cost-saving new technology and new management techniques. Even the middlemen's real costs declined due to greater efficiency. When, in the 1890s, the Russians sought to make their grain more competitive in the world market, they sent a delegation to the United States to learn how American brokers and grain handlers managed to get the American wheat crop to market at such low cost. Even scholars who believe that late-nineteenth-century price declines can be traced to an excessively slow increase in the money supply doubt that this was deliberately engineered by a cabal of conspirators.

Agrarianism.   And yet we are left with the reality of turbulent farm discontent in the generation following the Civil War. How can we explain it?

First, let us note that the agrarian insurgency of the period was confined primarily to the wheat- and cotton-growing areas. As we saw, dairy farmers, corn-hog farmers, and truck farmers who sold their products to domestic consumers in the fast-growing cities had little reason to respond to the insurgent appeal. Though their prices declined like all others, they were more stable than many.

Instability, indeed, is one possible answer to the riddle of insurgency in the wheat and cotton belts. Grain and cotton farmers were subject to greater uncertainty than other producers. These cultivators sold their crops in a world market where they competed fiercely with other nations. By the end of the nineteenth century the entire world had been knit together in a single market for nonperishable agricultural goods, and prices in this market were established by countless impersonal transactions between buyers and sellers. The system was a tremendous boon to consumers. Everywhere they benefited from the declining cost of food and fabric. But it produced disturbing price fluctuations. A bumper wheat crop in the American Plains could be expected to lower world grain prices. But it might be more than offset by a dearth in, say, Argentina, that would push prices up. And, of course, the reverse might also occur: An American farmer, expecting good prices after a short crop, might be bitterly disappointed if Australia or the Ukraine had a bounteous harvest. The net effect was that farmers found themselves on a roller coaster over which they could exercise no control. The villains were actually impersonal market forces, but these were not as satisfactory as flesh-and-blood villains of the sort that farmers saw or heard about every day—the bankers, railroad officials, politicians, and farm machinery manufacturers. In some ways the late-nineteenth-century farmer's plight and response resemble that of many American workers and manufacturers today confronting the globalization of the world economy for industrial goods.

Clearly, American farmers as a group faced difficult problems adjusting to the demands and circumstances of a new industrialized, urbanized era. Besides price instability, one cannot deny the distress of sharecroppers in the South, penalized often by a vicious social and racial system that placed them at the mercy of powerful and privileged planters and landowners. Land in America, moreover, bore a disproportionate share of the national tax burden; personal property and personal income were lightly taxed or entirely tax-exempt. Then there was the legitimate concern of shippers for transportation gouging. Though railroad rates generally went down, in noncompetitive areas, usually in the West and South, the railroad managers tried to make up for the "cutthroat" competition on major trunk lines by charging all that the local traffic would bear. Finally, as fuel for farm discontent, agriculture as a way of life had lost standing. More and more the cities had seized on the imaginations of Americans. This explained, in part, the exodus of young people from the rural areas. It also accounted for the increasing references to "rubes," "hayseeds," and "appleknockers" in the metropolitan press. As the nation urbanized, American farmers felt more and more disesteemed and neglected.

Moved by such forces and feelings, post-Civil War farm advocates, playing on resonant Jeffersonian chords, sought to create a social philosophy based on farm distress and rural rights that can best be labeled agrarianism.

Agrarianism exalted the farmer as the only true citizen, the backbone of the nation, the heart of the "producing masses." Agrarians gradually expanded the concept to include the ever-growing number of wage earners, and some sought to construct a farmer-labor alliance of producers, whose plight was said to be shared by the nation as a whole. On the other side, agrarians personalized the enemy as the "money power" or the "bloated middlemen." These "plutocrats," they said, had seized control of the economy and through various hidden financial arrangements had imposed their will on the nation. The United States was fast becoming the land of a rich few and an impoverished, exploited, and powerless many.

Though agrarian advocates sought to universalize their protest, much of their indictment had a sectional edge. Both the Great Plains and the South, as we noted, regarded themselves as colonies in bondage to the "East." It was the East that was the source of credit, and it was eastern moneylenders and bankers who charged the high interest rates the "producing sections" paid. The railroads had their headquarters in Boston, New York, Philadelphia, or Chicago, and it was in these eastern and large midwestern cities that the freight rates that squeezed cotton and wheat farmers were set. Easterners—or Europeans—also owned the land and marketed the crops, the agrarians said. The farm-machinery manufacturers, the barbed-wire producers, and the other industrialists who made the equipment western and southern farmers needed to survive were easterners. Furthermore, the East dominated the major political parties and through them the government. Policies regarding the Indians, finance, money, tariffs, and land were not made by the people of the West and South, who were most directly concerned. They were made by the representatives of the eastern "money interests," who sought only their own gain, or by eastern reformers who did not know the problem first hand.

Whether true or false, whether exaggerated or exact, the agrarian indictment of plutocracy and the East had become a powerful political force by the end of the century. The agrarian reformers were never enemies of private property and the profit system. Their complaint was with the way capitalism had supposedly been rigged in favor of the few and against the many. Their desire was not to end profit and property but to make sure that the benefits of both were more widely distributed among the masses of the people.

The Grangers

In the early 1870s restless prairie farmers flocked to local "Granges" of the Patrons of Husbandry, a fraternal order founded in 1876. At first the Granges were primarily social and educational organizations. Farm life was isolated and lonely, and farmers and their wives welcomed the chance to socialize and listen to lectures at the local Grange hall. The Granges soon became politically active. Joining with eastern merchants and businesspeople who also disliked the railroads' high and often arbitrary freight charges, in farm belt states including Illinois, Iowa, Wisconsin, and Minnesota the Grangers were able to enact railroad and grain elevator regulatory laws.

The Patrons were also active in various cooperative ventures to improve the economic standing of farmers. In several midwestern states Grange agents negotiated purchases of large quantities of supplies from merchants or manufacturers at special low prices. In 1872 a group of merchants formed Montgomery Ward and Company for the specific purpose of dealing with the Grangers. Efforts to produce farm machinery cooperatively failed, however; the managers of Grange manufacturing enterprises lacked experience and were unable to meet the aggressive competition of established private firms.

The Alliances.

By the late 1870s the Grange had ceased to be anything more than a social-educational organization, but by this time a more militant force had appeared.

The Alliance movement began in the mid-1870s when small rancher-farmers in central Texas organized a private club to catch horse thieves, collect stray cattle, and fight the large ranchers who ignored the rights of their smaller neighbors. The organization soon spread to the rest of the state and grew in strength and ambition. In 1886 the Texas Alliance, borrowing ideas from the Greenback party of 1884, adopted a platform of opposition to landholding by foreigners, for stiff taxes on railroads, and for abundant paper money. Under Charles W. Macune the Alliance expanded into a regional Southern Alliance that incorporated the Arkansas Wheel and a large Colored Alliance composed of black tenant farmers and sharecroppers. By 1890 the Southern Alliance had a million members. Farm discontent in the prairies and Great Plains led to similar efforts. By 1890 the Northwest Alliance, organized a decade earlier, had spread to fifteen states, with particularly heavy concentration of membership in Kansas, Nebraska, the Dakotas, and Minnesota.

Toward the end of the 1880s the Alliances began to emphasize politics rather than cooperatives. Alliance-affiliated candidates won election as either Democrats or Republicans to state legislatures in the South and West. In several states they captured one of the major parties and compelled it to endorse farmers' programs. Alliance-controlled state legislatures enacted some legislation regulating railroads and businesses, but these measures were largely ineffective. Alliance-dominated state governments were frequently led by political novices who were easily outmaneuvered by the seasoned politicians of the regular parties. Frustrated by their initial experiences with politics, Alliance leaders concluded that the fault lay in relying on the Democrats and Republicans. Instead, the farmers should organize their own party, one that would be free of the old-line politicos, who seemed indifferent at heart to the needs of rural people.

Conclusions

The development of the last American frontier made an enormous difference in the nation's history. The exploitation of the trans-Missouri West added immense resources to the country's economic base. The cattle and mining frontiers also supplied raw material for American literature and legend. For the American Indian, development of this area was the final defeat in almost three centuries of bitter conflict with people of Old World origins.

The Last West was also the focus for the last truly serious threat of sectional disunity. Along with the cotton South, it was indeed in some ways a colony of the Northeast. Eastern money controlled its resources; eastern attitudes affected its Indian policy; eastern politicians decided its political fate. By the end of the century, moreover, western and southern grievances had created a sense of apartness, of distinctiveness, that contributed to a mighty political revolt. This sense was reinforced and given focus by a group of agrarian thinkers who drew their ideas from the Jefferson-Jackson tradition of the early Republic. Scholars may argue over the validity of western grievances or whether western leaders properly identified the causes of their section's difficulties. But there can be no question that by 1890 in the West and the South a powerful wave of discontent was gathering force. Before the new century began, it would sweep over the nation, threatening to push aside long-standing political alignments and shift the country's balance of power.

ONLINE RESOURCES

"We Have Got a Good Friend in John Collier: A Taos Pueblo Tries to Seal the Indian New Deal" *http://historymatters.gmu.edu/d/26* In a letter to his friend John Collier, Taos Pueblo Indian Antonio Lunan describes his progress in persuading the Indians to accept New Deal federal policy. He describes the Indians' questions and concerns.

Little Bighorn Battlefield Archeology and History *http://www.cr.nps.gov/mwac/libi/index.html* This site provides information about this well-known battle though narratives, a chronology, photos, and artwork. Artifacts from the battlefield lend insights about this type of warfare and the people who waged it.

California Notes: Museum of the City of San Francisco *http://www.sfmuseum.org/hist9/turrillgold.html* Providing detailed explanations of the terminology and technology, this site details the process of gold mining in California in the late 1800s. Links to the San Francisco History Index lead to a collection of sketches and primary-source documents about the excavations and miners.

Photographs of the American West, 1861–1912 *http://www.archives.gov/research/american-west/* See how people transformed the West into an organization of settlements through this large collection of photographs whose subjects include training at Indian schools, the first continental railroad, and scenes of life on the homestead.

20

The Gilded Age

How "Gilded" Was It?

1851	The YMCA is established in the United States
1858	The National Association of Baseball Players is founded
1859	Darwin's *The Origin of Species* published in England
1870–82	Printing process improves, enabling newspapers to print more news daily; The Associated Press and the United Press are founded; Pulitzer begins yellow journalism in the *New York World*
1870–90	American school of art, led by Winslow Homer
1873	The Coinage Age ("Crime of 73"); Congress drops silver from coinage system
1875	The Whiskey Ring scandal
1876	American Library Association founded, lobbies for support of free public libraries
1877	Rutherford B. Hayes is elected president in Compromise of 1877
1878	The Bland–Allison Act
1879	The United States returns to gold standard
1880s	More than 80 percent of the electorate votes in presidential elections
1880	James Garfield elected president; William Le Baron Jenney designs first skyscraper
1881–82	The Star Route scandals
1881	Garfield is assassinated; Chester A. Arthur becomes president
1883	The Pendleton Act establishes Civil Service Commission; Brooklyn Bridge is completed; Metropolitan Opera House opens
1884	Mark Twain's *Adventures of Huckleberry Finn* published; Grover Cleveland elected president
1886	*Wabash, St. Louis and Pacific Railway Co. v. Illinois*
1887	The Interstate Commerce Act creates the Interstate Commerce Commission (ICC)
1888	Benjamin Harrison elected president
1890	Sherman Silver Purchase Act; Sherman Antitrust Act; McKinley Tariff Act
1892	People's Party (Populist) formed; Grover Cleveland elected president for the second time
1893	The Chicago World's Fair; financial panic leads to depression
1894	The Wilson–Gorman Tariff Act
1895	Stephan Crane's *The Red Badge of Courage* published
1896	First showing of a commercial motion picture in a legitimate theater; William McKinley elected president, defeating William Jennings Bryan

1897	Almost half of federal employees are under Civil Service rules
1900	Theodore Dreiser's *Sister Carrie* published; Tin Pan Alley marks beginning of popular music; Frank Lloyd Wright begins functional modernism in architecture
1903	First World Series of baseball
1904	Pragmatist philosopher John Dewey changes educational system; The Henri–Ashcan school marks trend toward modernism in painting
1913	Armory exhibition shows Cézanne, Van Gogh, Picasso, Matisse, Duchamp in US
1915	Over 80 percent of all children attend school due to compulsory laws

"Golden ages" are eras of cultural creativity, innovative thought, high ethical ideals, and benevolent political relationships. By contrast the generation following the Civil War has acquired the name the "Gilded Age," suggesting a thin veneer of gilt applied to cultural, intellectual, and moral base metal.

The disparaging label comes from an 1873 novel written by Mark Twain and Charles Dudley Warner. *The Gilded Age* deals with human types who came to the top of the social pile in the post-Civil War era. The characters are self-seeking, insincere, corrupt, hypocritical, coarse, materialistic. They seem to epitomize the new era when greed, gain, and good times dominated the nation's political, economic, and cultural life. Mark Twain and his collaborator were writing primarily about the tawdry, mercenary national politics of the day. Other observers of the post-Civil War years, however, were just as harsh about the cultural scene. In 1874 Edwin L. Godkin, a transplanted Anglo-Irishman who edited the prestigious *The Nation*, declared that his adopted country was a "chromo civilization"; like the inexpensive, popular prints of the day (chromolithographs), its colors were gaudy and false.

How "gilded" was the political and cultural life of America in the generation following Appomattox? Did it, perhaps, contain some nuggets of real gold?

Politics in the Gilded Age

American voters during the Gilded Age were passionate political participants. Voter turnouts during these years were spectacular. Except in the South, where thousands of black male citizens were effectively deprived of the right to vote after 1877, a far larger proportion of the eligible voters cast ballots than today. In 1896, for example, the turnout was more than 95 percent in the five states of the Old Northwest.

These citizens were steadfast partisans. In those years, "Independents"— voters without party allegiances—were treated with contempt as people without spirit or commitment. Few voters were willing to accept the label. Obviously Americans considered it important whether one party or the other won. But we must ask: why?

Politics as Recreation.   One non-trivial explanation for the public's interest in politics was its entertainment value. Americans of this era enjoyed relatively little leisure time. Besides the Fourth of July and Washington's Birthday, there were few legal holidays. A political rally gave working people one of their few occasions to take time off. Few employers dared say no when an American male citizen asserted his God-given right to hear a political speech. Besides an excuse to avoid work, political rallies were diverting. In the absence of television, motion pictures, and professional athletics (except baseball, already the national game), politics provided lively amusement. One reporter described a Republican political rally in Cambridge City, Indiana, in 1876 as "a spectacle no foreign fiesta could equal." Even though most people could not hear the distant speaker, General Benjamin Harrison, they were perfectly content, for it was "the holiday diversion, the crowds, the bravery of the procession, the music and the fun of the occasion they came chiefly to enjoy."

In part the excitement and fun derived from the closeness of the contests, which, like a tight baseball pennant race, brought out the partisans of both sides in record numbers. Between the 1870s and the late 1890s, neither party could dominate national politics. True, every president during these years except Grover Cleveland was a Republican, but almost all federal elections were close. In 1880 Republican James Garfield defeated his Democratic opponent, Winfield Scott Hancock, by only 7,000 popular votes. Four years later Cleveland, a Democrat, defeated James G. Blaine by under 25,000 votes out of 10 million cast. Only for three short periods during this era did the same party control the presidency and both houses of Congress. In only one midterm national election between 1878 and 1888 inclusively did more than 2 percentage points separate the total Democratic and Republican votes. When, after 1896, the Republicans forged ahead of their Democratic rivals in presidential races and the excitement declined, voter turnouts dropped off sharply.

Like all exciting and well-patronized spectator sports, Gilded Age politics had to have its stars, its heroes, its villains. Many of the national politicians of the day were colorful characters. There was the magnetic, charming, combative, brilliant, and corrupt "plumed knight," James G. Blaine, Republican senator from Maine. His sworn enemy from New York was Roscoe Conkling, a strutting "turkey-gobbler," who wore yellow shoes, scarlet coat, waistcoat with gold lace, and green trousers. Thomas B. Reed, the 300-pound Speaker of the House, tossed off aphorisms as funny as Mark Twain's: "A statesman is a dead politician"; "One with God is always a majority, but many a martyr has been burned at the stake while the votes were being counted." Men like these alternately delighted and dismayed the voting public and helped sustain the enthusiasm for Gilded Age politics.

Politics as Morality Play.

The metaphor of Gilded Age politics as a sport is useful up to a point. To some Americans, however—the so-called "best men"— politics during these years seemed rather to be a profound moral drama, a contest between good and evil. The evil was personified by the political rogues who had risen to the top after the Civil War and had perverted the once-virtuous republic. The good was personified by men like themselves—disinterested, dedicated, scrupulous, and competent, who wished only the public good and who, if allowed to govern, would restore America to a state of grace.

Almost all the "best men" were young. Many came from the country's most distinguished families: Charles Francis Adams, Jr., and his younger brother, Henry, were the grandsons of one president and great-grandsons of another.

Several, however—such as the righteous Carl Schurz and the self-righteous E. L. Godkin—were self-made or foreign-born. Almost all were people of cultivation and refinement. They were never more than a small minority, but they were an influential group. Through the pages of Edwin L. Godkin's *The Nation* and other journals of criticism and opinion, their views entered the homes of the educated middle class. The independents became a sort of conscience for the country, and few well-read Americans could entirely resist the feeling that what they supported was virtuous and what they opposed evil.

Corruption.   The "best men" believed that both parties were corrupt, and almost alone among the politically active people of the era, they voted for candidates and platforms rather than parties and gloried in being "independent." Their tone was one of almost constant outrage—an attitude that often amused the general public. One subscriber to the independent *New York Evening Post* noted that she always felt safe with the paper on her doorstep: "It just lay there and growled all night."

However exaggerated or humorless, this indignation had much to feed on. Scandal after scandal marred state and national politics in the Gilded Age. In many states rings of dishonest businessmen allied themselves with corrupt politicians to achieve their private ends. In New York the Erie Ring of Jay Gould and his allies bought and sold legislators like cattle. In Pennsylvania it was said that when Thomas A. Scott, president of the Pennsylvania Railroad, finished his business with the state government, the legislature at Harrisburg adjourned. At the federal level the Whiskey Ring, an alliance of federal officials and distillers, bilked the treasury of millions of dollars in revenue taxes. In 1881–1882 the federal authorities uncovered a gang of Post Office personnel that awarded generous contracts to private parties to deliver mail to remote areas (the "Star Routes") in return for kickbacks.

Corruption spread even to elections. Every year, following some local or national political contest, the newspapers carried long accounts of bribery, ballot box stuffing, illegal voting by aliens, and the use of "floaters," who, to tip a close election, crossed state or county lines to vote illegally. Most of the electoral chicanery took place in the cities, where the foreign-born were often blamed. But in fact, one of the most flagrant instances of chronic electoral dishonesty in this era occurred in Adams County, Ohio, a rural community composed mostly of old-stock Americans where virtually the entire voting population sold their votes to the highest bidder. Given the near-equal strength of parties, it is likely that more than one presidential election was won by voting fraud.

The Spoils System.   Besides outright corruption, the independents also deplored the spoils system, or patronage system, which had emerged during the 1820s and 1830s but came to full flower during the Gilded Age. The practice grew out of a problem that Americans have never fully solved: how to pay for political campaigns and party government. Many citizens today are still concerned that parties are financed by the rich and the powerful to the detriment of the common public good.

Under the Gilded Age spoils system, parties were in effect financed by the government, largely in the form of job patronage. And vast amounts of patronage were available. Between 1865 and 1891 the federal payroll expanded from

53,000 to 166,000 employees. Even the lowest-paid federal workers earned from two to three times the annual income of privately employed unskilled workers, and they normally spent only eight hours a day at their jobs, in contrast with the ten- to twelve-hour workdays common in private business.

Men and women, not surprisingly, eagerly sought federal employment. Would-be officeholders worked hard for political candidates and expected patronage appointments in return. Once on the job, appointees were willing to contribute further effort and a portion of their salaries ("assessments") to keep their party in office lest a victorious opposition deprive them of their positions.

The system was wasteful and inefficient. Although government was becoming ever more complex and technical, the spoils system made flattery, party loyalty, and political know-how the sole criteria for appointment and promotion. Moreover, when competent people did gain office, they seldom kept their jobs long enough to learn their duties and perfect their skills. At the beginning of each administration the civil service, and with it the whole federal government, was immobilized while the president sorted out the patronage claims of party supporters all over the country. The spoils system also encouraged outright corruption. Men and women bribed influential politicians to get choice jobs and even advertised in the newspapers their willingness to pay cash to obtain federal employment.

The independents demanded civil service reform that would substitute merit, determined by competitive examination, for party loyalty, and security in office for constant replacement. But the spoils system was so deeply entrenched in American politics that it was difficult to eradicate. Then, in 1883, after the assassination of President James Garfield by Charles Guiteau, a disappointed office seeker, Congress passed the first federal civil service law, the Pendleton Act. The law forbade the assessment of federal employees, made appointments contingent on examinations, regularized promotions and linked them to demonstrated competence. Presidents Arthur and Cleveland placed some 20,000 federal jobs on the "classified list" of those covered by the new rules. By 1897, when William McKinley became president, 86,000 employees—almost half the federal civil service—were recruited by examination, promoted by merit, and protected by tenure.

The Bases for Party Affiliation

Viewing Gilded Age politics as an exciting game or as a moral drama tells us something about how and why the political system worked. But it does not tell us what distinguished the average Democrat from the average Republican.

The Civil War Legacy.
One distinction was attitudes toward the Civil War. The war, its antecedents, its Reconstruction aftermath, and the long memories of these emotion-stirring events helped forge links both of shared affection and of antagonisms that contributed to party identification.

Republican politicians worked hard to keep former Union sympathizers in the Grand Old Party. Republicans leaders regularly "waved the bloody shirt" to appeal to Union veterans and northerners generally. In a typical bloody-shirt tirade, Republican Oliver Morton of Indiana roared: "The Democratic party may be described as a common sewer, and loathsome receptacle, into which is emptied every element of treason North and South, every element of inhumanity and barbarism which has dishonored the age."

Even when they abandoned the black population of the South to the conservative white "redeemers" in the 1870s, Republicans were quick to react when southern mistreatment of blacks became too blatant. As late as 1890 a Republican House of Representatives passed a "force bill" designed to reimpose federal supervision of national elections so that blacks were not totally disfranchised by the southern states. Republicans also furiously denounced Grover Cleveland, the first Democratic president since Buchanan, and forced him to retreat when he threatened to return captured Confederate battle flags to the southern states as a gesture of sectional reconciliation. Black voters, for their part, though not numerous in either section due to disenfranchisement in the South and sparse numbers generally in the North, remembered their champions, Abraham Lincoln and Thaddeus Stevens, and were among the most loyal Republicans in the entire nation.

The Democrats, too, capitalized on Civil War and Reconstruction memories. In the white South, hatred of "Black Republican" emancipation and later Radical Reconstruction policies created a powerful and long-lasting Democratic solidarity. Any white man who voted Republican was branded a traitor to his race by Democratic politicians. By the 1880s, except for a few small dissenting pockets in the former anti-secession mountain regions, it was hard to find a Republican voter in the South. In local contests, winning the Democratic nomination for office became tantamount to election.

One key component of the Republican coalition was Union veterans. Not only were they energized by bloody-shirt appeals; they were also shamelessly bribed by Republican administrations. Prodded by the Union veterans' organization, the Grand Army of the Republic (GAR), successive Republican Congresses appropriated millions of dollars in pensions for former Union soldiers and their widows and dependents. By 1899 the total paid annually to these people by the U.S. Treasury amounted to almost $157 million. So pervasive were these grants that one scholar has called the Union veteran pension policy the beginning of the social welfare state in America.

Religion, Race, and Nationality.   With each passing year the political hold of the Civil War became a little weaker, especially among northern voters. Yet party loyalty remained intense, and only the most extraordinary scandal or the most lackluster candidate could drive the average voter away from his traditional allegiance. What tied the voters to their individual parties so firmly after the Civil War issues had dimmed?

Some historians now believe that ethnic and religious factors forged the tightest bonds of Gilded Age party loyalty. By the 1880s the German, Irish, and Scandinavian immigrants of the 1830–1870 period had put down roots and emerged as an important political force. In addition, there were now many second-generation, American-born children who combined an understanding of the American political system with a continuing loyalty to their ethnic and religious traditions. It is no surprise, then, that in the generation following the Civil War, cultural loyalties and tensions played a special role in political life.

Religion apparently shaped party loyalties more than nationality or ethnic background by themselves. Whatever their national origins, members of the "liturgical" churches, which emphasized "right belief" over personal regeneration, were generally Democrats. The most numerous of the liturgical church groups were the Catholics who, since the days of Jefferson, had found a political refuge in the more "popular" of the two parties. Members of other churches that similarly emphasized ritual and well-defined dogma—Lutherans, Jews, Episcopalians—frequently voted the same way. The Democrats had welcomed the Catholic French, Germans, and Irish who crossed the Atlantic before the Civil War, and had catered to their needs. These needs, in part, had been material and practical, and, as we have seen, the predominantly Democratic machines in the cities helped the immigrants with jobs, handouts, and legal aid.

Both parties played this game, but concessions to cultural differences were more difficult for the Republicans to make. Republicans, like their Whig forebears, shared a latter-day puritanism that generally opposed the cultural and religious values of the liturgical faiths. Both Whigs and Republicans, each in its own day, were drawn heavily from members of evangelical churches that emphasized inner regeneration, personal reformation, and "right behavior." They were mostly native-born Baptists, Methodists, Presbyterians, and Congregationalists; but some were foreign-born Pietists who, like their native-born counterparts, tended to consider politics a vehicle for imposing their moral vision.

In the 1850s evangelicals had helped found the Republican party dedicated to the containment and ultimate extinction of sinful slavery. Through the remainder of the century Republican zeal for public and private virtue was expressed in demands for blue laws and restrictions on the manufacture and sale of liquor and the suppression of "blood" sports such as cockfighting and boxing. Republicans also insisted on strict separation of church and state, since the alternative, they felt, was to allow Catholic ascendency in public institutions.

Catholics, as well as many Lutherans, resented these efforts to restrict their personal freedoms and limit their influence. Unlike evangelicals, they held that what citizens did in their personal lives was no business of the state. They also believed that far too many state-supported institutions, though supposedly nonsectarian, were actually dominated by pietistic Protestants. The Democrats naturally played on these resentments. John ("Bathouse") Coughlin, a Chicago Democrat, warned the voters: "A Republican is a man who wants you t' go t' church every Sunday. A Democrat says if a man wants t' have a glass of beer on Sunday he can have it. Be Democrats unless you want t' be tied t' a church, a schoolhouse, or a Sunday school."

Political puritanism went beyond blue laws and mild expressions of religious intolerance. In the 1880s the antiforeign, anti-Catholic American Protective Association (APA) demanded the exclusion of noncitizens from American political life, attacked "the diabolical works of the Roman Catholic Church," and pledged to fight for the "cause of Protestantism." During the 1890s the APA intruded into several local campaigns as an unacknowledged, but not unrecognized, ally of the Republicans and a champion of "true Americanism" against "aliens" and "papists." However impatient liturgical voters might become at times with their traditional party allegiances, or however tempted to vote for a particularly attractive Republican candidate, anti-Catholic and antiforeign sentiment confirmed their view "that personal liberty . . . [was] surely only safe with the Democratic party in power."

Party Realignments

For fifty years, then, cultural values and memories of the Civil War had forged bonds between the voters and the two major parties. In the 1890s the discontented westerners and southern farmers discussed in Chapter 19 would form a new party, and in the process unintentionally created a new political era dominated by the Republicans.

The Populist Party. The People's Party of the U.S.A., or Populists, was launched in 1892 by leaders of the Farmers' Alliances (see Chapter 19) and assorted political dissidents at a convention held at Omaha, Nebraska. The preamble to the new party's platform delivered an agrarian message. Wealth concentration and the power of bondholders, usurers, and millionaires had brought the nation to the verge of ruin. "A vast conspiracy against mankind" had been "organized on two continents" and was "rapidly taking possession of the world." The conspirators had reduced the nation's money supply to an amount totally inadequate for its business, and the consequences were "falling prices, the formation of combines and rings, and the impoverishment of the producing class." The two traditional parties had failed the voters and now, in the impending political campaign, they proposed "to drown out the outcries of a plundered people with the uproar of a sham battle over the tariff, so that capitalists, corporations, national banks, rings, trusts, watered stock, the demonetization of silver, and the oppression of the usurers may be lost sight of."

To counter the people's oppressors, the Populists called for "free and unlimited coinage of silver" at a sixteen-to-one ratio with gold, a money supply of at least $50 per capita, a graduated income tax, and a postal savings bank for small savers afraid of private banks. The government should own the railroads and the telephone and telegraph systems, and aliens and the railroads should be compelled to give up excess land. Tacked on as a platform afterthought was a section calling for a secret ballot, restrictions on immigration, an eight-hour workday for government workers, the "initiative" and "referendum" as ways of furthering direct democracy, and direct election of the president and United States senators without the intermediaries of the electoral college or the state legislatures.

Several provisions of the 1892 Populist platform foreshadowed the program of the early-twentieth-century progressives and even presaged the modern social welfare state. Its overall thrust was the desire to make government more responsive to the popular will, limit the power of large corporations, and reduce some of the worst disparities of wealth. At the same time, it did not directly challenge the existing regime of private property. It is not surprising that several leading socialists of the day dismissed the Populists as a "bourgeois party" composed of petty rural capitalists.

In 1892 the Populists faced the difficult task of overcoming traditional party allegiances. The problem was especially difficult in the South, where a third party threatened the unchallenged Democratic dominance established by the redeemers

in the 1870s and maintained by their equally conservative successors, the Bourbons. Still worse, the Populists might open the door to black suffrage, erased so
successfully after 1877.

The latter fears seemed valid. Some southern Populists were eager to gain
black votes. In Georgia Tom Watson, a leading Populist, promised black voters
that if they stood "shoulder to shoulder" with the Populists, they would have "fair
play and fair treatment as men and citizens, irrespective of color." But in fact, the
Populist commitment to racial equality was limited. Populists in southern state
legislatures did not differ noticeably from the Bourbons in their desire to keep
blacks "in their place," nor were they particularly sensitive to the special social
problems that blacks faced beyond those they shared with poor whites. Yet many
white southerners feared the third party endangered white dominion.

In the 1892 presidential election the Populist candidate, James B. Weaver, a
former Union general, campaigned effectively for his party's platform. Unfortunately for the People's Party, Weaver's Union record aroused deep suspicion in
the South. On the western Plains the new party did better. In the end the Populist
ticket won over 15 percent of the vote in the Deep South and higher percentages in
the silver-producing mountain states and parts of the Great Plains. Weaver received over 1 million out of 12 million votes cast, or about 8.5 percent. Cleveland
won, but the Populist vote promised—or threatened—much for the future.

Unrest Under Cleveland.   Grover Cleveland's second presidential term
(1893–1897) was marked by social unrest more threatening than anything the
country had seen since the Civil War. In the spring of 1893 the stock market
crashed, ushering in a devastating depression. Strikes, labor demonstrations, and
riots erupted in many parts of the country as workers struggled desperately to
keep their jobs or prevent cuts in pay. This climate of fear and anger set off the
Pullman strike of 1894 (described in Chapter 17).

Another manifestation of the hard times was Coxey's Army, a march on Washington of the unemployed in 1894. Led by Jacob S. Coxey, an ex-Greenbacker, the
demonstrators sought to dramatize the plight of the jobless and advertise Coxey's
plan for a federal works program financed by a paper-money issue of $500 mil-
lion. The experts of the day ridiculed the idea, and when Coxey's 400 bedraggled
men finally arrived in Washington, federal officials arrested their leaders for
trampling the Capitol grass.

The reaction of the Cleveland administration to the distress of the laboring
population was at best unimaginative. The president believed that Populist agitation and the government's piling up of silver—required by the Sherman Silver
Purchase Act of 1890—had set off the panic and the resulting slump by shaking
public confidence in the ability of the government to pay its obligations in gold.
And, in fact, there was reason for concern. Hoarders were withdrawing gold from
the banks and the treasury and threatening to force the nation off the gold standard. To stop the gold drain and reassure public creditors, Cleveland asked Congress to repeal the Sherman Silver Act. Simultaneously he sought to shore up the
treasury's gold reserve by selling bonds to the public for gold coin. The public
bought the bonds, but then brought more paper money to the treasury to be

redeemed for gold. Gold went in one treasury door and out the other. Ultimately Cleveland was able to save the gold standard by inducing the international investment bankers to guarantee delivery of foreign gold. But his tactics only convinced millions of southerners and westerners that J. P. Morgan, "Wall Street," and the Rothschilds, the prominent European banking family, owned the country.

Bankruptcies, unemployment, and suspicious dealings with the international financiers form the background of the important election of 1896. By 1895 many Americans, especially in the West and South, believed that the United States was fast falling under the sway of the "money power." These sections could not be ignored. In the generation since the Civil War the South had regained some of its self-confidence and the West had become an important force in the nation's economic and political life. In 1889–1890, North Dakota, South Dakota, Montana, Washington, Idaho, and Wyoming had been admitted to the Union, adding to Congress twelve senators who endorsed the West's view of politics and increasing the political power of the silver-mine owners, the chief financial backers of free-silver candidates.

"Bryan! Bryan! Bryan!"   Despite the Populists, the arena in which the contending forces fought out their differences was the Democratic party. On one side were the Democratic goldbugs, mostly from the Northeast and the Midwest, who believed that civilization itself rode on the gold standard. On the other side were the many western and southern Democrats, who were equally convinced that humanity could survive and prosper only if silver were restored to the currency system. The Republicans also had silver and gold wings, representing western and eastern attitudes, respectively. But the proponents of silver were far stronger among the Democrats.

In June 1896 the Republicans nominated William McKinley of Ohio on a platform pledged to a high tariff, a gold standard (although promising to consider monetizing silver as well if acceptable by international agreement), and an aggressive foreign policy. The gold-standard plank was a bitter disappointment to the Republican silverites, and Senator Henry M. Teller of Colorado and his western friends walked out of the convention.

At the Democratic convention in Chicago the silverites were in the majority. Senator Richard ("Silver Dick") Bland of Missouri was the front-runner as the delegates arrived. But a young ex-congressman from Nebraska, William Jennings Bryan, was also a serious contender. Bryan had spent many months writing letters to influential politicians, speaking before silverite audiences and Democratic groups, and cultivating the Farmers' Alliances to win support for himself and his cause. Rising as the last speaker before the convention voted on whether to endorse a gold-standard or a free-silver platform, he launched into the most influential convention address in American party history.

Bryan sought to make silver the cause of the masses everywhere. In answer to the previous speaker, a defender of gold as essential to sound business, he pointed out that the man who worked for wages, the "merchant at the crossroads store," the farmer, and the miner were also "businessmen." All were the same and must be treated the same. But he quickly made clear that the money question inevitably drove a wedge between Americans. "We say not one word against those who live

Though they criticized Bryan's religious rhetoric, the Republicans had their own pious slogan: "In God we trust, in Bryan we bust."

upon the Atlantic Coast, but the hardy pioneers who had braved all the dangers of the wilderness . . . are as deserving of the consideration of their party as any people in this country. . . . It is for these that we speak." He continued:

> "You came to tell us that the great cities are in favor of the gold standard; we reply that the great cities rest upon our broad and fertile prairies. Burn down the cities and leave our farms, and the cities will spring up again as if by magic; but destroy our farms and the grass will grow in the streets of every city in the country."

Now followed the soaring conclusion that gave the name "Cross of Gold" to the address. If the gold men insisted on the gold standard, the silverites, supported by the "producing masses" and the "toilers everywhere," would fight them to the end. Pressing his hands to the sides of his head, Bryan thundered: "You shall not press down upon the brow of labor this crown of thorns, you shall not crucify mankind upon a cross of gold." As Bryan finished, he stretched his arms out horizontally, as if crucified himself. For several seconds the crowd was silent, then it burst into frenzied shouts and cheers: "Bryan! Bryan! Bryan!" Amid flying hats and waving handkerchiefs, the delegates lifted the speaker onto their shoulders and carried him off the platform. On July 10, 1896, the Democrats chose Bryan as their candidate and Arthur Sewall, a silverite Maine businessman, as his running mate.

The Election of 1896.

At their convention in St. Louis soon after the Democrats had adjourned, the Populists faced a dilemma. Many saw free silver as an exaggerated issue. According to the Populist journalist Henry Demarest Lloyd, silver was the "cowbird" of the insurgent movement. It would deposit its eggs in another bird's nest and when its young were born they would evict the offspring of the original parents. In effect, silver would crowd out the other important issues. Bryan, moreover, was a Democrat. To southern Populists especially, the Democrats were the enemy. After fighting the Bourbons for so long, how could they now fuse with them on the candidate at the top of the ticket? Despite misgivings, delegates to the St. Louis People's Party convention gave Bryan their nomination as president. Unable to support banker Arthur Sewall, however, they selected Georgia's fiery Tom Watson, one of their own, as their vice presidential nominee.

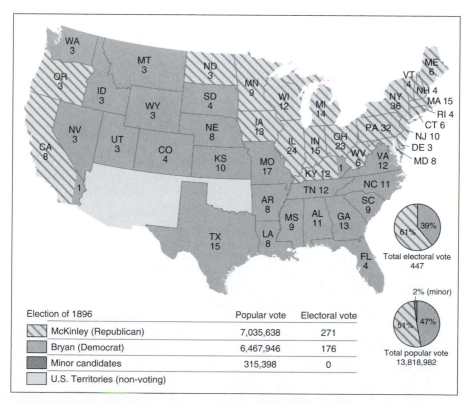

Election of 1896	Popular vote	Electoral vote
McKinley (Republican)	7,035,638	271
Bryan (Democrat)	6,467,946	176
Minor candidates	315,398	0
U.S. Territories (non-voting)		

The Election of 1896

The campaign that followed was one of the bitterest on record. Both major parties split. A large group of conservative Democrats refused to endorse Bryan and organized a separate "gold" Democratic ticket with John M. Palmer of Illinois at its head. "Silver" Republicans endorsed the Democratic candidates, Bryan and Sewall.

Obviously the underdog, Bryan campaigned hard. Consciously or not, he sought to change the foundation of Gilded Age party alignments. Playing on the hard times, he worked to overcome evangelical allegiance to the Republicans by appealing to class and economic interests. With silver, he declared, times would get better, prosperity would return, and wealth inequalities would be reduced. At the same time Bryan appealed to traditional Republicans by speaking the language that Americans of pious Protestant background understood. A devout Protestant himself, raised on the Bible and old-time religion, he saw free silver as more than an economic position; it represented justice and virtue. Gold, on the other hand, was not just the metal of the creditors; it was the source of injustice and oppression. "Every great economic question," Bryan declared as he crisscrossed the country, was "in reality a great moral question." Through the Midwest he called on goldbug sinners to "repent." In the South and on his beloved prairies, the people treated his rallies like great religious camp meetings. The Democratic campaign of 1896 was a moral crusade.

The Republican campaign was a countercrusade. To conservative Americans, Bryan and his forces were dangerous radicals. Postmaster General William L. Wilson declared that the silver leaders were "socialists, anarchists and demagogues of a dangerous type. . . ." A writer to the *New York Times* asserted that "within six months of Bryan's election mobs would be rushing up and down our streets howling for bread." If Bryan tried to make the free-silver cause a moral issue, so did his opponents. The *Chicago Tribune* declared that the gold position was a matter of simple honesty. "It is in no respect a question of politics, but of moral principle. It is taking the commandment, 'Thou Shalt not Steal' . . . , and applying it to the Nation."

The goldbugs had the tremendous advantage of deep pockets. The Republican national chairman, Ohio industrialist Mark Hanna, was spectacularly effective in convincing the business community to write checks for McKinley and other antisilver candidates. The one important business group that might have contributed to Bryan, the silver-mine owners of the mountain states, proved surprisingly stingy (the price of silver having dropped). To make up for the lack of money, Bryan had only his own fierce energy and dazzling eloquence.

In the end these were not enough. The public perceived the election as the most critical since 1860 and turned out in record numbers. But the consequence was a resounding defeat for Bryan. The Democratic candidate won 6.5 million popular and 176 electoral votes to McKinley's 7.1 million and 271.

The nature of the vote reveals much about the social and sectional divisions of the 1890s. Bryan did not carry a single state in New England, the Middle Atlantic region, and the Old Northwest. On the Pacific Coast he carried only Washington. In the Great Plains he did much better, taking Kansas, Nebraska, South Dakota, and Missouri. Bryan's real support, however, came from the South and the mountain states. In the South traditional Democratic voters gave Bryan the large majorities that Democratic candidates could invariably count on from the former Confederacy. In the mountain states, however, the Bryan sweep represented a major shift, best explained by the Democratic focus on silver.

Despite Bryan's appeal to all "producers," city people voted strongly Republican. Republicans who normally offended Catholic and other liturgical voters were careful this time to emphasize unity and tolerance. "We have always practiced the Golden Rule," declared McKinley: "the best policy is to 'live and let live'." There were also economic factors. Rather than splitting the rich from the poor, the self-employed and professional classes from the wage earners, the threat of free silver forged a bond across class lines. Eastern working men saw no advantage for themselves in cheap money. The Republican promise that a new tariff would bring prosperity and "the full dinner pail" seemed more likely than the millennium promised by Bryan.

Bryan's partisans have charged that the Republicans used coercion to win wage-earner votes for McKinley. And, in fact, many businessmen were panicked by the prospect of free silver and made extravagant statements expressing their fears. But this pressure was probably not decisive. In the end, Bryan and free silver lost because their appeal was confined primarily to southern and western voters.

Culture in the Age of the Dynamo

The nation's political life in the post-Civil War era was not, then, notably golden (except in the financial sense!). What about America's cultural life? Was it equally gilded?

In fact, in the half-century following Appomattox the United States produced a flood of authors, painters, architects, thinkers, and educators who made it one of the vital cultural centers of the Western world. There was also an exuberant and vigorous growth of "low" culture—the song, dance, theater, and amusements of average men and women—that helped make America a cultural beacon to people of other lands.

Literature. Post-Civil War Americans had an impressive literary heritage to build on. But many of the outstanding figures of the prewar days were gone by 1865. The Boston-Cambridge area continued to be the literary capital of the nation and its major journals of culture, the *Atlantic Monthly* and the *North American Review*, along with the *The Nation* and *Harper's Weekly*, published in New York, remained the arbiters of literary taste among the educated elite.

These publications defended the "genteel tradition" in literature. Fiction and poetry, they held, must represent the spiritual, the pure, and the elevated, for literature was a moral medium. It should not seek to report life as it actually was, but help to transform it into something nobler and more refined. As the poet James Russell Lowell noted, no man should write what he was unwilling for his young daughter to read. Evil existed in the fiction of the genteel authors, of course, but it was without detectable social cause and always, in the end, defeated. Sex was so buried under flowery romanticism that a traveler from another planet who read a genteel novel might not have known that men and women were biologically different.

But even in the 1870s and 1880s these pallid principles were being left behind by writers who insisted on depicting American regional reality with all its coarse vigor and liveliness. One of the new voices came from the mining camps of California and depicted a way of life that had just recently passed. In 1867 Bret Harte, a transplanted easterner, published a short story "The Luck of Roaring Camp," in the San Francisco-based *Overland Monthly*. It concerned the hard-bitten miners and dance-hall girls of a Sierra Nevada mining camp who are, disconcertingly, bequeathed a baby. The plot was less important, however, than the cast of characters; each has a rough exterior and speaks the way people in the mining camps probably did speak. Few are "good" people in the usual sense. It was this quality of apparent authenticity that made the story an instant sensation and turned Harte into a celebrity. In the next few years his other stories about the mining camps, including "The Outcasts of Poker Flat," "The Idyl of Red Gulch," and "Tennessee's Partner," were widely applauded as examples of honesty in literature.

Over the next few decades "regionalism" attracted other authors. Edward Eggleston's books depicted rural Indiana with a sharp eye for local color and a true ear for regional speech. George Washington Cable wrote brilliantly about Creole New Orleans. The southern mountain people of the Great Smokies and the Cumberland plateau found their literary portrait painter in Mary Noailles Murfree. Joel Chandler Harris's "Uncle Remus" stories depicted poor Georgia whites and even poorer Georgia blacks. The East, too, had its "local colorists." Sarah Orne Jewett began to write stories of the village and farm people of southern Maine during the 1860s.

The most talented of all the regional authors, one who exceeded them in depth and universality, was Samuel Langhorne Clemens, alias Mark Twain. Mark Twain shared with the local colorists their love of dialect, their focus on rural and small-town "types," their humorous emphasis. But Twain was more talented than the local colorists. Combining the traditions of the frontier tall tale with an uncanny ear for speech, and at times a sense of the tragic, he became an author of international stature. At the beginning of his career, however, he capitalized on his capacity to make people laugh. In books such as *Innocents Abroad* (1869) and on the lecture circuit, which occupied much of his time and earned him large fees, he told jokes and funny stories and in general seemed to be interested solely in amusing people.

Mark Twain's more serious side became evident in his later books. In three of these he turned to the upper South before the Civil War, describing the joys and the agonies of youth. *Tom Sawyer* (1876) is about a boy growing up in a town very much like Sam Clemens's own Hannibal, Missouri. *Life on the Mississippi* (1883) is a superb nonfiction account of the great days before the Civil War when the steamboat dominated commerce on the South's rivers and the steamboat captain was almost a Renaissance prince. Mark Twain's greatest novel, *Adventures of Huckleberry Finn* (1885), was a sequel to *The Adventures of Tom Sawyer*. But Huck is a more interesting boy than Tom—less conventional, more genuine, less spoiled by romantic illusion, more spontaneous.

Despite his genius and his willingness at times to choose truth over romantic convention, Mark Twain never fully escaped from the literary conventions of the Gilded Age. Even his best works contain much sentimentality and cheap farce. He eventually turned to vapid historical romance and developed a tendency to flaunt an adolescent melancholy.

As the century progressed, "realism," employing more modern materials, would supersede the older style. Leader of the new genre was William Dean Howells, a midwesterner who edited the Boston-published *Atlantic Monthly*.

Though he never fully liberated himself from the prudishness of the day, Howells insisted a novel must by "true to the motives, the impulses, the principles that shape the life of actual men and women." As editor and critic, he welcomed newer talents such as Hamlin Garland, whose bitter stories of western farm life, *Main-Travelled Roads*, appeared in 1891. He also introduced to American readers the realism of Émile Zola in France and Henrik Ibsen in Scandinavia. As a novelist, Howells practiced what he preached. The hero of *The Rise of Silas Lapham* (1885) was a self-made millionaire manufacturer who finds that his simple western ways cause social difficulties for himself and his family in Boston. The violent Haymarket affair in Chicago awakened Howells's social conscience and in *A Hazard of New Fortunes* (1890), his business characters are less amiable and sympathetic, and his canvas expands to include poor working people, a German-American socialist, and a violent streetcar strike. *A Traveler from Altruria* (1894) and *Through the Eye of the Needle* (1907) raised socialist alternatives to what seemed a dog-eat-dog economic system.

A major American literary figure not easy to classify is Henry James, brother of the philosopher William James. Acutely aware of the nuances in human relationships, James wrote about men and women in comfortable circumstances whose lives revolved about the subtleties of taste, class, and nationality, and crises of personal integrity. The tensions in many of his best works—*The American* (1877), *Portrait of a Lady* (1881), *The Wings of the Dove* (1902), and *The Golden Bowl* (1904)—arise between simple but honest and intelligent Americans, often young women, and sophisticated but corrupt and devious Europeans. James seemed little interested in the vast social changes sweeping the Western world. Yet he escapes the false sentimentality of the genteel authors. His people, though well-bred and worldly, are recognizably real human beings with the complex personalities found in actual life.

By the 1890s a new breed of women authors had made gender an issue in literature. American women had been successful and admired authors as far back as the colonial era. During the early nineteenth century women had dominated the field of the popular novel. After the Civil War several entered the front ranks of literature.

The female local colorists at times expressed the emotions of the "New Woman" beginning to emerge as the century wound down. In Jewett's *A Country Doctor* (1884), one character protests against society's effort to "bury the talent that God has given me." Other women authors went beyond the local colorist genre in expressing the full range of women's yearnings. Among the novelists, Ellen Glasgow, a Virginian, wrote about her native section with special attention to the false gentility of southern womanhood. Edith Wharton, a descendant of New York's old Knickerbocker families, depicted heroines caught between the vulgar new rich and the decaying upper class. But the novelist who best exemplified the New Woman was Kate O'Flaherty Chopin, a widow and mother of six, who despite her own experience—or because of it—raised explicit questions about women's roles as wives, mothers, and lovers. Chopin's novel, *The Awakening* (1899), offended the more prudish critics as "sex fiction" for its focus on women's sexual feelings. The hostile response, including refusal of librarians in her native St. Louis to circulate it, crushed Chopin's spirit.

As the end of the century approached, Howells's mild realism gave way to something more vigorous and more brutal. The realists retained an essentially sunny view of life; the "naturalists" often perceived it as sordid and vicious. In their novels men and women are mere atoms in the grip of forces beyond their control or even understanding. Their endings are generally tragic. Naturalist novels often focused on the emerging industrial-urban order, and even their rural characters are people whose lives are entangled in the vast social changes that characterized the closing years of the nineteenth century.

One young writer who explored the relationship between large social currents and the lives of rural Americans was Hamlin Garland, a "son of the middle border," the prairie region undergoing momentous and jarring change during the 1870s and 1880s. In *Prairie Folks* (1893), Garland told of the bitter failures and intense hardships of rural life, and of farm people crushed both by cruel nature and by even crueler human oppressors. Stephen Crane's *Maggie: A Girl of the Streets* (1893) concerns a young woman who is destroyed by the poverty, drunkenness, and crime of her environment. The picture is one of brutality and sordidness so frankly rendered that Crane had to finance its publication himself under a pseudonym. Crane, who died young of tuberculosis, would write one masterpiece, *The Red Badge of Courage* (1895), the story of a young soldier in the Civil War experiencing his first taste of battle.

Theodore Dreiser, an Indianan from a background of poverty, was a crude stylist but a writer of great cumulative power. His characters are often at the mercy of their appetites, their drives, their yearnings. Carrie, of *Sister Carrie* (1900), is an ambitious young woman who uses men, is corrupted by them, and then destroys them in turn as she claws her way up the social ladder. Frank Cowperwood of *The Financier* (1912) and *The Titan* (1914), modeled after business tycoon Charles Yerkes, is an unprincipled big businessman driven by a lust for power who allows nothing and no one to stand in his way; although he triumphs over all his enemies, he is no more master of his destiny than Crane's tragic Maggie.

Other authors of these years who played on the theme of powerful social forces molding people include two Californians, Frank Norris and Jack London. In *McTeague* (1899) Norris depicted a simple-minded San Francisco dentist who is gradually overwhelmed by material failure and tragically driven to murder. *The Octopus* (1901) concerns the wheat farmers of California's Central Valley and their struggles with the railroad. London, though an avowed socialist, worshiped the power of the individual, and in adventure books set in Alaska—*The Call of the Wild* (1903) and *White Fang* (1905)—as well as in works dealing with driven men—*The Sea Wolf* (1904)—he glorified the superman. Modeled on philosopher Friedrich Nietzsche's "blond beast," these brutal, arrogant, commanding characters, acting like elemental forces, sweep lesser beings aside.

Painting and Architecture.   In two other areas of the arts, painting and architecture, we encounter the same movement from romantic gentility to an attempt to incorporate the emerging twentieth-century world. In both, as in literature, some of the results are lasting and impressive achievements.

American painting during the 1860s and 1870s was dominated by borrowed European romanticism, and Europe of the "Old Masters" remained for many years the measure of good taste. During the 1880s a more distinctively American school appeared. Led by Winslow Homer, John La Farge, and Thomas Eakins, their work was direct and vivid, but its subject matter lacked relevance to the world in which most Americans lived. Not until the beginning of the new century did a group of American painters come to terms with the emerging urban-industrial America.

The core of this group consisted of former newspaper illustrators from the Philadelphia area. Trained to capture events in quick, vivid pen and pencil images, Everett Shinn, George Luks, John Sloan, and William Glackens developed keen eyes for city scenes and city types. In the early 1890s they came under the tutelage of Robert Henri, a teacher at the Pennsylvania Academy of Fine Arts, who had been influenced by the French impressionists. Impressionists relied on the sort of visual shorthand that the eye in real life detects and the mind converts into reality. Toward the end of the decade Henri and his four disciples, one by one, moved to New York, where they were joined by Maurice Prendergast, Arthur B. Davies, and Ernest Lawson.

The Henri circle considered the conventional American painting of the day anemic and feeble, suitable for interior decoration, "merely an adjunct of plush and cut glass," as one of them said. Their own work they intended to be vigorous and real. They depicted prize fights, ordinary people waiting for taxis and streetcars, pigeons wheeling over tenement roofs, urban backyards, children at play in city streets, and the New York "el" at rush hour. Their technique often bordered on caricature. People were fat, frumpy, often coarse-looking. The critics attacked their work as harsh and vulgar. Before long the Henri group was being derided as the "Ashcan School." Offended by the tight rein imposed on artists by the conservative National Academy of Design, which excluded them from its prestigious exhibitions, eight Ashcan painters held their own show at the MacBeth Gallery in New York in 1908. The show immortalized "The Eight" and marked a new era in American painting.

In 1913 the Henri group, and the still more radical postimpressionists, sponsored a major showing of the best new European and American work at the Sixty-Ninth Regiment Armory in New York. Here for the first time a large number of Americans saw the works of Cézanne, Van Gogh, Picasso, Matisse, and the cubists, who seemed to have abandoned representation entirely. The sensation of the show was Marcel Duchamp's *Nude Descending a Staircase,* a cubist painting that, by a succession of overlapping cut-out figures, suggested the motion of a woman walking down a flight of stairs. One critic called the Duchamp painting "an explosion in a shingle factory." Another labeled the whole exhibit an exercise in "incomprehensibility combined with symptoms of paresis."

Despite the attacks, the Armory show was a profoundly influential event in American art. The paintings attracted immense crowds wherever they were shown. Most people came to smirk, but many stayed to marvel and appreciate. In all, 235 of the paintings were eventually sold. The market for modern art boomed, and American taste was given a tremendous push toward modernism.

The years immediately following the Civil War found American architecture particularly out of tune with contemporary life. Designers of public buildings were still creating Greek temples or combining elements of so many traditional European styles that no clear label could be given them. Meanwhile, the ordinary middle-class family bought a balloon-frame house constructed of wood uprights and siding stuck together with nails, and decorated, if at all, with wooden "gingerbread" trim.

By the 1880s and 1890s critics began to call for a finer aesthetic. The plea was answered by a group of young men—including Stanford White, Charles McKim, Daniel Burnham, and William Robert Ware—who had studied in Paris and could reproduce the fine detail of Renaissance and Elizabethan homes and Gothic libraries and churches. But, the carpers asked, in what sense were these American buildings? The first signs of change came in the 1880s when a group of Chicago architects began to look at building in a new way. During this decade the Windy City was caught up in a frenzy of construction, both to restore structures destroyed in the devastating fire of 1871 and to meet the space needs of the nation's fastest-growing metropolis. In the midst of this building boom William Le Baron Jenney designed the first true skyscraper.

In the past, tall buildings had not served commercial purposes well. Their walls had to be very thick at the base to bear the enormous weight of the masonry above, thereby reducing the usable space. The many flights of stairs made space at upper floors virtually unrentable. In the new buildings of Jenney, Louis Sullivan, Ernest Flagg, and Cass Gilbert, instead of heavy, weight-bearing walls, thin outer walls of brick or stone veneer were attached to a frame of light, interlocked steel beams. With electricity and fast elevators, such a building could provide convenient, usable space at much lower cost than an equivalent masonry structure. Because the skyscraper could be erected to virtually any height, designers could go up rather than out and so reduce the outlay on expensive downtown real estate.

At first skyscrapers were made to look like overblown Gothic cathedrals. Gradually, however, architects began to insist that a structure's design and appearance honestly reflect its technology and function. In the words of Louis Sullivan, "Over all the coursing sun, form ever follows function, and that is the law." A building should not disguise its use, but proclaim it boldly and honestly. Sullivan's best works were the Schiller Building (1891–1892) in Chicago and St. Louis's Wainwright Building (1890–1891).

Frank Lloyd Wright, Sullivan's pupil, translated his mentor's theories into domestic architecture. Wright made the close relation of form, use, materials, and site the basis for his famous prairie houses—low structures to match the terrain of the flat Midwest. He avoided traditional elements of exterior design and built the homes of local stone and timber that suited their locations. Critics hailed Wright's work as strikingly innovative, yet at first few patrons came to him. Not until the 1920s did his form of architectural modernism begin to attract widespread public acclaim.

Popular Culture.   The gradual response of the arts to the realities of the American social and economic scene was matched in popular culture, entertainment, sports, and recreation.

As more and more Americans moved to the cities, they found that the world of play as well as the world of work had changed. In the larger cities space for people seeking physical exercise was often unavailable. As we have seen, few American cities had preserved open space in their congested centers. Not until the very end of the nineteenth century did cities open playgrounds for children and add sports and exercise programs to school curricula. Insufficient leisure remained a deterrent to sports for a longer time. Most wage earners worked every day except Sunday, and in many cities evangelical Protestant groups imposed blue laws that kept theaters and ball parks closed on the Sabbath. Only gradually as the old century gave way to the new did pressure from Catholics, nonbelievers, working people, and various secular groups force city officials to permit Sunday sports and amusements. Increasingly, sports became incorporated into city life. But most urbanites were caught up in the movement as paid spectators rather than personal participants.

The first of the nineteenth-century sports to be commercialized was baseball. By the 1850s amateur baseball clubs had become common in the cities and towns. Their matches soon attracted spectators, and reports of their encounters began to appear in the newspapers. Before long the teams were erecting high fences around their playing fields and charging spectators for admission to underwrite the cost of equipment, uniforms, and travel to rival communities.

In 1858 promoters organized the National Association of Baseball Players, and in 1869 the Cincinnati Red Stockings began to pay salaries to players. In 1876 the National League of Professional Baseball Clubs—with teams in New York, Philadelphia, Hartford, Boston, Chicago, Louisville, Cincinnati, and St. Louis— superseded the amateur organization. In the next few years more professional teams joined the National League, and in 1901 entrepreneurs organized the American League. In 1903 the champions of each met in the first World Series; the American League's Boston Red Sox beat the National League's Pittsburgh Pirates. Baseball attendance grew rapidly in the early part of the new century, and in the 1913 World Series gate receipts for the five games reached $326,000. In 1908 the song "Take Me Out to the Ball Game" became a popular hit and marked the triumph of baseball as the country's "national" sport.

Football and boxing, though popular, failed to match baseball's audience during these years. Until the 1920s football remained primarily a game played at colleges by amateurs and patronized by upper-middle-class people, often graduates of one of the schools. Yet toward the end of the century college rivalries encouraged active recruiting of players, often poor sons of immigrants. By 1917 critics were charging that the supposedly amateur game had become commercialized with hidden subsidies to players, vulgar hoopla, and expensive stadiums—in addition to excessive violence.

Because of its brutality, boxing carried a stigma as a "blood" sport in these years. Few women and few middle-class men attended matches, and in some cities boxing was forbidden. Yet the sport was popular among working men, especially recent immigrants and second-generation Americans in the big cities. When John L. Sullivan returned to his native Boston after knocking out Jake Kilrain in a harrowing seventy-five-round bare-knuckle fight in 1889, the city's Irish turned out in force to honor him as an ethnic hero.

Professional sports were relatively democratic. The lists of star players or champions in a particular sport record the growing assimilation and acceptance of newer-stock Americans. At the beginning the names are Anglo-Saxon; by the 1890s they are German and Irish; by 1910 or 1920 they are increasingly Italian, Spanish, and Slavic. Clearly, professional sports provided an escalator upward for each new European group in America.

Most professional sports retained the "color bar," however. Black baseball players were forced to play in segregated black leagues, where salaries were low, equipment poor, and ballparks mere fenced fields. College football was somewhat more open in the North, though when northern teams played rivals in the South, they benched their black players in deference to southern prejudices. The least segregated major spectator sport was prizefighting; in 1908 Jack Johnson, a black man, defeated Tommy Burns, a white Canadian, to become heavyweight champion of the world. But even boxing was not free of prejudice. The white public resented Johnson's reign as champion and yearned for a "white hope" to defeat him. Johnson's marriage to a white woman made him even more unpopular, and when he was defeated by Jess Willard, a white American, the white public cheered.

Music, the theater, the circus, and the amusement park were other ways in which city people in the half-century following the Civil War filled their limited leisure time and softened the sharp edges of their daily lives.

The amusement park was largely the invention of the streetcar companies, which, to encourage weekend business, established resorts on the outskirts of the towns they served. On Sundays city people flocked to these parks to hear concerts, watch balloon ascensions and bicycle races, and patronize the "rides," including the Ferris wheel, the roller coaster, and others. Here Americans learned the culinary delights of hamburgers and hot dogs for the first time.

Before World War I "classical" music was the music of an elite, composed—and often performed—by foreigners. Popular music was homegrown. During the post-Civil War years, songwriting, composing popular songs to be sold as sheet music and played and sung at the parlor piano, became a successful profession for a score of composers. By 1900 most of the songwriters and their agents were located along New York's Twenty-eighth Street, "Tin Pan Alley." The label soon became the nickname for the lucrative popular music business.

Some of the most successful composers, Gussie Davis and Scott Joplin, for example, were black. An unusually large contingent, including Edward Marks, Monroe Rosenberg, and Irving Berlin, were Jewish. During the 1890s Joplin and other black composers introduced ragtime to a wider public. "Rags" were instrumental pieces written for either piano or band. They combined elements of traditional white music, the syncopation of urban black music, and the street music of the white underclass. In the hands of Joplin, a Texas-born black man with formal musical training, they were often complex, sophisticated works. Joplin wrote thirty-nine rags and was widely imitated by other composers, black and white alike.

Jazz, like ragtime, had roots in the black city ghettos. Its original home was New Orleans, where blacks had been a vital part of the cultural scene even before the Civil War. Black wind musicians played at important public occasions—parades, funerals, and political gatherings—both solemn and joyous. They freely improvised on melodies from traditional French and American marches and popular songs, combining them with ragtime-style syncopation drawn from the black musical experience. Black singers, pianists, and instrumentalists also played in the saloons and brothels of Storyville, the New Orleans red-light district. Here one heard both ragtime and "the blues," a mournful vocal form related to rural black spirituals, but usually concerned with less uplifting themes: crime, betrayal, sexual passion. It was in Storyville that such inspired performers as Ferdinand ("Jelly Roll") Morton, Louis Armstrong, Joseph ("King") Oliver, and "Ma" Rainey got their start.

When military authorities closed the Storyville brothels in 1917, supposedly to protect servicemen from venereal disease, New Orleans musicians scattered in all directions. Eventually many settled in the emerging black neighborhoods of Chicago, St. Louis, Kansas City, Memphis, and New York, where they played in the nightclubs and speakeasies that Prohibition had spawned. Young white musicians found "Jass" an exciting new form and began to imitate the black players. Their lively new Chicago Style, like the original, relied on improvisation and spontaneity. At its worst, as in the music of Paul Whiteman, the "King of Jazz," white adaptation was a slick, contrived sort of popular music that suited the palates of a middle-class white audience.

Popular music in this period often shared billing with other entertainment on stage. The minstrel show, a form of "review" dating from before the Civil War, featured songs, dances, and comedy routines that exploited black stereotypes and black musical themes. By the 1880s vaudeville had replaced the minstrel show. A typical vaudeville performance consisted of as many as thirty brief acts—dances, comic skits, songs, acrobatics, animal stunts, juggling, magic. Like the minstrel show, it was a showcase for popular songs. It also offered talented young men and women from newer immigrant stock—Jewish, Hispanic, Italian, Irish—opportunities to win fame and fortune as performers. The vaudeville show was especially popular among the new urban audiences. Even if they knew no English, they could enjoy a juggler or a magician, and the costumes and music created a glamorous image, briefly transforming their narrow, impoverished world.

The motion picture was even better suited to the growing urban audience. Many of its technical elements emerged from the laboratory of Thomas A. Edison, but at first the great inventor considered it an amusing toy and was happy to license exhibitors to show thirty-second films in penny arcades. The first films were merely scenic views or bits of action. Soon the exhibitors discovered more profit in such racy material as *Taking a Bath, What the Bootblack Saw,* and *Dolorita's Passion Dance.*

The audience for the new medium proved enormous. Live theater was expensive and relied on conventions that sometimes baffled untutored audiences. There was also no language barrier in the new medium. The early movies were silent and told their simple stories with broad gestures and large images. Once the medium's success was assured, Edison attempted to impose a monopoly by insisting his patent rights be respected and charging movie makers high fees to use his cameras and projectors. He could not stop the tide. Dozens of small picture makers, using equipment of their own make or imported from Europe, were soon shooting films in backyards and makeshift studios. Many were Jewish small businessmen who, excluded from other enterprises, were quick to recognize the potential of the new medium.

There was a similar proliferation of exhibitors. By 1900, hundreds were showing films in empty stores, town halls, school auditoriums, almost any place they could assemble some chairs in a darkened room. These early movie houses, often

called "nickelodeons," charged five cents for an eight-minute showing of a humorous, exciting, or exotic incident. Most of these primitive sketches were created
on the spur of the moment by directors, camera operators, or other employees of
the many small firms formed to provide material for the exhibitors.

This impromptu approach to filmmaking soon gave way to more careful
and deliberate efforts. In 1903 Edwin Porter of the Edison company produced
The Great Train Robbery, which told a story of some complexity, in almost a full reel
of film. Soon other firms were imitating Porter. Equipment became better, theaters
more permanent and comfortable, and films more impressive artistically. By 1905
producers had established many of the classic film types—western, comedy-
romance, crime, travelogue, science fiction.

At first many of the film companies were located in the East, close to the established pool of actors and technicians. But land for studios in the big eastern cities
was expensive and the cold and rainy eastern weather often hindered "shooting"
outdoors. The East was also close to the Edison "film trust," which pursued a policy
of suing every company that did not pay a substantial fee for the privilege of making films. In 1907, to escape the trust and to take advantage of cheap space and
sunny climate, William Selig, a Chicago producer, moved his company to southern
California. Soon Selig was joined by others. By 1912 the Los Angeles suburb of
Hollywood had become the nation's filmmaking capital.

Motion picture viewers eventually came to expect more sophisticated fare than
purveyed by the pioneers. After 1910 they could count on D. W. Griffith, working for
the Biograph studio. Griffith was the first producer-director who truly understood the
new medium and successfully exploited its unique potential. In 1915 he produced, for
the then-immense figure of $100,000, *The Birth of a Nation.* Concerned with the tribula-
tions of Reconstruction, the movie was blatantly racist and pro-Ku Klux Klan. Wherever it was shown it aroused fierce opposition among blacks and white liberals, but it
was an immense popular success, and from a purely artistic perspective deservedly
so. Twelve reels long, it made use of the fadeout, the dissolve, crosscutting, the close-
up, and the long-shot. In the special theaters where it was shown, orchestras accompanied the action. However deplorable ideologically, *The Birth of a Nation* set a new
standard of artistic and technical excellence for the entire film industry.

Education.

In their various ways, then, the arts, both "high" and "low," responded to the transformation of America from a rural and agricultural society to one
dominated by cities and industry. The educational life of the nation between the
Civil War and World War I revealed a similar shift.

The greatest change in education in the half-century following 1865 was its
sheer expansion. In 1870 about 7 million pupils were enrolled in public day schools;
by 1915 there were over 18 million, with another 1.5 million in private schools,
mostly Catholic parochial institutions. By 1915 well over 80 percent of all young
people were attending classes of some sort. School outlays rose even faster than
enrollments, growing to $605 million in 1915, or $31 annually per pupil.

The expansion had many sources. In 1860 few states in the South had systems
of public education. During Reconstruction, however, southern states had joined
the rest of the country in accepting responsibility for supporting elementary
schools. Meanwhile, in the large cities a parallel system of parochial schools

sprang up, largely to serve the nation's growing Catholic population. More and more states also made school attendance compulsory. In 1881 nineteen states and territories in the North and West had compulsory attendance laws; by 1898 there were thirty-one. At the same time legislatures raised minimum school-leaving ages and made the school year longer.

These changes added substantially to the taxpayers' bills, but education seemed well worth the cost to this generation of Americans. A larger and more complex economy not only made education easier to pay for; it also made it more essential. Business needed more and more young men and women who could calculate receipts, add figures, write letters, and follow written instructions. Assured of well-paying jobs requiring literacy, the young found staying in school more attractive.

Secondary education particularly benefited from the increased demand for clerical and managerial skills. Before the Civil War, only Massachusetts had a system of high schools supported by public funds. Secondary education elsewhere was the domain of the private "academy." After 1865 several states followed Massachusetts's lead. By 1915 the United States had more than 11,000 public high schools, with over 1.3 million pupils. Initially the curricula of the public high schools emphasized the same liberal arts and classic languages that were dominant in the private academies. School administrators soon introduced commercial programs, including typing, bookkeeping, and accounting. Latin and Greek gave way to modern foreign languages. Even more "practically" oriented were the vocational classes that began to invade the high schools under the prodding of the National Society for the Promotion of Industrial Education. In 1917 Congress passed the Smith–Hughes Act providing subsidies to the states to underwrite vocational and industrial skills courses for high school students.

During these same years the United States began the transformation that would make it a world leader in college and university education. Before the Civil War the typical American college was a small church-related institution that prepared young men for the ministry or for the learned professions. Most had a few hundred students, a single classroom building, a museum containing stuffed and preserved animals, and a library of a few hundred books, mostly on religion, tucked into some corner. Faculties were small, and many of the professors were clergymen who doubled in science and modern languages—if these subjects were taught at all.

After 1865 change came swiftly. The Morrill Land Grant College Act (1862) provided funds for a new class of agricultural and technical colleges, many of which developed into major universities. At the same time vast sums to establish new colleges and universities and revive old ones flowed from the swollen fortunes of post-Civil War business tycoons. During these years Rockefeller, Leland Stanford, Andrew Carnegie, James B. Duke, and others contributed millions to establish new universities or upgrade old ones. Under the guidance of a new breed of college president, curricula altered rapidly to provide students with training in the sciences, modern languages, and the new social sciences, as well as vocational courses such as accounting and engineering. In the 1880s, President Charles W. Eliot of Harvard introduced the elective system, ending the requirement of tightly prescribed courses and allowing students to choose their own programs within broad limits.

Higher education for women also expanded. Before 1860 only a handful of institutions allowed women to take college degrees. After the Civil War women's colleges proliferated and state universities opened their doors to men and women on an equal basis. In the older elite schools—the so-called Ivy League—women were admitted to sister institutions with separate faculties, courses, and buildings. In the state schools they sat in the same classrooms with men, though they used separate dormitories and were subject to stricter rules of decorum.

This period also witnessed the appearance of the research university and the graduate school. Before the Civil War American college faculty were not expected to advance the frontiers of knowledge as part of their duties. Then, in 1876 Johns Hopkins in Baltimore opened on the German model, as a graduate school where the sciences, social sciences, and humanities were treated as scholarly disciplines. The new university taught by the seminar system, where a prominent scholar and a small group of advanced students worked on a common set of problems. The result for the student was published research and the degree of Ph.D. (Doctor of Philosophy).

Hopkins was soon widely imitated. Several new institutions were founded on the same model, while many existing colleges set up graduate schools for training scholars and scientists. In 1900 some 240 Ph.D.s were conferred on American students, and the degree was well on its way to becoming the "union card" of the college teaching profession. Meanwhile, however imperfectly, the best American universities were being transformed into communities of creative men—and some women—dedicated to the quest for new fundamental understanding as well as important practical knowledge.

Other professions followed college teaching from a field for amateurs to one dominated by trained and "credentialed" experts. The trend was fueled by the sheer accumulation of knowledge, which forced each field to divide into ever-narrower specializations. Professionalization was also a consequence of efforts by occupational groups to raise their status and income by restricting entry into the field, usually by credentialing procedures in the name of higher professional standards.

In law and medicine, training through apprenticeship gave way in these years to formal education in law schools and medical schools. In medicine, at first, this led to an enormous proliferation of inferior schools, some mere diploma mills where students acquired M.D. degrees for a fee and perfunctory clinical and course work. In 1910 a report by Abraham Flexner, supported by the Carnegie Foundation, exposed widespread abuses in medical education and led the American Medical Association to push for the closing of inferior schools and the upgrading of others. The effects were drastic. The number of medical graduates dropped from over 5,000 yearly between 1900 and 1906 to about half that number in 1922. Critics charged that the true purpose of the upgrading was to restrict the number of physicians in order to prevent overcompetition. Yet the changes did indeed improve the level of skills among doctors.

Legal training also improved, though the overall effect was less restrictive. During these years more and more universities established law schools with three-year courses of study. At first, students could begin legal training after high school. Gradually, however, the better law schools insisted on college preparation, and in the 1870s Harvard introduced the case method—learning legal principles by studying actual cases decided by the courts.

The process of professionalization soon spread to many other areas. The usual pattern was for some occupational group, dissatisfied with its income, social status, and prevailing intellectual level, to band together in a professional association. The association then set new standards for education and training and established a degree program to be required of all future entrants into the profession. Another step in many cases was a state-administered examination imposed on those seeking to practice the profession under state license. In this way such diverse groups as teachers, nurses, engineers, accountants, social workers, dentists, pharmacists, optometrists, and others raised themselves to professional status. As in the case of doctors, professionalization improved the level of service for the public, but also increased the cost of those services. A final beneficiary of professionalization was the universities, which acquired crowds of students eager to gain degrees and the training needed to pass professional licensing exams.

The New Journalism.

In 1865 newspapers were very different from their counterparts today. They were smaller, usually only sixteen to twenty pages long. News-gathering facilities were primitive. Foreign news, in the absence of the transatlantic cable (which was not successfully laid until 1866), took weeks to arrive. Domestic news was transmitted by telegraph, but only a few of the very largest urban papers had reporters outside their home cities. For coverage of any American community but their home towns, newspaper editors were forced to copy stories from other newspapers received by "exchange" in the mail.

The newspaper of 1865 had no pictures. The few illustrated weeklies relied on woodcuts or copper engravings, which could not be prepared quickly enough for the daily press. There were also no comic strips, syndicated news columnists, food columns, horoscopes, or "advice to the lovelorn." Anyone reading an 1860 newspaper today would also be impressed by the relative sedateness of the coverage. Editors reported crimes and disasters, but usually in a sober, matter-of-fact way. Most of their space was filled with political news from Washington, D.C., the state capital, and the local board of aldermen. Reported in enormous detail, these stories are valuable for a political historian today, but may well have induced instant sleep in contemporary readers.

During the next generation new technology improved the gathering, packaging, and distributing of news and transformed the newspaper industry. The new technology came through widely scattered developments. The modern typewriter, capable of printing both upper- and lower-case letters, appeared in the 1870s. A decade later Ottmar Mergenthaler's linotype machine eliminated the need to set type for presses laboriously by hand. Cheap pulp paper came into wide use about the same time, as did processes for fast reproduction of illustrations and photographs. The telephone, invented in the 1870s by Alexander Bell, a Scottish-born teacher of the deaf, was in wide use by the 1890s and proved an invaluable tool for information gathering.

New sorts of news-collecting and news-packaging agencies also facilitated change. In the 1840s a group of New York editors began to pool information and sell it to subscribers. Out of this grew the Associated Press, with information-gathering facilities in major foreign capitals and in many American news centers. The United Press followed in 1882. In 1884, S. S. McClure, an inventive publisher, established "Newspaper Features," providing ready-made syndicated columns, short stories, and a "woman's page" for subscribing papers.

Taking advantage of these changes was a group of aggressive publishers. One of them, Joseph Pulitzer, a Hungarian immigrant who arrived in the United States in 1864 with hardly a penny, acquired the ailing *St. Louis Post-Dispatch* in 1878, and made the paper a success. With the money he accumulated he next bought the *New York World*, in the nation's press capital. Pulitzer helped create what critics would call "yellow journalism." The *World* emphasized "human-interest" stories—crime, corruption, disasters, strange reversals, sudden luck, and the like. It printed illustrations showing "X—Where the Body Was Found." Its headlines ran to: "Baptized in Blood" and "Death Rides the Blast." Pulitzer also attracted readers by promotional schemes. In one of these he sent the "girl reporter" Nellie Bly on a world-circling race to beat Jules Verne's fictional hero of *Around the World in Eighty Days*. He was also the first editor to publish a comic strip, R. F. Outcault's "The Yellow Kid," printed in yellow ink. Thereafter Pulitzer's approach to the newspaper business came to be called "yellow journalism."

Pulitzer soon acquired a flock of imitators, including the Scripps brothers, with papers in Detroit, Cleveland, St. Louis, and Cincinnati, and William Randolph Hearst in San Francisco. In 1895 Hearst came to New York, determined to outdo Pulitzer. He introduced his own comic strips, "The Katzenjammer Kids" and "Happy Hooligan," and then stole "The Yellow Kid" from Pulitzer. Before many months his *New York Journal* was engaged in a full-scale circulation war with the *World*, with each editor attempting to out-sensationalize the other. In later years Hearst acquired or established newspapers all over the nation and even set up his own press service. By the early years of the twentieth century he had become the nation's most powerful "press lord," using a formula of sensationalism plus human interest that usually lacked Pulitzer's saving grace of concern for the underdog.

New Ideas and Modes of Thought.

In the half-century following the Civil War a substantial group of urban, educated men and women adjusted their thinking to a flood of new ideas, many of them derived ultimately from the theories of the English naturalist Charles Darwin. Darwin's ideas often served as a prop for the social and economic status quo. Yet Darwinism also had a radically dislocating tendency, unsettling old attitudes and ways of thinking about society.

American social thought at the end of the Civil War was "formalistic." Attitudes toward society were often rooted in received wisdom, based on universal principles that changed little over time. To understand the world, to prescribe policies for society, one merely had to reason logically from these first principles. Formalistic thinkers assumed a static, rather than dynamic, reality and held tight to precedent and tradition when considering the lot of humankind. The advent of Darwin, stressing change and flux, seriously challenged this way of thinking. Institutions, like species, were not static; they evolved. Institutions, said these "reform Darwinists," must indeed be encouraged to change so as to maximize human welfare.

One man who found progressive and humane lessons in Darwinism was the sociologist Lester Ward. A man who had spent many years as a federal civil servant, Ward did not fear government. Society's ultimate goal, he believed, should be "the scientific control of the social forces by the collective mind of society." Similarly, Richard T. Ely used Darwinism to support the idea that government should play a positive role in the economy. Ely endorsed trade unions and believed the state was "an educational and ethical agency whose positive aid is an indispensable condition of human progress."

A still more radical break with the formalism of the past emerged from the fertile mind of the Norwegian-American Thorstein Veblen. Veblen rejected the economic "first principles" associated with the laissez-faire economists. These assumed that people made decisions based on rational self-interest and that their efforts to maximize material advantages explained how the economy operated. In fact, Veblen said, people were more often impelled by inherited drives and historically transmitted cultural values than by the desire to maximize wealth or profit. In *The Theory of the Leisure Class* (1899) Veblen sought to show that the great business magnates of the day were impelled as much by the primitive drives for status and emulation as by rational calculation. In later books he spoke about the "instinct of workmanship" as the wellspring of true economic progress. Veblen's major intellectual contribution, however, was to create a new school of "institutional" economics that substituted the study of economic practices evolving over time for model-making based on supposed first principles.

Legal thinking, too, felt the impact of the evolutionary revolt against formalism. Here the outstanding figure was Oliver Wendell Holmes, Jr., associate justice of the Supreme Court (1902–1932) and one of the great legal minds of his generation. Holmes attacked the idea that the law was a static set of rules struck off by some great intellect in the past or the incontestable collective wisdom of the ages. Such a view, he stated in *The Common Law* (1881), was merely a convenient defense of the past. All law, even law embodied in revered documents such as the federal Constitution, had evolved gradually in response to the needs of particular periods and groups. "The felt necessities of the time, the prevalent moral and political theories, institutions of public policy, avowed or unconscious, even the prejudices which judges share with their fellow men," he declared, "have a good deal more to do than the syllogism in determining the rules by which men should be governed." The law must evolve with the times, said Holmes. When it was out of touch with modern conditions and needs, it merely served as a brake on progress.

In the discipline of history we find the same critical spirit during the years following 1890. American historical studies had emphasized the extent to which characteristic American institutions were planted as "germs" (seeds) by northern European settlers. Thus the New England town meeting and ultimately the nation's democratic legislatures were survivals of ancient German peoples' assemblies. There was no sense in the work of scholars that the American environment had substantially altered those germs. Then in 1893 Frederick Jackson Turner famously informed the American Historical Association that "American democracy was born of no theorist's dream; it was not carried in the *Susan Constant* to Virginia, nor in the *Mayflower* to Plymouth. It came out of the American forest, and it gained new strength each time it touched a new frontier." This was an evolutionary view of American institutions, one that took seriously the three centuries of experience on American soil. Turner eventually developed a theory of change that emphasized the molding effect of the physical environment.

The new spirit of dissent from static and excessively abstract ways of viewing social institutions also affected philosophy, the most abstract area of thought. The new approach was Pragmatism, and its major practitioners were John Dewey and William James.

The pragmatists dealt with the issue of "what is true?" The old view, they noted, held that truth was some ultimate measuring rod to which statements or beliefs corresponded. But this was not so. Truth, in reality, was a quality that changed, evolved, as relationships were viewed from different perspectives or as an idea was employed for different purposes. To the pragmatists, most of the ideas about ultimate realities that had concerned philosophers and thinkers over the centuries simply had no real answers, except formal and inconsequential ones. What men and women needed to know was what difference did it make whether this was "true" or that was "false." The "value" of an idea, then, was not in its truth or falsity in the traditional sense, but in what consequences flowed from believing it or applying it. In a vivid but misunderstood phrase, William James declared that it was "the cash value" of an idea that really counted.

Because true ideas were those that had desirable effects in the world around us, the purpose of thought was not to contemplate eternity but to solve problems and serve as a guide to some practical course of action. In John Dewey's version of Pragmatism the model of all truth-seeking was the experimental method of the natural sciences. Social and political ideas could not be tested by rigorous experiments, perhaps, but social and political thinkers, like natural scientists, could ask about the consequences of choosing course "A" as opposed to course "B," and act accordingly.

The pragmatic approach was experimental, practical, relativistic, and evolutionary. To the pragmatists the world was not rigidly laid out and determined. It was, rather, incomplete, ongoing, open, diverse, and turbulent—very much, they said, like the urban-industrial America of the day—and the task of philosophers and other thinkers was to find solutions to the problems of real people in the real world.

As a whole, Pragmatism was a method or approach rather than a fully rounded system with precise prescriptions. Yet in one area, education, Dewey sought to apply his ideas directly. He believed that the education of the day was excessively static, mechanical, and irrelevant to the new society he saw emerging around him. Rather than memorizing by rote, he wanted students to be actively involved in learning. Dewey's disciples, the "progressive" educators, called this kind of teaching "learning by doing." Dewey also believed that teachers should spend less time on books and more on showing students how to get along with one another so that they could ultimately make society less competitive and exploitive. In 1904 Dewey joined the faculty of Teacher's College at Columbia University. There his teachings profoundly influenced an entire generation of professors of education and through them thousands of student teachers who spread the message of progressive education to virtually every school system in the country.

Evolutionary ideas were profoundly disturbing to many people. Not all scientists accepted Darwin. But most hostile were traditional Christians, both laypeople and ministers.

In the half-century after the Civil War, Christian ideas still powerfully affected the way Americans thought about the world and their place in it. Most Christians, but especially Protestants, placed the Bible at the center of their faith as God's revealed word. To the orthodox the account in Genesis of how God created the world and all its creatures in six days and how all humans were descendants of Adam and Eve was literally true. Darwinian ideas challenged the Bible's authority by proposing slow, natural processes for events that Scripture describes as under the immediate guidance of God and as happening in a brief period of time. Evolution also connected humankind to lower creatures in the biological realm. If Darwin was right, the Bible could not be literally true. In itself this conclusion was unthinkable to many, but its human consequences were also disturbing. If humans were part of the "brute creation," they could not be creatures made in God's own image and set above other living things as the Bible said. Evolution not only contradicted the Bible; it also seemed to strip humans of their unique dignity.

Traditional Christian belief also came under attack as scholars in England, France, and Germany began to examine the Bible as a historical document. Exponents of the so-called Higher Criticism depicted the Holy Scriptures as a work of men living in distinctive historical settings and compiled over generations. It did not represent God's exact words, they said, so much as the thoughts of inspired poets, chroniclers, philosophers, and prophets. As such it was not infallible, nor was it to be taken literally. Though the Higher Criticism originated abroad, it quickly won disciples among the American Protestant clergy and laity.

Religious modernism was often linked to another new current in religious thought: the social gospel. During the 1870s and 1880s many clergymen and laypeople began to believe that Protestantism had retreated too far from the old Puritan zeal to make the world a better place and had lost contact with the urban poor. To ministers such as Washington Gladden, William Bliss, and Walter Rauschenbusch, it appeared that Christianity had failed the poor by emphasizing the problem of personal salvation excessively. To traditional Christians, Gladden explained, religion was "too much a matter between themselves and God." Yet true Christianity was social as much as individual. It required righteous dealings with other people, not merely concern for personal salvation. To the social gospel preachers it seemed essential that the churches take stands on social issues and defend the weak and oppressed from those who exploited them. As early as the 1880s Gladden endorsed trade unions and the right to strike. Bliss, an Episcopal minister influenced by the Christian socialism of England, organized an American society of Christian socialists in 1889. Rauschenbusch denounced the competitive economic system and supported one based on the cooperative ideal.

Social gospel ideas were especially powerful among the Unitarians, Episcopalians, Methodists, and Congregationalists—the denominations that were also most open to the Higher Criticism and new scientific ideas generally. In 1905, thirty-three social gospel-oriented denominations, representing millions of communicants, banded together in the Federal Council of Churches of Christ in America. The council endorsed the abolition of child labor and the adoption of the six-day workweek, workers' compensation for injury, old-age insurance, a living wage for workers, and other social reforms.

The new views were not universally accepted. Many traditionalists worried that they substituted "relativism" for absolute truth, encouraged immorality, and undermined faith in God. Numerous Christians, including clergymen, found it possible to accept both the essential truth of Christian teachings and the views of

Darwin. Yet many, especially among the more evangelical Protestant denominations with rural roots, saw Darwin's ideas and the Higher Criticism as deplorable theories that endangered true religion. After 1910, to counter these views, a group of conservative Protestant clergy and theologians published a series of pamphlets, the "Fundamentals," that enumerated five points as the irreducible foundation of Christian faith: the infallibility of the Bible, Jesus' virgin birth, His resurrection, His atonement for humankind, and the inevitability of His second coming. In the following decades those who accepted the "Five Points" would wage a mighty battle to halt the erosion of traditional Protestantism and the growth of the modernism they perceived as false, dangerous to society, and threatening to human salvation.

Conclusions

How tawdry and corrupt, then, was the Gilded Age? The cultural and intellectual life of the United States underwent a colossal transformation in the half-century following the Civil War. On every level, from the heights of academic philosophy to the everyday amusements of ordinary men and women, culture adapted to the new urbanism and to the changes in technology and in political and economic institutions that swept the nation.

Were the cultural adaptations to the new forces cheap and vulgar? Was Gilded Age America a "chromo civilization"? So many changes are involved that it would be difficult under any circumstances to answer these questions. The problem is made worse by the fact that we are seeking to evaluate ideas as well as artistic expression.

In the case of the arts, surely the changes of the period 1865–1915 were "progressive." It is difficult not to applaud the eclipse of insipid literary gentility by robust realism; it is difficult to defend the imitative architectural old guard against the innovative Louis Sullivan and Frank Lloyd Wright. In the area of popular culture, too, the changes of the period were surely advances, ultimately making accessible whole new worlds of enjoyment and knowledge to masses of ordinary people.

Changes in the realm of ideas, however, cannot be seen as a simple matter of progress. The struggle between the progressive thinkers and the formalists, for example, represents merely one round in a battle between competing views of the world, humanity, and God that has been fought in the Western world for hundreds of years. If the formalists were often too rigid, their opponents were often so flexible that they weakened all moral and intellectual guideposts.

The political system, on the other hand, clearly lagged behind. America was often admired for its freedom and democracy, but few at home or abroad believed it enjoyed a government of honest, principled leaders who gave the public what it deserved. In the political realm, the gilt was highly visible.

Meanwhile, as the twentieth century began, a new awareness of neglected needs and higher standards began to stir beneath the surface, inspired in part by the social gospel, reform Darwinism, and the pragmatic philosophers. Before long the nation would embark on a new, transforming political crusade.

Online Resources

"1896: The Presidential Campaign, Cartoons, and Commentary—The Populists" *http://projects. vassar.edu/1896/populists.html* This site provides extensive information about the Populist Party, including explanations about dueling Populist factions, the party's platform, and primary news accounts.

"The Cross of Gold Speech" *http://www.kancoll.org/articles/speeches/bryan.htm* Read the full text of William Jennings Bryan's speech at the 1896 Democratic National Convention in which he attacks the notion of the gold standard.

Northwestern Industrial Army Marches to Join Coxey's Army *http://www.historylink.org/ essays/output.cfm?file_id=2181* The unemployment that plagued men of Coxey's Washington army also stretched to the West Coast. This Web site describes the efforts of men from Seattle, Washington, to join in the demonstrations in the nation's capital.

"Money Matters: The American Experience with Money *http://www.chicagofed.org/consumer_ information/money_matters.cfm* This Web site of the Federal Reserve Bank of Chicago explains the history of money in the United States and sheds light on the late-nineteenth-century debate over silver, gold, and paper currencies.

21

The American Empire

Why Did the United States Look Abroad?

1853–54	Commodore Perry opens American–Japanese trade
1867	Secretary of State Seward negotiates the purchase of Alaska and American control of the Midway Islands
1868	Ulysses S. Grant elected president
1869–70	Grant attempts to annex Santo Domingo
1877	Rutherford B. Hayes becomes president
1878	Coaling station at Pago Pago established
1880	James A. Garfield elected president
1881	Garfield is assassinated; Chester A. Arthur becomes president
1883	Congress appropriates funds to build modern naval vessels
1884	Grover Cleveland elected president
1887	The United States secures a naval base at Pearl Harbor
1888	Benjamin Harrison elected president
1890	The McKinley Tariff Act; Alfred Thayer Mahan's *The Influence of Sea Power upon History* published
1892	Grover Cleveland elected president
1893	American planters organize coup d'état in Hawaii; Frederick Jackson Turner's *The Significance of the Frontier in American History* published
1895	The United States disputes British claims in Venezuela
1896	William McKinley elected president
1898	The *Maine* is sunk in Havana harbor; Congress declares war on Spain; Congress votes to annex Hawaii; Treaty of Paris; Spain surrenders the Philippines, Puerto Rico, and Guam, and frees Cuba
1899–1900	Secretary of State Hay writes the *Open Door Notes;* The Boxer Rebellion
1899–1902	Emilio Aguinaldo leads a guerrilla war against the American occupation of the Philippines
1901	McKinley assassinated; Theodore Roosevelt becomes president; The Platt Amendment affirms American right to intervene in Cuba; The Hay-Pauncefote Treaty allows the United States to build a Central American interocean waterway
1903	Hay-Bunau-Varilla Treaty gives the United States the Canal Zone
1904	Roosevelt states Monroe Doctrine Corollary

In April 1898 Albert Beveridge, a young Indiana Republican soon to go to the United States Senate, spoke to Boston's Middlesex Club on the occasion of former President Grant's birthday. The Spanish-American War had just been declared, and although the fighting had scarcely begun, Beveridge looked ahead to what would follow the expected American victory.

> American factories are making more than the American people can use; American soil is producing more than they can consume. Fate has written our policy for us; the trade of the world must and shall be ours. . . . We shall establish trading posts throughout the world as distributing points for American products. We will cover the ocean with our merchant marine. We will build a navy to the measure of our greatness. Great colonies governing themselves, flying our flag and trading with us, will grow about our posts of trade. Our institutions will follow our flag on the wings of our commerce. And American law, American civilization, and the American flag will plant themselves on shores hitherto bloody and benighted, but by those agencies of God henceforth to be made beautiful and bright.

In this brief burst of oratory Beveridge summarized virtually every motive that contemporaries and later scholars would advance for America's overseas thrust during the generation following the Civil War. The American people need-ed markets for their surplus manufactures and farm products. They envisioned the glorious Stars and Stripes waving around the globe, with American civiliza-tion conferring immense benefits on the "benighted" peoples fortunate enough to fall under United States dominion. All this was to be accomplished by the "agen-cies of God." Glory, Gold, and God all justified an American empire in 1898—as they had a Spanish empire in 1498 and a British empire in 1598.

The resemblance between historical phenomena spread over 400 years is striking, and it is tempting to assume that not much had changed in the interval. But nineteenth-century Americans were not fifteenth-century Spaniards or six-teenth-century Englishmen. Even if they had the same general self-serving mo-tives for expansion as their predecessors, these were expressed in different ways and present in different proportions. How can we explain America's expansionist impulse during the years immediately preceding the twentieth century?

The Background

Viewed one way, post-Civil War expansionism seems merely an extension of the American past. For 250 years following the first permanent English settlements along the Atlantic Coast, Americans had pushed steadily westward toward the Pacific. This was not the filling in of an empty continent. The vast interior of North America was occupied by Native Americans who resisted the settlers' thrust and were pushed aside, often brutally. Parts of what later became the United States, moreover, were under the sovereignty of European nations, and Americans used aggressive diplomacy and military force to incorporate these areas into the United States. In this sense, the overseas thrust following 1865 was simply a continuation of what had preceded.

Any theory of post-Civil War expansionism must also consider the immediate international context. Expansionism is an expression of unequal power. As the Western world's advantage in technology and wealth grew during the nineteenth century, the temptation to use that edge became irresistible. The closing decades of the century witnessed the last burst of European colonialism until, with few exceptions, the remotest regions of the Earth were firmly under European control. America in these years surpassed its competitors on every index of wealth; inevitably, this view holds, it felt the same urge as the other western nations to impose its will on others.

And we must consider a common Marxist theory of capitalist imperialism that has long been influential in intellectual circles. Marxists hold that advanced capitalist societies inevitably develop "contradictions" taking the form of insufficient markets at home for their goods and outlets for their capital, and so turn to weaker societies abroad to exploit. Imperialism, then, derives from the capitalist need to stave off crisis and social upheavals.

The Beginnings of Overseas Expansion

The story of American overseas expansion does not begin abruptly in 1865. Before the Civil War southern pressures had induced President Franklin Pierce to offer Spain $130 million for the island of Cuba. In the same era American adventurers and soldiers of fortune had fomented revolutions in Central America for the purpose of annexing territory to the United States. In the mid-1850s, an aggressive policy of encouraging foreign trade culminated in the visits of an American naval squadron to Japan under Commodore Matthew Perry, forcing Japan to open its doors to commerce and traditional diplomatic relations with other nations. The Civil War brought these expansionist activities to a sudden halt. But after Appomattox Americans began once again to look with interest toward the surrounding oceans and the lands that dotted and bordered them.

Foreign Policy Under Seward.   The man at the forefront of this revived concern with the outside world was William Henry Seward, Andrew Johnson's secretary of state. Seward's interest in American expansion had its practical, strategic side. The difficulties in dealing with the Confederate ships raiding northern commerce during the Civil War had convinced him that the United States must have naval bases and coaling stations scattered around its perimeter to fend off any future naval aggressor. He also had a romantic vision of a benevolent American empire that resembled the Manifest Destiny of the 1840s. In 1867, in a burst of poetry surprising in a man so practical and businesslike, Seward announced:

> Our nation with united interests blest,
> Not content to pose, shall sway the rest;
> Abroad our empire shall no limits know,
> But like the sea in boundless limits flow.

But first Seward had to deal with the problem of European intrusion into the Western Hemisphere. In 1863, while the United States was preoccupied by the Civil War, the French had established a puppet regime in Mexico under Archduke Maximilian of Austria and had sent troops to support him against Mexican patriots led by Benito Juárez. The French occupation of Mexico was a clear challenge to the Monroe Doctrine of 1823, and when the war ended, Seward told Napoleon III, the French emperor, that the United States would no longer tolerate Maximilian's rule in Mexico. Growing opposition at home, the cost of maintaining troops in America, and the threat of the seasoned Union army just across the border induced the French to withdraw their support of the puppet regime in 1867. Shortly thereafter, Maximilian was captured by Juárez's soldiers and executed.

Seward's success in driving the French from Mexico was applauded by Americans and Mexicans alike. For once, the Monroe Doctrine had served Latin Americans as an effective shield against European aggression. But Americans did not greet Seward's own expansionist moves as warmly. Most were either indifferent or stubbornly opposed to empire building. When Seward tried to buy land for a coaling station in Santo Domingo (the Dominican Republic), Congress refused to back him. He also could not get Congress to approve a treaty to purchase the Danish West Indies (now the U.S. Virgin Islands). Critics of the secretary had a field day with these island-shopping trips. A mock advertisement in a New York newspaper ran: "A Few West India Islands Wanted.—Any distressed persons having a few islands to dispose of in the Spanish Main can find a purchaser by applying to Washington D.C. . . ." The only islands that Seward ever managed to acquire were specks of land a thousand miles west of Hawaii: the Midway group. Seward's only major expansionist success was the vast northwestern edge of North America, Alaska.

"Seward's Folly."   A Russian possession, Alaska had been exploited for many years by the Russian-American Company primarily for its furs. By the mid-nineteenth century the fur trade had begun to decline, and the Russian government faced the prospect of having to rescue the company from bankruptcy. The Russians also feared that in a war with Great Britain, they would not be able to protect their distant colony. Unsure of Alaska's defenses and unwilling to support it financially, the czar decided to sell it to the United States.

The American secretary of state was more than willing to talk terms. Seward saw Alaska not only as a base for American naval defense in any Pacific war, but also as a way-station to the Far East and the potential markets of China. But many outspoken Americans were opposed to acquiring a distant, unknown, and apparently worthless chunk of land. Those who had ridiculed Seward's Caribbean interests promptly called his new scheme "Seward's Folly" and the territory itself "Seward's Icebox." A weekly newspaper reported that the benefits of buying Russian America included a bracing climate, a promising ice crop, and cows that gave ice cream instead of milk. At the very least, the $7.2 million that the Russians wanted was a high price for half a million square miles of desolate mountains, icefields, tundra, and pine forest.

Seward quickly mounted a sales campaign to change his fellow citizens' minds. He secured expert testimonials describing the region's vast natural resources and collected 1803 newspaper attacks on the Louisiana Purchase to show his opponents as timid men without vision or foresight. Aided by Charles Sumner, the influential chairman of the Senate Foreign Relations Committee, he induced the Senate to pass the Alaska annexation treaty. When the House of Representatives balked at appropriating the necessary money, the Russian minister plied the reluctant members with cash. In the end it all worked out. On October 18, 1867, the American flag was raised over the Russian fort at Sitka. Alaska was now American territory.

A Stronger Navy. For almost two decades following Seward's retirement, the American people turned inward. In 1869–1870 the Senate rejected President Grant's attempt to annex all of Santo Domingo, and thereafter the expansionist impulse subsided. During the 1870s and 1880s much of the nation's energy was consumed in filling in the rest of the continent with farms, railroads, mines, factories, and new cities and towns. So remote and unimportant did America's foreign relations appear that as late as 1889 the *New York Sun* could half seriously suggest doing away with the diplomatic service as "a costly humbug and sham" that did "no good to anybody."

Yet even during this low point, there were rumblings of a revived interest in foreign concerns and a new aggressiveness toward the outside world. The new mood manifested itself initially as anxiety about American naval impotence. Of the 1,900 vessels in the fleet in 1880, only 48 could fire a gun. As the joke went the American navy was "too weak to fight; too slow to run." Citizens began to wonder how the country could protect itself against foreign attack. To remedy the problem, in 1883 Congress authorized four new steel coast defense warships, adding the battleships *Texas* and *Maine* to the fleet several years later. Americans breathed a little easier, but still the navy remained primarily a defensive force.

Then, in the 1890s, the United States began to build a high-seas fleet capable of supporting an ambitious foreign policy. The inspiration for the "new navalism" was the writings of Captain Alfred Thayer Mahan, a career naval officer who taught at the Naval War College at Newport, Rhode Island. In *The Influence of Sea Power upon History,* published in 1890, he described how Britain had become the mightiest nation in the world by seizing command of the seas. America must now strive to equal Great Britain or accept eventual decline.

Mahan's popular book convinced many that the country must have a navy second to none. Spurred on by his ideas, during the 1890s the United States built a flotilla of fast warships with long cruising ranges, capable of meeting an enemy anywhere in the world. By the end of the decade the naval building program had created a high-seas force consisting of seventeen steel-hulled battleships, along with six armored cruisers and numerous modern smaller craft.

"Jingo Jim" Blaine. Still, Americans as a whole remained uninterested in foreign concerns. James G. Blaine, secretary of state under James Garfield (1881) and again under Benjamin Harrison (1889–1892), felt differently. Blaine was not a man to sit at his desk and shuffle papers. "Jingo Jim" was particularly interested in Latin America. Like many Americans since Monroe's day, he believed that the United States had a special big-brother role to play in the Western Hemisphere and he advocated stronger ties among the nations of the New World, a policy he referred to as "Pan-Americanism."

Blaine's interest in Latin America combined altruism and economic gain in roughly equal parts. Although the United States bought large quantities of foodstuffs and raw materials from its southern neighbors, Latin America continued to buy most of its manufactured goods from Europe. Blaine hoped to divert the flow of Latin American trade from Europe to the United States, but he feared that improved economic relations would be impossible so long as the Latin American nations continued to squabble constantly among themselves. If the United States could act as a peacemaker and a stabilizing influence in the Western Hemisphere, everyone would benefit. Good deeds would bring good profits.

In 1881 Blaine called an inter-American conference to meet in Washington to further these goals. Before it could assemble, President Garfield was assassinated. Blaine soon resigned as secretary of state, and his successor in the State Department canceled the conference. Blaine got another chance during the second round of his "spirited diplomacy" when he again became secretary of state under President Benjamin Harrison. In October 1889 representatives of seventeen Latin American states convened in Washington at Blaine's invitation. The results, from Blaine's point of view, were mixed. The delegates rejected the secretary's pet project, a Western Hemisphere customs union to increase United States–Latin American trade and curtail trade with Europe. They also turned down his proposal for establishing procedures to handle inter-American disagreements. The conference, however, did establish the Pan American Union as a clearinghouse to distribute information and further hemispheric cooperation.

A New Frontier.

Thus, even during this low point in diplomacy, Americans never completely lost their interest in international affairs. In the last two decades of the century, thoughtful men and women began to reconsider their country's place in the world. During the 1880s and 1890s a sense of crisis seized many middle-class Americans. The nation, it seemed, was threatened with serious instability in the form of Populism, labor unrest, and political radicalism. Why was discontent so rife and what could be done about it? As they struggled for answers, Americans encountered a persistent theme: The United States had run out of physical space.

The most influential spokesman for this idea was the historian Frederick Jackson Turner, who in 1893 announced that the frontier experience was over. For almost three centuries the "West" had provided a constructive outlet for social discontents and had encouraged social and political democracy. Now it was gone, he said, and a vital safety valve had closed. Turner did not propose moving the American frontier overseas, but he raised in the minds of the educated the frightening prospect of growing inequality and social chaos if America could not find some alternative to continental expansion.

The Reverend Josiah Strong made the overseas expansion solution explicit. His views in some ways parallel those of the Marxists. In his popular book *Our Country* (1885) he asserted that since the free land was gone, the United States would soon "approximate European conditions of life," marked by class conflict and gross inequality. To avoid these afflictions, America must leap the oceans and find new frontiers abroad where its civilization would have room to expand. Though Strong's vision combined Protestant missionary zeal and American expansionism, his advocacy of expanded foreign Christian missions was lost in the defense of American destiny.

Strong and Turner used history and sociology to justify expansion; another group of expansionist thinkers relied on science, or pseudo-science. Social Darwinists, as we saw, viewed the competition among nations and peoples as a necessary continuation of the struggle for survival that fueled biological evolution. In this struggle the strong would win and gain dominion over the weak. Imperialism then was condoned by nature. At its most extreme, social Darwinism tipped over into the "scientific" racism of Madison Grant, John Fiske, John W. Burgess, and others who believed in the "natural superiority" of the Nordic and Anglo-Saxon peoples. Grant, who was associated with the Museum of Natural History in New York, used notions of Nordic superiority primarily to justify immigration restriction. But other racists insisted that this superiority gave Americans the right to rule "inferior peoples." Anglo-Saxons had always been conquerors, declared philosopher and historian Fiske, and would continue to assert their "sovereignty of the seas" and "their commercial supremacy." Burgess, a professor of political science at Columbia University, taught his students that people of English origin were particularly well suited to the establishment of national states and were destined to impose their political institutions on the rest of the world.

The Foreign Policy Elite.   The literate, middle-class Americans who read the works of Turner, Strong, Grant, and the other expansionist thinkers were an important part of the political community. But closer to the process of decision making in foreign affairs was what one scholar has called "the foreign policy elite." This was a small group of people who were seriously, and often personally, concerned with what went on in the outside world. Strategically located in government, journalism, the universities, the professions, and business, they influenced public opinion, Congress, and the State Department out of proportion to their numbers. Undoubtedly their concerns were in part economically derived. But there were also elements of nationalism, cosmopolitanism, and broad cultural and intellectual interest in world affairs. To many of this elite it seemed a shame that the United States, as strong as any of the great European colonial powers, had so far held back. America's restraint, they said, had encouraged Europe to consider this nation unimportant in international affairs outside the Western Hemisphere. Few European countries, they noted, assigned ambassadors to Washington, being content with ministers or lesser diplomatic representatives. A colonial empire promised to end this undeserved inferiority and propel the United States into the ranks of the world powers, where the foreign policy elite believed it belonged.

Hawaii and Venezuela

Toward the end of the 1880s, then, expansionist sentiment and national assertiveness began to reemerge among the decision makers and the public at large. Early in the 1890s the phrase "Manifest Destiny" began to appear once more in political platforms; in 1893 Congress created the rank of ambassador to replace that of minister in the diplomatic service. Yet for some years Americans' interest in overseas matters would continue to vacillate, as the experience with Hawaii illustrates.

Ambivalence About Expansion.   The strategic value of the Hawaiian Islands in the Pacific had been recognized ever since the English explorer, Captain James Cook, had encountered them in 1778. In the early nineteenth century American merchant ships en route to China often stopped at the beautiful islands for fresh water and supplies. In 1820 the first American missionaries arrived and devoted themselves to bringing their Christian faith to the native Polynesian peoples. Whalers soon came

Queen Liliuokalani was actually less benevolent than this picture suggests.

to the island kingdom, and the whaling crews, long without female companion-ship, helped to undo the missionaries' efforts to change Hawaiian morals. The sons of the missionaries, along with other American settlers attracted to the is-lands, made sugar-growing rather than soul-saving their chief concern and even-tually came to own much of the land. The strong American presence and the strategic location of the island chain inevitably aroused the interest of the United States government. Seward soon added the annexation of Hawaii to his other am-bitious schemes. But few Americans were interested and nothing was done at this time. Then, in 1875 the United States agreed to allow Hawaiian sugar, unlike that from other foreign lands, to enter the United States duty free. As a result, the is-lands' economy soon became dependent on the profitable American market. The Hawaiian government, meanwhile, came under the influence of the American planters and businessmen who had brought prosperity to the kingdom. In 1887 the United States renewed the sugar agreement and received the right to use Pearl Harbor at Honolulu as a naval base.

Suddenly the rosy Hawaiian economic situation changed. The McKinley Tar-iff of 1890 removed the duty on all sugar entering the United States, thus ending Hawaii's advantage over its competitors in the American market. The islands' economy took a nosedive. Almost simultaneously Queen Liliuokalani succeeded her brother to the Hawaiian throne, determined to restore much of the royal power he had surrendered to American advisers. The new queen was anti-American. Adopting the battle cry "Hawaii for the Hawaiians," she launched a campaign to end all foreign influence in her kingdom. In 1893 she issued a new constitution that disenfranchised all Europeans, except those married to native Hawaiian women, and gave herself dictatorial powers.

The Americans in Hawaii promptly organized a "Committee of Safety," staged a coup d'état, and established a provisional government. The American minister to Hawaii, John L. Stevens, used the pretext of protecting American property to deploy marines from the cruiser U.S.S. *Boston* outside the queen's palace. Unable to resist this show of force, the queen abdicated. Stevens then proclaimed the islands an American protectorate and triumphantly wrote the State Department: "The Hawaiian pear is now fully ripe and this is the golden hour for the United States to pluck it." Repeating the process of Texan-Americans sixty years before, the provisional government leaders soon applied for annexation to the United States.

President Harrison quickly signed an annexation treaty with representatives of the rebel government. Unfortunately for the annexationists, Grover Cleveland became president before the Senate could act on the treaty. Upright, principled, conscientious, Cleveland opposed territorial acquisition and doubted the morality of the American residents' takeover. He withdrew the treaty from the Senate and sent James H. Blount as his personal representative to the islands to investigate the circumstances of the queen's downfall.

When the Blount report arrived in Washington, it confirmed Cleveland's worst suspicions. Stevens, it said, had high-handedly interfered in Hawaii's internal affairs; a large majority of native Hawaiian voters opposed annexation. For a time, Cleveland considered restoring the queen to her throne. But when she declared her intention to decapitate the revolutionaries as soon as she regained control, he withdrew his support, allowed the Americans to remain in power, and recognized the provisional government as the legitimate authority of the Republic of Hawaii. But he refused to join the islands legally with the United States. Until its annexation in 1898, Hawaii remained an independent republic controlled by its American residents.

The Monroe Doctrine Reasserted.   The Hawaiian affair points up the still-cautious side of American foreign policy. But as the century approached its end the jingoist, aggressive side took hold. This more combative attitude was displayed in the Venezuela incident of 1895. Independent Venezuela and the English colony of British Guiana, on the Caribbean coast of South America, had long disputed their common boundary. From the beginning of this controversy, the Venezuelans had sought American support and had taken pains to depict the British as callous aggressors against a weaker nation. The American State Department had become suspicious of renewed European interest in Latin America. The Royal Navy had recently landed troops in Nicaragua on the pretext that the British consul had been insulted. The incident, made doubly offensive to Americans by the British admiral's remark that the Monroe Doctrine was a myth, had set off a strong anti-British response in the American press. American anxiety over European colonial ambitions in the Western Hemisphere was reinforced by the desire to prevent British commercial dominance in the large area of the continent drained by the Orinoco River. Matters came to a head in 1894 when the British government refused President Cleveland's offer to arbitrate the dispute.

Early in 1895 Congress passed a resolution denouncing British claims in Venezuela. Secretary of State Richard Olney backed the resolution in an aggressive letter to the American minister in London. Defending the right of the United States under the Monroe Doctrine to guarantee the independence of Latin American republics, the secretary launched into a blunt declaration of American power that startled the British. "Its infinite resources," he boasted, "combined with its isolated position render [the United States] the master of the situation and practically invulnerable against any or all other powers." Olney concluded by demanding arbitration and insisting that Britain respond before Congress met later in the year. Offended by Olney's tone, the British prime minister, Lord Salisbury, rejected the call for arbitration with a brusqueness almost equal to Olney's. President Cleveland replied that if Britain refused arbitration, the United States would impose a boundary line and defend it with military force if necessary. Amid a wave of anti-British enthusiasm throughout the United States and Latin America, Congress approved Cleveland's plan and quickly appropriated $100,000 for a boundary commission. Anglophobes and jingoes eagerly awaited war with Great Britain.

Fortunately for world peace, sober second thoughts soon took hold on both sides of the Atlantic. By now Britain had begun to fear Germany's growing challenge to its naval supremacy and its recent support of the Boer settlers in South Africa in their dispute with them. Rather than take on both the United States and imperial Germany, Lord Salisbury chose to placate the Americans. In the United States a peace faction composed of clergy, business leaders, financiers, and journalists was able to cool down heated tempers. Britain and Venezuela eventually agreed to accept arbitration; but by the time a decision was handed down in 1899, the whole dispute had been virtually forgotten.

Cuba Libre

Cleveland's second administration (1893–1897) marked a transition from an isolationist to a more expansionist attitude toward the world. The shift was triggered by events in Cuba. That rich Caribbean island, along with Puerto Rico, had remained under Spanish rule long after the rest of Spain's New World empire had disintegrated. The Cubans, however, were dissatisfied with Spanish rule and in 1868 launched an insurrection to gain independence. During the ten-year uprising Cuban rebels, some of them naturalized American citizens, appealed to the United States for help. But despite a number of minor diplomatic brushes with Spain, the United States refused to be drawn in, and the revolt eventually subsided.

Revolution in Cuba. For seventeen years the Cuban revolutionary spirit remained dormant. Then, in the early 1890s, harsh Spanish rule, its effects amplified by a severe crisis in the Cuban sugar industry, goaded the Cubans to revolt once again. The insurrectionists set fire to sugar plantations and cattle ranches in the countryside, hoping that Spain would capitulate if nothing of value was left on the island. Cuban patriots living in the United States organized "juntas" to aid the rebels and provoke trouble between Spain and the United States. The Spanish authorities under General Valeriano Weyler (called "the butcher" in the anti-Spanish press) struck back by rounding up thousands of suspected rebels and sympathizers, including women and children, and confining them in concentration camps. Weyler did not intend mass murder, but unsanitary conditions and rebel interference with the food-supply systems made the concentration areas death camps.

American Sympathies. As in virtually all revolutions and civil wars, both sides were brutal and destructive, yet almost without exception the American people condemned Spain and supported the Cuban rebels. It used to be said that our sympathies were determined by our economic interests in the island. But there is little evidence to support this assertion. In reality, with the depression of 1893–1897 finally coming to an end, involvement in Cuba that might lead to war was the last thing the business community wanted. As relations with Spain worsened, the business press attacked any drastic action that would "impede the march of prosperity and put the country back many years." Farmers were more interventionist. Agricultural spokesmen favored policies to expand overseas markets for American crops, but few favored war with Spain. As for labor, working people usually shared the views of their employers: A war with Spain would depress business and therefore hurt the working class. And yet by April 1898 most Americans—farmers, businesspeople, wage earners, and others—had come to favor intervening in Cuba despite the risk of war with Spain. Why?

In part, Americans were moved by age-old sympathies for underdogs and identified the Cuban insurrection with their own struggle for freedom from a European power 120 years before. Fortunately for the Cuban rebels, American sympathies were strongly reinforced by the activities of the "yellow press," especially William Randolph Hearst's *New York Journal* and Joseph Pulitzer's *New York World*. During the late 1890s the two press lords were fighting a bitter circulation war. In these clashes truth often took a back seat to profit. Each sought to provide a daily diet of atrocity stories detailing Spanish brutality, for that sold papers. Both were unscrupulous, though Hearst was probably even less principled than his rival. According to one story, when an American artist sent to Cuba to illustrate the insurrection reported that things were currently quiet, Hearst shot back: "You furnish the pictures and I'll furnish the war."

War Becomes Unavoidable.   Yet war seemed only a remote possibility when William McKinley was inaugurated in March 1897. The new president shared the business community's reluctance to jeopardize returning prosperity and declared in his inaugural address that war must be avoided "until every agency of peace has failed; peace is preferable to war in almost every contingency." But McKinley could not control events. Ordinary public opinion was running against him, and the foreign policy elite considered his course cowardly and unworthy. The chauvinist New Yorker Theodore Roosevelt, for one, believed McKinley was as spineless "as a chocolate éclair." Early in 1898 a key group of congressional Republicans agreed to push the president for a war resolution, promising to join with the Democrats and sponsor one themselves if he did not comply. The religious press, viewing the issue in Cuba as a fight between Cuban virtue and Spanish beastliness, also demanded that the American government intervene to end the atrocious situation.

The Spaniards seemed to be their own worst enemies. In January 1898 the Spanish minister to the United States, Enrique Dupuy de Lôme, a well-meaning but indiscreet grandee, wrote an imprudent letter to a friend in Cuba expressing his contempt for McKinley and admitting that Spain was negotiating in bad faith over a proposed trade treaty with America. A Cuban patriot stole the letter from the desk of the recipient in Havana and sent it to Hearst, who promptly published it in his newspapers. The outraged public demanded that de Lôme be sent home. The minister instantly resigned in hope of mending the situation, but the damage was done. The American people now had even more reason than before to picture the Spaniards as arrogant and deceitful.

De Lôme's blunder was soon followed by an even bigger blow to Spanish–American relations. In January 1898 the American government sent the battleship *Maine* to Havana. The visit was officially "friendly"; the ship was supposedly only there to protect American lives and property following a serious local riot. The captain and the crew of the vessel were treated courteously by Spanish officials in Havana, though the visit naturally aroused some suspicion. Then, on February 15, a tremendous explosion rocked the ship, sending it to the bottom of the harbor with the loss of over 260 lives.

A modern investigation of the sunken ship has confirmed the view that the *Maine* was destroyed by an internal boiler explosion. But contemporaries disagreed. Spanish authorities denied responsibility for the sinking. American divers at the time concluded that the explosion had come from outside. Regardless of who

A contemporary artist's horrific vision of what the destruction of the battleship *Maine* looked like.

or what sank the ship, most Americans considered it an act of war. Agreeing with Theodore Roosevelt's theory that the *Maine* had been "sunk by an act of dirty treachery on the part of the Spaniards," they demanded immediate retaliation. Jingoes had a field day. Mass rallies were held all over the country at news of the atrocity. People marched through the streets, chanting, "Remember the *Maine*. To Hell with Spain!" The yellow press, of course, insisted that Spain be punished with all the force of America's might.

McKinley could not resist the growing pressure to intervene. He promptly instructed the American minister in Madrid to demand that the Spanish government grant an armistice to the rebels and end the cruel concentration camp policy. If Spain did not accept these terms by October, the United States would impose a settlement. The Spanish government was caught in a dilemma. Domestic public opinion would be outraged by surrender to the United States; but war seemed the certain alternative. For a while it wavered, but finally, on the advice of the pope, it agreed to grant an armistice and abolish the concentration camps.

Spain had given the United States virtually everything it had asked for, but it was not enough to avoid war. American opinion now would not be satisfied with anything less than an independent Cuba—"Cuba Libre." The president was still reluctant to intervene, but he, too, was caught in a dilemma. In Congress the pressure to declare war was becoming irresistible; even if he did not request a declaration of war, there were signs that Congress would go ahead without him. Moreover, if he held back, the Democrats would charge him with weakness and jeopardize his chances of winning reelection in 1900.

On April 11 McKinley sent a war message to Congress. The United States, he said, must protect the lives and property of American citizens and put an end to the "barbarities, bloodshed, starvation, and horrible miseries . . . right at [its] door." Intervention was justified, the president claimed, by the "very serious injury to commerce, trade, and business of our people, and by the wanton destruction of property and devastation of the island." In addition, it was of "utmost importance" to end a disturbance that was a "constant menace to our peace and entails upon this Government an enormous expense."

On April 19 Congress passed four resolutions defining the nation's war policy: (1) Cuba must be free; (2) Spain must withdraw from the island; (3) the president could use the armed forces to obtain these ends; and (4) the United States would not annex Cuba. The commitment to nonannexation—the Teller Amendment—was approved without a dissenting vote. On April 25, 1898, Congress formally declared war on Spain.

The Spanish-American War

The war with Spain was short and cheap. Few American lives were lost; more soldiers died at "Custer's Last Stand" than from battle wounds in the entire Spanish-American conflict. Moreover, the war was over in a few months and peace concluded by December 1898. As wars go, this one was also a bargain: It cost the United States only $250 million. John Hay, soon to be secretary of state, called it a "splendid little war," and from the point of view of most Americans, the successes of their country's armed forces, particularly the navy, were splendid indeed.

Quick Victory.

As assistant secretary of the navy, Theodore Roosevelt had anticipated war with Spain and, acting in the temporary absence of his superior, he had dispatched Commodore George Dewey and the navy's Asiatic squadron to China even before McKinley delivered his war message. With the official war declaration, Dewey sailed for the Philippines, a Spanish possession in the China Sea. Commanding six modern vessels of the new fleet, Dewey attacked and sank the whole Spanish Asiatic squadron in Manila Bay without losing a ship and hardly a man. The navy soon repeated Dewey's Pacific triumph in the Caribbean. In July the main United States naval force in Cuban waters under Admiral William T. Sampson defeated the Spanish fleet in a brief battle off Santiago. American losses were one sailor killed, one wounded.

The army's performance was considerably less impressive. For years its main job had been to contain and control the Indians in the West. When war came, the War Department had to recruit and train a large number of volunteers, including Roosevelt's band of western cowboys and eastern gentlemen who, along with Roosevelt himself, enlisted as the "Rough Riders." Secretary of War Russell A. Alger botched the job of organizing and supplying the new recruits. Amid incredible confusion, 17,000 ill-equipped soldiers were embarked from Tampa, Florida, and landed near Santiago in southeastern Cuba. After several sharp skirmishes with the Spaniards, including the Rough Riders' famous charge up San Juan Hill, the Americans captured the heights overlooking the city. On July 17, following Sampson's naval victory, the Spanish military commander in Santiago surrendered. Soon after the American army occupied Puerto Rico without opposition.

The Spoils of War.

By the end of July the Spanish government was ready to sue for peace. In October delegates from the United States and Spain met in Paris to work out final details. Spain had already agreed to give Cuba its independence and to cede Puerto Rico and the Pacific island of Guam to the United States. The issue that blocked final terms was the fate of the Philippines. Although Dewey had sunk the Spanish Asiatic fleet, he lacked occupation troops and waited offshore for reinforcements before taking Manila, the capital city. Meanwhile, Britain and Germany assembled naval squadrons nearby, ostensibly to protect the interests of their citizens in the Philippines but actually to claim the islands if the United States proved uninterested.

Before the war few Americans had paid attention to the Philippines; most did not even know where they were. Now, suddenly, they were up to their ears in international complications over these exotic islands. What should they do with them? Many were disturbed by German designs. Since its unification twenty years before, imperial Germany had become an aggressive colonial power, rummaging around for new properties all over the world. This had seldom disturbed Americans before, but the United States had fought for the islands; the Germans had expended nothing for them. Why allow them to fall into undeserving hands?

And there were also practical matters to consider. Though initially skeptical of war, the business community was now convinced that the islands could serve as a base for trade with China. In July 1898, moved by a new, war-generated expansionist fever, Congress had finally annexed Hawaii. Add the Philippines as well and the United States would have a convenient set of steppingstones across the Pacific to the Asian mainland. As Senator Henry Cabot Lodge noted, controlling the port of Manila would be "the thing which will give us the eastern trade."

There seemed serious moral considerations as well. Could we rescue Cuba from Spanish tyranny and return the Filipino people to Spain's colonial rule? Besides, what a field for missionary effort the islands promised to be! Ignoring the fact that most Filipinos were already Catholics, McKinley found this opportunity to advance Christian civilization a compelling reason to hold on to the islands. He had been troubled by the fate of the Philippines and its people, he later told a church group, until in answer to his prayers for divine guidance he had suddenly seen what must be done:

> We could not give them back to Spain—that would be cowardly and dishonorable. . . .
> There was nothing left for us to do but take them all and to educate the Filipinos, and
> uplift and civilize them and Christianize them, and by God's grace do the very best by
> them, as our fellowmen for whom Christ also died.

After reaching this conveniently inspired and practical conclusion, McKinley told the American negotiators in Paris to insist that the whole island chain be ceded to the United States as part of the peace agreement. Spain resisted at first, but in exchange for $20 million it surrendered the Philippines (along with Puerto Rico and Guam), and at the same time confirmed Cuban independence.

The Anti-Imperialists.   The Treaty of Paris, especially the provision ceding the Philippines, triggered a storm of protest in the United States. The war had undoubtedly legitimized imperialism, but many opponents of expansion remained unconvinced. Mugwump reformers, along with many intellectuals and clergymen, believed that acquiring colonies was immoral and damaging to American traditions. By searching for colonies, lamented professor Charles Eliot Norton of Harvard, America had "lost her unique position as a potential leader in the progress of civilization" and had "taken her place simply as one of the grasping and selfish nations of the present day." Other anti-imperialists were more angry than sad about the nation's desertion of its ideals. "God damn the United States for its vile conduct in the Philippine Isles," wrote the philosopher William James. If the United States made the islands a colony, it would leave the Filipinos with nothing: we could "destroy their own ideals," he declared, "but we can't give them ours." Many anti-imperialists feared that racial problems would overwhelm the United States if it incorporated the Philippines and parts of the Caribbean into its domain. Could the nation, asked Carl Schurz, absorb territories inhabited by "savages and half-savages" all "animated with the instinct, impulses and passions bred by the tropical sun." If we attempted to do so, "what will become of American labor and the standards of American citizenship?" Banded together as the Anti-Imperialist League, the opponents of colonies tried to block American negotiators from signing the Treaty of Paris. When this effort failed, the league turned its attention to the Senate, where the fight for ratification promised to be long and bitter. In the course of a few months it badgered senators and other politicians to stop the treaty and mailed thousands of propaganda pieces denouncing colonialism.

Ratification of the Treaty of Paris. In the end the anti-imperialists failed. Under a barrage of cajolery, persuasion, and pressure from McKinley and other administration leaders, almost all Senate Republicans pledged to support the treaty. But Democratic votes, too, were needed for passage and William Jennings Bryan seemed to hold the key to success. Though defeated for president in 1896 and now a private citizen, he continued to exert great influence among fellow Democrats. Bryan was not an imperialist, but he threw his support behind the treaty, believing that ending the war was more important than the details of the settlement. He also naively assumed the United States would give the Philippines its freedom almost immediately. Enough Democrats went along with Bryan to carry the treaty 57 to 27, just one vote more than needed for ratification.

Imperial America

Yet this did not end the controversy over expansionism. Bryan still opposed overseas colonies and hoped to make the election of 1900 a referendum favoring return to the country's old, non-imperial ways. But American presidential elections seldom revolve about a single issue. In the end, the election of 1900 turned on silver, reform, prosperity, and the achievements of the first McKinley administration. Bryan's resounding defeat revealed little of what the American public felt about overseas expansion: Even the anti-imperialists split their votes between the two candidates.

Meanwhile, events in the Philippines were demonstrating the dangers and costs of America's new imperial course. Two days before ratification of the Spanish treaty, full-scale fighting broke out between the Filipinos, led by Emilio Aguinaldo, and the forces seeking to impose American sovereignty. Aguinaldo and his followers proclaimed Filipino independence in June 1898 and resisted American annexation. Eventually the United States was forced to fight a full-scale colonial war to put down the Filipino patriots. The "insurrection" required more than 125,000 American troops to quell after a four-year fight that cost 4,000 American lives and many more Filipino. The fighting was often savage with atrocities on both sides. Not until mid-1902 were the army regulars able to capture Aguinaldo and pacify the islands. The Philippines Insurrection was America's first land war in Asia, and like Vietnam in the 1960s, it called into question America's democratic values.

In the years following, the United States sought to make amends in the Philippines by introducing land reform, establishing local self-government, and improving educational facilities. In 1902 Congress created a Philippine legislative assembly, though the governor of the islands remained an American. But the ugly war experience was a disturbing one and made Americans all the more uneasy in the role of colonial power.

During the next twenty years the nation vacillated between its liberal and its imperial tendencies. In 1900, under the Foraker Act, Congress authorized limited self-government for Puerto Rico. By the Platt Amendment to the Army Appropriation Bill of 1901, it directed the president to withdraw American forces from Cuba. Yet Cuba was not to be truly free. It could not enter into any treaty that would impair its sovereignty, nor could it contract debts beyond its capacity to pay. Also, the United States might intervene in the island's internal affairs to maintain law and order.

Relations with Latin America.

America's attitude toward its closest neighbors in Latin America during these years was that of a strict, disapproving older brother: It would protect them against outsiders, but they must behave or face American wrath. This policy worried and offended Latin Americans; Yankees considered it necessary for their peace of mind. The United States was the only great power in the Western Hemisphere, and Americans found this situation comfortable. Any hint that a European country was trying to extend its influence into the Western Hemisphere set off immediate alarm bells in Washington.

Sometimes this proprietary attitude operated to the advantage of America's smaller neighbors. Without American protection, a number of the weaker Latin American states would almost certainly have fallen again into the hands of one or another of the great European powers. Yet Latin America undoubtedly paid a high price for this protection. The United States insisted that its own strategic, political, and economic interests came first, and often acted in ways that left a legacy of resentment.

Events in Panama early in the century vividly illustrate this highhandedness. During the conflict with Spain the Pacific-based U.S.S. *Oregon* had been forced to sail around Cape Horn to come to the defense of the East Coast, exposed, it was feared, to a possible attack by the Spanish navy. The delay had underscored the advantages of a canal across the narrow isthmus that joined North and South America. With the war over and America the uneasy owner of a new Pacific empire, a canal seemed even more imperative.

Two obstacles blocked the way. The Clayton-Bulwer Treaty, signed with Great Britain in 1850, had denied the United States exclusive control over an isthmian canal. This hurdle was overcome by the 1901 Hay-Pauncefote Treaty with Britain, which gave sole right to the United States to build, control, and fortify a Central American waterway. Location was the second problem. Two routes were possible: one through Nicaragua and one at Panama. Favoring Panama was the enormous labor already expended by the French under Ferdinand de Lesseps, builder of the Suez Canal, who had been hacking their way unsuccessfully through the fever-ridden jungles and mountains of the isthmus since the 1880s. When the French offered to sell their rights and equipment for $40 million, Congress accepted.

But another difficulty now loomed. Panama was a province of Colombia. Before construction could begin, that nation would have to agree to the arrangement. In January 1903 the United States concluded a treaty with Tomás Herrán, the Colombian minister in Washington, giving the South American republic a one-time $10 million payment and $250,000 annually for the rights to build the canal and to lease a canal zone six miles wide along the right-of-way for ninety-nine years. When the treaty reached the Colombian Senate, however, it was defeated. The Colombians had two major objections: The treaty gave the Americans too much power over a portion of their territory; it also failed to give them, rather than the French canal company, the $40 million Congress had promised.

President Theodore Roosevelt considered the Colombians' action outrageous. These people, he shouted, were "contemptible little creatures" who were "imperiling their own future." The United States might have to teach them a lesson for their own good. Equally upset were the agents of the French canal company, who saw the promised $40 million escaping their grasp, and those residents of Panama who looked forward to the prosperity that the canal would bring and feared that it would now be built in Nicaragua.

In the end, the French agents, the Panamanians, and Theodore Roosevelt combined to assure a Panama route. Although they had revolted against Colombia in the past, the Panamanians had never succeeded in gaining their independence. Now, encouraged and financed by the French canal company, they rose once again. Fortunately for the insurgents, the U.S.S. *Nashville,* an American warship, had conveniently arrived just a day before the revolt broke out and was docked at Colón on Panama's Caribbean coast. Inspired by this scarcely disguised support, the rebels quickly overcame the feeble Colombian military forces and in a matter of hours proclaimed an independent Panamanian republic. To no one's surprise, Roosevelt immediately concluded an accord with the new government. For the same financial terms offered Colombia, the United States was granted the right to build a canal through a ten-mile-wide zone where it would exercise "all the rights, power, and authority" it would possess "if it were the sovereign of the territory."

With the political details out of the way, work on the gigantic engineering project began. Using mammoth steam shovels and thousands of black laborers drawn from the Caribbean islands, American engineers chopped their way across the isthmus. Hundreds of lives were lost to yellow fever until Colonel William C. Gorgas wiped out the mosquito-breeding places at Colón and Panama City and eliminated the disease from the country. On August 15, 1914, the interocean canal connecting the Atlantic and Pacific, the dream of three centuries, was formally opened to world shipping.

Roosevelt also acted aggressively elsewhere in Latin America. Many of the smaller Latin American countries, he felt, by defaulting on their debts and failing to control internal political turmoil, were inviting European nations to intervene in the Western Hemisphere to protect their citizens and their investments. By American reasoning, if the Caribbean and Central American republics expected the United States to defend them against the European powers they could not expect their protector to ignore their misdeeds. In 1904, when several European nations threatened to blockade the Dominican Republic until it paid its debts, Roosevelt decided to lay down the law. In his "corollary" to the Monroe Doctrine, he announced that "chronic wrongdoing" by Latin American countries or political "impotence" that resulted in serious disorder might force the United States to "exercise . . . police power, and compel it to intervene in the offending nation's internal affairs." While the Roosevelt Corollary prevented takeovers by European nations, it also gave the United States an excuse to intrude at will into Latin American affairs.

The Open Door in China.

The United States often took advantage of its power to overawe its weaker hemispheric neighbors, but its role in the Far East was, on the whole, more benign. After acquiring Hawaii and the Philippines, the nation eagerly awaited the opening of the supposedly vast China market. It failed to materialize. In those years the Chinese people neither wanted the major American exports nor could they pay for them. Nevertheless, Americans remained hopeful and were anxious to prevent China from being carved up by Japan and the major European powers into exclusive "spheres of influence" where others could not trade. But American interest in China went beyond trade. Educated Americans were fascinated by China's ancient civilization, art, and customs. Many also considered the Celestial Empire a promising field for Christian missionary effort. The first American missionaries had arrived in China before the Civil War, bringing Western science and learning along with the Protestant faith. However much they deplored Chinese "heathenism," the missionaries deeply sympathized with the long-suffering Chinese people and conveyed their compassionate feelings to pious churchgoers at home. By the end of the nineteenth century millions of Americans considered China an arena for Christian benevolence, not for crass economic and political exploitation.

For many years American policy toward China was marked by this combination of self-interest and compassion. After China's defeat by Japan in the First Sino-Japanese War (1894–1895), the great powers renewed their demands for political and economic concessions. The United States, which had no designs on Chinese territory, feared that the Western nations would completely carve up the decaying empire, destroying Chinese sovereignty while excluding the United States commercially. Encouraged by the British, Secretary of State John Hay in 1899 sent notes to the major colonial powers asking for assurances that they would not demand special trading privileges in China. Most gave Hay evasive answers, but he chose to interpret these as acceptance of his "open door" principle, which rejected exclusive "spheres of influence" and held that all nations must be free to trade throughout China. In 1900, following suppression of the violently antiforeign Chinese Boxers by an international army, the United States converted the principle of economic parity into one of defending the Chinese nation against European annexation. In a circular letter of July 1900 Hay declared that it was "the policy of the United States government" to "bring about . . . peace to China" and to "preserve Chinese territorial and administrative entity. . . ."

The Open Door policy was a perfect mirror of American ambivalence. Unprepared by its history and traditions to take up the burdens and responsibilities of blatant overseas colonialism, the United States sought to protect its share of the Chinese market in some less costly way than political control. At the same time, Americans sincerely sympathized with the Chinese people and sought to preserve Chinese sovereignty. But whatever the motives, the concern of the United States for an independent China would serve on more than one occasion to keep it from being dismembered by the European colonial powers and an expansionist Japan.

Conclusions

Many elements contributed to the outward thrust of the post-Civil War generation. The impulse that had carried the American people 3,000 miles across the North American continent continued to operate even after the Pacific was reached. Much as the earlier expansion had been fortified by the quest for gain, so the later one was reinforced by the desire for trade and expanded investment opportunities. Altruism, however misguided and arrogant, also influenced America's interest in foreign lands. Americans continued to believe that they had unique gifts—political freedom and material abundance—to offer other peoples. The American role in China, Hawaii, and the Philippines, in particular, expressed this mixture of the crass and the idealistic.

But post-Civil War expansionism also contained new ingredients. The desire to achieve great-power status by collecting colonies on the model of the western European imperialists augmented the older Manifest Destiny. So did the fear that now that continental expansion had ended, the United States must seek out new territory or cease to prosper and grow. It is not true, as some believed, that American capitalism could only survive if fed by imperial expansion. But that does not mean that some contemporaries did not hold to something that resembles this idea.

The aggressiveness of the American government, particularly toward Latin America, reflected the new mood of big-power assertiveness: Great powers cut a wide swath in their own neighborhoods; they did not allow themselves to be defied by troublesome pygmies. And yet Americans never wore the mantle of imperialism very comfortably. A rich nation of continental proportions, the United States inevitably threw its weight around, but less so than nations that had fewer natural resources and smaller home markets. The United States was also more restricted by its traditional liberal anticolonial values and by its fears that overseas acquisitions could not be incorporated into the Union as equal partners with the older states. In the new century just opening, the world would see many further instances of American forbearance and even generosity toward weaker nations combined with manifestations of self-serving interest, and would be puzzled by the inconsistent course of the Great Republic.

ONLINE RESOURCES

The Age of Imperialism *http://smplanet.com/imperialism/toc.html* Through narrative text, maps, and illustrations, this site lends insight into American expansion into the Pacific as well as involvement in Latin America.

William Jennings Bryan: "The Paralyzing Influence of Imperialism" *http://mtholyoke.edu/acad/intrel/bryan.htm* Offering a negative view of American imperialism, Bryan's speech to the 1900 Democratic Convention contended that American expansionism was against the very nature of a republican democracy.

A War in Perspective: Public Appeals, Memory, and the Spanish-American Conflict *http://www.nypl.org/research/chss/epo/spanexhib/page_2.html* This exhibit site examines the public sentiment about the Spanish-American War from the viewpoints of Cuban, Spanish, and U.S. citizens.

22

Progressivism

What Were Its Roots and What Were Its Accomplishments?

1874	Women's Christian Temperance Union established
1890	Jane Addams's Hull House opens in Chicago; National American Woman Suffrage Association is formed in a merger of two older groups
1892	Grover Cleveland elected president
1895	Booker T. Washington's Atlanta Compromise Address
1896	*Plessy v. Ferguson* legalizes segregation; William McKinley elected president
1899	The National Consumers' League is formed
1900–06	Governor La Follette of Wisconsin establishes state primaries and taxes railroads
1901	McKinley assassinated; Theodore Roosevelt becomes president
1902	Roosevelt's antitrust campaign begins
1903	Congress establishes the Department of Commerce and Labor and the Bureau of Corporations
1904	Roosevelt elected president
1905	W. E. B. Du Bois launches the Niagara Movement
1905–07	Most states limit or outlaw child labor
1906	Congress passes Hepburn Act, Meat Inspection Act, and Pure Food and Drug Act
1908	William H. Taft elected president; Aldrich-Vreeland Emergency Currency Act
1909	Ballinger-Pinchot controversy; The Payne-Aldrich Tariff; National Association for the Advancement of Colored People (NAACP) founded
1910	The Mann-Elkins Act; The Mann Act
1911	*Standard Oil Co. v. United States*
1912	Woodrow Wilson elected president
1913	The Sixteenth and Seventeenth amendments allow a federal income tax and direct election of senators; The Federal Reserve Act; Underwood Tariff
1914	The Federal Trade Commission Act; The Clayton Antitrust Act; World War I begins in Europe
1916	Wilson sponsors the Federal Farm Loan Act, the Kern-McGillicuddy Act for federal employees, and the Keating-Owen Act limiting child labor

"Slowly, as the new century began its first decade," wrote editor William Allen White from the vantage of 1946, "I saw the Great Light. Around me in that day scores of young leaders in American politics and public affairs were seeing what I saw, feeling what I felt. . . . All over the land in a score of states and more, young men in both parties were taking leadership by attacking things as they were in that day."

White's "Great Light" was the urge to change American society that historians have called the Progressive movement. In the years between the beginning of the new century and America's entrance into World War I, men and women of all national backgrounds and all classes felt the yearning to improve life for themselves and for their fellow citizens. They did not join any one organization; they had no single leader, no neat, well-defined set of goals. Their support of change was not always unselfish. Most groups—whether intellectuals, professionals, wage earners, or farmers—understandably placed their own concerns first or believed their own concerns were truly everybody's. Nevertheless, many progressives displayed broad social sympathies, encompassing many groups besides their own.

The new views first appeared in the cities during the 1890s. A little later they came to the statehouses. Finally, about 1904 or 1905, they arrived in Washington, D.C. When they did, they were given the name "Progressivism," and they helped transform the nation. How can we explain this sudden passion for reform? What made so many people conclude that things had to change? What did the reformers want, and what did they accomplish?

Uncertainties

Fear of Bigness. If any single concern united the forces of reform during the opening years of the twentieth century, it was the fear of uncontrolled private economic power. The sense of being at the mercy of great aggregations of private wealth and privilege was not new; it was as old as the republic and had never ceased to affect political perceptions. In each of the early instances—whether Jeffersonian, Jacksonian, or Populist—the opposition to "monopolists" had come predominantly from small producers such as farmers, independent artisans, and small manufacturers. That was inevitable; until late in the nineteenth century most Americans had belonged to one of these economically defined groups. By the 1880s and 1890s the nation had spawned a large class of urban wage earners, salaried professionals, and white-collar workers, but by and large they had refused to join the populistic movements of the period; it had been the small farmers of the South and West who had formed the backbone of the People's Party and the free-silver movement.

Progressivism, the new, early-twentieth-century attack on concentrated power and wealth, originated in, and found its chief support among, groups that Populism and Bryanism had failed to ignite. Rural Americans would consider themselves progressives in these years, but the movement would be led by middle-class urbanites widely supported by the city working class. What had happened in one short decade to change the perceptions of millions of city dwellers, blue collar and middle class?

The Growth of Trusts. One plausible answer is that the attitude change was sparked by the speed-up of business consolidation during the closing years of the nineteenth century. In the generation following the Civil War the nation's economic integration was brought to swift completion by the final wave of railroad building. As the cost of shipping goods to distant customers declined, local markets evolved into regional markets and then into national markets. Firms grew larger as they sought to serve growing numbers of customers, many now living in the burgeoning cities. For a time business competition intensified. And for a time prices dropped. However beneficial to consumers, this regime did not please producers and, as we saw, they tried to stabilize market shares and prices through pools, trusts, mergers, and other arrangements to avoid "cutthroat" competition.

Late-nineteenth-century business consolidation came in two bursts. The first began in the 1870s and culminated in the formation of the Standard Oil Company. It was this round that had spurred the anxiety of the Grangers and the Alliances. It ended abruptly with the panic of 1893 and the depression that followed. Then, beginning in 1896, the merger movement revived, primarily among industries that catered to the exploding urban market. As midwifed by J. P. Morgan and other investment bankers, this second merger wave came to a grand climax between 1898 and 1902. In those five years 2,500 large firms combined into huge ones. In 1901 the process reached its peak with the formation of United States Steel, the world's first billion-dollar corporation.

Americans watched the consolidation process with apprehension. Trusts seemed to be everywhere. In 1904 financial analyst John Moody counted 318 trusts, with total capital of over $7.2 billion, "covering every line of productive industry in the United States."

The New Urban Consumers.   Almost all Americans deplored the trend toward ever-greater concentrations of private economic power. But to urbanites the trusts appeared particularly threatening. Many city people remained producers who turned out manufactured goods in small or large shops. But many others were now white-collar workers—professionals, clerks, accountants, office workers—whose connections with a physical product were indirect at best. To an increasing extent urban Americans, especially those of the middle class, viewed themselves more as consumers than producers.

When most Americans were farmers they had been able to supply many of their own needs. They had slaughtered their own hogs and cattle, raised their own fruits and vegetables, and produced their own eggs and milk. Even urban folk had been less dependent on others in the simpler days before 1900. They had been closer to the country suppliers of their needs, and these needs had been less complicated. Through most of the nineteenth century average Americans had burned wood from their own woodlots in their stoves, read by candlelight or firelight, communicated with their friends face to face, gone to work on foot, and doctored themselves with nostrums from their own gardens or from a local medical practitioner. In all these matters they had relied on themselves or on someone they knew well personally.

For city dwellers in 1900 this self-reliance was a thing of the past. The food they consumed, for instance, was now supplied by remote corporations—meat-packers, canners, millers, and other food processors whose products could not be trusted. Dishonest meat packers could and did doctor spoiled beef to make it appear fresh. Firms disguised lard and suet as butter and packed turnips in syrup to be sold as canned peaches or pears.

Nor was this all. City dwellers now relied on public utilities to light their houses, fuel their stoves, and transport them from their homes to their offices and shops. But the gas and lighting companies had legal monopolies through franchises and could squeeze customers as they pleased. The "traction" companies that ran the streetcars and elevated railroads corrupted city officials to secure exclusive charters, and then provided poor and expensive service to riders.

Personal health care too now frequently depended on others. When ill, city dwellers counted on over-the-counter "patent medicines"—bottled or packaged concoctions they saw advertised in the newspapers and magazines. These were generally useless and sometimes harmful potions, fortified with alcohol or even opium. Nevertheless, the drug companies claimed their value for every disease known, and for several invented by the patent medicine purveyors themselves.

In short, urban consumers were at the mercy of others and were vulnerable to deception and exploitation without precedent. As the economist Richard Ely expressed it in 1905: "Under our present manner of living, how many of my vital interests must I entrust to others! Nowadays the water main is my well, the trolley car is my carriage, the banker's safe is my stocking, and the policeman's billy is my fist."

Dependence and deception were bad enough, but consumers of this period also faced remorselessly rising prices. For a whole generation after 1897 the nation would escape major depressions such as those of the 1870s and 1890s. But the income gains that Americans made in these years were partly offset by the steady inflation that reversed the trend of the previous decades. Beginning about 1902, consumer prices started a steady climb that did not end until the early 1930s. Deflation following the Civil War had hurt farmers and other producers; now inflation hurt consumers. Everyone who went to the corner grocery store or butcher or who paid a utility bill or bought a load of coal soon became painfully aware of the new trend. Who was responsible for the "high cost of living"? The answer seemed inescapable to many: the monopolies.

The new consumerism was a particularly effective political glue. As one journalist pointed out in 1913: "In America to-day the unifying . . . force is the common interest of the citizen as a consumer of wealth. . . . " The producers were "highly differentiated," but "all men, women, and children who buy shoes (except only the shoe manufacturer) are interested in cheap, good shoes." Because consumers were "overwhelmingly superior in numbers than producers," consumer consciousness, this writer was certain, formed the basis for a political revolt of vast proportions that the politicians would not fail to note.

Besides their exposed position as consumers, urban people also confronted the special hazards of the city environment. Large cities provided men and women with more opportunities to learn, grow, and amuse themselves. But for wage earners they were also places where crime, vice, loneliness, and poverty flourished. In the 1870s and 1880s, as we have seen, the city poor had often turned to the political machines to protect them against the hard edges of urban life; by the 1890s many had come to believe that urban reform might be in their interests. The urban middle class, meanwhile, saw city government as inefficient and wasteful.

Why could not cities be run like businesses, though obviously ones dedicated to the public interest rather than to profit? Dissatisfaction with city government further fueled the desire for progressive reform.

Farmers, Blacks, and Women.   The addition of urbanites to the ranks of the nation's uneasy and discontented citizens may well have been the crucial trigger to Progressivism. But farmers still faced many difficult problems. Railroad officials and farm machinery manufacturers remained arrogant and arbitrary. Credit for farmers was still in short supply. Country life continued to fall behind city life in its amenities. The voice of dissatisfied rural Americans would at times imbue Progressivism with a strong agrarian tinge reminiscent of Populism.

In these years many women, especially urban middle-class women, found their lives constrained in ways that no longer seemed acceptable. By now there were thousands of women high school and college graduates, but there were still only limited professional outlets for their talents and energies. As late as 1910 women in only Wyoming, Colorado, Utah, and Idaho could vote; several other states had rejected referenda to establish woman suffrage. Many educated women with unused talents and energies joined women's clubs and spent their time discussing art, high culture, and great ideas. Women were active in church affairs. A few middle-class or wealthy women also did "charity work" among the poor. Yet as the new century opened, many talented women felt that society was not properly using their skills and brains, and it made them receptive to social and political change.

Black Americans, too, found much to complain of as the new century dawned. In the South blacks were deprived of voting rights either by intimidation or by ingenious legal dodges. All through Dixie, where in 1900 two-thirds of the country's 10 million black citizens still lived, the system of legal segregation prevailed. In many ways, in fact, southern "Jim Crow" was more powerfully entrenched as the twentieth century began than at the end of Reconstruction. Worst of all was the brutal regime of lynchings. Each year blacks accused of criminal offenses were taken from local jails and maimed, burned, or hanged by white mobs unwilling to wait for the slow processes of law. From 1900 to 1920 there were on average 75 lynchings a year, mostly in the South. Blacks were better treated in the North. Few were lynched; they could vote in national and local elections. But unofficial segregation, especially in housing, and discrimination in jobs, college admissions, and professional education were commonplace. And even African-Americans in the North did not fully escape violence. In Springfield, Illinois, in 1908 a white mob went on a rampage, attacking blacks and destroying black business property. Order had to be restored by 5,000 state militia.

Until now most of the black community had accepted the leadership of educator Booker T. Washington. Born a slave in 1856, Washington had risen to prominence in the 1890s as a protégé of southern whites. White philanthropists had sent him to Hampton Institute in Virginia, one of the few all-black institutions of higher education. In 1881 they chose him to head a school for black youths at Tuskegee, Alabama. Washington made Tuskegee into a flourishing institution emphasizing industrial education, modeled on the work-ethic, self-help principles of Hampton. In 1895 he achieved national prominence with an electrifying address at the Atlanta Cotton States Exposition. Speaking to a predominantly white audience, he proposed that blacks accept disenfranchisement and racial segregation in exchange for the right to advance economically and be secure in their persons and property. This so-called Atlanta Compromise immediately impressed influential white southerners. Opposed equally to disorder and black equality, they saw it as a formula for a peaceful status quo. Thereafter the white establishment made Washington the "spokesman" for his race and the quasi-official dispenser of white philanthropy and political patronage to blacks.

Washington's Atlanta Compromise acquiesced in segregation and appeared to encourage black passivity in the face of mistreatment. But in truth, while projecting a public image of meekness, behind the scenes Washington quietly fought segregation, lynching, and debt peonage. When President Theodore Roosevelt gave dishonorable discharges in 1906 to three companies of black soldiers for refusing to identify the leaders of a riot in Brownsville, Texas, Washington went to the White House to intercede for the wronged men, though without success.

At all events, as the twentieth century began, a new generation of college-educated black urban leaders appeared, determined to make white Americans grant black citizens their constitutional and God-given rights.

Some historians have seen Progressivism as a predominantly middle-class movement. Yet it is clear that it recruited recent immigrants, factory workers, and slum dwellers as well. In fact, for a time almost all Americans came to consider themselves progressives in some sense. Progressivism by about 1910 was definitely "in the air," a fact that helps to explain its complexity and its seeming inconsistencies. No coalition so large could have been all of a piece or definable in a single sentence.

The Opinion Makers

But we cannot reduce Progressivism to a list of group fears and discontents. The Progressive movement owed much to the anti-formalistic intellectual currents that had appeared in the last decades of the nineteenth century. Many of the new thinkers—including Oliver Wendell Holmes, Jr., John Dewey, and Charles Beard—were also reformers. It was through their intellectual challenges to the social pieties of the day, however, rather than their personal activities that they made their contribution to change.

The Muckrakers.   Contributing more directly to the timing of the new reform surge was a group of talented editors, journalists, and essayists known as the muckrakers who aimed dazzling spotlights into every dark cranny of American political and social life to reveal a multitude of abuses. They owed their name to Theodore Roosevelt, who often sympathized with their aims but considered their passion for uncovering dirt and wrongdoing excessive. TR likened them to a morose character in John Bunyan's "Pilgrim's Progress" who "continued to rake to himself the filth of the floor" even when offered a "celestial crown."

The hard-hitting newspaper or magazine exposé was not invented in the Progressive Era. Yet it was not until after 1900—when lower printing costs, the new mass audience educated by the public high schools, and the capacity to produce long runs of magazines cheaply and quickly, all came together—that true exposé journalism appeared.

Samuel S. McClure, an ebullient but shrewd Irish-American, was the first publisher to take advantage of the new opportunity. McClure's instinct for profitable journalism was sound, if at times disconcerting. He would have paid well, one wit observed, for a "snappy life of Christ." McClure did not consciously intend to create a new kind of journalism; he wanted to sell magazines. But his practice of hiring talented writers and reporters to investigate various aspects of American life produced a media revolution. In October 1902 *McClure's* carried an article by a young Californian, Lincoln Steffens, describing the efforts of a young district attorney to prosecute the corrupt St. Louis Democratic machine. The November issue carried the first installment of a series by Ida Tarbell exposing the monopolistic practices of the Standard Oil Company. Early in 1903 Ray Stannard Baker's article on unfair labor practices appeared. The public took notice of these articles, and McClure was soon selling more magazines than he had ever believed possible. Other publishers, observing their rival's success, rushed to hire men and women with a talent for uncovering wrongdoing and writing about it in a colorful and exciting way.

What followed was the greatest outpouring of crusading journalism in American history. Eventually the muckrakers probed into every national abuse: uncontrolled sale of patent medicines; the shady doings of stock market manipulators; businessmen's efforts to corrupt legislatures, city councils, and Congress; the harsh treatment of labor; the disgusting and unsanitary conditions in the meatpacking industry; the profiteering of the "beef trust"; the exploitation of child workers; the savage treatment of defenseless young women by purveyors of vice; the behind-the-scenes effort of the "money trust" to manipulate the entire American economy. Some of the muckrakers' output does not stand up to careful rechecking. But it touched the contemporary public's exposed nerves, confirmed its uneasiness, and gave direction to its fears.

Progressivism Enters Politics

The Cult of Efficiency in City Government.   The first expressions of progressivism appeared at the local level. In the cities the "reform with a heart" that emerged in the 1890s (discussed in Chapter 18) was one aspect of the new political mood. Later, a group of city reformers emerged with somewhat different goals and a different clientele. Most of these were professionals—engineers, lawyers, doctors, teachers, journalists—who believed that cities were much like large business firms and could be run effectively if subject to scientific management principles. Their motto, and their god, was efficiency.

This "cult of efficiency" reflected the growing prestige of science and technology in these years. In the view of the efficiency reformers there was no Democratic or Republican way to clean the streets or provide police protection or pure water. City government, accordingly, should be headed by nonpartisan "managers" or "commissioners" who would run them on scientific and business principles designed to provide good value for the taxpayers' money.

In the 1890s the new city reformers organized the National Municipal Reform League and formulated a model city charter, which they hoped cities and state legislatures would adopt. Their first actual success came in 1901 when Galveston, Texas—following a catastrophic hurricane—adopted the commission plan. City government was turned over to a board of five commissioners chosen on a non-partisan basis and at-large, rather than by wards, to eliminate old-fashioned politics from the selection process. The board combined the role of mayor and city council in one body. By merging functions and by eliminating partisan politics, the commissioners could run city government like an efficient business. Still another idea was the city manager scheme first adopted in Staunton, Virginia, in 1908. City managers were professionals selected by an elected city council and paid to manage the city much as a corporation might hire an executive to run the firm. By the 1920s several dozen cities, usually small or middle-sized, had adopted one or the other of the new municipal government schemes.

The Social Progressives.   The Progressive movement reached beyond city hall, down into the neighborhoods and slums. There men and women dedicated to changing the urban environment established networks of neighborhood voluntary associations designed to improve the lives of the poor. These "social" progressives formed the most militant wing of the Progressive movement. Many were inspired by the social gospel of Walter Rauschenbusch or the Christian socialism of Washington Gladden. They were for the most part recruited from among the idealistic young people who poured from the secondary schools and colleges in the last years of the nineteenth century. Particularly prominent among them were young college women who sought to use their skills, education, and energies for something more fulfilling than the self-improvement of women's clubs. Many of these young people became voluntary charity workers or took up the new profession of "social work." An especially dedicated contingent went to live in settlement houses in the noisome slums that dominated the cities' centers.

Settlement houses were places where slum children could go for recreation and entertainment; where mothers could learn about nutrition, scientific child care, and household management; and where fathers could learn vocational skills, improve their English, prepare for citizenship, and discuss city or community problems. Beginning with the Neighborhood Guild on New York's Lower East Side and Hull House in Chicago, settlements sprang up during the 1890s in all the major cities. Hull House, under the leadership of Jane Addams, and New York's Henry Street Settlement, run by Lillian Wald, were the most prominent, but there were scores of others in every large city. Most of the people who used the settlements were European immigrants and their children, but the settlement workers were also concerned with the problems of black city dwellers. Frances Kellor of New York's College Settlement helped organize the National League for the Protection of Negro Women after she discovered how young black rural women were lured to the cities by promises of good jobs and then harshly exploited by employers or forced into prostitution. Another white social worker, Mary White Ovington, established a settlement in a New York black slum.

The settlements soon became springboards of social reform. In Chicago Jane Addams and her Hull House colleagues worked for the election of reform politicians who dared to challenge the machines. Addams also supported improved tenement housing and better educational and recreational opportunities for the urban working class. She and her counterparts in other communities regularly joined in citywide efforts to eliminate vice and reduce crime.

Women's clubs too became sources of reform in neighborhoods and cities. The clubs were especially active in the fight for honest city government, but middle-class women also took up consumers' issues and worked to help the urban poor. In 1899 a group of upper-middle-class women established the National Consumer's League, which threatened boycotts of employers who did not adhere to fair employment practices. The league also labored to improve community health through licensing of food vendors, and supported measures to protect urban consumers against retail fraud.

Progressivism in the States.
Only so much could be accomplished on the neighborhood or city level, however, and in the end the reformers had to turn to the state legislatures to achieve their goals. Until the 1890s state governments all too often had been little more than junior partners of large business corporations. Legislators often took money from businesspeople and did their bidding without concern for the public interest. For years reformers had denounced the "unholy alliance" of state government and big business characteristic of the Gilded Age. Their voices went unheeded. Then the panic of 1893 exposed many of the flaws in the country's economy and pointed up the dangers of unregulated economic power as never before.

The revelation came with particular force to the people of Wisconsin, a state dominated by a Republican machine that had always worked hand-in-glove with the major corporations. The depression of 1893–1897 severely jolted Wisconsin's economy. By the winter of 1893–1894 more than a third of the state's wage earners were unemployed. Meanwhile, the hard-pressed utility firms refused to pay their taxes and raised their rates to city consumers to offset declining revenue. To make matters worse, the distress of the unemployed and consumers was accompanied by revelations that a clique of bankers had been embezzling funds from depositors and stockholders.

No Wisconsinite better understood the growing public outrage than the ambitious young Republican lawyer Robert M. La Follette. As governor after 1900 La Follette made Wisconsin the nation's "laboratory" for progressive lawmaking. His first reform measure was a state "primary" system that allowed the voters to bypass the party bosses and nominate their own candidates for state office. He next pushed through a railroad tax that shifted some of the burden of supporting government from farmers and wage earners to the previously untaxed railroad corporations and their stockholders. He later supported a state railroad commission to regulate the rates that the railroads could charge.

In 1902 La Follette ran for reelection. In his first successful campaign he had stressed his Republicanism, albeit a reform variety. This time he appealed for nonpartisan support and got it. Virtually all Wisconsin citizens, not just Republicans, by now feared the power of the "interests." The sense of insecurity in the face of irresponsible wealth cut across ethnic lines, and many Catholic voters abandoned their earlier allegiance to the Democratic party to vote for the reformer. La Follette's resounding reelection victory helped eclipse the old party politics of the Gilded Age.

Wisconsin continued to be a center of progressive reform even after "Battle Bob" went to Washington as United States senator. Under his successors, the state adopted two new instruments of "direct democracy." The first, the initiative, was a procedure enabling voters to introduce legislation without waiting for legislators to do so. The referendum allowed voters to accept or reject, by a direct ballot, certain laws passed by the legislature. Progressives hoped that these innovations would allow the voters to bypass or overrule legislatures controlled by powerful economic interests and gain a greater say in the political process. The state also established a public utility commission to protect consumers against gouging by gas companies and power and light companies. Working closely with social scientists from the University of Wisconsin, successive state administrations enacted a workers' compensation act for injured or disabled wage earners and a state income tax to make wealthier citizens bear a larger part of the community's tax load. They established a board of public affairs to protect vital natural resources from corporate exploiters. All told, under the "Wisconsin Idea," ordinary citizens, it was hoped, would be protected against the hazards of an exploitive business-dominated economy through the agency of a benevolent and responsive state government.

The Wisconsin experiment captured the attention of millions of Americans. Other states soon adopted Wisconsin's program. Much of the new legislation was designed to protect citizens in general. A good deal of it was aimed specifically at weaker groups in society. Beginning with Illinois in 1899, for example, many states established special courts for juvenile offenders. Between 1905 and 1907 two-thirds of the states enacted laws limiting the hours of child labor or outlawing paid labor for young children. Both juvenile offenders reform, and child labor restrictions were part of a larger "child saving" movement, which also included the goals of making widely available germ-free milk and play facilities. Working women, too, were increasingly surrounded by state regulations intended to prevent employer exploitation and abuse. The states also limited the working hours of men employed in exhausting or hazardous occupations such as baking and mining. More and more states joined Wisconsin in adopting workers' compensation insurance schemes, though, in part, this was at the behest of business firms increasingly beset by lawsuits instigated by injured workers. As an expression of the most advanced social vision there was even talk of publicly funded health and unemployment insurance.

Southern Progressivism.

In 1912 Robert La Follette remarked that he "did not know of any progressive sentiment of any progressive legislation in the South." But he was wrong. Beginning early in the century, progressive southern governors launched attacks against railroads, utility companies, insurance firms, and other business groups that seemed to be exploiting the region and its citizens. In Alabama Braxton Bragg Comer, a wealthy Birmingham manufacturer, banker, and landowner, expanded the authority of the state railroad commission and beat down passenger and freight rates. In Arkansas, Attorney General Jeff Davis initiated scores of suits against insurance companies, tobacco firms, and oil companies, charging them with unfair, monopolistic practices and price-fixing.

Southern progressives were often openly anti-Yankee, aiming their sharpest barbs at "Wall Street" and "foreign"—that is, northeastern—corporations, which were accused of sucking profits out of the region while giving back nothing in return. At times skeptical southern progressives twitted their colleagues for reluctance to attack such home-grown abuses as child labor, when doing so might discourage the growth of local industry. But the South had its advanced social reformers, too. The Southern Sociological Congress—composed of ministers, urban humanitarians, and middle-class clubwomen—worked to improve the lot of the region's children, the handicapped, consumers, and prisoners. The congress could claim credit for only a small amount of advanced social legislation, but it brought together men and women of like mind and helped to create the "southern liberal" type, whose efforts would help transform the region in later years.

Black Americans.   The Sociological Congress worked to improve race relations, but by and large southern progressivism was "for whites only." A number of prominent southern politicians—James K. Vardaman and Theodore G. Bilbo of Mississippi, for example—managed to combine sympathy for white yeomen farmers exploited by corporations with a violent antiblack rhetoric that poisoned the racial atmosphere. Even southern primary laws often injured black southerners. Arguing that the conservative southern Bourbons used the black vote to reinforce privilege, southern progressives often excluded blacks from the primaries.

Meanwhile, as progressive laws poured from southern state legislatures, the "Jim Crow" system, which kept the races strictly segregated, expanded into every corner of the region's daily life. Blacks and a few white liberals tried to check the process through legal action. But the Supreme Court ruling in the landmark *Plessy v. Ferguson* (1896) decision that segregation did not violate the equal protection clause of the Fourteenth Amendment as long as the facilities provided each race were equal in quality, frustrated their efforts. Far worse, lynching continued and even grew as a savage weapon of terror to keep southern blacks in "their place."

A new generation of African-American leaders blamed black acquiescence for the South's continued oppression of its black citizens. To a new group of urban black intellectuals Booker T. Washington's willingness to surrender fundamental constitutional rights and to consent to permanent second-class citizenship came to seem intolerable. Led by the Boston editor William Monroe Trotter, T. Thomas Fortune of the *New York Age,* by the Jacksonville minister J. Milton Waldron, and, most prominently, by W. E. B. Du Bois, they launched a movement to make blacks equal citizens of the republic.

An early advocate of black liberation from white economic and cultural domination, a Ph.D. in history from Harvard, the Massachusetts-born Du Bois insisted that black Americans must run their own businesses, provide their own professional services, write their own books, and create their own art. In 1903, in *The Souls of Black Folk,* he attacked Washington as a man who had "practically accepted the alleged inferiority of the Negro," and urged prominent black Americans to cease flattering the white South and to speak out on the race issue.

In 1905 Du Bois and Trotter convened a meeting at Fort Erie, Ontario, near Niagara Falls, to raise a militant voice against black oppression. The convention issued a manifesto demanding true manhood suffrage, the end of racial discrimination, the freedom of blacks to criticize American society, and free access for black Americans to liberal education as well as to vocational training. Incorporated as the Niagara Movement, the group continued to meet annually for several years to defend black rights and demand that white America practice its professed principles of equality.

In 1909 the Niagara Movement militants merged with a group of white progressives, including Oswald Garrison Villard, Jane Addams, Clarence Darrow, William Dean Howells, and John Dewey, to establish the National Association for the Advancement of Colored People (NAACP). The NAACP quickly came to the forefront of the battle to defend the legal and constitutional rights of blacks wherever they were threatened or denied. By 1914 the NAACP had 6,000 members, mostly middle-class blacks in the cities. However small at first, the modern movement for racial equality was now underway.

Women Progressives.
Women were among the most active workers for social reform before and during the Progressive Era. Nowhere were they more effective than in the cause of temperance.

The battle to end the social and moral evil of drunkenness had engaged the attention of American women for many years. In 1874 female reformers organized the Women's Christian Temperance Union (WCTU), which allied itself after 1900 with the predominantly male Anti-Saloon League. Together the two organizations propagandized in the schools and churches against alcohol and lobbied for state laws outlawing the production, sale, and consumption of beer, wine, and whiskey. In later years the temperance movement would often be associated with social and political conservatism, but in the early years of the twentieth century temperance reformers like Frances Willard and Anna Shaw were champions of child-labor laws and other progressive legislation.

No cause, however, engaged the energies of women reformers so completely as the issue of suffrage for women themselves. For decades women suffragists had been struggling for the right to vote. But most men—and many women—dismissed women suffrage as a violation of nature and a threat to the family. The battle proved long and hard. During the Gilded Age, Susan B. Anthony and Elizabeth Cady Stanton, both pre-Civil War suffrage leaders, working through the National Woman Suffrage Association, scored some successes in the West. By 1896 Wyoming, Utah, Colorado, and Idaho had granted women the vote. Meanwhile, a more conservative group, including Lucy Stone and Julia Ward Howe, had formed the American Woman Suffrage Association. In 1890 the two organizations merged under the presidency of Stanton as the National American Woman Suffrage Association (NAWSA).

To NAWSA's left was a cluster of "social feminists" who insisted that true gender equality depended on deep changes in women's relations with men, on shifts in the economy, and on alteration of the traditional family. Charlotte Perkins Gilman argued in *Women and Economics* (1898) that women's subordinate economic role had stunted their personalities and damaged their effectiveness as wives and mothers. Crystal Eastman, an active suffragist, also advocated sexual emancipation of women and free dissemination of birth-control information and devices. In 1914, Eastman and Alice Paul, a young Quaker activist, organized the Congressional Union to agitate for a suffrage amendment to the Constitution in place of a state-by-state approach. The new militants adopted the flamboyant protest tactics of English suffragists, which included mass marches, chaining themselves to

Throughout his long life (1868–1963), W. E. B. Du Bois's thinking anticipated developments in black positions on race. The first black to receive a Ph.D. from Harvard, he helped start the Niagara Movement and then the NAACP, advocated Pan-Africanism, lost faith in integration, became a Communist, supported Black Power, and finally moved to Africa.

lampposts, and prison fasts when arrested. In the elections of 1914 and 1916, Paul's group (organized as the National Women's Party in 1916) campaigned to punish the Democrats, the party in power, for failure to support a suffrage amendment.

Progressivism Goes National

Progressivism was at first largely a local political phenomenon. Until about 1900 all was quiet along the Potomac.

In 1898, four months after his much-publicized charge up San Juan Hill in the war with Spain, Theodore Roosevelt was elected governor of New York. Although he had been the hand-picked candidate of Thomas C. Platt, the state's Republican boss, as governor Roosevelt appointed honest men to office and supported bills to tax public utilities. Unhappy with his choice, and anxious to get him out of New York, Platt maneuvered Roosevelt into accepting second place on the 1900 Republican presidential ticket with William McKinley. McKinley and Roosevelt won a landslide victory in 1900 over Democrats William Jennings Bryan and Adlai Stevenson. On September 6, 1901, while on a visit to the Pan-American Exposition in Buffalo, McKinley was shot by Leon Czolgosz, a demented anarchist. The president died a week later. Suddenly, at forty-two, Roosevelt found himself the youngest man yet to occupy the presidential office.

The new president was a remarkable person. A graduate of elite Groton School and Harvard College, "TR" was a highly literate man whose histories, *The Naval*

War of 1812 and *Winning of the West,* though bellicose, can still be read with profit today. He was also a man of frenetic action who forced even the most distinguished guests at his Long Island home, and later at the White House itself, to join him on jogs about the countryside while he shouted his views of politics, art, and economics. Though capable of dashing off reviews, speeches, books, and articles, and holding his own with distinguished scholars, he also enjoyed living with the cowboys of western Dakota and spent long, happy months in the wilds of three continents hunting, exploring, and collecting zoological specimens. TR had a juvenile streak that often led him to snap judgments. One distinguished foreign observer remarked to an American friend: "You know your president is really six." An intense nationalist, Roosevelt identified the United States with virtue and tended to see non-"Anglo-Saxons" as inherently inferior. Despite his failings—or perhaps partly because of them—Roosevelt charmed and delighted the American public, and his personal appeal would rub off on the programs he supported.

Roosevelt's First Term.

The conservative Republican "Old Guard" did not trust Roosevelt. When his name was first proposed for vice president on the 1900 Republican ticket, Senator Mark Hanna warned that if the governor received the nomination, only one life would stand between the country and a "madman." Yet as president TR at first adopted a moderate course. In his first annual message to Congress he recommended a cabinet-level department of commerce and labor to protect labor's rights and to publicize inflated corporate earnings; stronger measures to protect the country's forests and conserve its natural resources; and increased power for the feeble Interstate Commerce Commission to help guarantee fair treatment to shippers. None of this was revolutionary.

Congress eventually gave TR much of what he asked for. In 1902 it passed the Newlands Act, which set aside money from federal land sales in the arid West for dams and canals to irrigate the land (see Chapter 19). In 1903 it established the Department of Commerce and Labor, incorporating a Bureau of Corporations empowered to subpoena information from industry that could then be used for antitrust suits under the Sherman Antitrust Act. That same year Congress passed the Elkins Act outlawing rebates to favored shippers and giving the federal courts the power to issue injunctions ordering railroads to desist from practices that benefited some shippers at the expense of others.

Despite these advances, reform-minded observers considered Roosevelt's initial legislative performance timid. In his executive capacity, however, he proved bolder and startled the nation in 1902 by ordering Attorney General Philander Knox to file suit against the Northern Securities Holding Company for violating the Sherman Antitrust Act.

The Northern Securities Company, put together by J. P. Morgan, James J. Hill, E. H. Harriman, and the Rockefellers, merged most of the railroads in the northwestern corner of the nation into one giant firm. If ever a business trust promised to "restrain trade" and impose an economic stranglehold on millions, this was it. Now, after twelve years, the Sherman Antitrust Act, gutted by the Supreme Court, was finally to be used for its intended purpose. Soon after, Knox also indicted Swift and Company, the Chicago meat-packers, for conspiring with its competitors to fix prices for beef and pork.

The liberal press and the growing contingent of reform-minded citizens hailed the antitrust suits with delight. Morgan, however, was dismayed by the Northern Securities indictment. How could the president act in such an arbitrary way? The uncrowned king of Wall Street did not see himself as a mere private citizen subject to ordinary law, and he told the president: "If we have done anything wrong send your man to my man to fix it up." Roosevelt was not swayed and the suit proceeded to a successful conclusion in 1904, when the Supreme Court ordered the dissolution of the Northern Securities Company.

The Northern Securities case, the Swift suit, and later suits against Standard Oil and the American Tobacco Company gave TR the reputation of being a "trust-buster" and an uncompromising foe of big business. Actually, Roosevelt distinguished between "good trusts" and "bad trusts." The first, though they dominated a given industry, obeyed the law and did not use their power to squeeze the consuming public; the latter exercised no such restraint. "Bad trusts" should be punished, but "good trusts" should be left alone because large firms were more efficient than small ones. Besides, TR felt, the country could not stop the processes of corporate growth. Instead, it could "regulate and control them," to prevent misuse of corporation power. In fact, though he rejected Morgan's overtures, TR was not adamantly opposed to negotiations with big business. In 1905, for example, he struck a bargain with Elbert Gary, board chairman of giant U.S. Steel. If Gary cooperated with a federal investigation of his company's practices, then any wrongdoing detected would be reported to him to correct before the government commenced a suit.

Clearly TR was at most a qualified opponent of big business. He was an equally qualified friend of organized labor. Like most middle-class Americans of the day, the president feared socialism and at times confused it with trade union activity. Yet far more than most of his predecessors, TR believed that unions had a legitimate place as agencies to protect wage earners.

Roosevelt demonstrated his sympathetic attitude early in his first term. In May 1902, after months of arguing with the coal mine owners in eastern Pennsylvania over higher wages, union recognition, and an eight-hour day, members of the United Mine Workers, led by John Mitchell, walked off their jobs. The anthracite coal they produced was the major source of heating fuel along much of the Atlantic Coast. If the strike dragged on through the summer and fall, there would be no coal for winter and millions of householders would suffer. Yet for months the mine owners arrogantly refused to negotiate. In reply to critics, George F. Baer, spokesman for the owners, haughtily declared that the "rights and interests of the laboring man will be protected and cared for not by labor agitators but by the Christian men to whom God has given control of the property rights of the country."

Roosevelt and a majority of the voters were offended by the owners' arrogance and indifference to the public's welfare. In early October, as winter approached, Roosevelt invited the union leaders and the mine operators to the capital to discuss a settlement. At an all-day conference Mitchell declared his willingness to negotiate with the owners directly or to abide by the decision of a presidential arbitration commission—if the owners also agreed to accept its decision. The owners refused to budge. Their spokesman denounced Mitchell personally and demanded that the president use federal troops to end the strike.

Outraged by the stubbornness of the operators and their discourtesy toward Mitchell, Roosevelt threatened to seize the mines and run them as federal property. Faced with the president's determination, the mine owners finally yielded. At another White House conference, representatives of the miners and the operators agreed to a settlement. The men would go back to work; and a five-man commission consisting of an army engineer, a mining engineer, a businessman, a federal judge, and an "eminent sociologist" would be appointed by the president to arbitrate differences. The eminent sociologist Roosevelt selected was a union leader: E. E. Clark of the Brotherhood of Railroad Conductors, a novel choice for the day. The commission granted the miners their wage increase and some reduction in hours, but not union recognition. It was at best a mixed result, but to many Americans it was, as TR described it, a "square deal." The settlement established an important new precedent: From now on, the national government would be a factor to reckon with in disputes between capital and labor that vitally affected consumer interests.

The New Nationalism.   With "a Square Deal for all Americans" as his rallying cry, Roosevelt ran for reelection in 1904. Tired of two defeats in succession under Bryan's banner, the Democrats nominated the conservative New York judge Alton B. Parker to oppose him. The change did not help them. TR won an impressive victory with 56 percent of the popular vote.

Roosevelt soon moved significantly to the left, responding to the changing mood of the American people, as well as to his growing political confidence now that he had been elected president in his own right. By this time a contingent of Republican progressives, including La Follette, Senators Albert Cummins of Iowa, Albert Beveridge of Indiana, Moses Clapp of Minnesota, Joseph Bristow of Kansas, and William E. Borah of Idaho, had arrived in Washington, D.C., from the states where they had long been active in local reform movements. In later years they would be joined by other Republican progressives such as Hiram Johnson of California and George Norris of Nebraska. In addition, an increasing number of Democrats, caught up like their rivals in the surge of reform zeal, were prepared to support legislation to protect the public against "the interests." The opposition promised to be formidable, however. The Republican stand-pat Old Guard—led by Senators Nelson W. Aldrich, Orville Platt, and John C. Spooner—were still powerful and would fiercely resist every attempt to alter the status quo.

Despite the stand-patters, during his second term Roosevelt was able to get some notable progressive legislation on the books. In 1906 he induced Congress to pass the Hepburn Act, for the first time giving a government agency—the Interstate Commerce Commission, in this case—the power to set rates for a private business. The bill allowed the commission to inspect the books of interstate railroads before setting rates and outlawed the practice of issuing free passes with which the railroads had bribed politicians. The bill was not a complete victory for the reformers. The railroads, through Aldrich, succeeded in inserting a provision giving the courts power to overturn commission-set rates. Nevertheless, the law was an important addition to the federal arsenal against business abuses.

Pure Food and Drug Legislation.

Two other important regulatory measures passed in 1906 provided direct federal protection to consumers. For years reformers had attacked irresponsible meat-packers and food processors. In the government itself Dr. Harvey Wiley, chief of the Department of Agriculture's Bureau of Chemistry, had long warred against the patent medicine quacks and demanded that drug preparations be labeled to show their contents. Wiley supplied most of the data for "The Great American Fraud," a sensational muckraking article on the drug companies by Samuel Hopkins Adams, published in *Collier's* in 1905. An even more effective brief for consumer protection came in 1906, when Upton Sinclair published his lurid novel *The Jungle*. Sinclair's description of the filth of the Chicago meat-packing plants, of men falling into the lard vats and being rendered into cooking fat, and of packers injecting spoiled meat with chemicals to improve its appearance and then selling it to city saloons for their free lunch counters revolted the public and turned the stomach of the president himself.

After checking Sinclair's facts, TR threw his support behind a meat inspection bill then in Congress. Although the bad reputation of American beef had hurt their sales abroad, the meat-packers resisted the bill's passage strenuously. Only when the president warned them that he would publish the results of his own investigation of Sinclair's charges did they yield, though not without extracting concessions. The bill that Roosevelt signed into law as the Meat Inspection Act on June 30, 1906, provided for government supervision of sanitary practices in meat-packing plants, but the cost of the inspection would be borne by the treasury. On the same day, the years of agitation for drug regulation also bore fruit when TR approved the Pure Food and Drug Act requiring that the contents of food and drug preparations be described on their labels. Now at least the public could tell what it was getting when it bought "Brown's Iron Bitters" or "Horsford's Acid Phosphate."

Conservation.

Progressives strongly favored policies to protect and conserve the nation's natural resources and endowment.

Their efforts appealed to a wide range of citizens. Lovers of nature considered the unspoiled wilderness a delight in itself, one capable of renewing the soul and the spirit. Led by Scottish-born naturalist John Muir and groups such as the Sierra Club of California, these "preservationists" insisted that the country's natural heritage be protected against any sort of defilement and preserved intact. Another group—the "conservationists"—was more pragmatic in its goals. Led by Chief Forester Gifford Pinchot, a Pennsylvanian trained in forestry and land management, they worshiped efficiency and sought the "best use" of resources. Best-use conservationists of the Pinchot variety believed the natural endowment must be exploited, but exploited rationally, scientifically, so that it would remain available to future generations. They noted the destruction of the buffalo, the disappearance of the enormous Great Lakes forests, the erosion of the soil everywhere, and the neglect of usable resources, and called for scientific resource management. At times the preservationists and the conservationists fought one another, but they also cooperated to battle the great lumber and mining companies, which they accused of putting profit ahead of the nation's long-term interests. At times, too, they found themselves at odds with ranchers and other western groups that resented eastern attempts to interfere with the traditional free-wheeling way they exploited the land.

Both preservationists and conservationists embodied the growing realization, as the nineteenth century closed, that the country's last frontier was rapidly filling in. As we saw, the emerging new sense of finite unspoiled space inspired creation of Yellowstone National Park in 1872. Yellowstone would be the precedent for setting aside other tracts of exceptionally scenic land as permanent recreation areas. In 1890, after strenuous efforts by Muir and other preservationists, Congress created Yosemite National Park in California, embracing one of the most beautiful natural spots in North America. Eventually the United States would create a national park system unequaled in the world. And the conservationist–preservationist impulse to protect resources from exploitation went beyond scenic sites. In 1891, the Forest Reserve Act withdrew acreage in federally owned forests from the public domain and exempted them from private purchase.

As an authority on wildlife and a lover of the outdoors, Roosevelt naturally championed the conservation movement. Closer to Gifford Pinchot than to John Muir, he approved such "best-use" projects as the 1902 Newlands Act. In 1905 he transferred the government's forest reserves from the Department of the Interior to the Department of Agriculture, where Chief Forester Pinchot could supervise their management. Two years later he and Pinchot saved millions of additional acres of public-domain forest and several important power sites from western timber companies by placing them in the forest reserves or designating them as ranger stations. In 1908 the president called a National Conservation Conference of forty-four state governors and hundreds of experts to consider resource-management problems.

The Panic of 1907.   Although the economy generally was healthy during the Progressive Era, in 1907 the country only narrowly averted a serious depression when a major New York bank closed its doors, setting off a wave of panicky deposit withdrawals from other banks. If matters had taken their usual course, the panic would have spread to the stock market and, in the absence of a central bank, would have tripped off a major depression. Fortunately, the combined action of the treasury, which deposited $35 million of the government's surplus in various private banks, and large loans by J. P. Morgan and other private bankers to troubled financial institutions, stopped the panic in its tracks. A business downturn did follow, but it was both brief and shallow.

Morgan and the treasury had saved the day; but in the wake of the scare, Congress considered what could be done to avoid future panics. In 1908 it passed the Aldrich-Vreeland Emergency Currency Act, making $500 million in new currency available to certain national banks that deposited bonds with the treasury, and establishing a congressional commission to investigate the deficiencies in the country's banking system and recommend changes.

Taft's Misfortunes.   Theodore Roosevelt left the White House in March 1909 convinced that William Howard Taft, his hand-picked successor, would carry on in his progressive steps. He had reason to be confident. The 350-pound Taft—a former federal jurist, Commissioner of the Philippines, and secretary of war—had campaigned in 1908 on his predecessor's record. With the popular Teddy behind him, Taft defeated William Jennings Bryan, once again the Democratic candidate.

Affable, well-liked, but ponderous and indolent, Taft did not really want to be president. His was a judicial rather than an executive temperament. At one point he said that if he could be made a common pleas judge in Hamilton County, Ohio, he would be content to remain there all his life. His obesity hampered him. He ate gargantuan meals and then fell asleep at the table even with guests present. It made him a figure of derision.

Taft was pledged to continue TR's progressive policies, but at heart he was a conservative. He and his attorney general, George W. Wickersham, would be reasonably energetic in enforcing the Sherman Antitrust Act, for it was the law of the land. Indeed, Taft brought more suits against trusts than either Roosevelt or Wilson, Taft's progressive successor. But he was at best a timid reformer who refused to dramatize his policies or rally public opinion in their favor. When opposed by the party's Old Guard, Taft usually retreated.

Roosevelt had scarcely left office to go big-game hunting in Africa when the new president managed to alienate the progressives in his own party, turning them into fierce opponents. Taft's problems with the Republican "insurgents" began when, in fulfillment of a campaign pledge, he asked Congress to consider lowering tariffs. By 1909 tariff revision seemed long overdue. With brief and minor exceptions, taxes on foreign imports had risen steadily since the Civil War. Reformers charged they had been costly to the American consumer. The Dingley Tariff of 1897 had pushed import duties to their highest level in history and had inflated the price of everything the public wore, ate, and used. Indeed, some critics insisted that the Dingley Tariff explained the rising prices that Americans had been experiencing since the turn of the century. To make matters worse, they said, the high tariff was the "mother of trusts," encouraging the great industrial combinations that further gouged the public.

TR chooses his successor. Carrying the mountainous William Howard Taft on his shoulder this way would have been quite a feat!

Prompted by the party's recent campaign pledge and the president's request, in 1909 the Republican House of Representatives passed a tariff revision bill sponsored by Sereno E. Payne, cutting rates sharply. This bill ran afoul of Rhode Island's Nelson Aldrich when it came to the Senate. A businessman himself as well as a stand-patter, Aldrich threw out most of the House bill's lowered schedules. Taft was appalled by the Payne-Aldrich bill, but he left the fight against it to the Senate Republican progressives.

Day after day, during the hot Washington summer, La Follette, Beveridge, Dolliver, Clapp, and other midwestern Republican progressives attacked the Payne-Aldrich bill. Taking up each of the schedules in turn, they showed how the Senate version would raise costs to the consumer and benefit only the trusts. The Aldrich measure, La Follette declared, would encourage monopoly, and with competition gone the results would be "shoddy in everything we wear and adulteration in everything we eat." Beveridge acknowledged that the country had to protect wage earners and manufacturers, but "a just and equal consideration . . . [must] be shown the consuming public."

The insurgents' fight was futile; the Aldrich rates prevailed. The results might have been different if the president had intervened, but Taft refused to use his influence to defeat the measure. When it came to his desk with the Aldrich changes intact, he signed it into law. Soon afterward he called it "the best tariff measure the Republican party has ever passed."

The president's response shocked progressives. The midwestern Republican insurgents considered Taft's performance a repudiation of TR's policies and betrayal of the party's promises to the public. In short order the reformers found new cause for dismay in the president's handling of conservation policies. Taft's secretary of the interior was Richard A. Ballinger, a Seattle attorney with close ties to western mining and lumbering interests. As secretary, Ballinger restored lands to commercial exploitation that Roosevelt had removed from entry, interfered with the Reclamation Service, and canceled an agreement giving the Forest Service control over forest preserves on Indian lands. Each of these actions offended Pinchot, who was still Chief Forester, and who, somewhat self-righteously, considered himself the special guardian of the public against selfish business interests The argument between Ballinger and Pinchot came to a head when the secretary of the interior transferred government-owned coal lands in Alaska to a Morgan-Guggenheim syndicate. Briefed by John Glavis, an Interior Department agent, Pinchot condemned this as a blatant giveaway of public resources and accused Ballinger of being in cahoots with the despoilers of the public domain. The president defended Ballinger, but Pinchot persisted. Rather than confining his criticism to private memos to the president, he made speeches attacking his department chief and sent a letter to Senator Dolliver denouncing Ballinger. When Dolliver read it to his Senate colleagues in open session, the angry Taft fired Pinchot while retaining Ballinger. Pinchot was now a Progressive martyr and his treatment another reason to distrust Taft.

The insurgent Republicans also clashed with Taft over congressional reorganization. They had long feuded with the Republican Speaker of the House, the profane, hard-drinking "Uncle Joe" Cannon, a man fiercely opposed to progressive legislation. Soon after Pinchot's dismissal, Cannon began to deprive the party rebels of committee chairmanships they had earned by seniority. The insurgent Republicans resolved to break his power and turned to the president for support. Taft disliked Cannon but declined to help the insurgents, claiming that the Speaker was too deeply entrenched to be ousted. The rebels refused to give up. At the opening of the March 1910 congressional session, led by George Norris, a young progressive Republican from Nebraska, they joined with anti-Cannon Democrats to strip Cannon of his power to appoint members to the all-important House Rules Committee and deprived him of his own place on it.

By mid-1910, then, Taft had thoroughly alienated the progressive, largely midwestern wing of his party. In truth, the president's record on progressive measures was not all bad. He supported the Mann-Elkins Act (1910), which gave the Interstate Commerce Commission the power to suspend railroad-initiated rate changes if they seemed excessive and also authorized government supervision of telephone, wireless, and telegraph companies. That same year he endorsed a "postal savings" scheme to allow small savers, often victimized by private bank failures, to place their money in the safekeeping of the federal post office. He also threw his considerable weight behind the Sixteenth Amendment to the Constitution, which authorized a federal income tax, and signed the Mann Act (1910), which prohibited the interstate transportation of women for purposes of prostitution. Yet on most of these issues Taft so equivocated that he received little credit from the insurgents. Perhaps worst of all, in their eyes, the lethargic, dull chief executive was not the dynamic, joyous, charismatic TR. One progressive publication put its dismay into verse:

> Teddy, come home and blow your horn,
> The sheep's in the meadow, the cow's in the corn.
> The boy you left to tend the sheep,
> Is under the haystack fast asleep.

Republican Split.   The progressive Republican leaders rapidly deserted Taft. In May 1910 Pinchot met with Roosevelt in Europe, as he was returning from Africa, and filled his ears with news of Taft's transgressions. By the time TR arrived back in the United States, his cordial feelings for his protégé had decidedly cooled. The last straw was the administration's revelation, in the course of an antitrust suit, that during the 1907 panic Roosevelt had allowed U.S. Steel to buy the Tennessee Coal and Iron Company without protest, though the purchase enhanced the firm's monopoly position in steel. Roosevelt believed that the move had been justified to restore business confidence when it was badly shaken, but the leak made him appear a tool of Morgan. He deeply resented the administration's effort to smear him.

Besides his growing doubts about Taft's political wisdom and loyalty, TR simply could not abandon politics. In 1910 he was only fifty-two and still overflowing with energy. Permanent retirement seemed unthinkable. He had served only one elected term, even though he had been president for almost eight years, so tradition did not bar his reelection. Under the barrage of the anti-Taft insurgents, Roosevelt quickly warmed to the idea of opposing the president for the 1912 Republican nomination.

By this time Herbert Croly's book *The Promise of American Life* (1909) had crystallized the activist view of the government's role that he had considered for some years. In a speech at Osawatomie, Kansas, in August 1910, TR used Croly's phrase, "the New Nationalism," to describe a federal government that, rather than forbidding combinations or attempting to break them up, would seek to "control them in the interest of the public." This New Nationalism would also place the well-being of the public ahead of property rights. "Every man," TR told his Kansas audience, "holds his property subject to the general right of the community to regulate its use to whatever degree the public welfare may require." Here was an endorsement of government paternalism and control beyond anything previously espoused by a major-party candidate. It distanced Roosevelt still further from the president.

Not all Republican progressives favored Roosevelt. Many, especially in the Midwest, preferred Wisconsin's La Follette. In January 1911 the midwesterners had organized the National Republican Progressive League to advance progressive ideas and promote La Follette's candidacy. Roosevelt refused to join. For a while the two men jockeyed for leadership of the party's progressive wing, but then, unable to compete with TR's broad national appeal, La Follette dropped out of the race.

Throughout the spring of 1912 Roosevelt and Taft battled for Republican convention delegates. TR won in the states, mainly western, that used the new presidential primaries to choose convention delegates. Taft swept the states in the South and East where tightly controlled conventions, dominated by party regulars, made the delegate choice. At the national convention in Chicago the Republican National Committee, controlled by the Taft men, refused the Roosevelt partisans' claim to a large block of disputed convention seats, giving almost all to Taft. The Roosevelt delegates walked out, leaving the convention firmly in the president's hands.

But Roosevelt and his friends were not through. Early in August, 2,000 men and women, many of them social workers, settlement house leaders, and state and local reformers, assembled in Chicago to organize the Progressive party and nominate Roosevelt for president. The delegates selected Hiram W. Johnson of California as their vice presidential candidate. The platform of the Progressive party—or Bull Moose party, as it was called after TR's remark that he felt as energetic as a bull moose—was the most radical ever proposed by a major party, foreshadowing almost all of the modern American social welfare state. Taking many of the emerging progressive ideas and carrying them several steps further, the platform endorsed popular election of United States senators; presidential primaries; the initiative, referendum, and recall in federal matters; women's suffrage; the recall (by citizens' petitions) of state court decisions; tariff reduction; a commission to regulate interstate industry as well as interstate commerce; a more stringent pure food and drug law; old age pensions; minimum wage and maximum hours laws; and the prohibition of child labor. The closing words of TR's acceptance speech conveyed the crusading mood of the new organization. "Our cause," the candidate thundered, "is based on the eternal principles of righteousness, and even though we who now lead for the first time fail, in the end the cause itself will triumph. . . . We stand at Armageddon and we battle for the Lord."

The Election of 1912.

Meanwhile, the Democrats had nominated Woodrow Wilson, former president of Princeton University and, most recently, progressive governor of New Jersey. The son of a Presbyterian minister from Virginia, Wilson was a slender, scholarly man who joined stubborn self-righteousness with an

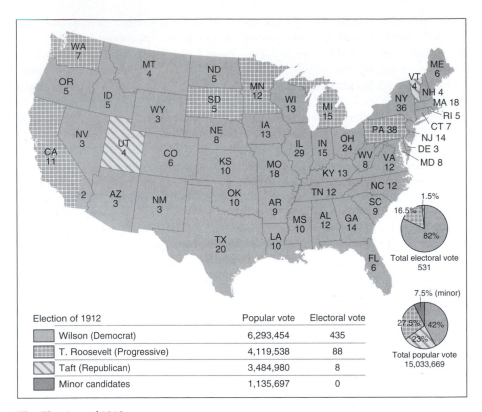

The Election of 1912

Election of 1912	Popular vote	Electoral vote
Wilson (Democrat)	6,293,454	435
T. Roosevelt (Progressive)	4,119,538	88
Taft (Republican)	3,484,980	8
Minor candidates	1,135,697	0

eloquence unequaled since Lincoln and a vision of human potential unmatched since Jefferson. In 1910 the New Jersey Democratic bosses had selected him as a figurehead candidate for governor, but he had gone on after the election to repudiate his sponsors and make an impressive record as a strong, liberal leader who brought staunchly conservative New Jersey into the progressive era. At the 1912 Democratic convention in Baltimore, with Bryan's support, Wilson defeated Speaker of the House, Missouri's Champ Clark, in a grueling forty-six ballots.

During the next few months the country experienced the liveliest presidential battle since 1896. The contest was really between Roosevelt and Wilson, with Taft lagging badly from the beginning. During the weeks of campaigning the conflicting ideologies of the two front-runners were thrown into sharp relief. TR trumpeted the message of the New Nationalism: Bigness as such was not bad; it only became bad when it injured the public and the national interest. Government could, and should, regulate private economic interests. Government also had a responsibility to protect citizens in many other aspects of daily life and reduce life's uncertainties and hazards. Wilson, a man from the Jeffersonian tradition of limited government, fought back with his New Freedom, much of it inspired by the liberal Boston lawyer Louis D. Brandeis. The New Nationalism was "big-brother government," Wilson charged. "You will find," he told a Buffalo audience of working men, "that the programme of the new party legalizes monopolies and systematically subordinates workingmen to them and to plans made by the Government. . . . " Like the Bull Moosers, Wilson believed that concentrated private economic power was a danger to the American public; he differed from them in holding that the way to salvation lay in breaking up these monopolies by vigorous antitrust action. TR's response to the New Freedom was blunt: It was "rural toryism," he declared, more suitable for a simpler age than for the twentieth-century world.

Wilson won with an electoral majority but did not receive a majority of the popular vote. The public loved Teddy, but many progressives were suspicious of his newfound radicalism, especially since he had allowed a Morgan partner, George Perkins, to play an important role in his campaign as fund-raiser and organizer. In the end TR received the votes largely of the Republican progressives; Taft, of the Republican stand-pat core. Wilson, on the other hand, won the votes of both Democratic progressives and traditional conservative Democrats. (Eugene V. Debs took 900,000 votes for the Socialists.) For the first time since 1897 a Democrat would occupy the White House, but only because a third party had split the opposition.

The Wilson Administration

The New Freedom in Action.
Woodrow Wilson proved to be a strong president. Disregarding the precedent established by Jefferson in 1801, he appeared before Congress in person to read his first annual message. His first major concern was the tariff, which, he reminded Congress, had long fostered monopolies and exposed the consuming public to oppressive prices. The structure of "privilege" and "artificial advantage" derived from the tariff must be destroyed and American businesses compelled to compete with their rivals in the rest of the world. Wilson was determined to do what Taft had failed to achieve in 1909.

The fruit of the president's efforts was the 1913 Underwood Tariff. This measure substantially lowered the nation's tariff walls for the first time since the Civil War. To make up for the expected loss of federal revenue, Congress took advantage of the recently adopted Sixteenth Amendment and included a graduated income tax in the legislation. Lobbyists for manufacturing and other special-interest groups resisted passage of the tariff bill, but Wilson fought back. Lashing out at the "industrious and insidious" lobbyists, he accused them of seeking to "create an artificial opinion and to overcome the interests of the public" for their own selfish ends. His counterattack jarred the Senate, and the bill passed.

Wilson's next important achievement was the Federal Reserve Act. The national Banking Acts of the Civil War Era had failed to create a central bank to regulate the supply of money and credit and extend help to hard-pressed local commercial banks in time of crisis. Nor had the national banking system provided a flexible currency that could expand to meet the needs of the economy during peak periods and then contract during quiet months. Farmers condemned the system for forbidding federally chartered banks to lend on land, the only security for loans that they generally possessed. Yet agrarians feared a system that would be centralized in New York City and tightly controlled by Wall Street.

As finally passed in 1913, the Federal Reserve Act was a compromise between the centralizers and agrarians, the supporters of government rule and those who favored private control. It created twelve district banks, whose directors were chosen by both private bankers and the government. The entire system was placed under the weak overall supervision of a central Federal Reserve Board in Washington, D.C. The district banks would hold the reserves of member banks—the commercial banks that did the day-to-day business of the nation. By lending money to member banks at low interest rates, or alternately by limiting such loans by charging high interest rates (through the "rediscount" process), the district banks could regulate credit and the money supply to suit the economy's seasonal needs and head off financial crises. The new system also allowed member banks to lend on farm mortgages. Despite the serious failings that time would reveal, the new system seemed a great improvement over the old.

The third major item on Wilson's first-term agenda was antitrust legislation to fulfill his campaign promise to break up the monopolies. Over the years the government's antitrust drive had been blunted by the federal courts. Most recently, in its 1911 "rule of reason" decision (*Standard Oil v. United States*), the Supreme Court had declared that only "unreasonable" restraints on interstate commerce were illegal; from now on an instance of monopoly must be blatant to be subject to antitrust prosecution. But that was not all. For over a decade the federal courts had been treating labor unions as "combinations in restraint of trade," and hence subject to antitrust prosecution. They had even issued injunctions (as in the 1894 Pullman strike) compelling unions to cease strikes and boycotts or face federal contempt-of-court charges. In the hands of the courts the Sherman Antitrust Act had become a union-busting weapon.

To protect organized labor's rights, help consumers, and get around the courts' limitations on antitrust actions, Wilson proposed two new measures. The first established the Federal Trade Commission (1914) to replace Roosevelt's Bureau of Corporations. The FTC was given powers to procure data from corporations and issue cease-and-desist orders against abuses such as mislabeling, adulteration of products, trade boycotts, and combinations to fix wholesale prices. The new commission would be the public's watchdog against the trusts. The second measure, the Clayton Antitrust Act (1914), strengthened the Sherman Antitrust Act by prohibiting firms from charging one price to one customer and a different price to another when such discrimination tended to foster monopoly, and forbidding contracts that required buyers not to do business with sellers' competitors. It also declared illegal most "interlocking directorates," a device by which one group of corporate directors headed several firms simultaneously. Similarly, a corporation was prohibited from acquiring stock in other corporations when the transaction threatened to reduce competition. A final provision—called by AFL president Samuel Gompers "labor's Magna Carta"—declared both labor unions and farmers' cooperatives exempt from the antitrust laws and limited the right of federal courts to issue injunctions in labor disputes.

Another important change during Wilson's first months in office—one that was a general progressive initiative rather than Wilson's alone—was the adoption of the Seventeenth Amendment to the Constitution (1913). Henceforth all

United States senators would be elected by direct vote of the people in each state rather than by the state legislators. No longer, the reformers felt, would the Senate be a bastion of conservatism that could ignore public opinion and protect the big corporations.

Wilson's Failings.

Despite the president's legislative successes, his first few years disappointed some of the most advanced progressives. He declined to support women's suffrage and at first refused to fight for a child-labor law. Nor was he as fierce an opponent of trusts as he had promised to be during the campaign. Like TR before him, he bargained with big corporations, agreeing not to prosecute them for combining to restrain trade if they would modify their behavior in some acceptable way.

But the most conspicuous defect of Wilson's first administration was its attitudes toward black Americans. The new president was a Virginian by birth and had lived much of his early life in the South. His party, moreover, was strongly southern in its makeup, and many of his closest advisers were white southerners. The new administration had few ties to the black community. Once in office, it abruptly cut off much of the political patronage that the Republicans had always conferred on black supporters. In addition, one by one, federal departments and agencies in Washington began to segregate their remaining black workers, imposing on the federal government the Jim Crow system that permeated the South. Eventually, following loud protests from black leaders and their white progressive allies, the president tried to undo some of the damage. But it was too late. By the end of his administration the nation's capital had become a full-blown southern city in its biased racial practices.

Wilson Shifts Left.

Wilson's first three years in office produced mixed results from the progressive perspective. After passage of the Clayton Act of 1914, the president appeared to lose interest in pushing further progressive legislation. Then, as the 1916 election approached, his reformist enthusiasm revived.

The change was politically expedient. Wilson had won in 1912 because the Republicans had been split between Taft and Roosevelt. By 1916 TR had returned to the GOP of his youth, virtually killing the Bull Moose party. To win reelection, Wilson concluded, he would have to attract former Bull Moosers, and this meant moving to the left. Hitherto his New Freedom brand of reform had avoided the social legislation that required expansion of federal authority. Now Wilson shifted ground.

To further aid farmers, he pushed the Federal Farm Loan Act of 1916, which established twelve Federal Farm Loan banks to lend money at low rates to farmers who joined certain farm loan associations. A bolder innovation was the Keating-Owen Act (1916), which prohibited interstate traffic in goods manufactured by the labor of children under sixteen years of age, and was intended to end child labor. The president also pushed the Kern-McGillicuddy Compensation Act (1916) providing workers' compensation for injured federal employees, and the Adamson Act (1916) establishing an eight-hour day and time-and-a-half overtime pay for railroad workers. Though these new laws applied to only limited groups of employees, they represented a long step toward federal regulation of the labor market.

One additional move rounded out Wilson's shift to the left in 1916: the nomination of his friend Louis D. Brandeis as Supreme Court justice. For years Brandeis had been one of the best-known labor lawyers in the country. His work in establishing arbitration procedures in the New York garment industry had been hailed as a model approach to labor–capital relations. In 1908, in the case *Muller v. Oregon*, Brandeis had mustered arguments drawn from sociology to demonstrate that long work hours were detrimental to the health of women and seriously injured society as a whole. The "Brandeis brief" had convinced the court and saved the Oregon law. It established an important precedent for defending future social legislation.

The nomination of Brandeis now raised a storm. The Supreme Court in 1916 had only one progressive member, Oliver Wendell Holmes, Jr., and the nation's liberals cheered the prospect of Brandeis joining him. But conservatives, including ex-president Taft and the American Bar Association, fought the nomination with every ounce of their strength. Running through much of the opposition was a barely disguised streak of anti-Semitism. Despite the powerful opposition, Wilson fought hard for his friend and adviser, pulling all the strings he could. His success earned him additional gratitude from progressives of both parties.

Despite the list of accomplishments, by late summer of 1916 the Progressive movement had largely run its course. By now the public's attention had shifted from domestic issues to the question of war or peace. In a few months the country would embark on a crusade to make the whole world safe for the kind of liberal society that the progressives had been trying for a decade or more to construct at home. In the process the domestic reform impulse would go into eclipse until another era.

Conclusions

Between 1890 and 1917, then, more and more Americans became uneasy over unrestrained private power. As the nation became ever more tightly knit together, giant corporations had become essential to provide the products people needed for a comfortable life. Meanwhile, growing numbers living in the cities became dependent on large firms for virtually everything they consumed. Seeking to protect themselves, urban Americans of all classes adopted a new political outlook, one that resembled views earlier held by rural reformers such as the Populists and the free-silver Democrats.

The progressives took much from Populism. Their primary enemy was similar—the trusts, the monopolies—and they borrowed the familiar rhetoric of an earlier rural age when they attacked "the interests." Especially in Wilson's New Freedom, we find echoes of Jefferson and Jackson in attitudes and ideas. Progressives also revived the Populist concern for direct democracy to bypass corrupt legislatures. Yet the addition of urban people to the reform cause altered its quality. Progressivism was more sophisticated than Populism. Borrowing from the liberal social Darwinists and the new efficiency-oriented professionals, progressives abandoned monetary cure-alls and developed new ideas of direct government action to solve social ills. Inevitably they focused on city problems and on wage earners, though rural grievances were not ignored. Especially in its New Nationalism guise, which emphasized a powerful regulatory federal government, progressivism foreshadowed future reform in a complex urban society.

Progressivism was not a complete success even in its own terms. It did not end the abuses inherent in a society with large inequalities of wealth and power; it did not end the insecurity that afflicted many Americans. It would remain to a later generation to tackle these problems again, with, perhaps, somewhat greater success.

Progressivism had inherent limitations. The prophets of efficiency clearly had a restricted vision of a better society. Nor were progressives as a whole free of the racial and ethnic prejudice that marked their predecessors. Today, moreover, many would question their faith in the efficacy of federal and state paternalism. Nevertheless, the reformers of 1900–1917 were the first generation to grapple with the problems of an urbanized nation. For all their failings, they laid the foundation for much of the reform that would follow.

ONLINE RESOURCES

"Racial Prejudice" http://projects.vassar.edu/1896/prejudice.html This informative Web site includes many primary-source documents that speak to racial issues in the New South period. These documents include the full text of a public address by Booker T. Washington, African–American and white responses to African-Americans' quest for civil rights, and links to African-American pamphlets published from 1880–1920.

"The Triangle Shirtwaist Factory Fire" http://www.ilr.cornell.edu/trianglefire/ This rich and informative site details this now-infamous workplace disaster. Through the use of an interpretative introductory essay, photographs, oral histories of survivors, and contemporary newspaper accounts, this source explains the impact of the industrial accident on workplace safety reform.

"The Evolution of the Conservation Movement" http://memory.loc.gov/ammem/amrvhtml/ conshome.html Explore this area of progressive reform through timelines that link to important documents in conservation history, such as Teddy Roosevelt's addresses on the subject and acts of Congress.

"The Urban Log Cabin" http://www.wnet.org/tenement/logcabin.html See what living conditions were like in a 1915 tenement house. This site describes the many conditions progressives were battling, including overcrowding, poor sanitary conditions, and disease.

"How the NAACP Began" http://www.naacp.org/about/library/library_began.html This site offers Mary White Ovington's 1914 history of the organization's beginnings. As a former executive secretary and chairperson of the organization, Ovington outlined in the document the NAACP's original platform, acts of civil injustices against blacks, and the role of W. E. B. DuBois.

Child Labor in America, 1908–1912 http://www.historyplace.com/unitedstates/childlabor/index.html Showcasing the photographs of Lewis Hine, this site shows the realities of children at work in mines and textile mills and on city streets. Used to help encourage social reform, Hine's original captions accompany his photographs.

In the Shadow of the IWW http://www.reuther.wayne.edu/exhibits/iww.html Visit this site to explore the IWW, one of the Progressive Era's most radical labor unions. Featuring the union platform, IWW illustrations, and the lyrics to the union's organizing songs, this site chronicles the creation and downfall of the union.

23

World War I

Idealism, National Interest, or Neutral Rights?

1914	American marines occupy Veracruz, Mexico; World War I begins in Europe; Wilson calls for American neutrality
1915	Marines occupy Haiti; Germany declares a war zone around the British Isles; U-boats sink the *Falaba*, the *Lusitania*, and the *Arabic*, all with loss of American lives; Wilson initiates the preparedness program to enlarge the army and the navy
1916	Wilson orders General John Pershing and 6,000 troops to Mexico to capture Pancho Villa; Colonel Edward House promises American intervention if deadlock on Western Front continues; U-boat sinks the *Sussex* with resulting American injuries; Germany suspends submarine warfare; Wilson reelected on "He kept us out of war" platform; Marines occupy the Dominican Republic
1917	Germany resumes submarine warfare and the United States severs diplomatic relations; British intelligence intercepts the Zimmermann telegram; Wilson orders the arming of American merchant ships; The Russian Revolution; Congress declares war on Germany; the War Industries Board, the War Labor Board, and the Committee of Public Information manage the war effort at home; Congress passes the Espionage Act
1918	The Sedition Act; Postmaster General Albert Burleson excludes publications critical of the war from the mails; The Justice Department indicts socialist leaders Eugene Debs and Victor Berger on charges of advocating draft evasion; Wilson announces his Fourteen Points; Germany collapses and armistice ends the war
1919	Peace conference at Versailles; League of Nations incorporated into treaty
1919–20	Congress rejects the Versailles Treaty
1920	The states ratify the Nineteenth Amendment providing for women's suffrage; Warren G. Harding elected president; Harding signs separate peace treaty with Germany in lieu of Versailles Treaty

As Americans read their newspapers over morning coffee on June 29, 1914, many must have wondered, "Where is Sarajevo?" The day before, in that remote Balkan town in present-day Bosnia, a fanatical Serbian nationalist had shot and killed Archduke Francis Ferdinand, heir to the Austro-Hungarian throne. Few people could have anticipated how their lives and those of millions of others would be affected by the archduke's murder in that unruly corner of southeastern Europe.

Within six weeks the major European powers were at war. Tied together by a bewildering tangle of alliances and agreements, both public and secret, all the large nations of Europe were quickly drawn into the dispute, with France, Russia, and Great Britain (the Allies) on one side, and Germany and Austria-Hungary (the Central Powers) on the other. Before many months Japan and Italy had joined the Allies; and the Ottoman Empire (Turkey) and Bulgaria had allied themselves with the Central Powers. By the end of 1914, using the most lethal weapons that twentieth-century technology had yet devised, enormous armies, navies, and air fleets grappled in ferocious combat in Europe and around the world.

President Wilson quickly announced United States neutrality. Americans must be "neutral in fact as well as in name during these days that are to try men's souls," he proclaimed. We must "be impartial in thought as well as in action, must put a curb on our sentiments as well as upon every transaction that might be construed as a preference of one party to the struggle before another." Thirty-one months later the same man would appear before a joint session of Congress to ask for a declaration of war against the Central Powers.

What had happened in those months to bring the peaceful and self-satisfied republic into this "most terrible of wars"? Why did the United States and its people not heed the president's early advice and remain neutral both "in thought" and "in action"?

Wilson and the World Order

To understand American involvement in World War I, we must consider Wilson's view of America's place in the world. Some progressives—internationalists such as Theodore Roosevelt and Albert J. Beveridge—believed the United States must play a vigorous role in world affairs and serve as a force for honorable behavior among nations. Isolationists within the progressive group, such as Senators Robert La Follette of Wisconsin and Hiram W. Johnson of California, feared that United States involvement in concerns beyond its borders would interfere with reform at home. Neither group doubted that enlightened, liberal capitalism was the most benevolent social system in the world.

Wilson's foreign-policy views fluctuated between these poles. At times he seemed to believe progressive democracy was for domestic consumption only. On other occasions he acted as if it was for export as well. In addition, his attitudes were infused with an intense moralism. To complicate matters further, like every national leader, he had to consider first his country's vital interests and defend them against any threatening power. To satisfy all these differing imperatives Wilson walked a tightrope, and his resulting unsteadiness and hesitation led to charges of inconsistency and even hypocrisy.

Moral Diplomacy.   Wilson chose William Jennings Bryan as his first secretary of state. Bryan had worked long in the cause of peace and shared Wilson's view that America must serve as the world's "moral inspiration." In 1913 and 1914 he negotiated conciliation treaties with twenty-one nations, binding the parties to submit all international disputes to permanent investigating commissions and to forgo armed force until the commission had completed its report.

A similar idealism infused other aspects of Wilson's early diplomacy. Both Bryan and his chief opposed using the American government to serve the interests of American businesses abroad. Under Taft, Wilson's predecessor, the United States had supported the participation of American bankers in a multinational consortium to build railroads in China. Feeling that the arrangement might undermine China's fragile sovereignty, Bryan withdrew the government's support. Wilson and Bryan also induced Congress to repeal a 1912 law that had exempted American coastal vessels from paying tolls on the Panama Canal, a law that violated the Hay-Pauncefote Treaty and its promise of equal treatment for all nations using the canal.

But Wilson never forgot the country's "vital interests"; where they seemed at stake, and where the risks appeared minor, he was sometimes insensitive to moral considerations. In the Caribbean, which the United States considered an American lake, Wilson and his chief lieutenant proved as overbearing as Roosevelt. In 1913 Bryan negotiated a treaty with Nicaragua giving that small nation $3 million for exclusive American rights to construct a second Atlantic–Pacific canal. The Bryan-Chamorro agreement, not ratified until 1916, made the strategically located Central American republic a virtual satellite of the United States, with little control over its own international economic relations. In 1915 and 1916 the United States intervened militarily in Haiti and the Dominican Republic—in the first to put down disorder, in the second to prevent the European powers, especially Germany, from landing troops to protect their citizens and collect unpaid debts. In each of these cases Wilson believed that he was merely holding America's less scrupulous neighbors to universal standards of order and honesty. To outsiders, the United States seemed to be imposing its will on countries too weak to resist the American giant.

Mexico.

In Mexico the United States managed to combine blatant self-interest and idealism in a particularly confusing way. For a generation following 1880 Mexico was ruled by strongman Porfirio Díaz. Determined to modernize his nation, Díaz had encouraged foreign investment in Mexican mines, oil wells, and railroads; by 1913 American businesses had poured over a billion dollars into his country. Though this infusion of capital helped the middle class, ordinary Mexicans remained as poor, illiterate, and oppressed as in Montezuma's day. Mexico remained an authoritarian nation without a functioning party system.

In 1911 Díaz's enemies among the country's liberal intellectuals toppled him from power and made Francisco Madero president. Madero tried to effect sweeping democratic reforms and restore constitutional liberties denied by Díaz. His policies aroused the hostility of the Mexican landed aristocracy, the army, and the Catholic Church. Two years later Victoriano Huerta, Madero's chief military adviser, seized power and had Madero murdered.

Great Britain, Germany, and France had already officially recognized Huerta when Wilson took office. Many Americans, including businesspeople with investments in Mexico, advised Wilson to follow suit. He refused. Despite the tradition of nations, including the United States, recognizing established governments no matter how they gained power or what their internal policies were, in Wilson's eyes Huerta was a "butcher." Instead of according diplomatic recognition to the Huerta government, Wilson proclaimed a new policy toward revolutionary regimes in

Latin America: The United States would not recognize any new government unless it was "supported at every turn by . . . orderly processes . . . based upon law, not upon arbitrary or irregular force."

Wilson sought to isolate the new Mexican tyrant by pressuring the British into withdrawing their recognition. He also stationed American naval vessels off Mexico's major ports to stop arms shipments to Huerta while allowing weapons to reach his enemies. Eventually, he hoped, Huerta might be pushed out by some champion of liberal rule such as Venustiano Carranza, an associate of Madero who had raised the banner of revolt in the northern part of the country.

Wilson's policies led to trouble. In April 1914 crewmen of an American naval vessel were arrested by a Huertista officer when they went ashore at Tampico. Although they were soon released, the American naval commander, Admiral Henry Mayo, demanded that the Mexican officer be punished and that the commander of the port give the American flag a twenty-one-gun salute as a sign of respect. The Mexican commandant apologized and promised disciplinary action against his subordinate, but refused the salute.

The incident now seems trivial, but Wilson made it an issue of principle. Appearing before Congress, he asked for authority to compel the Mexicans to show respect for American rights. At this point, a German vessel began to land arms for Huerta at Veracruz. To prevent this, Admiral Mayo shelled the city and ordered it occupied by marines. In the fighting that followed, over a hundred Mexicans lost their lives.

In explaining the Veracruz disaster, the president maintained that he meant only the best for the Mexican people and hoped to see them establish a new order based on "human liberty and human rights." The Mexicans would have to equalize the condition of rich and poor and keep foreign corporations from exerting excessive power and influence. This worthy prescription for Mexico's future ignored its heritage of bitter class antagonism and ideological conflict, and assumed that fundamental social change in such a nation might be effected as peaceably and amicably as progressive legislative reform in the United States. Still more imperceptive was the president's conclusion that the United States had the right to prescribe for Mexico at all. The Veracruz incident illustrated how American intrusion, even in a good cause, could produce damaging consequences for its intended beneficiary.

Meanwhile, the Veracruz attack had outraged all patriotic Mexicans, raised Huerta's stock among his own people, and cast the United States in the role of a brutal aggressor. It looked as if the Wilson administration would now be forced into the folly of war with Mexico. The president was rescued from this fate when Argentina, Brazil, and Chile offered to mediate. In May 1914 the United States, Mexico, and the so-called "ABC powers" met at Niagara Falls, Canada, and thrashed out a compromise that averted war.

But war with Mexico soon threatened again. Unable to resist the growing pressure at home and abroad, Huerta finally resigned, and control in Mexico City passed to Carranza. Once in office, however, Carranza was challenged by Francisco ("Pancho") Villa. Hoping to goad the United States into some overt action against Mexico that would unite the Mexican people against the "gringos" and help his chances to seize power, Villa ordered his men to attack American citizens both in Mexico and across the border.

WOODROW WILSON, THE SCHOOL TEACHER.

A minister's son and a historian, Wilson had been president of Princeton University. As president of the United States, he continued to lecture and preach. Here, symbolically, he instructs a rather skeptical Mexico in the principles of true democracy.

American indignation quickly reached a new peak. Whatever they felt following Tampico and Veracruz, virtually all Americans now agreed that the United States must take strong action. In March 1916, after 35 Americans had been murdered by Villista soldiers on both sides of the border, Wilson ordered General John J. Pershing to cross into Mexico with 6,000 troops. The wily Villa eluded the American army, however, while drawing it deeper and deeper into Mexican territory.

Carranza had reluctantly given the Americans permission to enter Mexico to capture Villa. But he soon came to regard the American penetration as a virtual invasion. War was averted at the last minute only when Wilson, realizing that the United States had far more pressing concerns in Europe, ordered Pershing to return to Texas. The president then sent Ambassador Henry Fletcher to Mexico and formally recognized the Carranza administration.

With this move Wilson ended the threat of war with Mexico. Though his bungling caused anti-American feeling to run high in Mexico for years, his support for Carranza and his newfound determination to avoid war despite sharp provocations allowed the revolutionaries to establish control. The Mexican involvement revealed the principal elements of the Wilson foreign policy: moralism, self-interest, missionary interventionism, and a deep reluctance to make war. These contradictory urges would also be apparent in the American approach to the war in Europe.

Neutrality and Public Opinion

Wilson's call for neutrality in August 1914 had summoned a loud "amen" from the American public. Americans had a traditional distaste for the complicated alliances formed among the European nation-states and almost no one wanted to become directly entangled in Europe's quarrels. Moreover, war promised to arouse conflicting sympathies and create domestic social tensions and unrest.

Americans Take Sides.   Yet how could Americans remove themselves from European concerns as the president hoped? Millions of citizens had been born in one or another of the belligerent nations, or were recently descended from such people, and found they could not escape the emotional commitments of their heritage. Arrivals from England, Scotland, and Wales retained their affection for Britain and hoped to see it remain mistress of the seas. On the other side, the large German-American population still had strong attachments to the "Fatherland." The picture was complicated by the immigrants from Austria-Hungary and Russia, sprawling empires containing millions of Poles, Czechs, South Slavs, Finns, Jews, and many other groups denied their national aspirations or actively persecuted. Irish-Americans further complicated this tangle of responses; many hated Britain as their homeland's centuries-long oppressor and hoped that England's troubles could be turned to Ireland's advantage.

Old-stock Americans looked askance at the continued attachment of immigrants to their native lands and accused the "hyphenates" of putting European concerns ahead of America's. Yet even they took sides. Aside from a small group of intellectuals who respected German culture and scholarship or disliked the pervasive English influence on American life, most old-stock Americans were pro-Ally. Such people read the classics of English literature and admired English law and parliamentary institutions. Many of them tended to feel affection for France as well, remembering with gratitude French aid during the Revolution, and fascinated with French fashions, food, and culture.

Beyond these considerations, however, England and France were tied to the United States by a common bond of democracy and rule of law. This natural sympathy was to some extent offset by the revulsion Americans felt toward tyrannical and backward czarist Russia, but Russia was very remote and seemed, at most, a junior partner of the western Allies. Meanwhile, Germany's conservatism, militarism, and arrogance confirmed American preferences. A nation dominated by Prussian militarism since its unification in 1871, Germany had allowed its imperial ambitions to swell to gigantic proportions under Kaiser Wilhelm II. Since 1898 American military and naval leaders had become increasingly worried about a German threat to the Western Hemisphere. As recently as 1910 the Navy General Board had estimated that Germany was probably America's most dangerous potential enemy. Opinion makers and the foreign policy elite shared the fear of German aggressiveness and power, and many other citizens could not help feeling that Germany's defeat would benefit America and democratic principles everywhere.

All told, a majority of Americans were pro-Ally from the outset. At no time would intervention to help Germany be a conceivable option. The best that the Central Powers could expect was American neutrality. From the beginning, however, the British and French had reason to hope that the United States could be turned into an active ally, willing to supply arms and perhaps even men to help them defeat their opponents.

The Propaganda War.

Both sides sought to sway American opinion, the Allies for intervention, the Central Powers for neutrality. They were soon waging a fierce propaganda battle in which truth often took a back seat to expediency.

In the passionate struggle for America's mind, the Germans labored under serious handicaps. The British and French controlled the transatlantic cables, which transmitted European news to the American press, leaving the Germans with only the still-primitive wireless for getting their message out. The Central Powers were also inept. German war propaganda emphasized hate and destruction—an approach that often aroused more revulsion than sympathy abroad. Some of the most effective Allied efforts to win American approval consisted of reprinting German hate propaganda against Britain and France.

German deeds offended American opinion even more than German words. Germany opened its military campaign against France and Britain on the Western Front in 1914 by invading little Belgium, thereby violating an international agreement of long standing. The German chancellor then contemptuously referred to the agreement as a "scrap of paper." When patriotic Belgians challenged the invaders, the German authorities retaliated by executing Belgian civilians and by burning the old university town of Louvain.

If the Germans were clumsy propagandists, the Allies were adroit. The British in particular spoke the language of Americans, literally and figuratively. Instinctively, they knew how to arouse American sympathies for their cause and to make their enemy seem bestial. They were quick to blow up German atrocities to enormous proportions. In 1915 the British government issued an official report signed by James Bryce, a distinguished historian and respected former British ambassador to Washington, which concluded that under the German occupation "murder, lust, and pillage prevailed . . . on a scale unparalleled in any war between civilized nations in the last three centuries." Many of the atrocity stories were unfounded; others were grossly exaggerated. Nevertheless, the Bryce Report convinced many Americans that the Germans were savage "Huns" who deserved the condemnation of the entire civilized world.

The Wilson Administration's Partisanship.

In some ways the Allies' strongest supporter in America was the president himself, despite his appeal for neutrality. Ever since his early career, when he wrote *Congressional Government*, praising the English parliamentary system, Wilson had been an Anglophile. As president he felt close to the leaders of the Liberal party in England, whose program of social welfare in the years immediately preceding the war had closely paralleled his own. The president tried to be neutral, but his true feelings often showed through his reserve. At one point he told the British ambassador that everything he loved most in the world depended on Allied victory. He remarked at another point to his private secretary that "England is fighting our fight. . . . I will not take any action to embarrass England when she is fighting for her life and the life of the world."

In addition, Wilson and his closest advisers, Colonel Edward M. House and later Robert Lansing, took the threat of German expansionism seriously and looked to Britain and France to check the German emperor's ambitions. Ever since the Spanish-American War, when Britain alone among the European powers had supported the United States against Spain, makers of American foreign policy had regarded England as a bulwark against the ambitions of expansionist Germany. This feeling remained a major, though unspoken, cornerstone of American foreign policy from the late 1890s onward and would influence American policymakers after August 1914.

Neutral Rights

Despite the pro-Ally bias of the American people and their government, the United States could have avoided the war if not for neutral rights. Once more, as during the Napoleonic Wars a century before, the United States found itself the major neutral power in a world divided into two warring camps, each determined to defeat the other no matter what the cost to bystanders. This country insisted that the European belligerents observe the rights traditionally due neutral nations in wartime. Under these rules, vessels owned by neutrals had the right to carry unmolested all goods except contraband. Contraband normally meant arms and munitions, with commodities such as food, textiles, and naval stores explicitly excluded. Neutrals also had the right to trade freely with all belligerents, although their ships might be legitimately intercepted and turned back by an effective surface blockade maintained outside a belligerent port. If a neutral merchant or passenger ship was stopped by such a blockade, however, the blockading power was responsible for the safety of the passengers and crew of the detained vessel.

Wilson, in his characteristic way, gave the longstanding American policy of defending neutral rights a new moral emphasis. The right of neutral citizens to go wherever they pleased, sell whatever they pleased, to whomever they pleased, subject only to the recognized rules of war, he said, was more than a legal abstraction or a matter of profit. What was at stake was the fundamental structure of the international order. This structure must be based on well-defined inviolable rules, which in turn must be derived from the basic principles of respect for human life and fair treatment of all peoples and nations.

Still, no matter how pro-British or how determined he was to guarantee American rights, for many months following the outbreak of the war, Wilson saw no reason to intrude into European affairs. By remaining neutral, America might exert a strong moral force to end the fighting quickly and then help establish new relations among nations based on disarmament, arbitration, and international justice. A neutral America, Wilson declared, would be "fit and free to do what is honest and disinterested and truly serviceable for the peace of the world."

Allied Violations of American Rights.   From the beginning, both the British and the Germans disregarded American "rights" in international trade. The British extended the definition of contraband to include almost everything that might be useful to Central Powers survival. They stopped American vessels and forced them to go to British ports for thorough and time-consuming searches. They planted mines in the North Sea, endangering all neutral ships routed through the area. They set up blacklists of American firms suspected of trading with Germany and Austria-Hungary through other neutral nations, and threatened these firms with the loss of English business.

The United States possessed the power to retaliate against the British and force them to relent. Soon after the war broke out, the British and the French had placed immense orders with American firms for arms, grain, cotton, and other supplies. In the beginning the Allies paid cash; but when cash ran low, they requested loans from American bankers. Secretary of State Bryan at first considered credits to the Allies a breach of neutrality and refused to sanction them. Gradually he retreated, and in October 1914 Wilson informed National City Bank and the Morgan Company that he would not oppose bankers' credits to finance Allied war orders. By early 1917 Americans had lent Great Britain over $1 billion and France $300 million more.

Had Wilson wished, he might have discouraged loans or asked Congress to embargo munitions to belligerents unless the Allies complied with American demands. He justified his failure to use this powerful weapon of coercion—one employed by Thomas Jefferson in 1807—on the grounds that neutralizing the Allied advantage of control of the shipping lanes to Europe would be equivalent to helping the Central Powers. But it is difficult to avoid the conclusion that the president was less willing to enforce neutral rights against the Allies than against their enemies.

But there were strong reasons other than pro-Ally feelings for discriminating between British and German violations of American rights. England avoided injuring too many American interests simultaneously for fear that a general outcry would force retaliation. The English were also careful to blunt the edge of their actions. When placing cotton on the contraband list produced a loud protest from southern cotton growers, for example, the British agreed to buy enough cotton to make up for the lost German-Austrian market. But the most compelling reason for distinguishing between the Allies and the Central Powers was that Allied policies toward neutrals hurt only their pocketbooks; German policies took lives.

Submarine Warfare.   The chief German naval weapon against the Allies was the U-boat (*Unterseeboot*), a submarine armed with torpedoes and one small deck gun. U-boats could creep up on their targets unseen and sink them without warning. But because they were small and thin-skinned, they could not risk surfacing to warn of their intentions, to search for contraband, or to care for civilians aboard the vessels they attacked. German U-boats could strangle England, which relied on overseas sources for vital food and munitions, but only by "unrestricted" U-boat warfare—attacking all shipping, naval or merchant, enemy or neutral, found in the waters off the British Isles, thereby endangering civilians and deeply offending international opinion.

Chancellor Theobald von Bethmann-Hollweg and a few other German leaders foresaw that a "shoot-on-sight" U-boat policy would lead to serious problems with the United States. Nevertheless, in February 1915 the German government announced that it would authorize its submarines to sink without warning all ships found within a large war zone surrounding the British Isles.

The American State Department immediately denounced these "unprecedented" tactics and declared that the German government would be held to "a strict accountability" for any action that injured Americans or their property. The Berlin authorities were unmoved. A month later a German submarine sank the British passenger liner *Falaba,* killing an American citizen. Bryan urged the president to forbid Americans to travel in the war zones, at least on belligerent ships; but Wilson refused on the grounds that to do so would surrender a valid American right. A far worse tragedy took place in May when the large British passenger liner *Lusitania* was sunk off the Irish coast by a German submarine, with a loss of 1,198 lives, 128 of them American. Before the vessel left New York, the German authorities had advised Americans to avoid belligerent ships, but the actual attack had come totally without warning.

The sinking of an unarmed passenger liner, with such wholesale destruction of life, profoundly shocked Americans. "From the Department of State," the *New York Times* trumpeted, "there must go to the imperial Government in Berlin a demand that the Germans shall no longer make war like savages drunk with blood." For days afterward American press editorials denounced the attack as "criminal," "bestial," "uncivilized," and "barbarous." "Condemnation of the act," the *Literary Digest* summarized, "seems to be limited only by the restrictions of the English language."

For a time there was some loose talk of war with Germany. But the public was not ready to plunge into the European bloodbath, and most Americans concluded that strong words would be sufficient. On May 13 Wilson dispatched a note to the German government demanding an apology for the brutal act and a statement renouncing future attacks on merchant and passenger vessels. The Germans expressed regret for the American dead, but defended the sinking as an act of "self-defense" because the *Lusitania* had carried arms that would have been used against German soldiers. In a second, stiffer note, Wilson insisted that the Germans give up unrestricted submarine warfare entirely. A third note threatened to sever diplomatic relations if another passenger ship was attacked.

Bryan considered the second Lusitania note a threat of war against Germany. He resigned in protest. Wilson replaced him with Robert Lansing, a man of a very different stripe, who believed that German victory "would mean the overthrow of democracy . . ., the suppression of individual liberty, the setting up of evil ambitions . . ., and the turning back of the hands of human progress two centuries." Lansing's leadership of the State Department strengthened the pro-Ally groups in the government and undoubtedly helped steer the country into war.

The conflict over the *Lusitania* remained unresolved when, in August 1915, the U-boats struck again, sinking the *Arabic,* another unarmed British passenger liner, and causing the death of two Americans. The sinking brought to a climax the battle between the cautious Chancellor Bethmann-Hollweg and the German admirals, who wanted to continue unrestricted submarine warfare. This time the German emperor sided with the moderates and assured the American State Department that his navy would stop attacking passenger ships without warning and in the future would provide for the safety of passengers and crews. The German government now suspended submarine warfare against passenger vessels.

The War Spirit Rises.   The *Arabic* pledge prevented a break in diplomatic relations with Germany, but it did not fully comply with Wilson's demands. The German government had not agreed to exempt neutral cargo vessels from attack and had not apologized for the *Lusitania* sinking. It also had not offered reparations for lost American lives.

While these grievances festered, Americans were treated to new demonstrations of seemingly outrageous German behavior. Shortly after the *Arabic* sinking, an American Secret Service agent picked up a briefcase carelessly left by a man on the Sixth Avenue el in New York. The contents revealed that its owner, Dr. Heinrich F. Albert, was head of a widespread covert German operation in the United States to influence American opinion and sabotage munitions factories and shipyards producing war materiel for the Allies. At almost the same time, the British released captured documents that disclosed German-Austrian plans to foment labor stoppages at American armament plants. Soon afterward the United States accused two German diplomatic attachés of spying and sent them home; another German agent was indicted for blowing up a bridge; and still others were held responsible for various unexplained explosions and accidents in American factories and war plants.

The sensational revelations of German undercover activities deeply antagonized the American public. Bombings and espionage brought the terrible war to America's shores. By mid-1915 many citizens had begun to fear that the nation could not avoid entering the fight.

The changing public mood manifested itself in a "preparedness" movement to rearm the United States for any eventuality. Some preparedness advocates believed that if the country was strong militarily, it would not have to fight. But many thought war with Germany unavoidable, or even desirable, and wanted to ensure that when it came, the country could fight effectively. The most militant leader of the preparedness-interventionist group was former president Theodore Roosevelt, who toured the country calling Wilson "yellow" for holding back on rearmament and for not taking a stronger line against the Germans. At one point, in his typically intemperate way, TR recommended that if war came, peace advocate Senator Robert La Follette should be hanged forthwith.

A strong peace contingent, however, resisted the preparedness movement. The peace advocates included Quakers and members of other traditional "peace churches," and many progressives who believed that domestic reform would be forgotten if the country became embroiled in war. Women progressives were particularly prominent in the peace movement. War represented the male principle of physical force, asserted Harriot Stanton Blatch, and world peace would prevail only when the "mother viewpoint" predominated in international diplomacy. Socialists were even more strongly opposed to the preparedness campaign and intervention than progressives. The war in Europe, they held, was a struggle between rival capitalist imperialists. Its outcome was only of marginal interest to the world's working class.

At first Wilson was skeptical of the preparedness movement, but his growing anger at Germany and belief that preparedness was politically popular soon changed his mind. In mid-summer 1915 the president finally asked his naval and military advisers to draw up plans for an enlarged army and navy. On the basis of these proposals, in November he recommended that Congress approve a $500 million naval building program and expand the army to 400,000 men.

Even as he readied the nation for the possibility of war, however, Wilson struggled to avoid it. In early 1915 he had sent Colonel House to Europe to try to bring the belligerents together around the peace table. House was ignored. In January 1916 Wilson sent the colonel back to Europe for the same purpose, determined this time that if either side refused to parley, the United States would use its "utmost moral force" to compel the reluctant party to accept compromise terms that would include disarmament and a world peacekeeping organization. Once again, House accomplished little. The warring nations wanted no part of peace except on their own terms. Despite the stubbornness of both Allied and German leaders, House made some startling promises to Britain and France that exceeded the president's instructions. If the 1916 Allied effort to break the military deadlock on the Western Front failed, and if Germany appeared to be winning, the United States, House told the British and French leaders, would intervene to prevent Allied defeat.

The Sussex Pledge. German–American relations took a turn for the better early in February 1916 when the Kaiser's government finally expressed regret for the sinking of the *Lusitania* and offered to pay an indemnity for lost lives. But the pendulum soon shifted once more when a U-boat torpedoed the unarmed French steamer *Sussex,* injuring a number of Americans.

Wilson now shot off a note to the German government declaring that unless it ceased all attacks on cargo and passenger ships, the United States would immediately break off diplomatic relations. With the moderates still in control, the German government gave the so-called Sussex pledge: It would abandon its practice of shoot-on-sight in all cases except those involving enemy warships. The pledge was qualified, however. The Germans would honor it only if the United States compelled the Allies to abide by the rules of international law. Wilson accepted the Sussex pledge, knowing that it would be impossible to force the Allies to comply with Germany's conditions. But peace was preserved for the moment at least.

For some time following the Sussex pledge, the Germans acted in exemplary fashion. Meanwhile the British seemed determined to arouse the wrath of the American public. They seized American packages and parcels sent abroad by mail to look for contraband, opened and read letters to and from America, and refused to allow American shipowners to use British coaling facilities unless they submitted to British inspection. They also brutally suppressed the Easter Rebellion in Ireland. The execution of the Irish rebels appalled Americans and seriously damaged Britain's image as a defender of democracy. War talk ebbed as Americans had second thoughts about the Allied cause.

The Election of 1916.

For the next few months public interest in foreign af-
fairs was eclipsed by the excitement of a presidential election. In 1916, with the
Progressive party virtually dead, Wilson faced a single opponent, Supreme Court
Justice Charles Evans Hughes, an attractive candidate who had established a solid
reputation during two terms as progressive Republican governor of New York.
Despite Hughes's appeal, Wilson was reelected. The president's success in part
derived from his late turn to the left, as discussed in Chapter 22. But even more,
the campaign outcome turned on the issue of war and peace.

Hughes had the difficult task of holding together a party with a substantial
number of pro-Ally interventionists and a large number of German-American
Central-Powers supporters. A poor speaker, he seemed to waver on the issues to
please every segment of the voting public. The Democrats were more forthright.
"He kept us out of war" was their campaign slogan. A Democratic ad in the New
York Times reminded voters:

> You are working;
> —*Not Fighting!*
>
> Alive and Happy;
>
> —*Not Cannon Fodder!*
> Wilson and Peace with Honor?
>
> or
>
> *Hughes with Roosevelt, and War?*

The election was close. Hughes carried the Northeast and much of the Midwest. Wilson took the South, the mountain states, and most of the Pacific coast. Because of slow returns from California, not until the Friday following the Tuesday
balloting was Wilson assured of four more years in the White House.

The Road to War.

Wilson's reelection was a vote for peace. However sympa-
thetic to the Allies, most Americans still wanted very much to keep out of the war.
In the wake of his victory Wilson decided to make one last effort to force both
sides to hammer out a compromise settlement. Late in December 1916 he sent
notes to the belligerents asking them to state their war aims and offering again to
mediate. He warned both sides that only a "peace without victory" would last.
Any other "would leave a sting, a resentment, a bitter memory upon which terms
of peace would rest . . . only as upon quicksand." The president's words were
prophetic, but neither side was willing to stop the fighting and talk terms.

German–American relations now moved swiftly toward a final crisis. By the
end of 1916 the military stalemate in Western Europe was becoming intolerable to
the German leaders. Continued frustration weakened the moderates in Berlin and
strengthened the military. At a momentous conference in January 1917 the aggressive generals told Kaiser Wilhelm that because the United States was already providing the Allies with as much war materiel and financial aid as it could, it would
make little difference if it formally joined the enemy. Moreover, Germany was
now so well supplied with U-boats that if the submarine captains were not required to observe the rules imposed by neutral opinion, they could deliver a
knockout blow to the Allies in short order. The generals' analysis was convincing:
Germany chose unlimited submarine warfare.

On January 31, 1917, the German ambassador in Washington informed Secretary of State Lansing that Germany would direct its U-boats to sink without warning all ships, both neutral and enemy, found in the eastern Mediterranean and in the waters surrounding Great Britain, France, and Italy. The new German order repudiated the Sussex pledge. True to his promise, Wilson severed diplomatic relations with Germany. Most Americans, even many of Wilson's former critics, supported his decision. Volunteers began to show up at army enlistment centers.

Wilson still hoped to avoid hostilities, and refused Lansing and House's advice to prepare for war. While he deliberated, rallies all over the country demanded American forbearance and further negotiations before taking the final step. Much of the president's and the public's remaining doubt was dispelled by the revelation of a secret note from the German foreign secretary, Arthur Zimmermann, to the German minister in Mexico proposing that if the United States and Germany came to blows, Mexico ally itself with Germany and help persuade Japan to switch its allegiance to the Central Powers. In the event of German victory, Mexico would be rewarded with its lost territory in Texas, New Mexico, and Arizona. Intercepted by British intelligence, the "Zimmermann telegram" pushed Wilson over the line. The day following the receipt of the incriminating document he asked Congress for authority to arm American merchant ships and employ "any other instrumentalities or methods" to protect American interests on the high seas. When the isolationists in the Senate, led by La Follette and George W. Norris of Nebraska, threatened to talk the measure to death, Wilson released the telegram to a shocked and furious public. Carried along by a wave of public indignation, the House gave Wilson the power he wanted. But the Senate isolationists blocked action despite Wilson's condemnation of them as a "little group of willful men, representing no opinion but their own."

On March 9 Wilson announced that he was arming American merchant vessels under his authority as commander in chief. Public outrage against Germany reached a new pitch when, soon after, three American merchant ships were sunk by submarines, with heavy loss of life. In the minds of many Americans, final doubts about the Allied cause evaporated when a liberal uprising in Russia overthrew the autocratic government of the czar. Now if the United States joined the Allies, it would be able in good conscience to claim it was fighting on the side of democracy.

Wilson's War Message.   On the evening of April 2, 1917, the president appeared before a joint session of Congress to ask for a declaration of war. German contempt for American rights and American lives, displayed by brutal, unrestricted U-boat war, left no other course, he said. But there were higher moral considerations than self-defense. The United States would be fighting for all people, for the "vindication of right, of human right" against "autocratic governments backed by organized force." As the American people faced the months of "fiery trial and sacrifice" ahead, they would not forget that they were struggling

> for the things which we have always carried nearest our hearts—for democracy, for the right of those who submit to authority to have a voice in their own Governments, for the rights and liberties of small nations, for a universal dominion of rights by a concert of free peoples as shall bring peace and safety to all nations and make the world at last free.

The Senate passed the war declaration on April 4. House approval followed on April 6.

The War

America was finally in! In London, Rome, and Paris, crowds cheered the news and drank toasts to the United States and its great president. Sagging Allied spirits soared. At home most socialists and a number of midwestern isolationists denounced the war. Senator Norris charged that the war's sole cause was greed and that Americans would be "sacrificing millions of . . . [their] countrymen's lives in order that other countrymen may coin their lifeblood into money." Many German-Americans, Irish-Americans, and a small minority of intellectuals remained skeptical of the Allied cause. But on the whole the American people embraced the war wholeheartedly and accepted the sacrifices it required.

Combat.   Now, the nation's resources had to be mobilized. Americans had not expected at first to send large numbers of men to the fighting fronts, but it soon became clear that the Allies could not fight on without American troops. The liberal Russian Revolution of March 1917 had been followed by the Bolshevik Revolution of October 1917. The Bolsheviks soon concluded peace with the Germans, freeing the German troops fighting Russia to move to the western front. Only American forces could offset the surge in German strength in France.

The first military draft since the Civil War provided the needed manpower. It worked surprisingly well. Scrupulously administered by local civilian draft boards, it did not arouse the feeling of class favoritism that had appeared fifty years before. With its help the army grew from 200,000 to 4 million men. Draftees were sent to thirty-two training camps and were quickly transformed into soldiers.

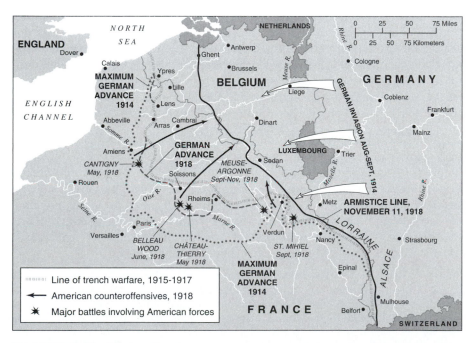

World War I: The Western Front

Over 2 million American troops eventually went to France, and 1.4 million of them saw action on the front lines. The lot of American "doughboys" on the Western Front was as miserable as that of their European counterparts. They faced mud, rain, cold, vermin, and constant risk of death or dismemberment. They huddled in the trenches while fierce artillery bombardments shook the earth for days at a time. They "went over the top" in savage assaults on the enemy's positions, sacrificing their lives for a few hundred yards of ground. About 50,000 died in combat; an equal number succumbed to disease.

The American navy, under Admiral William S. Sims, escorted troop and supply vessels to France and, in cooperation with the British, helped end the U-boat threat. For every American soldier it brought safely to the fighting front, the navy had to guarantee the arrival of fifty pounds of supplies and equipment daily. Ultimately millions of tons of food, munitions, vehicles, medicines, clothing, guns, horses, and fuel were ferried from American ports to Le Havre, Bordeaux, Calais, Brest, and Boulogne, with minimal loss from U-boats.

"Over There."   American troops made a major difference in the war's outcome. The American Expeditionary Force (AEF) under the command of General John J. Pershing saw little fighting before early spring 1918. In March 1918 the Germans, strengthened by the armies brought west from defeated Russia, attacked on a broad front, engaging the Americans in May and June around the town of Chateau-Thierry and at Belleau Wood, fifty miles from Paris. In September the American First Army, some 500,000 strong, pushed back a German salient at Saint-Mihiel. Between late September and the armistice, 1.2 million Americans were committed in the Meuse-Argonne campaign around Verdun.

The War Effort at Home

Mobilization.   This enormous military and logistical effort was made possible by the effective mobilization of economic and emotional resources at home. The war cost the United States $33 billion, including $9 billion of loans to the Allies. About a quarter of this huge sum was raised by taxes. The war taxes were highly progressive, taking up to 75 percent of the largest incomes. Inheritance taxes of 25 percent, an excess-profits tax of 65 percent, and a variety of excise taxes also helped spread the burden through the population. The rest of the money came from banks and from campaigns to sell Liberty Bonds, which not only provided needed funds, but also helped whip up enthusiasm for the war effort.

The billions, however, had to be effectively deployed. For this purpose the Wilson administration borrowed a page from the New Nationalism progressives by setting up a cluster of new federal agencies. In 1917 the administration created the War Industries Board (WIB) to mobilize the country's productive resources. Under financier Bernard Baruch the WIB-established production priorities instituted measures to save rubber, copper, and steel and establish fair prices for raw materials. To conserve fuel used for lighting, the government instituted daylight saving time. Agriculture, too, got a "czar" in the person of Herbert Hoover, a millionaire mining engineer of Quaker background. Hundreds of government groups intruded into the private economy to expedite production and conserve raw materials. By the end of the war these administrative bodies were exerting many new powers and had achieved extraordinary control over the economy. They also anticipated a number of governmental structures and measures of the New Deal and provided precedents for the mobilization effort of World War II.

Food production burgeoned under the direction of Food Administrator Herbert Hoover, who had supervised food relief to ravaged Belgium earlier in the war. Americans voluntarily observed "wheatless" and "meatless" days in a remarkably effective campaign to conserve food. The Food Administration guaranteed an attractive price for the entire 1917 wheat crop, causing a dramatic jump in the number of acres planted with wheat. Vegetable gardens appeared everywhere, and exotic meats such as horse and rabbit were introduced into the wartime diet. Hoover launched a campaign for Americans to conserve food that included catchy slogans: "Don't Let Your Horse Be More Patriotic Than You Are—Eat a Dish of Oatmeal"; "Serve Beans by All Means." The Food Administration was a great success, and it helped boost Hoover's popularity after the war.

The War Industries Board, headed by Baruch, performed relatively well after a slow start. American arms and clothing factories equipped the American doughboy better than any other soldier in the world. American shipyards struggled, not always successfully, with the crucial task of replacing Allied vessels sunk by U-boats.

Montgomery Flagg, a popular illustrator of the day, produced this saccharine poster urging boys and girls in 1917 to help the American war effort by saving money.

The board built new production facilities and converted existing ones for war purposes, developed new sources of raw materials, served as purchasing agent for the Allies, standardized thousands of necessary items, and established strict economic priorities. Despite the immense effort American industry failed to provide all the equipment that the armed forces needed. American pilots would be forced to fly British or French fighter and reconnaissance planes. Much of the AEF's artillery consisted of French "seventy-fives." Meanwhile, the United States Railroad Administration took tight control of the country's rail transportation, now called on to carry millions more passengers and tons of freight than in peacetime. The administration combined railways into regional units, limited unnecessary passenger travel, standardized rates and schedules, and gave priority to munitions and war matériel over nonessential goods. Harry A. Garfield became a virtual dictator over the nation's fuel supply. When a coal shortage immobilized thirty-seven munitions ships in New York harbor during the bitterly cold winter of 1917–1918, he closed down all civilian manufacturing plants to release their coal for the ships' use.

The war overstimulated the economy. Unemployment melted away, and men and women were soon working long hours at good pay. But despite high taxes and the Liberty and Victory Loans that drained off much excess purchasing power, prices rose sharply and offset many of the workers' gains. It soon became apparent that labor would have to be regulated, along with other sectors of the economy, to ensure uninterrupted work, prevent strikes for higher wages, and provide the highest priority for war industry. To attain these goals, Wilson created the War Labor Policies Board. By granting recognition to labor unions and establishing generally favorable working conditions for wage earners, the board purchased labor peace during the war. It prohibited strikes, but it also forced management to negotiate with the unions. Under these policies the AFL and other unions expanded their membership to over 4 million, a 50 percent increase over 1914.

Women and the War.   One firm principle of the War Labor Policies Board was that women should have equal pay for equal work in war industries. High wages, encouraged by wartime labor shortages and labor board policies, soon drew thousands of women into the labor force. Many also went "over there" to France with the doughboys, working as ambulance drivers and nurses and representing organizations such as the Salvation Army and Red Cross. The war accustomed many American women to working outside the home and accelerated their economic independence.

The war also gave a massive push to the women's suffrage movement. During the 1916 presidential election Alice Paul and her new National Woman's Party (NWP) attacked Wilson and the Democrats for failure to act on the suffrage issue. Meanwhile, using gentler means, Carrie Catt of the National American Woman Suffrage Association managed to convert the president himself to the women's suffrage cause. Still, Congress and much of the male public resisted. The suffragists appealed to the nation's conscience with slogans like "Democracy Begins at Home," and advertised the giant contributions women were making to the war effort. Alice Paul and her group picketed the White House. When District of Columbia officials carted the demonstrators off to jail they became martyrs whose treatment aroused sympathy for their cause. Eventually, even Wilson relented, feeling women had earned the right to vote. "The services of women during the supreme crisis," he noted in 1918, "have been of the most signal usefulness and distinction; it is high time that part of our debt should be acknowledged."

At last, in January 1918, the House of Representatives, anxious to further national unity during wartime, passed the women's suffrage amendment (the Nineteenth) to the Constitution by precisely the two-thirds majority needed. The Senate took another year and a half to approve the amendment, and not until August 1920 was it ratified by three-fourths of the states. But without the impetus of war, women would have been forced to wait longer for the right to vote.

Black Americans and the War.   Blacks also made economic gains during 1917–18. With millions of men in the armed forces and European immigration at an all-time low, the supply of civilian labor tightened just when the economy needed labor most. To meet the shortage, employers were forced to lower their barriers to black workers. Thousands of black men and women were soon leaving southern farms for the high wages of the northern war plants. Thousands more took jobs in the coal mines and the railroads. Most poured into the large industrial cities. Chicago's black population leaped from 44,000 in 1910 to 110,000 in 1920. Cleveland's grew from 8,000 to 34,000.

Yet the war did not fundamentally disturb the racial status quo in the United States. Segregation continued in America wherever it had existed before. This included the armed services. The 367,000 blacks in the military forces were kept apart from whites and largely led by white officers. The black migration north, meanwhile, created serious tensions between new black arrivals and people who felt challenged or displaced. In 1917 thirty-eight blacks lost their lives in lynchings; the following year the number rose to fifty-eight. In East Saint Louis a race riot triggered by employment of blacks in a factory producing war materiel resulted in the death of at least forty blacks. The Germans sought to take advantage of racial tensions in the United States. They kept close track of racial incidents and urged black Americans to refuse to help the country that permitted these atrocities. Black Americans did not respond. Indeed, they were among the most patriotic groups in the nation. But the threat of disunity goaded Wilson into denouncing lynching and mob violence.

The Propaganda War.   To lead the propaganda war, the government created the Committee on Public Information (CPI) and chose George Creel, a progressive journalist with a gift for storytelling and platform oratory, as its head. Creel mobilized thousands of people in the arts, advertising, and motion pictures to "advertise America." Some of the most talented painters and graphic artists in the country designed Liberty Loan and recruiting posters. An army of lecturers, called "Four-Minute Men," delivered pithy patriotic talks all across the country on subjects like "Maintaining Morals and Morale," "Why We Are Fighting," and "The Meaning of America." "There was no part of the great war machinery that we did not touch," Creel wrote after the war, "no medium of appeal that we did

not employ . . . to make our own people and all other peoples of the world understand the causes that compelled America to take up arms."

Civil Liberties during the War.

Creel's campaign was immensely effective in whipping up enthusiasm for the war and Wilson's goal of making the world "safe for democracy." War fervor also unleashed a wave of intolerance against those who did not show the proper patriotic spirit or who harbored pacifist or socialist attitudes.

Quick to sense the new superpatriotic mood, in 1917 Congress passed the Espionage Act and the Trading with the Enemy Act. The first imposed severe penalties on persons found guilty of obstructing military recruitment, aiding the enemy, or encouraging anyone to be disloyal or insubordinate or to refuse duty in the armed forces. Under it the postmaster general could exclude from the mails any material he deemed treasonable or seditious. The Trading with the Enemy Act authorized the government to confiscate and run German-owned businesses and to censor international communications and the foreign-language press. In 1918 Congress passed the Sedition Act, declaring "disloyal" or "seditious" all talk against the war and making the use of "profane, scurrilous, or abusive language" about the Constitution, the flag, or the armed forces a crime.

Wilson had warned that war might bring intolerance and repression, and it did, with administration officials often at the forefront of the hysteria. Attorney general Thomas Gregory fanned the flames of intolerance with his assertion that opponents of the war should expect no mercy "from an outraged people and an avenging government." Postmaster General Albert S. Burleson excluded from the mails publications opposed to the war. The federal courts also failed to bolster the right to dissent. In *Schenck v. The United States* the Supreme Court upheld the conviction of a man for mailing circulars that urged draftees to refuse military induction. In war, said Justice Oliver Wendell Holmes, Jr., speaking for the majority of the Court, such material posed a "clear and present danger" to the nation and therefore could by law be suppressed. In 1918 the Justice Department indicted and secured the convictions of Eugene V. Debs and Victor L. Berger, two Socialist party leaders, on the charge of encouraging draft evasion. Kate O'Hare, a socialist firebrand, went to federal prison for a speech claiming that "the women of the United States are nothing more than brood sows, to raise children to get into the army and be made into fertilizer."

Local officials joined the repressive chorus and fined and imprisoned those who spoke out against the war. Meanwhile, vigilante groups and self-appointed "patriots" intimidated supposed subversives and "slackers" who failed to don their country's uniform. In the Pacific Northwest their target was often the Industrial Workers of the World (IWW), a radical labor group with a strong following among western miners and loggers.

One of the war's casualties was ethnic tolerance. Many schools and colleges suspended the teaching of the German language. Bigots renamed sauerkraut "liberty cabbage" and German measles "liberty measles." Superpatriots attacked their German-American neighbors. One group of jingoes even thought it desirable to change the names of American cities borrowed from Germany, such as Berlin, Frankfort, and Potsdam, to Anglo-Saxon names.

Making the Peace

On November 1 the American and Allied armies broke the German line of defense. Beaten on the battlefield and on the verge of collapse at home, the Germans began talking of peace.

The Fourteen Points. The Central Powers' defeat was in part military. But it also stemmed from deteriorating morale. By late 1918 the overstretched German will to resist had been seriously undermined by expectations of a generous peace as laid out in Wilson's Fourteen Points. Announced in a January 1918 speech while the fighting was still at an indecisive stage, the Fourteen Points was a blueprint for the postwar world. Wilson addressed several immediate, war-connected issues: Germany must abandon all occupied territories in France, Russia, and Belgium; Austria must surrender territorial gains in the Balkans; all nations must agree to respect neutral rights on the high seas. The American president also sought to remedy the fundamental causes of the war still raging: Armaments must be sharply reduced to prevent future destabilizing arms races; Serbia should be given access to the sea; the repressed aspirations for nationhood among the peoples of the Turkish, Austrian, and German empires should be satisfied; Italy's frontiers should be altered to incorporate Italian-speaking people living outside its existing borders; the conflicting colonial claims of the great powers must be adjusted with due regard to the rights of the colonial populations themselves.

On a more abstract level, Wilson proposed to remake the international order so that future disputes among nations could be kept from deteriorating into war. The president was here expressing American liberal idealism and, critics would say, American naiveté. He denounced "private international understandings," that is, secret treaties, and demanded in their place "open covenants of peace, openly arrived at." He called for "the removal, as far as possible," of all international economic barriers and the establishment of "equality of trade conditions among all the nations consenting to the peace." The most visionary "point" of the fourteen was "a general association of nations . . . for the purpose of affording mutual guarantees of political independence and territorial integrity to great and small states alike." Wilson concluded with an assurance to the Germans that the United States did not desire their destruction or humiliation. America would welcome them into the family of "peace-loving nations" if they demonstrated their clear desire for peace by overruling the "military party and the men whose creed is imperial domination."

Central Powers' spokesmen initially derided the Fourteen Points as propaganda and almost a year more of fighting and dying would follow. Then, following the 1918 German military failure on the western front, Wilson's hopeful and generous terms pushed Germany over the line to peace. That fall events moved swiftly. On October 27 the Austrians notified Wilson that they would be willing to conclude a separate peace. The next day the sailors of the German Imperial Navy mutinied at their base in Kiel when ordered to sail for a desperate showdown battle against the British fleet. The revolt soon spread to other German garrisons and towns. On November 9 the German kaiser abdicated and went into exile; Germany was proclaimed a republic. By this time German officials had already agreed to surrender terms at Compiègne in northern France. These incorporated much of the Fourteen Points but also imposed on Germany punitive reparations for war damages. On November 11 at 11 A.M. the guns fell silent; World War I, the Great War, was over.

Versailles.   On January 18, 1919, the victorious Allied leaders met at Versailles, near Paris, to determine the shape of the peace. Wilson was there in person. Although widely criticized for his precedent-shattering decision to leave the United States while in office, the president insisted that only his physical presence could ensure that the victors would accept a just and secure peace.

Wilson was received like a savior when he arrived in Europe. Wherever he went, enormous crowds turned out to cheer him. In Paris 2 million people lining the Champs-Elysées rained flowers and bouquets on his open car as he drove down the boulevard. The people of Europe were honoring not only the man; Wilson represented American idealism and the possibility of a more decent and democratic world system. Even the defeated Germans seemed willing to entrust their future to his hands.

But while the common people of Europe applauded the president, his chief Allied colleagues—Georges Clemenceau of France, David Lloyd George of Britain, and Vittorio Orlando of Italy—remained skeptical. To these unsentimental men Wilsonian idealism was all very well to shore up faltering Allied morale and weaken the German will to fight, but it seemed impractical as the basis for an international settlement. The major Allied powers wanted Germany condemned as a war criminal, totally disarmed, and forced to pay stiff indemnities that could be used to rebuild the devastated Allied economies. France, in particular, feared the might of a restored Germany and demanded guarantees that the attack of 1914 would not be repeated. The European Allies were also determined not to surrender any of their gains, including the German colonies that they had seized during the war. Finally, they were suspicious of the principle of self-determination. Could the confused patchwork of nationalities in eastern Europe really be sorted out into functioning nations? Reinforcing all anxieties and doubts was the specter of Bolshevism, already victorious in Russia, hovering over a continent devastated by war and shaken by the breakup of old empires. As the victorious Allied leaders conferred amid the splendors of Louis XIV's palace at Versailles, it seemed vital to move quickly or face Bolshevik-inspired revolutions throughout eastern and central Europe.

Wilson soon discovered that he could not force the European powers to accept his Fourteen Points without drastic modification. The French refused to consider any treaty provision that threatened their quest for secure borders. The British would not hear of the "freedom of the seas" that might challenge Britain's naval supremacy. Several of the European Allies wanted a slice of the overseas German empire, and they all wanted the German aggressor punished and forced to pay financial compensation for the losses they had incurred. The president was not happy with the changes his colleagues demanded, but he went along with most of them, convinced that his "general association of nations" would eventually right many of the injustices of the peace settlement.

The terms of the resulting treaty were a severe disappointment to idealists all over the world. The agreement allowed many German-speaking peoples to be absorbed into the newly created nations of Poland and Czechoslovakia. Italy acquired the German-speaking Tyrol. The German possessions in Africa and Asia were greedily parceled out among the European Allies. And, disastrously, Germany was forced to accept complete responsibility for the war—"war guilt," it was called—to disarm completely and pay reparations (ultimately set at $33 billion) to the victors. Unmentioned in the treaty were Wilson's idealistic calls for world disarmament, tariff reductions, and freedom of the seas.

Throughout the Versailles deliberations Wilson worked tirelessly for the League of Nations, the provision he considered the cornerstone of his peace proposals. As finally hammered out, the League would consist of a general assembly of all member nations, with an executive council to consist of the United States, the British Empire, France, Italy, Japan, and four other countries to be elected by the assembly. These bodies would listen to disputes among member nations and dispense international justice. The League's decisions could be enforced by economic sanctions against the international wrongdoers and, if necessary, by the use of military forces contributed by member nations. In addition, the League would help adjust minor disputes between citizens of different countries through a permanent International Court and seek to improve world social standards through an International Bureau of Labor.

As Wilson labored at Versailles during the winter of 1919, his support at home eroded. Before leaving for Europe he had asked the American public to vote for his party in the 1918 congressional elections as a mandate for his policies. When the voters gave the Republicans control of the Senate, his enemies claimed that they had repudiated the president's leadership. Wilson had further antagonized his political opponents by appointing only one Republican to the peace commission that accompanied him to Paris, although treaty ratification in the Senate would require the support of both parties.

Now, as news of the treaty's provisions filtered back to the United States, his opponents took sharp aim at its specific proposals. Irish-Americans were soon attacking the failure of the treaty to further the cause of Irish freedom from Britain. Italian-Americans complained because Italy had not been awarded the Adriatic city of Fiume (now Rijeka). German-Americans denounced the war-guilt clause that made their ancestral land a self-confessed criminal nation. Jingoes and super-patriots claimed that the treaty would compromise American sovereignty. Isolationists insisted that the League would entangle the United States in affairs abroad in which it had no true interest.

After two months of hard negotiating at Versailles, Wilson returned briefly to the United States to discover that the still-uncompleted treaty had come under withering fire. Thirty-seven senators, led by Henry Cabot Lodge of Massachusetts, had signed a "round robin" declaring that they would not vote for the treaty without amendment. Lodge and his fellow dissenters feared the loss of American autonomy under the League. Lodge himself also personally despised Wilson. "I never thought I could hate a man as I hate Wilson," he once said. The treaty had enough No votes to defeat it; clearly, a bitter battle over ratification was in prospect.

The president returned to Europe for further negotiations certain that the American people, if not the Senate, shared his vision of a new world order. To accommodate his critics, however, he had the League Covenant modified to allow any member nation to withdraw from the organization and to refuse colonial trusteeships if it so wished. The League would also keep hands off member nations' domestic tariff and immigration policies and avoid intruding into regional security arrangements such as the Monroe Doctrine. The treaty, incorporating the revised League Covenant, was ratified by the delegates in the Hall of Mirrors at Versailles on June 28, 1919. Soon afterward Wilson departed for home to fight for Senate approval.

The Battle for the League.

Scores of newspapers, many labor leaders, and representatives of farm and women's organizations—much of the old progressive coalition—supported Wilson's League, fearing that the peace would otherwise prove fragile. Wilson counted on people like these to get the treaty through the balky Senate. But by this time Senator Lodge had developed a clever strategy to defeat it. He would not oppose it directly but would demand a series of "reservations." (Reservations, unlike amendments, would not have to be approved by other League members.) Most of these would be moderate enough to attract support from a number of fence-sitting senators. But Lodge foresaw that Wilson and his supporters would reject them. If he maneuvered adeptly, Lodge believed, he might get its own supporters to defeat the treaty in the Senate.

First, Lodge called hearings that consumed many weeks. By the time the interested parties had finished their wordy testimony, the protreaty public had begun to lose interest. Wilson fought back. Although thoroughly exhausted by the arduous negotiations in France, he decided to take his case directly to the American people. For three weeks the tired president toured the country, speaking before large audiences in support of his work at Versailles. Soon after a speech at Pueblo, Colorado, Wilson collapsed and had to cancel the remainder of his trip. Following his return to Washington, he suffered a severe stroke that partially paralyzed him. For months he was unable to work, and during this period his wife and the cabinet took over most of the duties of the presidential office. Though Wilson's strength gradually returned, he never fully recovered, and he remained irritable and quick to take offense. The illness exaggerated Wilson's stubbornness and heightened his belief in his cause.

The president's illness proved fatal for the treaty. By the time he returned to Washington, Senator Lodge had appended fourteen "reservations" to the Versailles agreement. These actually altered the document only in detail. But the obstinate Wilson believed they "emasculated" his work, and he insisted that his supporters vote against the modified treaty. They did. At the same time the isolationists refused to accept the original treaty. It looked as if the agreement hammered out at Versailles was finished.

The treaty and the League were not yet dead, however. Under public pressure the Senate was forced to reconsider its decision. In March 1920 the modified treaty was once more put to a vote. Wilson again proved unyielding. "Either," he declared, "we should enter the league fearlessly, accepting the responsibility and not fearing the role of leadership which we now enjoy, contributing our efforts towards establishing a just and permanent peace, or we should retire as gracefully as possibly from the great concert of powers by which the world was saved." Wilson's supporters were loyal to him again, but they did his cause a fatal disservice by helping to defeat the treaty for the last time.

The ailing Wilson sought to make the 1920 presidential election a referendum on the League. It was a wasted effort, for the public was tired of war and progressivism and great crusades at home and abroad. Campaigning for "normalcy," the Republican candidate Warren G. Harding won by a landslide of seven million votes over his opponent, enabling the isolationists to claim that the American people had repudiated internationalism. The new Harding administration eventually signed a separate peace treaty with Germany officially ending the hostilities, but the United States never entered the League of Nations.

Conclusions

The outcome of World War I was profoundly disillusioning to those Americans who shared Wilson's view of their country as a missionary nation ordained to carry the blessings of liberal democracy to every part of the world. Most citizens, however, were not deeply committed internationalists, and after 1918 were happy to return to the business of their daily lives. They might agree with Wilson that the world deserved a better international order, but far more than the idealist in the White House, they had supported the war as the only way to punish the nation that had brutally violated American "rights" as a neutral and murdered Americans on the high seas. Both the ordinary citizen's modest goal of fending off a savage attacker who used barbarous U-boat warfare to gain his ends and the president's more exalted vision of a "new world" were needed to bring the United States into the great conflict. But the simple defeat of Germany was enough to satisfy the average American, and Wilson's hopes remained unfulfilled. America, having entered the war from a position of self-proclaimed moral authority, was forced to recognize that there were limits to what could be accomplished with great wealth and missionary zeal. The unworkable settlement reached at Versailles, the failure of the League of Nations, and the resurgent American isolationism that followed World War I—all these contributed to the causes of World War II, an even more colossal tragedy.

By 1919 progressivism, which had dominated the first two decades of the twentieth century, was in deep shadow. The battle to defeat Germany had consumed the emotions that had helped fuel the crusade against injustice and unregulated private power. At home wartime intolerance had broken up the broad progressive coalition by pitting American against American. In the prewar decades the issues of trust control, more responsive government, consumer protection, and social justice had united Americans. Now the nation was about to enter an era when cultural issues and prejudices would deeply divide them from one another.

ONLINE RESOURCES

"War Message of World War I" *http://www.lib.byu.edu/~rdh/wwi/1917/wilswarm.html* The speech featured on this site was delivered to Congress by President Woodrow Wilson on February 3, 1917. In it, he severed diplomatic relations with Germany, drawing America into the Great War.

"World War I Document Archive" *http://www.lib.byu.edu/~rdh/wwi/* This archive consists of official primary documents such as conventions and treaties concerning World War I. Also, the site contains personal stories of men and women who were involved with the war.

Sow the Seeds of Victory! Posters from the Food Administration during World War I *http://www.archives.gov/research/arc/topics/ww1.html#posters* In an appeal to the public's sense of voluntarism and because of the need for rationing food for the war effort, the U.S. Food Administration produced posters to meet their goals. This site also explains other government methods of food rationing during the conflict.

The Influenza Epidemic of 1918 *http://www.pbs.org/wgbh/amex/influenza/filmmore/index.html* This portion of PBS's "The American Experience" Web site examines the influenza pandemic of 1918 and its social, psychological, and scientific effects in America. Read how the virus outbreak influenced life in Boston and San Francisco.

Sir, I will Thank You with All My Heart: Seven Letters from the Great Migration *http://historymatters.gmu.edu/d/5332* Millions of southern African Americans sought defense jobs in the North with the beginning of American involvement in World War I. This collection of letters, addressed to the editors of a national black newspaper and written by black men seeking such work, speaks to their desire for nonagricultural employment and for social and economic justice.

24

The Twenties

Happy Adolescence or Decade of Stress?

1913	Henry Ford introduces the moving assembly line in his automobile plant
1916	Wilson is reelected president; The Federal Highways Act
1917	The Eighteenth Amendment provides for national Prohibition
1919	The Volstead Act enforces Prohibition; Steelworkers strike unsuccessfully for union recognition; Attorney General Palmer breaks miners' strike; Race riot in Chicago
1920	Palmer orders Department of Justice agents to jail 4,000 aliens suspected of radical activities; Warren Harding elected president; Pittsburgh station begins commercial radio broadcasting
1920–21	Postwar recession
1920–29	Unemployment and low profits beset the New England textile industry, coal mining, railroads, and agriculture; 1.2 million leave farms for cities
1921	The Sacco and Vanzetti trial; The American Plan is designed by the National Association of Manufacturers to resist unions; The Immigration Act establishes national quotas for first time
1921–23	Congress exempts farmers' cooperatives from antitrust laws and regulates middlemen's rates
1921–31	Treasury Secretary Andrew Mellon shifts the tax burden from the rich to the middle class
1922	The Fordney-McCumber Act raises tariff rates
1923	Harding dies; Calvin Coolidge becomes president; The Teapot Dome scandal
1924	Coolidge elected president; The Johnson-Reed Immigration Act establishes stricter immigration quotas
1925	Scopes trial; Ku Klux Klan membership reaches 3 million
1927	Sacco and Vanzetti executed; Charles Lindbergh makes first transatlantic solo flight; Marcus Garvey, black leader of Back to Africa movement, is deported
1928	Herbert Hoover elected president
1929	Southern mill owners defeat United Textile Workers' union drive; Automobile production reaches five times that of 1915; National Origins Act further limits immigration; The stock market crashes, ushering in the Great Depression
1930	Union membership falls to 3.6 million, down from a high of 5 million in 1920

To many of the men and women who reached adulthood after Versailles, the 1920s would seem a wonderful time of vitality, zany creativity, and bounding affluence. Novelist F. Scott Fitzgerald called the twenties "an age of miracles, . . . an age of art," when world leadership "passed to America." It was "the greatest gaudiest spree in history." Joseph Wood Krutch, one of the decade's bright young men, later recalled that he and his fellow journalists and critics "were . . . fundamentally optimistic, . . . gay crusaders. . . . The future was bright and the present was good fun at least." Contemporaries were also delighted with its economy. "We are approaching equality of prosperity more rapidly than most people realize," declared Harvard economist Thomas N. Carver in 1925.

Contemporary judgment was not all favorable, however. The novelist Sinclair Lewis considered the nation's heart hollow and sick. H. L. Mencken, a persistent critic of American life, thought only a tiny minority escaped the sham and stupidity of daily life in twenties America. After months spent in Muncie, Indiana, during 1924 interviewing citizens and investigating social conditions, sociologists Robert and Helen Lynd, New York sophisticates and social liberals, concluded that "Middletown's" people had failed to adjust to rapidly changing technology. Change had produced serious "friction spots" that people tried to relieve with boosterism and police repression.

What were the 1920s really like? Was it an era of happy adolescence when Americans, released from puritanical restraints and blessed with newfound abundance, responded creatively and joyously to a new world? Or was it a period of friction, repression, and painful adjustment covered over with a thin shiny veneer? Was the twenties economy a truly "new era," or was prosperity a fragile, bubble certain to burst at almost any moment?

The Swing to the Political Right

One way to view the twenties is as a time when diversity replaced unity. During the Progressive Era there was broad harmony on the big political issues. As we have noted, Americans shared a fear of big business and joined together in the crusade to check irresponsible power and protect the "common man." World War I projected this crusading mood out to the rest of the world and reinforced the voluntary unity of the preceding decade and a half with overheated patriotism. But the war also exhausted the national zeal to right wrongs and opened ideological and cultural fissures. With the armistice the consensus came apart. Americans lost their sense of common danger and abandoned their concern for social justice. In its place they substituted pursuit of the good life as each individual defined that term.

The Retreat to Privatism.   The new mood of privatism was felt first in the political sphere. By 1919 many progressive reformers were tired and disillusioned. Much of the great progressive crusade, it seemed, had ended in triviality. Journalist Walter Weyl of *The New Republic* despaired that the person "who aspired to overturn society, ends by fighting . . . for the inclusion of certain books" in a village

library. Walter Lippmann, Weyl's colleague, summed up the new attitudes, and po-
etically expressed his own waning political faith: "The people are tired," he wrote,
"tired of noise, tired of politics, tired of inconvenience, tired of greatness, and longing for a place where the world is quiet and where all trouble seems dead leaves,
and spent waves riot in doubtful dreams of dreams."

Progressivism did not entirely disappear, however. Its focus on efficiency in
business and government survived in Herbert Hoover's Commerce Department,
which worked to eliminate wasteful practices in private industry and government. In New York Governor Alfred E. Smith's administration successfully continued many progressive welfare programs. And the conservation ideal, well
represented by Horace Albright, superintendent of Yellowstone National Park, remained before the public's mind. In Congress meanwhile some fifty representatives and senators from the Midwest and South—the "Farm Bloc"—regularly
fought big-business domination of political life and senators George Norris and
Robert La Follette continued to demand that government protect the weak from
the rich and powerful. But most of this dissent lacked a broad vision, and in the
case of the Farm Bloc, too often was a defense of narrow agricultural interests
against urban ones. These survivals were at best a remnant of the once-pervasive
progressive impulse.

In foreign relations, isolationism, which had been in eclipse since the 1890s, once
again became the dominant public sentiment. The country did not cut its ties with
the rest of the world. On the contrary, during the 1920s, under presidents Harding,
Coolidge, and Hoover, the government aggressively fostered outlets for American
goods and capital abroad. Meanwhile, the Republican administrations sought to promote stability in the Western Hemisphere by dispatching U.S. marines to several
small Latin American countries to put down disorders and protect American lives
and property. This interventionist policy did not last. Gradually, under the leadership
of Secretaries of State Charles Evans Hughes and Frank Kellogg, the United States
backed away from intruding in Latin America's domestic affairs.

A more significant sign of isolationism, however, was the response to Europe
and "collective security." The United States never joined the League of Nations
and, after long wavering, rejected membership in the League's Court of International Justice. The nation's one stab at collective international peace efforts was the
Kellogg-Briand Pact of 1928 to "outlaw war," jointly initiated by France and the
United States and signed by scores of nations. The pact provided no penalties for
violators and was little more than a pious expression of hope. Meanwhile, Americans alienated our former allies, Britain, France, Belgium and other nations, by insisting that they pay us back for money lent in fighting the common enemy.

Harding's Presidency.
The wide swing in political mood was best expressed
by Senator Warren G. Harding of Ohio. Speaking to a Boston audience early
in 1920, before his election as president, the senator declared that the country
needed "not heroism, but healing, not nostrums but normalcy, not revolution,
but restoration, not agitation but adjustment, not surgery but serenity, not the
dramatic but the dispassionate, not experiment but equipoise, not submergence
in international duty but sustainment in triumphant nationality." It is difficult to
say precisely what Harding meant by these alliterative pairings, but the general

drift was clear: Americans wished to retreat from reform to a quieter, less demanding, more private world. And Harding was right about the public mood. Americans indeed wanted "normalcy."

Harding reflected the best and the worst of postwar America. He was amiable, kind, and neighborly, as befitted a former small-town newspaper editor. But he also was morally shoddy, bringing illegal liquor and a mistress into the White House while president. His good cheer and easy-going ways suited the public mood, however, and in 1920, against Democrats James Cox of Ohio and Franklin Roosevelt of New York, Harding and his running mate, Calvin Coolidge of Massachusetts, scored the most sweeping victory in a presidential election to that time.

Harding was an indifferent president. He did select for his cabinet talented men such as Charles Evans Hughes, the 1916 Republican presidential candidate, and Herbert Hoover, wartime food czar and administrator of Belgian war relief. Americans no longer considered businessmen villains and Harding successfully carried out the public mandate to reconcile government and business interests. During his administration, Washington became the friend and ally of business. The president himself supported the Fordney-McCumber Tariff (1922), which raised import duties far above those of the Underwood Tariff of 1913, and pushed for a bill to subsidize the American merchant marine, which, now that the war was over, could not compete with the merchant fleets of other nations.

Though government–business reconciliation was probably inevitable after 1918, the administration tilted too far in giving capital its way. Secretary of the Treasury Andrew Mellon, a Pittsburgh industrial tycoon, saw the high taxes imposed to finance the war as restraints on enterprise, and persuaded Congress to eliminate the wartime excess-profits tax and reduce income tax rates at the upper levels while leaving those at the bottom untouched. Between 1920 and 1929 Mellon won further victories for his drive to shift more of the tax burden from high-income earners to the middle and wage-earning classes.

Hughes and Hoover excepted, many of Harding's executive appointments were deplorable. As attorney general, he chose his old crony Harry M. Daugherty, a man of loose principles who distributed government favors with a free hand. The "Ohio gang" presided over by Daugherty's close friend Jesse Smith dispensed unwarranted Justice Department pardons and paroles, granted businessmen immunity from antitrust prosecution, and bestowed government appointments on any who would pay the price. To head the Veterans' Bureau, the president selected Charles R. Forbes, whom he had met while on vacation and liked. Forbes sold off veterans' hospitals' supposedly surplus blankets, sheets, and medical supplies for a song—and a kickback. Worst of all, perhaps, was Albert B. Fall, secretary of the interior. Soon after taking office, Fall induced the secretary of the navy to turn over the government's naval oil reserves to the Interior Department. Then, disregarding the public's interests, he promptly leased the Elk Hills (California) oil reserve to Edward L. Doheny of the Pan-American Petroleum Company and the Teapot Dome (Wyoming) reserves to Harry F. Sinclair. In exchange Doheny "lent" Fall $100,000 in cash; Sinclair gave Fall's son-in-law $200,000 in government bonds.

Harding was probably unaware of the Teapot Dome frauds and the other unsavory doings of his subordinates. In subsequent months, Fall would be convicted of accepting bribes, and Forbes would be sent to prison. The president, however, would never learn about these events. In June 1923 he had set out on a speaking tour of the West Coast and Alaska. In San Francisco, on the way home, he suffered a stroke and died in his hotel bed.

Coolidge Does Little.   Calvin Coolidge, who now became president, was as inward and dour as Harding had been outgoing and cheerful. As governor of Massachusetts he had done little to attract attention outside the state and seemed merely another regional politician. Then, in September 1919, when the Boston police went on strike, leaving the city exposed to unchecked crime and chaos, Governor Coolidge captured national attention by declaring that there was "no right to strike against the public safety by anybody, anywhere, anytime." These blunt words expressed the public's own growing impatience with labor unrest and won Coolidge the Republican vice presidential nomination the following year.

As president, Coolidge restored the public's faith in the honesty of the executive branch. He appointed two outstanding attorneys as prosecutors of the government's case against the Teapot Dome culprits, thus bypassing Daugherty, the corrupt attorney general. He soon replaced Daugherty with the distinguished former dean of the Columbia University Law School, Harlan Fiske Stone. The White House itself, hitherto the scene of hard-drinking, poker-playing cronyism, became a more dignified place with Coolidge and his charming and cultivated wife, Grace, as its occupants.

Otherwise Coolidge virtually slept away most of his five years in office. During his term the watchword of government was "do nothing." The administration avoided new programs to achieve a balanced budget and reduce the national debt. This inaction pleased business, but it ignored pressing social and physical needs of the country. The nation acquired a major new road system and hundreds of new schools, courthouses, and other public facilities; but the burden of constructing them was thrown largely on the states. Farmers found the new president a disappointment. Hoping for substantial assistance from the government to help them out of economic difficulties brought about by the contraction of war-inflated agricultural prices, they were dismayed when Coolidge twice vetoed congressional farm assistance plans.

But to be fair, Coolidge suited the public mood. On balance, most Americans liked what they saw: dignity in the White House and a president who knew when to let well enough alone. When Coolidge ran for president in his own right in 1924, he won by a large majority over the combined votes for La Follette on the new Progressive Farmer–Labor ticket and Democrat John W. Davis, a conservative corporation attorney from New York.

"New Era" Prosperity

Republican electoral success in the twenties was assured by the country's booming economy. By 1925 the United States was producing a flood of commodities beyond anyone's dreams, and most Americans could see little reason to challenge the party that stood watch over this affluent "New Era."

In fact, the decade opened with a brief, sharp recession. Government spending during the war had produced a boom that poured money into the pockets of millions of Americans. For a year following the armistice, good times continued and eased the return of 4 million men to the civilian economy. The bubble burst in 1920. As Europe recovered and restored its devastated fields and factories, its reliance on American exports declined. At the same time American consumers, appalled by sky-high prices, held off buying. Down came prices with a resounding crash, a collapse that particularly hurt farmers.

The hard times soon passed, however, and the economy surged. Growth of total GNP reached an average of 7 percent a year between 1922 and 1927. By 1923 unemployment was only about 3 percent of the labor force. Total national product in 1929 would be 75 percent higher than in 1909. The income of the average American was a third higher in 1929 than in the last years before World War I.

The Consumer Durables Revolution.

The great economic boom of the middle and late 1920s was in part triggered by readily available credit. Interest rates remained low through the decade. Thousands of citizens could and did borrow money to invest in factories and productive machinery, buy houses, and acquire expensive goods "on the installment plan." Foreigners borrowed extensively from American bankers, and the borrowed dollars soon came back to pay for imported American automobiles, electrical equipment, petroleum, wheat, and corn.

More fundamental than cheap credit was a major structural change in the economy. Between 1910 and 1920 average family income reached the point where many Americans had substantial amounts of discretionary income (that is, money left over after buying necessities, such as food, clothing, and shelter). For the first time, a relatively large number of consumers could afford services and goods that had always been beyond their reach. Many middle- and working-class women could now buy silk, or at least rayon, stockings and pay for the services of beauty parlors and hairdressers. Middle-class families could "eat out" more often, go to the movies, and employ household help. Most important, American consumers could now buy expensive "durables" like radios, vacuum cleaners, washing machines, electric irons, refrigerators, and, above all, automobiles. In 1929 automobile production was five times greater than it had been fourteen years earlier, and there were over 23 million registered passenger cars in the country. This development in consumption patterns has been called a "consumer durables revolution."

The total impact of the new markets was immense. Demand for consumer durables called forth billions of dollars of investment in new factories and offices, creating jobs and income for building contractors, architects, electricians, bricklayers, and a host of people directly involved in construction. The indirect effects, especially of the automobile, were truly immense. Cars needed roads. Until the 1920s the typical American highway was a dirt track leading from the farm to the local railroad depot. Now the states, aided by matching federal outlays under the Federal Highway Act of 1916, poured billions into new, hard-surfaced, all-weather roads. At the end of the 1920s the nation had an unequaled network of 275,000 miles of asphalt and concrete intercity two-lane highways.

Investment in roads was only the beginning, however. To meet the needs of automobile manufacturers and users, capital poured into the steel, rubber, glass, and petroleum-producing industries. The automobile also gave birth to a new generation of suburban communities now made accessible to city wage earners

Cities had known traffic jams in the age of the horse and wagon. But they got much worse—and spread to the suburbs as well—after the automobile became supreme in the 1920s.

by the family car and the paved highway. Within ten years new "automobile suburbs" grew up in rings around the cities, beyond the streetcar suburbs of an earlier period. There was a downside, undoubtedly, of this surge in automobile ownership and use. It was in many ways the first phase of the major problems of pollution and suburban sprawl that would worsen in our own day. But clearly it spurred the economy.

Growing industrial efficiency also fueled the economic boom. In 1913 Henry Ford had introduced the moving assembly line in his Detroit automobile plant. During the war the need for speed to supply the fighting fronts and offset labor shortages led to greater reliance on such mass-production techniques using standardized, interchangeable parts. Meanwhile, the principles of Frederick W. Taylor, which reduced management to a precise "science," spread to more and more industrial concerns. These elements combined to increase labor productivity dramatically. By one estimate, the amount of labor time needed for a given unit of industrial output shrank 21 percent between 1920 and 1929.

Business and Labor.   Still another cause—as well as effect—of prosperity was the new public attitude toward private enterprise. Americans celebrated business and businesspeople during the 1920s. At times their good opinion approached reverence. "The man who builds a factory builds a temple," intoned President Coolidge, and "the man who works there worships there." In a 1925–1926 bestseller

The Man Nobody Knows, an advertising executive could find no better way to convey the glory of Jesus than by describing him as a first-rate entrepreneur who "picked up twelve men from the bottom ranks of business and forged them into an organization that conquered the world." The clergy itself was saturated with business values. Typical sermon titles of the 1920s included "Christ: From Manger to Throne," "Public Worship Increases Your Efficiency," and "Business Success and Religion Go Together." Preachers were admonished by parishioners and church superiors to "preach the gospel and advertise."

This pro-business attitude inevitably hurt organized labor. Without public support, the unions suffered a succession of defeats when they attempted to organize sectors of industrial labor. In 1919, the steelworkers union lost a major strike to gain recognition from the large steel firms. In 1929, mill owners defeated the efforts of the United Textile Workers to unionize southern cotton workers. Encouraged by the changed environment, American business, under the auspices of the National Association of Manufacturers, adopted the "American Plan" to roll back trade unionism. Businessmen were encouraged to use labor spies to ferret out and report on union activities, to hire strikebreakers if unions tried to shut them down, and to spread propaganda among their employees to discourage union organizing.

An unfriendly federal government and biased federal courts also contributed to organized labor's declining fortunes. The steel strikers lost in 1919 in part because Attorney General A. Mitchell Palmer dispatched federal troops to the United States Steel plant at Gary, Indiana, to protect strikebreakers. Shortly thereafter Palmer broke a miners' strike. In 1922 Attorney General Daugherty ordered a federal judge to issue an injunction against idle railroad shopworkers, forcing them back to work. Under Chief Justice William Howard Taft, the former president, the Supreme Court gutted the provision of the Clayton Act exempting unions from antitrust prosecution and made it possible once again for employers to attack union activities as illegal restraints of trade.

The figures reflect these changes. In 1920, as a result of wartime expansion, the number of union members had reached over 5 million—almost 20 percent of all nonagricultural workers. It soon dropped to 3.6 million, hovering around this figure for the remainder of the decade while the labor force grew rapidly. By 1930 scarcely 10 percent of nonfarm workers belonged to unions.

The Depressed Industries.

The boom of 1923–1929 was wide and deep enough to validate the conservative, pro-business values of the day. But prosperity was by no means universal. Unemployment remained high and wages low in several chronically sick industries. Miners of soft coal experienced hard times throughout the decade. The railroad industry was depressed, and the railroad companies laid off many workers. Cotton manufacturing also failed to benefit from overall prosperity. To survive in the face of stiff competition, many textile companies had moved from New England to the southern Piedmont region of Virginia, the Carolinas, and Georgia, where labor and land were cheap and where they could put up new mills with the latest and most efficient equipment. The southern mill communities were often squalid places for their inhabitants. Upton Sinclair reported that at Marion, South Carolina, most mill workers' homes lacked running water or toilets. Old newspapers served as wallpaper.

The most seriously depressed of all economic sectors was the most competitive one: agriculture. In 1925 there were still 6.5 million American farms, and growers of wheat and cotton faced millions of foreign competitors as well. During the war farmers had borrowed heavily to buy more land and upgrade their machinery to cash in on high wartime prices. Then, at the end of 1920, farm prices dropped sharply leaving farmers with large interest payments but less income. During the remainder of the decade farmers continued to confront low prices and large debts.

Farmers adapted to the depression in different ways. During the 1920s over 1.2 million people abandoned agriculture, most of them going to the cities and their growing suburbs. The migration of black sharecroppers and farm laborers out of the rural South became a flood, though new opportunities in northern manufacturing was as much an incentive to move as the depressed conditions in the cotton fields. Farmers also turned to politics, as they had in the past. But except for La Follette's short-lived effort in 1924 to create a farmer–labor alliance, they relied on pressure-group politics rather than third parties. The congressional farm bloc extracted legislation from Congress to ease agricultural credit, exempt farmers' cooperatives from antitrust prosecution, and regulate the rates various middlemen charged. Their major program, however, the McNary-Haugen plan, stalled. This scheme obligated the federal government to buy domestic farm surpluses at prices that would guarantee growers a good income and then sell them abroad at the lower world price, with the loss made up from a small fee paid by each farmer. Twice Congress approved the McNary-Haugen Farm Relief Bill and twice Coolidge vetoed the measure as favoring a special class of citizens and unduly interfering with free markets. Though the scheme never passed, it familiarized Americans with the idea of farm price supports, which a more experimental decade would later enact into law.

Old and New America

During the 1920s, then, the United States was not exempt from economic difficulties and class antagonisms. Yet organized opposition to the class and economic arrangements of society remained weak. Support for the Socialist party dwindled as working- and middle-class citizens lost interest in radical action. In 1928 Norman Thomas, the Socialist party's presidential candidate, received only 267,000 votes; William Z. Foster, of the new Communist party, only 49,000.

Still, the 1920s were scarcely harmonious. Americans fought bitterly over many issues, but they were primarily social and cultural rather than political or economic. As in other periods of relative prosperity, including our own, the questions that most divided citizens involved religion, ethnicity, race, culture, and styles of life.

As we look at the twenties we can identify two broad divisions of cultural belief and style, separated by a chasm. Two contingents of Americans confronted one another. On one side were the forces of New America. New America was urban, and professed to be urbane. It was also modernist and free thinking in religion and was apt to be liberal or, occasionally, radical in politics. It was also culturally liberal. At the level of the "man-in-the-street" this often meant "fun-loving" hedonism. Among the better educated it was associated with avant-garde or modernist taste in the arts. New America accepted freer sexual standards and was "wet"—that is, it considered drinking a matter better left to private conscience than government regulation. On the issue of alcohol, though not necessarily on the others, New America found itself allied with urban Catholics.

Old America, by contrast, was rural or small town and proud of its traditional family-centered values. In religion it was Protestant, and often fundamentalist. Its politics tended to be conservative and strongly Republican in the North. It rejected the freer sexual practices of New America. Old America considered drinking both a social evil and a sin that should be discouraged by the authorities. Old America and New America were both loose clusters that at no point had any formal embodiment in a single organization. And yet, to a surprising degree, these two sets of attitudes can be found consistently ranged against each other in the passionate cultural war that raged throughout the twenties.

Wets Versus Drys.   Prohibition was a major cultural battlefield of the decade. During the Gilded Age, the Women's Christian Temperance Union (WCTU) and the Anti-Saloon League had launched a crusade against "demon rum." Early in the new century progressives took up the cause of restricting liquor to suppress a social evil. By 1915 fifteen states in the South, Midwest, and Far West had prohibited the production and sale of alcoholic beverages. In truth, not all rural Americans were drys. In the rural South, especially, there was a venerable tradition of illegal distilling—and consumption—of "moonshine." Yet it was the big cities in the industrialized states where the resistance to prohibition was most formidable. These were home to many New Americans—Catholics, sophisticates, and social liberals—who considered it tyrannical for the state to dictate what a person could or could not drink. Other enemies were the brewers and distillers, loudly seconded by the saloonkeepers and proprietors of hotels and restaurants, who stood to lose business, if not their very livelihoods, if Americans were not permitted their beer, wine, and whiskey.

World War I gave the campaign for national prohibition an enormous boost. Temperance organizations contended that brewing and distilling consumed badly needed grain. They played on the public's concern for the morals of the young men drafted into the army and took advantage of the fact that many brewers were of German origin. In 1917 Congress passed the Eighteenth Amendment, outlawing the manufacture, sale, and transportation of intoxicating liquors one year after its adoption. In January 1920, after state confirmation, national Prohibition went into effect.

The Volstead Act of 1919 implemented the Eighteenth Amendment by declaring illegal any beverage containing more than 0.5 percent alcohol and establishing a Prohibition Bureau for enforcing the law. But at no time during the Prohibition Era did Congress ever give the bureau enough money to do its job. Nor were city and state authorities particularly willing to spend resources to enforce the federal measure. Some states passed their own "baby Volstead acts," but their enforcement, too, was generally poorly funded and weak. Americans continued to drink.

Poor enforcement was as much a symptom as a cause of Americans' continuing homage to John Barleycorn. Many of those who supported Prohibition did so only for the sake of appearances or to guarantee someone else's good behavior.

In a famous quip humorist Will Rogers remarked that the people of one thoroughly dry state would "hold faithful and steadfast to Prohibition as long as the voters [could] stagger to the polls." In fact, by adding an element of the forbidden to the usual attractions of drinking, Prohibition made alcohol consumption appealing to new classes of people. In former days the "better" people seldom consumed hard liquor. Now whiskey, rum, and gin became a significant part of urban middle-class life. Alcohol consumption overall apparently declined during the 1920s and with it such diseases as cirrhosis and alcoholic psychosis as well as arrests for public drunkenness. But the "noble experiment" also replaced the tea party with the cocktail party as a social diversion and a mark of distinction between the urban sophisticate and the puritanical, small-town "rube."

It has been said that whenever a community forbids a practice that many favor, it encourages disregard for law in general. This formula held true in the 1920s. The United States might enjoin the manufacture and sale of intoxicants, but Canadians, Mexicans, and Europeans did not. Alcohol transported by truck across the borders or landed clandestinely by boat on the beaches produced huge profits for rumrunners. Once in the country, its distribution and sale were taken over by bootleggers, who were also happy to furnish customers with "moonshine," "white lightning," "bathtub gin," and other potent—and often dangerous—domestic concoctions.

Prohibition, along with the fast automobile and the Thompson submachine gun, helped create modern-day organized crime. To accommodate the thousands of citizens who were willing to pay good money to drink, enterprising and ruthless men organized liquor distribution networks that rivaled major legitimate business enterprises in their complexity and efficiency. Just as successful businessmen often diversified, successful bootleggers, organized into "families" under strong and brutal leaders, extended their operations into prostitution, gambling, and the "protection" racket.

The "mobs" brought new violence to the cities. When one gang tried to invade another's territory, the result was often warfare that left scores dead. In the 1929 St. Valentine's Day massacre, for example, six members of Bugs Moran's North Side gang were gunned down by unknown rivals in a Chicago garage while waiting for a shipment of bootleg liquor. Periodically, crusading district attorneys, goaded by the newspapers or citizens' groups, cracked down on the gangsters. But indictments and convictions were hard to get. Members of rival mobs refused to testify against their opponents; honest citizens were intimidated; officials, judges, and juries were bought off. Al Capone, the Chicago gang lord, foiled every attempt to bring him to justice and was only convicted when Eliot Ness of the U.S. Justice Department's special squad of "untouchables" found evidence against him of income tax evasion.

Throughout the 1920s millions of citizens continued to consider Prohibition a "noble experiment" worth supporting for the sake of national health and social order and moral purity. "Drys"agitated constantly to increase appropriations for Volstead Act enforcement; the Anti-Saloon League maintained lobbyists in Washington and the state capitals to ensure that lawmakers did not relax their vigilance. No group endorsed the noble experiment as vigorously as the Protestant clergy, especially those of the conservative evangelical denominations. Nevertheless, by the end of the decade the dry forces were losing ground, and each day more and more people came to believe that the noble experiment had failed.

Xenophobia.   During the war, as we saw, superpatriotism and xenophobia had tarnished the nation's liberal record on civil liberties and ethnic tolerance. Antiforeign tensions grew after the armistice as thousands of Europeans sought to escape the devastation of their homelands by fleeing to the United States. European immigration quadrupled between 1919 and 1920 and almost doubled again in 1921.The new wave of foreigners threatened Old America. The immigrants were largely Catholic and Jewish and hence religiously alien. They were also certain to be "wet" since neither Catholics nor Jews generally considered drinking sinful.

"Red Scare."   Some of the new arrivals were also radicals—or so many Old Americans believed. Ever since the war and the Bolshevik Revolution, the public had worried about radicals and social upheaval. This anxiety was magnified soon after the armistice by a wave of terrorist bombings. In early 1919 a series of bomb-laden packages arrived at the homes of public figures despised by the political far left. When opened by unsuspecting recipients they exploded, causing serious injuries. That April a clerk at the New York post office, alerted by the bombings, spotted sixteen suspicious packages about to be mailed to prominent people. Charles Kaplan notified his superiors who discovered that the packages indeed contained "infernal devices." In June a series of bombings ripped the homes of judges and public officials in cities across the country. The worst in its effects was the enormous explosion that detonated outside the home of Attorney General A. Mitchell Palmer in Washington on the night of June 2. The blast shattered the windows and destroyed the porch. One who came to the Palmers' aid was Assistant Secretary of the Navy Franklin Roosevelt, who lived across the street.

The public blamed the violence on alien extremists, and it was probably right. Palmer's response, however, was disproportionate. In January 1920 Department of Justice agents rounded up 6,000 men and women, mostly eastern European aliens, on suspicion of radical activities, and threw them into unsanitary, overcrowded cells. There they were kept for weeks without explicit charges placed against them. Despite Palmer's assertion that a radical uprising was imminent, the police discovered no explosives and only three handguns among the hapless radicals. Eventually the courts released most of the prisoners.

As the ordeal of Nicola Sacco and Bartolomeo Vanzetti illustrates, even after Palmer's term, fear of radicalism remained a central component of anti-foreign feeling among traditional Americans. The two men, both Italian-born and both admitted anarchists, were convicted in 1921 of killed a shoe factory paymaster and his guard in South Braintree, Massachusetts, in the course of a robbery. Scholars still disagree over whether the two men were guilty of the crime, but it is clear that judge Webster Thayer, who officiated at their trial and presided over a number of the review hearings, was strongly prejudiced against foreigners and radicals. And he was not alone. To many Old Americans the men were aliens, both in their "race" and their views.

On the other side, the liberal community rallied around the two Italian radicals. Led by journalist Walter Lippmann and law professor Felix Frankfurter, liberals and intellectuals turned the defense of Sacco and Vanzetti into a crusade for free speech and common justice. Meetings, petitions, lobbying, and civil disobedience were deployed to drum up support for retrial or pardon of the two prisoners.

The issue so deeply divided public opinion that one Sacco-Vanzetti supporter, the novelist John Dos Passos, described the opposing sides as "two nations." The liberals succeeded in getting the case reconsidered several times. But on August 22, 1927, after final appeals for clemency were rejected, both men were sent to the electric chair. Whatever most Americans believed, to the political left, in both America and around the world, their execution was accounted judicial murder.

The Door Is Closed.   Antiforeign feeling fueled a powerful drive for immigration restriction. It would be unfair to dismiss the arguments for restriction as mere bigotry. The United States could not have continued an open-door policy on immigration indefinitely. Yet restriction need not have been so extreme nor have so sharply discriminated along ethnic lines. In 1921, as a preliminary move, Congress limited for a one-year period the number of new arrivals of each nationality to 3 percent of that group present in the country in 1910. In 1924 it passed the Johnson-Reed Immigration Act limiting total immigration to 154,000 persons annually and assigning national quotas that strongly favored northern and western over southern and eastern Europe. Italy, Poland, and Russia—the major sources of recent immigrants—were left with ludicrously small quotas.

The Johnson-Reed Act ended the three centuries of free European immigration to America. It also enshrined into law the prejudices of native-born Old America against persons who, by their mere presence, seemed to be endangering the customs, habits, and beliefs of the United States.

Black Achievement.   The growing assertiveness of blacks disturbed much of Old America. During the war thousands of black soldiers had served their country in France, where they had encountered a racially more liberal society than their own. When they returned home, some sought to defy the segregation and bigotry of their own country and, in the South, became targets of violence. In 1919 alone, ten black veterans were lynched in southern states, several while still in uniform. Less dramatic, but far more important, thousands of southern blacks left for the North, continuing the wartime exodus. By 1930 Chicago would have over 230,000 black residents; New York, over 327,000; Philadelphia, over 219,000; and Detroit, over 120,000.

Few black Americans who came north found work beyond unskilled or semi-skilled labor. The typical black worker in the North during the 1920s was a factory hand or a day laborer. In increasing numbers black women replaced Irish and German women as domestics in middle-class urban homes.

The mass movement of rural blacks to northern slums worsened urban social problems. Black families experienced many of the same strains as the immigrant families of the recent past. Children, once physically close to parents, now lost touch as fathers and mothers went to work away from the home. Poverty in the northern city seemed worse at times than in the rural South, where a family could at least raise part of its food and was spared many city costs. The black migration to northern cities brought racial tensions in its wake. Many whites resented and feared the new arrivals and fought to exclude them from their neighborhoods. In Chicago racial antagonisms built during the summer of 1919 and exploded in a furious race riot in late July when a black teenager, swimming off a Lake Michigan beach that whites considered their preserve, was stoned and drowned. Within hours gangs of white and black youths were battling one another and beating innocent bystanders. For thirteen days the city was torn by riot, arson, and vandalism, with the authorities unable to stop the destruction. When the casualties were finally counted, the death toll stood at almost 40, with over 500 injured.

Despite the troubles and difficulties, some blacks found new opportunities in northern cities. Sociologist and historian W. E. B. Du Bois, poet and critic James Weldon Johnson, and painter Henry Ossawa Tanner already had established reputations in professional circles. But the black achievements of the 1920s outshone anything earlier. Harlem, in upper Manhattan, became a black Athens where poets, writers, painters, musicians, and intellectuals gathered from all over the country and from other parts of the world. Among the Harlem Renaissance authors were Jamaican-born Claude McKay who wrote eloquently and bitterly about the repression of blacks; Jean Toomer, an author of realistic stories about black life; and Countee Cullen, a master of delicate lyric poetry. Most impressive of all was Langston Hughes, a poet, novelist, and short-story writer of rare power who could employ humor as well as satire and argument to defend his race and express its hopes.

The 1920s was also an era when black musicians and music began to attract the attention of white Americans. Although they seldom gave it a second thought, whenever a white "flapper" and her "lounge lizard" boyfriend danced the Charleston or Black Bottom, they were affirming the vitality of black musical creativity in the 1920s. This was the decade when jazz broke out of the black community and began to find an appreciative audience around the world. Within the black community itself, great performing artists like the trumpeter Louis Armstrong, trombonist Kid Ory, and the powerful blues singer Bessie Smith were immensely popular. Their records sold millions of copies among the "cliff-dwellers" of Harlem, Chicago's South Side, and the other developing urban black neighborhoods.

Marcus Garvey.   The new urban environment was fertile soil for a Back-to-Africa movement led by Marcus Garvey, a native of the Caribbean, who came to New York in 1916 to establish a branch of his Universal Negro Improvement Association. Garvey appealed especially to working-class urban blacks who did not feel at home in the NAACP, the middle-class black defense organization. Garvey told blacks to be proud of their race. Everything black, he declared, was admirable and beautiful. Because America was unalterably racist, black people should return to Africa and there erect a new empire befitting their potential. The black middle class considered these ideas unsound; but among the urban immigrants from the rural South, Garvey's message was beguiling. Many joined the movement to become knights of the Nile, dukes of the Niger and Uganda, and members of the Black Eagle Flying Corps or the Universal Black Cross Nurses.

Federal officials eventually accused Garvey of mail fraud. Tried by a liberal white judge, a member of the rival NAACP, he was sentenced to five years in jail and died in obscurity in 1940. Despite his failure, he had blazed a black separatist trail that other black leaders would follow over a generation later.

The Sexual Revolution.   Sexual behavior was yet another issue that divided the two Americas. No matter how fiercely traditionalists might protest, the nation's sexual values were changing, especially among the young.

Women were at the forefront of this transformation. Once the battle for female suffrage was won, the woman's rights movement began to retreat. The League of Women Voters succeeded the National American Woman Suffrage Association, but failed to arouse the same enthusiasm for expanded economic opportunity for women as it had for suffrage. Alice Paul's more militant National Woman's party, with an equal rights amendment to the Constitution as its major goal, survived into the 1920s, but with only 8,000 members it had little influence. But having won the right to vote, women activists and dissenters now challenged the status quo in the social realm. Young urban, middle-class women began to demand in ever-larger numbers that they be treated as adult individuals, not as overgrown children or fragile dolls. In the 1920s many respectable wives, mothers, and daughters began to smoke, a habit that till then had been confined to men or to women of ill-repute. They also began to drink as never before. The new cocktail party introduced a feminine element to social drinking, previously an all-male preserve. However dubious for health, the changes marked a new level of feminine independence.

More shocking was the new female sexual assertiveness. For women who reached their late teens or twenties between 1919 and 1929, sex was not so obviously linked to marriage and children as it had been for their mothers. Influenced by a popularized version of Sigmund Freud's theories concerning the emotional dangers of sexual repression, many young women began to insist that they were as entitled as men to the pleasures of physical love and the free choice of sexual partners. The incidence of premarital sex increased sharply, especially among well-educated women. Adultery also became more common. Even when young women did not "go all the way," they were far more relaxed in their social relations with men than before. Young women of respectable families "petted"; they refused to be chaperoned; they danced "cheek-to-cheek."

The "flapper," as the liberated young woman of the 1920s was called, also insisted on greater freedom in her dress and appearance. In contrast to the "womanly" long skirt, sweeping picture hat, rounded bosom, tight natural waist, and petticoats of the past, her skirt was cut off at the knee to reveal a long stretch of silk- or rayon-stockinged leg. Her waistline was high, her bosom flattened, her underclothes minimal, her cloche hat brimless. In 1913 a typical woman's outfit consumed nineteen and a half yards of cloth. In 1925 it required a scant seven. Hair, previously grown long and worn down the back or pinned up, was cut short and "bobbed" or "shingled." To offset the tomboy effect of her dress and reassert her femininity, the flapper painted her face as respectable women never had before.

Traditional Americans predictably deplored the new trends in dress and behavior among the female young. Smoking by women was the "beginning of the end," according to one male social critic. Dr. Francis Clark of the Christian Endeavor Society denounced modern dances as "impure, polluting, corrupting, debasing." One clergyman proclaimed: "We get our [dress] styles from New York, New York from Paris, and Paris from Hell." Legislators joined the disapproving chorus. In 1921 the Utah legislature considered a bill to fine or imprison any woman whose skirts were higher than three inches above the ankle.

The Media Assault on the Small Town.

In explaining the erosion of the traditional sexual code, moralists often pointed to the debasing effects of the media.

Novels like Walter Fabian's *Flaming Youth* (1923), F. Scott Fitzgerald's *This Side of Paradise* (1920), and Floyd Dells' *Moon-Calf* (1920) glorified the pursuit of pleasure by the young. Early in the decade Hollywood produced a flood of films with such suggestive titles as *Up in Mabel's Room, A Shocking Night, Sinners in Silk,* and *Her Purchase Price.* One producer described his films as replete with "neckers, petters, white kisses, red kisses, pleasure-mad daughters, sensation-seeking mothers . . . the truth—bold, naked, sensational." Though this was pretty tame compared to recent "X-rated" films, it brought down the wrath of the moralists and censors. To avoid legal repression, the movie industry in 1922 chose a "czar"—Warren Harding's postmaster general, Will H. Hays—to lay down guidelines of taste and decorum. The Hays Office rules ended the rash of cheap exploitation movies. Critics charged that they also lowered the intellectual and artistic level of Hollywood films to that suitable for a sheltered child of twelve. In 1930 the movie industry adopted a "production code" to guarantee that motion pictures would not offend the most prudish tastes.

The moralists undoubtedly exaggerated the social impact of the movies. But they were not entirely mistaken. Popular media undoubtedly helped to undermine the values and culture of Old America even when they did not directly

A 1922 cover of George Jean Nathan and H. L. Mencken's "The Smart Set" featuring a story by F. Scott Fitzgerald. It touches on a set of famous twenties cultural icons: jazz music and flappers.

attack them. Good roads and the automobile had reduced the isolation of America's farms and small towns. Now the movies brought to the smallest communities an image of sophisticated urban life that appealed intensely to American youth. Young people learned what passed for romantic technique among worldly men and women. "It was directly through the movies that I learned to kiss a girl on her ears, neck, and cheeks, as well as her mouth," wrote one young man. After long exposure to the fantasies of Hollywood, one small-town girl told a social researcher that her "daydreams . . . consist of clothes, ideas on furnishings, and manners." Such young people were not easily induced to accept the sexual taboos, dress customs, and social values of their small town and rural communities.

Radio, too, challenged small-town values. The basic technology of radio was invented before World War I, but the medium did not come into its own until 1920, when Station KDKA in Pittsburgh began to broadcast commercial programs. In 1927 General Electric, Westinghouse, and the Radio Corporation of America joined to create the first radio network, the National Broadcasting Company. The Columbia Broadcasting Company appeared the next year. By 1929 over 10 million American families owned receiving sets. Radio broadcasting was not placed under government control, as in most of Europe. Instead, it became a private industry dependent on advertising for revenue. In 1927 the federal government did intrude by assigning station wavelengths to avoid chaos, but it did little to compel broadcasters to serve the public. Advertisers who paid the stations' bills and naturally wished to attract the largest audiences were far more inclined to sponsor "Roxy and His Gang" or "Amos 'n Andy" than serious intellectual or political discussion or the Metropolitan Opera, programming with limited public appeal.

But if commercial broadcasting failed to promote serious discourse or elevate public taste, it exposed listeners to a high level of professionalism that did much to unintentionally undermine the confidence and morale of village America. How could a community amateur hour outdo the "Ipana Troubadours"? How could the local high school dance band compete with Paul Whiteman, coming "live from New York"?

Rebel Artists. Nor was the decade free from more direct assaults on traditional cultural values. The big cities, especially New York, were the havens of sophisticates who projected a barely disguised contempt for rural, small-town America. The bohemians of the shabby-chic apartments and refurbished townhouses of Greenwich Village in lower Manhattan felt themselves escapees from small-town culture. They expressed their new freedom through hard drinking, free sex lives, socialism, and devotion to the avant-garde in the arts and in thought.

The bohemians of the twenties considered American culture hopelessly provincial. Europe, with its greater intellectual and artistic depth, seemed far more interesting. Many of the decade's writers, including Ernest Hemingway, F. Scott Fitzgerald, Edna St. Vincent Millay, and Gertrude Stein, felt so alienated that they left the country, most to live in Paris for long periods. There a vibrant expatriate community developed that cross-pollinated creative communities in New York, Boston, San Francisco, and the better college campuses.

Some who stayed, as well as a few who left, wrote novels that ridiculed and condemned the life of the American small town. Sinclair Lewis's *Main Street* (1920) recounts the story of a young woman who moves to Gopher Prairie, a typical midwestern small town. There she resolves to reform her neighbors' tastes, values, and politics, but is instead defeated by their ignorance and materialism. Sherwood Anderson's *Winesburg, Ohio* (1919) depicts the small-mindedness, hypocrisy, and secret vice that Anderson believed afflicted provincial Americans.

American writers and intellectuals ridiculed not only the small towns but also the entire culture of Old America. H. L. Mencken, the acid-tongued social critic of the *Baltimore Evening Sun*, turned his guns on almost everything in his native land and shocked traditional Americans by his irreverence, elitism, and ridicule of established beliefs. Mencken reserved his sharpest barbs for the "booboisie," the crass and puritanical middle class he claimed inhabited the country's heartland. Sinclair Lewis followed *Main Street* with *Babbitt* (1922), a novel about a businessman in a middle-sized midwestern city whose material success and irrepressible boosterism masked deep doubt about his own worth. Its hero's name became a byword for conformity. Another powerful indictment of the nation's materialism was *An American Tragedy* (1925) by Theodore Dreiser, a tale of the corrupting effect of ambition for wealth and position on a weak young man.

F. Scott Fitzgerald was a more subtle denigrator of America's predominant values. Fitzgerald was alternately attracted and repelled by the life of the American upper bourgeoisie in the 1920s. He never lost his fascination for the rich and their doings, but in *The Great Gatsby* (1925) he brilliantly depicted the dry rot at the heart of America's business civilization in the person of Jay Gatsby, a man who destroys himself in pursuit of wealth and glamor.

A representative young man of the "Lost Generation," who had fought in World War I and had returned to find "all Gods dead, all wars fought, all faiths shaken," Ernest Hemingway was still another mordant critic of American civilization. In *The Sun Also Rises* (1926) he portrays a group of young Americans wandering through Europe after World War I seeking a substitute for the ideals of the past that now seemed hollow and insincere. In this first book and such later works as *A Farewell to Arms* (1929), in muscular, unadorned prose, Hemingway depicts characters struggling against the hypocrisies of the world and forced to find heroism and authenticity in their private lives.

Drama also became a vehicle of protest against the conventionality of the decade. Eugene O'Neill, the most important figure of the "little theater" movement, was the first American playwright of international distinction. O'Neill and the stage designers, producers, and other writers connected with the Provincetown Players sought to make the American theater into a vehicle for expressing serious ideas. With such productions as Elmer Rice's *The Adding Machine* (1923), satirizing the emptiness of modern commercial life, and O'Neill's *Desire Under the Elms* (1924), debunking American puritanism, the little theater groups looked critically at American life.

Confrontation

Old America watched with pain, frustration, and anger the influx of immigrants, the new assertiveness of blacks, the frivolous and "immoral" behavior of the young, the rise of organized crime, and the ridicule and naysaying of the writers and intellectuals. The "intellectuals and liberals," declared one defender of the old

ways, had "betrayed Americanism" and created "confusion in thought and opinion, a groping and hesitancy about national affairs and private life alike." Old
America seized on every sign that all was not lost. The successful solo flight of
Charles Lindbergh to Paris in 1927 touched off a wave of hero worship unequaled
since Washington's day. "Lindy," the tall, clean-cut, blond young American
from the Midwest, demonstrated that something survived of the noble past. His
achievement, noted one social critic, showed "that we are not rotten at the core,
but morally sound and sweet and good!" Old America fought back against
modernity, setting off a series of confrontations that alternately disturbed and
fascinated the nation.

The Klan Reborn.

The Klan Reborn.   At its most angry and extreme, Old America's counterattack took the form of a revived Ku Klux Klan. The Klan of Reconstruction days
lived on in the South's collective memory as the heroic savior of white culture and
the bulwark against "ignorant" blacks and their villainous carpetbagger allies.
This view was reinforced and widely disseminated by a popular historical novel,
The Clansman, published in 1905 by Thomas Dixon. In 1915 the novel became the
basis for D.W. Griffith's groundbreaking film *The Birth of a Nation.*

The movie stirred the imagination of William Simmons, an Atlanta Methodist
preacher and professional organizer of fraternal orders and lodges. Soon after seeing it, he set about establishing a new "high class order for men of intelligence and
character," which he named after its Reconstruction predecessor. The war's superpatriotism and intolerance helped swell the new Klan's ranks to several thousand,
all dedicated to defending white Protestant America against blacks, aliens, and
dissenters. After 1918, with the help of Edward Young Clarke and Elizabeth Tyler,
two skilled publicists, Simmons capitalized on the pervasive postwar anxiety over
social change to recruit members for his new organization.

The Klan represented the most extreme fringe of traditional, white, native-
born America. Utterly devoted to white supremacy, it also condemned Catholics
and Jews as aliens, under obligation in the first case to the pope and in the second
to an international anti-Christian conspiracy. The Klan also became the defender
of traditional public morals. It endorsed Prohibition and denounced the illegal
liquor traffic; it attacked prostitution and sexual laxity; it warned wife beaters and
criminals to cease their nefarious doings; it stood for "100 percent Americanism"
and opposed all radical ideology.

During the 1920s the Klan became a political force in the rural parts of the nation, especially in the South, Midwest, and Far West. It even penetrated the big
cities, where it appealed to white Protestants recently arrived from rural areas,
who felt lost amid the social and ethnic diversity that surrounded them. The "Invisible Empire" entered politics in many states and cities. At one time it virtually
controlled the governments of Indiana and Oregon. Denver and Dallas fell under
its sway; in Denver it succeeded in defeating the reelection bid of the famous liberal judge, Ben Lindsey.

By 1925 there were 3 million Klansmen, and their presence was felt almost
everywhere. Daytime Klan parades of sheeted, robed men, and nighttime rallies
under immense fiery crosses became common in many American communities.

Some Klansmen, no doubt, were well-meaning if misguided men who sincerely believed they were upholding decency and traditional values. Others joined the Klan because it was economically or politically expedient. Yet many lawless and viciously racist people hid behind Klan regalia to commit crimes against blacks, supposed radicals or social deviants, and Jews and Catholics. Intimidation, boycotts, tar and feathering, and even murder were all part of the Klan arsenal. Outraged by Klan atrocities, various Catholic, Jewish, black, and liberal groups fought back. Many big-city newspapers, led by the *New York World*, denounced it. Even many conservative Protestants, frightened by its divisive influence on the nation, resisted the Klan.

This counterassault was aided by the hypocrisy of Klan leaders. Thousands of dollars poured into Klan coffers as dues or from sale of regalia, but much of the money stuck to the fingers of Klan officials. Even more damaging were instances of sexual laxity by several prominent Klan leaders. For an organization that denounced the ethical slackness of the times and appointed itself the guardian of community morals, public revelations of the financial and carnal weaknesses of its own leaders were damaging blows. By 1930 the Klan was practically dead. But in later years, when social tensions once more intensified, it would again become a vehicle for hate, intolerance, and mindless superpatriotism.

The Klan fight was only one of many clashes pitting Old and New Americans against each other. Two others were the Scopes trial in Dayton, Tennessee, in 1925, and the presidential election of 1928.

The Scopes Trial.

During the 1920s education became a major battleground between conservative fundamentalists and liberal modernists. Religious conservatives held that the schools had to be kept from purveying skepticism and irreligion; modernists held that teachers had to be free to teach the latest theories of science, wherever they led. Inevitably, the teaching of Darwinism and evolution ignited a furious confrontation between the Old and the New America.

The struggle came to a head in 1925 when the Tennessee legislature passed the Butler Law, making the teaching of Darwin's theory of evolution illegal in state-supported public schools and colleges. In the small town of Dayton, John Scopes, a young high school teacher, following a meeting with local rebels at Robinson's drug store, agreed to say that he had reviewed a biology text which taught Darwinism and had thus violated the law. Scopes was arrested and brought to trial.

The response of outsiders to Scopes's arrest was startling. The venerable William Jennings Bryan volunteered to help the prosecutor protect traditional America from the theory that humanity had evolved from lower forms of life. The American Civil Liberties Union (ACLU), an organization dedicated to free speech, had looked forward to a test case on the Butler law; when the prominent liberal lawyer Clarence Darrow volunteered to defend Scopes, the ACLU joined him in the defense. All the major news services set up shop in sleepy Dayton. Curiosity seekers and hundreds of local farmers poured into the town for the legal showdown. The square in front of the courthouse became a bustling fair with hawkers of soft drinks, souvenirs, fans, books, and religious tracts everywhere.

Scopes's technical guilt was not in question; he had violated the letter of the law. But Darrow and the ACLU were more interested in attacking what they saw as the irrationality and ignorance of traditional America than in establishing their client's legal innocence. At one point during the trial Darrow declared that his purpose was to "show up Fundamentalism . . . to prevent bigots and ignoramuses from controlling the educational system of the United States." Enraged at the attack, Bryan responded that his purpose was to "protect the word of God against the greatest atheist and agnostic in the United States."

Neither side came off well in the encounter. Bryan appeared as grossly misinformed about modern science; Darrow showed himself to be a cocky smart aleck. The trial ended in a draw. The jury found Scopes guilty and fined him $100, but the state supreme court later threw out the verdict on a technicality. The law remained on the books, and its violator went free. The legal results were anticlimactic, but the Scopes trial proved a setback to conservative religion and provided a window into the forces contending for America's cultural soul.

The Election of 1928.

More momentous for the country was the 1928 presidential election. The contestants were Secretary of Commerce Herbert Hoover and Alfred E. Smith, the Democratic governor of New York.

The two men seemed complete opposites. Smith was an extrovert who loved clubhouse politics and enjoyed the company of men and women from all walks of life. Hoover was a painfully shy man who seldom evoked warm personal affection. Smith was a natty dresser who made his trademark the striped suit and the brown derby that had been high fashion in his youth. Hoover's clothes were always well cut and black. Smith's formal education was minimal. Hoover was a mining engineer, a graduate of Stanford University, and a world traveler. Most important of all, Smith's origins were urban, Irish-Catholic, and wet. Hoover was a Quaker from the tiny hamlet of West Branch, Iowa, who believed Prohibition was "a great social and economic experiment, noble in motive and far-reaching in purpose."

Smith was a controversial figure to many Americans. Good government voters had reservations about his Tammany Hall affiliations. Drys deplored his stand on liquor and the Volstead Act. Snobs winced at his imperfect English pronunciation and education. Rural voters questioned his knowledge of farm problems. Westerners doubted he cared about their section. But among traditional voters it was his Catholicism that awakened the most misgivings. Sophisticated critics charged that Catholics did not accept American traditions such as the separation of church and state and did not support secular public education. At the lowest social level there was the Klan's unthinking prejudice against Catholicism as a perversion of Gospel Christianity and an evil international conspiracy. One Vermonter expressed the anti-Smith position succinctly when he prayed that "the good Lord and the Southland [might] keep us safe from the rule of the Wet, Tammany, Roman Catholic Booze Gang."

In fact, no Democrat could have won in 1928. Most Americans agreed that the country had never been so prosperous, and during the campaign, while some

Republicans attacked Smith's religion and his personal attributes, others played up the blessings of good times. "Given a chance to go forward with the policies of the last eight years," Hoover intoned in his acceptance speech, "we shall with the help of God be in sight of the day when poverty will be banished from this nation." Elect the "Great Engineer," Republican campaign slogans declared, and there would be a "chicken in every pot and two cars in every garage." Good times, added to the fear of Catholicism, made the Republican ticket unbeatable in November 1928.

Nevertheless, the Democratic candidate won wide support in the cities. If thousands in the South and the rural West and North voted against him because of his Catholicism, thousands of others in the big cities voted for him for the same reason. In some Irish and Italian election districts in New York City, Smith received 98 percent of the total vote! If one views the campaign in the context of American party history from the Civil War to the present, Smith's candidacy marks a point where the urban immigrant vote, which had been loosened from its nineteenth-century Democratic moorings by World War I and Republican New Era prosperity, became more strongly fastened to the Democrats than ever before. Hoover carried 40 of the 48 states, with 444 electoral votes and over 21 million popular votes, to Smith's 87 electoral votes and 15 million popular ones. For the first time since Reconstruction, Texas, Florida, North Carolina, Tennessee, and Virginia went Republican. On the face of it, it was a Democratic disaster. In reality, it was the beginning of a great resurgence that would soon make the Democrats the party of the normal American majority.

Conclusions

In his 1929 inaugural address Herbert Hoover told the American people that the years ahead were "bright with hope." He was expressing the optimism that many Americans felt, and he and they apparently had good reason for their sunny expectations.

The decade was a period of unusual achievement. For the middle class and upper levels of American wage earners, it was a breakthrough into a new affluence. It was also a time of expanding freedom for women, young people, and intellectuals, and it was a creative age in the arts.

But the decade had a darker side. It was a time of contraction for farmers and of severe material limits for the semiskilled and unskilled. But above all it was also a decade of bitter cultural and social strife. Between 1919 and 1929 an older, rural, traditional, native, fundamentalist America collided with a newer, urban, modernist, foreign-born, non-Protestant America. The Klan, immigration restriction, Prohibition, political intolerance, and organized crime were all ugly manifestations of that cultural clash.

And now a new force was about to intrude into the cultural battleground. Seven months into Hoover's term the stock market collapsed, altering the lives of millions of Americans and the course of the nation's history.

Online Resources

"The Red Scare" *http://newman.baruch.cuny.edu/digital/redscare/* This site consists of some 300 images, including political cartoons, that depict Americans' distrust of immigrants and radicals following World War I.

"Talking History" *http://www.albany.edu/talkinghistory/archive/goinnorth.ram* Beginning with part 2 of "Goin' North, Great Tales of the Great Migration," hear African Americans talk through audio files about their experiences in going to Philadelphia for jobs during World War I. (This is an audio file and requires the common audio player feature.)

American Cultural History 1920–1929 *http://kclibrary.nhmccd.edu/decade20.html* This site lists numerous links to articles describing art, literature, music, fashions, fads, and films from the 1920s.

"Prosperity and Thrift: The Coolidge Era and the Consumer Economy, 1921–1929" *http://memory.loc.gov/ammem/coolhtml/coolhome.html* This site is a compilation of numerous primary sources, ranging from mass advertising and presidential addresses to short films. It tracks the nation's transition to a consumer society and examines the role of the government in that change. It also discusses life for those who did not enjoy the emerging fruits of the economy.

"Famous Trials in American History. Tennessee vs. John Scopes: The Monkey Trial" *http://www.law.umkc.edu/faculty/projects/ftrials/scopes/scopes.htm* This site details the famous legal battle, which testifies to the challenges to tradition that were prevalent in the 1920s. The site includes eyewitness accounts, excerpts from the trial, photographs, and more.

"Harlem: Mecca of the New Negro" *http://etext.lib.virginia.edu/harlem/index.html* The e-text of the historical 1925 *Survey Graphic,* a journal of social work, featured on this site is an example of one of the first attempts to understand the social, cultural, and political significance of the Harlem community in New York.

25

The New Deal

Too Far or Not Far Enough?

1929	Depression begins with financial panic on Wall Street; President Hoover increases federal spending on current projects but avoids deficit spending
1930	4 million Americans are unemployed; Hawley-Smoot Tariff
1932–35	Drought makes Great Plains a dust bowl
1932	Congress establishes the Reconstruction Finance Corporation (RFC); Dispersal of the Bonus Army; Franklin D. Roosevelt elected president
1933–35	First New Deal
1933	Roosevelt orders a four-day bank holiday; New Deal legislation and agencies: Emergency Banking Act, Agricultural Adjustment Act (AAA), National Industrial Recovery Act (NIRA), Public Works Administration (PWA), National Recovery Administration (NRA), Home Owners Loan Corporation (HOLC), Federal Emergency Relief Act, Civilian Conservation Corps (CCC), Federal Deposit Insurance Corporation (FDIC), Tennessee Valley Authority (TVA), Civil Works Administration (CWA)
1934	Securities and Exchange Commission established; Conservative Democrats and wealthy Republicans form the anti-Roosevelt Liberty League
1935–38	Second New Deal
1935	Legislation: Emergency Relief Act, National Labor Relations (Wagner) Act, Social Security Act, Public Utility Holding Company Act, Revenue (Wealth Tax) Act, Banking Act, Frazier-Lemke Farm Mortgage Moratorium Act, Resettlement Administration Act, Rural Electrification Act; The Supreme Court strikes down the NIRA; Committee on Industrial Organizations (CIO) formed; The Supreme Court invalidates the AAA; Huey Long is assassinated; Benny Goodman organizes his own orchestra
1936	Roosevelt reelected president; Soil Conservation and Domestic Allotment Act
1937	Roosevelt's attempt to pack the Supreme Court; General Motors Corporation and United States Steel recognize unions as the bargaining agents for their employees; Chicago police kill ten while breaking up a strike against Republic Steel; The Farm Security Administration established; Wagner-Steagall Housing Act
1938	Agricultural Adjustment Act; Food, Drug, and Cosmetic Act; Fair Labor Standards Act

The New Deal, that wide-ranging political response to the massive social and economic crises of the 1930s, has always been controversial. Contemporary conservatives called it "socialistic" and denounced it for destroying fundamental American liberties. Contemporary radicals condemned it for preserving America's capitalist institutions and the inequalities of wealth and power that went with capitalism. Critics from both ends of the political spectrum continue to attack it today. Conservative scholars believe the New Deal delayed recovery from the Great Depression by frightening the business class that might have invested their capital and restored economic momentum. They have also attacked it as the source of the bloated federal presence in American life and the source of the demoralizing welfare state. At the other end of the political spectrum, historian Barton J. Bernstein critically notes that the "liberal reformers of the New Deal . . . conserved the protected American corporate capitalism. . . . There was no significant redistribution of power in American society, only limited recognition of other organized groups, seldom of unorganized people."

Was the New Deal's role in American life positive or negative? Did it fall short of the goals it set for itself? Were its goals too limited? Did it really create as many problems for our society as it solved? To answer these questions we must look at the difficulties the nation faced during the Great Depression, and for this purpose we must turn back to the closing months of the twenties' New Era.

Boom and Bust

American capitalism racked up a dazzling year in 1929. By almost every measure the economy had never performed so well. Automobile production reached almost 4.5 million units, 800,000 more than in 1928; steel production climbed to 5 million tons above the year before. Manufacturing output as a whole reached an all-time peak. Late in the summer the stock market soared to a historic high, with shares in American corporations selling for prices never before attained. When economists got around to figuring out the gross national product for 1929, they would put it at over $104 billion, or $857 for every man, woman, and child— 25 percent higher than a decade before.

Life for many Americans seemed good as the 1920s drew to a close. Over 20 million of the nation's 30 million families had automobiles. Radios were prized possessions in over 10 million households; many people were beginning to acquire electric washing machines and refrigerators. Almost half of all American families owned their own homes, and over two-thirds had home electric power— twice the proportion of the previous decade. Never before had so many enjoyed so much. Few Americans doubted that 1929 was a charmed year.

Abruptly, the spell broke. In the weeks following Labor Day, the stock market plunged, paused, and then plunged again. On Thursday, October 24, a record-breaking 13 million shares changed hands at prices so sharply deflated that $9 billion in investment values were wiped out in that single day. Thousands of investors and speculators now scrambled to sell stocks for whatever they could get. On October 29, 16 million shares were sold, with prices down an average of 40 points.

For the next two and a half years the 1920s "bull market" deflated. At times there were rallies, but they were short-lived. By July 1932 stock prices had reached bottom at a fraction of their former value and would take years to recover. During the long slide over $70 billion of investments and paper wealth were wiped out, $616 for every person in the country!

Causes of the Depression.
Americans have often blamed the stock market collapse for their plight during the 1930s. The blame is not entirely misplaced. The Crash wiped out billions in paper wealth and replaced the buoyant optimism of the New Era with fear and caution. It badly unnerved the people who made the economy's decisions to invest. By 1932 gross private domestic investment had sunk to one-ninth the 1929 amount. Although far fewer Americans proportionately than in recent times then owned stock, the Crash also destroyed the confidence of consumers, who sought to protect themselves by tightening their belts and, when possible, delaying buying. If the blind optimism of stock market investors during the New Era had helped cause the Crash, the equally blind pessimism following it undoubtedly prolonged the Great Depression.

The stock market tumble, however, was only the most visible cause of the economic collapse. True, the 1920s had been a time of economic growth, but that growth had depended on an unstable balance of factors. New markets for automobiles, radios, refrigerators, and other durables had induced businesses to invest vast sums to expand production. In addition, governments had poured more billions into roads, bridges, and other capital improvements, while private citizens, now able to rely on the family automobile for quick transportation to city jobs, bought homes in the burgeoning suburbs. Pushed by the consumer durables surge, construction, steel, cement, petroleum, rubber, and scores of other industries boomed, creating jobs and income for millions of urban Americans. Most people came to see the new affluence as normal and to assume that it would never end.

But they were wrong, of course. The end of the surge was inevitable. With 50 percent of the nation's income going to only 20 percent of its families, the market for expensive consumer durables, though wider than in the past, was limited. When all those who could afford the new car or the new radio had satisfied their needs, demand had to decline. By 1927 or 1928 these effects were already being felt and manufacturers were beginning to cut production and lay off workers. A spiral was now set in motion: Fewer new orders for goods led to fewer jobs; in turn, the unemployed could not buy what the factories produced, and so orders further declined. Overall, the massive push to invest, which had fed the economy since World War I, had lost its momentum.

The instability of the international economy also contributed to the decline. The burdens of World War I war debts and tariff barriers were becoming harder to bear as the decade neared its end. England and France had emerged from the war owing enormous sums to America. To pay they needed to export to the United States. But, as we have seen, this country raised tariffs during the 1920s, making it increasingly difficult to sell foreign goods to Americans. The $33 billion indemnity imposed on Germany by the postwar Allied Reparations Commission could potentially have made up the Allied payments gap with America. But the Germans could not pay it, and in two successive stages (the Dawes Plan, 1924, and the Young Plan, 1929) the payments were pared down and stretched out. For a while, large-scale lending by American banks took up the slack, enabling the former

Allies to buy American goods on credit. Indeed, American banks invested heavily in nations around the world, helping to fuel the worldwide 1920s boom. By 1928, however, the bankers were beginning to have second thoughts about foreign loans. The whole shaky structure of foreign trade was now in jeopardy.

The Great Depression.   The collapse of the stock market triggered an avalanche of disaster. Credit became tight, and interest rates soared. The Federal Reserve Board could have eased the situation by lowering interest rates, but foolishly took no action. To save themselves, commercial banks cut off credit to businesses and foreign borrowers. All trade slowed, but foreign commerce, which had been sustained by constant infusions of American credit, was especially hard hit.

To sustain their exports and reduce their imports, many nations imposed strict foreign trade barriers and raised tariffs. The world's trading nations had used a currency exchange system pegged to the price of gold that had encouraged international trade and investment. Now, many abandoned the gold standard, allowing the values of goods and currencies to fluctuate wildly and further disturbing international commerce. Under the combined blows of trade restrictions and currency instability, commerce among the world's nations declined precipitously. By mid-1930 the Great Depression had become virtually worldwide.

Meanwhile, the domestic banking system faced collapse. As the economy worsened, frightened depositors rushed to withdraw their savings. Bank after bank failed as "runs" forced even solvent institutions into bankruptcy. In November 1930 alone a total of 256 banks with deposits of $180 million closed their doors. Most severely affected in this round were the financial institutions of the farm areas, where bank failures had been numerous even in the 1920s.

The decline of consumption was a key factor in worsening and prolonging the Depression. The collapse of the bull market in stocks frightened consumers of luxury goods, whose sense of well-being often depended on their paper profits and wealth. But even ordinary consumers, who had not "played the market" during the twenties, turned timid after the Crash and ceased to make their indispensable contribution to the economy. Here the nation's very affluence hurt it. In former times, when most consumers' income went for necessities, they had limited choices whether to spend or not when times turned bad. But in this rich era they could put off vacation trips and decide not to buy new radios, cars, or refrigerators. The most durable of all durable goods—houses—could be deferred the longest, and new housing sales dropped off disastrously.

Deferring purchases and investment at first was largely voluntary, but it soon became inescapable. As unsold inventories built up in stores and showrooms, retailers reduced their orders to manufacturers and suppliers. They in turn lowered their investment goals, cut back on production, slashed wages, and fired employees. Unemployment shot up. By the end of 1930 over 4 million men and women were out of work. Many more were working part-time or for sharply reduced wages. Families whose breadwinners lost their jobs in turn cut their budgets to the bone. Total demand now declined still further, establishing a vicious downward spiral of economic deflation.

If commodity prices had fallen as far and as fast as consumer income, goods might have continued to move, and workers might have kept their jobs.

In areas where there were many competitive producers prices did fall. Between 1929 and 1933 agricultural prices dropped 56 percent, while output remained virtually the same. The plunge was unfortunate for farmers, but it kept farm production and farm employment high and prevented widespread hunger. In segments of the economy where competition was limited, however, prices stayed high. Automobiles remained expensive—about $600 for the average vehicle both in 1929 and in 1932. Because most people could not buy cars, production—and employment—fell. By 1932 automobile output had dropped to 25 percent of the 1929 figure, and the number of automobile workers had declined to under 40 percent of the 1929 total.

The Human Toll.

The Great Depression was a human disaster of colossal proportions. Despair spread through every part of the country and penetrated every walk of life. By the winter of 1932–1933 a quarter of those Americans willing to work were without jobs. The plight of blue-collar wage earners, who had few resources to cushion them against adversity, was the worst. Millions of factory hands and construction workers tramped the streets looking for jobs or waited in lines for handouts from charity organizations. But hard times did not respect class lines. Small business owners went bankrupt as their customers dwindled. Lawyers had fewer clients; doctors and dentists discovered that their patients put eating before health care. The sharp decline in building and construction left architects without commissions.

Private agencies were not equipped to handle the thousands of destitute families who applied for help. Nor could state and local governments provide sufficient relief. During the Depression three states and hundreds of municipalities went bankrupt trying to cope with widespread want at a time when tax revenues were declining sharply. Few, if any, Americans died of starvation during these appalling years. But many went hungry, and doctors saw thousands of cases of malnutrition.

What did the unemployed do to survive? When a family's savings had been exhausted, day-to-day survival became precarious. Families pawned valuables, or borrowed from friends, or against insurance policies, until no one would lend anymore. As in past periods of hard times, many jobless young men and women became "hobos," traveling by freight train, dodging railroad police, begging, or working at odd jobs. Some of the unemployed set up small, undercapitalized stores. Others sold apples on the streets. These pathetic efforts became symbols of pluck and determination, but they seldom succeeded.

One of the most urgent problems of the unemployed was housing. Many families could not pay their rent or their mortgage and were evicted from their homes. A common sight on city streets was the "dispossessed" family sitting disconsolately on the street curb, their furniture besides them, not knowing where to go. (A joke that made the rounds in 1933 was a version of an old classic. Bill asks Mike: "Who was that lady I saw you with last night at the sidewalk café?" Mike replies: "That was no lady; that was my wife. And that was no sidewalk café; that was my apartment furniture.") Thousands of Americans moved in with friends or relatives. On the outskirts of every large city the unemployed and their families took shelter in squatters' settlements thrown together from loose boards, packing crates, tin sheets, and cardboard. For the first time migration from country to city was reversed as young adults returned in droves to the rural homestead where at least there was enough food.

The Special Plight of Black Americans.

Among the most unfortunate victims of the Great Depression were many of the nation's 12.5 million African-Americans. In the North, where black people had only recently found a toehold in industry, they were often the first to lose their jobs when employers cut back their workforce. In April 1931 some 35 percent of the black workers in Philadelphia were unemployed, compared with 24 percent of white wage earners. In the South the economic crisis provided a new excuse for white bigotry. In Houston black and Mexican-American relief applicants were regularly turned down by local officials. In Atlanta in 1930, a group of Klanlike "Black Shirts" paraded downtown carrying banners inscribed "Niggers, back to the cotton fields—city jobs are for white folks." But things were no better in the cotton fields. In 1931 the price of cotton slumped to 4.6 cents a pound, the lowest since 1894. Early that year a Red Cross worker in a rural cotton-growing area of Arkansas found that more than half the homes he visited did not have enough food to last forty-eight hours.

Women and Families.

Women, of course, shared the fate of their families, but the Depression imposed special burdens as well. With so many male "breadwinners" without work, employers, public and private, often sought to discourage women from taking or keeping jobs. There were also new male competitors for jobs formerly considered "women's work," such as elementary school teaching.

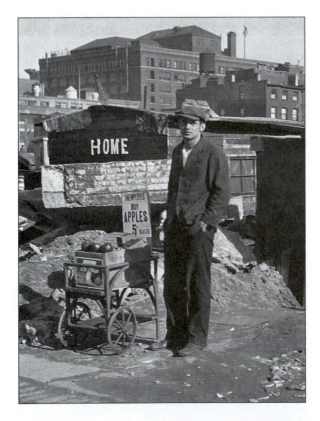

The Great Crash and ensuing Great Depression spared neither working-class nor middle-class people, though clearly the former suffered more absolute deprivation. The Depression's near-universality made it an exceptionally potent political force.

Yet the Depression, if anything, increased the proportion of women, even married women, who joined the labor market. As the wages for men fell and as male family heads lost their jobs, more women looked for and found work. By the end of the Depression there were 25 percent more women working than in the late 1920s.

Family life was inevitably affected by the hard times. On the one hand divorce rates declined; it was simply too expensive to break up established matrimonial relationships. Better a less-than-perfect marriage than alimony, child support, and the rest. (Though there were many informal marriage breakups in the form of desertion.) On the other hand, birth rates plummeted. Children were costly to raise and, in an urban society, could not be put to work for their families at an early age as on the farm in previous eras.

Life Goes on.   Yet a majority of Americans continued to work and to provide their families with the necessities of life. They even managed to enjoy themselves. During the winter of 1929–1930 a craze for miniature golf took hold, and by the summer of 1930 thousands of Americans were tapping golf balls through little tunnels and over tiny bridges. By 1930 radio had produced its first superstars: Freeman F. Gosden and Charles J. Correll, both whites, who amused listeners with their comic stereotypes of the uneducated but shrewd black characters Amos 'n Andy. The theater flourished as well. In the fall of 1931 the big Broadway hit was *Of Thee I Sing*, a musical spoof of American politics. Through the worst years of the Depression, Hollywood continued to prosper. During the 1930s, 85 million Americans went to the nation's 17,000 movie houses each week to seek escape from the drabness and worries of their lives.

Popular music, too, helped people, especially the young, get through the hard days. New Orleans-type jazz had gone into eclipse with the end of good times. By the early 1930s black arrangers, including Edward ("Duke") Ellington, Fletcher Henderson, and Sy Oliver, had adapted jazz to a big-band format. Then, in 1935, clarinetist Benny Goodman created a sensation with a new sort of big-band dance music, called "swing." Thousands were soon dancing the Lindy Hop, the Suzie-Q, and the Big Apple to the arrangements of Tommy Dorsey, Glenn Miller, and Count Basie, as well as of Goodman, the "King of Swing," himself. In 1938 swing became a part of "culture" when the Goodman band gave a sensational concert at New York's Carnegie Hall.

Hoover and the Depression

Viewing the 1930s from the present, the initial reaction of the federal government to the economic disaster seems inexplicably limited and slow. But we must recognize that it took months before anyone could assess how serious the damage was. There was, moreover, a strong conviction among contemporaries that government could, or should, play only a limited role in financial crises and that self-righting forces would soon assert themselves.

Federal Inaction.   Though Hoover had never been an extreme laissez-faireist, he and his administration initially rejected an active interventionist role in the economy. Secretary of the Treasury Andrew Mellon proposed doing nothing whatsoever and allowing the downturn to bottom out by itself. "Liquidate labor," Mellon advised, "liquidate the farmers, liquidate real estate. It will purge the rottenness out of the system. . . . Values will be adjusted and enterprising people will pick up the wreck from less competent people." Fortunately, the president was never as committed to inaction as his treasury secretary. In November 1929 Hoover called a series of conferences of business and labor leaders and local government officials to consider the economic crisis. At his urging they pledged to maintain wages, desist from strikes, and continue the existing level of investment and local public works spending. Simultaneously, Hoover went to great pains to project optimism. The "fundamental business of the country," he told the worried public several days after the Crash, "is on a sound and prosperous basis."

As the dreary months passed with no improvement, voluntary efforts to maintain spending, employment, and investment levels became grossly inadequate. The obvious solution was public works programs to get the unemployed back on the job and put money into the hands of consumers and investors. Hoover did increase the federal government's planned outlays for public projects, and because federal tax revenues had dropped sharply, he could not avoid a budget deficit in doing so. But, believing it would compete with private industry for limited investment funds, he refused to allow the government to borrow money to finance public works. Actually, with business prospects so shaky, there was no need for the president to worry about the government's outbidding private industry for limited capital.

Hoover was even more reluctant to use federal funds to relieve human misery than to stimulate recovery. For a man who had served as relief administrator for Europe during and immediately following World War I, he seemed strangely insensitive to his fellow citizens' misfortunes. It was dangerous to make people dependent on federal handouts, he argued; aid to the unemployed must come from voluntary organizations and local governments, not from Washington. Hoover's view disregarded realities. Private religious and charitable organizations could not come close to meeting the needs of the vast army of the unemployed; cities, counties, and states found themselves, as their revenues declined, overwhelmed by demands for social relief. Only the federal government could deal with a disaster that deprived millions of the nation's families of their fundamental means of support.

Hoover's Programs.   The president never endorsed direct federal outlays for relief, but gradually he came to see that something more than pep talks was needed to check the economic slide. To help restore the international economy, in 1931 he proposed a one-year moratorium on German reparations and the intergovernmental debts of the former Allies. This was a wise, if limited, move. But Hoover was inconsistent. The previous year, against the advice of the country's best economists, he had accepted a traditional Republican solution to economic difficulties and signed the Hawley-Smoot Tariff Act, which raised the already high American protective wall and further undermined international trade.

By late 1931 Hoover finally recognized that the federal government must intervene directly in the domestic economy to get the country moving again. In his State of the Union message to Congress that year, he proposed establishing an agency to lend federal funds to business to restore confidence, encourage growth, and increase employment. In compliance, Congress created the Reconstruction Finance Corporation (RFC) in 1932 and gave it a $500 million appropriation with authority to borrow $1.5 billion more. The new RFC could lend these funds to faltering banks, railroads, savings and loan associations, and industrial firms. In addition, the president signed into law measures providing new capital to federal land banks, liberalizing the credit-granting powers of the Federal Reserve System, and establishing home-loan banks to refinance home mortgages.

Hoover's liberal opponents labeled his program, particularly the RFC, a "breadline for big business" that only indirectly touched the predicament of ordinary men and women. To be fair to Hoover, his moves—though tardy and insufficient—were steps in the right direction. But the president got little credit from the public for more vigorous actions in the last two years of his administration. Herbert Hoover lacked the popular touch. Characteristically, through the worst years of his term, he continued to wear formal clothes when dining at the White House, even when he and his wife were eating alone. As the economic clouds became ever darker, the president's popularity plummeted. Soon people were referring to empty pockets turned inside out as "Hoover flags," shantytowns on the outskirts of cities as "Hoovervilles," and newspapers wrapped around the body for warmth as "Hoover blankets."

The Bonus Expeditionary Force.

Most difficult to forgive, in the public's estimate, was the president's callous treatment of the Bonus Army. World War I veterans were among the "forgotten men" of the Depression. In 1924 Congress had authorized a "delayed bonus" for veterans, to be paid in 1945. In 1931, over Hoover's veto, Congress liberalized the law to allow former doughboys to borrow immediately up to 50 percent of the amount ultimately due them. This money was quickly spent, and veterans wondered why they should wait fifteen years for the rest of it. In June 1932 several thousand veterans, calling themselves the Bonus Expeditionary Force (BEF), arrived in Washington, D.C., to demand immediate payment of the remainder of the bonus.

The veterans camped out in tents and shacks at Anacostia Flats, a vacant area on the edge of the city. They asked to see the president, but he refused to have anything to do with them. When Congress rejected a new bonus bill, 15,000 veterans resolved to "stay till 1945." The men, many of whom had brought their wives and children, were orderly and sober. Most were prepared to wait patiently for Congress to act. As the congressional session drew to a close without action, however, tensions mounted. Though reluctant to involve the federal government in what he considered a local police problem, Hoover called in the army when the District of Columbia officials asked for federal help.

The troops under General Douglas MacArthur evicted the veterans from some abandoned buildings in the city and then, despite Hoover's orders, MacArthur ordered his men to sweep Anacostia Flats. Firing tear gas in every direction, the soldiers put the tents and the shanties to the torch and drove the BEF out of the camp with bayonets and sabers. Over a hundred people were injured in the melee, and two infants died of tear-gas inhalation.

The scene at Anacostia shocked many Americans. Men who had served their nation bravely had been treated like dangerous revolutionaries. Hoover's standing, already low, dropped still further. The president was not responsible for ordering the attack; but he had refused to see the BEF leaders and he shared the blame for the outcome.

Hoover Defeated.   The Bonus Army was not the only episode of confrontation during the first years of the Depression. In mid-1932 desperate midwestern farmers, to stem the collapse of agriculture, organized a "farm holiday" that stopped shipments of food to cities, halted the forced sale of farms whose impoverished owners had fallen behind in tax payments, and dumped underpriced milk into gutters. In parts of the country, meanwhile, hungry men looted stores and food delivery trucks. Early 1932 saw 3,000 unemployed men march on Henry Ford's River Rouge plant to demand jobs. Police used tear gas to stop them and then opened fire with revolvers and a machine gun, killing four.

Still more ominous to conservatives was rising public interest in socialism as a solution to the crisis. Big business, which had claimed so much credit for good times, now bore the brunt of the public's wrath when times turned bad, and angry voices began to denounce capitalism as a cruel fraud against humanity. In September 1932 the Marxist journal *New Masses* published a symposium in which prominent intellectuals Edmund Wilson, Clifton Fadiman, Sherwood Anderson, Upton Sinclair, and others declared that socialism alone could save the country. Two months later the Socialist party candidate for the presidency, Norman Thomas, received 880,000 votes, the largest Socialist vote since 1920.

There is no way of telling how much change in the existing social order Americans might have demanded if the nation had been forced to endure four more years of Hoover. Despair might have pushed Americans into communism or into a right-wing dictatorship such as emerged in central Europe in response to similar pressures. Fortunately, the two-party system provided orderly constitutional ways to express the public's anguish.

In the congressional elections of 1930 the Democrats came close to winning control of both the House and Senate. At this point they did not offer drastic ideological or programmatic alternatives to the Republicans. Many Democrats, in fact, were as conservative as Hoover. Yet surely they would be an improvement over the failed incumbent. Who would they chose as their presidential candidate and what would he do to relieve the nation's plight? In the end the public got more than it expected.

By early 1931 the Democratic presidential front-runner was Franklin D. Roosevelt, the governor of New York. An only child born to comfort in Hyde Park, New York, Roosevelt had developed the confidence and poise that came with an assured position in society and the love of a doting mother. Though from an upper-class family, he was an ancestral Democrat who had supported Wilson for president. In 1913 he became assistant secretary of the navy, and in 1920 he received the vice presidential nomination of his party. During the 1920s he contracted polio, and for the rest of his life was unable to walk or stand without assistance. Though he failed to recover his mobility, the experience confirmed FDR's sense that any obstacle could be overcome with enough determination. Encouraged by his strong-willed wife, Eleanor, Theodore Roosevelt's niece, he refused to give up politics. In 1928 he ran for governor of New York and was elected, although Smith, the party's presidential candidate, went down to defeat.

In 1930 Roosevelt was reelected governor in a landslide. During his second term, as the Depression spread, he proved to be a vigorous and compassionate leader who used his power to alleviate the plight of the state's unemployed. Surrounded by astute political managers, and a proven vote-getter in the nation's then most populous state, FDR won the 1932 Democratic presidential nomination handily. In a lackluster convention, the Republicans renominated Hoover without opposition.

The campaign was not an inspiring one. Neither party platform was especially bold or innovative. Nevertheless, Roosevelt promised increased aid to the unemployed and endorsed government involvement in electric power generation, national resource planning, and federal regulation of utilities and the stock market. The Democrats also favored the repeal of Prohibition. Hoover warned that Roosevelt's election would worsen the country's economic crisis; but everywhere he went, he was greeted with hoots, catcalls, and hostile demonstrators accusing him of killing veterans or of personally causing the country's economic problems. He soon became his party's worst liability, a man exuding gloom from every pore. On election day, as expected, Roosevelt and the Democrats were swept in with 23 million votes to Hoover's 16 million. FDR captured 282 counties that had never gone Democratic before. Both House and Senate also went overwhelmingly for the Democrats.

FDR's New Deal

In the four months between the election and Roosevelt's inauguration, the economy plunged to new lows. During the early weeks of 1933 virtually every bank in the country stopped paying its depositors or tottered on the edge of doing so. To stave off legal bankruptcy, by March 4 the governors of thirty-eight states had been forced to declare "holidays," allowing the banks to close their doors rather than acknowledge insolvency. By the eve of the inauguration it seemed that the whole financial structure on which American capitalism rested was about to crumble.

During these dismal lame-duck weeks, Hoover tried to enlist Roosevelt's cooperation on emergency measures. The president-elect listened to Hoover's suggestions but, unwilling to tie his hands, refused to commit himself and his administration to anything specific.

The First Hundred Days. Roosevelt's inaugural address of March 4 set the tone for the early months of what would be called the New Deal. He proposed federal public works measures, legislation to redistribute population from the cities to the country, to raise the prices of agricultural products, to end home and farm mortgage foreclosures, to cut spending at all levels of government, to improve and make more efficient relief measures, and finally, to tighten federal regulation of banking and stock speculation. His specific proposals were less important than his tone and manner, however. In a resonant, upper-class voice the president told the American people that "fear itself" was the chief danger and that if they submitted to sacrifice and discipline, all would be well. If necessary he was prepared to ask for broad emergency powers similar to those he would need if the nation were facing a foreign invasion.

The response to the address was remarkable. In the succeeding days the White House received a half million letters and telegrams from people who were cheered by the president's words. "It was the finest thing this side of heaven," wrote one citizen. "It seemed to give the people, as well as myself, a new hold on life," exclaimed another. Actually, Roosevelt had not moved much beyond his campaign proposals, but he had conveyed some of his own jaunty optimism and given people the feeling that there was now a strong hand at the helm.

Yet Roosevelt had few specific remedies in hand. Although influenced by the progressivism of his youth, he was not a brilliant economist or a man with a clear-cut set of principles to guide him. At times these deficiencies would create confusion and lead to serious mistakes. But FDR had some impressive assets, notably his open-mindedness and willingness to experiment. "Take a method and try it," he advised. "If it fails, admit it frankly and try another." And he had gathered around him a talented array of advisers, a so-called Brain Trust—drawn from the universities, from law, and from the social work profession—who could supply him with the ideas he himself lacked.

The new president's first move, on March 5, was to order the nation's banks closed. The four-day federal bank holiday was accompanied by an order that, in effect, took the country off the gold standard. Four days later, acting with the enthusiasm it had never shown Hoover, Congress passed the Emergency Banking Act, confirming the bank closings and providing for an orderly reopening of those that proved sound. The administration's bold action reassured the American people, who expressed their confidence in the president when the banks reopened by redepositing the cash they had earlier withdrawn in panic.

The bank holiday was the first shot of a whirlwind hundred-day war on defeatism, despair, and decline such as Americans had never witnessed before. The assault was marked by confusion and contradiction and did not end the Depression. But it did check the decline and restore a sense of forward motion to the American people.

The Agricultural Adjustment Act of 1933, the AAA, was the New Deal's major effort to deal with the acute farm crisis. Farmers would be encouraged to reduce their output or acreage of seven basic commodities by a fee from the proceeds of a special tax levied on food processors (millers, meat-packers, canners, and so on). Scarcity would check the price slide and ultimately raise farm income. The parallel National Industrial Recovery Act (NIRA) was designed to further industrial recovery. It established the National Recovery Administration (NRA) with the power to negotiate codes of "fair competition" with representatives of the nation's major industries. These codes would set prices and assign production quotas to individual firms. Though the authors of the law added language expressing concern over creating monopolies that might squeeze consumers, in reality the measure represented a suspension of antitrust principles. Labor, too, was handed a gift. Section 7(a) of the NIRA required that every code provide for collective bargaining for labor and comply with presidential guidelines for minimum pay rates and maximum working hours. Tacked on to the NIRA as Title II was a provision establishing a Public Works Administration (PWA) with a $3.3 billion budget to undertake large-scale public construction projects.

The two major recovery measures fell short of achieving their goals. By the time the AAA went into effect in the spring of 1933, southern farmers and sharecroppers had already planted many acres of cotton, and in the corn belt millions of sows had produced their annual litters. To keep this supply of fiber and food from coming to market and further weakening prices, the Department of Agriculture had to persuade cotton growers to uproot a quarter of their crop. In September 1933 it induced farmers to destroy 6 million pigs. Some of the pork was given to people on relief. Nevertheless, the wholesale destruction of commodities at a time when people were hungry and ill-clothed seemed irrational to many Americans. More serious was an unanticipated social effect. Reducing cotton production squeezed sharecroppers off the land. Those who remained, both black and white, were often deprived by landlords of the federal cash due them.

Despite the AAA's failings, during the two years following its passage, farm income more than doubled. Some of the gains represented direct payments to farmers for cutting production; some came from the higher prices that reduced output encouraged. But the AAA was responsible for only a part of the advance. Higher wheat prices, for example, owed as much to the severe drought that parched the Great Plains between 1932 and 1935 as to government programs. The drought turned a vast area stretching from Texas to the Dakotas into a "dust bowl," where the skies were obscured by blowing topsoil and crops withered. Meanwhile, thousands of tenant farmers in Oklahoma and Arkansas were uprooted. Imprecisely called "Okies," many became "gasoline gypsies" and set off in jalopies for the warmth, jobs, and presumed easy living of southern California. The sharp drop in wheat production added substantially to the impact of the AAA wheat program. When the federal judiciary declared the tax on food processors unconstitutional, the AAA's major crop-reduction features were reincorporated into a new law, the Soil Conservation and Domestic Allotment Act (1936).

Unlike the AAA, the NIRA was almost a complete disappointment. The flamboyant NRA administrator, General Hugh S. Johnson, had hoped to use the PWA to beef up demand by putting people to work. But Roosevelt handed over the agency to Secretary of the Interior Harold Ickes, depriving Johnson of one of his tools for success. Working with what he had, Johnson bullied the nation's largest industries into writing codes of fair practices that included mandatory collective bargaining for employees and limitations on child labor. In return for these, however, the NRA authorized price-fixing and output limitations and allowed big business to adopt policies that injured small firms.

But the greatest disappointment of the NIRA was that it failed to revive industry. The government gave its program a symbol—a blue eagle—and a slogan—"We Do Our Part." Blue eagle parades wound through the downtowns of a score of cities; blue eagle stickers were plastered over store fronts and factory windows. For a time the ballyhoo boosted investor confidence and consumer morale and probably kept the Depression from worsening. But the agency established no effective machinery for restarting silent mills and factories, and industrial production remained stalled. When in May 1935 the Supreme Court struck down the code-making sections of the NIRA as unconstitutional, few people, even in the administration, mourned the agency's passing.

Fiscal Stimulus.

Today, it is easy to see why the two major recovery measures failed. In addition to their unfortunate side effects, they did not do enough to increase investment rates or consumer spending. Under the circumstances of the day, only large scale government spending could have jump-started the economy. The treasury under Roosevelt did expend more money than under Hoover. The RFC lent money to the banks to help them expand their loans. The Home Owners Loan Corporation (HOLC) dispensed billions of dollars to savings and loan associations to refinance mortgages. The PWA, which survived the Supreme Court's invalidation of the NIRA, poured millions into major federal works projects. Between 1933 and 1939 the agency built 70 percent of the nation's new schools and 65 percent of its new city halls, sewage plants, and courthouses. It was responsible for more than a third of all the new hospitals. It funded university libraries, the Lincoln Tunnel connecting New York and New Jersey, the causeway linking the Florida Keys to the mainland, and many other outstanding construction projects. But all these outlays were not enough.

Whatever his critics charged, Roosevelt was never a deliberate "big spender." He believed that a little "pump priming" by government could be useful, but he worried about running the treasury consistently in the red. Federal spending exceeded federal income in every year of the New Deal, but the deficits were always incidental to relief; they were never part of a deliberate program. Nor were they ever large enough to spark a complete recovery. Few in the Roosevelt administration had read the works of the apostle of deliberate deficit spending, English economist John Maynard Keynes, though Marriner Eccles, a Utah banker who headed the Federal Reserve Board, was an instinctive Keynesian. The administration thus lacked the tools needed to offset the collapse of private investment and consumer demand.

Relief.   By far the largest outpouring of federal funds throughout the New Deal Era went to jobs and relief for the unemployed. Although conservative in fiscal matters, FDR, unlike Hoover, put the welfare of ordinary men and women before a balanced budget.

To relieve unemployment among urban youths, as part of the First Hundred Days, Congress established the Civilian Conservation Corps (CCC). The corps took 2.5 million idle young men on relief rolls and put them to work on public lands at $30 a month planting trees, building forest ranger stations, clearing brush, and restoring historic battlefields. Congress also created the Federal Emergency Relief Administration (FERA) and appropriated $500 million for local and state relief agencies to distribute to the unemployed. Administering the program was a fast-talking, poker-playing young social worker, Harry L. Hopkins, who believed that jobs, rather than outright charity, were needed to restore individual morale and self-respect. In late 1933 Hopkins persuaded Roosevelt to establish the Civil Works Administration (CWA) with funds drawn from FERA and the PWA to put the unemployed directly on the federal payroll. By mid-January 1934 the CWA was providing 4 million men and women with a steady paycheck averaging $15 a week. But the president worried that it was too expensive and would create a permanent class of government dependents. By summer Roosevelt had shut down the program and returned relief to the local governments.

It did not remain there for very long, for the local authorities simply did not have the means to carry the burden. In January 1935 Roosevelt asked Congress for $5 billion to support other work relief programs. The men would be employed on various government projects at wages higher than the straight dole under FERA, but lower than the amount paid by CWA. Congress responded to the president's request and made the largest single appropriation in the nation's history. Secretary Ickes wanted it devoted to long-term projects under his PWA. Hopkins wanted it

The WPA under Harry Hopkins sought to rescue people in the arts, as well as other Americans, from idleness during the Depression. Moses Soyer here, in Artists on WPA, depicts a room full of WPA painters using their skills and earning some money in the process.
(Moses Soyer, "Artists on WPA" (1935). Oil on canvas, 36 1/8" × 42 1/8" (91.7 × 107 cm). National Museum of American Art, Smithsonian Institution, Washington, DC/Art Resource, NY)

for short-term projects like those of his CWA. In the end Roosevelt allotted most of the money to a new agency, the Works Progress Administration (WPA), under Hopkins's direction.

For the remainder of the Depression, the WPA was the major distributor of government funds to the unemployed. It, and the other relief agencies, were also significant stimulants to the economy. Government spending, however incidental, pushed up the GNP and cut into unemployment. By 1935 the number of jobless had declined from almost 13 million, or 24.9 percent of the labor force, to 10.6 million, a little over 20 percent of those seeking work.

The relief programs cannot be measured solely by their statistical consequences, however. True, much of the WPA outlay went to make-work projects. But Hopkins was an imaginative man who saw that artists, writers, intellectuals, and performers were also victims of the economic collapse. Under his direction the WPA sponsored programs to put these people to work enriching community life, while preserving their own skills. Hundreds of musicians were paid to perform in school auditoriums and community halls. Artists were hired to paint murals for the new federal courthouses and post offices built with PWA funds. Writers were set to work compiling state guidebooks. Many talented writers—including Saul Bellow, Ralph Ellison, Richard Wright, and Arthur Miller—owed their starts to the Federal Writers Project or the Federal Theater Project under the WPA. The WPA also established a National Youth Administration to give part-time work to college and high school students to enable them to complete their studies.

Reform and Innovation.   The president had promised reform and innovation along with relief and recovery, and he came through on his promises. A series of New Deal measures sought to end stock market abuses by placing the management of Wall Street under the new Securities and Exchange Commission (SEC). The banking system was made more secure and stable by creation of the Federal Deposit Insurance Corporation (FDIC) to insure depositors' accounts and prevent the sort of panic withdrawals that had almost destroyed the banking system following the Crash.

The most original program of the First Hundred Days was the Tennessee Valley Authority. In May 1933 FDR secured congressional approval of the TVA, a resource-management project long advocated by Senator George Norris of Nebraska and other conservationists who were dismayed at the physical and social deterioration of the potentially rich Tennessee River valley and the waste of its precious water resources. The agency was given the authority to build dams, manufacture fertilizer, undertake soil conservation and reforestation measures, and join with local authorities within the seven-state valley in various social improvement projects. Between 1933 and 1944 the authority built nine major dams, bringing low-cost lighting and power to valley homes and farms and providing new recreational facilities on the man-made lakes created. Cheap power attracted large industries to the region, especially during World War II. Together with reforestation and soil conservation, inexpensive electricity helped reverse the valley's long decline, turning it into one of the more prosperous parts of the South.

For all its benefits the TVA represented an old-fashioned sort of conservation. From a modern ecological point of view its virtues seem limited. Its disruption of the natural environment and its focus on maximizing energy use would not get high marks today. In fact, it is doubtful if the project could have passed the environmental impact tests imposed on new developments in the twenty-first century. But for decades the TVA would be cited as a triumph of the New Deal at its best.

Friends and Enemies

The early months of the New Deal was a tumultuous time. The public wavered between fear and hope, still stunned by the economic catastrophe but encouraged by the new surge of energy in the nation's capital. Congress gave Roosevelt almost everything he wanted without looking too closely at the cost or questioning the wisdom of his proposals. As the months passed, however, opposition mounted at both ends of the political spectrum, and by 1935 Roosevelt and the New Deal were beset by critics and enemies.

Thunder on the Right.

Despite the new legislation to regulate and constrain the banks and Wall Street, FDR was not a foe of business. Many of his advisers were conservative men who endorsed business–government cooperation. Their views had been incorporated into the NIRA. Unfortunately for FDR, once the worst of the economic crisis had passed and businesspeople lost their fear of total collapse, many began to accuse the New Deal of unwarranted interference with the economy, fiscal irresponsibility, and socialist leanings. In August 1934 a group of conservative Democrats and executives of Du Pont, General Motors, and other large corporations organized the Liberty League to fight the "further aggrandizement of an ever-spreading governmental bureaucracy."

At the same time a more formidable conservative challenge came from the Supreme Court. Composed of men whose average age was over seventy, the Court was dominated by some of the most tradition-bound lawyers in the American bar. On May 27, 1935, in the Schechter case, it struck down the NIRA on the grounds that it unconstitutionally conferred legislative power on the executive branch. Shortly after, in *United States v. Butler,* the Court invalidated the AAA on the grounds that the processing tax to pay farmers was primarily a means to regulate production and exceeded Congress's powers under the Constitution. If the principles of the AAA were allowed to stand, the Court said, federal taxing power could be used to regulate industry throughout the United States.

The Attack of the Left.

Roosevelt also came under attack from the political left. Most Americans retained their faith in private property and a market economy during the Depression years, but an influential segment of intellectuals, artists, journalists, academics, and trade union leaders came to believe that the only hope for America lay in a socialist state. The apparent success of the Soviet "experiment" clinched the argument. While capitalism was reeling in the United States, the Soviet economy seemed to be forging ahead under Joseph Stalin's bold Five-Year Plans. Capitalism appeared to be in its death throes while Soviet socialism had solved the problems of growth, unemployment, and economic inequality.

American Marxists attacked the New Deal as too little, too late. The Socialist party leader, Norman Thomas, at first was friendly to Roosevelt. By 1935, however, the socialists were denouncing the New Deal as "the greatest fraud among all the utopias." Whether right or wrong, the American socialists were at least their own masters. Not so the communists. In 1934 Earl Browder, head of the Communist Party of the United States, called the New Deal "a program of hunger, fascization, and imperialist war." When, after 1935, the Soviet Union sought a policy of cooperation with the western democracies to stop Hitler and Nazi Germany, Browder and his colleagues ceased their attacks. Under a new "United Front" policy, the New Deal and Roosevelt became acceptable.

The Neopopulists.

The Socialists and Communists were at most an annoyance to Roosevelt. The real political challenge from the left came from a collection of neopopulists in the dissenting tradition of the West and South.

Closest to the Populist heritage was Senator Huey Long, the Louisiana "Kingfish." An earthy man who wore pink suits, called fellow officeholders "dime-a-dozen punks," and conducted public business in pajamas and a silk bathrobe, Long was also a shrewd politician who knew that the times cried out for a savior. As governor of Louisiana during the late twenties he had raised taxes on the state's corporations and used the money to build bridges, hospitals, mental institutions, and schools. Long had employed any weapon at hand to carry out his program, including physical intimidation, political blackmail, even kidnapping. His opponents in Louisiana considered him a dictator.

In 1932 Long came to Washington as a Democratic senator. He had supported Roosevelt during the election, but within six months he had turned against him and the new Deal. In part the argument between Long and Roosevelt was a clash between two strong and ambitious men. But they also disagreed ideologically. The Kingfish wanted to "share the wealth" by taxing away all large incomes and fortunes and giving every citizen a lump sum gift of $5,000 and a guaranteed income of $2,000 a year. Long's proposal to make "every man a king" appealed to millions of ordinary people, but Roosevelt, as many others, considered him a rabble-rousing demagogue and one of the most dangerous men in America. The Senator and the administration were soon at war.

Another outspoken critic of the New Deal was Father Charles E. Coughlin, a Catholic priest from Royal Oak, Michigan. Coughlin's radio broadcasts of sermons and commentary had begun in the late 1920s, and by 1933 the golden-voiced "radio priest" had an audience of millions. Like Long, he first supported the New Deal, but turned against FDR when the president refused to endorse inflationary measures to end the Depression. In late 1934 Coughlin formed the National Union for Social Justice, a pressure group advocating silver inflation and the nationalization of power, oil, light, and natural gas companies, and ultimately the seizure of the banks as well. At various times he was denounced by Catholic prelates for his rhetorical excesses, especially his anti-Semitism; but secure in the support of his own bishop, he continued to attack Roosevelt and those he called the "money-lenders."

A third populistic challenge came from an aging California physician, Francis E. Townsend. A man with a tender heart, Townsend was outraged by the lack of public concern for the elderly victims of the Depression. To rescue them and aid the distressed nation generally, he proposed that all persons over sixty be given pensions of $200 a month on condition that they retire from their jobs and "spend the money as they get it." The scheme, he declared, would simultaneously remove thousands of older workers from the overcrowded job market and inject millions of dollars of fresh purchasing power into the economy.

The Townsend Plan quickly won a following among older people and was incorporated into a bill introduced in Congress in early 1935. Critics attacked the measure as unworkable and unfair to the great majority of Americans under sixty. Many of its opponents were conservatives who saw the plan as socialistic, but Frances Perkins, FDR's secretary of labor, also derided it as a crackpot scheme. The *Townsend Weekly,* the doctor's editorial voice, soon responded with an angry attack on the administration.

The Roosevelt Coalition.   Fortunately for Roosevelt, he had also won many friends. By 1935 millions of Americans had reason to thank the New Deal and the Democratic party for their help. Artists, writers, and musicians were grateful for the opportunity under the WPA to do productive work and maintain their skills and talents. Young people were grateful for the subsidy from the National Youth Administration that allowed them to stay in school and prepare for careers. Middle-class homeowners sang Roosevelt's praises for sparing them the humiliation of eviction from their homes through a timely HOLC loan. Unemployed factory workers could thank the president for the relief payments that kept them from hunger. Farmers welcomed cash under AAA and its replacements. For many millions of citizens, the federal government for the first time seriously touched their lives and the contact seemed protective and benign.

Black Americans were especially grateful to Roosevelt and his party. Not since Reconstruction had African-Americans received as good a shake from their government as now. Not that the administration's policies were ideal in racial terms. Recent research has shown that in the South African-Americans were often denied the benefits they deserved under the federal relief laws. The AAA programs, as administered, had, for example, hurt black sharecroppers. Moreover, needing southern votes in Congress, Roosevelt was unwilling to attack head-on the racial caste system of the South. He sponsored a federal antilynching bill but allowed it to be filibustered to death in the Senate. Nonetheless, blacks shared in WPA programs; the National Youth Administration helped many hundreds of young black men and women. When the New Deal adopted a slum-clearance program, blacks would become prominent beneficiaries of the new public housing. New Dealers, moreover, were often solicitous of black pride. Eleanor Roosevelt and Secretary Harold Ickes, particularly, accorded recognition to talented black men and women, supported black aspirations, and sought to further the cause of civil rights. When the Daughters of the American Revolution refused to allow the distinguished black contralto Marian Anderson to sing at their convention in Washington's Constitution Hall, Secretary Ickes invited her to use the steps of the Lincoln Memorial for an open-air concert. Black Americans appreciated the benefits of the New Deal and ignored its deficiencies. Many broke their traditional Republican ties and shifted their votes to the Democratic column.

By late 1935 organized labor had also joined the Roosevelt camp. During the 1920s, as we saw, the unions had declined in power and numbers. After 1924 leadership of the labor movement rested in the conservative hands of William Green, Samuel Gompers's successor as head of the American Federation of Labor. Green did little to counteract the decline in union membership and influence; nor was he interested in bringing the millions of new industrial wage earners into organized labor's house. There were a few industrial unions in the nation—the feeble United Mine Workers under the unpredictable John L. Lewis and two unions of garment workers under Sidney Hillman and David Dubinsky. But these were exceptional. Unlike skilled craftspeople, most factory workers and miners were unorganized.

Then came the NIRA and its Section 7a, authorizing collective bargaining in industries that adopted NIRA fair-practice codes. To enforce the NIRA labor provision the administration pursued a vigorous policy of encouraging labor unions and collective bargaining. Soon thousands of workers, inspired by labor organizers' claim that "the president wants you to unionize," were flocking into both old and new labor organizations, glad to oblige the president and certain that he wished them well. Roosevelt was at first indifferent to organized labor. But many prominent New Dealers, particularly Senator Robert F. Wagner of New York and Secretary of Labor Frances Perkins (the first woman cabinet member), were strongly pro-union. Whether he deserved it or not, FDR would come to be seen as the champion of the working man and woman against their enemies, the "bosses" and the "economic royalists."

The Social Welfare State

The first New Deal had been devoted largely to recovery and relief. Of the two goals, only the second had met with much success. In 1935 growing opposition, particularly from the neopopulists, and the sense that the New Deal had stalled, pushed Roosevelt into a new program to weaken the power of big business, equalize opportunity, and increase economic security. In a burst of energy known as the Second Hundred Days, or the Second New Deal, the administration transformed the nation into a modern social welfare state.

The stimulus for the new tack may have been immediate problems, but the inspiration was derived from the reform impulse of the early twentieth century. The Second New Deal elevated the progressive social welfare programs, largely confined to the states before 1917, to the national level. Now the federal government would not only complete the job of subduing the "vested interests" but also make Washington the guardian of the weak and unfortunate and the source of security for all Americans.

In June 1935 the president sent Congress a list of "must" legislation consisting of four crucial items: a social security bill, a measure to replace the collective bargaining provision of the defunct NIRA, a banking regulation proposal, and a new income tax with rates that rose sharply as income increased. In addition, he demanded that Congress pass several important secondary measures to expand social and economic benefits for various segments of the nation.

Labor's New Charter.   Over the next few months FDR got most of what he asked for. In July Congress passed the National Labor Relations Act (also called the Wagner Act, after its chief sponsor, Senator Robert Wagner of New York), establishing a permanent National Labor Relations Board with the authority to supervise elections to determine whether workers in an industry wanted union representation. The union, if approved, would become the legal collective bargaining agent for its members, whether employers liked it or not.

The Wagner Act would prove a powerful weapon in the struggle to organize the nation's industrial workers. But many obstacles remained. For years employers had successfully used labor spies, strikebreakers, strong-arm methods, and legal injunctions to defeat unionization in the mines and factories, and they were certain to fight back now. Nor could the industrial union organizers expect much help from the AFL, whose leaders considered the growth of industrial unionism a threat to their own power and were contemptuous of the semiskilled workers of immigrant stock who labored in the factories and mines. When, at the 1935 annual AFL convention, president William Green and his friends refused to support the principle of industrial unionism, dissenters Sidney Hillman, David Dubinsky, and John L. Lewis set up the Committee for Industrial Organization. In 1938, under the name Congress of Industrial Organizations (CIO), it became a separate and competing national labor federation.

The steel industry was the first target of CIO organizers. Several of the smaller steel firms ferociously resisted unionization. On Memorial Day 1937, outside Republic Steel, strikers and the police clashed violently, leaving several strikers dead and many injured. The giant of the industry, United States Steel, however, quickly capitulated, signing an agreement with the steelworkers in March 1937 that recognized the union as their collective bargaining agent. The automobile industry was tougher, but it, too, yielded. In February 1937, after a series of dramatic sit-down strikes in which workers refused to leave the plants until their demands were met, General Motors surrendered and recognized the United Automobile Workers. Ford Motor Company, under the fiercely individualistic Henry Ford, held out for many more months, using hoodlums and spies to help break the union drive. But in 1940 Ford, too, capitulated. By the eve of World War II the entire auto industry had been unionized.

By 1941, as a result of the Wagner Act and the doggedness of Lewis, Hillman, and other leaders of industrial labor, the number of men and women belonging to unions had swelled to a record 8.4 million—23 percent of the nonfarm labor force. It would not be easy for the politicians to ignore labor representatives again. The successful organizing of industrial labor seemed a power shift as dramatic as any that had taken place since the Civil War.

Social Security.

The next installment of Second Hundred Days "must" legislation had consequences that were even more far-reaching than the Wagner Act. Advanced progressives had long championed a system of social security for the unemployed, the handicapped, the sick, and the aged. Other nations had adopted such schemes, but in the United States health costs, job loss, and retirement uncertainties were problems left to the individual or to private charities to solve. The Social Security Act of 1935 established a system of unemployment insurance under the joint administration of the states and the federal government, financed by a payroll tax levied on employers. It set up a pension scheme for retired people over sixty-five and their survivors to be paid for by a tax levied equally on both employers and employees. The working generation would pay for retirees and so there would have to be enough employed people to support the existing cohort of retirees if the system was to work. Finally, the Social Security Act provided federal funds to the states to aid the destitute blind and provide support for delinquent, crippled, dependent, and homeless children, and for establishing public health and maternity care programs, and vocational rehabilitation services.

The United States had finally joined the ranks of the other advanced industrial nations in providing a measure of economic security for its citizens. But it was at best a qualified commitment. Roosevelt backed off including a comprehensive health insurance plan in his Social Security package when the American

Medical Association, speaking for the nation's doctors, attacked it as "socialized medicine" that would damage the doctor–patient relationship and make the medical system heavy with bureaucracy. And even within its limited scope the original Social Security legislation was imperfect. The old-age pension plan as enacted excluded farm workers and the self-employed, for example. The sums provided were often skimpy. A later generation would plug some of the gaps and beef up the amounts but would also allow the aid-to-dependent-children provision to become a dole for a permanent class of healthy adult "welfare" clients unwilling to take care of themselves. And in the long run, demographic changes would make chancy the ability of the pension fund to take care of the growing number of retirees taking money out of the system compared to employed workers still paying money into it.

Additional "Must" Legislation.
Still other legislation of the Second Hundred Days fulfilled or reinforced old progressive promises. The Public Utility Holding Company Act gave the federal government control over interstate transmission of electricity and gas. It also conferred on the new Security and Exchange Commission power over monopolistic corporate holding companies. The Wealth Tax Act increased estate and gift tax rates and imposed stiffer levies on high-income recipients. The final "must" law was the Banking Act of 1935, which strengthened the federal government's control over the Federal Reserve System and gave the hitherto weak Federal Reserve Board a more effective voice in the management of the country's monetary affairs.

Several measures of the Second New Deal were designed specifically to improve the quality of rural life. In May 1935 Congress established a Rural Electrification Administration (REA). In a few years this agency brought electricity to millions of the nation's farms, created large new markets for electrical appliances, and dramatically changed the lives of farm families. The Soil Conservation and Domestic Allotment Act of 1936 rescued the crop-limitation features of the disallowed AAA by paying farmers not to grow "soil-depleting" crops. The Frazier-Lemke Farm Mortgage Moratorium Act extended farm mortgages for three years to save hard-pressed farmers from foreclosures.

Conservatives often criticized New Dealers as "planners," a term equivalent among some critics to "socialists." In reality, besides the Tennessee Valley Authority, the Resettlement Administration (RA) was one of the few deliberate New Deal attempts at social planning, in this case to eliminate the chronic problem of rural poverty. Established by Roosevelt as part of Federal Emergency Relief Administration, the RA sought to move farmers from unfertile, "submarginal" land where they lived at bare subsistence levels to farms where they could support themselves in modest comfort. The federal government would provide subsistence farmers with better acreage, low-cost loans, and expert advice. Under Rexford Tugwell, one of Roosevelt's liberal brain trusters, the underfunded agency succeeded only in relocating some 4,000 poor farmers and sharecroppers. The RA's successor, the Farm Security Administration (established by the 1937 Bankhead-Jones Farm Tenancy Act), took on the special task of converting tenant farmers into farm owners. It, too, was starved for money and made only a little dent in the problem of rural poverty.

End of the New Deal

By the end of the Second Hundred Days the 1936 presidential campaign was well underway. Roosevelt easily won his party's renomination. The Republicans turned to Governor Alfred M. Landon of Kansas, a modest, likable man with progressive leanings. To the left of the Democrats—or to the right, some insisted—was the Union party, whose nominee, William Lemke of North Dakota, was a farmer-laborite in the Populist tradition. In all likelihood Huey Long would have headed the third-party ticket had he not been assassinated by one of his many Louisiana enemies in September 1935.

The campaign outcome was never really in doubt. By now a new political coalition had formed around Roosevelt, composed not only of the Democratic party's traditional southern whites, Catholics, and urban ethnics, but also of blacks, Mexican-Americans, intellectuals, organized labor, and a big slice of the Protestant lower middle class. Many of these voters were beneficiaries of New Deal programs. But they also revered FDR as a man and a leader. Millions listened to his "fireside chats" on the radio and felt that their government cared.

During the campaign conservatives called Roosevelt a dictator who had seized unheard-of powers over every aspect of American life. They denounced the "bloated" federal bureaucracy and warned that "big government" would soon dominate every other institution. They were not entirely wrong. No president had ever achieved such power over the economy and over so many people's lives. The combination of big government and a vigorous leader who had a rare rapport with the people focused more attention on Washington, D.C., than ever before.

Whatever drawbacks time would disclose in this arrangement, in 1936 only a minority of Americans took the conservatives' warnings seriously. In November the voters turned out in record numbers and expressed their enthusiastic support of the New Deal. Roosevelt carried every state in the union except rock-ribbed Republican Maine and Vermont and won the most impressive popular mandate in American political history: almost 28 million votes to Landon's 17 million. In the congressional contest the results were equally lopsided. When the new Congress convened, the Democratic side of the House would be so crowded that many of the new Democrats were forced to sit with the opposition.

In his second inaugural address Roosevelt promised to extend the New Deal's social and economic programs to meet the needs of the "one third of a nation" that was "ill-housed, ill-clad, ill-nourished." It was a call for a new burst of reform, and he secured a part of what he wanted from the new Congress. In September 1937 the National Housing Act (Wagner-Steagall Act) initiated a generation of federal slum clearance and public housing projects for the urban poor. The Agricultural Adjustment Act of 1938, without the unconstitutional processing tax, restored the crop-limitation provisions of the first AAA and made farm price supports a permanent feature of the American economy. The Food, Drug, and Cosmetic Act of June 1938 strengthened the consumer-protection features of the progressives' Pure Food and Drug Act of 1906. The Fair Labor Standards Act established for the first time a federally mandated minimum hourly wage and a maximum workweek for millions of workers in occupations involved in interstate commerce. But the Fair Labor Standards Act was the last important piece of New Deal legislation. Thereafter New Deal initiatives ceased. The effort to overhaul America and promote recovery had run out of steam.

Given Roosevelt's overwhelming vote of confidence in the election and the top-heavy Democratic majority in Congress in 1937 and 1938, this outcome is startling. Yet it is understandable if we consider where the nation was at this point. Despite every New Deal effort, the economy had failed to make a complete recovery. In 1937, though the nation's output forged ahead, unemployment remained at 14.3 percent of the labor force. Growth, moreover, had been accompanied by sharp price rises. Fearing inflation, in June Roosevelt cut back sharply on federal spending, throwing the economy into an unexpected tailspin. By the following year unemployment was back to 19 percent of the workforce. Roosevelt checked the descent by quickly increasing relief and other outlays, but it was clear to everyone that the country had not solved its chronic unemployment problem.

The persistence of hard times undoubtedly damaged New Deal zest and morale. Nothing seemed to work—or work well—and the administration seemed to have no new ideas. FDR's inability to get the economy going again injured his prestige within his own party. Divisions between northern liberals and southern conservatives, which had been papered over by the mutual concern for recovery, now broke through. Within months of the November electoral victory, the Democrats were in disarray, squabbling with one another and uncertain which way to turn.

At this point Roosevelt launched an ill-considered attack on the Supreme Court. FDR saw the Court as a bastion of judicial conservatism. It had struck down the AAA and the NIRA and had declared unconstitutional the Frazier-Lemke Act as well as several other New Deal measures. Roosevelt feared that it would wipe from the books the major social legislation of 1935–1936.

The justices were almost all elderly men, and Roosevelt might have allowed resignations and deaths to change the Court's profile. Instead, in February 1937 he asked Congress for the power to name up to six new judges, one for each incumbent who refused to resign after reaching seventy years of age. This scheme to "pack the Court" with more liberal judges stirred up a storm. Predictably, conservatives saw it as an attempt to subvert the Constitution. But even liberals balked at the proposal to undermine the Court's independence. When the "nine old men," perhaps intimidated by the president's stand, unexpectedly sustained several crucial pieces of New Deal legislation and several liberal state laws, the Court-packing bill's congressional support melted away. In late July the Senate sent the bill back to the Judiciary Committee, where it quietly died. The president had suffered a major legislative defeat, almost his first, and the blow to his prestige was damaging. Thereafter, as confidence in Roosevelt's leadership waned, southern Democrats would increasingly side with conservative Republicans against their own party's leader.

The loss of support was also expressed by the public at the polls. In the 1938 congressional elections, hoping to strengthen the liberal contingent in Congress, Roosevelt urged Democrats to defeat conservatives in the party congressional primaries. Many voters, resenting interference in local politics, ignored the president's wishes. In the congressional elections themselves the Democrats lost eighty-one seats in the House and eight in the Senate. Losses in midterm national elections are not unusual for the party in power, and in any case the 1936 Democratic congressional majority was too lopsided to last. Nevertheless, it was clear that many citizens had lost confidence in the man and the party they had turned to in order to save the country. In the turbulent years that followed, Roosevelt continued to be admired as the country's savior; but for all intents and purposes the New Deal was incapable of further successful innovation.

Conclusions

The New Deal failed to bring the Great Depression to an end. As the decade of the 1930s drew to a close, the government's ability to restore full employment by massive deficit spending was still unproved. But after 1939 it would be difficult for any president to insist that the business cycle had to work itself out no matter what the human cost. Moreover, Roosevelt's policies did check the frightening downward slide and, more important, saved millions of citizens from the catastrophic effects of an economy gone haywire.

Roosevelt and his colleagues did not usher in a revolution. The United States remained a capitalist nation after 1938. But it would be capitalist with a difference. In the words of economist John Maynard Keynes, Roosevelt had made himself "the trustee" for all those who sought "to mend the evil of our condition by reasoned experiment within the framework of the existing social system." Later conservative administrations would seek to trim and partially reverse the New Deal but never again would Americans be completely exposed to the uncertainties of a freewheeling economy qualified only in favor of business.

The New Dealers have been criticized for failing to use the crisis of American capitalism to create a more egalitarian society. Perhaps more rigorous progressive taxation and more extensive social welfare programs might have reduced inequality. But that FDR could have converted America to socialism—assuming he had wished to do so—is doubtful. Public fear in 1933 gave Roosevelt a broad mandate for change and experiment. Yet few Americans would have supported anything so much against the national grain as federal ownership of industry and the banks. And if, in panic, the voters had endorsed such measures, they certainly would have regretted and reversed their action once they had regained their confidence.

In the process of creating the modern social welfare state, there were undoubtedly losses as well as gains. Federal power and executive authority were both greatly expanded. Only the hidebound conservatives, who opposed virtually every New Deal measure, saw the dangers in this change as the 1930s came to an end. Time would reveal to what extent FDR had encouraged an "imperial presidency." Time would also disclose unanticipated failings in a number of New Deal programs. Yet few political movements would have such a benign impact on the quality of American lives.

Meanwhile, as the 1940s loomed, the country began to turn its attention to the threatening events taking place beyond its shores.

ONLINE RESOURCES

"The History of Mexican Americans in California: Revolution to Depression" *http://www.cr.nps.gov/history/online_books/5views/5views5c.htm* Explore the subject of immigration from Mexico to America. Through this site, learn about Mexican-Americans' lives in the barrios in California and their struggle for a better life through mutual aid and work.

"The Great Depression" *http://xroads.virginia.edu/~1930s/PRINT/newdeal/intro3.html* This in-depth site examines all facets of the economic crisis, from its causes to the reactions in the United States and from the government to the populace.

"Fireside Chats of Franklin D. Roosevelt" *http://www.mhric.org/fdr/fdr.html* Learn about FDR's New Deal programs much like many Americans did in the late 1930s through these radio addresses known as fireside chats. Read transcripts of these broadcasts that spanned from 1933 to 1944.

"Labor Unions During the Great Depression and the New Deal" *http://memory.loc.gov/ammem/ndlpedu/features/timeline/depwwii/depwar.html* In addition to an overview of the status of labor unions during the era, this site provides documents and interviews from Americans who belonged to these unions. The site discusses the importance of the New Deal to unionization and to workers' lives and also contains union songs and chants that reflect this period of unionization.

"TVA: Electricity for All" *http://newdeal.feri.org/tva/index.htm* On this site, read the Tennessee Valley Authority Act, explore letters from the field that tell of the social and environmental impact of the expansive federal project, and learn about rural electrification.

New Deal Network Library *http://newdeal.feri.org/library/index.htm* This site offers a first-hand glimpse into the world of the Great Depression and the New Deal era with more than 4,000 photographs online.

The Great Flint Sitdown *http://www.reuther.wayne.edu/exhibits/sitdown.html* This online exhibit provides just one example of the strength of labor unions during the New Deal era with its discussion of the UAW strike in Flint, Michigan. See photos of strikers in action, and read a compelling narrative of the strike.

26

World War II

Blunder, or Decision in the National Interest?

1904	Japan defeats Russia, takes control of Korea and Manchuria
1908	Root-Takahira Agreement
1921–22	Washington Conference; Benito Mussolini rises to power in Italy, imposing Fascist regime
1928	Kellogg-Briand Pact
1931–32	Japan reoccupies Manchuria
1932	Franklin D. Roosevelt elected president
1933	Adolf Hitler ends Weimar Republic and becomes German chancellor, imposing Nazi rule
1936	Hitler occupies the Rhineland; FDR reelected
1937–38	Japan invades China
1938	Hitler annexes Austria; Munich Pact cedes Czechoslovakia's Sudetenland to Germany
1939	Germany occupies the remainder of Czechoslovakia; The Soviet Union and Germany sign a nonaggression pact; Germany invades Poland; Great Britain and France declare war on Germany
1940	Germany conquers Norway, Denmark, Belgium, Luxembourg, Holland, and France; Japan, Italy, and Germany sign a military and economic agreement forming the Axis alliance; FDR reelected
1941	Lend-Lease Act; Germany invades the Soviet Union; Roosevelt and Churchill issue Atlantic Charter; Japan bombs Pearl Harbor; United States declares war on Japan; Germany and Italy declare war on United States; Manhattan Project begins; Fair Employment Practices Act; Hitler begins extermination of Jews
1942	Roosevelt orders the War Department to confine Japanese-Americans on West Coast; Battle of Midway checks Japanese Pacific advance; Women's Army and Navy corps (WACS, WAVES) established
1943	Allies defeat the German Afrika Korps, invade Sicily; Soviets stop Germans at Stalingrad; "Big Three" meet in Teheran; MacArthur and Nimitz close in on Pacific islands; California and Detroit race riots
1944	Normandy invasion; Japanese launch first kamikaze attacks; FDR reelected
1945	Yalta Conference; MacArthur recaptures Philippines; Germany defeated; FDR dies; Harry S. Truman becomes president; Atomic bombing of Hiroshima and Nagasaki; Soviets declare war on Japan; Japan surrenders

December 7, 1941, dawned partly cloudy over the Hawaiian island of Oahu, 2,200 miles southwest of San Francisco. At Pearl Harbor, base of the United States Pacific Fleet, eight battleships, nine cruisers, twenty destroyers, and forty-nine other naval vessels lay at their berths or in dry dock. It was Sunday, and many of the sailors were on weekend liberty. At the airfields, Army Air Corps planes were parked in tight clusters, almost wing to wing, on the runways to prevent possible sabotage. The air crews were mostly away or asleep in the barracks. Suddenly at 7:55 A.M. Pearl Harbor erupted in flames as tons of explosives, released by Japanese torpedo planes and bombers, slammed into the American ships tied up at Battleship Row. At the military airfields American planes became sitting ducks for the attackers; only forty American pursuit planes rose to challenge the enemy. Meanwhile, several Japanese midget submarines, having sneaked through the harbor's protective net, were launching torpedoes at every target in sight. Two hours later, when the attack ended, much of America's naval and air power in the Pacific had been destroyed. In that brief, hellish interval 2,400 American sailors, marines, soldiers, airmen, and civilians died; 8 battleships were sunk or badly damaged; and 183 planes were lost. Fortunately the aircraft carrier force had been at sea and so escaped intact. Still, it was the worst naval disaster in American history.

On December 8, shortly after noon Eastern Standard Time, President Roosevelt appeared before a joint session of Congress to ask for a declaration of war against Japan. The country, he declared, would never forget that the Japanese had attacked while their emissaries were in Washington talking peace. December 7 was a date that would "live in infamy." With only one dissenting vote, Congress declared war against Japan. On December 11 Germany, Japan's Axis ally, declared war against the United States; Italy, the third Axis power, immediately followed. The crowded and tragic events of four days had finally brought the United States into World War II, the greatest war in history.

How did the country arrive at this tragic point? In the weeks and months following Pearl Harbor, few Americans doubted that they had any choice but to defend themselves against a treacherous attack. The war stilled the discordant voices that for three years or more had debated war or peace. But after 1945 Americans would resume the argument. A majority saw Pearl Harbor as the logical culmination of Axis plans to enslave all free peoples. A minority concluded that the United States had blundered into an unnecessary war or had even been pushed into it by scheming men. Some accused Franklin Roosevelt of deception to achieve his misconceived interventionist ends.

Who was right? Was American entrance into war in December 1941 a mistake that might have, and should have, been avoided? Or was war against the Axis powers, however triggered, the only way the United States could have protected itself and its vital interests against dangerous predators intent on destroying democracy and freedom and enslaving the American people?

Seeds of Conflict

The Japanese attack and the great war that followed brought to a head events that began a century earlier and involved the relations of one half of the industrialized world with the other.

Friction with Japan.   American interests in the Far East dated from late in the eighteenth century when China became an important United States trading partner and an object of philanthropic and missionary concern. American–Japanese relations commenced in the 1850s when Captain Matthew Perry of the United States Navy forced the Japanese to abandon their traditional isolation and open trade relations with the West. Perry's visit propelled Japan into the modern world. To fend off Western domination the Japanese were soon imitating not only the West's parliamentary institutions, universal education, and industrialization but also its aggressive nationalism and imperialism. In 1895 Japan wrenched Korea from China. In 1904 it challenged czarist Russia over China's loosely attached northern provinces and defeated the Russian giant in a brief and bloody war.

In the early twentieth century American–Japanese relations were often bumpy. The United States supported the Japanese against the Russians in 1904–1905. But when President Theodore Roosevelt helped bring the Russo-Japanese War to an end by compromise, the Japanese blamed the United States for depriving them of the gains they considered their due. Matters worsened two years later when the San Francisco Board of Education placed Japanese-American students in segregated schools. A proud people, the Japanese were outraged by this assertion of inferiority. Theodore Roosevelt patched things up with the so-called Gentlemen's Agreement: The school board would cancel its order, and the Japanese government would not issue any more passports to would-be immigrants to the United States. The issue was superficially settled, but by this time feelings between the two nations had been rubbed raw. In succeeding years there would be talk, particularly in the Hearst newspapers, of the "yellow peril" in the Far East.

In the next few years Japanese and American interests would frequently clash in east Asia. In the 1908 Root-Takahira Agreement, Japan accepted the American position that China must remain independent and retain its territorial integrity. But resentments continued to fester. Japan coveted the natural resources of China and Southeast Asia. Japanese nationalists were certain that the United States and the other Western powers—"have" nations with abundant resources either at home or within their empires—were trying to keep Japan—a "have-not" nation, without oil, coal, rubber, iron, and copper—from becoming the great power it deserved to be.

In 1915 Japan took advantage of Europe's preoccupation at home during World War I to present China with the so-called Twenty-One Demands. Negating the Root-Takahira Agreement, these would have reduced China to a Japanese protectorate. American protest forced the Japanese to back off. The Washington Armament Conference of 1921–1922 further constrained Japan. Called by Secretary Hughes to help stabilize international relations in the Far East, the conference resulted in the Four Power Treaty by which France, the United States, England, and Japan pledged to respect one another's possessions in the Pacific. A Nine Power Treaty signed by the same four powers and four smaller European nations plus China promised to respect Chinese territorial integrity and the Open Door principle.

For a while Japanese ambitions diminished, and relations with the United States improved. At the end of the 1920s, however, Japanese militarists and extreme nationalists came to power in Tokyo and launched a more aggressive policy toward

China. In 1931–1932 the militarists provoked an "incident" with China and seized its rich northern province of Manchuria, converting it into a puppet kingdom, re-named Manchukuo. The United States viewed Japan's aggression against its weak-er neighbor as a violation of Japan's international agreements. But distracted by the Depression and unwilling to take action stronger than the American public would then support, Washington limited itself to diplomatic protests. In January 1932 Sec-retary of State Henry L. Stimson, reasserting John Hay's Open Door policy of a gen-eration before, announced that the United States would not recognize any act that impaired the "territorial and administrative integrity of the Republic of China."

The Stimson Doctrine did not deter the Japanese military leaders. Early in 1932 Japanese army units clashed with Chinese troops in Shanghai, and during the fighting that ensued thousands of Chinese civilians were killed. In 1937, following a shooting incident at the Marco Polo Bridge near Peking, the Japanese began a piecemeal occupation of the Chinese Republic. Before long their armies had seized major Chinese cities and torn large chunks of the republic from the control of Chiang Kai-shek, leader of the Kuomintang, China's ruling party. In 1938 the Japanese announced a "new order" in the Far East based on thinly disguised Japanese domination of the whole region.

The Rise of Fascism in Europe.
Meanwhile, an even more dangerous group of aggressors had appeared in Europe. In Italy, where bitter conflict between Communists and conservatives and the losses of World War I had undermined the parliamentary system, Benito Mussolini seized power in 1922 in the name of law and order. "Il Duce" and his Fascists brutally eliminated their opponents, established a centralized totalitarian regime, and launched an aggressive foreign policy. In 1935 Fascist Italy attacked Ethiopia, one of the few still-independent African nations, and brutally conquered it. The moving plea to the League of Nations of Ethiopia's emperor, Haile Selassie, brought economic sanctions against Italy. But weakly supported by member nations and the United States, these did not deter Mussolini.

Authoritarian governments resembling Fascist Italy's spread through eastern and southern Europe following the collapse of the international economy in the early 1930s. The boundaries drawn by Wilson and his colleagues had created several small nations out of the ruins of Austria-Hungary and the Russian empire; few besides Czechoslovakia of these had democratic traditions or the social insti-tutions to support parliamentary government. By the early 1930s Hungary, Poland, Yugoslavia, and the Baltic states, along with Bulgaria, Romania, Albania, and Greece, all had despotic regimes. Many of the new states were not viable economically, and their weaknesses would be a permanent temptation to their greedy, more powerful neighbors.

Most dangerous of all, the post-World War I settlement failed to create a stable German democracy. By blaming Germany for the war, imposing vast indemnities on the German economy, and forcing the German nation to disarm, the Versailles treaty left a legacy of intense bitterness. German nationalists held the democratic Weimar Republic, successor to Kaiser Wilhelm II's imperial regime, responsible for the degrading treaty and never became reconciled to it. Despite these prob-lems, for a few years in the late 1920s the German people experienced a period of prosperity and cultural creativity under their new democratic regime. When the bottom fell out of the world economy in 1929, however, the inability of the Weimar government to stop Germany's downward economic spiral destroyed the German public's fragile confidence in democracy. Right-wing and Communist groups quickly took advantage of the situation to attack liberal parliamentary government. By 1930 Weimar's enemies, on both the extreme left and the extreme right, were engaged in a life-or-death struggle to see who could destroy the republic first and impose its own ideology, Communist or Fascist, on the German people.

The victor in the competition was the National Socialists (Nazis) under Adolf Hitler, a fanatical right-wing nationalist who proclaimed his intention to repudiate Versailles and the galling military restraints and financial burdens it had imposed on Germany. The new "Third Reich" would restore German pride and German might. Like Italy's Fascists, the Nazis glorified the state and expressed contempt for democracy and parliamentary institutions and for the "degenerate" culture that the liberal Weimar regime had fostered.

Indeed, Hitler's hatred of liberal values went beyond even Mussolini's. The Nazis were rabid racists who carried ideas of Nordic supremacy to a chilling conclusion: All other peoples were inferior beings who must bow to the *Herrenvolk*, the superrace of northern Europe. In Hitler's view the Jews, especially, were malign beings who were responsible for most of Germany's calamities, including the defeat in 1918. Elevated to Chancellor in 1933, Hitler promised the German people that he would punish the Jews, destroy the Communists, repudiate Versailles, and make Germany the most powerful nation in Europe once more.

Few Americans had paid much attention to events in Germany before 1933, but Hitler and the Nazis could not be ignored. Once in control of the German state, Hitler renounced the armaments limitations of the Versailles treaty and began to rearm Germany. He quickly swept away parliamentary government and either assassinated his democratic and leftist opponents or threw them into concentration camps. Finally, he deprived Germany's Jewish population of all their civil rights and sent thousands of the nation's most talented scientists, writers, musicians, doctors, and scholars fleeing as refugees to western Europe and the United States.

From the outset Hitler scarcely concealed his lust for European dominance. In 1936 he reoccupied the Rhineland, which had been demilitarized by the Versailles treaty. That same year he and Mussolini concluded an alliance of mutual support (the Rome-Berlin Axis). In 1937 the two dictators intervened in the civil war in Spain, siding with the Fascist strongman Francisco Franco against the coalition of liberals, socialists, Communists, and anarchists (the Loyalists) who supported the Spanish Republic. In 1938 Hitler began his campaign to reincorporate all German-speaking territories in Europe into "Greater Germany" by annexing Austria. Hitler's next target was Czechoslovakia, a democratic republic formed from parts of the Austro-Hungarian Empire, which contained several million Germans within its Sudetenland region.

Not all Americans saw fascism-nazism as a serious danger. Some Catholics and conservatives, for example, preferred Hitler's client, Franco, to the Spanish Loyalists. Small numbers of Italian-Americans and German-Americans endorsed the dictators of their respective mother countries. There was even a small group of intellectuals who believed that Nazism represented the "wave of the future."

Yet undoubtedly the great majority of Americans deplored and feared what they saw taking place in central and southern Europe.

Nazi Germany clearly threatened the balance of power in Europe. Yet England and France, traumatized by their enormous human and financial losses in World War I and weakened by the worldwide Depression, were reluctant to take a strong stand against the German threat. When, in early 1938, Hitler demanded that Czechoslovakia turn over the Sudetenland to Germany, the Czechs asked Britain and France for support. British Prime Minister Neville Chamberlain and French Premier Édouard Daladier refused. Believing they could successfully appease the Germans, they agreed, at a conference with the German dictator at Munich in September 1938, to support Hitler's demands on the Czechs. Unable to confront Germany alone, the Czechs were forced to surrender the Sudetenland to preserve the rest of the republic.

Chamberlain returned home to Britain from Munich convinced that appeasement would work and that the Munich Pact would bring "peace in our time." It did not. In March 1939, defying the Munich agreement, German forces occupied the rest of now defenseless Czechoslovakia and set up a puppet regime. Hitler soon made territorial demands on Germany's large eastern neighbor, Poland. By this time only the near-blind could believe that Hitler and Mussolini did not pose a serious threat to the peace and stability of Europe. In April 1939 Britain and France signed a mutual assistance pact with Poland, promising to come to its aid if attacked.

Roosevelt and the Interventionists.

Though most Americans deplored the rise of the dictators, they did not agree on the implications for the United States. Liberals and leftists saw the rising tide of authoritarianism as a danger to free government everywhere. Even many middle-of-the road Americans feared that German, Italian, and Japanese expansionism would throw the world into turmoil. After the fall of Czechoslovakia, Americans were forced to confront the possibility that the aggressors could be stopped only by force.

Yet few Americans wished to see the United States become directly involved in Europe's troubles. By the late 1930s isolationism had hardened into an ideology that denied American vital interests abroad and insisted that, in the past, Americans had been duped into foreign wars by munitions manufacturers, bankers, and other cunning, self-serving manipulators. Between 1934 and 1936 isolationist views were reinforced by the Senate Munitions Investigating Committee hearings probing the origins of World War I. The committee, chaired by Senator Gerald P. Nye, concluded that those who profited from munitions manufacture had encouraged United States intervention. In the wake of the Nye Committee hearings, Congress passed a series of Neutrality Acts requiring the president in the event of war to embargo arms shipments to belligerents, forbid American citizens to sail on belligerent ships, and deny bankers the right to extend credit to the warring powers. By avoiding the entangling policies of 1914–1917, they believed, the United States could stay out of any future war. By 1937, according to an opinion poll, 94 percent of the American people favored nonintervention abroad regardless of who the combatants were or how just their cause.

From the outset President Roosevelt was more interventionist than most Americans. FDR believed in America's responsibility as a great power to cooperate with other nations to achieve a stable world order. During the 1920s he moved with the drift of American public opinion to isolationism, but the rise of the dictators quickly revived his internationalist convictions. At what moment Roosevelt and his advisers concluded that the dictators must be stopped at all cost is unclear. As early as 1933 he tried to induce Congress to prohibit the sale of arms to aggressor nations. In 1935, in the interest of world security, he asked Congress to approve admitting the United States to the World Court. Congress, dominated by isolationists, rejected both schemes.

Frustrated in Europe, Roosevelt worked to strengthen the United States by establishing closer ties with Latin America. His Good Neighbor Policy, built on the earlier initiatives of his immediate Republican predecessors, was designed to create "hemispheric solidarity." During his first term of office FDR renounced the Platt Amendment, which had allowed the United States to intervene in Cuban affairs. At two Latin American conferences in 1933 and 1936, the United States reinforced the pledge (given in the 1928 Clark Memorandum) to cease intervening in the affairs of Central and South America. Before long the United States had removed its last troop contingents from Caribbean nations. The Good Neighbor policy would pay dividends: When war came, almost all the Latin American countries would support the United States against its enemies.

During his second term, as the international situation darkened, the president turned to face the aggressors directly. In 1937, following Japan's attack on China, he denounced "international lawlessness" and proposed that nations contributing to "international anarchy" be "quarantined"—isolated and walled off by the rest of the world. By this time the president clearly considered Germany, Italy, and Japan potentially dangerous adversaries; in private conversations he referred to them as the "three bandit nations."

In the emerging international crisis, ideology inevitably influenced Roosevelt's views. The totalitarian and militaristic regimes of Germany, Italy, and Japan represented everything a liberal democrat despised: repression, racism, and brutality. The president, moreover, was surrounded by advisers who saw Hitler as embodying the most primitive, irrational, reactionary currents in Western society. But there were also more self-interested motives at play. Ever since the late nineteenth century the United States had relied on the Western European nations, especially Britain, to impose stability in the world outside the Americas. With England and France threatened by Germany, and the Japanese on the rampage in the western Pacific, the president feared for the safety of the United States. What would happen if Britain and France could not check Hitler? A triumphant Germany to the east, allied with a triumphant Japan to the west, would leave the United States a besieged outpost in the middle of a hostile and dangerous world.

By 1938 most Americans shared FDR's opinion of the dictators. A Gallup poll, following Germany's occupation of Czechoslovakia, showed that 65 percent of Americans endorsed a boycott of Germany and Italy, and 55 percent wanted the Neutrality Acts revised to aid the democracies. But there seemed little need as yet for direct American involvement. If war were to erupt, Britain and France would surely prevail, but in any case, safe behind its ocean moats, the American fortress could hold out indefinitely against the dictators.

The Erosion of American Neutrality

American complacency would be put to the test in the fall of 1939. On September 1, after signing a nonaggression pact with the Soviet Union's Joseph Stalin, his former archenemy, Hitler attacked Poland. Two days later Britain and France, fulfilling their pledge to Poland, declared war on Germany. World War II had begun.

On September 3 Roosevelt delivered a fireside chat to the American people. Like Wilson in 1914, he promised to expend "every effort" to avoid war. Consciously diverging from his predecessor, however, he refused to ask Americans to "remain neutral in thought" as well. As required by the neutrality legislation, he forbade the export of arms to the belligerents. But on September 21 he called a special session of Congress to ask for repeal of the arms embargo.

Roosevelt kept out of sight while others carried the burden of getting repeal through Congress. Meanwhile, behind the scenes he used his patronage to bring fellow Democrats into line. The strategy worked. On October 27, by a vote of 63 to 30, the Senate replaced the arms embargo with a "cash-and-carry" policy that permitted the British and French to buy war matériel as long as they paid cash and transported their purchases in their own ships. A week later the House accepted the revision, 243 to 181.

Hitler Conquers Europe.   Had the war against Hitler gone well for the Allies, the United States could have remained aloof. It went badly. Poland, invaded from the east by the Soviet Union, fell to the German invaders from the west in five weeks. The Germans established an occupation government and began the monstrous process of murdering Poland's elites and its Jewish population. For several months thereafter an ominous quiet hung over Europe with neither side engaged in military action. During the "phony war," as isolationists contemptuously called this period, nothing suggested that the major European powers were locked in a life-or-death struggle. Then on April 9, 1940, the German army struck at neutral Norway and Denmark. Denmark fell virtually without a shot; Norway, though aided by Britain and France, was quickly subdued. On May 10 German armored units smashed across the borders into Belgium, Luxembourg, and Holland aiming for the heart of France. In a week German armored columns were sweeping toward Paris.

The British and French armies were quickly overwhelmed by the fast-moving German tank columns supported by terrifying Stuka dive bombers. The German *Blitzkrieg* destroyed French military resistance in a few weeks. By the end of May the British forces in France were pinned against the English Channel near Dunkirk by a tightening ring of German troops and artillery. They were able to hold the German tanks at bay long enough for an armada of small ships to rescue the entrapped forces from the flaming beaches, but most of their equipment had to be left behind. On June 10 Paris surrendered and Italy entered the war as Germany's ally. On June 22, with more than half their country in German hands, the French, now led by Marshal Henri Philippe Pétain, a hero of World War I but a conservative enemy of the French Third Republic, signed an armistice with the Germans that allowed the invaders to occupy the whole northern half of the country and France's Atlantic coast. A few Frenchmen rallied around the free French leader, Charles de Gaulle, who established a London-based government-in-exile.

The Free French and the Pétain government, located at Vichy, were soon battling for control of the French overseas empire.

Hitler had now conquered Norway, Denmark, Luxembourg, France, Belgium, and Holland and had almost destroyed the power of mighty Britain. In a few weeks he had achieved what his imperial predecessor, Wilhelm II, had been unable to do in four years of war. Americans were shocked by the rush of catastrophic events, and for the first time some began to see war as inevitable. Roosevelt's reaction to the Nazi triumph was swift in coming. In mid-May he asked Congress for vast sums for rearmament, including funds to produce 50,000 planes a year and a "two-ocean navy." By October Congress had appropriated $17 billion to strengthen the nation's neglected defenses. In September it would authorize peacetime compulsory military service for the first time in American history. On October 16, 1940, some 6.5 million young men registered for the draft and soon went off to training camps to become soldiers.

Meanwhile, the Germans had launched an all-out air campaign to soften England up for a cross-Channel invasion (Battle of Britain). During the summer of 1940 German aircraft bombarded and strafed the British Isles in daylight until the losses exacted by the gallant, but badly stretched, Royal Air Force made these raids too costly. In early September the *Luftwaffe* began night raids that set London and scores of other English cities ablaze. The British people held on. Sustaining them were the words of their eloquent prime minister, Winston Churchill, who had succeeded Chamberlain after the Allied defeat in Norway. A master of English prose, Churchill declared that if the British Empire lasted a thousand years, men would say: "This was their finest hour." He promised ultimate victory though the cost would be "blood, toil, tears, and sweat."

Britain's brave struggle aroused the admiration of virtually all Americans. In 1940–1941 news from Europe for the first time was being relayed instantaneously to the United States by short-wave radio, creating a sense of participation impossible in an earlier day. From London Americans heard Edward R. Murrow of CBS and other American correspondents describe the Nazi air attacks while sounds of air-raid sirens, anti-aircraft guns, and exploding bombs filled the background. As they listened, many Americans found it impossible not to feel that they themselves were cowering under the storm of German bombs.

Roosevelt's Third Term.

By mid-1940 few Americans doubted that Britain's plight was desperate, and many had come to believe that their country was next on Hitler's list. That spring, supporters of England—mostly eastern liberals—organized the Committee to Defend America by Aiding the Allies, with the old Kansas progressive editor, William Allen White, as head. In the fall a Gallup poll showed that half the voters were now willing to help England "even at the risk of getting into war." Yet the isolationist voice remained powerful and insistent. In early September 1940 a group of isolationists organized the America First Committee, composed of philosophical isolationists and conservatives with a fringe of Anglophobes, Roosevelt haters, and pro-Nazi anti-Semites. For the next year the two groups waged a bitter war for the minds of the American people.

Meanwhile, the country found itself in the middle of another presidential campaign. After keeping everyone guessing for months, FDR concluded that the survival of liberal policies and the nation's safety during the international crisis required his strong hand at the helm. Having effectively eliminated all potential party rivals, he left the Democrats with no choice but to break with the two-term tradition and nominate him for a third time.

The 1940 Republican nominee was Wendell Willkie, a utility magnate from Indiana whose sincerity and boyish charm appealed to younger, less conservative Republicans. Fortunately for the country's unity, Willkie proved to be as much of an interventionist as Roosevelt. He denounced the president's gift of fifty overage destroyers to England in exchange for bases in British North American possessions (September 3) as "the most dictatorial and arbitrary act of any President in the history of the United States." But on the whole, the two candidates were careful to avoid arguing over foreign policy. Toward the end of the campaign, however, Roosevelt uttered some words that would later make his friends cringe. "I have said this before," he told a Boston audience in October, "but I shall say it again and again and again: Your boys are not going to be sent into any foreign wars." FDR would have been elected in any case; in the midst of the grave world crisis Americans were not inclined to exchange the veteran leader for a novice. But the promise helped. On election day Roosevelt carried 38 states to Willkie's 10 and won a popular majority of 27.2 million votes to his opponent's 22.3 million.

Lend-Lease.

During the next full year of peace Roosevelt maneuvered the country ever closer to war. A month following the election Churchill laid out Britain's plight in stark outline to the president in a private letter. He warned that the well-being of the American people was "bound up with the survival and independence of the British Commonwealth of Nations." British sea power protected the United States and the Americas against their enemies. But it was spread very thin and might collapse entirely if the Pétain government at Vichy turned over the French navy to the Nazis. Nor was this all. In the Far East Japan was taking advantage of French, Dutch, and British weakness and inability to protect their Asian possessions by expanding its power and influence. Japanese aggression directly threatened American interests. Britain did not require American manpower to fight on, said Churchill, but it did need that American supplies get through the tightening German submarine blockade. He pleaded for American naval assistance and for an end to the cash-and-carry system. Cash-and-carry was better than the embargo, but Britain was running out of money and more direct help was needed if it was to survive as a bulwark against the Nazi scourge.

Churchill's letter played effectively on Roosevelt's deepest fears. Soon afterward the president prepared the ground for his new aid scheme by warning the public of the critical danger to civilization posed by the Axis powers and explaining the need for the United States to become the "arsenal of democracy." In January 1941 he submitted a "lend-lease" bill to Congress authorizing him to "lend" military equipment to any country "whose defense the President deems vital to the defense of the United States" and providing $7 billion for the purpose, the largest single appropriation in the nation's history. The bill immediately came under withering attack. Isolationist Senator Burton K. Wheeler of Montana called lend-lease the "New Deal's Triple A foreign policy" that would "plow under every fourth American boy." The *Chicago Tribune* called it "a bill for the destruction of the American

Republic . . . [and] a brief for an unlimited dictatorship . . . with power to make war and alliances forever." Administration officials retorted that Britain faced invasion within three months and without such aid would be defeated. If the British navy were destroyed or seized, the United States would be in serious danger.

Both sides had a point. Wheeler's remarks were grossly unfair and the *Tribune*'s attack was as much an anti-New Deal tirade as a legitimate defense of the Constitution. But in later years many Americans would come to regret the erosion of congressional control over foreign policy that began under FDR. Yet the president was not consciously attempting to usurp power; he and his advisers were expressing their honest fears. And most informed citizens supported them. After a furious battle the congressional isolationists were defeated. On March 11 Roosevelt signed the lend-lease bill into law. In a few weeks the $7 billion of war matériel that Congress had authorized began flowing to Britain.

United States Aid Increases.   The additional American aid had little immediate effect on the fortunes of war. During the spring of 1941 Americans gasped as Germany and Italy conquered the Yugoslavs and Greeks in the Balkans and forced the British in North Africa to retreat almost to the Nile. Britain was also losing the vital Battle of the Atlantic, as German submarines sent vast quantities of American munitions and supplies to the bottom of the ocean. Could nothing be done to stop the Axis?

In Washington, Roosevelt moved cautiously to provide further aid to Britain. On April 9 he concluded an agreement putting Greenland, a Danish colony, under United States protection, aiding the Royal Navy by extending American naval patrols partway to Britain. His advisers urged him to go further—use the United States Navy to convoy arms all the way to Britain. But the president held back. On May 13 he agreed to shift part of the Pacific Fleet to the Atlantic. On May 27 he announced an unlimited "national emergency" giving him expanded powers over the economy. In June he issued an executive order freezing Axis assets in the United States and placing German and Italian ships in American ports under federal control. Each action brought the nation a little closer to outright belligerency, but still the president was reluctant to throw the country's full weight behind Britain. He believed war must come but felt unable to start it himself. In mid-May he told Secretary of the Treasury Henry Morgenthau, Jr.: "I am waiting to be pushed into the situation."

Hitler carefully avoided a showdown with America, for he had other things in mind. Four thousand miles from Washington, on the vast plains of eastern Europe, German and Soviet troops faced one another along an extended common border that ran through what had once been the independent republic of Poland. For almost two years the two countries had maintained an uneasy marriage of convenience. Then, on June 22, 1941, in fulfillment of his long-cherished ambition to destroy communism and expand German power eastward, the Nazi dictator sent his tanks, aircraft, and troops across the border, hurtling toward the heart of the Soviet Union.

In London and Washington the Nazi attack provoked a quick response. The British and Americans could have ignored Russia's plight. Many people in both countries considered the USSR little better than Nazi Germany. Yet neither the

British nor the American government hesitated very long in offering help to the Russians. Two days after the German attack, Roosevelt promised aid to the Soviet Union. In the fall a British-American mission traveled to Moscow to determine Soviet war needs. Soon afterward the United States pledged $1 billion in lend-lease matériel to the embattled Russians; by the end of the war American aid would grow to $11 billion in value.

Although he welcomed Russia as a new ally against Hitler, Roosevelt could not lose sight of Britain and the Atlantic. In July he sent troops to occupy Iceland and announced that the American navy would escort British-bound supplies as far east as that strategic island. The following month the president met Churchill face-to-face on a ship off Newfoundland. Out of that meeting came the Atlantic Charter linking Britain and America in a common set of war goals. This document affirmed and expanded upon the Wilsonian ideals of self-determination for all people, freer international trade, cooperative efforts for world prosperity, freedom of the seas, disarmament, and "freedom from fear and want."

Bit by bit, Roosevelt was pushing the United States toward an alliance with Britain and a direct confrontation with Germany. He did not confide his plans to the American people, and that lack of candor has troubled even his firmest admirers. Yet the president was not seeking power or personal glory. FDR was certain that the fate of civilization depended on Hitler's defeat. But he feared taking a divided people into war and was still convinced that the enemy must act first.

By the fall of 1941 events seemed to be moving the way FDR hoped. Soon after his return from Newfoundland, a German U-boat commander off the coast of Iceland, believing his vessel to be under British attack, launched two torpedoes at the United States destroyer *Greer*, which had been tracking the submarine and radioing its location to the British. The *Greer* returned the fire. Roosevelt (neglecting to mention that the *Greer* had been engaged in unneutral activities) called the incident an act of "piracy legally and morally," adding that from now on American naval vessels would "shoot on sight" at any German submarine found between Iceland and North America. On October 9, 1941, he asked Congress to modify the Neutrality Acts further to permit the arming of American merchant vessels. Early in November, after the Germans had torpedoed the destroyer *Kearney* and sunk the U.S.S. *Reuben James* with heavy loss of life, Congress authorized the arming of American merchant vessels and removed restrictions on their carrying cargoes to belligerent ports.

By mid-November the United States was in a virtual naval war with the Germans. Yet a substantial minority of the American people still hoped to avoid full-scale military intervention. As recently as August the House had voted to extend the draft period an additional eighteen months by a margin of only a single vote. Isolationist sentiment in Congress was powerful enough to prevent easy passage of the modifications of the Neutrality Acts. In the Senate the president's majority was only 50 to 37; in the House, 212 to 194.

The continuing strength of isolationism troubled Roosevelt. What if the Germans avoided further serious incidents? How could Americans be brought, united, to the point of war? The president was stumped. As his friend and biographer Robert Sherwood later wrote: "He had no tricks left. . . . The bag from which he had pulled so many rabbits was empty." Fate—and the Japanese—would soon solve the problem for the undecided nation.

Miscalculations in the East.
Roosevelt and his advisers misunderstood and underestimated the Japanese. Convinced that without the resources of Manchuria, China, and the East Indies, it could not survive as a great power, Japan had a deep commitment to its expansionist policies. It would not be easy to get the Japanese to back down in China, or the Far East generally, without the use of military force. In addition, the American government did not take Japan seriously as a military opponent. Americans knew that Japanese industry was capable of producing the shoddy trinkets and gewgaws that flooded the five-and-dime stores of the day, but doubted that it could produce modern weapons in quantity.

Until the fall of France, the United States, over the protest of China's many American friends, supplied much of the steel and petroleum that supllied Japan's war machine. Then, when the Japanese began to pressure the Vichy French for bases in Indochina and threatened the Dutch in the oil-rich East Indies, the American government imposed licensing requirements on the export of American oil and scrap metal and forbade the export of aviation gasoline. These moves goaded the Japanese into seeking allies elsewhere. In September 1940 Japan signed an agreement with Italy and Germany, converting the Rome-Berlin Axis into the Rome-Berlin-Tokyo Axis. The agreement pledged the three nations to support one another's plans to establish a "new order" in Europe and a "Greater East Asia" in the Far East. If any one of them was attacked by a fourth power—with which it was not then already at war—the others would go to its aid. The Soviet Union, which the Japanese feared, was specifically exempted from this provision, making it clear that it was aimed at the United States. In effect, if the United States attacked either Japan or one of the European Axis nations, it would find itself with a two-ocean war. The American government responded to this threat by finally prohibiting the export of scrap iron and steel outside the Western Hemisphere.

As yet, however, neither the Americans nor the Japanese were prepared for a showdown. In March 1941 the moderate government of Prince Fumimaro Konoye opened conversations with Secretary of State Hull in Washington to prevent an irreparable break between the two countries. The Japanese were willing to make minor concessions but not, as Hull demanded, to evacuate China. As the talks dragged on, the Japanese, who already controlled northern Indochina, moved to seize the rest of the French colony. In July 1941 Japan forced the Vichy government to grant it bases in southern Indochina, close to the East Indies and British Malaya. Shortly thereafter, Roosevelt ordered all Japanese assets in the United States frozen, virtually ending trade between the two nations. This move was quickly followed by the order of the governor of the Dutch East Indies embargoing the shipment of Dutch oil to Japan.

By showing Japan how dependent it was on foreign sources of raw material, the Americans and Dutch hoped to give the Japanese pause. Their moves had the opposite effect. During the remaining months of peace two groups of Japanese leaders—the military chiefs on one hand and the royal family on the other—battled over what policy to pursue toward the United States. The army generals were confident they could defeat the United States in any war. The admirals hoped that a massive surprise blow would so damage American naval power that the United States would be forced to give Japan a free hand in East Asia. If Japan did not act soon, the American oil embargo would cripple the Japanese war machine, they argued. Prince Konoye and Emperor Hirohito opposed this aggressive course except as a last resort.

In August, Konoye proposed a meeting with President Roosevelt to iron out Japanese–American differences. Secretary Hull distrusted the Japanese, however, and refused the offer. But the American government was not yet anxious for a showdown, and for a while strung Prince Konoye along. In October, his credibility with his own people damaged by American delays, Konoye resigned in favor of the more militant war minister, Hideki Tojo.

Tojo was determined to break the deadlock between the two nations or attack. On November 5 the Japanese government decided to adopt the admirals' policy unless the United States and Great Britain halted their aid to the Chinese and allowed Japan access to oil and other vital raw materials from America and Southeast Asia. In return, Japan would agree to withdraw its troops from the French possessions when the war with China was over and would eventually leave China itself. On November 25 Admiral Isoroku Yamamoto ordered the navy strike force secretly to put to sea, subject to last-minute recall. The United States refused to accept the final Japanese terms. America could not, Hull believed, end its aid to Chiang Kai-shek; we were too firmly committed to a stable Chinese republic to desert him. Moreover, the Japanese could not be trusted to evacuate China.

The American government had broken the top-secret Japanese "purple cipher" code by this time and knew from intercepted messages that unless a settlement with the United States was soon reached, Japan would launch an attack against American or British-Dutch forces somewhere in the Pacific. The American government assumed that the blow would land in Southeast Asia and alerted military commanders in Hawaii and the Philippines. On the morning of December 7, Washington time, Army Chief of Staff General George C. Marshall sent radiograms to military commanders in San Francisco, the Canal Zone, Hawaii, and the Philippines, warning of an imminent attack. Electrical interference delayed the radio message to Hawaii, and it had to be sent by cable. By the time it arrived at the Western Union office in Honolulu, the bombs were falling over Pearl Harbor.

On December 8 the United States declared war on Japan. Three days later the Germans and Italians ended American uncertainty regarding the European conflict by declaring war on the United States. The titanic struggle over intervention was finally over. Their country was now at war and a united American people were now heart and soul in the crusade to stop Hitler and the other aggressors.

The Home Front

Mobilization.   World War II was the most costly war in American history. Between December 1941 and the Japanese surrender in the late summer of 1945, the war effort cost the treasury almost $300 billion. Sixteen million men and women served in the armed forces. Of these, almost 300,000 died in combat; another 700,000 were wounded.

The government, as we saw, had begun raising a military force before Pearl Harbor. Late in 1940 the first peacetime draftees were inducted into service.

After induction the new GI—so called because of his "government issue" uniform and gear—was shipped off to a training camp for eight weeks or more of "basic training," followed by either advanced infantry training or, if qualified, instruction in some military specialty. The voluntary branches of the service—Navy, Marine Corps, Coast Guard, and Army Air Corps—conducted similar training operations.

Most young Americans found it difficult at first to adjust to the armed forces. They were fed well, and the transformation of many once-skinny adolescents into well-muscled young men amazed their families and friends when they returned home on their first leave. But they did not like military discipline and despised the hard, dirty jobs of obstacle-course running, calisthenics, bivouacking, and marching—not to speak of KP ("kitchen police") and guard duty. The War and Navy departments tried to make the hardships acceptable by providing libraries, movies, and religious services to trainees. Church and volunteer organizations sponsored camp dances to which young women were invited. Yet complaints about the military's stupidities and foul-ups became the mark of the wartime citizen-soldier; SNAFU, an acronym usually politely translated as "situation normal, all fouled up," was added to the American vocabulary. Nevertheless, as time would show, American youths would make fine soldiers when well led.

Racism on the Home Front.

Pearl Harbor was a tremendous shock to American confidence. For days after the frightening news from Hawaii, Americans peered anxiously at the skies, expecting to see bombers overhead with Japan's rising-sun emblem on their wings. In the early weeks following December 7 there were air-raid scares in several cities.

The fears were aggravated by an unbroken string of Japanese victories in the Pacific that followed the initial Pearl Harbor attack. On the West Coast something close to panic seized Americans in these early weeks. Jittery citizens, certain that the resident Japanese-American population was a potential "fifth column," demanded their removal from the exposed Pacific Coast. Fear was reinforced by racism and greed. Long the targets of bigotry, the Japanese in America were envied for their economic success. Many whites coveted their property, much of it rich farmland in California and Washington.

For a time federal officials resisted the pressure for relocation by West coast congressmen and state officials. But they soon yielded. On February 19, 1942, Roosevelt signed an executive order allowing the War Department to "prescribe military areas . . . from which any or all persons may be excluded." Within weeks thousands of Issei (immigrant Japanese) and Nisei (their American-born children) were forced to sell their homes, businesses, and farms, often at a fraction of their true value, and move to detention centers in isolated areas of inland states such as Utah, Arizona, and Arkansas.

Though these centers were a far cry from the concentration camps of Nazi Europe, they were a disgrace to American democratic principles. Despite harsh living conditions, most of the imprisoned people survived the war; remarkably, many of them retained their loyalty toward the United States.

By comparison, the government treated other enemy nationals generously. Italians and Germans, even those not citizens, were left alone. Leaders of the pro-Nazi German-American Bund, along with a handful of native-born Fascists, were indicted under the antisubversive Smith Act of 1940, which imposed tighter controls over aliens and made it a crime for any person or group to teach the overthrow of the government by violent means. But the extreme anti-Germanism that characterized World War I did not surface. Nor did the antiradicalism that flourished during the earlier war. The Communist party, which had denounced Roosevelt as a warmonger during 1940 and early 1941, hailed him as a hero after Hitler attacked the Soviet Union. During the war itself American Communists were among the most fervent patriots. Combined with the heroic struggle of the Russian people against Hitler, this enthusiasm deflected antiradical excesses.

Of course, the war did not turn the country into a tolerant social paradise. In June 1943 some young Mexican-Americans (Chicanos), wearing characteristic "zoot suits"—flashy outfits with broad-shouldered jackets, tightly pegged trousers, and wide-brimmed flat hats—attacked U.S. sailors on liberty in Los Angeles. The sailors retaliated by beating up every zoot-suiter they could find. It was, *Time* magazine said, "the ugliest brand of mob action" in California "since the coolie riots of the 1870s." Hundreds were injured before the violence ended.

Black Americans.   Blacks, too, fell victim to wartime social stresses. War brought a mixture of good and bad to black Americans, much as it had in 1917–1918. During the peacetime arms buildup, defense contractors had resisted hiring black workers. When A. Philip Randolph, president of the all-black Brotherhood of Sleeping Car Porters, threatened in May 1941 to organize a mass march on Washington to protest this exclusion, Roosevelt established the Fair Employment Practices Committee. Thereafter, the FEPC and the pressure of urgent war orders forced open the employment doors to black Americans. Black men and women by the thousands found jobs in the tank factories of Detroit, the steel mills of Pittsburgh, the shipyards of Puget Sound, and the aircraft factories of southern California, Texas, and Kansas.

Economic opportunities for blacks during the war was not equaled by advances in other areas of American life, however. More black soldiers than ever before became commissioned officers, and for the first time blacks were admitted to the Marine Corps and to the navy at ranks higher than mess boy. But through most of the war black servicemen were kept in segregated military units. Their obvious second-class status injured black military morale. In the South and at army camps in the North, serious tensions developed between black servicemen and neighboring white civilians. In Detroit, where thousands of blacks and newly arrived southern whites lived and worked side by side, racial friction set off a bloody race riot in mid-1943 that left 30 people dead, 800 injured, and over $2 million in property destroyed.

Despite their mistreatment, black Americans were loyal and patriotic during the war. Hitler's virulent racism, of course, was particularly repulsive to black Americans; but many of them might have been attracted to the Japanese who were nonwhites fighting the white European nations. A tiny minority did find the Japanese cause appealing; the overwhelming majority, however, supported the war effort. Like other Americans, black citizens bought bonds, worked in war plants, and collected scrap metal and rubber. Thousands of black troops fought in

Europe and the Pacific, albeit in segregated units. In Italy the all-black Ninety-Ninth Fighter Squadron achieved a distinguished record in air combat against the German *Luftwaffe*.

Despite their overall support of the war effort, black leaders put the nation on notice that it could not indefinitely treat African-Americans as it had in the past. Their watchword was the "Double V"—"victory over our enemies at home and victory over our enemies on the battlefields abroad." Yet ultimately, they recognized, black Americans would have to fight for their own civil rights. As Walter White, head of the NAACP, declared, the majority of black soldiers would "return home determined to use these efforts [fighting the Axis] to the utmost."

Pressures on Women and Families.

The war was hard on American families. Married men had been exempted from the peacetime draft; but in 1943 even fathers were inducted. The wartime industrial boom also strained family relations. Whole families from the Northeast and Midwest migrated to distant parts of the nation to work in war plants. Sometimes male workers left their wives and children behind to move in with parents or other relations. Between 1940 and 1945 the number of families headed by a married woman with her husband absent rose from 770,000 to almost 3 million.

Young wives and mothers made the best of a difficult situation, but the best was often not very good. Women were lonely and sought out one another's company. Some inevitably found other male companionship, and marriages broke up. More than a few GIs received "Dear John" letters telling them that other men had taken their place.

Some young women found military service an attractive option. In 1942 Congress authorized the Women's Auxiliary Army Corps (the WACS, after "auxiliary" was dropped from the title), and later established the WAVES, the navy equivalent. In all, a quarter of a million young women donned military uniforms and served in noncombatant jobs at home and overseas.

Many women took jobs in the civilian sector to keep busy, to supplement their incomes, or to help the war effort. "Rosie the Riveter," in overalls and protective snood, became a familiar figure in every American industrial community. The nation valued her, but working mothers compounded the problems caused by absent fathers. Children often did not get proper care. During the war juvenile delinquency leaped. In San Diego, a major aircraft-manufacturing center and naval base, 55 percent more boys were charged with crimes in 1945 than in the previous year; the arrest rate for girls climbed 355 percent.

The pressures on families were particularly severe where there was a heavy concentration of war industry. Housing inevitably was in short supply and families had to live in trailers or Quonset huts. Schools were forced to hold double sessions. The government provided money for education in "war-impacted" areas, but it was not enough to improve conditions created by the influx of new people.

To a degree, all civilians paid a price for the war. After Pearl Harbor the government drastically cut automobile production and housing construction. It soon began to ration rubber tires and later restricted gasoline consumption. Metals, deflected into war production, were replaced by wood or plastic. Rationing of meat, sugar, coffee, butter, and cooking fats began in 1942. Rationing of clothing began

Woman war workers made up for the manpower shortage
during World War II. Here two women are helping to bulild aircraft.

at about the same time. The housing, gasoline, and rubber shortages produced hardships, but the food and clothing restrictions were relatively easy to accept. Consumers often discovered that they had ration "points" for more items than they either needed or could afford. Compared with the bitter experiences of Britain or Russia, life in wartime America remained easy.

The Wartime Economy.   The war gave an immense boost to the home front economy. By 1941 lend-lease and defense spending had reduced unemployment to less than 10 percent of the civilian labor force, the lowest figure since 1930. By 1943 it was down to a miniscule 1.9 percent. By 1943 the country enjoyed a per capita GNP some 70 percent higher than in the "miracle" year 1929. Even when purely military items are subtracted, Americans enjoyed more consumer goods by the middle of the war than in the most prosperous peacetime era. In essence, by forcing the government to forsake a balanced budget, the war made up for lagging private consumption and investment. The Depression was over!

Everyone welcomed the return of prosperity, but a new danger, inflation, soon appeared. The public had billions of extra dollars to spend, but relatively little to spend it on. The absence of expensive consumer durables such as automobiles, household appliances, and new homes put great added pressure on the prices of those goods that were available. To deal with this imbalance of commodities and cash, the government raised taxes drastically. Beginning with the first "defense" budgets in 1940, Congress lowered the personal income tax exemption, raised tax rates sharply, and established the excess-profits tax for business firms. In June 1943 the treasury began withholding income taxes from paychecks. Forty-four percent of the cost of the war was paid with tax money; for the first time most working Americans paid income taxes.

To further reduce the danger of inflation, the government, as in World War I, issued war bonds. In September 1942 the treasury launched its first war-bond drive with a massive advertising campaign in print and on radio. The most effective support for these drives came from Hollywood stars, who were credited with selling bonds worth $834 million in the first drive alone.

Neither taxes nor bond sales were sufficient to skim off all the excess purchasing power, and prices soon began to rise. Then in 1942 Congress established the Office of Price Administration (OPA) and the War Production Board, with the power to ration scarce raw materials, set wage rates, and fix wholesale and retail commodity prices, rents, and other charges. From April 1943 to August 1945 retail prices rose only 4.2 percent, a remarkably low figure for wartime.

Arsenal of Democracy.   The most important role of the American home front was to supply the fighting fronts. The role was magnificently performed; American industrial might proved to be a decisive factor in Allied victory. Under a succession of "dollar-a-year" men called in from private industry to run various superagencies, war production soared despite bottlenecks, labor and raw material shortages, strikes,

An artist depicts the 1944 Allied invasion of Normandy for a war-bond drive. The casualties are difficult to find, an omission typical of wartime propaganda.

and union disputes. Between 1940 and 1945 United States factories churned out 300,000 aircraft, 5,425 merchant ships, 72,000 naval vessels, 87,000 tanks, 2.5 million trucks, 372,000 artillery pieces, and 44 billion rounds of small-arms ammunition. Far more than in 1917–1918, the country met all its own military needs, and beyond that truly became, as Roosevelt had promised, the arsenal of democracy.

The Fighting Fronts

The months immediately following Pearl Harbor were a time of disastrous American and Allied military retreat. In quick succession, the Japanese captured Singapore, Hong Kong, the Dutch East Indies, and Burma. In May 1942, after a long siege of the Bataan Peninsula and Corregidor Island, near Manila, they forced the surrender of a combined force of Americans and Filipinos and occupied the Philippine archipelago. Before the final collapse, however, the navy rescued the American commander, General Douglas MacArthur, and brought him to Australia to lead the defense and reconquest of the South Pacific. Despite these critical Pacific losses, Roosevelt and his advisers, believing Hitler the more dangerous

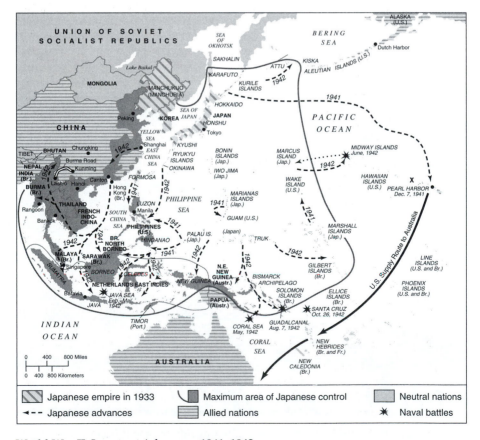

World War II: Japanese Advances, 1941–1942

enemy, accepted the policy, strongly favored by the British, of "Europe first." The war against Japan would be a holding operation until American factories and training camps had provided enough arms and men to deal with Hitler and the Japanese simultaneously.

Wary of heavy human losses, the British favored an attack on Germany either through Africa or through Europe's "soft underbelly," the Mediterranean. But Roosevelt and Chief of Staff Marshall preferred a direct thrust across the English Channel into France and the heart of German-occupied Europe. In the end British and American strategies were combined, but the decision spread Allied strength too thinly and probably lengthened the war.

Early in 1942 the first American GIs arrived in Britain, the vanguard of millions of American soldiers and airmen who came for the delayed cross-Channel attack. At the end of the year the United States and Britain undertook Operation Torch, an invasion of North Africa that pitted Allied troops against combined German and Italian forces commanded by General Erwin Rommel.

Meanwhile, the Allies were slowly winning the vital battle against the U-boats in the Atlantic. America's entrance into the war initially provided German submarine commanders with easy pickings in coastal Atlantic waters. During 1942 millions of tons of Allied shipping went to the bottom. By 1943 new techniques using destroyers, aircraft, and innovative submarine-detection equipment cut losses to enemy submarines drastically while the sheer productivity of American shipyards began to offset losses.

The year 1942 was the darkest of the war, but also marked the turning of the tide. On May 7–8 American carrier planes turned back the Japanese advance toward Australia by sinking a Japanese aircraft carrier and damaging two others at the Battle of the Coral Sea. A month later, alerted to enemy plans by code-breakers, they inflicted a stunning defeat on the Imperial Navy at the Battle of Midway, sinking 4 Japanese carriers and shooting down 275 enemy aircraft. Midway shifted the balance of naval strength in the Pacific permanently to the United States. In August American marines, soldiers, and naval forces invaded the Japanese base on Guadalcanal Island, opening a three-year "island-hopping" counteroffensive against the Pacific enemy. The struggle on Guadalcanal, and in the waters surrounding it, proved bitter and costly. Not until early February did the Japanese abandon their efforts to hold on.

In Europe the Germans were equally tenacious. By 1942 the Nazi regime had enslaved millions of people, from France in the west to Russia in the east. The German treatment of virtually all these people was bestial, but none were subjected to the horrors inflicted on the millions of Jews who had fallen into Nazi hands in Poland, western Europe, and the Soviet Union. Hitler marked the Jewish population of Europe for total extermination. Many were shipped to slave-labor camps where they were worked to death. In late 1941 the Nazis initiated the "final solution to the Jewish problem": the mass slaughter of all of Europe's Jews—men, women, and children. By the time the war ended, almost 6 million—along with hundreds of thousands of Russians, Poles, Gypsies, and other "inferior beings"— had been shot, hanged, tortured, starved, or gassed to death in such camps as Auschwitz, Treblinka, and Majdanek. This monstrous event—the Holocaust— remains as one of the most appalling atrocities in human history.

Wartime Diplomacy.   The "United Nations" war effort required complex interactions among countries allied as much by necessity as by admiration and shared values. Relations among the Western Allies were relatively good. Roosevelt did not get along with the touchy Free French leader de Gaulle, but overall Britain and the Commonwealth countries (Canada, South Africa, Australia, and New Zealand) cooperated closely with the United States. With its vast manpower and industrial output, America was clearly the senior partner. If the British resented that seniority, they recognized its inevitability.

Generally speaking, relations with China were good, too. Roosevelt believed that under Chiang Kai-shek China had the makings of a great power, once freed of the Japanese yoke. In 1942 he and Churchill agreed to abandon the remaining special privileges their nations' citizens held in China. In November 1943, at Cairo, the two Western allies and China agreed to exact "unconditional surrender" peace terms from Japan and resolved to return to the Chinese Manchuria, Formosa (Taiwan), and the Pescadores, which Japan had wrenched from them in past years.

Relations between the Western partners and the Soviet Union were not as cordial. In 1943 the Russians dissolved the Comintern, the central body of the revolution-provoking international Communist movement, as a gesture of friendship with the West. Yet Stalin remained suspicious of Britain and the United States, and they of him. Though Hitler's invasion of Russia temporarily papered over East–West differences, the war itself created grounds for mutual distrust. From the outset Stalin suspected that Roosevelt and Churchill would be content to see the Soviet Union and Nazi Germany destroy each other on the Eastern Front. Starting in late 1941, he repeatedly demanded that Britain and America open a second front in Western Europe to relieve the excruciating pressure on Soviet troops and the Soviet people. Aware of German military prowess, the Allies insisted on sufficient planning and build-up, and the delay became a sore point with the Soviet Union.

Still, suspicion did not prevent cooperation. In October 1943 Secretary of State Hull, British Foreign Secretary Sir Anthony Eden, and Vyacheslav M. Molotov, the Soviet foreign minister, met in Moscow to discuss wartime problems and consider postwar reconstruction. The ministers agreed to establish a European Advisory Commission to formulate policy for Germany after victory and to set up a world organization to maintain international peace. One problem they could not solve was the postwar fate of Poland. Britain and the United States were committed to returning the Polish government-in-exile, then in London, to power when the war ended. The Soviet Union preferred a pro-communist government friendlier to itself. The issue was not settled at the Moscow meeting and continued to fester; but as a token of good faith, Stalin promised to join the war against Japan as soon as Germany was defeated. At Teheran, Iran, a month later, Churchill, Roosevelt, and Stalin met personally to confirm the results at Moscow and plan joint military operations against the common foe.

The Defeat of Germany.   By the time of the Teheran meeting, Soviet fortunes had begun to improve. The initial German offensive against Russia had carried Hitler's armies to the gates of Moscow by September 1941. In the course of their eastward drive the Germans killed, captured, or wounded some 2.5 million Soviet troops, virtually wiped out the Soviet air force and tank corps, destroyed enormous quantities of war matériel, and laid waste hundreds of Russian cities and towns. At first many Soviet citizens, despising the communist regime, had welcomed the German invaders. But the Nazis imposed a regime of such naked brutality on the Russian people that it left them no choice but resistance. The anti-German struggle soon became for Russian people the "Great Patriotic War."

During the winter of 1941–1942 Soviet forces counterattacked the invaders, forcing the Germans to retreat at a few points. In the spring the German offensive eastward resumed, and by fall Hitler's armies had penetrated to Stalingrad, on the Volga River, and Maikop, deep in the Caucasus. During this critical period of the war vast British and American air fleets based in England dropped tons of bombs on Germany and German-occupied territories. These raids devastated the civilian population of Germany but did little to relieve pressure on the Russians or impair the German war effort.

World War II: Closing the Ring, 1942–1945

The turning point of the European war came in February 1943 when the Russian army enveloped thousands of German troops in a vast pocket near Stalingrad on the Volga and forced them to surrender. In August the renewed German eastern offensive was stopped dead by the Soviet armies and then reversed. Meanwhile, in the spring of 1943, in North Africa, the combined British and American forces led by generals George S. Patton and Bernard Montgomery, under the overall command of General Dwight D. Eisenhower, dealt the final blow to Rommel's Afrika Korps. The wily Rommel escaped to fight again, but on May 13 some 250,000 Axis troops surrendered to the British and Americans. In early July the Allies invaded Sicily. The king of Italy soon announced the resignation of Mussolini and negotiated the surrender of Italy. Mussolini was rescued by German troops and placed at the head of a puppet Italian regime. Meanwhile, British and American forces had crossed the Straits of Messina to the Italian boot only to encounter fierce and effective opposition from the entrenched Germans, who retreated slowly northward while inflicting heavy casualties on the Allies.

In 1944 Germany began to crumble. In January the Russians liberated Leningrad, their second city, from a devastating two-and-a-half-year siege and began their major westward drive toward the heart of the Reich. By February they had crossed the 1939 Polish-Russian frontier. In Italy the stalled Allied advance resumed, and on June 4 the American Fifth Army liberated Rome; in August the British marched into Florence.

By this time Eisenhower had launched Operation Overlord, the long-awaited second front in France. The cross-Channel attack began before dawn on the morning of "D-Day," June 6, when a colossal armada of Allied warships, transports, landing craft, and massive artificial ports approached the French coast in Normandy. Overhead, the Allied air forces dropped thousands of paratroopers at strategic points across northern France. After several days of ferocious fighting, the beachheads were secured. For six weeks the Germans were able to contain the Allies in a shallow pocket in Normandy. Then, at the end of July, the American Third Army under George Patton, the swashbuckling tank commander, broke out and began a swift drive east toward Germany. On August 15 the United States Seventh Army landed on the French Mediterranean coast and advanced north to attack the Germans from behind. On August 25 the Free French Second Armored Division liberated Paris.

Wherever the British and Americans encountered the German Wehrmacht there can be no doubt that man-for-man the German soldiers were more skilled and effective. As military historian Max Hastings has said, the soldiers of the democratic nations expected to survive the war and return home to happy personal lives. This hope encouraged caution. German soldiers, often Nazi-inspired, proved more disciplined and stoical, more willing to accept death. In the end, victory for the United Nations depended more on the volume of guns, tanks, planes, and vehicles that the United States brought to the fighting fronts than the superiority of their fighting men. And we must remember that the Soviet army bore the brunt of the military losses incurred in wearing Germany down, sparing the civilians-turned-soldiers who filled the ranks of the U.S. and British military.

After the fall of Paris the end of Hitler's empire seemed in sight. In October American troops crossed onto German soil. The Germans rallied briefly in December in a desperate counterattack at the Battle of the Bulge in the snowy

Ardennes Forest that stopped the allied advance. The defending American troops had to be rescued by George Patton's Third Army shifting direction, but in March 1945 American armies crossed the Rhine in force and dashed eastward. Meanwhile, the Russians, too, had crossed into Germany. On April 22, 1945, they reached Berlin. Rather than face defeat, Hitler committed suicide in his underground Berlin bunker. On April 25 American and Russian troops met at Torgau on the Elbe. On May 7 the German military commander accepted unconditional surrender at Allied headquarters. The war in Europe was over.

Yalta. In February 1945, as Germany's collapse approached, Stalin, Churchill, and Roosevelt had met once again, this time at Yalta in the Soviet Crimea. Out of their deliberations emerged a set of important agreements that helped mold the postwar world.

In their public pronouncements the three leaders agreed to cooperate militarily until Germany's unconditional surrender. They would then establish four occupation zones in the defeated nation, one for each of the major powers plus France. These would remain under military control until a final peace settlement with Germany down the road. They also pledged to root out all Nazis influence from Germany so that its people could eventually join the community of peaceful nations. In the countries liberated from the Nazi yoke, provisional governments would

"The Big Three" met for the last time at Yalta in February 1945. There they discussed the United Nations, the partition of Germany, boundaries, and political arrangements in eastern Europe. Two months later, Roosevelt, already looking frail, died.

be established composed of all "democratic elements" to be chosen by free elections. The future Polish government, they declared, would be made up largely of the pro-Soviet provisional government established at Lublin, rather than the London-based, pro-Western government-in-exile. Poland's postwar boundaries would be shifted westward at the expense of Germany. The Soviets would annex parts of prewar Polish territory in the east, and in Yugoslavia, the pro-Soviet guerrilla leader, Josef Tito, would lead the future provisional government. Looking ahead, they announced that they would meet in San Francisco in April 1945 to draw up the charter for a new "United Nations" world organization to replace the League of Nations.

The secret clauses, not revealed until later, included an agreement on mutual repatriation of Soviet and American prisoners of war recaptured by the respective UN armies, a voting formula for the Big Four nations in the UN Security Council to come after the San Francisco meeting, and, most important of all to the Americans, an agreement by the Soviet Union to declare war on Japan "in two or three months after Germany . . . surrendered." In return for helping Britain and the United States, the USSR would receive from Japan the Kurile Islands and the southern half of Sakhalin Island off the Siberian coast. In addition, it would be assigned an occupation zone in the northern half of Korea, could establish a Soviet protectorate over Outer Mongolia, and would be allowed special privileges in Manchuria and other parts of northern China.

Roosevelt's concessions to the Soviet Union at Yalta have been sharply criticized as a sell-out. Eventually the Soviet Union would establish puppet regimes in Poland and in all the other eastern European countries and strengthen its position in the Far East. But the Yalta Conference cannot be blamed for these Soviet gains. By the time the "Big Three" met in the Crimea, Soviet troops were already entering Germany in great force. Nothing could have kept the Soviet Union from imposing its will on Poland or the Balkan and Danube regions. As for the concessions in the Far East, the American atomic bomb had not been successfully tested and no one could foresee that by the time Germany surrendered, Japan would be on its knees and Soviet aid not needed. Roosevelt knew that the Russians had driven a hard bargain at Yalta, but he did not see how it could have been avoided. As he told a close adviser shortly after the conference: "I didn't say it was good. . . . I said it was the best I could do."

The Last Days of the Pacific War.

Meanwhile, there was still a war to win in the Pacific. From 1943 to 1945 the United States mounted a score of bloody and expensive amphibious operations against the over-extended Japanese empire. Moving from the east, American naval task forces, under the command of Admiral Chester Nimitz, thrust deep into Japanese-controlled areas of the central Pacific. Under cover of carrier aircraft and the guns and rockets of battleships and cruisers, waves of marines and army troops landed on enemy beaches and crushed often-fierce resistance. After Midway the Japanese navy no longer controlled the open seas, but it continued to be a danger to amphibious landings, especially as American forces neared Japan itself. On October 25, 1944, the Japanese launched their first *kamikaze* attacks—suicide missions by pilots flying their bomb-loaded planes directly into American invasion ships. Meanwhile, MacArthur's forces, coming from their bases in Australia to the south, made a series of brilliant end runs around Japanese-controlled islands, leaving large pockets of imperial troops behind to be mopped up at leisure. In late 1944 the American and Japanese navies fought a series of battles off the Philippines that virtually destroyed the Imperial Navy as a fighting force. Soon after, American troops, led by MacArthur, landed in the Philippines, fulfilling the general's promise to "return."

The Japanese fought desperately for every scrap of coral reef. Even when overwhelmingly outnumbered they refused to surrender. Whole Japanese garrisons went to their deaths in suicide charges against the Americans. Where the terrain permitted, Japanese troops retreated to interior caves and mountains and fought to the last man. The Pacific fighting was always on a smaller scale than in Europe or North Africa, but it was more vicious and proportionately more costly. At Iwo Jima, 775 miles from the main Japanese island of Honshu, over 4,500 Americans lost their lives early in 1945 in a few days of ferocious battle. Japanese casualties were even greater: Over 21,000 of the emperor's finest troops died defending the small dot of land.

In late February 1945 MacArthur's forces marched into Manila, the wrecked Philippine capital. On April 1 U.S. marines and army units invaded Okinawa, 360 miles from the Japanese main islands. This attack was the largest amphibious

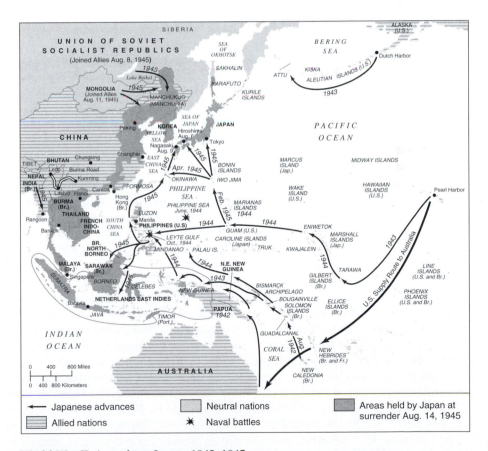

World War II: Assault on Japan, 1942–1945

operation of the Pacific war and also one of the costliest. *Kamikaze* planes sank or badly damaged 30 American vessels, and Japanese ground troops inflicted almost 40,000 casualties, including over 11,000 deaths, on the American invaders before they could take the island.

Once in American hands, Okinawa was converted into an immense air base in preparation for the invasion of the Japanese home islands. By now Japan was in desperate straits. Many Japanese cities were in ruins from massive American air raids that incinerated the flimsily built Japanese houses, often with their inhabitants inside. The Imperial Navy rested on the bottom of the Pacific and the surviving parts of the empire that supplied Japan with vital raw materials were cut off from the home islands by American submarine attacks on vital Japanese shipping lanes. Yet the Japanese still had the will and the means to fight. On the main islands 2 million troops and 8,000 kamikaze planes awaited the final American assault. If the experiences of Okinawa, Iwo Jima, Guadalcanal, and the other islands seized by American troops was an accurate foretaste of Japanese determination to resist, the United States, military strategists concluded, could expect hundreds of thousands of casualties in any invasion attempt.

The First Nuclear Attack.

The B-29 Superfortress air raids on Japanese cities culminated in the destruction of the cities of Hiroshima and Nagasaki by atomic attack in August 1945. The long road to these devastating events began in 1939 when a group of scientists-exiled from Hitler's Germany, led by Albert Einstein, informed Roosevelt that the Nazis were developing a new bomb of unimaginable destructiveness, based on the newly discovered process of uranium fission. To save the civilized world the United States must beat the Nazis to the punch. In mid-1940 Roosevelt turned the proposal over to a newly formed National Defense Research Committee. After Pearl Harbor the government created the Manhattan District project. At three major centers hundreds of scientists and technicians, supervised by physicist J. Robert Oppenheimer, set to work to build an atom bomb. At the cost of almost $2 billion, the engineering problems were gradually solved.

As the war approached its end in 1945, Einstein, Niels Bohr, and other prominent scientists concluded that the bomb would not be needed and, fearing a postwar atomic weapons arms race, they tried to stop the Manhattan Project. By the time the first atomic bomb was exploded experimentally at Alamogordo, New Mexico (July 16, 1945), the decision to use the bomb against Japan had been the subject of much heated debate in high government circles and among atomic scientists. Opponents of the bomb argued that the Japanese were on their last legs and would sue for peace shortly with or without the atomic bomb, especially if the Allies allowed the emperor to remain on the throne. Proponents of dropping the bomb noted that Japan had spurned as "unworthy of public notice" the American warning in July of "prompt and utter destruction" unless it accepted Allied "unconditional surrender" peace terms. And if American invasion casualties had been high in the outlying islands, what would they be like when American troops landed on the sacred home islands?

The decision to use the bomb would not be made by FDR. In 1944 Roosevelt had been elected to a fourth term. His running mate was Senator Harry S. Truman of Missouri, who had achieved prominence as Senate investigator of abuses in war production. Roosevelt barely survived two months of his new term. In early

April 1945 he died of a cerebral hemorrhage in Warm Springs, Georgia, worn down by twelve years of leadership during some of the nation's most trying and momentous times.

Truman scarcely knew the atomic bomb existed when he took the presidential oath of office. Once he learned of the bomb's power, he decided to use it, convinced that invading Japan could be a colossal bloodbath.

At dawn on August 6, 1945, the Superfortress *Enola Gay* and two escorts arrived over southern Honshu. At 8:15 its pilot released his bomb over Hiroshima. Sixty seconds later the *Enola Gay* crew watched in disbelief as an immense fireball rose over the city and slowly turned into a luminous mushroom cloud.

For the bustling Japanese city it was a moment of unspeakable horror. Hundreds of people simply vanished from the face of the earth, incinerated by the intense heat. Others were torn to pieces. Thousands, unshielded from the flash, were severely burned. All told, over 60,000 people died in the first few minutes of the attack. Others, exposed to high radiation levels, sickened and died later. The entire center of the city was flattened except for a few reinforced concrete structures.

Now the war moved swiftly toward a conclusion. Two days after the Hiroshima attack, the Soviet Union declared war on Japan and sent thousands of troops across the Manchurian frontier. On August 9 a second atomic bomb killed another 35,000 Japanese in Nagasaki. By this time the Japanese leaders were meeting to consider surrender. The military advised fighting to the bitter end, but the emperor vetoed the idea. Assured at the last minute that Hirohito would not be forced to abdicate, the Japanese accepted Allied surrender terms. On September 2, aboard the battleship *Missouri* anchored in Tokyo Bay, the Japanese signed the capitulation agreement. MacArthur presided over the ceremony that ended the most devastating war in history.

Conclusions

During the days of jubilation that marked VJ (Victory-Japan) Day, few people asked themselves why the nation had gone to war. But as the country settled into the comfort, and the problems, of peace, those who had at first opposed the war sought to justify their positions or to even the score with their interventionist opponents.

Those critics believed that the United States had no vital reason to join the anti-Axis coalition. Only Roosevelt's need to escape the political and economic impasse confronting the New Deal or, alternately, his unwarranted and grossly exaggerated fear of Hitler's designs, led him to favor American involvement. Nor was the president honest in his actions, they said. While denying that he wanted war, he was actively turning the United States into the anti-Axis arsenal and maneuvering the Japanese into a position where they had to attack the United States or surrender their vital interests. Pearl Harbor was the result of a dishonest scheme by the administration to overcome antiwar public opinion and force America's hand.

As we have seen, these charges are, at best, partial truths. By 1941 FDR undoubtedly believed that war was unavoidable. But he wanted to fight Hitler, not Tojo; the Japanese could be attended to eventually after Germany's defeat. The Pacific war was a blunder, but only in the sense that Roosevelt preferred to contain the Japanese while taking care of the Nazis first, and Pearl Harbor forced the United States to fight both simultaneously.

Nor was the president seeking primarily to escape a political impasse. Roosevelt's fear of the dictators predated the New Deal's political and economic difficulties. FDR was a Wilsonian who believed in collective security and detested authoritarian regimes long before the problems of his second term stopped the New Deal in its tracks. It was Hitler's astonishing and frightening successes that awakened his concern after 1937, not political frustration. The president was indeed less than candid in his tactics. While denying that he favored war, he was goading the Nazis into attacking American ships. But however mistaken he was in not taking the voters into his confidence, his purpose was governed by his concern for free American institutions.

And still another qualification is in order. Roosevelt's view of the Axis danger was not his alone; it was eventually shared by a large majority of Americans. The president was more eager than many of his fellow citizens to intervene, but the public was treading closely on his heels. In the end it was Germany's utter contempt for humanity and its obvious threat to every nation's independence, not Roosevelt's duplicity, that was responsible for America's intervention in World War II. As we look back at the evil unleashed by Hitler and his allies in Europe and East Asia we can only be grateful that the United States massively intervened. In the end, there is good reason to accept the judgment of history that the anti-Axis struggle of 1941–45 was the "good war."

ONLINE RESOURCES

"Rosie Pictures: Select Images Relating to American Women Workers During World War II" *http://www.loc.gov/rr/print/list/126_rosi.html* See U.S. government-issued posters designed to encourage women to become defense workers. Some feature African-American women and speak to one of the earliest possibilities for women of color to work on production jobs in factories.

"Japanese Internment, Camp Harmony" *http://www.lib.washington.edu/exhibits/harmony/Exhibit/default.htm* This site tells the story of Seattle's "Camp Harmony" Japanese-American community, including information on housing, daily life in the camp, photographs, maps, and excerpts from the camp newsletter.

"Double Victory" *http://www.pbs.org/blackpress/educate_event/treason.html http://www.pbs.org/blackpress/news_bios/index.html* Read about the "Double V" campaign and the African-American newspaper that started the campaign for freedom abroad and freedom at home for the nation's African-American citizens.

The Rutgers Oral History Archives of World War II *http://oralhistory.rutgers.edu/Interviews/indexes/conflictindex.html* This site contains transcripts of almost 150 oral history interviews of men and women who experienced World War II, either on the front lines or on the home front.

Japanese Internment: "War Relocation Authority Camps in Arizona, 1942–1946" *http://parentseyes.arizona.edu/wracamps/* On this site read about life for Japanese Americans held in relocation camps during the war. More than 140 photographs are compiled on this site and testify to daily life in the camps.

United States Holocaust Museum *http://www.ushmm.org* Explore virtually every facet of the Holocaust experience for Jews during World War II through online exhibits.

27
Postwar America

Why So Security Conscious?

1944	Bretton Woods Conference; Congress passes the GI Bill of Rights
1945	United Nations charter approved; Potsdam Conference; Roosevelt dies; Truman becomes president
1946	Winston Churchill's Iron Curtain speech; The Chinese civil war resumes; United States gives $3.75 billion in aid to Britain and $11 billion to the United Nations Relief and Rehabilitation Administration
1947	Truman orders the FBI to locate bad security risks in government; Congress endorses the Truman Doctrine, voting $400 million in military and economic aid to Greece and Turkey; Taft-Hartley Act; Congress creates the Central Intelligence Agency (CIA); Cold War begins
1948	Congress approves the Marshall Plan; Berlin Airlift supports West Berlin against Soviet takeover; Executive order desegregates the armed forces; Truman elected president
1949	North Atlantic Treaty Organization (NATO) organized; The Soviet Union explodes its first atomic bomb; People's Republic of China established under Mao Tse-tung; Nationalists retreat to Taiwan
1950	GNP rises above its wartime peak; Alger Hiss convicted of perjury; Senator Joe McCarthy begins campaign against alleged American Communists; McCarran Internal Security Act passed over Truman's veto
1950–53	The Korean War
1952, 1953	The United States and the Soviet Union explode hydrogen bombs
1952	Dwight D. Eisenhower elected president
1954	*Brown v. Board of Education*; Army-McCarthy hearings; Senate condemns McCarthy
1954–59	Housing legislation makes credit available for home buying, accelerating the middle-class move to the suburbs
1955	Montgomery bus boycott; Martin Luther King, Jr., rises to national prominence
1956	Interstate Highway System construction begins; Eisenhower reelected
1957	Federal troops enforce desegregation of Little Rock, Arkansas, Central High School
1960	John F. Kennedy elected president

Sometimes a book expresses the essence of a time so well that it captures the imagination of a wide public. *The Lonely Crowd: A Study of the Changing American Character*, by David Riesman, Reuel Denney, and Nathan Glazer, published in 1950, was one such work.

According to the authors, Americans had once been "inner-directed" people, guided through life by values learned and incorporated in their youth. Now most were "other-directed." How they acted depended on the opinions of their peers; they were anxious to fit in, to conform to a group average. Using the technology imagery of the new postwar era, Riesman, the senior author, described the change as the shift from internal gyroscopes to radar sets.

The Lonely Crowd claimed that the spirit of innovation had gone out of American life, replaced by conformity. And there was much truth to this conclusion. Some intellectual naysayers survived from an earlier era. Yet many of the thinkers of the "fifties" (as for convenience's sake we may refer to the decade and a half following VJ Day) were celebrators. Writers and intellectuals had often been sharp critics of their society during the 1920s and 1930s and hopeful that it could be improved. Some had been Marxists with unmoveable faith in the possibility of constructing a socialist utopia. But during the postwar decade-and-a-half this mood changed. In religious thought, beliefs emphasizing humanity's limitations and the inevitability of imperfection and injustice in this world became more common. In political thought a narrow pragmatism became a force for rejecting ambitious change and reform. In history, sociology, and political science American scholars ceased to be adversaries and began to praise their society, sometimes uncritically. When former Marxist Daniel Bell published *The End of Ideology* in 1960, he delivered a swan song for the intellectual life of a generation.

And even young people now seemed sedate, committed primarily to security. Theirs was the "silent generation," it was said, aspiring to little more than early marriage, a suburban house, a secure job, and a new car in the garage. Moralists lamented that young people seemed listless and dull.

Why had Americans become so fainthearted? Why had they lost their taste for political change and social reform? Why did they fear bold self-expression? What made this the decade of the safe thought, the safe course, the safe life?

The Politics of Dead Center

The public in these years seemingly had little interest in political movements to reduce inequalities, expand opportunities, or erect further safeguards against life's mischances. Yet liberalism did not die. The trade unions continued to work for higher minimum wages, expanded Social Security, federal health insurance, and racial justice. A liberal press, although a minority voice, survived from the previous decade. And the universities continued to be bastions of liberal thought, though some of the more stylish campus intellectuals became conservatives. In 1947 Eleanor Roosevelt and others organized Americans for Democratic Action (ADA), a group dedicated to greater social justice and an expanded social welfare state. But these groups and individuals were small in numbers and on the defensive through most of the decade.

The Man from Missouri. Harry S. Truman, who inherited Roosevelt's job, was a throwback to an earlier, more liberal era. Though a protégé of Thomas J. Pendergast, boss of the corrupt Kansas City Democratic machine, he was an honest man who came to the United States Senate in 1934, where he identified himself with the New Deal wing of his party. During the war he achieved national stature by uncovering sensational cases of waste and corruption in defense procurement, and in 1944, to please the party regulars, Roosevelt chose him, instead of the erratic and visionary Henry Wallace, as his running mate.

Truman was unprepared for his abrupt elevation to the presidency in April 1945. He had not been admitted to the inner war councils of the administration, and with FDR's death, he later declared, he felt as if "the moon, the stars, and the planets" had landed on his head. Nevertheless the new president moved quickly to take up the reins of domestic policy. Days after the Japanese surrender he submitted to Congress a legislative program that contained the main features of what he would later call the Fair Deal. Truman asked for an extension of unemployment benefits to ward off a new depression; continued support of the U.S. Employment Service to help returning veterans get jobs; a permanent Fair Employment Practices law to ensure equal job rights to minorities; retention of price and wage controls to prevent runaway inflation; an increase in the minimum wage from 40 to 65 cents an hour to maintain consumers' purchasing power; a large public works program to build roads, hospitals, and airports to provide jobs; "broad and comprehensive housing legislation" to give returning GIs places to live; government aid for small business; continued agricultural price supports for farmers; an expanded Social Security system; a bill to guarantee full employment; and, down the road, a national health insurance program. Liberals applauded Truman's agenda, but they deplored his rejection of Roosevelt's New Deal advisers in favor of old cronies from his Kansas City days, men who seemed to one liberal editor "a lot of second-rate guys trying to function in an atom bomb world."

A crucial test of the president's liberalism came with the Employment Act of 1946, a measure mandating "full employment" through federal spending and taxing policies, inspired by the disciples of John Maynard Keynes. Truman failed to push Congress hard for votes and the law as finally passed did not commit the government to deficit spending to guarantee full employment. Rather, it merely established a Council of Economic Advisors to inform the president about the state of the economy and recommend economic policies, and set up a Joint Economic Committee of Congress to perform similar functions. As the disappointed liberal magazine *The New Republic* wrote: "Alas for Truman, there is no bugle in his voice."

A pressing, immediate problem, in the months after VJ Day, was price controls. Liberals hoped that wartime price regulations would be retained to protect middle- and lower-income consumers against the serious threat of postwar inflation. Conservatives claimed that price controls merely fostered government bureaucracy and guaranteed shortages. When Congress passed a weak price-control bill, the president vetoed it, leaving the country without any price regulation at all. Costs of still-scarce civilian commodities, especially beef, quickly soared. Congress now became more receptive to a stronger bill, but Truman failed to fight effectively for one and signed a measure not much better than the first one.

When his control board ordered a roll-back of beef prices, ranchers refused to ship cattle, creating a beef famine that had the public up in arms. Truman held out for a few weeks, then ordered the end of price controls on beef. Meat reappeared in stores, but at prices that shocked consumers. The president once more seemed an ineffectual, confused, and inexperienced man.

The steady and rapid rise in prices in the postwar months injured all consumers, but few expressed their grievances as effectively as trade unionists. During the war the unions had agreed to hold the line on wages. Now union workers felt they deserved to catch up. In January 1946 the steelworkers demanded a wage increase and when industry management refused, they struck. On January 19 some 800,000 workers walked off the job, not to return for eighty crippling days. The following April John L. Lewis of the United Mine Workers led 400,000 coal miners out of the mines to force the coal operators to meet his demands for a miners' welfare fund. Truman ordered the government to take over the mines but then caved in to the union's wage demands, though he considered them inflationary. He was more decisive when, soon afterward, the railroad workers threatened to strike. This time he promised to seize the rail lines and have the army run them if they did. When this did not work, he went before Congress to announce that he would draft the striking railroad workers into the army if they did not return to their jobs. Dramatically, as he was addressing Congress, news reached him that the strike had been settled.

All told, the labor troubles left a bad taste in everyone's mouth. The union leaders felt Truman had been too hard; the middle-class public felt he had not been hard enough. Many people also resented his public profanity and his tendency to shoot verbally from the hip. In the 1946 off-year congressional elections the Republicans made "Had Enough?" their party's slogan. The voters responded with a resounding "yes," electing a Republican Congress for the first time since 1930.

Election: 1948. They quickly discovered that they had gotten more than they bargained for. The public was undoubtedly more conservative than before the war. But when the Eightieth Congress started to dismantle the New Deal, it provoked the wrath of important blocs of voters.

In June 1947, furious over recent strikes and strike threats, Congress passed the Taft-Hartley Act. This measure made the "closed shop" and secondary boycotts illegal; labor unions, that is, were forbidden to compel employers to hire only union members, nor could they prevent employers from doing business with other employers on a union hit list. The act permitted states to adopt "right to work" laws forbidding "union shops," that is, agreements where workers, after being hired, had to join the union. The law allowed the government to impose a sixty-day cooling-off period on would-be strikers, legalized injunctions against strikes that threatened national health and safety, ended the practice whereby employers could be forced to collect dues for the unions (the "check-off"), required unions to disclose their financial practices, and imposed an anti-Communist loyalty oath on union officials. The law represented a major check to the power conferred on unions by the New Deal, and organized labor would make its repeal its chief legislative target for the next twenty years.

The same Eightieth Congress frustrated the president on civil rights issues by refusing to abolish racial segregation in the armed forces by statute and rejecting his recommendations for a fair employment practices act to eliminate job discrimination in firms with federal contracts.

Truman improved his liberal credentials by vetoing the Taft-Hartley measure, though Congress easily overrode his veto. He also cheered the liberals by desegregating the armed forces and establishing a fair employment hiring practices commission, both by executive order.

The president capitalized brilliantly on the conservative record of the Eightieth Congress in his campaign for a full presidential term in 1948. His major opponent was the governor of New York, Thomas E. Dewey, a member of the northeastern liberal Republican establishment. But he also faced challenges from both ends of the political spectrum. To his right was Senator J. Strom Thurmond of South Carolina, candidate of the States' Rights Democratic party ("Dixiecrats"), a new organization of conservative Southern Democrats strongly opposed to racial equality. To his left was the former vice president, Henry Wallace, running on the Progressive party ticket, supported by left-liberals, Soviet sympathizers, and those who feared that Truman's interventionist foreign policies would lead to war.

Neither Thurmond nor Wallace had a chance, but at the outset Dewey appeared impossible to beat. Fortunately for Truman, Dewey was a stiff, overcontrolled man with a small, fussy moustache, who reminded one observer of the little spun-sugar groom on top of a wedding cake. The Republican candidate's chief difficulty, however, was the unusually conservative, and often negative, record of the Republican Eightieth Congress. Truman took brilliant advantage of that record. Through the late summer and into the fall, he criss-crossed the country by train and spoke 271 times, often to small audiences at whistle stops from the back of his observation car. The president attacked the "do-nothing Congress" and warned that those who had benefited from New Deal programs—farmers, wage earners, ethnic Americans, and blacks—would lose all their gains if Dewey and his party won. The public took heed of his words and came to admire his pluck. Across the country, as the campaign progressed, the crowds began to shout "Give 'em hell, Harry!" at the game little man with the awkward gestures and rough syntax. The result was one of the most remarkable upsets in American presidential history. All the polls had predicted that Truman would lose; he beat Dewey by a popular plurality of 2 million votes.

The Fair Deal.   The American people had announced that they did not want to return to the "bad old days" of Herbert Hoover. It soon became clear that they did not want to go forward very far or very fast, either. The next four years disappointed those who looked for further liberal change. In his State of the Union message soon after the election, the president unveiled his agenda for domestic reform, a developed and augmented version of the program he had earlier outlined. Labeled a "Fair Deal," it aimed at rounding out the limited welfare state Roosevelt inaugurated. But Congress, dominated by a coalition of conservative northern Republicans and Dixiecrat Democrats, refused to give him what he wanted. Little of the Fair Deal passed. Congress defeated Truman's farm program (the Brannan Plan), which sought to replace farm price supports with a system of farm income subsidies; rejected the administration's effort to add federal health insurance to the Social Security system; and ignored its scheme to provide federal aid for education. The only concessions that Truman could squeeze from the legislative branch were a higher minimum wage, an extension of Social Security coverage to an additional 9 million citizens, and a Housing Act (1949) for slum clearance and low-cost federal housing. All chance of significant domestic change evaporated when high administration officials, including the president's chief aide, Harry Vaughan, St. Louis Collector of Internal Revenue James Finnegan, and Assistant Attorney General T. Lamar Caudle, were accused of selling their influence to people who wanted government favors. Truman was innocent of these misdeeds, but in the midterm elections of 1950 the Republicans picked up many additional seats in Congress.

The Republican Decade Begins.   In March 1952 Truman announced that he would not be a candidate for reelection. In the Democratic free-for-all that followed, the nomination went to the one-term governor of Illinois, the articulate, witty, patrician Adlai E. Stevenson, the man favored by the party's liberal northern wing.

Among Republicans the party regulars and conservatives supported Senator Robert A. Taft of Ohio, son of the twenty-seventh president and a man of acute intelligence but little personal warmth. The moderate wing wanted Dwight D. Eisenhower, the hero of the great victory in Europe over the Nazis. "Ike" was an attractive figure politically. Benevolent in mien, bumbling but reassuring in speech, he seemed to be everyone's kindly uncle. The general had no known party affiliation; but he was clearly a patriot and a moderate, and he seemed certain to prove an irresistible candidate. After adopting a conservative platform, the Republican convention nominated Eisenhower. As its vice presidential candidate it chose an eager young senator from California, Richard M. Nixon, whose reputation as an aggressive campaigner and hard-line anti-Communist had recently brought him to national prominence.

The race that followed had more than its share of surprises. It looked as if the Democrats had a winning issue when it was disclosed that Nixon was the beneficiary of a dubious businessmen's fund to help pay his political expenses. Appearing on nationwide television, he explained that he had not received any personal gain from the fund. He was not a rich man, he told his viewers. His wife, Pat, unlike the mink-coated wives of Truman administration officials, wore a "Republican cloth coat." He had accepted one gift while in office: a black-and-white cocker spaniel, which one of his two young daughters had named Checkers. No matter what anyone said about that transaction, he was not going to give Checkers back!

Most voters liked the homey, sentimental quality of the "Checkers" speech, and the public response guaranteed that Nixon would not be dropped from the ticket. In fact, the entire Republican campaign sounded a note of wholesome domesticity and traditionalism that the 1950s public found congenial. By contrast, Stevenson seemed an "egg-head," an intellectual—and a divorced man at that. By the end of the campaign the Republicans were making the Democratic candidate and the men around him seem vaguely un-American. The campaign clincher came in October, when Eisenhower promised that if elected he would go to the Far East to help end the Korean War, then still in progress. In the end the Eisenhower–Nixon ticket won with a 7-million-vote margin.

"I Like Ike."   As president, Eisenhower allowed his staff, headed by Sherman Adams, former governor of New Hampshire, to conduct most day-to-day business while he saved himself for the important events. In later years he declared that he had intended to "create an atmosphere of greater serenity and mutual confidence," and he accomplished his end. His opponents attacked him for his indolence, but most voters found it soothing. Eisenhower has been described as "a hidden hand" president who hid behind a benign passive image to better achieve his ends. Even his sometimes garbled syntax, it has been said, was deliberate, allowing him to avoid clarity when he had not yet made up his mind.

Ideologically, "Ike" was moderately conservative. He opposed deficit spending as "fiscal irresponsibility" and once described New Deal–Fair Deal social programs as "creeping socialism." On the other hand he fought off efforts of the ultra-conservatives of his own party to dismantle the welfare state. His cabinet

Here "Ike" is making a campaign speech to the Republican National Convention in 1952. The slogan was platform enough for victory in November.

was heavily weighted with businessmen, one of whom, Defense Secretary Charles E. Wilson of General Motors, offended many liberals by his remark that "what is good for the country is good for General Motors, and what's good for General Motors is good for the country."

Eisenhower's domestic policies tended to favor business and the growing suburban middle class over blue-collar wage earners and city dwellers. Between 1954 and 1959 a series of housing acts made credit for home buying more readily available, accelerating the middle-class flight to the suburbs. In 1956 Congress passed the Highway Act, which authorized $32 billion for an immense interstate highway system financed by a federal gasoline tax. The measure, though much needed in an era of fast-growing motor car ownership, further drained the central cities and, by destroying the passenger traffic of the railroads, made Americans still more dependent on the wasteful, polluting private automobile.

In 1956 the general ran for reelection with Stevenson his opponent once more. The team of Eisenhower and Nixon won an even greater victory than in 1952, despite the misgivings many Americans had about Ike's shaky health following his heart attack in 1956. During his second term the president spent more time on the golf course. Yet at times Ike could rise above his indolence and natural conservatism. In his parting words to his fellow citizens, he warned against the "military-industrial complex." This close alliance of defense industry and government was in some ways unavoidable, he noted, but it was also a potential danger to the country's liberties. This was a strange conclusion for a military man, but his warning would be remembered and often praised by dissenting citizens in later years.

The Good Life

Prosperity was a major prop of 1950s conservatism. And its impact was all the greater for being unexpected and hard-won.

Between 1941 and 1945, 12 million young Americans had worn their country's uniform in military theaters of conflict around the world. They had yearned for the day when they could return to the tranquility and happy pursuits of family, home, and careers. On the industrial front, many women, after months on the "swing shift" and living with parents and in-laws in temporary accommodations, looked forward to starting families and enjoying domestic routines in their own homes.

This vision of private satisfaction left a deep impression on the values of the postwar generation. After 1945 the average age for marriage dropped sharply, birth rates soared, and family sizes swelled. The nation experienced a "baby boom" that lasted until the early 1960s and created a generation of Americans numerically larger than both the one before and the one after. In 1945 the country had 37.5 million households; by 1960 there were almost 53 million. In 1954 *McCall's* magazine would coin the word "togetherness" to describe the new commitment to a close family life revolving about children, the private suburban house, and home entertainment.

Avoiding a New Depression.   Prosperity made it possible for most GIs to make the difficult adjustment to peace. During the final stages of the war Americans had begun to worry about what the defeat of Germany and Japan would mean for the economy. To avoid disaster, in 1944 Congress passed a measure popularly known as the GI Bill of Rights. This law extended to all honorably discharged veterans generous monthly allowances for education; loans to purchase farms, businesses, or homes; and unemployment compensation of $20 a week for a maximum of fifty-two weeks. Millions of veterans became members of the "fifty-two, twenty club" until they were able to find jobs. Thousands started small businesses financed by government loans. Veterans flocked to the nation's colleges and universities. The "GI Bill" ultimately cost the government $14.5 billion, but it cushioned the economy, eased the postwar transition, and, most significantly perhaps, created a giant pool of educated, trained people that would serve the economy well in the years to come.

The Rage to Consume.   Luck also helped the economy avoid disaster. During the war high wages combined with acute shortages of new homes and consumer durables had forced the public to save. By the end of 1945 the American people had piled up $134 billion in cash, bank accounts, and government bonds. Having gone without the good things of life for so long through the Depression and war, Americans now seemed unwilling to deny themselves anything. In the closing months of the war advertisers reminded their customers that civilian products would shortly become available. "There's a Ford in your future," announced the car manufacturer. A month before Japan's surrender, General Electric advertised its "all-electric kitchen-of-the-future." The breathless advertising copy noted that the dishwasher "washes automatically in less than 10 minutes. And the Disposall disposes of food electrically—completely eliminates garbage."

The immense pent-up demand helped ensure that there would be no repetition of the economic collapse of 1929–1933. After an initial period of scarce consumer goods and climbing prices, industry completed its conversion to peacetime production and caught up with demand. During the first full year of peace only a little more than 2 million cars were produced—fewer than in 1934. Two years later output would almost double. Americans soon came to consider many new items essential for the good life. General Electric's prophecy came true: By the end of the decade the public was buying 225,000 automatic dishwashers and 750,000 electric Disposalls a year. In 1946 the first electric laundry dryers appeared, and housewives began to order them enthusiastically.

Television.   One electronic gadget not foreseen by GE would be even more momentous. The first experiments with television transmission had begun in the 1920s. In 1939 the Radio Corporation of America offered for sale the first home television sets. The war stopped further growth in the industry, but after Japan's surrender the market took off. In 1948 RCA and other domestic manufacturers turned out a million sets; in 1956, almost 7.5 million. By 1960 almost half of all American homes had one or more black-and-white television receivers.

The standard Levittown house with the standard
Levittown family (3 children) in 1950.

Besides its boost to the economy, the new industry had a powerful social and
cultural impact. Sports were transformed as lucrative broadcasting contracts converted both the college and the professional variety into immensely profitable big
businesses. The way Americans amused themselves was transformed. Hollywood shuddered as families gave up their Saturday nights at the movies to watch
TV "sitcoms" or variety shows. Television proved to be more than an entertainment medium, however. Parents complained that its reliance on dramas steeped
in violence was dangerous to young children, and educators and professors were
certain that young TV viewers were losing their capacity to read. But it was also
capable of providing serious instruction and enlightenment. Local as well as
national and international events came "live" into the living rooms of millions of
viewers. Television affected how the public perceived politicians. It made a
difference in the 1960 election and also helped bring down Senator Joseph
McCarthy, as we shall see.

The drastic increase in the number of families made new housing the nation's most pressing postwar need. At first thousands of returned veterans and
their spouses lived in army surplus Quonset huts or moved in with their parents. Then came William J. Levitt and his imitators. Levitt used standardized
construction components and automatic equipment to create housing "developments" on a giant scale. His houses were virtually all the same, but they had
the indispensable modern conveniences and a price tag of $10,000, payable in
thirty years on an FHA or GI home mortgage. Levitt's two largest developments

were on Long Island and in eastern Pennsylvania, but before long there were "Levittowns" in every part of the country, each boasting the same rows of houses with picture windows, small front lawns, and tree-bordered streets full of playing children.

And so the postwar depression did not materialize. Despite brief recessions—in 1949, 1953–1954, and 1959–1960—the GNP grew at a high average annual rate of 3.2 percent during the fifties. Prices rose at less than 2 percent a year for the remainder of the decade after 1950. The good health of the postwar economy owed most to factors that were unforeseen. Most important of these were the enormous pent-up domestic demand, cheap international raw materials, and America's unique position after 1945 as the only undamaged industrial power, the only nation capable of meeting the needs of war-ravaged Europe and Asia. But the contribution of government was not negligible. The GI Bill of Rights provided millions of young men and women with the cash and credit to consume the products of the factories and the services of schools and colleges. Over the entire post-1945 period, moreover, the sheer size of the government sector of the economy and the existence of unemployment insurance, old-age pensions, and federal deposit insurance provided a cushion against the instability of the years before 1933.

Suburbia Triumphant.   Economic expansion dramatically altered the quality of American life. As the economy grew, its structure changed. By 1960 occupations such as farming, mining, and even manufacturing had sharply declined in relative importance; more and more Americans worked at service jobs like advertising, technical, medical, and clerical services, publishing, accounting, and teaching. Particularly dramatic was the drop in farm workers: from 9 million to 5.2 million between 1940 and 1960. By 1960 there were more white-collar than blue-collar Americans.

The new white-collar class—and many skilled blue-collar workers—developed a characteristic lifestyle centered around suburban living. The pattern was home- and child-oriented. Wives became experts in house decoration, gardening, and meal planning. Husbands took up handicraft hobbies like carpentry and boat building. A "do-it-yourself" craze swept the suburbs as much to accommodate the new domestic interests of men as to help keep down the high cost of home repairs. The doings and problems of children became major new concerns of suburban parents. They worried about their offspring perhaps more than in the recent past, when simple economic survival had overshadowed difficulties about schools, dating patterns, orthodontia, and "cultural advantages." With so many children in the house and some money to spare, many parents discovered the babysitter problem for the first time.

The suburban pattern often imposed a heavy financial burden. Many married women went to work to help pay the bills, especially after 1950. Between 1950 and 1970 the percentage of married women employed went from 23.8 to 40.8. During the 1950s most of these wives took jobs to supplement the family income until husbands completed school on the GI Bill or received a promotion. Such labor seemed unavoidable if the precious new lifestyle was to be maintained.

The Other Half

The shift of population from city to suburb was one of the dramatic social developments of the 1950s. Yet millions of people remained in the central cities; many rural or semirural folk moved into the urban neighborhoods emptied by the lure of the suburbs.

Urban Poverty.   Some of the newcomers were, as in the past, Europeans— refugees from the war's devastation and disorder. During the decade Congress passed a number of special immigration measures that admitted GI "war brides" and several hundred thousand displaced persons, refugees from Europe's postwar wasteland. Most of the new arrivals in the central cities, however, were African Americans from the South and people of Hispanic background. Their experiences in some ways repeated those of earlier newcomers to American cities. Largely unskilled, they, too, took the lowest-paying jobs; they, too, moved into housing rejected by the middle class; they, too, were victims of prejudice and discrimination. Like their predecessors, they often found themselves caught in a web of poverty, crime, and family disruption and were blamed for their afflictions.

Most Americans assumed that the latest arrivals would move up in society as they acquired skills. It took longer than expected. Mid-twentieth-century America did not offer as many unskilled jobs as in the past. A construction worker now had to know how to operate a bulldozer; he could no longer merely wield a pick and shovel. Thousands of Puerto Rican, Mexican, and black women found jobs as domestics, waitresses, and hospital attendants; but their husbands, brothers, and sons often looked vainly for decent-paying work. And even when newcomers had some skill, they often found that their way up was blocked by unions whose members were hostile to them as a group or who wanted to save the declining number of skilled blue-collar jobs for their own relatives.

Civil Rights.   Though poverty continued to afflict minorities, the 1950s did see major advances in civil rights. The war had made a considerable difference for America's racial and religious minorities. By throwing into ghastly relief the fruits of Nazi racism, it shamed many Americans into reconsidering their own behavior and attitudes. Hostility toward Japanese-Americans, whose impressive fighting record in Italy during the war was widely acclaimed, rapidly dissipated. Jews, the Nazis' chief victims, also experienced a new kind of acceptance. And the wartime mingling of Americans of all kinds in a common struggle reduced traditional anti-Catholic prejudice. The war helped consolidate the sense of a shared American nationality.

Black Americans, the most afflicted by prejudice, benefited the least from the wartime changes. In the South state and local ordinances continued to require hospitals, theaters, buses, trains, playgrounds, parks, and other public accommodations to maintain separate facilities for blacks and whites. Prodded by a new generation of liberal federal judges, southern states by the 1950s were making an effort to upgrade black schools so that they could meet the "separate-but-equal" test of *Plessy v. Ferguson.* But almost everywhere they remained both separate and inferior. Nor could blacks yet vote in most of the South. Intimidation, poll taxes, and rigged registration laws kept most eligible blacks from going to the polls in state and national elections. Worst of all, lynching and other kinds of racial violence survived as a brutal method of social control.

The situation for African–Americans in the North was better. The movement of thousands of black people out of the South, where they were effectively disenfranchised, to northern cities, where they could vote, enormously increased their political influence. In most northern communities there was no legal bar to the schools that black citizens could attend or theaters, hotels, restaurants, or sports events they could patronize. On the other hand, many white northerners continued to believe that blacks were inherently inferior. Their prejudice informally accomplished many of the same ends that statutes did in the South. Whites excluded blacks from private social clubs; restaurant and hotel managers refused to accept black patrons. Landlords' and home owners' prejudice forced blacks to accept inferior housing even when they could afford better. Few blacks, no matter how well qualified, could find skilled professional work. The AFL craft unions, making up the building trades, informally excluded black workers. Although black talent was often recognized in the arts and in sports, even there bigotry persisted. In baseball, presumably the "national sport," there were no black players in the major leagues until after World War II. In 1947 Branch Rickey, the courageous owner of the Brooklyn Dodgers, signed Jackie Robinson to play second base, finally breaking the major leagues' longtime color bar.

The struggle for black civil rights engaged many white liberals, but African–Americans carried much of the burden themselves. During the 1940s Walter F. White, secretary of the NAACP, and A. Phillip Randolph, president of the Brotherhood of Sleeping Car Porters, fought for a federal antilynching bill, an end to poll taxes in federal elections, and the outlawing of discrimination in work under government contract. The NAACP initiated a succession of suits aimed at breaking down segregation sanctioned by southern state and local laws.

By 1950 black citizens were growing ever more restive as they watched the snaillike pace of change in race relations. The political system, however well it responded to the wishes of the white middle class, seemed incapable of meeting blacks' needs. Congress was paralyzed by the resistance of the well-organized southern Democratic bloc to any change in the racial order. The Republicans owed little to black voters and seemed indifferent to their problems.

Brown v. Board of Education.

Into this void stepped the branch of government traditionally the least democratic and the least responsive to public pressures: the federal courts. Beginning in 1953, the Supreme Court was led by Chief Justice Earl Warren, an Eisenhower appointee. A liberal Republican himself, he presided over a court composed of "judicial activists," holdovers from the New Deal who were willing to extend the Court's power into areas hitherto considered legislatures' concerns or beyond the reach of law. The Warren Court would expand the realm of personal rights as against the government in many areas of life. But its most momentous decisions targeted the legal barriers to racial equality and change.

Even before Warren's appointment, the federal courts, under NAACP goading, had begun to restrict segregation in housing and in graduate and professional education. Then, in 1954, came the Supreme Court's landmark ruling in the case of *Brown v. The Board of Education of Topeka,* brilliantly argued for the NAACP by black attorney Thurgood Marshall. Resting its decision on the findings of sociologists and psychologists that separate schooling inevitably harmed black children, the Court declared that segregation in the public schools was a denial of the Fourteenth Amendment's requirement that the states accord to every person "equal protection of the laws." "We conclude," chief justice Warren wrote, "that in the field of public education the doctrine of 'separate but equal' has no place. Separate educational facilities are inherently unequal." Hoping to give the Court's words their maximum moral authority, he had lobbied his colleagues intensely and the decision had been unanimous.

The road to actual color-blind schools would be long and difficult. In the southern border states compliance with the Brown decision was generally good. In Washington, D.C., the schools immediately desegregated. In the lower South the decision produced a storm of resistence. The more respectable conservatives of the region organized White Citizens' Councils—"uptown Ku Klux Klans," their critics called them—to defeat the Court's order by boycotts and other economic weapons directed against both black and white supporters of desegregation. The Klan itself revived and used violence and threats of violence to prevent compliance with the Brown decision. Everywhere in the lower South school boards dragged their feet in meeting the federal mandate. In 1955, in the so-called *Brown II* decision, the Court ruled that local communities must comply with the desegregation decision with "all deliberate speed," though it left specific timetables to the lower federal courts to decide.

The order had minimal effect. In the lower South "massive resistance" continued. At Little Rock, Arkansas, in 1957 the Klan backed Arkansas Governor Orval Faubus when he defied a court order that black students be admitted to Central High School. Mobs of angry white protesters gathered outside the school, blocking entrance by the black pupils. Faubus refused to remove them. President Eisenhower, though not a civil rights enthusiast, could not allow such blatant disregard of the law of the land and dispatched federal troops to protect the black children seeking admission. Ike was willing to march with the times, but he did not want to lead the parade. He would later call his appointment of Earl Warren as chief justice "the biggest damnfool mistake" he ever made.

Civil Disobedience.

Legal action was the preferred tactic of the NAACP against segregation and denial of voting rights. Other civil rights leaders, however, believed that the white South would only respond to civil disobedience.

This strategy was associated with a new black leadership. There was now a substantial southern black middle class of clergymen, teachers, students, small-business owners, and professionals—men and women better prepared by education and income to defend their race than their predecessors. Such leaders identified their cause with the struggles of oppressed colonial peoples around the world and concluded that the tactics used to evict the European imperialists from Africa and Asia might be applied to the American South.

The new approach first attracted national attention in December 1955, when Rosa Parks, a black seamstress and activist, weary from her day's work in a downtown department store, refused to give up her seat on a crowded Montgomery, Alabama, bus to a white man as the local Jim Crow law required. Mrs. Parks was arrested and fined $10. Black community leaders, waiting for a case to test Montgomery's segregation ordinances, quickly organized a boycott of the city bus company. The city authorities arrested the boycott leaders, including the twenty-seven year-old Reverend Martin Luther King, Jr., a Georgia-born, northern-educated Baptist minister. The Klan bombed King's house and burned several black churches.

Despite the reprisals, day after day, Montgomery's black community refused to patronize the buses; dedicated people got to work on foot or by car-pooling. Some Montgomery blacks were tempted to meet violence with violence, but King, an adherent of *Satyagraha*, Indian leader Mohandas Gandhi's doctrine of nonviolent civil disobedience, headed them off. "We must love our white brothers," he advised, "no matter what they do to us." A year after the boycott began the U.S. Supreme Court ordered the end of segregation on the Montgomery bus system. The black protesters had won.

The Montgomery boycott raised King, whose eloquence and courage had sustained the protesters through difficult times, to the front rank of civil rights leadership. It also made nonviolent civil disobedience the central strategy of the civil rights movement. In 1957 King and his followers established the Southern Christian Leadership Conference (SCLC) in Atlanta as agent of a concerted nonviolent, biracial campaign to challenge the remaining bastions of Jim Crow and restore the voting rights the white South had denied its black citizens for almost a hundred years. The grass-roots efforts were intended to keep southern race discrimination clearly before the court of public opinion. King and his colleagues on the SCLC never doubted that white support was needed to defeat racism. As the civil rights hymn proclaimed: "White and black together" would "overcome some day." Fortunately the civil rights leaders could at first count on broad white support. By the 1950s many middle-class whites, especially in the North, had come to accept the conclusions of social scientists and anthropologists that race differences were culturally determined and that discrimination was costly, irrational, and unjust. With his dazzling eloquence, cultivated mind, and disarming message of Christian love, King was particularly well equipped to capitalize on liberal white attitudes.

Meanwhile, civil rights leaders continued to press for reform on the level of federal law and policy. In September 1957 Congress passed the first of several measures designed to restore voting rights to black southerners. The Civil Rights Act of 1957, the first such legislation since Reconstruction, set up a Civil Rights Commission to investigate complaints of voting rights violations, and a Civil Rights Division of the Department of Justice to prosecute officials found responsible. A relatively modest measure, without sharp teeth to enforce its goals, it was strengthened by the 1960 Civil Rights Act, which required voting registrars to retain their records for some months following an election so that they could be examined by federal officials. Both laws provided the government with weapons to end black disenfranchisement. But as the 1960s began, the slow and painful process of restoring rights guaranteed to black Americans by the Fourteenth and Fifteenth Amendments almost a century before had just begun.

The Cold War

The retreat of Americans to private satisfactions during the 1950s can be explained in part by the payoff that fulfilled people's material hopes. Yet as millions surrendered to the pleasures of a consumer society, a great collective anxiety remained: the threat of nuclear holocaust. This fear, like affluence, would encourage a political and social philosophy that avoided criticism of the nation and its dominant private enterprise, middle-class values.

The United Nations.   During the war itself internationalists, fearing another American retreat from international responsibility, had succeeding in committing the United States to world cooperation. In 1944, at Bretton Woods, New Hampshire, American and other anti-Axis diplomats signed agreements for an international bank and a world monetary fund to stabilize international currencies and rebuild war-torn economies. In November 1945 the Senate endorsed "an international authority to preserve peace," an act, noted the *New York Times*, in a reference to the defeat of the Versailles treaty, that undid "a twenty-four-year-old mistake."

The internationalists' goal took definitive form at the conference at San Francisco in April–June 1945. There, by the bay, 282 delegates representing the 50 nations arrayed against the Axis powers created the United Nations, modeled after the failed League of Nations. The UN charter established a General Assembly composed of all member nations to serve as the ultimate UN policy-making body. An eleven-nation Security Council, consisting of five permanent members—the United States, Great Britain, the Soviet Union, France, and China—and six others elected by the General Assembly for two-year terms—would actually make the major decisions for settling disputes among member nations. Each permanent member was given the power to veto Security Council decisions.

The creation of the UN was a triumph for the Wilsonian ideal of international cooperation to preserve world peace. But it could not disguise the discord that had long been growing between the Soviet Union and the West or settle all the conflicts brewing in the troubled postwar world.

An Unsettled World.   Clearly, the international balance following VJ Day was very different from the past. Western Europe, long the world's power center, emerged after 1945 profoundly enfeebled. France, defeated by the Nazis in 1940, was demoralized and faced with the serious problems of reestablishing national unity and confidence and a political consensus. Germany and Italy were shattered societies where children begged on the streets and women sold themselves to American GIs or Soviet soldiers for packs of cigarettes and chocolate bars. Most disruptive of all, victorious Britain was impoverished and incapable of holding its vast empire together. All over the former Nazi-occupied territories misery prevailed. Millions of displaced persons wandered across the continent looking for a place to live and ways to reconstruct their lives. The physical scars of war marked every city and town. Hunger and disease afflicted populations weakened by wartime privations and continuing shortages. Winston Churchill scarcely exaggerated when he described Europe in 1945 as "a rubble heap, a charnel house, a breeding ground of pestilence and hate."

Society in Eastern Europe was even more unsettled than in the West. Millions of Russians, Jews, Poles, and others had lost their lives in combat or been shot, gassed, or starved to death by the Nazi conquerors. Twenty million Soviet citizens had died. The political equilibrium had also been profoundly altered. Before 1939 a group of independent nations, including the Baltic states (Lithuania, Latvia, and Estonia), Finland, Poland, and Romania, had walled the Soviet Union off from the rest of Europe. The regimes in these countries, as well as the next tier to the west, had been generally suspicious of the USSR before the war and held it at arm's length. After 1945 the picture was completely transformed. Now the Soviets shared occupation zones in Germany and Austria with the Western Allies; had established pro-Soviet "satellite" regimes in Poland, Hungary, Romania, Bulgaria, Albania, and Yugoslavia; incorporated the Baltic states into the Soviet Union as Soviet republics; and had extended the USSR's official borders westward by annexing eastern Poland and compensating the Poles with former German territory. Finland and Czechoslovakia remained independent, but the former did so only at the price of avoiding policies that offended the Soviet Union, while the latter's autonomy would be short-lived.

Meanwhile, the decline of Western Europe had created a power vacuum in Asia and Africa. In the Far East the Japanese military successes of 1941–1943 had stripped away the myth of European invincibility and awakened dormant nationalist feelings in Indonesia, Ceylon (Sri Lanka), Indochina, Burma, India, and Malaysia. In the Middle East and North Africa, Arab nationalism, long held in check by France and Britain, began to seethe. In sub-Saharan black Africa, too, by 1945 Western-educated elites were demanding an end to European colonial rule.

Especially troubling in Asia was the turmoil in China, the world's most populous nation. During the war the United States, Great Britain, and even the Soviet Union had supported the Kuomintang, the Chinese Nationalist government under Chiang Kai-shek. But Chiang's regime had increasingly come under the domination of corrupt bureaucrats, privileged landlords, and rich merchants. It had failed to win the support of the Chinese peasantry and after the war seemed unable to deal with China's economic backwardness and social inequalities.

For many years Chiang's chief adversary had been the Communists led by Mao Tse-tung. In the portion of north China they controlled, the Communists had established an authoritarian administration, though one reputedly less corrupt than Chiang's. In December 1945 President Truman sent General George C. Marshall to China to end the Nationalist–Communist rift. Marshall failed, and by mid-1946 China had descended into a devastating civil war.

And even in the Americas there were churning discontents. In the Latin countries to the south of the United States, resentment of authoritarian regimes run by generals, combined with gross inequalities of wealth and power, encouraged radical movements and political restlessness.

Sources of the Cold War.

The postwar instability in Europe, Asia, Africa, and the Americas set the stage for world competition between the only two nations that still possessed substantial international power—the United States and the Soviet Union. Eventually all five major continents would become arenas for unremitting rivalry between the two and their respective allies. Their conflict would become a worldwide struggle waged by diplomacy, propaganda, economic rivalry, and military threat and intimidation. Occasionally the Cold War would erupt in actual combat, though fortunately for humanity, only through surrogates, never between the two nuclear-armed superpowers directly.

Each of the two nations contributed to the conflict. In both, the leaders and public were certain that their country alone stood for social justice and world peace. Both believed that their system must ultimately prevail. Viewed objectively, the Cold War was the attempt of the leaders and elites of the two superpowers to ensure their own safety and protect what they perceived as their vital interests in the dramatically transformed international environment after 1945.

Yet the positions of the two sides were not symmetrical. The Soviet Union was an outsider nation, aggrieved by a sense of exclusion from a central role in world affairs. It resembled, after 1945, a new-made millionaire blackballed from the best private clubs by the established elite and determined to achieve his rightful place at all costs. The belligerence of Soviet leaders was exacerbated by their sense of inferiority toward America. The United States, on the other hand, felt itself the world's power hub, inevitable successor to Britain and France as the balance wheel to the world international order. The relation of outsider to insider was unavoidably confrontational. The Soviet Union, to achieve its goals, had to alter the existing world order; the United States need only preserve it.

The asymmetry went beyond differing strategic locations, however. The two systems were not morally equivalent. America, for all its imperfections, was a democratic society with a functioning multiparty political system and a large private sphere protected by traditions of individual liberty and personal rights incorporated into fundamental law. The Soviet Union was an oppressive, totalitarian society where boundaries between the public and private spheres were weak and political and economic control was centralized at the top in a single, all-powerful Communist Party and an unresponsive, rigid bureaucracy. To make matters worse, during the immediate postwar years the ruler of the sprawling, untidy, monolithic Soviet Union, Josef Stalin, for all his skill, was a ruthless, paranoid dictator who had swept aside or massacred all his domestic enemies and imposed a regime on the Soviet people that made the czars' autocratic reign seem benevolent by comparison. Before, during, and after the war, Stalin's secret police arrested thousands of men and women who were accused, usually on the flimsiest evidence, of being enemies of the state and sent to brutal Siberian prison camps (the *Gulag*), or summarily executed. During his last years he became a half-mad recluse who locked himself in the Kremlin and imagined plots against his rule. Even after Stalin's death in 1953, his successors, though never as bad, continued to repress their own people and support the tyrants in the Soviet satellite nations who imitated their masters in Moscow. The USSR continued to be a prison for scores of national groups conquered by the czars and compelled to accept the domination of the Slavic Great Russians who ruled from Moscow.

This moral asymmetry, however, does not mean that the United States was not capable of coercive, arbitrary, and ruthless actions in the pursuit of its interests. At home, the Cold War was fought at times at the expense of civil liberties and repression of dissent. Abroad it often involved self-serving behavior that harmed neutrals and perpetuated injustice and tyranny.

The Emerging Conflict. As we saw, the leader of the Soviet Union and the Western powers had maintained a show of friendship during the war that papered over serious disagreements. Many ordinary Americans had sincerely admired the brave Soviet people in their fierce struggle with the Nazi invaders. Then, as Soviet troops broke the back of the German army and pushed westward, questions of postwar boundaries, spheres of influence, and relations between the Soviet Union and its immediate neighbors became sources of contention.

By the time of the Big Three's Potsdam Conference in July 1945, the postwar world was already taking shape. Churchill, defeated for reelection by the British voters before Japan surrendered, was replaced at the conference by British Labour Party head, Clement Atlee, as prime minister. President Harry Truman came in place of the recently deceased Roosevelt. During the conference, Truman received word that the scientists of the Manhattan Project had successfully tested an atomic bomb. Roosevelt had believed he could charm Stalin. Truman, influenced perhaps by the sense of America's awesome new strength, took a more skeptical attitude toward the Soviet dictator. The conferees agreed to little of consequence, and most pending issues between the democracies and the Soviet Union remained unresolved.

Meanwhile, determined to eliminate all unfriendly regimes from the Soviet Union's western borders, Stalin moved rapidly toward establishing political dominion over Eastern Europe and permanent division of conquered Germany. With the Red Army holding all the territory Stalin coveted, his allies had no choice but to concede Soviet gains. The American people, led by Roosevelt to believe that he could handle Stalin, were bitterly disappointed when Truman "lost" Eastern Europe to the Communists.

Most western Europeans and Americans, except those who sympathized with Communist ideology, were alarmed by this shift of Soviet power to the heart of Central Europe, too close to the West for comfort. For their part, the Soviets and their friends argued that they could not allow the "Socialist Motherland" to be surrounded by hostile states as in the past. And, in any event, they said, the new Communist regimes within the Soviet orbit expressed the will of the local people far better than the aristocratic and semifascist ones that had existed in 1939.

The Third World—as the undeveloped countries of Asia, Africa, and the Americas would be called—presented both opportunities and dangers to both superpowers. With France, Britain, Holland, and Japan too weakened to maintain empires, who would benefit from the political changes bound to come in their former colonies? The United States had never been a major colonial power like France or Britain, and during the post-1945 occupation of Japan it had demonstrated a commendable zeal for encouraging free, liberal institutions abroad. Could it now capitalize on the goodwill it possessed to win the emerging Third World nations over to Western-style liberal capitalism? But the Soviet Union also had advantages in the competition. It, too, had taken little part in the earlier race for overseas colonies, and so could claim to be free of imperialist taint. The people in almost all these emerging societies were desperately poor and would be attracted by drastic schemes to redistribute land and end the privileged status of local elites. The Soviet Union sought to identify itself with these changes. Communism would be the vehicle for creating equitable societies after national independence was achieved, they claimed. Many Third World intellectuals were strongly influenced by Marxist ideas, which promised quick modernization without the complexities and inconveniences of democratic struggles.

In any struggle over the "nonaligned" world, then, it was not clear who would win. Some Americans, and perhaps some Soviet leaders, did not see the world as a simple polar division of "East" versus "West." But during the immediate postwar period most Americans and Russians found it difficult to imagine that nations could be permanently nonaligned. Either "they were for us, or against us," opinion leaders on both sides seemed to believe.

Containment.   If Soviet aggression had been confined to its immediate western borders in Europe, its opponents might not have rallied so quickly to resist it. It was not. In 1945 the Moscow government demanded that neighboring Turkey cede to it several frontier districts and concede Soviet control over the Dardanelles, the all-important strait connecting Soviet Black Sea ports with the Mediterranean. In the following year Greece was torn apart by a Communist-led and inspired revolt sustained by supplies sent by Stalin and Marshal Josip Broz Tito, the leader of the Yugoslav Communists. Meanwhile, in the months following German surrender, Soviet agitation, intrigue, and propaganda in war-damaged, impoverished, and demoralized Western Europe seemed a preliminary to Soviet political penetration. Perhaps the Soviet Union never expected direct conquest and occupation of France, Italy, or Great Britain, but Moscow seemed determined to build pro-Soviet parties within each that would ally these nations with the USSR. Even a neutral Europe would be an enormous defeat for the United States and a corresponding victory for the Soviet Union and its ideology.

From the outset alert Americans and Britons were aware of the Soviet threat. In March 1946 Winston Churchill told an audience at Fulton, Missouri, that an "iron curtain" had "descended across the continent of Europe" behind which Communist tyranny reigned supreme. Elsewhere "Communist fifth columns" were threatening Christian civilization. A year later George F. Kennan, an influential senior American diplomat, cabled his State Department superiors from Moscow that the Soviet Union was committed to an "aggressive intransigence with respect to the outside world." American policy, he advised, must be one of "long-term, patient, but firm and vigilant containment of Russian expansive tendencies." In 1946 Congress authorized a $3.75 billion loan to Great Britain and contributed to the United Nations Relief and Rehabilitation Administration (UNRRA), an agency formed to funnel money and supplies to starving Europeans. These efforts were not enough, however, and by 1947 Europe seemed on the verge of an economic collapse that would deliver it into the hands of local communist parties.

The first significant move to wall in the spreading "red tide" came during the cruel winter of 1946–1947 when western Europe seemed to touch bottom. In February 1947 the financially besieged British told George Marshall, now Truman's secretary of state, that communist pressure in Greece and Turkey was reaching a crisis and Britain could no longer perform its traditional stabilizing role in the eastern Mediterranean. To counter Soviet pressure, on March 12 Truman asked Congress for $400 million in aid for the two beleaguered nations. Under the leadership of Republican Senator Arthur H. Vandenberg of Michigan, Congress endorsed the Truman Doctrine and made the appropriation. Massive aid to Greece

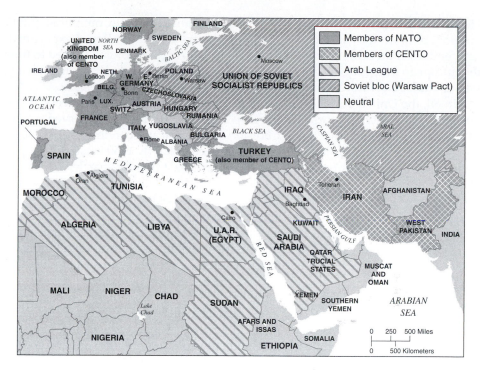

Postwar Alliances in Europe and the Middle East

and Turkey, combined with the break in 1948 between Tito and the Soviet Union, blocking Russian arms and supplies to the Greek guerrillas, soon ended the Communist threat in both countries. The Truman Doctrine established a precedent that would inspire American foreign policy for the next forty years.

The Marshall Plan.   The next, and far bigger, installment of containment was the Marshall Plan. A joint U.S.–European economic recovery program first broached by Secretary of State Marshall in June 1947 at the Harvard commencement, it sought to restore "the confidence of the European people in the economic future of their own country and of Europe as a whole." That July an all-European conference convened in Paris, formed the Committee for European Economic Cooperation, and agreed on the shape of the program. The American call for a cooperative effort did not exclude the Soviet Union, although the prospect of Soviet participation made American officials uneasy. Suspicious of the United States and wanting no part in any program that would strengthen Western capitalism, the Soviets came to the conference but walked out when they discovered that they could not disrupt the meeting.

Americans did not support containment unanimously. Walter Lippmann, the dean of American journalism, called it a "strategic monstrosity" and feared that it was a blank check for American entanglement in every conflict around the globe. Critics on the left and friends of the Soviet Union considered it a scheme to preserve capitalist injustice and a danger to world peace. Former Vice President

Henry Wallace, for one, dubbed it the "Martial Plan." But anti-Communist public opinion, reinforced by farmers' and manufacturers' zeal for enlarged export markets, endorsed the administration proposal. In March 1948 Congress voted to fund the European Recovery Program, and in a few weeks vessels laden with grain and vital manufactures were steaming for Europe.

In all, the United States contributed $12.5 billion to European recovery. It was not pure generosity, of course. Shoring up Western Europe clearly served America's strategic interests and helped bolster the American economy. But however motivated, the Marshall Plan's results were spectacular. By 1950 Western Europe's economic output had outstripped that of 1939, the last prewar year, by 25 percent. Noncommunist Europe was beginning a dramatic economic surge that would carry living standards far beyond anything dreamed of before the war. As poverty receded, so did communism. By 1950 the voters in the fast-recovering West European nations were confident once again. The Communist parties of France, Italy, and Germany would survive with the support of many intellectuals and industrial workers, but their takeover of the governments of these nations would be effectively checked.

The Marshall Plan was accompanied by other moves to stiffen European resistance to Soviet and internal Communist pressures. Britain, France, and the United States were determined to restore an independent German state. In 1948 they stabilized the German currency and soon after created out of their occupation zones a West German Federal Republic with its capital at Bonn. Fearful of a revived and militant anti-communist Germany, the Russians reacted strongly. In June 1948 they imposed a land blockade on all traffic into the western sector of Berlin, a city deep inside Soviet-occupied eastern Germany. To save Berlin and prevent its complete takeover by the Soviets, the United States and Britain airlifted vital supplies into the city. The Berlin Airlift lasted for more than ten months until, conceding defeat, the Russians withdrew their barricades and allowed the city to be supplied once more by rail and truck. Although for the moment Berlin had been saved, until 1971 the city would remain a western hostage in Soviet-East German hands, periodically triggering dangerous East-West confrontations. In October 1949 the Soviets transformed their own German occupation zone into the German Democratic Republic (East Germany) under firm local Communist control.

NATO. During these critical early postwar years the two superpowers played a deadly game across the chessboard of Europe. In February 1948 a Communist coup d'état in Prague, Czechoslovakia, turned the only Eastern European country with a surviving democratic regime into another Soviet satellite. In September 1949 the USSR exploded its first atomic bomb. Knowledge that the Soviets were now capable of waging atomic war sent shock waves through the Western nations.

The Prague coup and the Berlin blockade goaded the Western powers into a defensive alliance. In April 1949 Belgium, Canada, Denmark, France, Great Britain, Iceland, Italy, Luxembourg, the Netherlands, Norway, Portugal, and the United States joined together in the North Atlantic Treaty Organization (NATO). Each NATO member pledged to defend any other member if attacked by the Soviet Union or any other enemy. Isolationist Republican senators sought to defeat confirmation of the NATO treaty, but with the support of Senator Arthur Vanden-burg, the leading Republican internationalist, it passed. For the first time the Unit-ed States had committed itself to an international alliance in time of peace. The Soviets soon responded in kind to what they considered a Western provocation. Fearing especially a western move to include West Germany in NATO, in 1955 they countered with the Warsaw Pact, a military alliance of Albania, Bulgaria, Czechoslovakia, East Germany, Hungary, Poland, and Romania with the USSR.

American opinion was slow to accept Soviet domination in Eastern Europe. In January 1953 Secretary of State John Foster Dulles declared in a television broad-cast that people behind the Iron Curtain, in the Soviet satellite nations, could "count on" the United States. This seemed a pledge that they could rely on Amer-ican aid if they rose up against their Soviet oppressors. Soon afterward Dulles's supporters in Congress introduced the "captive peoples" resolution deploring the "aggressive despotism" imposed on those behind the Iron Curtain and providing further encouragement for them to resist their masters. The promise was empty. When soon after, Soviet troops put down riots and protests against the Russians in several East German cities, the United States made no move to intervene. Again, in 1956, when the Hungarians rose in revolt against their satellite regime and de-manded the departure of Soviet troops and an end to Soviet control, the United States allowed the Hungarian "freedom fighters" to be brutally crushed by Soviet troops and tanks. The tragic failure of the Hungarian uprising clarified the limits of American commitment: The United States would go to war for the NATO coun-tries and West Germany; it would not fight to liberate the "captive peoples" be-hind the Iron Curtain.

The Arms Race.

Adding to the uncertainties of balance-of-power politics, and coloring almost every international event, was the threat of a direct nuclear ex-change between the two superpowers and the possibility of world cataclysm. Stal-in had professed indifference when Truman had alluded to the atom bomb at the Potsdam conference. But the Soviets were actually terrified by their adversary's new weapon. During the war, to help create their own bomb, they had spied on British and American atomic weapons developments. After 1945 they stepped up their drive to produce atomic weapons. When the United States proposed interna-tional control of such weapons in 1946, the USSR rejected it on the grounds that it would freeze the status quo while the Americans were still ahead. The Russians seemed sure to acquire a working bomb sooner or later, but in September 1949 when President Truman announced that the Soviet Union had exploded its first atomic weapon, many Americans were startled.

The Soviet race for the bomb was only the first phase of a prodigious super-power struggle to achieve arms supremacy by every means possible. At first each side sought bigger and better nuclear weapons. In 1950, over the protests of Robert Oppenheimer and other prominent scientists, the American government authorized development of the hydrogen bomb, a far more destructive weapon that the atomic bombs dropped on Japan. On November 1, 1952, the first of these was exploded at Eniwetok, an atoll in the Marshall Islands. Within ten months the Soviet Union exploded its own H-bomb, thus ending America's brief nuclear advantage.

Over the next few years both sides set off dozens of H-bombs to test their effectiveness and improve their reliability. It soon became obvious that the device was indeed a "hell" bomb that made it theoretically possible to destroy humanity. Each test explosion, moreover, released large amounts of radioactive strontium-90 into the atmosphere, threatening to cause thousands of deaths from cancer in future generations.

Once both superpowers had acquired explosive weapons of unimagined power, the arms race shifted to delivery systems. During the early 1950s the United States maintained a 270,000-person Strategic Air Command, which kept a constant patrol of B-29 bombers in the air, each one carrying H-bombs, to retaliate against any Soviet attack. The Russians sought to outflank the United States by developing guided missiles. Soviet engineers soon succeeded in producing unmanned, radar-guided rockets that could travel great distances and hit their targets within an error of a few miles. To counteract the Russian intercontinental ballistic missiles (ICBMs), the United States established a chain of radar stations, the DEW (distant early warning) line across northern Canada. At the same time American scientists worked furiously to close the "missile gap."

Missiles and H-bombs did not preclude heavy investment in conventional weapons. American budget outlays for planes, tanks, artillery, atomic submarines, and other defense items went from $13 billion in 1950, when it was about one third of the total federal budget, to $46 billion in 1960, when it was half.

Added to the outlays on military hardware were vast disbursements for other Cold War safeguards. In July 1947 Congress passed the National Security Act unifying the army, navy, and air force under a single secretary of defense, establishing the National Security Council (NSC) to advise the president on issues necessary to American safety, and setting up a Central Intelligence Agency (CIA) to gather information deemed essential to American security abroad. Over the next three decades the CIA became the major American spy agency, and its epic battle of wits with its East Bloc counterparts became legendary, reviving the whole genre of spy novels and movies. Along with other Cold War agencies, such as Radio Free Europe and the Voice of America, the CIA cost billions of dollars, though its budgets were hidden in other federal expenditures to conceal the extent of its activities from the Soviet enemy.

A vocal minority of Americans deplored the economic costs of the Cold War. Conservatives believed that it might be possible to achieve economies in military outlays without weakening American defense. During the Eisenhower administration, Secretary of State John Foster Dulles advanced the doctrine of "massive retaliation," including the use of atomic weapons against any Soviet attack, as a way of keeping down costs. Rather than trying to match the Soviet Union man for man, gun for gun, and tank for tank, we should build up an H-bomb arsenal that would deter our adversary from threatening our vital interests. Critics of the secretary's views noted that it would turn every confrontation with the USSR into a possible atomic war. Given another Dulles policy, "brinkmanship"—bringing each crisis with the Soviet Union to the edge of war—the emphasis on atomic weapons seemed a certain prescription for world disaster.

The arms race awakened a tenacious peace movement. Pacifists, women's civic groups, liberal scientists and academics, and political radicals denounced most arms outlays, nuclear and otherwise, as wasteful and dangerous. Some of the "stop-the-arms-race" groups—including SANE (National Committee for a Sane Nuclear Policy) and the Committee for Nonviolent Action—emphasized the dangers of nuclear fallout from atmospheric testing. Others underscored the draining effect of armaments expenditures on civic life. Still others insisted that the arms competition was certain to trip off a full-scale superpower war. Their solutions differed. Some peace protesters advocated strict international arms controls agreements; others believed the only way to save the world was for the West to set an example by disarming first ("unilaterally"), even if that entailed risks.

The resistance affected the course of the weapons competition. Neither the United States nor the Soviet Union abandoned the arms race, but public concerns induced the superpowers in 1963 to sign a treaty (the Limited Nuclear Test Ban Treaty) forbidding atmospheric testing of nuclear weapons. The continued pressure of peace groups, moreover, helped create a widespread international demand for arms limitations that would eventually bear fruit.

Containment in Asia.   In Asia, meanwhile, the United States found itself facing a new danger. Since the end of World War II Washington had sent $2 billion in aid to Chiang Kai-shek in China with little result. Much of the war matériel was sold off by corrupt Kuomintang (Nationalist) officials and ended up in the hands of either profiteers or the Chinese Communists. The Kuomintang soon lost the confidence of the Chinese people. The Communists rushed to fill the gap. By 1948 Mao Tse-tung's army was advancing triumphantly south from their northern base, sweeping their Nationalist enemies before it. In December 1949 Chiang, his entourage, and his remaining troops fled the mainland to reestablish the "Republic of China" on Taiwan (Formosa), off the south coast of China. Supreme on the mainland, Mao and his supporters proclaimed the People's Republic of China (PRC) with its capital at Beijing. Many Americans concluded that Mao's victory had added hundreds of millions more adversaries to the Communist side of the scales.

During the Chinese civil war Americans associated with the "China lobby" and an Asia-first policy had supported direct military intervention to prevent the Communist takeover. The Truman administration rejected the idea, convinced that a land war in Asia would be a bottomless quagmire. Even after the Communist victory the American government sought to avoid a direct military role in East Asia as an insupportable position. In January 1950 Secretary of State Dean Acheson declared that the United States did not consider Taiwan, mainland Southeast Asia, or South Korea essential to American security. If any of these places were invaded, the "initial resistance" would have to come from those attacked.

Acheson inadvertently gave the Asian Communists the green light for further expansion. Korea, under the brutal rule of Japan for many years, had been divided after World War II into Soviet and American zones at the thirty-eighth parallel, pending its eventual reunification. By 1948 there were two governments in Korea: a Republic of Korea (ROK) in the South led by Syngman Rhee, elected president under UN supervision, and a communist People's Republic in the North, closely allied with the Soviet Union. In 1949 the United States withdrew its last remaining troops from the South, leaving the pro-western ROK unprotected.

Soon after Acheson's statement, the North Koreans—apparently with Soviet approval—concluded that it was time to unite Korea under Communist rule by force. On June 25, 1950, 95,000 Soviet-armed North Korean troops crossed the thirty-eighth parallel in a full-scale invasion of the Republic of Korea, still formally under United Nations control. Reversing his administration's position as stated by Acheson, Truman moved quickly to stop the aggression. The United States called an emergency session of the UN Security Council, from which the USSR had temporarily withdrawn its representative. On June 27, unimpeded by a Soviet veto, the Security Council asked all members of the United Nations to contribute "such assistance to the Republic of Korea as may be necessary to repel the armed attack and restore international peace and security in the area." By this time a small force of American troops under the command of General Douglas MacArthur, Supreme Allied Commander in Japan, had been dispatched to South Korea. The UN resolution made the Korean War a "police action" in which the United States acted technically as agent of the UN.

The initial North Korean attack quickly overwhelmed the small army of the Republic of Korea and the weak and untested force of Americans initially sent from Japan. Seoul, the South Korean capital, fell to the invaders on June 28 and the ROK and Americans were soon forced into a tight pocket around the port of Pusan. There they held on desperately until reinforcements began to arrive from the United States and other UN countries. In September the UN forces at Pusan under MacArthur's overall command made a surprise end run by sea around the North Koreans at Inchon and were soon driving the enemy north, back the way they had come. By October the UN forces reached the thirty-eighth parallel. Here the American Joint Chiefs of Staff advised MacArthur to stop, but the overconfident general believed that the Chinese would not intervene, or if they did, that they would be pushovers. He ordered his troops to advance rapidly toward the Korean–Chinese border at the Yalu River to evict the Communists from the whole of Korea.

MacArthur's army drove into a trap. On November 26 masses of Communist Chinese troops hit the ROK and UN forces in the Yalu valley. For a time they threatened to capture thousands of South Korea's defenders, and General Walton Walker, MacArthur's field commander, was forced into a headlong retreat south. The Chinese advance was finally checked by General Matthew Ridgeway, who succeeded Walker after he was killed in a jeep accident. Thereafter the two sides settled down to months of cruel and costly trench warfare close to the thirty-eighth parallel, resembling the military stalemate on the Western Front during World War I.

From the moment the Chinese intervened, MacArthur proposed bombing Chinese military bases in Manchuria and "unleashing" Chiang Kai-shek in Taiwan to invade the People's Republic. President Truman warned the general to desist from his bellicose pronouncements, but he refused. When Truman sought to open peace negotiations with the Communists in March 1951, MacArthur publicly threatened to escalate the war, thereby scuttling the talks. Several weeks later the general addressed a public letter to House Republican leader Joseph Martin declaring "there is no substitute for victory," and urging the United States to shift its strategic priorities from Europe to Asia. Truman now concluded that the general

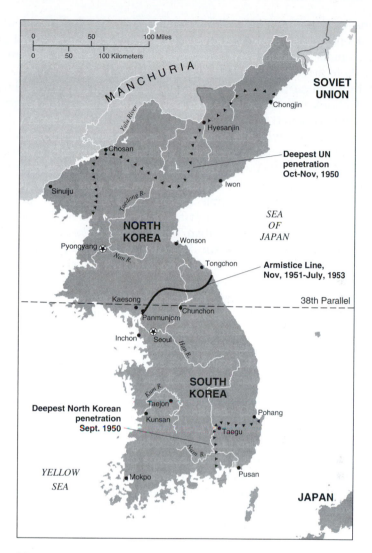

The Korean War Arena

had allowed his years as benevolent dictator in Japan to go to his head, and re-moved him from overall command, replacing him with Ridgeway, a man who obeyed orders.

To many conservatives MacArthur's dismissal was a sign of administration weakness in the global struggle against the Communist threat. When the general returned home he was welcomed as a hero. Thousands lined the streets of various cities as he passed through on his way to Washington and Congress invited him to speak to a joint session. A talented actor, the general eloquently defended his policies and bade a tearful farewell to the American people that concluded with the words of an old army song: "Old soldiers never die; they just fade away."

Republicans were soon talking about nominating him for president in 1952. The general's popularity waned after hearings before a congressional committee where the administration made an effective case for prudence in Korea He soon retired quietly to private life.

MacArthur's departure cleared the way for Korean peace talks. In July 1951 the United Nations and the Communist regime opened armistice negotiations at Kaesong, soon transferred to Panmunjom. The cease-fire discussions dragged on fruitlessly for two years while hundreds of Americans died in vicious small-scale patrol actions along the static front line. At home, frustrations grew. Not until after Stalin's death in March 1953 was a cease-fire agreement reached. On July 26 the fighting finally ceased.

Meanwhile, the American people had paid dearly for the "police action." At home the country returned to a war footing. Congress revived the draft and expanded the armed forces to more than 3 million men. The decision to rebuild a conventional military force pushed the defense budget to over $50 billion by 1952. The economy, which had been in the doldrums in 1949, quickly revived and then began to overheat. By 1951 the cost of living had risen about 12 percent despite the government's efforts to hold it down by price controls like those of World War II. The total cost in lives and wealth was immense for a struggle that accomplished so little. The United States had suffered 135,000 military casualties (including 33,000 killed) and spent an estimated $54 billion to achieve a stalemate. More than fifty years later Korea remains divided along a line just a few miles from the June 1950 border. And several thousand American troops remain in South Korea to deter the bellicose Communist North, and now nuclear-armed, from invading once again.

A Second "Red Scare"

The Cold War sorely tried the patience of Americans. The new enemy was elusive. The danger from Hitler and Tojo had been clear for all to see, and could be directly confronted and then defeated. But the United States could not take direct military action against the chief Cold War enemy, for that threatened nuclear catastrophe. Instead, the means deployed on both sides were prolonged campaigns of subversion, espionage, and propaganda, all unsuited to the American temperament. Few Americans knew much about the emerging Third World of former colonial states, and most tended to see the Soviet Union behind every social upheaval in Asia, Africa, or Latin America. And indeed, the Soviet Union did use wars of "national liberation" to expand its power and influence. During much of the 1950s, moreover, the Communists appeared to be winning the struggle for world control. Disinclined to make distinctions among Chinese Communists, Yugoslav Communists, and Soviet Communists, many Americans thought the whole world was turning uniformly "red."

The Enemy Within.   Because Communism seemed so obviously evil, atheistic, and abhorrently brutal, its Cold War successes awakened suspicions among Americans that along with the visible enemy in China and the Soviet Union there must be a disguised and hidden one operating internally to undermine anti-Communist resistance. Many suspected that Communists were hiding behind familiar American institutions, secretly supported by respectable people in high places here and in Europe. However simplistic this analysis of the Cold War might be, it gained currency among Americans during the 1950s and beyond.

The distrustful public mood was reinforced by real Soviet espionage operations in the United States. In 1950 the British uncovered the doings of Klaus Fuchs, a German refugee atomic physicist who had been employed at Los Alamos on the Manhattan Project during the war and had transmitted atomic secrets to the Soviet Union. Fuchs's detection led to an enlisted man at the Los Alamos Atomic energy center who, when questioned, accused his brother-in-law and sister, Julius and Ethel Rosenberg, of passing atomic secrets to the Russians. Although the political left believed them innocent, the Rosenbergs were eventually convicted of espionage and executed in what had become an international cause célèbre. In March 1950 Judith Coplon and her Soviet agent-lover, Valentin Gubitchev, were convicted of spying. Gubitchev was deported and Coplon sentenced to jail.

Most disturbing of all the espionage cases was the apparent betrayal of the country by a prominent public servant, Alger Hiss. Hiss had served in the State Department during the 1930s and was part of the staff that accompanied Roosevelt to Yalta. In 1948 journalist Whittaker Chambers, an admitted former Communist, told the House Committee on Un-American Activities (HUAC) that he and Hiss had been members of a prewar Soviet spy ring in Washington and that Hiss had given secret government documents to the Russians. Summoned before HUAC and closely questioned by Congressman Richard Nixon, Hiss denied that he had ever known Chambers or stolen official secrets. Because of the statute of limitations, Hiss could no longer be indicted for espionage. He sued Chambers for libel, however, and in the trial Chambers produced documents that he claimed Hiss had stolen. The federal government now tried Hiss for perjury, and in the second of two trials he was found guilty of lying under oath and sentenced to five years in prison.

Conservatives seized on the Hiss case to attack the New Deal of which he had been a part. Alien to the American way, it represented, they said, "twenty years of treason." Nor were the Democrats any better now. They were still protecting traitors, they charged. The Truman administration, noted Congressman Nixon, "was extremely anxious that nothing happen to Mr. Hiss." The political left, by contrast, came to Hiss's defense as another innocent martyr to Cold War hysteria. Liberals at times responded to the charges against Hiss, and other accused spies, as if Soviet espionage against the United States was inconceivable or incapable of posing a threat to the nation.

McCarthyism.
But in truth, the public often confused spying with subversion. Many Americans failed to distinguish between stealing government secrets and merely advocating ideas that were, or seemed to be, "un-American." Before long the country was in the grip of a full-scale panic that endangered the civil liberties of many Americans.

The Truman administration was not innocent of encouraging the hysteria. Afraid to appear "soft on communism," Truman in March 1947 issued Executive Order 9835 establishing a program to eliminate "disloyal" federal employees who, because of their politics or their personal or sexual habits, might pose security risks. As part of the same executive order, he authorized the attorney general to indict eleven top officials of the American Communist Party on charges of violating the Smith Act of 1940 by advocating overthrow of the government by force. After a tumultuous trial in New York, in which the Communist Party sought to indict the government for its Cold War policies, all the defendants were convicted and sentenced to prison.

Truman did not want the antisubversive drive to go too far, however. In 1950 he vetoed the McCarran Internal Security Act requiring registration of Communist and Communist-front organizations, excluding from the country would-be immigrants who belonged to a totalitarian party, forbidding the employment of Communists in defense work, and providing for the internment of radicals during national emergencies. "In a free country," Truman declared in his veto message, "we punish men for the crimes they commit, but never for the opinions they have." These were stirring words, but Congress overrode his veto. Whether he acted out of conviction or from fear, Truman cannot escape blame then for having stimulated the excessive reaction to internal subversion that marked the decade.

It was perhaps inevitable that a demagogue would appear to exploit Americans' fears and suspicions for his own purposes. The man was Joseph R. McCarthy, the Republican junior senator from Wisconsin. Like many demagogues, McCarthy had his attractive side. He genuinely liked people and could never understand why they often despised him. Though he was a scrappy man, willing to take on anyone, he did not make his political foes into personal enemies. But he was also a liar, a petty tyrant, a crude opportunist, and an insensitive boor who could not comprehend that a democratic society required a modicum of civility and political decency to function.

In early 1950 McCarthy was in political trouble. Elected to the Senate over a weak opponent in the 1946 Republican sweep, he had acquired a reputation as an opportunist who exchanged votes and influence for favors from business groups and had even championed the Nazi SS in a case involving the murder of American prisoners-of-war during World War II. Clearly, the junior senator had to find an issue that would give him broad exposure and a good press if he wanted to stay in Washington. He quickly found his issue in the country's rising anti-Communist concerns.

In Wheeling, West Virginia, on February 9, McCarthy opened his reelection drive with a speech devoted to the dangers of communism at home and abroad. The United States, he told the local Republican women's club, found itself "in a position of impotency" in international affairs because of "the traitorous actions" of men in high government posts. The State Department, especially, was "thoroughly infested with Communists," bright young men from the privileged classes who had betrayed their country. He could, he said, name 205 members of the State Department whom the secretary of state knew to be members of the Communist Party.

McCarthy could do nothing of the sort. His list was based on sources long out of date. But the press began to take notice of his sensational charges, and the country was soon in an excited mood. Soon afterward, while testifying before a Senate subcommittee, McCarthy announced dramatically that the "top Soviet espionage

Senator Joseph McCarthy uses "visuals" to show supposed power of communism in the United States as Joseph Welch expresses his skepticism.

agent" in the United States was Owen Lattimore, a professor of Far Eastern affairs at Johns Hopkins University, who had been a State Department adviser on China policy. The testimony of witnesses failed to support McCarthy's claims, but many Americans, deeply chagrined at the recent "loss" of China, were willing to believe that Lattimore and men like him had betrayed the nation. For days the senator made the headlines. In a few short months the word "McCarthyism" had been added to the language as a term for irresponsible mudslinging and defamation.

McCarthy and his cause were at first genuinely popular. Opinion polls in 1950 showed that the senator had the approval of 50 percent of the American people. McCarthy's strong political base was confirmed when, in the 1950 congressional election, he helped defeat for reelection Democratic Senator Millard Tydings of Maryland, one of his severest critics. His strength with the voters made McCarthyism an effective weapon for conservative Republicans to use against liberals and Democrats. As such it was sanctioned by many GOP leaders, including "Mr. Republican" himself, Robert Taft. So pervasive was McCarthy's popularity that even liberal Democrats had to reckon with it. In the early 1950s the young Massachusetts congressman John F. Kennedy noted that "Joe . . . may have something."

McCarthyism became a mood and an attitude that penetrated many layers of American life in these years, with malign consequences. Besides McCarthy's own probes, the House Committee on Un-American Activities and the Senate Internal Security Subcommittee regularly investigated Communist infiltration of American institutions. HUAC's well-publicized public hearings usually focused on very visible areas such as the movies, the universities, the churches, and the unions. The committee forced men and women under subpoena to answer charges, often anonymous, that they had been members of "subversive" organizations. These groups need not be formally Communist; they could be "Communist fronts" included on the "Attorney General's List" of several hundred suspect organizations. HUAC did not punish offenders directly, but many of those called before the committee were injured professionally and lost their jobs.

Private organizations and local officials quickly joined the antisubversive clamor. The broadcasting industry refused to hire anyone for radio or television work who was listed in *Red Channels*, a volume compiled by three former FBI agents that claimed to identify entertainers and media writers with past or existing radical affiliations. In Hollywood there were unofficial blacklists of performers, screenwriters, and directors whom no studio would employ. The theater, too, was rife with accusers and lists of "disloyal" people. Universities imposed loyalty oaths on faculty; states and local governments required clerks, typists, laborers, and officials to swear they had never been members of the Communist Party.

The prevailing hysteria over Communism and subversion cast a shadow over American life. The fear of attack and the possible consequences for their careers and personal lives undermined creative men and women. Many former political activists retreated to conservatism or became apolitical, a process that reinforced the shift of the political spectrum to the right. Even ordinary citizens were deeply affected. When vigilantes were attacking every dissenting view and every dissenter as Communist, it seemed wise to keep silent and repress opinions that could be considered irreverent. Fear of attack as a dangerous subversive, then, undoubtedly reinforced the 1950s American retreat into privatism.

After Eisenhower's victory and McCarthy's reelection in 1952, observers expected the senator to quiet down. The Republicans were now in office, and attacks on government officials would hurt McCarthy's own party. But he refused to stop. In February 1953 he accused officials of the United States Information Agency, the information arm of the State Department, of attempting to undermine the American propaganda war against the Soviet Union. Panicked, Secretary of State John Foster Dulles ordered dozens of books by authors of "doubtful loyalty" removed from the agency's shelves.

McCarthy's Downfall.

In 1954, with his popularity at its peak, the Wisconsin senator accused Secretary of the Army, Robert T. Stevens, of approving the promotion of Irving Peress, an army dentist who had once been a member of the radical American Labor Party. The promotion was actually a routine reranking of all drafted medical personnel, but in the next few weeks McCarthy made "Who promoted Peress?" a rallying cry for dedicated anti-Communists. The army responded by accusing McCarthy of using his influence to gain preferential treatment at Fort Monmouth for G. David Schine, a draftee who had been a member of the senator's staff and a protégé of Roy Cohn, his committee counsel.

Eventually Congress voted to hold an investigation of the charges before McCarthy's own committee with Republican Senator Karl Mundt of South Dakota presiding. On April 22, 1954, the hearings commenced, and when they were over eight weeks later, McCarthy had run his course. Before the glaring lights of the television cameras, the senator seemed like a scowling Hollywood villain. He badgered witnesses and insulted them; he constantly interrupted the proceedings with points of order and irrelevancies. Many television viewers in their living rooms concluded he was a hateful man.

McCarthy's stock quickly plummeted. On December 2, 1954, the Senate passed a resolution condemning him for bringing the Senate into disrepute. The censure motion entailed no legal penalties, but from that day on, his colleagues shunned him, and when he rose to speak, they left the Senate chamber. Worst of all, the media began to ignore him. No matter what he said, he could no longer make the headlines. On May 2, 1957, he died of a liver ailment, unlamented by most Americans.

McCarthy's Legacy.   McCarthy was gone, but in various guises the feelings he fed on and the movement he helped launch survived. In 1958 Robert Welch, a Massachusetts candy manufacturer, founded the John Birch Society, a far-right anti-Communist organization that claimed the entire nation was riddled with secret Communists. Well-supplied with money from southwestern oil, cattle, and electronics magnates, the Birch Society attracted people obsessed with the Communist danger and every opponent of change or novelty. Its local chapters fought against the fluoridation of drinking water, instigated recall elections against liberal school board members, attacked "subversive" college professors, demanded the impeachment of Chief Justice Earl Warren, and resisted efforts to impose gun controls. Even more extreme was George Lincoln Rockwell's American Nazi Party and similar neo-Nazi hate groups, and semisecret paramilitary organizations such as the Minute Men, which collected arms and held drills in expectation of an imminent Soviet invasion or an internal Communist takeover.

McCarthyism also affected United States foreign policy. America's refusal to accord diplomatic recognition to Communist China, for example, was in part a response to pressure from the McCarthyite Communist hunters. Even more serious, perhaps, fear of being attacked for "losing Indochina," as Truman had "lost China," would help propel Lyndon Johnson into one of the most unfortunate military episodes in American history.

The Election of 1960.   With the popular Ike about to retire, 1960 seemed a promising year for the Democrats, and from the outset they fielded an array of eager and able candidates—the liberal Minnesota senator, Hubert Humphrey; the still popular Adlai Stevenson; Lyndon Johnson, the powerful Senate Majority Leader from Texas; and the young senator from Massachusetts, John F. Kennedy.

Kennedy's qualifications for president were not entirely convincing. The oldest surviving son of Wall Street operator Joseph Kennedy, he seemed more interested in wine, women, and song than in public service. He had returned from the war a young navy hero and had been pushed by his ambitious father to run for Congress. As a member of the House and then the Senate, Kennedy had been a mediocre legislator, not generally admired by his colleagues. But his most serious disqualification to many voters was his religion. The Kennedys were Catholics and the last time a Catholic had run for president—Al Smith in 1928—he had been badly beaten. Anti-Catholicism, though it had diminished since 1928, still ran strong in the rural Midwest and the South, and it did not seem likely that a Catholic, even in 1960, could overcome the ingrained religious prejudice of the heartland.

But Kennedy had several things going for him as well. He was handsome, well-spoken, well-educated, and rich. The rich part was important, for money talked eloquently in politics even in 1960. The Kennedys could pay for chartered jets, TV time, and newspaper advertisements far beyond their opponents' means. When Kennedy defeated Hubert Humphrey in the West Virginia primary, the nomination was all but clinched. Kennedy won on the first ballot at the Los Angeles Democratic convention and, in a stunning show of political pragmatism, turned to Texan Lyndon Johnson to balance the ticket.

The Republican candidate was Vice President Richard Nixon. Liberals considered him unprincipled and had long called him "Tricky Dick." But as vice president he had acquired some stature as a foreign-policy expert, in part for the "kitchen debate" with Soviet leader Khrushchev, when, at a gleaming model American kitchen on exhibition at a Moscow trade fair, he had scored points for American capitalism. Henry Cabot Lodge, Jr., the UN ambassador, got the Republican vice presidential slot.

The contest was the most exciting in a decade. Nixon plugged his own experience, especially in foreign affairs, and called his opponent a lightweight. The vice president never mentioned Kennedy's Catholicism, but clearly it was on the minds of many traditional Protestants. Kennedy partially neutralized the issue by appearing before the Greater Houston Ministerial Association in September and eloquently endorsing the separation of church and state. The contest may have been decided by a set of TV debates between the two candidates during September and October. In the first one especially, the more telegenic Kennedy, though the younger man, seemed poised and articulate. Nixon, looking unshaven, appeared nervous and tired. The election marked the true onset of the "tube" as the key media instrument in American politics.

The election was one of the closest on record. The Massachusetts senator received only 100,000 more popular votes than Nixon out of almost 69 million cast, and he carried fewer, though larger, states than did his adversary. There is some evidence, moreover, that in both Texas and Illinois the Democratic machines altered the popular votes in favor of the party's candidate. Nixon might have challenged the results but chose to accept them rather than force a major constitutional crisis.

Conclusions

During the 1950s Americans sought escape from public problems in private pursuits. Having suffered through the nation's worst depression and its most agonizing war, they could not help regarding the postwar era as an improvement. With all its flaws, prosperity was real, and they turned from politics to revel in the pleasures of growing abundance and domestic life. The pursuit of private goals and satisfactions and the avoidance of controversy after 1945 was to some extent, then, a predictable consequence of the surprising success of the postwar economy.

It was also the result of fear. Communism loomed over half the planet and seemed to be expanding daily. Moreover, for the first time since the Ottoman threat to Christendom in the seventeenth century, the West had to reckon with the competition of non-Europeans with values and cultures different from its own.

It was difficult to deal with this challenge from abroad. An all-out military response, in the era of nuclear weapons, was precluded by considerations of both humanity and self-preservation. The only valid answer, we can now see, was patient diplomatic and intellectual struggle. But Americans are not a patient people, and the resulting frustration and anxiety brought out their worst side as expressed in McCarthyism. McCarthyism in turn engendered further fear and insecurity. Intimidated by public events that seemed to threaten their safety, and exposed to the pleasures of consumerism as never before, Americans turned inward and sought personal, safe satisfactions.

Yet despite the appeal of privatism and prudence, by the mid-1950s acute observers could detect signs of change. In 1956 a popular sociologist, John Keats, wrote *The Crack in the Picture Window*, attacking suburbia as deadening to the mind and spirit. By the end of the decade a new cultural bohemia composed of "Beat" poets and novelists had begun to appear in San Francisco and New York. For bohemians, the Beats were unusually apolitical and "cool," but they took drugs, wore sandals, and were sexually promiscuous. Clearly, the times were beginning to change.

ONLINE RESOURCES

"Readings in the 1950s" *http://www.english.upenn.edu/~afilreis/50s/home.html* This site contains primary sources that reflect the anti-Communist ideology that permeated the Cold-war era. Sources on the site include transcripts from testimony from anti-Communist hearings, magazine articles that address the cultural anxiety of nuclear threat, and numerous links to other sites.

"The Truman Doctrine" *http://www.yale.edu/lawweb/avalon/trudoc.htm* Read President Harry Truman's address before a joint session of Congress in which the "Truman Doctrine," or using U.S. economic power to ensure the freedom of all nations, was born.

"Korean War" *http://www.nps.gov/kwvm/war/korea.htm* On this site sponsored by the National Park Service, read about the origins of the Korean War, the conflict year by year, and the context of the homefront. It also features information on the Korean War veterans' memorial.

"Levittown: Documents of an Ideal Suburb" *http://www.uic.edu/~pbhales/Levittown.html* Discover the cultural history of Levittown through contemporary photographs of the suburb and its inhabitants, construction of the houses, family life, and suburb-centered recreation.

"Rebel Poets of the 1950s" *http://www.npg.si.edu/exh/rebels/poets.htm* Part of an exhibit on the Beat movement, this site interprets the Beats and their impact. Also, see paintings and photographs of Beat poets.

"NSC68" *http://www.mtholyoke.edu/acad/intrel/nsc68.htm* This site features a National Security Council report ordered by President Eisenhower that examines U.S. programs for national defense, the risks of nuclear war, and Soviet preparedness.

Beyond the Playing Field: Jackie Robinson, Civil Rights Advocate *http://www.archives.gov/education/lessons/jackie-robinson/* Through this Web site, see the activist side of baseball great Jackie Robinson. Through letters written to American presidents and his numerous quotes, these archives record Robinson's quest for racial justice.

The Cold War and Red Scare in Washington State *http://www.washington.edu/uwired/outreach/cspn/curcan/main.html* Produced by the Center for the Study of the Pacific Northwest, this site explains how McCarthyism played out in Washington State and affected the lives of many of its citizens. The site contains a national overview as well as documents that pertain to statewide anti-Communist committees.

The Fifties at Home *http://www.sos.state.mi.us/history/museum/explore/museums/hismus/1900-75/fifties/50shome.html* Take a virtual tour of a typical 1950s home on the Michigan Historical Museum System Web page. See photos and read about how 1950s consumerism shaped the home and its contents.

History and Politics Out Loud: I Have a Dream Speech *http://hpol.org/record.php?id=72* Hear the speech of Martin Luther King, Jr., delivered at the March on Washington in 1963. A transcript of this speech and other of King's addresses are also available at this site.

28

The Dissenting Sixties

Why Protest in the "Great Society"?

1954	French defeated at Dien Bien Phu; Geneva Accords
1957	Russians launch Sputnik into orbit; Martin Luther King, Jr., founds the Southern Christian Leadership Conference (SCLC)
1959	Castro overthrows Batista regime in Cuba; U-2 incident
1960	Student Nonviolent Coordinating Committee (SNCC) founded; Birth-control pill introduced; John F. Kennedy elected president
1961	Peace Corps founded; Kennedy announces the Alliance for Progress; CIA and anti-Castro Cubans launch the Bay of Pigs invasion of Cuba; Berlin Wall built; Kennedy sends American troops to Vietnam
1962	Cuban Missile Crisis
1962, 1963	Attorney General Robert Kennedy enforces integration of state universities in Mississippi and Alabama
1963	Civil rights demonstrators numbering 250,000 march on Washington; Kennedy assassinated; Lyndon Johnson becomes president
1964	Johnson launches the War on Poverty; China explodes its first atom bomb; Congress passes the Civil Rights Act; Tonkin Gulf Resolution
1964–65	Berkeley Free Speech Movement sets precedent for major campus revolts
1965	Johnson orders the bombing of North Vietnam; Great Society legislation and agencies: Elementary and Secondary Education Act, Medicare, Department of Housing and Urban Development (HUD), Omnibus Housing Act, Voting Rights Act, National Foundations of the Arts and Humanities, Higher Education Act, Metropolitan Area Redevelopment Act, Truth in Lending Act
1965–67	Black riots in Los Angeles, Detroit, Newark
1966	Highway Safety Act; Betty Friedan organizes the National Organization for Women (NOW)
1968	My Lai Massacre; Martin Luther King and Robert Kennedy assassinated; Street riots at Democratic National Convention in Chicago; Richard Nixon elected president
1969	American Indian activists occupy Alcatraz Island; Woodstock and Altamont rock festivals; Americans land on the moon

In April 1968 a group of young actors appeared in a new musical at the Biltmore Theater in New York. The play, *Hair*, glorified every rebellious, nonconformist theme of the decade. *Hair* proclaimed that the "Age of Aquarius" was at hand, that "harmony and understanding" and "crystal revelation" would soon prevail. A song called "Sodomy" described the presumed delights of oral sex and masturbation; "Air" detailed the horrors of air pollution; and "Walking in Space" was simultaneously about the space program and "tripping" on mind-altering drugs. The musical theme of "Hare Krishna" was borrowed from a Hindu sect whose orange-robed adherents could be seen ringing bells and chanting on the streets and airports of American cities in these years. The high point of the play's performance came at the end of the first act, when members of the biracial cast removed all their clothes while singing "Beads, Flowers, Freedom and Happiness."

To a Rip Van Winkle of 1948 awakening twenty years later, *Hair* would have been a profound shock. Radical in politics, "liberated" in social vision, ecstatic and orgiastic in cultural texture, it was almost the antithesis of the values Americans had accepted in the years between 1945 and 1960. Only in the darkest corners of American life at the time had there been a hint that such things even existed. But in 1968 the members of the *Hair* cast became culture heroes who, according to theater critic Clive Barnes of the *New York Times*, expressed "the authentic voice of today."

How had this startling transformation come about? America in the 1950s was a prosperous, self-satisfied, cautious society. Why did it change so drastically, so quickly? Was it primarily the inexorable swing of the cultural pendulum: having moved so far toward conformity, it could only move toward revolt? Did prosperity, as in the past, breed its special forms of discontent with the status quo? Were outside forces and events responsible?

Politics in Camelot

The decade began with a breath of fresh political air. The thousand days of the Kennedy presidency have been likened to Camelot, the mythical court of King Arthur where, "for one brief shining moment," there flourished an enchanted realm of brave men and beautiful women worthy of the world's admiration. The new president was handsome, articulate, and young, the first chief executive born in the twentieth century. We now know that he was not the personal paragon of the Camelot legend. But for the first time since FDR, the White House became a lively and interesting place, and the public delighted in the change.

Kennedy appealed especially to the idealism of young people. One of his first moves was to propose a Peace Corps of young men and women who would invest their skills and part of their lives in working abroad among the sick and poor of Third World nations. Soon afterward he announced the Alliance for Progress, a foreign aid proposal to pump $20 billion into Latin America to raise economic output and redistribute it among the hemisphere's poor and oppressed.

Kennedy Foreign Policy.   However idealistic in tone, Kennedy's Alliance for Progress did not fundamentally alter "containment" as the core of American foreign policy. Yet Kennedy and his advisers brought new ideas to the American conduct of foreign affairs.

In his 1960 campaign Kennedy had warned that his Republican predecessor had allowed the Soviet Union to build more missiles than the United States and that this "missile gap" threatened the nation's security. After taking office he found that the gap did not exist. But the new president had more substantial objections to Eisenhower's weapons policy as well. Ike and his chief foreign-policy adviser, John Foster Dulles, had neglected conventional weapons and built up stockpiles of hydrogen bombs. This meant that in the event of a serious international challenge, America's only credible response was nuclear attack. While this might be appropriate for a full-scale Soviet assault on NATO, would we use "massive deterrence" against Soviet aggression at such pressure points as Berlin, the Middle East, Africa, or southeast Asia? Clearly, the risks of nuclear holocaust were simply too great for the interests at stake. In effect, then, the lack of conventional American military forces only invited Soviet subversion all over the world.

To avoid these unacceptable alternatives of doom or surrender, Kennedy and Secretary of Defense Robert McNamara proposed a "flexible response." The United States must build up its conventional forces and prepare itself to use counterinsurgency tactics to tailor its response to the extent of the threat. To implement the new policy, the administration expanded the army from eleven to sixteen combat divisions and began retraining troops for jungle and guerrilla fighting. These innovations were expensive, and during the Kennedy years the defense budget grew by 25 percent.

Early Tests.

The first attempt at counterinsurgency was a humiliating fiasco. In April 1961 Kennedy gave the green light to an operation conceived under Eisenhower to land a small force of armed insurgents at the Bay of Pigs in Cuba to overthrow Fidel Castro, the charismatic young leader who had toppled the strongman Fulgencio Batista in 1959 and installed an anti-American government in Havana. According to the CIA, even a small invasion would trigger a general uprising that would knock the Castro regime to the ground, but the predicted uprising did not occur; the invaders were quickly pinned down on the beach by Castro's forces. To avoid deeper involvement in an embarrassing enterprise, the president refused to provide American air and military support to rescue them. In a matter of days they were all killed or captured, and the United States found itself condemned as a bully, and an ineffectual one at that.

Kennedy's first direct contact with the Soviets was not much happier. Soviet Premier Nikita Khrushchev, Stalin's successor, though not a paranoid tyrant like his predecessor, did not intend to surrender any of his nation's interests. His 1955 meeting with Eisenhower at Geneva—the first U.S.–Soviet "summit"—had produced nothing concrete, but its cordial and cooperative tone (the "Spirit of Geneva") cheered the world, uneasy over the superpower rivalry. This quickly dissipated, however, when, in November 1958, Khrushchev escalated Cold War tensions over Berlin.

That city, divided between east and west zones, was a Communist sore point. Between 1949 and 1958 almost 3 million Germans had fled Communist East Germany for West Germany, and to prevent further loss of productive people the

Communist authorities had sealed off most of the two Germanies' common frontier. Berlin, however, remained open, and its Western zone continued to be a magnet for disaffected East Germans. Hundreds escaped daily to West Berlin, and each person who fled the German Democratic Republic advertised the superiority of the capitalist over the Communist way of life. Related to the problem of Berlin was the refusal of the Western powers to sign a peace treaty that accepted the division of Germany, and their insistence that they would deal only with the Soviet Union, not the East German officials, in matters concerned with Berlin. On November 10, 1960, Khrushchev announced that the Soviet Union intended to transfer authority over the eastern zone of Berlin to the East German authorities, thus forcing the Western powers to deal with them. Implied was the possibility of another Berlin blockade.

Fortunately, the Soviet premier withdrew his threat soon after, and for a time the danger of superpower confrontation over Berlin receded. Then in May 1960, just prior to a scheduled summit conference between Eisenhower and Khrushchev, the Soviets announced that they had shot down an American U-2 spy plane over the Soviet Union and captured its CIA civilian employee pilot, Francis Gary Powers. Caught with the goods, Ike reluctantly admitted that the U.S. had sponsored the spying mission. Khrushchev denounced the spy flight and, in effect, canceled the summit meeting. In January the next year he ominously declared his country's "unlimited support" to "peoples fighting for their liberation." The Cold War, in the form of "wars of national liberation," would now be extended around the world.

Kennedy's encounter with Khrushchev at Vienna in June 1961 was an unnerving experience. The Bay of Pigs fiasco led the Soviet leader to conclude that the young American president was weak and inexperienced and could be bullied. At Vienna Khrushchev was abrupt, even insulting. Berlin was a "bone in the throat" of the Soviet Union, he said. If the Western powers failed to sign an agreement that accepted the legitimacy of the communist German Democratic Republic, he would turn over administration of Berlin to its authorities, who could well end free communication between the city and West Germany. If the United States chose to go to war over this, so be it. When Khrushchev returned to Moscow he delivered a number of warlike speeches and raised the Soviet military budget.

Though shaken by Khrushchev's threats, Kennedy refused to be intimidated. He asked Congress for an additional $3.5 billion for defense, announced the call-up of army reserves and National Guard units, and urged Americans to build bomb shelters against a possible nuclear war. Public anxiety soared.

Meanwhile, in Berlin the stream of refugees to the West became a flood. To staunch this hemorrhage, on August 14, 1961, East German authorities began to erect a high wall of brick, concrete blocks, and barbed wire between their sector and the western powers'. Anyone caught trying to scale this wall would be shot. For the next twenty-eight years the Berlin Wall would symbolize the barriers separating the two Cold War antagonists.

For a while longer the tension continued. In early September the Soviets defiantly resumed above-ground nuclear testing on a massive scale, releasing enormous quantities of radioactive matter into the atmosphere. In retaliation Kennedy authorized the resumption of American nuclear testing, though only under-ground. Then Khrushchev backed down. At the end of the month in Moscow he told a visiting diplomat from Belgium, a NATO nation: "I'm not trying to put you in an impossible situation; I know very well that you can't let yourself be stepped on." In mid-October he informed the Communist Party Congress that the Western powers appeared conciliatory and he, accordingly, would defer a peace treaty with East Germany. The second Berlin crisis was over.

The Cuban Missile Crisis.

But Khrushchev recklessly forced one more major confrontation in his war of nerves against the United States and its president. The Soviet leader knew that the United States actually surpassed the Soviet Union in its ability to deliver nuclear weapons. Hoping to equalize the imbalance and to protect Cuba, his new ally, against American attack, a year and a half after the Bay of Pigs invasion he quietly dispatched Soviet troops and missile techni-cians to Cuba. These Soviet forces brought with them two sorts of missiles: strate-gic SS-4s of medium range, capable of reaching Washington, D.C., and New York, and short-range tactical missiles that could destroy any American invasion force landing on Cuba's beaches. The strategic missiles remained under Moscow's di-rect control, but the Soviet commander in Cuba was authorized, without Moscow's approval, to launch the tactical missiles to stop an American invasion if he felt it necessary. As military experts—Soviet, Cuban, and American—concluded thirty years later, after the Cold War had ended, this was a prescrip-tion for world nuclear disaster.

Even without full knowledge of the risks, Kennedy and his advisers recog-nized that the world stood on the edge of catastrophe. From the moment Ameri-can intelligence revealed the presence of the missiles in mid-October, a special executive committee of the National Security Council (Excom) met in continuous session to debate what course to take. The bellicose Air Force General Curtis LeMay favored an immediate attack on Cuba to capture and destroy the missiles. Defense Secretary Robert McNamara and the president's brother, Attorney Gener-al Robert F. Kennedy, warned that such an attack would probably kill Soviet citi-zens and be viewed as well as an assault by a giant against a weak neighbor. Instead, he advised a blockade of the island to prevent missiles still on their way by ship from being landed. The president rejected the aggressive LeMay course. On the evening of October 22, 1962, he appeared on national television to tell the American people about the Soviet missiles and explain that the government had decided to "quarantine" Cuba to prevent delivery of more. If the Soviets tried to run the blockade, the American navy would shoot.

The announcement startled the nation and the world. A wrong move by ei-ther of the superpowers might plunge the world into nuclear war. Americans generally supported the president's course, but outside the United States many people charged that the American president was gambling with the very exis-tence of humanity.

What would the Soviets do when their missile-carrying ships, fast ap-proaching Cuba, encountered the American blockade vessels? For four days the world held its breath. In Cuba, Soviet technicians worked feverishly to complete the missile launch pads, and began to assemble crated Soviet bombers. Washington kept NATO leaders informed of minute-by-minute developments. Then the break came. On October 26 Khrushchev sent a long message to the American government admitting for the first time that Soviet missiles were being installed in Cuba. The Soviet Union, Khrushchev stated, would send no more missiles if the United States agreed not to attack Cuba. At the same time he publicly released an offer to remove the missiles in Cuba if the United States removed its missiles from NATO member Turkey, close to the USSR. Overtly ignoring the issue of Turkish bases, Kennedy agreed not to attack Cuba if the Soviet missiles were taken out. Khrushchev did not insist on his initial terms.* Soviet vessels nearing Cuba stopped and reversed course. The crisis was over. The world sighed with collective relief.

Vietnam Intervention Begins.   Even as world attention focused on Cuba and Berlin, a disastrous U.S.–Communist confrontation was unfolding in Southeast Asia. The setting for the debacle was Vietnam, Cambodia, and Laos, nations carved out of French Indochina in the years following the Japanese surrender in 1945 and made "associated states" of the French Union—that is, dependent French protectorates. In the northern part of Vietnam, however, Ho Chi Minh, a Communist nationalist, refused to accept continued French rule. Ho established a "Democratic Republic" with its capital in Hanoi and claimed to speak for all Vietnamese, including those in the south. The French attempted to subdue Ho and his Vietminh forces, but in 1954 they suffered a major military defeat at Dien Bien Phu. Soon after, they agreed to a division of Vietnam along the seventeenth parallel, pending a 1956 election that would decide the future government for a united country. This decision was ratified by a meeting of the major powers at Geneva, but the election was never held. Fearing that a free ballot might topple his anti-Communist regime, South Vietnamese Premier Ngo Dinh Diem, an American client, dithered and delayed and, when the Eisenhower administration failed to exert pressure to coerce him, postponed the election indefinitely.

The French military defeat awakened American fears of further Communist expansion in Southeast Asia. As Eisenhower explained in 1954, the countries of the region were like "dominos"; if "you knock over one . . . the last one . . . will go over very quickly." That September the United States negotiated a treaty with Australia, Great Britain, France, New Zealand, Thailand, the Philippines, and Pakistan pledging joint action against Communist aggression in the region. Though designed to emulate NATO, SEATO (the South East Asia Treaty Organization) lacked a unified military command and proved ineffectual in checking East Asian Communist expansion.

Though pressured to do so, Eisenhower refused to send troops to the region. But the United States supplied war matériel and economic aid on a large scale to pro-Western or neutral regimes in Laos, Cambodia, and South Vietnam to help them resist Communist takeovers. American policy was at best a partial success.

*We now know that Kennedy promised in private, however, to remove the Turkish missiles at some later time.

In Laos the Pathet Lao, a Communist-led nationalist movement, grew more powerful and threatened to overthrow the neutralist government. In South Vietnam the Diem regime in Saigon failed to pacify the country. Diem and his supporters proved corrupt and unpopular with the country's Buddhists and peasants, and before long the "National Liberation Front" (Vietcong), a Communist guerrilla movement supplied with arms by Ho Chi Minh in North Vietnam, attracted a following among the rural people. Allied with Ho, the Vietcong would seek to unite both Vietnams under the Communist government in Hanoi.

Kennedy, like Eisenhower, adopted a containment policy for Asia and, despite misgivings, for a time continued to help Diem against his Communist enemies. Unlike his predecessor, however, JFK was willing to send American personnel as well as money and supplies. In May 1961 he dispatched 400 Special Forces troops, trained in counterinsurgency tactics, to South Vietnam. By October 1962 over 16,000 Americans, military and civilian, were in South Vietnam advising assisting the Diem government, and, though none of these were combat troops, the number of Americans injured or killed had reached almost 600.

The Kennedy administration could not refrain from intervening in South Vietnamese affairs in other ways. In late 1963, convinced that Diem, who favored his family and persecuted the Buddhists, had lost the support of his people and could no longer effectively defend South Vietnam against the Communists, the president gave the green light for a coup to a group of South Vietnamese generals. Diem was captured fleeing the presidential palace in Saigon and assassinated. Unfortunately, the military men who replaced him soon proved no more competent, tolerant, or honest—and no more capable of rallying the South Vietnamese people to the side of the Saigon regime and against the Vietcong.

JFK and Civil Rights.

On civil rights the Kennedy administration's record was mixed. JFK had received his margin of victory in 1960 from blacks in the North. But he feared driving white southerners out of the Democratic party if he acted too aggressively to advance civil rights. Under the aegis of his brother, Robert, the Attorney General, the Justice Department enforced provisions of the 1957 and 1960 Civil Rights Acts and helped get thousands of black southerners on the voting rolls. Yet many civil rights leaders believed the administration lagged in its commitment to racial justice and was moving too slowly. The government's caution particularly offended the young civil rights activists who were coming to the fore as the sixties unfolded.

The new militancy dated from early 1960, when four black students at North Carolina Agricultural and Technical College at Greensboro took seats at the lunch counter of the local Woolworth's. They were denied service. The next day the students returned with friends and resumed their sit-in. Day after day they continued their protest against segregation despite the catcalls and jeers of unfriendly whites. In a few days press reports helped spread the sit-in movement all over the South. The new activism encouraged the formation, with Martin Luther King, Jr.'s sponsorship, of the Student Nonviolent Coordinating Committee. At the outset SNCC accepted King's commitment to a nonviolent, biracial approach to civil rights, but it was not clear how long the young militants would agree to the guidance of their elders.

A major test of the administration's dedication to civil rights came with the "freedom rides." Seeking to challenge segregation at depots, white and black civil rights activists, under the auspices of the Congress of Racial Equality (CORE), traveled through the South by bus during May 1961. White supremacists threatened the freedom riders wherever they stopped, and in South Carolina and Alabama white toughs beat them severely. The activists appealed to the Justice Department to protect them from their assailants. The government complied, but too slowly to suit the young firebrands. The riders had to cut their plans short.

Yet at times the administration's intervention served the civil rights cause well. In 1963 King and the SCLC launched a campaign in Birmingham to end downtown segregation of eating places and other public facilities and create jobs for qualified blacks. The SCLC leaders shrewdly estimated that to succeed they must arouse the liberal conscience of the nation by showing the brutal face of racism.

Birmingham seemed the ideal setting. The city was thoroughly segregated and racist. At one point Martin Luther King declared that when in Birmingham he felt he was "within a cab ride of being in Johannesburg, South Africa," the capital of the viciously racist Afrikaner regime. As anticipated, the city authorities cooperated. The police threw King in jail where he composed an eloquent 19-page letter in reply to white ministers who had urged the civil rights leaders to go slow in their demands. King chided the ministers for urging delay, noting that it was easy enough for them but not for people who had "seen vicious mobs lynch [their] mothers at will and drown [their] sisters and brothers at whim," who had seen "hate-filled policemen curse, kick, and even kill [their] brothers and sisters." Smuggled out of jail, the "Letter from a Birmingham Jail" became one of the most effective documents of the civil rights movement.

Even more effective in arousing the conscience of white America was the brutal behavior of Birmingham's police chief, Eugene "Bull" Connor. On May 2, 6,000 black children marched into downtown Birmingham to protest the city's policies. The police arrested a thousand of them. The next day Connor's men used high-pressure water hoses and snarling attack dogs against another group of protesters, including children, in another unauthorized march. The public watched the TV images in horror. The president was appalled and dispatched to the city Justice Department officials who succeeded in negotiating a settlement with the business community and city authorities that gave the SCLC most of what it wanted.

In the summer of 1963 the nonviolent, biracial phase of the civil rights movement reached its culmination when more than 200,000 civil rights supporters, black and white, came to Washington to demonstrate for "jobs and freedom" and to express their support of a pending new federal civil rights bill. At the Lincoln Memorial the enthusiastic and orderly crowd was deeply moved by King's "I Have A Dream" address, a speech that expressed the noblest aspirations of the civil rights movement for a society where skin color would no longer have any significance. Many white Americans would be moved by his vision of a future America that would be "a beautiful sympathy" of "little black boys and girls holding hands with little white boys and girls" and "the sons of former slaves and

The 1963 March on Washington was for civil rights, but as several of these signs show, it was also a demonstration for jobs.

former slaveholders sitting down together at the table of brotherhood." The president had feared that the march, especially if the militants in the movement were allowed free rein, would hurt the chances of a pending new civil rights bill. Actually the demonstration helped win passage of the measure, but not until after Kennedy was dead.

The New Frontier.   Kennedy's New Frontier, the collective name for his domestic programs, was at best a modest success. At his behest, Congress expanded the number of workers covered by the minimum wage levels, increased those levels as well as Social Security payments, and passed the Housing Act of 1961, which pumped nearly $5 billion over four years into preserving urban open spaces, developing mass transit, and building middle-income housing. Congress also raised unemployment compensation benefits and provided aid to economically depressed areas.

Yet most of Kennedy's major New Frontier initiatives either died in Congress or were delayed until after his death. He had at best only narrow Democratic majorities in Congress, and the administration was unable to bring to its side the conservative Democrats, primarily from the South, who often neither liked nor respected him and his brash associates. Congress defeated his bill to provide funds for school construction and scholarship aid for college students.

It refused to pass a health insurance plan for the aged and to enact measures to help unemployed youth, migrant workers, and commuters. One of the most important Kennedy proposals was a tax cut to stimulate the economy by putting more money into the hands of consumers. A year after its introduction the bill was still wending its way through Congress.

It would be hard to give the Kennedy administration the highest grades for its handling of domestic and foreign affairs. Yet despite his mixed record, Kennedy's popularity grew with the passing months. The public remembered his successes and forgot his failures or blamed them on Congress. Young Americans identified with him and his beautiful wife. In late 1963 Camelot was still untarnished.

The president was not universally loved and admired, however. The far right, particularly strong in the South and Southwest, despised him. The reemerging left saw him as too conservative and a cold warrior besides. When, in November 1963, the president and his wife set off on a political peacemaking trip to Texas, advisers warned that he might encounter trouble. Shortly before, Adlai Stevenson, then ambassador to the United Nations, had been verbally abused and spat on in Dallas.

Kennedy ignored the advice and went to Texas, accompanied by Vice President Johnson. In Dallas, while his motorcade moved slowly through downtown streets lined with friendly crowds, he was shot through the head by a sniper. Rushed to Parkland Memorial Hospital, he was pronounced dead a half hour later.

His killer, Lee Harvey Oswald, was an unstable leftist who had spent some years in the Soviet Union and had been active in the pro-Castro Fair Play for Cuba organization. Oswald had admitted nothing when, two days later as he was being escorted from jail, before the eyes of millions of horrified television viewers, he was shot by Jack Ruby, a shady Dallas nightclub owner who apparently saw himself as an avenging angel.

Few events in a decade rife with catastrophic shocks so appalled the American people. The assassination in Dallas had not only killed an American president but had also struck down a young hero who had come to symbolize to many contemporaries all that was best and most worthy in American life. To the young, especially, his death seemed a bitter tragedy. In the somber hours between the murder and the burial at Arlington National Cemetery, television's uninterrupted coverage of the events helped draw the nation together as a family united by a shared grief.

In the months that followed, sorrow over the assassination gave way to uneasiness and frustration. President Lyndon Johnson, hoping to allay public doubts about the murder, appointed a commission headed by Chief Justice Earl Warren to investigate the assassination. In September 1964 the commission reported that Oswald was indisputably the culprit and had acted alone. Most Americans probably accepted the Warren Report, but a large minority suspected that it was incomplete or even a cover-up. There were too many loose ends, they insisted; too many questions unanswered. In the next few years, as the toll of assassinated American leaders grew, more and more Americans would conclude that there was an evil plot afoot, a conspiracy or several of them, to kill off the nation's great popular champions.

"Jackie" and "Jack," a glamorous couple. Taken during the 1960 presidential campaign. The picture foreshadows "Camelot."

The Affluent Society

During the 1960s the country enjoyed what was till then the longest sustained economic boom in its history, with Gross National Product growing at the average rate of 4 percent annually, well above that for the preceding fifteen-year period. Between 1960 and 1970 average per capita real income increased by 48 percent. Compared to recent years, moreover, the gap between the most affluent and other Americans was relatively modest. The major American industries were still unchallenged at home and still enjoyed large markets abroad. No American worker needed to worry about his or her job going overseas. Unions were strong and regularly bargained successfully for higher pay for their members. Some unemployment persisted, and toward the end of the decade prices began to rise at a fast clip. Yet through most of the 1960s, the public's sense of economic well-being surpassed even that of the previous decade.

The Knowledge Industries.
The accumulation and diffusion of knowledge helped fuel the decade's economic boom. In some ways this knowledge explosion was the payoff from years of previous scientific advances. It also owed

much to the great postwar outlays for research and higher education. In 1950 Congress had established the National Science Foundation to encourage research, especially in areas related to national defense. By 1957 outlays for research and development (R&D) by public and private organizations together had reached almost $10 billion annually. Meanwhile, the country's higher education system surged dramatically. In 1940, the last full peacetime year, there were 1.5 million college students; by 1950, 2.6 million. From the mid-1950s on, the country's support of what would later be called the "knowledge industries" was dazzling by any previous standard.

Below the college level, however, American education seemed flawed. Americans complained that the public schools were not teaching children to read or to calculate and many blamed it on John Dewey's disciples, the "progressive educators." But most citizens were proud of the job the nation was doing training the young. Their complacency was suddenly shattered when, in October 1957, the Russians put a hollow steel ball called Sputnik into orbit around the earth. Having long considered their nation the world's scientific and technological leader, Americans were dismayed to discover that they had been abruptly pushed off their pinnacle by their chief international rival.

For the next few years Americans subjected themselves to one of their periodic agonizing reappraisals of education. A dozen books were soon echoing the complaints of earlier critics about American educational failings. Public dismay over Sputnik induced Congress in 1958 to pass the National Defense Education Act, providing large federal outlays for scientific and language training for college students. By 1970 federal appropriations for research had almost tripled, and federal funding of higher education was four times as high as it had been ten years earlier. Industrial firms, universities, and foundations also invested billions in basic scientific research and the development of new products.

Booming research and industrial growth made a college education even more valuable than in the past, and with the postwar "baby-boom" generation reaching their late teens, there were also more eligible college-age students. By 1970 some 7 million young men and women were enrolled in colleges and universities, an increase of nearly 500 percent in little more than a generation.

The Impact of Science and Technology.   The scientific and technological advances that flowed from the laboratories were often dramatic. Linus Pauling, James Watson, H. Gobind Khorana, and others discovered how the gene, the basic unit of heredity, was constructed. Besides solving some of nature's great mysteries, genetics bore fruit—literally—in a great surge in the output per acre of rice, corn, and wheat, the so-called Green Revolution that benefited Third World nations especially. During this decade, the electronic computer first became a powerful tool for solving mathematical and scientific problems and controlling production processes. The textile industry adopted new high-speed looms and developed new synthetic fibers. A long list of thermoplastics filled needs hitherto met at higher cost by metals and other natural materials. The subsonic passenger jet, first introduced in the early 1950s, replaced the propeller plane in the 1960s and shrank the world to half its former size. Meanwhile, the space program, begun under the auspices of the National Aeronautics and Space Administration

One of the greatest feats of modern technology was the landing of
men on the moon in July 1969. This picture of astronaut Edwin
"Buzz" Aldrin was taken by fellow moonwalker Neil Armstrong,
whose reflection is visible in the visor of Aldrin's helmet.

(NASA) to challenge the Soviet Union, yielded unexpected scientific dividends.
Communications satellites were launched, and new metals and alloys and miniaturized computer elements developed to solve the problems of space travel found
surprisingly down-to-earth commercial and technical uses.

Medicine, too, made giant strides in these years. An arsenal of new antibiotic
drugs, X-ray techniques, isotope tracers, computerized studies of environmental
factors in disease, and other applications of the new science markedly improved
the nation's and the world's health. In the 1950s researchers developed vaccines to
fight polio. In 1963 they introduced a measles vaccine. Heart disease and cancer
remained major killers, and indeed lung-cancer deaths from smoking soared, but
the death rate from infectious diseases plummeted.

These medical advances, combined with better nutrition, produced a healthier, longer-lived population than ever before. Life expectancy for a newborn baby rose from 68.2 years in 1950 to 70.9 years in 1970. At the later date it was considerably higher for women (74.8) than for men (67.1) and for whites (71.7) than for blacks (65.3). Still, the improvement was substantial for every segment of the population.

The rapid expansion of the economy and the great surge in technology were not cost-free. American life became increasingly bureaucratized as the federal government expanded its power and size and as ever more private businesses consolidated into giant corporations. Much of the new technology was damaging to the land, to water supplies, and to the air people breathed. By the end of the decade these environmental drawbacks would produce a powerful impulse to protect the public, which came to be called the ecology movement.

The Johnson Years

Lyndon Johnson took office at a time of affluence and optimism when most citizens still trusted government and believed it could make a significant difference in the nation's life. Abundance made the plight of those left out seem especially unacceptable, while the surge in government revenues from a soaring economy made spending for new federal programs relatively easy to bear. The "Great Society" of Lyndon Johnson floated on a sea of prosperity that allowed Americans, without too much sacrifice, to indulge their periodic yearning for a just and benevolent nation.

The Great Society.   Lyndon B. Johnson was in many ways the antithesis of his predecessor. Middle-aged, rugged, earthy, and self-made rather than young, elegant, and patrician, Johnson lacked the glamour of Kennedy. Yet he was incomparable as a legislative manager. His long years as Senate leader had honed his talent for getting laws enacted. As president his skills were put to good use. A congressman or official who resisted the president's demands was marched into Johnson's office, seated next to the towering Texan, and subjected to a powerful verbal assault of jokes, promises, threats, cajolery, and ego stroking, along with thumps, squeezes, and pokes. Few politicians could hold out against the "Johnson treatment" for very long, and in the course of his five years as president, Johnson initiated more significant domestic legislation than any chief executive since Franklin D. Roosevelt.

Johnson's program was an expression of liberalism's faith in a powerful nurturing and managerial government. The president was a long-time admirer of Franklin Roosevelt and hoped to complete and round out the social welfare state that FDR had launched between 1933 and 1938 and that his Democratic successors, Truman and Kennedy, had been unable to complete.

Johnson wasted no time in pushing his liberal agenda. Invoking the memory of his martyred predecessor, he quickly induced Congress to enact stalled legislation of the Kennedy administration: the tax reduction bill, an Urban Mass Transportation Act, and a Wilderness Preservation Act. In January 1964, following through on a half-developed Kennedy initiative, Congress passed the Economic Opportunity Act establishing an Office of Economic Opportunity (OEO) to reduce illiteracy, find jobs for inner-city youths, improve depressed conditions in the Appalachian area, sharpen skills among the poor, and provide capital to minority businesses. With a mandate to wage a "war on poverty," OEO was authorized to create "community-action" groups to give local-area people a hand in designing and running new antipoverty programs and instill in the poor a new sense of confidence that would enable them to help themselves.

LBJ's impressive early leadership guaranteed his party's 1964 nomination, with Hubert H. Humphrey, Minnesota's liberal senator, as his running mate. The Republicans chose Senator Barry Goldwater of Arizona, who selected an obscure New York congressman, William Miller, as second on the ticket.

Goldwater represented the extreme right wing of his party. His supporters claimed that they were offering the country "a choice, not an echo." The choice, it seemed to many voters, was to dismantle the Social Security system, sell the New Deal's Tennessee Valley Authority to private interests, and return to Hooverism. Given the Republican candidate's bellicose foreign-policy statements and his affection for uniforms and air force bombers, his election also promised an enlarged Vietnam involvement that few Americans wanted. Goldwater made matters worse by inept public statements. When many moderate Americans were still worried about the far-right John Birch Society, Goldwater told them, "extremism in the defense of liberty is no vice! And . . . moderation in the pursuit of justice is no virtue!" The Democrats did not play fair in their criticism of Goldwater's bellicose responses. At the very time Johnson was considering escalating the American commitment in Vietnam, he was denouncing Goldwater as a warmonger and promising to "seek no wider war" in Southeast Asia. Johnson won with 61 percent of the popular vote, better even than FDR's 1936 triumph. A year later a bitter joke would make the rounds: "I was told if I voted for Goldwater we would be at war in six months. I did—and we were!"

With a landslide victory to work with, LBJ pushed beyond his predecessor's initiatives. His Great Society sought to do more than just improve material security and well-being. As the president had described it in May 1964 at the University of Michigan, the Great Society was a domain where the "order of plenty" Americans now enjoyed could be used "to enrich and elevate our national life and to advance the quality of our American civilization." In the Great Society every child would find "knowledge to enrich his mind and . . . enlarge his talents." There leisure would be a "welcome chance to build and reflect." It would be a place where "the city of man serves not only the needs of the body but the desire for beauty and the hunger for community," and where people could "renew contact with nature." With the spectacular Democratic majorities in Congress to back him up, he made remarkable progress in converting his vision into law.

In the spring of 1965, overcoming longstanding Catholic–Protestant disagreements over public aid to parochial education, Congress passed the $1.3 billion Elementary and Secondary Education Act appropriating federal money for the direct support of local public schools for the first time in history. Catholic opposition was neutralized by providing that even if students were enrolled in Catholic schools, they, though not the schools themselves, would be eligible for federal aid. In July, it swept aside the opposition of the organized medical profession and enacted the first federal health insurance programs—Medicare for old-age pensioners and Medicaid for the poor. A month later the Omnibus Housing Act set up a rent supplement program for low-income families. Recognizing the cities' special needs, Congress established the Department of Housing and Urban Development (HUD) in September. The president promptly appointed as its head Robert C. Weaver, who became the nation's first black cabinet member. Soon after, the president signed a measure establishing the National Endowments for the Arts and for the Humanities to subsidize artists, writers, composers, painters, and scholars and provide aid to local cultural institutions. Clean air and clean water acts to improve the environment followed soon afterward, as did a Higher Education Act providing the first federal scholarships for college students; the Highway Safety Act to make automobile travel safer; an anti-billboard highway beautification act; and a Truth-in-Lending Act to protect consumers in credit transactions. In October, in the 1965 Immigration Act, Congress replaced the discriminatory national quota system for immigrants (established in the 1920s) with rules to facilitate family reunification and encourage the immigration of skilled workers and professionals.

Some of these laws were hastily drawn; some were ultimately ineffective or even harmful. The OEO anti-poverty programs, critics charged, created unrealistic expectations that only aroused frustration and anger among its anticipated beneficiaries. Federal school aid did not make American children more literate. Nor did the National Endowments produce a golden age of the arts or of scholarship. Medicare and Medicaid, it was claimed, helped fuel a runaway inflation of medical costs and would prove impossibly expensive to a later generation. By the 1990s many Americans would blame the flood of poor, unskilled immigrants from Latin America on the family reunification provision of the 1965 immigration bill.

But the Great Society had its successes as well. Head Start, a War on Poverty program that paid for educational enrichment of poor preschool children, made a difference in the success of those children in later years. Great Society programs helped low- and moderate-income students pay for college, made automobiles safer, and provided recreation facilities for millions of Americans taking their leisure. Medicare and other programs for the aged and retired virtually ended the serious problem of poverty among older Americans. However costly, federal health programs did make Americans healthier and extended their life spans. Much of the consumer protection and environmental legislation was overdue and produced long-term aesthetic and health benefits.

Space Exploration.

Johnson must also be given credit for major progress in space exploration. In May 1961 Kennedy had set the goal of, within the decade, "landing a man on the moon and returning him safely to earth." Hoping to show the superiority of democratic capitalism to communism by beating the Soviet Union in the space race, Johnson pushed the moon-landing program hard. The competition was attacked by some liberals for starving needed social programs here on earth. Many black Americans considered it a white man's enterprise of no great interest to them. And there were critics among the scientists as well: We could have learned as much about the solar system, they said, by using far cheaper unmanned rockets. But LBJ kept the appropriations coming for the Apollo moon launches. By the end of his presidency, three astronauts had transmitted television Christmas greetings to earth from seventy miles above the moon's forbidding surface. It was now only a matter of months before the first human beings would place their feet on some other part of the universe besides Mother Earth.

Johnson and Civil Rights.

Lyndon Johnson was if anything more committed to racial justice than his predecessor. Though born and raised in a former Confederate state, he had never accepted the racial attitudes of the white South. Senator Johnson was one of only three southern senators who refused to sign a 1956 "Southern Manifesto" opposed to the Supreme Court's Brown school-desegregation decision.

With his incomparable command of parliamentary maneuver, Johnson helped win passage in July of the 1964 Civil Rights Act that Kennedy had originated. The sweeping new law barred discrimination in public accommodations, authorized the Justice Department to initiate suits to force desegregation of schools and other public facilities, outlawed job discrimination based on race, color, religion, national origin, or sex, and reduced the power of local voter registration boards to disqualify black registrants on the basis of literacy. It would change the face of race relations in the nation, especially in the South.

After election in his own right that November, LBJ continued to push for progress on the civil rights front. When, in early 1965, Governor Wallace denied the right of King and Alabama civil rights protesters to stage a march on the Alabama state capital, Johnson intervened forcefully. The president called Wallace to the White House and subjected him to his standard treatment of cajolery and brow-beating that had worked so well with federal politicians. Wallace yielded to the federal authorities. On March 15 Johnson went before Congress to support a bold new voting rights bill. The civil rights issue, he asserted, was not a black problem or a white problem. "There is only an American problem," and Congress was now assembled to solve it. The whole nation must "overcome the crippling legacy of bigotry and injustice." The president brought members of Congress to their feet with his ringing peroration that ended with the words of the moving civil rights anthem "And We Shall Overcome."

In August 1965 Johnson signed the Voting Rights Act, the last of the major civil rights bills of the sixties. The measure authorized federal voter registration in districts where local officials had kept the number of registered voters below half the voting-age population. Under its terms the equal franchise promised black southerners a century before was finally fulfilled.

Judicial Activism.

The liberal activism of the decade was amplified by major decisions of the Supreme Court under Chief Justice Earl Warren. An exponent of "judicial activism," Warren believed that the federal courts must not only attack segregation; it must also defend individual rights against intrusive state control, promote political equality, and help uphold a liberal secular society. In a cascade of decisions the Court took stands on controversial issues that Congress and the state legislatures had long avoided. In *Mapp v. Ohio* (1961) the justices ruled that evidence collected illegally could not be used in court against an accused criminal.

In *Gideon v. Wainright* (1963) and *Miranda v. Arizona* (1966), the Court insisted that accused criminals had the right to remain silent when questioned, had the right to consult a lawyer, and had to be provided with a lawyer by the state if they lacked the money to hire one themselves. *Engel v. Vitale* (1962) forbade prayer in the public schools, on the grounds of separation of church and state. *Griswold v. Connecticut* (1964) struck down state laws banning birth control because they violated the right to marital privacy. In *A Book Named . . . "Memoirs of a Woman of Pleasure" v. Attorney General of Massachusetts* (1966), the Court virtually lifted the legal ban on pornography. Hailed by liberals as the great tribune of the disenfranchised and the oppressed, and defender of free speech, the Warren Court was denounced by conservatives as an abettor of crime, pornography, and atheism.

The Rise of Dissent

By most measures of well-being and social progress the sixties should rank as a golden age. Americans were affluent; government seemed relevant and effective; the lot of the disadvantaged was getting better. And yet no period of the twentieth century would ring with such loud, intemperate cries of protest and dissent as the second half of that momentous decade. Ironically, as some observers noted, affluence and freedom had produced more discontent than poverty and tyranny.

From Civil Rights to Black Power.   After 1965 the civil rights movement drastically shifted ground. At mid-decade Martin Luther King, Jr., was at the very peak of his career. In January 1964 *Time* had named him Man of the Year. In October he won the Nobel Peace Prize. With passage of the Voting Rights Act, King's formula of black–white cooperation and nonviolent civil disobedience seemed triumphant.

But white participation and the tactic of nonviolence would not last much longer. From the outset black nationalism, or black separatism, which rejected cooperation with whites and what were perceived as white values, had been an undercurrent in the postwar civil rights movement. During the forties and fifties the Black Muslims (the Nation of Islam) had won disciples for a set of beliefs that labeled Christianity a "slave religion," denounced whites as "blue-eyed devils," and proclaimed the superiority and primacy of black people. Led by Elijah Muhammad, the Black Muslims, much like Marcus Garvey before them, sought to foster black racial pride and black separatism. By the early sixties the Black Muslims' most articulate spokesman was Malcolm X, a former convict converted to the Nation of Islam while in prison. Malcolm denied he was a racist, but his rhetoric was often angry and frightened many whites.

Black separatism might have remained a "fringe" if not for the growing frustration of many African-Americans over the slow advance toward racial equality. By 1965 virtually all of the legal barriers to black public access in the South had been swept away. Jim Crow was virtually dead. Blacks, moreover, were voting in record numbers in the South. Nationally, there was also a great surge of black college students and of black workers in retail sales, public services, banking, and other white-collar areas where few had ever served before. Yet major inequalities remained. Black Americans were still poorer, sicker, less literate, and more badly housed than whites. Thousands of black youths were unemployed and, seemingly, unemployable. The disparity between promise and fulfillment created intense strains. In the ghettos high expectations often coexisted with modest actual achievement. It was an explosive combination.

Five days after Johnson signed the Voting Rights Act a riot exploded in the black Los Angeles suburb of Watts, tripped off by charges of police brutality. During the violence, twenty-eight blacks died; property damage reached $200 million. The fury of Watts shook Martin Luther King and confirmed his resolve to shift his focus from the South to the northern urban ghettos and their problems of jobs and housing. In January 1966 King conducted a series of marches through white Chicago neighborhoods in support of equal housing laws. The Chicago campaign failed. Many white Chicagoans perceived a threat to their neighborhoods and jeered the marchers and pelted them with stones and other missiles. The marchers were forced to retreat. King admitted afterward that he had "never seen anything as hostile and as hateful as I've seen here today." Meanwhile, violent ghetto protest seemed to become institutionalized after Watts. During the "long, hot summers" of 1966 and 1967 the black neighborhoods of Newark, Cleveland, Detroit, Chicago, and scores of other cities erupted in paroxysms of burning, looting, and attacks on whites and the police. Many of the casualties were black victims of poorly trained, trigger-happy police, National Guards units, or federal troops.

The ghetto upheavals helped polarize the civil rights movement. Despite his efforts, King came to be seen by younger activists as too timid and too ineffectual. In 1966 SNCC replaced its moderate head John Lewis with militant Stokely Carmichael; CORE replaced James Farmer with militant Floyd McKissick. Both new leaders endorsed "black power," a position that had first surfaced during a civil rights "walk against fear" from Memphis to Jackson. In mid-1966 SNCC, led by Carmichael, rejected nonviolence and black-and-white-together in favor of black separatism and black self-defense. SNCC and CORE quickly told their white members to quit and continue the fight for racial equality through their own all-white organizations. That same year, in the Oakland, California, ghetto, two students at a local community college, Huey Newton and Bobby Seale, formed the "Black Panther Party for Self-Defense," a paramilitary organization initially dedicated to compelling the Oakland police to respect black community rights. Dressed in shiny leather jackets and black berets and openly carrying rifles, the Panthers frightened many whites and enraged the police. Their existence attracted national attention when in May 1967 a group of 30 Panthers, bearing rifles, shotguns, and pistols, marched into the California State capitol in Sacramento to protest a bill forbidding the carrying of loaded weapons. Before long the Panthers were engaged in murderous shoot-outs with police in Oakland, Chicago, and other cities.

The Great Insurgency.

The civil rights movement was one sector of a war against the "establishment" of white middle-class America that erupted in the second half of the sixties. Before the decade ended, the country would experience other insurgent movements—by students, women, gays, Latinos, American Indians, environmentalists, and many other groups.

The revolt had tangled roots. In the political realm it was fed by the decline of repressive McCarthyism and the emergence of a new generation of Americans less complacent about good times than their elders and less certain that the Cold War was inevitable. Many of these young people had been raised in the affluence of postwar suburbia and took for granted that America was capable of providing all of its people with the means to lead fulfilling and interesting lives. Yet as they looked around them they perceived racism, blight, despair, repression, and international belligerence that seemed to belie the nation's professed values. With so many of these idealistic and dissatisfied young people going to college, the nation's campuses became potentially explosive.

Socially and culturally, too, the nation was ripe for dissent by the mid-1960s. A new, more permissive attitude toward sex was foreshadowed by the investigations in the late 1940s and early 1950s of Dr. Alfred C. Kinsey and his associates, which showed Americans as far less traditional in their sexual behavior than the conventional wisdom taught. Even more important, perhaps, was the advent of oral contraceptives in 1960. Besides reducing the birth rate, "the pill" lowered the chances of unwanted pregnancies and so reduced the dangers and inconveniences of sex outside traditional marriage.

The more permissive sexual values were reflected in the declining power of communities to censor books, movies, and magazines. Beginning with a 1952 decision holding that films were covered by the First Amendment's guarantee of free speech, the Supreme Court extended the principle so that a book, play, or motion picture had to be "utterly without redeeming social value" to be regarded as obscene. Soon long-banned erotic classics were available at bookstores, and before long it became clear that even works with social values no one could detect could be legally published and sold. In 1968, in recognition of the new situation, Hollywood adopted a rating system that placed films in categories ranging from "G" for family movies to "X" for out-and-out pornography.

Meanwhile, a new school of radical social thinkers, such as the sociologist C. Wright Mills, the social psychologist Paul Goodman, and the neo-Marxist philosopher Herbert Marcuse, provided intellectual ammunition to attack existing society and its values. In their individual ways, each of these men condemned existing society as oppressive, repressive, and rife with inequalities of wealth and power. In 1960 Mills gave currency to the term "New Left" to describe a new radical mood among the young intellectuals and students that he detected emerging in the United States and around the world.

Popular culture, too, especially music, both expressed and encouraged the new dissent. Rock-and-roll, a merger of black rhythm and blues and electronic instruments, burst on the scene in the mid-1950s with Bill Haley's recording "Rock Around the Clock." Soon after, Elvis Presley, a white southerner who borrowed from black musicians, gave rock a strong sexual cast.

Rock was the music of the rebellious young. The most successful rock group of the sixties, the Beatles, wore the long hair and mod clothes of angry English working-class adolescents. The Rolling Stones, also an English group, and various whimsically named American groups, wore the "love beads," Indian headbands, and gaudy jeans that soon became trademarks of youthful cultural revolt. Eventually some rock bands began to dabble directly in political matters. Groups like the Grateful Dead, Jefferson Airplane, and Country Joe and the Fish became active propagandists for sexual freedom, mind-expanding drugs, and the anti-Vietnam War movement. Folk singers like Joan Baez and Bob Dylan also became increasingly political. Dylan's "The Times They Are A-Changin'" would become an anthem of youth rebellion.

Student Activists.   Unlike many other nations, the United States had never had a significant protest movement run primarily by the young. During the sixties this changed when the proportion of young adults reached an all-time record and many of these amassed on college campuses.

Youth is naturally adventurous and rebellious, but the insurgency of the 1960s had its own special accelerant. Many younger white activists were radicalized by their experiences in the civil rights movement. When excluded by Black Power from direct participation in the militant civil rights movement, they turned their eyes to their home turf. Student militancy, moreover, was encouraged by the campus physical setting. Colleges were crowded and classes were large. To handle the load administrations became more impersonal and bureaucratic. Students soon felt that they were numbers rather than human beings.

But probably the most potent trigger of student radicalism was the accelerating and ever-expanding war in Vietnam. At first young men were excused from the military draft merely for attending college. Then they had to pass a test and maintain good grades to be exempt. This system provoked profound anxieties and fed student guilt about evading danger while nonstudents, both black and white, were sent off to Southeast Asia to fight and die. The cast of *Hair* announced the injustice of this arrangement when they sang: "War is white people sending black people to make war on yellow people to defend the land they stole from red people." Some students tried to avoid the war personally by seeking conscientious objector status or wrangling medical exemptions. Others escaped to Canada. Many channeled their personal dilemma into an angry movement to get the United States out of the Vietnam conflict in any way possible. Broader in its effect than these, the war in Vietnam undermined the nation's leadership and inspired attacks on the whole "system" as unresponsive, corrupt, repressive, and cruel.

The liberal campus of the University of California at Berkeley was the setting for the first of the major student rebellions. When, in the fall of 1964, the administration withdrew the right to use university property as a free-speech enclave, student activists, many of whom had worked for civil rights both in the South and in the Bay Area, rebelled. On December 2 a thousand students took over the administration building and refused to leave until the university agreed to cancel its directive. The authorities called in the police, who arrested hundreds of protestors. In the end the Free Speech Movement rebels got the ban rescinded, but for the remainder of the decade Berkeley student activists and the university would struggle over free expression and a wide range of issues including university government, classroom overcrowding, restrictions on students' private lives, ethnic studies, and university–community relations.

Berkeley became the precedent for a wave of campus upheavals that soon spread from coast to coast. Impatient with hierarchies and authority, many students came to see university administrations as prototypes of all oppressive agencies in society and so worthy of assault. The supposed complicity of universities in the Vietnam war effort amplified the sense that they were legitimate targets.

Organized student opposition to the war began in early 1965 with campus "teach-ins," marathon sessions in which students and faculty examined the roots of the American intervention and invariably denounced the administration's policies. Teach-ins were followed by "peace marches" in which students paraded with pacifists, antiwar liberals, radicals, and other concerned citizens to protest U.S. policies. As the antiwar movement accelerated, radical students began to burn draft cards and mob campus recruiters from the armed forces and from businesses, such as Dow Chemical Company, engaged in weapon production.

From 1965 on, many of the campus upheavals were led by Students for a Democratic Society (SDS), an organization that initially condemned both capitalism and Soviet-style communism, proclaimed the need for personal freedom and individual autonomy, and called for a "democracy of participation" to replace the prevailing bureaucratic democracy of the day. SDS became more militant and intolerant as the sixties advanced. By 1968 it had begun to glorify violence toward the oppressive "system" of "Amerika," and had replaced "participatory democracy" by Marxist-Leninism that emphasized a "vanguard party" to lead the inevitable revolution.

The Counterculture.   The New Left sought political change primarily, but simultaneously American youth were in revolt against bourgeois behavior, dress, values, and expression. Middle-class conventions, the rebels claimed, were repressive tools by which a timid, hidebound society repressed people's instinctual drives and diminished human potential. Unlike the New Left, the counterculture lacked an organizational center, though at different times the Yippies, the Mayday Tribe, and other colorfully named groups would claim to speak for it.

The counterculture's chief practitioners were called "hippies," from "hip," a jazz musicians' expression meaning knowledgeable or "with it." Hippies displayed their contempt for middle-class values by wearing tattered jeans, sandals, and beads; displaying an abundance of hair; and cultivating an elliptical way of speaking that used such expressions as "like," "groovy," and "dig it." Hippies adopted an aesthetic outlook that emphasized natural things. They wore flowers in their hair and around their necks and referred to themselves as "flower children." They considered material possessions fetishes of the "straight culture" and furnished their own "pads" with a few castoffs.

Old sexual values were already changing when the hippies appeared on the scene. But the counterculture amplified these trends. Gatherings of counterculture people at times included displays of mass nudity and even public sexual intercourse, as at the mammoth rock-and-roll festival near Woodstock, New York, in August 1969. Hippies also experimented with communes where everything, including sexual partners, was shared, and accepted cohabitation without marriage as normal.

As the 1960s unfolded, counterculture values invaded the cultural mainstream. By mid-decade practices that previously were seldom mentioned and mainly relegated to the sexual underground were publicly exhibited. In Tom O'Horgan's play *Futz,* one character has sexual intercourse with a pig. "X-rated" movies, now permitted, brought the depiction of oral sex acts to every large city's downtown theaters. Homosexuality, too, ceased to be a shameful aberration in the eyes of many Americans.

The counterculture was steeped in psychedelic, mood-altering drugs. In the early 1960s two Harvard psychology instructors, Timothy Leary and Richard Alpert, experimented with a new chemical substance, lysergic acid diethylamide (LSD), which they believed capable of "expanding" consciousness and enabling people to conquer their "inner space." Soon LSD and other consciousness-altering drugs were incorporated into the hippie revolt against bourgeois society. As in the case of sexual behavior, the drug culture expanded beyond hippiedom. Large numbers of middle-class white youths were soon experimenting with substances that had only been used in the ghettos or bohemian enclaves before.

The counterculture had its characteristic music, "acid rock." Thousands of young people flocked to mammoth rock concerts where flashing strobe lights and heavy use of "grass" and LSD augmented the music on stage. It also had its characteristic psychedelic art and a host of counterculture, "underground" publications, including *The Berkeley Barb,* the *East Village Other,* and the *Chicago Seed.* Few lasted more than a year or two, but during that time they enjoyed wide readership, especially among college students.

The hippie phenomenon was short-lived. During the 1967 "summer of love" hippies flocked to the Haight-Ashbury district of San Francisco and to the East Village in New York, neighborhoods that catered to their special needs. These quickly deteriorated into squalid youth slums. When the larger culture adopted the hippie style of talk, dress, and behavior, it became tainted in the eyes of counterculture purists. Meanwhile, the great rock music festivals degenerated into saturnalias of drugs and violence. The commune movement for a while became the refuge for the more idealistic counterculture people. But then it, too, deflated.

The student political left soon followed the counterculture in a downward spiral. Frustrated by the never-ending Vietnam War, infiltrated by rigid, orthodox Marxists, under attack by radical feminists, in June 1969, at its annual convention in Chicago, SDS split in two over who would lead the expected revolution. One faction, the Weathermen, adopted violence and fought with the Chicago police during the "Days of Rage" in October 1969. Thereafter its members became underground terrorists determined to attack "imperialist Amerika" from within. Over the next few years the Weathermen would be responsible for dozens of bombings of government facilities and corporate offices. In February 1970 a Weathermen bomb factory in a Greenwich Village townhouse exploded when someone connected a wrong wire, killing three Weathermen leaders. The resort to violence, the declining economy, and a recognition that revolution was still a long way off combined to finish off what remained of the New Left.

Liberation

The 1960s insurgency stirred to life a new yearning for freedom, for liberation, for redress among ethnic minorities and others who saw themselves as outside the inner circle of privilege.

Chicanos.   Mexican-Americans, mostly recent immigrants, were the largest of these minorities, numbering over 6 million in California, the Southwest, and the Chicago area. Called "Chicanos," they worked as domestics and unskilled factory hands, and as migrant farm laborers, picking lettuce, tomatoes, fruit, and other crops in the fertile valleys of California and Texas. They were often the victims of social and economic discrimination by the prevailing "Anglo" culture.

Beginning in the 1960s, a new generation of Chicano leaders began to demand better treatment for their people. In New Mexico, Reies Tijerina's Alianza organization demanded that lands in the Southwest that had originally belonged to Mexican-Americans be returned to them. In California, union leader César Chavez sought to compel the grape and lettuce growers to accept unionization of their largely Chicano workforce. In his struggle he was helped by consumer boycotts of nonunion grapes and lettuce by sympathetic liberals and radicals.

Native Americans.   The 1960s was a decade of revived self-awareness and assertiveness for American Indians too. Even after passage of the 1934 Wheeler-Howard Act (see Chapter 19) Indians remained a depressed group in America. Whites continued to treat them as second-class citizens; traditional Indian values continued to erode; mortality rates for children on the reservations remained appalling. In 1946 Congress established the Indian Claims Commission to reimburse Indians for financial injustices against them from the very beginning of the federal government. In 1953, by a joint resolution, it authorized "termination" of all federal benefits and controls over the tribes. Though termination was intended to make Indians equal to other citizens, the National Congress of American Indians protested that it became primarily a way to lower federal costs at the expense of the Indians. The termination process was soon slowed, but not before it had raised up a new class of Indian leaders more militant than any in the recent past.

These leaders were often young urban activists inspired by the civil rights movement of blacks and Chicanos. They demanded that they be called "Native Americans" rather than Indians, a name imposed on them by Europeans. David Edmunds and Vine Deloria, Jr., wrote Native American history from a Native American viewpoint, siding with Sitting Bull against Custer and with the Apaches against the cavalry. In 1969 a group of young activists occupied the abandoned federal prison on Alcatraz Island in San Francisco Bay and demanded that it be converted into an Indian cultural center. In 1970 the American Indian Movement (AIM) emerged as the center of the young urban militants.

The New Feminism.   The most consequential of the liberation movements was the new feminism. From a feminist perspective, the immediate post-1945 period had been depressing. The fifties ideals of domesticity and togetherness had confined women to the home to a greater degree than at any time since before the first

World War. Women who worked seldom had rewarding or well-paid jobs and although many women lacked the training and work experience of men, clearly they were also victims of what would be called sexism. Sex discrimination, feminists would later note, was often indirect and subtle. Female children, they said, were "programmed" from the earliest age to assume that they were emotionally and mentally weaker than men, and came to absorb this view themselves.

As the 1950s drew to a close, gender perceptions and attitudes began to change. By 1960 millions of women had gone through college, where they had been exposed to psychological, anthropological, and sociological concepts that identified many supposedly feminine characteristics as primarily the result of upbringing. Educated women were confronted with the contrast between their training and the routine lives they led, either as housewives or as "gals Friday" to some male executive. By this time, too, the precedent of black liberation had illuminated the path that the nation's largest "minority" could take.

The new feminism surfaced in 1963 with a report by the Kennedy-appointed President's Commission on the Status of Women urging job equality, day-care centers, and paid maternity leave for women. The intellectual breakthrough came that same year when Betty Friedan, a suburban housewife, published *The Feminine Mystique*. The book described dissatisfaction with the narrow life of the housebound wife and mother as "the problem that has no name." Domesticity was a trap that had diminished women's lives. Like most feminist activists of the past, Friedan, a Smith College graduate and former labor activist, spoke mainly for the educated middle class. But among this group her message reverberated loudly and the book became an immense bestseller. In 1964 the emerging new mood was further encouraged by the Civil Rights Act, which forbade job discrimination based not only on race, but also on sex. The law unleashed a flood of complaints by women to the Equal Employment Opportunity Commission established under the act to monitor compliance with its provisions. When the commission proved resistant to women's complaints, feminists decided to act. In June 1966, they organized NOW, the National Organization for Women, with Friedan as its first president.

NOW was a moderate voice of the new feminism. It worked through the courts and the legislatures to bring "women into full participation in the mainstream of American society" with the right to exercise "all the privileges and responsibilities thereof in truly equal partnership with men. . . ." It did not target men as the enemy or seek to fundamentally restructure the family or society as a whole. To the left of NOW more militant groups would soon appear, derived primarily from the student New Left. These "women's liberationists" developed a radical critique of Western society as hopelessly male-dominated. "Patriarchy," rather than capitalism, they held, was the source not only of female oppression but of all oppression in the world, and its destruction was a prerequisite for the liberation of all humankind. Radical feminists sometimes seemed to have little respect for conventional women or for the conventional family. A vocal minority were lesbians with an agenda separate from more traditional women.

Women's liberationists employed such attention-getting tactics as "guerrilla theater"—street demonstrations in the form of political drama—and disruption of "sexist" rituals. In September 1968 radical feminists picketed the Miss America

Pageant in Atlantic City as a woman-degrading event. Though they did not burn their bras, as myth would have it, they did toss other supposed symbols of female bondage—corsets, eyelash curlers, high-heeled shoes—into a "freedom ash can."

The radical feminists also introduced as part of their arsenal "consciousness-raising"—small, intense meetings of women for personal self-examination and disclosure of male oppression. These sessions doubtless helped women to face painful marriages and other unhealthy relationships with men; they also provided a steady stream of recruits for the new women's liberation movements.

Gay Liberation.   The gay rights movement was another late manifestation of the new liberationist mood. Homosexuality had always existed, of course, but in modern times gay men and lesbian women had carefully hidden their sexual preferences to avoid "straight" society's stern disapproval and laws that made many homosexual practices criminal offenses. In many large cities homosexuals congregated in their own neighborhoods and developed their own cultural and social institutions where they could be comfortable. Gays often led double lives: one at home, where they felt free; and one at work, where they felt compelled to conform to the straight world's expectations. This enforced concealment, added to the legal hazards of being gay, created a deep sense of resentment and the feeling among homosexuals that they, too, constituted an oppressed minority.

By the mid-1960s male and female homosexuals had formed organizations for mutual support and defense such as the Mattachine Society and the Daughters of Bilitis. Then came a crucial event in Gay Liberation. In June 1969 the police raided the Stonewall Inn, a homosexual bar in New York's Greenwich Village. Gays, who usually accepted such raids as a normal part of existence, this time fought back. The battle against the police lasted far into the night and continued the next day. Stonewall marked the end of homosexual acquiescence and the beginning of the Gay Liberation Movement. In its wake militant gays began to "come out of the closet" and demand that the laws against free sexual expression and practice, and those denying gays equal employment and other rights, be removed from the statute books.

Quagmire In Vietnam

Lyndon Johnson was a novice in foreign affairs who relied on the advice of better-informed men to guide his policy. He kept on Kennedy's foreign-policy advisers and accepted their view that the United States had no other choice than to support the pro-American regime in Saigon to prevent the Communists from conquering the South. Later he would accept his military advisers' views of how to fight the war and their estimates of progress being made in defeating the Vietcong and North Vietnamese forces.

Johnson was also a captive of his own past. Like many of his generation, he viewed Vietnam in terms of the "lessons" of the 1930s when the dictators were riding a wave of success: If you appeased aggressors, as Chamberlain had appeased Hitler at Munich, they would force you ultimately to fight on more difficult

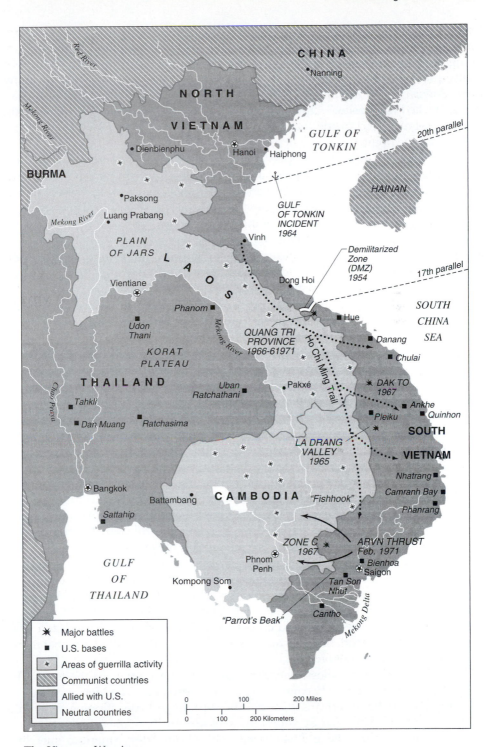

The Vietnam War Arena

ground. "I knew," Johnson later told his biographer Doris Kearns, "that if the aggression succeeded in South Vietnam, then the aggressors would simply keep on going until all of Southeast Asia fell into their hands, slowly or quickly." However faulty for Vietnam, the formula was convincing to the president and to many other Americans as well. Johnson also feared the precedent of Truman, who had been attacked for "losing" China after the Communist takeover in the late 1940s. "I don't want it said of me that I was the president who lost Vietnam," he remarked at one point.

LBJ's first step down the slippery path in Vietnam was the Gulf of Tonkin Resolution he extracted from Congress in August 1964 following a reported North Vietnam attack on American naval vessels off the Vietnam coast. Passed almost unanimously, it authorized the president to "take all necessary measures to repel any armed attack against the forces of the United States." Johnson would treat the resolution as the virtual equivalent of a declaration of war.

During the 1964 presidential campaign, as we saw, Johnson muted the Vietnam issue. Then, early in 1965, following a damaging Vietcong attack on a U.S. airbase at Pleiku, the administration launched "Operation Rolling Thunder," a massive aerial bombing campaign against North Vietnam to induce the Ho Chi Minh government to abandon its effort to overthrow the pro-American regime in South Vietnam. When it proved ineffective, Johnson increased the number of American military advisers to the South Vietnamese army and in April 1965 took the fatal step of dispatching the first American ground combat troops to Vietnam. When asked at a press conference at the time whether the decision represented a sharp change of direction, he denied it vehemently.

All through 1965 and 1966 Johnson increased the pressure on the Vietcong and North Vietnamese in hopes of forcing a settlement that would preserve South Vietnam as an anti-Communist bastion under the pro-American leaders Nguyen Van Thieu and Nguyen Cao Ky. In April 1966 the United States sent B-52s to bomb Hanoi, the North Vietnamese capital, and Haiphong, the major North Vietnamese port of entry for supplies from the Soviet Union. Meanwhile, on the ground, United States marines and army units fought a vicious war in the Vietnamese jungles and rice paddies under terms imposed by Vietcong guerrillas. By the end of 1966 there were 385,000 American troops in Vietnam; by the end of 1967 over 485,000.

While pouring men and materiel into Vietnam, the administration sought to avoid a total war, such as an actual invasion of North Vietnam, the base of Communist operations in the south. Such a move might bring the Soviet Union or China in and trip off World War III. It might also reveal that the American people had no heart for the casualties and costs of a full commitment. Confronted with these dangers, the president chose the awkward course of a limited war that many would later say could not be won.

The fighting, nevertheless, was dirty work in every sense of the term. The American military used body counts to chart their progress. The Vietcong, usually refusing to meet the Americans head-on, chose to hit and run, slipping away into the jungle when confronted by superior forces. South Vietnamese villagers were often caught in the middle and were attacked by both sides. American guerrilla-warfare experts tried to establish secure areas free of "the Cong," but the villages seldom remained secure for long. Too many Vietnamese peasants considered the guerrillas less dangerous than the Americans or the corrupt officials of the Saigon government, or simply could not resist Vietcong threats. There were atrocities on both sides. The Vietcong set off bombs on the streets of Saigon that killed innocent civilians. They tortured and murdered South Vietnamese villagers, policemen, teachers, and Catholics who opposed them. Americans also committed atrocities, though they were never officially condoned. In March 1968 an American army unit under Lieutenant William L. Calley, Jr., attacked My Lai, a village of 600 people suspected of harboring Vietcong, and massacred virtually every inhabitant. The Defense Department attempted to cover up this crime, but it became known when a former member of Calley's unit informed several high government officials. Calley was eventually tried, but received a light sentence.

By 1968 the United States had sunk deeply into a dirty, divisive, expensive war. As in the Korean conflict, there seemed to be no way to conclude the fighting without surrender. Reassuring government statements were undercut daily by television broadcasts from the battlefields that showed no cause for optimism.

As the war dragged on month after month, it began to damage the economy. Johnson was at first afraid to ask Americans to pay for the war directly, lest economic sacrifice encourage further opposition. Yet by 1967 it was costing the country $25 billion a year. This sum, on top of Great Society domestic programs, produced what then seemed large budget deficits: $8.7 billion in 1967 and $25.2 billion in 1968. Finally, the president asked for higher taxes to siphon off excess purchasing power, but by then the harm was done. Until 1966 yearly consumer price increases had remained below 2 percent. In 1966 they rose to 3.4 percent and in 1968 to 4.7 percent. The dollar was becoming one of the war's casualties.

Organized protests against the war by college students, pacifist groups, and various peace organizations began in 1965. In early 1966, a congressional "dove," J. William Fulbright of Arkansas, chairman of the Senate Foreign Relations Committee, conducted televised hearings on the war during which he grilled Secretary of State Dean Rusk remorselessly and exposed many of the weaknesses of the prowar "hawk" position. Fulbright denounced the war as displaying the "arrogance of power." Before long, liberal and radical clergy began to demand an end to the Vietnam slaughter. In early 1967 Martin Luther King, Jr., made a "Declaration of Independence" from the war, announcing that it was "time to break silence." In 1967 Father Daniel Berrigan and his brother, Philip, organized the Catholic Ultra-Resistance.

Yet most Americans continued to support the war. Many considered the protesters traitors to their country. Bumper stickers reading "America: Love it or Leave it" began to appear on the streets and highways. Even many anti-Communist liberals continued to believe that abandoning South Vietnam would destroy the credibility of American foreign policy and play into Soviet hands.

After 1967, however, support for the president's Vietnam policies eroded rapidly. The greatest blow to "hawk" confidence came in early 1968 when, during the Vietnamese Lunar New Year (Tet), the Vietcong launched a major offensive against Saigon and scores of other South Vietnamese cities. One squad of Vietcong commandos broke into the American embassy compound in Saigon and threatened to capture the embassy itself. After fierce and bloody fighting, the Communist assault was checked. The Vietcong suffered thousands of casualties. But Tet made a mockery of the administration's confident propaganda. Until this point many Americans had found it possible to believe that the war, however protracted, was being won. Tet seemed to show that the enemy was, if anything, growing in strength.

By early 1968 administration leaders were beginning to have doubts themselves. Early in the year a discouraged and disillusioned defense secretary Robert McNamara left the Pentagon to become head of the World Bank. Johnson himself began to have second thoughts. The war seemed to be getting out of hand and threatening to rip the country apart. The president found himself personally under siege. Whenever he appeared in public he was surrounded by protesters carrying signs denouncing him and chanting "Hey! Hey! LBJ, How Many Kids Did You Kill Today?" On top of his other troubles, as the presidential election of 1968 approached Johnson found himself facing a formidable challenge for renomination from within his own party.

The 1968 Election

McCarthy v. Kennedy. The president's challengers were Senators Eugene McCarthy of Minnesota and Robert F. Kennedy of New York. A former Catholic seminarian, McCarthy attracted many students and academics who appreciated his ethical stance. Kennedy could communicate more readily with blue-collar workers and blacks. Wearing the still-shining mantle of Camelot, he projected a warmer image as friend of the masses. McCarthy was first in the field against Johnson. When the "dump Johnson" leaders initially failed to entice Kennedy into running, the Minnesota senator reluctantly announced his candidacy. Few expected that he could make much headway against an incumbent president, but in the New Hampshire Democratic primary in March 1968 thousands of student volunteers turned out to ring doorbells, make phone calls, and stuff envelopes for him. Many "cleaned for Gene," shaving off beards, abandoning jeans and T-shirts to avoid offending the state's conservative voters. The primary results were startling: The challenger received only a few hundred votes fewer than the president. Having concluded that Johnson was beatable, Kennedy now also entered the race.

By early 1968 Johnson had decided to renounce another full term. His new Defense Secretary, the debonair Clark Clifford, and the informal group of foreign-policy elder statesmen known as the "Wise Men," told him after Tet that the war was unwinnable. He should, they said, gradually reduce the American military commitment. Reluctantly accepting their position, Johnson refused to grant the request of General William Westmoreland, U.S. commander in Vietnam, for an additional 206,000 troops. He also concluded that he could encourage a negotiated peace if he ceased the bombing campaign and withdrew himself from public life. In an address to the nation on March 31 announcing a bombing halt and a major peace initiative, he concluded with the words: "I shall not seek, and will not accept, the nomination of my party for another term as your president." The two Democratic antiwar candidates now began the long struggle through the state primaries to secure the party nomination.

Before the campaign's end two tragedies intervened. The first took place in Memphis, where Martin Luther King, Jr., had gone to support a local strike of the predominantly black city garbage collectors. King's nonviolent approach to racial change, as we saw, was under powerful attack by black-power militants, but he was about to open a new phase of his career by leading a "poor people's campaign" to compel the government to revive its flagging effort to end poverty. He never did. On April 4, 1968, he was shot and killed by James Earl Ray, an escaped white convict who may have been in the pay of white supremacists. Black ghettos around the country exploded in rage and despair. From their offices on Capitol Hill congressmen could see the flames and smoke from Washington's burning buildings and stores.

The second tragedy came on June 6 in Los Angeles minutes after Kennedy's victory over McCarthy in the California primary. As he left his cheering supporters in the Embassy Room of the Ambassador Hotel, Kennedy was assassinated by a Palestinian immigrant named Sirhan Bishara Sirhan. These two events magnified the public's agony over violence and reinforced the sense that the nation must extricate itself from the contaminating brutality of Vietnam. The United States now seemed to be at the edge of anarchy.

The forces that converged on Chicago for the Democratic presidential nominating convention in late August represented an explosive mixture. Now that Johnson was out of the running, the hawks had gathered around Vice President Humphrey, who, however much he personally disliked the war, had become Johnson's heir apparent, tied to his policies by loyalty and dependence. On the other side were the combined antiwar groups representing McCarthy and the delegates who had supported Kennedy. On the streets and in the parks of the Windy City were the Yippies (Youth International Party), politicized counterculture protestors led by activists Jerry Rubin and Abbie Hoffman, along with New Left radicals, antiwar students, and pacifists, who were determined to replace the Democrats' "convention of death," with their own "festival of life."

Within the convention hall itself the Humphrey forces won. Supported by the remaining hawks, by union leaders, by party regulars, and by the big-city power brokers, Humphrey overcame the insurgent peace forces and was nominated on the first ballot. In the streets of Chicago, meanwhile, Mayor Richard Daley's police clashed violently with the antiwar activists before the eyes of the delegates and the TV cameras. To many viewers the contrast between political business-as-usual in the convention hall and the images of burly policemen hurling young people and reporters through plate glass windows was final evidence that America was out of control. Many voters blamed the chaos on the Democrats and on Hubert Humphrey; his campaign was in deep trouble from the start.

The Backlash.   The chaotic events in Chicago reinforced the view of many white voters that the decade's permissiveness and toleration had gotten out of hand. The ghetto riots, the anti-Americanism of peace protesters, the hippie disregard of public decency, the courts' acceptance of pornography and rejection of school prayer—in fact, the whole thrust of the decade—were sickening, they felt, and should be reversed. Called "backlash" voters, they were disproportionately white males of working-class background who felt left behind by government and a culture they believed was run by elitists who favored society's crazies and extremists over themselves. Many saw a savior in George Wallace, the segregationist governor of Alabama, who had challenged Lyndon Johnson in several of the Democratic primaries in 1964 and done surprisingly well among blue-collar registered Democrats.

Meanwhile, in Miami, in a convention as bland as the Democrats' was tumultuous, the Republicans nominated Richard M. Nixon. The nomination represented a spectacular comeback for the candidate. In 1962 Nixon had run for governor of California and had been beaten by the incumbent, Edmund Brown. After his defeat, in an intemperate outburst accusing the press of "kicking him around" during the campaign, he had promised never to run for office again. Soon after, he joined a high-powered New York law firm to spend his remaining days making money and enjoying the pleasures of private life. He could not stay out of politics, however, and soon started the comeback campaign that finally brought him victory at the Miami convention.

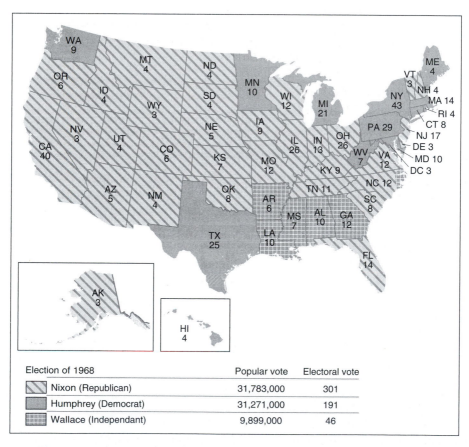

Election of 1968	Popular vote	Electoral vote
Nixon (Republican)	31,783,000	301
Humphrey (Democrat)	31,271,000	191
Wallace (Independant)	9,899,000	46

The Election of 1968

The 1968 presidential contest was a close one. Many observers felt that the Democrats had destroyed themselves in Chicago by their bitter, divisive in-fighting and the rioting in the streets. The Republicans, on the other hand, worried about defections in the South and among white blue-collar males to Wallace, running as the American Independent Party candidate on a platform of law and order, total victory in Vietnam, clamping down on dissenters and civil rights activists, and reducing the power of federal bureaucrats over people's lives. To avoid losing the South and the backlash voters to Wallace, Nixon promised conservative Senator Strom Thurmond of South Carolina that if elected he would keep the nation strong militarily, work for a less activist Supreme Court, and slow the pace of desegregation. It was with Thurmond's urging that Nixon selected Spiro T. Agnew, the little-known governor of Maryland, as his running mate.

The Republicans were well in the lead as the campaign opened. Humphrey was handicapped by his association with the administration's Vietnam policy and not until September did he free himself from this onus by proposing a more "dovish" approach to a negotiated peace in Vietnam. He was also in trouble because many blue-collar male Democrats threatened to defect to Wallace. Then, as November approached, the traditional Democratic coalition of ethnics, blacks, eastern liberals, and union members began to rally around Humphrey. Had the campaign gone on for just a few days longer, the ticket of Humphrey and Senator Edmund S. Muskie of Maine might have pulled ahead. But the surge came too late. On November 5 Nixon won by 31.7 million votes (301 electoral) to Humphrey's 31.2 million (191 electoral) and Wallace's 9.9 million (46 electoral). Richard Nixon would be the thirty-seventh president of the United States.

Conclusions

During the 1960s the United States attained a level of material well-being beyond anything dreamed of in the past. Affluence transformed the public mood. The middle class, initially, experienced a new spirit of generosity. Generosity, reinforced perhaps by guilt, and underscored by the sweeping 1964 victory of Lyndon Johnson over Barry Goldwater, in turn unleashed a surge of social reform not equaled since the New Deal.

And, ironically, prosperity also encouraged an unprecedented wave of dissent and social criticism. Minorities, even more keenly than in the past, felt resentment at long-denied basic civil rights and exclusion from the benefits of abundance. To the privileged young, who took America's bounding wealth for granted, American society seemed an ugly place of bureaucratic rigidity, meaningless relationships, racism, manipulation, and aesthetic squalor. With affluence so readily attainable the dissenters could experiment, indulging their yearnings for alternative ways of living their lives.

But there was also the war. The dissenters' disgust with their society was reinforced by a distant and apparently pointless war. Vietnam undermined the legitimacy of many of the nation's established institutions: government, the universities, the mainstream press, the churches.

Thus, some of the chief beneficiaries of prosperity were the very people who despised it the most. Their excesses in turn would outrage those who still held to traditional values and attitudes and force the dissenters on the defensive. The election of Richard Nixon in 1968 expressed that outrage. The sixties were, in effect, over. What would replace it?

ONLINE RESOURCES

"The Cuban Missile Crisis" *http://www.gwu.edu/~nsarchiv/nsa/cuba_mis_cri/* *http://www.gwu.edu/~nsarchiv/nsa/cuba_mis_cri/cmcchron.html* This site provides an introduction and overview of events of the Cuban Missile Crisis, including declassified documents, air reconnaissance photographs, audio clips, and minute-by-minute chronologies.

"The Great Society Speech" *http://comm.tamu.edu/pres/speeches/lbjgreat.html* At this online speech archive, read Lyndon B. Johnson's "Great Society" speech and many others of his presidency.

"The History of NOW" *http://www.now.org/history/history.html* Visit the National Organization of Women's Web site and read about the group's founding, its involvement in the Equal Rights Amendment drive, and its advocacy for issues concerning working women. Also, read primary-source documents addressing woman's liberation at Duke University's online collection "Documents from the Women's Liberation Movement" at *http://scriptorium.lib.duke.edu/wlm/*

"The Wars of Vietnam: An Overview" *http://vietnam.vassar.edu/* Offering an extensive overview of military conflicts in Vietnam from 1945 up through U.S. engagement, this site offers the full texts of historical documents including the Tonkin Gulf Resolution and excerpts from American presidential speeches.

"The History of GATT and the Structure of the WTO" *http://www.econ.iastate.edu/classes/econ355/choi/wtoroots.htm* On this Web site, read more about the fundamental policies of the General Agreement on Tariffs and Trade (GATT), the 1947 economic policy intended to reduce trade barriers and regulate commerce.

The Psychedelic '60s: Literary Tradition and Social Change *http://www.lib.virginia.edu/exhibits/sixties/index.html* An online exhibit that explores the counterculture of the 1960s addressing issues such as the war in Vietnam and the civil rights movement through poetry, literature, and pop art of the day.

29
The Uncertain Seventies

Why Did the Right Fail?

1960	Organization of Petroleum Exporting Countries (OPEC) is formed
1969	Paris peace talks on Vietnam begin; Nixon orders the secret bombing of Cambodia; Strategic Arms Limitation Talks (SALT) begin in Helsinki; Americans land on the moon; Nuclear Nonproliferation Treaty
1970	United States invades Cambodia; Four students killed by National Guard in antiwar demonstration at Kent State University in Ohio; Congress repeals the Gulf of Tonkin Resolution
1971	The *New York Times* publishes the "Pentagon Papers"; Nixon imposes wage and price controls; Berlin Accord
1972	Nixon visits China; Congress passes the Federal Election Campaign Act; Nixon visits Moscow; The United States and the Soviet Union ratify arms limitation treaties; Watergate break-in; Nixon reelected in landslide
1973	Truce in Vietnam; Senate Select Committee holds public hearing on Watergate; House Judiciary Committee begins hearings on impeachment resolutions; Vice President Agnew resigns in disgrace; Gerald Ford becomes vice president; Israel and Egypt go to war, touching off Arab oil embargo; Abortion legalized by Supreme Court in *Roe v. Wade*
1974	Arab oil embargo ends, but OPEC raises oil prices drastically; House Judiciary Committee recommends impeachment of Nixon; Nixon resigns; Ford becomes president; Ford pardons Nixon
1975	North and South Vietnam are reunited
1976	Bicentennial celebrations; Jimmy Carter elected president
1977	SALT II talks collapse; Carter launches "moral equivalent of war" on United States dependency on foreign oil; Camp David Accords
1978	Panama Canal treaties
1979	SALT II agreement; Three Mile Island nuclear power plant disaster; Shah of Iran exiled; 66 American hostages taken by Khomeini's followers in Iran; Russia invades Afghanistan
1980	Ronald Reagan elected president

In January 1969 a new Republican administration came to power in Washington apparently determined to dismantle the Great Society, slow the pace of social change, and vigorously push back the tide of world Communism. Between that date and the end of the 1970s American public opinion would, by and large, support such a conservative agenda. Yet very little of it would be achieved. Indeed, by the opening of the 1980s the United States, in the eyes of many committed conservatives, had retrogressed: The social welfare state had expanded, the federal courts had pushed into new areas of social change, and the United States was embarked on a course of accommodation to the Communist world.

How had such results come about? How had Richard Nixon, the man who seemed to epitomize conservative anti-Communism, managed to perpetuate big government and the social welfare state that he and his followers despised and to replace the hard-line anti-Communism of recent American policy with a more flexible approach?

The Nixon Presidency

Richard Nixon was one of the most puzzling and inconsistent men to occupy the White House. His father was an angry, abusive man and a financial failure; his mother a sweet-tempered Quaker lady. The contrasting personalities of his parents helped mold the extremes of Nixon's own character: one side self-pitying and vindictive, particularly in the face of frustration; the other generous, even idealistic. Both facets of the new president's nature could be detected in his approach to public issues. He could support welfare reform, environmental protection laws, and reconciliation with Red China and the Soviet Union, for example. But he also sought to weaken civil rights protection, was unscrupulous in confronting his political adversaries, and inspired the illegal political acts we call Watergate.

Nixon's tough, partisan side was reflected in his inner circle of Attorney General John Mitchell, White House Chief of Staff H. R. Haldeman, and chief adviser on domestic affairs John Ehrlichman. Coming from outside the normal American political culture of give-and-take, these men, like the president, believed that winning was all that counted. They also shared with their boss a deep suspicion of the "eastern establishment," a vaguely defined circle of liberal leaders who, they claimed, dominated the press, the universities, and the upper reaches of the professions, and would do anything to malign and frustrate the president if they could.

Nixon also appointed better advisers, however. Daniel Moynihan, assistant for urban affairs, was one of the more imaginative men in American political life. Henry Kissinger, Nixon's national security adviser and later secretary of state, was an unusually adept diplomat with a vision influenced by his deep knowledge of history, though he harbored a streak of deviousness. Other competent Nixon appointees included Treasury Secretary John Connally and Secretary of Defense Melvin Laird. Unfortunately, the inner circle of White House aides under Haldeman and Ehrlichman often exerted disproportionate influence on administration policy.

Détente.   Nixon was far more interested in foreign policy than domestic affairs; it was as an international statesman that he hoped to make his mark in history. Foremost, he and Kissinger sought to stabilize relations with the Communist world by withdrawing from Vietnam, recognizing the People's Republic of China, and reducing rivalry with the Soviet Union.

However commendable their goals, the Nixon-Kissinger diplomatic style disturbed many observers. Initially the president's national security adviser, Kissinger had little respect for Secretary of State William Rogers, and often employed secret "back channel" negotiations with foreign representatives that bypassed the State Department. This awkward situation was rectified in 1973 when the German-born Kissinger became Rogers's successor. Yet even as Secretary of State, Kissinger continued to rely on what his opponents considered devious stratagems.

Though controversial, the Nixon–Kissinger policy made substantial progress toward reducing world tensions. One source of Soviet–American competition ended during the summer of 1969 when astronaut Neil A. Armstrong took the first steps on the moon while millions around the world watched on television. The United States had undeniably won the "space race," set off by the Soviet launching of Sputnik in 1957. Then, in November 1969, Nixon and Soviet president Nikolai Podgorny signed the Nuclear Nonproliferation Treaty to prevent the spread of dangerous nuclear weapons to nations that did not yet possess them. In 1971 and 1972 the perennial problems of Berlin and the two Germanies (The Federal Republic in the west and the Democratic Republic in the east) were finally settled by the Berlin Accord: Britain, France, the United States, and the Soviet Union agreed to cease threatening communications between the non-Communist zone of Berlin and the Federal Republic, and formally recognized the existence of two separate German nations.

Another step in the process of accommodation with America's chief rival ("détente") came in May 1972 when Nixon visited the Soviet Union, the first American president ever to do so. The visit produced a set of agreements pledging the two nations to facilitate commercial relations and cooperate in the scientific, medical, and environmental realms. More significantly, it led to the signing of the SALT I (Strategic Arms Limitation Treaty) agreements negotiated over several years by the two powers. SALT I confirmed MAD ("mutually assured destruction") as superpower policy: The check on nuclear war would be deterrence guaranteed by the ability of either side to massively retaliate against any nuclear attack. The core agreement of SALT I was the Anti-Ballistic Missile (ABM) Treaty forbidding virtually all defensive weapons capable of shooting down hostile incoming ICBMs. It also included agreements to limit the construction and deployment of new offensive missiles.

The People's Republic of China.

Even more remarkable in some ways than détente with the Soviet Union was the breakthrough in relations with the People's Republic of China. Until now the United States had refused to recognize the Chinese mainland regime of Mao Tse-tung and had vetoed every attempt to admit the

People's Republic to the United Nations. In Washington's view, "China" was the Republic of China on Taiwan where Chiang Kai-shek's Nationalists had fled after the Communist mainland victory in 1949. American troops were stationed on Taiwan to provide military support if the Chinese Communists should ever attempt to invade the island across the Strait of Formosa.

There were good reasons to dislike the regime in Beijing. On attaining power, the Communists had executed thousands of people as class enemies and imposed a harsh, authoritarian regime on the Chinese people. To restore flagging revolutionary zeal, in the 1960s they had unleashed a wave of murderous anarchy (the Cultural Revolution) against all traces of the bourgeois past, all western influences, and all dissenting opinion. Yet, with its 800 million people, China's existence could not be wished away. Not only did America's China policy seem unrealistic; it was also probably not in America's best interests. Nixon perceived that since Stalin's death in the early 1950s, China and the Soviet Union, once closely allied, had become adversaries whose armies at times violently clashed along their common Asian border. It seemed foolish not to take advantage of the Sino–Soviet rift and use one Communist nation to check the goals and ambitions of the other. Indeed, an opening to China seemed an essential ingredient of achieving stable relations with the Soviet Union.

Soon after the 1968 American presidential elections, Beijing indicated its desire to smooth over Sino–American differences. Both countries were soon holding secret meetings in Warsaw. Another signal of friendship came in early 1971 when the Chinese invited an American ping-pong team then visiting Japan to tour the People's Republic and play Chinese teams. In July 1971, after a secret visit by Kissinger to Beijing, Nixon startled the world by announcing that he had been invited to visit the People's Republic of China and would go there sometime in the early part of the following year. In October the United States for the first time abstained from vetoing the admission of Red China to the United Nations. The Beijing government was promptly seated and the Taiwan regime's representatives expelled.

On February 21, 1972, Nixon, his wife, and a large presidential entourage arrived in Beijing by plane. Scores of American reporters and the TV media were present, and millions of viewers in the United States watched the American president shake hands with Premier Chou En-lai, Mao's right-hand man. The discussions that followed with Chou and Communist party chairman, the aging Mao, were largely exploratory; little of a concrete nature was accomplished during the visit except for an agreement to withdraw the American troops from Taiwan. Much of Nixon's time was spent in sightseeing and banqueting. But the meeting was momentous symbolically. Television pictures of Nixon toasting Chou, quoting Chairman Mao, and strolling along the Great Wall made clear to the American people that the policy of ignoring the world's most populous nation was finally ended.

The far right considered the settlement with the People's Republic and abandonment of Taiwan a surrender to Communism. Most Americans, however, accepted the move as sensible and long overdue. Many of Nixon's liberal critics noted ruefully that only a conservative with a reputation as a militant anti-Communist could have gotten away with the abrupt change of policy.

Richard Nixon and Chinese Premier Chou En-lai at a banquet during Nixon's famous 1972 trip to Beijing. Nixon looks dubious about his food.

"Peace with Honor" in Vietnam.

Until the middle of Nixon's second term, however, America remained trapped in the Vietnam morass, the worst of the foreign policy past. In January 1969 serious peace talks between North Vietnam and the United States, initiated by Johnson, opened in Paris. They quickly deadlocked. North Vietnam had no intention of abandoning its goal of evicting the Saigon regime and reuniting Vietnam under its sole control; the United States did not intend to desert its ally.

The new American administration had little interest in continuing the war. But, like his predecessor, Nixon did not want to be charged with "losing" Vietnam. America must disengage, but it must preserve an independent South Vietnam to keep its reputation and pride intact. Nixon called this "peace with honor"; his critics called it foolish, among other things.

Nixon was willing to use any means to force the Communists to bargain. At one point he spread the story that he was a Communist-obsessed nuclear madman capable of blowing up the world if he did not get his way. In March 1969 he secretly ordered the massive bombing of Vietnam's neighbor, Cambodia—a supposedly neutral nation—to hamper Communist military operations in South Vietnam. At the same time, however, he announced that the United States would adopt the policy of "Vietnamization": It would gradually shift responsibility for military defense to the South Vietnamese and begin to withdraw American combat troops.

The antiwar forces at home gave little credit to the president for Vietnamization. Nixon talked peace, they said, but the fighting and dying continued. America should leave Vietnam immediately. "Out Now" was the only valid policy. Then, in late April 1970, Nixon sent American forces on a sweep through Cambodia to attack bases that, he claimed, were refuges for Vietcong guerrillas. A seeming escalation of fighting, this move electrified the antiwar movement. Demonstrations erupted on scores of college campuses. At Kent State University in Ohio, National Guardsmen fired live ammunition at student antiwar demonstrators, killing four and wounding eleven. Hundreds of American campuses shut down to protest the killings and to allow students to mobilize against the detested war. In June Congress reacted to the revived antiwar surge by repealing the 1964 Gulf of Tonkin resolution that Johnson had used as a legal equivalent of a declaration of war.

By now antiwar feeling had spread far beyond the original circle of activists. Seeking to show the war's nefarious roots, in June 1971 Daniel Ellsberg, a former Pentagon official, made public a collection of classified Defense Department documents describing the slow steps to American entrapment in the Vietnam swamp and the deception that accompanied the process. The Justice Department indicted Ellsberg for unauthorized use of government material and sought a court injunction to stop publication of the "Pentagon Papers" in the *New York Times* and *Washington Post*. The Supreme Court denied the injunction.* Meanwhile, in Vietnam the promised withdrawal undermined the morale of American troops still in Vietnam. Determined to avoid danger now that departure was on the way, more and more disobeyed direct orders or "fragged" officers by rolling live hand grenades into their tents while they slept. Others turned to drugs to make the time until their tour of duty ended pass more quickly. The war, it seemed, was destroying the American military.

In 1972, with only a few thousand American combat troops remaining in South Vietnam, the Communists launched a major offensive to topple the Saigon government. In retaliation, Nixon ordered the resumption of massive bombing of North Vietnam and the mining of Haiphong harbor, the port of entry for most of the arms and supplies from the Soviet Union. It looked as if the escalation pattern of the past would be repeated once more despite Vietnamization. Fortunately, by this time, both the Chinese and the Russians were more anxious for better relations with the United States than for North Vietnamese victory, and they told Hanoi that it must act more reasonably. Meanwhile, the Saigon government, reassured by a billion-dollar gift of American military hardware to help it defend itself against a Communist takeover, also proved more amenable to negotiation.

These events finally broke the peace negotiation logjam in Paris. In January 1973 the United States, South Vietnam, and the Vietcong-North Vietnamese signed an agreement that included (1) a cease-fire between Hanoi and Saigon, (2) the release of all American prisoners of war, (3) the withdrawal of all remaining U.S. military personnel, (4) massive American economic aid to South Vietnam, and (5) several complicated arrangements intended to reconcile the South Vietnamese government and the Vietcong. Nixon and Kissinger claimed that the terms would preserve the separate existence of South Vietnam. Whether they truly believed this or merely hoped for "a decent interval" before Saigon fell is not clear. In any event, despite the supposed safeguards, by April 1975 Communist forces had

---

*As part of the fallout from Watergate, in May 1973 the charges against Ellsberg were dismissed.

overwhelmed the South Vietnamese army and occupied all of Vietnam, forcibly uniting North and South under their harsh regime. The Communists had finally achieved their goal of thirty years.

Few Americans could extract satisfaction from the result. Vietnam was devastated—physically, economically, socially. Literally millions of Vietnamese, civilians and soldiers, had died. The United States too had paid a high cost. Over 46,000 Americans had lost their lives and the country had squandered over $150 billion. Hawks saw the outcome as a humiliation for the United States. It was the first war that America had lost, and it would weaken the nation's self-confidence. At first, those who had opposed the war could boast that they had helped end the killing and replaced a corrupt, undemocratic Asian government with a more popular one. It was soon obvious, however, that the Communist regime was as benighted as its enemies had long charged. The North Vietnamese conquerors rounded up thousands of the Saigon regime's friends and sent them to forced labor or "reeducation" camps. Over 1.4 million refugees fled the country, many in small boats. Thousands of Vietnamese refugees settled in the United States. For decades Vietnam would remain one of the poorest, most backward nations in all of East Asia, an embarrassment to all who had supported Hanoi's struggle to reunite the country.

The war's outcome would color the debate over future American foreign policy. Some citizens would see it as a lesson in limits: The United States must confine itself to matters that affected its vital interests closer to home. Others would view it as an instance of how defeat would inevitably follow loss of nerve and confidence. For a time the limits group would predominate, and during the mid-1970s American foreign policy would enter a phase that observers called neo-isolationist.

Courting the Backlash Vote.

In domestic affairs Nixon looked two ways. He had based his 1968 election campaign on the existence of a "silent majority," composed mostly of nominal Democrats who were fed up with many of the social trends of the day. Their disgust could be used to forge a new and unbeatable Republican majority. This resembled George Wallace's "backlash" strategy, though it was not as strident or overtly racist.

Nixon and his advisers found many backlash views personally congenial. Administration officials wore patriotic American flag pins on their lapels and cultivated a reverent demeanor toward traditional American values. After 1969 the administration set out to woo "Middle Americans," whether Democrats or Republicans, by echoing their views. Nixon described campus radicals as "bums." When it came to crime and disorder, ordinary citizens he said, "have had it up to here." The most hard-line conservative rhetoric came from Vice President Spiro Agnew, who toured the nation denouncing "rad-libs," the "nattering nabobs of negativism," and "troglodytic leftists." "The disease of our time," he said, "is an artificial and masochistic sophistication—the vague uneasiness that our values are false, and there is something wrong with being patriotic, honest, moral and hard-working."

The campaign to turn back the clock went beyond words. Federal officials eased up on the enforcement of desegregation in the South. In March 1971 Nixon asked Congress to halt "forced busing" of children from neighborhood schools to more distant ones to achieve racial balance. In April he directed veterans' hospitals to cease abortions for ex-servicewomen. The president frequently called for "law and order" and sponsored several bills to strengthen the hand of judges and the police. Nixon and his advisers believed, as had Johnson, that antiwar and New Left dissenters were encouraging the Vietcong and the North Vietnamese to continue their fight. The administration cracked down hard. During a May 1970 antiwar march on Washington, Attorney General Mitchell threw thousands of demonstrators into jail and detention compounds. The Justice Department indicted leading pacifists and student activists, including the Yippies and the baby-doctor, Benjamin Spock, for crimes or conspiracy to commit crimes. The defendants won most of these cases, but the legal defenses depleted the energies and financial resources of the antiwar movement.

Unlike Republicans in the past, Nixon counted on support from the white, formerly solid Democratic South. At the 1968 Republican convention he had promised conservative Dixie leaders to defer to traditional white southern feelings and wishes in regard to administrative and judicial appointments. In early 1969 he nominated to the Supreme Court Judge Clement F. Haynsworth, Jr., of South Carolina, a man suspected of segregationist views. The Democratically controlled Senate used Haynsworth's dubious conflicts of interest on the bench as the basis for rejecting his nomination. Nixon then sent forward the name of Florida federal judge G. Harrold Carswell. Antilabor and racially conservative, the new nominee was a man whose decisions had frequently been reversed by higher courts. The Senate rejected this appointment too. Nixon eventually succeeded in getting confirmed another presumed conservative, Harry Blackmun. Blackmun was a northerner, but the president's efforts on behalf of southerners Haynsworth and Carswell were appreciated by conservative white voters in Dixie.

Nixon presided over the change to a less turbulent and socially liberal society. On his watch the student revolt subsided; the hippies gradually disappeared; antiwar protest ceased. Still, these results did not satisfy backlash voters for other abuses remained or soon appeared. Drug abuse reached into the high schools of suburban America, teenage pregnancies soared, crime spread, and movies and books continued to deal with sexually explicit themes.

Worst of all to some conservatives was the continued judicial activism of the Supreme Court. Earl Warren retired in 1968 and Nixon appointed as the new Chief Justice Warren Burger, a man opposed to his predecessor's liberal and activist views. Yet the Supreme Court continued to dismay conservatives. In *Swann v. Charlotte-Mecklenburg Board* (1971), the justices condoned busing children to distant schools for the purpose of "racial balance," undermining local control over public schools, in the view of traditionalists.

More momentous in its consequences was *Roe v. Wade* (1973). For many years abortion had been illegal in the United States under state laws. Women got abortions nevertheless, but these were often performed by medically unskilled men and women or were even crudely self-induced. Women sometimes died or were permanently rendered incapable of ever bearing children. With the rise of feminism in the 1960s public opinion shifted against the prohibition of legal termination of pregnancies and a number of states repealed their anti-abortion laws. Then, in 1973, in the name of expanding the right to privacy, the Supreme Court struck down the remaining state anti-abortion laws and allowed abortion on demand during the first trimester of pregnancy. Conservatives charged the justices with condoning baby murder. The decision would reap a whirlwind of passionate controversy.

Domestic Moderation.   Many of Nixon's conservative constituents, then, remained dissatisfied and would continue to search for ways to restore the nation to old-fashioned virtue. Yet Nixon did not send the American ship of state into full reverse. Those who had hoped that the Republican president would decrease the size and reach of the federal government or use it to roll back the social legislation of his liberal predecessors were disappointed.

In 1969 he proposed a "New Federalism" intended to downsize the federal government by transferring many domestic "entitlement" programs to the states, but in the end, he said, owing to resistance by the Democratic-controlled Congress and liberal federal bureaucrats, he succeeded only modestly. Nixon also left intact most Great Society welfare programs. In fact, during his administration, many received better funding than before. In 1968 federal social welfare expenditures had totaled $142 billion; in 1974 they reached $229 billion. Nixon even added programs to the Johnson roster. He signed into law the Supplementary Security Income Act that guaranteed a check each month for elderly, blind, and disabled Americans who were not otherwise entitled to a federal pension. He also endorsed a drastic welfare reform proposal by Daniel Moynihan to provide a guaranteed $1,600-a-year minimum income to each poor family from federal funds. The measure, many hoped, would end forever the inequalities and indignities that beset the existing "welfare system" and cut through the bureaucratic tangle that encumbered it. The Family Assistance Program never made it through both houses of Congress, in part because liberals felt it was not generous enough, but it was a bold departure for a president marked as a conservative.

Nixon's management of the economy was another surprise to those who expected him to pursue traditional conservative policies. By 1971 inflation was running about 5 percent a year, at the same time the economy was in a slump. On the recommendation of Treasury Secretary John Connally, in August the president announced a ninety-day freeze on all wages and prices, to be enforced by appointed control boards. The United States would also end the convertibility of the American dollar into gold in international exchanges. Closing the "gold window" ended the era of fixed international exchange rates that had helped to mend and then stimulate the world economy after 1945. Experts would later say that it accelerated inflation and retarded economic growth.

The New Environmentalism.   In some ways the most unexpected of all Nixon's domestic policies was his endorsement of the new environmentalism, if only in a qualified way. Drawing on new scientific insights regarding the interrelatedness of all living things, by the 1970s scientists saw humans as part of a complex "ecosystem," a web of life that extended far beyond our own species. This mandated esteem for living creatures and respect for the balances of nature. The public mind was alerted to many of the new ideas by Rachel Carson, a naturalist with the U.S. Fish and Wildlife Service, whose 1962 book, *Silent Spring*, described the long-term lethal effects of the insecticide DDT on wildlife, especially birds, and the dangers of carelessly introducing such potent poisons into the natural environment. For every reader of the bestseller who caught the message of nature's interrelatedness there were many more undoubtedly roused by the threat to human health. *Silent Spring* was followed by a flood of books, magazine articles, and TV reports informing the public of how humans interacted with the natural environment and advertising the dangers of pollution from a host of industrial and agricultural processes.

Many of the new views went on display on Earth Day, April 22, 1970, a one-day nationwide celebration of nature that proclaimed the need to stop the environment-despoiling "development" juggernaut. It is not likely that Nixon personally absorbed much of the advanced new ecological sensibility, but he did respond to growing public fears of environmental hazards. Soon after Earth Day he approved the Clean Air Act of 1970, establishing a billion-dollar air pollution control program and imposing tighter emission standards on automobiles. He also signed the Occupational Safety and Health Act establishing an agency to oversee new standards of health and safety for workers in the job environment. Following a serious tanker oil spill off Santa Barbara, California, he approved the Water Quality Improvement Act of 1970 imposing penalties for pollution of ocean and inland waters. In October of that year he created the Environmental Protection Agency (EPA) to administer the various government antipollution programs. In later years the EPA would be in the thick of the battle to preserve and upgrade the natural environment.

The 1972 Election.

Many of Nixon's domestic policies—the price control measures particularly—were driven by short-term political considerations. Nothing, including inflation and a weak dollar, must stand in the way of his reelection in 1972.

In retrospect it is difficult to understand why the administration was so politically insecure. The Democrats' choice for president in 1972 was Senator George McGovern of South Dakota who represented the party's most liberal wing. McGovern had won the nomination under new convention rules, adopted in 1968, requiring each state delegation to reflect individual voter blocs—youth, women, minorities, as well as white males—in approximate proportion to their numbers in the general populace. The Democratic delegates at Miami were probably a better cross section of the country's citizens than at past conventions, but traditional Democrats—white southerners, blue-collar Catholics, older people, trade unionists—felt left out. It soon appeared that many of them either would not vote or would vote Republican.

McGovern also proved to be an inept campaigner. He selected Senator Thomas Eagleton of Missouri as his running mate without conducting a careful background check. When Eagleton admitted that he had been hospitalized for mental illness, McGovern first rallied to Eagleton's side and then dropped him for former Peace Corps director Sargent Shriver. The Democratic candidate also stumbled over his welfare reform plan, revealing his own uncertain grasp of a guaranteed annual income scheme that many found extravagant. By early fall the polls were pointing to a Democratic disaster.

With the Democrats obviously fumbling away the election, Nixon could avoid the political rough-and-tumble and act "presidential." By fall the economy was firmly in hand under phase one of Nixon's wage and price control program. The results were predictable. Nixon won 60.8 percent of the popular vote, a tiny fraction below Lyndon Johnson's 1964 landslide, and took all the nation's electoral votes except those of the District of Columbia and Massachusetts.

Watergate

The stunning November victory seemed a mandate for four more years of presidential achievement. It was not to be. On June 17, five months before, five men had been arrested at the Washington, D.C., headquarters of the Democratic National Committee in the Watergate housing complex; two accomplices were caught outside. To this day their motives are unclear, but the best guesses are that either they were trying to recover information on an illegal gift by millionaire Howard Hughes to a close Nixon friend; or they were hoping to find some dirt on the Democrats that could be used to prevent disclosure of the Hughes transaction.

Although three of the burglars were connected either to the White House or the Committee to Reelect the President (CRP), no information damaging to the administration came to light before the election. When questioned by reporters in mid-June, White House press secretary Ron Ziegler called the Watergate break-in a "third-rate burglary" that had nothing to do with the administration. McGovern struggled to make a campaign issue of Watergate but could prove little, and it did not affect the outcome. Then, by the time of Nixon's second inauguration, the story behind the break-in began to emerge.

In January 1973 the Watergate burglars came before federal District Court judge John Sirica. Dissatisfied with the unaggressive questioning of the prosecutors, Sirica grilled the defendants himself. After conviction by a jury, to avoid stiff sentences from "Maximum John," James McCord revealed to the court that the break-in had involved others besides the defendants and that perjury had been committed at the trial.

It was unfortunate for the administration that the Democrats were in the majority of both houses of Congress; a Republican House and Senate would undoubtedly have been less aggressive in pursuing the president. In February the Senate established a Select Committee on Presidential Campaign activities under the chairmanship of Senator Sam Ervin, Jr., of North Carolina. In May the Ervin committee began to hear testimony on the Watergate matter from a parade of administration officials including Jeb Stuart Magruder, deputy director of CRP; John Dean, the president's counsel; former Attorney General John Mitchell; and Alexander Butterfield, former deputy presidential assistant.

Both Dean and Magruder had already begun to tell the federal prosecutors all they knew, disclosing that Haldeman, Ehrlichman, and Mitchell had tried to hide the administration's role in the break-in. In effect, three of Nixon's closest associates were seeking to obstruct justice, a clearly indictable crime. On April 30, the president learned that Dean intended to accuse him of attempting to hide the administration's responsibility for Watergate. Nixon announced that he had accepted the resignations of Haldeman, Ehrlichman, and Attorney General Richard Kleindienst, and had fired Dean. He also directed the new attorney general, Elliot Richardson, to appoint a special prosecutor to probe Watergate. Richardson named Archibald Cox of the Harvard Law School to the post.

Further Disclosures.

As the televised Ervin committee hearings proceeded, an appalled and fascinated public watched a steady parade of witnesses reveal the administration's disreputable efforts, through CRP (called CREEP by the unfriendly media), to crush its political opponents and illegally hide its acts. Led by *Washington Post* reporters Bob Woodward and Carl Bernstein, the press exposed other serious misdeeds.

The list of unethical and illegal Watergate actions eventually uncovered was a long one. Though it began as part of a "plumbers" operation to "plug" information leaks damaging to the administration, it soon ballooned far beyond this.

> Administration operatives had broken into the office of Daniel Ellsberg's psychiatrist looking for evidence to use against him in his trial for leaking the classified "Pentagon Papers."

> Ehrlichman had sought to influence the presiding judge in the Ellsberg case by hinting that he might be appointed FBI director if he made the right decision. (The White House effort backfired; when the attempt to suborn the judge came out, charges against Ellsberg were dismissed.)

> White House representatives had paid large sums of cash to the Watergate burglars after they were arrested to keep them silent on the connection between the break-in and CRP. Acting director of the FBI, L. Patrick Gray, under pressure from the White House, had destroyed evidence in the Watergate case. The FBI had also shared information from its Watergate investigation with White House counsel Dean, though the White House itself was clearly the target of the investigation.

> The Nixon reelection committee had engaged in "dirty tricks" to disrupt the campaigns of several Democratic candidates during the 1972 primaries. CRP had collected large sums of cash from corporations with promises of favors, or threats of retaliation, in violation of federal law, and had then tried to conceal it.

> The White House had drawn up an "enemies list" of adversaries in the media, the universities, and the entertainment world. These people were to be harassed by Internal Revenue Service audits and by other means.

> One of the Watergate burglars, E. Howard Hunt, had forged State Department messages to implicate the late President John F. Kennedy in the assassination of Vietnamese leader Ngo Dinh Diem. This was designed to besmirch the reputation of President Kennedy' brother, Ted, a potential Nixon presidential rival.

> The administration had engaged in illegal wiretapping, even of its own officials, to ferret out political and national security leaks.

> The president himself had taken dubious tax breaks for contributing his personal papers to the Library of Congress and had used federal funds to make improvements on his personal homes in Florida and California.

The most telling testimony before the Ervin committee came from John Dean, who claimed that Nixon had known of the illegal break-in for eight months and had tried to cover it up, even offering executive clemency to the burglars if they would keep quiet. But Dean's testimony could not be corroborated. Then, on July

16 Alexander Butterfield revealed that since 1971 all conversations in the president's Oval Office and in the Executive Office Building had been taped, and all the president's phones had been linked to recording devices. Now, everything that John Dean and others had disclosed could be checked against the actual record. The president immediately tried to block access to the tapes. For a full year his lawyers asserted that "executive privilege," needed to preserve the president's freedom of action, permitted him to keep the tapes of vital White House conversations confidential.

When the Ervin committee hearings concluded, the burden of uncovering the remaining facts about the break-in and the cover-up shifted to special prosecutor Archibald Cox. In July, Cox subpoenaed nine tapes. Nixon refused to surrender them, and Cox went before Judge Sirica to demand that they be produced. In late August, Sirica ordered Nixon to comply. The president's lawyers promptly appealed to the District of Columbia Circuit Court, which upheld Sirica's order.

Nixon Fights Back. On October 20, 1973, Nixon ordered Richardson to fire Cox. The Attorney General refused, as did his deputy, and both resigned. Solicitor General Robert Bork, as acting attorney general, finally performed the deed.

This "Saturday Night Massacre" produced a storm of criticism. The White House was deluged with telegrams denouncing the president and his actions. *Time* magazine, a conservative journal, in the first formal editorial in its fifty-year history, declared "the President should resign." On October 30 the House Judiciary Committee began to consider impeachment charges against Nixon.

Taken aback by this ferocious reaction, Nixon retreated. On October 23 he agreed to obey Sirica's order to deliver the tapes. On November 1 he appointed a new special prosecutor, Leon Jaworski, a conservative Texas attorney. But then the president's lawyers revealed that two of the tapes requested did not exist and that another, of a crucial June conversation with Dean, contained an 18-minute gap as the result of an "accidental" erasure. By this time few Americans believed anything the president said, and most doubted that the erasure had been unintended.

Meanwhile, Vice President Agnew was having his own troubles with the law. Accused of income tax evasion and of accepting payoffs for favors to contractors when he was governor of Maryland, he resigned from office on October 10, 1973. Under terms of the recently adopted Twenty-fifth Amendment to the Constitution, Nixon nominated House Minority Leader Gerald Ford of Michigan as Agnew's successor. Ford took the oath of office on December 6, 1973, as the new vice president. Now, if Watergate did force Nixon out, the country would at least have an honest man in his place.

Impeachment. Other bombs soon went off. In late April 1974 Nixon released 1,200 pages of edited transcripts of White House tapes. This was the public's first glimpse of what the president and his advisers had actually been saying and doing about Watergate in private. The view was appalling. The transcripts revealed Nixon as a profane, confused, and peevish man, willing to use any tack against his enemies and prone to mean-spirited and bigoted remarks. Worse than this, several conversations seemed to confirm his role in abetting a cover-up, though a "smoking gun" was not yet visible.

On May 1 the House Judiciary Committee denied that the release of the edited transcripts constituted full compliance with its subpoena. Jaworski's office had also subpoenaed tapes, and on May 20 Judge Sirica ordered Nixon once more to comply. The president's counsel appealed his decision to the Supreme Court.

That uneasy summer as Americans watched the unfolding drama, matters came to a head. First, the Supreme Court unanimously ruled that Nixon must release all the tapes Jaworski asked for. For reasons that would soon become clear, the president resisted the Court's order, but then relented. The process of transcribing the tapes began. On July 24 the House Judiciary Committee opened televised debates on articles of impeachment. A few days later it voted to recommend to the full House of Representatives three articles of impeachment: (1) that Nixon had obstructed justice by his role in the Watergate cover-up; (2) that he had misused federal agencies in violation of the rights of American citizens; and (3) that he had withheld information subpoenaed by the Judiciary Committee.

On August 5, 1974, Nixon released transcripts of three conversations between himself and Haldeman recorded on June 23, 1972, a scant week after the break-in. They clearly showed that the president had tried to squelch the FBI investigation of the burglary; he had in effect conspired to obstruct justice. Here was the "smoking gun" that could not be explained away, and Nixon's remaining congressional supporters now abandoned him. Facing almost certain impeachment by the full House, Nixon resigned as president on August 8 effective at noon the next day. On August 9, 1974, Gerald Ford took the oath of office as the new president.

Causes and Effects.   Observers pondered the roots of Watergate long after the president flew off to retirement in California. Some pointed their fingers at "the imperial presidency." Powers granted FDR and his successors to deal with the Great Depression, World War II, and the Cold War, they said, had raised the chief executive above the other branches of government and tempted the White House inner circle to consider the administration as the American government itself and its political opponents little better than national traitors. Some saw Nixon and his advisers primarily as victims of the paranoid Cold War mentality that at times excused unacceptable activities if done for the sake of "national security." Critics noted that the FBI and CIA had grown into fiefdoms that collected vast files on private citizens considered disloyal, opened private mail, and engaged in dirty tricks operations of their own against suspected subversives. In such an atmosphere it was no wonder that the White House itself should adopt a no-holds-barred attitude toward its opponents.

In the postmortems on Watergate, some Americans saw reasons for optimism in the outcome. The "system had worked," they said; the villains had been caught and punished, and honest, constitutional government had been restored. Others noted that Nixon had, after all, been reelected in a landslide and might easily have gotten away with it all if a few events had happened differently. Overall, Americans could not avoid feeling more cynical than ever about the honesty of politicians and more skeptical about the effectiveness of the nation's political system.

One thing is perfectly clear: Watergate ended whatever hope remained that Nixon would turn back the clock politically. Those voters who had believed that Nixon would return the country to traditional values felt bitterly betrayed. Liberals rejoiced that "Tricky Dick" had got his comeuppance.

The Ford Interlude.

America's only nonelected president, Gerald Ford, assumed office at a time when the nation desperately craved an end to distrust and uncertainty. Ford seemed the right man to start the healing process. A stolid legislator who had served in the House of Representatives for many years without special distinction, he was nevertheless an open, decent, and generous man whom most Americans quickly came to like.

The public's respect for Ford the man was not, however, matched by its view of Ford the president. Ford squandered much of the public's trust at the start of his presidency by granting a pardon to Nixon, thereby cutting off any further legal action against the ex-president. Though in his remarks announcing the pardon he emphasized personal compassion toward the former president and his determination to end the controversy and distrust caused by Watergate, many citizens suspected a secret deal whereby Ford, if chosen as Agnew's successor, would agree to pardon Nixon if he was forced to resign.

In foreign affairs Ford continued the initiatives of the recent past, retaining Kissinger as secretary of state and continuing to push détente. Gradually, however, high hopes for mutually advantageous arrangements with the Soviet Union dissipated. Soviet–American cultural exchanges helped dispel Cold War views that Russians were ogres, but Soviet violations of its own citizens' rights and mistreatment of its Jewish population offset such gains. Besides, the Soviet Union seemed determined more than ever to pursue expansionist ends through surrogates. When, for example, the African nation of Angola, newly independent from Portugal, collapsed into civil war, Soviet-armed Cuban troops supported the Angolan Marxists' drive to take control.

In domestic affairs Ford was even less successful. In response to a serious business recession following the spectacular hike in oil prices that accompanied the fourth Arab-Israeli war in 1973, he endorsed a tax cut and sought lower interest rates. By the fall of 1975 national output began once more to rise, but large pockets of unemployment remained.

In his early months as president, Ford had shown little interest in running for a full term. But as he settled into the job, he changed his mind and announced his candidacy for the 1976 election.

The 1976 Election.

Ford's supporters believed the president deserved a vote of confidence for having restored Americans' faith in their government. But the bad smell of Watergate lingered on and many Americans were more convinced than ever that Washington was tightly controlled by wheeler-dealers and politicians on the take.

The public's disgust with the "mess in Washington" helped the nomination campaigns of two outsiders, Ronald Reagan of California and Jimmy Carter of Georgia. Reagan, a former Hollywood actor turned conservative politician, had been an effective governor of California. Though a committed conservative, he had often placed ideology aside and compromised with his opponents to get things done. Carter was an Annapolis graduate who had served a single term as his state's governor. Unlike many southern politicians of the past, he had worked to reduce discrimination against blacks. Both candidates could claim to be untouched by the dirt that besmirched Washington insiders.

Despite the Reagan challenge, Ford got the Republican nomination at Kansas City and selected Senator Robert Dole of Kansas as his running mate. Carter won the Democratic nomination on the first ballot in New York and balanced his ticket by choosing as his partner Senator Walter Mondale of Minnesota, a liberal and a close former associate of Hubert Humphrey. In November, the support of black voters and white southerners, along with traditionally Democratic Catholic and Jewish voters, helped carry the Carter-Mondale ticket to victory. At the time many observers saw the Carter-Mondale vote as a reassembly of the old New Deal coalition, and a return of the voters to a more liberal outlook. It is now clear that Northern voters were reacting to Watergate while many white southerners were determined to elect the only one of their kind since Zachary Taylor in 1848 to win a major party nomination (if we except Lyndon Johnson, a Texan).

Seventies Discontents

President Jimmy Carter had his work cut out for him. The nation he would lead was buffeted by crosscurrents, uncertainties, and uncomfortable challenges to its self-confidence and its leading position in the free world.

The celebration of the two-hundredth anniversary of American independence on July 4, 1976, was symbolic of the public's insecurities and hesitations. There had been talk of a major international exposition at Philadelphia to proclaim, as a century before, America's achievements to all the world. It proved impossible to bring off such a celebration. The America of 1976 was far richer than in 1876, but it lacked the easy confidence in the political and economic future that had prevailed a century earlier. The bitterness of Vietnam lingered, and thousands of antiwar veterans doubted that America had much to boast about. Spokespersons for blacks, Indians, and other minorities insisted that they, the perennial outsiders, had scant reason to celebrate 200 years of nationhood. The country, of course, did not let the day go unmarked. In New York City a fleet of sailing ships from all over the world drew throngs of spectators to the harbor and banks of the Hudson River. In San Antonio a longhorn cattle drive, commemorating the days of the Texas cattle trails, was the celebration centerpiece. In Washington, D.C., half a million people watched a parade down Pennsylvania Avenue. Other communities had their own moving and eye-catching ways of commemorating the great event. Still, to critics, it seemed a party by the traditional white middle class, with millions of skeptics standing on the sidelines.

African–Americans.   As the 1970s advanced the predominant mood among black Americans was one of disappointment. The previous decade had promised so much and, in truth, some of it had been achieved. Nowhere could the law be used to bolster exclusion of blacks from public places or services or to enforce separation of the races. Even in the South blacks voted without restraint and were

becoming a force to be reckoned with in southern politics. By the early 1980s, the mayors of many big cities—Cleveland, Chicago, Washington, D.C., Los Angeles, Philadelphia, and Atlanta—would be black.

There had also been sweeping economic and social advances for black Americans. The number of black college students had risen from 141,000 in 1960 to 718,000 in 1980. Black median family income had grown from $3,230 in 1960 to $12,674 in 1980. Yet the picture was at best mixed. The gains since 1960 had not ended black poverty; nor had they eliminated the differences between black and white family incomes. At the end of the 1970s the average black family was still only 60 percent as rich as its white counterpart.

A new disturbing feature of the racial picture was the appearance of a two-tier social structure in the black community itself. By 1980 there was a new black middle class of professionals, government workers, skilled white-collar employees, and business managers. But at the same time there was a persistent "underclass" of unemployed ghetto-dwellers who seemed stuck in the groove of poverty, welfare, drug dependence, and—at times—crime.

Many sociologists blamed faulty family structure for this unfortunate result. Successful blacks came primarily from intact, two-parent families; the underclass were primarily mothers without husbands—many mere teenagers—and their children. Since the 1960s, single-parent, female-headed families had grown disproportionately among all social sectors in the United States as a result of soaring divorce rates and teenage pregnancy. But the phenomenon was more severe among blacks than other groups. In such one-parent families—especially those headed by young, poorly educated women—the processes of child nurture and social conditioning needed to produce competent young people were apparently limited.

Unfortunately, it was not certain why the traditional family was becoming less prevalent. Conservative observers often blamed it on the welfare system: By encouraging dependency, the federal welfare system, a heritage of New Deal days, accelerated the breakup of families. They also blamed the cultural excesses of the 1960s, which, they said, had undermined conventional sexual morality and family values and condoned teenage premarital sex and teenage pregnancies. Liberals and black spokespeople often ascribed family failure to persistent racism that made it difficult for young black males to get decent jobs and undermined incentives to remain with the families they had created. Still other analysts believed it derived from structural change in the economy. Factory work and semiskilled labor that had served as ladders upward for wage earners in the past no longer worked. Now the economy needed men and women who could program computers, sell financial securities, draw up plans for sales campaigns, and design sophisticated machines. Those without the necessary skills were relegated to dead-end jobs that provided neither the income for a reasonable family life nor the psychological and emotional bases it required.

Immigrants.   Some observers of race relations saw the freer entry of aliens following the 1965 Immigration and Nationality Act as a factor in the slow economic progress of African–Americans. Immigration of people from poor lands, particularly Latin America, they said, had depressed wages for unskilled black labor.

And immigration had indeed soared after passage of the 1965 Great Society measure. A large majority of the newcomers were from Latin America, with Mexico far in the lead. Many of them were legal immigrants. But there was also a very large group of "undocumented" immigrants without visas or immigration clearances who had fled the poverty of their countries for a better life in the United States. Many undocumented Hispanics worked at low-paying jobs in hospitals, restaurants, or offices, and in unskilled construction and factory work. In fact, many of these industries could not survive without them. Though most Hispanic-Americans were poor, there were pockets of notable Latin economic success. In the Miami area, for example, Cuban exiles from Castro's Marxist regime—mostly middle-class people with skills and capital—had reestablished themselves comfortably in their new American homes and were respected if not always liked by their "Anglo" neighbors.

Immigration during the 1970s also resulted in spectacular increases in the number of Asians in the United States. By 1980 there were 800,000 Chinese, 700,000 Japanese, 774,000 Filipinos, 350,000 Koreans, and 260,000 Vietnamese in the country. As in the case of Hispanics, some of the new arrivals were illegals. Many repeated the experience of early twentieth-century European immigrants by working in ill-paying garment industry "sweat shops" in New York and other cities. But on the whole, Asians did well in their new country. Many opened small businesses—delis, restaurants, dry cleaning establishments; others succeeded as musicians, scientists, and computer experts. Like some white groups before them, Asians benefited from supportive families and respect for education. Asian students worked hard and gained admission in disproportionate numbers to the country's best colleges and universities.

As in past eras, however, the newcomers to America in the sixties and seventies were not integrated into American society without friction. On the Texas Gulf Coast, competing "Anglo" and Vietnamese fishermen clashed in a series of violent incidents. Some middle-class people resented the academic success of Chinese and Japanese students. Hispanics, too, aroused rancor. In Miami blacks often felt bitter about the success of the Cubans. In the Southwest and California some whites feared that Anglo ways would be submerged under a wave of illegal Hispanic immigration. In many communities in the Northeast and Southwest programs to fund the use of Spanish as a language of instruction in the public schools became a divisive issue. Whites feared the displacement of English. Some Hispanic-Americans, on the other hand, worried about their children's loss of the Spanish language and with it their cultural heritage.

During the seventies and eighties public resentment focused especially on illegal immigration. Many Americans demanded tighter controls on immigration, and the Immigration and Naturalization Service deployed massive resources to stem the flood of immigrants crossing the U.S. border, especially from Mexico. Success was limited. In 1986 Congress passed the Simpson-Rodino Act imposing fines on employers who hired undocumented immigrants, but at the same time granting a general amnesty to all illegal immigrants who had arrived in the United States before January 1, 1982. The law was not enforced, however, and failed to end the frustration many Americans felt about unregulated immigration.

Women.   In many ways the most revolutionary social issues of the 1970s concerned women. In the 1960s feminists had argued that women should be free to choose roles other than that of "homemaker." By the late 1970s they had entered the labor market in record numbers. In 1965, 37 percent of all women over sixteen were employed; by 1978 the figure was 50 percent. Single women had worked in substantial numbers for many years. The new working woman contingent for the first time, however, included many thousands of married women with children. Only 19 percent of women with children under age six worked in 1960; by 1980 the figure had reached 45 percent.

Many of these women were engaged in serious careers. Educated women flooded into law, medicine, science, college teaching, journalism, computer programming, and other professional fields. By the mid-1980s, the list of women who had attained prominent positions in business, professional life, and government service had grown long: Jeane Kirkpatrick, Ambassador to the United Nations; Ella Grasso, Governor of Connecticut; Mayor Jayne Byrne of Chicago; Sandra Day O'Connor, associate justice of the U.S. Supreme Court; Geraldine Ferraro, Democratic vice presidential candidate in 1984; Hannah Gray, President of the University of Chicago; Sherry Lansing, high executive of Twentieth-Century-Fox. Even the military service academies at West Point, Annapolis, and Colorado Springs opened their doors to women in the 1970s, as did the armed services in all their branches, except those involving direct combat.

Yet women did not achieve full equality with men in the job market. Women's salaries were lower than for equally qualified men, and relatively few women were to be found in top executive positions. In many businesses there seemed to be a "glass ceiling" beyond which women could not rise. Women activists charged that the major cause of this shortfall was sex discrimination. And clearly "sexism" existed, especially in subtle forms. But others pointed to women's often delayed professional educations, greater job instability, and overall lower expectations as important factors in slowing their career advance.

The flood of women into the labor market imposed additional strains on the family already reeling from the effects of soaring divorce and illegitimacy. Less and less did the "typical" American family consist of dependent children, a working father, and a mother at home to do the family cooking and cleaning and socializing of young children. By the late 1970s only one in five families followed this pattern, and many conservative observers warned that the change would undermine effective child-rearing practices and damage the health of society as a whole. Feminists and liberals, on the other hand, defended the changes and demanded better and cheaper child-care facilities so that mothers could work without fear that their children's health, safety, and development would suffer.

Families were not only less stable; they were also smaller. By the seventies the baby boom of the 1950s and 1960s was over. In 1960 there had been almost 24 births per thousand Americans. In 1970 they were down to 18.4 and by 1976 had further fallen to 14.8. Social observers speculated on the reasons for the birthrate decline. Some blamed it on a new class of affluent young adults, "baby boomers," who seemed unusually self-centered. Children cost money and interfered with career goals, and female professionals and managers, especially, sought to postpone pregnancies until well into their thirties and then often experienced infertility. Others were less willing to blame individuals. Rather, it was part of a long-term trend, they said, only briefly interrupted by the post-World War II baby boom, and in any case the falling birth rate was worse in other rich industrial nations such as West Germany and Japan than in the United States.

Affirmative Action.   Despite progress toward equality, then, racial minorities and women continued to stand below white males on the economic ladder. Merely leveling the playing field was not enough, argued some activists and social critics. Minorities and women had suffered so much from past bias that even if existing overt discrimination were totally eliminated these groups could not catch up in the foreseeable future. What was needed was not merely equal opportunity, but equal results. This required, at least as a temporary measure, "affirmative action"—that is, preferential treatment for ethnic minorities and women in hiring, promotions, admissions to training and apprenticeship programs, and to colleges and professional schools. Such practices would compensate for the past and, in addition, balance the moral account. Elite groups had long had the deck stacked in their favor. Why not women and minorities now?

Affirmative action was beset by difficulties. Should all employers or institutions be automatically compelled to give preferential treatment to minorities, or only those that were proved to have practiced discrimination in the past? And how could such proof be established? Was it sufficient to show that given employers, for example, had fewer minority employees than their general proportion of the population, or did intent to discriminate have to be demonstrated? And what about assigning definite percentages—quotas—to minority members who must be hired or admitted to comply with the rules?

Many Americans disliked affirmative action. Opponents called it "reverse discrimination." Not only did it disregard "merit" as the key to reward; it also hurt those who, by accident of birth, did not belong to officially designated disadvantaged groups. In some fields, claimed opponents, it was impossible for a qualified white male to get a decent job. Affirmative action was, moreover, inherently sexist and racist because it assumed that members of disadvantaged groups could not make it on their own in America as others had in the past. It effect, it stigmatized those accorded special treatment as people who did not fully deserve their success.

Despite opposition, under Nixon's labor secretary, George Shultz, the government established affirmative action plans for blacks and selected ethnic groups in all firms submitting bids for government contracts (the Revised Philadelphia Plan). These firms, as well as labor unions, would have to seek out minority workers or members aggressively. During the 1970s the policy was further extended by federal court interpretation to women and then applied to a host of additional private firms, to universities, to foundations, and to other employers. Opponents challenged the principle in court with mixed results. In the *Bakke* decision of 1978 the Supreme Court struck down a University of California Medical School affirmative action rule that denied admission to a white applicant—Allan Bakke—while accepting less qualified nonwhites. Yet the Court did not declare affirmative action invalid, only that the university's method of achieving it through a rigid quota system was not permissible. The following year, in the Weber case, the Court ruled that private employers could adopt voluntary affirmative action plans to eliminate "manifest racial imbalance."

ERA and Abortion.
The hottest social issues of the seventies and eighties were the Equal Rights Amendment and abortion, both "women's issues." First official-ly proposed by Alice Paul's National Woman's Party in the 1920s, the ERA stated simply that "equality of rights under the law shall not be denied on account of sex." Introduced into every session of Congress from 1923 onward, it had been re-jected many times. In 1972, with the new feminism gathering momentum, Con-gress finally approved it by the constitutionally required two-thirds' majority and sent it along for ratification to the legislatures of the states.

The ratification process moved swiftly at first. Thirty-two of the necessary thirty-eight states approved the amendment in a little over a year. Then the oppo-sition began to rally. In early 1973 Phyllis Schlafly, a lawyer and mother of six, or-ganized a "Stop ERA" campaign. Schlafly and her allies said the amendment would hurt women's rights in divorce, that it mandated women's military service in the event of war, and that it even precluded separate male and female public bathrooms. The opponents of ERA touched a deep pool of antifeminist feeling in women themselves. Studies would show that wives and mothers not working outside the home, and even many who did solely for the income, often viewed feminists as hostile to the family values and personal relationships that gave their own lives worth.

Under the impact of the counterattack, state ratifications soon ceased and sev-eral states even rescinded their earlier approval. By 1979, the original expiration date, ERA had still not gotten the three-fourths vote it needed. Congress extended the deadline for another three and a half years, but it still failed to get the requisite adoptions. In 1982 ERA was declared dead, though it remained on the feminist agenda for the future.

The abortion issue provoked still stronger reactions, for it literally involved matters of life or death. On one side was a "pro-choice" coalition of feminists and liberals who considered the 1973 Supreme Court decision, *Roe v. Wade*, legalizing abortion during the first three months of pregnancy, to be a long overdue confir-mation of women's right to "control their own bodies." The "pro-life" opponents of abortion—traditional Catholics, evangelical Protestants, Orthodox Jews, and political conservatives—considered *Roe* an invitation to infant murder. There were many positions between these extremes, and most Americans probably accepted abortion as necessary under some circumstances but deplored easy recourse to it.

From 1973 on, anti-abortionists sought to limit women's access to abortion in several ways: by requiring that minors obtain prior parental consent to the procedure; by denying welfare recipients the right to federally subsidized abor-tions; by trying to limit conditions under which abortions could be legally obtained to cases where the pregnancy resulted from rape or incest, or where the birth threatened the life of the mother. By the end of the 1970s pro-lifers were demanding passage of the Human Life Amendment, a constitutional mea-sure to prohibit abortion and place it beyond the jurisdiction of the courts and also to forbid some forms of birth control.

"Pro-Choice" advocates parading in 1970s.

The "Me" Generation.   While some Americans continued to battle over major social and political issues in the 1970s, others turned away from public concerns. Some retreat was probably inevitable given the intense social activism of the previous decade, but it was also encouraged by the unusual difficulty of the problems of the seventies and early eighties. The journalist Tom Wolfe called the mid-1970s the era of the "me generation," a period when people placed personal fulfillment and pleasure before other considerations.

One sign of the new narcissism was the extraordinary interest in personal physical culture. Americans had long allowed their health to suffer through lack of exercise and poor eating habits, and no doubt reformation was long overdue. But the remarkable new interest in "natural" diets, "working out," and jogging that appeared in the late 1970s was closely connected with the new obsession with self. Still another manifestation of this "me" mood was the growth of a multitude of new mental health therapies. Affluent young urbanites flocked to teachers of "primal scream," EST, Rolfing, and other therapeutic programs that promised emotional comfort or personal fulfillment. Others sought satisfaction in one of the new religious cults such as Sun Myung Moon's Unification Church, L. Ron Hubbard's Scientology, the Hari Krishnas, or Jim Jones's People's Temple. Cults provided many young men and women with a sense of purpose and community. They also lent themselves to fraud, manipulation, charlatanism, and fanaticism.

Americans would be deeply shocked when, in November 1979, over 900 of Jones's American followers committed mass suicide in their settlement in Guyana at the behest of their unbalanced leader.

Sun Belt versus Snow Belt.

One of the most important social trends of the seventies and early eighties was the shift of population, wealth, and leadership from the long-dominant northeastern quarter of the country—the so-called Snow Belt—to the Sun Belt of the South and West.

For more than a century the region stretching from southern New England to northern Virginia and then across the upper midwest to the Mississippi had been the richest, most populous, and most culturally creative part of the United States. It had harbored the nation's most productive industries—clothing, steel, textiles, automobiles, pharmaceuticals, electronics, rubber. Its large cities had been the centers of the nation's cultural life, sheltering its major museums, universities, publishing houses, symphony orchestras, theater, and dance companies. It had been the hub of financial services and insurance.

The balance began to shift during the 1960s and accelerated thereafter. As more and more Americans retired to live on pensions, they chose to leave behind the cold winters of the Northeast and Midwest. Immense retirement communities sprang up in California, Florida, Arizona, and Nevada. Industry, too, particularly light industry and industry connected with defense, found the warmer climate, abundant land, cheaper nonunionized labor, and lower taxes of the South and West an advantage. Under four presidents from the region— Lyndon Johnson of Texas, Richard Nixon and Ronald Reagan of California, and Jimmy Carter of Georgia—government seemed to favor the Sun Belt through tax and defense-contract policies. Texas, Louisiana, and California, for a time, would also profit from the energy crisis of the late 1970s. With their still large reserves of oil and natural gas, these states could offer cheap energy to business and individuals alike. Congress magnified this advantage when it decontrolled most natural gas and petroleum prices in 1978.

Much of this process was anticipated by economists as early as the 1960s, but the message was driven home by the figures provided by the twentieth census. The preliminary results, announced on the last day of 1980, showed small increases, or even declines, in the populations of the northeastern and midwestern states during the previous decade. By contrast, already massive California grew by 17.7 percent; Nevada by almost 64 percent; Texas by 26.4 percent; Arizona by almost 53 percent, and Florida by more than 41 percent. While the population of many older Snow Belt cities stagnated or declined, Phoenix, Albuquerque, Tucson, Houston, Dallas, San Antonio, Las Vegas, Tampa, San Diego, and San Jose leaped ahead. For the first time in history, moreover, the nation's population statistical center had moved west of the Mississippi River, to southeast Missouri.

The figures both confirmed previous trends and foreshadowed new ones. Political power would clearly shift with population. When Congress was reapportioned, New York, Illinois, Ohio, and Pennsylvania would lose seats in the House of Representatives, and Texas, California, Florida, and Arizona would gain several seats each. Because the newer regions were more conservative politically than the older Snow Belt, this meant a rightward trend in the nation's political climate.

Besides politics, the nation's cultural life was certain to be affected. Already the Snow Belt's near-monopoly of high culture—painting, music, dance, and theater—had been loosened, partly through the National Endowment for the Arts and its counterpart in scholarship and literature, the National Endowment for the Humanities. Since their founding in 1965 as part of Lyndon Johnson's Great Society, these two federally funded bodies had pumped large sums of money into universities, theatrical and dance companies, and orchestras located outside the old cultural centers. By the early 1980s, universities in the Mountain states, Texas, and the Far West were matching the prestige and creativity of those of the East, while local culture in the Sun Belt was flourishing as never before.

The Energy Crisis and Economic Malaise

The growth of the Sun Belt and decline of the Snow Belt were tied to new resource problems facing the United States in the 1970s. For the first time in its history the country faced an acute energy crisis.

Oil and the American Way of Life.   For Americans, the "pursuit of happiness" has traditionally meant the quest for increasing income and physical comfort. Success has often depended on access to cheap natural resources as well as advanced technology. For a time in the 1970s, however, the world's industrialized nations confronted growing resource dearth. Supplies of such crucial metals as platinum, silver, tin, copper, and nickel—all needed in modern industrial products and processes—seemed to grow scarcer. The real crisis, however, was the oil shortage. To many Americans in the late 1970s, the blocks-long lines to buy scarce gasoline at prices soaring into the stratosphere seemed to foretell the end of an affluence they had come to accept as their national birthright.

The energy problem had evolved over several decades. By the post-World War II era, the rich industrial nations had become increasingly dependent on oil, and by the 1950s much of the world's supply came from the Middle East. The richest oil wells themselves were located in places like Saudi Arabia, Kuwait, Iran, and Iraq, but their contents were extracted, refined, and marketed by seven giant western oil companies, five of them American. These companies had helped finance and develop the oil fields and for many years took the lion's share of the revenues they yielded.

After 1945, under the influence of Arab nationalism, the Middle Eastern rulers of oil-rich countries began to reconsider their agreements with the western oil companies. At first they demanded increased royalties from the companies. Then, in 1960, the major oil-producing nations organized a cartel, the Organization of Petroleum Exporting Countries (OPEC), for the purpose of setting world petroleum prices and thereby expanding the profit for themselves.

Political and economic events of the early seventies abetted OPEC's monopoly pricing effort. First, the western nations, including the United States, became ever more reliant on imported energy sources. In the years between 1971 and 1973 alone, America quadrupled its oil imports, mostly from the Middle East. The flood of American demand would help create a world seller's market. Then, in October

1973, two Arab nations, Egypt and Syria, suddenly attacked Israel. The OPEC nations were meeting in Vienna during the "October War," and when the United States backed Israel they responded by boosting the price of oil from $3 to $5 a barrel and announcing an oil embargo against the United States and other nations supporting Israel. Suddenly the United States faced its first peacetime oil shortage since the discovery of petroleum in Pennsylvania more than a century before.

The uncomfortable winter of 1973–1974, with its cold homes and long gas lines, passed. But the embargo made it clear that America now relied for energy on the Arab world. The October War itself had other effects on America's energy situation. After heavy casualties on both the Arab and Israeli sides, the conflict ended with a United Nations-supervised cease-fire but no decrease in the hostility between the enemies and no prospect for a long-term peace settlement. Though the Egyptians and Syrians had not won the war, their limited success had increased Arab unity and buoyed Arab self-confidence. In the years that followed, the OPEC nations promised to be far more effective than in the past at acting in concert to control the oil market.

Energy Alternatives.

For a time the energy crisis forced Americans to consider their future as a people of plenty. Some concluded that we must accept "limits." The United States, they said, had been living beyond its means for many years. Now the age of abundance was over. Some of this school of thought predicted that the country would face years of rising social tensions as groups fought over their respective slices of a diminished economic pie. Environmentalists were prominent within the "limits" group. Some seemed almost to welcome the oil crunch, believing it proved the need to keep population growth low, find ways to conserve resources, and generally reduce the human impact on Mother Nature. By changing our goals from crude expansion of GNP to other, more ecologically sound priorities, we could avoid disappointment and frustration, they promised. Other Americans denied the need for belt-tightening. Some believed that the oil companies had contrived the energy shortage to increase their profits. Others blamed the continuing dearth on the environmentalists, who, they said, resisted every attempt to find alternative energy sources in the name of their precious ideology.

The energy crisis reinforced Americans' sense of malaise already kindled by the Vietnam debacle and Watergate. The soaring price of energy drained immense amounts of income and capital from the industrial nations and transferred it to the oil producers. Some of it came back in the form of investments by the OPEC nations in Europe and America and lavish spending on western goods by Saudi sheiks and Kuwaiti businessmen. But it also slowed western economic growth rates. For the western world, including the United States, 1973 would be a significant economic watershed marking a division between eras of faster and slower economic expansion. Besides impotence abroad and corruption at home, then, it seemed we now had to face for the first time the possibility of long-term material limits. To pessimists America appeared to have passed its prime; it could no longer achieve all the goals it set for itself.

The nation struggled to contain the energy crisis. Congress clamped a fifty-five-mile-per-hour speed limit on drivers and prescribed minimum gas mileage requirements for car manufacturers. It offered tax credits to homeowners who insulated their houses to conserve fuel. It also passed measures to encourage the development of alternative energy sources, such as geothermal, wind, and solar power. In July 1979, President Carter would ask Congress to fund a synthetic fuels program to free Americans from dependence on foreign energy sources.

The oil shock triggered a major debate over nuclear power. Lauded at one time as the complete solution to the world's energy needs, nuclear power had come under increasing fire on environmental and safety grounds as the seventies advanced. The critics' arguments were given frightening immediacy by an accident at the Three Mile Island nuclear power plant near Harrisburg, Pennsylvania, in March 1979, which for a time threatened to produce a "meltdown" of the reactor's nuclear core. Had that occurred, thousands of lives might have been lost and property worth billions contaminated for decades.

Fortunately, the reaction was contained and no lives and little property lost, but the near disaster intensified the nuclear power debate. Supporters of nuclear energy pointed out that the overall safety record of the industry had been good. Opponents insisted that the accident confirmed the unsuitability of the nuclear solution to the energy problem. Moreover, power from the atom raised difficult issues of nuclear waste disposal. During the next few years environmentalists, organized in various "alliances," conducted a crusade against nuclear power that helped delay construction of new plants and imposed stricter safety standards on old ones. The assault raised the costs of construction so high that by the 1980s the building of new nuclear power plants ceased, and several almost completed plants had to be abandoned. By 1980 nuclear power no longer was an energy option in the United States.

Turmoil in the Economy.   The relentless rise in general consumer prices reinforced the public's disquiet and sense of crisis. By mid-1979 the average American family had to earn almost double its 1970 dollar income to achieve the same standard of living. In effect, the value of the dollar had fallen to half its worth from a decade before.

By the end of the decade inflation had become self-perpetuating. Americans rushed to department stores and discount houses to snap up appliances, clothing, sports equipment, and goods of every kind with their credit cards before prices rose further. The buying spree not only aggravated the inflationary surge; it also reduced personal savings. There was little incentive to put dollars into savings accounts when the gain from interest earned was certain to be more than offset by their loss of value. The drop in personal savings made the United States increasingly dependent on foreign sources of capital for financing private industry and to help service the large federal debt.

Experts puzzled over the causes of the inflation. Clearly, skyrocketing energy costs were a factor. But many economists placed even more blame on rising wages not offset by equivalent increases in labor productivity. Labor costs were simply passed along to consumers, they claimed, because in many areas competition was nonexistent. Still others took their cue from the conservative economist Milton Friedman, who insisted that an excess of cheap money and credit, permitted by the Federal Reserve system and reinforced by large federal deficits, explained the powerful inflation surge.

One difficulty in dealing with inflation was that stable prices seemed to depend on keeping unemployment high. Price rises would cease only if the economy flattened. By cutting back government spending and raising interest rates, private investment and consumer spending could be curtailed. This would push up the jobless rate, but at the same time reduce inflation. Conservatives accepted the trade-off as unavoidable. But liberals and organized labor did not. Better higher prices than mass unemployment, they argued.

But the argument soon came to seem pointless. By mid-decade unemployment was accompanied by continued inflation. The combination, called "stagflation" by phrasemakers, could not easily be explained, though some experts believed unemployment figures were exaggerated and others emphasized that millions of Americans, especially minorities, were without the skills needed to find a place in the new "high-tech" economy. No matter what the nation's growth rate, low or high, they would not find work. Whatever the reason, clearly the nation faced a dilemma: It could have full employment, but apparently only at the expense of more severe inflation.

The Carter Years

Jimmy Carter would be forced to shoulder much of the blame for the economic troubles of the late 1970s. Yet when he took office in January 1977, many people were optimistic that this ex-peanut farmer, who had come from nowhere to win the presidency, would be an effective leader. They would be disappointed.

Carter as President.   Americans at first were impressed by Jimmy Carter. The Carter style seemed refreshingly informal. He broke with precedent by walking in his own inaugural parade with his wife, Rosalynn, and his daughter, Amy, by his side. From the White House he answered citizens' phoned-in questions on TV and wore blue jeans and old sweaters around the Oval Office. Amy went to a Washington public school, like other unpretentious residents of the District of Columbia, rather than a private school. Carter also tried to reduce the number of White House officials and cut back on staff limousines and television sets.

The politicians on Capitol Hill found him less enchanting than the public. Having run against the Washington "establishment," Carter had trouble achieving a working relationship with Congress. He also experienced the congressional backlash against presidential leadership following Watergate and the abrasive years of the imperial presidency. Inexperienced in the ways of Washington, he and his staff fumbled badly.

Carter's first mistake was to attack a congressional sacred cow by cutting off federal funding for eighteen dams and other water projects in the West. His arguments that the projects were wasteful were valid, but he had not reckoned with the importance of the "pork barrel" to members of Congress and the significance of irrigation in the West. Faced with a storm of protest, he retreated. He did little better in his early relations with key congressional leaders, failing to consult Senate Majority Leader Robert Byrd on which senators to brief on energy policy, and announcing federal appointments in House Speaker Thomas ("Tip") O'Neill's own Massachusetts district without first informing him. Eventually, Carter and his advisers improved relations with Congress, but they were never able to establish an effective partnership with those who enacted the nation's laws.

Domestic Policies.   Carter's gravest challenge was how to end the nation's dependence on foreign oil. The issue aroused all the president's considerable moral fervor. At one point, (borrowing from philosopher William James) he called the battle to make the United States oil-independent "the moral equivalent of war." Unfortunately, his actual recommendations to Congress in February 1977 were disproportionately modest: a small federal tax on crude oil imports and on "gas-guzzling" cars. Given the president's dire warnings, this program struck many Americans as ludicrous. Humorist Russell Baker abbreviated the "moral equivalent of war" to MEOW. Congress was similarly unimpressed and acted slowly, though eventually giving the president much of what he asked for.

In the summer of 1979 another grave oil "shock" was triggered by the turmoil in Iran. During the confusion of the Islamic fundamentalist revolution that overthrew the Shah, Iranian oil production dropped drastically. The oil-importing nations were soon bidding against one another for the reduced world supply, tripping off a panic that created new gas lines through June and July. By now many Americans had concluded that here, as in other areas, Carter was an ineffectual leader.

The oil crisis of 1979–1980 pushed inflation into high gear. In 1979 consumer prices leaped 13.3 percent in a single year. In early 1980 they began to rise still faster, threatening to reach an astronomical 18 percent per annum if not stopped. The Federal Reserve, under its new head, Paul Volcker, raised interest rates to discourage spending with borrowed money. The president established a Council on Wage and Price Stability to monitor wage and price guidelines. Neither move worked at first. Interest rates were pushed to 20 percent in early 1980, but prices continued to rise. The council proved ineffective. Its orders were unenforceable and its fruitless "jawboning" only made the administration again seem feeble and incompetent.

Carter's Foreign Policy.   Carter had an idealist's view of foreign affairs. He hoped to distance the United States from aggressive Vietnam-era policies and make the nation a force for benevolence in the world. The president and many of his advisors believed at the outset that the United States had subordinated too many other considerations to winning the Cold War. A more important destabilizing force than the continuing East–West conflict, they said, was the disparities between the wealthy nations of the world's northern industrial belt and the poor ones of the southern agricultural portion of the globe. In a 1977 speech at Notre Dame University the president noted that "an inordinate fear of communism" had "led us to embrace any dictator who joined us in our fear." Reflecting these sunny views, the first two Carter defense budgets, already down from the Vietnam War, fell to the lowest proportion of total federal outlays since 1960. In June 1979 the president signed the SALT II agreement, further limiting U.S. and Soviet nuclear arsenals, and sent the treaty to the Senate for ratification. In 1979 also, going beyond the Nixon initiatives, he established formal American diplomatic relations with the People's Republic of China. Meanwhile, to avoid a confrontation with Panamanian nationalists and to raise America's stock in Latin America, he helped push through the Senate a treaty with Panama ending exclusive American control of the Canal Zone. As part of the new respect for international morality Carter also mobilized America's good offices on behalf of victims of government oppression around the world. He called this his "human rights" policy.

Conservatives charged the Carter initiatives weakened America and helped our enemies abroad. The "human rights" policies, they said, were a slap at many foreign allies who helped us contain communism. The Panama Canal treaties cravenly surrendered American rights in the Canal Zone of seventy years' standing. As for SALT II, it was a Soviet trick. Its predecessor, SALT I, had lulled the United States into a false sense of security while the Soviets had surpassed us in conventional weapons.

There was one foreign-policy area, however—Arab–Israeli relations— where Carter got high marks from everyone. In November 1977 Egyptian President Anwar Sadat had made an unprecedented visit to Jerusalem, the Israeli capital. For the first time the head of an Arab state had made a friendly gesture toward the Jewish nation and it looked as though peace between Egypt and Israel might be at hand. Unfortunately, the peace process soon bogged down over the thorny problem of Palestinian self-rule, and it appeared that Sadat's bold initiative would come to nothing. To break the impasse, in September 1978 Carter induced both Sadat and Israeli Prime Minister Menachem Begin to come to Camp David, the presidential hideaway in the Maryland mountains, to discuss the differences between the two countries. Carter used every means to get these two stubborn men to agree and finally succeeded in squeezing a joint peace statement from them. As a result of the Camp David Accords, in March 1979 Israel and Egypt signed a peace treaty that bound the two nations to full diplomatic relations, to phasedevacuation by Israel of the Sinai Peninsula conquered during the 1967 war, and to some form of autonomy for the Palestinians living in the West Bank and Gaza Strip. The treaty did not bring peace to the Middle East. None of the other Arab nations followed Egypt's lead, and the Palestinian issue continued to fester. But for the first time in its history Israel was at peace with one of its Arab neighbors.

The Hostage Crisis.

Whatever credit Carter won from the Camp David accords was squandered by his handling of the hostage crisis with Iran. Iran was a distant, exotic place to most Americans in 1979. Islamic though not Arabic, located on the oil-rich Persian Gulf, it was ruled despotically by Shah Mohammed Reza Pahlevi, a close friend of America. The CIA had helped the Shah gain his throne in 1953 by a coup against his enemies, and the United States considered him a bulwark of anti-Soviet stability in the Middle East. In January 1979 he was ousted by internal enemies who simultaneously despised his repressive methods, his friendship with the west, and his attempts to aggressively modernize his conservative land. The Shah fled to Mexico, leaving behind a nation in turmoil. In October he was admitted to a New York hospital for treatment of cancer. This show of American hospitality outraged the faction now dominant in Iran, the Islamic fundamentalists led by the ultraorthodox religious leader, the Ayatollah Ruhollah Khomeini.

On November 4, 1979, a group of pro-Khomeini Iranian students, probably with the Ayatollah's approval, invaded the American Embassy in Teheran and took hostage more than sixty American citizens, mostly embassy employees.

Months of protest, negotiation, and maneuver would follow, but to no avail. Seizing the embassy of a country that one was not at war with was contrary to all civilized practice, and no government could have condoned it. But America found itself dealing with a regime ruled by extremists. The Islamic fundamentalists considered America "the Great Satan" and demanded ransom to release the hostages. The United States must surrender the Shah to his enemies, apologize for supporting him in the past, and agree to turn over to the Iranian government all the assets that he supposedly had taken with him when he fled his homeland. If the United States did not comply, not only would the Americans remain prisoners, they might well be tried for espionage and executed.

The United States refused to accept these extreme conditions. The administration froze billions of dollars of Iranian assets in the United States, cut off all trade with Teheran, and appealed to the United Nations and the World Court to condemn the hostage-taking. Nothing worked. As the weeks passed, outraged Americans became obsessed with the hostage crisis. Public frustration and anger at American impotence grew and voices were soon raised demanding retaliation. Some people called for a declaration of war against Iran and a blockade of the Persian Gulf. Irate citizens attacked Iranian students attending American universities. The administration, too, became consumed with the hostage crisis to the neglect of other important matters. In late April 1980 the president ordered a military rescue operation from U.S. naval vessels in the Persian Gulf against the advice of Secretary of State Cyrus Vance. This maneuver failed dismally and eight men died in the attempt. Vance resigned. The public's level of frustration rose to new heights.

The Cold War Resumes.   Conservative Americans from the outset questioned Carter's optimism about the Cold War. In 1976 a coalition of anti-Soviet hawks from government, business, the universities, and the intellectual community, skeptical of Nixon's détente policy, had organized the Committee on the Present Danger. The committee warned that "the principle threat to our nation and the cause of human freedom" was "the Soviet drive for dominance based on an unparalleled military build-up." The United States must not be lulled into a false sense of security.

Events would shortly confirm the committee's fears. All hope of preserving détente collapsed in late December 1979 when Soviet troops and tanks poured across the border into Afghanistan, the Islamic country bordering Iran, to save a Soviet puppet leader from his domestic enemies. The Soviet invasion substantiated the hard-liners' contentions but shocked Carter. Indignant at what he considered the deception of Soviet premier Leonid Brezhnev, he told the American people that the United States must once more seek to contain Soviet expansionism and be prepared to defend the free flow of oil to the west from the Persian Gulf region. To implement this policy (quickly labeled the "Carter Doctrine"), he cut off sales of wheat and advanced technology to the Soviet Union, withdrew the United States team from the 1980 summer Olympics in Moscow, shelved SALT II for the foreseeable future, and asked Congress to enact legislation requiring all nineteen- and twenty-year-olds to register for the military draft.

The 1980 Election.

Despite this vigorous response, the public came to perceive the Carter administration as feckless and impotent. Americans grew weary of the president's homilies about energy belt-tightening and international morality. Whenever he spoke, it seemed, he sounded the dreary theme of an American "malaise."* Meanwhile, inflation continued; the energy shortage persisted; and, overseas, America seemed to lose force and direction. The voters' gloom about events at home and abroad determined the outcome of the 1980 election.

Though the incumbent, Carter had to fight for his party's renomination against Senator Edward Kennedy of Massachusetts. The youngest of the Kennedy brothers, "Ted" had seriously damaged his reputation for honesty and courage in 1969 when he failed to save the life of a young woman aide when their car went into the water off Chapaquiddick Island. Despite the Chapaquiddick incident, the senator had the support of the party's liberal wing and mounted an energetic campaign to deny Carter the nomination. In the end Carter defeated his challenger and became his party's nominee for the second time.

The Republican nominee was Ronald Reagan, the sixty-nine-year-old spokesman for the new southern and western political right. The former California governor appealed to many of the same backlash voters who had supported George Wallace and Richard Nixon in 1968, with the added backing of business groups associated with the exploding industry and enterprise of Texas, southern California, the Mountain States, and the South.

Though divorced and a former actor, Reagan had been raised in an evangelical Protestant household and endorsed the conservative social agenda of the new religious right. By the mid-1970s this rapidly growing segment of Protestantism had become a formidable challenge to the mainstream, predominantly liberal, Protestant groups. In 1979 Baptist minister Jerry Falwell organized the Moral Majority to bring the nation's evangelicals into the political arena. The Moral Majority favored abortion restriction, traditional family values, heterosexuality, tougher laws against drugs, lower taxes, school prayer, expanded defense spending, and a more aggressive anti-Communist foreign policy. Its supporters claimed to favor pluralism and separation of church and state, but their opponents saw them as intolerant and determined to use government to encourage their own religious values. Along with a cluster of secular "New Right" groups, the new religious right operated through political action committees (PACs) funded by money raised through direct-mail appeals.

During the campaign the Carter administration looked for a breakthrough in the hostage crisis to give it an electoral boost. But the Iranians toyed with the American negotiators, reinforcing the impression of administration weakness.

---

*In fact, he never used the term, which seems to have been a media creation.

When election day arrived the hostages were still captive. The result was an impressive Republican victory. Reagan received 43 million popular votes to 35 million for Carter. Going down to defeat along with the president were a flock of liberal Democratic senators and representatives targeted by the New Right and the Moral Majority. Reagan would have a Republican Senate to work with and, though the House of Representatives would remain in Democratic hands, it was doubtful if it could check the new conservative surge.

Conclusions

It had taken twelve years for the conservative promise of 1968 to finally be realized. In 1968 the voters had rejected one of its most liberal political leaders and endorsed one of its most conservative. Americans, it seemed, had repudiated the liberal Great Society and all it represented.

But conservatives had been disappointed. Richard Nixon turned out to be a pragmatist and a compromiser. Perhaps, during his second term, he would have taken the conservative agenda more seriously. But the disaster of Watergate kept him from achieving anything after 1973. Gerald Ford, by pardoning the ex-president, kept alive the disgrace of Watergate and damaged his own administration. Yet the conservative current continued to run under the surface. In 1976 the public did not endorse an ideological shift; it merely repudiated the party responsible for Watergate. Yet Carter could have reversed the conservative current if he had been adept and likable. He was neither, and in 1980 conservative voters turned him out of office to try once more to get what they had failed to do in 1968. In the end it was Ronald Reagan, rather than Richard Nixon, who would launch the conservative experiment in Washington.

ONLINE RESOURCES

"May 4 Kent State" *http://www.library.kent.edu/exhibits/4may95/index.html* Through the "May 4" collection, learn more about the Kent State student shootings. The site includes photos, links to various other sites, chronologies, and information on the aftermath of the incident.

Revisiting Watergate *http://www.washingtonpost.com/wp-srv/national/longterm/watergate/front.htm* Read about the Watergate crisis through timelines and biographies of the key players in the affair. Also, the site provides newspaper articles that correspond to the Watergate chronology.

30

The "Reagan Revolution"

What Was It?
What Did It Accomplish?

1980	Ronald Reagan elected president; Republicans gain control of Senate
1981	Beginning of Reagan era; Conservative agenda put into place; Cutbacks in domestic social programs; Huge increases for defense; Tax cuts seen as stimulus to economic growth; Deregulation of industries; Reagan fires striking air traffic controllers
1982	Budget deficits mount; Breakup of AT&T; Midterm elections see Democrats pick up seats in House while GOP retains Senate control; Contra aid a political issue
1983	Reagan continues to stress military build-up; Adds new missiles in Europe; American marines sent to Lebanon; President pushes "Star Wars" to counter Soviet missile threat; 241 marines killed in Beirut terrorist attack; Soviets shoot down Korean airliner, killing 269; U.S.–Soviet relations worsen
1984	Reagan reelected in landslide; AIDS crisis grows ever larger
1985	Stock market continues to be bullish
1986	Space shuttle disaster; Trade imbalance worsens; U.S. jets attack Libya; Reagan–Gorbachev summit in Iceland ends on chilly note; Iran-Contra scandal breaks
1987	Congress probes Iran-Contra affair, televised hearings begin; Bork nomination to Supreme Court defeated in Senate; Stock market crash; Reagan and Gorbachev meet in Washington and sign agreement eliminating medium-range missiles from Europe; Scandals beset religious right
1988	Reagan era winds down

Reagan's inaugural address on January 20, 1981, was a display case for the new president's conservative agenda. "Government" is "not the *solution* to our problem. Government *is* the problem," he announced. He would "get the government back within its means and . . . lighten our punitive tax burden." He would check runaway inflation and get the economy moving again. His administration would restore America's standing in the world. While Americans craved peace, we would "maintain sufficient strength to prevail if need be." Finally, in his conclusion, he tipped his hat to his conservative religious constituency. "We are," he declared, "a nation under God," and "God intended for us to be free." He hoped that in future years Inauguration Day would be "declared a day of prayer."

The next eight years have been perceived as a major rightward shift in consonance with the new president's inaugural address, a so-called "Reagan Revolution." Was there a Reagan Revolution? Did the nation reverse its political direction? Did the Reagan victory usher in marked changes in the economy, in America's role in the world, in the nation's predominant cultural and religious values?

The First Term

The American Economy.   Reagan was speaking for millions of voters when he deplored high taxes. In many communities home owners were dismayed by soaring property taxes tied to the inflation of real estate values. Steep income taxes incensed high earners who believed they deserved to keep more of what they made. Business executives were not happy at what seemed exorbitant state and federal levies on corporations.

These were pragmatic tax cutters; they hoped to avoid the personal burden of taxation. But there was a broader case to be made for tax cuts. "Libertarians," disciples of novelist-social thinker Ayn Rand or of economists Frederick Hayek or Milton Friedman, opposed taxation because they considered virtually all government a denial of personal freedom. Taxes were merely another manifestation of this bondage. During the late 1970s the "supply-side" theories of economist Arthur Laffer became a core component of the conservative creed. Laffer denounced the dominant Keynesian concepts that emphasized augmented *demand* to achieve growth. Instead, it was essential to augment *supply* by cutting taxes to encourage effort and enterprise now confined by excessive burdens. There was no need to worry about government deficits, insisted the Lafferites. As production, profits, and jobs grew the government would be able to cover its expenses even at the lower tax rates since total revenues would rise.

Laffer had made a deep impression on several members of Congress including the young Republicans Jack Kemp of New York and David Stockman of Michigan. In 1976 Kemp, joined by Senator William Roth of Delaware, introduced a bill to reduce income taxes 30 percent across-the-board to restore the economy and encourage growth. During the 1980 presidential campaign Reagan had tentatively embraced the Kemp-Roth, supply-side proposal, believing that the new economics expressed, more truly than the liberals' timid talk of limits and no-growth, the American spirit of enterprise and expansion. Many traditional, no-deficit Republicans disagreed. George Bush, Reagan's chief opponent during the Republican nomination race, referring primarily to the revenue increase aspect, called the Laffer theory "voodoo economics." But in any case, abroad in the land was a growing aversion to high taxes that would soon have major political consequences.

As the new president took office in January 1981, the country faced other economic problems besides high taxes. Inflation was running at double-digit rates, the steepest since the Civil War. Unemployment was high and overall economic growth rates were down from previous decades. Most shocking of all, the United

States seemed to be losing its international competitiveness. In the 1950s the United States had been a towering economic giant surrounded by pygmies. By 1980 Western Europe had recovered, thanks to American aid, and far surpassed its pre-war levels. East Asia, moreover—Korea, Taiwan, Singapore, and above all Japan—had become an economic dynamo. Germany and Japan, especially, had become more efficient than the United States in many areas of production, and whole classes of American manufactures—consumer electronics, cameras, even automobiles—were being replaced on the domestic market by foreign imports.

By the opening years of the 1980s the problems of taxation, inflation, and un-employment, and America's international slippage, had convinced many people that the country must try new economic policies.

The Tax Cuts.   The administration's first order of business was a federal tax-cutting bill that expressed the new supply-side theory. Prepared by David Stock-man, now head of the Office of Management and Budget, the cuts were the deepest and broadest on record. The Democrats controlled the House of Representatives by a small margin and might have defeated the bill, but many House members accepted the 1980 election as a mandate for change and were willing to go along. Reagan, moreover, proved to be an effective parliamentary leader. His charm, his good humor, his rugged manliness appealed especially to southern Democrats ("Boll Weevils") and many proved willing to support the president. Much of the remaining opposition collapsed when an unbalanced young man shot and seriously wounded Reagan on March 30 as he was leaving a Washington hotel. The president's courage and good humor while recovering aroused the admiration of the country and expedited the bill's passage.

The Economic Recovery Act of 1981 mandated a 25 percent cut in the personal income tax over a three-year period and a sharp reduction of the maximum tax on "unearned" income from appreciation of real estate and other investments. It also authorized a drastic cut in corporate taxes—the "largest tax cut in the history of American business," one Reagan official described it—to stimulate investment.

It is difficult to assess the short-term effects of the tax cuts for their enactment coincided with a sharp recession. By December 1982 unemployment had soared to 10.8 percent of the labor force; 12 million Americans were out of work. This was the highest jobless level since the Great Depression. Yet it is clear that the recession was not related to the Economic Recovery Bill. The slide had been brought on by the tight money policies adopted by head of the Federal Reserve, Paul Volker, de-signed to bring down the ruinous inflation of the late seventies. Though wage earners felt considerable pain, the Fed's policies were followed by the easing of inflation. By 1983 price rises were down from 13 percent per year in 1980 to a little over 3 percent. Toward the end of Reagan's second term pessimists would warn that inflation was still an untamed dragon, but in fact it would never again become the frightening monster of the late 1970s.

Undoubtedly Volcker's tight money policy deserves much credit for ending the ruinous inflation of the previous decade. But other forces also contributed to the new price stability. By the early 1980s conservation measures had begun to reduce world petroleum demand, while at the same time total world oil output, stimulated by high prices in the 1970s, surged. The world was soon awash in oil capacity. Low energy prices removed a major component of the seventies' inflation wave. Wage pressures also eased. By the later 1980s unions found it difficult to extract wage increases from management. Once powerful bargaining agents for American labor, they lost power as the "smokestack industries"—steel, coal, and automobiles—were downsized under the remorseless pressure of foreign competition. Loss of numbers in industry was offset to some extent by gains in the service trades, especially government employment. But at best union membership, as a percentage of all employees, stagnated. In 1980 it was the same 24 percent as it had been in 1960.

The Reagan administration seriously undercut the remaining power of organized labor. The president himself, though former head of the Screen Actors' Guild, took a tough line on work stoppages. In August 1981, when the Professional Air Traffic Controller Organization (PATCO) called an illegal strike against the government, Reagan fired all 11,000 members and refused to hire them back even when they relented. PATCO disbanded. PATCO was not a large organization, but the attack by a popular president helped undermine the entire trade union movement. Between 1980 and 1984 total membership dropped by over 2.7 million members. By 1988 only 17 percent of American full-time workers were members of trade unions, a 6 percentage-point decline since the beginning of the decade.

The Welfare State.

The administration hoped that cutting domestic social programs would reduce taxpayers' burdens. But Reagan and his advisers also believed that the many welfare "entitlements" from the 1960s and early 1970s had only made poverty and dependency worse. As conservative social thinker Charles Murray would write in 1984, the nation's poverty programs had "tried to provide more for the poor and produced more poor instead." The figures seemed to confirm the view. In 1968, 13 percent of Americans had been classified as poor. After billions of dollars of federal largesse the proportion in 1980 was exactly the same 13 percent!

The president promised that his policies would maintain a "safety net" for the most vulnerable and disadvantaged groups in society. But he would get rid of the "welfare cheats" who received federal money though not eligible under the law; he would eliminate programs that had proved ineffective; he would reduce high administrative costs. Wherever possible he would demand that the able-bodied work rather than receive handouts. Liberals were not reassured and called the proposed cuts in welfare selfish and cruel. Nevertheless, Congress went along with many of the administration's proposals. It cut outlays for food stamps, child nutrition, Aid to Families with Dependent Children, Supplemental Security Income, Low Income Energy Assistance, financial aid for needy students, job training, health block grants, and many other programs. The president and his colleagues claimed that none of these cuts seriously harmed the poor; his critics claimed that their effects were devastating.

But the coin had another side as well. Whether from the effect of the tax cuts or the natural rebound from recession, by the late 1980s unemployment had fallen below 6 percent nationally. The administration could also point with pride to job creation in the 1980s. At no time in the past, its friends noted, had the country created jobs for so many people in so short a period as under the Reagan watch. Though the job market had been flooded by the baby-boomers born after 1945 and by women in larger numbers than ever before, it had absorbed them all. Critics countered that far too many of these were unskilled, minimum-wage positions that forced workers to rely on two or more family wage earners to achieve a reasonable living standard. In many cases their parents had been able to achieve the same standard with only one. All told, critics noted, American real wages were not rising. Many Americans could buy no more with their incomes in 1985 than in 1975. For the first time in memory, they said, adult Americans could not assume that their children would be better off than they were.

Meanwhile, by mid-decade a new class of deprived Americans were to be found living on the streets, under bridges, in parks and public squares, and in municipal shelters in many American cities. Critics of the administration charged that cuts in welfare and housing appropriations explained the surge in homelessness. But the problem was more complex than that. Many of the street people were single men and women afflicted with alcoholism or drug addiction. Others were mentally ill persons who, in a previous period, would have been admitted to state mental hospitals. These institutions, often squalid "snake pits," were now largely shut down, however, and those formerly warehoused in them, out of sight, were now blocking doorways, begging on the streets, using telephone booths and elevators as toilets, and sometimes insulting or assaulting pedestrians.

Yuppies.   While some sank, others rose. A substantial group of well-educated young men and women were forging ahead of the pack. These "Yuppies"—young upwardly mobile professionals—were the social phenomenon of the decade. As depicted by the media, they were brash, materialistic, self-centered, politically and socially insensitive, and greedy. Many were self-indulgent people who used their quick riches to buy luxury apartments, high-performance cars, imported wines, gourmet foods, class A restaurant meals, and illegal drugs, especially cocaine. For a time cocaine became a major "recreational drug" in yuppie circles. In some of the more prosperous cities of the Northeast and West coast by the late 1980s whole neighborhoods catered to yuppie tastes. Food emporia carried quiche and Brie cheese; car dealers sold Mercedes and BMWs; wine merchants offered imported chablis and champagne.

Social Security.   One "entitlement" program the Reagan administration found untouchable was Social Security. It was now clear that the aged as a class were no longer underprivileged. Thanks to Medicare and federal old-age pensions as well as private savings, people over sixty-five had higher incomes than average Americans. Most of those classified as poor were now families with young children, especially those headed by single parents. Children, in effect, were the new poor. To some conservatives it seemed foolish to coddle the elderly when so many of them were well off. Why not limit the benefits of those over sixty-five in the name of social equity?

Meanwhile the Social Security system was becoming more expensive and fiscally unstable. In the view of some conservatives it should be replaced entirely with a system of private annuities financed by each individual wage earner. Others wanted it drastically downsized. Neither reckoned with the power of the seniors' lobby. When the president proposed revisions to hold down soaring Social Security outlays and help, presumably, to make the system fiscally sound, the outcry from elderly voters forced him to drop the issue like a hot potato.

Eventually it required a bipartisan congressional commission to apply some actuarial restraint by increasing Social Security taxes, skipping some projected increases in payments, and mandating a gradual rise in the minimum retirement age. The working public was soon complaining that Social Security taxes had become more burdensome than income taxes.

All told, though Reagan and his supporters sought drastic changes in the existing welfare system, they butted their heads against a stone wall. Congress, fearing public wrath, refused to budge. The overall public mood had become less generous than in the past, but many entitlement beneficiaries, particularly when numerous and well-organized, were able to protect their interests against the budget cutters. A drastic overhaul of the Depression-era welfare system, if needed, would have to wait for a later day.

Defense Policy.   Defense was an even worse budget-buster than the welfare system. During the 1980 presidential campaign Reagan had described a "window of vulnerability" in nuclear arms as well as deficiencies in conventional arms that had to be corrected if America was to remain strong and safe. He took office pledged to a massive arms build-up that would increase American military power relative to the Soviet Union. Reagan was intensely suspicious of the Soviets and in the first news conference of his administration attacked détente as "a one-way street" that the Soviet Union had "used to pursue its own aims." At a later point in his presidency he would call the Soviet Union an "evil empire" and "the focus of evil in the modern world." The label "evil empire" would dismay the Soviet Union and become a shorthand expression for a reheated Cold War confrontation.

Among the earliest Reagan proposals as president was a five-year, $1.7 trillion increase in defense spending, supposedly to catch up with the Soviets. Congress scaled down the administration's military shopping list despite the determined resistance of Secretary of Defense Caspar Weinberger, but defense outlays leaped from $135 billion in 1980 to $210 billion in 1983 and to $231 billion in 1984. All told, the Reagan administration would engineer the largest American military buildup in peacetime history.

Budget Deficits.   The explosion in defense spending more than offset the modest cuts in domestic programs. If the supply-siders had been right, the soaring defense costs could have been covered by the revenue gains from tax cuts. But Vice President Bush had been right: The Laffer theory was indeed "voodoo economics." Federal revenues declined, and combined with the surge in defense spending, produced the largest budget deficits Americans had ever experienced. The results were ironic. As Democratic critics quickly pointed out, for decades the Republicans had denounced their opponents as wild spenders who had mortgaged the nation's future to gratify their urge to throw money at problems. Now, a Republican president had raised the annual federal deficit from Carter's $60 billion in 1980 to over $180 billion in 1984. By the final year of his first term, Reagan's shortfalls had increased the national debt by an additional $650 billion. This vast sum was equal to the cumulative total of all the deficits run by every president from Franklin Roosevelt to Jimmy Carter.

Deregulation and the Environment.

Deregulation of business was an important part of the president's economic program. Conservatives believed if America was to become more productive, entrepreneurs must be unshackled. Public safety and consumer interests would be taken care of primarily by free market forces.

The process of deregulation had already begun in the Carter administration when, in 1978, Congress passed the Airline Deregulation Act phasing out the regulatory Civil Aeronautics Board, allowing free choice by airlines of routes, and permitting them to set their fares competitively. In 1980 the deregulation process was extended to truckers and, to a more limited extent, to railroads. That same year the Depository Institutions and Monetary Control Act allowed "thrifts"—Savings and Loan Associations (S&Ls)—to pay market interest rates to depositors and lend on more kinds of security than the traditional real estate. Commercial banks too could, under the new rules, pay depositors higher interest to attract savings and could also enter the business of trading in stocks and bonds. In 1982, as a result of an antitrust suit initiated by the Carter administration, the courts ordered the breakup of the American Telephone and Telegraph Company, which had enjoyed a legal near-monopoly on telephone services in many parts of the country. There would now be twenty-two local Bell Companies for local calls plus a scaled-down AT&T, which would retain its long-distance services but would now have to compete with newly formed long-distance companies.

Under Reagan, deregulation accelerated. To free business from what they claimed were crippling chains, Reagan officials reduced the government's role in consumer protection. The Department of Agriculture stopped printing booklets describing poor dietary habits and detailing good ones. Administration appointees allowed a dubious mixture of fat, meat scraps, gristle, and ground bone to be sold to consumers as ground beef without the warnings previously required. The administration transformed the Occupational Safety and Health Administration from a federal watchdog of the workplace to "a cooperative regulator" of business. Transportation secretary Drew Lewis revoked safety standards mandating automatic seat belts or airbags for automobiles by 1984.

The most controversial change in the regulatory climate was the administration's effort to reduce the government's role in environmental protection. Reagan officials complained that every project to increase the country's energy output, improve its roads and highways, provide new office space, lower the cost of raw materials, or exploit its natural resources inevitably crashed into a wall of environmental regulation or was buried under a wave of environmental lawsuits. The presence of some obscure "endangered species," like the tiny snail-darter fish, could bring to a grinding halt a major dam project; the claim that a new building might cast a shadow over a park could stop a skyscraper from going up. Every major construction scheme was invariably burdened with reams of "environmental impact" statements and other elaborate documentation that added to costs. During the early 1980s a joke went the rounds among Reaganites: "How many Americans does it take to replace a light bulb? Answer: Five—one to change the bulb and four to write an environmental impact statement." The administration claimed, then, that its chief concern was to lower costs and raise productivity. Its critics insisted that its anti-environmentalism was primarily a payoff to the business groups whose support it counted on.

The chief federal agency for safeguarding the public health against pollution and contaminants was the Environmental Protection Agency (EPA), established under Richard Nixon in 1970 and given jurisdiction over a wide range of environmental concerns. During the Reagan administration, the EPA's budget was steadily cut, falling from $5.6 billion in fiscal 1980 to $4.1 billion in fiscal 1984. Reagan's appointee as EPA head was Anne Burford, who administered a $1.4-billion "superfund" to clean up toxic waste dumpsites that dotted the nation. Burford, however, was not an effective guardian of the public's health and she came under attack for delaying the vast task of ridding the environment of dangerous hot spots. In March 1983 she resigned under fire.

Reagan's secretary of the interior, James Watt, also antagonized environmentalists. A Denver lawyer, Watt had been head of the Mountain States Legal Foundation, a public interest law firm financed by the conservative Colorado brewer, Joseph Coors. The foundation was a legal arm of the so-called Sagebrush Rebellion, a movement of western ranchers, mine owners, timber barons, and irrigation farmers who opposed federal control of western resources and favored transferring public lands to state management. Under Watt the firm had initiated lawsuits challenging federal regulation of public land use for the sake of ecological balance, recreational use, and resource conservation.

The environmentalists had opposed his selection to head the Interior Department but, in the wake of the Reagan 1980 election sweep, were unable to stop it. Watt turned out to be just what they feared. Pleading the need to encourage economic growth, he authorized oil drilling in four areas off the Carolina coast that his predecessors had declared off-limits, opened up millions of acres of federal land to prospecting and exploitation by mineral and timber companies, and proposed to sell 35 million acres of federal land to private companies. Environmental pressure groups such as the Wilderness Society, the Sierra Club, the Audubon Society, and the National Wildlife Association denounced Watt, but, despite misgivings, the president kept him. Then, in October 1983, Watt made a remark to a public gathering that managed to offend blacks, Jews, the handicapped, and women simultaneously. Reagan forced him to resign and replaced him with William Clark, a close White House adviser.

First-Term Foreign Policy.   Reagan's first term coincided with a gap in the leadership of the Soviet Union. Following the death of Leonid Brezhnev in November 1982 there was a succession of short-term, interim Soviet leaders. Not until Mikhail Gorbachev, a vigorous man of fifty-four, became Communist Party Chairman in March 1985 did the United States have a steady leader to deal with.

In the interim, Soviet–American relations deteriorated. The Soviet invasion of Afghanistan and the hostage-taking episode in Teheran, as we saw, had compelled the Carter administration to assume a more aggressive stance toward America's adversaries. But Reagan went still further. The president and his closest foreign-policy advisers believed the Soviet Union to be the author of virtually all the turmoil and tension in the world. The USSR, they said, had cheated on SALT I and other arms agreements. Either directly, or through surrogates, it was responsible for upheavals in Africa, Latin America, and East Asia. The USSR and its satellites and allies, moreover, were behind the wave of bombings, airplane hijackings, and hostage-taking around the world. They were also the ultimate source of Arab intransigence against Israel in the Middle East. Retreating from Carter's policies, the administration also sought to make a distinction between "authoritarian" regimes, capable of reform, which we should be willing to support if they were anti-Communist, and totalitarian societies, like China and the Soviet Union, which could not be expected to change and had to be contained.

Shortly after taking office, Reagan found himself forced to deal with a possible Soviet invasion of Poland. In mid-1980 Solidarity, an anti-Communist union started by rebellious Polish shipyard workers, challenged the corrupt and repressive puppet regime in Warsaw and its Soviet masters. As Reagan took up the reins of office in early 1981 it looked as if Soviet troops would march once more to put down a popular uprising in one of the satellite nations, as they had in Hungary, Czechoslovakia, and previously in Poland itself. The Soviets managed to avoid an invasion, but in mid-December 1981 they installed in Warsaw a still more repressive regime under Marshall Jaruzelski that imposed martial law and imprisoned Solidarity's leader, Lech Walesa. Like his predecessors, Reagan was not prepared to take military action against the Soviets. Yet the president used the occasion to drive home his theme of the Soviet Union as the source of the world's turmoil. During the 1981 Christmas season he ordered lighted candles placed in the White House windows to attest to America's concern for the Polish people and imposed several new economic sanctions on the Soviet Union.

Much of the anti-Soviet campaign was a war of words. A more serious Soviet–American confrontation, however, developed over deploying intermediate-range nuclear missiles in Europe.

At best, neither SALT I nor SALT II was expected to stop totally the nuclear arms race. Both sides continued to add to their nuclear delivery systems: long-range ICBMs, bombers, nuclear-carrying submarines, tactical nuclear weapons, and intermediate-range nuclear weapons. In Europe the Warsaw Pact countries and NATO confronted each other with a variety of middle-range nuclear weapons as part of the balance of terror that lay at the heart of the Cold War deterrence policy. In 1980 the Soviets upgraded its Intermediate Nuclear Force (INF) weapons aimed at western Europe with a new, better rocket. At the urging of America's NATO ally, West Germany, Carter promised to send new, upgraded American weapons to restore the balance. But his term ended before he could act, leaving the issue to his successor.

Reagan accepted the commitment to send new "cruise" and Pershing II missiles to Europe. The Soviets reacted with outrage. The Americans, they charged, were threatening the Soviet Union and heating up the Cold War. The issue of the new missiles became the chief concern of the American and Soviet negotiators at Geneva who had been trying to work out a mutual intermediate-range nuclear arms accommodation. The Russians threatened to "walk out in indignation" and hinted at still more dire, if unspecified, consequences if the United States actually deployed the new Pershing II missiles on German soil as scheduled in late 1983. Talks at Geneva on the Pershings soon reached an impasse, and it looked as if Soviet–American relations were once more reaching a crisis point.

The pressure on the Reagan administration to rescind deployment of the Pershings ballooned to enormous proportions in late 1982 and 1983. In Western

Europe a new generation of young men and women now feared nuclear war more than the Soviet threat. Marches and rallies to protest the missile deployment and demand the arms race cease once and for all erupted in many cities of America's NATO allies in the wake of Reagan's resolve. In the United States, too, the INF crisis fed fears of nuclear holocaust. During 1983 the antiwar and nuclear disarmament movements, in eclipse since the end of the Vietnam War, revived explosively. As in Europe there were demonstrations in major American cities to protest the arms race and demand a "nuclear freeze." Public jitters were amplified by Jonathan Schell's best-selling book *The Fate of the Earth*, which described the likely catastrophic effects on the entire globe of nuclear war. The "no nukes" media campaign culminated in ABC television's "The Day After," a graphic and horrifying depiction of what a nuclear attack would do to one midwestern community.

The administration resisted the pressure to draw back. It also upped the arms race ante. In March 1983 the president had proposed, almost as an afterthought, that the United States abandon MAD (Mutually Assured Destruction) as its sole reliance for nuclear peace. Instead, he asked, why not try to find some high-tech defense against enemy missiles, some system to shoot them down before they could reach their targets? Called the Strategic Defense Initiative (SDI) by its friends and "Star Wars" by its enemies, the proposal was unsettling. Many scientists announced that the scheme was simply not possible technically; so why waste billions on such a science fiction operation? Cold War doves insisted that SDI would only encourage further Soviet fears and hence further Soviet militancy.

For the Soviet leaders the Star Wars proposal, apparently, was a profound shock. We now know how far behind the West the Soviet economy and technological prowess were in the 1980s. To compete with NATO and to maintain its allies abroad, the USSR was already spending as much as 25 percent of its GNP on defense. Even with the Reagan arms build-up of the early 1980s, Americans were spending only one quarter as much proportionately. And nowhere was the Soviet economy so far behind the capitalist nations as in high-tech programs. Star Wars now threatened the Soviets with another giant round of arms competition with the West—and in the very area where they were most deficient.

In late November 1983 the American Pershing missiles were finally deployed on West German soil. The Soviets, as threatened, now walked out of the ongoing Geneva arms talks, declaring that "changes in the global strategic situation" had made it "necessary for the Soviet side to review all problems under discussion." For the first time in many years the United States and the USSR would not be discussing at some forum how to contain the arms race. U.S.–Soviet relations had reached a low point, and many people around the world feared they would get still worse.

Reagan was equally aggressive in other corners of the world, although when real danger appeared, prudence often overcame his hard line rhetoric. In the Middle East the president maintained close ties with Israel and was rumored to have encouraged the Israeli invasion of Lebanon in 1982. In September 1983, in the hope of pacifying the chronically chaotic country, Reagan sent American marines to Lebanon. Rather than bringing peace, the marines became targets of warring Lebanese factions, several of them representing violently anti-American, pro-Iranian terror groups. Earlier in the year a Muslim fanatic had detonated an explosives-laden truck next to the American embassy in Beirut, killing forty-seven people, including sixteen Americans. In October 1983, soon after the marines arrived, another Islamic terrorist carried out a similar attack against the marine barracks in Beirut, killing 241 American servicemen. In February 1984 Reagan removed the remaining troops from the scene of the violence. In later years it was said that this timid response to attack had encouraged terrorists. Meanwhile, ominously, the same militant anti-American groups in Lebanon had begun to take hostages among the Americans residing in Beirut, and the media began to pressure the administration to do something to recover the kidnapped men.

Nicaragua.   The president and his advisers saw the work of the Soviets and their Western Hemisphere surrogate, Fidel Castro's Cuba, behind much of the social and political unrest in Latin America. Fearing Marxist beachheads in the Western Hemisphere, the administration intervened in El Salvador to help the conservative-to-moderate regime of Napoleon Duarte against a Marxist-led insurgency. In October 1983 American troops invaded the tiny island republic of Grenada, ostensibly to ensure the safety of several hundred American students studying for their medical degrees on the island, but actually to keep the Cubans from getting a toehold.

The most inflamed spot in the Americas was Nicaragua, another small republic in Central America. The country was ruled by the Sandinistas, a leftist group responsible for the overthrow in 1979 of the American-supported strongman, Anastasio Somoza. Since coming to power, the Sandinistas, led by Daniel Ortega, had established a one-party political system governed by increasingly dogmatic and authoritarian Marxist principles. The administration accused the Sandinistas of aiding the Salvadorean rebels and stirring up anti-American discontent in Latin America generally. To undermine the Sandinista regime the United States provided arms, logistical support, and intelligence to the "Contras," made up mostly of Nicaraguan exiles who despised Ortega and his regime.

American public opinion was divided on the civil wars raging in Central America. Many Americans, like the administration, feared another Marxist bridgehead in the Americas, but others worried about a replay of the Vietnam quagmire. In 1983 a Vietnam-shy Congress passed, over the president's protest, the Boland Amendment requiring the chief executive to consult Congress before using any more Defense Department money to supply the Contras. Thereafter, Congress blew hot and cold over the anti-Sandinista rebels, at times refusing them funds of any sort, at other times restricting their use entirely to "humanitarian" aid—food, clothing, medical supplies, and the like. Frustrated by congressional anti-Contra actions, dedicated anti-Communist hardliners within the CIA and the National Security Council soon began to consider ways to evade Congress's intentions. Their schemes would precipitate a political crisis.

Reelection.   None of Reagan's missteps affected his standings in the polls. The president's personal charm, his relaxed manner, and his good looks sugar-coated his actions. The "great communicator" seemed tough toward America's enemies while avoiding confrontations. He remained a "good guy" while cutting programs for the poor. A generation raised on media images took his words and manner more seriously than his deeds. Exasperated opponents would dub him the "Teflon president," because nothing adverse seemed to stick to his political skin.

In 1982, however, the Republicans had faced, and failed, their first electoral challenge. The 1982 midterm elections found the economy still lagging badly, with unemployment at a lofty 9.7 percent. The Democrats made substantial gains in the House, though they did not regain control in the Senate. By 1984 the economy had sprung back. There remained soft spots in the old Snow Belt industrial areas and—owing to declining world oil prices—the "Oil Patch" of Texas, Oklahoma, and Louisiana began to suffer as well. But on the Pacific coast and in parts of the Northeast, massive defense spending and the transition to computers pushed the economy to new highs. Middle-class America began to feel flush and confident again.

As the 1984 presidential election approached, the Democrats faced a popular president who could claim he had ended the decade-long inflation surge and brought renewed prosperity. Yet there was no lack of Democratic challengers. In the end, the Democratic race came down to Senator Gary Hart of Colorado and former Vice President Walter Mondale of Minnesota. Hart claimed to speak for the younger voters who were coming of age in the 1980s. Mondale represented a more traditional New Deal, bread-and-butter sort of liberalism. To the left of both was Jesse Jackson, a black minister sprung from the civil rights movement, who sought to create a "Rainbow Coalition" of blacks, Hispanics, feminists, gays, and other minorities and social outsiders. Jackson was the first serious black presidential contender, and his candidacy had special meaning for black voters.

The presidential primaries had by now become a long, expensive obstacle course, and for months the Democrats slugged it out. In the end Mondale did well and won on the first ballot at the Democratic convention in San Francisco. Hoping to take advantage of a "gender gap" between the parties, he boldly chose a woman, Representative Geraldine Ferraro of New York, as his running mate. In a fit of rare political honesty, he also promised, if elected, to raise taxes to bring down the escalating budget deficits. The contest was no contest. By the fall the economy was booming and many Americans felt that Reagan had restored America's standing in the world. Underscoring the new pride was the American sweep at the Summer Olympics in Los Angeles, in part because of a Soviet-bloc boycott. The Republican campaign slogan, "It's Morning in America," proclaimed in a raft of TV ads, proved effective. As the race reached the home stretch, one Reagan adviser noted that he "almost felt sorry for Mondale, . . . it's like running against America."

It was indeed a Reagan landslide. The Republican presidential ticket won every state except Minnesota, Mondale's home state, and garnered 59 percent of the popular vote. The Republicans had done well in almost every sector of the population. There was one bit of good news for the Democrats, however. Despite the Reagan landslide, the new House of Representatives would remain under Democratic control.

The Second Four Years

Few presidents accomplish as much in their second term as in their first. By the beginning of their fifth year they have achieved most of their agenda and depleted their good will. In Reagan's case the problems would be compounded by the 1986 midterm elections, when the Democrats regained control of the Senate, making it even more difficult for the administration to win congressional cooperation than before.

Second-term problems were aggravated by the president's age and health. Reagan was already seventy when he became president, the oldest man to hold the presidential office. In addition, he had survived an assassination attempt in 1981, and by 1987 he had undergone surgery for colon cancer and an enlarged prostate. At times in his second term he seemed to be tired, distracted, and forgetful. He still read prepared speeches magnificently, but did poorly at extemporaneous press conferences where he had to think on his feet, and so avoided them. Some Americans believed he had lost his grip.

The Aids Crisis.   Troubles and conflicts would come in shoals during Reagan's second four years. In 1981 the calamity of AIDS burst on the scene when scientists discovered that a hitherto unknown viral agent was attacking the immune systems of thousands of victims and destroying their resistance to cancer and infectious diseases. It was soon learned that the disease was transmitted through infected bodily fluids including semen and blood. In 1984 French and American scientists identified the disease-causing agent as a virus that entered the bloodstream and over time destroyed the body's ability to manufacture antibodies.

AIDS (Acquired Immune Deficiency Syndrome) was not a gay disease as such. But at first it was largely confined to the gay community. AIDS ran through New York's Greenwich Village, the Castro district in San Francisco, and other gay urban neighborhoods, cutting down young men in the hundreds and undermining the hard-won self-confidence that gays had acquired since the late 1960s. It also produced a sharp upsurge of antigay feeling. Though the disease obviously afflicted other groups, social conservatives, including many supporters of the Moral Majority, saw it as a sign of God's displeasure at homosexuality.

Medical experts insisted that the disease could not be transmitted by casual contact, but many people initially feared AIDS victims, however they had acquired the disease. People began to avoid contact with gays; they demanded that AIDS-infected children be kept from school. Medical personnel took to wearing masks and gloves in the presence of AIDS patients. Fear of AIDS also began to affect relations between heterosexual men and women; experts claimed that all sexual contact with infected people created the risk of infection. Combined with a surge of genital herpes and other sexually transmitted diseases, the advent of AIDS took its toll on the permissive sexual revolution of the 1960s and 1970s.

The president was caught in the middle of the controversies that swirled around the AIDS scourge. Gay activists accused him of refusing to mobilize the nation's medical resources against AIDS out of homophobia. The president endorsed mandatory testing of federal and state prisoners, patients admitted to VA hospitals, and marriage-license applicants. These programs fell far short of the mass-testing programs demanded by a few far right advocates, but gays and civil libertarians claimed they would place the jobs and insurance coverage of AIDS patients in jeopardy and were preliminary to an official policy of quarantine. Never highly popular in the homosexual community, the administration probably lost whatever support it had among an emerging self-conscious social minority.

Retreat of the Religious Right.   As his second term approached its end Reagan also found his support among the religious right less sustaining. As we saw, he had benefited from the surging political activism of fundamentalist Protestant groups. The Moral Majority coalition and similar groups had applauded the president's pronouncements on abortion, on school prayer, on traditional family values, but they had been less impressed with his actions. Reagan, some said, talked a good Christian game but did little to implement it.

In 1987 the president sought to appease his supporters on the religious and political right by nominating Robert Bork to the Supreme Court. As a federal appeals court judge, Bork had opposed the judicial activism of many of his liberal predecessors on the bench and denied that the "right to privacy" could be found in the Constitution, the principle on which many of the Court's liberal social decisions were based. Not surprisingly, liberals resisted having him entrenched for life at the nation's judicial center. After widely watched televised hearings, the Senate rejected him. The administration defiantly nominated another far right judge, Douglas Ginsburg. Ginsburg soon confessed to having smoked marijuana while a law professor, and in a matter of days agreed to withdraw his name. The president then nominated Anthony Kennedy of Sacramento, a man closer to the center, whom the Senate finally confirmed. But the ill-conceived initial selections underscored for many social conservatives how little the administration had accomplished in actually reversing the liberal trends of the day.

But by 1987 the religious right itself had become a victim of its own excesses. The chief culprit was Jim Bakker, one of a number of fundamentalist "televangelists" who, during the decade, learned to use the electronic media to disseminate their messages of good works, salvation, righteous living, and anti-modernism. Bakker, along with his blonde wife, Tammy Faye, sponsored a large resort in Fort Mill, South Carolina, that combined the features of Disneyland, a revival camp, and a country club. There the devout, who paid the requisite sum, could spend their vacations soaking up the sun and God's word at the same time. In March 1987 Bakker resigned as head of his "Praise the Lord" ministry after the media revealed he had made sexual advances to both men and women. In 1989 after investigation of dubious sales practices at Fort Hill, he was tried for fraud and sentenced to forty-five years in prison.

The Jim and Tammy scandal damaged the evangelical movement as a whole. Many sincere followers of fundamentalist preachers became disillusioned. Contributions to TV evangelism dropped; membership growth in fundamentalist churches slowed. Jerry Falwell, discouraged by the un-Christian squabbling and infighting that had erupted over PTL, announced in late 1987 that he was abandoning political activism and would hereafter focus on his pastoral duties as minister at the Thomas Road Baptist church in Lynchburg, Virginia. In 1989 the Moral Majority officially disbanded though other, less visible, groups continued to represent the evangelical voice in the political arena. The retreat was not a rout, however. In the next decade the religious right would rally and become an even more formidable force in American Protestantism and politics.

Economic Abuses.   During Reagan's second term the economy's performance continued strong. Unemployment continued to decline, reaching 6 percent in December 1986 and dropping another percentage point by the end of the administration. The inflation rate remained low. Most impressive of all was the stock market boom. In 1985 the Dow Jones Index of leading industrial stocks rose by over 20 percent; in 1986 it leaped by another 15 percent; in the first half of 1987 it soared into the stratosphere.

The bull market in part reflected the successes of several American industries during the 1980s. In 1983 the advent of IBM's "personal computer" produced a breakthrough in individualizing computing power. Already begun by Apple, a Silicon Valley firm established by Stephen Wozniak and Steven Jobs, the miniaturizing of silicon processors made desktop personal machines at moderate price practical. By mid-decade the little box with keyboard and screen, began to affect almost every aspect of daily life—the way people banked, wrote letters, kept accounts, and even spent their leisure time. Hundreds of businesses and whole industries—computer magazines, computer retailers, software manufacturers, computer consultants—grew up around the new PC. High-tech stocks would be the engine that helped push the stock market to greater highs.

But the bull market also expressed other, less admirable, elements of the 1980s business culture. The Reagan victory and tax reforms did unleash enterprise, but clearly not all was of the constructive sort. The administration's message that government was there to befriend business, not to restrain it, encouraged a frenzy to get rich without the painful necessity of making a better product or providing a better service.

One aspect of this mood was "insider trading," the use of information not available to the general public for private speculative gain. Great fortunes were made during the bull market years by such traders as Ivan Boesky using illegal means of manipulating the stock market. Junk bonds and leveraged buyouts also expressed the new attitude. Junk bonds were risky corporate securities that paid high interest rates. Previously scorned by investors, they gained popularity when a young Los Angeles financier, Michael Milken, convinced the public that they were actually a lucrative investment. Before long Milken's firm, Drexel, Burnham, Lambert, was selling many millions of dollars of junk bonds to private and corporate investors.

Able to tap this new source of funds, other shrewd financiers, with relatively little money of their own, bought up large companies, often engaging in fierce bidding wars with their existing managers and stockholders. The battles for control took on the dimensions of financial epics that resembled the struggles of Gould, Fisk, Vanderbilt, and other robber barons to manipulate Gilded Age corporate finance for their own ends. If successful, the "corporate raiders" were seldom interested in improving the efficiency of the new firm or the quality of its product. Usually, they sold off the profitable pieces of the firm, often receiving more from sales of the parts than the whole company had cost them. The remaining husk was not only deprived of its money-making subsidiaries; it was also saddled with millions of dollars of high-interest junk-bond debt.

Still another dubious aspect of business during the 1980s was the mismanagement of the nation's savings and loan associations (S&Ls) that hitherto had provided much of the mortgage money for home buyers. As we saw, these institutions had been closely regulated until 1980 when, to counteract high interest rates paid elsewhere, Congress allowed them to pay higher rates and invest in many other instruments besides houses, offices, and real estate. This helped stem the outflow of deposits from the firms. But it required higher-paying and more liquid investments—like the junk bonds that Drexel, Burnham, Lambert and its competitors were offering, or grandiose commercial projects of dubious profitability. Some S&Ls simply fell into the hands of con artists who made loans to friends, family, or even disguised versions of themselves, without real security. Much of this high flying was confined to the fastest-growing sections of the country—California, the Mountain States, Texas, and Florida. When, during the mid-1980s, the economies of some of these places crashed, many S&Ls found themselves with millions of dollars of worthless IOUs, unable to pay their depositors.

The public would have been outraged at such practices in any case, but matters were made much worse by the fact that billions of dollars of S&L deposits were insured by the federal government. This meant that the American taxpayer would have to make good on the troubled thrifts' depositors' claims. By the last months of Reagan's second term, a few experts close to the events warned that a crisis was building. Few took it seriously. It failed to become an issue during the 1988 campaign, but remained a ticking bomb waiting to detonate.

Trade Deficits.   One of the most serious economic worry from the mid-1980s on was America's deteriorating international trade position. For the previous three-quarters of a century the United States had exported huge amounts of farm and manufactured goods, valued at far more than our imports. In 1971, for the first time since 1914, the U.S. ran a trade deficit. It was not until the 1980s, however, that this trade gap began to expand at a dangerous rate. By 1984 the American trade shortfall had reached $107 billion a year. In 1986 it had gone to $170 billion, by far the largest in our history.

No nation can continue to run international trade deficits for very long unless other nations are willing to lend it money. And so it was now. By 1984, for the first time since World War I, seventy years before, the United States had become a net debtor nation, owing its foreign creditors billions more than they owed us. By 1990, one estimate held, Americans would be paying interest to lenders abroad of over $100 billion a year.

The nation's debtor status had humiliating and unsettling effects. Increasingly foreigners came to own ever larger amounts of American assets—stocks, bonds, factories, and real estate. In 1990 Americans were startled and dismayed when a Japanese company bought Rockefeller Center in New York, long considered an American icon. Bit by bit, worried critics said, we were selling our heritage for a mess of Sonys, Toyotas, and Nikons.

The reasons for the sweeping change in America's international economic position were complex. The quality of American manufactured products relative to their foreign competition had clearly slipped. Through the mid-1980s American industrial and university laboratories continued to lead the world in cutting-edge research. But American companies no longer seemed able to convert this research into attractive, competitively priced consumer goods. Some experts blamed the failure on the excessive focus of American business managers on short-range corporate profit and their own personal financial advantage, versus long-range company growth. Others blamed American workers: They were, it was said, careless, undisciplined, and ill-educated. Still others blamed the high cost of capital in the United States. Americans were not saving; they were spending a larger proportion of their income than ever before. With little domestic saving, investment capital was higher priced here than overseas.

During the 1980s perceptions like these spawned a flood of self-critical analyses that blamed one aspect or another of American culture or policy. One popular candidate for censure was our poor educational system, especially at the lower levels. The results of various international tests confirmed that young Americans ranked behind their peers in many other industrial nations in their knowledge of geography, math, science, history, art, and virtually everything needed to excel. The message seemed clear: How could such a collection of ignoramuses expect to compete with the rest of the world?

But it was also possible to point the finger of blame for America's feeble competitive performance at others. The nation's chief trade rival in the 1980s was Japan, and Japan, many critics said, did not play fair. While the United States remained open to foreign imports, the Japanese refused to buy American goods even when they were indisputably superior to the domestic product. Moreover, said the "Japan bashers," the Japanese government, though professing to favor open markets, actually raised a multitude of phony barriers to foreign goods while at the same time dumping such Japanese products as computer microchips at below cost on foreign markets to destroy the local industry and thereafter become the sole supplier. Japan, in fact, considered international trade a form of warfare and, said some critics, its enormous trading surplus with the United States was a kind of revenge for military defeat in 1945.

Still another economic worry was the size of the domestic public debt. As we saw, the tax cuts of 1981 and after, combined with the defense build-up of the early eighties, produced unparalleled annual federal deficits. By 1988 the deficit had pushed the total national debt to over $2.6 trillion, more than $10,500 for every man, woman, and child. The interest alone on this sum amounted to $214 billion each year. Such an interest payout deprived the private capital markets of an enormous amount of badly needed investment funds. The deficit also thwarted every proposal for additional federal programs, no matter how meritorious or cost-effective. Whether intended or not, Reaganomics had incapacitated the government, the only agency that could tackle many of the problems that faced the American people.

"Irangate." In 1986–1987 Ronald Reagan finally seemed to lose his Teflon coating. The event that changed his luck was a secret deal with Iran instigated, apparently, by CIA director William Casey; National Security Council staffer Lt. Colonel Oliver North; and North's chief at the NSC, Vice Admiral John Poindexter. The deal promised to solve two problems simultaneously: how to fund the Contras and how to win freedom for Americans taken hostage in Lebanon by anti-American Muslim extremists.

All three men were determined to defeat the Nicaraguan Sandinistas. But, as we saw, Congress resisted supplying the Contras with funds and at times had cut these off entirely. Meanwhile, the Lebanese hostage problem had been blown out of proportion by the media and the public was clamoring for their release. Iran seemed the key to both difficulties. As North, Casey, and Poindexter perceived the facts, the

Iranians were desperate for weapons to defeat Iraq, with whom they had been at war since 1980. They would pay any price to get American guns, missiles, and aircraft parts, and in gratitude they would use their good offices with the Muslim extremists to release their American prisoners. There would also undoubtedly be cash profits from the deal and these did not have to be made public. Instead, they could just be handed over to the Contras, thus getting around Congress's unwillingness to fund the "freedom fighters" struggling to overthrow the Marxist Nicaraguan regime.

The Iran-Contra scheme was launched in mid-1985 when the president authorized the then-National Security Adviser, Robert McFarlane, to contact Iranian officials and offer to sell them arms. Soon after, he approved sending American-owned missiles to the Iranians. At first the American negotiators were unable to secure the release of any of the captives. Finally, on November 2, the day before a Lebanese magazine published details of the arms sales and McFarlane's visit to Teheran, the extremists released the first of a small group of kidnapped Americans. The actual arms deals took place through intermediaries, who took a share of the profits. An uncertain portion of the remainder, as intended, ended up in the coffers of the Contras, where it paid for arms and supplies in the anti-Sandinista guerrilla war.

Most Americans were shocked when they learned of the Iran-Contra deal at the end of 1986. Ronald Reagan had promised to be tough on terrorists and on America's enemies generally. He would never, he said, pay ransom to kidnappers. In April 1986, after a number of airplane hijackings, airport bombings, and an attack on an American servicemen's discotheque in West Berlin that implicated the Libyans, he had ordered an air raid against the Libyan cities of Tripoli and Benghazi from aircraft carriers and from air bases in Britain. Over 77 percent of the American public endorsed the retaliatory raids. But after this bold act, what was the public to make of the deal with the Iranians, the worst terrorists in the entire Mideast? Americans from all parts of the political spectrum were appalled by the Iran-Contra affair. Aside from the dubious legality of the scheme, who was running American foreign policy? Congress had cut off funds for the Contras. Did the administration or, more accurately, a small cabal within the administration, have the right to ignore the nation's constitutional policy-making processes?

At first the president denied that there had been an arms-for-hostages deal. Few people believed him. Attorney General Edward Meese admitted that profits from the arms sales had been diverted to the Contras and soon after the president announced that he had fired Oliver North and accepted the resignation of Admiral Poindexter. During the weeks of new revelations that followed, Reagan seemed confused and ill-informed about what had been done in his name and under his very nose. Chief of Staff Donald Regan, to save his own reputation, soon disclosed a White House where chaos reigned and where, he said, only his own rearguard actions had prevented open scandal.

Moderates and liberals were especially dismayed. As more information surfaced, it became clear that a rogue operation had been mounted by quite junior officials in the government, in violation of federal law. Once again, as under Nixon, an administration had violated public trust and ridden roughshod over the Constitution. In mid-December Reagan authorized a special prosecutor to investigate the Iran-Contra matter. The president also appointed a commission headed by former Republican Senator John Tower of Texas to uncover what had happened.

In late February 1987 the Tower Commission issued a report condemning the administration's operations as "chaotic" and "amateurish." It expressed dismay at Reagan's lax "personal management style" and criticized him for allowing his concern for the hostages to get in the way of his good sense. But it absolved him of actual wrongdoing. According to the Tower Commission Report the chief culprit was Donald Regan, who had failed to keep the president informed of White House operations. Regan, now under heavy attack, fought to keep his job, but the First Lady, Nancy Reagan, highly protective of her husband, turned against him and helped force him out. Soon after, Howard Baker, the respected former senator from Tennessee, assumed the role of White House chief of staff. Many people, skeptical of the president's grasp of complexity, applauded the change. At least now the aging chief executive would have a skilled and savvy man to back him up.

Congressional hearings on the Iran-Contra affair began in early May 1987 with a parade of witnesses who described the complex negotiations and intrigues of Iran–Contra. The two chief witnesses were Colonel North and Admiral Poindexter. CIA director Casey could not be examined; he had died of a brain tumor, taking his knowledge of the intrigue to the grave. During the televised hearings the young, crisp, articulate North made an eloquent case for his actions and managed to indict his critics as people of dubious patriotism. The public at first ate it up. For a week or two the nation found itself in the grip of "Ollimania," an uncritical acceptance of North as a patriot and a hero.

Meanwhile, the president's reputation and standing slipped badly. A December 1986 poll showed that Reagan's approval rating had dropped from 67 percent to 46 percent in one month. In late April 1987 two-thirds of those asked by a *Washington Post*–ABC poll believed the president was not telling the truth about his role in the Iran-Contra fiasco. The Teflon, it seemed, had finally worn off the country's chief executive.

Nicaragua Resolved.

The polls also showed that the public remained unwilling to become deeply involved in Nicaragua. In early 1986, 62 percent opposed giving aid to the Contras. Even among those who considered themselves Reagan partisans, only 35 percent favored Contra assistance. Yet the president and his advisers continued to seek the overthrow of Daniel Ortega and his government. Liberals, as well as activists on the left, continued to liken Nicaragua to Vietnam and warned against becoming bogged down in another military and political swamp, this one nearer home.

Toward the end of 1987 it began to look as if a peaceful solution might emerge in Central America after all. Five Central American nations, led by the president of Costa Rica, agreed on a peace plan that would bring the Contras and Sandinistas together, introduce democratic practices into Nicaragua, and end the threat of superpower intervention in that country. In the United States most Democrats also approved of it as a way out of the Central American impasse, but the administration remained skeptical and for a time it seemed that the peace plan had stalled. Then, in late March 1988, the Sandinistas and the Contras signed a cease-fire. In 1990 an anti-Sandinista coalition led by Violetta Chamorro won a surprise victory over the Sandinistas in a free election. It finally looked as if the Nicaragua problem would be peacefully resolved.

The Soviet Union and Arms Reduction. For months following emplacement of U.S. Pershing missiles in Germany, the United States and the Soviet Union sniped at one another. But vast changes were underway in the Soviet Union that would soon transform worldwide international relations.

The author of these changes was the new Soviet leader, Mikhail Gorbachev, a Communist reformer who sought to revive a society increasingly corrupt, rigid, and inefficient. For a brief time in the 1960s Communism had seemed capable of exceeding capitalism in material production. By the 1980s, however, it was clear that the USSR could not provide the consumer products its people craved and the economic strength and technological capacity it needed to compete against the capitalist nations in the world arena. Gorbachev understood the weaknesses of the Soviet system and sought to rectify them. Through *Glasnost* (openness) and *Perestroika* (economic restructuring), the Soviet Union might be transformed into an efficient, tolerant, and productive state.

The Soviet leader was impelled primarily by domestic concerns. But he recognized that the Soviet Union's commitment to expansionist foreign initiatives imposed unbearable economic burdens and must be reduced if Soviet restructuring was to succeed. Perhaps, as some observers believed, the prospect of another arms race with the United States, especially a Star Wars high-tech competition, was a significant factor in his decision to contract Soviet power around the world.

The two men—President Ronald Reagan and Soviet Premier Mikhail Gorbachev—who arguably ended the Cold War. Gorbachev was on a visit to the United States.

The first fruit of Gorbachev's new foreign policy initiatives was the resumption of U.S.–Soviet arms talks, broken off in 1983. These proved fruitful, and in December 1987 Gorbachev and Reagan signed an agreement in Washington eliminating all medium-range missiles in Europe, thereby accepting the main ingredients of the American position at Geneva three years before. For the first time, a whole class of nuclear missiles would actually be removed from superpower arsenals. During his visit to the United States the affable, balding, Soviet leader delighted the American public. He joked and smiled and stopped his limousine on a Washington street to shake hands with pedestrians. Americans even liked his wife, Raisa, though Nancy Reagan, it seemed, did not. The trim and stylish Raisa Gorbachev was the first Kremlin "First Lady," one wag remarked, who weighed less than her husband.

"Black Monday."   In some sense the Reagan era ended on October 19, 1987, when the stock market plummeted over 500 points in a few hours. This was the most catastrophic one-day decline in the history of Wall Street. In the estimate of experts, a trillion dollars in paper wealth were wiped out between August 25, when stocks had reached their all-time Dow Jones peak of 2722, and October 20, with most of the loss on Black Monday itself.

For a time the air was abuzz with dire predictions that the nation, and perhaps the world, was staring another Great Depression in the face. This disaster did not happen. Stocks soon recovered and by mid-1990 had risen above their 1987 high.

Nor did the nation go into an economic tailspin. Modest growth continued; unemployment remained low; price increases neither slowed nor accelerated. And yet something significant had happened. Black Monday dissipated the air of cocky economic confidence that surrounded the Reagan era. Thereafter there would be less flaunting of wealth and less facile defense of crude financial wheeling-dealing. For many high-flying Yuppies the stock crash represented a whiff of mortality, and it was sobering.

Conclusions

Ronald Reagan and his supporters hoped to launch a "revolution," a conservative revolution. They achieved at least part of what they sought to accomplish.

They wished to limit the size and scope of government, and they succeeded to a point. Domestic programs for the non-working poor were reduced, restrained, or eliminated. Few new ones were adopted. The federal government reduced its oversight role in many areas of business activity. Federal participation in a wide range of activities was replaced by control by the states instead. More important, however—whether the result was intended or fortuitous—the drastic tax cuts created unprecedented deficits that promised to tie the hands of the federal government for years to come.

Yet the conservative ideologues were never able to dismantle big government as they hoped. There were too many constituents for Head Start, water and air pollution controls, resource conservation, health research, and the many other functions and roles that modern government had assumed even in the United States. Federal budget outlays on existing domestic programs continued to grow, though at a slower pace.

The Reaganites had promised to revive the American economy and tap new sources of economic productivity. The United States would once more become the economic locomotive that pulled the free world. And the average American, not just the rich, would benefit, for a booming economy would scatter its blessings over all. The administration could point to some economic successes. Reaganite economic policies helped break the dangerous inflationary cycle of the 1970s. During the 1980s, moreover, the economy absorbed millions of new workers entering the job market. Once past the 1982–1983 slump, the economy began a growth phase that lasted longer than any before it.

Yet the economic downside of Reaganomics was undeniable. Contrary to the Laffer theory, cutting federal tax rates did not increase total federal tax takes. Combined with extravagant outlays for arms, the cuts created large budget shortfalls. During the decade federal budget deficits ballooned. The Reagan era also witnessed the shift of income shares from the poorest groups to the richest, with the very richest 1 percent of families improving their relative standing more than any other sector of the public. Administration policies alone did not explain this outcome; world economic trends were surely in part responsible as well. Still, Reaganite tax policy and deregulation encouraged the unequal result. Nor did the administration's economic policies stem America's relative international decline. Indeed, many experts believed that the massive federal budget deficits imposed severe limitations on any possibility for improving the country's competitiveness. Too much of the nation's savings, they said, was absorbed by the persistent deficits; they prevented needed federal expenditures for education, roads and bridges, research, and many other things required for the United States to catch up to its chief world rivals.

The Reaganites came to office resolved to strengthen old-fashioned family structures. Their immediate success was limited. There was little that any administration in Washington could do in the short run about the drastic changes in American sexual mores and family patterns. Illegitimacy, divorce, and broken families continued to plague the nation.

Reagan pledged to restore world respect for the United States and reduce Soviet power and political influence. He left office with America and its allies on the verge of an astonishing victory over their Communist adversaries. Two years into his successor's administration, the Soviet Union had ceased to be a threat to Western Europe or, for that matter, to any nation around the world. Everywhere communism was collapsing; the Cold War was over and it would be hard to refute the claim that the West had won. Obviously the Reagan arms build-up and the stubborn resolve to deploy new nuclear weapons on NATO soil do not by themselves explain the stupefying result. The containment policy went back to the late 1940s and had been supported by half a dozen administrations. Yet it would be difficult to dismiss the influence of the Reagan administration's hard-line policies in inducing Kremlin leadership to reconsider aggressive Soviet international commitments.

Was there a Reagan Revolution? Keeping in mind the normal inertia of America's political culture, its resistance to quick shifts, the term may be valid. The years 1981–1989 witnessed more rapid change than most equal intervals of the past. Inevitably, however, Americans would disagree over whether to cheer or to scoff.

ONLINE RESOURCES

"Possible Soviet Responses to the U.S. Strategic Defense Initiative" *http://www.fas.org/spp/ starwars/offdocs/m8310017.htm* From the office of the Director of Central Intelligence, this report seeks to ascertain Soviet military strength and intentions during the Reagan era.

"Reagan" *http://www.pbs.org/wgbh/amex/reagan/filmmore/index.html* This comprehensive site contains information on the Iran-Contra affair, a timeline of Reagan's presidency, in-depth coverage of the 1982 recession and the Grenada invasion, and text copies of many of Reagan's presidential speeches. A companion site to a documentary on the president, this site also contains transcripts of interviews with scholars about the Reagan presidency.

"The History of Silicon Valley" *http://www.ocf.berkeley.edu/~kenken/svhis.htm* This site details the beginnings of the information age through electronics. Read about the beginnings of Silicon Valley as a research center and how the industry was propelled by the revolutions of the personal computer and the World Wide Web.

"The Intermediate Nuclear Force Agreement (INF)" *http://www.state.gov/t/isn/trty/18432.htm* Read the full text of the INF agreement between the United States and the Soviet Union, an agreement that was the first true nuclear disarmament treaty.

31

A United America?

Would Diversity and the War on Terror Change America?

2001	President Bush succeeds in getting a gigantic tax cut bill passed over Democrats' resistance; Bush seeks to weaken environmental protection policies of Clinton administration; Terrorists linked to Osama bin Laden hijack American commercial airliners and crash them into New York's World Trade Center twin towers and the Pentagon in Washington and over 3,000 die; Bush declares "war" on bin Laden and terrorism; American forces begin campaign to oust bin Laden and his network from Afghanistan
2002	American-led forces oust Taliban regime in Afghanistan; Homeland Security Act consolidates 22 federal agencies into new Department of Homeland Security; Israelis sweep West Bank and Gaza; Corporate scandals shake public confidence in business community
2003	U.S. and British forces invade Iraq, occupy Baghdad, capture Saddam Hussein but find no WMDs; Congress enacts further tax cuts and raises debt limit
2004	Iraqi unrest mounts; Bush defeats Democratic challenger John Kerry; Republicans attain majority in both House and Senate
2005	Iraqis vote in large numbers in parliamentary elections but public support for Iraq policies declines; Israelis announce withdrawal from West Bank and Gaza; Bush abandons efforts to restructure Social Security; Hurricane Katrina devastates Gulf coast and floods New Orleans
2006	Hamas party wins Palestinian elections; key Enron executives tried and convicted

The Presidency of George Herbert Walker Bush

The 1988 Presidential Election.   As the 1988 presidential election approached, Democrats took heart. The "Great Communicator" would soon be off to California and trouble them no more. In the end the Democratic nomination went to the governor of Massachusetts, Michael Dukakis, a brainy technocrat who claimed to have made his state into a model of high-tech efficiency. Dukakis chose Senator Lloyd Bentsen of Texas, a conservative Democrat, as his running mate. On the Republican side, in the nomination race, Vice President George Bush quickly leaped ahead of his chief adversary, Senator Minority Leader Robert Dole. Winning on the first ballot at New Orleans, he chose a young senator from Indiana, Dan Quayle, to share the ticket.

The campaign was no credit to the American political process. Dukakis sought to emphasize "competence" over ideology; he would make America competitive again in the world economy. But the Democrats also harped on the fact that Quayle had ducked active military duty in Vietnam in favor of safe and comfortable National Guard service and had a feeble academic record to boot. The Republican campaign was even more negative. The most telling Republican campaign ad was a TV spot featuring a convicted black murderer, Willie Horton, who, while on furlough under a Massachusetts prison release program during Dukakis's administration, had raped a white woman. Dukakis, it implied, was soft on crime. The Democrats also charged that the Republicans were appealing to racial bigotry. The spot seemed to be effective with some white voters.

Dukakis proved to be an awkward, wooden campaigner who struck few sparks. Bush, however, made effective use of the public's deep aversion to taxes. His most memorable campaign line was: "Read my lips; no new taxes." On November 8 the Bush–Quayle ticket won forty states to ten, with a popular vote of 48.8 million to 41.8 million, and an electoral vote of 426 to 112. Dukakis had carried a small group of the most liberal states of the Northeast, the Midwest, and the Pacific coast, but had lost everywhere else.

The Domestic Scene.

As president, George Bush was marginally less conservative than his predecessor. During the campaign he had talked about a "kinder, gentler nation" and a "thousand points of light," phrases that suggested that compassion would replace rugged individualism as the administration watchword. As president he made stabs at strengthening environmental safeguards, raising educational standards, and providing help for working mothers. In 1990 he signed the Americans With Disabilities Act, which promised new access for disabled people to mainstream facilities and protected them against discrimination. But he often did not follow through. Bush was a captive of Reagan's legacy of enormous federal deficits. There was simply no money for new initiatives even if the president had favored them.

Early on Bush had to deal with the snowballing S&L crisis. Besides the sheer magnitude of the disaster, it soon became obvious that more than incompetence and inattention were involved. Each day brought new revelations of how federal regulators, as well as prominent members of Congress, had abetted the S&L manipulators in exchange for favors and campaign contributions.

Abortion was another prickly domestic problem that surfaced during the first months of the administration. Social conservatism remained a powerful force in the nation and by the early 1990s it had come to focus most of its energies on reversing the 1973 Supreme Court decision in *Roe v. Wade*.

By the end of the 1980s it was clear that the Supreme Court was the key to the pro-life campaign's success. The expectation that a conservative majority would overthrow the liberal abortion rules made each new Supreme Court nomination a battleground between pro-life and pro-choice proponents. The appointments of Justices Anthony Kennedy and Antonin Scalia had already tipped the balance toward the pro-life side, and in *Webster v. Reproductive Health Services* (1989) the court decided by a five-to-four margin that Missouri could limit the right to abortion more strictly than did *Roe v. Wade*.

In the summer of 1990 Justice William Brennan, the Court's most liberal member, retired. Bush nominated, and the Senate confirmed, an obscure, but presumably conservative New Hampshire judge, David Souter, to succeed him. Soon after, Thurgood Marshall, the only black justice and an outstanding liberal, joined Brennan in retirement. The overturn of *Roe v. Wade*—and much else the liberal Court had made the law of the land—appeared possible.

The Clarence Thomas–Anita Hill Affair.

Bush nominated Judge Clarence Thomas to succeed Marshall. Thomas was an African-American, but he was also a conservative. Bush claimed that he was the person best qualified for the job, but more than a few Americans suspected that as a black man, Thomas could not be "Borked" by the liberals, who would be chary of voting against a man of his race.

But the confirmation process proved to be more than usually rocky. The Bush strategy seemed to be working until Anita Hill, a black woman law professor at the University of Oklahoma, told the Senate Judiciary Committee that when she worked for Thomas on the Equal Employment Opportunity Commission eight years before he had harassed her by making sexually suggestive remarks and overtures.

Hill's complaints highlighted a long-simmering issue: sexual harassment in the workplace. Many women believed that it was a serious problem all too often ignored. Ardent feminists claimed it was another example of the subordination of women that permeated all of American life. On the other side were those who believed the issue exaggerated. Many men were puzzled about what constituted sexual harassment.

Thomas categorically denied the charges. He was, he said, like so many black males in the past, being "lynched." Most of the senators, recognizing that two of the most delicate subjects in American life—gender and race—were involved, treated the two participants warily. But some feminists saw the all-male inquisitors as insensitive to Anita Hill's concerns. In the end Thomas was confirmed and as Associate Justice on the Court fully substantiated his conservative reputation.

The Cold War Ends.   If Bush seemed beleaguered at home, abroad he could glory in the fruits of good luck and his predecessors' policies. In Eastern Europe Soviet leader Mikhail Gorbachev was dismantling the Communist military alliance, the Warsaw Pact, and discarding the entire repressive political regime that the Soviets had imposed in Eastern Europe after 1945. The Iron Curtain was soon gone. In 1989 popular movements in Poland, Hungary, Romania, Bulgaria, Czechoslovakia, and the German Democratic Republic replaced corrupt and tyrannical Communist regimes with administrations professing democracy and respect for free market economics. No other episode of the miraculous year would match the razing of the Berlin Wall as a symbol of change. The world watched transfixed as cheering crowds tore the detested wall apart, and Germans on both sides of the line joyously mingled as one people for the first time since 1945. Propelled by Chancellor Helmut Kohl of West Germany, the Communist collapse in East Germany was quickly converted into an economic merger of the two Germanies, soon followed by full political union. For good or ill, Germany would be reunited into one powerful nation for the first time since 1945.

Meanwhile the Soviet leader, bedeviled by a fast-sinking economy, was making further cooperative arrangements with the United States. In May 1989 the United States and the Soviets agreed to reopen the START nuclear disarmament talks, and Gorbachev and Bush both proposed substantial cutbacks in the troops and conventional weapons each deployed against the other in Europe. By this time the Soviets had withdrawn their military forces from Afghanistan after admitting that the 1979 invasion had been a blunder that had cost them thousands of lives and enormous resources. An apparent victory for the United States, the consequences would in reality prove disastrous. The Taliban, a fanatically fundamentalist student-led Islamic party, backed initially by the United States, soon moved into the country's power vacuum. Elsewhere, however, the results of Soviet decline were benign. The Russians began to reduce their support for revolutionary client regimes in Africa, Asia, the Middle East, and Latin America, including Cuba. Deprived of Soviet subsidies and arms, many of the left wing insurrections around the world subsided.

Even the People's Republic of China felt the effects of the "freedom wind" that began to blow through the world in the late 1980s. After his death Mao's successors had jettisoned the hard-line Communist micro-management of the economy, and foreign capital and technology began to pour into the country. Though liberalizing the economy, the aging Chinese leaders, Deng Xiaoping and Li Peng, refused to permit a democratic, multiparty system and a free press. Among a brave core of students and intellectuals, inspired by Soviet reforms and western values, the mood soon turned bitter.

On May 17, 1989, during a visit to China by Soviet leader Gorbachev, a million protesters camped out in Beijing's Tiananmen Square to demand political change. The protesters proclaimed their democratic agenda in massive posters and in a large plaster statue that resembled the Statue of Liberty in New York harbor. In early June the hard-line regime ordered the army to clear the square and put down the rebellion. The brutal operation, caught on tape for the world to see, cost many hundreds of lives and was followed by the trial and conviction of many Tiananmen Square demonstrators.

Americans had applauded the Chinese "Pro-Democracy Movement" as a promise that the world's largest nation was about to be liberated from the Communist yoke. The crackdown outraged westerners and many Americans demanded economic and diplomatic sanctions against the People's Republic. In the end, caution prevailed. The Bush administration condemned the repression and called for liberalization of Chinese political life, but refused to break off the profitable new economic ties with Beijing. Critics accused the administration of putting dollars before democracy.

Chinese backsliding notwithstanding, the Cold War was clearly over. Containment, it seemed, had worked! In the first flush of jubilation, foreign-policy expert Francis Fukuyama published a much-noticed article entitled "The End of History," proclaiming that all the world's dangerous confrontations were finally at an end and the system of liberal capitalism was now universally triumphant.

The Gulf War

In the summer of 1990 the euphoria was quickly dissipated by a major international crisis. Suddenly it became clear that the world was still an uncertain and dangerous place, perhaps more unstable than ever, and that Americans could not afford to bury their heads in the sand.

Iraq Invades Kuwait.   During the drawn-out Iraq–Iran War of 1980–1988, the United States had tilted toward Iraq. Although it was the aggressor in the war and although its leader, Saddam Hussein, was a brutal tyrant who used terror tactics, including poison gas, against his own people, Iraq seemed preferable to an Iran controlled by the hostile Shiite Muslim fundamentalists under Ayatollah Khomeini, who had overthrown the Shah and ordered the taking of American embassy hostages in 1979. American arms support had helped prevent Iraqi defeat, and by 1988 the two Mideast countries had negotiated a cease-fire.

The Iraqi urge to dominate the oil-rich Persian Gulf, which had inspired the attack on Iran, had not subsided with the peace, however. In fact, Iraq's need to pay the billions of debt incurred by the war gave Saddam a new reason for aggression against his Gulf neighbors. Yet it was a complete surprise when, on August 2, 1990, Iraqi troops and tanks thrust across the border into the small, oil-rich kingdom of Kuwait and seized control of the country. After watching Hussein gobbling up that small country, the world wondered what would keep him from further conquests in the Persian Gulf including Saudi Arabia, the oil-rich though militarily weak kingdom on the Arabian peninsula. The Persian Gulf was the world's richest producer of petroleum, with Saudi Arabia by itself the largest supplier. Could the United States, having allowed itself to become utterly dependent on petroleum, permit Saddam to have a choke hold on much of the world's supply? There was also the frightening matter of nuclear arms. Saddam had long sought to acquire nuclear weapons. Set back for years by an Israeli air attack on his nuclear facilities in 1981, he had, it was believed, resumed the quest to make Iraq a nuclear power. Now that Saddam had revealed his aggressive policies, the nuclear issue became urgent. If he succeeded in constructing an atomic arsenal the entire Mideast, even the world, would be destabilized in ways too frightening to contemplate.

Reacting quickly to the occupation of Kuwait, the United Nations Security Council, with strong American support, passed resolutions condemning the aggression and demanding that the Iraqis withdraw their troops. UN members pledged to embargo all goods and supplies to Iraq and refuse to buy Iraqi oil. If Saddam refused to comply, the UN itself lacked the military power to force him. In that case, clearly, the United States would have to bear the primary burden of blocking his imperial designs.

Despite the American public's fears of military involvement in distant lands, Bush quickly dispatched 125,000 troops to Saudi Arabia. Meanwhile, Secretary of State James Baker and Defense Secretary Richard Cheney criss-crossed the Atlantic to line up military, diplomatic, and financial support for American intervention. Egypt, Syria, and other Arab nations, as well as Britain, France, Italy, and other NATO allies pledged troops and financial help for "Operation Desert Shield." Even Russia endorsed the sanctions against Iraq, though the Soviet government remained uneasy about the massive intrusion of United States military forces into the sensitive Mideast.

During the fall and early winter of 1990 troops, supplies, munitions, and weapons piled up in Saudi Arabia for an invasion. Thirty-four nations contributed to the military personnel of the international "Coalition" that the administration was able to assemble. More than 500,000 were American, however, and they reflected the new, revitalized post-Vietnam military. All-volunteer, the services included many black and Hispanic soldiers and, for the first time, a substantial proportion of women, though not generally in combat positions.

Meanwhile, despite the UN embargo and oil sanctions, Saddam's army defiantly dug in along the Kuwait–Saudi border, prepared to fight the kind of defensive war that had served them so effectively against Iran. Playing to fears of the American public, Saddam thundered that he would turn any coalition attack into

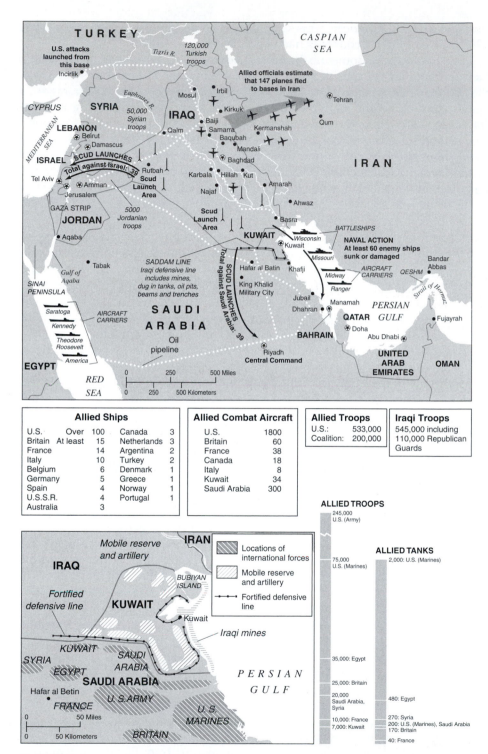

Gulf War

a bloodbath and would not reject the use of poison gas and germ warfare against his opponents if necessary. Appealing to the discontented Arab masses over the heads of their pro-Western leaders, he depicted himself simultaneously as a Robin Hood who would share Gulf oil wealth with the poor and a champion of the Palestinian people in their struggle against Israel.

As a military confrontation approached, the American public debated the Gulf crisis. A majority was convinced from the outset that Saddam was a major threat to world peace and nothing except actual force would deter him. A small minority considered intervention a shameful instance of American imperialism and war-mongering. A much larger bloc of Americans, while deploring Iraqi aggression, favored waiting to see if economic sanctions worked. On January 12 Congress authorized the president to use force against Iraq if in his judgment the facts warranted it.

War and Victory.   The actual shooting war, called "Desert Storm," began soon after when, on signal from General Norman Schwartzkopf, the United States and its coalition partners launched a massive air offensive against Iraq employing sophisticated new electronically guided weapons. The targets of the initial attacks were Iraqi command headquarters, communications centers, electric power stations, Scud missile launchers, chemical weapons factories, and suspected nuclear bomb development facilities. Though later questioned, the results seemed a spectacular success at the time. The war, it seemed, might be won with air power alone without the need to use ground forces and risk heavy casualties.

Once the fighting started, patriotic sentiment swept the nation and Americans took to wearing bits of red, white, and blue bunting and tying yellow ribbons around curbside trees to indicate support for the troops. In the Middle East, meanwhile, day after day coalition bombers, fighters, and missiles hurtled across the desert to drop their explosives on Iraqi troops, tanks, artillery, bridges, and communications facilities. Inevitably Iraqi civilians died.

The Iraqis retaliated by firing off Scud missiles targeting Riyadh, the Saudi capital, and Tel Aviv, Haifa, and other Israeli cities. Israel was not a coalition nation, but Saddam believed that if he could goad the Israelis into retaliation, their response would so offend the Arab world that the hastily forged Gulf coalition would fall apart. Fortunately, powerful pressure from the United States deterred the Israelis from counterattacking. Yet the Scuds were more than an annoyance. One disastrous missile killed twenty-eight American service troops in Riyadh. The need to take them out tied up many coalition planes and troops.

The long-awaited ground assault came on February 23. General Schwartzkopf had deceived the Iraqis into believing that he would attack across the beaches from the Gulf and head-on from the south across the Saudi–Kuwaiti border. Instead, he sent his main armored units in a swing to the west, and then north and east, around the Iraqi defensive line, cutting off the elite Republican Guards and the bulk of Iraqi armor from retreat to Baghdad. Meanwhile, Saudi, Egyptian, and Kuwaiti troops, bolstered by U.S. marines, crossed directly from Saudi territory into occupied Kuwait.

The armored sweep around their right end smashed the Republican Guard in a brief, one-sided tank battle. In a day or two the vaunted Guard was cut off and

Armored personnel carriers going into battle during Desert Storm.

forced into a pocket around Basra. Thousands of Iraqis, waving coalition surrender leaflets, gave up without firing a shot. Meanwhile, in sharp fighting south of
Kuwait City, the marines and coalition troops forced the main Iraqi army into
headlong retreat northward. As they fled, they were mercilessly pounded by
coalition planes from the air. Yielding to humanitarian pressure, President Bush
ordered a cease-fire rather than continue the slaughter. Before they fled Kuwait,
the Iraqis looted the kingdom's capital and ignited thousands of oil wells.

Only 125 American soldiers died in the fighting in the Gulf in the seven weeks
of active air and ground conflict. The Iraqis, however, had suffered thousands of
casualties and had lost most of their military equipment. Saddam would be able to
replace some of the loss in the months ahead, but the victory was one of the most
complete and total in the history of modern warfare.

The Election of 1992

Victory in the Gulf War did wonders for Bush's popularity. As the price of defeat,
Saddam was forced to accept UN inspectors to monitor his attempts to build
weapons of mass destruction and to allow coalition planes to patrol his air space.
Many Americans believed that the president should have ordered the coalition
troops on to Baghdad, the Iraqi capital, to oust Saddam Hussein from power. But
the president and his advisers, afraid to encourage chaos in the defeated country,
balked at continuing the war. One unfortunate consequence was that Saddam was

able to brutally suppress an uprising by the Kurds in the country's north encouraged by the United States. The Kurds had to be rescued from massacre and starvation by UN forces and relief workers. Still, the public admired the president's overall handling of the Gulf crisis as resolute and effective. A major opinion poll in March 1991 showed that 91 percent of the American people, a truly extraordinary proportion, believed that Bush was doing a good job.

The approval did not last. The American people had never loved George Herbert Walker Bush as they had Ronnie Reagan. He seemed an aloof patrician who tried too hard to affect the common touch. With the onset of the longest recession since the end of World War II his popularity quickly faded.

The Economic Slump.

By late 1989 many of the standard economic indicators began to turn down. The real estate boom, fueled by lavish credit from savings and loan associations and by the bounding optimism of the Reagan era, flattened soon after Bush took office. Fear of debt also undermined consumer confidence. Many Americans had gone into hock for cars, boats, VCRs, home computers, second homes, and travel. Once the economic clouds began rolling in, many consumers felt it wiser to save than spend. In short order, the crowds in the shopping malls dwindled and a flock of venerable stores, including the Macy's chain, found themselves in bankruptcy.

The end of the Cold War probably contributed to the recession as well. Congress slashed billions from the budget formerly spent on ships, planes, rockets, tanks, and other weapons. Simultaneously, a congressional Base Closure and Realignment Commission marked military bases for shut down all over the country. Many communities were economically devastated when the factories and bases closed.

The Bush administration committed a serious political blunder by discounting the severity of the economic downturn and the worries of the voters. The recession would be short and self-righting, the president said. The government must not do anything to worsen the federal deficit, and so should avoid major public works programs or large tax cuts. The public soon accused the president of obsession with foreign affairs and indifference to domestic problems. In November 1991 a *New York Times*–CBS poll showed Bush's job performance rating down to 51 percent, a drop of 16 percentage points in a month.

The Nomination Battles.

The economic dip formed the background of the 1992 presidential campaign. By the early months of 1992 five Democrats were battling for their party's nomination. The front-runner almost from the beginning, however, was Bill Clinton, former governor of Arkansas.

A southerner of working-class origins, William Jefferson Clinton attended Georgetown University and then, in 1968, went to Oxford in England on a prestigious Rhodes Scholarship. These were the turbulent years when many male college students, opposed to the war in Vietnam, resisted being drafted. Clinton was an antiwar activist at Oxford and avoided military service by some dubious maneuvering. Returning from Britain, he entered Yale Law School where he met fellow student Hillary Rodham, a young woman from Illinois. In 1975 they were married.

After teaching and practicing law in Arkansas, Clinton ran for governor, and in 1978, at the age of thirty-three, he was elected to head his home state. In his five terms in the Arkansas statehouse he won plaudits from his fellow governors for effective leadership. On the other hand he also made serious enemies, some of whom were appalled by his lax personal morals, others by his moderate-to-liberal policies.

Clinton belonged to the Washington, D.C.-based Democratic Leadership Council (DLC), a group of middle-of-the-road Democrats. The DLC favored cutting federal welfare rolls, encouraging family preservation, holding down deficits, and making the United States strong internationally. Such policies, the DLC leaders believed, would enable the Democrats to recapture the blue-collar voters they had lost to Ronald Reagan and the Republicans.

Clinton won the nomination for president on the first ballot in New York and delivered a long-winded "Clinton Special" acceptance speech. He made up for this lapse by choosing the personable young senator from Tennessee, Albert Gore, as his running mate.

President Bush, meanwhile, had to fend off the challenge of Patrick Buchanan, a combative right-wing journalist and TV personality, who claimed to speak for "working people." During the primaries, Buchanan attacked the president as too concerned with overseas problems and at most an ersatz conservative. His most effective jab was that Bush had repudiated his 1988 no-tax pledge, when he had supported a bipartisan 1990 tax bill designed to raise federal revenues by $164 billion over five years. Still, Buchanan could not win more than one third of the vote in any of the Republican state primaries and failed to stop Bush's renomination. He did force the Republican National Convention in Houston to give him a hearing, however. In a prime-time speech, Buchanan denounced Hillary Clinton as a "radical feminist" and called the coming campaign a religious and cultural war. Moderate Republicans winced at these remarks, and to many voters they seemed strident and divisive.

The Campaign.   The 1992 presidential campaign marked the political debut of Ross Perot, a self-made Texas billionaire whose chief asset was that he was not a politician. The public had become skeptical of the professional "pols" who seemed incapable of governing. During the previous dozen years a Republican president and a Democratic Congress had been at loggerheads, and few of the country's pressing problems had been addressed. Political life in Washington had also been tarnished by a succession of scandals. In 1990 five United States senators were accused of using their political influence to help the business interests of Charles Keating, head of the Lincoln Savings and Loan Association of California, who was later sent to jail for fraud. Soon after, the public heard that House members had used overdraft checks at the House of Representatives bank, in effect taking interest-free loans for themselves.

Perot profited from the public disgust with politics-as-usual. But in fact, his political views were not easy to define. He favored fiscal restraint and deficit reduction and talked about making America more competitive in the world economy. But he did not seem to possess any core vision. Still, when he announced that if he could get on the ballot in all fifty states he would run for president, many voters responded enthusiastically. As much as a third of the American public initially saw Perot as a real alternative to a corrupt and ineffective party system that had failed the nation. Unfortunately for his followers, Perot was a volatile personality. On July 16 he abruptly announced his withdrawal from the race. Then, on October 1, having sat out much of the campaign, he decided to reenter. He later explained that Bush administration threats to injure his business and disrupt the wedding of his daughter had driven him from the contest. The excuse seemed eerie and many of his followers wondered if the man was not too eccentric to trust. His candidacy was kept alive, however, by the continuing scorn of many voters for both of the major party nominees.

The job of James Baker, who left the State Department to head the flagging Republican campaign, was formidable. Week after week the economic indicators reinforced the sense of economic malaise. Everyone knew that the slumping economy was the Republicans' albatross. James Carville, the Democratic campaign manager, had prepared a large sign that he prominently displayed at campaign headquarters—"It's the Economy, Stupid!"—to keep his party's task in clear focus. And generally it remained on target. The Democrats promised tax breaks for the middle class, deficit reduction, a more efficient health care system, and heavy investment in education and long-neglected infrastructure to increase America's international competitiveness.

To deflect his opponent's attacks, Bush offered one-time economic payoffs to key constituencies. But outbidding the Democrats economically took second place to undermining Clinton's reputation and character. Just before the New Hampshire Democratic primary, a former nightclub singer, Gennifer Flowers, had told a supermarket tabloid that she and Clinton had had a twelve-year affair during his governorship. The accusations almost derailed the Clinton nomination campaign and many voters were left with a sense that Clinton had been less than fully candid. The adultery charge had been contained by the time the presidential race itself began, but the Republicans probed other weak spots in Clinton's personal armor. George Bush had been a navy pilot in World War II and been shot down by the Japanese over the Pacific. Clinton, though the right age for combat in Vietnam, had, as we saw, evaded service.

But nothing worked for the Republicans. In November Clinton took 32 states with 370 electoral votes and 43 percent of the popular vote (43.7 million). Bush won 168 electoral votes from the remaining 18 states with 38 percent of the popular vote (38 million). Perot did not carry a single state but received 19 percent of the popular vote (19.2 million).

Clinton's First Term

The American public was initially more than willing to give the young, affable president the benefit of the doubt. Perhaps he could revive the economy, create a better health-care system, improve education, tame the burgeoning deficit, and usher in an era of international stability and justice. It did not take long for Clinton to dissipate much of this initial hope and goodwill.

Early Gaffes.   The public gave mixed reviews at best to his choices for cabinet- and subcabinet-level posts. Clinton made no bones about the demographic goals of his appointment agenda. He wanted, he said, to have a cabinet that "looked like America," and he succeeded. Of fourteen people nominated for cabinet positions, two were Hispanic, three were black, and three were women.

By his second term half of these appointees had come under legal scrutiny for public or private transgressions. Clinton seemed particularly inept in his effort to find a female attorney general. His initial choices, both women, had employed illegal aliens to take care of their children, in violation of the immigration laws, and were disqualified. Not until mid-March did unmarried Florida state attorney Janet Reno, his third choice, make it through to confirmation.

By now many people had begun to question both the administration's political judgment and its competence. At the end of May, in a major damage-control move, he appointed David Gergen, an ex-Reagan strategist, as White House adviser.

Gergen's steadying presence may explain what many observers considered a very shrewd selection for Supreme Court justice in mid-1993. Clinton's choice settled on Judge Ruth Bader Ginsburg of New York. Ginsburg was a liberal, but not an ideologue. She supported a woman's right to abortion but rejected judicial activism. Her nomination sailed through the Senate without serious demurrer. The appointment helped protect *Roe v. Wade* for the foreseeable future, but it did not end the picketing outside abortion clinics and the attempts by pro-life activists to disrupt their operations. In fact, the rancor over abortion seemed to be getting worse. In March 1993 an abortion clinic doctor was shot to death in Pensacola, Florida, by a 37-year-old pro-life activist. Pro-choice proponents were soon warning that legal abortion was being nullified by violence and intimidation.

Gays in the Military.

In the midst of the attorney general fiasco, Clinton issued a series of executive orders that offended many conservative Americans, though they clearly pleased liberals. In short order the president lifted the so-called gag rule that forbade federally funded family planning clinic personnel from discussing the abortion option with clients; rescinded restrictions on using fetuses from elective abortions in federally funded medical research; and ordered Secretary of Health and Human Services Donna Shalala to review a Bush-era prohibition on the French-developed RU-486 abortion pill. In the environmental area Clinton ordered the Forest Service to halt clear-cutting by loggers in the Sierra Nevada region to protect the endangered spotted owl. He also canceled the Bush-created Council on Competitiveness, an agency designed to facilitate business by loosening the restrictions on environmental practices. Meanwhile, Interior Secretary Bruce Babbitt sought to raise the fees paid by ranchers, loggers, and miners for the use and exploitation of federal lands.

The most controversial executive order of all, however, related to homosexuals in the military. For many years gay men and lesbians had quietly served in the nation's armed forces. Few doubted that they had made as good soldiers, sailors, or airmen as heterosexuals. But open acknowledgment of gay preferences had been punished by dismissal from the military. Clinton had made a promise during the campaign to lift the discrimination against gays in the services if elected and had won the support of gay voters. Soon after the inauguration, he sought to follow through on his promise by executive order.

Social conservatives objected to a move they considered giving homosexuality moral and legal parity with heterosexuality. In Congress, the Senate Republican minority leader, Robert Dole of Kansas, and Democrat Sam Nunn of Georgia, head of the Senate Armed Services Committee, threatened to override Clinton's executive order by statute if he persisted. After much backing and filling, the president arranged a compromise. Called by the media "don't ask, don't tell," it provided that the military authorities would not question new recruits on their sexual orientation and would not investigate the sexual preferences of military personnel already serving. For their part, gays and lesbians would not make public their sexual identity and would not engage in sexual activities while on duty on pain of discharge from the service. It seemed a makeshift solution and it pleased few completely. Most Americans, however, polls showed, believed the agreement an acceptable solution to a difficult problem.

Foreign Affairs. Clinton's early unsteadiness in domestic matters was matched by his waffling on foreign policy. By 1993 the former Soviet Union had completely dissolved as a political entity following an attempted coup by old-line Communists against the reformer Mikhail Gorbachev. Democratic forces, led by Boris Yeltsin, the president of the Russian Federation, rushed to Gorbachev's support and quelled the revolt, but Gorbachev himself did not long remain in power. Yeltsin became head of the Russian state and moved quickly to establish a market economy, abolish the Communist party, create democratic institutions, a free press, and an independent judiciary. Soviet troops were removed from the non-Russian parts of the old USSR, allowing a flock of nationalities—Ukrainians, Kazakhs, Uzbeks, Georgians, Armenians, and others—to create their own independent nation-states. The Soviet Union itself disappeared as a political entity.

None of these secessions from the Soviet Union was accompanied by serious violence. Not so the breakup of another Communist nation, the former Yugoslavia. Located in the chaotic Balkan peninsula, Yugoslavia had been cobbled together after World War I out of a hodgepodge of ethnic and religious groups. Fierce antagonisms among these had been held in check by the Communist regime under Marshal Josip Broz Tito, but after Tito's death in 1980 the country quickly fell apart. The core, Serbia, with its capital in Belgrade, remained under the control of the largest ethnic group, the Orthodox Christian Serbs. Other groups, however, formed their own independent states. In the midsection of the former Yugoslavia, with their capital in Sarajevo, were the Bosnians, many of whom were Muslims, despised by the Christian Croats and Serbs alike. In 1992 the Bosnians too proclaimed their independence. The European nations and the United States recognized the independence of all the Yugoslav successor states except Macedonia, to which Greece, a NATO member, objected, fearing designs on its own territory.

Coveting its territory and hostile to Muslims, neither the Serbs nor the Croats were willing to accept an independent Bosnia, at least not with its generous initial boundaries. Serbs and Croats soon launched a campaign to destroy the new Bosnian nation or at least compress it into a mini-state composed almost entirely of Muslims. The Serbs, especially, employed "ethnic cleansing" terror tactics to either kill or drive the Muslim population out of regions they coveted. The process reeked of the Nazi Holocaust and sent a shudder through the European and American publics.

But West Europeans and Americans initially refused to become entangled in the age-old hatreds of the Balkans. During the 1992 presidential campaign Clinton scolded the Bush administration for timidity and promised to use American influence and, if needed, its military power, to stop the atrocities in Bosnia. After his inauguration, however, he refused to authorize the use of force until and unless the

West European nations, closer than the United States to the killing fields, were willing to intervene directly. They refused, and Clinton threw up his hands in frustration. Some observers depicted the response as another sign of Clinton's weakness and indecisiveness on the foreign-policy front.

Americans did not need to look any further than Somalia to see the dangers of foreign intervention when humanitarian considerations, rather than vital U.S. interests, were the primary concern. The Somalia difficulty was not of Clinton's making. Back in December 1992, just after his election defeat, the lame duck Bush had sent a force of U.S. marines into the East African nation to prevent mass starvation due to severe drought and political chaos. The mission—Operation Restore Hope—was purely humanitarian, Bush said, and American troops would be back home in two or three months.

The troops restored order and ended the famine. Announcing that the mission had been accomplished, Bush ordered withdrawal of most American armed personnel. In May 1993 the UN took over the job of protecting the relief workers and medical personnel who remained in the country. Some 5,000 Americans were assigned to the UN forces.

After Clinton took office, the picture in Somalia changed. During the summer warlord Mohammed Farah Aidid, initially cowed, attacked and killed fifty Pakistani UN peacekeepers. The UN forces, including Americans, soon gave chase to capture him and destroy his power. In September Aidid's forces ambushed a group of Americans soldiers under UN command, killed fifteen, and dragged their bodies with glee through the streets. The American public, having enthusiastically supported Operation Restore Hope, now screamed with pain. American troops must be brought home immediately! In Congress, Republicans, though hawkish under their own president, now sounded like isolationists. Clinton was risking American lives unnecessarily, they announced, and for a time Congress threatened to limit his power to send troops into danger zones or place Americans under UN command.

To many observers, the Somali affair seemed a cautionary tale that must be heeded in the future: The United States could not be the world's emergency rescue squad. Speaking before the United Nations in New York in September 1993 Clinton finally acknowledged the reality by calling for well-defined missions for the world organization and distinct plans for pull-outs when these were accomplished. Unfortunately, we now know, the American retreat in Somalia encouraged terrorists into believing the United States was too cowardly to defend itself.

Domestic Accomplishments.

By the summer of 1993 the administration finally seemed to be moving on the domestic front. On February 17 the president asked Congress for increased long-term government outlays on education, job training, and research in line with Labor Secretary Robert Reich's views that the United States needed a skilled and educated labor force to compete in the globalized economy. He also asked for investment in the nation's dilapidated transportation system and in a high-speed national computer network to make it a leader in "the information age." On this occasion Clinton broached the important issue of national health care. The public liked the speech and the outlines of the health plan. But the succession of White House missteps, including the mysterious mass

Hillary Clinton, the First Lady, and Bill Clinton in a happy moment.
Not all moments of his presidency were this sunny.

firing of the White House travel office, continued to undermine the public's confidence in the administration.

By this time Clinton could count on some solid victories. In early February the president signed into law a Family Leave Bill allowing employees several months of unpaid leave from their jobs to care for young children or sick relatives. Soon after, he approved the "Motor Voter" bill easing the complicated voter registration process in federal elections by automatically registering voters at the time they applied for state auto licenses. Congress passed the president's National Service Plan for Youth, a scheme to help pay education costs for thousands of young Americans who signed up to serve the elderly, the poor, the homeless, and other disadvantaged groups as part of a domestic Peace Corps.

More significant was passage of the North American Free Trade Agreement (NAFTA), a major addition to the economic globalization process now underway.

By lowering trade barriers, this pact merged Canada, the United States, and Mexico into a single market of over 350 million consumers and producers. Many Americans feared that it would accelerate the departure of factories and jobs south of the border, and several of the major U.S. industrial unions opposed it bitterly. The treaty had been negotiated by the Bush administration, and at first Clinton seemed reluctant to support it, especially because so many Democrats were beholden to trade union political support. But by the fall of 1993, he had concluded that he must stand up for freer international trade generally if the United States was to compete in the global economy. In November, after a major administration show of political muscle, the treaty won by a narrow vote. Though the victory margin included more Republican than Democratic yeas, many informed observers gave Clinton an "A" for presidential leadership.

National Health Insurance.   Clinton's most ambitious domestic initiative during his first year was his health insurance scheme. Drawn up by a Health Task Force headed by First Lady Hillary Clinton, it was submitted to Congress in late September 1993.

By this time the country's health delivery system seemed in crisis. Health costs as a proportion of total domestic national product were already close to 15 percent, about $1 trillion annually, and climbing steadily higher. America's outlays on health care were larger proportionately than any other country's. Whole sectors of the economy would inevitably contract if health care costs expanded much further. Already many American business firms were complaining bitterly that a large part of the price of their product represented health care outlays for their workers and retirees.

But even at these bloated levels the system did not do a consistently good job. Many Americans were indeed adequately insured against illness. The millions with private health insurance or on Medicare generally received competent medical attention. But there were an estimated 37 million Americans who had no coverage at all. Such people, usually the working poor, did without medical services entirely or were thrown on the dubious resources of public charity hospitals or of private hospital emergency rooms. The public paid for these services indirectly, either through higher community taxes or through medical charges passed along to insured patients. But even the insured often could not count on health coverage to protect them adequately. Many health plans excluded preexisting conditions or serious chronic disease. People often forfeited their coverage when they lost or left their jobs. Retirees on Medicare had to pay for their medicines, often a major cost for people living on pensions.

The Health Task Force under the First Lady held hearings around the country seeking advice from experts. Fearing that leaks would enable the lobbyists and the skeptics to pick apart any plan before it could be submitted, the task force kept its meetings and its deliberations private, a procedure that aroused criticism. When the 246-page health plan was finally submitted to Congress in late September 1993, it set off one of the most intense policy debates, in Congress and out, since the 1960s.

The plan rejected "single-payer" national health insurance administered by the government and paid for largely by taxes, an approach widely used in Europe. Instead, the Clinton plan proposed "managed competition" by which regional health alliances would represent consumers in striking bargains with drug companies, doctors, and hospitals for the lowest costs. All citizens would be covered whether they worked for large corporations, which normally paid employees' health insurance, or for small firms, which often did not. People would not be denied health insurance for preexisting conditions or dumped from the insurance rolls because they lost their jobs. Employers and patients would pay much of the cost. The self-employed would pay their costs themselves, but could deduct these outlays from their income tax. The remaining funding would come from a tax on cigarettes and perhaps hard liquor, two items that contributed to poor health in the first place.

Most Americans initially favored the president's proposals. His televised presentation to Congress was agile and convincing. But as the measure worked its way through the legislative process the public began to have doubts. In Congress conservatives attacked it as likely to expand the already excessive federal bureaucracy. Some liberals continued to prefer the single-payer scheme. Outside Congress every group with a stake in the nation's health care system weighed in. The insurance companies, certain that they would be deprived of profits, mounted major TV advertising campaigns to convince the public that the bill was unworkable. Small business attacked it as a crippling burden that they could not afford. Physicians' groups also took potshots at the administration measure as likely to limit their professional freedom. As the bill wended its way through Congress it was eroded by successive concessions of the White House and the Democratic leadership.

And in the end the bill did not pass. In late September 1994 Senate Majority Leader George Mitchell of Maine declared the health care reform drive dead for the 103rd Congress. He and other administration supporters vowed to take the measure up again the following year but, with Republican gains in the forthcoming elections likely, few believed it possible to achieve major revision of the nation's health care system in the foreseeable future.

Scandals.   By mid-point in his first term the Clinton record was, in fact, a mixed bag. Yet the public had the decided impression that the president was not a strong leader. Some of the same people who were attacking him for weak leadership were also decrying his character. Undoubtedly Clinton was less than a saint. Even after he became president various young women showed up at press conferences and on talk shows to accuse him of sexual indiscretions while he was governor of Arkansas.

One of these was Paula Jones, an Arkansas state employee who claimed that, while governor, Clinton had summoned her to a hotel room and then asked her for sex. She asserted, she has uffered severe psychological trauma. In May 1994, just before the statute of limitations went into effect, Jones filed a lawsuit for sexual harassment against the president. Clinton's attorneys sought to have the suit delayed until after the president left office on the grounds that it would interfere with the vital business of the country's Chief Executive, but in mid-1997 the Supreme Court decided that even the president was not exempt from civil legal action.

More serious, it seemed, were charges that the Clintons had used their powerful position in Arkansas during his governorship to advance their own financial interests. The chief claim was that they had concocted a complicated real estate deal to develop a tract of land for housing and recreation in the Ozarks. Critics claimed that the "Whitewater" development involved illegal relations with business groups, including savings and loan promoters. The Clintons said that there had been nothing illegal about the venture; and they had actually lost money on the deal.

Attorney General Janet Reno, under pressure from the Republicans, finally appointed a special prosecutor to look into Whitewater. He was replaced during the summer of 1994 by Kenneth Starr, a conservative lawyer less friendly to the Clintons than his predecessor. In July Congress began hearings on the role of the Treasury Department and the White House in trying to fend off investigators. If the president and his wife had been more forthcoming, observers said, they might have been believed. Instead, they seemed determined to cover up the details of the scheme and did everything they could to avoid an investigation.

The 1994 Midterm Elections.

By the midterm congressional elections many voters were disappointed with the president's leadership. The Republicans for their part conducted a vigorous campaign based on a conservative manifesto, "The Contract for America," that pilloried liberalism and promised an "end of government that is too big, too intrusive, and too easy with the public's money." The election produced a major shift rightward in Congress. Twenty-three incumbent House Democrats, including the scandal-ridden Speaker, Tom Foley, were defeated and the Republicans gained some 50 House seats in all, giving them control of the lower house. Many of the new Republican freshmen were conservative firebrands determined to rigorously apply their small-government, balanced-budget, anti-welfare and anti-entitlement principles. The new House Speaker would be Representative Newt Gingrich of Georgia.

A highly partisan Republican, who in previous Congresses had savaged the Democrats, Gingrich pledged to enact the Contract for America. In short order the Republicans introduced a balanced-budget constitutional amendment, a tougher crime bill, a major welfare reform bill, a measure to boost savings, a proposal to discourage product liability law suits, a law to set term limits for members of Congress, and a capital gains tax cut to encourage business growth. Unfortunately for the conservative agenda, Gingrich proved to be no match for the president in political maneuver. He lacked the capacity to please and his image as a harsh ideologue was further blackened by charges that he had used tax-deductible donations to fund an American history course he taught at a small Georgia college. Not long after this he was also charged with accepting a $4 million advance from a large publisher for writing two books while in office, an act that seemed a blatant attempt to capitalize on the power and prestige of his office. (Gingrich canceled the book contract, but in December 1996 the House Ethics Committee would censure him for the misuse of campaign funds, and in 1997 fine him $300,000 for breaking the House's ethics rules.)

Meanwhile, Clinton moved adroitly toward what he perceived as the vital center. During 1995 and 1996 the president and the Republican Congress jockeyed over the conservative agenda. Clinton proved remarkably flexible—some liberals called it spinelessness. He accepted with only minor demurrers the Republican plan to overturn the sixty-year-old federal welfare system instituted during New Deal days. The welfare bill he signed in July 1996 replaced federal cash payments to the poor with block grants to the states to administer welfare programs of their own individual devising. Recipients of food stamps and other aid would have to work and any aid given would be subject to time limits. The bill also ended welfare payments to all immigrants, even legal ones.*

The president got the better of the Republicans on the budget. Clinton accepted the need to achieve a balanced federal budget in the not-too-distant future. But he disagreed with his opponents on how soon the goal should be reached, what programs should be cut to achieve it, and whether any new budget should include tax cuts, especially those like lower estate and capital gains taxes that primarily benefited the prosperous. Twice during the 1995 session of Congress, the White House and Capitol Hill reached an impasse on the federal budget. To pressure the president the Republican-led Congress refused to enact stopgap spending bills and various offices of the federal government simply closed their doors, causing inconvenience for millions. The Republicans had miscalculated. The public blamed Gingrich and his party in Congress and supported Clinton's refusal to yield. By the summer of 1996 Clinton's dismal approval ratings had recovered. By contrast the polls showed that many moderate Americans had lost patience with the Speaker and the conservative partisans elected to Congress in 1994.

Race, Gender, and Nationality

As the millennium's end approached, major population changes, long underway, began to alter the texture of American life. The new demographics were reflected in Clinton appointment policy, noted above; they played out even more significantly on the nation's cultural and intellectual stages.

Demographic Change.   The social profile of the American people altered rapidly in the 1980s and 1990s. During these decades birth rates fell, health improved, men and women lived longer. As the net effect of these trends, between 1980 and 1997 the median age of the American people rose from 30 years to 34.9, the highest it had ever been, and promised to go still higher in the years ahead as the baby boomers of the post-1945 era moved past middle age.

The rise in average age was certain to affect American life in profound ways. An aging population was unavoidably a more ailing population. Much of the soaring costs of medicine were incurred at the end of life, as doctors employed heroic methods to delay death by a few weeks or months. In the years ahead, demographers predicted, the flood of people in their eighties and nineties would put intense new pressure on the already overloaded health care system.

The problem encouraged new approaches to the last years of life. The "living will" movement sought to guarantee the legal right for victims to reject life support systems when all hope for recovery from serious illness had passed. The euthanasia movement sought to allow people with terminal illnesses to choose suicide—to "die with dignity"—rather than linger hopelessly comatose or in pain. Living wills offended relatively few; legal suicide made many Americans uncomfortable. The activities of Dr. Jack Kervorkian, the "Suicide Doctor," to assist seriously ill patients to end their lives, scandalized many and led the Michigan legislature and others in 1993 to make assisted suicide a crime.

---

*Later revised to preserve payments to legal immigrants.

An aging population raised non-medical problems as well. As the ratio of re-tired people to workers rose, the need to support the retired promised to become a drag on the incomes of the economically most productive. Younger workers feared that the Social Security system would become bankrupt and would simply not be there for them when they were ready to retire. In 1983 a bipartisan revision of the Social Security Act had increased Social Security taxes and raised the age at which future pensioners would receive full benefits. But to some that measure seemed only a stopgap and down the road there promised to be further actuarial difficulties. The problem raised the specter of a generational battle between younger workers and retirees that few people welcomed.

And there was the matter of a geriatric society's psychology. How would the country deal with a population with an increasingly foreshortened horizon? "Seniors" could not be faulted for special concern about their own immediate cir-cumstances and the here-and-now. But that was not necessarily the best thing for the country as a whole. An aging population was surely a less innovative and less socially conscious population. Would America, as it grayed, become less creative and less compassionate?

The most significant new demographic trends were changes in the nation's ethnic and racial makeup. Overall, United States birth rates had been dropping for some time. Unlike the citizens of several other advanced industrial countries, Americans still had enough babies each year to offset aggregate mortality. But these birth rates were not equal across the ethnic and racial board. Whites had birth rates of 64.7 per thousand women in 1989; blacks had birth rates of 90.4. His-panic groups, too, especially Mexican-Americans and Puerto Ricans, had higher birth rates than people of European antecedents. By themselves these differentials meant that the population of both blacks and Hispanics would inevitably increase faster than "Anglo" whites.

Immigration.   But there was immigration to consider as well. The growing numbers of European-Americans and African-Americans derived mostly from natural increase. Much of the Hispanic—as well as the Asian—growth came from immigration, rather than domestic births. America remained a magnet for millions around the world, and during the 1980s immigration was responsible for a third of the country's net population increase.

As we saw, as early as the 1970s, the major sources of immigration had switched from Europe to Latin America and Asia. By 1990 three times as many Asians as Europeans came to America each year, and eight times as many people from Latin America, primarily Mexico, the Caribbean, and Central America. These figures, however, described only legal immigration. Many experts held that the illegal immigration from the newer sources was at least as great. Already the dif-ferential birth rates of blacks, European whites, Asians, and Hispanics were chang-ing the overall profile of Americans. By the 1990 census almost 25 million Americans were Hispanic, and they were the fastest growing group, with increases during the 1980s of a startling 6.1 percent annually. The continuing wave of immi-grants was certain to shift the racial and ethnic balance still further as time passed. In 1993 a Census Bureau report predicted that the Hispanic population of the Unit-ed States would exceed the black population by the year 2010. It also projected a total population of 392 million in 2050, of which only 53 percent would be "Non-Hispanic White," while 16 percent would be black and 22.5 percent Hispanic. At that date Asians-Chinese, Koreans, Indians, Arabs, Indians, Pakistanis—totaling about 3 percent in 1990—would make up 10 percent of the total population.

The magnitude of non-European immigration was in part the result of relaxed American immigration practices. The Immigration Reform and Control Act of 1986, modifying the expansive 1965 immigration law, sought to reduce "illegals" by threatening to punish any employer who offered work to someone without the precious "green card" attesting to lawful residence. The law was not effectively enforced, however, and did little to deter illegal entry. Virtually anyone who set foot on American soil could claim asylum from religious or political persecution and stay in the United States if the claim seemed minimally valid. Many came on student visas and never registered for college classes. The Immigration and Naturalization Service investigation of claims was slow, and the immigrant was allowed to move into the community at large while waiting. Few if any ever returned to learn what the INS had determined. Students who used their visas as de facto immigration passes were seldom investigated.

Still another leak in the system allowed illegal immigrants to stay if they had children born in the United States. Under the federal Constitution these children were American citizens and there was no humane way to deport their parents. Many immigrant couples, critics said, came to the United States and conceived children before the authorities could expel them. They then remained, courtesy of their American-born offspring. In 1990, reflecting the white public's ethnic and economic anxieties, Congress passed a new measure to encourage immigration of Europeans and trained, educated workers.

Despite what Americans considered low wages, long hours, and the absence of benefits, immigrants sought to reach and stay in the United States in every way possible. In some cases Chinese immigrants offered as much as $30,000 to unscrupulous entrepreneurs to smuggle them in and were then, often, kept in near-slavery, toiling at menial jobs or even working as prostitutes, until they repaid their debt. This deplorable traffic was highlighted in June 1993 when a small freighter, the *Golden Venture,* carrying 300 ill-fed, sick Chinese aliens, grounded on a New York beach and the illegals and their exploiters were taken into custody.

The loose immigration policies of the United States were thrown into still more vivid relief by the events of early 1993 in lower Manhattan. Suddenly, on February 26, 1993, an explosion ripped through the lower floors of one of the twin towers of the World Trade Center, the second-tallest buildings in the nation. Six people died in the explosion in the underground parking garage and thousands had to be hurriedly evacuated by stairs to escape the suffocating smoke. (No one guessed that the event foreshadowed a far worse catastrophe in the same place eight and a half years later.)

In a matter of days combined federal and local police forces arrested the culprits, a group of Muslim immigrants from North Africa and the Middle East who worshiped at mosques in Brooklyn and New Jersey under the spiritual guidance of Sheik Omar Abdel-Rahman, a fundamentalist Egyptian cleric who despised the secular Arab government of his homeland and preached violence against the perceived enemies of Islam, including America. He had been carelessly allowed to enter the United States, even though his extreme views were well documented by the Egyptian authorities. In the next months the FBI uncovered plots among the Sheik's other adherents to blow up the UN, plant bombs in the major tunnels and bridges connecting New York and New Jersey, and assassinate American politicians and American Jewish leaders considered unfriendly to Islamic causes. Four of the defendants in the World Trade Center bombing were convicted in May 1994 and sentenced to long terms in prison. In the summer of 1993 the conspirators in the larger plot were indicted. Ten, including Sheik Rahman, were convicted in October 1995 and sentenced to long prison terms. In late 1997 Ramzi Ahmed Yousef, an admitted terrorist captured in Pakistan two years before, was convicted of masterminding the 1993 World Trade Center bombing.

Without doubt the feelings of native-born Americans toward the newest immigrants were, as in the past, tainted by prejudice. Arab-Americans, for example, clearly suffered from the anti-Muslim attitudes of some, intolerance reinforced by the World Trade Center bombing and the activities of Sheik Rahman; crude racism obviously played a part in biases against people from Asia and Latin America. But the swelling immigration tide raised reasoned concerns as well. What was the net economic impact, for example, of the flood of immigrants? Did the newcomers take more from the economy in the way of free public education, medical services, and "welfare" than they contributed in taxes and needed skills? Did they displace poor, but striving, native-born Americans from necessary entry-level jobs? Did they depress the wages of unskilled native-born Americans? The answers were not clear, but the governor of California, a state hard-hit by defense cutbacks and soaring unemployment rates in the early 1990s, concluded that they did. The United States must tighten its immigration laws, declared Governor Pete Wilson, even if this meant repealing the existing citizenship provision of the Fourteenth Amendment.

Nor was Governor Wilson the only one concerned about the costs of uncontrolled immigration. Many black leaders complained that foreigners were undermining the wages of, and stealing jobs from, black American citizens. Some American-born Hispanic citizens also thought that the deluge from Latin America and the Caribbean hurt them economically. Middle-class white Americans seldom competed directly with foreign-born workers from Latin America, but Asians were another case. Many, it seemed, and especially their American-born children, were nosing out white Americans for top professional jobs and elite college admissions. At the prestigious University of California at Berkeley, Asians in turn complained that university officials had put a lid on their admission in order to guarantee blacks, Hispanics, and whites a prescribed proportion of new freshman admissions. When criticized by Asian spokespersons, the Berkeley administration noted that the university "must provide effective leadership in an increasingly multiethnic society. . . ." In effect, "diversity" took precedence over "merit."

The Struggle over Culture.
Would the changing profile of the American population produce shifts in American values and culture? If so, what would these be? And would they substantially alter the quality of American life?

Some effects were already apparent. At colleges and universities around the country non-white students and faculty, often led by blacks, were demanding curriculum changes to refocus courses on the achievements, values, and histories of non-European peoples. Ever since the 1960s, colleges had offered black history, Asian culture, Latin American studies, and the like. But the Western tradition continued to be the core of the cultural and intellectual curriculum. The new "multicultural" mood on campuses, especially the more cosmopolitan ones, sought to replace this emphasis. At Stanford, for example, the administration dropped the long-term required course "Western Culture" in 1988 in favor of a three-course sequence "Cultures, Ideas, Values," that pared down the European component of the core. Defending the decision, President Donald Kennedy of Stanford announced: "We confirm that many minority issues and concerns are not the special pleadings of interest groups, but are Stanford issues—ones that engage all of us."

Curriculum revisions like Stanford's assumed a common core for all Americans to share, though a different one from the past. Some multiculturalists, however, rejected the idea of a shared tradition entirely. Americans had no truly common experience, they seemed to say, and each component of the country's population needed to understand and appreciate only its own cultural heritage.

The new cultural offensive on campus was directed not only against Euro-centered education. There was a parallel feminist drive to change the campus intellectual and cultural environment. If the conventional curriculum gave excessive attention to Europe and its traditions, feminists declared, it was also dominated by male views of the world.

Feminist scholarship and thought had been evolving ever since the late 1960s toward a view of culture, history, science, and politics that broke with mainstream approaches in several of the disciplines. Some feminist scientists, for example, claimed that "male" science ignored the intuitive nature of much knowledge; feminist literary critics denounced the exclusion of talented women and their insights from the standard literary "canon"; feminist historians noted that half the world's population had been ignored by the male-led discipline. Feminist social scientists and psychologists also sought to change basic perspectives on the nature of men and women. They distinguished "sex," a biological category, from "gender," a socially and historically "constructed" entity. The observable differences between the way men and women thought and behaved, they said, derived primarily from the cultural environment of a particular time and place, not from body parts and hormones.

The new perspectives of race, ethnicity, and gender were strongest in the academic world, where they were particularly influential in the humanities and social science disciplines. There, they appealed not just to black and female faculty and students but also to younger men and women who had been influenced by the ideological shifts of the late 1960s and 1970s. In the field of American history, a woman's perspective, an ecological perspective, and a Native American perspective were added to the previously adopted black perspective, to alter the traditional emphases.

One effect of these new currents was to polarize student bodies. Observers of campus life noted that, increasingly, black and white students ate separately, partied separately, and studied separately. On some campuses, black students demanded their own residences and student centers, and university administrations often obliged. Defenders of the self-segregation tendency claimed that it was necessary to protect black students, many from poor inner-city backgrounds, against a hostile, predominantly white university environment. Critics said that it created resentment and encouraged the ghettos it was designed to prevent.

There were also growing tensions on campus between men and women as feminists redefined rape and sexual harassment to include long-tolerated male practices and behavior. Some observers felt that the new concern was long overdue. For far too long men had imposed their wills on women in the guise of "boys will be boys." Now men must be made to accept "no" for an answer. Traditionalists often questioned the new attitudes. The evils were exaggerated, they said. Some of the practices proscribed were inevitable parts of the "mating game" and not offenses at all. The university's attempts to protect women, some critics insisted, treated them as children. More than a few men professed to be thoroughly confused about what they could or could not do.

It is hard to say what was cause and what effect, but the new multiculturalism, feminist sensibility, and "political correctness" made some campuses acrimonious places during the early 1990s. At Dartmouth, where an off-campus, student-run, conservative paper frequently attacked "politically correct" views of the college's faculty and students, there were frequent clashes over the whole range of cultural issues. At the University of Pennsylvania nine black students, offended by a *Daily Pennsylvanian* editorial attacking affirmative action, destroyed 14,000 copies of the student newspaper. Modern campuses, one Ivy League professor remarked, had "the cultural diversity of Beirut. There are separate armed camps. The black kids don't mix with the white kids. The Asians are off by themselves. Oppression is the great status symbol."

The new cultural and ideological styles and tensions went beyond the universities. A gay sensibility began to alter the tone and content of the performance and visual arts. One manifestation was a flock of moving plays about the devastation wrought by AIDS on the homosexual community. There was also a growing irreverence toward mainstream "square" values and culture informed by a gay perspective. At times the influence was subtle and nuanced. At other times, however, it challenged "square" moral and aesthetic values by flaunting extreme aspects of the gay sensibility. The photographs of Robert Mapplethorpe, for example, showed men engaged in undisguised sadomasochistic homosexual acts. Even more extreme was an occasional "in your face" confrontational quality apparently designed to offend and provoke. One of the works of Andres Serrano, called "Piss Christ," was a photograph of a crucifix immersed in Serrano's own urine.

Race Relations.   Academe and the intellectual and artistic worlds are rather remote from the lives of most Americans. But the widening national divisions both affected and reflected the way many Americans regarded their fellow citizens.

Race relations during the late 1980s and 1990s in many ways became more tense. Following the successes of the civil rights movement, racial reconciliation and mutual acceptance seemed to spread widely across groups, sections, and classes. But the process soon reversed. Economic stagnation and even retreat in the inner cities created a degree of hopelessness and frustration that fed black racial resentments. In some ghetto communities these feelings were directed not just at whites but also at Asian storekeepers, who were accused of treating black customers with suspicion and discourtesy. In New York, Los Angeles, and other cities Korean grocers and black customers engaged in feuds that led to boycotts and picketing.

The late 1980s and 1990s also witnessed an eruption of white racism that frightened many moderate Americans. White supremacist and anti-Semitic groups—"skinheads" and neo-Nazis—proliferated in the Northwest, Mountain States, and the South. In 1991 David Duke, former Grand Wizard of the Louisiana Ku Klux Klan, placed second in the state gubernatorial primary and, in the general election, came frighteningly close to defeating the Democratic candidate.

Serious violence would mar the nation's record of racial tolerance through the period. In 1986, in New York's Howard Beach, a group of white youths attacked some young black men whose presence in their neighborhood they resented, leading to the death of one. The black community demanded and got a special prosecutor to push the case. Violence was narrowly averted when the jury convicted three of the youths of second-degree murder. In another New York neighborhood, where a close-knit community of orthodox Hassidic Jews lived close by a black community, the death of a young black boy in an automobile accident led to several days of racial violence aimed at Jewish residents of Crown Heights, in Brooklyn. In Miami, the shooting of two black motorcyclists in 1989 by a Hispanic policeman set off three days of riots in the black Overtown and Liberty City districts. Six people were shot, 27 stores burned, and 400 people arrested.

It was Los Angeles, however, where the most serious racial explosion of all took place. The city had never solved the problems that triggered the Watts riots of 1965. In the South-Central district poverty remained as ingrained as ever; crack-cocaine had brought wholesale gang violence and murder; family disintegration and out-of-wedlock births had become the norm for thousands of residents. Relations between the black community and the Los Angeles police, never very good, had worsened under police chief Daryl Gates, a man who seemed to have little respect for the city's minority population.

The trigger for massive community violence was the arrest of black motorist Rodney King in early March 1991 after a high-speed freeway chase. The cops kicked and beat King mercilessly for fifteen minutes. The brutal attack on a single unarmed civilian was recorded by a citizen on his video recorder. Played over and over on the local and national airwaves, the tape outraged millions of Americans of all races. The authorities indicted four Los Angeles Police Department members for using excessive force.

The trial, in April 1992, was not held in Los Angeles where the jury was apt to be multiracial but in predominantly white and conservative Simi Valley. On April 29, to the amazement of many Americans, the jury of ten whites, one Asian, and one Hispanic acquitted three of the officers completely and convicted one on a minor charge.

South-Central Los Angeles erupted within minutes in a fountain of rage and violence. White truckers and motorists passing through the community were pulled from their vehicles and beaten and stomped. Hundreds of stores, offices, and shops were torched and looted, with Korean-owned businesses particular targets, though even black establishments were not spared. Latinos and others joined the riots, which threatened to spill over into affluent white neighborhoods. The violence spread to several other cities including San Francisco, Atlanta, Seattle, Miami, and Las Vegas. As they watched the TV images of smoke, flame, broken glass, looting, and tear gas, many Americans feared a reprise of the sixties' "long

The explosion of violence in South Central Los Angeles following the acquittal of
white police officers for a brutal attack on a black driver shocked the country.
The rioters beat whites and Hispanics and destroyed property—especially white-
or Korean-owned stores.

hot summers." After five days, physical and emotional exhaustion, the voices of
responsible community leaders, and National Guard and federal troops put a stop
to the disorders. A final tally listed 58 lives lost and a billion dollars of property
damage. More than 11,900 people were arrested, mostly for burglary and for
receiving stolen goods, a few for beating innocent bystanders.

In the wake of the catastrophe, the presidential candidates visited Los Angeles
and made promises of improved conditions. Los Angeles replaced Police Chief
Gates with a man more sensitive to the feelings of the inner city community. In
early 1993 the Justice Department indicted the acquitted police on federal charges
that they had violated Rodney King's civil rights. This time the trial was held in
Los Angeles before a less racially uniform jury, and this time the jury voted to convict two of the four officers.

O. J. Simpson and the Racial Divide.

But concern over the differing black and
white perception of justice was revived by the jury decision in the trial of O. J. Simpson for murder of his ex-wife, Nicole Brown and a companion, Ronald Goldman, in
June 1994. The case of *The People v. O. J. Simpson* riveted the attention of Americans,
and millions around the world, as no other criminal trial in recent history.

An imposing African-American, Simpson was a former football hero who had
enjoyed a spectacular career playing for the Buffalo Bills professional team. After
football, "OJ" had become a film actor and a celebrity endorser for the Hertz rental
car agency. In 1985 he had married a pretty blond "trophy wife" with whom he had

two children. But OJ and Nicole were not happy. Some eight times during the 1980s the Los Angeles police had been summoned to their home by Nicole to keep her husband from beating her. In 1992, the two were divorced and Nicole went to live with her children at an apartment not far from OJ's house.

In the late evening of June 12, 1994, a dog walker found the brutally slashed, bloody bodies of Nicole and Ronald Goldman, an employee of the restaurant where she had recently dined. The case against Simpson was "circumstantial"; no one had seen him commit the two murders. But it was powerful. There was also believable motivation: Simpson was a ferociously jealous man and a confessed wife beater.

However convincing by the usual measures, not all Americans accepted his guilt. The public divided along racial lines. White Americans as a group were certain that Simpson was a brutal murderer. But a large majority of African-Americans rejected this view. OJ was a hero of African-Americans and his plight an instance of a famous "brother" whom white America wanted to destroy as it had so many others before. In the wake of the Rodney King beating, it was easy for African Americans to doubt the evidence the Los Angeles police had gathered and to believe the L.A.P.D was determined to frame OJ for a crime he did not commit.

The televised trial played to high ratings for 11 months. The prosecution made many mistakes including failing to monitor the jury selection process carefully enough. In the end a majority of the jurors were black women, a group that, as a whole, were natural partisans of OJ. The defense, on the other hand, proved immensely skilled in shifting the focus of the trial from the defendant to the supposed misdeeds of the Los Angeles police, who were accused of an elaborate conspiracy to frame OJ for racist reasons. The so-called "dream-team," led by talented black criminal lawyer Johnny Cochrane, was able to nail detective Mark Fuhrman as a blatant bigot who probably planted a bloody glove simply to destroy the black hero.

The trial concluded on September 29, 1996, and after two hours of deliberation the jurors declared O. J. Simpson "not guilty." Black Americans from all walks of life cheered the verdict. Most white Americans were amazed and appalled. Given the makeup of the jury, many were certain that OJ's acquittal was proof that race, rather than innocence, had decided the outcome. The social pundits wondered whether this was a glimpse of a future when white and black perceptions of reality would have little in common.

The Attack on Affirmative Action.

One sore spot in black–white relations was affirmative action. As we saw, this effort to ensure more equal results in hiring, promotion, college and professional school admissions, and other areas, provoked resentment among some whites who felt it was "discrimination in reverse." Even some black Americans felt it placed a stigma on their achievements and created a permanent dependence among blacks. Beginning in the early 1990s, opponents of affirmative action launched a major drive to replace it with "color-blind" selection based on "merit" alone.

The issue came to a head in the nation's two largest states, California and Texas. In July 1995 the University of California's Board of Regents dropped affirmative action for admissions to university programs. In March 1996 a federal appeals court declared illegal University of Texas Law School admissions policies favoring black and Hispanic applicants over others. Later that year, California voters approved Proposition 209 forbidding the state government to establish race or gender preferences in educational admissions, public hiring, and public contracting. In August 1997, after an unsuccessful court challenge, it went into effect.

By this time the results of dropping affirmative action recruitment at the law schools of California and Texas had become known. Black enrollments plummeted at both institutions; the number of new Hispanic students also dropped drastically. The outcome was so disappointing that even opponents of affirmative action were dismayed. The two schools trained only a fraction of the nation's lawyers, but was this a portent of what would follow if racial policies changed? Virtually no one wanted to see a return to the days when professional schools had no black students, but it was not clear how the system could be "fixed" to produce results that most Americans would judge "fair."

Meanwhile, in a further blow against the preferential policies of the recent past, the Supreme Court in mid-1995 struck down federal rulings that mandated Congressional redistricting in the states to guarantee one or more predominantly black districts. By a 5-to-4 decision the Court ruled that race could not be used as a decisive factor in laying out the boundaries of Congressional districts. At virtually the same time, in *Adar and Constructors v. Pena*, it restricted the federal government's right to confer preferences in the awarding of contracts to minority businesses.

Balkanization.

In fact, there were many signs during the early 1990s that Americans were losing their sense of common identity and beginning to define themselves primarily as part of some smaller, more cohesive, quasi-tribal group. Some Americans felt that the federal mandate of bilingual education aided and abetted the process. However benign in its intentions, it discouraged foreign-born children from acquiring English and perpetuated group separateness. In Milwaukee, the school board sought to establish a publicly financed high school just for black males. The curriculum would emphasize the black experience and so, it was said, raise the self-esteem of the young black men, a group who often failed in the regular schools. Critics insisted it was divisive and should not be paid for out of public taxes.

The multicultural trend disturbed many Americans who prized what they perceived as the civic unity of the past. In 1992 Arthur Schlesinger, Jr., a distinguished liberal historian, published *The Disuniting of America,* deploring the divisive effects of the new sensibility. Schlesinger lauded the discovery of ethnic and racial "roots" by Americans and credited it with giving neglected groups their proper due. But he also praised, with qualification, the assimilationist ethic of the past. Noting the growing tribalism around the world and its often murderous effects, he warned that denial of common values and sense of the past might well propel the United States along the same dangerous, divisive path as Yugoslavia, the former Soviet Union, and language-torn Canada. Americans should be wary of replacing the focus on the individual, which had long been central to the country's tradition, with the concept of group identity so common elsewhere in the world. Yet other intellectuals praised the new trends. Ronald Takaki, an American historian of Japanese ancestry, in *A Different Mirror,* described how Americans "have been constantly redefining their identity" and lauded the retention of strong ties with ancestral cultural and intellectual roots. As if to overcome the assimilationist forces, Takaki, like other multiculturalists, emphasized the victimization through history of ethnic and nonwhite Americans by the old-stock, Anglo-Saxon elite.

Cults and Militias.

The new cultural divisions brought to the surface a pool of resentment and paranoia among some white Americans that resembled the reactions to social change by the Ku Klux Klan in the 1920s and by backlash voters in the 1960s. At its most extreme these feelings transmuted into the formation of "militias," paramilitary organizations dedicated to resisting the supposed seizure of the federal government by nonwhites, led in many cases they said, by Jews or some other "alien" group. The bible of the militia movement was a science fiction novel, *The Turner Diaries*, by William Pierce, a neo-Nazi. The book advocated guerrilla war against blacks, Jews, and the federal government in the name of personal freedom.

The militia groups demonized the federal government and its agents as tyrannical and inimical to the exercise of unfettered personal rights. The most sacred of these, it seemed, were the rights to bear arms in defiance of gun control laws and to abstain from paying taxes. Several militia groups denied all legitimacy to the government and claimed the right to establish their own sovereign states beholden to no other. They refused to obey local laws, denied the legality of commercial contracts, and threatened state, local, and federal officials.

At times federal law enforcement agencies were grossly heavy-handed in their response to those who defied federal weapons laws and denied the sovereignty of the United States government. In August 1992, the wife of Randall Weaver, a white supremacist and militia sympathizer who had refused to appear for trial on illegal weapons charges, was killed by an FBI sharpshooter during a standoff with federal agents at her family's cabin in Idaho. The FBI tried to cover up the details of the Ruby Ridge assault, but the facts that came out during Weaver's trial and at congressional hearings confirmed government mismanagement. Weaver was acquitted and the FBI official who was responsible for the siege was fired.

The consequences of government ineptitude were even more lamentable at Waco, Texas, where a religious sect calling itself the "Branch Davidians," led by a religious zealot, David Koresh, had established a community, Mt. Carmel, housed in a cluster of wooden structures. The Davidians believed Koresh was a prophet who could point the way of repentance to society and so hasten the return of Jesus. The Davidians helped pay their expenses by buying and selling guns and were rumored to have accumulated an arsenal of weapons in their compound. They were also said to be practitioners of dissolute sexual behavior and Koresh, it was believed, had created a virtual harem of young women who catered to his pleasures.

In February 1993 federal agents, trying to arrest Koresh on charges of illegal weapons and explosives possession, engaged in a shoot-out with the Branch Davidians in which four agents were killed. The FBI surrounded Mt. Carmel and tried to negotiate a peaceful surrender of the perpetrators. After 51 days the authorities lost patience and stormed the compound. Tear gas canisters lobbed into the buildings apparently ignited the wooden structures, burning to death 80 people, including women and children.

The government defended its actions. Attorney General Janet Reno said she had ordered the attack only when she heard that children were being abused by

Koresh. Though many Americans supported the government, others believed federal agents should not have launched the assault. To members of the militias the disaster at Waco was proof of the government's arbitrary, despotic behavior.

Their loathing for the federal government took murderous form in the bombing of the federal office building in Oklahoma City in April 1995. The instigator was Timothy McVeigh, a veteran of the Gulf War who sought revenge against the federal government for the Waco disaster by exploding an enormous truck bomb in front of the building. The most ghastly terrorist attack in American history until then, the blast killed 168 people, many of them children and visitors to the building rather than federal employees. Seized while fleeing the city, McVeigh. it turned out, was a fringe member of the militia movement and had long talked of avenging Waco. Tried in Denver in the spring of 1997, he was sentenced to death and executed in the summer of 2001.

Election 1996.

As the 1996 presidential election year approached Clinton's position had greatly improved. The budget impasse with the Republicans had worked in his favor. The Democrats also had good times on their side. By mid-1996 the economy had recovered from the slump of 1989–1990 and was booming. There was never any question that Clinton would be renominated. The Republicans turned to Senate Majority Leader Bob Dole, who chose as his running mate former Congressman and cabinet officer Jack Kemp.

The campaign was a walkover for the Democrats. Many Americans had doubts about "Slick Willy," as his enemies labeled the president. He could charm the birds out of the trees, but he seemed to some an unprincipled manipulator. Liberals were dismayed by his collaboration with the Congressional Republicans on welfare reform and a balanced budget, which seemed to repudiate the Democratic party's New Deal legacy. Moreover, the Whitewater scandal and Paula Jones's accusations of sexual harassment remained unresolved. Yet the public liked Clinton personally and, more important, the economy was making unprecedented gains. And there were also Dole's negatives. He was 73, the oldest man ever to run for president, and at times his age showed. The Republican candidate ran a lackluster campaign and was badly behind from the beginning.

Campaign finance was a worse scandal than ever. Both parties tapped foreign sources to pay their bills, but the Democrats did so on a more massive scale. Particularly disturbing was the money that flowed to them from the Chinese government, clearly intended to influence American policies. In July 1997 the Senate began a major investigation into the finances of the 1996 election that promised, but failed to deliver, some serious effort at campaign finance reform.

In the end Clinton won by a vote of 45.6 million popular votes (379 electoral) to Dole's 37.9 million (159 electoral). Perot, who ran again in a lackluster campaign, got almost 8 million popular votes. The Republicans retained control of both houses of Congress by about the same margins as in 1994.

Second Term.

After his second inauguration Clinton continued to face challenges in foreign policy. In the Middle East, Saddam Hussein, chaffing under the UN cease-fire terms imposed by the victors at the Gulf War's end, seemed determined to foil UN inspectors monitoring his programs to develop nuclear, chemical, and biological weapons—"weapons of mass destruction." Saddam refused to let the inspectors visit suspicious sites and singled out the Americans on the inspection teams as unacceptable observers. In the end, he succeeded in ousting the UN inspectors as a preliminary step, it was generally assumed, to resuming his build-up of weapons, including so-called "weapons of mass destruction."

The former Yugoslavia also remained a trouble spot. In November 1995 Clinton had brokered an agreement among the contending parties to solve the Bosnian problem that included the dispatch of NATO troops, Americans among them, to serve as peacekeepers in the tumultuous former Yugoslav province. In deference to the American public's reluctance to become entangled in Balkan problems, Clinton had promised to remove the Americans in a year. The continuing tensions in the region forced him to renege; American troops stayed on. Meanwhile, a new danger appeared in the Serbian province of Kosovo. There, ethnic Albanians, a majority, were demanding autonomy from the oppressive Serbs and a new round of violence broke out with the Serbs determined to rid the province of Kosovan Muslims through another brutal campaign of ethnic cleansing. European and American opinion bridled at the slaughter, which reminded them of Hitler's "Final Solution" for the Jews. In March 1999, Clinton induced NATO to launch a bombing campaign against Serbia to force it to desist. Seventy-eight days later, with Serbia in ruins, Premier Slobodan Milosevic surrendered. In the arrangement that followed, the Serbs agreed to withdraw their troops, allow the return of refugees, and accept an independent interim government for Kosovo.

On the domestic front, during Clinton's second term, legislative war continued between the president and the Republican leadership in Congress. With the economy booming, the Treasury faced, for the first time in many decades, a budget surplus. The president proposed that the surplus be used to strengthen Social Security so that future retirees would not be shortchanged. The Republicans in Congress preferred that the public benefit in the short run by a tax cut. The issue remained unresolved during the remainder of Clinton's presidency.

Monica Lewinsky.

By this time Bill Clinton's womanizing tendencies had come to threaten his presidency. His behavior was certainly immoral and reckless. Most Americans considered it deplorable that the president of the United States would violate his marriage vows in the White House with a love-smitten woman half his age. As the scandal intensified, evidence turned up that as president Clinton may have made sexual overtures to other women as well. To make his behavior still more lamentable, Clinton could not bring himself to confess his errors. Instead, over the course of the scandal, he evaded the truth and took refuge in semantic nitpicking that even dismayed many of his supporters.

The squalid story began in November 1995 when the president initiated a sexual liaison with Monica Lewinsky, a young White House aide. In April 1996 a protective White House official had her removed from her job. She did not leave government, however. Instead, the presidential staff found a place for her in the Pentagon. Clinton terminated the relationship completely in late March 1997 when even he judged it too risky to continue. Unreconciled, Lewinsky sought without success to return to the White House from the Pentagon and the president, seeking to appease her, asked his friend Vernon Jordan, an influential lawyer, to find her a job in

New York. Jordan failed, but his efforts seemed to be a thinly disguised attempt to keep Lewinsky from blabbing to the media about her affair with the president.

In any event, the move did not work. Lewinsky told her story to Linda Tripp, a new friend at the Pentagon. A former White House aide herself, Tripp despised the entire Clinton circle and encouraged Monica to confide in her while she secretly taped her words. By now the writing of articles and books about the Clintons' supposedly unethical doings had became a profitable minor industry and Tripp, apparently, saw no reason why she should not cash in by publishing Monica's juicy story.

When he learned of the Lewinsky affair, special prosecutor Kenneth Starr, hired to investigate Whitewater, leaped at the chance to nail the president on a new count. In January 1998, members of Starr's staff waylaid Lewinsky and hustled her off to a room at the Ritz-Carlton hotel in Washington where they pressured her to testify about what she knew of Clinton's sexual peccadillos. Only when promised immunity from prosecution did she agree to tell her story. On July 19 she turned over to Starr a semen-stained dress from one of her meetings with the president. Now the special prosecutor had a sample of Clinton's DNA to refute him if he should deny his liaison with the former White House aide.

Meanwhile, Clinton had been deposed by the attorneys for Paula Jones, the woman who was suing him for sexual harassment during his governorship. Her lawyers asked him about his contacts with Jones, Gennifer Flowers, White House volunteer Kathleen Willey, and Monica Lewinsky. Clinton denied the charges categorically. At one point he declared: "I have never had sexual relations with Monica Lewinsky,"

Americans were both shocked and dismayed when they learned about the Lewinsky affair. Clinton bashers saw it as confirmation that he was a debauched and unprincipled man. Religious conservatives judged his behavior proof of every charge ever made against the moral laxity of the 1960s, the decade when Clinton had reached manhood. Loyalists, however, defended the president. Appearing on the "Today" show, First Lady Hillary Clinton repeated the president's denial of the Lewinsky affair and called the Kenneth Starr investigation part of a "vast right-wing conspiracy" against her husband that had begun "the day he announced for president." The First Lady's charge ignored Clinton's actual wrong-doing. It also suggested a degree of close coordination among Clinton's enemies that did not exist. Yet it was not an incorrect description of the unusual array of ferociously partisan and dogged forces, predominantly regional, determined to demolish Clinton politically. Clinton's defenders would claim that his enemies, unable to accept his popularity, were in fact seeking to nullify the elections of 1992 and 1996 through litigation. It seemed to many another sign of the deep divisions within the country.

Impeachment.   During the months that followed, the Lewinsky scandal and its meaning for Clinton's presidency dominated the nation's domestic news. The independent counsel's office considered the Lewinsky affair a godsend. After expending three years of labor and $30 million of public money on Whitewater and ancillary issues, Starr and his colleagues had come up with very little they could use to legally impugn the president. Now they thought they had finally caught Clinton in an attempt to obstruct justice, an indictable offense.

On August 17, 1998, the president was forced to testify to the grand jury in the Lewinsky affair. Never before had a sitting president been called before such a body. He now admitted he had "engaged in conduct that was wrong." On the other hand, he stated, neither he nor Vernon Jordan had sought to keep Monica Lewinsky from telling the truth. Shortly after his testimony he confessed on TV that his relations with Lewinsky had been "inappropriate" and that he had misled his wife. But he attacked the independent counsel and noted that it was "time to stop the pursuit of personal destruction and prying into private lives and get on with our national life." A portion of the press treated his failure to provide a full apology to the American people as a serious moral lapse. The public did not share the journalists' outrage, however. By this time there was a distinct gap between the views of the press and the general public. To the chagrin of Clinton's opponents, the polls continued to show the president with a high public approval rating.

But neither Starr nor partisan Republicans were willing to desist. The Republican leadership was determined to remove Clinton from office and on December 19, 1998 the House voted to impeach on the count of perjury before the grand jury, by a vote of 228 to 206. The ballot was highly partisan: only five Democrats voted for the motion; only five Republicans opposed it.

The trial of the president before the Senate for "High Crimes and Misdemeanors," the first such event since 1868, began on January 7, 1999. Clinton's attorneys denied that he had obstructed justice. The president's misdeeds were entirely of a personal nature and impeachment represented "a total lack of balance" in dealing with them. The results were a foregone conclusion since a two-thirds majority was required to convict. But in the end even some Republican senators defected. The final vote on the crucial first count of lying to the grand jury was 45 guilty, 55 not guilty. Five moderate Republicans had voted with the president. As in 1868, conviction had failed, but this time by a much wider margin.

The New Economy

The Lewinsky scandal played out against a background of unprecedented prosperity for America and the world. In less than a year, helped by loans from the International Monetary Fund, the economies of Asia, which had recently fallen into a slump, began to rebound. Meanwhile, at home, the economy soared. Between 1993 and 1998 Gross Domestic Product leaped from $6.6 trillion to $8.5 trillion.* Real growth rates in the last years of the 1990s averaged well over 3.5 percent annually, a high figure by historical terms. The revival that began in 1993 continued through Clinton's second term, and by 2000 the economic expansion had lasted longer than any in the past, even exceeding the surge of the 1960s. One feature of the boom was the apparently remarkable rebound of American productivity. As the nineties progressed the output per capita of American workers, so long stagnant, finally forged ahead, helping to reduce inflationary pressures. The expanding economy fostered rapid job growth. Between 1993 and 1997 it generated 13.5 million new jobs. By the

---

*In standard 1992 dollars, which discount for inflation, the increase was from $6.4 trillion to $7.6 trillion, a smaller figure but impressive nonetheless.

last quarter of 1998 the unemployment rate touched 4.4 percent, the lowest since the 1960s and the lowest for any contemporary large industrial country in the world. By early 2000 it was below 4 percent. The surge was a boon to many, even those who, in the past, seemed to belong to the "hard core" unemployed group. Though new federal legislation slashing welfare eligibility clearly played a role, the buoyant job market was probably the most important reason for the sharply reduced welfare rolls by the end of the century.

Sources of 1990s Prosperity.

The sources of the sustained boom were, as is usual, matters of dispute. Many observers emphasized the restructuring of the American and world economy through "globalization" that reduced the economic importance of national boundaries and created a unified world market. During these last years of the twentieth century international trade was expedited through the tariff-lowering General Agreement on Tariffs and Trade (GATT), the World Trade Organization (WTO), the World Bank, the European Economic Union, and NAFTA—the North American Free Trade Agreement. These pacts and agencies expedited the free movement across borders of technical knowledge, skilled management, and technical personnel and drastically reduced protective duties and regulations that impeded free transfer of products between countries. Not since before World War I had people, goods, services, and ideas moved so freely without regard to borders. Taken together, these worked to create global markets for goods and services.

The globalization process operated in several way, said economists. For "developing" nations—India, China, and Brazil, for example—it helped trigger the transition to high-level manufacturing and to modernity. These countries became vibrant markets for American goods and in turn produced cheap staple products—clothing, electronics, housewares—for American consumers. In the developed nations themselves, including the United States, said globalization advocates, it compelled firms to become more efficient and innovative to confront increasing competition abroad. Faced with unfettered world rivalry each nation would, they asserted, find its optimum mix of agriculture, commerce, finance, and manufacturing and use its "comparative advantage" to trade with others what they did better. The benign domestic effects of this international specialization, it followed from this analysis, ultimately registered in the declining American unemployment rate and the nation's GDP surge of the period.

Some observers emphasized the innovative technologies that facilitated globalization as the key to the boom. Most important of these was the Internet, the "information superhighway," as Vice-President Gore and others had quaintly called it early in the decade. By the end of the century business firms and millions of ordinary Americans were able to access from their personal computers vast pools of useful information and engage in buying and selling without leaving their homes or offices. Internet service providers like America Online, CompuServe, and Yahoo had acquired millions of clients and become multibillion dollar companies. Meanwhile, "e-mail" provided a new way for individuals and family members to keep in touch and companies to knit together their operations. By the end of the century "dot-com" companies such as Amazon, eBay, Priceline, and others had established Internet systems for the purchase of books, toys, computers, even groceries. Though in fact traditional marketing remained larger in volume, in part it was the investing public's expectation that "e-commerce" was the wave of the future that led to the extraordinary boom in the NASDAQ stock index that measured the value primarily of high-tech securities.

Biotechnology was another innovation that contributed to the success of the so-called New Economy. By the end of the century, "bio-tech" promised to provide breakthroughs in medicine, agriculture, and even psychology. Among its many merits, its practitioners declared, was its potential for producing hardier and more productive food plants and animals, thereby making cheaper food and fiber available to the world's consumers. One amazing bio-tech development of the 1990s was animal cloning, a form of asexual reproduction that produced living organisms identical genetically to their parents. During the Clinton administration, the advances in the new field were encouraged by the federal government, which, beginning in the early 1990s, subsidized a major scientific project, the Human Genome Project, to decipher the genetic "code" that defined human beings physically, and perhaps behaviorally as well. Meanwhile, a private firm, Celera, led by J. Craig Venter, set out on the same quest using different techniques. In June 2000 the two competitors announced completion of the first "rough draft" of the human genome. The media reported it as one of the greatest scientific breakthroughs in history. And perhaps it was, though practical applications in the form of new drugs and new medical knowledge probably remained years away.

But if globalization and the new technologies were boons, they also created problems. Some societies fell further behind the world leaders. At home, American businesses now competed with the best that the world had to offer, with bankruptcy the price of failure. Firms felt compelled to become "lean and mean" by cutting out layers of management and reducing workers' fringe benefits. Over and over, during the 1990s the public would be dismayed by yet another headline announcing that a major firm—TWA, AT&T, Sears, Eastman Kodak, IBM, American Airlines, GM—was "downsizing," shucking off thousands of workers, white-collar as well as blue-, and closing less efficient plants or abandoning less profitable routes, to remain competitive. Many companies transferred their entire operations offshore, or "outsourced" a portion of them to cheap-labor countries in Latin America or Asia . Americans consumers often found that their telephoned or emailed "customer service" complaints were being answered by technicians in Mumbai or Bangalore. Even the most highly skilled professional services did not seem immune from outsourcing. By the early years of the new century, for example, medical diagnoses were being farmed out to doctors overseas.

Even workers not directly affected wondered how long they would continue to draw a paycheck. Clearly, if the American economy overall benefited from globalization and the new technology that sustained and reinforced it, particular segments of the workforce were injured. (It did not apparently reduce the compensation of top executives, whose salaries often seemed to rise despite mediocre company performance.)

The Bubble Economy.

One component of the extraordinary 1990s economic surge, said cautious observers, was the "irrational exuberance" that gripped investors. Based on the "hype" of a world transformed by computers and the Internet, the public poured its savings into stocks, especially of firms expected to profit from the new high-tech devices and the new high-tech way of doing things. By the mid-nineties the stock markets had rebounded from the frightening 1987 sell-off and in 1990 the Dow Jones index of industrial stocks stood at about 2700. By mid-1999 it had reached 11,000, a quadrupling in less than ten years. The NASDAQ, a new securities market primarily for technical stocks, reached a spectacular peak in mid-2000.

By the end of the decade with almost half of American households invested in "the market", either through pension funds or through individual accounts, the extraordinary performance of stocks made many Americans feel rich. The "wealth effects" on consumers of soaring stock prices translated into lively business at the department stores, the malls, the automobile showrooms, the travel agencies, the restaurants, vacation resorts, and theaters. The economic expansion of the late 1990s also floated on a sea of rising credit. Millions of Americans "maxed out" their credit cards that banks issued , often carelessly. They borrowed on their homes, took out bank loans. "Why not?" they asked; the booming economy would provide the means to repay these debts when they came due.

Optimists proclaimed that the "New Economy" was exempt from the normal business cycle. Recessions were things of the past. The old rules no longer applied. The gains were not temporary, moreover; they were permanent. Everyone who invested in the new "dot-coms" was likely to get rich. Prudent observers were skeptical, however. The recent stock prices, they said, often bore little relationship to company earnings. However productive workers had become and however much lowered trade barriers had stimulated world economic growth, this was, they warned, a "Bubble Economy" based on speculation that would sooner or later collapse. And when it did trillions in paper wealth would evaporate, jobs would disappear, and millions of people would find themselves in deep debt.

Winners.   In fact, the boom of the 1990s produced both winners and losers. Some Americans profited exorbitantly from the New Economy. Programmers, mathematicians, electrical engineers, and geneticists found employers bidding competitively for their skills and services. Labor shortages developed in these areas, and American firms welcomed with open arms a flood of foreign-born and trained technicians, mostly from India, Taiwan, Korea, China, and other parts of Asia. Men and women working as scientists, technicians, and managers for high-tech firms frequently took modest salaries in exchange for options that allowed them to buy their companies' stock at bargain levels. Then, when the companies made their "initial public offering," their stock often soared and these young employees found themselves rich overnight. In 1997 an extraordinary 21,000 employees of Microsoft Corporation in Seattle, two-thirds of its personnel, had become millionaires through such a process. Silicon Valley, the region south of San Francisco Bay in California, where many of the most successful computer software firms were located, probably had more millionaires per square yard than any other spot on earth. Elsewhere around the country—in Austin, Boston, New York, and other places—there were pocket versions of Silicon Valley with thousands of established and would-be high-tech millionaires.

Losers. Yet however impressive the economy's performance, many Americans were left behind in these boom years. The native-born unskilled and undereducated, recent immigrants from less developed nations, as well as the unambitious and the unlucky, were left in the rear. In fact, for those whose incomes fell in the bottom percentiles, life scarcely improved materially over the 1960s. Until the very end of the decade, when the growth of labor productivity and the tight job market finally changed the picture, "real wages," measuring actual buying power, scarcely rose at all for many categories of wage earners. In 1998 almoost 13 percent of American families were considered below the poverty level, scarcely better than in 1970.

Resisters. Inevitably some Americans deplored aspects of the New Economy. Labor leaders complained that globalization undermined the living standards of American workers now forced to compete with cheaper foreign labor and fend off employers' threats to move jobs offshore. Democrats with ties to the labor unions sought to impose restrictions on goods made with foreign labor to protect American workers, but they were seldom successful. By the new century globalization had also stirred to life an international coalition of younger activists, whose attitudes and tactics resembled those of 1960s student rebels. The proponents of globalization got a wake-up call in December 1999 at the meeting in Seattle of the World Trade Organization. WTO was the successor to GATT, the General Agreement on Tariffs and Trade formed to implement freer international trade after World War II. WTO came under fire for failing to protect the environment and for neglecting the working conditions of factory labor in undeveloped parts of the world who produced cheap goods for the consumers of rich nations. Beyond this, however, WTO had become the symbol of those forces, cultural as well as economic, that were changing the world at speeds that many found dismaying. During the Seattle conference, trade unionists, environmentalists, and anti-capitalist radicals picketed meetings and harassed delegates. In places, radical anti-establishment activists rampaged through the city, smashing store windows, setting fires, and looting. In later years no meeting of the WTO or other bodies representing pro-globalization policies could assemble without confronting demonstrators, many of them angry and some violent. Before long such meetings were scheduled only for remote venues where the police could tightly control the environment.

Nor did everyone admire and welcome the scientific breakthroughs of the New Economy. Critics were especially skeptical of biotechnology which promised to increase agricultural output but at the same time posed potential health dangers and opened the door to changes that violated many people's sense of a God-given natural order. The possibility of human cloning, for example, disturbed many Americans and in March 1997 President Clinton, noting the "troubling prospect" of making humans through cloning processes, banned the use of federal funds for experiments in the field. More significant was the growing fear that genetic alteration of plants and animals would create grave health dangers or cause unforeseen hazards to the environment. Environmentalists, led by such activists as Jeremy Rifkin and Ralph Nader, pressured the American government to bar genetically altered seeds and plants. They met little success at home, but since the United States was the leader in genetic alteration, European environmentalists were able to insulate their consumers from the supposed dangers of the new technology by raising import barriers to genetically altered foods and seeds. The pressure of the environmentalists, domestic and foreign, induced a number of seed companies and major bio-tech firms to limit or abandon their plans to market genetically engineered products. Defenders of the new technology called the naysayers "Luddites," backward-looking people whose exaggerated fears would abort benefits to mankind, especially to the poor in the Third World who needed sources of cheap food. Yet their counterattacks seldom convinced the activists.

Election 2000

The surge of economic growth during the mid-1990s seemed likely to redound to the Democrats' advantage in the 2000 presidential election, especially since the Democratic front-runner, Al Gore, Clinton's vice president, was a man closely associated with the new technology and related institutional change. On the other side of the Democrats' ledger, however, was Clinton's personal disgrace. Although the public, by and large, had opposed the impeachment drive, it had not forgiven Clinton for his personal transgressions. And Gore himself carried some dubious ethical baggage. No one accused him of sexual immorality, but there was evidence that he had violated the election laws in raising money for the 1996 campaign by soliciting funds from within the White House.

As the campaign season opened the Republican front-runner was George W. Bush, oldest son of former president George Herbert Walker Bush. Often referred to as "W" or "Dubya" to distinguish him from his father, Bush had been educated at elite schools in the Northeast but had cast his lot in with the business culture of Texas as an oil company executive and a baseball team owner. He supporters called him a "compassionate conservative," and as governor of Texas he had seemed a moderate. Yet he appealed to conservative Republican contributors and power brokers who, exiled for eight years from the White House, were anxious for a winner. Through their efforts Bush accumulated what quickly became the largest campaign war chest on record.

Bush's chief opponent for the Republican party nomination was Senator John McCain of Arizona, a former navy pilot and Vietnam prisoner-of-war. For a time, McCain gave the Bush forces a scare, but was unable to make inroads into the loyal party core. By the early spring of 2000 he had been eliminated from the nomination race.

With the respective presidential candidates in effect already chosen, the national conventions themselves failed to fascinate the public and the major TV networks refused to cover them from "gavel to gavel," as in the past. Only the vice presidential nominations aroused much attention. Gore made the unusual choice of Senator Joseph Lieberman of Connecticut, an orthodox Jew. Bush's selection of Richard Cheney, the secretary of defense under Bush's father during the Gulf War period, seemed motivated by the candidate's own inexperience with national issues and his need for veteran guidance around Washington if elected.

The campaign was not notable for new ideas. But it was the most expensive on record by far. Together the two parties spent a billion dollars to get their messages across to the public. These costs confirmed for many Americans the worrisome reality of money's critical role in political life. One problem for the Democrats was the candidacy of Ralph Nader on the Green Party ticket. The hero since the 1960s of environmentalists and anti-establishment activists, Nader accepted the nomination though many liberals warned that he would draw votes from Gore and help assure the election of Bush, the more conservative and less environment-friendly major candidate. An interesting lesser race during the fall election was the senatorial contest in New York in which the Democratic candidate was Hillary Clinton, the First Lady. Never before had a president's wife run for national office, and the contest attracted attention all over the country.*

The Disputed Election of 2000.
The outcome of the voting was almost unprecedented. When all the ballots were counted Al Gore had won a half-million more popular votes than Bush out of over 100 million cast. But as we know, it is the electoral college that legally chooses a president, and this time—the first occasion since 1876—the electoral college outcome was contested. Gore carried most of the Northeast, the upper Midwest, and the Pacific coast, the region that would become identified as the "Blue States." Bush swept the South, the Mountain states, and the farm belt, the "Red States." In many places, however, the results were very close. On election eve, as important the votes from contested states like Pennsylvania, Michigan, Wisconsin, and Florida seesawed back and forth, the TV networks often made "too close to call" announcements based on exit polls.

One key state, Florida, where Jeb Bush, George W.'s younger brother was governor, was called for Gore by the networks early in the evening count. As the tally continued, however, and most of the "undecideds" fell into place, Florida seemed to move into the Bush column. A populous state with 25 electoral votes, this result, if valid, guaranteed a Bush majority in the electoral college and made the Texas governor president-elect. Assuming he had lost Florida, on election eve Gore congratulated Bush on his victory. But then, unexpectedly, the vote counters changed their minds. Florida, it seemed, was too close to call after all. Gore now withdrew his concession.

For the next month the Florida count, and with it the choice of president, remained in doubt. Early unofficial vote totals gave Bush a 1,700 vote majority, out of over six million cast. A machine recount soon reduced this to fewer than 400. In Florida, Nader's 97,000 votes, many of which almost certainly would have gone for Gore, were far more than enough to have put the vice president over the top. In some sense, then, as Democrats had feared, the Nader candidacy had kept the vice president from a victory.

But even more disturbing to Democrats were the apparent "irregularities" in the count. In populous and heavily Democratic Palm Beach County, for example, a confusing "butterfly" paper ballot had probably led several thousand Democratic voters to unwittingly mark their ballots for Pat Buchanan, the candidate of the far right Reform Party. In other counties, several thousand punch-card ballots

*In November Hillary Clinton won the Senate race in New York.

failed to register any choice for president because the small paper "chad" had remained attached. If the tally had not been so close these imperfect results would have meant little. But with the final outcome dependent on so few votes, the Florida anomalies promised momentous consequences.

Who would decide the final popular vote in the Sunshine State and so determine Florida's slate of presidential electors? Both sides sent teams of lawyers and spokespersons to Tallahassee and other Florida cities to oversee the final tabulations. While the nation and the world looked on aghast, both the legal struggles and the contest in the court of public opinion seesawed back and forth. On November 26, refusing to accept the results of ongoing hand recounts in several counties, the Florida secretary of state, the Republican Katherine Harris, declared Bush the winner in Florida by 537 votes. Bush declared that he had been legally elected and called on Gore to concede. The vice president refused. The Gore legal team asked the courts to force Harris to wait for further hand counts.

The contest was finally resolved on December 12 when the United States Supreme Court overruled the Florida Supreme Court's decision authorizing hand counts, thereby letting Harris's ruling in favor of Bush stand. The federal Supreme Court decision was by a narrow five-to-four majority strictly along party and ideological lines. As critics pointed out, the decision was ironic. Though the grounds for overruling the Florida court was that time was running out, and that the hand recounts, lacking standards, in effect deprived some voters of their equal protection under the law, the justices who most strongly advocated state over federal power had in effect nullified a decision of a state's highest court.

However dubious the decision, Gore now withdrew his challenge and acknowledged defeat. In a brief nationally televised speech he announced that "now that the U.S. Supreme Court has spoken, let there be no doubt, while I strongly disagree with the court's decision I accept it. And for the sake of the unity of the people and our democracy, I concede." An hour later Bush, now president-elect, appeared on the same forum. He thanked his rival for his concession and promised to be the president of all Americans, not just his partisans.

Bush and the War Against Terrorism

Bush's domestic policies.   Despite his "president of all Americans" pledge, in his first moves in office Bush made clear that he did not intend to continue the centrist-to-liberal policies of his predecessor. He quickly rolled back Clinton's environmental-friendly resource decisions, many made just before he left office. Citing rising petroleum prices, he and Vice President Cheney, both previously connected to the oil and gas industry, recommended that the oil reserves of Alaska's pristine North Slope be opened to oil drilling and commercial exploitation. He also rejected the treaty negotiated by most of the world's nations at Kyoto, Japan, to address global warming by long-term reductions in carbon dioxide emissions. Global warming, he declared, was only speculation, not a proven phenomenon.

Bush also sought to please his conservative Christian supporters. Less than a month into his presidency he announced the creation of the White House Office of Faith-Based Initiatives along with centers in five cabinet departments for faith-based activities. These organizations would become the agencies to deliver social services, under existing programs, and presumably future programs, to those entitled to such services. In effect, designated religious groups would share with secular federal agencies the task of administering the nation's social welfare laws. The proposal aroused opposition among secular groups and those who insisted that it violated the principle of separation of church and state, but it was welcomed by conservative religious organizations.

The keystone of Bush's early agenda was a massive cut in federal taxes. Like his conservative predecessor, Ronald Reagan, Bush justified the proposed cut in income taxes of $1.5 trillion over ten years as means to revive the economy and encourage growth. And there was reason for public economic concerns. In these opening months of the new administration output, markets, and employment were slumping badly.

Though he had coined the phrase "irrational exuberance" to describe the stock bubble of the 1990s, Federal Reserve chairman Alan Greenspan had been slow to use his powers to restrain the runaway expansion. Stocks reached their peak in January 2000 with the Dow Jones index at over 11,000. Then, as long predicted, the bubble burst. Unsupported by sufficiently high earnings, corporate stocks plummeted. By mid-2002 the Dow index had dropped to 8000; the decline in the NASDAQ, which measured the stock market's high-tech component, was even more drastic. Thousands of investors, both big and small, now saw their assumed wealth, in whole or in part, wiped out. In the two years following January 2000 some $8.5 trillion of paper assets evaporated. The stock crash soon spread its toxin to other parts of the economy. Beginning in July 2000 industrial production plunged. In twelve months two million jobs disappeared, raising the unemployment rate from an enviable 3.8 percent to 6 percent.

As usual the first line of economic defense was the "Fed." Chairman Greenspan, a man virtually idolized when the New Economy was in full flower, cut short-term interest rates steadily by quarter- and half-point increments. By the fall of 2001 the rediscount rate was down to 2.5 percent, a forty-year low. But the economy did not respond. Consumer spending for a time held up, but business investment took a nose dive since, during the Bubble period, many firms had already overinvested in new products and technologies. Thousands of miles of optical cable, for example, had been laid by telecom companies that expected unlimited markets for their services, but these had not developed. By late summer 2001 companies, especially "dot-coms," many in recently booming Silicon Valley, were shedding workers by the thousands or closing their doors. During the collapse newspapers carried stories of bibulous dot-com bankruptcy parties where the former high-tech paper millionaires ironically celebrated the collapse of their recent high hopes.

However doleful, the slump provided an immediate rationale for Bush's tax cuts. They would, he could claim, stimulate the economy and end the recession. Yet many critics doubted the president's antirecession motives. Rather the cuts were an excuse by conservatives to "starve the beast," to scale down government programs including education enrichment, better highways, and upgraded facilities in national parks. They also seemed a payoff to Bush's rich supporters, a conclusion seemingly confirmed by a parallel Republican push to repeal the inheritance tax, or, as its critics preferred to call it, the "death tax." This levy applied only to a tiny fraction of the very largest estates, though its repeal promised to cost the treasury many billions over the years to come. Finally, critics of the president's tax cut proposals charged, they were reckless. They were so huge that they threatened the Clinton-era treasury surplus and the money set aside to sustain the Social Security system in later years. Yet despite the storm of criticism, much of it from fiscal conservatives, the disciplined Republican majorities in Congress gave the president what he asked. In June Bush signed the measure mandating a $1.35 trillion tax cut spread over a ten-year period. It included a gradual reduction of the estate tax. The administration would soon try to induce Congress to repeal the estate tax entirely, but with federal deficits growing at a furious pace, even Republicans balked. The House approved total repeal, but the Senate refused to go along.

September 11, 2001.

Though the effects of the administration's domestic policies were not yet apparent, Bush's standing at the polls in early September 2001 was at best mediocre. Many Democrats continued to believe his election invalid. Other Americans had come to doubt his abilities. The president often appeared uninformed and unsure of himself. Despite his Yale education, he had trouble with his syntax, pronunciation, and verbal delivery. His top aides–Colin Powell as secretary of state, Donald Rumsfeld as secretary of defense, Paul O'Neill as secretary of treasury, and Condoleezza Rice as national security advisor–were respected leaders in their fields, but the president himself at times seemed at sea.

The world changed abruptly for Bush and most other Americans on the morning of September 11, 2001. At 8:46 A.M. an American Airlines jet carrying 81 passengers from Boston bound for Los Angeles crashed into the north tower of the World Trade Center on the southern tip of Manhattan island. Less than 20 minutes later another airliner with 65 passengers and crew hit the south tower. Both planes were carrying thousands of gallons of aviation fuel, which instantly ignited. The passengers on the planes and many in the buildings died in the initial impact; many others, including over three hundred New York firefighters and police who had arrived as rescue personnel, perished when the skyscrapers collapsed into piles of choking rubble. At 9:37 another civilian jet slammed into the Pentagon, seat of the U.S. Defense Department in Washington, slicing a large wedge from the building and killing almost 200 occupants. Meanwhile, still another hijacked civilian jet, apparently aimed at some target in the nation's capital, probably the White House, crashed into an open field in Pennsylvania before it could reach its destination. The authorities immediately grounded all civilian planes to prevent further hijackings and put the FBI, the CIA, federal marshals, and the military on high alert. All told 3,000 innocent people, in the target structures and on the planes, had died in the hellish hour of terrorism.

The perpetrators' *modus operandi* soon became known. Armed with knives and box cutters, the hijackers had seized control from the pilots and turned the planes into giant flying projectiles. The case of the Pennsylvania misfire, deduced from cell phone calls by frightened passengers who had heard on their radios of the World Trade Center attacks, suggested a brave, but failed, attempt by some of the passengers to take back control from the plane's hijackers. As more and more was learned it became clear that the 19 suicide terrorists—most from Saudi Arabia; others from Egypt, Lebanon, and the United Arab Emirates—had long planned the blow. Many had hidden in the United States for months living apparently quiet, normal lives while taking flying lessons and maturing their plans.

Though in shock, Americans responded vigorously. The CIA and other security agencies quickly identified the culprits and detained scores of people suspected of being part of the plot or helping those involved. The trail led back to Osama bin Laden, a rich, violently anti-American Saudi. Bin Laden and his followers in the extremist terror network called Al Qaeda despised the United States for what it had done and what it represented. In their view America was a Godless land and the source of the immoral, hedonistic values of the western world. It was also a friend of Israel and an enemy of the Palestinians, a foe of Islam, and an exemplar of chaotic democracy and unfettered capitalism. Bin Laden had been implicated in attacks on American military bases in Saudi Arabia in 1995 and 1996 and in the August 1998 bombing of two American embassies in East Africa, which had caused the death of more than 200 people. He had probably planned the attack on the USS *Cole*, an American naval vessel moored in Aden harbor in October 2000, causing the deaths of 17 sailors.

Initially bin Laden and his terrorist circle had based their operations in the Sudan, an Islamic country in north Africa. When, bowing to American pressure, the Sudanese expelled them in 1996, they transferred their headquarters and training camps to Afghanistan where they were given refuge by the Taliban, a group of brutally repressive ultra-fundamentalist Moslems who had seized control of the country after the expulsion of the Soviets in 1989. One of the ironies of the bin Laden case, and of this wave of Islamic terrorism in general, was that many of the most violent activists had been originally armed and trained by the United States to defeat the Soviet intrusion into Afghanistan during the 1980s.

For many days after September 11, the nation mourned its losses. Although most of the dead or missing were from the New York City area they represented an enormous range of nationalities attesting to the diversity of the nation. Hearts went out particularly to the city's firefighter and police rescuers who had died as the buildings collapsed. Americans from all over identified with the tragedy that overwhelmed New York City and its environs and thousands came to personally help or contributed blood, food, medical supplies, or money during the days following 9/11 when hopes still remained that some people might have survived the attacks. Many who followed the tragedy hour by hour came to admire New York's mayor, Rudy Giuliani, whose management skills and quiet determination seemed masterful. The giant smoking hole where the buildings had collapsed would become a place of pilgrimage.

The tragedy stirred to life a great wave of patriotism and national solidarity. Millions of citizens raised American flags on their houses and applied patriotic decals to their cars. Others wore red, white, and blue ribbons on their lapels. Quick polls showed that an overwhelming majority of Americans demanded forceful action to punish the guilty, not just bin Laden and his associates, but those that gave them safe-haven as well. Meanwhile abroad, the European nations, particularly Britain, pledged to back the United States in its efforts to capture and punish the culprits and eradicate terrorism. Even in Asia many expressed sympathy for New York and for Americans generally. Congress voted several billion dollars as compensation for the victims of the catastrophe and appropriated other billions to aid New York and the airlines which suffered extraordinary losses in the post "nine-eleven" period when passenger traffic plummeted.

The War Against Terrorism.   President Bush's combative first responses after 9/11 suited the outrage almost all Americans felt. Bin Laden, he declared, was wanted "dead or alive." The United States now declared "war" against terrorism that would be carried through to the bitter end. His strong, unqualified words reassured many Americans. The public's gratitude and admiration at this moment of crisis would stand the president and his administration in good stead and sugarcoat many of his missteps in the months ahead. Yet some informed observers demurred from the outset. The metaphor of war, they said, was invalid for the circumstances. Unlike most previous wars, the enemy in this case had no capital city, no organized military force, no industrial or commercial infrastructure—no "assets," that is—that could be seized or destroyed. There could be no set battles in this "war" and probably no clean victory. When and if located, bin Laden and his associates would undoubtedly be punished, but that would not necessarily end the terrorist attacks on the United States. And, finally, the war would clearly have to be fought as much through diplomacy, financial countermeasures, and intelligence gathering as through guns and bombs. It would take years and require patience similar to the long Cold War era.

One immediate problem the administration faced was how to keep the conflict from appearing to be a latter-day Crusade, an assault by the Christian West on Islam. The president and his advisors had no desire to align the United States against the more than one billion Muslims in the world. Soon after 9/11 Bush visited several local mosques to assure American Muslims that the government and most citizens respected their faith. Theologians and experts on the Mideast were quick to assure Americans that Islam was a peaceful and compassionate religion that did not condone the murder of innocent people. But some Americans seemed to welcome a religious confrontation. After the 9/11 attacks hotheads vandalized Islamic symbols and beat people who were identified, often mistakenly, as Arabs or Muslims. Evangelical minister Pat Robertson declared that Muhammad, the revered founder of the Islamic faith, "was an absolute wide-eyed fanatic" and his religion was dedicated to terrorism. Yet in the end, most non-Muslim Americans proved tolerant of the Mideasterners in the United States. For their part, an overwhelming majority of Muslim-Americans pledged their loyalty to their adopted country. The administration's task was complicated by the post-9/11 reaction of Muslims abroad, however. Many in the Islamic world refused to accept the guilt of Al Qaeda. Some even cheered the attack on America. Yet despite the anti-Americanism the administration was able to forge a coalition of moderate Muslim states in the Mideast to support the United States and, in varying degrees, help with the counter-offensive against bin Laden and the terrorist networks.

For a time at least, the terrorist attacks brought Americans together. In Congress Democrats joined Republicans to provide the president with the legislation he desired to pursue the "war" on terrorism. One necessity was strengthening the nation's security apparatus. According to the National Commission on Terrorist Attacks Upon the United States, created in late 2002 to investigate 9/11, the assault "should not have come as a surprise." The nation's security agencies had failed to focus on terrorism and to share with one another information they had garnered. Many Americans had been shocked by the lax security measures at the nation's airports on September 11. Immediately after the attack airport safeguards were tightened and other measures adopted to overhaul the entire program of security. The president appointed Governor Tom Ridge of Pennsylvania as head of a new Office of Homeland Security to improve security for Americans and coordinate counter measures against terrorism. Congress quickly passed the Homeland Security Act creating a cabinet-level Department of Homeland Security, incorporating some 22 agencies from other parts of the government, including FEMA, the Federal Emergency Management Agency. Meanwhile, Attorney General John Ashcroft proposed major changes in the legal code to permit more rigorous federal surveillance of people suspected of endangering national security. Incorporating Ashcroft's views, in October 2001 Congress passed the "USA Patriot Act" greatly expanding the federal government's surveillance and detention powers in the case of suspected terrorists. The measure established a long list of new terrorist crimes including use of biological weapons, attacks on mass transportation systems, harboring terrorists and giving them support, and engaging in money laundering to disguise terrorist financial transactions. It gave the FBI and other agencies new power to monitor private electronic communications, to detain foreigners suspected of terrorist intentions, and to deport those accused of such goals. It permitted the government to collect personal records from organizations for purposes of detecting terrorist activities and impeding such activities.

The president's new security measures were carried along by the wave of public anxiety and patriotism. But civil libertarians, liberals and conservatives alike, worried that the Patriot Act went too far in allowing government agencies to violate privacy rights and breach constitutional protections against arbitrary arrest and detention. In 2006 they were further dismayed when it became known that the administration had secretly authorized wiretaps of some overseas telephone calls and the accumulation of massive databases concerning domestic calls without approval by the appropriate federal court. As for the Department of Homeland Security, some critics feared that it was too unwieldy and would be ineffective in protecting Americans from disasters, whether from terrorism or nature's calamities.

The Anthrax Scare.   The 9/11 shock was barely past when the American public suffered another blow to its sense of security. In mid-September the Washington office of Senate majority leader Tom Daschle received a letter with a mysterious white powder that proved to be the deadly anthrax virus. Similar packets arrived at the offices of all three television network news divisions as well as the *New York Post* and America Media, a Florida publisher. Another batch of anthrax-laced envelopes was received at various addresses in the following month. The second round of mailings, fortunately, was the last, but in all 22 people developed anthrax infections and eight or nine died of the disease. For months Americans cowered in fear. Was this another phase of the terrorist campaign against America? Meanwhile, the FBI, the Defense Department, the Environmental Protection Agency, and other government agencies launched massive investigations to determine the possible sources of the anthrax powder and the possible culprits. Besides the deaths of innocent people and the public panic, the investigations, the cleanups, and the disruptions, especially of postal services, cost the nation millions of dollars. The powder, it was eventually determined, was concocted in America, not abroad. But to this day the perpetrators and their motives remain a mystery.

War in Afghanistan.   The administration also took decisive action to confront terrorists abroad. The first overseas arena of the anti-terrorist war was Afghanistan, a poor, mountainous Muslim nation northwest of India where, as we saw, the repressive, ultra-orthodox Taliban regime had given refuge to bin Laden and his Al Qaeda circle. On October 7, the U.S. and Britain mounted "Operation Enduring Freedom." Flying from aircraft carriers in the Arabian Sea and land bases worldwide, American and allied planes launched a ferocious bombing campaign against Taliban and Al Qaeda targets in Afghanistan. The U.S. and Britain supplied only a few hundred special forces ground troops for the campaign, but the combination of Afghani fighters led by the anti-Taliban Northern Alliance and overwhelming western air power decimated the Taliban. On November 12 they fled the capital, Kabul, and soon after abandoned other parts of the country. The war was not over, however. Taliban fighters, as well as bin Laden and many of the foreign fighters supporting Al Qaeda, retreated to the mountainous region bordering Pakistan where they dug in at the Bora Bora caves. With relatively few ground troops of their own the Americans and their Afghan allies found it difficult to clear the caves and by the time they did many Taliban, including bin Laden, had escaped to the remote western provinces of Pakistan where the populace shielded them from their enemies. Though several of his lieutenants were killed or captured, as of this writing bin Laden is still at large.

In December delegates from Afghanistan's main parties established a provisional government with Hamid Karzai, a western-educated tribal leader, to head the administration. In June 2002 Karzai was elected interim president of Afghanistan and set about the difficult task of rebuilding the country and establishing the central government's control over large regions ruled by local chieftains. An international force remained in the country to protect the Kabul government, and continue the fight against remaining Taliban. Unfortunately, American economic aid to the new regime proved limited, and the Afghan economy remained depressed. Impoverished Afghan farmers soon discovered that growing poppy plants, the source of opium, was a lucrative way of rebuilding their personal fortunes.

The War In Iraq

The Genesis of War.   The attacks of 9/11 profoundly influenced the Bush administration's perception of the world. During the 2000 presidential campaign Bush had attacked as sentimental do-goodism the Democrats' willingness to intrude into the internal affairs of distant places for the purposes of "nation building" and preventing atrocities. Nine-eleven turned his administration around. The horrific attack apparently unleashed feelings hitherto buried in Bush himself and inspired a group of influential administration advisors and officials—usually referred to as the "Neoconservatives"—to see in the event an opportunity to settle issues in the Middle East that had long festered. In his State of the Union speech of January 2002, four months after 9/11, Bush included three nations—North Korea, Iran, and Iraq—in an "axis of evil" that were developing weapons of mass destruction (WMD)—biological, chemical, and nuclear—and providing havens for terrorists. He singled out for special denunciation the brutal regime of Saddam Hussein in Iraq that had, some years past, used poison gas against Iraq's rebellious Kurdish citizens, killing many hundreds of men, women, and children.

But Bush's loathing of Saddam may well have predated 9/11. The administration would claim that there was no need to look past Saddam's own actions to explain the president's response. The Iraqi leader had undermined efforts to monitor and limit his arms programs by harassing UN arms inspectors assigned to Iraq after the Gulf War to the point where, in 1998, they were compelled to leave Iraq. In violation of the agreement at the end of that war, he had siphoned off money from sequestered Iraqi oil revenues to line his own pockets and provide his regime with the means to rearm. He had, the administration claimed, given refuge to Al Qaeda terrorists and had subsidized them with funds. Most telling of all, they insisted, he was engaged in a concerted drive to develop weapons of mass destruction that would threaten the survival of his neighbors, and undermine needed stability in the oil-rich Mideast, and the peace and safety of the United States itself. Some observers believed that there were more personal motives for the administration's response as well. Bush and his closest advisors, they noted, had long brooded over the first president Bush's failure in 1990, at the Gulf War's end, to topple Hussein's Baathist regime in Baghdad and replace it with one less aggressive and more friendly to the United States. They now saw a chance to complete the job. Several critics noted that the president personally seethed over Saddam's failed plot to assassinate his father in 1993. Now, it seemed, was the time to settle old scores with the cruel dictator in Baghdad.

The very day of the September 11 attack, still covered with dust and debris from the plane strike at the Pentagon, Defense Secretary Donald Rumsfeld raised the question with his staff and with Paul Wolfowitz,, his closest aide, whether or not the United States should "hit" Saddam at the same time it went after bin Laden. Their answer was positive. But if the Defense Department—along with Vice President Richard Cheney—was eager to secure a "regime change" in Baghdad, Secretary of State Colin Powell was not. Unlike Wolfowitz and other neoconservative Bush advisors, Powell was skeptical of the claim that Saddam had weapons of mass destruction, that he would be a military pushover, or that the United States should go it alone against him if other nations refused to cooperate with us.

Up to a point, the administration preferred the support of world opinion and the aid and cooperation of other nations as during the Gulf War. It proved difficult to attain. Most nations endorsed the American attack on the Taliban in Afghanistan as a legitimate pursuit of terrorism. But many foreign leaders considered an assault on Iraq another matter. In September 2002 Bush appeared before the UN to ask for a resumption of suspended weapons inspections and support by the Security Council for military action against Iraq if it was found to be in "material breach" of the weapons restrictions imposed in 1990. Led by France, Russia, and China, the Security Council balked at giving the American president what amounted to a blank check to attack Iraq. It took weeks to get UN agreement on a new resolution and the one that passed altered the "all necessary means" phrase the U.S. wanted if Saddam refused to comply, to a weaker "serious consequences." Yet faced with overwhelming world pressure the Iraq government agreed to allow the readmission of UN weapons inspectors.

Soon after the UN speech, Bush introduced a resolution in Congress authorizing the president to "use all means that he determines to be appropriate, including force" to deal with the presumed Iraqi threat. On October 10 the House, by a vote of 296 to 133, gave the president the powers he requested. The Senate the next day seconded the motion by a vote of 77 to 23. Bush now had the equivalent, he would claim, of a congressional war declaration against Iraq whenever he chose to invoke it. In the House 126 Democrats, a party majority, had opposed the resolution; in the Senate 29 of 50 Democrats had voted no.

UN on-site inspections of Iraq's weapons programs resumed under the direction of UN official Hans Blix, a Swedish diplomat, in mid-November 2002. Blix's interim report of results, on January 27, criticized the Saddam regime for its lack of cooperation but did not claim that it had discovered any WMD. A parallel report by the head of the International Atomic Energy Agency declared that the Baghdad government had apparently not resumed its nuclear weapons program dismantled after the Gulf War. Determined to topple Saddam, and impatient with the delay, the administration pushed for another UN resolution authorizing an attack. In addition to Britain, Spain and some of the newer members of NATO in eastern Europe were also willing to endorse such a move, but France, Germany, Russia, and China insisted that the inspections should be allowed to run their course before taking military action. In anger, Secretary Rumsfeld, referring to France and Germany, dismissed "Old Europe" as tired and enfeebled compared to "New Europe," the nations that favored our policies.

In a final push to get UN endorsement of immediate military action, Secretary of State Powell appeared before the Security Council on February 5 to make the American case. Personally a skeptic regarding the grounds for immediate war, he had insisted on thorough intelligence briefings from George Tenet, director of the CIA, and other American intelligence officials before the event. The secretary made the administrations's case for covert Iraqi WMD programs, using transcriptions of intercepted messages, photographs of supposed weapons sites, reports of defectors, and graphic visuals showing "mobile production facilities used to make biological agents." Powell also claimed that the Iraqi government was harboring "a deadly terrorists network" that was collaborating with bin Laden and Al Qaeda. However skillful, Powell's presentation did not convince the skeptical members of the Security Council. Once more, only Britain sided with America.

Though without the UN authorization they wanted, on March 20 U.S. and British troops crossed the border into Iraq and began to push northward toward Baghdad. Meanwhile, guided bombs and cruise missiles rained down on Iraqi military units and command centers. Believing large numbers unnecessary, Rumsfeld deployed far fewer troops than had invaded Iraq in the First Gulf War. Yet the initial attack, led by general Tommy Franks, proved overwhelming. Faced with the professional, high-tech skills of the U.S. military, the Iraqi army quickly collapsed. In a matter of days, the British and Americans had seized the rich oil fields in both the south and north of the country. In early April U.S. troops entered Baghdad and were greeted with joy by crowds of Shia Muslims, who, like the Iraqi Kurds in the northern part of the country, had long been oppressed by Saddam's Sunni Muslims. On April 9 the media carried images of a twenty-foot statue of Saddam in Baghdad being toppled from its base by Shia Iraqis helped by nearby American troops. On May 1, a triumphant, smiling president, alighted from a plane on the deck of aircraft carrier USS *Abraham Lincoln,* and declared that combat operations in Iraq were over. Behind him, on the carrier bridge, the navy had placed a huge sign: "Mission Accomplished."

The War Drags On.   It was a moment of extraordinary hubris. If the initial military campaign had been conducted with skill, its aftermath was badly bungled. The administration apparently had given little thought to the future of Iraq beyond "regime change." Saddam was still alive and although many of his Baath Party lieutenants were soon rounded up, he remained in hiding, a rallying point for Baathists and many Sunni Muslims. When the coalition authorities foolishly disbanded the Iraqi army many of its fighters went underground to launch a guerrilla war against the occupation forces.

Still another mistake soon became apparent. Following Rumsfeld's doctrine that in future wars the American military needed fewer but better trained and equipped troops, fewer than 200,000 troops had been sent to defeat Saddam and occupy the country. Having also disbanded the Saddam-era police force, the sparse American army could not check the orgy of looting and crime that erupted after the regime's fall. In the weeks that followed criminals stole hospital equipment, rifled public buildings, and pilfered treasures from Baghdad's museums and libraries. Iraq soon become a maelstrom of vandalism, robbery, kidnapping, rape, and murder. Almost daily suicide bombings, mounted by angry Sunni dissidents reinforced by terrorist, anti-American "foreign fighters," took a heavy toll of lives. So did ambushes and shoot-outs. Most of the victims were Iraqis, often members of the reestablished Iraqi army or of the new police forces cooperating with the occupation forces. But many were U.S. soldiers or marines, many of whom were killed by roadside bombs as their motorized convoys passed. By mid-2006 almost 2500 members of the American military had died through hostile action in Iraq; more than 17,000 had been wounded. More might have been lost if American troops had not often been sequestered in highly fortified enclaves from which they made forays against the insurgents.

The fighting took a toll beyond the casualty lists. After the initial friendly response, many Iraqis turned against the American occupation, and demanded its end. Some of the countries that had agreed to help in Iraq—Spain and Poland, for example—withdrew their troops to avoid the human cost. After coming under lethal attack the UN and the International Red Cross withdrew their missions too. The administration soon found it difficult to maintain troop strength. Many of the soldiers and marines in Iraq were reservists or National Guard troops, citizens who had joined units before the war to earn some money and acquire some skills while maintaining their civilian lives. Now they were in the middle of a shooting war on long tours of duty. Generally speaking their morale remained good, but the Defense Department soon encountered major problems recruiting new men and women for the services. Not too many Americans, apparently, wished to die or be maimed in a hot, distant country.

The United States appointed several proconsuls to administer the occupation and try to bring peace and stability to the country. In July 2003 Paul Bremer, Iraq's civilian administrator, selected a Governing Council of Iraqis and prepared a road map of transition to a presumed secular, democratic state which Iraqi s would accept as legitimate. In November the council mandated elections in 2005 for a provisional parliament. This body would select a committee to write a new constitution. Meanwhile, the killing and disruptions continued. The capture of Saddam Hussein in December 2003 did not noticeably reduce them, as some had hoped. In fact, in 2004 the insurgency intensified. By this time Iraq had become a magnet pulling anti-Western "Jihadists" from all over the Islamic world to take on the Western "Crusaders."

Meanwhile, now that the United States occupied Iraq, the administration launched a comprehensive search for weapons of mass destruction to prove its case for the invasion. The effort was for naught. In January 2004 David Kay, head of the official Iraq Survey Group, reported that he had found no evidence that Saddam had any ongoing WMD programs at the time of the coalition invasion. Kay placed responsibility for the administration's erroneous claims at the door of the CIA and other U.S. intelligence agencies. Yet another administration claim was laid to rest in September 2004 when the national commission appointed to investigate 9/11 reported that it had found "no credible evidence that Iraq and Al Qaeda [had] cooperated on attacks" against the United States. The administration claimed that here too it had been misled by faulty information. But these results created a quandary for Bush. With its two chief claims now declared invalid, how could the invasion be defended? Administration officials soon came up with two answers: the U.S. was serving humanity by evicting a cruel tyrant from power and protecting innocent Iraqis from his torture and murder; in addition, we would make Iraq a model democratic nation that would provide an example for the rest of the seething, unstable Muslim world to emulate. Such a Mideast would be a more peaceful and stable region. Neither argument squared with the president's rejection of "nation building" during the 2000 political campaign.

One of the ironies of Bush administration policy, ostensibly aimed against a cruel tyrant, was the use of brutal methods to extract information from Iraqi prisoners and other Mideast captives. Several hundred captured Taliban and suspected Al Qaeda from Afghanistan had been brought to Guantanamo, the American military base in Cuba, for interrogation. They were called "enemy combatants" and considered ineligible for prisoner-of-war status. They were held without charges, denied legal counsel, and subject to intense questioning to extract information about terrorist personnel and plans. Human rights groups and civil libertarians charged that the Guantanamo authorities employed torture and intimidation in their questioning procedures. Attorney General Ashcroft insisted that the captives were being treated humanely, but the administration continued to deny them the rights that others believed they deserved under both American and international law. The administration also, it seems, had sent captives to locations abroad where American allies might employ harsh interrogation methods that squeamish Americans preferred to avoid.

A far worse prisoner scandal erupted when in April 2004 CBS News released photographs of Iraqi captives being abused and sexually humiliated by American guards at Abu Ghraib prison near Baghdad. Widely distributed over the Internet, the pictures sent a wave of outrage around the world and, in the eyes of America's enemies and even some friends, made the Bush administration claims to a democratic and humanitarian mission in Iraq seem utter hypocrisy. Though Bush and Rumsfeld denounced the abuses and ordered an investigation, in the end only a handful of low-ranking American military police were court-martialed. No one in high office, either civilian or military, was officially blamed or punished.

Israel and the Palestinians.

In any event, the likelihood of winning friendship for America in the Arab Middle East seemed virtually nil so long as the Israeli-Palestinian conflict remained unresolved. The Bush administration, which initially had avoided intervention into that thorny issue, now found itself compelled to seek a solution if only to bolster its rationale for the war in Iraq.

Unfortunately, the problem of competing Israeli-Palestinian interests and aspirations was dauntingly intractable. President Clinton, as we saw, had tried to forge a compromise that would satisfy Palestinian statehood aspirations while assuring Israel that its security would be protected. Some observers believed that the two parties had come close to agreement at that time, but soon after, the Second Intifada, a campaign of suicide bombings by Palestinian militants against Israeli civilians, had begun. The Israeli public's response was to throw out the moderate prime minister Ehud Barak and replace him with the hard-liner Ariel Sharon. Sharon used harsh tactics against Yasser Arafat and his Palestinian Authority, held responsible for the campaign. In the spring of 2002 he sent the Israeli army into West Bank Palestinian communities, previously granted autonomy under the Oslo Accords, and destroyed much property and killed suspected supporters of terrorism. Israel sought to associate its struggle with America's post-9/11 war against terrorism. The campaign met with some success among Americans. President Bush, for one, seemed to tilt strongly against Arafat and in favor of Israel. But in the Islamic world, the United States' apparent pro-Israel bias, aroused anger and further encouraged anti-American feelings. Meanwhile, both sides seemed to become more intransigent. More and more Israelis concluded that a Palestinian state would work from the outset for Israel's destruction. The Palestinians in turn were confirmed in their view that the Israelis intended to continue indefinitely their occupation of Gaza and the West Bank and had no intention of ever allowing them to achieve national statehood.

A possible breakthrough came in the summer of 2005 when Sharon agreed unilaterally to remove Jewish settlers from enclaves in the occupied Gaza Strip and in several locations on the West Bank. These settlements had been established years before by Israel in hope of frustrating Palestinian independence ambitions and to accommodate orthodox Jewish extremists who claimed the land by biblical right. It eventually became clear to Sharon and many Israelis that the costs in manpower and money to keep these exposed settlers safe from Palestinian attack had become exorbitant. But at the same time removing them could be offered as a concession to Palestinian aspirations and a token of Israel's willingness to accept a Palestinian state. Israel would expect Mahmoud Abbas, the successor of the deceased Arafat as Palestinian prime minister, to reciprocate by controlling the extremist factions in his own land that had launched murderous attacks against Israel. In August 2005, under Sharon's orders, Israeli troops and police compelled the settlers, many of whom resisted fiercely, to leave their homes and abandon businesses and synagogues. The Bush administration had helped broker the evacuation and now hoped that it would lead to further progress toward eventual Israeli-Palestinian peace.

The promising beginning soon ground to a halt. In early 2006 Sharon suffered a massive stroke that ended his political career. Soon after, following America's strong urging, the Palestinians held free elections that, to everyone's surprise, resulted in the victory of the extremist party, Hamas, a group that denied Israel's legitimacy and had sponsored numerous terrorist acts against Israeli civilians. It looked to many as if the Bush administration's vaunted effort to bring democracy to the Mideast had failed miserably. It was, they said, serving only as an instrument for the most extreme Islamist groups that preferred terrorist tactics and an intransigent attitude to compromise with Israel.

Enron and the End of the "New Economy" Era

The stock market slump after 2000 had been worsened by the attacks of 9/11. But the market might have quickly rebounded, and with it the economy as a whole, if not for a deluge of bad news from the business world in late 2001. These stories revealed an unprecedented level of financial fraud and chicanery during the boom years of the late 1990s.

The prototype of the swindles was the performance of one of the largest American energy conglomerates, the Enron Corporation of Houston. The firm's officials had falsified its earnings reports to inflate its stock value, the chief marker in those years of a company's success, and often directly tied to the CEO's financial compensation. Prompted by this system, top Enron executives, including Kenneth Lay and Jeffrey Skilling, with the connivance of the company's outside auditor, the Arthur Andersen accounting firm, had manipulated its financial statements to show profits where there were really losses. By late 2001, unable to cook the books any longer, Enron's executives managed to sell off much of their stock holdings before they plummeted while urging their employees to hold on to their own. Enron soon declared bankruptcy of over $60 billion. Many Enron employees, with their pensions invested in the company's stock, lost most of their life savings.

The Enron collapse not only outraged its employees, but also triggered deep populistic responses among Americans generally. Congress soon opened hearings on the Enron debacle. When questioned, Lay and Skilling pleaded the Fifth Amendment right against self-incrimination, but were finally brought to trial in early 2006 and found guilty of almost all the charges prosecutors brought against them. Congressional committees began to consider new regulatory legislation to strengthen the Securities and Exchange Commission. The administration seemed implicated in the Enron debacle. At least one member of the Bush administration,

Secretary of the Army Thomas White, had close ties to Enron. Critics charged that he had sought to help the firm through dubious use of his influence. And he too had somehow managed to cash out his investment before the downfall.

The Enron collapse brought down the major accounting firm, Arthur Andersen of Chicago. Andersen was supposed to supply judicious accounting oversight for Enron and the other firms it audited. But Andersen had financial reasons to accept Enron's dubious accounting practices and failed in its duties. Indeed, when Enron's malpractices began to emerge, Andersen officials destroyed mountains of documents to avoid implicating themselves and their company in the scandal. In mid-2002 a Houston jury found Andersen guilty of obstructing justice and imposed a large fine. It soon went out of business. The Enron-Anderson affair raised serious doubts about the honesty of the nation's corporate accounting methods. It seemed to make a mockery of the "transparency" of American business methods that, during the New Economy era, was held to be one of the sterling merits of the American economy.

The Enron scandal proved to be the first of a series. In subsequent months huge firms like TYCO, QWEST, and WorldCom, all emblems of the 1990s New Economy, were found to have used various tricks to inflate their profit statements so as to hike the value of their stock. WorldCom, a conglomerate that included the telecommunications giant MCI, admitted that it had inflated its profits of 2001–2002 by $3.8 billion. In late July 2002 the company declared bankruptcy. At $107 billion it was the largest business failure in American history. In the summer of 2002 even General Electric, the poster boy of New Economy corporate management, fell under suspicion that its success was due as much to accounting manipulation as to the genius of its long-time CEO, Jack Welch.

The scandals of 2001–2002 undermined the faith of many Americans in the business system that had been so triumphant in the 1990s. Though into mid-2002 basic economic indicators continued to look fairly good, the stock market refused to respond. Unable to tell whether a company was making money or not when so many officials were committing fraud, how could investors be expected to buy or hold their stock? By mid-July hundreds of billions of dollars of private and institutional wealth had evaporated and the media circulated stories of retirees being forced to return to work because their pensions had been drastically undercut, or men and women, counting on early retirement, being forced to postpone it indefinitely, or parents losing the savings they had put away for their children's college tuition.

The pressure for Congress and the administration to restore public trust and to prevent a repetition of the post-1929 economic debacle grew urgent. President Bush sought to get ahead of the curve by recommending a strengthened SEC and greater legal accountability of CEOs. His critics said his proposals were feeble. The stock market refused to respond favorably.

Reelection and Second Term

Midterm Elections.   Despite predictions, the Republicans, still perceived as the country's bulwark against terrorists, made substantial gains in the 2002 midterm elections, increasing their majority in the House of Representatives by five seats and winning a majority in the U.S. Senate. Now, for the first time in many years, they would have control of both the White House and both houses of Congress simultaneously. Some observers wondered if this would this be an invitation to political excess and irresponsibility.

Presidential Campaign 2004.

The Democrats understood that they had to avoid the appearance of weakness in the face of the world terrorist threat. Yet for a time the Democratic front-runner was the antiwar former governor of Vermont, Howard Dean, whose supporters, many of them younger liberal enthusiasts, were mobilized and financed by a campaign conducted on the Internet. The other Democratic candidates were critical of the administration's conduct of the war, but many had supported it at the outset and were careful to avoid labeling it a mistake. In the end they nominated the junior senator from Massachusetts, John Kerry, who was a decorated hero of the Vietnam War and so seemed proof against any charge of weakness in the face of national enemies. Kerry selected as his running mate, the eloquent young senator from North Carolina, John Edwards.

Despite his record as a veteran of Vietnam, Kerry proved to be a vulnerable candidate. Son of a State Department diplomat, he came from a cosmopolitan background which included education in Switzerland, and then Yale, where he was elected to the elite Skull and Bones society. He was a divorced man whose second wife, the Portuguese-born Teresa Heinz, was the widow of John Heinz, a former Senator from Pennsylvania and heir to the great Heinz food products fortune. Though he had received both a Bronze Star and a Silver Star, as well as three Purple Hearts, for his service in Vietnam, Kerry had turned against the war in 1970 after discharge from the navy and became a highly visible antiwar protester.

During the campaign the Swift Boat Veterans for Truth, composed of pro-Bush Vietnam veterans, succeeded in undermining Kerry's war record. Other pro-Bush groups attacked Kerry's supposedly unpatriotic anti-Vietnam war stance after his discharge. Beneath the surface was an unspoken campaign to make the Democratic candidate seem an un-American, ultra-liberal elitist, someone who had little in common with the average American voter. The Democrats pointed out that Bush himself came from a rich and powerful family and had received an elite education at Yale. They also sought to cast doubt on Bush's own Vietnam-era war record. He had avoided dangerous service in Southeast Asia, they said, by joining the Air National Guard and then had not even fulfilled the terms of his enlistment.

The Democrats appealed to voters worried about the economy, which remained sluggish despite the massive tax cuts. But it was the "war against terrorism" that was probably decisive for the outcome. Anxious Americans retained their faith in the administration's ability to protect them against extremists and were unsure that Kerry would do as well. Despite the failure to discover WMDs and despite the growing insurgency in Iraq, many voters still believed the administration's claims that the overthrow of the Iraqi regime had advanced the war on terrorism. In three televised debates Kerry appeared more adept and better informed than his opponent, but many viewers considered him glib and preferred the plain, mid-American manner and delivery of the president. Though the terrorism issue was an important element in the Republican victory, so was the religious-cultural factor. Kerry was

Catholic. White evangelical Protestants, who made up 23 percent of the electorate, voted for Bush by 78 percent to 22 percent. Those "faith-based" initiatives, and equivalent administration moves, had paid dividends at the polls.

The vote was a substantial, if not spectacular, victory for the Bush-Cheney ticket. This time the Republican candidate won a popular majority of 59 million to 55.4 million for his opponent, a 3.6 million margin. In the electoral college it was Bush-Cheney 274 to Kerry-Edwards 252. In Congress the Republicans increased their majority slightly in the House and by a larger number in the Senate. For the first time since 1924 an incumbent president had won a second term with majorities in both houses of Congress. Once again the country had split into the Republican Red State–Democrat Blue State division with the Northeast, the West coast, and the upper Great Lakes states going for Kerry, and the South and Midwest for Bush. One victory that Republicans particularly relished was the defeat for reelection of Tom Daschle, head of the Senate Democrats.

Second Term

As we have seen before, presidential second terms are seldom as productive and trouble-free as first ones. And so it was for Bush. As usual, there were several significant changes of administration personnel between terms. Secretary of State Colin Powell, who had never been happy with the president's Iraqi plans, retired soon after the election and was replaced by Condoleezza Rice, the former national security advisor, who was more attuned to the president's international goals. Attorney General John Ashcroft, seen by liberals as indifferent to civil liberties concerns, was replaced by Bush's White House Counsel, Alberto Gonzales, the first Hispanic attorney general. Many opponents of the administration hoped the president would replace Donald Rumsfeld, but he decided to retain him despite the sharp criticism of his alleged failures in managing the Iraq war.

And these failures continued to plague Iraq. The country remained a cauldron of sabotage, kidnappings, assassinations, and suicide bombings. If anything, the pace of these attacks accelerated as "Jihadists," Muslim fanatics from all over the Mideast, converged on Iraq determined to drive out the perceived western enemies of Islam. In early 2006 the extremists, assumed to be Sunnis, destroyed a holy Shia mosque, pushing the country to the edge of a vicious sectarian war between Shiites and Sunnis that threatened to tear the already chaotic country apart. The Sunnis, formerly the chief supporters of Saddam though a minority, felt deeply aggrieved that they had lost the 2005 parliamentary elections to the Shias and could no longer rule the country. A particularly vicious leader of the insurgents was Abu Musab al Zarqawi, a Jordanian who boasted of ordering the on-video camera beheading of foreign hostages to discourage European and Asian nations cooperating with the United States. Although the Bush administration continued to claim that Saddam Hussein had provided a base for international terrorism, critics insisted that it was only after the American invasion that Iraq became a haven for anti-Western fanatics. Meanwhile, terrorists succeeded in driving one of America's European allies, Spain, from Iraq by a vicious attack on

Spanish train commuters in Madrid which killed almost 200 people. The attack turned Spanish voters against the pro-American ruling party and in the national election soon following, they voted into power the antiwar opposition party. The new government promptly removed all Spanish troops from Iraq.

The administration sought to put the best face on events in Iraq. It claimed that the scars of war were being quickly removed and the Iraqi economy was recovering. It also claimed that the intense effort to train Iraqi soldiers and police to take over safety and security in the country from the Americans was beginning to bear fruit. Critics, including many ordinary Iraqis, responded that adequate clean water, regular electric service, and free flow of oil from the country's rich wells were still impaired. Worst of all was the crime, disorder, and danger to life and limb resulting from the insurgency.

At home public confidence in the Iraq venture sharply declined in 2005. A *Washington Post*-ABC News poll in June, after a particularly lethal month for American troops, showed that for the first time since the Iraq invasion began more than half the American public believed that the war had not made the United States safer. Two-thirds of Americans now concluded that the military was bogged down in Iraq; sixty percent said the war was not worth fighting. In August Cindy Sheehan, a California woman whose soldier son had been killed in Iraq the year before, began a vigil near the president's ranch at Crawford, Texas, while Bush was on a "working vacation." Sheehan demanded that the President see her personally and explain the purpose of the war, a fight that she claimed did not have "anything to do with the war on terror." Sheehan became the focus of a growing antiwar movement composed of other "Gold Star" mothers and other opponents of the Iraq venture. By mid-2005 some members of Congress, including several prominent Republicans, began to question the Iraq war and proposed assigning a date for withdrawing American troops.

The president and his allies fought back. Bush pointed out how self-defeating a withdrawal date would be. The insurgents would merely wait us out before toppling the friendly Iraqi government and replacing it with one they alone controlled. No, we must stay the course, assuming that with proper training and equipment, the Iraqi police and army would be able to defeat the insurgency by themselves. To do otherwise would be to break faith with those young Americans who had sacrificed in the war. Bush also pointed to the hopeful progress being made toward establishing a democratic regime in Baghdad. In January 2005, despite threats of insurgents' violence, a large proportion of Iraqis had gone to the polls and elected a provisional parliament. It was a heartening sign. And many Americans hoped that it was, as the president said, the beginning of a new democratic era in the country. But then the process toward a permanent government stalled. In August, the constitutional convention found it impossible to reconcile fully the opposing views of Shias, Kurds, and Sunnis and the disagreements between secular and Islamist delegates. The Sunnis, fearing the new frame of government gave too many advantages to the Kurds and Shias, were especially disaffected. As of early 2006 Iraq remained without a full-fledged administration and the country seemed to be drifting into a sectarian civil war between Shias and Sunnis.

Yet many of Bush's political adversaries found themselves caught in a dilemma. Though skeptical of the war and dubious of its motivation, they agreed that now that we were embroiled in Iraq we could not just "cut and run."

Second Term Domestic Agenda.   During Bush's second term many of the adverse effects of his tax policies became apparent. As critics had anticipated, the monumental cuts, combined with skyrocketing costs of national security, a major foreign war, and recession-reduced tax revenues, dried up the surpluses of the Clinton years and pushed the treasury decisively into the red. In fiscal 2002, for the first time in five years, the federal budget was in deficit. Still, on the grounds that a sagging economy needed fiscal stimulation to recover, Bush had demanded further cuts in both income taxes and levies on capital gains. In May 2003 Congress, firmly in republican control, would grant most of what he requested, pushing the deficit that fiscal year to $374 billion. Soon after, Congress granted the treasury's request to raise the national debt limit by almost a trillion dollars to an all-time record of $7.4 trillion.

Growing Economic Inequality.   As the results of the Bush tax policies became more apparent, critics from both ends of the political spectrum denounced them. The conservative Federal Reserve Chairman Alan Greenspan warned in May 2004 that the federal budget deficit, expected to reach $500 billion by the end of the year, was "a significant obstacle to long term stability." Liberals noted how unequal the tax-cut benefits were proving to be. As of 2004 each of the households in the middle fifth of the income range received an average cut of $647. The top one percent of American households, by contrast, averaged $35,000, while for those 260,000 families with annual incomes over one million dollars, the gain would be $123,000, or a full 6.4 percent of their income. All told, the tiny cohort of million-dollars-a-year families would receive a total tax boon of more than $30 billion.

Critics also attacked the tax cut policy for its detrimental effects on the overall distribution of income and wealth. From a country that had long boasted of relative economic equality compared to its European counterparts, the United States had become one of the most unequal. In 2005 the Census Bureau reported that over fifty percent of total annual income had gone to the top twenty percent of households. For the fifth year in a row, moreover, the median household income of Americans had remained stuck at the equivalent of about $44,000. Only five percent of households in 2004 had experienced rising incomes. Income inequality was now at the level of the Gilded age at the end of the nineteenth century.

In truth the adverse trend had begun before 2000 and had multiple causes. In an age when the "knowledge industries"—computers, aerospace, financial services, bio-tech—were expanding and superseding agriculture, mining, and industry as sources of jobs and income, the rewards were going primarily to men and women with advanced training and educations. Brawn and manual skills were no longer sufficient to provide a man or woman with a middle-class standard of living. Yet another long term factor was the attrition of trade union power. Formerly, workers in steel, autos, textiles, and other industries were able to protect their jobs and their wages through collective bargaining. But after the 1970s unions had lost leverage especially in the older manufacturing industries. These were "sunset" industries, losing customers as public tastes changed or management became incapable of adapting to new challenges. Unions feared to push such weakened firms into bankruptcy by insisting they maintain jobs, wages, and benefits. The process was accelerated by globalization and foreign "out-sourcing." Employers could now threatened workers with replacement by cheap overseas labor. Here too a weak trade union movement was in no position to fight employers for that course risked the company shifting its operations to Mexico, China, or some other low-wage country with a complete loss of jobs for its members.

Few of these factors could be laid solely at the administration's door; they were part of world-ranging processes that transcended any administration. But the Bush tax policies clearly amplified the trend and reinforced the views of liberal critics that the administration favored the wealthy.

Social Security "Reform"   The major item of Bush's second term domestic agenda was "reform" of the Social Security system. Initiated by the New Deal and expanded by other presidents, Social Security had served Americans well. Under it millions of older citizens had been saved from poverty through federal pensions and from ill-health through Medicare and Medicaid. The basic law, seventy years old, had failings, however. The pension scheme relied on younger working citizens to pay for seniors' retirements. But as more and more people lived to their late seventies and beyond, and as the birthrate declined, reducing the number of contributors to the pension fund, the burden on younger workers promised to become too great to bear. The Social Security trust fund remained substantial, but by various estimates it would run out either in 2042 or 2052. Other failings could be found in the health care provisions under Medicare and Medicaid. The first lacked a drug payment provision. The administration sought to fill this gap with the "Medicare Modernization Act" of late 2003. This measure promised, beginning in 2006, to pay for seniors' prescription drug bills. Supposed to cost some $400 billion over time, by early 2005 the likely cost was estimated at $1.2 trillion during the decade ahead. The scheme relied on many different plans arranged by private insurers and when put into effect in early 2006, produced mass confusion among seniors eligible for benefits.

Bush claimed that his pension reform plan would save the system from "bankruptcy." But its major feature was to allow younger workers, still paying Social Security taxes, to divert a proportion of their contribution into "personal retirement accounts," These, it was said, would enable workers to manage some of their money before pension time, to withdraw it as they wished, and to use it for any purpose they chose. In line with his goal of "an ownership society," the president was appealing to the individualistic side of the American tradition. He also noted, correctly, that the returns from stock and bond investment, historically, were far better than the returns workers could expect from Social Security pensions. But critics were quick to jump on the scheme's flaws. First, they said, it did not solve the problem of excess withdrawals from the trust fund. Real solutions to trust fund depletion might include reduction in payout benefits, a gradual rise in the retirement age, or an increase in Social Security taxes, none, admittedly, likely to be politically popular. They also pointed out that the stock market was as capable of falling as of rising. If it were to be in decline at the time a worker retired, he or she could lose a major part of their pension. The critics also suspected that the administration was only doing the bidding of the bankers, financial advisers, and stock brokers who stood to profit enormously with the shift of hundreds of billions of Social Security dollars into the private financial markets.

Bush embarked on a campaign to sell his plan by speeches and meetings around the country, but failed to arouse much enthusiasm. Seniors' organizations, including the powerful American Association of Retired Persons (AARP), roundly condemned it as a "privatization" of Social Security that would make it less protective. The original system, they said, had served seniors well. Why change it? Many younger Americans, remembering the stock market disaster of 2000–2001, wondered whether it was not too risky. By late 2005, observers agreed, the plan was essentially dead.

Bush was more successful in enacting other items in his domestic agenda. In August 2005 he signed the Transportation Act appropriating billions for highways, bridges, public transportation. He was also able to cram though Congress a measure to create CAFTA (Central American Free Trade Agreement). This established, on the model of NAFTA, a free trade zone between the Central American Republics and the United States. The 109th Congress also passed the Energy Policy Act providing tax breaks to encourage the production and conservation of energy and granted modest subsidies to producers of ethanol, a gasoline additive.

Each of these measures contained beneficial features, but all came under attack. The Transportation Act, for example, contained $24 billion of "pork" projects introduced by members to benefit their districts, including bridges to nowhere, unneeded roads, tourist sidewalks, snowmobile trails, and graffiti cleanup programs. Despite a growing world energy crunch and rapidly rising prices for gasoline, natural gas, and heating oil, the energy bill, critics pointed out, lacked a fuel conservation feature with any real bite and any provision for shifting from dependence on fossil fuels to renewable energy sources. Its most serious defect was that it failed to reduce American dependence on foreign oil, and so limited America's freedom to pursue desirable foreign policy goals for fear of offending countries in the Middle East and triggering an international oil crisis. Just such a constraint tied our hands in the confrontation with Iran's bellicose regime hell-bent, it seemed, to make the Persian gulf nation a power capable of wielding nuclear weapons. As for CAFTA, some said it was just another case of the administration's indifference to the transfer of American manufacturing and jobs to other, low-wage, nations.

Hurricane Katrina.

Bush's popularity suffered a further massive blow when "Katrina," a Category 4 hurricane, struck the Gulf coast of Louisiana, Mississippi, and Alabama, in late August 2005. The storm devastated the coastal communities of Mississippi and Alabama, but it was New Orleans, a city of half a million sitting in a shallow bowl below sea level, that suffered the most. As the storm approached, thousands of citizens left the city by cars, buses, and planes. Many thousands, however, either chose to, or were compelled to, remain and ride out the hurricane in their homes. Far worse than the wind damage, most of the city was turned into a shallow lake when the levees protecting it from the Mississippi River and Lake Pontchartrain were breached.

For many New Orleanians help was slow in coming. Thousands had been told by the mayor to go to the city's Superdome, the covered sports arena near downtown to escape the flooding. Others were sent to the city's Convention Center. The stranded were forced to wait days, with little food, water, or medical attention, in heat, squalor, and filth. Hundreds died of drowning, disease, or exposure. Meanwhile, in the major shelters, and on the flooded streets, lawlessness erupted as gangs of young men with stolen guns looted, mugged, and raped. The city's police and rescue personnel at times were forced to call off rescue and evacuation efforts. National Guard troops moved to take their place, but with agonizing sluggishness. Thousands of lives were saved by the outpouring of aid from the Red Cross, the Salvation Army, FEMA, the U.S. military, state and local agencies, and volunteers from all over the country. But the total of human misery and social disruption was enormous. By mid-September the city was mostly empty and refugees were scattered around the country where they were provided with food, shelter, and medical and financial help. But jobless, their possessions destroyed, they could only guess at what their futures would bring. Meanwhile, the fate of a great American city seemed in doubt. It would cost many billions of dollars to restore New Orleans and more than a few observers called for abandoning it entirely.

The calamity was the worst natural disaster in American history. The rescue operation could not avoid being difficult. But critics could make a good case for overly slow reaction and mismanagement by the Bush administration. The vulnerability of New Orleans to just such a catastrophic blow had been understood for many years, they said, yet the federal government was unprepared to provide quick relief and slow and uncoordinated when disaster struck. Beyond this, the administration had cut, rather than increased, the budget for levee improvement, though the Army Corps of Engineers had long recommended it. Some environmentalists also faulted the administration for failing to prevent coastal development projects in Louisiana that had depleted the protective wetlands. Others noted that the hurricane, one of an unusually long series during the 2005 season, was quite possibly a product of the long-predicted global warming, the reality of which the administration had refused to acknowledge. Many critics zeroed in on the incompetence of FEMA, the Federal Emergency Management Agency, whose head, Michael Brown, and other high officials, were all inexperienced Bush patronage appointees. Still others said the disaster highlighted the administration's indifference to the poor citizens of America. Some critics contended that if the white inhabitants of New Orleans had been the prime victims of Katrina, rather than its black citizens, the administration would have done a better job of rescue than it did. Bush's defenders either praised the president's leadership or sought to deflect much of the blame on to Brown, who soon resigned. Bush and other high administration officials also sought to recoup by frequent trips to the disaster areas to show their concern. But all told the president's approval rating took another serious hit.

By the spring of 2006 some sixty percent of polled voters thought the president had not done a good job overall, a conclusion that incorporated the public's feelings that he had mismanaged the Iraqi war, the rescue effort along the Gulf Coast, the nation's foreign trade, and a host of domestic problems. Republicans worried that the public's misgivings would produce a party disaster in the looming mid-term elections for Congress and the state governorships.

Conclusions

It is difficult, of course, to reach firm conclusions about events that are still unfolding. Historians properly deal with the past, not the present; they need perspective. Yet it is obvious that in the new twenty-first century the United States and the American people faced immense challenges unforseen in the immediate euphoria that followed the end of the Cold War.

The years that began with Bill Clinton's taking office were a roller coaster ride. In 1992 the United States economy was still in the doldrums. The experts worried that the country had lost its talent for creating wealth, and they looked to Japan for lessons on how to succeed in manufacturing and trade. By 2000 Japan too had lost its economic luster, and America once more led the world in innovation and economic efficiency, its budget balanced and unemployment at an all-time low. Then the bubble burst. In the fall of 2001 the economy was already in retreat when terrorists destroyed the World Trade Center towers and damaged the Pentagon. In the first half of 2002, moreover, as one disclosure of business malfeasance after another made the headlines, the whole concept of a breakthrough New Economy, and the inherent superiority of the American business model, was called into question.

In the new century the country also confronted a new enemy, Islamic terrorism. This adversary seemed more insidious and elusive than others in the past. As unchallenged leader in the post-Cold War era the United States had become the target of forces that deplored all that it seemed to represent in the modern world. America's new enemies, however, could not be confronted directly and it was unclear whether the trials ahead would not overtax the nation's patience and resolve. For a time, the ousting of the Taliban in Afghanistan seemed likely to strike a fatal blow to Osama bin Laden and Al-Qaeda. Then U.S. energies were deflected into an invasion of Iraq ostensibly to prevent development of weapons of mass destruction and to shut down a haven for terrorists. By mid-2006 a majority of Americans were convinced that the invasion of Iraq had been a mistake and was unlikely to make them more secure. Yet few had any idea how to disengage in Iraq without giving aid and comfort to terrorists and extremists around the world.

Meanwhile, the country faced severe internal social and cultural stresses as well. During the 1990s, demographic change, racial antagonisms, feminist activism—all churning for two decades—broke through to the surface. The America that appeared to be emerging—rancorous, exasperated, bigoted, at times violent—was not a pretty picture. For a time the events of September 11, 2001 jarred awake the nation's buried sense of its common identity. An overwhelming majority of Americans pledged anew their allegiance to the United States of America. But the mood did not last. Racial wounds and grievances reopened over the rescue efforts in the wake of hurricane Katrina. The culture issues promised to revive over the make-up of the Supreme Court. The resignation of Justice Sandra Day O'Connor and the death shortly thereafter of Chief Justice William Rehnquist reopened the issue of abortion, the relations of church and state, and the nature of federalism.

The future also promised to make economic inequality a new source of conflict. It appeared that the rich were getting richer and the relative economic progress of everyone else had stalled, if not reversed. Although the process had begun earlier, many critics blamed the Bush administration's tax policies and pro-business attitudes for the unfortunate trend.

In the end, however, it is impossible to tell how the uncertainties of the early twenty-first century will play out, for we, like every generation of Americans, can see the future only "through a glass darkly."

ONLINE RESOURCES

"The Gulf War" *http://www.pbs.org/wgbh/pages/frontline/gulf/* Read about the Gulf War commanders, read testimonies of American soldiers in combat, and learn about the events leading up to the invasion by consulting the timeline of events.

Appendix

The Declaration of Independence
The Unanimous Declaration of the Thirteen United States of America

When in the Course of human events, it becomes necessary for one people to dissolve the political bands which have connected them with another, and to assume among the powers of the earth, the separate and equal station to which the Laws of Nature and of Nature's God entitle them, a decent respect to the opinions of mankind requires that they should declare the causes which impel them to the separation.

We hold these truths to be self-evident, that all men are created equal, that they are endowed by their Creator with certain unalienable Rights, that among these are Life, Liberty, and the pursuit of Happiness.

That to secure these rights, Governments are instituted among Men, deriving their just powers from the consent of the governed.

That whenever any Form of Government becomes destructive of these ends, it is the Right of the People to alter or to abolish it, and to institute new Government, laying its foundation on such principles and organizing its powers in such form, as to them shall seem most likely to effect their Safety and Happiness. Prudence, indeed, will dictate that Governments long established should not be changed for light and transient causes; and accordingly all experience hath shewn, that mankind are more disposed to suffer, while evils are sufferable, than to right themselves by abolishing the forms to which they are accustomed.

But when a long train of abuses and usurpations, pursuing invariably the same Object evinces a design to reduce them under absolute Despotism, it is their right, it is their duty, to throw off such Government, and to provide new Guards for their future security.

Such has been the patient sufferance of these Colonies; and such is now the necessity which constrains them to alter their former Systems of Government. The history of the present King of Great Britain is a history of repeated injuries and usurpations, all having in direct object the establishment of an absolute Tyranny over these States. To prove this, let Facts be submitted to a candid world.

He has refused his Assent to Laws, the most wholesome and necessary for the public good.

He has forbidden his Governors to pass Laws of immediate and pressing importance, unless suspended in their operation till his Assent should be obtained; and when so suspended, he has utterly neglected to attend to them.

He has refused to pass other Laws for the accommodation of large districts of people, unless those people would relinquish the right of Representation in the Legislature, a right inestimable to them and formidable to tyrants only.

He has called together legislative bodies at places unusual, uncomfortable, and distant from the depository of their public Records, for the sole purpose of fatiguing them into compliance with his measures.

He has dissolved Representative Houses repeatedly, for opposing with manly firmness his invasions on the rights of the people.

He has refused for a long time, after such dissolutions, to cause others to be elected; whereby the Legislative powers, incapable of Annihilation, have returned to the People at large for their exercise; the State remaining in the mean time exposed to all the dangers of invasion from without, and convulsions within.

He has endeavoured to prevent the population of these States; for that purpose obstructing the Laws for Naturalization of Foreigners; refusing to pass others to encourage their migrations hither, and raising the conditions of new Appropriations of Lands.

He has obstructed the Administration of Justice, by refusing his Assent to Laws for establishing Judiciary powers.

He has made judges dependent on his Will alone, for the tenure of their offices, and the amount and payment of their salaries.

He has erected a multitude of New Offices, and sent hither swarms of Officers to harass our people, and eat out their substance.

He has kept among us, in times of peace, Standing Armies without the Consent of our legislatures.

He has affected to render the Military independent of and superior to the Civil power.

He has combined with others to subject us to a jurisdiction foreign to our constitution, and unacknowledged by our laws; giving his Assent to their Acts of pretended Legislation:

For quartering large bodies of armed troops among us:

For protecting them, by a mock Trial, from punishment for any Murders which they should commit on the Inhabitants of these States:

For cutting off our Trade with all parts of the world:

For imposing Taxes on us without our Consent:

For depriving us in many cases, of the benefits of Trial by Jury:

For transporting us beyond Seas to be tried for pretended offences:

For abolishing the free System of English Laws in a neighbouring Province, establishing therein an Arbitrary government, and enlarging its Boundaries so as to render it at once an example and fit instrument for introducing the same absolute rule into these Colonies:

For taking away our Charters, abolishing our most valuable Laws, and altering fundamentally the Forms of our Governments:

For suspending our own Legislatures, and declaring themselves invested with power to legislate for us in all cases whatsoever.

He has abdicated Government here, by declaring us out of his Protection and waging War against us.

He has plundered our seas, ravaged our Coasts, burnt our towns, and destroyed the Lives of our people.

He is at this time transporting large Armies of foreign Mercenaries to complete the works of death, desolation and tyranny, already begun with circumstances of Cruelty & perfidy scarcely paralleled in the most barbarous ages, and totally unworthy the Head of a civilized nation.

He has constrained our fellow Citizens taken Captive on the high Seas to bear Arms against their Country, to become the executioners of their friends and Brethren, or to fall themselves by their Hands.

He has excited domestic insurrections amongst us, and has endeavoured to bring on the inhabitants of our frontiers, the merciless Indian Savages, whose known rule of warfare, is an undistinguished destruction of all ages, sexes and conditions.

In every stage of these Oppressions We have Petitioned for Redress in the most humble terms: Our repeated Petitions have been answered only by repeated injury. A Prince, whose character is thus marked by every act which may define a Tyrant, is unfit to be the ruler of a free people.

Nor have We been wanting in attentions to our British brethren. We have warned them from time to time of attempts by their legislature to extend an unwarrantable jurisdiction over us. We have reminded them of the circumstances of our emigration and settlement here. We have appealed to their native justice and magnanimity, and we have conjured them by the ties of our common kindred to disavow these usurpations, which would inevitably interrupt our connections and correspondence. They too have been deaf to the voice of justice and of consanguinity. We must, therefore, acquiesce in the necessity, which denounces our Separation, and hold them, as we hold the rest of mankind, Enemies in War, in Peace Friends.

We, therefore, the Representatives of the United States of America, in General Congress, Assembled, appealing to the Supreme Judge of the world for the rectitude of our intentions, do, in the Name, and by Authority of the good People of these Colonies, solemnly publish and declare, That these United Colonies are, and of Right ought to be Free and Independent States; that they are Absolved from all Allegiance to the British Crown, and that all political connection between them and the State of Great Britain, is and ought to be totally dissolved; and that as Free and Independent States, they have full Power to levy War, conclude Peace, contract Alliances, establish Commerce, and to do all other Acts and Things which Independent States may of right do.

And for the support of this Declaration, with a firm reliance on the protection of divine Providence, we mutually pledge to each other our Lives, our Fortunes and our sacred Honor.

JOHN HANCOCK

NEW HAMPSHIRE
Josiah Bartlett
William Whipple
Matthew Thorton

MASSACHUSETTS BAY
Samuel Adams
John Adams
Robert Treat Paine
Elbridge Gerry

RHODE ISLAND
Stephen Hopkins
William Ellery

CONNECTICUT
Roger Sherman
Samuel Huntington
William Williams
Oliver Wolcott

NEW YORK
William Floyd
Philip Livingston
Francis Lewis
Lewis Morris

NEW JERSEY
Richard Stockton
John Witherspoon
Francis Hopkinson
John Hart
Abraham Clark

PENNSYLVANIA
Robert Morris
Benjamin Rush
Benjamin Franklin
John Morton
George Clymer
James Smith
George Taylor
James Wilson
George Ross

DELAWARE
Caesar Rodney
George Read
Thomas M'Kean

MARYLAND
Samuel Chase
William Paca
Thomas Stone
Charles Carroll,
    of Carrollton

VIRGINIA
George Wythe
Richard Henry Lee
Thomas Jefferson
Benjamin Harrison
Thomas Nelson, Jr.
Francis Lightfoot Lee
Carter Braxton

NORTH CAROLINA
William Hooper
Joseph Hewes
John Penn

SOUTH CAROLINA
Edward Rutledge
Thomas Heyward, Jr.
Thomas Lynch, Jr.
Arthur Middleton

GEORGIA
Button Gwinnett
Lyman Hall
George Walton

Resolved.   *That copies of the Declaration be sent to the several assemblies, conventions, and committees or councils of safety, and to the several commanding officers of the continental troops; that it be proclaimed in each of the United States, at the head of the army.*

The Constitution of the United States of America

PREAMBLE

We the People of the United States, in Order to form a more perfect Union, establish Justice, insure domestic Tranquility, provide for the common defence, promote the general Welfare, and secure the Blessings of Liberty to ourselves and our Posterity, do ordain and establish this Constitution for the United States of America.

ARTICLE I

Section 1. All legislative Powers herein granted shall be vested in a Congress of the United States, which shall consist of a Senate and House of Representatives.

Section 2. The House of Representatives shall be composed of Members chosen every second Year by the People of the several States, and the Electors in each State shall have the Qualifications requisite for Electors of the most numerous Branch of the State Legislature.

No Person shall be a Representative who shall not have attained to the Age of twenty-five Years, and been seven years a Citizen of the United States, and who shall not, when elected, be an Inhabitant of that State in which he shall be chosen.

Representatives and direct Taxes shall be apportioned among the several States which may be included within this Union, according to their respective Numbers. [which shall be determined by adding to the whole Number of free Persons, including those bound to Service for a Term of Years, and excluding Indians not taxed, three fifths of all other Persons.][1] The actual Enumeration shall be made within three Years after the first Meeting of the Congress of the United States, and within every subsequent Term of ten Years, in such Manner as they shall by Law direct. The Number of Representatives shall not exceed one for every thirty Thousand, but each State shall have at Least one Representative; and until such enumeration shall be made, the State of New Hampshire shall be entitled to chuse three; Massachusetts eight; Rhode Island and Providence Plantations one; Connecticut five; New York six; New Jersey four; Pennsylvania eight; Delaware one; Maryland six; Virginia ten; North Carolina five; South Carolina five; and Georgia three.

When vacancies happen in the Representation from any State, the Executive Authority thereof shall issue Writs of Election to fill such Vacancies.

The House of Representatives shall chuse their Speaker and other Officers; and shall have the sole Power of Impeachment.

Section 3. The Senate of the United States, shall be composed of two Senators from each state, [chosen by the Legislature thereof,][2] for six Years; and each Senator shall have one Vote.

Immediately after they shall be assembled in Consequence of the first Election, they shall be divided as equally as may be into three Classes. The Seats of the Senators of the first Class shall be vacated at the Expiration of the second year, of the second Class at the Expiration of the fourth Year, and of the third Class at the Expiration of the sixth Year, so that one third may be chosen every second Year; [and if Vacancies happen by Resignation, or otherwise, during the Recess of the Legislature of any State, the Executive thereof may make temporary Appointments until the next Meeting of the Legislature, which shall then fill such Vacancies.][3]

---

[1]Bracketed material superseded by Section 2 of the Fourteenth Amendment.

[2]Bracketed material superseded by Clause 1 of the Seventeenth Amendment.

[3]Bracketed material modified by Clause 2 of the Seventeenth Amendment.

No Person shall be a Senator who shall not have attained to the Age of thirty Years, and been nine Years a Citizen of the United States, and who shall not, when elected, be an Inhabitant of that State for which he shall be chosen.

The Vice-President of the United States shall be President of the Senate, but shall have no Vote, unless they be equally divided.

The Senate shall chuse their other Officers, and also a President pro tempore, in the Absence of the Vice-President, or when he shall exercise the Office of President of the United States.

The Senate shall have the sole Power to try all Impeachments. When sitting for that Purpose, they shall be on Oath or Affirmation. When the President of the United States is tried, the Chief Justice shall preside: And no Person shall be convicted without the Concurrence of two thirds of the Members present.

Judgment in Cases of Impeachment shall not extend further than to removal from Office, and disqualification to hold and enjoy any Office of honor, Trust or Profit under the United States: but the Party convicted shall nevertheless be liable and subject to Indictment, Trial, Judgment and Punishment, according to Law.

Section 4. The Times, Places and Manner of holding Elections for Senators and Representatives, shall be prescribed in each State by the legislature thereof; but the Congress may at any time by Law make or alter such Regulations, except as to the Places of chusing Senators.

[The Congress shall assemble at least once in every Year, and such Meeting shall be on the first Monday in December, unless they shall by Law appoint a different Day.]⁴

Section 5. Each House shall be the Judge of the Elections, Returns and Qualifications of its own Members, and a Majority of each shall constitute a Quorum to do Business; but a smaller Number may adjourn from day to day, and may be authorized to compel the Attendance of absent Members, in such Manner, and under such Penalties as each House may provide.

Each House may determine the Rules of its Proceedings, punish its Members for disorderly Behaviour, and, with the Concurrence of two thirds, expel a Member.

Each House shall keep a Journal of its Proceedings, and from time to time publish the same, excepting such Parts as may in their Judgment require Secrecy; and the Yeas and Nays of the Members of either House on any questions shall, at the Desire of one fifth of those Present, be entered on the Journal.

Neither House, during the Session of Congress, shall, without the Consent of the other, adjourn for more than three days, nor to any other Place than that in which the two Houses shall be sitting.

Section 6. The Senators and Representatives shall receive a Compensation for their Services, to be ascertained by Law, and paid out of the Treasury of the United States. They shall in all Cases, except Treason, Felony and Breach of the Peace, be privileged from Arrest during their Attendance at the Session of their respective Houses, and in going to and returning from the same; and for any Speech or Debate in either House, they shall not be questioned in any other Place.

No Senator or Representative shall, during the Time for which he was elected, be appointed to any civil Office under the Authority of the United States, which shall have been created, or the Emoluments whereof shall have been encreased during such time; and no Person holding any Office under the United States, shall be a Member of either House during his Continuance in Office.

Section 7. All Bills for raising Revenue shall Originate in the House of Representatives; but the Senate may propose or concur with Amendments as on other Bills.

Every Bill which shall have passed the House of Representatives and the Senate, shall, before it becomes a Law, be presented to the President of the United States; If he approve he shall sign it, but if not he shall

---

⁴Bracketed material superseded by Section 2 of the Twentieth Amendment.

return it, with his Objections to that House in which it shall have originated, who shall enter the Objections at large on their Journal, and proceed to reconsider it. If after such Reconsideration two thirds of that House shall agree to pass the Bill, it shall be sent, together with the Objections, to the other House, by which it shall likewise be reconsidered, and if approved by two thirds of that House, it shall become a Law. But in all such Cases the Votes of both Houses shall be determined by Yeas and Nays, and the Names of the Persons voting for and against the Bill shall be entered on the Journal of each House respectively. If any Bill shall not be returned by the President within Ten Days (Sundays excepted) after it shall have been presented to him, the Same shall be a Law, in like Manner as if he had signed it, unless the Congress by their Adjournment prevents its Return, in which Case it shall not be a Law.

Every Order, Resolution, or Vote to which the Concurrence of the Senate and House of Representatives may be necessary (except on a question of Adjournment) shall be presented to the President of the United States; and before the Same shall take effect, shall be approved by him, or being disapproved by him, shall be repassed by two thirds of the Senate and House of Representatives, according to the Rules and Limitations prescribed in the Case of Bill.

Section 8. The Congress shall have Power To lay and collect Taxes, Duties, Imposts, and Excises, to pay the Debts and provide for the common Defence and general Welfare of the United States; but all Duties, Imposts and Excises shall be uniform throughout the United States;

To borrow Money on the credit of the United States;

To regulate Commerce with foreign Nations, and among the several States, and with the Indian Tribes;

To establish an uniform Rule of Naturalization, and uniform Laws on the subject of Bankruptcies throughout the United States;

To coin Money, regulate the Value thereof, and of foreign Coin, and fix the Standard of Weights and Measures;

To provide for the Punishment of counterfeiting the Securities and current Coin of the United States;

To establish Post Offices and post Roads;

To promote the Progress of Science and useful Arts, by securing for limited Times to Authors and Inventors the exclusive Right to their respective Writings and Discoveries;

To constitute Tribunals inferior to the supreme Court;

To define and punish Piracies and Felonies committed on the high Seas, and Offences against the Law of Nations;

To declare War, grant Letters of Marque and Reprisal, and make Rules concerning Captures on Land and Water;

To raise and support Armies; but no Appropriation of Money to that Use shall be for a longer Term than two years;

To provide and maintain a Navy;

To make Rules for the Government and Regulation of the land and naval Forces;

To provide for calling forth the Militia to execute the laws of the Union, suppress Insurrections and repel Invasions;

To provide for organizing, arming, and disciplining, the Militia, and for governing such Part of them as may be employed in the Service of the United States, reserving to the States respectively, the Appointment of the Officers, and the Authority of training the Militia according to the discipline prescribed by Congress;

To exercise exclusive Legislation in all Cases whatsoever, over such District (not exceeding ten Miles square) as may, by Cession of particular States, and the Acceptance of Congress, become the Seat of the Government of the United States, and to exercise like Authority over all Places purchased by the Consent of the Legislature of the State in which the Same shall be, for the Erection of Forts, Magazines, Arsenals, dock-Yards, and other needful Buildings;—And

To make all Laws which shall be necessary and proper for carrying into Execution the foregoing Powers, and all other Powers vested by this Constitution in the Government of the United States, or in any Department or Officer thereof.

Section 9. The Migration or Importation of such Persons as any of the States now existing shall think proper to admit, shall not be prohibited by the Congress prior to the year one thousand eight hundred and eight, but a Tax or duty may be imposed on such Importation, not exceeding ten dollars for each Person.

The Privilege of the Writ of Habeas Corpus shall not be suspended, unless when in Cases of Rebellion or Invasion the public Safety may require it.

No Bill of Attainder or ex post facto Law shall be passed.

No Capitation, or other direct, Tax shall be laid, unless in Proportion to the Census or Enumeration herein before directed to be taken.[5]

No Tax or Duty shall be laid on Articles exported from any State.

No Preferences shall be given by any Regulation of Commerce or Revenue to the Ports of one State over those of another; nor shall Vessels bound to, or from, one State, be obliged to enter, clear, or pay Duties in another.

No Money shall be drawn from the Treasury, but in Consequence of Appropriations made by Law; and a regular Statement and Account of the Receipts and Expenditures of all public Money shall be published from time to time.

No Title of Nobility shall be granted by the United States: And no person holding any office of Profit or Trust under them, shall, without the Consent of the Congress, accept of any present, Emolument, Office, or Title, of any kind whatever, from any King, Prince, or foreign State.

Section 10. No State shall enter into any Treaty, Alliance, or Confederation; grant Letters of Marque and Reprisal; coin Money; emit Bills of Credit; make any Thing but gold and silver Coin a Tender in Payment of Debts; pass any Bill of Attainder, ex post facto Law, or Law impairing the Obligation of Contracts, or grant any Title of Nobility.

No State shall, without the Consent of the Congress, lay any Imposts or Duties on Imports or Exports, except what may be absolutely necessary for executing its inspection Laws: and the net Produce of all Duties and Imposts, laid by any State on Imports or Exports, shall be for the Use of the Treasury of the United States; and all such Laws shall be subject to the Revision and Control of the Congress.

No State shall, without the Consent of Congress, lay any Duty of Tonnage, keep Troops, or Ships of War in time of Peace, enter into any Agreement or Compact with another State, or with a foreign Power, or engage in War, unless actually invaded, or in such imminent Danger as will not admit of delay.

ARTICLE II

Section 1. The executive Power shall be vested in a President of the United States of America. He shall hold his Office during the Term of four Years, and, together with the Vice-President, chosen for the same Term, be elected, as follows.

Each State shall appoint, in such Manner as the Legislature thereof may direct, a Number of Electors, equal to the whole Number of Senators and Representative to which the State may be entitled in the Congress; but no Senator or Representative, or Person holding an Office of Trust or Profit under the United States, shall be appointed an Elector.

[The Electors shall meet in their respective States, and vote by Ballot for two Persons, of whom one at least shall not be an Inhabitant of the same State with themselves. And they shall make a List of all the Persons voted for, and of the Number of Votes for each; which List they shall sign and certify, and transmit sealed to the Seat of the Government of the United States, directed to the President of the Senate. The President of the Senate shall, in the Presence of the Senate and House of Representatives, open all the Certificates, and the Votes shall then be counted. The Person having the

---

[5]Modified by the Sixteenth Amendment.

greatest Number of Votes shall be the President, if such Number be a Majority of the whole Number of Electors appointed; and if there be more than one who have such Majority, and have an equal Number of Votes, then the House of Representatives shall immediately chuse by Ballot one of them for President; and if no Person have a Majority, then from the five highest on the List the said House shall in like Manner chuse the President. But in chusing the President, the Votes shall be taken by States, the Representation from each State having one Vote; A quorum for this Purpose shall consist of a Member or Members from two thirds of the States, and a Majority of all the States shall be necessary to a Choice. In every Case, after the Choice of the President, the Person having the greatest Number of Votes of the Electors shall be the Vice-President. But if there should remain two or more who have equal Votes, the Senate shall chuse from them by Ballot the Vice-President.][6]

The Congress may determine the Time of chusing the Electors, and the Day on which they shall give their Votes; which Day shall be the same throughout the United States.

No Person except a natural born Citizen, or a Citizen of the United States, at the time of the Adoption of this Constitution, shall be eligible to the Office of President; neither shall any Person be eligible to that Office who shall not have attained to the Age of thirty-five Years, and been fourteen Years a Resident within the United States.

[In Case of Removal of the President from Office, or of this Death, Resignation, or Inability to discharge the Powers and Duties of the said Office, the Same shall devolve on the Vice-President, and the Congress may by law provide for the Case of Removal, Death, Resignation or Inability, both of the President and Vice-President, declaring what Officer shall then act as President, and such Officer shall act accordingly, until the Disability be removed, or a President shall be elected.][7]

The President shall, at stated Times, receive for his Services, a Compensation, which shall neither be encreased nor diminished during the Period for which he shall have been elected, and he shall not receive within that Period any other Emolument from the United States, or any of them.

Before he enter on the Execution of his Office; he shall take the following Oath or Affirmation—"I do solemnly swear (or affirm) that I will faithfully execute the Office of the President of the United States, and will to the best of my Ability, preserve, protect and defend the Constitution of the United States."

Section 2. The President shall be Commander in Chief of the Army and Navy of the United States, and of the Militia of the several States, when called into the actual Service of the United States; he may require the Opinion, in writing, of the principal Office in each of the executive Departments upon any Subject relating to the Duties of their respective Offices, and he shall have Power to grant Reprieves and Pardons for Offences against the United States, except in Cases of Impeachment.

He shall have Power, by and with the Advice and Consent of the Senate, to make Treaties, provided two thirds of the Senators present concur, and he shall nominate, and by and with the Advice and Consent of the Senate, shall appoint Ambassadors, other public Ministers and Consuls, Judges of the supreme Court, and all other Officers of the United States, whose Appointments are not herein otherwise provided for, and which shall be established by Law; but the Congress may by Law vest the Appointment of such inferior Officers, as they think proper, in the Presidents alone, in the Courts of Law, or in the Heads of Departments.

The President shall have Power to fill up all Vacancies that may happen during

---

[6]Bracketed material superseded by the Twelfth Amendment.

[7]Bracketed material modified by the Twenty-fifth Amendment.

the Recess of the Senate, by granting Commissions which shall expire at the End of their next Session.

Section 3. He shall from time to time give to the Congress Information of the State of the Union, and recommend to their Consideration such Measures as he shall judge necessary and expedient; he may, on extraordinary Occasions, convene both Houses, or either of them, and in Case of Disagreement between them, with Respect to the Time of Adjournment, he may adjourn them to such Time as he shall think proper; he shall receive Ambassadors and other public Ministers; he shall take Care that the Laws be faithfully executed, and shall Commission all the Officers of the United States.

Section 4. The President, Vice-President and all civil Officers of the United States, shall be removed from Office on Impeachment for, and Conviction of, Treason, Bribery, or other high Crimes and Misdemeanors.

ARTICLE III

Section 1. The judicial Power of the United States, shall be vested in one supreme Court, and in such inferior Courts as the Congress may from time to time ordain and establish. The Judges, both of the supreme and inferior Courts, shall hold their Offices during good Behaviour, and shall, at stated Times, receive for their Services, a Compensation, which shall not be diminished during their Continuance in Office.

Section 2. The judicial Power shall extend to all Cases, in Law and Equity, arising under this Constitution, the Laws of the United States, and Treaties made, or which shall be made, under their Authority;—to all Cases affecting Ambassadors, other public Ministers and Consuls;—to all Cases of admiralty and maritime Jurisdiction;—To Controversies to which the United States shall be a Party;—to Controversies between two or more States;—between a State and Citizens of another State;—between Citizens of different States;—between Citizens of the same State claiming Lands under Grants of different States, and between a State, or the Citizens thereof, and foreign States, Citizens or Subjects.[8]

In all Cases affecting Ambassadors, other public Ministers and Consuls, and those in which a State shall be Party, the supreme Court shall have original Jurisdiction. In all the other Cases before mentioned the supreme Court shall have appellate Jurisdiction, both as to Law and Fact, with such Exceptions, and under such Regulations as the Congress shall make.

The Trial of all Crimes, except in Cases of Impeachment, shall be by Jury; and such Trial shall be held in the State where the said Crimes shall have been committed; but when not committed within any State, the Trial shall be at such Place or Places as the Congress may by Law have directed.

Section 3. Treason against the United States, shall consist only in levying War against them, or in adhering to their Enemies, giving them Aid and Comfort. No Person shall be convicted of Treason unless on the Testimony of two Witnesses to the same overt Act, or on Confession in open Court.

The Congress shall have Power to declare the Punishment of Treason, but no Attainder of Treason shall work Corruption of Blood, or Forfeiture except during the Life of the person attained.

ARTICLE IV

Section 1. Full Faith and Credit shall be given in each State to the public Acts, Records, and judicial Proceedings of every other State. And the Congress may by general Laws prescribe the Manner in which such Acts, Records and Proceedings shall be proved, and the Effect thereof.

Section 2. The Citizens of each State shall be entitled to all Privileges and Immunities of Citizens in the several States.

A Person charged in any State with Treason, Felony, or other Crime, who shall flee from Justice, and be found in another

---

[8]This paragraph modified in part by the Eleventh Amendment.

State, shall on Demand of the executive Authority of the State of which he fled, be delivered up, to be removed to the State having Jurisdiction of the Crime.

[No Person held to Service or Labour in one State, under the Laws thereof, escaping into another, shall, in Consequence of any Law or Regulation therein, be discharged from such Service or Labour, but shall be delivered up on Claim of the Party to whom such Service or Labour may be due.][9]

Section 3. New States may be admitted by the Congress into this Union; but no new State shall be formed or erected within the Jurisdiction of any other State; nor any State be formed by the Junction of two or more States, or Parts of States, without the Consent of the Legislatures of the States concerned as well as of the Congress.

The Congress shall have Power to dispose of and make all needful Rules and Regulations respecting the Territory or other property belonging to the United States; and nothing in this Constitution shall be so construed as to Prejudice any Claims of the United States, or of any particular State.

Section 4. The United States shall guarantee to every State in this Union a Republican Form of Government, and shall protect each of them against Invasion; and on Application of the Legislature, or of the Executive (when the Legislative cannot be convened) against domestic Violence.

ARTICLE V

The Congress, whenever two thirds of both Houses shall deem it necessary, shall propose Amendments to this Constitution, or, on the Application of the legislatures of two thirds of the several States, shall call a Convention for proposing Amendments, which, in either Case, shall be valid to all Intents and Purposes, as Part of this Constitution, when ratified by the Legislatures of three fourths of the several States, or by Conventions in three fourths thereof, as the one or

the other Mode of Ratification may be proposed by the Congress; Provided that no Amendment which may be made prior to the Year One thousand eight hundred and eight shall in any Manner affect the first and fourth Clauses in the Ninth Section of the first Article; and that no State, without its Consent, shall be deprived of its equal Suffrage in the Senate.

ARTICLE VI

All Debts contracted and Engagements entered into, before the Adoption of this Constitution, shall be as valid against the United States under this Constitution, as under the Confederation.

This Constitution, and the Laws of the United States which shall be made in Pursuance thereof; and all Treaties made, or which shall be made, under the Authority of the United States, shall be the supreme Law of the Land; and the Judges in every State shall be bound thereby, any Thing in the Constitution or Laws of any State to the Contrary notwithstanding.

The Senators and Representatives before mentioned, and the members of the several State Legislatures, and all executive and judicial Officers, both of the United States and of the several States, shall be bound by Oath or Affirmation, to support this Constitution; but no religious Test shall ever be required as a Qualification to any Office or public Trust under the United States.

ARTICLE VII

The Ratification of the Conventions of nine States, shall be sufficient for the Establishment of this Constitution between the States so ratifying the Same.

DONE in Convention by the Unanimous Consent of the States present the Seventeenth Day of September in the Year of our Lord one thousand seven hundred and eighty seven and of the Independence of the United States of America the Twelfth. IN WITNESS whereof We have hereunto subscribed our Names.

---

[9]Bracketed material superseded by the Thirteenth Amendment.

GEORGE WASHINGTON—*President and deputy from Virginia*

NEW HAMPSHIRE
John Langdon
Nicholas Gilman

CONNECTICUT
William Samuel
*   Johnson*
Roger Sherman

NEW YORK
Alexander Hamilton

NEW JERSEY
William Livingston
David Brearley
William Paterson
Jonathan Dayton

PENNSYLVANIA
Benjamin Franklin
Thomas Mifflin
Robert Morris
George Clymer
Thomas FitzSimons
Jared Ingersoll
James Wilson
Gouverneur Morris

DELAWARE
George Read
Gunning Bedford, Jr.
John Dickinson
Richard Bassett
Jacob Broom

MASSACHUSETTS
Nathaniel Gorham
Rufus King

MARYLAND
James McHenry
Daniel of St. Thomas
*   Jenifer*
Daniel Carroll

VIRGINIA
John Blair
James Madison, Jr.

NORTH CAROLINA
William Blount
Richard Dobbs
*   Spaight*
Hugh Williamson

SOUTH CAROLINA
John Rutledge
Charles Cotesworth
*   Pinckney*
Charles Pinckney
Pierce Butler

GEORGIA
William Few
Abraham Baldwin

Attest: William
   Jackson, *Secretary*

THE AMENDMENTS

ARTICLES in addition to, and Amendment of the Constitution of the United States of America, proposed by Congress, and ratified by the Legislatures of the several States, pursuant to the fifth Article of the original Constitution.

ARTICLE I

[Articles I through X, now known as the Bill of Rights, were proposed on September 25, 1789, and declared in force on December 15, 1791.]

Congress shall make no law respecting an establishment of religion, or prohibiting the free exercise thereof; or abridging the freedom of speech, or of the press; or the right of the people peaceably to assemble, and to petition the Government for a redress of grievances.

ARTICLE II

A well regulated Militia, being necessary to the security of a free State, the right of the people to keep and bear Arms, shall not be infringed.

ARTICLE III

No Soldier shall, in time of peace be quartered in any house, without the consent of the Owner, nor in time of war, but in manner to be prescribed by law.

ARTICLE IV

The right of the people to be secure in their persons, houses, papers, and effects, against unreasonable searches and seizures, shall not be violated, and no Warrants shall issue, but upon probable cause, supported by Oath or affirmation, and particularly describing the place to be searched, and the persons or things to be seized.

ARTICLE V

No person shall be held to answer for a capital, or otherwise infamous crime, unless on a presentment or indictment of a Grand Jury, except in cases arising in the land or naval forces, or in the Militia, when in actual service in time of War or public danger; nor shall any person be subject for the same offence to be twice put in jeopardy of life or limb; nor shall be compelled in any criminal case to be a witness against himself, nor be deprived of life, liberty, or property, without due process of law; nor shall private property be taken for public use, without just compensation.

ARTICLE VI

In all criminal prosecutions, the accused shall enjoy the right to a speedy and public trial, by an impartial jury of the State and district wherein the crime shall have been committed, which district shall have been previously ascertained by law, and to be informed of the nature and cause of the accusation; to be confronted with the witnesses against him; to have compulsory process for obtaining witnesses in his favor, and to have the Assistance of Counsel for his defence.

ARTICLE VII

In Suits at common law, where the value in controversy shall exceed twenty dollars, the right of trial by jury shall be preserved, and no fact tried by a jury shall be otherwise reexamined in any Court of the United States, than according to the rules of the common law.

ARTICLE VIII

Excessive bail shall not be required, nor excessive fines imposed, nor cruel and unusual punishments inflicted.

ARTICLE IX

The enumeration in the Constitution, of certain rights, shall not be construed to deny or disparage others retained by the people.

ARTICLE X

The powers not delegated to the United States by the Constitution, nor prohibited by it to the States, are reserved to the States respectively, or to the people.

ARTICLE XI

[Proposed March 4, 1794; declared ratified January 8, 1798]

The Judicial power of the United States shall not be construed to extend to any suit in law or equity, commenced or prosecuted against one of the United States by Citizens of another State, or by Citizens or Subjects of any Foreign State.

ARTICLE XII

[Proposed December 9, 1803; declared ratified September 25, 1804]

The Electors shall meet in their respective states and vote by ballot for President and Vice-President, one of whom, at least, shall not be an inhabitant of the same state with themselves; they shall name in their ballots the person voted for as President, and in distinct ballots the person voted for as Vice-President, and they shall make distinct lists of all persons voted for as President, and of all persons voted for as Vice-President, and of the number of votes for each, which lists they shall sign and certify, and transmit sealed to the seat of the government of the United States, directed to the President of the Senate;—The President of the Senate shall, in the presence of the Senate and House of Representatives, open all the certificates and the votes shall then be counted;—The person having the greatest number of votes for President, shall be the President, if such number be a majority of the whole number of Electors appointed; and if no person have such majority, then from the persons having the highest numbers not exceeding three on the list of those voted for as President, the House of Representatives shall choose immediately, by ballot, the President. But in choosing the President, the votes shall be taken by states, the representation from each state having one vote; a quorum for this purpose shall consist of a member or members from two-thirds of the states, and a majority of all the states shall be necessary to a choice. [And if the House of Representatives shall not choose a President whenever the right of choice shall devolve upon them, before the fourth day of March next following, then the Vice-President shall act as President, as in the case of the death or other constitutional disability of the President.][10]—The person having the greatest number of votes as Vice-President, shall be the Vice-President, if such number be a majority of the whole number of Electors appointed and if no person have a majority; then from the two highest numbers on the list, the Senate shall choose the Vice-President; a quorum for the purpose

---

[10]Bracketed material superseded by Section 3 of the Twentieth Amendment.

shall consist of two-thirds of the whole number of Senators, and a majority of the whole number shall be necessary to a choice. But no person constitutionally ineligible to the office of President shall be eligible to that of Vice-President of the United States.

ARTICLE XIII

[Proposed January 31, 1865; declared ratified December 18, 1865]

Section 1. Neither slavery nor involuntary servitude, except as a punishment for crime whereof the party shall have been duly convicted, shall exist within the United States, or any place subject to their jurisdiction.

Section 2. Congress shall have power to enforce this article by appropriate legislation.

ARTICLE XIV

[Proposed June 13, 1866; declared ratified July 28, 1868]

Section 1. All persons born or naturalized in the United States, and subject to the jurisdiction thereof, are citizens of the United States and of the State wherein they reside. No State shall make or enforce any law which shall abridge the privileges or immunities of citizens of the United States; nor shall any State deprive any person of life, liberty, or property, without due process of law; nor deny to any person within its jurisdiction the equal protection of the laws.

Section 2. Representatives shall be apportioned among the several States according to their respective numbers, counting the whole number of persons in each State, excluding Indians not taxed. But when the right to vote at any election for the choice of electors for President and Vice-President of the United States, Representatives in Congress, the Executive and Judicial officers of a State or the members of the Legislature thereof, is denied to any of the male inhabitants of such State, being twenty-one years of age, and citizens of the United States, or in any way abridged, except for participation in rebellion, or other crime, the basis of representation therein shall be reduced in the proportion which the number of such male citizens shall bear to the whole number of male citizens twenty-one years of age in such State.

Section 3. No person shall be a Senator or Representative in Congress, or elector of President and Vice-President, or hold any office, civil or military, under the United States, or under any State, who, having previously taken an oath as a member of Congress, or as an officer of the United States, or as a member of any State legislature, or as an executive or judicial officer of any state, to support the Constitution of the United States, shall have engaged in insurrection or rebellion against the same, or given aid or comfort to the enemies thereof. But Congress may by a vote of two-thirds of each House, remove such disability.

Section 4. The validity of the public debt of the United States, authorized by law, including debts incurred for payments of pensions and bounties for services in suppressing insurrection or rebellion, shall not be questioned. But neither the United States nor any State shall assume or pay any debt or obligation incurred in aid of insurrection or rebellion against the United States, or any claim for the loss or emancipation of any slave; but all such debts, obligations and claims shall be held illegal and void.

Section 5. The Congress shall have power to enforce, by appropriate legislations, the provisions of this article.

ARTICLE XV

[Proposed February 26, 1869; declared ratified March 30, 1870]

Section 1. The right of citizens of the United States to vote shall not be denied or abridged by the United States or by any State on account of race, color, or previous condition of servitude.

Section 2. The Congress shall have power to enforce this article by appropriate legislation.

ARTICLE XVI

[Proposed July 12, 1909; declared ratified February 25, 1913]

The Congress shall have power to lay and collect taxes on incomes, from whatever source derived, without apportionment among the several States, and without regard to any census or enumeration.

ARTICLE XVII

[Proposed May 13, 1912; declared ratified May 31, 1913]

The Senate of the United States shall be composed of two Senators from each State, elected by the people thereof, for six years; and each Senator shall have one vote. The electors in each State shall have the qualifications requisite for electors of the most numerous branch of the State legislatures.

When vacancies happen in the representation of any State in the Senate, the executive authority of such State shall issue writs of election to fill such vacancies: *Provided,* That the legislature of any State may empower the executive thereof to make temporary appointments until the people fill the vacancies by election as the legislature may direct.

This amendment shall not be so construed as to affect the election or term of any Senator chosen before it becomes valid as part of the Constitution.

ARTICLE XVIII

[Proposed December 18, 1917; declared ratified January 29, 1919; repealed by the Twenty-first Amendment December 5, 1933]

Section 1. After one year from the ratification of this article the manufacture, sale, or transportation of intoxicating liquors within, the importation thereof into, or the exportation thereof from the United States and all territory subject to the jurisdiction thereof for beverage purposes is hereby prohibited.

Section 2. The Congress and the several States shall have concurrent power to enforce this article by appropriate legislation.

Section 3. This article shall be inoperative unless it shall have been ratified as an amendment to the Constitution by the legislatures of the several States, as provided in the Constitution, within seven years from the date of the submission hereof to the States by the Congress.

ARTICLE XIX

[Proposed June 4, 1919; declared ratified August 26, 1920]

The right of citizens of the United States to vote shall not be denied or abridged by the United States or by any State on account of sex.

Congress shall have power to enforce this article by appropriate legislation.

ARTICLE XX

[Proposed March 2, 1932; declared ratified February 6, 1933]

Section 1. The terms of the President and Vice-President shall end at noon on the 20th day of January, and the terms of Senators and Representatives at noon on the 3d day of January, of the years in which such terms would have ended if this article had not been ratified; and the terms of their successors shall then begin.

Section 2. The Congress shall assemble at least once in every year, and such meeting shall begin at noon on the 3d day of January, unless they shall by law appoint a different day.

Section 3. If, at the time fixed for the beginning of the term of the President, the President elect shall have died, the Vice-President elect shall become President. If a President shall not have been chosen before the time fixed for the beginning of his term, or if the President elect shall have failed to qualify, then the Vice-President elect shall act as President until a President shall have qualified; and the Congress may by law provide for the case wherein neither a President elect nor a Vice-President elect shall have qualified, declaring who shall then act as President, or the manner in which one who is to act shall be elected, and such person shall act accordingly until a President or Vice-President shall have qualified.

Section 4. The Congress may by law provide for the case of the death of any of the persons from whom the House of Representatives may choose a President whenever the right of choice shall have devolved upon them, and for the case of the death of any of the persons from whom the Senate may choose a Vice-President whenever the right of choice shall have devolved upon them.

Section 5. Sections 1 and 2 shall take effect on the 15th day of October following the ratification of this article.

Section 6. This article shall be inoperative unless it shall have been ratified as an amendment to the Constitution by the legislatures of three-fourths of the several States within seven years from the date of its submission.

ARTICLE XXI

[Proposed February 20, 1933; declared ratified December 5, 1933]

Section 1. The eighteenth article of amendment to the Constitution of the United States is hereby repealed.

Section 2. The transportation or importation into any State, Territory, or possession of the United States for delivery or use therein of intoxicating liquors, in violation of the laws thereof, is hereby prohibited.

Section 3. This article shall be inoperative unless it shall have been ratified as an amendment to the Constitution by conventions in the several States, as provided in the Constitution, within seven years from the date of the submission hereof to the States by the Congress.

ARTICLE XXII

[Proposed March 24, 1947; declared ratified March 1, 1951]

Section 1. No person shall be elected to the office of the President more than twice, and no person who has held the office of President, or acted as President, for more than two years of a term to which some other person was elected President shall be elected to the office of the President more than once. But this Article shall not apply to any person holding the office of President when this Article was proposed by the Congress, and shall not prevent any person who may be holding the office of President, or acting as

President, during the term within which this Article becomes operative from holding the office of President or acting as President during the remainder of such term.

Section 2. This article shall be inoperative unless it shall have been ratified as an amendment to the Constitution by the legislatures of three-fourths of the several States within seven years from the date of its submission to the States by the Congress.

ARTICLE XXIII

[Proposed June 16, 1960; declared ratified April 3, 1961]

Section 1. The District constituting the seat of Government of the United States shall appoint in such manner as the Congress may direct:

A number of electors of President and Vice-President equal to the whole number of Senators and Representatives in Congress to which the District would be entitled if it were a State, but in no event more than the least populous state; they shall be in addition to those appointed by the States, but they shall be considered, for the purposes of the election of President and Vice-President, to be electors appointed by a State; and they shall meet in the District and perform such duties as provided by the twelfth article of amendment.

Section 2. The Congress shall have power to enforce this article by appropriate legislation.

ARTICLE XXIV

[Proposed August 27, 1962; declared ratified February 4, 1964]

Section 1. The right of citizens of the United States to vote in any primary or other election for President or Vice-President, for electors for President or Vice-President, or for Senator or Representative in Congress, shall not be denied or abridged by the United States or any State by reason of failure to pay any poll tax or other tax.

Section 2. The Congress shall have power to enforce this article by appropriate legislation.

ARTICLE XXV

[Proposed July 6, 1965; declared ratified February 23, 1967]

Section 1. In case of removal of the President from office or of his death or resignation, the Vice-President shall become President.

Section 2. Whenever there is a vacancy in the office of the Vice-President, the President shall nominate a Vice-President who shall take office upon confirmation by a majority vote of both Houses of Congress.

Section 3. Whenever the President transmits to the President pro tempore of the Senate and the Speaker of the House of Representatives his written declaration that he is unable to discharge the powers and duties of his office, and until he transmits to them a written declaration to the contrary, such powers and duties shall be discharged by the Vice-President as Acting President.

Section 4. Whenever the Vice-President and a majority of either the principal officers of the executive departments or of such other body as Congress may by law provide, transmit to the President pro tempore of the Senate and the Speaker of the House of Representatives their written declaration that the President is unable to discharge the powers and duties of his office, the Vice-President shall immediately assume the powers and duties of the office as Acting President.

Thereafter, when the President transmits to the President pro tempore of the Senate and the Speaker of the House of Representatives his written declaration that no inability exists, he shall resume the powers and duties of his office unless the Vice-President and a majority of either the principal officers of the executive department or of such other body as Congress may by law provide, transmit within four days to the President pro tempore of the Senate and the Speaker of the House of Representatives their written declaration that the President is unable to discharge the powers and duties of his office. Thereupon Congress shall decide the issue, assembling within forty-eight hours for that purpose if not in session. If the Congress, within twenty-one days after receipt of the latter written declaration, or, if Congress is not in session, within twenty-one days after Congress is required to assemble, determines by two-thirds vote of both Houses that the President is unable to discharge the power and duties of his office, the Vice-President shall continue to discharge the same as Acting President; otherwise, the President shall resume the powers and duties of his office.

ARTICLE XXVI

[Proposed March 23, 1971; declared ratified July 5, 1971]

Section 1. The right of citizens of the United States, who are eighteen years of age or older, to vote shall not be denied or abridged by the United States or by any State on account of age.

Section 2. The Congress shall have power to enforce this article by appropriate legislation.

Presidential Elections

Year	Candidates Receiving More than One Percent of the Vote (Parties)	Popular Vote	Electoral Vote
1789	GEORGE WASHINGTON (No party designations)		69
	John Adams		34
	Other Candidates		35
1792	GEORGE WASHINGTON (No party designations)		132
	John Adams		77
	George Clinton		50
	Other Candidates		5
1796	JOHN ADAMS (Federalist)		71
	Thomas Jefferson (Democratic-Republican)		68
	Thomas Pinckney (Federalist)		59
	Aaron Burr (Democratic-Republican)		30
	Other Candidates		48
1800	THOMAS JEFFERSON (Democratic-Republican)		73
	Aaron Burr (Democratic-Republican)		73
	John Adams (Federalist)		65
	Charles C. Pinckney (Federalist)		64
	John Jay (Federalist)		1
1804	THOMAS JEFFERSON (Democratic-Republican)		162
	Charles C. Pinckney (Federalist)		14
1808	JAMES MADISON (Democratic-Republican)		122
	Charles C. Pinckney (Federalist)		47
	George Clinton (Democratic-Republican)		6
1812	JAMES MADISON (Democratic-Republican)		128
	De Witt Clinton (Federalist)		89
1816	JAMES MONROE (Democratic-Republican)		183
	Rufus King (Federalist)		34
1820	JAMES MONROE (Democratic-Republican)		231
	John Quincy Adams (Independent-Republican)		1
1824	JOHN QUINCY ADAMS (Democratic-Republican)	108,740	84
	Andrew Jackson (Democratic-Republican)	153,544	99
	William H. Crawford (Democratic-Republican)	46,618	41
	Henry Clay (Democratic-Republican)	47,136	37
1828	ANDREW JACKSON (Democratic)	647,286	178
	John Quincy Adams (National Republican)	508,064	83
1832	ANDREW JACKSON (Democratic)	687,502	219
	Henry Clay (National Republican)	530,189	49
	William Wirt (Anti-Masonic)	33,108	7
	John Floyd (National Republican)		
1836	MARTIN VAN BUREN (Democratic)	765,483	170
	William H. Harrison (Whig)		73
	Hugh L. White (Whig)	739,795	26
	Daniel Webster (Whig)		14
	W.P. Mangum (Anti-Jackson)		11

Year	Candidates Receiving More than One Percent of the Vote (Parties)	Popular Vote	Electoral Vote
1840	WILLIAM H. HARRISON (Whig)	1,274,624	234
	Martin Van Buren (Democratic)	1,127,781	60
1844	JAMES K. POLK (Democratic)	1,338,464	170
	Henry Clay (Whig)	1,300,097	105
	James G. Birney (Liberty)	62,300	0
1848	ZACHARY TAYLOR (Whig)	1,360,967	163
	Lewis Cass (Democratic)	1,222,342	127
	Martin Van Buren (Free Soil)	291,263	0
1852	FRANKLIN PIERCE (Democratic)	1,601,117	254
	Winfield Scott (Whig)	1,385,453	42
	John P. Hale (Free Soil)	155,825	0
1856	JAMES BUCHANAN (Democratic)	1,832,955	174
	John C. Fremont (Republican)	1,339,932	114
	Millard Fillmore (American)	871,731	8
1860	ABRAHAM LINCOLN (Republican)	1,865,593	180
	Stephen A. Douglas (Democratic)	1,382,713	12
	John C. Breckinridge (Democratic)	848,356	72
	John Bell (Constitutional Union)	592,906	39
1864	ABRAHAM LINCOLN (Republican)	2,206,938	212
	George B. McClellan (Democratic)	1,803,787	21
1868	ULYSSES S. GRANT (Republican)	3,013,421	214
	Horatio Seymour (Democratic)	2,706,829	80
1872	ULYSSES S. GRANT (Republican)	3,596,747	286
	Horace Greeley (Democratic)	2,843,446	—*
	Other Candidates		63
1876	RUTHERFORD B. HAYES (Republican)	4,036,572	185
	Samuel J. Tilden (Democratic)	4,284,020	184
1880	JAMES A. GARFIELD (Republican)	4,453,295	214
	Winfield S. Hancock (Democratic)	4,414,082	155
	James B. Weaver (Greenback-Labor)	308,579	0
1884	GROVER CLEVELAND (Democratic)	4,879,507	219
	James G. Blaine (Republican)	4,850,293	182
	Benjamin F. Butler (Greenback-Labor)	175,370	0
	John P. St. John (Prohibition)	150,869	0
1888	BENJAMIN HARRISON (Republican)	5,447,129	233
	Grover Cleveland (Democratic)	5,537,857	168
	Clinton B. Fisk (Prohibition)	249,506	0
	Anson J. Streeter (Union Labor)	146,935	0

*Greeley died shortly after the election: the electors supporting him then divided their votes among other candidates.

Year	Candidates Receiving More than One Percent of the Vote (Parties)	Popular Vote	Electoral Vote
1892	GROVER CLEVELAND (Democratic)	5,555,426	277
	Benjamin Harrison (Republican)	5,182,690	145
	James B. Weaver (People's)	1,029,846	22
	John Bidwell (Prohibition)	264,133	0
1896	WILLIAM McKINLEY (Republican)	7,102,216	271
	William J. Bryan (Democratic)	6,492,559	176
1900	WILLIAM McKINLEY (Republican)	7,218,491	292
	William J. Bryan (Democratic; Populist)	6,356,734	155
	John C. Wooley (Prohibition)	208,914	0
1904	THEODORE ROOSEVELT (Republican)	7,628,461	336
	Alton B. Parker (Democratic)	5,084,223	140
	Eugene V. Debs (Socialist)	402,283	0
	Silas C. Swallow (Prohibition)	258,536	0
1908	WILLIAM H. TAFT (Republican)	7,675,320	321
	William J. Bryan (Democratic)	6,412,294	162
	Eugene V. Debs (Socialist)	420,793	0
	Eugene W. Chafin (Prohibition)	253,840	0
1912	WOODROW WILSON (Democratic)	6,296,547	435
	Theodore Roosevelt (Progressive)	4,118,571	88
	William H. Taft (Republican)	3,186,720	8
	Eugene V. Debs (Socialist)	900,672	0
	Eugene W. Chafin (Prohibition)	206,275	0
1916	WOODROW WILSON (Democratic)	9,127,695	277
	Charles E. Hughes (Republican)	8,533,507	254
	A.L. Benson (Socialist)	585,113	0
	J. Frank Hanly (Prohibition)	220,506	0
1920	WARREN G. HARDING (Republican)	16,143,407	404
	James M. Cox (Democratic)	9,130,328	127
	Eugene V. Debs (Socialist)	919,799	0
	P.P. Christensen (Farmer-Labor)	265,411	0
1924	CALVIN COOLDIGE (Republican)	15,718,211	382
	John W. Davis (Democratic)	8,385,283	136
	Robert M. La Follette (Progressive)	4,831,289	13
1928	HERBERT C. HOOVER (Republican)	21,391,993	444
	Alfred E. Smith (Democratic)	15,016,169	87
1932	FRANKLIN D. ROOSEVELT (Democratic)	22,809,638	472
	Herbert C. Hoover (Republican)	15,758,904	59
	Norman Thomas (Socialist)	881,954	0
1936	FRANKLIN D. ROOSEVELT (Democratic)	27,752,869	523
	Alfred M. Landon (Republican)	16,674,665	8
	William Lemke (Union)	882,479	0
1940	FRANKLIN D. ROOSEVELT (Democratic)	27,307,819	449
	Wendell L. Willkie (Republican)	22,321,018	82

Year	Candidates Receiving More than One Percent of the Vote (Parties)	Popular Vote	Electoral Vote
1944	FRANKLIN D. ROOSEVELT (Democratic)	25,606,585	432
	Thomas E. Dewey (Republican)	22,014,745	99
1948	HARRY S. TRUMAN (Democratic)	24,179,345	303
	Thomas E. Dewey (Republican)	21,991,291	189
	J. Strom Thurmond (States' Rights)	1,176,125	39
	Henry Wallace (Progressive)	1,157,326	0
1952	DWIGHT D. EISENHOWER (Republican)	33,936,234	442
	Adlai E. Stevenson (Democratic)	27,314,992	89
1956	DWIGHT D. EISENHOWER (Republican)	35,590,472	457
	Adlai E. Stevenson (Democratic)	26,022,752	73
1960	JOHN F. KENNEDY (Democratic)	34,226,731	303
	Richard M. Nixon (Republican)	34,108,157	219
1964	LYNDON B. JOHNSON (Democratic)	43,129,566	486
	Barry M. Goldwater (Republican)	27,127,188	52
1968	RICHARD M. NIXON (Republican)	31,785,480	301
	Hubert H. Humphrey (Democratic)	31,275,166	191
	George C. Wallace (American Independent)	9,906,473	46
1972	RICHARD M. NIXON (Republican)	45,631,189	521
	George S. McGovern (Democratic)	28,422,015	17
	John Schmitz (American Independent)	1,080,670	0
1976	JAMES E. CARTER, JR. (Democratic)	40,274,975	297
	Gerald R. Ford (Republican)	38,530,614	241
1980	RONALD W. REAGAN (Republican)	42,968,326	489
	James E. Carter, Jr. (Democratic)	34,731,139	49
	John B. Anderson (Independent)	5,552,349	0
1984	RONALD W. REAGAN (Republican)	53,428,357	525
	Walter F. Mondale (Democratic)	36,930,923	13
1988	GEORGE H. BUSH (Republican)	48,881,221	426
	Michael Dukakis (Democratic)	41,805,422	112
1992	WILLIAM J.B. CLINTON (Democratic)	44,908,254	370
	George H. Bush (Republican)	39,102,343	168
	H. Ross Perot (Independent)	19,741,065	—
1996	WILLIAM J. CLINTON (Democratic)	45,590,703	379
	Robert Dole (Republican)	37,816,307	159
	H. Ross Perot (Reform)	7,874,283	
2000	GEORGE W. BUSH (Republican)	50,459,624	271
	Albert Gore (Democratic)	51,003,328	266
	Ralph Nader (Green)	2,882,985	0
2004	GEORGE W. BUSH (Republican)	59,117,523	286
	John Kerry (Democratic)	55,557,584	252
	Ralph Nader (Green)	405,623	0

Chief Justices of the Supreme Court

Term	Chief Justice
1789–1795	John Jay
1795	John Rutledge
1795–1799	Oliver Ellsworth
1801–1835	John Marshall
1836–1864	Roger B. Taney
1864–1873	Salmon P. Chase
1874–1888	Morrison R. Waite
1888–1910	Melville W. Fuller
1910–1921	Edward D. White
1921–1930	William H. Taft
1930–1941	Charles E. Hughes
1941–1946	Harlan F. Stone
1946–1953	Fred M. Vinson
1953–1969	Earl Warren
1969–1986	Warren E. Burger
1986–2005	William Rehnquist
2005–	John G. Roberts, Jr.

Presidents, Vice-Presidents, and Cabinet Members

President and Vice-President	Secretary of State	Secretary of Treasury	Secretary of War	Secretary of Navy	Postmaster General	Attorney General	Secretary of Interior
1. George Washington (1789) John Adams (1789)	Thomas Jefferson (1789) Edmund Randolph (1794) Thomas Pickering (1795)	Alexander Hamilton (1789) Oliver Wolcott (1795)	Henry Knox (1789) Timothy Pickering (1795) James McHenry (1796)		Samuel Osgood (1789) Timothy Pickering (1791) Joseph Habersham (1795)	Edmund Randolph (1789) William Bradford (1794) Charles Lee (1795)	
2. John Adams (1797) Thomas Jefferson (1797)	Timothy Pickering (1797) John Marshall (1800)	Oliver Wolcott (1797) Samuel Dexter (1801)	James McHenry (1797) John Marshall (1800) Samuel Dexter (1800) Roger Griswold (1801)	Benjamin Stoddert (1798)	Joseph Habersham (1797)	Charles Lee (1797) Theophilus Parsons (1801)	
3. Thomas Jefferson (1801) Aaron Burr (1801) George Clinton (1805)	James Madison (1801)	Samuel Dexter (1801) Albert Gallatin (1801)	Henry Dearborn (1801)	Benjamin Stoddert (1801) Robert Smith (1801) J. Crowninshield (1805)	Joseph Habersham (1801) Gideon Granger (1801)	Levi Lincoln (1801) Robert Smith (1805) John Breckinridge (1805) Cesar Rodney (1807)	
4. James Madison (1809) George Clinton (1809) Elbridge Gerry (1813)	Robert Smith (1809) James Monroe (1811)	Albert Gallatin (1809) George Campbell (1814) Alexander Dallas (1814) William Crawford (1816)	William Eustis (1809) John Armstrong (1813) James Monroe (1814) William Crawford (1815)	Paul Hamilton (1809) William Jones (1813) Benjamin Crowninshield (1814)	Gideon Granger (1809) Return Meigs (1814)	Caesar Rodney (1809) William Pinckney (1811) Richard Rush (1814)	
5. James Monroe (1817) Daniel D. Thompkins (1817)	John Quincy Adams (1817)	William Crawford (1817)	Isaac Shelby (1817) George Graham (1817) John C. Calhoun (1817)	Benjamin Crowninshield (1817) Smith Thompson (1818) Samuel Southard (1823)	Return Meigs (1817) John McLean (1823)	Richard Rush (1817) William Wirt (1817)	
6. John Quincy Adams (1825) John C. Calhoun (1825)	Henry Clay (1825)	Richard Rush (1825)	James Barbour (1825) Peter B. Porter (1828)	Samuel Southard (1825)	John McLean (1825)	William Wirt (1825)	

Presidents, Vice-Presidents, and Cabinet Members (continued)

President and Vice-President	Secretary of State	Secretary of Treasury	Secretary of War	Secretary of Navy	Postmaster General	Attorney General	Secretary of Interior
7. Andrew Jackson (1829) John C. Calhoun (1829) Martin Van Buren (1833)	Martin Van Buren (1829) Edward Livingston (1831) Louis McLane (1833) John Forsyth (1834)	Samuel Ingham (1829) Louis McLane (1831) William Duane (1833) Roger B. Taoney (1833) Levi Woodbury (1834)	John H. Eaton (1829) Lewis Cass (1831) Benjamin Butler (1837)	John Branch (1829) Levi Woodbury (1831) Mahlon Dickerson (1834)	William Barry (1829) Amos Kendall (1835)	John M. Berrien (1829) Rober B. Taney (1831) Benjamin Butler (1833)	
8. Martin Van Buren (1837) Richard M. Johnson (1837)	Louis McLane (1833)	Levi Woodbury (1837)	Joel L. Poinsett (1837)	Mahlon Dickerson (1837) James K. Paulding (1838)	Amos Kendall (1837) John M. Niles (1840)	Benjamin Butler (1837) Felix Grundy (1838) Henry D. Gilpin (1840)	
9. William H. Harrison (1841) John Tyler (1841)	Daniel Webster (1841)	Thomas Ewing (1841)	John Bell (1841)	George E. Badger (1841)	Francis Granger (1841)	John J. Crittenden (1841)	
10. John Tyler (1841)	Daniel Webster (1841) Hugh S. Legaré (1843) Abel P. Upshur (1843) John C. Calhoun (1844)	Tomas Ewing (1841) Walter Forward (1841) John C. Spencer (1843) George M. Bibb (1844)	John Bell (1841) John McLean (1841) John C. Spencer (1841) James M. Porter (1843) William Wilkins (1844)	George E. Badger (1841) Abel P. Upshur (1841) David Henshaw (1843) Thomas Gilmer (1844) John Y. Mason (1844)	Francis Granger (1841) Charles A. Wickliffe (1841)	John J. Crittenden (1841) Hugh S. Legaré (1841) John Nelson (1843)	
11. James K. Polk (1845) George M. Dallas (1845)	James Buchanan (1845)	Robert J. Walker (1845)	William L. Marcy (1845)	George Bancroft (1845) John Y. Mason (1846)	Cave Johnson (1845)	John Y. Mason (1845) Nathan Clifford (1846) Isaac Toucey (1848)	
12. Zchary Taylor (1849) Millard Fillmore (1849)	John M. Clayton (1849)	William M. Meredith (1849)	George W. Crawford (1849)	William B. Preston (1849)	Jacob Collamer (1849)	Reverdy Johnson (1849)	Thomas Ewing (1849)

President / Vice President							
13. Millard Fillmore (1850)	Daniel Webster (1850) Edward Everett (1852)	Thomas Corwin (1850)	Charles M. Conrad (1850)	William A. Graham (1850) John P. Kennedy (1852)	Nathan K. Hall (1850) Sam D. Hubbard (1852)	John J. Crittenden (1850)	Thomas McKennan (1850) A.H.H. Stuart (1850) Robert McClelland (1853)
14. Franklin Pierce (1853) William R. King (1853)	William L. Marcy (1853)	James Guthrie (1853)	Jefferson Davis (1853)	James C. Dobbin (1853)	James Campbell (1853)	Caleb Cushing (1853)	
15. James Buchanan (1857) John C. Breckinridge (1857)	Lewis Cass (1857) Jeremiah S. Black (1860)	Howell Cobb (1857) Philip F. Thomas (1860) John A. Dix (1861)	John B. Floyd (1857) Joseph Holt (1861)	Isaac Toucey (1857)	Aaron V. Brown (1857) Joseph Holt (1859)	Jeremiah S. Black (1857) Edwin M. Stanton (1860)	Jacob Thompson (1857)
16. Abraham Lincoln (1861) Hannibal Hamlin (1861) Andrew Johnson (1865)	William H. Seward (1861)	Salmon P. Chase (1861) William P. Fessenden (1864) Hugh McCulloch (1865)	Simon Cameron (1861) Edwin Stanton (1862)	Gideon Welles (1861)	Horatio King (1861) Montgomery Blair (1861) William Dennison (1864)	Edward Bates (1861) Titian J. Coffey (1863) James Speed (1864)	Caleb B. Smith (1861) John P. Usher (1863)
17. Andrew Johnson (1865)	William H. Seward (1865)	Hugh McCulloch (1865)	Edwin M. Stanton (1865) Ulysses S. Grant (1867) Lorenzo Thomas (1868) John M. Schofield (1868)	Gideon Welles (1865)	William Dennison (1865) Alexander Randall (1866)	James Speed (1865) Henry Stanbery (1866) William M. Evarts (1868)	John P. Usher (1965) James Harlan (1865) O.H. Browning (1866)
18. Ulysses S. Grant (1869) Schuyler Colfax (1869) Henry Wilson (1873)	Elihu B. Washburne (1869) Hamilton Fish (1869)	George S. Boutwell (1869) William A. Richardson (1873) Benjamin H. Bristow (1874) Lot M. Morrill (1876)	John A. Rawlins (1869) William T. Sherman (1869) William W. Belknap (1869) Alphonso Taft (1876) James Cameron (1876)	Adolph E. Bone (1869) George M. Robeson (1969)	John A.J. Creswell (1869) James W. Marshall (1874) Marshall Jewell (1874) James N. Tyner (1876)	Ebenzer R. Hoar (1869) Amos T. Akerman (1870) G.H. Williams (1871) Edwards Pierrepont (1875) Alphonso Taft (1876)	Jacob D. Cox (1869) Columbus Delano (1870) Zachariah Chandler (1875)

Presidents, Vice-Presidents, and Cabinet Members (continued)

President and Vice-President	Secretary of State	Secretary of Treasury	Secretary of War	Secretary of Navy	Postmaster General	Attorney General	Secretary of Interior
19. Rutherford B. Hayes (1877) William A. Wheeler (1877)	William M. Evarts (1877)	John Sherman (1877)	George W. McCrary (1877) Alexander Ramsey (1879)	R.W. Thompson (1877) Nathan Golf, Jr. (1881)	David M. Key (1877) Horace Maynard (1880)	Charles Devens (1877)	Carl Schurz (1877)
20. James A. Garfield (1881) Chester A. Arthur (1881)	James G. Blaine (1881)	William Windom (1881)	Robert T. Lincoln (1881)	William H. Hunt (1881)	Thomas I. James (1881)	Wayne MacVeagh (1881)	S.I. Kirkwood (1881)
21. Chester A. Arthur (1881)	E.T. Frelinghuysen (1881)	Charles J. Folger (1881) Walter Q. Gresham (1884) Hugh McCulloch (1884)	Robert T. Lincoln (1881)	William E. Chandler (1881)	Timothy O. Howe (1881) Walter Q. Gresham (1883) Frank Hatton (1884)	B.H. Brewster (1881)	Henry M. Teller (1881)
22. Grover Cleveland (1885) T.A. Hendricks (1885)	Thomas E. Bayard (1885)	Daniel Manning (1885) Charles S. Fairchild (1887)	William C. Endicott (1885)	William C. Whitney (1885)	William F. Vilas (1885) Don M. Dickinson (1888)	A.H. Garland (1885)	L.Q.C. Lamar (1885) William F. Vilas (1888)
23. Benjamin Harrison (1889) Levi P. Morgan (1889)	James G. Blaine (1889) John W. Foster (1892)	William Windom (1889) Charles Foster (1891)	Redfield Procter (1889) Stephen B. Elkins (1891)	Benjamin F. Tracy (1889)	John Wanamaker (1889)	W.H.H. Miller (1889)	Jon W. Noble (1889)
24. Grover Cleveland (1893) Adlai E. Stevenson (1893)	Walter Q. Gresham (1893) Richard Olney (1895)	John G. Carlisle (1893)	Daniel S. Lamont (1893)	Hilary A. Herbert (1983)	Wilson S. Bissel (1893) William L. Wilson (1895)	Richard Olney (1893) Judson Harmon (1895)	Hoke Smith (1893) David R. Francis (1896)
25. William McKinley (1897) Garret A. Hobart (1897) Theodore Roosevelt (1901)	John Sherman (1897) William R. Day (1897) John Hay (1898)	Lyman J. Gage (1897)	Russell A. Alger (1897) Elihu Root (1899)	John D. Long (1897)	James A. Gary (1897) Charles E. Smith (1898)	Joseph McKenna (1897) John W. Griggs (1897) Philander C. Knox (1901)	Cornelius N. Bliss (1897) E.A. Hitchcock (1899)

President / Vice President	Secretary of State	Secretary of Treasury	Secretary of War	Secretary of Navy	Postmaster General	Attorney General	Secretary of Interior
26. Theodore Roosevelt (1901) Charles Fairbanks (1905)	John Hay (1901) Elihu Root (1905) Robert Bacon (1909)	Lyman J. Gage (1901) Leslie M. Shaw (1902) George B. Cortelyou (1907)	Elihu Root (1901) William H. Taft (1904) Luke E. Wright (1908)	John D. Long (1901) William H. Moody (1902) Paul Morton (1904) Charles J. Bonaparte (1905) V.H. Metcalf (1906) T.H. Newberry (1908)	Charlese E. Smith (1901) Henry Payne (1902) Robert J. Wynne (1904) George B. Cortelyou (1905) George von L. Meyer (1907)	Philander C. Knox (1901) William H. Moody (1904) Charles J. Bonaparte (1907)	E.A. Hitchcock (1901) James R. Garfield (1907)
27. William H. Taft (1909) James S. Sherman (1909)	Philander C. Knox (1909)	Franklin McVeagh (1909)	Jacob M. Dickinson (1909) Henry Stimson (1911)	George von L. Meyer (1909)	Frank H. Hitchcock (1909)	G.W. Wickersham (1909)	R.A. Ballinger (1909) Walter L. Fisher (1911)
28. Woodrow Wilson (1913) Thomas R. Marshall (1913)	William I. Bryan (1913) Robert Lansing (1915) Bainbridge Colby (1920)	William G. McAdoo (1913) Carter Glass (1918) David F. Houston (1920)	Lindley M. Garrison (1913) Newton D. Baker (1916)	Joephus Daniels (1913)	Albert S. Burleson (1913)	J.C. McReynolds (1913) T.W. Gregory (1914) A. Mitchell Palmer (1919)	Franklin K. Lane (1913) John B. Payne (1920)
29. Warren G. Harding (1921) Calvin Coolidge (1921)	Charles E. Hughes (1921)	Andrew W. Mellon (1921)	John W. Weeks (1921)	Edwin Denby (1921)	Will H. Hays (1921) Hubert Work (1922) Harry S. New (1923)	H.M. Daugherty (1921)	Albert B. Fall (1921) Hubert Work (1923)
30. Calvin Coolidge (1923) Charles G. Dawes (1925)	Charles E. Hughes (1923) Frank B. Kellogg (1925)	Andrew W. Mellon (1923)	John W. Weeks (1923) Dwight F. Davis (1925)	Edwin Denby (1923) Curtis D. Wilbur (1924)	Harry S. New (1923)	H.M. Daugherty (1923) Harlan F. Stone (1924) John G. Sargent (1925)	Hubert Work (1923) Roy O. West (1928)
31. Herbert C. Hoover (1929) Charles Curtis (1929)	Henry L. Stimson (1929)	Andrew W. Mellon (1929) Ogden L. Mills (1932)	James W. Good (1929) Patrick J. Hurley (1929)	Charles F. Adams (1929)	Walter F. Brown (1929)	W.D. Mitchell (1929)	Ray L. Wilbur (1929)
32. Franklin D. Roosevelt (1933) John Nance Garner (1933) Henry A. Wallace (1941) Harry S. Truman (1945)	Cordell Hull (1933) E.R. Stettinius, Jr. (1944)	William H. Woodin (1933) Henry Morgenthau, Jr. (1934)	George H. Dern (1933) Harry H. Woodring (1936) Henry L. Stimson (1940)	Claude A. Swanson (1933) Charles Edison (1940) Frank Knox (1940) James V. Forrestal (1944)	James A. Farley (1933) Frank C. Walker (1940)	H.S. Cummings (1933) Frank Murphy (1939) Robert Jackson (1940) Francis Biddle (1941)	Harold L. Ickes (1933)

Presidents, Vice-Presidents, and Cabinet Members (continued)

President and Vice-President	Secretary of State	Secretary of Treasury	Secretary of War/Defense	Secretary of Navy	Postmaster General	Attorney General	Secretary of Interior
33. Harry S. Truman (1945) Alben W. Barkley (1949)	James F. Byrnes (1945) George C. Marshall (1947) Dean G. Acheson (1949)	Fred M. Vinson (1945) John W. Snyder (1946)	Robert P. Patterson (1945) Kenneth C. Royal (1947) *Secretary of Defense* James V. Forrestal (1947) Louis A. Johnson (1949) George G. Marshall (1950) Robert A. Lovett (1951)	James V. Forrestal (1945)	R.E. Hannegan (1945) Jesse M. Donaldson (1947)	Tom C. Clark (1945) J.H. McGrath (1949) James P. McGranery (1952)	Harold L. Ickes (1945) Julis A. Krog (1946) Oscar L. Chapman (1949)
34. Dwight D. Eisenhower (1953) Richard M. Nixon (1953)	John Foster Dulles (1953) Christian A. Herter (1959)	George M. Humphrey (1953) Robert B. Anderson (1957)	Charles E. Wilson (1953) Neil H. McElroy (1957) Thomas S. Gates (1959)		A.E. Summerfield (1953)	H. Brownell Jr. (1953) William P. Rogers (1957)	Douglas McKay (1953) Fred Seaton (1950)
35. John F. Kennedy (1961) Lyndon B. Johnson (1961)	Dean Rusk (1961)	C. Douglas Dillon (1961)	Robert S. McNamara (1961)		J. Edward Day (1961) John A. Gronouski (1963)	Robert F. Kennedy (1961)	Stewart L. Udall (1961)
36. Lyndon B. Johnson (1963) Hubert H. Humphrey (1965)	Dean Rusk (1963)	C. Douglas Dillon (1963) Henry H. Fowler (1965) Joseph W. Barr (1968)	Robert S. McNamara (1963) Clark M. Clifford (1968)		John A. Gronouski (1963) Lawrence F. O'Brien (1965) W. Marvin Watson (1968)	Robert F. Kennedy (1963) N. deB. Katzenbach (1965) Ramsey Clark (1967)	Stewart L. Udall (1963)
37. Richard M. Nixon (1969) Spiro T. Agnew (1969) Gerald R. Ford (1973)	William P. Rogers (1969) Henry A. Kissinger (1973)	David M. Kennedy (1969) John B. Connally (1970) George P. Schultz (1972) William E. Simon (1974)	Melvin R. Laird (1969) Elliot L. Richardson (1973) James R. Schlesinger (1973)		Winton M. Blount (1969)	John M. Mitchell (1969) Richard G. Kleindienst (1972) Elliot L. Richardson (1973) William B. Saxbe (1974)	Walter J. Hickel (1969) Rogers C.B. Morton (1971)

38. Gerald R. Ford (1974) Nelson A. Rockefeller (1974)	Henry A. Kissinger (1974)	William E. Simon (1974)	James R. Schlesinger (1974) Donald H. Runsfeld (1975)	William B. Saxbe (1974) Edward H. Levi (1975)	Rogers C.B. Morton (1974) Stanley K. Hathaway (1975) Thomas D. Kleppe (1975)
39. James E. Carter, Jr. (1977) Walter F. Mondale (1977)	Cyrus R. Vance (1977) Edmund S. Muskie (1980)	W. Michael Blumental (1977) G. William Miller (1979)	Harold Brown (1977)	Griffin B. Bell (1977) Benjamin R. Civiletti (1979)	Cecil D. Andrus (1977)
40. Ronald W. Reagan (1981) George H. Bush (1981)	Alexander M. Haig, Jr. (1981) George P. Schultz (1982)	Donald T. Regan (1981)	Caspar W. Weinberger (1981)	William French Smith (1981)	James G. Watt (1981) William Clark (1983) Donald P. Hodel (1985)
Ronald W. Reagan (1985) George H. Bush (1985)	George P. Schultz (1985)	James A. Baker III (1985)	Caspar W. Weinberger (1985)	Edwin Meese III (1985)	
41. George H. Bush (1988) James D. Quayle III (1988)	James A. Baker III (1988)	Nicholas Brady (1988)	Richard B.Cheney (1988)	Richard L. Thornburgh (1988)	Manuel Lujan, Jr. (1988)
42. William J.B. Clinton (1993) Albert Gore, Jr. (1993)	Warren Christopher (1993)	Lloyd Bentsen (1993)	Les Aspin (1993)	Janet Reno (1993)	Bruce Babbit (1993)
William J. B. Clinton (1996) Albert Gore, Jr. (1996)	Madeleine K. Albright (1997)	Robert Rubin (1995) Lawrence Summers (1999)	William J. Perry (1994) William S. Cohen (1997)	Janet Reno (1997) William J. Henderson (1998)	Bruce Babbit (1997)
43. George W. Bush (2000) Richard Cheney (2000)	Colin Powell (2001)	Paul H. O'Neill (2001)	Donald Rumsfeld (2001)	John Ashcroft (2001) William J. Henderson (1998)	Gail Norton (2001)
George W. Bush (2004) Richard Cheney (2004)	Condoleezza Rice (2005)	John Snow (2003) Henry Paulson (2006)	Donald Rumsfeld (2005)	Alberto Gonzales (2005) William J. Henderson (1998)	Gail Norton (2005) Dirk Kempthorne (2006)

Bibliographies

CHAPTER 1   *The New World Encounters the Old*

Alvin M. Josephy.   *The Indian Heritage of America* (1968). An overall survey of the Indian peoples of both American continents, region by region and era by era.

Brian M. Fagan.   *The Great Journey: The Peopling of Ancient America* (1987). How Asian peoples first settled the Americas across "Baringia," the land bridge that once connected the Old World to the New.

Francis Jennings.   *The Invasion of America: Indians, Colonialism, and the Cant of Conquest* (1975). Jennings seeks to redress the traditional story that makes the Indians into "savages" and the Europeans into the civilized party to the Old World-New World encounter after 1492.

Alfred W. Crosby.   *The Columbian Exchange: Biological and Cultural Consequences of 1492* (1972). Crosby sees the contacts between Europeans and the native peoples of America as a two-way street—both for good and ill.

J.H. Parry.   *The Age of Reconnaissance: Discovery, Exploration, and Settlement. 1450–1650* (1963). An excellent review of the roots and course of late medieval-early modern European overseas expansion.

Samuel Eliot Morison.   *The European Discovery of America: The Northern Voyages, 400–1600* (1971); and *The Southern Voyages, 1492–1616* (1974). Both of these volumes are superb blends of lucid text, maps, and photographs by a sailor-historian who was a master of his craft.

Samuel Eliot Morison.   *Christopher Columbus, Mariner* (1955). This is the condensed paperback edition of one of the great biographies in American historical literature, *Admiral of the Ocean Sea.*

Charles Gibson.   *Spain in America* (1966). An informative and tightly written analysis and interpretation of Spanish-American history from the earliest explorations to the nineteenth century.

C.R. Boxer.   *The Portuguese Seaborne Empire, 1415–1825* (1969). This is by far the best modern account of that epic expansion.

Carlo M. Cipolla.   *Before the Industrial Revolution: European Economy and Society, 1000–1700* (1980). A first-rate survey of the economy of early modern Europe.

J.H. Parry.   *The Spanish Seaborne Empire* (1966). The best work on the subject, complementing Parry's broader *Age of Reconnaissance.*

G.V. Scammell.   *The World Encompassed: The First European Maritime Empires, 800–1650* (1981). The best, and most recent, treatment of European expansion in the Middle Ages and early modern period.

Charles C. Mann.   *1491: New Revelations of the Americas Before Columbus* (2005). A recent work on pre-Columbian American societies which reveals their sophistication, their complexity, their creativity, and the details of their often warlike histories.

Diarmaid McCulloch.   *Reformation: Europe's House Divided, 1490–1700* (2003). Describes not only the Reformation, but also the Counter-reformation. Makes lucid the complex theological as well as political and social elements of both.

CHAPTER 2   *The Old World Comes to America*

Thomas J. Wertenbaker.   *The First Americans, 1607–1690* (1927). Still an excellent and well-written survey of the early settlement patterns of British America.

James Morton Smith, editor.   *Seventeenth Century America: Essays in Colonial History* (1959). Includes several important essays on early colonization as well as good chapters on early Indian–white relations in North America.

Carl Bridenbaugh.   *Vexed and Troubled Englishmen, 1590–1642* (1974). A social history of ordinary English people during the early years of American colonization.

Edmund Morgan.   *The Puritan Dilemma: The Story of John Winthrop* (1958). A fine biography of the early Puritan leader of Massachusetts who did so much to make that colony a success.

Alden T. Vaughan.   *American Genesis: Captain John Smith and the Founding of Virginia* (1975). The early history of the Jamestown colony approached through the biography of the colorful soldier John Smith.

Edmund S. Morgan.   *American Slavery, American Freedom: The Ordeal of Colonial Virginia* (1975). An excellent account of the early years of the Virginia colony, which also deals interestingly with the issues of race and labor relations between whites and Indians and between whites and black slaves in the first permanent British North American colony.

Abbot Emerson Smith.   *Colonists in Bondage: White Servitude and Convict Labor in America, 1607–1776* (1947). Tells how indentured servants and convicts were induced, seduced, kidnapped, and "spirited" to America.

Daniel Mannix and Malcolm Cowley.   *Black Cargoes: A History of the Atlantic Slave Trade* (1962). An eye-opener for readers who have accepted the conventional wisdom about early black Africa and the international slave trade.

John Barth.   *The Sot-Weed Factor* (1964). A long historical novel which spoofs the heroic accounts of early American settlement.

David Galenson.   *White Servitude in Colonial America: An Economic Analysis* (1981). Traces the shift in the colonial workforce from indentured servitude to slavery and relates it to changing costs of both skilled and unskilled labor.

Barnard Bailyn.   *Voyagers to the West: A Passage in the Peopling of America on the Eve of the Revolution* (1986). Deals with immigration from Britain on the eve of the Revolution.

Philip D. Curtin.   *The Atlantic Slave Trade: A Census* (1969). A detailed demographic examination of the Africa–America slave trade.

CHAPTER 3   *Colonial Society*

Daniel Boorstin.   *The Americans: The Colonial Experience* (1958). A bold attempt to demonstrate how the American environment altered transplanted Old World institutions and culture.

John Demos.   *A Little Commonwealth: Family Life in Plymouth Colony* (1970). A fascinating study of family life in Plymouth Colony, drawn from both the written records and the archeological evidence of surviving artifacts, houses, and utensils.

Philip Greven.   *Four Generations: Population, Land, and Family in Colonial Andover, Massachusetts* (1970); and *The Protestant Temperament* (1977). The first is a demographic study of a seventeenth-century New England town that shows the remarkable longevity and prosperity of the early settlers. The second deals with child-rearing practices in America from 1600 to 1830.

Kenneth Lockridge.   *A New England Town, The First Hundred Years: Dedham, Massachusetts, 1636–1736* (1970). A brilliant study of one New England town during its first century. A model study.

Carl Bridenbaugh.   *Myths and Realities: Societies of the Colonial South* (1952). A brief and readable treatment of the often neglected southern colonial heritage.

James R. Lemon.   *The Best Poor Man's Country: A Geographical Study of Early Southwestern Pennsylvania* (1972). An interesting study of the interplay of the institutions and physical environment of early Pennsylvania.

Peter Wood.   *Black Majority* (1975). One of the best treatments we have of colonial slavery. Wood believes that transplanted Africans contributed significantly to the culture and institutions of early southern society.

Louis B. Wright, editor.   *The Cultural Life of the American Colonies, 1607–1763* (1957). Summarizes developments in colonial religion, literature, education, science, architecture, theater, and music.

Henry F. May.   *The Enlightenment in America* (1976). Sees the American Enlightenment as a complex three-part development, with the phase described in this chapter (the defense of balance and order) as the most characteristically American.

Charles Sydnor.   *Gentlemen Freeholders: Political Practices in Washington's Virginia* (1952). Emphasizes the "popular" features of colonial Virginia's political life by contrast with the aristocratic ones given prominence by earlier authors.

Robert E. Brown and B. Katherine Brown.   *Virginia 1705–1786: Democracy or Aristocracy?* (1964). The authors see colonial Virginia as a remarkably democratic society in a political sense.

Robert E. Brown.   *Middle-Class Democracy and the Revolution in Massachusetts, 1691–1780* (1955). Massachusetts described as a middle-class democratic society by the eve of the Revolution.

Jack P. Green.   *The Quest for Power: The Lower Houses of Assembly in the Southern Royal Colonies, 1689–1763* (1963). Deals with the struggle of the southern provincial assemblies to become independent legislatures rather than rubber stamps of royal governors or Parliament.

Nathaniel Hawthorne.   *The Scarlet Letter* (1850). An incomparable introduction to the gloomy, brooding, morbid side of Puritan New England.

Michael Zuckerman.   *Peaceable Kingdoms: New England Towns in the Eighteenth Century* (1970). Emphasizes the consensus aspect of New England towns.

Christine Leigh Heyrman.   *Commerce and Culture: The Maritime Communities of Colonial Massachusetts, 1690–1750* (1984). A fine description of colonial life in Marblehead and Gloucester, two major New England ports.

David Freeman Hawke.   *Everyday Life in Early America* (1988). An interesting depiction of daily life in colonial America.

Darrett B. Rutman and Anita H. Rutman.   *A Place in Time: Middlesex County, Virginia, 1650–1750* (1984). The Rutmans demonstrate that the colonial Chesapeake region was not the structureless, individualistic place that scholars had formerly believed.

Gloria Main.   *Tobacco Colony: Life in Early Maryland, 1650–1720* (1982). Deals with the social abstractions of colonial Maryland—demographic processes and the impact of market forces on development—and also with the concrete details of daily life.

David Hackett Fischer.   *Albion's Seed: Four British Folkways in America* (1989). Advances the view that four distinctive cultural patterns were transmitted from Britain to colonial

America and that they persisted relatively intact and unblended, through the colonial period and beyond.

Jon Butler.   *Awash in a Sea of Faith: The Christianization of the American People* (1990). Butler says that the "Great Awakening" phenomenon has been greatly exaggerated.

Russell Shorto.   *The Island at the Center of the World* (2004). An entertaining history of Dutch New Netherland, but makes exaggerated claims for the city's importance.

CHAPTER 4   *Moving Toward Independence*

John H. McCusker and Russell Menard.   *The Economy of British America, 1607–1789: Needs and Opportunities* (1985). A recent survey of the colonial economy that pulls together much of the newest research and suggests new directions and new areas of investigation for future scholars.

Alice H. Jones.   *Wealth of a Nation to Be: The American Colonies on the Eve of the Revolution* (1980). The definitive study of just how wealthy Americans were in the late eighteenth century and how their wealth was distributed among the various members of society.

Arthur M. Schlesinger.   *The Colonial Merchants and the American Revolution, 1763–1776* (1917). A good older work that examines the contribution of colonial traders to the origins of the Revolution.

James Henretta.   *The Evolution of American Society, 1700–1815: An Interdisciplinary Analysis* (1973). An interesting attempt by a social historian to integrate the social, economic, and political history of early America.

Jackson T. Main.   *The Social Structure of Revolutionary America* (1965). Main depicts the colonists as prosperous and socially mobile. Colonial America, he says, was indeed "the best poor man's country in the world."

Edmund S. Morgan and Helen M. Morgan.   *The Stamp Act Crisis: Prologue to Revolution* (1953). The best short treatment of this crucial step along the road to independence.

Bernard Bailyn.   *The Ideological Origins of the American Revolution* (1967). Shows how the libertarian ideas forged in the seventeenth- and early eighteenth-century English struggle with the crown helped mold the actions of American Patriots after 1763.

Robert A. Gross.   *The Minutemen and Their World* (1976). This study of the town of Concord, Massachusetts, before 1776 captures the hopes, frustrations, and fears of a small American community caught in the vortex of great imperial changes.

Pauline Maier.   *From Resistance to Revolution: Colonial Radicals and the Development of American Opposition to Great Britain, 1765–1776* (1972). Views the "radical" leaders of the American independence movement as orderly and prudent men who opposed mob violence.

Bernard Bailyn.   *The Ordeal of Thomas Hutchinson* (1974). A fine study of the mind and views of a leading American Tory.

Merrill Jensen.   *The Founding of a Nation: A History of the American Revolution, 1763–1776* (1968). A long and well-written study of the whole sweep of events, from the French and Indian War onward, that culminated in the Declaration of Independence.

John C. Miller.   *Sam Adams: Pioneer in Propaganda* (1936). A classic older study of a major Revolutionary radical.

Dumas Malone. *Jefferson the Virginian* (1948). The best treatment of Jefferson during the years he was intimately involved in the colonial struggle with Great Britain.

Carl Van Doren. *Benjamin Franklin* (1941). A classic of American biography by a brilliant stylist.

Douglas Southall Freeman. *Washington: An Abridgment* (1968). This is the one-volume condensation of Freeman's monumental seven-volume life of Washington.

Fred Anderson. *Crucible of War: The Seven Years' War and the Fate of Empire in North America, 1754–1766* (2000). The French and Indian War seen in global context as worldwide battle of empires.

CHAPTER 5   *The Revolution*

Howard H. Peckham. *The War for Independence: A Military History* (1958). A brief narrative of the military aspects of the Revolution.

Samuel Eliot Morison. *John Paul Jones: A Sailor's Biography* (1959). This portrait of the Revolutionary War sea captain also describes the growing pains of the tiny American navy.

Henry S. Commager and Richard B. Morris, editors. *The Spirit of '76: The Story of the American Revolution as Told by Participants* (1958). A vast miscellany of letters, diaries, journals, diplomatic correspondence, parliamentary debates, and more.

Alfred F. Young, editor. *The American Revolution* (1976). A volume of essays emphasizing class conflict in several states during the Revolution.

James Franklin Jameson. *The American Revolution Considered as a Social Movement* (1925). The classic statement of the social dimensions of the American Revolution.

Richard B. Morris. *The American Revolution Reconsidered* (1967). An attempt to update Jameson.

Mary Beth Norton. *Liberty's Daughters: The Revolutionary Experience of American Women, 1750–1800* (1980). An important and interesting book that supports the view that the Revolution helped to improve the lot and increase the freedom of women.

Arthur Zilversmit. *The First Emancipation: The Abolition of Slavery in the North* (1967). The best study of the process by which the northern states excluded slavery from their borders.

Jack Sosin. *The Revolutionary Frontier, 1763–1783* (1967). Tells the important story of the West in both the origins and the course of the Revolution.

Gordon Wood. *The Creation of the American Republic, 1776–1787* (1968). An important reinterpretation of the Revolutionary period as well as the Confederation era that emphasizes the rise of a republican ideology.

Kenneth Roberts. *Arundel* (1930) and *Rabble in Arms* (1933). Benedict Arnold is a principal character in these two entertaining historical novels and he is sympathetically portrayed.

John R. Alden. *A History of the American Revolution* (1969). This is probably the best single-volume history of the Revolution.

Richard Morris. *The Peacemakers: The Great Powers and American Independence* (1965). Deals with the diplomacy of the Revolution.

Arthur Bowler. *Logistics and the Failure of British Arms in America, 1775–1783* (1975). A specialized study of the military aspects of the Revolution that points the finger at supply problems as the reason for British defeat.

Gordon S. Wood. *The Radicalism of the American Revolution* (1992). A sophisticated restatement of the thesis that a real revolution took place in 1775–1783.

CHAPTER 6   *The Origins of the Constitution*

Merrill Jensen.   *The New Nation: A History of the United States During the Confederation, 1781–1787* (1948). Seeks to refute the notion that the Confederation era was a critical period.

Marion Starkey.   *A Little Rebellion* (1955). An entertaining account of Shay's Rebellion.

Jackson Turner Main.   *The Anti-Federalists: Critics of the Constitution, 1781–1788* (1961). Main sees the opponents of a stronger central government in the 1780s as largely isolated farmers who were not tied to the sale of commercial crops and so had little interest in foreign trade.

Irving Brant.   *James Madison: The Nationalist, 1780–1787* (1948). Describes government under the Articles of Confederation and Madison's dismay at the weaknesses of his country during the 1780s and his efforts that culminated in the federal Constitution.

Charles A. Beard.   *An Economic Interpretation of the Constitution of the United States* (1913). Beard's thesis is that the fathers of the Constitution constructed a frame of government that was designed to serve the economic needs of their class.

Robert E. Brown.   *Charles Beard and the Constitution* (1956). A reexamination of Beard's thesis that finds it seriously wanting.

Forrest McDonald.   *We the People: The Economic Origins of the Constitution* (1958); and *E Pluribus Unum: The Formation of the American Republic, 1776–1790* (1965). The first of these two books challenges Beard's description of the economic factors and groups behind a stronger central government in the 1780s. The second is an interesting if sometimes highly personal discussion of the drive toward the Constitution and the formation of a new national government.

Benjamin F. Wright, editor.   *The Federalist* (1961). *The Federalist Papers*, written by Madison, Hamilton, and John Jay, are essential to understanding the thinking of the Constitution's supporters.

Robert A. Rutland.   *The Ordeal of the Constitution: The Anti-Federalists and the Ratification Struggle of 1787–88* (1966). Sympathetic to the anti-Federalists who opposed ratification of the Constitution, Rutland explains the strategy of the two opposing groups and the reasons for anti-Federalist defeat.

Irving Brant.   *The Bill of Rights: Its Origin and Meaning* (1965). This full treatment (515 pages) of the first ten amendments to the Constitution deals with the Bill of Rights' roots in both English and American experience, its creation early in the new republic, and its application over the many years that have ensued.

Amar Reed Akhil.   *America's Constitution: A Biography* (2005). A fascinating account by a Yale legal scholar of the Constitution's origins and role in American life.

CHAPTER 7   *The First Party System*

John C. Miller.   *The Federalist Era, 1789–1801* (1960). One of the best short political histories of the administrations of Washington and Adams.

Lance Banning.   *The Jeffersonian Persuasion: Evolution of a Party Ideology* (1978). Banning sees the Jeffersonian Republicans as men whose view of the political world was largely a product of "real Whig" ideology—which also influenced those who led the Revolution.

Richard Hofstadter.   *The Idea of a Party System, 1780–1840* (1969). Deals with the emergence of parties in the United States as a part of our intellectual history.

Joseph E. Charles. *The Origins of the American Party System* (1956). The first modern interpretation of the first party system by a promising scholar who died young.

John C. Miller. *Alexander Hamilton: Portrait in Paradox* (1959). Miller considers Hamilton's preoccupation with the creation and maintenance of a strong Union, the key to all his ideas and policies.

Paul A. Varg. *Foreign Policies of the Founding Fathers* (1963). Analyzes the economic and ideological factors in early foreign policy, the conflict between moralism and realism in policy-making, and the contribution of foreign-policy disagreements to the early formation of national political parties.

Harry Ammon. *The Gênét Mission* (1973). A brief, pro-Jefferson account of Edmond Genét's mission to enlist American support for republican France against England.

Leland Baldwin. *The Whiskey Rebels: The Story of a Frontier Uprising* (1939). The Whiskey Rebellion and its background treated with special attention to the feelings of those involved.

Manning J. Dauer. *The Adams Federalists* (1953); and Stephen G. Kurtz. (*The Presidency of John Adams: The Collapse of Federalism, 1795–1800* (1957). These are two essential monographs on the Federalist party after the departure of Washington from the political scene.

Paul Goodman. *The Democratic Republicans of Massachusetts: Politics in a Young Republic* (1964). A superior state study of the Jeffersonians in a commonwealth where it was an uphill fight for the followers of the Sage of Monticello.

James T. Flexner. *George Washington and the New Nation, 1783–1793* (1969); and *George Washington: Anguish and Farewell, 1793–1799* (1972). These two volumes cover Washington's presidency and last years as completely as the student could wish.

Reginald Horsman. *The Frontier in the Formative Years, 1783–1815* (1970). Tells the important story of the West during the early years of the republic.

James M. Smith. *Freedom's Fetters: The Alien and Sedition Laws and American Civil Liberties* (1956). Written during the era of Joe McCarthy, it sees the 1790s as a rehearsal for the later age of repression.

Joyce Appleby. *Capitalism and a New Social Order: The Republican Vision of the 1790s* (1984). Appleby seeks to depict the Jeffersonians as forward-looking democratic innovators rather than nostalgic agrarians.

Stanley Elkins and Eric McKitrick. *The Age of Federalism: The Early American Republic, 1788–1800* (1993). A long, but readable and insightful review of the years of Federalist ascendancy.

CHAPTER 8   *The Jeffersonians in Office*

Merrill Peterson. *Thomas Jefferson and the New Nation: A Biography* (1970). Peterson relates Jefferson's private life and his thought to his public role, and is lucid on the political issues of the day.

Fawn Brodie. *Thomas Jefferson: An Intimate History* (1973). Criticized by many scholars for suggesting an intimate relationship between Jefferson and his female slave, Sally Hemmings, this work is a superior psychobiography of our third president.

Forrest McDonald. *The Presidency of Thomas Jefferson* (1976). This brief, well-written volume has a strong point of view that not every scholar can accept.

Bernard De Voto, editor. *Journals of Lewis and Clark* (1953). The chronicle of the twenty-eight-month-long search for an overland route to the Pacific.

Leonard Levy. *Thomas Jefferson and Civil Liberties: The Darker Side* (1963). A revisionist study that depicts the third president as a man who often violated his own precepts in matters of civil liberties.

Henry Adams. *History of the United States During the Administrations of Jefferson and Madison* (1881–1891). This nine-volume work is a classic of American historical literature.

Reginald Horsman. *The War of 1812* (1969). The best one-volume history of the war.

Bernard Sheehan. *Seeds of Extinction: Jeffersonian Philanthropy and the American Indian* (1973). Describes how the Indian reformers of Jefferson's day, hoping to lead the tribes from "savagery" to "civilization," only managed to drive them brutally into the interior, thereby making way for white speculators and settlers.

Bernard Mayo. *Henry Clay: Spokesman of the New West* (1937). The story of Clay's life to 1812, when he was the thirty-five-year-old Speaker of the House of Representatives and leader of the War Hawks.

Bradford Perkins. *Prologue to War: England and the United States, 1805–1812* (1961). Perkins ascribes the drift of Britain and America toward war to the condescending attitude of the English and to American insistence on neutral trade in a world beset by war.

Julius Pratt. *Expansionists of 1812* (1925). Emphasizes how American interest in acquiring Canada, Florida, and possibly Mexico influenced the decision for war in 1812.

Gore Vidal. *Burr* (1973). A historical novel about Aaron Burr in the form of a memoir. Vidal is very much biased toward Burr.

CHAPTER 9   *The American Economic Miracle*

George R. Taylor. *The Transportation Revolution, 1815–1860* (1951). Still the best single-volume treatment of the American economy during the period covered by this chapter.

Stuart Bruchey. *The Roots of American Economic Growth, 1607–1861: An Essay in Social Causation* (1965). More up-to-date in its reliance on modern economists' growth theory than the Taylor book, though Bruchey also stresses the importance of national values and political, scientific, and technological developments.

Alan Dawley. *Class and Community: The Industrial Revolution in Lynn* (1976). Describes the shoemakers of Lynn, Massachusetts, as strongly opposed to the emerging industrial values and practices of the age and determined to preserve a preindustrial working-class ethic even if that meant resisting "progress."

H.J. Habakkuk. *American and British Technology in the Nineteenth Century* (1962). Compares English and American technology during the early industrial revolution.

Ronald Shaw. *Erie Water West: A History of the Erie Canal, 1792–1854* (1966). The social and political history of the great canal.

Mark Twain. *Life on the Mississippi* (1883). A beautifully written narrative of Twain's experiences as apprentice to a Mississippi River steamboat pilot before the Civil War.

Norman Ware.   *The Industrial Worker, 1840–1860: The Reaction of American Industrial Society to the Advance of the Industrial Revolution* (1924). An older work that examines the roots of the American labor movement and sees it as a reaction to the loss of skill and autonomy ushered in by the factory system.

Hannah Josephson.   *Golden Threads: New England Mill Girls and Magnates* (1949). A well-written social and economic history of the early New England textile industry.

Anthony Wallace.   *Rockdale: The Growth of an American Village in the Early Industrial Revolution* (1978). A fascinating study of an early textile community near Philadelphia, written by an anthropologist.

Paul E. Johnson.   *A Shopkeeper's Millennium: Society and Revivals in Rochester, New York, 1815–1837* (1979). Describes the religious roots of the pre-Civil War work ethic.

Merritt Roe Smith.   *Harpers Ferry Armory and the New Technology: The Challenge of Change* (1977). Smith shows how the cultural milieu of a community affected its industrial performance.

Sean Wilentz.   *Chants Democratic: New York City and the Rise of the American Working Class, 1788–1850* (1984). An interesting account of what the author considers a class-conscious labor movement in pre-Civil War New York.

CHAPTER 10   *Jacksonian Democracy*

George Dangerfield.   *The Era of Good Feelings* (1952). An elegantly written narrative history of the years between the War of 1812 and the rise of Jackson as a major political figure.

Robert Remini.   *Andrew Jackson* (1966). Concentrates on Andrew Jackson's role in strengthening the presidency, his deft handling of the Calhounites, the nullification crisis, and his battle with the BUS.

Thomas Govan.   *Nicholas Biddle, Nationalist and Public Banker* (1959). The public life of the BUS president during the years when the "Monster Bank" was locked in combat with "King" Andrew. Govan is pro-Bank and anti-Jackson.

John William Ward.   *Andrew Jackson: Symbol for an Age* (1955). Deals with Jackson's popular image as a folk hero.

Arthur M. Schlesinger, Jr.   *The Age of Jackson* (1945). The classic defense of Jacksonian democracy by a master of historical prose.

Marvin Meyers.   *The Jacksonian Persuasion: Politics and Belief* (1957). Meyers concludes that the Jacksonians were moralistic rather than materialistic, a conservative set of men who pined for an America already past.

Richard P. McCormick.   *The Second American Party System: Party Formation in the Jacksonian Era* (1966). McCormick describes how the second party system actually came together during the 1820s and 1830s.

Lee Benson.   *The Concept of Jacksonian Democracy: New York as a Test Case* (1961). Benson claims that religion, culture, and ethnicity were more important determinants of party affiliation in New York during the second party system than class or occupation.

Ronald Formisano.   *The Birth of Mass Political Parties: Michigan, 1827–1861* (1971). A study of the second party system in a state where the ethnocultural interpretation of party choice works exceptionally well.

William W. Freehling. *Prelude to Civil War: The Nullification Controversy in South Carolina, 1816–1836* (1966). Treats nullification primarily as a frightened reaction of the South Carolina planter class to abolitionism.

Richard N. Current. *John C. Calhoun* (1963). A short, well-written biography of the 1812 "War Hawk" who eventually became secretary of war, vice president, and ardent defender of southern minority "rights."

Grant Foreman. *Indian Removal: The Emigration of the Five Civilized Tribes of Indians* (1932). The sympathetic story of the forced migration of the Choctaws, Creeks, Chickasaws, Cherokees, and Seminoles from their homes in the Southeast to Oklahoma.

Marvin E. Gettleman. *The Dorr Rebellion: A Study in American Radicalism, 1833–1849* (1973). A sympathetic attempt to find native American radical roots, but not uncritical of the Dorr rebels.

Edward Pessen. *Jacksonian America: Society, Personality, and Politics* (1978). A highly critical view of Jackson and the Jacksonians. Pessen denies most of the egalitarian virtues usually ascribed to both.

Charles Sellers. *The Market Revolution: Jacksonian America, 1815–1846* (1991). Restores Jackson as the champion of the masses in the effort to hold back the forces of all-conquering capitalism.

CHAPTER 11   *The Mexican War and Expansionism*

Bernard De Voto. *Across the Wide Missouri* (1947). De Voto delightfully chronicles the Rocky Mountain fur trade that flourished in the 1820s and 1830s.

Francis Parkman. *The Oregon Trail* (1849). This is a fascinating contemporary depiction of the trans-Mississippi West by a literary artist. A classic.

John David Unruh. *The Plains Across: The Overland Emigrants and the Trans-Mississippi West, 1840–1860* (1978). The best overall treatment of emigration by way of the various overland "trails" from the settled areas of the East to the West coast before the Civil War.

Henry Nash Smith. *Virgin Land: The American West as Symbol and Myth* (1950). Examines how the nineteenth-century West influenced the life and helped to shape the character of American society as a whole.

George R. Stewart. *Ordeal by Hunger: The Story of the Donner Party* (1936). The harrowing story of eighty-nine California-bound people who were stranded in the High Sierra during the winter of 1846–1847.

Ray Allen Billington. *The Far Western Frontier, 1830–1860* (1956). A colorful survey of the Far West in the generation before the Civil War.

Frederick Merk. *Manifest Destiny and Mission in American History* (1963). The best discussion of this important topic by one of the deans of western history.

David M. Pletcher. *The Diplomacy of Annexation: Texas, Oregon, and the Mexican War* (1973). Treats the background of the Mexican War and the economic and political interests of the United States, Mexico, Britain, and France during the 1830s and 1840s.

Norman A. Graebner. *Empire on the Pacific: A Study in American Continental Expansion* (1955). Graebner concludes that it was not Manifest Destiny or the "pioneering spirit," but rather the desire of eastern commercial interests for ports on the Pacific that explains American expansion to the Pacific Coast.

Eugene Genovese. *The Political Economy of Slavery: Studies in the Economy and Society of the Slave South* (1965). Depicts expansionism as the effort of a southern planter elite to save slavery from a trap of soil exhaustion and declining profitability.

Otis Singletary. *The Mexican War* (1960). A good, brief treatment of the war against Mexico.

Julie Roy Jeffrey. *Frontier Women: The Trans-Mississippi West, 1840–1880* (1979). A fresh, entertaining discussion of women along the way to, and in, the Far West, from Oregon onward.

Oakah Jones, Jr. *Santa Anna* (1968). Depicts the Mexican leader as an honest patriot rather than the rank opportunist of other portraits.

CHAPTER 12   *Americans Before the Civil War*

Roger Brown. *Modernization: The Transformation of American Life, 1600–1865* (1976). An attempt to place social change in America within the framework of "modernization" where custom and personal, face-to-face relations among people are replaced by impersonal, contractual relations.

Keith Melder. *The Beginnings of Sisterhood* (1977). A fine, brief treatment of the social background and early course of the women's rights movement.

Nancy Cott. *The Bonds of Womanhood: "Women's Sphere" in New England, 1780–1835* (1977). Sees women's lives being transformed by the growing separation of family and work during the early years of the Republic.

Linda Gordon. *Woman's Body, Woman's Right: A Social History of Birth Control in America* (1976). A book with a strong thesis: "Birth control represented the single most important factor in the material basis of woman's emancipation in the course of the last century."

Russel B. Nye. *Society and Culture in America, 1830–1860* (1974). A superior intellectual and cultural history.

Oscar Handlin, editor. *This Was America* (1949). Contains excerpts from many of the accounts by foreign travelers that scholars have used to paint antebellum America's portrait.

John Kasson. *Rudeness and Civility: Manners in Nineteenth-Century Urban America* (1990). An interesting discussion of the role of the arbiters of manners, especially the authors of etiquette books, on standards of behavior in nineteenth-century American cities.

Ray Allen Billington. *America's Frontier Heritage* (1966). Billington examines Turner's frontier thesis and revises it in light of relatively recent scholarship.

Oscar Handlin. *Boston's Immigrants, 1790–1880* (1968). Catches the essence of the urban immigrant experience primarily before the Civil War in microcosm.

Ray Billington. *The Protestant Crusade, 1800–1860: A Study of the Origins of American Nativism* (1938). This case study of mass reaction describes the development of anti-Catholic and antiforeign feeling that reached its peak in the 1850s.

Leon F. Litwack. *North of Slavery: The Negro in the Free States, 1790–1860* (1961). Litwack's thesis is that by 1860 most blacks in the states where slavery was forbidden were segregated from whites, economically oppressed, and without civil rights.

David Rothman. *The Discovery of the Asylum: Social Order and Disorder in the New Republic* (1971). Rothman sees the origin of much of the antebellum reform impulse in the attempt by society to make up for the deficiencies of the American family.

Richard Wade. *The Urban Frontier: The Rise of Western Cities, 1790–1830* (1959). Wade makes the point that the antebellum West consisted of fast-growing urban centers as well as farms.

Milton Brown, Sam Hunter, John Jacobus, Naomi Rosenblum, and David Sokol. *American Art: Painting, Sculpture, Architecture, Decorative Arts, Photography* (1979). This large, beautiful, and expensive volume covers all the visual arts from the beginning of colonial settlement through the 1960s.

Leonard Arrington. *Great Basin Kingdom: An Economic History of the Latter-Day Saints, 1830– 1900* (1958). An economic history of the Mormons from their beginnings in upstate New York to the twentieth century.

Jack Larkin. *The Reshaping of Everyday Life, 1790–1840* (1988). How Americans of all classes, all occupations, and both races and genders lived day-to-day before the Civil War.

CHAPTER 13   *The Old South*

William R. Taylor. *Cavalier and Yankee: The Old South and American National Character* (1961). Examines the myth of the southern cavalier—a symbol of the agrarian South and the opposite, supposedly, of the money-minded, unchivalrous Yankee.

Frederick Law Olmsted. *The Cotton Kingdom: A Traveler's Observations on Cotton and Slavery in the American Slave States* (1861). Edited and introduced by Arthur M. Schlesinger, Sr. (1953). In this colorful report, the planner of New York's Central Park demonstrates, to his own satisfaction at least, that dependence on slave-grown cotton fostered "lazy poverty" and was a barrier to the South's broad economic progress.

Grady McWhiney. *Cracker Culture: Celtic Ways in the Old South* (1988). Seeks to explain the yeoman culture of the white Old South by tying it to the origins of much of its population in the Celtic fringe of the British Isles rather than the English-speaking parts.

Benjamin A. Botkin, editor. *Lay My Burden Down: A Folk History of Slavery* (1945). This one-volume oral history was compiled from the Slave Narrative Collection made by the U.S. government during the 1930s.

John W. Blassingame. *The Slave Community: Plantation Life in the AnteBellum South* (1972). Demonstrates the extent to which slaves were able to create islands of freedom in which to conduct their personal lives.

Robert W. Fogel and Stanley L. Engerman. *Time on the Cross: The Economics of Negro Slavery* (1974). An econometric study of Old South slavery that suggests that it was profitable. It has drawn a lot of criticism both for its methods and for its conclusions.

Herbert Gutman. *The Black Family in Slavery and Freedom, 1750–1925* (1976). An important study of the evolving black family from the colonial era until well after emancipation. Gutman supports the view that black slave families were strong units.

Eugene Genovese. *Roll Jordan Roll: The World the Slaves Made* (1974). According to Genovese, American slaves did more than merely survive; they formed a "black nation" in the South based on religion and strong family ties.

Clement Eaton. *Freedom of Thought in the Old South* (1940). This older work presents a critical view of antebellum southern intolerance of intellectual dissent.

Ulrich B. Phillips. *Life and Labor in the Old South* (1929). Now seventy years old, this is the nearest thing we have to a scholarly version of the moonlight and magnolias view of the Old South.

Robert Fogel.   *Without Consent or Contract: The Rise and Fall of American Slavery* (1989). This is Fogel's "second thoughts" about the institution of slavery. It seeks to alter the slavery-was-not-so-bad impression of his earlier work.

Frank Owsley.   *Plain Folk of the Old South* (1949). The best summation of the school of southern history, which emphasizes the small farmers rather than the slaves and large planters.

Ann F. Scott.   *The Southern Lady from Pedestal to Politics, 1830–1930* (1970). Makes the point that in the Old South white middle-class women were indeed pampered and patronized.

William Styron.   *Confessions of Nat Turner* (1967). Nat Turner, the black preacher who instigated the 1831 Virginia slave uprising, tells his own story in this widely acclaimed, though flawed, historical novel.

Eugene Genovese and Elizabeth Fox Genovese.   *The Mind of the Master Class* (2005). An analysis of the Old South's defense of slavery and of its culture. Critical but respectful.

CHAPTER 14   *The Coming of the Civil War*

Michael Holt.   *The Political Crisis of the 1850s* (1978). Holt believes that the breakup of the Union can be ascribed to the need of the two parties to define themselves in different and opposed ways.

Holman Hamilton.   *Prologue to Conflict: The Crisis and Compromise of 1850* (1964). Hamilton provides a dramatic and incisive analysis of the strategy of the factions that drew up the Compromise of 1850.

David Potter.   *The Impending Crisis, 1848–1861* (1976). A masterful analysis of the political turmoil that ended with the secession of the South.

Robert E. May.   *The Southern Dream of a Caribbean Empire, 1854–1861* (1973). May concludes that sectional conflict increased when the Republican-controlled Congress refused to support southern expansion into Central America and the Caribbean.

Eugene Berwanger.   *The Frontier Against Slavery: Western Anti-Negro Prejudice and the Slavery Extension Controversy* (1967). The author weighs the effects of this bigotry on the laws and politics of the old Northwest, as well as Iowa, Kansas, Nebraska, Oregon, and California.

James A. Rawley.   *Race and Politics: "Bleeding Kansas" and the Coming of the Civil War* (1969). In this analysis of the free-soilers' motives, Rawley emphasizes their race prejudice.

Eric Foner.   *Free Soil, Free Labor, Free Men: The Ideology of the Republican Party Before the Civil War* (1970). According to Foner, Republican leaders viewed the North–South conflict as one between two very different societies.

Stephen B. Oates.   *To Purge This Land with Blood: A Biography of John Brown* (1970). Oates depicts Brown as a nineteenth-century Calvinist in a time made violent and fanatic by the slavery controversy.

David H. Donald.   *Charles Sumner and the Coming of the Civil War* (1960). An excellent, perceptive biography of a major figure in the rise of political antislavery. It is critical of Sumner as intolerant, ambitious, and at times self-deceived.

Harriet Beecher Stowe.   *Uncle Tom's Cabin* (1852). Stowe's major theme is not the day-to-day brutality of slavery, but its more indirect consequences in the break-up of black families and the corruption of slaveholders themselves.

J. Mills Thornton III.   *Politics and Power in a Slave Society: Alabama, 1800–1860* (1978). Thornton believes that Alabama's secession in 1860 ultimately derived from its white citizens' fear that the North's actions endangered equality and freedom for the South's white people.

William L. Barney.   *The Secessionist Impulse: Alabama and Mississippi in 1860* (1974). Barney ties the secession of two key slave states to fear of abolitionist plots, racial anxieties, the work of firebrands, and uneasiness over severe food shortages during the months of crisis.

Kenneth Stampp.   *And the War Came* (1950). A close analysis, by an outstanding Civil War scholar, of the final secession crisis and Lincoln's part in it.

Don E. Fehrenbacher.   *The Dred Scott Case: Its Significance in American Law and Politics* (1978). The best treatment of the Dred Scott decision.

Kenneth Stampp.   *America in 1857: A Nation on the Brink* (1990). A dean of Civil War history examines the state of the American Union in a single year, "probably the year when the North and South reached the political point of no return."

William E. Gienapp.   *The Origins of the Republican Party, 1852–1856* (1987). The best recent study of this important subject.

CHAPTER 15   *The Civil War*

David H. Donald, editor.   *Why the North Won the Civil War* (1960). Five historians discuss the social and institutional structure of the Confederacy, the war-making potentials of North and South, northern political parties, military affairs, and Civil War diplomacy.

David H. Donald.   *Lincoln* (1995). The best one-volume biography of our sixteenth president.

Richard N. Current.   *The Lincoln Nobody Knows* (1958). What was Lincoln really like as a person? Current discusses Lincoln's domestic life, religious view, and political goals.

Clement Eaton.   *Jefferson Davis* (1977). The best recent biography of the Confederate president. Written by a southern scholar, it is objective and fair.

Bruce Catton.   *Mr. Lincoln's Army* (1951); *Glory Road* (1952); and *A Stillness at Appomattox* (1956). Catton captures the sights, sounds, and smells of battle, besides telling us what went on in the minds of the military commanders. The view is from the Yankee side of the line.

T. Harry Williams.   *Lincoln and His Generals* (1952). Williams deals with Lincoln "as a director of war and his place in the high command and his influence in developing a modern command system for this nation."

Adrian Cook.   *The Armies of the Streets* (1974). Spiraling inflation, racial and class resentments, and opposition to the new Union draft brought four days of looting, burning, and lynching of blacks to New York in July 1863.

George M. Frederickson.   *The Inner Civil War* (1965). The war, says Frederickson, induced reformers to reject their anti-institutional, individualistic attitudes as "feeble sentimentalities" and to favor an uncritical nationalism.

Frank L. Klement.   *The Copperheads in the Middle West* (1960). Sees the Copperheads as the forerunners of Gilded Age agrarian dissenters.

Margaret K. Leech.   *Reveille in Washington, 1860–1865* (1941). A panorama of life, society, and politics in wartime Washington.

Bell I. Wiley. *The Life of Johnny Reb: The Common Soldier of the Confederacy* (1943); and *The Life of Billy Yank: The Common Soldier of the Union* (1952). Drawn from ordinary enlisted men's letters, diaries, and other records, these are vivid, down-to-earth accounts of the amusements and inconveniences of camp life and the brutal experience of battle as it appeared to the ordinary soldier.

Benjamin Quarles. *The Negro and the Civil War* (1953). Deals with black Americans in both North and South, and with black soldiers as well as black civilians.

Emory M. Thomas. *The Confederate Nation, 1861–1865* (1979). This study of the Confederacy claims that if the South had won its independence, it would have been as thoroughly transformed by the wartime experience as the North.

Martin Duberman. *Charles Francis Adams, 1807–1886* (1960). An exemplary biography of a moderate antislavery leader who became United States minister to England during the Civil War and Lincoln's most important diplomatic representative abroad during the years of Union crisis.

MacKinlay Kantor. *Andersonville* (1955). This historical novel is about the infamous Confederate prison near Americus, Georgia, where almost 13,000 Union soldiers died in the last months of the war.

James McPherson. *Battle Cry of Freedom* (1988). Each generation feels the need to retell the epic of the Civil War. This is the best of the recent crop.

Ralph Andreano, editor. *The Economic Impact of the American Civil War* (1959). A collection of articles on the subject of the Civil War as an accelerator of economic growth.

CHAPTER 16   *Reconstruction*

Eric L. McKitrick. *Andrew Johnson and Reconstruction* (1960). Andrew Johnson, says the author, failed to see that the North needed evidence of southern contrition before it could forgive and allow a return to normal relations between the two regions.

Clement Eaton. *The Waning of the Old South Civilization, 1860–1880* (1968). Eaton concludes that the New South retained much of the old, especially its devotion to states' rights, white supremacy, and the cult of southern womanhood.

Albion W. Tourgée. *A Fool's Errand: A Novel of the South During Reconstruction* (1879). Edited by George M. Frederickson (1966). An autobiographical novel by a "carpetbagger" lawyer from Ohio who settled in North Carolina after the Civil War and became a Radical superior court judge.

Allen W. Trelease. *White Terror: The Ku Klux Klan Conspiracy and Southern Reconstruction* (1971). The definitive study of the first Klan after the Civil War and a potent indictment of all its doings.

Joel Williamson. *After Slavery: The Negro in South Carolina During Reconstruction, 1861–1877* (1965). Williamson concludes in this detailed study of race relations in one key Reconstruction state that racial segregation was not wholly a product of "redemption."

Willie Lee Rose. *Rehearsal for Reconstruction: The Port Royal Experiment* (1964). Though the ex-slaves ultimately lost the rich cotton lands to their former owners, the temporary success of the Port Royal experiment tells us what might have been if the northern commitment to black freedom and racial justice had been stronger.

Roger Ransom and Richard Sutch. *One Kind of Freedom: The Economic Consequences of Emancipation* (1977). An important book by two "cliometricians" about how emancipation affected the economic well-being of the freedmen and the South as a whole.

LaWanda Cox and John Cox. *Politics, Principles, and Prejudice, 1865–1866: Dilemma of Reconstruction America* (1963). A study of presidential Reconstruction that gives the Radicals much credit for idealism and suggests how much personal political advantage actually entered into Andrew Johnson's decisions.

Leon Litwack. *Been in the Storm So Long: The Aftermath of Slavery* (1980). Professor Litwack tells us what black men and women felt about the new world of freedom after 1863.

Herbert Gutman. *The Black Family in Slavery and Freedom, 1750–1925* (1976). Excellent social history, not only of the slavery period but also of the postslavery experience of black families.

Kenneth Stampp. *The Era of Reconstruction, 1865–1877* (1965). An excellent overall view of the "new" Reconstruction history by a man who helped pioneer it.

C. Vann Woodward. *Reunion and Reaction: The Compromise of 1877 and the End of Reconstruction* (1951). Concludes that the agreement to end the presidential election dispute of 1876–1877 was a behind-the-scenes agreement to exchange continued Republican supremacy for major economic favors to southern business groups.

Jonathan Wiener. *Social Origins of the New South, 1860–1885* (1978). A Marxist-oriented study of postbellum southern society that emphasizes the continued domination of the planter class and the near-slavery of the freedmen.

Eric Foner. *Reconstruction, America's Unfinished Revolution, 1863–1877* (1988). A long history of Reconstruction that reflects the revisionist research of the past generation as well as the political and cultural perceptions of today. (The reader could substitute Foner's briefer version, *A Short History of Reconstruction* (1990)).

CHAPTER 17   *The Triumph of Industrialism*

Edward C. Kirkland. *Dream and Thought in the Business Community, 1860–1900* (1956). This intellectual history of Gilded Age businessmen is based on their private correspondence, congressional testimony, and published writings.

Matthew Josephson. *Edison* (1959). According to Josephson, Edison's Menlo Park laboratory was his greatest invention: It was the first industrial research laboratory, applying scientific theory and technical knowledge to practical problems.

Harold C. Livesay. *Andrew Carnegie and the Rise of Big Business* (1975). This brief book—not a full biography—makes Carnegie's role in the post-Civil War economic surge clear.

Frederick Lewis Allen. *The Great Pierpont Morgan* (1949). A breezy, entertaining biography of Morgan that succeeds in defining his place in American economic life.

Irvin G. Wyllie. *The Self-Made Man in America: The Myth of Rags to Riches* (1954). Wyllie follows the myth of the self-made individual from colonial times to 1929.

Theodore Dreiser. *The Financier* (1912). The hero of this novel is modeled after the Gilded Age streetcar magnate Charles Yerkes.

Herbert Gutman. *Work, Culture, and Society in Industrializing America* (1976). A collection of essays by a leading social historian emphasizing the experience of working-class life in the half century following 1865.

Stephen Thernstrom. *Progress and Poverty: Social Mobility in a Nineteenth-Century City* (1964); and *The Other Bostonians: Poverty and Progress in the American Metropolis* (1973). Both books deal with social mobility for working people and the middle class in nineteenth-century America. The results were mixed: In Newburyport movement up the social and occupational ladder for wage earners was modest and difficult; in Boston it was remarkably easy, especially for native-born Americans, Northern Europeans, Protestant immigrants, and Jews.

Stanley Buder. *Pullman: An Experiment in Industrial Order and Community Planning, 1880–1930* (1967). As much urban as labor history, this book tells the story of the town of Pullman and views it as an example of unsuccessful paternalism.

David Montgomery. *Beyond Equality: Labor and the Radical Republicans, 1862–1872* (1967). An interesting attempt to connect the Gilded Age labor movement to the egalitarian ideas of the 1860s Radical Republicans.

Daniel Walkowitz. *Worker City, Company Town: Iron and Cotton Worker Protest in Troy and Cahoes, New York, 1855–1884* (1978). A study of two New York industrial towns with different ethnic mixes and with different property distribution patterns.

David Brody. *Steelworkers in America: The Nonunion Era* (1960). Brody shows not only what produced discontent among American steelworkers before 1919, but also what encouraged labor's stability and acquiescence.

Harold C. Livesay. *Samuel Gompers and Organized Labor in America* (1978). Goes beyond biography and tells us much of the evolving labor movement, particularly the AFL, during the years 1890 to 1920.

Daniel T. Rogers. *The Work Ethic in Industrial America, 1850–1920* (1975). Examines the intellectual defense of hard work and steady application that accompanied industrialization in the United States.

Daniel Bell. *Marxian Socialism in the United States* (1962). Bell, a former Marxist, is critical of socialism in this short history.

Nick Salvatore. *Eugene V. Debs: Citizen and Socialist* (1982). Written by a scholar sympathetic to, but not uncritical of, the Socialist leader.

Charles Francis Adams, Jr., and Henry Adams. *Chapters of Erie* (1866). The classic account of the chicanery of Jay Gould and his confederates. The work of patrician descendants of Presidents John Adams and John Quincy Adams.

Maury Klein. *The Life and Legend of Jay Gould* (1986). Professor Klein attempts the difficult here: rehabilitating the reputation of Jay Gould.

Ron Chernow. *Titan: The Life of John D. Rockefeller, Sr.* (1998). A new, first rate biography of the man who parlayed business acumen and rigid, puritan morals into the country's largest fortune.

CHAPTER 18   *Age of the City*

Maury Klein and Harvey A. Kantor. *Prisoners of Progress* (1976). The authors briskly describe American industrialization and the growth of cities between 1850 and 1920.

Sam B. Warner. *Streetcar Suburbs: The Process of Growth in Boston, 1870–1900* (1962). Warner describes the developing economic and social segregation of city and suburbs as the middle and upper classes left Boston, spurred on by the "rural ideal."

Thomas Kessner. *The Golden Door: Italian and Jewish Immigrant Mobility in New York City, 1880–1915* (1977). A case study of urban social mobility for two important New Immigrant groups.

Philip Taylor. *The Distant Magnet: European Immigration to the U.S.A.* (1971). This volume by an English scholar deals with European immigration to the United States for the whole period from 1830 to 1930.

Stanford Lyman. *Chinese Americans* (1974). Tells of the constant tension in Chinese-Americans between desires for community and ethnic integrity and acceptance in the wider world of Caucasian America.

Matt S. Meier and Feliciano Rivera. *The Chicanos: A History of Mexican Americans* (1972). A brief survey of the whole sweep of Mexican-American history.

John Higham. *Strangers in the Land: Patterns of American Nativism, 1860–1925* (1955). Higham demonstrates how the post-Civil War European immigrant often became a scapegoat when Americans suffered a loss of confidence as a result of depression, war, or some other crisis.

Abraham Cahan. *The Rise of David Levinsky* (1917). Written by a Jewish immigrant journalist and editor who settled in New York's Lower East Side, it vividly describes sweatshops, problems between the established German Jews and the newer arrivals from eastern Europe, and conflicts between generations in immigrant families.

Seymour Mandelbaum. *Boss Tweed's New York* (1965). Tweed was not a good man, but he was a useful one—as Professor Mandelbaum shows in this study of Thomas Nast's favorite villain.

Zane Miller. *Boss Cox's Cincinnati* (1968). Cox, too, was useful, but more enlightened and honest than Tweed.

Humbert Nelli. *The Italians in Chicago, 1880–1930* (1970). A model study of an urban ethnic group of the New Immigration following 1880.

Melvin Holli. *Reform in Detroit: Hazen Pingree and Urban Politics* (1969). Pingree was the "potato-patch mayor" of Detroit who fought the transit magnates and brought reform with a heart to his city.

Theodore Dreiser. *Sister Carrie* (1900). Recounts the experiences of a young rural woman who comes to Chicago to make her fortune and succeeds primarily by choosing, and using, the right lovers.

Gunther Barth. *City People: The Rise of Modern City Culture in Nineteenth-Century America* (1980). A fine treatment of the culture of Gilded Age American cities.

CHAPTER 19   *The Trans-Missouri West*

Walter P. Webb. *The Great Plains* (1931). The classic study of the Great Plains. Webb shows the important ways in which geography and climate modified transplanted institutions.

Fred A. Shannon. *The Farmer's Last Frontier: Agriculture, 1860–1897* (1945). This older work is still the indispensable study of agriculture in the generation following the Civil War.

Allan G. Bogue. *Money at Interest: The Farm Mortgage on the Middle Border* (1955); and *From Prairie to Corn Belt* (1963). Bogue denies that eastern moneylenders made excessive profits from western farmers. He also claims that corn belt farmers did very well for themselves in the late nineteenth century.

Everett Dick. *The Sod-House Frontier, 1854–1890* (1954). The subtitle of this book is: "A Social History of the Northern Plains from the Creation of Kansas & Nebraska to the Admission of the Dakotas."

Rodman W. Paul. *Mining Frontiers of the Far West, 1848–1880* (1963). Combines excellent scholarship with a sense of the romantic aspect of the great western mining bonanzas.

R.K. Andrist. *The Long Death: The Last Days of the Plains Indians* (1964). A skillful overview of the tragic destruction of the Plains tribes by the encroachment of "civilization."

Robert W. Mardock. *Reformers and the American Indian* (1970). Surveys the Indian reformers through to the Dawes Act of 1887 and sees them as sincere but limited and culture-bound.

Ernest Staples Osgood. *The Day of the Cattlemen* (1929). A brief classic study of the range cattle industry of the northern Plains.

Robert Utley. *The Lance and the Shield: The Life and Times of Sitting Bull* (1993). An impressive new scholarly treatment of Sitting Bull and his tribe and also, along the way, a re-examination of Indian–white relations after the Civil War.

Robert Dykstra. *The Cattle Towns* (1968). A study of the cattle towns between 1876 and 1885 that emphasizes the nature of town life in the cattle communities and talks as much of drygoods merchants as of cowboys and dance-hall girls.

Gene M. Gressley. *Bankers and Cattlemen* (1966). The subtitle of this book is "The Stocks-and-Bonds, Havana-Cigar, Mahogany-and-Leather Side of the Cowboy Era."

Hamlin Garland. *Main-Travelled Roads* (1891). Garland, who settled with his parents on the Iowa prairie, learned early that "farming is not entirely made up of berrying, tossing the new-mown hay, and singing 'The Old Oaken Bucket' on the porch by moonlight."

Frank Norris. *The Octopus* (1901). In this description of California wheat growers in the Central Valley, the Southern Pacific Railroad is depicted as "a giant parasite fattening upon the lifeblood of an entire commonwealth."

Robert Utley. *The Last Days of the Sioux Nation* (1963). The best, most complete treatment we have of the Ghost Dance uprising and the Wounded Knee massacre.

CHAPTER 20   *The Gilded Age*

H. Wayne Morgan, editor. *The Gilded Age: A Reappraisal* (1970). Twelve contributors write on civil service reform, labor, the robber barons, science, the currency question, the party system, Populism, foreign policy, popular culture, and the arts.

Richard Jensen. *The Winning of the Midwest: Social and Political Conflict, 1888–1896* (1971). Using statistical data, Jensen demonstrates how political affiliations during the Gilded Age were often determined by social and religious values rather than by pocketbook issues.

John G. Sprout. *"The Best Men": Liberal Reformers in the Gilded Age* (1968). A fine study of Gilded Age reform focusing on the Liberal Republican movement of 1872 and the later Mugwumps.

Irwin Unger. *The Greenback Era: A Social and Political History of American Finance, 1865–1879* (1964). Deals with post-Civil War finance as an example of who controlled political power in the Gilded Age. The author of *These United States* tends to be partial to this work.

Morton Keller.   *Affairs of State: Public Life in Late-Nineteenth-Century America* (1977). Shows how the social and economic transformation of the nation between 1865 and 1900 was reflected in its political life.

Matthew Josephson.   *The Politicos, 1865–1896* (1938). The classic older treatment of Gilded Age politics. According to Josephson, the political leadership of the period was thoroughly unprincipled.

Allan Nevins.   *Grover Cleveland: A Study in Courage* (1932). One of the best political biographies for the era remains this older work by a master of narrative history, Allan Nevins.

Ari Hoogenboom,   *Rutherford B. Hayes* (1996). Another fine biography of a Gilded Age political leader.

Mark Twain and Charles Dudley Warner.   *The Gilded Age* (1873). This satire on the "all-pervading speculativeness" in business life and corruption in politics gave the Gilded Age its name.

Mary R. Dearing.   *Veterans in Politics: The Story of the G.A.R.* (1952). A study of the Civil War Union veterans' organization, the Grand Army of the Republic, as a political pressure group and a bulwark of the Republican party after 1865.

John D. Hicks.   *The Populist Revolt: A History of the Farmers' Alliance and the People's Party* (1931). This is the standard older treatment of late-nineteenth-century agrarian insurgency. Hicks sees the Populists as the forerunners of twentieth-century American liberalism.

O. Gene Clanton.   *Populism: The Humane Preference in America, 1890–1990* (1991). A strong defense of Populism as a humane alternative to mainstream politics of the 1890s.

Lawrence Goodwyn.   *Democratic Promise: The Populist Movement in America* (1976). An impassioned defense of the Populists against their detractors.

Louis W. Koenig.   *Bryan: A Political Biography of William Jennings Bryan* (1971). The best one-volume biography of Bryan. Fair without being enthusiastic.

Paul Kleppner.   *The Cross of Culture: A Social Analysis of Midwestern Politics 1850–1900* (1970). Kleppner's book is the pioneer study of Gilded Age cultural politics.

Morton White.   *Social Thought in America: The Revolt Against Formalism* (1957). Written by a Harvard philosopher who has made American thought his province, it is by far the best study of the changes in social thought as molded by Darwinism in these years.

Richard Hofstadter.   *Social Darwinism in American Thought* (1944). This work deals not only with the conservatives who used Darwin to defend the social and economic status quo, but also with those who used evolutionary ideas to defend reform.

Lawrence Vesey.   *The Emergence of the American University* (1965). The best one-volume study of the new currents in graduate and professional training that arose during this period.

Lawrence A. Cremin.   *The Transformation of the School: Progressivism in American Education, 1876–1957* (1961). Examines the roots, the course, and the eventual transformation of the "progressive movement" in education that John Dewey helped to launch.

Arthur M. Schlesinger.   *The Rise of the City, 1878–1898* (1933). This older book is still one of the few good treatments of popular culture as a whole during the Gilded Age.

Oliver W. Larkin.   *Art and Life in America* (1949). This work covers far more than the period of this chapter, and so can be consulted selectively by the student of the Gilded Age.

John Burchard and Albert Bush-Brown. *The Architecture of America: A Social and Cultural History* (1966). What applies to Larkin's book also applies to this work.

Lewis Mumford. *The Brown Decades: A Study of the Arts in America, 1865–1895* (1931). This still readable and useful book was a ground-breaking attack on Victorian architecture and a defense of the "modern" trend.

W.A. Swanberg. *Citizen Hearst* (1961). A colorful, critical biography of William Randolph Hearst, one of the creators of yellow journalism, by an outstanding popular biographer.

Sidney Hook. *John Dewey* (1939). An intellectual biography of Dewey by one of his most articulate disciples.

Burton Bledstein. *The Culture of Professionalism: The Middle Class and the Development of Higher Education in America* (1976). Bledstein makes a linkage between the ambition of the mid-nineteenth-century American middle class, the development of the professions, and the rise of the university.

Justin Kaplan. *Mr. Clemens and Mark Twain* (1966). As the title suggests, Kaplan sees Mark Twain as a deeply divided personality, a man who wanted both wealth and success and yet despised all they represented.

Gunther Schuller. *Early Jazz* (1968). The best discussion of jazz from its origins to the early 1930s—by a fine modern composer.

CHAPTER 21   *The American Empire*

Walter LaFeber. *The New Empire: An Interpretation of American Expansion, 1860–1898* (1963). A study of late-nineteenth-century American expansionism by a scholar who believes that "economic forces [were] the most important causes" of the expansionist impulse.

Ernest R. May. *American Imperialism* (1968). May ascribes American expansionism at the end of the nineteenth century to the appearance of a foreign policy elite inspired by the example of Britain, France, and Germany.

Walter Millis. *The Martial Spirit: A Study of Our War with Spain* (1931). Sees the war's origins in the gradual development of a warlike spirit that derived from a mixture of boredom, greed, politics, and the yearning for glory.

Julius W. Pratt. *Expansionists of 1898: The Acquisition of Hawaii and the Spanish Islands* (1936). Pratt criticizes the view, common in his day, that the Spanish-American War was the work of business groups anxious to acquire markets.

Graham A. Cosmas. *An Army for Empire: The United States Army in the Spanish-American War* (1971). This study of the army and the War Department during the war with Spain seeks to refute the usual picture of bungling and general incompetence.

Kenton J. Clymer. *John Hay: The Gentleman as Diplomat* (1975). A study of Secretary of State John Hay's thought about such matters as race, expansion, England, and China.

Howard K. Beale. *Theodore Roosevelt and the Rise of America to World Power* (1956). An effective, if not always fair, attack on TR for his jingoism and imperialistic arrogance.

Joseph Wisan. *The Cuban Crisis as Reflected in the New York Press* (1934). Wisan probably exaggerates the significance of the Hearst–Pulitzer circulation battle in New York as a cause of the Spanish-American War, but this study does tell us much about American values and prejudices, and how prowar groups played on them.

Frank A. Freidel. *Splendid Little War* (1958). The words and pictures of news correspondents, artists, and photographers tell the story of the war in Cuba.

Robert Beisner. *Twelve Against Empire: The Anti-Imperialists, 1898–1900* (1968). Beisner studies twelve prominent Americans who opposed the Spanish-American War. All upper-class Republicans or former Mugwumps, they believed that acquiring unwilling colonies ran counter to American principles and would threaten democracy at home.

Leon Wolff. *Little Brown Brother* (1961). War in the Philippines lasted from 1898 to 1902, but after 1898 the United States, as explained in this work, fought not Spain but Filipino guerrillas.

Thomas J. McCormick. *China Market: America's Quest for Informal Empire, 1893–1901* (1967). Informed by Vietnam era views, this book claims America's China policies were intended to solve the problems of domestic economic overproduction through an Open Door agreement to assure American domination of the China market.

David C. McCulloch. *The Path Between the Seas: The Creation of the Panama Canal, 1870–1914* (1977). A lively account of the building of the great isthmian canal, from the early French effort to the final success under the auspices of the United States.

CHAPTER 22   *Progressivism*

Richard Hofstadter. *Age of Reform: From Bryan to F.D.R.* (1955). Urban and middle-class in origin, according to Hofstadter, the progressive movement failed to achieve real reform because its members distrusted organized labor and immigrants and were obsessed with threats to their own status from both the left and the right.

Lincoln Steffens. *Autobiography* (1931). The famous muckraker eventually became disillusioned with the liberal values that motivated progressivism, concluding that capitalism itself was responsible for political corruption and social oppression.

James Harvey Young. *The Toadstool Millionaires: A Social History of Patent Medicines in America Before Federal Regulation* (1962). This funny and tragic tale of the gullible, hypochondriacal public and the patent-medicine manufacturers will tell you something about modern advertising.

Allen F. Davis. *Spearheads for Reform: The Social Settlements and the Progressive Movement, 1890–1914* (1967). Shows the frustration of settlement workers' efforts for social justice in the wards. Davis evaluates their success in citywide and national politics, especially their influence on education, housing, unions, and female and child labor.

David Thelen. *The New Citizenship: Origins of Progressivism in Wisconsin, 1885–1900* (1972). This well-written monograph on progressivism in Wisconsin emphasizes the role consumer anger and frustration played in launching the new reform movement.

August Meier. *Negro Thought in America, 1880–1915* (1963). Analyzes what Booker T. Washington, W.E.B. Du Bois, and other black leaders' thought about contemporary politics, economics, migration, colonization, racial solidarity, and industrial and elite education.

James Weldon Johnson. *Autobiography of an Ex-Coloured Man* (1912). This is a fictional composite autobiography of blacks before World War I by a real black composer and lyricist, lawyer, a founder of the NAACP, and chronicler of Harlem.

Henry F. Pringle.   *Theodore Roosevelt* (1931). Pringle's long and graceful biography follows the many TRs: sickly boy, university dude, reformer in New York City, Dakota rancher, Washington office seeker, Rough Rider in Cuba, president, Bull Mooser, and anti-Wilsonite.

Upton Sinclair.   *The Jungle* (1906). Sinclair, a socialist, intended this novel to arouse the nation's indignation about the meatpackers' working conditions. Instead, his nauseatingly detailed descriptions of the meat prepared for public consumption turned the nation's stomach.

Roy Lubove.   *The Progressives and the Slums* (1962). Focusing on New York City, Lubove has written a fine study of how the progressives dealt with one of the key social problems of the day—the slums.

William Harbaugh.   *The Life and Times of Theodore Roosevelt* (1975). Harbaugh's, biography of TR is more up-to-date and more in tune with recent scholarship than Pringle's.

Samuel P. Hays.   *Conservation and the Gospel of Efficiency: The Progressive Conservation Movement, 1890–1920* (1959). This was a ground-breaking book when it appeared and is still important for the serious student of progressivism. Emphasizes the progressives' obsession with efficiency.

John D. Buenker.   *Urban Liberalism and Progressive Reform* (1973). Buenker believes that we must not ignore the interest in, and support of, progressivism by urban working people and their political spokespersons in Congress and the state legislatures.

George Mowry.   *The California Progressives* (1951). This study of progressivism in a banner progressive state helped introduce the thesis that the progressives were middle-class citizens suffering from acute social anxiety as a result of threats to their status.

Arthur Link.   *Woodrow Wilson and the Progressive Era* (1954). Still the best study of the Wilsonian phase of progressivism. Link admires his subject, but he can also see his flaws.

Aileen Kraditor.   *The Ideas of the Woman Suffrage Movement, 1890–1920* (1965). A study of the thought of the women's suffrage movement leaders during the final drive that brought success.

William O'Neill.   *Everyone Was Brave: A History of Feminism in America* (1971). A lively, intelligent discussion of feminism with an especially good section on feminist politics in the Progressive Era.

CHAPTER 23   *World War I*

N. Gordon Levin.   *Woodrow Wilson and World Politics: America's Response to War and Revolution* (1968). Levin maintains that the "effort to construct a stable world order of liberal-capitalist internationalism"—safe from "imperialism of the Right" and "revolution of the Left"—was basic to Wilson's foreign policy and all subsequent American policy-making.

Robert E. Quirk.   *An Affair of Honor: Woodrow Wilson and the Occupation of Veracruz* (1962). Quirk's treatment of the Tampico incident and the shelling and occupation of Veracruz by American marines is brief and well written.

Walter Millis.   *Road to War: America, 1914–1917* (1935). Writing when most citizens believed that America's entry into World War I was a mistake, Millis blames Allied propaganda, American businessmen, and anti-German prejudice for dragging the nation into an unnecessary conflict.

Arthur S. Link.   *Woodrow Wilson and the Progressive Era, 1910–1917* (1954). Half of this book is devoted to Wilson's foreign policy and the advent of war with the Central Powers. Link sees the president as motivated by idealism and a sincere desire to stop brutal aggression.

Frederick Luebke.   *Bonds of Loyalty: German-Americans and World War I* (1974). Luebke describes the unfair treatment of German-Americans during 1917–1918.

Ralph Stone.   *The Irreconcilibles: The Fight Against the League of Nations* (1970). This is the best study of Lodge and his anti-League colleagues.

Randolph S. Bourne.   *War and the Intellectuals: Collected Essays, 1915–1919*. Edited and introduced by Carl Resek (1964). Bourne, a brilliant political commentator, ridicules the tendency of many of his fellow intellectuals to justify American intervention in progressive and moral terms. Why did the United States fight? Because, Bourne says, "War is the health of the State."

John Dos Passos.   *Three Soldiers* (1921). Three young men of very different temperaments and backgrounds meet in an army training camp and go to war. Dos Passos traces their spiritual destruction in this novel.

Erich Maria Remarque.   *All Quiet on the Western Front* (1929). The author of this novel was a German private serving in the trenches of the Western Front. He recounts the death of spirit and passion in living men under the extreme conditions of trench warfare.

Florette Henri.   *Black Migration: Movement North, 1900–1920* (1975). A sympathetic survey of the migration of 1.25 million blacks from the South, the "hard-luck place," to northern cities, where wages were higher and jobs more plentiful.

Ernest May.   *The World War and American Isolation, 1914–1917* (1959). A balanced study of American entrance into World War I that uses the German as well as the Allied archives.

Robert Ferrell.   *Woodrow Wilson and World War I, 1917–1921* (1985). Ferrell celebrates Wilson's soaring idealism but also criticizes his stubbornness and racial bigotry.

CHAPTER 24   *The Twenties*

Frederick Lewis Allen.   *Only Yesterday: An Informal History of the 1920s* (1931). This 1932 bestseller vividly sketches the politics, morals, fashions, heroes, business, and arts of the "bally-hoo" twenties.

Irving Bernstein.   *The Lean Years* (1960). Bernstein describes the very different responses of organized and unorganized 1920s workers to change, the role played by employer associations, and the courts' use of injunctions to break strikes.

Ray Ginger.   *Six Days or Forever? Tennessee v. John Thomas Scopes* (1958). Ginger's sharp, witty portraits of Darrow and Bryan are entertaining, and quotations from the court proceedings make this book valuable for research as well as good general reading.

William E. Leuchtenburg.   *The Perils of Prosperity, 1914–1932* (1958). Leuchtenburg treats the cultural conflicts of the 1920s, industrial development, labor, morals, and the nature and limits of the decade's prosperity. He emphasizes the confrontation of the city and the small town.

Robert S. Lynd and Helen M. Lynd.   *Middletown: A Study in Modern American Culture* (1929). In this classic sociological study of Muncie, Indiana, during the 1920s, the Lynds examine the effects of mass production, the car, electricity, and advertising on attitudes toward work, leisure, education, the family, and the community.

Robert K. Murray.   *Red Scare: A Study in National Hysteria, 1919–1920* (1955). A fine study of the post-World War I Palmer raids. Murray is highly critical of the attorney general's brutal disregard of civil liberties.

William Manchester.   *Disturber of the Peace: The Life of H.L. Mencken* (1951). Superpatriots, public officials, intellectuals, reformers, and "homo boobiens"—none were safe from Mencken's gibes.

Roderick Nash.   *The Nervous Generation: American Thought, 1917–1930* (1970). Nash writes of the uncertainty and contradiction in American thinking about war, democracy, the nation, aesthetics, nature, humanity, and ethics during the 1920s.

Andrew Sinclair.   *Prohibition: Era of Excess* (1962). Sinclair explores the social and psychological forces behind the enactment and repeal of Prohibition.

Edmund Moore.   *A Catholic Runs for President, 1928* (1956). A good treatment of the Smith-Hoover battle.

Joan Hoff Wilson.   *Herbert Hoover, Forgotten Progressive* (1975). Portrays Hoover as a progressive, rather than the reactionary New Dealers believed him to be.

Norman Furniss.   *The Fundamentalist Controversy, 1918–1931* (1954). Discusses the Scopes trial and much else regarding the conservative Protestant surge of the twenties.

Paula Fass.   *The Damned and the Beautiful: American Youth in the 1920s* (1977). The title is misleading; this is really a book about college youth in the twenties. But on that subject it is the last word.

Geoffrey Perrett.   *America in the Twenties: A History* (1982) A brilliant account of a period that has often inspired brilliant writing.

Ann Douglas.   *A Terrible Honesty: Mongrel Manhattan in the 1920s* (1995). The book's thesis is that during the 1920s the nation's metropolis profited from a rare blend of blacks and whites, Jews and Christians, men and women who joined together to create a tolerant, sophisticated, culture that quickly conquered the western world.

CHAPTER 25   *The New Deal*

John Kenneth Galbraith.   *The Great Crash, 1929* (1955). This account of the great Wall Street panic of 1929 explains its causes and effects without resorting to technical jargon.

Peter Temin.   *Did Monetary Forces Cause the Great Depression?* (1976). Tackles the question: Was it money mismanagement that produced the Depression? Author says no, and accepts instead the Keynesian view that weak investment was the culprit.

William E. Leuchtenburg.   *Franklin D. Roosevelt and the New Deal, 1932–1940* (1963). In this excellent short history of Roosevelt and the New Deal, Leuchtenburg maintains that Roosevelt assumed "that a just society could be secured by imposing a welfare state on a capitalist foundation."

Richard H. Pells.   *Radical Visions and American Dreams: Culture and Social Thought in the Depression Years* (1973). In a well-written analysis of articles, books, novels, plays, and films of the 1930s, Pells seeks to demonstrate an underlying conservatism in the thought of the intellectual elite.

Studs Terkel.   *Hard Times: An Oral History of the Great Depression* (1970). Terkel interviews miners, farmers, migrant farm workers, corporation presidents, a "Share Our Wealth" organizer, hobos, and teachers. Depression poverty created feelings of confusion, shame, and guilt in many of these people.

Robert S. Lynd and Helen M. Lynd. *Middletown in Transition: A Study in Cultural Conflict* (1937). Returning to Muncie, Indiana in the 1930s, the Lynds found that its citizens believed the Depression to be a temporary problem that did not require radical changes.

James Agee and Walker Evans. *Let Us Now Praise Famous Men* (1941). Evans's photography complements Agee's sensitive, compassionate record of the daily lives of three white tenant cotton farmers in Alabama during the hard years of the 1930s.

Theodore Rosengarten. *All God's Dangers: The Life of Nate Shaw* (1974). An aged black Alabama cotton farmer tells of his years as a sharecropper in a world dominated by white landlords, bankers, fertilizer agents, gin operators, sheriffs, and judges.

Robert E. Sherwood. *Roosevelt and Hopkins: An Intimate History* (1948). Only about a third of this dual biography concerns the New Deal years, but that third is one of the best brief histories of political leadership during the Depression.

James M. Burns. *Roosevelt: The Lion and the Fox* (1956). The best discussion of Roosevelt as a domestic leader. Burns describes FDR's early life and his preparation for ultimate greatness.

Paul Conkin. *The New Deal* (1967). Conkin sees the New Deal as a lost opportunity to equalize wealth and power in the United States.

John Steinbeck. *The Grapes of Wrath* (1939). Recounts the story of midwestern farmers fleeing the Depression by heading west to California, and their reception there.

Michael Bernstein. *The Great Depression: Delayed Recovery and Economic Change in America, 1929–1939* (1989). The most recent discussion of the causes of the Great Depression. Rather technical at times.

Frank Freidel. *Franklin D. Roosevelt: A Rendezvous with Destiny* (1990). A one-volume distillation of decades-long research and writing on Roosevelt by the dean of Roosevelt scholars.

Lizabeth Cohen. *Making a New Deal: Industrial Workers in Chicago, 1919–1939* (1990). A first-rate study of ethnic life and ethnic politics in Chicago during the New Deal era and the decade immediately preceding.

CHAPTER 26   *World War II*

William Langer and S. Everett Gleason. *Challenge to Isolation, 1937–40* (1952); and *Undeclared War, 1940–41* (1953). These weighty studies are defenses of Roosevelt's foreign policy and support the view that war between Germany and the United States was inevitable.

James M. Burns. *Roosevelt: The Soldier of Freedom* (1970). Also sees foreign policy before and during the war through Roosevelt's eyes.

Robert Dallek. *Franklin D. Roosevelt and American Foreign Policy, 1932–1945* (1979). A monumental study (540 pages) covering all of Roosevelt's foreign policy.

Charles A. Beard. *President Roosevelt and the Coming of the War, 1941* (1948). Written by the dean of American progressive historians just before his death, this book indicts Roosevelt for bringing on an unnecessary war in 1941 to revive the flagging fortunes of his party and the New Deal.

Samuel Eliot Morison. *The Two-Ocean War: A Short History of the United States Navy in the Second World War* (1963). Morison had the good fortune to witness much actual sea action in both the Atlantic and Pacific, so this well-written account is based on some firsthand knowledge.

Barbara Tuchman. *Stilwell and the American Experience in China, 1911–1945* (1971). General "Vinegar Joe" Stilwell brilliantly commanded American forces in China until 1944, when Chiang Kai-shek had him recalled for advocating increased aid to Chinese Communist forces.

Dwight D. Eisenhower. *Crusade in Europe* (1948). An account in Eisenhower's own words of the American war effort in Europe that led to the final defeat of the Germans.

John Morton Blum. *V Was for Victory: Politics and American Culture During World War II* (1976). Shows the greed, bigotry, dishonesty, and stupidity as well as the selflessness, goodwill, patriotism, and intelligence of Americans "back home" during the war.

Richard Lingeman. *Don't You Know There's a War On? The American Home Front, 1941–45* (1970). Lingeman's book is lighter fare than Blum's and better at catching the flavor of American civilian life during the war.

Audrie Gardner and Anne Loftis. *The Great Betrayal: The Evacuation of the Japanese-Americans During World War II* (1969). A critical account of an event that weakened the moral position of the United States in a war against the enemies of freedom.

James P. Baxter. *Scientists Against Time* (1946). This popular history of the Office of Scientific Research and Development tells how industrial and university scientists worked with the military to develop improved radar, antisubmarine devices, rockets, blood substitutes, and medicines.

John Hersey. *Hiroshima* (1946). A gripping account of how the first atomic bombing affected six survivors: a clerk, two doctors, a poor widow with three children, a German missionary priest, and the pastor of a Japanese Methodist church.

John Toland. *The Rising Sun: The Decline and Fall of the Japanese Empire, 1936–1945* (1970). An American journalist-scholar tells the story of Japan's tragic try for world greatness. Rather sympathetic to Japan.

Robert Leckie. *Delivered from Evil: The Saga of World War II* (1987). A vivid, well-written journalistic history of the war on all fighting fronts.

CHAPTER 27   *Postwar America*

Dean Acheson. *Present at the Creation* (1969). Acheson's own account of his State Department experiences from 1941 to 1953, it is, not surprisingly, a strong defense of the Truman Doctrine, the Marshall Plan, NATO, and the Korean intervention.

Athan Theoharis. *Seeds of Repression: Harry Truman and the Origins of McCarthyism* (1971). Theoharis blames the liberals, rather than the political right, for McCarthyism.

Thomas C. Reeves. *The Life and Times of Joe McCarthy: A Biography* (1982). A masterly and unfailingly interesting biography by a careful scholar.

William F. Buckley, Jr., and L.B. Bozell. *McCarthy and His Enemies* (1954). A favorable view of Joe McCarthy by two conservatives associated with the *National Review.*

Alan Weinstein. *Perjury: The Hiss-Chambers Case* (1978). A definitive study that concludes that Hiss was guilty as charged.

Walter LaFeber. *America, Russia, and the Cold War* (1975); and David Horowitz, editor, *Containment and Revolution* (1967). "Revisionist" studies of the Cold War that strongly endorse the view that American policy was the predominant, and avoidable, cause of the confrontation with the Soviet Union.

Daniel Yergin. *Shattered Peace: The Origins of the Cold War and the National Security State* (1977). The United States after 1945, says Yergin, vacillated between the position that it could accommodate to the Soviet Union and that it was impossibile to compromise with an aggressive, expansionist power.

Alonzo Hamby. *Beyond the New Deal: Harry S. Truman and American Liberalism* (1973). This solid volume is a defense of Truman and Truman liberalism.

Charles C. Alexander. *Holding the Line: The Eisenhower Era, 1952–1959* (1975). The title suggests the author's view of the Eisenhower administration.

Douglas T. Miller and Marion Nowak. *The Fifties: The Way We Really Were* (1977). The authors see the fifties as a time of real but neglected problems.

David Riesman, Reuel Denney, and Nathan Glazer. *The Lonely Crowd: A Study of the Changing American Character* (1950). The influential study that made Americans worry about the loss of "inner direction." An important cultural document.

Scott Donaldson. *The Suburban Myth* (1969). Suburbs, Donaldson believes, were the most realistic solution of the mid-twentieth-century housing problem—the negative attitudes of American intellectuals notwithstanding.

Richard O. Davies. *The Age of Asphalt: The Automobile, the Freeway, and the Condition of Metropolitan America* (1975). Davis describes the reason for the 1956 Highway Act and discusses the neglected alternatives that might have eased our energy and urban crises.

Richard Kluger. *Simple Justice: The History of Brown v. Board of Education and Black America's Struggle for Equality* (1975). The best single volume on the civil rights movement in the 1950s. Focuses on the famous 1954 school desegregation decision of the Supreme Court.

Bruce Cook. *The Beat Generation* (1971). Cook's thesis is that the Beat movement of the 1950s anticipated much of the cultural and political radicalism of the 1960s.

Jack Kerouac. *On the Road* (1957). A Beat novel of characters frantically moving across the American landscape of the 1950s.

Ralph Ellison. *Invisible Man* (1952). A beautifully written, convincing, and often amusing novel of the coming of age of a young black man who is caught up in—and then dumped by—the Communist party.

Max Hastings. *The Korean War* (1987). This lively review of the Korean "police action" depicts the conflict as a dress rehearsal for Vietnam, with many of the same frustrations and confusions as the later war.

J. Ronald Oakley. *God's Country: America in the Fifties* (1986). Oakley shows that all was not necessarily well in the Garden of Eden, what with racism, the Cold War, and Joe McCarthy.

CHAPTER 28   *The Dissenting Sixties*

William O'Neill. *Coming Apart: An Informal History of America in the 1960s* (1971). A witty, highly readable, and opinionated overview of the mores, politics, culture, and thought of the 1960s.

Irwin Unger and Debi Unger.   *1968: Turning Point* (1988). A panorama of the 1960s from the perspective of its culminating year. Strongly recommended.

Allen Matusow.   *The Unraveling of America: A History of Liberalism in the 1960s* (1984). A critical examination of 1960s political liberalism as seen from the moderate left.

Arthur M. Schlesinger, Jr.   *A Thousand Days: John F. Kennedy in the White House* (1965). A highly sympathetic portrait of the Kennedy presidency by a professorial participant in it.

Herbert Parmet.   *Jack: The Struggles of John F. Kennedy* (1980); and *JFK: The Presidency of John F. Kennedy* (1983). A more balanced assessment of Kennedy and his administration than Schlesinger's.

Lyndon B. Johnson.   *The Vantage Point: Perspectives of the Presidency, 1963–69* (1971). Johnson defends his administration's policies—not only the Great Society programs, but also the intervention in Vietnam.

Michael Harrington.   *The Other America: Poverty in the United States* (1962). In this influential book, Harrington rediscovered poverty in America after the experts had said it no longer existed.

Irving Bernstein.   *Guns Or Butter: The Presidency of Lyndon Johnson* (1996). A compendious survey of the Johnson presidency with particularly good sections on the Great Society.

Irwin Unger.   *The Best of Intentions: The Triumph and Failure of the Great Society Under Kennedy, Johnson, and Nixon* (1996). Reviews the origins of the Great Society programs of the Sixties and gives them mixed reviews.

Doris Kearns.   *Lyndon Johnson and the American Dream* (1976). A fascinating combination of psychological study, biography, and memoir, written by a scholar who enjoyed Johnson's trust and confidence from 1967 to his death in 1973.

Eric Goldman.   *The Tragedy of Lyndon Johnson* (1969). Written by the White House "intellectual in residence," this critical book catches the tragic downfall of Lyndon Johnson.

Norman Podhoretz.   *Why We Were in Vietnam* (1982). The author, a leading neoconservative intellectual, makes the best case possible for American involvement in Vietnam.

George Herring.   *America's Longest War: The United States and Vietnam, 1950–1975* (1986). Herring was a dove who believed that America's containment policy, as displayed in Vietnam, was "fundamentally flawed in its assumptions."

Frances Fitzgerald.   *Fire in the Lake: The Vietnamese and the Americans in Vietnam* (1972). Discusses the Vietnamese people and their history to provide the setting for the Vietnam War.

David Halberstam.   *The Best and the Brightest* (1972). A sharply critical account of the foreign policy "establishment" under Kennedy and Johnson and how its members entangled the United States in the Vietnam War.

Nancy Zaroulis and Gerald Sullivan.   *Who Spoke Up? American Protest Against the War In Vietnam, 1963–1975* (1984). A blow-by-blow account of the anti-Vietnam War movement. Encyclopedic.

Betty Friedan.   *The Feminine Mystique* (1963). Friedan devastatingly attacks the 1950s cult of female domesticity and leaves it a shambles among most intellectuals and a large proportion of college-educated women. Helped launch the Sixties New Feminism.

Alice Echols.   *Daring to Be Bad: Radical Feminism in America, 1967–1975* (1989). The author considers radical feminism "the most vital and imaginative force within the women's liberation movement."

David Garrow.   *Bearing the Cross: Martin Luther King, Jr., and the Southern Christian Leadership Conference* (1986). Not so eloquent as Stephen Oats's *Let the Trumpet Sound* (1982), but better balanced on King.

Taylor Branch.   *Parting the Waters: America in the King Years, 1954–63* (1988). An effective invocation of the early, more successful years of the civil rights movement.

Morris Dickstein.   *Gates of Eden: American Culture in the Sixties* (1977). Written by a professor of literature who is young enough to have been at the center of things himself during the 1968 student uprising at Columbia University.

Theodore Roszak.   *The Making of a Counter Culture: Reflections on the Technocratic Society and Its Youthful Opposition* (1969). Both a description of the 1960s counterculture phenomenon and an influential force in its emergence.

Charles Perry.   *The Haight-Ashbury: A History* (1984). A depiction of "hippie heaven" during its brief glory period.

W.J. Rorabaugh.   *Berkeley at War: The 1960s* (1989). The best treatment of the free speech movement as well as the later struggles in Berkeley between the young radicals and the university and political authorities.

James Miller.   *Democracy Is in the Streets: From Port Huron to the Siege of Chicago* (1987). A sympathetic treatment of the student New Left during its heyday.

Todd Gitlin.   *The Sixties* (1987). A positive, and nostalgic, treatment of the Sixties' insurgencies by a founder of SDS who became a journalism professor.

CHAPTER 29   *The Uncertain Seventies*

Richard Nixon.   *Six Crises* (1962). Tells Nixon's own version of major early crises in his life, including the Hiss case, the Checkers Speech, Eisenhower's heart attack, his near-catastrophic visit to Caracas, the "kitchen debate" with Khrushchev, and the 1960 presidential contest with Kennedy.

Gary Wills.   *Nixon Agonistes: The Crisis of the Self-Made Man* (1970). One of the best analyses of Richard Nixon and his place in American political history.

Theodore White.   *Breach of Faith: The Fall of Richard Nixon* (1975). An excellent summary of Watergate by a master of political journalism who once admired Nixon.

Richard Nixon.   *Memoirs* (1978). Not ultimately convincing, perhaps, but it does make it clear that Nixon was a fallible human being, not some inhuman monster. Written after Watergate.

Joan Hoff Wilson.   *Nixon Reconsidered* (1994). Seeks to rehabilitate Nixon as a kind of liberal who expanded the Great Society programs of his predecessor.

Henry Kissinger.   *The White House Years* (1979). A fascinating inside report on the making of American foreign policy during Nixon's first four years, by his national security adviser at the time.

John Osborne.   *White House Watch: The Ford Years* (1977). A moderate appreciation of the Ford administration by a liberal journalist.

Robert Shogan.   *Promises to Keep: Carter's First Hundred Days* (1977). A journalist's favorable report on the Carter administration's first three months in office.

Haynes Johnson.   *In the Absence of Power: Governing America* (1980). An indictment of the Carter administration for its feebleness and lack of competence.

Studs Terkel. *Working People Talk About What They Do All Day and How They Feel About What They Do* (1974). Here 130 people from a wide range of American types talk about the frustrations and gratifications of earning a living in the 1970s while maintaining their sense of individual worth.

Barry Commoner. *The Politics of Energy* (1979). An indictment of American energy policy by a man who believes that most of the nation's energy difficulties have been caused by big-business groups greedy for profits.

Robert B. Stobaugh and Daniel Yergin, editors. *Energy Future: Report of the Energy Project at the Harvard Business School* (1978). The authors of these essays consider the 1970s energy crisis real and urge strict conservation as the way to deal with it.

William Quandt. *Decade of Decision: American Policy Toward the Arab-Israeli Conflict* (1977). The single best volume on this important subject.

Christopher Lasch. *The Culture of Narcissism: American Life in an Age of Diminishing Expectations* (1979). A pessimistic and somewhat carping book about what has gone wrong with American culture in the 1970s.

Ralph E. Smith, editor. *The Subtle Revolution: Women at Work* (1979). A survey of the enormous changes that have taken place in women's roles in the American economy since 1945, with special emphasis in the 1970s.

Kirkpatrick Sale. *Power Shift: The Rise of the Southern Rim and Its Challenge to the Eastern Establishment* (1975). A good analysis of the political rise of the Sun Belt and its significance for national affairs.

CHAPTER 30 *The "Reagan Revolution"*

Ronnie Dugger. *On Reagan: The Man and His Presidency* (1983). A highly critical view of Reagan and his administration by the publisher of the *Texas Observer,* a liberal magazine.

Elizabeth Drew. *Campaign Journal: The Political Events of 1983–1984* (1985). This volume is not as readable as Theodore White's *The Making of the President* series, but it is probably better reportage.

Charles Murray. *Losing Ground: American Social Policy, 1950–1980* (1984). Though this work deals with the years before Reagan's presidency, it conveys many of the conservative attitudes toward social policy that characterized the Reagan administration.

Sidney Blumenthal. *The Rise of the Counter-Establishment: From Conservative Ideology to Political Power* (1986). A critical, liberal-oriented analysis of the conservative surge of the 1970s and 1980.

Thomas Ferguson and Joel Rogers. *Right Turn: The Decline of the Democrats and the Future of American Politics* (1986). The authors conclude that Reaganism triumphed, not because public opinion shifted right, but because a new elite, composed of rich businesspeople, manipulated the electoral process successfully to achieve their conservative ends.

Robert S. McElvaine. *The End of the Conservative Era: Liberalism After Reagan* (1987). Placing his faith in a theory of conservative–liberal cycles, McElvaine believes the impetus behind the Reagan Revolution had waned by the mid-1980s.

Randy Shilts. *And the Band Played On: Politics, People, and the AIDS Epidemic* (1987). A San Francisco reporter chronicles the AIDS plague, both as an unfolding human tragedy and as a story of folly and error.

Garry Wills. *Reagan's America* (1988). An impressionistic, skeptical view of Ronald Reagan's life and career by a liberal scholar of the American presidency.

Jack W. Germond and Jules Witcover. *Wake Us When It's Over: Presidential Politics of 1984* (1985). This description of the 1984 election emphasizes the work of professional media and campaign advisers who packaged the candidates and brainwashed, misled, and deceived the voting public in the process.

David Stockman. *The Triumph of Politics: The Inside Story of the Reagan Revolution* (1986). The Reagan budget director's account of how he sold the president and his advisers an economic policy that he himself was unsure of and how, in his estimate, it failed.

Martin Anderson. *Revolution* (1988). A "supply-side," true-believer's view of the Reagan Revolution.

Donald Regan. *For the Record: From Wall Street to Washington* (1988). Bitter at being made the scapegoat for the Iran-Contra fiasco, Reagan chief-of-staff Don Regan reveals the confusion in the White House, Nancy Reagan's influence on the president, and various astrologers' influence on her.

Peggy Noonan. *What I Saw at the Revolution* (1990). A witty and wry account of what it was like to be a speechwriter for Ronald Reagan.

Nancy Reagan. *My Turn: The Memoirs of Nancy Reagan* (1989). The former First Lady gets her licks in here in this volume—after taking it on the chin herself.

Clyde Prestowitz. *Trading Places: How We Allowed Japan to Take the Lead* (1988). Japan-bashing at its most convincing by a former U.S. trade official who had to negotiate with the Japanese.

Laurence Tribe. *Abortion: The Clash of Absolutes* (1990). A sophisticated history and analysis of the abortion war by a strong pro-choice constitutional lawyer at Harvard Law School.

Kevin Phillips. *The Politics of Rich and Poor: Wealth and the American Electorate in the Reagan Aftermath* (1990). Phillips, a conservative political analyst, is disillusioned by Reaganomics and foresees a new populist uprising based on class resentment just down the road.

Paul Freiberger and Michael Swaine. *Fire in the Valley: The Making of the Personal Computer* (1984). The best single-volume history of a subject so new that the ancient past is 1975.

CHAPTER 31   *A United America?*

Arthur M. Schlesinger, Jr. *The Disuniting of America* (1992). A noted liberal expresses fear that recent tribalism will undermine a shared history and set of values among Americans.

Ronald Takaki. *A Different Mirror: A History of Multicultural America* (1992). Himself a Japanese-American, Takaki celebrates the diversity of America and emphasizes the plight of ethnics and people of non-European ancestry in a society dominated mostly by people of North European background.

Robert Hughes. *The Culture of Complaint: The Fraying of America* (1992). A prominent Australian-born art critic who finds both the purveyors of political correctness and many of their shriller conservative critics rather foolish people.

Katherine Roiphe. *The Morning After: Fear, Sex and Feminism* (1993). A young Ivy League graduate who condemns what she considers the excesses of feminist responses on campus to male behavior toward women.

Catherine MacKinnon.   *Only Words* (1993). A leading feminist attorney attacks pornography as demeaning to women and calls for strict laws against it.

Dinesh D'Souza.   *Illiberal Education: The Politics of Race and Sex on Campus* (1991). A sharp indictment of "politically correct" attitudes and teachings on American campuses by a young conservative, Asian by birth, who rejects the philosophy behind affirmative action and other forms of ethnic preference.

Joe Klein.   *Primary Colors* (1996). An amusing novel about a presidential campaign, featuring a thinly disguised Bill Clinton, by "Anonymous," a thinly disguised political reporter, Joe Klein.

David Maraniss.   *First in His Class: A Biography of Bill Clinton* (1995). A critical review of Clinton's early life. Shows the talents and the failings.

Joseph Stiglitz.   *The Roaring Nineties* (2003). A history of the 1990s economy from the perspective of a liberal former Clinton economic advisor. At times critical of the Clinton administration for not being liberal enough.

Joseph Stiglitz.   *Globalization and Its Discontents* (2002). A critical examination of the effects of globalization.

Thomas Friedman.   *The World Is Flat* (2005). Friedman, a columnist for *The New York Times*, defends globalization against its critics.

Thomas Frank.   *What's the Matter with Kansas?* (2004). The author, a liberal, analyses the Republican surge of the late 1990s and early twentieth century and blames much of it on liberal ineptitude.

Samuel P. Huntington.   *Who Are We?* (2004). Huntington insists that the American sense of identity is WASP in derivation and that the immigration deluge of recent years is threatening to dilute that heritage with the loss of Americans' sense of who they are as a people.

Bob Woodward.   *Plan of Attack* (2004). One of America's most renowned reporters describes the evolution of the Bush administration's decision to attack Iraq to overthrow Saddam Hussein.

Michael Gordon and Bernard Trainor.   *Cobra II: The Inside Story of the Invasion and Occupation of Iraq* (2006). A military as well as political account of the Iraq war. Highly critical of Rumsfeld for miscalculating troop requirements and the Bush administration for lack of planning for the period after Saddam's defeat.

Photo Credits

3 American Museum of Natural History.   12 The Granger Collection.   19 The Granger Collection.

27 The Granger Collection.   37 American Antiquarian Society.

47 The Granger Collection.   67 Library of Congress.

76 Library of Congress.   80 The Saint Louis Art Museum, Museum Purchase.

103 Library of Congress.   121 The Granger Collection.

129 The Historic New Orleans Collection.   141 Independence National Historical Park.

152 John Trumbull (1756–1843). "Alexander Hamilton" (1755/57–1804), 1806. Oil on canvas, 76.2 × 61 cm. (30 × 24 in.). Gift of Henry Cabot Lodge. National Portrait Gallery, Smithsonian Institution/Art Resource, NY   156 The New-York Historical Society.

173 Library of Congress.   176 New Haven Colony Historical Society.

192 (Top and bottom) Carnegie Library of Pittsburgh.   196 Corbis/Bettmann.   204 The New-York Historical Society.

225 AP Wide World Photos.   228 Art Resource, N.Y.

250 The Granger Collection.   253 The Granger Collection.

263 Art Resource/The New York Public Library.

285 The Granger Collection.   290 SuperStock, Inc.

298 Matthew Brady photographer, Art Resource, N.Y.   306 Library of Congress.   317 Courtesy of Library of Congress.

330 The Granger Collection.   337 Library of Congress.

355 Currier & Ives, Nath. & James, American, "Fall of Richmond, Virginia" (A. 1857–1907). Private Collection/Bridgeman Art Library, London/SuperStock, Inc.   361 Arthur Stumpf, "Andrew Johnson," 1808–1875. National Portrait Gallery, Smithsonian Institution/Art Resource, N.Y.   363 Library of Congress.   369 Corbis/ Bettmann.   376 Library of Congress.   378 Corbis/Bettmann.   379 Rutherford B. Hayes Presidential Center.   381 Corbis/Bettmann.

391 Art Resource/The New York Public Library.   400 State Historical Society of Wisconsin, International Harvester Collection, WHi(X3)30648.

418 William H. Rau photographer, Library of Congress.   428 The Granger Collection.   430 Museum of the City of New York.

443 Library of Congress.   446 From the collections of Henry Ford Museum & Greenfield Village.

470 Judge, September 19, 1896 V.31, no.779/Library of Congress.

499 Library of Congress.   503 Chicago Historical Society.

524 Corbis/Bettmann.   530 Culver Pictures, Inc.

544 The Granger Collection.   556 The Granger Collection.

572 Brown Brothers.   581 The Granger Collection.

594 Culver Pictures, Inc.   603 Art Resource, N.Y.

632 Corbis/Bettmann.   633 National Archives and Records Administration.   639 Franklin D. Roosevelt Library.

651 Corbis/Bettmann.   654 Bernard Hoffman/Life Magazine/© 1950 Time Pix.   675 UPI/Corbis/Bettmann.

689 Library of Congress.   691 Berinsky, Burton photographer, Omni-Photo Communications, Inc.   693 Neil Armstrong photographer, The Granger Collection.

719 UPI/Corbis/Bettmann.   736 Michael Abramson photographer, Black Star.

766 AP Wide World Photos.

778 AP Wide World Photos.   785 J. Scott Applewhite photographer, AP Wide World Photos.   796 Steve Grayson/ Riverside Press-Enterprise/Getty Images, Inc – Liaison.

Index

U.S. History Documents CD-ROM

Over 300 Primary Source Documents

SINGLE PC LICENSE AGREEMENT AND LIMITED WARRANTY

READ THIS LICENSE CAREFULLY BEFORE OPENING THIS PACKAGE. BY OPENING THIS PACKAGE, YOU ARE AGREEING TO THE TERMS AND CONDITIONS OF THIS LICENSE. IF YOU DO NOT AGREE, DO NOT OPEN THE PACKAGE. PROMPTLY RETURN THE UNOPENED PACKAGE AND ALL ACCOMPANYING ITEMS TO THE PLACE YOU OBTAINED THEM.

1. GRANT OF LICENSE and OWNERSHIP: The enclosed computer programs <<and data>> ("Software") are licensed, not sold, to you by Pearson Education, Inc. publishing as Pearson Prentice Hall ("We" or the "Company") and in consideration of your purchase or adoption of the accompanying Company textbooks and/or other materials, and your agreement to these terms. We reserve any rights not granted to you. You own only the disk(s) but we and/or our licensors own the Software itself. This license allows you to use and display your copy of the Software on a single computer (i.e., with a single CPU) at a single location for *academic* use only, so long as you comply with the terms of this Agreement. You may make one copy for back up, or transfer your copy to another CPU, provided that the Software is usable on only one computer.

2. RESTRICTIONS: You may *not* transfer or distribute the Software or documentation to anyone else. Except for backup, you may *not* copy the documentation or the Software. You may *not* network the Software or otherwise use it on more than one computer or computer terminal at the same time. You may *not* reverse engineer, disassemble, decompile, modify, adapt, translate, or create derivative works based on the Software or the Documentation. You may be held legally responsible for any copying or copyright infringement that is caused by your failure to abide by the terms of these restrictions.

3. TERMINATION: This license is effective until terminated. This license will terminate automatically without notice from the Company if you fail to comply with any provisions or limitations of this license. Upon termination, you shall destroy the Documentation and all copies of the Software. All provisions of this Agreement as to limitation and disclaimer of warranties, limitation of liability, remedies or damages, and our ownership rights shall survive termination.

4. LIMITED WARRANTY AND DISCLAIMER OF WARRANTY: Company warrants that for a period of 60 days from the date you purchase this SOFTWARE (or purchase or adopt the accompanying textbook), the Software, when properly installed and used in accordance with the Documentation, will operate in substantial conformity with the description of the Software set forth in the Documentation, and that for a period of 30 days the disk(s) on which the Software is delivered shall be free from defects in materials and workmanship under normal use. The Company does *not* warrant that the Software will meet your requirements or that the operation of the Software will be uninterrupted or error-free. Your only remedy and the Company's only obligation under these limited warranties is, at the Company's option, return of the disk for a refund of any amounts paid for it by you or replacement of the disk. THIS LIMITED WARRANTY IS THE ONLY WARRANTY PROVIDED BY THE COMPANY AND ITS LICENSORS, AND THE COMPANY AND ITS LICENSORS DISCLAIM ALL OTHER WARRANTIES, EXPRESS OR IMPLIED, INCLUDING WITHOUT LIMITATION, THE IMPLIED WARRANTIES OF MERCHANTABILITY AND FITNESS FOR A PARTICULAR PURPOSE. THE COMPANY DOES NOT WARRANT, GUARANTEE OR MAKE ANY REPRESENTATION REGARDING THE ACCURACY, RELIABILITY, CURRENTNESS, USE, OR RESULTS OF USE, OF THE SOFTWARE.

5. LIMITATION OF REMEDIES AND DAMAGES: IN NO EVENT, SHALL THE COMPANY OR ITS EMPLOYEES, AGENTS, LICENSORS, OR CONTRACTORS BE LIABLE FOR ANY INCIDENTAL, INDIRECT, SPECIAL, OR CONSEQUENTIAL DAMAGES ARISING OUT OF OR IN CONNECTION WITH THIS LICENSE OR THE SOFTWARE, INCLUDING FOR LOSS OF USE, LOSS OF DATA, LOSS OF INCOME OR PROFIT, OR OTHER LOSSES, SUSTAINED AS A RESULT OF INJURY TO ANY PERSON, OR LOSS OF OR DAMAGE TO PROPERTY, OR CLAIMS OF THIRD PARTIES, EVEN IF THE COMPANY OR AN AUTHORIZED REPRESENTATIVE OF THE COMPANY HAS BEEN ADVISED OF THE POSSIBILITY OF SUCH DAMAGES. IN NO EVENT SHALL THE LIABILITY OF THE COMPANY FOR DAMAGES WITH RESPECT TO THE SOFTWARE EXCEED THE AMOUNTS ACTUALLY PAID BY YOU, IF ANY, FOR THE SOFTWARE OR THE ACCOMPANYING TEXTBOOK. BECAUSE SOME JURISDICTIONS DO NOT ALLOW THE LIMITATION OF LIABILITY IN CERTAIN CIRCUMSTANCES, THE ABOVE LIMITATIONS MAY NOT ALWAYS APPLY TO YOU.

6. GENERAL: THIS AGREEMENT SHALL BE CONSTRUED IN ACCORDANCE WITH THE LAWS OF THE UNITED STATES OF AMERICA AND THE STATE OF NEW YORK, APPLICABLE TO CONTRACTS MADE IN NEW YORK, EXCLUDING THE STATE'S LAWS AND POLICIES ON CONFLICTS OF LAW, AND SHALL BENEFIT THE COMPANY, ITS AFFILIATES AND ASSIGNEES. THIS AGREEMENT IS THE COMPLETE AND EXCLUSIVE STATEMENT OF THE AGREEMENT BETWEEN YOU AND THE COMPANY AND SUPERSEDES ALL PROPOSALS OR PRIOR AGREEMENTS, ORAL, OR WRITTEN, AND ANY OTHER COMMUNICATIONS BETWEEN YOU AND THE COMPANY OR ANY REPRESENTATIVE OF THE COMPANY RELATING TO THE SUBJECT MATTER OF THIS AGREEMENT. If you are a U.S. Government user, this Software is licensed with "restricted rights" as set forth in subparagraphs (a)-(d) of the Commercial Computer-Restricted Rights clause at FAR 52.227-19 or in subparagraphs (c)(1)(ii) of the Rights in Technical Data and Computer Software clause at DFARS 252.227-7013, and similar clauses, as applicable.

Should you have any questions concerning this agreement or if you wish to contact the Company for any reason, please contact in writing: Legal Department, Prentice Hall, 1 Lake Street, Upper Saddle River, NJ 07450 or call Pearson Education Product Support at 1-800-677-6337.